Regulation of Lawyers:
Statutes and Standards

2013 Edition

ISBN 978-1-4548-1363-7
ISSN 1082-8583

Regulation of Lawyers:
Statutes and Standards

2013 Edition

Stephen Gillers

Elihu Root Professor of Law
New York University

Roy D. Simon

Distinguished Professor of Legal Ethics Emeritus
Hofstra University

Andrew M. Perlman

Professor of Law
Suffolk University Law School

Wolters Kluwer
Law & Business

About Wolters Kluwer Law & Business

Wolters Kluwer Law & Business is a leading global provider of intelligent information and digital solutions for legal and business professionals in key specialty areas, and respected educational resources for professors and law students. Wolters Kluwer Law & Business connects legal and business professionals as well as those in the education market with timely, specialized authoritative content and information-enabled solutions to support success through productivity, accuracy and mobility.

Serving customers worldwide, Wolters Kluwer Law & Business products include those under the Aspen Publishers, CCH, Kluwer Law International, Loislaw, Best Case, ftwilliam.com and MediRegs family of products.

CCH products have been a trusted resource since 1913, and are highly regarded resources for legal, securities, antitrust and trade regulation, government contracting, banking, pension, payroll, employment and labor, and healthcare reimbursement and compliance professionals.

Aspen Publishers products provide essential information to attorneys, business professionals and law students. Written by preeminent authorities, the product line offers analytical and practical information in a range of specialty practice areas from securities law and intellectual property to mergers and acquisitions and pension/benefits. Aspen's trusted legal education resources provide professors and students with high-quality, up-to-date and effective resources for successful instruction and study in all areas of the law.

Kluwer Law International products provide the global business community with reliable international legal information in English. Legal practitioners, corporate counsel and business executives around the world rely on Kluwer Law journals, looseleafs, books, and electronic products for comprehensive information in many areas of international legal practice.

Loislaw is a comprehensive online legal research product providing legal content to law firm practitioners of various specializations. Loislaw provides attorneys with the ability to quickly and efficiently find the necessary legal information they need, when and where they need it, by facilitating access to primary law as well as state-specific law, records, forms and treatises.

Best Case Solutions is the leading bankruptcy software product to the bankruptcy industry. It provides software and workflow tools to flawlessly streamline petition preparation and the electronic filing process, while timely incorporating ever-changing court requirements.

ftwilliam.com offers employee benefits professionals the highest quality plan documents (retirement, welfare and non-qualified) and government forms (5500/PBGC, 1099 and IRS) software at highly competitive prices.

MediRegs products provide integrated health care compliance content and software solutions for professionals in healthcare, higher education and life sciences, including professionals in accounting, law and consulting.

Wolters Kluwer Law & Business, a division of Wolters Kluwer, is headquartered in New York. Wolters Kluwer is a market-leading global information services company focused on professionals.

Summary of Contents

Dedications

Stephen Gillers dedicates this edition of the book to the memory of his mother, Sylvia Gillers Wadler, who was born February 20, 1914, and died April 18, 2007, age 93. Sylvia didn't have much use for lawyers until her son became one and then gained an even greater appreciation when he married a lawyer. Nor did Sylvia need to think much about legal ethics. Like mothers everywhere, she intuitively knew right and wrong, good behavior and bad, so far as her children were concerned, which is what mostly mattered. And she had a powerful sanctioning system, usually implicit and summarized at the end of a description of a particular course of conduct that her children were expected to obey, or refrain from, with such words as "if you know what's good for you." We mostly did know. And it mostly was.

Roy Simon (Jr.) dedicates this edition of the book to the memory of his father, the original Roy Simon, who aspired to be a lawyer and studied pre-law subjects at the University of Illinois. But in 1929, when the Great Depression hit, Roy (Sr.) left college in the middle of his junior year to help out at his father's clothing store in Chicago. A few years later, when the clothing store went bankrupt, my father began selling life insurance, and continued doing so for the next fifty years. My father taught me ethics by example throughout his life, and I continue to think about him every day, twenty-eight years after his untimely death in 1984 at age 73.

Andrew Perlman dedicates this edition of the book to the memory of his father, Murray Perlman, who died in 1986 at the age of 68. Murray became a father at an older age than most men, and I benefited enormously from his accumulated wisdom. He had a strong moral compass that was forged during the Great Depression and his time as a paratrooper in World War II. He taught me many lessons, but one of my lasting impressions of him was his strong sense of what was right. I like to think that he would have found some value in my work on legal ethics, so I dedicate this edition of the book to him.

Acknowledgments

The authors appreciate the time and effort of the dozens of people and organizations that have helped the authors keep this book accurate and up-to-date.

We begin by thanking the outstanding personnel of the ABA Center for Professional Responsibility and other ABA entities: Jeanne Gray, Director of the ABA Center for Professional Responsibility and Senior Director of Public Services; Art Garwin, Deputy Director of the ABA Center for Professional Responsibility; George Kuhlman, former Ethics Counsel, and Eileen Libby, Associate Ethics Counsel to the ABA Standing Committee on Ethics and Professional Responsibility; Ellyn Rosen, Lead Senior Counsel to the Center for Professional Responsibility and Counsel to the ABA Commission on Ethics 20/20; Martin Whittaker, Senior Counsel at the American Bar Association and Counsel to the Technology Working Group of the ABA Commission on Ethics 20/20; Will Hornsby, ABA Staff Counsel, Delivery of Legal Services; John Holtaway, Lead Senior Counsel, Client Protection and Policy Implementation; and Becky Stretch, who served as Special Counsel to the ABA Ethics 2000 Commission.

We also received assistance from lawyers in all parts of the country. We thank Randall Difuntorum of the California State Bar; Professor Kevin Mohr, a Professor at Western State College of Law and a consultant to the California Commission for the Revision of the Rules of Professional Conduct; Professor Byron Stier of Southwestern Law School; William P. Smith III, General Counsel to the State Bar of Georgia; Dennis Rendleman, former General Counsel to the Illinois State Bar Association; Alice Neece Mine of the North Carolina State Bar; Cynthia Kuhn of the District of Columbia Bar; Robert Bloom, who works at the Supreme Judicial Court of Massachusetts; John Rabiej, Chief of the Rules Committee Support Office of the Administrative Office of the United States Courts; Kathleen Mulligan Baxter, Counsel to the New York State Bar Association; Jim McCauley, Ethics Counsel to the Virginia State Bar; Betsy Brandborg and Chris Manos of the State Bar of Montana; and many others who provided us with helpful information about changes in the standards and statutes governing lawyers.

Acknowledgments

The authors also thank the editors of the ABA/BNA Lawyer's Manual on Professional Conduct, whose biweekly Current Reports are indispensable to keeping up with state and national developments in the legal profession.

Stephen Gillers is, as always, grateful to Shirley Gray for her yearly help in bringing this book to press. He also expresses much thanks to Barbara S. Gillers for eliminating errors in his portion of the book.

We deeply appreciate the exceptional work done by our developmental editor, Kathy Langone of Aspen Publishers; and our editor, Troy Froebe of The Froebe Group.

The authors are enormously grateful to the American Bar Association for its permission to use numerous items, including all of the following:

- ABA Model Rules of Professional Conduct, 2011 Edition, available online at *http://www.americanbar.org/groups/professional_responsibility/publications/ model_rules_of_professional_conduct/model_rules_of_professional_conduct_table_of_ contents.html.* Copyright © 2011 by the American Bar Association. Reprinted with permission. Bound copies of ABA Model Rules of Professional Conduct, 2011 Edition are available from the American Bar Association's Service Center, 321 North. Clark Street, Chicago, IL 60654; 1-800-285-2221; *http://apps.americanbar. org/abastore/books/WebOrdFrm.pdf.*
- Excerpts from the Ethics 2000 Commission Report, published online at *http://www.americanbar.org/groups/professional_responsibility/policy/ethics_2000_ commission.html.* Copyright © 2000 by the American Bar Association. Reprinted with permission.
- Reporter's Explanation of Changes, by the Ethics 2000 Commission, published online at *http://www.americanbar.org/content/dam/aba/migrated/cpr/e2k/ 10_85rem.authcheckdam.pdf.* Copyright © 2000 by the American Bar Association. Reprinted with permission.
- *Excerpts from Client Representation* in the 21st Century, a Report of the ABA Commission on Multijurisdictional Practice (August 2002), published online at *http://www.americanbar.org/content/dam/aba/migrated/final_mjp_rpt_121702_2. authcheckdam.pdf.* Copyright © 2002 by the American Bar Association. Reprinted with permission.
- Excerpts from ABA Model Code of Professional Responsibility (1981), available online at *http://www.americanbar.org/content/dam/aba/migrated/cpr/ mrpc/mcpr.authcheckdam.pdf.* Copyright © 1981 by the American Bar Association. Reprinted with permission. In 1983, the ABA Model Rules of Professional Conduct replaced the ABA Model Code of Professional Responsibility.
- Black Letter Standards were excerpted from the ABA Standards for Criminal Justice: Prosecution Function and Defense Function, 3rd Edition (1993), available online at *www.americanbar.org/groups/criminal_justice/policy/standards. html.* Copyright © 1993 by the American Bar Association. Reprinted with permission.
- Excerpts from the ABA Standards for Imposing Lawyer Sanctions (1992), by the ABA Joint Committee on Professional Sanctions, available online at *http://www.americanbar.org/content/dam/aba/migrated/cpr/regulation/standards_ sanctions.authcheckdam.pdf.* Copyright © 2005 by the American Bar Association. Reprinted with permission.

- ABA Canons of Professional Ethics (1956), available online at *http://www.americanbar.org/content/dam/aba/migrated/cpr/mrpc/Canons_Ethics.authcheckdam.pdf.* Copyright © 1956 by the American Bar Association. Reprinted with permission.
- ABA Model Code of Judicial Conduct, 2008 Edition, available online at *http://www.americanbar.org/content/dam/aba/migrated/judicialethics/ABA_MCJC_approved.authcheckdam.pdf.* Copyright © 2008 by the American Bar Association. Reprinted with permission. Bound copies of ABA Model Code of Judicial Conduct, Second Edition 2011, are available for purchase from the American Bar Association's Service Center, 321 North Clark Street, Chicago, IL 60654; 1-800-285-2221; *http://apps.americanbar.org/abastore/books/WebOrdFrm.pdf.*
- Guideline C was excerpted from Guidelines for the Selection and Performance Standards of Retained Counsel, by the ABA Tort Trial & Insurance Practice Section's Special Task Force on Selection and Performance Standards of Retained Counsel. Copyright © 1992 by the American Bar Association. Reprinted with permission.
- Preface excerpted from the ABA Commission on Billable Hours Report, 2001-2002. Copyright © 2002 by the American Bar Association. Reprinted with permission.
- Model Court Rule on Insurance Disclosure, located online at *http://www.americanbar.org/content/dam/aba/migrated/cpr/clientpro/Model_Rule_InsuranceDisclosure.authcheckdam.pdf.* Copyright © 2005 by the American Bar Association. Reprinted with permission.
- Excerpts from the Preliminary Report of the American Bar Association Task Force on Corporate Responsibility (2002), available online at *http://www2.law.mercer.edu/lawreview/files/54310.pdf.* Copyright © 2002 by the American Bar Association. Reprinted with permission.

The authors also thank the following other copyright holders for their permission to reprint the materials in this book. The copyright holders reserve all rights to the following materials:

The American Law Institute, for permission to reprint the black letter sections from the Restatement (Third) of the Law Governing Lawyers © 2000.

The American Trial Lawyer's Association, for permission to reprint its 1988 Code of Conduct and its 1986 Victim's Bill of Rights.

The Federal Bar Association, for permission to reprint excerpts from the Model Rules of Professional Conduct for Federal Lawyers © 1990.

The American Academy of Matrimonial Lawyers (AAML), for permission to reprint excerpts from the Bounds of Advocacy.

The Roscoe Pound Foundation (formerly the Roscoe Pound-American Trial Lawyers Foundation), for permission to reprint excerpts from the 1982 Revised Draft of the American Lawyer's Code of Conduct.

The National Association of Legal Assistants, Inc., 1516 S. Boston, Tulsa, OK 74119, for permission to reprint excerpts from the NALA's Model Standards and Guidelines for Utilization of Legal Assistants.

Finally, Roy Simon is grateful to his wife, Karen, and their four children, Daniel, Nicole, Joshua, and Rebecca, for their interest and support through all 24 editions of this book.

Introduction to the Regulation of Lawyers

This book contains rules regulating the behavior of lawyers and judges. These rules come from many sources: statutes, administrative regulations, rules of evidence and procedure, and—most prominently—ethical codes. These rules continue to grow and change, and this book tries to capture a sense of the breadth, pace, and direction of the changes.

What's New Since Our Last Edition?

This is the twenty-fourth edition of *Regulation of Lawyers: Statutes and Standards*. Like all of our previous editions, this edition has dozens of new items and many updates to older materials. We provide here an overview of the major changes that have occurred since our last edition, as well as a summary of some possible future changes that were formally or informally under consideration when we went to press in September 2012.

American Bar Association Developments

ABA Model Rules of Professional Conduct: The ABA amended numerous provisions of the ABA Model Rules of Professional Conduct at its August 2012 Annual Meeting. (These were the first changes since August 2009.) All of the changes were recommended by the ABA Commission on Ethics 20/20, which was created in 2009 to undertake a comprehensive review of the ABA Model Rules of Professional Conduct and the American system of lawyer regulation in light of globalization and changes in technology. Specifically, the ABA House of Delegates approved changes to the following provisions of the ABA Model Rules:

- Rule 1.0 (Terminology): Black letter and Comments
- Rule 1.1 (Competence): Comments only
- Rule 1.4 (Communication): Comments only

- Rule 1.6 (Confidentiality of Information): Black letter and Comments
- Rule 1.17 (Sale of Law Practice): Comments only
- Rule 1.18 (Duties to Prospective Client): Black letter and Comments
- Rule 4.4 (Respect for Rights of Third Parties): Black letter and Comments
- Rule 5.3 (Responsibilities Regarding Nonlawyer Assistants): Title and Comments
- Rule 5.5 (Unauthorized Practice of Law; Multijurisdictional Practice of Law): Comments only
- Rule 7.1 (Communications Concerning a Lawyer's Services): Comments only
- Rule 7.2 (Advertising): Comments only
- Rule 7.3 (Direct Contact with Prospective Clients): Title, Black letter, and Comments

In addition, the House of Delegates approved the Commission's recommendations to amend the ABA Model Rule on Admission by Motion and to create a new ABA Model Rule on Practice Pending Admission (see separate entries below). Separately, in October 2012 the Ethics 20/20 Commission decided to propose amendments to the ABA Model Rule for Registration of In-House Counsel and the ABA Model Rule on Pro Hac Vice Admission at the ABA's 2013 Mid-Year Meeting (see separate entries below).

More changes will be considered during 2013. In September 2012, the Ethics 20/20 Commission circulated two sets of draft proposals for public comment. Those proposals are as follows:

- Rule 1.5 (Fees): Comments only
- Rule 1.7 (Conflict of Interest: Current Clients): Black letter and Comments
- Rule 5.5 (Unauthorized Practice of Law; Multijurisdictional Practice of Law): Black letter and Comments
- Rule 8.5 (Disciplinary Authority; Choice of Law): Comments only

The Commission had not decided whether to file these proposals with the ABA House of Delegates for consideration at the ABA's February 2013 Mid-Year Meeting, but planned to make that decision at its October 25-26, 2012 meeting after considering the comments received in response to the drafts and engaging in further research and deliberations. We have not attempted to summarize the draft proposals or the supporting reports, but they are available online at *http://www.americanbar.org/groups/professional_responsibility/aba_commission_on_ethics_20_20.html*.

The Ethics 20/20 Commission also decided not to go forward with a proposal to amend Rule 5.4 to allow limited non-lawyer ownership of law firms, under specified circumstances. In December 2011, the Ethics 20/20 Commission circulated a "Discussion Paper on Alternative Law Practice Structures," and the Commission conducted informal hearings on the concept of non-lawyer ownership during the next few months. The concept, however, met with substantial resistance, and in April 2012, the Ethics 20/20 Commission abandoned the idea of proposing a change to the Rules on non-lawyer ownership. The Commission issued a statement saying, "Based on the Commission's extensive outreach, research, consultation and the response of the profession, there does not appear to be a sufficient basis for recommending a change to the ABA policy."

In the same statement, the Commission noted that it would continue to study a variety of choice of law issues associated with non-lawyer ownership. Thereafter, the Illinois State Bar Association and Senior Lawyers Division of the American Bar Association asked the ABA House of Delegates to adopt the following resolution (Resolution 10A):

> RESOLVED, That the American Bar Association reaffirms the following policy, adopted July 2000:
> The sharing of legal fees with non-lawyers and the ownership or control of the practice of law by non-lawyers are inconsistent with the core values of the legal profession. The law governing lawyers that prohibits lawyers from sharing legal fees with non-lawyers and from directly or indirectly transferring to non-lawyers ownership or control over entities practicing law should not be revised.

At the ABA's August 2012 Annual Meeting, the Resolution was "postponed indefinitely" by a vote of approximately 2-1.

On a separate track relating to the ABA Model Rules, the ABA Standing Committee on Ethics and Professionalism, and the ABA Standing Committee on Professional Responsibility have jointly circulated a proposed new Rule 5.1A obligating a firm to supervise lawyers more closely regarding contributions to judicial campaigns. Proposed ABA Model Rule 5.1A would provide as follows:

> Rule 5.1A *Responsibility of Partners, Managers, and Supervisory Lawyers Regarding Contributions to Judicial Campaigns*
> A lawyer who individually or together with other lawyers possesses managerial authority in a law firm shall institute procedures pursuant to which all lawyers and other employees in the firm report to the firm all financial and other support provided, directly or indirectly to any judge or judicial candidate running for election. Records of such reports shall be retained for at least [number] years.
> (1) The aggregate information compiled by the firm shall be reported to the agency, if any, designated by Court Rule.

An alternative Proposal for subparagraph (1) of Rule 5.1A would provide as follows:

> (1) When a lawyer appears before an elected judge, the lawyer shall inform the judge of the aggregate financial or other support the lawyer, the lawyer's firm, or other lawyers or employees in the firm have provided to the [most recent] election campaign of the judge.

For more background information, including related proposals to amend the ABA Model Code of Judicial Conduct, see the next entry.

ABA Model Code of Judicial Conduct: At the ABA's August 2011 Annual Meeting, the House of Delegates approved Resolution 107, which stated:

> [T]he Standing Committee on Ethics and Professional Responsibility and the Standing Committee on Professional Discipline should proceed on an expedited basis to consider what amendments, if any, should be made to the ABA Model Code of Judicial

Conduct or to the ABA Model Rules of Professional Conduct to provide necessary additional guidance to the states on disclosure requirements and standards for judicial disqualification.

In response to Resolution 107, in January 2012, the Standing Committee on Ethics and Professional Responsibility and the Committee on Professional Discipline jointly circulated for comment a package of proposals including proposed amendments to various advisory comments and a proposed new Model Supreme Court Rule on Maintenance of Records Regarding Contributions to Judicial Campaigns.

If adopted, the amendments would add seven new comments to Rule 2.11 explaining that a campaign contribution by itself does not warrant automatic disqualification. Instead, judges should evaluate the amended comments for further guidance on factors that might mandate disqualification. Under those factors, the dollar amount of a contribution is not as important as the significance of the contribution to the judge's campaign. The timeliness of a contribution is also a significant factor. A contribution made many years ago is less likely to cause the judge's disqualification than a recent contribution.

The comments also point out that financial contributions alone are not the only potential grounds for disqualification. Any "substantial support" could create a conflict and lead to disqualification. Substantial support is defined to include "assistance that a reasonable person would believe is intended to influence the election or defeat of a particular judicial candidate, such as fund-raising, letter-writing, emailing, assisting in telephone banks, managing (including directing or supporting the management of) a campaign, endorsing a judge's candidacy, getting-out-the-vote efforts, and other advocacy services."

The package of proposals relating to the Code of Judicial Conduct was the subject of a public hearing at the ABA's Mid-Year Meeting in New Orleans on February 3, 2012. For more background, see *ABA Groups Float New Disclosure Rule on Contributions to Judicial Campaigns*, 28 Law. Man. Prof. Conduct 20 (Jan. 4, 2012).

ABA Model Rule on Practice Pending Admission: At its August 2012 Annual Meeting, on the recommendation of the ABA Commission on Ethics 20/20, the ABA adopted a new Model Rule on Practice Pending Admission. The rule provides that a lawyer who holds an active license to practice law in another U.S. jurisdiction, and who has been engaged in the active practice of law for three of the last five years, "may provide legal services in this jurisdiction through an office or other systematic and continuous presence for no more than [365] days" (a time period each state can adjust), provided that the lawyer:

a. is not disbarred or suspended from practice in any jurisdiction and is not currently subject to discipline or a pending disciplinary matter in any jurisdiction;

b. has not previously been denied admission to practice in this jurisdiction or failed this jurisdiction's bar examination;

c. notifies Disciplinary Counsel and the Admissions Authority in writing prior to initiating practice in this jurisdiction that the lawyer will be doing so pursuant to the authority in this Rule;

d. submits within [45] days of first establishing an office or other systematic and continuous presence for the practice of law in this jurisdiction a complete application for admission by motion or by examination;

e. reasonably expects to fulfill all of this jurisdiction's requirements for that form of admission;

f. associates with a lawyer who is admitted to practice in this jurisdiction;

g. complies with Rules 7.1 and 7.5 of the Model Rules of Professional Conduct [or jurisdictional equivalent] in all communications with the public and clients regarding the nature and scope of the lawyer's practice authority in this jurisdiction; and

h. pays any annual client protection fund assessment.

According to Comment [1] to the new rule, the Model Rule on Practice Pending Admission "recognizes that a lawyer admitted in another jurisdiction may need to relocate to or commence practice in this jurisdiction, sometimes on short notice," but the admissions process can take "considerable time, thus placing a lawyer at risk of engaging in the unauthorized practice of law and leaving the lawyer's clients without the benefit of their chosen counsel." The new rule "closes this gap" by authorizing the lawyer to practice in the jurisdiction for "a limited period of time . . . while the lawyer diligently seeks admission." The full text of the Model Rule on Practice Pending Admission and the report submitted in support of the rule are available online at *http://www.abanow.org/2012/06/2012am105d.* (The same report recommended amendments to Rule 5.5 and its Comment, which the House of Delegates approved.)

ABA Model Rule on Admission by Motion: At its August 2012 Annual Meeting, on the recommendation of the ABA Commission on Ethics 20/20, the ABA amended the ABA Model Rule on Admission by Motion. The prior version of the rule (as amended in 2011) required that an applicant for admission on motion have been primarily engaged in the active practice of law in a state, territory, or D.C. for "five of the seven years" immediately preceding the application. The 2012 amendments shortened this to "three of the <u>five</u> years" immediately preceding the application. The amendments also added a clause stating that "in no event shall any activities that were performed pursuant to the Model Rule on Practice Pending Admission" be accepted toward the durational requirement. The Resolution accompanying the 2012 amendments "urges jurisdictions that have not adopted the Model Rule on Admission by Motion to do so, and urges jurisdictions that have adopted admission by motion procedures to eliminate any restrictions that do not appear in the Model Rule on Admission by Motion." The Model Rule on Admission by Motion (as amended in 2012) and the proposed resolution and report that led to the 2012 amendments are available online at *http://www.abanow.org/2012/06/2012am105e.*

ABA Model Rule for Registration of In-House Counsel: On September 4, 2012, after studying comments on earlier proposals, the ABA Ethics 20/20

Commission released revised proposals to amend the ABA Model Rule for Registration of In-House Counsel. The revised draft would permit in-house registration not only by U.S. lawyers but also by "a foreign lawyer, who is employed as a lawyer by an organization and has a continuous presence in this jurisdiction. . . ." The proposal defines a "foreign lawyer" for purposes of this Rule as "a member in good standing of a recognized legal profession in a foreign jurisdiction, the members of which are admitted to practice as lawyers or counselors at law or the equivalent and subject to effective regulation and discipline by a duly constituted professional body or a public authority." The proposal also provides that a foreign in-house lawyer shall not "provide advice on the law of this or another U.S. jurisdiction, other than international law, except in consultation with a U.S. lawyer authorized to provide such advice." The Commission decided at its October 25-26, 2012 meeting to bring the revised proposal (or something similar) before the ABA House of Delegates at its 2013 ABA Mid-Year Meeting.

ABA Model Rule on Pro Hac Vice Admission: On September 4, 2012, in response to public comments on earlier proposals, the ABA Ethics 20/20 Commission released revised proposals to amend the ABA Model Rule on Pro Hac Vice Admission. The revised proposals add limited authority for foreign lawyers to obtain admission pro hac vice, subject to two main conditions: (a) the foreign lawyer may only appear as a co-counsel, alongside a U.S. lawyer or in an advisory or consultative role in the proceeding; and (b) the U.S. lawyer is responsible to the court and the client for the conduct of the proceeding and for independently advising the client on the substantive law of a United States jurisdiction as well as procedural issues. The court may limit the activities of the foreign lawyer or require further action by the U.S. lawyer, such as requiring the U.S. lawyer to sign all pleadings and documents submitted to the court or to other parties, to be present at all depositions and conferences, and to attend all proceedings. The Commission decided at its October 25-26, 2012 meeting to bring the revised proposal (or something similar) before the ABA House of Delegates at its 2013 ABA Mid-Year Meeting.

ABA Model Rules for Fee Arbitration: The ABA's influential Model Rules for Fee Arbitration were amended in relatively minor ways at the ABA's February 2012 Mid-Year Meeting. For details, see *ABA Delegates Update Fee Arbitration Rules; Proposed Guidance on Experts Is Withdrawn*, 28 Law. Man. Prof. Conduct 97 (Feb. 15, 2012).

ABA Standards for Imposing Lawyer Sanctions: At the ABA's February 2012 Mid-Year Meeting, on the recommendation of the ABA Standing Committee on Discipline, the House of Delegates adopted a resolution (Resolution 107) reaffirming the black letter ABA Standards for Imposing Lawyer Sanctions (which were originally adopted in 1986 and amended in 1992), but rescinding the ABA's adoption of the Commentary to those Standards. The Commentary collected case summaries but did not provide guidance the way the Comments to the ABA Model Rules of Professional Conduct do.

The Standing Committee on Professional Discipline plans to replace the old Commentary with "Annotations," and will update the Annotations at regular intervals. The Standing Committee on Discipline also will undertake a comprehensive review of the black letter Sanctions Standards themselves to ensure their currency, and will then consider whether true Comments (such as those in the ABA Model Rules of Professional Conduct) should eventually be adopted.

ABA Resolution on Military Spouses Who Are Lawyers: At its February 2012 Mid-Year Meeting, the ABA House of Delegates approved a resolution (Resolution 108) urging states to allow military spouses to practice law without taking the bar exam as long as the spouse (i) "demonstrates presence in that jurisdiction due to a spouse's military service," (ii) is admitted in at least one U.S. jurisdiction, (iii) is in good standing (and not facing disciplinary charges) in all jurisdictions where admitted, (iv) pays the jurisdiction's annual client protection fund assessment, and (v) "complies with all other ethical, legal and continuing legal education obligations." The resolution was the brainchild of a relatively new organization (founded in June of 2011) called the Military JD Spouse Network, and was co-sponsored by the ABA Commission on Women in the Profession and more than a dozen other ABA entities. Admission by endorsement lasts only "while" the spouse is in the jurisdiction—the word "while" was added during the ABA meeting to make clear that admission by endorsement is temporary, not permanent—but the resolution recognizes that gaining admission via the bar exam route is costly, and may take so long that the JD spouse has to move again on military orders before obtaining admission via the bar exam. Resolution 108 and the supporting report are available online at *http://www.abanow.org/issue/?midyear-meeting-2012&view=hod.* (In April 2012, Idaho became the first state to adopt an admission rule tailored to military spouses. In June 2012, the New York State Bar Association House of Delegates recommended the military spouse provision to the Courts, but the Courts had not acted on it by our press deadline.)

ABA Resolution on Qualified Immunity: On January 17, 2012, the United States Supreme Court heard oral argument in *Filarsky v. Delia,* a case brought by a fireman against a private attorney who had been hired by a city in California to investigate the fireman's alleged wrongdoing. The Ninth Circuit had held that the defendant attorney was not entitled to qualified immunity because he was a private attorney, not a city employee. The ABA submitted an amicus brief advocating qualified immunity for the defendant lawyer. At the ABA's February 2012 Mid-Year Meeting, acting on a proposal by the Section on State and Local Government Law, the House of Delegates approved Resolution 302, which essentially summarized the ABA's amicus position. Resolution 302 provides as follows:

> RESOLVED, That the American Bar Association supports the principle that "private" lawyers representing governmental entities are entitled to claim the same qualified

immunity provided "government" lawyers from 42 U.S.C. Section 1983 claims when they are acting "under color of state law."

The report submitted in support of Resolution 302 argued that if outside counsel could not claim qualified immunity for actions taken under color of state law, then fewer attorneys would be willing to serve the public in these roles—and those who did serve might be chilled in their representation or charge higher fees to reflect the potential risks of liability. On April 17, 2012, in *Filarsky v. Delia,* 132 S. Ct. 1657 (2012), the Supreme Court reversed the Ninth Circuit and held that the defendant attorney was entitled to seek the protection of qualified immunity. The Court's opinion, which was consistent with the ABA's amicus brief, stated that qualified immunity for private lawyers protects the government's ability to perform its traditional functions by (i) "helping to avoid 'unwarranted timidity' in performance of public duties, (ii) ensuring that talented candidates are not deterred from public service, and (iii) preventing the harmful distractions from carrying out the work of government that can often accompany damages suits." Resolution 302 and the supporting report are available at *http://www.abanow.org/issue/?midyear-meeting-2012&view=hod.*

ABA Guidelines for Conduct of Experts Retained by Lawyers (rejected): In 2012, the ABA Section of Litigation sought but failed to gain ABA approval for a set of proposed Guidelines for Conduct of Experts Retained by Lawyers. The aim, according to the accompanying report, was to "to create uniform best practices of what lawyers should seek from experts who are retained by lawyers on behalf of their clients for litigated or contested matters." The Guidelines cover five aspects of lawyer-expert relationships: (i) integrity and professionalism; (ii) competence; (iii) confidentiality; (iv) avoiding conflicts of interest; and (v) avoiding contingent compensation. A resolution (Resolution 300) adopting the Guidelines was on the agenda for the ABA's February 2012 Mid-Year Meeting, but it was withdrawn before a vote to allow more time for other ABA entities to comment on them. After comments were received, the Guidelines were narrowed to cover only testifying experts (as opposed to consulting experts) and only civil matters (as opposed to criminal matters). At the ABA's August 2012 Annual Meeting, the House of Delegates voted not to adopt the revised Guidelines.

ABA Decision Not to Accredit Foreign Law Schools: During the ABA's August 2012 Annual Meeting, the ABA Council of Legal Education and Admissions to the Bar voted not to extend accreditation to law schools outside the United States. The question arose in 2008 when Peking University School of Transnational Law expressed an intention to pursue ABA accreditation. The ABA formed a committee to examine the issue, and in 2010 that committee recommended that the ABA seriously consider extending accreditation to some foreign schools. That recommendation was met with an uproar, so the ABA appointed a new committee, which reached the opposite conclusion, asserting that foreign accreditation would be expensive and difficult to administer. The ABA Council of Legal Education and Admissions to the Bar voted 15-0 (with two abstentions) to adopt the committee's recommendation not to accredit foreign law schools. For additional details, see Karen Sloan, *ABA Panel Votes 'No' on Accrediting Overseas Law Schools* (National Law Journal, Aug. 7, 2012), and Mark Hansen, *Legal Ed Section's Council Votes Not to Accredit Foreign Law Schools* (ABA Journal online, Aug 3, 2012).

Federal Statutes, Rules, and Regulations

Although the regulation of lawyers is primarily a matter of state law, Congress and federal rule makers and policy makers also sometimes regulate lawyers. This section reports on federal developments regarding the regulation of lawyers since our prior edition.

USPTO Time Limit for Filing Disciplinary Complaints Against Lawyers: The America Invents Act, which was signed into law by President Obama on September 16, 2011, requires that disciplinary proceedings relating to misconduct by lawyers who practice before the United States Patent and Trademark Office (USPTO) be commenced not later than the earlier of (i) 10 years after the date on which the misconduct occurred, or (ii) one year from the date on which the misconduct was made known to an officer or employee of the USPTO. To implement the America Invents Act, the USPTO adopted a new paragraph of 37 C.F.R. Part 11. The new paragraph, 37 C.F.R. §11.34(d), became effective on August 30, 2012. It provides as follows:

> (d) *Time for filing a complaint.* A complaint shall be filed within one year after the date on which the OED [Office of Enrollment and Discipline] Director receives a grievance forming the basis of the complaint. No complaint shall be filed more than ten years after the date on which the misconduct forming the basis for the proceeding occurred.

Proposed USPTO Rules of Professional Conduct: In October 2012, the U.S. Patent and Trademark Office (USPTO) issued for sixty days of public comment a notice of proposed rulemaking entitled "Changes to Representation of Others Before the United States Patent and Trademark Office." The proposed changes are intended to "align the USPTO's professional responsibility rules with those of most other U.S. jurisdictions" by replacing the current USPTO Code of Professional Responsibility (which was adopted in 1985, based on the ABA Model Code of Professional Responsibility) with a version of the ABA Model Rules. The new USPTO Rules of Professional Conduct would generally track the ABA Model Rules, but would omit provisions relating to domestic relations, criminal practice, and other matters irrelevant to patent practice, and would add some provisions specifically tailored to patent practice. For example, §11.106 (equivalent to ABA Model Rule 1.6) would amend subparagraph (b)(3) to permit disclosure necessary to "prevent, mitigate or rectify substantial injury to the financial interests or property of another that is reasonably certain to result or has resulted from the client's commission of a crime, fraud, *or inequitable conduct before the Office* [the USPTO] in furtherance of which the client has used the practitioner's services." (Emphasis added.)

The USPTO also proposes to revise the existing procedural rules governing disciplinary investigations and proceedings. The proposals are available online at *http://www.ofr.gov/OFRUpload/OFRData/2012-25355_PI.pdf.* For a thoughtful analysis of the proposed rules, see the Guest Post by Professor Lisa Dolak of Syracuse at *http://www.patentlyo.com/patent/2012/10/guest-post-new-uspto-proposed-ethics-rules-part-i.html.*

Proposed Fairness in Disclosure of Evidence Act of 2012: On March 15, 2012, Sen. Lisa Murkowski (R-Alaska) introduced a bill called the Fairness in Disclosure of Evidence Act of 2012 (S. 2197), which is a bill to "require the attorney for the Government to disclose favorable information to the defendant in criminal prosecutions brought by the United States, and for other purposes." The Act begins by defining the term "covered information" to mean all "information, data, documents, evidence, or objects that may reasonably appear to be favorable to the defendant in a criminal prosecution brought by the United States with respect to (A) the determination of guilt; (B) any preliminary matter before the court before which the criminal prosecution is pending; or (C) the sentence to be imposed." The heart of the bill says:

> (b) *Duty to Disclose Favorable Information*—In a criminal prosecution brought by the United States, the attorney for the Government shall provide to the defendant any covered information —
>> (1) that is within the possession, custody, or control of the prosecution team; or
>> (2) the existence of which is known, or by the exercise of due diligence would become known, to the attorney for the Government.
> (c) *Timing*—Except as provided in subsections (e) and (f), the attorney for the Government shall provide to the defendant any covered information —
>> (1) without delay after arraignment and before the entry of any guilty plea; and
>> (2) if the existence of the covered information is not known on the date of the initial disclosure under this subsection, as soon as is reasonably practicable upon the existence of the covered information becoming known, without regard to whether the defendant has entered or agreed to enter a guilty plea.

The bill was referred to the Senate Committee on the Judiciary, which held hearings on the bill in June 2012. For more information, see *Report on Lapses by Federal Prosecutors Spurs Calls for Reforms, New Legislation,* 28 Law. Man. Prof. Conduct 200 (March 28, 2012).

Proposed Consumer Financial Protection Board Rules: This item requires some background explanation. The Dodd-Frank Wall Street Reform and Consumer Protection Act established the Consumer Financial Protection Bureau (CFPB) as an independent agency within the Federal Reserve System. In 2011, the CFPB took over the authority to supervise banks with more than $10,000,000,000 (ten billion dollars) in assets. To carry out these supervisory responsibilities, the CFPB sometimes asks banks to provide information protected by the attorney-client privilege and/or attorney work product protection. Previous regulators (such as the FDIC) took the position that a supervised institution's submission of privileged information to its regulator would not waive any applicable privilege with respect to a third person. Congress codified that position in 2006 by amending the Federal Deposit Insurance Act (FDIC Act). The Dodd-Frank Act does not explicitly address whether banks waive the privilege by submitting privileged information to the CFPB, but Congress gave the CFPB all the powers and duties of the prior regulators, and Congress has delegated authority to the CFPB to "prescribe rules regarding the confidential treatment of information obtained from persons in connection with the exercise of its authorities under Federal consumer financial law."

In March 2012, the CFPB proposed a rule, to be codified at 12 CFR §1070.48, that would provide, in pertinent part, as follows:

> *§1070.48 Privileges not affected by disclosure to the CFPB.*
>
> *(a) In General.* The submission by any person of any information to the CFPB for any purpose in the course of any supervisory or regulatory process of the CFPB shall not be construed as waiving, destroying, or otherwise affecting any privilege such person may claim with respect to such information under Federal or State law as to any person or entity other than the CFPB.

The CFPB notes that the proposed rule is "substantively identical" to the statutory provisions that govern submission of privileged information to the FDIC and other financial regulators. However, in an April 12, 2012 comment letter, the ABA opposed the proposed rule on two grounds: (1) the CFPB lacks authority to demand privileged information; and (2) even if it has that authority, the proposed rule goes much further than existing rules because it applies not only to "depository institutions" such as banks and credit unions, but also to non-depository institutions such as payday lenders, private education lenders, debt collectors, and credit reporting companies. Instead, the ABA favors a legislative approach to the problem (see "Proposed Amendment to the FDIC Act" below).

A different CFPB rule will govern debt collection attorneys. In the "consumer debt collection market," the CFPB regulates "larger participants," defined as any "nonbank" person whose annual receipts from consumer debt collection exceed $10 million. On October 24, 2012, the CFPB issued a final rule defining the term "debt collector" to mean any person using interstate commerce or mail "in any business the principal purpose of which is the collection of any debts, or who regularly collects or attempts to collect . . . debts. . . ." This definition sweeps in all collection attorneys who collect more than $10 million annually. When read together with existing rules, the new rule empowers the CFPB to send field examiners to the offices of debt collection attorneys to review their procedures, evaluate their compliance with CFPB debt collection regulations, and identify risks to consumers. Objections to the proposed rule were filed by the American Bar Association, the Commercial Law League of America, and the National Association of Retail Collection Attorneys, who argued that federal regulation of attorneys was inappropriate and would interfere with state regulation. The CFPB expressly rejected those arguments. The final rule will be codified at §1090.105 (entitled "Consumer Debt Collection Market") and will take effect on January 2, 2013.

Proposed Amendment to the FDIC Act: H.R. 4014 would amend §18(x) of the FDIC Act in two ways: (a) it would specify that handing over privileged information to the CFPB during its examination process does not waive attorney-client privilege or attorney work product protection, and (b) it would expressly allow the CFPB to share that privileged information with other enumerated federal agencies without waiving the privilege as to third parties. The bill got off to a good start. In March 2012, the House of Representatives approved H.R. 4014 by unanimous consent (meaning without a roll call vote). But the consent route was blocked in the Senate when two unnamed senators objected to the Senate version of the bill (S. 3394) on grounds that other areas of the CFPB and the Dodd-Frank Act should be open for amendments as well. On April 12, 2012, the ABA wrote a letter supporting the legislative approach in H.R. 4014 rather than the CFPB's proposed rule on the same subject (see previous item). On September 20, 2012, ABA President Laurel Bellows wrote a letter supporting S. 3394, but Congress had not taken any further action by the time we went to press. See *Legislative Fix Urged as Best Solution for CFPB to Protect Privileged Materials*, 28 Law. Man. Prof. Conduct 259 (April 25, 2012); *Banks, Regulators Said to Be Near Crisis Point on Confidentiality*, 28 Law. Man. Prof. Conduct 611 (Sept. 26, 2012).

Proposed Amendments to FTC Disciplinary Rules: In the January 23, 2012 Federal Register, the Federal Trade Commission (FTC) published proposed rule changes for public comment. Many of the proposed changes address discovery problems created by the proliferation of electronically stored information (ESI). The introduction to the proposed changes summarizes some of the changes wrought by electronic discovery:

> Document discovery today is markedly different than it was only a decade ago. . . . [P]arties can no longer complete searches by merely looking in file cabinets and desk drawers. While searchers must still reach into file cabinets and desk drawers, they must also—and primarily—seek and retrieve information from mainframe computers, shared servers, computers, cell phones, smart phones, portable devices, and other media, as well as from third-party service providers. Third, because ESI is broadly dispersed and not always consistently organized by its custodians, searches, identification, and collection all require special skills and, if done properly, may utilize one or more search tools such as advanced key word searches, Boolean connectors, Bayesian logic, concept searches, predictive coding, and other advanced analytics. Fourth, because ESI may be readily altered, it must be preserved early in any discovery process—or even before discovery, when litigation is anticipated—and handled carefully at all stages to preserve its accuracy, authenticity, and ultimate admissibility. Fifth, even when

investigations are conducted cooperatively, and are both well organized and well managed, there remains a substantial risk that mistakes and delays will occur. . . .

These problems are causing delays in the FTC's ability to secure the information it needs to complete its investigations. To combat this delay, the FTC proposes changes to Part 2 of its Rules of Practice. The changes would expedite Commission investigations by "(1) Conditioning any extensions of time to comply with Commission processes on a party's continued progress in achieving compliance" and by "(2) conditioning the filing of any petition to quash or limit Commission process on a party having engaged in meaningful 'meet and confer' sessions with Commission staff. . . ."

In addition, changes to FTC Rule of Practice 4.1(e) would authorize the FTC to take disciplinary action if an attorney engages in conduct that is "contemptuous, obstructionist, or violates appropriate standards of professional conduct," or if the attorney "knowingly or recklessly provides false or misleading information" to the FTC or its staff. For details, see *FTC Floats Changes to Disciplinary Rules for Attorneys Who Practice Before Agency*, 28 Law. Man. Prof. Conduct 67 (Feb. 1, 2012).

Bankruptcy Fee Guidelines: In 1996, pursuant to 28 U.S.C. §586, the United States Trustee Program (USTP) promulgated Guidelines for Reviewing Applications for Compensation and Reimbursement of Expenses filed under 11 U.S.C. §330 (the "1996 guidelines"). The 1996 guidelines are statements of policy that the USTP follows when reviewing applications for compensation. In an effort to control steep fee increases in bankruptcy cases, the USTP is revising the 1996 guidelines in phases.

On November 4, 2011, the USTP posted for public comment proposed guidelines for reviewing applications for attorney compensation in "larger" Chapter 11 cases (*i.e.*, more than $50 million in combined assets and liabilities). The comment period on the proposed guidelines initially ended on January 31, 2012, but because of harsh criticism, the USTP opened a second comment period in April and May 2012, and conducted a public meeting on June 4, 2012. When we went to press, the USTP was still considering the proposed guidelines.

The proposed guidelines, together with all public comments, are available online at *http://www.justice.gov/ust/eo/rules_regulations/index.htm*. Until the USTP adopts superseding guidelines, the 1996 guidelines will continue in effect for the review of applications filed under 11 U.S.C. §330 in (1) larger Chapter 11 cases by non-attorneys seeking compensation, (2) all Chapter 11 cases below the $50 million threshold, and (3) cases under other chapters of the Bankruptcy Code. The 1996 guidelines are reprinted in an Appendix to 28 C.F.R. Part 58 and are available online at *http://www.justice.gov/ust/eo/rules_regulations/guidelines/docs/feeguide.htm*.

Proposed Federal Reserve Board Requirement on Reporting Litigation Reserves: On February 22, 2012, the Federal Reserve Board proposed changes to the Comprehensive Capital Analysis and Review (CCAR) schedules governing data collection from large bank holding companies. Among other things, the Federal Reserve Board proposed requiring bank holding companies to report the capital reserves they have set aside for pending litigation (see 77 FR 10525). Some banks expressed concern that the information on litigation reserves would become public.

On June 4, 2012, the Federal Reserve approved most of the proposed changes, but it delayed final action on requiring banks to report capital reserves for litigation, instead extending the time for public comment. On July 31, the ABA President wrote a letter opposing the proposal. The letter expressed concern that lawyers and their bank clients "may lose confidence that their private communications and the lawyers' professional analysis, judgment, and advice will remain confidential," and noted that requiring banks to report their litigation reserves "could harm the banks' position in litigation by informing their adversaries of how the banks and their lawyers weigh the strengths and weaknesses of the subject claims." When we went to press, the Federal Reserve's proposal was still pending.

Financial Accounting Standards Board: The Financial Accounting Standards Board (FASB) is a private body whose accounting standards are officially recognized by the Securities and Exchange Commission. One set of FASB standards, Accounting Standards Codification 450, entitled "Disclosures of Certain Loss Contingencies" ("Topic 450"), requires public companies to determine whether losses that may be incurred in anticipated or pending litigation are "probable," "reasonably possible," or "remote." Since these classifications provide little information, in 2008, the FASB embarked on a project to expand the disclosures required in Topic 450 to assist users in assessing the likelihood, timing, and amount of future cashflows associated with loss contingencies, including litigation. However, vigorous opposition to the FASB's 2008 and 2010 "exposure drafts"—including strong criticism from the ABA based on confidentiality concerns—led the FASB to abandon the project in July 2012. For details, see *http://www.fasb.org/cs/ContentServer? site=FASB&c=FASBContent_C&pagename=FASB%2FFASBContent_C%2FProject UpdatePage&cid=900000011071.*

DEVELOPMENTS IN THE STATES

Broad Trends in the States

Before discussing individual jurisdictions, we will discuss broad trends in the states. This data is available due to the invaluable work of the ABA Center for Professional Responsibility (CPR), the national nerve center for professional responsibility issues, which keeps track of federal, state, and ABA developments regarding professional responsibility. The Center's unmatched website, which links to current and historical resources about the ABA Model Rules of Professional Conduct and other regulatory models, is available at *http://www.americanbar.org/groups/professional_responsibility. html.*

Of particular interest for our readers is the CPR's Policy Implementation Committee, which promotes ABA policies to the bar and the public, assists jurisdictions in reviewing and implementing policies adopted by the ABA, and maintains a national clearinghouse of information on efforts to implement ABA policies. The website of the Policy Implementation Committee contains legislative history and up-to-date charts regarding state-by-state implementation of (a) the ABA Model Rules of Professional Conduct, (b) the policies of the ABA Multijurisdictional Practice Commission, (c) the August 2010 version of the ABA Model Code of Judicial Conduct, (d) the ABA Model Court Rule on Insurance Disclosure, (e) the ABA Model Court Rule on Provision of Legal Services Following Determination of Major Disaster (the "Katrina Rule" or "Major Disaster Rule"), and (f) the ABA Model Rule for Registration of In-House Counsel. The Policy Implementation Committee's fabulous website is available at *http://www.americanbar.org/groups/professional_ responsibility/policy.html.*

"Ethics 2000" reviews: Nationally, since the ABA Ethics 2000 Commission released its final report in 2001, nearly all states have studied and reacted to the work of the ABA Ethics 2000 Commission. Specifically:

- forty-seven (47) U.S. jurisdictions have significantly revised their Rules of Professional Conduct (AK, AL, AR, AZ, CO, CT, DE, DC, FL, GA, IA, ID, IL, IN, KS, KY, LA, MA, MD, ME, MI, MN, MO, MS, MT, NE, NC, ND, NH, NJ, NM, NY, NV, OH, OK, OR, PA, RI, SC, SD, TN, UT, VA, VT, WA, WI, WY);
- three (3) states have circulated proposed rules that remain pending (CA, HI, WV);
- one (1) state has voted in a statewide referendum to reject revised rules (TX).

For a state-by-state chart providing links to primary sources for these data, see *http://www.americanbar.org/content/dam/aba/migrated/cpr/pic/ethics_2000_ status_chart.authcheckdam.pdf.* In addition, states continue to revise their rules a few at a time. For example, Georgia amended a number of rules effective November 2011 (shortly after the press deadline for our 2012 edition).

Comments to the ABA Model Rules of Professional Conduct: With respect to adopting the Comments to the ABA Model Rules, the state high courts fall into three basic categories.

- *Category No. 1:* About forty (40) jurisdictions have formally adopted the Comments as part of their Rules of Professional Conduct, but all such jurisdictions have added a proviso: "The Comments are intended as guides to interpretation, but the text of each rule is authoritative," or similar words.
- *Category No. 2:* Four (4) state high courts (ME, MI, MN, NH) have authorized publication of the Comments as an "aid to understanding of the rules" or "as an aid to the reader" or "for convenience" but have not adopted the Comments.
- *Category No. 3:* Six (6) states (LA, MT, NV, NJ, NY, OR) have adopted the Rules of Professional Conduct without any Comments (but in Louisiana the State

Bar publishes the ABA Comments with the black letter Rules, and in New York the State Bar has adopted the Comments as "guides to interpretation").

For a state-by-state chart providing a more detailed analysis and links to primary sources for these data, see *http://www.americanbar.org/content/dam/aba/ migrated/cpr/pic/comments.authcheckdam.pdf.*

Malpractice Insurance Disclosure Rules: In 2004, when only a few states required lawyers to disclose their malpractice insurance coverage, the ABA adopted a Model Court Rule on Insurance Disclosure. Today, at least 24 states require some form of malpractice insurance disclosure. To be specific, eighteen (18) jurisdictions require disclosure on their bar registration statements (AZ, CO, DE, HI, ID, IL, KS, MA, MI, MN, NE, NV, NM, ND, RI, VA, WA, WV), while seven (7) states require disclosure directly to clients (AK, CA, NH, NM, OH, PA, SD). (NM is listed in both categories because it requires disclosure on the bar registration statement *and* directly to clients, so the total of those two categories is 24, not 25.) At least five additional states (ME, NY, SC, UT, VT) are considering some form of legal malpractice disclosure rule. However, five states (AR, CT, FL, KY, TX) have rejected the ABA Model Court Rule on Insurance Disclosure, and one state (NC) formerly required insurance disclosure but dropped the requirement effective January 1, 2010. Only one state (OR) requires lawyers to carry legal malpractice insurance. For a state-by-state chart, visit the ABA Policy Implementation Committee's website available at *http://www.americanbar.org/content/dam/aba/administrative/professional_responsibility/malprac_disc_chart.authcheckdam.pdf.*

Multijurisdictional Practice Rules: Forty-four (44) U.S. jurisdictions have adopted a multijurisdictional practice rule similar or identical to ABA Model Rule 5.5 (Unauthorized Practice of Law; Multijurisdictional Practice of Law). A proposal to adopt a version of Rule 5.5 is pending before the Mississippi Supreme Court, and proposed court rules closely modeled on ABA Model Rule 5.5 were approved by the New York State Bar Association's House of Delegates at its June 2012 Annual Meeting and are pending before New York's courts. For a state-by-state chart regarding the adoption of ABA Model Rule 5.5, see *http://www.americanbar.org/content/dam/aba/administrative/professional_responsibility/quick_guide_5_5.authcheckdam.pdf.*

In-House Counsel Registration Rules: Thirty-four (34) states have adopted some form of in-house registration rule. (An in-house registration rule authorizes in-house lawyers who are in good standing in at least one U.S. jurisdiction to engage in the practice of law without being fully admitted to the bar of the state where they work, subject to certain conditions.) Some other states have not adopted the ABA in-house registration rule but have adopted ABA Model Rule 5.5(d)(1) or other rules or policies that allow in-house lawyers to practice without being admitted. The ABA adopted the ABA Model Rule for Registration of In-House Counsel in August of 2008. (Some states adopted in-house registration rules before the ABA acted.) The most recent jurisdiction to adopt an in-house registration rule is New

York, which adopted its own unique version effective April 20, 2011. For a state-by-state chart, see *http://www.americanbar.org/content/dam/aba/administrative/professional_responsibility/in_house_rules.authcheckdam.pdf.*

Major Disaster ("Katrina") Rule: In 2007, to respond to unauthorized practice problems caused by the dislocation of lawyers and clients after Hurricane Katrina, the ABA adopted the so-called "Katrina Rule" or "Major Disaster Rule" (formally known as the Model Court Rule on Provision of Legal Services Following Determination of Major Disaster). In the same year, the Conference of Chief Justices adopted a resolution that "commends" the ABA Major Disaster Rule as the "foundation" upon which to create a rule regarding the provision of legal services following of major disaster. Where adopted, the Katrina Rule authorizes out-of-state lawyers to provide pro bono services in a stricken state, and allows lawyers from the stricken state to carry on their home state practices in jurisdictions that have adopted the Katrina Rule. To date, states have reacted to the Major Disaster Rule as follows:

- sixteen (16) U.S. jurisdictions have adopted the rule (AZ, CO, DE, IA, IL, LA, MN, MO, NH, NJ, NY, ND, OR, TN, WA, WI);
- fourteen (14) jurisdictions are considering the rule (CA, DC, GA, HI, MD, MA, MS, MT, NE, OK, TX, VT, VA, WV);
- seven (7) states have expressly decided to *not* adopt it (FL, MI, NC, OH, PA, UT, WY);
- one (1) jurisdiction seems "unlikely" to adopt it (AL).

The most recent state to act is Florida. The Florida State Bar recommended the rule, but on April 12, 2012, the Florida Supreme Court rejected it for unspecified reasons—see Florida entry below. For a state-by-state chart showing each jurisdiction's reaction to the Katrina/Major Disaster rule, visit *http://www.americanbar.org/content/dam/aba/administrative/professional_responsibility/katrina_chart.authcheckdam.pdf.*

Developments in Particular States

For detailed information about developments in particular jurisdictions, visit the websites given after each jurisdiction listed below, or click on a link to individual state resources available at *http://www.americanbar.org/groups/professional_responsibility/resources/links_of_interest.html.* The following items describe some of the more interesting developments in particular states since the press deadline for our 2012 edition.

Alabama (www.alabar.org): Effective March 26, 2012, the Alabama Supreme Court amended the Alabama Rules of Civil Procedure and the Alabama Rules of Professional Conduct to establish procedures for limited scope representation, often called "unbundling" but referred to in Alabama as LSR. The State Bar notes that LSR has always been permissible under Rule of Professional Conduct 1.2 but has been little used in Alabama because the state had not adopted procedures explaining how a lawyer should operate when engaging in unbundled representation. The new rules, which were drafted by the State Bar's Pro Bono Committee, regulate and codify how LSR should take place. The State Bar's website paints the following candid (and probably accurate) picture of how the new LSR rules may affect lawyers and middle class clients:

> The new LSR rule changes also provide an opportunity to expand your law practice. In other states which have adopted LSR rules, lawyers have profitably marketed a LSR practice to potential middle-income clients who would otherwise not be able to pay full freight. This is especially true in the area of family law, where motions regarding child support, visitation, and custody are suitable for both in-court and out-of-court limited scope representation. Under the new ACRP 87, *you can provide in-court LSR without fear of getting trapped in a case beyond the scope of your agreement with the client.* [Emphasis added.]

The amended rules and the Alabama State Bar's helpful summaries of the amended rules are available online at *http://www.alabar.org/media/03272012_LimitedScopeRepresentationRules.cfm.*

California (www.calbar.ca.gov, www.courtinfo.ca.gov, and www.leginfo. ca.gov): Since 2002, California's Commission for the Revision of the Rules of Professional Conduct has been studying ways to revise and update California's rules, which are the last rules in the country not based on the ABA Model Rules of Professional Conduct. On July 20, 2011, the State Bar submitted an initial group of six proposed Rules of Professional Conduct to the California Supreme Court for approval (Rule 1.0 and Rules 7.1-7.5). The original plan was for the State Bar to follow up with two or three additional groups of submissions until the full complement of recommended rules were before the Supreme Court, but on October 28, 2011, the California Supreme Court issued an order, requested by the State Bar, withdrawing the initial submission.

In October 2012, the State Bar filed a new submission with the Supreme Court consisting of only two provisions, Rule 1.1 (Competence) and Rule 1.8.10 (Sexual Relations with Client). A major purpose of this initial submission is to determine whether the format and content of the submission provide the Supreme Court with the kinds of information the court will need to make an informed decision on each proposed rule. After the State Bar receives the Supreme Court's feedback on the initial submission, it will most likely submit the remaining rules in stages, a few at a time, grouped by topic (e.g., conflicts, advertising). However, the decision to submit the proposed rules in stages is subject to change, and the State Bar could still decide to submit all of the proposed new rules in a single comprehensive petition. If the State Bar decides to submit all of the rules in a single petition, that petition is not expected to be filed until sometime in the summer of 2013. For more information, including links to 67 draft rules proposed in 2010, visit *http://ethics.calbar.ca.gov/Committees/RulesCommission/ProposedRulesofProfessionalConduct.aspx.*

Separately, on April 9, 2012, the California State Bar voted to appoint a 21-member Task Force on Admissions Regulation Reform (which includes three law professors) to consider whether to add a "practical skills" requirement—such as a law school clinic or externship—as a condition of admission to the California Bar. The task force is studying six broad questions: (i) should the state require preadmission training; (ii) if so, how much training should be required, and for how long; (iii) what kinds of skills training would improve the competence level of new lawyers; (iv) should the state require a uniform practical skills curriculum, or instead permit a variety of skills training; (v) how do the costs of such a mandate compare to the benefits; and (vi) how will a practical skills mandate affect the costs and availability of legal services in California? The task force will also examine regulations that would require California's accredited law schools to publish post-graduation employment data, and will consider whether bar admission should be limited to graduates of law schools accredited by California or the ABA. (Currently, a graduate of any law school—including California's many unaccredited proprietary law schools—can take the California Bar exam.) The task force is due to issue a final report on December 31, 2013. For more information, visit *http://www.calbar.ca.gov/AboutUs/BoardofTrustees/TaskForceonAdmissionsRegulationReform.aspx.*

Florida (www.flabar.org and www.floridasupremecourt.org): On April 12, 2012, the Florida Supreme Court approved an amendment to Florida Rule 8.3 that will exempt a lawyer from making a mandatory report about another lawyer's professional misconduct if the information was "gained by a lawyer while serving as a mediator or mediation participant." The amendment, which will create a new Rule 8.3(c)(2), took effect on July 1, 2012. The court also accepted the bar's proposals to revamp rules governing lawyer trust funds (which are governed not only by Rule 1.15 but also by a separate set of court rules).

However, the court also rejected two proposed amendments to the Florida Rules of Professional Conduct. One of the rejected amendments would have allowed lawyers in contingent fee cases to send clients to outside counsel for lien resolution services even though the combined fees of the personal injury (p.i.) lawyer and the lien resolution lawyer would exceed the mandatory cap on the contingent fees in p.i. cases. The Bar thought this was important because liens are increasingly complex and many p.i. lawyers do not have the necessary expertise. The other rejected amendment would have prohibited lawyers from allowing nonlawyers to sign checks drawn on trust accounts. The court apparently thought this would impose too big a burden on sole practitioners. (Two judges dissented and would have adopted the proposed rule.)

Outside the Rules of Professional Conduct, the court rejected the Bar's recommendation to adopt the ABA's Katrina/Major Disaster Rule that would have allowed lawyers from other jurisdictions to practice temporarily in Florida following a natural disaster. The court said simply: "Because we have concerns about how this rule would apply, we decline to adopt it." One Justice dissented and would have adopted the rule. For details, see *Rule Changes Adopted in Sunshine State, Sans Key Proposals Backed by Florida Bar*, 28 Law. Man. Prof. Conduct 256 (April 25, 2012).

The Florida Supreme Court is also currently considering proposed amendments to Florida's advertising rules. On July 5, 2011, the Florida Bar petitioned the court to approve comprehensive changes to Florida's rules governing lawyer advertising. The titles of the proposed rules are completely different from the titles of the ABA Model Rules governing lawyer advertising—and Florida would have thirteen separate rules on advertising, more than twice as many as in the ABA Model Rules. By February of 2012, the Bar had developed revised proposals for Rules 4-7.3 (Deceptive and Inherently Misleading Advertisements), 4-7.4 (Potentially Misleading Advertisements), and 4-7.5 (Unduly Manipulative or Intrusive Advertisements) that would prohibit the use of an "authority figure" in lawyer advertising. The term "authority figures" is not defined in the text, but the Comment to Rule 4-7.3 refers to "an authority figure such as a judge or law enforcement officer. . . ." Public comments were due by May 1st and the court gave the Bar until May 22nd to respond to the comments.

In the courts, the Florida Bar has lost a First Amendment challenge to various provisions of Florida's lawyer advertising rules. A few years ago, the Florida Bar won summary judgment in federal district court, but in *Harrell v. the Florida Bar*, 608 F.3d 1241 (11th Cir. 2010), the Eleventh Circuit reversed and remanded. On remand, the district court held that Rule 4-7.2(c)(3) (manipulative descriptions or portrayals), Rule 4-7.5(b)(1)(A) (manipulative features in TV and radio ads), and the Comment to Rule 4-7.1 (which says that advertisements should provide only useful, factual information) are unconstitutionally vague on their face, and held that Rule 4-7.5(b)(1)(C) (prohibiting TV and radio ads with any background sound other than instrumental music) and Rule 4-7.2(c)(2) (which the Bar said prohibited use of the statement "Don't Settle for Less Than You Deserve" in plaintiffs' advertisements) were unconstitutional as applied to plaintiffs.

Finally, the Florida Supreme Court's Commission on Professionalism has circulated for public comment a set of rules for resolving "professionalism complaints." The commission conducted a public hearing on the proposals at the Florida Bar Annual Convention June 21, 2012.

For up-to-date information and commentary on developments in Florida, see *www.sunethics.com*, which is maintained by former Florida Bar counsel Tim Chinaris, and hosted by Faulkner University, Thomas Goode Jones School of Law.

Georgia (*www.gabar.org*): On November 3, 2011, effective immediately, the Georgia Supreme Court amended many of the Georgia Rules of Professional Conduct. Although the State Bar of Georgia developed the amendments to bring Georgia's rules more closely into line with the ABA Model Rules, Georgia did not adopt many of the key changes in the ABA Model Rules over the past decade. For example, Georgia declined to adopt ABA Model Rules 1.8(j) (sexual relations with clients), 1.18 (prospective clients), 6.5 (limited legal services programs), or 7.6 (pay-to-play). Nor did Georgia adopt the screening amendments to ABA Model Rule 1.10(a).

However, Georgia adopted an interesting new Rule 9.2 that prohibits any agreement "that prohibits or restricts a person from filing a disciplinary complaint, or that requires the person to request dismissal of a pending disciplinary complaint." The full text of the amended rules is online at *http:// www.gabar.org/barrules/georgia-rules-of-professional-conduct.cfm.* For a helpful summary of the changes, see *Georgia Opts for Highly Selective Approach in Choosing Model Rule Updates to Borrow,* 28 Law. Man. Prof. Conduct 66 (Feb. 1, 2012).

Hawaii (www.hsba.org): In 2011, the Hawaii Supreme Court's Disciplinary Board proposed comprehensive amendments to the Hawaii Rules of Professional Conduct and sent them to the Supreme Court for its review. The Supreme Court allowed the State Bar and the Disciplinary Board to post the proposals for public comment. The comment period ended on October 31, 2011, and the proposals remain pending before the Supreme Court. The proposed rules and an executive summary are available at *http:// www.hsba.org/Hawaii_Rules_of_Professional_Conduct.aspx.*

Idaho (isb.idaho.gov): Effective July 1, 2012, a new Idaho rule entitled "Military Spouse Provisional Admission" will enable military spouses to obtain a provisional license to practice law in the state, under the supervision and direction of local counsel, for up to one year (renewable upon application), without taking the Idaho bar exam and without meeting an experience requirement. The new provision, Rule 229 of the Idaho Bar Commission Rules Governing Admission to Practice and Membership in the Idaho State Bar, is consistent with the resolution adopted by the ABA at its February 2012 Mid-Year Meeting (see entry above in the section on ABA Developments). Idaho is the first jurisdiction in the country to adopt a rule expressly governing bar admission for military spouses.

Maine: Effective January 1, 2012, the Maine Supreme Court amended Rules 1.15, 1.16, and 3.1 of the Maine Rules of Professional Conduct. The amendments to Rules 1.15 and 1.16 are relatively minor, but the amendment to 3.1 adds a new paragraph (b) that provides as follows: "A lawyer shall not report or threaten to report misconduct to a criminal, administrative or disciplinary authority solely to obtain an advantage in a civil matter." The Advisory Notes point out that former Maine Bar Rule 3.6(c) provided that a lawyer "shall not present, or threaten to present, criminal, administrative, or disciplinary charges solely to obtain an advantage in a civil matter," and pointed out that the ABA Model Rules of Professional Conduct do not directly prohibit that conduct. New Rule 3.1(b) "gives expression to the continuing prohibition," but also "clarifies that prosecutors may engage in good faith negotiations to resolve multiple related matters." The amended rules and the helpful Advisory Notes are online at *http://www.courts.state.me.us/ rules_adminorders/rules/comments_nov11/ProflCondProposedAmendJan2012.pdf.*

Michigan (www.michbar.org): On December 8, 2011, the Michigan Supreme Court closed the file on proposed changes to Rule 7.3 of the Michigan Rules of Professional Conduct that (i) would have imposed a 30-day prohibition on targeted written solicitations following an injury, death, or accident, and (ii) would have required the labeling of letters and circulars, whether targeted or non-targeted, as advertising material. The order closing the file, the proposed changes that were not adopted, and the Bar's comments on the dead proposal are all available via links on the Bar's website.

During the same week, the Supreme Court published for comment other proposed changes to Rule 7.3 of the Michigan Rules of Professional Conduct that would impose a 14-day ban on contacting or soliciting parties in a family law case, measured from the earlier of the date of filing or date of service. The comment period expired on March 1, 2012. The court is still considering the comments.

Additional proposed changes to the Michigan Rules of Professional Conduct, which the Michigan Supreme Court circulated for public comment way back on March 22, 2011, apparently are still pending. Language that protects clients would be moved from the Comments to the black letter text. The comment deadline was July 1, 2011. The language that would be moved to the black letter text does not appear in the text of the ABA Model Rules of Professional Conduct. A redlined version of the proposed amendments is available at *http://op.bna.com/mopc.nsf/r?Open=kswn-8fdrak.*

New Hampshire (www.nhbar.org): On January 25, 2012, effective immediately, the New Hampshire Supreme Court added a new Rule 1.10(c), which provides that screening of lateral lawyers can resolve conflicts that might otherwise arise due to the lateral attorney's possession of confidential information regarding clients at the lateral's former firm. The Ethics Committee Note points out that N.H. Rule 1.10(c) "differs from the ABA Model Rule, and draws on more restrictive procedures that have been adopted in Massachusetts and Oregon." In particular, under the N.H. version, screening will not cure conflicts for migrating lawyers "who had substantial involvement in, or acquired substantial material information about, a matter ongoing at the time of the transfer between firms." Also, N.H. Rule 1.10(c) requires that "separate affidavits be prepared by the personally disqualified attorney and by a partner, officer or shareholder of the new firm." The full text of the amended rule is available at *http://www.courts.state.nh.us/rules/pcon/pcon-1_10.htm.*

New Jersey (www.judiciary.state.nj.us/rules/apprpc.htm): On February 3, 2012, the New Jersey Supreme Court circulated for public comment various proposed rule changes developed by the court's Professional Responsibility Rules Committee (PRRC). One proposal would amend N.J. Court Rule 1:21-1, which now requires a lawyer to maintain a bona fide office somewhere in the United States. The amended rule would allow lawyers to practice in New Jersey without maintaining a traditional brick-and-mortar office, but would require them to designate a "fixed, physical location" in New Jersey for service, hand deliveries, and file inspection. These requirements would also apply to out-of-state lawyers engaging in multijurisdictional practice in New Jersey. A related amendment would tighten the rule that allows out-of-state lawyers to practice in the state by associating with a New Jersey attorney.

A proposed amendment to Rule 1.6 would allow lawyers to reveal a client's intent to commit suicide. Two other proposals relate to judges. One would forbid law firms to make political contributions from the firm's business account while a municipal court judge is associated with the firm. The other would prohibit a lawyer from contacting a judge to discuss the judge's post-retirement employment while the judge is personally participating in a case in which the lawyer or anyone in the lawyer's firm is involved.

The PRRC also recommended that the court set up a task force to study whether New Jersey should amend its ethics rule on aggregate settlements to authorize clients to give advance consent to settlement by majority vote. (Six years ago, the New Jersey Supreme Court held that the state's current lawyer conduct rules do not permit this.)

Written comments on the proposed changes were due by April 2, 2012. The court said it would act on the recommendations during the summer of 2012 and that any resulting amendments would take effect on September 1, 2012. For additional details, see *New Jersey Seeks Comment on Proposals to Allow Virtual Offices, Close MJP Loophole*, 28 Law. Man. Prof. Conduct 131 (Feb. 29, 2012).

Regarding legislation, on January 17, 2012, Governor Chris Christie signed a bill (A1050) intended to deter the unauthorized practice of law (UPL). The bill upgrades penalties for engaging in UPL (*e.g.*, from a disorderly persons offense to a fourth degree crime) and creates a civil cause of action for UPL for victims of UPL who incur damages. However, Gov. Christie also pocket-vetoed a tough anti-solicitation bill. The bill, which was backed by the New Jersey Association for Justice, would have criminalized solicitation of people identified in motor vehicle accident reports within 30 days following the accident. It would also have made immediate written solicitation a prohibited form of contact under N.J. Stat. §2C:40A-4, a 1999 law that already makes it a crime for lawyers and other professionals to solicit accident victims in person, by telephone, or electronically for 30 days after an accident. For additional details about the legislation, see *Unauthorized Practice New Jersey Legislation Stiffens UPL Laws, But Solicitation Bill Dies on Governor's Desk*, 28 Law. Man. Prof. Conduct 65 (Feb. 1, 2012).

Some older proposals remain under consideration. On April 6, 2011, the New Jersey Supreme Court circulated a notice to the bar seeking comments on a proposal to add the following new sentence to Rule 7.5: "Use of a trade name shall be permissible so long as it describes the nature of the firm's legal practice in terms that are accurate, descriptive, and informative, but not misleading, comparative, unprofessional, or suggestive of the ability to obtain results. Such trade names should be accompanied by the name of the attorney who is responsible for the management of the organization." A proposed new paragraph in the Comment to Rule 7.5 would provide the Bar with illustrative examples of acceptable and unacceptable trade names. Comments were due by May 6, 2011. A red-lined version of the proposal is available at *http://www.judiciary.state.nj.us/ notices/2011/n110408a.pdf.*

Also apparently still pending is a proposed new Advertising Guideline that would prohibit an attorney or law firm from including, on a website or other advertisement, "a quotation from a judge or court opinion (oral or written) regarding the attorney's abilities or legal services." The New Jersey Supreme Court's Committee on Attorney Advertising proposed the new Guideline after reviewing an attorney's website that included two quotations from unpublished judicial opinions praising the attorney's legal abilities.

New York (www.nysba.org and www.courts.state.ny.us): Effective July 1, 2012, the New York Courts amended Rule 3.8 (Special Responsibilities of Prosecutors and Other Government Lawyers) by adding two new paragraphs that impose duties on a prosecutor who "knows of new, credible and material evidence creating a reasonable likelihood that a convicted defendant did not commit an offense of which the defendant was convicted," or who "knows of clear and convincing evidence establishing that a defendant was convicted, in a prosecution by the prosecutor's office, of an offense that the defendant did not commit. . . ." The two new paragraphs are generally modeled on ABA Model Rule 3.8(g)-(h), but there are some differences. New York also added a third new paragraph, taken verbatim from Comment [9] to Rule 3.8, that provides as follows: "A prosecutor's independent judgment, made in good faith, that the new evidence is not of such nature as to trigger the obligations of [the new paragraphs], though subsequently determined to have been erroneous, does not constitute a violation of this rule." The amended version of Rule 3.8 was the outgrowth of many years of work by the New York City Bar Association, especially Professors Bruce Green of Fordham and Ellen Yaroshefsky of Cardozo. The version ultimately adopted in New York was the product of lengthy negotiations between the City Bar and state and federal prosecutors throughout New York.

Also effective July 1, 2012 is a technical amendment to New York Rule 1.2(g), a throwback to the old Code of Professional Responsibility that has no ABA counterpart.

The Courts also approved amendment to New York Rule 4.2 that the State Bar House of Delegates approved at its January 2012 meeting. The proposal would essentially codify N.Y. State Bar Ethics Op. 879 (2011), which said that lawyer-litigants—whether pro se or represented by counsel—must abide by Rule 4.2 when communicating with an adverse party who the lawyer knows to be represented by counsel. The Courts were expected to issue an Order making the change official in November 2012.

In June 2012, the New York State Bar House of Delegates approved proposed new court rules that would permit temporary law practice by out-of-state lawyers. The language of the proposed rules is modeled closely on ABA Model Rule 5.5, but includes some enhancements, such as a provision allowing temporary practice while an application for full admission to the New

York bar is pending. The State Bar has forwarded the proposed rules to the Courts for consideration, but the rules will not take effect unless the Courts approve them. The Courts rejected similar proposals in 2003 and 2008.

In *Hayes v. New York Attorney Grievance Committee of the Eighth Judicial District*, 672 F.3d 158 (2d Cir. 2012) (Jon Newman, J.), which marked the culmination of a decade-long battle over claims of specialty certification, the Second Circuit held unconstitutional Rule 7.4(c)'s requirement that every lawyer advertising specialty certification state: "Certification is not a requirement for the practice of law in the State of New York and does not necessarily indicate greater competence than other attorneys experienced in this field of law." New York's Courts responded to the Second Circuit's opinion by striking the unconstitutional language. The Courts were expected to issue an Order in November 2012 making the change official. (The *Hayes* Court also rejected a challenge to a different disclaimer in Rule 7.4(c), but held that a requirement that the surviving disclaimer be "prominently made" was unconstitutional as applied. The Courts have appointed a special committee to study the "prominently made" requirement.)

In an important development going beyond any particular proposal, in March 2012, the Courts quietly adopted a policy of posting proposed rules for public comment. The Courts have dedicated a new page of the Unified Court System's website to soliciting public comments—see *http://www.courts. state.ny.us/rules/comments/index.shtml.*

On the statutory front, amendments to New York Judiciary Law §§475 and 475-a took effect on January 1, 2013. The amendments provide that "charging liens," which protect attorney fees in litigation, will now also attach to the proceeds of out-of-court settlements and to awards obtained by arbitration or other means of alternative dispute resolution. The Legislature also passed a bill (A. 5700 and S. 1998-A) that would upgrade the unauthorized practice of law from a misdemeanor to a felony if the person committing UPL "(1) either impersonates an attorney or offers legal services to the public under a title other than attorney; and (2) causes another person to suffer monetary loss or damages exceeding one thousand dollars or other material damage resulting from impairment of a legal right to which he or she is entitled according to law." However, Governor Andrew Cuomo still had not signed the bill when we went to press, raising speculation that he might object to the bill in its current form.

In the federal courts, the Local Rules for the Eastern and Southern Districts of New York were significantly amended effective March 29, 2012.

Finally, in a historic development related to New York Rule 6.1 (Voluntary Pro Bono Service), New York became the first jurisdiction in the nation to require a minimum amount of pro bono work as a condition of bar admission. Chief Judge Jonathan Lipmann announced the general outlines of the new requirement in his Law Day speech on May 1, 2012, and the Courts soon appointed a special task force to recommend guidelines for implementing the requirement. In September 2012, the task force presented its report and the Courts soon promulgated a new rule, codified at 22 NYCRR §520.16, that will take effect January 1, 2013. Because this rule is likely to be of special interest to law students across the country who are planning to seek admission to the New York bar, we reprint the rule in full here:

§520.16 Pro Bono Requirement for Bar Admission

(a) **Fifty-hour pro bono requirement.** Every applicant admitted to the New York State bar on or after January 1, 2015, other than applicants for admission without examination pursuant to section 520.10 of this Part, shall complete at least 50 hours of qualifying pro bono service prior to filing an application for admission with the appropriate Appellate Division department of the Supreme Court.

(b) **Pro bono service defined.** For purposes of this section, pro bono service is supervised pre-admission law-related work that:

(1) assists in the provision of legal services without charge for

(i) persons of limited means;

(ii) not-for-profit organizations; or

(iii) individuals, groups or organizations seeking to secure or promote access to justice, including, but not limited to, the protection of civil rights, civil liberties or public rights;

(2) assists in the provision of legal assistance in public service for a judicial, legislative, executive or other governmental entity; or

(3) provides legal services pursuant to subdivisions two and three of section 484 of the Judiciary Law, or pursuant to equivalent legal authority in the jurisdiction where the services are performed.

(c) **Supervision required.** All qualifying pre-admission pro bono work must be performed under the supervision of:

(1) a member of a law school faculty, including adjunct faculty, or an instructor employed by a law school;

(2) an attorney admitted to practice and in good standing in the jurisdiction where the work is performed; or

(3) in the case of a clerkship or externship in a court system, by a judge or attorney employed by the court system.

(d) **Location of pro bono service.** The 50 hours of pro bono service, or any portion thereof, may be completed in any state or territory of the United States, the District of Columbia, or any foreign country.

(e) **Timing of pro bono service.** The 50 hours of pro bono service may be performed at any time after the commencement of the applicant's legal studies and prior to filing an application for admission to the New York State bar.

(f) **Proof required.** Every applicant for admission shall file with the appropriate Appellate Division department an Affidavit of Compliance with the Pro Bono Requirement, describing the nature and dates of pro bono service and the number of hours completed. The Affidavit of Compliance shall include a certification by the supervising attorney or judge confirming the applicant's pro bono activities. For each position used to satisfy the 50-hour requirement, the applicant shall file a separate Affidavit of Compliance.

(g) **Prohibition on political activities.** An applicant may not satisfy any part of the 50-hour requirement by participating in partisan political activities.

Pennsylvania: On March 19, 2012, the Pennsylvania Supreme Court issued an order amending Pennsylvania's Rules of Disciplinary Enforcement and adding two new Comments to Rule 8.3 to reflect those amendments. Under the amendments to Rule 214, an attorney convicted of any crime—not just a serious crime—must report the conviction to the Office of Disciplinary Counsel within 20 days. The definition of "crime" includes any offense punishable by imprisonment in the jurisdiction where the conviction occurred, whether or not the lawyer was actually imprisoned. (However, the definition excludes parking violations or summary offenses unless a term of imprisonment was actually imposed.) The Supreme Court also amended Rule 216, which specifies the procedures for reciprocal discipline against an attorney who has been suspended, disbarred, resigned, or otherwise removed from practice in another jurisdiction. The new Comment paragraphs to Rule 8.3 summarize the amended rules. Links to the amendments are available at *http://www.padisciplinaryboard.org/newsletters/2012/april.php#story2.*

Virginia (www.vsb.org): Effective December 1, 2012, the Virginia Supreme Court has amended Rules 7.1-7.5 of the Virginia Rules of Professional Conduct, which govern lawyer advertising and solicitation. Among other things, the amendments eliminate Rule 7.2 and add a new Rule 7.3(b)(4) permitting lawyers to "give nominal gifts of gratitude that are neither intended nor reasonably expected to be a form of compensation for recommending a lawyer's services." However, the Supreme Court rejected the Virginia State Bar's proposal to eliminate the required disclaimer in Rule 7.4(d), which permitted lawyers to communicate specialty certification "by a named organization, provided that the communication clearly states that there is no procedure in the Commonwealth of Virginia for approving certifying organizations." Instead, the Supreme Court deleted Rule 7.4(d) entirely. As a result, lawyers may no longer claim specialty certification by organizations approved only by the ABA. In October 2012, the State Bar asked the Supreme Court to reconsider the deletion of Rule 7.4(d). For more information, see Jeff Day, *Virginia Rejects Bar Proposals to Ease Attorney Advertising Rules,* 28 Law. Man. Prof. Conduct 637 (Oct. 10, 2012).

The Virginia State Bar circulated for public comment a proposed amendment to Rule 1.11(d)(1) to provide that a conflict created by a move from private to public employment can be cured with the consent of both the private client and the appropriate government agency. Currently, a lawyer may represent a private client in connection with a matter in which the lawyer participated personally and substantially as a public employee with the consent of the private client and the government agency, but the reverse conflict cannot be cured even with consent from both affected clients. The amendment parallels the existing provision in paragraph (b)(1) that provides for waiver of the conflict with consent of the affected clients.

Finally, the Virginia Supreme Court is still considering whether to adopt the ABA Model Court Rule on Provision of Legal Services Following Determination of Major Disaster (Katrina Rule), which the Bar recommended in July of 2008. The Virginia proposal generally follows the ABA model on this subject, with a few modifications.

Details and updates regarding changes and proposed changes in Virginia can be found at *http://www.vsb.org/pro-guidelines/index.php/rule_ changes*, which systematically lists the status of adopted, pending, and rejected rule amendments and provides links both to concise summaries and to primary sources.

Washington State: On September 1, 2012, a new Limited Practice Rule for Limited License Legal Technicians took effect, making Washington State the first U.S. jurisdiction to create a category of non-lawyers authorized to provide certain types of legal services in civil matters without the supervision of a lawyer. However, the rule does not allow legal technicians to represent clients in court or to negotiate with opposing parties. When we went to press, the Washington Supreme Court was seeking applications for a new Limited License Legal Technician Board (LLLT), which will oversee and administer the Limited License Legal Technician program. The new rule (Admission to Practice Rule 28), which was approved by the Washington Supreme Court over a strong dissent, is available online at *http://www.courts.wa.gov/content/ publicUpload/Press%20Releases/25700-A-1005.pdf.*

Legal Ethics Websites

Much of the information discussed above was obtained by using some of the remarkable online research sources that are available regarding lawyer regulation. Among the most useful of these websites are the following:

www.americanbar.org/groups/professional_responsibility.html: This website, which is constantly updated by the staff of the ABA Center for Professional Responsibility, collects and posts vital information from the ABA Ethics 20/20 Commission, the ABA Ethics 2000 Commission, the ABA Commission on Multijurisdictional Practice, the ABA Commission on Multidisciplinary Practice, and other ABA sources. It also provides the full text of the ABA Model Rules of Professional Conduct, legislative history of the Model Rules, and links to dozens of other ethics resources, including all of the states and the District of Columbia. The website's breadth and depth reflects the fact that the ABA Center for Professional Responsibility is the central national source for information and action regarding ethics developments in the United States.

www.law.cornell.edu/ethics: This website, maintained by Cornell Law School, contains Cornell's American Legal Ethics Library, which links to ethics resources from every state. In addition, Cornell has commissioned lengthy narratives about the legal ethics rules in about 18 states, including most of the largest states (though most are unfortunately not kept up-to-date).

www.legalethicsforum.com: This free website is a legal ethics blog at which many law professors and practitioners who work in the field of professional responsibility (including all three co-authors of this book) describe and comment on new developments and interesting news stories relevant to the regulation of lawyers.

www.legalethics.com: This website concentrates on the ethics of electronic communications and posts important new developments in that area on its home page. The site also links to resources from every state and to many other useful sources.

www.americanbar.org/groups/criminal_justice/policy/standards.html: This website, which is maintained by the ABA Criminal Justice Section, contains links to all of the ABA Standards for Criminal Justice, which we often cite and sometimes quote in our Related Materials following each ABA Model Rule of Professional Conduct.

www.lawprofessors.typepad.com/legal_profession: This blog, known as the Legal Profession Blog, covers various issues relating to the legal profession and legal ethics, and is a particularly good source of information for new developments in the area of lawyer discipline.

Areas of Regulation Deserving Special Attention

Several areas of variation among the ABA Model Rules of Professional Conduct and most state ethics rules deserve special attention. These areas include confidentiality, corporate representation, multijurisdictional practice, and lawyer advertising and solicitation. ABA Model Rules 1.6, 1.8(b), 1.9(c), 1.13(c), 3.3, and 4.1(b) prominently address confidentiality issues. Rule 1.13 addresses the responsibilities of a lawyer whose client is an organization. Rules 5.5 and 8.5 address multijurisdictional practice. Rules 7.1 through 7.6 concern advertising, solicitation, and other methods for marketing legal services.

Other areas in which we see significant variation among jurisdictions include conflicts of interest (Rules 1.7, 1.8, 1.9, 1.10, 1.11, 1.12, 1.13, and 1.18); fairness to opposing parties and counsel (Rule 3.4); relationships between lawyers and non-lawyers (Rule 5.4); and pro bono service (Rule 6.1).

Two dominant concerns underlie the provisions containing these variations. The first concern is the proper scope of the lawyer's loyalty to current and former clients, including the scope of the lawyer's duty to protect client confidential information. Competing demands on this loyalty come from the justice system, third persons, other clients, and the lawyer's personal or financial interests.

The second concern is competition, both from within and from outside the profession, in marketing and profiting from legal services. One question is whether nonlawyers should be permitted to invest in or share profits from organizations that sell legal services for a profit. This question brings up competition between lawyers and persons or entities outside the legal profession. Another question is what limits should be placed on the ways in which lawyers compete with other lawyers. This question addresses issues of lawyer advertising and solicitation.

Another issue, which was fiercely debated within the ABA in the early 1990s, was whether lawyers should be permitted to own "ancillary" non-law businesses (such as title insurance companies, investment advisors, and real estate developers) that serve both clients and non-clients. By a slim vote, the ABA said "no" when it originally adopted Rule 5.7 in 1991. But only a year later, again by a thin margin, the ABA repealed Rule 5.7. In 1994, the ABA adopted a redrafted version of Rule 5.7 that permits lawyers to own ancillary non-law businesses if the lawyers satisfy certain conditions. The 1994 rule remains in effect today.

Some Special Features of Our Book

The areas of special concern that we have just identified generated controversy within the legal profession prior to adoption of the Model Rules, and they have generated the most frequent and pronounced variations among the states. But other provisions of the ABA Model Rules have sparked serious debate during the drafting phase and have resulted in disagreements among the states. Every ABA Model Rule has its own history, and U.S. jurisdictions have put many twists on each ABA Model Rule. Moreover, the ABA continuously studies and monitors the rules to determine whether amendments or new rules are needed, and various committees, commissions, and task forces within and outside of the ABA frequently suggest amendments and new rules. In addition, many sources other than the ABA Model Rules directly or indirectly regulate or influence the conduct of lawyers.

To capture the history, complexity, and variety of the ABA Model Rules and their state counterparts, we have developed many special features for this book. In our past editions, we have included these special features after each ABA Model Rule of Professional Conduct. This year, in an effort to make the ABA Model Rules themselves easier to use, we have gathered many of our special features in a new section entitled "Annotations on the ABA Model Rules of Professional Conduct," which immediately follows the Index at the end of the Model Rules. Here are the most important of our special features, with an asterisk after the ones that we have relocated to our new "Annotations" section:

- *Editors' Introductions.* At the beginning of each set of materials in this book, we have written an Editors' Introduction that provides an overview of the materials in the chapter and alerts readers to any significant changes since our last edition and to pending or anticipated proposals for significant change.
- *Editors' Notes.* To provide background or to highlight changes to particular items, we have written Editors' Notes throughout the book.
- *Canon and Code Antecedents.* * The ABA has been drafting rules of ethics for the legal profession for more than 100 years. The earlier efforts (the 1908 Canons of Professional Ethics and the 1969 Code of Professional Responsibility) often differ sharply from the current ABA Model Rules, but they also often reveal common and enduring themes. For each ABA Model Rule, therefore, we

unlock this history by quoting the most closely related provisions from the ABA Canons of Professional Ethics and by citing the most closely related provisions of the old Model Code of Professional Responsibility. (The Disciplinary Rules of the Model Code are reprinted in full later in this volume.)

- *Cross-References in Other Rules.** The meaning and impact of a given ABA Model Rule are often illuminated by the number and content of cross-references to that rule elsewhere in the Model Rules. For each ABA Model Rule, therefore, we have compiled a complete list of "Cross-References in Other Rules." This list quotes every other place in the Rules and Comments where the rule at hand is mentioned.

- *Legislative History.** Alternative ways of phrasing the Model Rules are difficult to imagine in the abstract, but they become concrete when we examine earlier drafts of the same rule and read ABA committee reports supporting and explaining specific amendments since the Model Rules were originally adopted. We have therefore sifted through the four major drafts circulated by the Kutak Commission (which drafted the original ABA Model Rules between 1977 and 1983), as well as the comprehensive proposals by the ABA Ethics 2000 Commission (which reviewed the rules from 1997 to 2002), and we have assembled interesting variations showing what might have been. In our Legislative History for each Model Rule, we excerpt each Kutak Commission draft and each Ethics 2000 proposal that differs significantly from the rule now in force. Our Legislative History also frequently provides the text of a rule as originally adopted, or notes significant differences between the original version and the current version. Perhaps most important, our Legislative History describes *every* amendment and proposed amendment to each Model Rule since the Model Rules were originally adopted in 1983, and we often reprint excerpts from ABA committee reports submitted in support of proposed amendments.

- *Selected State Variations.** The ABA Model Rules are not binding on the states in any way, so each state is free to accept, reject, or modify the ABA Model Rules. The states have taken advantage of this freedom by adopting rules that reflect local conditions, politics, and values. Because the states differ sharply from the ABA and from each other, for each ABA Model Rule we gather Selected State Variations that differ in important ways from the equivalent ABA Model Rule. These variations are by no means comprehensive or exhaustive. Rather, they merely illustrate some possible alternative approaches to a particular issue. We have drawn these variations from dozens of jurisdictions, large and small, but we have systematically compared the ABA Model Rules to the ethics rules in the following 16 jurisdictions: Arizona, California, the District of Columbia, Florida, Georgia, Illinois, Massachusetts, Michigan, Missouri, New Jersey, New York, North Carolina, Ohio, Pennsylvania, Texas, and Virginia. (If our Selected State Variations regarding a particular ABA Model Rule omit any of these 16 jurisdictions, that indicates that the omitted jurisdiction's rule is identical to or substantially similar to the equivalent ABA Model Rule.)

- We also frequently describe variations in states that have amended their rules since our last edition went to press about a year ago, or in which amendments are scheduled to take effect before our next edition goes to press about a year from now.

- Finally, in separate chapters in the expanded edition of this book (but not the Concise Edition), we reprint in full the legal ethics rules of California, the District of Columbia, and New York.
- The wide variety of samples from different jurisdictions should dispel any notion that the ABA Model Rules of Professional Conduct are "the rules" of professional conduct. The ABA Model Rules have been and continue to be highly influential, but the ABA is only one voice among many on the subject of professional conduct rules for lawyers.
- *Related Materials.** Just as the ABA Model Rules of Professional Conduct is only one voice among many, so are the rules of legal ethics adopted by the states just one of many sources of regulation and guidance for the legal profession. Many other authorities and resources—some binding and some merely advisory—influence or mandate the conduct of lawyers. Among these other sources are state and federal statutes and court rules, common law doctrines, federal regulations, the United States Constitution, ethics opinions, ABA entities that regularly deal with particular types of issues (*e.g.*, the ABA Commission on Lawyer Assistance Programs or the ABA Commission on Multijurisdictional Practice), and United States Supreme Court cases. In addition, competing codes and guidelines have been drafted by other groups to guide lawyers in all areas of practice (*e.g.*, the Restatement of the Law Governing Lawyers), or to guide lawyers in particular fields of law (*e.g.*, the ABA Standards for Criminal Justice). Finally, our Related Materials always cite the most comparable provisions of the American Law Institute's Restatement of the Law Governing Lawyers and the most relevant ABA formal ethics opinions.
- *Updated Index.* At the end of the ABA Model Rules, we include an index updated to reflect all amendments through our press date. We have based this index on the index prepared by the ABA Center for Professional Responsibility, but we have added some of our own index terms as well.

Finally, judges are subject to special regulations beyond those that govern practicing lawyers. Some of these are in statutory law, while others are in state codes of judicial conduct. This book therefore includes a selection of judicial conduct materials, including the 2007 ABA Model Code of Judicial Conduct (which is the most recent version) and two federal statutes (28 U.S.C. §§144 and 455) governing disqualification and discipline of federal judges.

We always appreciate news about developments and proposals in the field of legal ethics, as well as suggestions for improving this book. If you have news about developments in the field of legal ethics or ideas for improving the book, please contact us by e-mail at *stephen.gillers@nyu.edu, roy.simon@hofstra.edu,* and *aperlman@suffolk.edu.*

Stephen Gillers
Roy D. Simon
Andrew M. Perlman

October 2012

Model Codes and Standards

ABA Model Rules of Professional Conduct*
As amended through August 2012

Editors' Introduction. The rules that govern lawyer conduct in the United States are based primarily on the ABA Model Rules of Professional Conduct. Forty-nine states and the District of Columbia have adopted the Model Rules numbering system and most of the language suggested by the Model Rules. California is the lone holdout, having adopted its own system. But even California appears likely to adopt the Model Rules framework and much of its content in the foreseeable future.

Students need to understand three important points about the Model Rules. First, although nearly every state has adopted the format and much of the wording of the Model Rules, the Model Rules themselves are not binding on lawyers in any jurisdiction. They are merely suggested rules for each individual state to consider. The courts of each state adopt the jurisdiction's rules of professional conduct, and each state has the power to discipline its own lawyers. The American Bar Association—a voluntary, private organization with no government affiliation—has no power to discipline lawyers and no control over a state's rules of professional conduct beyond the power of persuasion.

Second, no state has adopted all of the ABA Model Rules verbatim. Many states still differ sharply from the ABA—and from each other—with respect to difficult issues, including confidentiality, conflicts of interest, advertising, trust accounts, pro bono service, and business relationships between lawyers and nonlawyers. Moreover, although the highest courts of nearly all jurisdictions have adopted the numbering system of the ABA Model Rules, in about ten jurisdictions the courts have not formally adopted the Comments. Because of all of these variations, no two states have adopted exactly the same ethics rules. Thus, the ABA Model Rules are merely a starting point for discussing the rules of legal ethics and represent only one of many possible approaches to the regulation of lawyers. For this reason, we have compiled "Selected State Variations" in the "Annotations on the Model Rules" portion of this book to illustrate divergent approaches that states have taken to particular issues.

Third, although states have adopted different approaches to specific issues, the ABA Model Rules nevertheless reflect a broad consensus about lawyer conduct, including how the rules should be organized and formatted and what topics they should address. This consensus exists because the ABA's House of Delegates, which has the authority to adopt and amend the Model Rules, includes representatives from every state and from many different practice settings. Moreover, many jurisdictions defer to the organization and formatting of the Model Rules to ensure uniformity with other jurisdictions. Thus, although the wording of particular rules varies from state to state, few jurisdictions have added rules on subjects that the ABA Model Rules do not address, and few jurisdictions have declined to adopt more than a handful of the ABA Model Rules.

Historical background. The ABA Model Rules of Professional Conduct represent the third generation in the ABA's long tradition of drafting model ethics codes for the legal profession. In 1908, the ABA promulgated the ABA Canons of Professional Ethics, a broadly worded set of guidelines that most states adopted with few variations. These Canons, with periodic amendments, governed the profession for more than 60 years and consisted primarily of general aspirational goals rather than specific legal obligations.

In 1969, after five years of study by a special committee (the Wright Committee), the ABA adopted the ABA Model Code of Professional Responsibility, which was far more specific than the Canons. The Code used a three-part structure: (1) nine "axiomatic" Canons that stated basic principles and themes, (2) numerous "aspirational" Ethical Considerations (ECs) for each Canon, and (3) "mandatory" Disciplinary Rules (DRs) organized by Canon. The Model Code quickly replaced the Canons of Professional Ethics in nearly every state, again with few variations.

The Code's shortcomings—including its confusing structure and its failure to address a number of common ethical problems—soon became apparent. In 1977, only eight years after adopting the Model Code, the ABA appointed another special commission (the Kutak Commission) to recommend revisions to the rules. The Kutak Commission's Chairperson was the late Robert Kutak of Omaha, and its Reporter was Professor Geoffrey Hazard, Jr., then of Yale Law School. The Kutak Commission soon decided that the Model Code should be completely rewritten and reorganized. Between 1979 and 1982, the Kutak Commission circulated four major drafts of its proposed Model Rules of Professional Conduct—the 1979 Unofficial Pre-Circulation Draft, the 1980 Discussion Draft, the 1981 Draft, and the 1982 Draft. After significantly revising some of the proposed rules, the ABA House of Delegates formally adopted the Model Rules in 1983. The rules abandoned the Model Code's confusing three-part formula in favor of a Restatement-style formula, with each black letter rule followed by its own explanatory Comment.

The ABA Ethics 2000 Commission. The ABA Model Rules of Professional Conduct have been amended many times since their original adoption in 1983. From 1987 through 2001, the ABA amended at least one or two Model Rules or Comments nearly every year. By the late 1990s, the ABA recognized that a more systematic approach to amending the Rules was required. Changes to the Rules were needed to account for the rapid development of technology, the globalization of the profession, and the extensive debate over the Restatement of the Law Governing Lawyers (which was written between 1986 and 2000). In 1997, therefore, the ABA appointed a new select body, the Ethics 2000 Commission, whose Mission Statement charged it with conducting "a comprehensive study and evaluation of the ethical and professionalism precepts of the legal profession" and "examining and evaluating the ABA Model Rules of Professional Conduct. . . ." The Chair of the Ethics 2000 Commission was the Honorable E. Norman Veasey, then Chief Justice of the State of Delaware. The Commission's Reporters were Professor Nancy Moore (who served as Chief Reporter), Professor Carl Pierce, and Professor Thomas Morgan.

From 1997 to 2001, the Ethics 2000 Commission held public hearings around the country and solicited public comments on various drafts of proposed amendments to the Model Rules. After debating the proposed changes in 2001 and 2002, the ABA House of Delegates adopted nearly all of the changes proposed by the Ethics 2000 Commission. The result was the most comprehensive revision of the Model Rules since their original adoption in 1983. The ABA added three new rules—Rule 1.18 (Duties to Prospective Clients), Rule 2.4 (Lawyer Serving as Third-Party Neutral), and Rule 6.5 (Nonprofit and Court-Annexed Limited Legal Services Programs)—and deleted one old rule, Rule 2.2 (Intermediary). The Ethics 2000 revisions also included scores of significant amendments to the existing Rules and Comments. (For a detailed chart of state-by-state responses and ongoing projects relating to the work of the Ethics 2000 Commission, visit the website for the ABA Center for Professional Responsibility.)

The ABA House of Delegates rejected three of the Ethics 2000 Commission's most controversial proposals. With respect to Rule 1.5 (Fees), the ABA voted against a proposal to require lawyers to put all fee agreements in writing except when the lawyer is charging a "regularly represented client" on the same basis as before, or when the reasonably foreseeable costs and fees in a given matter are $500 or less. With respect to Rule 1.6 (Confidentiality of Information), the ABA voted against a proposal to permit a lawyer to reveal information "to prevent, mitigate or rectify substantial injury to the financial interests or property of another that is reasonably certain to result or has resulted from the client's commission of a crime or fraud in furtherance of which the client has used the lawyer's services." (After the ABA voted against that proposal, the Ethics 2000 Commission withdrew a related proposal that would have permitted lawyers to reveal information necessary to prevent, mitigate, or rectify injury from a client's past financial frauds or crimes in which the lawyer's services had been used.) With respect to Rule 1.10 (Imputation of Conflicts of Interest: General Rule), the ABA rejected a proposal to permit timely screening and written notice to avoid disqualification based on a conflict with a lateral lawyer's former client. (As explained below, similar proposals regarding Rule 1.6 and Rule 1.10 were subsequently adopted by the House of Delegates in 2003 and 2009, respectively.)

The 2002 amendments to the Model Rules also included significant changes proposed by the ABA Commission on Multijurisdictional Practice (MJP Commission), which had been appointed in 2000 to study the practice of law by lawyers in jurisdictions where they are not admitted. In response to proposals by the MJP Commission, the ABA House of Delegates amended both Rule 5.5 (Unauthorized Practice of Law; Multijurisdictional Practice of Law) and Rule 8.5 (Disciplinary Authority; Choice of Law). The MJP Commission also proposed—and the ABA adopted—several new policies relating to multijurisdictional practice.

Finally, based on a proposal by the ABA's Standing Committee on Ethics and Professional Responsibility, the ABA amended Rule 7.2 (Advertising) in 2002 by adding a new subparagraph (b)(4), which permits lawyers to enter into nonexclusive reciprocal referral arrangements either with other lawyers or with nonlawyer professionals, provided the client is informed of the arrangement when a referral is made. The amendment was accompanied by a new Comment 8 to Rule 7.2 to explain the reciprocal referral provision, and by an amendment to Comment 1 to Rule 7.5 (Firm Names and Letterheads) branding it "misleading to use . . . the name of a nonlawyer" in a law firm's name.

Amendments after Ethics 2000. Significant changes to the Model Rules of Professional Conduct continued in 2003. In the wake of massive scandals at Enron, WorldCom, and other large corporations, and in the face of pressure from the Securities and Exchange Commission and from Congress's passage of the Sarbanes-Oxley Act of 2002, the ABA significantly amended Rule 1.6 (Confidentiality of Information) and Rule 1.13 (Organization as Client). Specifically, in 2003 the House of Delegates narrowly voted to amend Rule 1.6 by adopting the identical exceptions to confidentiality that the ABA had overwhelmingly rejected only two years earlier. The new paragraphs expanded the circumstances under which a lawyer may reveal client confidential information, especially to prevent, mitigate, or rectify injury from a client's crime or fraud in which the lawyer's services were used or are being used. At the same time, the House of Delegates amended Rule 1.13(b) to create a presumption that a lawyer must "report up" within an organization to expose wrongdoing by a corporate officer or employee, and the House amended Rule 1.13(c) to permit (but not require) a lawyer for an organization to "report out" by revealing client confidences outside the organization when the internal "reporting up" fails to stop certain serious wrongdoing.

In 2008 and 2009, the ABA made two other notable changes to the Model Rules. In 2008, the ABA House of Delegates amended Rule 3.8 and its Comment to impose significant post-conviction responsibilities on prosecutors. And in 2009, the ABA House of Delegates adopted and then fine-tuned significant amendments to Rule 1.10, which now permits law firms, in limited circumstances, to use "screens" to prevent a laterally hired lawyer's conflict of interest from being imputed to the rest of the firm, even without consent from the lateral's former client. This controversial rule change, which the ABA's House of Delegates had rejected during the Ethics 2000 process, will make it easier for law firms to hire attorneys from other private law firms in situations where amended Rule 1.10 applies.

The ABA Commission on Ethics 20/20. The ABA Commission on Ethics 20/20 was created in 2009 by then-ABA President Carolyn Lamm and was tasked with reviewing and proposing changes to the ABA Model Rules of Professional Conduct and the American system of lawyer regulation in light of advances in technology and the increasingly global nature of law practice. In August 2012, the ABA House of Delegates adopted numerous amendments to the Model Rules and related policies in response to the Commission's proposals. The changes affect rules relating to a lawyer's duty of confidentiality in a digital age, Internet-based advertising, outsourcing, and lawyer mobility. We have added Editors' Notes throughout the Model Rules to explain these recent changes. We also have underlined the new language in the Model Rules and have indicated where language was deleted. The Commission is expected to propose additional changes in February 2013.

The co-chairs of the Commission are Jamie Gorelick of Washington, D.C. (a former U.S. Deputy Attorney General) and Michael Traynor of California (the President-Emeritus and Chair of the Council of the American Law Institute). Professor Stephen Gillers (a co-author of this book) is a member of the Commission, and Professor Andrew Perlman (another co-author of this book) is the Commission's Chief Reporter. Professors Paul Paton, Anthony Sebok, and Bradley Wendel are also Commission Reporters. You can find additional information about the Commission at this website: *www.americanbar.org/ Ethics2020*.

How this book organizes materials related to the ABA Model Rules. The ABA Model Rules of Professional Conduct and all official ABA Comments to each Model Rule are reprinted below. At the end of the Model Rules, you will find an index to help you find Rules relating to particular subjects. These materials reflect all amendments through calendar year 2012.

Immediately after the Model Rules and the index, you will find a separate section called "Annotations on the Model Rules." The purpose of that section of the book is to capture the complexity, history, and variety of the Model Rules, to illustrate state approaches to the issues, and to put the Rules in context. In that section, you will find the following materials for each Model Rule:

(1) *Canon and Code Antecedents,* compiled especially for this book so that readers can trace the ABA's historical treatment of related issues in the ABA Canons of Professional Ethics and the ABA Model Code of Professional Responsibility;

(2) *Cross-References in Other Rules,* compiled especially for this book to show each place in the Rules and Comments where a particular Rule is mentioned in the Model Rules;

(3) *Legislative History of the Model Rule,* compiled especially for this book to describe the four Kutak Commission drafts and the frequent amendments and proposed amendments to particular Rules since their original adoption;

(4) *Selected State Variations,* compiled especially for this book to show some of the ways in which states have diverged from the ABA Model Rules. We have drawn these variations from many jurisdictions, but we have systematically noted significant differences, if any, between the ABA Model Rules of Professional Conduct and the ethics rules in the following 16 jurisdictions: Arizona, California, the District of Columbia, Florida, Georgia, Illinois, Massachusetts, Michigan, Missouri, New Jersey, New York, North Carolina, Ohio, Pennsylvania, Texas, and Virginia. (If the Selected State Variations do not point out any differences between the ABA Model Rule and the rules of one of these 16 jurisdictions, that generally means that the jurisdiction's rule is the same or substantially the same as the ABA Model Rule.); and

(5) *Related Materials,* compiled especially for this book to show cross-references to equivalent sections of the Restatement of the Law Governing Lawyers (which is reprinted later in this volume), descriptions of ABA entities and national organizations that regularly deal with particular types of issues, and references to statutes, cases, ABA ethics opinions, and other items that may shed light on a particular Rule.

For extensive historical materials regarding the ABA Model Rules of Professional Conduct, including commission reports, summaries of House of Delegates actions, written testimony from public hearings, minutes of commission meetings, and other materials documenting the work of the Ethics 2000 Commission, the Commission on Multijurisdictional Practice, and other ABA commissions, committees, and task forces, and for updated information about the ABA Model Rules, including the ongoing work of the Ethics 20/20 Commission, visit the website of the ABA Center for Professional Responsibility at *http://www.americanbar.org/groups/professional_responsibility.html.*

Contents

Preamble: A Lawyer's Responsibilities
Scope

Article 1. Client-Lawyer Relationship

Article 2. Counselor

Article 3. Advocate

Article 4. Transactions with Persons Other Than Clients

Article 5. Law Firms and Associations

PREAMBLE: A LAWYER'S RESPONSIBILITIES

[1] A lawyer, as a member of the legal profession, is a representative of clients, an officer of the legal system and a public citizen having special responsibility for the quality of justice.

[2] As a representative of clients, a lawyer performs various functions. As advisor, a lawyer provides a client with an informed understanding of the client's legal rights and obligations and explains their practical implications. As advocate, a lawyer zealously asserts the client's position under the rules of the adversary system. As negotiator, a lawyer seeks a result advantageous to the client but consistent with requirements of honest dealings with others. As an evaluator, a lawyer acts by examining a client's legal affairs and reporting about them to the client or to others.

[3] In addition to these representational functions, a lawyer may serve as a third-party neutral, a nonrepresentational role helping the parties to resolve a dispute or other matter. Some of these Rules apply directly to lawyers who are or have served as third-party neutrals. See, e.g., Rules 1.12 and 2.4. In addition, there are

Rules that apply to lawyers who are not active in the practice of law or to practicing lawyers even when they are acting in a nonprofessional capacity. For example, a lawyer who commits fraud in the conduct of a business is subject to discipline for engaging in conduct involving dishonesty, fraud, deceit or misrepresentation. See Rule 8.4.

[4] In all professional functions a lawyer should be competent, prompt and diligent. A lawyer should maintain communication with a client concerning the representation. A lawyer should keep in confidence information relating to representation of a client except so far as disclosure is required or permitted by the Rules of Professional Conduct or other law.

[5] A lawyer's conduct should conform to the requirements of the law, both in professional service to clients and in the lawyer's business and personal affairs. A lawyer should use the law's procedures only for legitimate purposes and not to harass or intimidate others. A lawyer should demonstrate respect for the legal system and for those who serve it, including judges, other lawyers and public officials. While it is a lawyer's duty, when necessary, to challenge the rectitude of official action, it is also a lawyer's duty to uphold legal process.

[6] As a public citizen, a lawyer should seek improvement of the law, access to the legal system, the administration of justice and the quality of service rendered by the legal profession. As a member of a learned profession, a lawyer should cultivate knowledge of the law beyond its use for clients, employ that knowledge in reform of the law and work to strengthen legal education. In addition, a lawyer should further the public's understanding of and confidence in the rule of law and the justice system because legal institutions in a constitutional democracy depend on popular participation and support to maintain their authority. A lawyer should be mindful of deficiencies in the administration of justice and of the fact that the poor, and sometimes persons who are not poor, cannot afford adequate legal assistance. Therefore, all lawyers should devote professional time and resources and use civic influence to ensure equal access to our system of justice for all those who because of economic or social barriers cannot afford or secure adequate legal counsel. A lawyer should aid the legal profession in pursuing these objectives and should help the bar regulate itself in the public interest.

[7] Many of a lawyer's professional responsibilities are prescribed in the Rules of Professional Conduct, as well as substantive and procedural law. However, a lawyer is also guided by personal conscience and the approbation of professional peers. A lawyer should strive to attain the highest level of skill, to improve the law and the legal profession and to exemplify the legal profession's ideals of public service.

[8] A lawyer's responsibilities as a representative of clients, an officer of the legal system and a public citizen are usually harmonious. Thus, when an opposing party is well represented, a lawyer can be a zealous advocate on behalf of a client and at the same time assume that justice is being done. So also, a lawyer can be sure that preserving client confidences ordinarily serves the public interest because people are more likely to seek legal advice, and thereby heed their legal obligations, when they know their communications will be private.

[9] In the nature of law practice, however, conflicting responsibilities are encountered. Virtually all difficult ethical problems arise from conflict between a lawyer's responsibilities to clients, to the legal system and to the lawyer's own interest in remaining an ethical person while earning a satisfactory living. The Rules of Professional Conduct often prescribe terms for resolving such conflicts. Within the

framework of these Rules, however, many difficult issues of professional discretion can arise. Such issues must be resolved through the exercise of sensitive professional and moral judgment guided by the basic principles underlying the Rules. These principles include the lawyer's obligation zealously to protect and pursue a client's legitimate interests, within the bounds of the law, while maintaining a professional, courteous and civil attitude toward all persons involved in the legal system.

[10] The legal profession is largely self-governing. Although other professions also have been granted powers of self-government, the legal profession is unique in this respect because of the close relationship between the profession and the processes of government and law enforcement. This connection is manifested in the fact that ultimate authority over the legal profession is vested largely in the courts.

[11] To the extent that lawyers meet the obligations of their professional calling, the occasion for government regulation is obviated. Self-regulation also helps maintain the legal profession's independence from government domination. An independent legal profession is an important force in preserving government under law, for abuse of legal authority is more readily challenged by a profession whose members are not dependent on government for the right to practice.

[12] The legal profession's relative autonomy carries with it special responsibilities of self-government. The profession has a responsibility to assure that its regulations are conceived in the public interest and not in furtherance of parochial or self-interested concerns of the bar. Every lawyer is responsible for observance of the Rules of Professional Conduct. A lawyer should also aid in securing their observance by other lawyers. Neglect of these responsibilities compromises the independence of the profession and the public interest which it serves.

[13] Lawyers play a vital role in the preservation of society. The fulfillment of this role requires an understanding by lawyers of their relationship to our legal system. The Rules of Professional Conduct, when properly applied, serve to define that relationship.

SCOPE

[14] The Rules of Professional Conduct are rules of reason. They should be interpreted with reference to the purposes of legal representation and of the law itself. Some of the Rules are imperatives, cast in the terms "shall" or "shall not." These define proper conduct for purposes of professional discipline. Others, generally cast in the term "may," are permissive and define areas under the Rules in which the lawyer has discretion to exercise professional judgment. No disciplinary action should be taken when the lawyer chooses not to act or acts within the bounds of such discretion. Other Rules define the nature of relationships between the lawyer and others. The Rules are thus partly obligatory and disciplinary and partly constitutive and descriptive in that they define a lawyer's professional role. Many of the Comments use the term "should." Comments do not add obligations to the Rules but provide guidance for practicing in compliance with the Rules.

[15] The Rules presuppose a larger legal context shaping the lawyer's role. That context includes court rules and statutes relating to matters of licensure, laws defining specific obligations of lawyers and substantive and procedural law in general. The Comments are sometimes used to alert lawyers to their responsibilities under such other law.

[16] Compliance with the Rules, as with all law in an open society, depends primarily upon understanding and voluntary compliance, secondarily upon reinforcement by peer and public opinion and finally, when necessary, upon enforcement through disciplinary proceedings. The Rules do not, however, exhaust the moral and ethical considerations that should inform a lawyer, for no worthwhile human activity can be completely defined by legal rules. The Rules simply provide a framework for the ethical practice of law.

[17] Furthermore, for purposes of determining the lawyer's authority and responsibility, principles of substantive law external to these Rules determine whether a client-lawyer relationship exists. Most of the duties flowing from the client-lawyer relationship attach only after the client has requested the lawyer to render legal services and the lawyer has agreed to do so. But there are some duties, such as that of confidentiality under Rule 1.6, that attach when the lawyer agrees to consider whether a client-lawyer relationship shall be established. See Rule 1.18. Whether a client-lawyer relationship exists for any specific purpose can depend on the circumstances and may be a question of fact.

[18] Under various legal provisions, including constitutional, statutory and common law, the responsibilities of government lawyers may include authority concerning legal matters that ordinarily reposes in the client in private client-lawyer relationships. For example, a lawyer for a government agency may have authority on behalf of the government to decide upon settlement or whether to appeal from an adverse judgment. Such authority in various respects is generally vested in the attorney general and the state's attorney in state government, and their federal counterparts, and the same may be true of other government law officers. Also, lawyers under the supervision of these officers may be authorized to represent several government agencies in intragovernmental legal controversies in circumstances where a private lawyer could not represent multiple private clients. These Rules do not abrogate any such authority.

[19] Failure to comply with an obligation or prohibition imposed by a Rule is a basis for invoking the disciplinary process. The Rules presuppose that disciplinary assessment of a lawyer's conduct will be made on the basis of the facts and circumstances as they existed at the time of the conduct in question and in recognition of the fact that a lawyer often has to act upon uncertain or incomplete evidence of the situation. Moreover, the Rules presuppose that whether or not discipline should be imposed for a violation, and the severity of a sanction, depend on all the circumstances, such as the willfulness and seriousness of the violation, extenuating factors and whether there have been previous violations.

[20] Violation of a Rule should not itself give rise to a cause of action against a lawyer nor should it create any presumption in such a case that a legal duty has been breached. In addition, violation of a Rule does not necessarily warrant any other nondisciplinary remedy, such as disqualification of a lawyer in pending litigation. The Rules are designed to provide guidance to lawyers and to provide a structure for regulating conduct through disciplinary agencies. They are not designed to be a basis for civil liability. Furthermore, the purpose of the Rules can be subverted when they are invoked by opposing parties as procedural weapons. The fact that a Rule is a just basis for a lawyer's self-assessment, or for sanctioning a lawyer under the administration of a disciplinary authority, does not imply that an antagonist in a collateral proceeding or transaction has standing to seek enforcement of the Rule. Nevertheless, since the Rules do establish standards of conduct by lawyers, a lawyer's violation of a Rule may be evidence of breach of the applicable standard of conduct.

[21] The Comment accompanying each Rule explains and illustrates the meaning and purpose of the Rule. The Preamble and this note on Scope provide general orientation. The Comments are intended as guides to interpretation, but the text of each Rule is authoritative.

> **Editors' Note.** In August 2012, the ABA House of Delegates adopted changes to Rule 1.0(n) and Comment 9 in response to proposals by the ABA Commission on Ethics 20/20. The definition of a "writing" in Rule 1.0(n) was updated to include all "electronic communications," not just "email." Comment 9 was amended to emphasize that, when employing a screen under Rule 1.0(k), lawyers need to take appropriate measures with regard to electronic information. To alert readers to the changes, we underscore the new language and strike through deleted language. For more information regarding these changes, see the Legislative History for this Rule in the "Annotations on ABA Model Rules" section of this book.

ARTICLE 1.   CLIENT-LAWYER RELATIONSHIP

Rule 1.0   Terminology

(a) "Belief" or "believes" denotes that the person involved actually supposed the fact in question to be true. A person's belief may be inferred from circumstances.

(b) "Confirmed in writing," when used in reference to the informed consent of a person, denotes informed consent that is given in writing by the person or a writing that a lawyer promptly transmits to the person confirming an oral informed consent. See paragraph (e) for the definition of "informed consent." If it is not feasible to obtain or transmit the writing at the time the person gives informed consent, then the lawyer must obtain or transmit it within a reasonable time thereafter.

(c) "Firm" or "law firm" denotes a lawyer or lawyers in a law partnership, professional corporation, sole proprietorship or other association authorized to practice law; or lawyers employed in a legal services organization or the legal department of a corporation or other organization.

(d) "Fraud" or "fraudulent" denotes conduct that is fraudulent under the substantive or procedural law of the applicable jurisdiction and has a purpose to deceive.

(e) "Informed consent" denotes the agreement by a person to a proposed course of conduct after the lawyer has communicated adequate information and explanation about the material risks of and reasonably available alternatives to the proposed course of conduct.

(f) "Knowingly," "known," or "knows" denotes actual knowledge of the fact in question. A person's knowledge may be inferred from circumstances.

(g) "Partner" denotes a member of a partnership, a shareholder in a law firm organized as a professional corporation, or a member of an association authorized to practice law.

(h) "Reasonable" or "reasonably" when used in relation to conduct by a lawyer denotes the conduct of a reasonably prudent and competent lawyer.

(i) "Reasonable belief" or "reasonably believes" when used in reference to a lawyer denotes that the lawyer believes the matter in question and that the circumstances are such that the belief is reasonable.

(j) "Reasonably should know" when used in reference to a lawyer denotes that a lawyer of reasonable prudence and competence would ascertain the matter in question.

(k) "Screened" denotes the isolation of a lawyer from any participation in a matter through the timely imposition of procedures within a firm that are reasonably adequate under the circumstances to protect information that the isolated lawyer is obligated to protect under these Rules or other law.

(l) "Substantial" when used in reference to degree or extent denotes a material matter of clear and weighty importance.

(m) "Tribunal" denotes a court, an arbitrator in a binding arbitration proceeding or a legislative body, administrative agency or other body acting in an adjudicative capacity. A legislative body, administrative agency or other body acts in an adjudicative capacity when a neutral official, after the presentation of evidence or legal argument by a party or parties, will render a binding legal judgment directly affecting a party's interests in a particular matter.

(n) "Writing" or "written" denotes a tangible or electronic record of a communication or representation, including handwriting, typewriting, printing, photostating, photography, audio or videorecording, and ~~e-mail~~ __electronic communications__. A "signed" writing includes an electronic sound, symbol or process attached to or logically associated with a writing and executed or adopted by a person with the intent to sign the writing.

COMMENT

Confirmed in Writing

[1] If it is not feasible to obtain or transmit a written confirmation at the time the client gives informed consent, then the lawyer must obtain or transmit it within a reasonable time thereafter. If a lawyer has obtained a client's informed consent, the lawyer may act in reliance on that consent so long as it is confirmed in writing within a reasonable time thereafter.

Firm

[2] Whether two or more lawyers constitute a firm within paragraph (c) can depend on the specific facts. For example, two practitioners who share office space and occasionally consult or assist each other ordinarily would not be regarded as constituting a firm. However, if they present themselves to the public in a way

that suggests that they are a firm or conduct themselves as a firm, they should be regarded as a firm for purposes of the Rules. The terms of any formal agreement between associated lawyers are relevant in determining whether they are a firm, as is the fact that they have mutual access to information concerning the clients they serve. Furthermore, it is relevant in doubtful cases to consider the underlying purpose of the Rule that is involved. A group of lawyers could be regarded as a firm for purposes of the Rule that the same lawyer should not represent opposing parties in litigation, while it might not be so regarded for purposes of the Rule that information acquired by one lawyer is attributed to another.

[3] With respect to the law department of an organization, including the government, there is ordinarily no question that the members of the department constitute a firm within the meaning of the Rules of Professional Conduct. There can be uncertainty, however, as to the identity of the client. For example, it may not be clear whether the law department of a corporation represents a subsidiary or an affiliated corporation, as well as the corporation by which the members of the department are directly employed. A similar question can arise concerning an unincorporated association and its local affiliates.

[4] Similar questions can also arise with respect to lawyers in legal aid and legal services organizations. Depending upon the structure of the organization, the entire organization or different components of it may constitute a firm or firms for purposes of these Rules.

Fraud

[5] When used in these Rules, the terms "fraud" or "fraudulent" refer to conduct that is characterized as such under the substantive or procedural law of the applicable jurisdiction and has a purpose to deceive. This does not include merely negligent misrepresentation or negligent failure to apprise another of relevant information. For purposes of these Rules, it is not necessary that anyone has suffered damages or relied on the misrepresentation or failure to inform.

Informed Consent

[6] Many of the Rules of Professional Conduct require the lawyer to obtain the informed consent of a client or other person (e.g., a former client or, under certain circumstances, a prospective client) before accepting or continuing representation or pursuing a course of conduct. See, e.g., Rules 1.2(c), 1.6(a) and 1.7(b). The communication necessary to obtain such consent will vary according to the Rule involved and the circumstances giving rise to the need to obtain informed consent. The lawyer must make reasonable efforts to ensure that the client or other person possesses information reasonably adequate to make an informed decision. Ordinarily, this will require communication that includes a disclosure of the facts and circumstances giving rise to the situation, any explanation reasonably necessary to inform the client or other person of the material advantages and disadvantages of the proposed course of conduct and a discussion of the client's or other person's options and alternatives. In some circumstances it may be appropriate for a lawyer to advise a client or other person to seek the advice of other counsel. A lawyer need

not inform a client or other person of facts or implications already known to the client or other person; nevertheless, a lawyer who does not personally inform the client or other person assumes the risk that the client or other person is inadequately informed and the consent is invalid. In determining whether the information and explanation provided are reasonably adequate, relevant factors include whether the client or other person is experienced in legal matters generally and in making decisions of the type involved, and whether the client or other person is independently represented by other counsel in giving the consent. Normally, such persons need less information and explanation than others, and generally a client or other person who is independently represented by other counsel in giving the consent should be assumed to have given informed consent.

[7] Obtaining informed consent will usually require an affirmative response by the client or other person. In general, a lawyer may not assume consent from a client's or other person's silence. Consent may be inferred, however, from the conduct of a client or other person who has reasonably adequate information about the matter. A number of Rules require that a person's consent be confirmed in writing. See Rules 1.7(b) and 1.9(a). For a definition of "writing" and "confirmed in writing," see paragraphs (n) and (b). Other Rules require that a client's consent be obtained in a writing signed by the client. See, e.g., Rules 1.8(a) and (g). For a definition of "signed," see paragraph (n).

Screened

[8] This definition applies to situations where screening of a personally disqualified lawyer is permitted to remove imputation of a conflict of interest under Rule 1.10, 1.11, 1.12 or 1.18.

[9] The purpose of screening is to assure the affected parties that confidential information known by the personally disqualified lawyer remains protected. The personally disqualified lawyer should acknowledge the obligation not to communicate with any of the other lawyers in the firm with respect to the matter. Similarly, other lawyers in the firm who are working on the matter should be informed that the screening is in place and that they may not communicate with the personally disqualified lawyer with respect to the matter. Additional screening measures that are appropriate for the particular matter will depend on the circumstances. To implement, reinforce and remind all affected lawyers of the presence of the screening, it may be appropriate for the firm to undertake such procedures as a written undertaking by the screened lawyer to avoid any communication with other firm personnel and any contact with any firm files or other ~~materials~~ information, including information in electronic form, relating to the matter, written notice and instructions to all other firm personnel forbidding any communication with the screened lawyer relating to the matter, denial of access by the screened lawyer to firm files or other ~~materials~~ information, including information in electronic form, relating to the matter, and periodic reminders of the screen to the screened lawyer and all other firm personnel.

[10] In order to be effective, screening measures must be implemented as soon as practical after a lawyer or law firm knows or reasonably should know that there is a need for screening.

Editors' Note.   In August 2012, the ABA House of Delegates added two new Comments to Rule 1.1 and revised an existing Comment. The two new Comments were proposed by the ABA Commission on Ethics 20/20 and are designed to give lawyers more guidance regarding their ethical obligations when retaining lawyers in other firms to work on client matters. The revision to what was previously Comment 6 (and is now Comment 8) was also proposed by the Commission and is intended to emphasize that a lawyer's duty of competence includes a duty to understand the risks and benefits from using relevant technology. To alert readers to these changes, we underscore the new language and strike through deleted language. For more information regarding these changes, see the Legislative History for this Rule in the "Annotations on ABA Model Rules" section of this book.

Rule 1.1   Competence

A lawyer shall provide competent representation to a client. Competent representation requires the legal knowledge, skill, thoroughness and preparation reasonably necessary for the representation.

COMMENT

Legal Knowledge and Skill

[1] In determining whether a lawyer employs the requisite knowledge and skill in a particular matter, relevant factors include the relative complexity and specialized nature of the matter, the lawyer's general experience, the lawyer's training and experience in the field in question, the preparation and study the lawyer is able to give the matter and whether it is feasible to refer the matter to, or associate or consult with, a lawyer of established competence in the field in question. In many instances, the required proficiency is that of a general practitioner. Expertise in a particular field of law may be required in some circumstances.

[2] A lawyer need not necessarily have special training or prior experience to handle legal problems of a type with which the lawyer is unfamiliar. A newly admitted lawyer can be as competent as a practitioner with long experience. Some important legal skills, such as the analysis of precedent, the evaluation of evidence and legal drafting, are required in all legal problems. Perhaps the most fundamental legal skill consists of determining what kind of legal problems a situation may involve, a skill that necessarily transcends any particular specialized knowledge. A lawyer can provide adequate representation in a wholly novel field through necessary study. Competent representation can also be provided through the association of a lawyer of established competence in the field in question.

[3] In an emergency a lawyer may give advice or assistance in a matter in which the lawyer does not have the skill ordinarily required where referral to or consultation or association with another lawyer would be impractical. Even in an emergency, however, assistance should be limited to that reasonably necessary in the circumstances, for ill-considered action under emergency conditions can jeopardize the client's interest.

[4] A lawyer may accept representation where the requisite level of competence can be achieved by reasonable preparation. This applies as well to a lawyer who is appointed as counsel for an unrepresented person. See also Rule 6.2.

Thoroughness and Preparation

[5] Competent handling of a particular matter includes inquiry into and analysis of the factual and legal elements of the problem, and use of methods and procedures meeting the standards of competent practitioners. It also includes adequate preparation. The required attention and preparation are determined in part by what is at stake; major litigation and complex transactions ordinarily require more extensive treatment than matters of lesser complexity and consequence. An agreement between the lawyer and the client regarding the scope of the representation may limit the matters for which the lawyer is responsible. See Rule 1.2 (c).

Retaining or Contracting with Other Lawyers

[6] Before a lawyer retains or contracts with other lawyers outside the lawyer's own firm to provide or assist in the provision of legal services to a client, the lawyer should ordinarily obtain informed consent from the client and must reasonably believe that the other lawyers' services will contribute to the competent and ethical representation of the client. See also Rules 1.2 (allocation of authority), 1.4 (communication with client), 1.5(e) (fee sharing), 1.6 (confidentiality), and 5.5(a) (unauthorized practice of law). The reasonableness of the decision to retain or contract with other lawyers outside the lawyer's own firm will depend upon the circumstances, including the education, experience and reputation of the nonfirm lawyers; the nature of the services assigned to the nonfirm lawyers; and the legal protections, professional conduct rules, and ethical environments of the jurisdictions in which the services will be performed, particularly relating to confidential information.

[7] When lawyers from more than one law firm are providing legal services to the client on a particular matter, the lawyers ordinarily should consult with each other and the client about the scope of their respective representations and the allocation of responsibility among them. See Rule 1.2. When making allocations of responsibility in a matter pending before a tribunal, lawyers and parties may have additional obligations that are a matter of law beyond the scope of these Rules.

Maintaining Competence

[68] To maintain the requisite knowledge and skill, a lawyer should keep abreast of changes in the law and its practice, including the benefits and risks associated with relevant technology, engage in continuing study and education and comply with all continuing legal education requirements to which the lawyer is subject.

Rule 1.2   Scope of Representation and Allocation of Authority Between Client and Lawyer

(a) Subject to paragraphs (c) and (d), a lawyer shall abide by a client's decisions concerning the objectives of representation and, as required by Rule 1.4, shall consult with the client as to the means by which they are to be pursued. A lawyer may take such action on behalf of the client as is impliedly authorized to carry out the representation. A lawyer shall abide by a client's decision whether to settle a matter. In a criminal case, the lawyer shall abide by the client's decision, after consultation with the lawyer, as to a plea to be entered, whether to waive jury trial and whether the client will testify.

(b) A lawyer's representation of a client, including representation by appointment, does not constitute an endorsement of the client's political, economic, social or moral views or activities.

(c) A lawyer may limit the scope of the representation if the limitation is reasonable under the circumstances and the client gives informed consent.

(d) A lawyer shall not counsel a client to engage, or assist a client, in conduct that the lawyer knows is criminal or fraudulent, but a lawyer may discuss the legal consequences of any proposed course of conduct with a client and may counsel or assist a client to make a good faith effort to determine the validity, scope, meaning or application of the law.

COMMENT

Allocation of Authority Between Client and Lawyer

[1] Paragraph (a) confers upon the client the ultimate authority to determine the purposes to be served by legal representation, within the limits imposed by law and the lawyer's professional obligations. The decisions specified in paragraph (a), such as whether to settle a civil matter, must also be made by the client. See Rule 1.4(a)(1) for the lawyer's duty to communicate with the client about such decisions. With respect to the means by which the client's objectives are to be pursued, the lawyer shall consult with the client as required by Rule 1.4(a)(2) and may take such action as is impliedly authorized to carry out the representation.

[2] On occasion, however, a lawyer and a client may disagree about the means to be used to accomplish the client's objectives. Clients normally defer to the special knowledge and skill of their lawyer with respect to the means to be used to accomplish their objectives, particularly with respect to technical, legal and tactical matters. Conversely, lawyers usually defer to the client regarding such questions as the expense to be incurred and concern for third persons who might be adversely affected. Because of the varied nature of the matters about which a lawyer and client might disagree and because the actions in question may implicate the interests of a tribunal or other persons, this Rule does not prescribe how such disagreements are to be resolved. Other law, however, may be applicable and should be consulted by the lawyer. The lawyer should also consult with the client and seek a mutually

acceptable resolution of the disagreement. If such efforts are unavailing and the lawyer has a fundamental disagreement with the client, the lawyer may withdraw from the representation. See Rule 1.16(b)(4). Conversely, the client may resolve the disagreement by discharging the lawyer. See Rule 1.16(a)(3).

[3] At the outset of a representation, the client may authorize the lawyer to take specific action on the client's behalf without further consultation. Absent a material change in circumstances and subject to Rule 1.4, a lawyer may rely on such an advance authorization. The client may, however, revoke such authority at any time.

[4] In a case in which the client appears to be suffering diminished capacity, the lawyer's duty to abide by the client's decisions is to be guided by reference to Rule 1.14.

Independence from Client's Views or Activities

[5] Legal representation should not be denied to people who are unable to afford legal services, or whose cause is controversial or the subject of popular disapproval. By the same token, representing a client does not constitute approval of the client's views or activities.

Agreements Limiting Scope of Representation

[6] The scope of services to be provided by a lawyer may be limited by agreement with the client or by the terms under which the lawyer's services are made available to the client. When a lawyer has been retained by an insurer to represent an insured, for example, the representation may be limited to matters related to the insurance coverage. A limited representation may be appropriate because the client has limited objectives for the representation. In addition, the terms upon which representation is undertaken may exclude specific means that might otherwise be used to accomplish the client's objectives. Such limitations may exclude actions that the client thinks are too costly or that the lawyer regards as repugnant or imprudent.

[7] Although this Rule affords the lawyer and client substantial latitude to limit the representation, the limitation must be reasonable under the circumstances. If, for example, a client's objective is limited to securing general information about the law the client needs in order to handle a common and typically uncomplicated legal problem, the lawyer and client may agree that the lawyer's services will be limited to a brief telephone consultation. Such a limitation, however, would not be reasonable if the time allotted was not sufficient to yield advice upon which the client could rely. Although an agreement for a limited representation does not exempt a lawyer from the duty to provide competent representation, the limitation is a factor to be considered when determining the legal knowledge, skill, thoroughness and preparation reasonably necessary for the representation. See Rule 1.1.

[8] All agreements concerning a lawyer's representation of a client must accord with the Rules of Professional Conduct and other law. See, e.g., Rules 1.1, 1.8, and 5.6.

Criminal, Fraudulent and Prohibited Transactions

[9] Paragraph (d) prohibits a lawyer from knowingly counseling or assisting a client to commit a crime or fraud. This prohibition, however, does not preclude the lawyer from giving an honest opinion about the actual consequences that appear likely to result from a client's conduct. Nor does the fact that a client uses advice in a course of action that is criminal or fraudulent of itself make a lawyer a party to the course of action. There is a critical distinction between presenting an analysis of legal aspects of questionable conduct and recommending the means by which a crime or fraud might be committed with impunity.

[10] When the client's course of action has already begun and is continuing, the lawyer's responsibility is especially delicate. The lawyer is required to avoid assisting the client, for example, by drafting or delivering documents that the lawyer knows are fraudulent or by suggesting how the wrongdoing might be concealed. A lawyer may not continue assisting a client in conduct that the lawyer originally supposed was legally proper but then discovers is criminal or fraudulent. The lawyer must, therefore, withdraw from the representation of the client in the matter. See Rule 1.16(a). In some cases, withdrawal alone might be insufficient. It may be necessary for the lawyer to give notice of the fact of withdrawal and to disaffirm any opinion, document, affirmation or the like. See Rule 4.1.

[11] Where the client is a fiduciary, the lawyer may be charged with special obligations in dealings with a beneficiary.

[12] Paragraph (d) applies whether or not the defrauded party is a party to the transaction. Hence, a lawyer must not participate in a transaction to effectuate criminal or fraudulent avoidance of tax liability. Paragraph (d) does not preclude undertaking a criminal defense incident to a general retainer for legal services to a lawful enterprise. The last clause of paragraph (d) recognizes that determining the validity or interpretation of a statute or regulation may require a course of action involving disobedience of the statute or regulation or of the interpretation placed upon it by governmental authorities.

[13] If a lawyer comes to know or reasonably should know that a client expects assistance not permitted by the Rules of Professional Conduct or other law or if the lawyer intends to act contrary to the client's instructions, the lawyer must consult with the client regarding the limitations on the lawyer's conduct. See Rule 1.4(a)(5).

Rule 1.3   Diligence

A lawyer shall act with reasonable diligence and promptness in representing a client.

COMMENT

[1] A lawyer should pursue a matter on behalf of a client despite opposition, obstruction or personal inconvenience to the lawyer, and take whatever lawful and ethical measures are required to vindicate a client's cause or endeavor. A lawyer must also act with commitment and dedication to the interests of the client and

with zeal in advocacy upon the client's behalf. A lawyer is not bound, however, to press for every advantage that might be realized for a client. For example, a lawyer may have authority to exercise professional discretion in determining the means by which a matter should be pursued. See Rule 1.2. The lawyer's duty to act with reasonable diligence does not require the use of offensive tactics or preclude the treating of all persons involved in the legal process with courtesy and respect.

[2] A lawyer's work load must be controlled so that each matter can be handled competently.

[3] Perhaps no professional shortcoming is more widely resented than procrastination. A client's interests often can be adversely affected by the passage of time or the change of conditions; in extreme instances, as when a lawyer overlooks a statute of limitations, the client's legal position may be destroyed. Even when the client's interests are not affected in substance, however, unreasonable delay can cause a client needless anxiety and undermine confidence in the lawyer's trustworthiness. A lawyer's duty to act with reasonable promptness, however, does not preclude the lawyer from agreeing to a reasonable request for a postponement that will not prejudice the lawyer's client.

[4] Unless the relationship is terminated as provided in Rule 1.16, a lawyer should carry through to conclusion all matters undertaken for a client. If a lawyer's employment is limited to a specific matter, the relationship terminates when the matter has been resolved. If a lawyer has served a client over a substantial period in a variety of matters, the client sometimes may assume that the lawyer will continue to serve on a continuing basis unless the lawyer gives notice of withdrawal. Doubt about whether a client-lawyer relationship still exists should be clarified by the lawyer, preferably in writing, so that the client will not mistakenly suppose the lawyer is looking after the client's affairs when the lawyer has ceased to do so. For example, if a lawyer has handled a judicial or administrative proceeding that produced a result adverse to the client and the lawyer and the client have not agreed that the lawyer will handle the matter on appeal, the lawyer must consult with the client about the possibility of appeal before relinquishing responsibility for the matter. See Rule 1.4(a)(2). Whether the lawyer is obligated to prosecute the appeal for the client depends on the scope of the representation the lawyer has agreed to provide to the client. See Rule 1.2.

[5] To prevent neglect of client matters in the event of a sole practitioner's death or disability, the duty of diligence may require that each sole practitioner prepare a plan, in conformity with applicable rules, that designates another competent lawyer to review client files, notify each client of the lawyer's death or disability, and determine whether there is a need for immediate protective action. Cf. Rule 28 of the American Bar Association Model Rules for Lawyer Disciplinary Enforcement (providing for court appointment of a lawyer to inventory files and take other protective action in absence of a plan providing for another lawyer to protect the interests of the clients of a deceased or disabled lawyer).

> **Editors' Note.** In August 2012, the ABA House of Delegates amended Comment 4 to Rule 1.4. The ABA Commission on Ethics 20/20 proposed this change to make clear that lawyers should respond promptly to all client communications, not just to "telephone calls." To alert readers to this change, we underscore the new language and strike through deleted language. For more information regarding this change, see the Legislative History for this Rule in the "Annotations on ABA Model Rules" section of this book.

Rule 1.4   Communication

(a) A lawyer shall:

(1) promptly inform the client of any decision or circumstance with respect to which the client's informed consent, as defined in Rule 1.0(e), is required by these Rules;

(2) reasonably consult with the client about the means by which the client's objectives are to be accomplished;

(3) keep the client reasonably informed about the status of the matter;

(4) promptly comply with reasonable requests for information; and

(5) consult with the client about any relevant limitation on the lawyer's conduct when the lawyer knows that the client expects assistance not permitted by the Rules of Professional Conduct or other law.

(b) A lawyer shall explain a matter to the extent reasonably necessary to permit the client to make informed decisions regarding the representation.

COMMENT

[1] Reasonable communication between the lawyer and the client is necessary for the client effectively to participate in the representation.

Communicating with Client

[2] If these Rules require that a particular decision about the representation be made by the client, paragraph (a)(1) requires that the lawyer promptly consult with and secure the client's consent prior to taking action unless prior discussions with the client have resolved what action the client wants the lawyer to take. For example, a lawyer who receives from opposing counsel an offer of settlement in a civil controversy or a proffered plea bargain in a criminal case must promptly inform the client of its substance unless the client has previously indicated that the proposal will be acceptable or unacceptable or has authorized the lawyer to accept or to reject the offer. See Rule 1.2(a).

[3] Paragraph (a)(2) requires the lawyer to reasonably consult with the client about the means to be used to accomplish the client's objectives. In some situations—depending on both the importance of the action under consideration and the feasibility of consulting with the client—this duty will require consultation prior to taking action. In other circumstances, such as during a trial when an immediate decision must be made, the exigency of the situation may require the lawyer to act without prior consultation. In such cases the lawyer must nonetheless act reasonably to inform the client of actions the lawyer has taken on the client's behalf. Additionally, paragraph (a)(3) requires that the lawyer keep the client reasonably informed about the status of the matter, such as significant developments affecting the timing or the substance of the representation.

[4] A lawyer's regular communication with clients will minimize the occasions on which a client will need to request information concerning the representation. When a client makes a reasonable request for information, however, paragraph (a)(4) requires prompt compliance with the request, or if a prompt response is not feasible, that the lawyer, or a member of the lawyer's staff, acknowledge receipt of the request and advise the client when a response may be expected. ~~Client telephone calls should be promptly returned or acknowledged.~~ <u>A lawyer should promptly respond to or acknowledge client communications.</u>

Explaining Matters

[5] The client should have sufficient information to participate intelligently in decisions concerning the objectives of the representation and the means by which they are to be pursued, to the extent the client is willing and able to do so. Adequacy of communication depends in part on the kind of advice or assistance that is involved. For example, when there is time to explain a proposal made in a negotiation, the lawyer should review all important provisions with the client before proceeding to an agreement. In litigation a lawyer should explain the general strategy and prospects of success and ordinarily should consult the client on tactics that are likely to result in significant expense or to injure or coerce others. On the other hand, a lawyer ordinarily will not be expected to describe trial or negotiation strategy in detail. The guiding principle is that the lawyer should fulfill reasonable client expectations for information consistent with the duty to act in the client's best interests, and the client's overall requirements as to the character of representation. In certain circumstances, such as when a lawyer asks a client to consent to a representation affected by a conflict of interest, the client must give informed consent, as defined in Rule 1.0(e).

[6] Ordinarily, the information to be provided is that appropriate for a client who is a comprehending and responsible adult. However, fully informing the client according to this standard may be impracticable, for example, where the client is a child or suffers from diminished capacity. See Rule 1.14. When the client is an organization or group, it is often impossible or inappropriate to inform every one of its members about its legal affairs; ordinarily, the lawyer should address communications to the appropriate officials of the organization. See Rule 1.13. Where many routine matters are involved, a system of limited or occasional reporting may be arranged with the client.

Withholding Information

[7] In some circumstances, a lawyer may be justified in delaying transmission of information when the client would be likely to react imprudently to an immediate communication. Thus, a lawyer might withhold a psychiatric diagnosis of a client when the examining psychiatrist indicates that disclosure would harm the client. A lawyer may not withhold information to serve the lawyer's own interest or convenience or the interests or convenience of another person. Rules or court orders governing litigation may provide that information supplied to a lawyer may not be disclosed to the client. Rule 3.4(c) directs compliance with such rules or orders.

Rule 1.5   Fees

(a) A lawyer shall not make an agreement for, charge, or collect an unreasonable fee or an unreasonable amount for expenses. The factors to be considered in determining the reasonableness of a fee include the following:

(1) the time and labor required, the novelty and difficulty of the questions involved, and the skill requisite to perform the legal service properly;

(2) the likelihood, if apparent to the client, that the acceptance of the particular employment will preclude other employment by the lawyer;

(3) the fee customarily charged in the locality for similar legal services;

(4) the amount involved and the results obtained;

(5) the time limitations imposed by the client or by the circumstances;

(6) the nature and length of the professional relationship with the client;

(7) the experience, reputation, and ability of the lawyer or lawyers performing the services; and

(8) whether the fee is fixed or contingent.

(b) The scope of the representation and the basis or rate of the fee and expenses for which the client will be responsible shall be communicated to the client, preferably in writing, before or within a reasonable time after commencing the representation, except when the lawyer will charge a regularly represented client on the same basis or rate. Any changes in the basis or rate of the fee or expenses shall also be communicated to the client.

(c) A fee may be contingent on the outcome of the matter for which the service is rendered, except in a matter in which a contingent fee is prohibited by paragraph (d) or other law. A contingent fee agreement shall be in a writing signed by the client and shall state the method by which the fee is to be determined, including the percentage or percentages that shall accrue to the lawyer in the event of settlement, trial or appeal; litigation and other expenses to be deducted from the recovery; and whether such expenses are to be deducted before or after the contingent fee is calculated. The agreement must clearly notify the client of any expenses for which the client will be liable whether or not the client is the prevailing party. Upon conclusion of a contingent fee matter, the lawyer shall provide the client with a written statement stating the outcome of the matter and, if there is a recovery, showing the remittance to the client and the method of its determination.

(d) A lawyer shall not enter into an arrangement for, charge, or collect:

(1) any fee in a domestic relations matter, the payment or amount of which is contingent upon the securing of a divorce or upon the amount of alimony or support, or property settlement in lieu thereof; or

(2) a contingent fee for representing a defendant in a criminal case.

(e) A division of a fee between lawyers who are not in the same firm may be made only if:

(1) the division is in proportion to the services performed by each lawyer or each lawyer assumes joint responsibility for the representation;

(2) the client agrees to the arrangement, including the share each lawyer will receive, and the agreement is confirmed in writing; and

(3) the total fee is reasonable.

COMMENT

Reasonableness of Fee and Expenses

[1] Paragraph (a) requires that lawyers charge fees that are reasonable under the circumstances. The factors specified in (1) through (8) are not exclusive. Nor will each factor be relevant in each instance. Paragraph (a) also requires that expenses for which the client will be charged must be reasonable. A lawyer may seek reimbursement for the cost of services performed in-house, such as copying, or for other expenses incurred in-house, such as telephone charges, either by charging a reasonable amount to which the client has agreed in advance or by charging an amount that reasonably reflects the cost incurred by the lawyer.

Basis or Rate of Fee

[2] When the lawyer has regularly represented a client, they ordinarily will have evolved an understanding concerning the basis or rate of the fee and the expenses for which the client will be responsible. In a new client-lawyer relationship, however, an understanding as to fees and expenses must be promptly established. Generally, it is desirable to furnish the client with at least a simple memorandum or copy of the lawyer's customary fee arrangements that states the general nature of the legal services to be provided, the basis, rate or total amount of the fee and whether and to what extent the client will be responsible for any costs, expenses or disbursements in the course of the representation. A written statement concerning the terms of the engagement reduces the possibility of misunderstanding.

[3] Contingent fees, like any other fees, are subject to the reasonableness standard of paragraph (a) of this Rule. In determining whether a particular contingent fee is reasonable, or whether it is reasonable to charge any form of contingent fee, a lawyer must consider the factors that are relevant under the circumstances. Applicable law may impose limitations on contingent fees, such as a ceiling on the percentage allowable, or may require a lawyer to offer clients an alternative basis for the fee. Applicable law also may apply to situations other than a contingent fee, for example, government regulations regarding fees in certain tax matters.

Terms of Payment

[4] A lawyer may require advance payment of a fee, but is obliged to return any unearned portion. See Rule 1.16(d). A lawyer may accept property in payment

for services, such as an ownership interest in an enterprise, providing this does not involve acquisition of a proprietary interest in the cause of action or subject matter of the litigation contrary to Rule 1.8(i). However, a fee paid in property instead of money may be subject to the requirements of Rule 1.8(a) because such fees often have the essential qualities of a business transaction with the client.

[5] An agreement may not be made whose terms might induce the lawyer improperly to curtail services for the client or perform them in a way contrary to the client's interest. For example, a lawyer should not enter into an agreement whereby services are to be provided only up to a stated amount when it is foreseeable that more extensive services probably will be required, unless the situation is adequately explained to the client. Otherwise, the client might have to bargain for further assistance in the midst of a proceeding or transaction. However, it is proper to define the extent of services in light of the client's ability to pay. A lawyer should not exploit a fee arrangement based primarily on hourly charges by using wasteful procedures.

Prohibited Contingent Fees

[6] Paragraph (d) prohibits a lawyer from charging a contingent fee in a domestic relations matter when payment is contingent upon the securing of a divorce or upon the amount of alimony or support or property settlement to be obtained. This provision does not preclude a contract for a contingent fee for legal representation in connection with the recovery of post-judgment balances due under support, alimony or other financial orders because such contracts do not implicate the same policy concerns.

Division of Fee

[7] A division of fee is a single billing to a client covering the fee of two or more lawyers who are not in the same firm. A division of fee facilitates association of more than one lawyer in a matter in which neither alone could serve the client as well, and most often is used when the fee is contingent and the division is between a referring lawyer and a trial specialist. Paragraph (e) permits the lawyers to divide a fee either on the basis of the proportion of services they render or if each lawyer assumes responsibility for the representation as a whole. In addition, the client must agree to the arrangement, including the share that each lawyer is to receive, and the agreement must be confirmed in writing. Contingent fee agreements must be in a writing signed by the client and must otherwise comply with paragraph (c) of this Rule. Joint responsibility for the representation entails financial and ethical responsibility for the representation as if the lawyers were associated in a partnership. A lawyer should only refer a matter to a lawyer whom the referring lawyer reasonably believes is competent to handle the matter. See Rule 1.1.

[8] Paragraph (e) does not prohibit or regulate division of fees to be received in the future for work done when lawyers were previously associated in a law firm.

Disputes over Fees

[9] If a procedure has been established for resolution of fee disputes, such as an arbitration or mediation procedure established by the bar, the lawyer must comply with the procedure when it is mandatory, and, even when it is voluntary, the lawyer should conscientiously consider submitting to it. Law may prescribe a procedure for determining a lawyer's fee, for example, in representation of an executor or administrator, a class or a person entitled to a reasonable fee as part of the measure of damages. The lawyer entitled to such a fee and a lawyer representing another party concerned with the fee should comply with the prescribed procedure.

> **Editors' Note.** In August 2012, the ABA House of Delegates added Rule 1.6(c), Rule 1.6(b)(7), and new Comment language in response to proposals by the ABA Commission on Ethics 20/20. The proposals address two distinct issues. First, Rule 1.6(c) was added to emphasize that lawyers have an obligation to protect their clients' confidential information from inadvertent or unauthorized disclosure and from unauthorized access. Comments 18 and 19 elaborate on this obligation. Second, Rule 1.6(b)(7) was added to address the following question: To what extent can lawyers in different firms disclose confidential information to each other to detect conflicts of interest that might arise when lawyers consider an association with another firm, two or more firms consider a merger, or lawyers consider the purchase of a law practice? Comments 13 and 14 elaborate on the new guidance offered in Rule 1.6(b)(7). To alert readers to these changes, we underscore the new language and strike through deleted language. For more information regarding these changes, see the Legislative History for this Rule in the "Annotations on ABA Model Rules" section of this book.

Rule 1.6   Confidentiality of Information

(a) A lawyer shall not reveal information relating to the representation of a client unless the client gives informed consent, the disclosure is impliedly authorized in order to carry out the representation or the disclosure is permitted by paragraph (b).

(b) A lawyer may reveal information relating to the representation of a client to the extent the lawyer reasonably believes necessary:

(1) to prevent reasonably certain death or substantial bodily harm;

(2) to prevent the client from committing a crime or fraud that is reasonably certain to result in substantial injury to the financial interests or property of another and in furtherance of which the client has used or is using the lawyer's services;

(3) to prevent, mitigate or rectify substantial injury to the financial interests or property of another that is reasonably certain to result or has resulted from the client's commission of a crime or fraud in furtherance of which the client has used the lawyer's services;

(4) to secure legal advice about the lawyer's compliance with these Rules;

(5) to establish a claim or defense on behalf of the lawyer in a controversy between the lawyer and the client, to establish a defense to a criminal charge or civil claim against the lawyer based upon conduct in which the client was involved, or to respond to allegations in any proceeding concerning the lawyer's representation of the client; ~~or~~

(6) to comply with other law or a court order~~.~~; or

(7) to detect and resolve conflicts of interest arising from the lawyer's change of employment or from changes in the composition or ownership of a firm, but only if the revealed information would not compromise the attorney-client privilege or otherwise prejudice the client.

(c) A lawyer shall make reasonable efforts to prevent the inadvertent or unauthorized disclosure of, or unauthorized access to, information relating to the representation of a client.

[handwritten margin note: State disclosure requirement if gov is involved]

COMMENT

[1] This Rule governs the disclosure by a lawyer of information relating to the representation of a client during the lawyer's representation of the client. See Rule 1.18 for the lawyer's duties with respect to information provided to the lawyer by a prospective client, Rule 1.9(c)(2) for the lawyer's duty not to reveal information relating to the lawyer's prior representation of a former client and Rules 1.8(b) and 1.9(c)(1) for the lawyer's duties with respect to the use of such information to the disadvantage of clients and former clients.

[2] A fundamental principle in the client-lawyer relationship is that, in the absence of the client's informed consent, the lawyer must not reveal information relating to the representation. See Rule 1.0(e) for the definition of informed consent. This contributes to the trust that is the hallmark of the client-lawyer relationship. The client is thereby encouraged to seek legal assistance and to communicate fully and frankly with the lawyer even as to embarrassing or legally damaging subject matter. The lawyer needs this information to represent the client effectively and, if necessary, to advise the client to refrain from wrongful conduct. Almost without exception, clients come to lawyers in order to determine their rights and what is, in the complex of laws and regulations, deemed to be legal and correct. Based upon experience, lawyers know that almost all clients follow the advice given, and the law is upheld.

[3] The principle of client-lawyer confidentiality is given effect by related bodies of law: the attorney-client privilege, the work-product doctrine and the rule of confidentiality established in professional ethics. The attorney-client privilege and work-product doctrine apply in judicial and other proceedings in which a lawyer may be called as a witness or otherwise required to produce evidence concerning a client. The rule of client-lawyer confidentiality applies in situations other than those where evidence is sought from the lawyer through compulsion of law. The confidentiality rule, for example, applies not only to matters communicated in confidence by the client but also to all information relating to the representation, whatever its source. A lawyer may not disclose such information except as authorized or required by the Rules of Professional Conduct or other law. See also Scope.

[4] Paragraph (a) prohibits a lawyer from revealing information relating to the representation of a client. This prohibition also applies to disclosures by a lawyer that do not in themselves reveal protected information but could reasonably lead to the discovery of such information by a third person. A lawyer's use of a hypothetical to discuss issues relating to the representation is permissible so long as there is no reasonable likelihood that the listener will be able to ascertain the identity of the client or the situation involved.

Authorized Disclosure

[5] Except to the extent that the client's instructions or special circumstances limit that authority, a lawyer is impliedly authorized to make disclosures about a client when appropriate in carrying out the representation. In some situations, for example, a lawyer may be impliedly authorized to admit a fact that cannot properly be disputed or to make a disclosure that facilitates a satisfactory conclusion to a matter. Lawyers in a firm may, in the course of the firm's practice, disclose to each other information relating to a client of the firm, unless the client has instructed that particular information be confined to specified lawyers.

Disclosure Adverse to Client

[6] Although the public interest is usually best served by a strict rule requiring lawyers to preserve the confidentiality of information relating to the representation of their clients, the confidentiality rule is subject to limited exceptions. Paragraph (b) (1) recognizes the overriding value of life and physical integrity and permits disclosure reasonably necessary to prevent reasonably certain death or substantial bodily harm. Such harm is reasonably certain to occur if it will be suffered imminently or if there is a present and substantial threat that a person will suffer such harm at a later date if the lawyer fails to take action necessary to eliminate the threat. Thus, a lawyer who knows that a client has accidentally discharged toxic waste into a town's water supply may reveal this information to the authorities if there is a present and substantial risk that a person who drinks the water will contract a life-threatening or debilitating disease and the lawyer's disclosure is necessary to eliminate the threat or reduce the number of victims.

[7] Paragraph (b)(2) is a limited exception to the rule of confidentiality that permits the lawyer to reveal information to the extent necessary to enable affected persons or appropriate authorities to prevent the client from committing a crime or fraud, as defined in Rule 1.0(d), that is reasonably certain to result in substantial injury to the financial or property interests of another and in furtherance of which the client has used or is using the lawyer's services. Such a serious abuse of the client-lawyer relationship by the client forfeits the protection of this Rule. The client can, of course, prevent such disclosure by refraining from the wrongful conduct. Although paragraph (b)(2) does not require the lawyer to reveal the client's misconduct, the lawyer may not counsel or assist the client in conduct the lawyer knows is criminal or fraudulent. See Rule 1.2(d). See also Rule 1.16 with respect to the lawyer's obligation or right to withdraw from the representation of the client in such circumstances, and

Rule 1.13(c) which permits the lawyer, where the client is an organization, to reveal information relating to the representation in limited circumstances.

[8] Paragraph (b)(3) addresses the situation in which the lawyer does not learn of the client's crime or fraud until after it has been consummated. Although the client no longer has the option of preventing disclosure by refraining from the wrongful conduct, there will be situations in which the loss suffered by the affected person can be prevented, rectified or mitigated. In such situations, the lawyer may disclose information relating to the representation to the extent necessary to enable the affected persons to prevent or mitigate reasonably certain losses or to attempt to recoup their losses. Paragraph (b)(3) does not apply when a person who has committed a crime or fraud thereafter employs a lawyer for representation concerning that offense.

[9] A lawyer's confidentiality obligations do not preclude a lawyer from securing confidential legal advice about the lawyer's personal responsibility to comply with these Rules. In most situations, disclosing information to secure such advice will be impliedly authorized for the lawyer to carry out the representation. Even when the disclosure is not impliedly authorized, paragraph (b)(4) permits such disclosure because of the importance of a lawyer's compliance with the Rules of Professional Conduct.

[10] Where a legal claim or disciplinary charge alleges complicity of the lawyer in a client's conduct or other misconduct of the lawyer involving representation of the client, the lawyer may respond to the extent the lawyer reasonably believes necessary to establish a defense. The same is true with respect to a claim involving the conduct or representation of a former client. Such a charge can arise in a civil, criminal, disciplinary or other proceeding and can be based on a wrong allegedly committed by the lawyer against the client or on a wrong alleged by a third person, for example, a person claiming to have been defrauded by the lawyer and client acting together. The lawyer's right to respond arises when an assertion of such complicity has been made. Paragraph (b)(5) does not require the lawyer to await the commencement of an action or proceeding that charges such complicity, so that the defense may be established by responding directly to a third party who has made such an assertion. The right to defend also applies, of course, where a proceeding has been commenced.

[11] A lawyer entitled to a fee is permitted by paragraph (b)(5) to prove the services rendered in an action to collect it. This aspect of the rule expresses the principle that the beneficiary of a fiduciary relationship may not exploit it to the detriment of the fiduciary.

[12] Other law may require that a lawyer disclose information about a client. Whether such a law supersedes Rule 1.6 is a question of law beyond the scope of these Rules. When disclosure of information relating to the representation appears to be required by other law, the lawyer must discuss the matter with the client to the extent required by Rule 1.4. If, however, the other law supersedes this Rule and requires disclosure, paragraph (b)(6) permits the lawyer to make such disclosures as are necessary to comply with the law.

Detection of Conflicts of Interest

[13] Paragraph (b)(7) recognizes that lawyers in different firms may need to disclose limited information to each other to detect and resolve conflicts of interest,

such as when a lawyer is considering an association with another firm, two or more firms are considering a merger, or a lawyer is considering the purchase of a law practice. See Rule 1.17, Comment [7]. Under these circumstances, lawyers and law firms are permitted to disclose limited information, but only once substantive discussions regarding the new relationship have occurred. Any such disclosure should ordinarily include no more than the identity of the persons and entities involved in a matter, a brief summary of the general issues involved, and information about whether the matter has terminated. Even this limited information, however, should be disclosed only to the extent reasonably necessary to detect and resolve conflicts of interest that might arise from the possible new relationship. Moreover, the disclosure of any information is prohibited if it would compromise the attorney-client privilege or otherwise prejudice the client (e.g., the fact that a corporate client is seeking advice on a corporate takeover that has not been publicly announced; that a person has consulted a lawyer about the possibility of divorce before the person's intentions are known to the person's spouse; or that a person has consulted a lawyer about a criminal investigation that has not led to a public charge). Under those circumstances, paragraph (a) prohibits disclosure unless the client or former client gives informed consent. A lawyer's fiduciary duty to the lawyer's firm may also govern a lawyer's conduct when exploring an association with another firm and is beyond the scope of these Rules.

[14] Any information disclosed pursuant to paragraph (b)(7) may be used or further disclosed only to the extent necessary to detect and resolve conflicts of interest. Paragraph (b)(7) does not restrict the use of information acquired by means independent of any disclosure pursuant to paragraph (b)(7). Paragraph (b)(7) also does not affect the disclosure of information within a law firm when the disclosure is otherwise authorized, see Comment [5], such as when a lawyer in a firm discloses information to another lawyer in the same firm to detect and resolve conflicts of interest that could arise in connection with undertaking a new representation.

[15] A lawyer may be ordered to reveal information relating to the representation of a client by a court or by another tribunal or governmental entity claiming authority pursuant to other law to compel the disclosure. Absent informed consent of the client to do otherwise, the lawyer should assert on behalf of the client all non-frivolous claims that the order is not authorized by other law or that the information sought is protected against disclosure by the attorney-client privilege or other applicable law. In the event of an adverse ruling, the lawyer must consult with the client about the possibility of appeal to the extent required by Rule 1.4. Unless review is sought, however, paragraph (b)(6) permits the lawyer to comply with the court's order.

[16] Paragraph (b) permits disclosure only to the extent the lawyer reasonably believes the disclosure is necessary to accomplish one of the purposes specified. Where practicable, the lawyer should first seek to persuade the client to take suitable action to obviate the need for disclosure. In any case, a disclosure adverse to the client's interest should be no greater than the lawyer reasonably believes necessary to accomplish the purpose. If the disclosure will be made in connection with a judicial proceeding, the disclosure should be made in a manner that limits access to the information to the tribunal or other persons having a need to know it and appropriate protective orders or other arrangements should be sought by the lawyer to the fullest extent practicable.

[175] Paragraph (b) permits but does not require the disclosure of information relating to a client's representation to accomplish the purposes specified in paragraphs (b)(1) through (b)(6). In exercising the discretion conferred by this Rule, the lawyer may consider such factors as the nature of the lawyer's relationship with the client and with those who might be injured by the client, the lawyer's own involvement in the transaction and factors that may extenuate the conduct in question. A lawyer's decision not to disclose as permitted by paragraph (b) does not violate this Rule. Disclosure may be required, however, by other Rules. Some Rules require disclosure only if such disclosure would be permitted by paragraph (b). See Rules 1.2(d), 4.1(b), 8.1 and 8.3. Rule 3.3, on the other hand, requires disclosure in some circumstances regardless of whether such disclosure is permitted by this Rule. See Rule 3.3(c).

Acting Competently to Preserve Confidentiality

[186] Paragraph (c) requires a A lawyer must to act competently to safeguard information relating to the representation of a client against unauthorized access by third parties and against inadvertent or unauthorized disclosure by the lawyer or other persons who are participating in the representation of the client or who are subject to the lawyer's supervision. See Rules 1.1, 5.1 and 5.3. The unauthorized access to, or the inadvertent or unauthorized disclosure of, information relating to the representation of a client does not constitute a violation of paragraph (c) if the lawyer has made reasonable efforts to prevent the access or disclosure. Factors to be considered in determining the reasonableness of the lawyer's efforts include, but are not limited to, the sensitivity of the information, the likelihood of disclosure if additional safeguards are not employed, the cost of employing additional safeguards, the difficulty of implementing the safeguards, and the extent to which the safeguards adversely affect the lawyer's ability to represent clients (e.g., by making a device or important piece of software excessively difficult to use). A client may require the lawyer to implement special security measures not required by this Rule or may give informed consent to forgo security measures that would otherwise be required by this Rule. Whether a lawyer may be required to take additional steps to safeguard a client's information in order to comply with other law, such as state and federal laws that govern data privacy or that impose notification requirements upon the loss of, or unauthorized access to, electronic information, is beyond the scope of these Rules. For a lawyer's duties when sharing information with nonlawyers outside the lawyer's own firm, see Rule 5.3, Comments [3]-[4].

[197] When transmitting a communication that includes information relating to the representation of a client, the lawyer must take reasonable precautions to prevent the information from coming into the hands of unintended recipients. This duty, however, does not require that the lawyer use special security measures if the method of communication affords a reasonable expectation of privacy. Special circumstances, however, may warrant special precautions. Factors to be considered in determining the reasonableness of the lawyer's expectation of confidentiality include the sensitivity of the information and the extent to which the privacy of the communication is protected by law or by a confidentiality agreement. A client may require the lawyer to implement special security measures not required by this Rule or may give informed consent to the use of a means of communication that would

otherwise be prohibited by this Rule. <u>Whether a lawyer may be required to take additional steps in order to comply with other law, such as state and federal laws that govern data privacy, is beyond the scope of these Rules.</u>

Former Client

[~~2018~~] The duty of confidentiality continues after the client-lawyer relationship has terminated. See Rule 1.9(c)(2). See Rule 1.9(c)(1) for the prohibition against using such information to the disadvantage of the former client.

Rule 1.7   Conflict of Interest: Current Clients

(a) Except as provided in paragraph (b), a lawyer shall not represent a client if the representation involves a concurrent conflict of interest. A concurrent conflict of interest exists if:

(1) the representation of one client will be directly adverse to another client; or

(2) there is a significant risk that the representation of one or more clients will be materially limited by the lawyer's responsibilities to another client, a former client or a third person or by a personal interest of the lawyer.

(b) Notwithstanding the existence of a concurrent conflict of interest under paragraph (a), a lawyer may represent a client if:

(1) the lawyer reasonably believes that the lawyer will be able to provide competent and diligent representation to each affected client;

(2) the representation is not prohibited by law;

(3) the representation does not involve the assertion of a claim by one client against another client represented by the lawyer in the same litigation or other proceeding before a tribunal; and

(4) each affected client gives informed consent, confirmed in writing.

COMMENT

General Principles

[1] Loyalty and independent judgment are essential elements in the lawyer's relationship to a client. Concurrent conflicts of interest can arise from the lawyer's responsibilities to another client, a former client or a third person or from the lawyer's own interests. For specific Rules regarding certain concurrent conflicts of interest, see Rule 1.8. For former client conflicts of interest, see Rule 1.9. For conflicts of interest involving prospective clients, see Rule 1.18. For definitions of "informed consent" and "confirmed in writing," see Rule 1.0(e) and (b).

[2] Resolution of a conflict of interest problem under this Rule requires the lawyer to: 1) clearly identify the client or clients; 2) determine whether a conflict of interest exists; 3) decide whether the representation may be undertaken despite the existence of a conflict, i.e., whether the conflict is consentable; and 4) if so, consult with the clients affected under paragraph (a) and obtain their informed consent, confirmed in writing. The clients affected under paragraph (a) include both of the clients referred to in paragraph (a)(1) and the one or more clients whose representation might be materially limited under paragraph (a)(2).

[3] A conflict of interest may exist before representation is undertaken, in which event the representation must be declined, unless the lawyer obtains the informed consent of each client under the conditions of paragraph (b). To determine whether a conflict of interest exists, a lawyer should adopt reasonable procedures, appropriate for the size and type of firm and practice, to determine in both litigation and non-litigation matters the persons and issues involved. See also Comment to Rule 5.1. Ignorance caused by a failure to institute such procedures will not excuse a lawyer's violation of this Rule. As to whether a client-lawyer relationship exists or, having once been established, is continuing, see Comment to Rule 1.3 and Scope.

[4] If a conflict arises after representation has been undertaken, the lawyer ordinarily must withdraw from the representation, unless the lawyer has obtained the informed consent of the client under the conditions of paragraph (b). See Rule 1.16. Where more than one client is involved, whether the lawyer may continue to represent any of the clients is determined both by the lawyer's ability to comply with duties owed to the former client and by the lawyer's ability to represent adequately the remaining client or clients, given the lawyer's duties to the former client. See Rule 1.9. See also Comments [5] and [29].

[5] Unforeseeable developments, such as changes in corporate and other organizational affiliations or the addition or realignment of parties in litigation, might create conflicts in the midst of a representation, as when a company sued by the lawyer on behalf of one client is bought by another client represented by the lawyer in an unrelated matter. Depending on the circumstances, the lawyer may have the option to withdraw from one of the representations in order to avoid the conflict. The lawyer must seek court approval where necessary and take steps to minimize harm to the clients. See Rule 1.16. The lawyer must continue to protect the confidences of the client from whose representation the lawyer has withdrawn. See Rule 1.9(c).

Identifying Conflicts of Interest: Directly Adverse

[6] Loyalty to a current client prohibits undertaking representation directly adverse to that client without that client's informed consent. Thus, absent consent, a lawyer may not act as an advocate in one matter against a person the lawyer represents in some other matter, even when the matters are wholly unrelated. The client as to whom the representation is directly adverse is likely to feel betrayed, and the resulting damage to the client-lawyer relationship is likely to impair the lawyer's ability to represent the client effectively. In addition, the client on whose behalf the adverse representation is undertaken reasonably may fear that the lawyer will pursue that client's case less effectively out of deference to the other client,

i.e., that the representation may be materially limited by the lawyer's interest in retaining the current client. Similarly, a directly adverse conflict may arise when a lawyer is required to cross-examine a client who appears as a witness in a lawsuit involving another client, as when the testimony will be damaging to the client who is represented in the lawsuit. On the other hand, simultaneous representation in unrelated matters of clients whose interests are only economically adverse, such as representation of competing economic enterprises in unrelated litigation, does not ordinarily constitute a conflict of interest and thus may not require consent of the respective clients.

[7] Directly adverse conflicts can also arise in transactional matters. For example, if a lawyer is asked to represent the seller of a business in negotiations with a buyer represented by the lawyer, not in the same transaction but in another, unrelated matter, the lawyer could not undertake the representation without the informed consent of each client.

Identifying Conflicts of Interest: Material Limitation

[8] Even where there is no direct adverseness, a conflict of interest exists if there is a significant risk that a lawyer's ability to consider, recommend or carry out an appropriate course of action for the client will be materially limited as a result of the lawyer's other responsibilities or interests. For example, a lawyer asked to represent several individuals seeking to form a joint venture is likely to be materially limited in the lawyer's ability to recommend or advocate all possible positions that each might take because of the lawyer's duty of loyalty to the others. The conflict in effect forecloses alternatives that would otherwise be available to the client. The mere possibility of subsequent harm does not itself require disclosure and consent. The critical questions are the likelihood that a difference in interests will eventuate and, if it does, whether it will materially interfere with the lawyer's independent professional judgment in considering alternatives or foreclose courses of action that reasonably should be pursued on behalf of the client.

Lawyer's Responsibilities to Former Clients and Other Third Persons

[9] In addition to conflicts with other current clients, a lawyer's duties of loyalty and independence may be materially limited by responsibilities to former clients under Rule 1.9 or by the lawyer's responsibilities to other persons, such as fiduciary duties arising from a lawyer's service as a trustee, executor or corporate director.

Personal Interest Conflicts

[10] The lawyer's own interests should not be permitted to have an adverse effect on representation of a client. For example, if the probity of a lawyer's own conduct in a transaction is in serious question, it may be difficult or impossible for the lawyer to give a client detached advice. Similarly, when a lawyer has discussions concerning possible employment with an opponent of the lawyer's client, or with a law firm representing the opponent, such discussions could materially limit the

lawyer's representation of the client. In addition, a lawyer may not allow related business interests to affect representation, for example, by referring clients to an enterprise in which the lawyer has an undisclosed financial interest. See Rule 1.8 for specific Rules pertaining to a number of personal interest conflicts, including business transactions with clients. See also Rule 1.10 (personal interest conflicts under Rule 1.7 ordinarily are not imputed to other lawyers in a law firm).

[11] When lawyers representing different clients in the same matter or in substantially related matters are closely related by blood or marriage, there may be a significant risk that client confidences will be revealed and that the lawyer's family relationship will interfere with both loyalty and independent professional judgment. As a result, each client is entitled to know of the existence and implications of the relationship between the lawyers before the lawyer agrees to undertake the representation. Thus, a lawyer related to another lawyer, e.g., as parent, child, sibling or spouse, ordinarily may not represent a client in a matter where that lawyer is representing another party, unless each client gives informed consent. The disqualification arising from a close family relationship is personal and ordinarily is not imputed to members of firms with whom the lawyers are associated. See Rule 1.10.

[12] A lawyer is prohibited from engaging in sexual relationships with a client unless the sexual relationship predates the formation of the client-lawyer relationship. See Rule 1.8(j).

Interest of Person Paying for a Lawyer's Service

[13] A lawyer may be paid from a source other than the client, including a co-client, if the client is informed of that fact and consents and the arrangement does not compromise the lawyer's duty of loyalty or independent judgment to the client. See Rule 1.8(f). If acceptance of the payment from any other source presents a significant risk that the lawyer's representation of the client will be materially limited by the lawyer's own interest in accommodating the person paying the lawyer's fee or by the lawyer's responsibilities to a payer who is also a co-client, then the lawyer must comply with the requirements of paragraph (b) before accepting the representation, including determining whether the conflict is consentable and, if so, that the client has adequate information about the material risks of the representation.

Prohibited Representations

[14] Ordinarily, clients may consent to representation notwithstanding a conflict. However, as indicated in paragraph (b), some conflicts are nonconsentable, meaning that the lawyer involved cannot properly ask for such agreement or provide representation on the basis of the clients consent. When the lawyer is representing more than one client, the question of consentability must be resolved as to each client.

[15] Consentability is typically determined by considering whether the interests of the clients will be adequately protected if the clients are permitted to give their informed consent to representation burdened by a conflict of interest. Thus, under paragraph (b)(1), representation is prohibited if in the circumstances the

lawyer cannot reasonably conclude that the lawyer will be able to provide competent and diligent representation. See Rule 1.1 (competence) and Rule 1.3 (diligence).

[16] Paragraph (b)(2) describes conflicts that are nonconsentable because the representation is prohibited by applicable law. For example, in some states substantive law provides that the same lawyer may not represent more than one defendant in a capital case, even with the consent of the clients, and under federal criminal statutes certain representations by a former government lawyer are prohibited, despite the informed consent of the former client. In addition, decisional law in some states limits the ability of a governmental client, such as a municipality, to consent to a conflict of interest.

[17] Paragraph (b)(3) describes conflicts that are nonconsentable because of the institutional interest in vigorous development of each client's position when the clients are aligned directly against each other in the same litigation or other proceeding before a tribunal. Whether clients are aligned directly against each other within the meaning of this paragraph requires examination of the context of the proceeding. Although this paragraph does not preclude a lawyer's multiple representation of adverse parties to a mediation (because mediation is not a proceeding before a "tribunal" under Rule 1.0(m)), such representation may be precluded by paragraph (b)(1).

Informed Consent

[18] Informed consent requires that each affected client be aware of the relevant circumstances and of the material and reasonably foreseeable ways that the conflict could have adverse effects on the interests of that client. See Rule 1.0(e) (informed consent). The information required depends on the nature of the conflict and the nature of the risks involved. When representation of multiple clients in a single matter is undertaken, the information must include the implications of the common representation, including possible effects on loyalty, confidentiality and the attorney-client privilege and the advantages and risks involved. See Comments [30] and [31] (effect of common representation on confidentiality).

[19] Under some circumstances it may be impossible to make the disclosure necessary to obtain consent. For example, when the lawyer represents different clients in related matters and one of the clients refuses to consent to the disclosure necessary to permit the other client to make an informed decision, the lawyer cannot properly ask the latter to consent. In some cases the alternative to common representation can be that each party may have to obtain separate representation with the possibility of incurring additional costs. These costs, along with the benefits of securing separate representation, are factors that may be considered by the affected client in determining whether common representation is in the client's interests.

Consent Confirmed in Writing

[20] Paragraph (b) requires the lawyer to obtain the informed consent of the client, confirmed in writing. Such a writing may consist of a document executed by the client or one that the lawyer promptly records and transmits to the client following an oral consent. See Rule 1.0(b). See also Rule 1.0(n) (writing includes

electronic transmission). If it is not feasible to obtain or transmit the writing at the time the client gives informed consent, then the lawyer must obtain or transmit it within a reasonable time thereafter. See Rule 1.0(b). The requirement of a writing does not supplant the need in most cases for the lawyer to talk with the client, to explain the risks and advantages, if any, of representation burdened with a conflict of interest, as well as reasonably available alternatives, and to afford the client a reasonable opportunity to consider the risks and alternatives and to raise questions and concerns. Rather, the writing is required in order to impress upon clients the seriousness of the decision the client is being asked to make and to avoid disputes or ambiguities that might later occur in the absence of a writing.

Revoking Consent

[21] A client who has given consent to a conflict may revoke the consent and, like any other client, may terminate the lawyer's representation at any time. Whether revoking consent to the client's own representation precludes the lawyer from continuing to represent other clients depends on the circumstances, including the nature of the conflict, whether the client revoked consent because of a material change in circumstances, the reasonable expectations of the other client and whether material detriment to the other clients or the lawyer would result.

Consent to Future Conflict

[22] Whether a lawyer may properly request a client to waive conflicts that might arise in the future is subject to the test of paragraph (b). The effectiveness of such waivers is generally determined by the extent to which the client reasonably understands the material risks that the waiver entails. The more comprehensive the explanation of the types of future representations that might arise and the actual and reasonably foreseeable adverse consequences of those representations, the greater the likelihood that the client will have the requisite understanding. Thus, if the client agrees to consent to a particular type of conflict with which the client is already familiar, then the consent ordinarily will be effective with regard to that type of conflict. If the consent is general and open-ended, then the consent ordinarily will be ineffective, because it is not reasonably likely that the client will have understood the material risks involved. On the other hand, if the client is an experienced user of the legal services involved and is reasonably informed regarding the risk that a conflict may arise, such consent is more likely to be effective, particularly if, e.g., the client is independently represented by other counsel in giving consent and the consent is limited to future conflicts unrelated to the subject of the representation. In any case, advance consent cannot be effective if the circumstances that materialize in the future are such as would make the conflict nonconsentable under paragraph (b).

Conflicts in Litigation

[23] Paragraph (b)(3) prohibits representation of opposing parties in the same litigation, regardless of the clients' consent. On the other hand, simultaneous

representation of parties whose interests in litigation may conflict, such as coplaintiffs or codefendants, is governed by paragraph (a)(2). A conflict may exist by reason of substantial discrepancy in the parties' testimony, incompatibility in positions in relation to an opposing party or the fact that there are substantially different possibilities of settlement of the claims or liabilities in question. Such conflicts can arise in criminal cases as well as civil. The potential for conflict of interest in representing multiple defendants in a criminal case is so grave that ordinarily a lawyer should decline to represent more than one codefendant. On the other hand, common representation of persons having similar interests in civil litigation is proper if the requirements of paragraph (b) are met.

[24] Ordinarily a lawyer may take inconsistent legal positions in different tribunals at different times on behalf of different clients. The mere fact that advocating a legal position on behalf of one client might create precedent adverse to the interests of a client represented by the lawyer in an unrelated matter does not create a conflict of interest. A conflict of interest exists, however, if there is a significant risk that a lawyer's action on behalf of one client will materially limit the lawyer's effectiveness in representing another client in a different case; for example, when a decision favoring one client will create a precedent likely to seriously weaken the position taken on behalf of the other client. Factors relevant in determining whether the clients need to be advised of the risk include: where the cases are pending, whether the issue is substantive or procedural, the temporal relationship between the matters, the significance of the issue to the immediate and long-term interests of the clients involved and the clients' reasonable expectations in retaining the lawyer. If there is significant risk of material limitation, then absent informed consent of the affected clients, the lawyer must refuse one of the representations or withdraw from one or both matters.

[25] When a lawyer represents or seeks to represent a class of plaintiffs or defendants in a class-action lawsuit, unnamed members of the class are ordinarily not considered to be clients of the lawyer for purposes of applying paragraph (a)(1) of this Rule. Thus, the lawyer does not typically need to get the consent of such a person before representing a client suing the person in an unrelated matter. Similarly, a lawyer seeking to represent an opponent in a class action does not typically need the consent of an unnamed member of the class whom the lawyer represents in an unrelated matter.

Nonlitigation Conflicts

[26] Conflicts of interest under paragraphs (a)(1) and (a)(2) arise in contexts other than litigation. For a discussion of directly adverse conflicts in transactional matters, see Comment [7]. Relevant factors in determining whether there is significant potential for material limitation include the duration and intimacy of the lawyer's relationship with the client or clients involved, the functions being performed by the lawyer, the likelihood that disagreements will arise and the likely prejudice to the client from the conflict. The question is often one of proximity and degree. See Comment [8].

[27] For example, conflict questions may arise in estate planning and estate administration. A lawyer may be called upon to prepare wills for several family members, such as husband and wife, and, depending upon the circumstances, a conflict

of interest may be present. In estate administration the identity of the client may be unclear under the law of a particular jurisdiction. Under one view, the client is the fiduciary; under another view the client is the estate or trust, including its beneficiaries. In order to comply with conflict of interest rules, the lawyer should make clear the lawyer's relationship to the parties involved.

[28] Whether a conflict is consentable depends on the circumstances. For example, a lawyer may not represent multiple parties to a negotiation whose interests are fundamentally antagonistic to each other, but common representation is permissible where the clients are generally aligned in interest even though there is some difference in interest among them. Thus, a lawyer may seek to establish or adjust a relationship between clients on an amicable and mutually advantageous basis; for example, in helping to organize a business in which two or more clients are entrepreneurs, working out the financial reorganization of an enterprise in which two or more clients have an interest or arranging a property distribution in settlement of an estate. The lawyer seeks to resolve potentially adverse interests by developing the parties' mutual interests. Otherwise, each party might have to obtain separate representation, with the possibility of incurring additional cost, complication or even litigation. Given these and other relevant factors, the clients may prefer that the lawyer act for all of them.

Special Considerations in Common Representation

[29] In considering whether to represent multiple clients in the same matter, a lawyer should be mindful that if the common representation fails because the potentially adverse interests cannot be reconciled, the result can be additional cost, embarrassment and recrimination. Ordinarily, the lawyer will be forced to withdraw from representing all of the clients if the common representation fails. In some situations, the risk of failure is so great that multiple representation is plainly impossible. For example, a lawyer cannot undertake common representation of clients where contentious litigation or negotiations between them are imminent or contemplated. Moreover, because the lawyer is required to be impartial between commonly represented clients, representation of multiple clients is improper when it is unlikely that impartiality can be maintained. Generally, if the relationship between the parties has already assumed antagonism, the possibility that the clients' interests can be adequately served by common representation is not very good. Other relevant factors are whether the lawyer subsequently will represent both parties on a continuing basis and whether the situation involves creating or terminating a relationship between the parties.

[30] A particularly important factor in determining the appropriateness of common representation is the effect on client-lawyer confidentiality and the attorney-client privilege. With regard to the attorney-client privilege, the prevailing rule is that, as between commonly represented clients, the privilege does not attach. Hence, it must be assumed that if litigation eventuates between the clients, the privilege will not protect any such communications, and the clients should be so advised.

[31] As to the duty of confidentiality, continued common representation will almost certainly be inadequate if one client asks the lawyer not to disclose to the

other client information relevant to the common representation. This is so because the lawyer has an equal duty of loyalty to each client, and each client has the right to be informed of anything bearing on the representation that might affect that client's interests and the right to expect that the lawyer will use that information to that client's benefit. See Rule 1.4. The lawyer should, at the outset of the common representation and as part of the process of obtaining each client's informed consent, advise each client that information will be shared and that the lawyer will have to withdraw if one client decides that some matter material to the representation should be kept from the other. In limited circumstances, it may be appropriate for the lawyer to proceed with the representation when the clients have agreed, after being properly informed, that the lawyer will keep certain information confidential. For example, the lawyer may reasonably conclude that failure to disclose one client's trade secrets to another client will not adversely affect representation involving a joint venture between the clients and agree to keep that information confidential with the informed consent of both clients.

[32] When seeking to establish or adjust a relationship between clients, the lawyer should make clear that the lawyer's role is not that of partisanship normally expected in other circumstances and, thus, that the clients may be required to assume greater responsibility for decisions than when each client is separately represented. Any limitations on the scope of the representation made necessary as a result of the common representation should be fully explained to the clients at the outset of the representation. See Rule 1.2(c).

[33] Subject to the above limitations, each client in the common representation has the right to loyal and diligent representation and the protection of Rule 1.9 concerning the obligations to a former client. The client also has the right to discharge the lawyer as stated in Rule 1.16.

Organizational Clients

[34] A lawyer who represents a corporation or other organization does not, by virtue of that representation, necessarily represent any constituent or affiliated organization, such as a parent or subsidiary. See Rule 1.13(a). Thus, the lawyer for an organization is not barred from accepting representation adverse to an affiliate in an unrelated matter, unless the circumstances are such that the affiliate should also be considered a client of the lawyer, there is an understanding between the lawyer and the organizational client that the lawyer will avoid representation adverse to the client's affiliates, or the lawyer's obligations to either the organizational client or the new client are likely to limit materially the lawyer's representation of the other client.

[35] A lawyer for a corporation or other organization who is also a member of its board of directors should determine whether the responsibilities of the two roles may conflict. The lawyer may be called on to advise the corporation in matters involving actions of the directors. Consideration should be given to the frequency with which such situations may arise, the potential intensity of the conflict, the effect of the lawyer's resignation from the board and the possibility of the corporation's obtaining legal advice from another lawyer in such situations. If there is material risk that the dual role will compromise the lawyer's independence of professional

judgment, the lawyer should not serve as a director or should cease to act as the corporation's lawyer when conflicts of interest arise. The lawyer should advise the other members of the board that in some circumstances matters discussed at board meetings while the lawyer is present in the capacity of director might not be protected by the attorney-client privilege and that conflict of interest considerations might require the lawyer's recusal as a director or might require the lawyer and the lawyer's firm to decline representation of the corporation in a matter.

Rule 1.8   Conflict of Interest: Current Clients: Specific Rules

(a) A lawyer shall not enter into a business transaction with a client or knowingly acquire an ownership, possessory, security or other pecuniary interest adverse to a client unless:

(1) the transaction and terms on which the lawyer acquires the interest are fair and reasonable to the client and are fully disclosed and transmitted in writing in a manner that can be reasonably understood by the client;

(2) the client is advised in writing of the desirability of seeking and is given a reasonable opportunity to seek the advice of independent legal counsel on the transaction; and

(3) the client gives informed consent, in a writing signed by the client, to the essential terms of the transaction and the lawyer's role in the transaction, including whether the lawyer is representing the client in the transaction.

(b) A lawyer shall not use information relating to representation of a client to the disadvantage of the client unless the client gives informed consent, except as permitted or required by these Rules.

(c) A lawyer shall not solicit any substantial gift from a client, including a testamentary gift, or prepare on behalf of a client an instrument giving the lawyer or a person related to the lawyer any substantial gift unless the lawyer or other recipient of the gift is related to the client. For purposes of this paragraph, related persons include a spouse, child, grandchild, parent, grandparent or other relative or individual with whom the lawyer or the client maintains a close, familial relationship.

(d) Prior to the conclusion of representation of a client, a lawyer shall not make or negotiate an agreement giving the lawyer literary or media rights to a portrayal or account based in substantial part on information relating to the representation.

(e) A lawyer shall not provide financial assistance to a client in connection with pending or contemplated litigation, except that:

(1) a lawyer may advance court costs and expenses of litigation, the repayment of which may be contingent on the outcome of the matter; and

(2) a lawyer representing an indigent client may pay court costs and expenses of litigation on behalf of the client.

(f) A lawyer shall not accept compensation for representing a client from one other than the client unless:

(1) the client gives informed consent;

(2) there is no interference with the lawyer's independence of professional judgment or with the client-lawyer relationship; and

(3) information relating to representation of a client is protected as required by Rule 1.6.

(g) A lawyer who represents two or more clients shall not participate in making an aggregate settlement of the claims of or against the clients, or in a criminal case an aggregated agreement as to guilty or nolo contendere pleas, unless each client gives informed consent, in a writing signed by the client. The lawyer's disclosure shall include the existence and nature of all the claims or pleas involved and of the participation of each person in the settlement.

(h) A lawyer shall not:

(1) make an agreement prospectively limiting the lawyer's liability to a client for malpractice unless the client is independently represented in making the agreement; or

(2) settle a claim or potential claim for such liability with an unrepresented client or former client unless that person is advised in writing of the desirability of seeking and is given a reasonable opportunity to seek the advice of independent legal counsel in connection therewith.

(i) A lawyer shall not acquire a proprietary interest in the cause of action or subject matter of litigation the lawyer is conducting for a client, except that the lawyer may:

(1) acquire a lien authorized by law to secure the lawyer's fee or expenses; and

(2) contract with a client for a reasonable contingent fee in a civil case.

(j) A lawyer shall not have sexual relations with a client unless a consensual sexual relationship existed between them when the client-lawyer relationship commenced.

(k) While lawyers are associated in a firm, a prohibition in the foregoing paragraphs (a) through (i) that applies to any one of them shall apply to all of them.

COMMENT

Business Transactions Between Client and Lawyer

[1] A lawyer's legal skill and training, together with the relationship of trust and confidence between lawyer and client, create the possibility of overreaching when the lawyer participates in a business, property or financial transaction with a client, for example, a loan or sales transaction or a lawyer investment on behalf of a client. The requirements of paragraph (a) must be met even when the transaction is not closely related to the subject matter of the representation, as when a lawyer drafting a will for a client learns that the client needs money for unrelated expenses

and offers to make a loan to the client. The Rule applies to lawyers engaged in the sale of goods or services related to the practice of law, for example, the sale of title insurance or investment services to existing clients of the lawyer's legal practice. See Rule 5.7. It also applies to lawyers purchasing property from estates they represent. It does not apply to ordinary fee arrangements between client and lawyer, which are governed by Rule 1.5, although its requirements must be met when the lawyer accepts an interest in the client's business or other nonmonetary property as payment of all or part of a fee. In addition, the Rule does not apply to standard commercial transactions between the lawyer and the client for products or services that the client generally markets to others, for example, banking or brokerage services, medical services, products manufactured or distributed by the client, and utilities' services. In such transactions, the lawyer has no advantage in dealing with the client, and the restrictions in paragraph (a) are unnecessary and impracticable.

[2] Paragraph (a)(1) requires that the transaction itself be fair to the client and that its essential terms be communicated to the client, in writing, in a manner that can be reasonably understood. Paragraph (a)(2) requires that the client also be advised, in writing, of the desirability of seeking the advice of independent legal counsel. It also requires that the client be given a reasonable opportunity to obtain such advice. Paragraph (a)(3) requires that the lawyer obtain the client's informed consent, in a writing signed by the client, both to the essential terms of the transaction and to the lawyer's role. When necessary, the lawyer should discuss both the material risks of the proposed transaction, including any risk presented by the lawyer's involvement, and the existence of reasonably available alternatives and should explain why the advice of independent legal counsel is desirable. See Rule 1.0(e) (definition of informed consent).

[3] The risk to a client is greatest when the client expects the lawyer to represent the client in the transaction itself or when the lawyer's financial interest otherwise poses a significant risk that the lawyer's representation of the client will be materially limited by the lawyer's financial interest in the transaction. Here the lawyer's role requires that the lawyer must comply, not only with the requirements of paragraph (a), but also with the requirements of Rule 1.7. Under that Rule, the lawyer must disclose the risks associated with the lawyer's dual role as both legal adviser and participant in the transaction, such as the risk that the lawyer will structure the transaction or give legal advice in a way that favors the lawyer's interests at the expense of the client. Moreover, the lawyer must obtain the client's informed consent. In some cases, the lawyer's interest may be such that Rule 1.7 will preclude the lawyer from seeking the client's consent to the transaction.

[4] If the client is independently represented in the transaction, paragraph (a)(2) of this Rule is inapplicable, and the paragraph (a)(1) requirement for full disclosure is satisfied either by a written disclosure by the lawyer involved in the transaction or by the client's independent counsel. The fact that the client was independently represented in the transaction is relevant in determining whether the agreement was fair and reasonable to the client as paragraph (a)(1) further requires.

Use of Information Related to Representation

[5] Use of information relating to the representation to the disadvantage of the client violates the lawyer's duty of loyalty. Paragraph (b) applies when the information

is used to benefit either the lawyer or a third person, such as another client or business associate of the lawyer. For example, if a lawyer learns that a client intends to purchase and develop several parcels of land, the lawyer may not use that information to purchase one of the parcels in competition with the client or to recommend that another client make such a purchase. The Rule does not prohibit uses that do not disadvantage the client. For example, a lawyer who learns a government agency's interpretation of trade legislation during the representation of one client may properly use that information to benefit other clients. Paragraph (b) prohibits disadvantageous use of client information unless the client gives informed consent, except as permitted or required by these Rules. See Rules 1.2(d), 1.6, 1.9(c), 3.3, 4.1(b), 8.1 and 8.3.

Gifts to Lawyers

[6] A lawyer may accept a gift from a client, if the transaction meets general standards of fairness. For example, a simple gift such as a present given at a holiday or as a token of appreciation is permitted. If a client offers the lawyer a more substantial gift, paragraph (c) does not prohibit the lawyer from accepting it, although such a gift may be voidable by the client under the doctrine of undue influence, which treats client gifts as presumptively fraudulent. In any event, due to concerns about overreaching and imposition on clients, a lawyer may not suggest that a substantial gift be made to the lawyer or for the lawyer's benefit, except where the lawyer is related to the client as set forth in paragraph (c).

[7] If effectuation of a substantial gift requires preparing a legal instrument such as a will or conveyance the client should have the detached advice that another lawyer can provide. The sole exception to this Rule is where the client is a relative of the donee.

[8] This Rule does not prohibit a lawyer from seeking to have the lawyer or a partner or associate of the lawyer named as executor of the client's estate or to another potentially lucrative fiduciary position. Nevertheless, such appointments will be subject to the general conflict of interest provision in Rule 1.7 when there is a significant risk that the lawyer's interest in obtaining the appointment will materially limit the lawyer's independent professional judgment in advising the client concerning the choice of an executor or other fiduciary. In obtaining the client's informed consent to the conflict, the lawyer should advise the client concerning the nature and extent of the lawyer's financial interest in the appointment, as well as the availability of alternative candidates for the position.

Literary Rights

[9] An agreement by which a lawyer acquires literary or media rights concerning the conduct of the representation creates a conflict between the interests of the client and the personal interests of the lawyer. Measures suitable in the representation of the client may detract from the publication value of an account of the representation. Paragraph (d) does not prohibit a lawyer representing a client in a transaction concerning literary property from agreeing that the lawyer's fee shall consist of a share in ownership in the property, if the arrangement conforms to Rule 1.5 and paragraphs (a) and (i).

Financial Assistance

[10] Lawyers may not subsidize lawsuits or administrative proceedings brought on behalf of their clients, including making or guaranteeing loans to their clients for living expenses, because to do so would encourage clients to pursue lawsuits that might not otherwise be brought and because such assistance gives lawyers too great a financial stake in the litigation. These dangers do not warrant a prohibition on a lawyer lending a client court costs and litigation expenses, including the expenses of medical examination and the costs of obtaining and presenting evidence, because these advances are virtually indistinguishable from contingent fees and help ensure access to the courts. Similarly, an exception allowing lawyers representing indigent clients to pay court costs and litigation expenses regardless of whether these funds will be repaid is warranted.

Person Paying for a Lawyer's Services

[11] Lawyers are frequently asked to represent a client under circumstances in which a third person will compensate the lawyer, in whole or in part. The third person might be a relative or friend, an indemnitor (such as a liability insurance company) or a co-client (such as a corporation sued along with one or more of its employees). Because third-party payers frequently have interests that differ from those of the client, including interests in minimizing the amount spent on the representation and in learning how the representation is progressing, lawyers are prohibited from accepting or continuing such representations unless the lawyer determines that there will be no interference with the lawyer's independent professional judgment and there is informed consent from the client. See also Rule 5.4(c) (prohibiting interference with a lawyer's professional judgment by one who recommends, employs or pays the lawyer to render legal services for another).

[12] Sometimes, it will be sufficient for the lawyer to obtain the client's informed consent regarding the fact of the payment and the identity of the third-party payer. If, however, the fee arrangement creates a conflict of interest for the lawyer, then the lawyer must comply with Rule 1.7. The lawyer must also conform to the requirements of Rule 1.6 concerning confidentiality. Under Rule 1.7(a), a conflict of interest exists if there is significant risk that the lawyer's representation of the client will be materially limited by the lawyer's own interest in the fee arrangement or by the lawyer's responsibilities to the third-party payer (for example, when the third-party payer is a co-client). Under Rule 1.7(b), the lawyer may accept or continue the representation with the informed consent of each affected client, unless the conflict is nonconsentable under that paragraph. Under Rule 1.7(b), the informed consent must be confirmed in writing.

Aggregate Settlements

[13] Differences in willingness to make or accept an offer of settlement are among the risks of common representation of multiple clients by a single lawyer. Under Rule 1.7, this is one of the risks that should be discussed before undertaking the representation, as part of the process of obtaining the client's informed consent.

In addition, Rule 1.2(a) protects each client's right to have the final say in deciding whether to accept or reject an offer of settlement and in deciding whether to enter a guilty or nolo contendere plea in a criminal case. The rule stated in this paragraph is a corollary of both these Rules and provides that, before any settlement offer or plea bargain is made or accepted on behalf of multiple clients, the lawyer must inform each of them about all the material terms of the settlement, including what the other clients will receive or pay if the settlement or plea offer is accepted. See also Rule 1.0(e) (definition of informed consent). Lawyers representing a class of plaintiffs or defendants, or those proceeding derivatively, may not have a full client-lawyer relationship with each member of the class; nevertheless, such lawyers must comply with applicable rules regulating notification of class members and other procedural requirements designed to ensure adequate protection of the entire class.

Limiting Liability and Settling Malpractice Claims

[14] Agreements prospectively limiting a lawyer's liability for malpractice are prohibited unless the client is independently represented in making the agreement because they are likely to undermine competent and diligent representation. Also, many clients are unable to evaluate the desirability of making such an agreement before a dispute has arisen, particularly if they are then represented by the lawyer seeking the agreement. This paragraph does not, however, prohibit a lawyer from entering into an agreement with the client to arbitrate legal malpractice claims, provided such agreements are enforceable and the client is fully informed of the scope and effect of the agreement. Nor does this paragraph limit the ability of lawyers to practice in the form of a limited-liability entity, where permitted by law, provided that each lawyer remains personally liable to the client for his or her own conduct and the firm complies with any conditions required by law, such as provisions requiring client notification or maintenance of adequate liability insurance. Nor does it prohibit an agreement in accordance with Rule 1.2 that defines the scope of the representation, although a definition of scope that makes the obligations of representation illusory will amount to an attempt to limit liability.

[15] Agreements settling a claim or a potential claim for malpractice are not prohibited by this Rule. Nevertheless, in view of the danger that a lawyer will take unfair advantage of an unrepresented client or former client, the lawyer must first advise such a person in writing of the appropriateness of independent representation in connection with such a settlement. In addition, the lawyer must give the client or former client a reasonable opportunity to find and consult independent counsel.

Acquiring Proprietary Interest in Litigation

[16] Paragraph (i) states the traditional general rule that lawyers are prohibited from acquiring a proprietary interest in litigation. Like paragraph (e), the general rule has its basis in common law champerty and maintenance and is designed to avoid giving the lawyer too great an interest in the representation. In addition, when the lawyer acquires an ownership interest in the subject of the representation, it will be more difficult for a client to discharge the lawyer if the client so desires. The Rule is subject to specific exceptions developed in decisional law and

continued in these Rules. The exception for certain advances of the costs of litigation is set forth in paragraph (e). In addition, paragraph (i) sets forth exceptions for liens authorized by law to secure the lawyer's fees or expenses and contracts for reasonable contingent fees. The law of each jurisdiction determines which liens are authorized by law. These may include liens granted by statute, liens originating in common law and liens acquired by contract with the client. When a lawyer acquires by contract a security interest in property other than that recovered through the lawyer's efforts in the litigation, such an acquisition is a business or financial transaction with a client and is governed by the requirements of paragraph (a). Contracts for contingent fees in civil cases are governed by Rule 1.5.

Client-Lawyer Sexual Relationships

[17] The relationship between lawyer and client is a fiduciary one in which the lawyer occupies the highest position of trust and confidence. The relationship is almost always unequal; thus, a sexual relationship between lawyer and client can involve unfair exploitation of the lawyer's fiduciary role, in violation of the lawyer's basic ethical obligation not to use the trust of the client to the client's disadvantage. In addition, such a relationship presents a significant danger that, because of the lawyer's emotional involvement, the lawyer will be unable to represent the client without impairment of the exercise of independent professional judgment. Moreover, a blurred line between the professional and personal relationships may make it difficult to predict to what extent client confidences will be protected by the attorney-client evidentiary privilege, since client confidences are protected by privilege only when they are imparted in the context of the client-lawyer relationship. Because of the significant danger of harm to client interests and because the client's own emotional involvement renders it unlikely that the client could give adequate informed consent, this Rule prohibits the lawyer from having sexual relations with a client regardless of whether the relationship is consensual and regardless of the absence of prejudice to the client.

[18] Sexual relationships that predate the client-lawyer relationship are not prohibited. Issues relating to the exploitation of the fiduciary relationship and client dependency are diminished when the sexual relationship existed prior to the commencement of the client-lawyer relationship. However, before proceeding with the representation in these circumstances, the lawyer should consider whether the lawyer's ability to represent the client will be materially limited by the relationship. See Rule 1.7(a)(2).

[19] When the client is an organization, paragraph (j) of this Rule prohibits a lawyer for the organization (whether inside counsel or outside counsel) from having a sexual relationship with a constituent of the organization who supervises, directs or regularly consults with that lawyer concerning the organization's legal matters.

Imputation of Prohibitions

[20] Under paragraph (k), a prohibition on conduct by an individual lawyer in paragraphs (a) through (i) also applies to all lawyers associated in a firm with the

personally prohibited lawyer. For example, one lawyer in a firm may not enter into a business transaction with a client of another member of the firm without complying with paragraph (a), even if the first lawyer is not personally involved in the representation of the client. The prohibition set forth in paragraph (j) is personal and is not applied to associated lawyers.

[handwritten annotation: If the lawyer could have obtained confid. info in the first rep. relevant to the 2nd. — analytical ease]

Rule 1.9   Duties to Former Clients

(a) A lawyer who has formerly represented a client in a matter shall not thereafter represent another person in the same or a substantially related matter in which that person's interests are materially adverse to the interests of the former client unless the former client gives informed consent, confirmed in writing.

(b) A lawyer shall not knowingly represent a person in the same or a substantially related matter in which a firm with which the lawyer formerly was associated had previously represented a client

(1) whose interests are materially adverse to that person; and

(2) about whom the lawyer had acquired information protected by Rules 1.6 and 1.9(c) that is material to the matter;

unless the former client gives informed consent, confirmed in writing.

(c) A lawyer who has formerly represented a client in a matter or whose present or former firm has formerly represented a client in a matter shall not thereafter:

(1) use information relating to the representation to the disadvantage of the former client except as these Rules would permit or require with respect to a client, or when the information has become generally known; or

(2) reveal information relating to the representation except as these Rules would permit or require with respect to a client.

COMMENT

[1] After termination of a client-lawyer relationship, a lawyer has certain continuing duties with respect to confidentiality and conflicts of interest and thus may not represent another client except in conformity with this Rule. Under this Rule, for example, a lawyer could not properly seek to rescind on behalf of a new client a contract drafted on behalf of the former client. So also a lawyer who has prosecuted an accused person could not properly represent the accused in a subsequent civil action against the government concerning the same transaction. Nor could a lawyer who has represented multiple clients in a matter represent one of the clients against the others in the same or a substantially related matter after a dispute arose among the clients in that matter, unless all affected clients give informed consent. See Comment [9]. Current and former government lawyers must comply with this Rule to the extent required by Rule 1.11.

[2] The scope of a "matter" for purposes of this Rule depends on the facts of a particular situation or transaction. The lawyer's involvement in a matter can also be a question of degree. When a lawyer has been directly involved in a specific transaction, subsequent representation of other clients with materially adverse interests in that transaction clearly is prohibited. On the other hand, a lawyer who recurrently handled a type of problem for a former client is not precluded from later representing another client in a factually distinct problem of that type even though the subsequent representation involves a position adverse to the prior client. Similar considerations can apply to the reassignment of military lawyers between defense and prosecution functions within the same military jurisdictions. The underlying question is whether the lawyer was so involved in the matter that the subsequent representation can be justly regarded as a changing of sides in the matter in question.

[3] Matters are "substantially related" for purposes of this Rule if they involve the same transaction or legal dispute or if there otherwise is a substantial risk that confidential factual information as would normally have been obtained in the prior representation would materially advance the client's position in the subsequent matter. For example, a lawyer who has represented a businessperson and learned extensive private financial information about that person may not then represent that person's spouse in seeking a divorce. Similarly, a lawyer who has previously represented a client in securing environmental permits to build a shopping center would be precluded from representing neighbors seeking to oppose rezoning of the property on the basis of environmental considerations; however, the lawyer would not be precluded, on the grounds of substantial relationship, from defending a tenant of the completed shopping center in resisting eviction for nonpayment of rent. Information that has been disclosed to the public or to other parties adverse to the former client ordinarily will not be disqualifying. Information acquired in a prior representation may have been rendered obsolete by the passage of time, a circumstance that may be relevant in determining whether two representations are substantially related. In the case of an organizational client, general knowledge of the client's policies and practices ordinarily will not preclude a subsequent representation; on the other hand, knowledge of specific facts gained in a prior representation that are relevant to the matter in question ordinarily will preclude such a representation. A former client is not required to reveal the confidential information learned by the lawyer in order to establish a substantial risk that the lawyer has confidential information to use in the subsequent matter. A conclusion about the possession of such information may be based on the nature of the services the lawyer provided the former client and information that would in ordinary practice be learned by a lawyer providing such services.

Lawyers Moving Between Firms

[4] When lawyers have been associated within a firm but then end their association, the question of whether a lawyer should undertake representation is more complicated. There are several competing considerations. First, the client previously represented by the former firm must be reasonably assured that the principle of loyalty to the client is not compromised. Second, the rule should not be so broadly cast

as to preclude other persons from having reasonable choice of legal counsel. Third, the rule should not unreasonably hamper lawyers from forming new associations and taking on new clients after having left a previous association. In this connection, it should be recognized that today many lawyers practice in firms, that many lawyers to some degree limit their practice to one field or another, and that many move from one association to another several times in their careers. If the concept of imputation were applied with unqualified rigor, the result would be radical curtailment of the opportunity of lawyers to move from one practice setting to another and of the opportunity of clients to change counsel.

[5] Paragraph (b) operates to disqualify the lawyer only when the lawyer involved has actual knowledge of information protected by Rules 1.6 and 1.9(c). Thus, if a lawyer while with one firm acquired no knowledge or information relating to a particular client of the firm, and that lawyer later joined another firm, neither the lawyer individually nor the second firm is disqualified from representing another client in the same or a related matter even though the interests of the two clients conflict. See Rule 1.10(b) for the restrictions on a firm once a lawyer has terminated association with the firm.

[6] Application of paragraph (b) depends on a situation's particular facts, aided by inferences, deductions or working presumptions that reasonably may be made about the way in which lawyers work together. A lawyer may have general access to files of all clients of a law firm and may regularly participate in discussions of their affairs; it should be inferred that such a lawyer in fact is privy to all information about all the firm's clients. In contrast, another lawyer may have access to the files of only a limited number of clients and participate in discussions of the affairs of no other clients; in the absence of information to the contrary, it should be inferred that such a lawyer in fact is privy to information about the clients actually served but not those of other clients. In such an inquiry, the burden of proof should rest upon the firm whose disqualification is sought.

[7] Independent of the question of disqualification of a firm, a lawyer changing professional association has a continuing duty to preserve confidentiality of information about a client formerly represented. See Rules 1.6 and 1.9(c).

[8] Paragraph (c) provides that information acquired by the lawyer in the course of representing a client may not subsequently be used or revealed by the lawyer to the disadvantage of the client. However, the fact that a lawyer has once served a client does not preclude the lawyer from using generally known information about that client when later representing another client.

[9] The provisions of this Rule are for the protection of former clients and can be waived if the client gives informed consent, which consent must be confirmed in writing under paragraphs (a) and (b). See Rule 1.0(e). With regard to the effectiveness of an advance waiver, see Comment [22] to Rule 1.7. With regard to disqualification of a firm with which a lawyer is or was formerly associated, see Rule 1.10.

Rule 1.10   Imputation of Conflicts of Interest: General Rule

(a) While lawyers are associated in a firm, none of them shall knowingly represent a client when any one of them practicing alone would be prohibited from doing so by Rules 1.7 or 1.9, unless

(1) the prohibition is based upon a personal interest of the disqualified lawyer and does not present a significant risk of materially limiting the representation of the client by the remaining lawyers in the firm; or

(2) the prohibition is based upon Rule 1.9(a) or (b), and arises out of the disqualified lawyer's association with a prior firm, and

(i) the disqualified lawyer is timely screened from any participation in the matter and is apportioned no part of the fee therefrom;

(ii) written notice is promptly given to any affected former client to enable the former client to ascertain compliance with the provisions of this Rule, which shall include a description of the screening procedures employed; a statement of the firm's and of the screened lawyer's compliance with these Rules; a statement that review may be available before a tribunal; and an agreement by the firm to respond promptly to any written inquiries or objections by the former client about the screening procedures; and

(iii) certifications of compliance with these Rules and with the screening procedures are provided to the former client by the screened lawyer and by a partner of the firm, at reasonable intervals upon the former client's written request and upon termination of the screening procedures.

(b) When a lawyer has terminated an association with a firm, the firm is not prohibited from thereafter representing a person with interests materially adverse to those of a client represented by the formerly associated lawyer and not currently represented by the firm, unless

(1) the matter is the same or substantially related to that in which the formerly associated lawyer represented the client; and

(2) any lawyer remaining in the firm has information protected by Rules 1.6 and 1.9(c) that is material to the matter.

(c) A disqualification prescribed by this rule may be waived by the affected client under the conditions stated in Rule 1.7.

(d) The disqualification of lawyers associated in a firm with former or current government lawyers is governed by Rule 1.11.

COMMENT

Definition of "Firm"

[1] For purposes of the Rules of Professional Conduct, the term "firm" denotes lawyers in a law partnership, professional corporation, sole proprietorship or other association authorized to practice law; or lawyers employed in a legal services organization or the legal department of a corporation or other organization. See Rule 1.0(c). Whether two or more lawyers constitute a firm within this definition can depend on the specific facts. See Rule 1.0, Comments [2]-[4].

Principles of Imputed Disqualification

[2] The rule of imputed disqualification stated in paragraph (a) gives effect to the principle of loyalty to the client as it applies to lawyers who practice in a law firm. Such situations can be considered from the premise that a firm of lawyers is essentially one lawyer for purposes of the rules governing loyalty to the client, or from the premise that each lawyer is vicariously bound by the obligation of loyalty owed by each lawyer with whom the lawyer is associated. Paragraph (a)(1) operates only among the lawyers currently associated in a firm. When a lawyer moves from one firm to another, the situation is governed by Rules 1.9(b) and 1.10(a)(2) and (b).

[3] The rule in paragraph (a) does not prohibit representation where neither questions of client loyalty nor protection of confidential information are presented. Where one lawyer in a firm could not effectively represent a given client because of strong political beliefs, for example, but that lawyer will do no work on the case and the personal beliefs of the lawyer will not materially limit the representation by others in the firm, the firm should not be disqualified. On the other hand, if an opposing party in a case were owned by a lawyer in the law firm, and others in the firm would be materially limited in pursuing the matter because of loyalty to that lawyer, the personal disqualification of the lawyer would be imputed to all others in the firm.

[4] The rule in paragraph (a) also does not prohibit representation by others in the law firm where the person prohibited from involvement in a matter is a nonlawyer, such as a paralegal or legal secretary. Nor does paragraph (a) prohibit representation if the lawyer is prohibited from acting because of events before the person became a lawyer, for example, work that the person did while a law student. Such persons, however, ordinarily must be screened from any personal participation in the matter to avoid communication to others in the firm of confidential information that both the nonlawyers and the firm have a legal duty to protect. See Rules 1.0(k) and 5.3.

[5] Rule 1.10(b) operates to permit a law firm, under certain circumstances, to represent a person with interests directly adverse to those of a client represented by a lawyer who formerly was associated with the firm. The Rule applies regardless of when the formerly associated lawyer represented the client. However, the law firm may not represent a person with interests adverse to those of a present client of the firm, which would violate Rule 1.7. Moreover, the firm may not represent the person where the matter is the same or substantially related to that in which the formerly associated lawyer represented the client and any other lawyer currently in the firm has material information protected by Rules 1.6 and 1.9(c).

[6] Rule 1.10(c) removes imputation with the informed consent of the affected client or former client under the conditions stated in Rule 1.7. The conditions stated in Rule 1.7 require the lawyer to determine that the representation is not prohibited by Rule 1.7(b) and that each affected client or former client has given informed consent to the representation, confirmed in writing. In some cases, the risk may be so severe that the conflict may not be cured by client consent. For a discussion of the effectiveness of client waivers of conflicts that might arise in the future, see Rule 1.7, Comment [22]. For a definition of informed consent, see Rule 1.0(e).

[7] Rule 1.10(a)(2) similarly removes the imputation otherwise required by Rule 1.10(a), but unlike section (c), it does so without requiring that there be

informed consent by the former client. Instead, it requires that the procedures laid out in sections (a)(2)(i)-(iii) be followed. A description of effective screening mechanisms appears in Rule 1.0(k). Lawyers should be aware, however, that, even where screening mechanisms have been adopted, tribunals may consider additional factors in ruling upon motions to disqualify a lawyer from pending litigation.

[8] Paragraph (a)(2)(i) does not prohibit the screened lawyer from receiving a salary or partnership share established by prior independent agreement, but that lawyer may not receive compensation directly related to the matter in which the lawyer is disqualified.

[9] The notice required by paragraph (a)(2)(ii) generally should include a description of the screened lawyer's prior representation and be given as soon as practicable after the need for screening becomes apparent. It also should include a statement by the screened lawyer and the firm that the client's material confidential information has not been disclosed or used in violation of the Rules. The notice is intended to enable the former client to evaluate and comment upon the effectiveness of the screening procedures.

[10] The certifications required by paragraph (a)(2)(iii) give the former client assurance that the client's material confidential information has not been disclosed or used inappropriately, either prior to timely implementation of a screen or thereafter. If compliance cannot be certified, the certificate must describe the failure to comply.

[11] Where a lawyer has joined a private firm after having represented the government, imputation is governed by Rule 1.11(b) and (c), not this Rule. Under Rule 1.11(d), where a lawyer represents the government after having served clients in private practice, nongovernmental employment or in another government agency, former-client conflicts are not imputed to government lawyers associated with the individually disqualified lawyer.

[12] Where a lawyer is prohibited from engaging in certain transactions under Rule 1.8, paragraph (k) of that Rule, and not this Rule, determines whether that prohibition also applies to other lawyers associated in a firm with the personally prohibited lawyer.

Rule 1.11   Special Conflicts of Interest for Former and Current Government Officers and Employees

(a) Except as law may otherwise expressly permit, a lawyer who has formerly served as a public officer or employee of the government:

(1) is subject to Rule 1.9(c); and

(2) shall not otherwise represent a client in connection with a matter in which the lawyer participated personally and substantially as a public officer or employee, unless the appropriate government agency gives its informed consent, confirmed in writing, to the representation.

(b) When a lawyer is disqualified from representation under paragraph (a), no lawyer in a firm with which that lawyer is associated may knowingly undertake or continue representation in such a matter unless:

(1) the disqualified lawyer is timely screened from any participation in the matter and is apportioned no part of the fee therefrom; and

(2) written notice is promptly given to the appropriate government agency to enable it to ascertain compliance with the provisions of this rule.

(c) Except as law may otherwise expressly permit, a lawyer having information that the lawyer knows is confidential government information about a person acquired when the lawyer was a public officer or employee, may not represent a private client whose interests are adverse to that person in a matter in which the information could be used to the material disadvantage of that person. As used in this Rule, the term "confidential government information" means information that has been obtained under governmental authority and which, at the time this Rule is applied, the government is prohibited by law from disclosing to the public or has a legal privilege not to disclose and which is not otherwise available to the public. A firm with which that lawyer is associated may undertake or continue representation in the matter only if the disqualified lawyer is timely screened from any participation in the matter and is apportioned no part of the fee therefrom.

(d) Except as law may otherwise expressly permit, a lawyer currently serving as a public officer or employee:

(1) is subject to Rules 1.7 and 1.9; and

(2) shall not:

(i) participate in a matter in which the lawyer participated personally and substantially while in private practice or nongovernmental employment, unless the appropriate government agency gives its informed consent, confirmed in writing; or

(ii) negotiate for private employment with any person who is involved as a party or as lawyer for a party in a matter in which the lawyer is participating personally and substantially, except that a lawyer serving as a law clerk to a judge, other adjudicative officer or arbitrator may negotiate for private employment as permitted by Rule 1.12(b) and subject to the conditions stated in Rule 1.12(b).

(e) As used in this Rule, the term "matter" includes:

(1) any judicial or other proceeding, application, request for a ruling or other determination, contract, claim, controversy, investigation, charge, accusation, arrest or other particular matter involving a specific party or parties, and (drafting legislation - Not included) *

(2) any other matter covered by the conflict of interest rules of the appropriate government agency.

COMMENT

[1] A lawyer who has served or is currently serving as a public officer or employee is personally subject to the Rules of Professional Conduct, including the prohibition against concurrent conflicts of interest stated in Rule 1.7. In addition, such a lawyer may be subject to statutes and government regulations regarding conflict of interest. Such statutes and regulations may circumscribe the extent to which

the government agency may give consent under this Rule. See Rule 1.0(e) for the definition of informed consent.

[2] Paragraphs (a)(1), (a)(2) and (d)(1) restate the obligations of an individual lawyer who has served or is currently serving as an officer or employee of the government toward a former government or private client. Rule 1.10 is not applicable to the conflicts of interest addressed by this Rule. Rather, paragraph (b) sets forth a special imputation rule for former government lawyers that provides for screening and notice. Because of the special problems raised by imputation within a government agency, paragraph (d) does not impute the conflicts of a lawyer currently serving as an officer or employee of the government to other associated government officers or employees, although ordinarily it will be prudent to screen such lawyers.

[3] Paragraphs (a)(2) and (d)(2) apply regardless of whether a lawyer is adverse to a former client and are thus designed not only to protect the former client, but also to prevent a lawyer from exploiting public office for the advantage of another client. For example, a lawyer who has pursued a claim on behalf of the government may not pursue the same claim on behalf of a later private client after the lawyer has left government service, except when authorized to do so by the government agency under paragraph (a). Similarly, a lawyer who has pursued a claim on behalf of a private client may not pursue the claim on behalf of the government, except when authorized to do so by paragraph (d). As with paragraphs (a)(1) and (d)(1), Rule 1.10 is not applicable to the conflicts of interest addressed by these paragraphs.

[4] This Rule represents a balancing of interests. On the one hand, where the successive clients are a government agency and another client, public or private, the risk exists that power or discretion vested in that agency might be used for the special benefit of the other client. A lawyer should not be in a position where benefit to the other client might affect performance of the lawyer's professional functions on behalf of the government. Also, unfair advantage could accrue to the other client by reason of access to confidential government information about the client's adversary obtainable only through the lawyer's government service. On the other hand, the rules governing lawyers presently or formerly employed by a government agency should not be so restrictive as to inhibit transfer of employment to and from the government. The government has a legitimate need to attract qualified lawyers as well as to maintain high ethical standards. Thus a former government lawyer is disqualified only from particular matters in which the lawyer participated personally and substantially. The provisions for screening and waiver in paragraph (b) are necessary to prevent the disqualification rule from imposing too severe a deterrent against entering public service. The limitation of disqualification in paragraphs (a)(2) and (d)(2) to matters involving a specific party or parties, rather than extending disqualification to all substantive issues on which the lawyer worked, serves a similar function.

[5] When a lawyer has been employed by one government agency and then moves to a second government agency, it may be appropriate to treat that second agency as another client for purposes of this Rule, as when a lawyer is employed by a city and subsequently is employed by a federal agency. However, because the conflict of interest is governed by paragraph (d), the latter agency is not required to screen the lawyer as paragraph (b) requires a law firm to do. The question of whether two government agencies should be regarded as the same or different clients for conflict of interest purposes is beyond the scope of these Rules. See Rule 1.13 Comment [9].

[6] Paragraphs (b) and (c) contemplate a screening arrangement. See Rule 1.0(k) (requirements for screening procedures). These paragraphs do not prohibit a lawyer from receiving a salary or partnership share established by prior independent agreement, but that lawyer may not receive compensation directly relating the lawyer's compensation to the fee in the matter in which the lawyer is disqualified.

[7] Notice, including a description of the screened lawyer's prior representation and of the screening procedures employed, generally should be given as soon as practicable after the need for screening becomes apparent.

[8] Paragraph (c) operates only when the lawyer in question has knowledge of the information, which means actual knowledge; it does not operate with respect to information that merely could be imputed to the lawyer.

[9] Paragraphs (a) and (d) do not prohibit a lawyer from jointly representing a private party and a government agency when doing so is permitted by Rule 1.7 and is not otherwise prohibited by law.

[10] For purposes of paragraph (e) of this Rule, a ''matter'' may continue in another form. In determining whether two particular matters are the same, the lawyer should consider the extent to which the matters involve the same basic facts, the same or related parties, and the time elapsed.

Rule 1.12   Former Judge, Arbitrator, Mediator or Other Third-Party Neutral

(a) Except as stated in paragraph (d), a lawyer shall not represent anyone in connection with a matter in which the lawyer participated personally and substantially as a judge or other adjudicative officer or law clerk to such a person or as an arbitrator, mediator or other third-party neutral, unless all parties to the proceeding give informed consent, confirmed in writing.

(b) A lawyer shall not negotiate for employment with any person who is involved as a party or as lawyer for a party in a matter in which the lawyer is participating personally and substantially as a judge or other adjudicative officer or as an arbitrator, mediator or other third-party neutral. A lawyer serving as a law clerk to a judge or other adjudicative officer may negotiate for employment with a party or lawyer involved in a matter in which the clerk is participating personally and substantially, but only after the lawyer has notified the judge or other adjudicative officer.

(c) If a lawyer is disqualified by paragraph (a), no lawyer in a firm with which that lawyer is associated may knowingly undertake or continue representation in the matter unless:

(1) the disqualified lawyer is timely screened from any participation in the matter and is apportioned no part of the fee therefrom; and

(2) written notice is promptly given to the parties and any appropriate tribunal to enable them to ascertain compliance with the provisions of this rule.

(d) An arbitrator selected as a partisan of a party in a multimember arbitration panel is not prohibited from subsequently representing that party.

COMMENT

[1] This Rule generally parallels Rule 1.11. The term "personally and substantially" signifies that a judge who was a member of a multimember court, and thereafter left judicial office to practice law, is not prohibited from representing a client in a matter pending in the court, but in which the former judge did not participate. So also the fact that a former judge exercised administrative responsibility in a court does not prevent the former judge from acting as a lawyer in a matter where the judge had previously exercised remote or incidental administrative responsibility that did not affect the merits. Compare the Comment to Rule 1.11. The term "adjudicative officer" includes such officials as judges pro tempore, referees, special masters, hearing officers and other parajudicial officers, and also lawyers who serve as part-time judges. Compliance Canons A(2), B(2) and C of the Model Code of Judicial Conduct provide that a part-time judge, judge pro tempore or retired judge recalled to active service, may not "act as a lawyer in any proceeding in which he served as a judge or in any other proceeding related thereto." Although phrased differently from this Rule, those Rules correspond in meaning.

[2] Like former judges, lawyers who have served as arbitrators, mediators or other third-party neutrals may be asked to represent a client in a matter in which the lawyer participated personally and substantially. This Rule forbids such representation unless all of the parties to the proceedings give their informed consent, confirmed in writing. See Rule 1.0(e) and (b). Other law or codes of ethics governing third-party neutrals may impose more stringent standards of personal or imputed disqualification. See Rule 2.4.

[3] Although lawyers who serve as third-party neutrals do not have information concerning the parties that is protected under Rule 1.6, they typically owe the parties an obligation of confidentiality under law or codes of ethics governing third-party neutrals. Thus, paragraph (c) provides that conflicts of the personally disqualified lawyer will be imputed to other lawyers in a law firm unless the conditions of this paragraph are met.

[4] Requirements for screening procedures are stated in Rule 1.0(k). Paragraph (c)(1) does not prohibit the screened lawyer from receiving a salary or partnership share established by prior independent agreement, but that lawyer may not receive compensation directly related to the matter in which the lawyer is disqualified.

[5] Notice, including a description of the screened lawyer's prior representation and of the screening procedures employed, generally should be given as soon as practicable after the need for screening becomes apparent.

Rule 1.13   Organization as Client

(a) A lawyer employed or retained by an organization represents the organization acting through its duly authorized constituents.

(b) If a lawyer for an organization knows that an officer, employee or other person associated with the organization is engaged in action, intends to act or refuses to act in a matter related to the representation that is a violation of a legal obligation to the organization, or a violation of law that reasonably might be imputed to the organization, and that is likely to result in substantial

injury to the organization, then the lawyer shall proceed as is reasonably necessary in the best interest of the organization. Unless the lawyer reasonably believes that it is not necessary in the best interest of the organization to do so, the lawyer shall refer the matter to higher authority in the organization, including, if warranted by the circumstances, to the highest authority that can act on behalf of the organization as determined by applicable law.

(c) Except as provided in Paragraph (d), if,

(1) despite the lawyer's efforts in accordance with paragraph (b), the highest authority that can act on behalf of the organization insists upon or fails to address in a timely and appropriate manner an action, or a refusal to act, that is clearly a violation of law, and

(2) the lawyer reasonably believes that the violation is reasonably certain to result in substantial injury to the organization, then the lawyer may reveal information relating to the representation whether or not Rule 1.6 permits such disclosure, but only if and to the extent the lawyer reasonably believes necessary to prevent substantial injury to the organization.

(d) Paragraph (c) shall not apply with respect to information relating to a lawyer's representation by an organization to investigate an alleged violation of law, or to defend the organization or an officer, employee or other constituent associated with the organization against a claim arising out of an alleged violation of law.

(e) A lawyer who reasonably believes that he or she has been discharged because of the lawyer's actions taken pursuant to Paragraphs (b) or (c), or who withdraws under circumstances that require or permit the lawyer to take action under either of those paragraphs, shall proceed as the lawyer reasonably believes necessary to assure that the organization's highest authority is informed of the lawyer's discharge or withdrawal.

(f) In dealing with an organization's directors, officers, employees, members, shareholders or other constituents, a lawyer shall explain the identity of the client when the lawyer knows or reasonably should know that the organization's interests are adverse to those of the constituents with whom the lawyer is dealing.

(g) A lawyer representing an organization may also represent any of its directors, officers, employees, members, shareholders or other constituents, subject to the provisions of Rule 1.7. If the organization's consent to the dual representation is required by Rule 1.7, the consent shall be given by an appropriate official of the organization other than the individual who is to be represented, or by the shareholders.

COMMENT

The Entity as the Client

[1] An organizational client is a legal entity, but it cannot act except through its officers, directors, employees, shareholders and other constituents. Officers,

directors, employees and shareholders are the constituents of the corporate organizational client. The duties defined in this Comment apply equally to unincorporated associations. "Other constituents" as used in this Comment means the positions equivalent to officers, directors, employees and shareholders held by persons acting for organizational clients that are not corporations.

[2] When one of the constituents of an organizational client communicates with the organization's lawyer in that person's organizational capacity, the communication is protected by Rule 1.6. Thus, by way of example, if an organizational client requests its lawyer to investigate allegations of wrongdoing, interviews made in the course of that investigation between the lawyer and the client's employees or other constituents are covered by Rule 1.6. This does not mean, however, that constituents of an organizational client are the clients of the lawyer. The lawyer may not disclose to such constituents information relating to the representation except for disclosures explicitly or impliedly authorized by the organizational client in order to carry out the representation or as otherwise permitted by Rule 1.6.

[3] When constituents of the organization make decisions for it, the decisions ordinarily must be accepted by the lawyer even if their utility or prudence is doubtful. Decisions concerning policy and operations, including ones entailing serious risk, are not as such in the lawyer's province. Paragraph (b) makes clear, however, that when the lawyer knows that the organization is likely to be substantially injured by action of an officer or other constituent that violates a legal obligation to the organization or is in violation of law that might be imputed to the organization, the lawyer must proceed as is reasonably necessary in the best interest of the organization. As defined in Rule 1.0(f), knowledge can be inferred from circumstances, and a lawyer cannot ignore the obvious.

[4] In determining how to proceed under Paragraph (b), the lawyer should give due consideration to the seriousness of the violation and its consequences, the responsibility in the organization and the apparent motivation of the person involved, the policies of the organization concerning such matters, and any other relevant considerations. Ordinarily, referral to a higher authority would be necessary. In some circumstances, however, it may be appropriate for the lawyer to ask the constituent to reconsider the matter; for example, if the circumstances involve a constituent's innocent misunderstanding of law and subsequent acceptance of the lawyer's advice, the lawyer may reasonably conclude that the best interest of the organization does not require that the matter be referred to higher authority. If a constituent persists in conduct contrary to the lawyer's advice, it will be necessary for the lawyer to take steps to have the matter reviewed by a higher authority in the organization. If the matter is of sufficient seriousness and importance or urgency to the organization, referral to higher authority in the organization may be necessary even if the lawyer has not communicated with the constituent. Any measures taken should, to the extent practicable, minimize the risk of revealing information relating to the representation to persons outside the organization. Even in circumstances where a lawyer is not obligated by Rule 1.13 to proceed, a lawyer may bring to the attention of an organizational client, including its highest authority, matters that the lawyer reasonably believes to be of sufficient importance to warrant doing so in the best interest of the organization.

[5] Paragraph (b) also makes clear that when it is reasonably necessary to enable the organization to address the matter in a timely and appropriate manner, the lawyer must refer the matter to higher authority, including, if warranted

by the circumstances, the highest authority that can act on behalf of the organization under applicable law. The organization's highest authority to whom a matter may be referred ordinarily will be the board of directors or similar governing body. However, applicable law may prescribe that under certain conditions the highest authority reposes elsewhere, for example, in the independent directors of a corporation.

Relation to Other Rules

[6] The authority and responsibility provided in this Rule are concurrent with the authority and responsibility provided in other Rules. In particular, this Rule does not limit or expand the lawyer's responsibility under Rule 1.8, 1.16, 3.3 or 4.1. Paragraph (c) of this Rule supplements Rule 1.6(b) by providing an additional basis upon which the lawyer may reveal information relating to the representation, but does not modify, restrict, or limit the provisions of Rule 1.6(b)(1)-(6). Under Paragraph (c) the lawyer may reveal such information only when the organization's highest authority insists upon or fails to address threatened or ongoing action that is clearly a violation of law, and then only to the extent the lawyer reasonably believes necessary to prevent reasonably certain substantial injury to the organization. It is not necessary that the lawyer's services be used in furtherance of the violation, but it is required that the matter be related to the lawyer's representation of the organization. If the lawyer's services are being used by an organization to further a crime or fraud by the organization, Rules 1.6(b)(2) and 1.6(b)(3) may permit the lawyer to disclose confidential information. In such circumstances Rule 1.2(d) may also be applicable, in which event, withdrawal from the representation under Rule 1.16(a)(1) may be required.

[7] Paragraph (d) makes clear that the authority of a lawyer to disclose information relating to a representation in circumstances described in paragraph (c) does not apply with respect to information relating to a lawyer's engagement by an organization to investigate an alleged violation of law or to defend the organization or an officer, employee or other person associated with the organization against a claim arising out of an alleged violation of law. This is necessary in order to enable organizational clients to enjoy the full benefits of legal counsel in conducting an investigation or defending against a claim.

[8] A lawyer who reasonably believes that he or she has been discharged because of the lawyer's actions taken pursuant to paragraph (b) or (c), or who withdraws in circumstances that require or permit the lawyer to take action under either of these paragraphs, must proceed as the lawyer reasonably believes necessary to assure that the organization's highest authority is informed of the lawyer's discharge or withdrawal.

Government Agency

[9] The duty defined in this Rule applies to governmental organizations. Defining precisely the identity of the client and prescribing the resulting obligations of such lawyers may be more difficult in the government context and is a matter beyond the scope of these Rules. See Scope [18]. Although in some circumstances

the client may be a specific agency, it may also be a branch of government, such as the executive branch, or the government as a whole. For example, if the action or failure to act involves the head of a bureau, either the department of which the bureau is a part or the relevant branch of government may be the client for purposes of this Rule. Moreover, in a matter involving the conduct of government officials, a government lawyer may have authority under applicable law to question such conduct more extensively than that of a lawyer for a private organization in similar circumstances. Thus, when the client is a governmental organization, a different balance may be appropriate between maintaining confidentiality and assuring that the wrongful act is prevented or rectified, for public business is involved. In addition, duties of lawyers employed by the government or lawyers in military service may be defined by statutes and regulation. This Rule does not limit that authority. See Scope.

Clarifying the Lawyer's Role

[10] There are times when the organization's interest may be or become adverse to those of one or more of its constituents. In such circumstances the lawyer should advise any constituent, whose interest the lawyer finds adverse to that of the organization of the conflict or potential conflict of interest, that the lawyer cannot represent such constituent, and that such person may wish to obtain independent representation. Care must be taken to assure that the individual understands that, when there is such adversity of interest, the lawyer for the organization cannot provide legal representation for that constituent individual, and that discussions between the lawyer for the organization and the individual may not be privileged.

[11] Whether such a warning should be given by the lawyer for the organization to any constituent individual may turn on the facts of each case.

Dual Representation

[12] Paragraph (g) recognizes that a lawyer for an organization may also represent a principal officer or major shareholder.

Derivative Actions

[13] Under generally prevailing law, the shareholders or members of a corporation may bring suit to compel the directors to perform their legal obligations in the supervision of the organization. Members of unincorporated associations have essentially the same right. Such an action may be brought nominally by the organization, but usually is, in fact, a legal controversy over management of the organization.

[14] The question can arise whether counsel for the organization may defend such an action. The proposition that the organization is the lawyer's client does not alone resolve the issue. Most derivative actions are a normal incident of an organization's affairs, to be defended by the organization's lawyer like any other suit.

However, if the claim involves serious charges of wrongdoing by those in control of the organization, a conflict may arise between the lawyer's duty to the organization and the lawyer's relationship with the board. In those circumstances, Rule 1.7 governs who should represent the directors and the organization.

Rule 1.14   Client with Diminished Capacity

(a) When a client's capacity to make adequately considered decisions in connection with a representation is diminished, whether because of minority, mental impairment or for some other reason, the lawyer shall, as far as reasonably possible, maintain a normal client-lawyer relationship with the client.

(b) When the lawyer reasonably believes that the client has diminished capacity, is at risk of substantial physical, financial or other harm unless action is taken and cannot adequately act in the client's own interest, the lawyer may take reasonably necessary protective action, including consulting with individuals or entities that have the ability to take action to protect the client and, in appropriate cases, seeking the appointment of a guardian ad litem, conservator or guardian.

(c) Information relating to the representation of a client with diminished capacity is protected by Rule 1.6. When taking protective action pursuant to paragraph (b), the lawyer is impliedly authorized under Rule 1.6(a) to reveal information about the client, but only to the extent reasonably necessary to protect the client's interests.

COMMENT

[1] The normal client-lawyer relationship is based on the assumption that the client, when properly advised and assisted, is capable of making decisions about important matters. When the client is a minor or suffers from a diminished mental capacity, however, maintaining the ordinary client-lawyer relationship may not be possible in all respects. In particular, a severely incapacitated person may have no power to make legally binding decisions. Nevertheless, a client with diminished capacity often has the ability to understand, deliberate upon, and reach conclusions about matters affecting the client's own well-being. For example, children as young as five or six years of age, and certainly those of ten or twelve, are regarded as having opinions that are entitled to weight in legal proceedings concerning their custody. So also, it is recognized that some persons of advanced age can be quite capable of handling routine financial matters while needing special legal protection concerning major transactions.

[2] The fact that a client suffers a disability does not diminish the lawyer's obligation to treat the client with attention and respect. Even if the person has a legal representative, the lawyer should as far as possible accord the represented person the status of client, particularly in maintaining communication.

[3] The client may wish to have family members or other persons participate in discussions with the lawyer. When necessary to assist in the representation, the

presence of such persons generally does not affect the applicability of the attorney-client evidentiary privilege. Nevertheless, the lawyer must keep the client's interests foremost and, except for protective action authorized under paragraph (b), must look to the client, and not family members, to make decisions on the client's behalf.

[4] If a legal representative has already been appointed for the client, the lawyer should ordinarily look to the representative for decisions on behalf of the client. In matters involving a minor, whether the lawyer should look to the parents as natural guardians may depend on the type of proceeding or matter in which the lawyer is representing the minor. If the lawyer represents the guardian as distinct from the ward, and is aware that the guardian is acting adversely to the ward's interest, the lawyer may have an obligation to prevent or rectify the guardian's misconduct. See Rule 1.2(d).

Taking Protective Action

[5] If a lawyer reasonably believes that a client is at risk of substantial physical, financial or other harm unless action is taken, and that a normal client-lawyer relationship cannot be maintained as provided in paragraph (a) because the client lacks sufficient capacity to communicate or to make adequately considered decisions in connection with the representation, then paragraph (b) permits the lawyer to take protective measures deemed necessary. Such measures could include: consulting with family members, using a reconsideration period to permit clarification or improvement of circumstances, using voluntary surrogate decisionmaking tools such as durable powers of attorney or consulting with support groups, professional services, adult-protective agencies or other individuals or entities that have the ability to protect the client. In taking any protective action, the lawyer should be guided by such factors as the wishes and values of the client to the extent known, the client's best interests and the goals of intruding into the client's decisionmaking autonomy to the least extent feasible, maximizing client capacities and respecting the client's family and social connections.

[6] In determining the extent of the client's diminished capacity, the lawyer should consider and balance such factors as: the client's ability to articulate reasoning leading to a decision, variability of state of mind, and ability to appreciate consequences of a decision; the substantive fairness of a decision; and the consistency of a decision with the known long-term commitments and values of the client. In appropriate circumstances, the lawyer may seek guidance from an appropriate diagnostician.

[7] If a legal representative has not been appointed, the lawyer should consider whether appointment of a guardian ad litem, conservator or guardian is necessary to protect the client's interests. Thus, if a client with diminished capacity has substantial property that should be sold for the client's benefit, effective completion of the transaction may require appointment of a legal representative. In addition, rules of procedure in litigation sometimes provide that minors or persons with diminished capacity must be represented by a guardian or next friend if they do not have a general guardian. In many circumstances, however, appointment of a legal representative may be more expensive or traumatic for the client than circumstances in fact require. Evaluation of such circumstances is a matter entrusted to the professional judgment of the lawyer. In considering alternatives, however, the lawyer should be aware of any law that requires the lawyer to advocate the least restrictive action on behalf of the client.

Disclosure of the Client's Condition

[8] Disclosure of the client's diminished capacity could adversely affect the client's interests. For example, raising the question of diminished capacity could, in some circumstances, lead to proceedings for involuntary commitment. Information relating to the representation is protected by Rule 1.6. Therefore, unless authorized to do so, the lawyer may not disclose such information. When taking protective action pursuant to paragraph (b), the lawyer is impliedly authorized to make the necessary disclosures, even when the client directs the lawyer to the contrary. Nevertheless, given the risks of disclosure, paragraph (c) limits what the lawyer may disclose in consulting with other individuals or entities or seeking the appointment of a legal representative. At the very least, the lawyer should determine whether it is likely that the person or entity consulted with will act adversely to the client's interests before discussing matters related to the client. The lawyer's position in such cases is an unavoidably difficult one.

Emergency Legal Assistance

[9] In an emergency where the health, safety or a financial interest of a person with seriously diminished capacity is threatened with imminent and irreparable harm, a lawyer may take legal action on behalf of such a person even though the person is unable to establish a client-lawyer relationship or to make or express considered judgments about the matter, when the person or another acting in good faith on that person's behalf has consulted with the lawyer. Even in such an emergency, however, the lawyer should not act unless the lawyer reasonably believes that the person has no other lawyer, agent or other representative available. The lawyer should take legal action on behalf of the person only to the extent reasonably necessary to maintain the status quo or otherwise avoid imminent and irreparable harm. A lawyer who undertakes to represent a person in such an exigent situation has the same duties under these Rules as the lawyer would with respect to a client.

[10] A lawyer who acts on behalf of a person with seriously diminished capacity in an emergency should keep the confidences of the person as if dealing with a client, disclosing them only to the extent necessary to accomplish the intended protective action. The lawyer should disclose to any tribunal involved and to any other counsel involved the nature of his or her relationship with the person. The lawyer should take steps to regularize the relationship or implement other protective solutions as soon as possible. Normally, a lawyer would not seek compensation for such emergency actions taken.

Rule 1.15   Safekeeping Property

(a) A lawyer shall hold property of clients or third persons that is in a lawyer's possession in connection with a representation separate from the lawyer's own property. Funds shall be kept in a separate account maintained in the state where the lawyer's office is situated, or elsewhere with the consent of the client or third person. Other property shall be identified as such and appropriately safeguarded. Complete records of such account funds and other property shall be kept by the lawyer and shall be preserved for a period of [five years] after termination of the representation.

(b) A lawyer may deposit the lawyer's own funds in a client trust account for the sole purpose of paying bank service charges on that account, but only in an amount necessary for that purpose.

(c) A lawyer shall deposit into a client trust account legal fees and expenses that have been paid in advance, to be withdrawn by the lawyer only as fees are earned or expenses incurred.

(d) Upon receiving funds or other property in which a client or third person has an interest, a lawyer shall promptly notify the client or third person. Except as stated in this rule or otherwise permitted by law or by agreement with the client, a lawyer shall promptly deliver to the client or third person any funds or other property that the client or third person is entitled to receive and, upon request by the client or third person, shall promptly render a full accounting regarding such property.

(e) When in the course of representation a lawyer is in possession of property in which two or more persons (one of whom may be the lawyer) claim interests, the property shall be kept separate by the lawyer until the dispute is resolved. The lawyer shall promptly distribute all portions of the property as to which the interests are not in dispute.

COMMENT

[1] A lawyer should hold property of others with the care required of a professional fiduciary. Securities should be kept in a safe deposit box, except when some other form of safekeeping is warranted by special circumstances. All property that is the property of clients or third persons, including prospective clients, must be kept separate from the lawyer's business and personal property and, if monies, in one or more trust accounts. Separate trust accounts may be warranted when administering estate monies or acting in similar fiduciary capacities. A lawyer should maintain on a current basis books and records in accordance with generally accepted accounting practice and comply with any recordkeeping rules established by law or court order. See, e.g., ABA Model Financial Recordkeeping Rule.

[2] While normally it is impermissible to commingle the lawyer's own funds with client funds, paragraph (b) provides that it is permissible when necessary to pay bank service charges on that account. Accurate records must be kept regarding which part of the funds are the lawyer's.

[3] Lawyers often receive funds from which the lawyer's fee will be paid. The lawyer is not required to remit to the client funds that the lawyer reasonably believes represent fees owed. However, a lawyer may not hold funds to coerce a client into accepting the lawyer's contention. The disputed portion of the funds must be kept in a trust account and the lawyer should suggest means for prompt resolution of the dispute, such as arbitration. The undisputed portion of the funds shall be promptly distributed.

[4] Paragraph (e) also recognizes that third parties may have lawful claims against specific funds or other property in a lawyer's custody, such as a client's creditor who has a lien on funds recovered in a personal injury action. A lawyer may have a duty under applicable law to protect such third-party claims against wrongful interference by the client. In such cases, when the third-party claim is not frivolous under applicable law, the lawyer must refuse to surrender the property to the client until the claims are resolved. A lawyer should not unilaterally assume to arbitrate a dispute between the client and the third party, but, when there are substantial grounds for dispute as to the person entitled to the funds, the lawyer may file an action to have a court resolve the dispute.

[5] The obligations of a lawyer under this Rule are independent of those arising from activity other than rendering legal services. For example, a lawyer who serves only as an escrow agent is governed by the applicable law relating to fiduciaries even though the lawyer does not render legal services in the transaction and is not governed by this Rule.

[6] A lawyers' fund for client protection provides a means through the collective efforts of the bar to reimburse persons who have lost money or property as a result of dishonest conduct of a lawyer. Where such a fund has been established, a lawyer must participate where it is mandatory, and, even when it is voluntary, the lawyer should participate.

Rule 1.16   Declining or Terminating Representation

(a) Except as stated in paragraph (c), a lawyer shall not represent a client or, where representation has commenced, shall withdraw from the representation of a client if:

(1) the representation will result in violation of the rules of professional conduct or other law;

(2) the lawyer's physical or mental condition materially impairs the lawyer's ability to represent the client; or

(3) the lawyer is discharged. (does not prevent a noisy withdrawal)

(b) Except as stated in paragraph (c), a lawyer may withdraw from representing a client if:

(1) withdrawal can be accomplished without material adverse effect on the interests of the client;

(2) the client persists in a course of action involving the lawyer's services that the lawyer reasonably believes is criminal or fraudulent;

(3) the client has used the lawyer's services to perpetrate a crime or fraud;

(4) the client insists upon taking action that the lawyer considers repugnant or with which the lawyer has a fundamental disagreement;

(5) the client fails substantially to fulfill an obligation to the lawyer regarding the lawyer's services and has been given reasonable warning that the lawyer will withdraw unless the obligation is fulfilled;

(6) the representation will result in an unreasonable financial burden on the lawyer or has been rendered unreasonably difficult by the client; or

(7) other good cause for withdrawal exists.

(c) A lawyer must comply with applicable law requiring notice to or permission of a tribunal when terminating a representation. When ordered to do so by a tribunal, a lawyer shall continue representation notwithstanding good cause for terminating the representation.

(d) Upon termination of representation, a lawyer shall take steps to the extent reasonably practicable to protect a client's interests, such as giving reasonable notice to the client, allowing time for employment of other counsel, surrendering papers and property to which the client is entitled and refunding any advance payment of fee or expense that has not been earned or incurred. The lawyer may retain papers relating to the client to the extent permitted by other law.

COMMENT

[1] A lawyer should not accept representation in a matter unless it can be performed competently, promptly, without improper conflict of interest and to completion. Ordinarily, a representation in a matter is completed when the agreed-upon assistance has been concluded. See Rules 1.2(c) and 6.5. See also Rule 1.3, Comment [4].

Mandatory Withdrawal

[2] A lawyer ordinarily must decline or withdraw from representation if the client demands that the lawyer engage in conduct that is illegal or violates the Rules of Professional Conduct or other law. The lawyer is not obliged to decline or withdraw simply because the client suggests such a course of conduct; a client may make such a suggestion in the hope that a lawyer will not be constrained by a professional obligation.

[3] When a lawyer has been appointed to represent a client, withdrawal ordinarily requires approval of the appointing authority. See also Rule 6.2. Similarly, court approval or notice to the court is often required by applicable law before a lawyer withdraws from pending litigation. Difficulty may be encountered if withdrawal is based on the client's demand that the lawyer engage in unprofessional conduct. The court may request an explanation for the withdrawal, while the lawyer may be bound to keep confidential the facts that would constitute such an explanation. The lawyer's statement that professional considerations require termination of the representation ordinarily should be accepted as sufficient. Lawyers should be mindful of their obligations to both clients and the court under Rules 1.6 and 3.3.

Discharge

[4] A client has a right to discharge a lawyer at any time, with or without cause, subject to liability for payment for the lawyer's services. Where future dispute about the withdrawal may be anticipated, it may be advisable to prepare a written statement reciting the circumstances.

[5] Whether a client can discharge appointed counsel may depend on applicable law. A client seeking to do so should be given a full explanation of the consequences. These consequences may include a decision by the appointing authority that appointment of successor counsel is unjustified, thus requiring self-representation by the client.

[6] If the client has severely diminished capacity, the client may lack the legal capacity to discharge the lawyer, and in any event the discharge may be seriously adverse to the client's interests. The lawyer should make special effort to help the client consider the consequences and may take reasonably necessary protective action as provided in Rule 1.14.

Optional Withdrawal

[7] A lawyer may withdraw from representation in some circumstances. The lawyer has the option to withdraw if it can be accomplished without material adverse effect on the client's interests. Withdrawal is also justified if the client persists in a course of action that the lawyer reasonably believes is criminal or fraudulent, for a lawyer is not required to be associated with such conduct even if the lawyer does not further it. Withdrawal is also permitted if the lawyer's services were misused in the past even if that would materially prejudice the client. The lawyer may also withdraw where the client insists on taking action that the lawyer considers repugnant or with which the lawyer has a fundamental disagreement.

[8] A lawyer may withdraw if the client refuses to abide by the terms of an agreement relating to the representation, such as an agreement concerning fees or court costs or an agreement limiting the objectives of the representation.

Assisting the Client upon Withdrawal

[9] Even if the lawyer has been unfairly discharged by the client, a lawyer must take all reasonable steps to mitigate the consequences to the client. The lawyer may retain papers as security for a fee only to the extent permitted by law. See Rule 1.15.

> **Editors' Note.** In August 2012, the ABA House of Delegates amended Comment 7 to Rule 1.17. The ABA Commission on Ethics 20/20 proposed this change to ensure that the Comment is consistent with the approach to conflicts detection set out in newly created Rule 1.6(b)(7). (See the Editors' Note before Rule 1.6.) To alert readers to this change, we underscore the new language in Comment 7 and strike through deleted language. For more information regarding this change, see the Legislative History for this Rule in the "Annotations on ABA Model Rules" section of this book.

Rule 1.17   Sale of Law Practice

A lawyer or a law firm may sell or purchase a law practice, or an area of law practice, including good will, if the following conditions are satisfied:

(a) The seller ceases to engage in the private practice of law, or in the area of practice that has been sold, [in the geographic area] [in the jurisdiction] (a jurisdiction may elect either version) in which the practice has been conducted;

(b) The entire practice, or the entire area of practice, is sold to one or more lawyers or law firms;

(c) The seller gives written notice to each of the seller's clients regarding:

(1) the proposed sale;

(2) the client's right to retain other counsel or to take possession of the file; and

(3) the fact that the client's consent to the transfer of the client's files will be presumed if the client does not take any action or does not otherwise object within ninety (90) days of receipt of the notice.

If a client cannot be given notice, the representation of that client may be transferred to the purchaser only upon entry of an order so authorizing by a court having jurisdiction. The seller may disclose to the court in camera information relating to the representation only to the extent necessary to obtain an order authorizing the transfer of a file.

(d) The fees charged clients shall not be increased by reason of the sale.

COMMENT

[1] The practice of law is a profession, not merely a business. Clients are not commodities that can be purchased and sold at will. Pursuant to this Rule, when a lawyer or an entire firm ceases to practice, or ceases to practice in an area of law, and other lawyers or firms take over the representation, the selling lawyer or firm may obtain compensation for the reasonable value of the practice as may withdrawing partners of law firms. See Rules 5.4 and 5.6.

Termination of Practice by the Seller

[2] The requirement that all of the private practice, or all of an area of practice, be sold is satisfied if the seller in good faith makes the entire practice, or the area of practice, available for sale to the purchasers. The fact that a number of the seller's clients decide not to be represented by the purchasers but take their matters elsewhere, therefore, does not result in a violation. Return to private practice as a result of an unanticipated change in circumstances does not necessarily result in a violation. For example, a lawyer who has sold the practice to accept an appointment to judicial office does not violate the requirement that the sale be attendant to cessation of practice if the lawyer later resumes private practice upon being defeated in a contested or a retention election for the office or resigns from a judiciary position.

[3] The requirement that the seller cease to engage in the private practice of law does not prohibit employment as a lawyer on the staff of a public agency or a legal services entity that provides legal services to the poor, or as in-house counsel to a business.

[4] The Rule permits a sale of an entire practice attendant upon retirement from the private practice of law within the jurisdiction. Its provisions, therefore, accommodate the lawyer who sells the practice on the occasion of moving to another state. Some states are so large that a move from one locale therein to another is tantamount to leaving the jurisdiction in which the lawyer has engaged in the practice of law. To also accommodate lawyers so situated, states may permit the sale of the practice when the lawyer leaves the geographical area rather than the jurisdiction. The alternative desired should be indicated by selecting one of the two provided for in Rule 1.17(a).

[5] This Rule also permits a lawyer or law firm to sell an area of practice. If an area of practice is sold and the lawyer remains in the active practice of law, the lawyer must cease accepting any matters in the area of practice that has been sold, either as counsel or co-counsel or by assuming joint responsibility for a matter in connection with the division of a fee with another lawyer as would otherwise be permitted by Rule 1.5(e). For example, a lawyer with a substantial number of estate planning matters and a substantial number of probate administration cases may sell the estate planning portion of the practice but remain in the practice of law by concentrating on probate administration; however, that practitioner may not thereafter accept any estate planning matters. Although a lawyer who leaves a jurisdiction or geographical area typically would sell the entire practice, this Rule permits the lawyer to limit the sale to one or more areas of the practice, thereby preserving the lawyer's right to continue practice in the areas of the practice that were not sold.

Sale of Entire Practice or Entire Area of Practice

[6] The Rule requires that the seller's entire practice, or an entire area of practice, be sold. The prohibition against sale of less than an entire practice area protects those clients whose matters are less lucrative and who might find it difficult to secure other counsel if a sale could be limited to substantial fee-generating matters. The purchasers are required to undertake all client matters in the practice or practice area, subject to client consent. This requirement is satisfied, however, even if a purchaser is unable to undertake a particular client matter because of a conflict of interest.

Client Confidences, Consent and Notice

[7] Negotiations between seller and prospective purchaser prior to disclosure of information relating to a specific representation of an identifiable client no more violate the confidentiality provisions of Model Rule 1.6 than do preliminary discussions concerning the possible association of another lawyer or mergers between firms, with respect to which client consent is not required. See Rule 1.6(b)(7). Providing the purchaser access to ~~client-specific~~ detailed information relating to the representation, ~~and to~~ such as the client's file, however, requires client consent. The Rule provides that before such information can be disclosed by the seller to the purchaser the client must be given actual written notice of the contemplated sale, including the identity of the purchaser, and must be told that the decision to consent or make other arrangements must be made within 90 days. If nothing is heard from the client within that time, consent to the sale is presumed.

[8] A lawyer or law firm ceasing to practice cannot be required to remain in practice because some clients cannot be given actual notice of the proposed purchase. Since these clients cannot themselves consent to the purchase or direct any other disposition of their files, the Rule requires an order from a court having jurisdiction authorizing their transfer or other disposition. The Court can be expected to determine whether reasonable efforts to locate the client have been exhausted, and whether the absent client's legitimate interests will be served by authorizing the transfer of the file so that the purchaser may continue the representation. Preservation of client confidences requires that the petition for a court order be considered in camera. (A procedure by which such an order can be obtained needs to be established in jurisdictions in which it presently does not exist.)

[9] All the elements of client autonomy, including the client's absolute right to discharge a lawyer and transfer the representation to another, survive the sale of the practice or area of practice.

Fee Arrangements Between Client and Purchaser

[10] The sale may not be financed by increases in fees charged the clients of the practice. Existing arrangements between the seller and the client as to fees and the scope of the work must be honored by the purchaser.

Other Applicable Ethical Standards

[11] Lawyers participating in the sale of a law practice or a practice area are subject to the ethical standards applicable to involving another lawyer in the representation of a client. These include, for example, the seller's obligation to exercise competence in identifying a purchaser qualified to assume the practice and the purchaser's obligation to undertake the representation competently (see Rule 1.1); the obligation to avoid disqualifying conflicts, and to secure the client's informed consent for those conflicts that can be agreed to (see Rule 1.7 regarding conflicts and Rule 1.0(e) for the definition of informed consent); and the obligation to protect information relating to the representation (see Rules 1.6 and 1.9).

[12] If approval of the substitution of the purchasing lawyer for the selling lawyer is required by the rules of any tribunal in which a matter is pending, such approval must be obtained before the matter can be included in the sale (see Rule 1.16).

Applicability of the Rule

[13] This Rule applies to the sale of a law practice by a deceased, disabled or disappeared lawyer. Thus, the seller may be represented by a non-lawyer representative not subject to these Rules. Since, however, no lawyer may participate in a sale of a law practice which does not conform to the requirements of this Rule, the representatives of the seller as well as the purchasing lawyer can be expected to see to it that they are met.

[14] Admission to or retirement from a law partnership or professional association, retirement plans and similar arrangements, and a sale of tangible assets of a law practice, do not constitute a sale or purchase governed by this Rule.

[15] This Rule does not apply to the transfers of legal representation between lawyers when such transfers are unrelated to the sale of a practice or an area of practice.

> **Editors' Note.** In August 2012, the ABA House of Delegates amended Rule 1.18 and several accompanying Comments. The ABA Commission on Ethics 20/20 proposed the changes to provide lawyers with greater guidance as to when a prospective client relationship arises as a result of electronic communications with the public. To alert readers to the changes, we underscore the new language and strike through deleted language. For more information regarding these changes, see the Legislative History for this Rule in the "Annotations on ABA Model Rules" section of this book.

Rule 1.18   Duties to Prospective Client

(a) A person who ~~discusses~~ <u>consults</u> with a lawyer <u>about</u> the possibility of forming a client-lawyer relationship with respect to a matter is a prospective client.

(b) Even when no client-lawyer relationship ensues, a lawyer who has ~~had discussions with~~ <u>learned information from</u> a prospective client shall not use or reveal <u>that</u> information ~~learned in the consultation,~~ except as Rule 1.9 would permit with respect to information of a former client.

(c) A lawyer subject to paragraph (b) shall not represent a client with interests materially adverse to those of a prospective client in the same or a substantially related matter if the lawyer received information from the prospective client that could be significantly harmful to that person in the matter, except as provided in paragraph (d). If a lawyer is disqualified from representation under this paragraph, no lawyer in a firm with which that lawyer is associated may knowingly undertake or continue representation in such a matter, except as provided in paragraph (d).

(d) When the lawyer has received disqualifying information as defined in paragraph (c), representation is permissible if:

(1) both the affected client and the prospective client have given informed consent, confirmed in writing, or:

(2) the lawyer who received the information took reasonable measures to avoid exposure to more disqualifying information than was reasonably necessary to determine whether to represent the prospective client; and

(i) the disqualified lawyer is timely screened from any participation in the matter and is apportioned no part of the fee therefrom; and

(ii) written notice is promptly given to the prospective client.

COMMENT

[1] Prospective clients, like clients, may disclose information to a lawyer, place documents or other property in the lawyer's custody, or rely on the lawyer's advice. A lawyer's ~~discussions~~ consultations with a prospective client usually are limited in time and depth and leave both the prospective client and the lawyer free (and sometimes required) to proceed no further. Hence, prospective clients should receive some but not all of the protection afforded clients.

[2] ~~Not all persons who communicate information to a lawyer are entitled to protection under this Rule.~~ A person becomes a prospective client by consulting with a lawyer about the possibility of forming a client-lawyer relationship with respect to a matter. Whether communications, including written, oral, or electronic communications, constitute a consultation depends on the circumstances. For example, a consultation is likely to have occurred if a lawyer, either in person or through the lawyer's advertising in any medium, specifically requests or invites the submission of information about a potential representation without clear and reasonably understandable warnings and cautionary statements that limit the lawyer's obligations, and a person provides information in response. See also Comment [4]. In contrast, a consultation does not occur if a person provides information to a lawyer in response to advertising that merely describes the lawyer's education, experience, areas of practice, and contact information, or provides legal information of general interest. ~~A person who communicates~~ Such a person communicates information unilaterally to a lawyer, without any reasonable expectation that the lawyer is willing to discuss the possibility of forming a client-lawyer relationship, and is thus not a "prospective client." ~~within the meaning of paragraph (a).~~ Moreover, a person who communicates with a lawyer for the purpose of disqualifying the lawyer is not a "prospective client."

[3] It is often necessary for a prospective client to reveal information to the lawyer during an initial consultation prior to the decision about formation of a client-lawyer relationship. The lawyer often must learn such information to determine whether there is a conflict of interest with an existing client and whether the matter is one that the lawyer is willing to undertake. Paragraph (b) prohibits the lawyer from using or revealing that information, except as permitted by Rule 1.9, even if the client or lawyer decides not to proceed with the representation. The duty exists regardless of how brief the initial conference may be.

[4] In order to avoid acquiring disqualifying information from a prospective client, a lawyer considering whether or not to undertake a new matter should limit ~~the initial interview~~ the initial consultation to only such information as reasonably appears necessary for that purpose. Where the information indicates that a conflict of interest or other reason for non-representation exists, the lawyer should so inform the prospective client or decline the representation. If the prospective client wishes to retain the lawyer, and if consent is possible under Rule 1.7, then consent from all affected present or former clients must be obtained before accepting the representation.

[5] A lawyer may condition ~~conversations~~ a consultation with a prospective client on the person's informed consent that no information disclosed during the consultation will prohibit the lawyer from representing a different client in the matter. See Rule 1.0(e) for the definition of informed consent. If the agreement expressly

so provides, the prospective client may also consent to the lawyer's subsequent use of information received from the prospective client.

[6] Even in the absence of an agreement, under paragraph (c), the lawyer is not prohibited from representing a client with interests adverse to those of the prospective client in the same or a substantially related matter unless the lawyer has received from the prospective client information that could be significantly harmful if used in the matter.

[7] Under paragraph (c), the prohibition in this Rule is imputed to other lawyers as provided in Rule 1.10, but, under paragraph (d)(1), imputation may be avoided if the lawyer obtains the informed consent, confirmed in writing, of both the prospective and affected clients. In the alternative, imputation may be avoided if the conditions of paragraph (d)(2) are met and all disqualified lawyers are timely screened and written notice is promptly given to the prospective client. See Rule 1.0(k) (requirements for screening procedures). Paragraph (d)(2)(i) does not prohibit the screened lawyer from receiving a salary or partnership share established by prior independent agreement, but that lawyer may not receive compensation directly related to the matter in which the lawyer is disqualified.

[8] Notice, including a general description of the subject matter about which the lawyer was consulted, and of the screening procedures employed, generally should be given as soon as practicable after the need for screening becomes apparent.

[9] For the duty of competence of a lawyer who gives assistance on the merits of a matter to a prospective client, see Rule 1.1. For a lawyer's duties when a prospective client entrusts valuables or papers to the lawyer's care, see Rule 1.15.

ARTICLE 2.   COUNSELOR

Rule 2.1   Advisor

In representing a client, a lawyer shall exercise independent professional judgment and render candid advice. In rendering advice, a lawyer may refer not only to law but to other considerations such as moral, economic, social and political factors, that may be relevant to the client's situation.

COMMENT

Scope of Advice

[1] A client is entitled to straightforward advice expressing the lawyer's honest assessment. Legal advice often involves unpleasant facts and alternatives that a client may be disinclined to confront. In presenting advice, a lawyer endeavors to sustain the client's morale and may put advice in as acceptable a form as honesty permits. However, a lawyer should not be deterred from giving candid advice by the prospect that the advice will be unpalatable to the client.

[2] Advice couched in narrow legal terms may be of little value to a client, especially where practical considerations, such as cost or effects on other people, are predominant. Purely technical legal advice, therefore, can sometimes be inadequate. It is proper for a lawyer to refer to relevant moral and ethical considerations in giving advice. Although a lawyer is not a moral advisor as such, moral and ethical considerations impinge upon most legal questions and may decisively influence how the law will be applied.

[3] A client may expressly or impliedly ask the lawyer for purely technical advice. When such a request is made by a client experienced in legal matters, the lawyer may accept it at face value. When such a request is made by a client inexperienced in legal matters, however, the lawyer's responsibility as advisor may include indicating that more may be involved than strictly legal considerations.

[4] Matters that go beyond strictly legal questions may also be in the domain of another profession. Family matters can involve problems within the professional competence of psychiatry, clinical psychology or social work; business matters can involve problems within the competence of the accounting profession or of financial specialists. Where consultation with a professional in another field is itself something a competent lawyer would recommend, the lawyer should make such a recommendation. At the same time, a lawyer's advice at its best often consists of recommending a course of action in the face of conflicting recommendations of experts.

Offering Advice

[5] In general, a lawyer is not expected to give advice until asked by the client. However, when a lawyer knows that a client proposes a course of action that is likely to result in substantial adverse legal consequences to the client, the lawyer's duty to the client under Rule 1.4 may require that the lawyer offer advice if the client's course of action is related to the representation. Similarly, when a matter is likely to involve litigation, it may be necessary under Rule 1.4 to inform the client of forms of dispute resolution that might constitute reasonable alternatives to litigation. A lawyer ordinarily has no duty to initiate investigation of a client's affairs or to give advice that the client has indicated is unwanted, but a lawyer may initiate advice to a client when doing so appears to be in the client's interest.

Rule 2.2   Intermediary [deleted in 2002]

Editors' Note. Rule 2.2 is no longer part of the ABA Model Rules of Professional Conduct. At its February 2002 Mid-Year Meeting, based on a recommendation by the ABA Ethics 2000 Commission, the ABA House of Delegates deleted Rule 2.2 and its Comment from the Model Rules. At the same time, also based on a proposal by the Ethics 2000 Commission, the House of Delegates added a new Rule 2.4 (Lawyer Serving as Third-Party Neutral). For more information about the amendments, see the entry entitled

"2002 Amendments" in the Legislative History for this Rule and Rule 2.4 in the Annotations portion of this book. For the text of Rule 2.2, see the entry entitled "1983-2002 Rule" in the Legislative History for Rule 2.2, which is also contained in the Annotations portion of this book.

Rule 2.3 Evaluation for Use by Third Persons

(a) A lawyer may provide an evaluation of a matter affecting a client for the use of someone other than the client if the lawyer reasonably believes that making the evaluation is compatible with other aspects of the lawyer's relationship with the client.

(b) When the lawyer knows or reasonably should know that the evaluation is likely to affect the client's interests materially and adversely, the lawyer shall not provide the evaluation unless the client gives informed consent.

(c) Except as disclosure is authorized in connection with a report of an evaluation, information relating to the evaluation is otherwise protected by Rule 1.6.

COMMENT

Definition

[1] An evaluation may be performed at the client's direction or when impliedly authorized in order to carry out the representation. See Rule 1.2. Such an evaluation may be for the primary purpose of establishing information for the benefit of third parties; for example, an opinion concerning the title of property rendered at the behest of a vendor for the information of a prospective purchaser, or at the behest of a borrower for the information of a prospective lender. In some situations, the evaluation may be required by a government agency; for example, an opinion concerning the legality of the securities registered for sale under the securities laws. In other instances, the evaluation may be required by a third person, such as a purchaser of a business.

[2] A legal evaluation should be distinguished from an investigation of a person with whom the lawyer does not have a client-lawyer relationship. For example, a lawyer retained by a purchaser to analyze a vendor's title to property does not have a client-lawyer relationship with the vendor. So also, an investigation into a person's affairs by a government lawyer, or by special counsel by a government lawyer, or by special counsel employed by the government, is not an evaluation as that term is used in this Rule. The question is whether the lawyer is retained by the person whose affairs are being examined. When the lawyer is retained by that person, the general rules concerning loyalty to client and preservation of confidences apply, which is not the case if the lawyer is retained by someone else. For this reason, it is essential to identify the person by whom the lawyer is retained. This should be made clear not only to the person under examination, but also to others to whom the results are to be made available.

Duties Owed to Third Person and Client

[3] When the evaluation is intended for the information or use of a third person, a legal duty to that person may or may not arise. That legal question is beyond the scope of this Rule. However, since such an evaluation involves a departure from the normal client-lawyer relationship, careful analysis of the situation is required. The lawyer must be satisfied as a matter of professional judgment that making the evaluation is compatible with other functions undertaken in behalf of the client. For example, if the lawyer is acting as advocate in defending the client against charges of fraud, it would normally be incompatible with that responsibility for the lawyer to perform an evaluation for others concerning the same or a related transaction. Assuming no such impediment is apparent, however, the lawyer should advise the client of the implications of the evaluation, particularly the lawyer's responsibilities to third persons and the duty to disseminate the findings.

Access to and Disclosure of Information

[4] The quality of an evaluation depends on the freedom and extent of the investigation upon which it is based. Ordinarily a lawyer should have whatever latitude of investigation seems necessary as a matter of professional judgment. Under some circumstances, however, the terms of the evaluation may be limited. For example, certain issues or sources may be categorically excluded, or the scope of search may be limited by time constraints or the noncooperation of persons having relevant information. Any such limitations that are material to the evaluation should be described in the report. If after a lawyer has commenced an evaluation, the client refuses to comply with the terms upon which it was understood the evaluation was to have been made, the lawyer's obligations are determined by law, having reference to the terms of the client's agreement and the surrounding circumstances. In no circumstances is the lawyer permitted to knowingly make a false statement of material fact or law in providing an evaluation under this Rule. See Rule 4.1.

Obtaining Client's Informed Consent

[5] Information relating to an evaluation is protected by Rule 1.6. In many situations, providing an evaluation to a third party poses no significant risk to the client; thus, the lawyer may be impliedly authorized to disclose information to carry out the representation. See Rule 1.6(a). Where, however, it is reasonably likely that providing the evaluation will affect the client's interests materially and adversely, the lawyer must first obtain the client's consent after the client has been adequately informed concerning the important possible effects on the client's interests. See Rules 1.6(a) and 1.0(e).

Financial Auditors' Requests for Information

[6] When a question concerning the legal situation of a client arises at the instance of the client's financial auditor and the question is referred to the lawyer,

the lawyer's response may be made in accordance with procedures recognized in the legal profession. Such a procedure is set forth in the American Bar Association Statement of Policy Regarding Lawyers' Responses to Auditors' Requests for Information, adopted in 1975.

Rule 2.4   Lawyer Serving as Third-Party Neutral

(a) A lawyer serves as a third-party neutral when the lawyer assists two or more persons who are not clients of the lawyer to reach a resolution of a dispute or other matter that has arisen between them. Service as a third-party neutral may include service as an arbitrator, a mediator or in such other capacity as will enable the lawyer to assist the parties to resolve the matter.

(b) A lawyer serving as a third-party neutral shall inform unrepresented parties that the lawyer is not representing them. When the lawyer knows or reasonably should know that a party does not understand the lawyer's role in the matter, the lawyer shall explain the difference between the lawyer's role as a third-party neutral and a lawyer's role as one who represents a client.

COMMENT

[1] Alternative dispute resolution has become a substantial part of the civil justice system. Aside from representing clients in dispute-resolution processes, lawyers often serve as third-party neutrals. A third-party neutral is a person, such as a mediator, arbitrator, conciliator or evaluator, who assists the parties, represented or unrepresented, in the resolution of a dispute or in the arrangement of a transaction. Whether a third-party neutral serves primarily as a facilitator, evaluator or decisionmaker depends on the particular process that is either selected by the parties or mandated by a court.

[2] The role of a third-party neutral is not unique to lawyers, although, in some court-connected contexts, only lawyers are allowed to serve in this role or to handle certain types of cases. In performing this role, the lawyer may be subject to court rules or other law that apply either to third-party neutrals generally or to lawyers serving as third-party neutrals. Lawyer-neutrals may also be subject to various codes of ethics, such as the Code of Ethics for Arbitration in Commercial Disputes prepared by a joint committee of the American Bar Association and the American Arbitration Association or the Model Standards of Conduct for Mediators jointly prepared by the American Bar Association, the American Arbitration Association and the Society of Professionals in Dispute Resolution.

[3] Unlike nonlawyers who serve as third-party neutrals, lawyers serving in this role may experience unique problems as a result of differences between the role of a third-party neutral and a lawyer's service as a client representative. The potential for confusion is significant when the parties are unrepresented in the process. Thus, paragraph (b) requires a lawyer-neutral to inform unrepresented parties that the lawyer is not representing them. For some parties, particularly parties who frequently use dispute-resolution processes, this information will be sufficient. For

others, particularly those who are using the process for the first time, more information will be required. Where appropriate, the lawyer should inform unrepresented parties of the important differences between the lawyer's role as third-party neutral and a lawyer's role as a client representative, including the inapplicability of the attorney-client evidentiary privilege. The extent of disclosure required under this paragraph will depend on the particular parties involved and the subject matter of the proceeding, as well as the particular features of the dispute-resolution process selected.

[4] A lawyer who serves as a third-party neutral subsequently may be asked to serve as a lawyer representing a client in the same matter. The conflicts of interest that arise for both the individual lawyer and the lawyer's law firm are addressed in Rule 1.12.

[5] Lawyers who represent clients in alternative dispute-resolution processes are governed by the Rules of Professional Conduct. When the dispute-resolution process takes place before a tribunal, as in binding arbitration (see Rule 1.0(m)), the lawyer's duty of candor is governed by Rule 3.3. Otherwise, the lawyer's duty of candor toward both the third-party neutral and other parties is governed by Rule 4.1.

ARTICLE 3.   ADVOCATE

Rule 3.1   Meritorious Claims and Contentions

A lawyer shall not bring or defend a proceeding, or assert or controvert an issue therein, unless there is a basis in law and fact for doing so that is not frivolous, which includes a good faith argument for an extension, modification or reversal of existing law. A lawyer for the defendant in a criminal proceeding, or the respondent in a proceeding that could result in incarceration, may nevertheless so defend the proceeding as to require that every element of the case be established.

COMMENT

[1] The advocate has a duty to use legal procedure for the fullest benefit of the client's cause, but also a duty not to abuse legal procedure. The law, both procedural and substantive, establishes the limits within which an advocate may proceed. However, the law is not always clear and never is static. Accordingly, in determining the proper scope of advocacy, account must be taken of the law's ambiguities and potential for change.

[2] The filing of an action or defense or similar action taken for a client is not frivolous merely because the facts have not first been fully substantiated or because the lawyer expects to develop vital evidence only by discovery. What is required of lawyers, however, is that they inform themselves about the facts of their clients' cases and the applicable law and determine that they can make good faith arguments in support of their clients' positions. Such action is not frivolous even though the lawyer believes that the client's position ultimately will not prevail. The action is frivolous, however, if the lawyer is unable either to make a good faith argument on the

merits of the action taken or to support the action taken by a good faith argument for an extension, modification or reversal of existing law.

[3] The lawyer's obligations under this Rule are subordinate to federal or state constitutional law that entitles a defendant in a criminal matter to the assistance of counsel in presenting a claim or contention that otherwise would be prohibited by this Rule.

Rule 3.2   Expediting Litigation

A lawyer shall make reasonable efforts to expedite litigation consistent with the interests of the client.

COMMENT

[1] Dilatory practices bring the administration of justice into disrepute. Although there will be occasions when a lawyer may properly seek a postponement for personal reasons, it is not proper for a lawyer to routinely fail to expedite litigation solely for the convenience of the advocates. Nor will a failure to expedite be reasonable if done for the purpose of frustrating an opposing party's attempt to obtain rightful redress or repose. It is not a justification that similar conduct is often tolerated by the bench and bar. The question is whether a competent lawyer acting in good faith would regard the course of action as having some substantial purpose other than delay. Realizing financial or other benefit from otherwise improper delay in litigation is not a legitimate interest of the client.

— codefendants?

Rule 3.3   Candor Toward the Tribunal

(a) **A lawyer shall not knowingly:**

(1) **make a false statement of fact or law to a tribunal or fail to correct a false statement of material fact or law previously made to the tribunal by the lawyer;**

(2) **fail to disclose to the tribunal legal authority in the controlling jurisdiction known to the lawyer to be directly adverse to the position of the client and not disclosed by opposing counsel; or**

(3) **offer evidence that the lawyer knows to be false. If a lawyer, the lawyer's client, or a witness called by the lawyer, has offered material evidence and the lawyer comes to know of its falsity, the lawyer shall take reasonable remedial measures, including, if necessary, disclosure to the tribunal. A lawyer may refuse to offer evidence, other than the testimony of a defendant in a criminal matter, that the lawyer reasonably believes is false.**

(b) **A lawyer who represents a client in an adjudicative proceeding and who knows that a person intends to engage, is engaging or has engaged in criminal or fraudulent conduct related to the proceeding shall take reasonable remedial measures, including, if necessary, disclosure to the tribunal.**

↳ *tell the client not to lie.*

↳ *extended responsibility even if its not your client.*

(c) The duties stated in paragraphs (a) and (b) continue to the conclusion of the proceeding, and apply even if compliance requires disclosure of information otherwise protected by Rule 1.6.

(d) In an ex parte proceeding, a lawyer shall inform the tribunal of all material facts known to the lawyer that will enable the tribunal to make an informed decision, whether or not the facts are adverse.

COMMENT

[1] This Rule governs the conduct of a lawyer who is representing a client in the proceedings of a tribunal. See Rule 1.0(m) for the definition of "tribunal." It also applies when the lawyer is representing a client in an ancillary proceeding conducted pursuant to the tribunal's adjudicative authority, such as a deposition. Thus, for example, paragraph (a)(3) requires a lawyer to take reasonable remedial measures if the lawyer comes to know that a client who is testifying in a deposition has offered evidence that is false.

[2] This Rule sets forth the special duties of lawyers as officers of the court to avoid conduct that undermines the integrity of the adjudicative process. A lawyer acting as an advocate in an adjudicative proceeding has an obligation to present the client's case with persuasive force. Performance of that duty while maintaining confidences of the client, however, is qualified by the advocate's duty of candor to the tribunal. Consequently, although a lawyer in an adversary proceeding is not required to present an impartial exposition of the law or to vouch for the evidence submitted in a cause, the lawyer must not allow the tribunal to be misled by false statements of law or fact or evidence that the lawyer knows to be false.

Representations by a Lawyer

[3] An advocate is responsible for pleadings and other documents prepared for litigation, but is usually not required to have personal knowledge of matters asserted therein, for litigation documents ordinarily present assertions by the client, or by someone on the client's behalf, and not assertions by the lawyer. Compare Rule 3.1. However, an assertion purporting to be on the lawyer's own knowledge, as in an affidavit by the lawyer or in a statement in open court, may properly be made only when the lawyer knows the assertion is true or believes it to be true on the basis of a reasonably diligent inquiry. There are circumstances where failure to make a disclosure is the equivalent of an affirmative misrepresentation. The obligation prescribed in Rule 1.2(d) not to counsel a client to commit or assist the client in committing a fraud applies in litigation. Regarding compliance with Rule 1.2(d), see the Comment to that Rule. See also the Comment to Rule 8.4(b).

Legal Argument

[4] Legal argument based on a knowingly false representation of law constitutes dishonesty toward the tribunal. A lawyer is not required to make a disinterested

exposition of the law, but must recognize the existence of pertinent legal authorities. Furthermore, as stated in paragraph (a)(2), an advocate has a duty to disclose directly adverse authority in the controlling jurisdiction that has not been disclosed by the opposing party. The underlying concept is that legal argument is a discussion seeking to determine the legal premises properly applicable to the case.

Offering Evidence

[5] Paragraph (a)(3) requires that the lawyer refuse to offer evidence that the lawyer knows to be false, regardless of the client's wishes. This duty is premised on the lawyer's obligation as an officer of the court to prevent the trier of fact from being misled by false evidence. A lawyer does not violate this Rule if the lawyer offers the evidence for the purpose of establishing its falsity.

[6] If a lawyer knows that the client intends to testify falsely or wants the lawyer to introduce false evidence, the lawyer should seek to persuade the client that the evidence should not be offered. If the persuasion is ineffective and the lawyer continues to represent the client, the lawyer must refuse to offer the false evidence. If only a portion of a witness's testimony will be false, the lawyer may call the witness to testify but may not elicit or otherwise permit the witness to present the testimony that the lawyer knows is false.

[7] The duties stated in paragraphs (a) and (b) apply to all lawyers, including defense counsel in criminal cases. In some jurisdictions, however, courts have required counsel to present the accused as a witness or to give a narrative statement if the accused so desires, even if counsel knows that the testimony or statement will be false. The obligation of the advocate under the Rules of Professional Conduct is subordinate to such requirements. See also Comment [9].

[8] The prohibition against offering false evidence only applies if the lawyer knows that the evidence is false. A lawyer's reasonable belief that evidence is false does not preclude its presentation to the trier of fact. A lawyer's knowledge that evidence is false, however, can be inferred from the circumstances. See Rule 1.0(f). Thus, although a lawyer should resolve doubts about the veracity of testimony or other evidence in favor of the client, the lawyer cannot ignore an obvious falsehood.

[9] Although paragraph (a)(3) only prohibits a lawyer from offering evidence the lawyer knows to be false, it permits the lawyer to refuse to offer testimony or other proof that the lawyer reasonably believes is false. Offering such proof may reflect adversely on the lawyer's ability to discriminate in the quality of evidence and thus impair the lawyer's effectiveness as an advocate. Because of the special protections historically provided criminal defendants, however, this Rule does not permit a lawyer to refuse to offer the testimony of such a client where the lawyer reasonably believes but does not know that the testimony will be false. Unless the lawyer knows the testimony will be false, the lawyer must honor the client's decision to testify. See also Comment [7].

Remedial Measures

[10] Having offered material evidence in the belief that it was true, a lawyer may subsequently come to know that the evidence is false. Or, a lawyer may be

surprised when the lawyer's client, or another witness called by the lawyer, offers testimony the lawyer knows to be false, either during the lawyer's direct examination or in response to cross-examination by the opposing lawyer. In such situations or if the lawyer knows of the falsity of testimony elicited from the client during a deposition, the lawyer must take reasonable remedial measures. In such situations, the advocate's proper course is to remonstrate with the client confidentially, advise the client of the lawyer's duty of candor to the tribunal and seek the client's cooperation with respect to the withdrawal or correction of the false statements or evidence. If that fails, the advocate must take further remedial action. If withdrawal from the representation is not permitted or will not undo the effect of the false evidence, the advocate must make such disclosure to the tribunal as is reasonably necessary to remedy the situation, even if doing so requires the lawyer to reveal information that otherwise would be protected by Rule 1.6. It is for the tribunal then to determine what should be done—making a statement about the matter to the trier of fact, ordering a mistrial or perhaps nothing.

[11] The disclosure of a client's false testimony can result in grave consequences to the client, including not only a sense of betrayal but also loss of the case and perhaps a prosecution for perjury. But the alternative is that the lawyer cooperate in deceiving the court, thereby subverting the truth-finding process which the adversary system is designed to implement. See Rule 1.2(d). Furthermore, unless it is clearly understood that the lawyer will act upon the duty to disclose the existence of false evidence, the client can simply reject the lawyer's advice to reveal the false evidence and insist that the lawyer keep silent. Thus the client could in effect coerce the lawyer into being a party to fraud on the court.

Preserving Integrity of Adjudicative Process

[12] Lawyers have a special obligation to protect a tribunal against criminal or fraudulent conduct that undermines the integrity of the adjudicative process, such as bribing, intimidating or otherwise unlawfully communicating with a witness, juror, court official or other participant in the proceeding, unlawfully destroying or concealing documents or other evidence or failing to disclose information to the tribunal when required by law to do so. Thus, paragraph (b) requires a lawyer to take reasonable remedial measures, including disclosure if necessary, whenever the lawyer knows that a person, including the lawyer's client, intends to engage, is engaging or has engaged in criminal or fraudulent conduct related to the proceeding.

Duration of Obligation

[13] A practical time limit on the obligation to rectify false evidence or false statements of law and fact has to be established. The conclusion of the proceeding is a reasonably definite point for the termination of the obligation. A proceeding has concluded within the meaning of this Rule when a final judgment in the proceeding has been affirmed on appeal or the time for review has passed.

Ex Parte Proceedings

[14] Ordinarily, an advocate has the limited responsibility of presenting one side of the matters that a tribunal should consider in reaching a decision; the conflicting position is expected to be presented by the opposing party. However, in any ex parte proceeding, such as an application for a temporary restraining order, there is no balance of presentation by opposing advocates. The object of an ex parte proceeding is nevertheless to yield a substantially just result. The judge has an affirmative responsibility to accord the absent party just consideration. The lawyer for the represented party has the correlative duty to make disclosures of material facts known to the lawyer and that the lawyer reasonably believes are necessary to an informed decision.

Withdrawal

[15] Normally, a lawyer's compliance with the duty of candor imposed by this Rule does not require that the lawyer withdraw from the representation of a client whose interests will be or have been adversely affected by the lawyer's disclosure. The lawyer may, however, be required by Rule 1.16(a) to seek permission of the tribunal to withdraw if the lawyer's compliance with this Rule's duty of candor results in such an extreme deterioration of the client-lawyer relationship that the lawyer can no longer competently represent the client. Also see Rule 1.16(b) for the circumstances in which a lawyer will be permitted to seek a tribunal's permission to withdraw. In connection with a request for permission to withdraw that is premised on a client's misconduct, a lawyer may reveal information relating to the representation only to the extent reasonably necessary to comply with this Rule or as otherwise permitted by Rule 1.6.

Rule 3.4 Fairness to Opposing Party and Counsel

A lawyer shall not:

(a) unlawfully obstruct another party's access to evidence or unlawfully alter, destroy or conceal a document or other material having potential evidentiary value. A lawyer shall not counsel or assist another person to do any such act;

(b) falsify evidence, counsel or assist a witness to testify falsely, or offer an inducement to a witness that is prohibited by law;

(c) knowingly disobey an obligation under the rules of a tribunal, except for an open refusal based on an assertion that no valid obligation exists;

(d) in pretrial procedure, make a frivolous discovery request or fail to make reasonably diligent effort to comply with a legally proper discovery request by an opposing party;

(e) in trial, allude to any matter that the lawyer does not reasonably believe is relevant or that will not be supported by admissible evidence, assert personal knowledge of facts in issue except when testifying as a witness, or state a personal opinion as to the justness of a cause, the credibility of a witness, the culpability of a civil litigant or the guilt or innocence of an accused; or

(f) **request a person other than a client to refrain from voluntarily giving relevant information to another party unless:**

(1) **the person is a relative or an employee or other agent of a client; and**

(2) **the lawyer reasonably believes that the person's interests will not be adversely affected by refraining from giving such information.**

COMMENT

[1] The procedure of the adversary system contemplates that the evidence in a case is to be marshalled competitively by the contending parties. Fair competition in the adversary system is secured by prohibitions against destruction or concealment of evidence, improperly influencing witnesses, obstructive tactics in discovery procedure, and the like.

[2] Documents and other items of evidence are often essential to establish a claim or defense. Subject to evidentiary privileges, the right of an opposing party, including the government, to obtain evidence through discovery or subpoena is an important procedural right. The exercise of that right can be frustrated if relevant material is altered, concealed or destroyed. Applicable law in many jurisdictions makes it an offense to destroy material for the purpose of impairing its availability in a pending proceeding or one whose commencement can be foreseen. Falsifying evidence is also generally a criminal offense. Paragraph (a) applies to evidentiary material generally, including computerized information. Applicable law may permit a lawyer to take temporary possession of physical evidence of client crimes for the purpose of conducting a limited examination that will not alter or destroy material characteristics of the evidence. In such a case, applicable law may require the lawyer to turn the evidence over to the police or other prosecuting authority, depending on the circumstances.

[3] With regard to paragraph (b), it is not improper to pay a witness's expenses or to compensate an expert witness on terms permitted by law. The common law rule in most jurisdictions is that it is improper to pay an occurrence witness any fee for testifying and that it is improper to pay an expert witness a contingent fee.

[4] Paragraph (f) permits a lawyer to advise employees of a client to refrain from giving information to another party, for the employees may identify their interests with those of the client. See also Rule 4.2.

Rule 3.5   Impartiality and Decorum of the Tribunal

A lawyer shall not:

(a) **seek to influence a judge, juror, prospective juror or other official by means prohibited by law;**

(b) communicate ex parte with such a person during the proceeding unless authorized to do so by law or court order;

(c) communicate with a juror or prospective juror after discharge of the jury if:

(1) the communication is prohibited by law or court order; or

(2) the juror has made known to the lawyer a desire not to communicate; or

(3) the communication involves misrepresentation, coercion, duress or harassment; or

(d) engage in conduct intended to disrupt a tribunal.

COMMENT

[1] Many forms of improper influence upon a tribunal are proscribed by criminal law. Others are specified in the ABA Model Code of Judicial Conduct, with which an advocate should be familiar. A lawyer is required to avoid contributing to a violation of such provisions.

[2] During a proceeding a lawyer may not communicate ex parte with persons serving in an official capacity in the proceeding, such as judges, masters or jurors, unless authorized to do so by law or court order.

[3] A lawyer may on occasion want to communicate with a juror or prospective juror after the jury has been discharged. The lawyer may do so unless the communication is prohibited by law or a court order but must respect the desire of the juror not to talk with the lawyer. The lawyer may not engage in improper conduct during the communication.

[4] The advocate's function is to present evidence and argument so that the cause may be decided according to law. Refraining from abusive or obstreperous conduct is a corollary of the advocate's right to speak on behalf of litigants. A lawyer may stand firm against abuse by a judge but should avoid reciprocation; the judge's default is no justification for similar dereliction by an advocate. An advocate can present the cause, protect the record for subsequent review and preserve professional integrity by patient firmness no less effectively than by belligerence or theatrics.

[5] The duty to refrain from disruptive conduct applies to any proceeding of a tribunal, including a deposition. See Rule 1.0(m).

Rule 3.6   Trial Publicity

(a) A lawyer who is participating or has participated in the investigation or litigation of a matter shall not make an extrajudicial statement that the lawyer knows or reasonably should know will be disseminated by means of public communication and will have a substantial likelihood of materially prejudicing an adjudicative proceeding in the matter.

(b) Notwithstanding paragraph (a), a lawyer may state:

(1) the claim, offense or defense involved and, except when prohibited by law, the identity of the persons involved;

(2) information contained in a public record;

(3) that an investigation of a matter is in progress;

(4) the scheduling or result of any step in litigation;

(5) a request for assistance in obtaining evidence and information necessary thereto;

(6) a warning of danger concerning the behavior of a person involved, when there is reason to believe that there exists the likelihood of substantial harm to an individual or to the public interest; and

(7) in a criminal case, in addition to subparagraphs (1) through (6):

(i) the identity, residence, occupation and family status of the accused;

(ii) if the accused has not been apprehended, information necessary to aid in apprehension of that person;

(iii) the fact, time and place of arrest; and

(iv) the identity of investigating and arresting officers or agencies and the length of the investigation.

(c) Notwithstanding paragraph (a), a lawyer may make a statement that a reasonable lawyer would believe is required to protect a client from the substantial undue prejudicial effect of recent publicity not initiated by the lawyer or the lawyer's client. A statement made pursuant to this paragraph shall be limited to such information as is necessary to mitigate the recent adverse publicity.

(d) No lawyer associated in a firm or government agency with a lawyer subject to paragraph (a) shall make a statement prohibited by paragraph (a).

COMMENT

[1] It is difficult to strike a balance between protecting the right to a fair trial and safeguarding the right of free expression. Preserving the right to a fair trial necessarily entails some curtailment of the information that may be disseminated about a party prior to trial, particularly where trial by jury is involved. If there were no such limits, the result would be the practical nullification of the protective effect of the rules of forensic decorum and the exclusionary rules of evidence. On the other hand, there are vital social interests served by the free dissemination of information about events having legal consequences and about legal proceedings themselves. The public has a right to know about threats to its safety and measures aimed at assuring its security. It also has a legitimate interest in the conduct of judicial proceedings, particularly in matters of general public concern. Furthermore, the subject matter of legal proceedings is often of direct significance in debate and deliberation over questions of public policy.

[2] Special rules of confidentiality may validly govern proceedings in juvenile, domestic relations and mental disability proceedings, and perhaps other types of litigation. Rule 3.4(c) requires compliance with such rules.

[3] The Rule sets forth a basic general prohibition against a lawyer's making statements that the lawyer knows or should know will have a substantial likelihood of materially prejudicing an adjudicative proceeding. Recognizing that the public

value of informed commentary is great and the likelihood of prejudice to a proceeding by the commentary of a lawyer who is not involved in the proceeding is small, the rule applies only to lawyers who are, or who have been involved in the investigation or litigation of a case, and their associates.

[4] Paragraph (b) identifies specific matters about which a lawyer's statements would not ordinarily be considered to present a substantial likelihood of material prejudice, and should not in any event be considered prohibited by the general prohibition of paragraph (a). Paragraph (b) is not intended to be an exhaustive listing of the subjects upon which a lawyer may make a statement, but statements on other matters may be subject to paragraph (a).

[5] There are, on the other hand, certain subjects that are more likely than not to have a material prejudicial effect on a proceeding, particularly when they refer to a civil matter triable to a jury, a criminal matter, or any other proceeding that could result in incarceration. These subjects relate to:

(1) the character, credibility, reputation or criminal record of a party, suspect in a criminal investigation or witness, or the identity of a witness, or the expected testimony of a party or witness;

(2) in a criminal case or proceeding that could result in incarceration, the possibility of a plea of guilty to the offense or the existence or contents of any confession, admission, or statement given by a defendant or suspect or that person's refusal or failure to make a statement;

(3) the performance or results of any examination or test or the refusal or failure of a person to submit to an examination or test, or the identity or nature of physical evidence expected to be presented;

(4) any opinion as to the guilt or innocence of a defendant or suspect in a criminal case or proceeding that could result in incarceration;

(5) information that the lawyer knows or reasonably should know is likely to be inadmissible as evidence in a trial and that would, if disclosed, create a substantial risk of prejudicing an impartial trial; or

(6) the fact that a defendant has been charged with a crime, unless there is included therein a statement explaining that the charge is merely an accusation and that the defendant is presumed innocent until and unless proven guilty.

[6] Another relevant factor in determining prejudice is the nature of the proceeding involved. Criminal jury trials will be most sensitive to extrajudicial speech. Civil trials may be less sensitive. Non-jury hearings and arbitration proceedings may be even less affected. The Rule will still place limitations on prejudicial comments in these cases, but the likelihood of prejudice may be different depending on the type of proceeding.

[7] Finally, extrajudicial statements that might otherwise raise a question under this Rule may be permissible when they are made in response to statements made publicly by another party, another party's lawyer, or third persons, where a reasonable lawyer would believe a public response is required in order to avoid prejudice to the lawyer's client. When prejudicial statements have been publicly made by others, responsive statements may have the salutary effect of lessening any resulting adverse impact on the adjudicative proceeding. Such responsive statements should be limited to contain only such information as is necessary to mitigate undue prejudice created by the statements made by others.

[8] See Rule 3.8(f) for additional duties of prosecutors in connection with extrajudicial statements about criminal proceedings.

Rule 3.7   Lawyer as Witness

(a) A lawyer shall not act as advocate at a trial in which the lawyer is likely to be a necessary witness unless:

(1) the testimony relates to an uncontested issue;

(2) the testimony relates to the nature and value of legal services rendered in the case; or

(3) disqualification of the lawyer would work substantial hardship on the client.

(b) A lawyer may act as advocate in a trial in which another lawyer in the lawyer's firm is likely to be called as a witness unless precluded from doing so by Rule 1.7 or Rule 1.9.

COMMENT

[1] Combining the roles of advocate and witness can prejudice the tribunal and the opposing party and can also involve a conflict of interest between the lawyer and client.

Advocate-Witness Rule

[2] The tribunal has proper objection when the trier of fact may be confused or misled by a lawyer serving as both advocate and witness. The opposing party has proper objection where the combination of roles may prejudice that party's rights in the litigation. A witness is required to testify on the basis of personal knowledge, while an advocate is expected to explain and comment on evidence given by others. It may not be clear whether a statement by an advocate-witness should be taken as proof or as an analysis of the proof.

[3] To protect the tribunal, paragraph (a) prohibits a lawyer from simultaneously serving as advocate and necessary witness except in those circumstances specified in paragraphs (a)(1) through (a)(3). Paragraph (a)(1) recognizes that if the testimony will be uncontested, the ambiguities in the dual role are purely theoretical. Paragraph (a)(2) recognizes that where the testimony concerns the extent and value of legal services rendered in the action in which the testimony is offered, permitting the lawyers to testify avoids the need for a second trial with new counsel to resolve that issue. Moreover, in such a situation the judge has firsthand knowledge of the matter in issue; hence, there is less dependence on the adversary process to test the credibility of the testimony.

[4] Apart from these two exceptions, paragraph (a)(3) recognizes that a balancing is required between the interests of the client and those of the tribunal and the opposing party. Whether the tribunal is likely to be misled or the opposing party is likely to suffer prejudice depends on the nature of the case, the importance and probable tenor of the lawyer's testimony, and the probability that the lawyer's testimony will conflict with that of other witnesses. Even if there is risk of such prejudice, in determining whether the lawyer should be disqualified, due regard must be given

to the effect of disqualification on the lawyer's client. It is relevant that one or both parties could reasonably foresee that the lawyer would probably be a witness. The conflict of interest principles stated in Rules 1.7, 1.9 and 1.10 have no application to this aspect of the problem.

[5] Because the tribunal is not likely to be misled when a lawyer acts as advocate in a trial in which another lawyer in the lawyer's firm will testify as a necessary witness, paragraph (b) permits the lawyer to do so except in situations involving a conflict of interest.

Conflict of Interest

[6] In determining if it is permissible to act as advocate in a trial in which the lawyer will be a necessary witness, the lawyer must also consider that the dual role may give rise to a conflict of interest that will require compliance with Rules 1.7 or 1.9. For example, if there is likely to be substantial conflict between the testimony of the client and that of the lawyer, the representation involves a conflict of interest that requires compliance with Rule 1.7. This would be true even though the lawyer might not be prohibited by paragraph (a) from simultaneously serving as advocate and witness because the lawyer's disqualification would work a substantial hardship on the client. Similarly, a lawyer who might be permitted to simultaneously serve as an advocate and a witness by paragraph (a)(3) might be precluded from doing so by Rule 1.9. The problem can arise whether the lawyer is called as a witness on behalf of the client or is called by the opposing party. Determining whether or not such a conflict exists is primarily the responsibility of the lawyer involved. If there is a conflict of interest, the lawyer must secure the client's informed consent, confirmed in writing. In some cases, the lawyer will be precluded from seeking the client's consent. See Rule 1.7. See Rule 1.0(b) for the definition of "confirmed in writing" and Rule 1.0(e) for the definition of "informed consent."

[7] Paragraph (b) provides that a lawyer is not disqualified from serving as an advocate because a lawyer with whom the lawyer is associated in a firm is precluded from doing so by paragraph (a). If, however, the testifying lawyer would also be disqualified by Rule 1.7 or Rule 1.9 from representing the client in the matter, other lawyers in the firm will be precluded from representing the client by Rule 1.10 unless the client gives informed consent under the conditions stated in Rule 1.7.

Rule 3.8   Special Responsibilities of a Prosecutor

The prosecutor in a criminal case shall:

(a) refrain from prosecuting a charge that the prosecutor knows is not supported by probable cause;

(b) make reasonable efforts to assure that the accused has been advised of the right to, and the procedure for obtaining, counsel and has been given reasonable opportunity to obtain counsel;

(c) not seek to obtain from an unrepresented accused a waiver of important pretrial rights, such as the right to a preliminary hearing;

(d) make timely disclosure to the defense of all evidence or information known to the prosecutor that tends to negate the guilt of the accused or mitigates the offense, and, in connection with sentencing, disclose to the defense and to the tribunal all unprivileged mitigating information known to the prosecutor, except when the prosecutor is relieved of this responsibility by a protective order of the tribunal;

(e) not subpoena a lawyer in a grand jury or other criminal proceeding to present evidence about a past or present client unless the prosecutor reasonably believes:

(1) the information sought is not protected from disclosure by any applicable privilege;

(2) the evidence sought is essential to the successful completion of an ongoing investigation or prosecution; and

(3) there is no other feasible alternative to obtain the information;

(f) except for statements that are necessary to inform the public of the nature and extent of the prosecutor's action and that serve a legitimate law enforcement purpose, refrain from making extrajudicial comments that have a substantial likelihood of heightening public condemnation of the accused and exercise reasonable care to prevent investigators, law enforcement personnel, employees or other persons assisting or associated with the prosecutor in a criminal case from making an extrajudicial statement that the prosecutor would be prohibited from making under Rule 3.6 or this Rule.

(g) When a prosecutor knows of new, credible and material evidence creating a reasonable likelihood that a convicted defendant did not commit an offense of which the defendant was convicted, the prosecutor shall:

(1) promptly disclose that evidence to an appropriate court or authority, and

(2) if the conviction was obtained in the prosecutor's jurisdiction,

(A) promptly disclose that evidence to the defendant unless a court authorizes delay, and

(B) undertake further investigation, or make reasonable efforts to cause an investigation, to determine whether the defendant was convicted of an offense that the defendant did not commit.

(h) When a prosecutor knows of clear and convincing evidence establishing that a defendant in the prosecutor's jurisdiction was convicted of an offense that the defendant did not commit, the prosecutor shall seek to remedy the conviction.

COMMENT

[1] A prosecutor has the responsibility of a minister of justice and not simply that of an advocate. This responsibility carries with it specific obligations to see that

the defendant is accorded procedural justice and that guilt is decided upon the basis of sufficient evidence, and that special precautions are taken to prevent and to rectify the conviction of innocent persons. The extent of mandated remedial action is a matter of debate and varies in different jurisdictions. Many jurisdictions have adopted the ABA Standards of Criminal Justice Relating to the Prosecution Function, which are the product of prolonged and careful deliberation by lawyers experienced in both criminal prosecution and defense. Competent representation of the sovereignty may require a prosecutor to undertake some procedural and remedial measures as a matter of obligation. Applicable law may require other measures by the prosecutor and knowing disregard of those obligations or a systematic abuse of prosecutorial discretion could constitute a violation of Rule 8.4.

[2] In some jurisdictions, a defendant may waive a preliminary hearing and thereby lose a valuable opportunity to challenge probable cause. Accordingly, prosecutors should not seek to obtain waivers of preliminary hearings or other important pretrial rights from unrepresented accused persons. Paragraph (c) does not apply, however, to an accused appearing pro se with the approval of the tribunal. Nor does it forbid the lawful questioning of an uncharged suspect who has knowingly waived the rights to counsel and silence.

[3] The exception in paragraph (d) recognizes that a prosecutor may seek an appropriate protective order from the tribunal if disclosure of information to the defense could result in substantial harm to an individual or to the public interest.

[4] Paragraph (e) is intended to limit the issuance of lawyer subpoenas in grand jury and other criminal proceedings to those situations in which there is a genuine need to intrude into the client-lawyer relationship.

[5] Paragraph (f) supplements Rule 3.6, which prohibits extrajudicial statements that have a substantial likelihood of prejudicing an adjudicatory proceeding. In the context of a criminal prosecution, a prosecutor's extrajudicial statement can create the additional problem of increasing public condemnation of the accused. Although the announcement of an indictment, for example, will necessarily have severe consequences for the accused, a prosecutor can, and should, avoid comments which have no legitimate law enforcement purpose and have a substantial likelihood of increasing public opprobrium of the accused. Nothing in this Comment is intended to restrict the statements which a prosecutor may make which comply with Rule 3.6(b) or 3.6(c).

[6] Like other lawyers, prosecutors are subject to Rules 5.1 and 5.3, which relate to responsibilities regarding lawyers and nonlawyers who work for or are associated with the lawyer's office. Paragraph (f) reminds the prosecutor of the importance of these obligations in connection with the unique dangers of improper extrajudicial statements in a criminal case. In addition, paragraph (f) requires a prosecutor to exercise reasonable care to prevent persons assisting or associated with the prosecutor from making improper extrajudicial statements, even when such persons are not under the direct supervision of the prosecutor. Ordinarily, the reasonable care standard will be satisfied if the prosecutor issues the appropriate cautions to law-enforcement personnel and other relevant individuals.

[7] When a prosecutor knows of new, credible and material evidence creating a reasonable likelihood that a person outside the prosecutor's jurisdiction was convicted of a crime that the person did not commit, paragraph (g) requires prompt disclosure to the court or other appropriate authority, such as the chief prosecutor

of the jurisdiction where the conviction occurred. If the conviction was obtained in the prosecutor's jurisdiction, paragraph (g) requires the prosecutor to examine the evidence and undertake further investigation to determine whether the defendant is in fact innocent or make reasonable efforts to cause another appropriate authority to undertake the necessary investigation, and to promptly disclose the evidence to the court and, absent court-authorized delay, to the defendant. Consistent with the objectives of Rules 4.2 and 4.3, disclosure to a represented defendant must be made through the defendant's counsel, and, in the case of an unrepresented defendant, would ordinarily be accompanied by a request to a court for the appointment of counsel to assist the defendant in taking such legal measures as may be appropriate.

[8] Under paragraph (h), once the prosecutor knows of clear and convincing evidence that the defendant was convicted of an offense that the defendant did not commit, the prosecutor must seek to remedy the conviction. Necessary steps may include disclosure of the evidence to the defendant, requesting that the court appoint counsel for an unrepresented indigent defendant and, where appropriate, notifying the court that the prosecutor has knowledge that the defendant did not commit the offense of which the defendant was convicted.

[9] A prosecutor's independent judgment, made in good faith, that the new evidence is not of such nature as to trigger the obligations of sections (g) and (h), though subsequently determined to have been erroneous, does not constitute a violation of this Rule.

Rule 3.9   Advocate in Nonadjudicative Proceedings

A lawyer representing a client before a legislative body or administrative agency in a nonadjudicative proceeding shall disclose that the appearance is in a representative capacity and shall conform to the provisions of Rules 3.3(a) through (c), 3.4(a) through (c), and 3.5.

COMMENT

[1] In representation before bodies such as legislatures, municipal councils, and executive and administrative agencies acting in a rule-making or policy-making capacity, lawyers present facts, formulate issues and advance argument in the matters under consideration. The decision-making body, like a court, should be able to rely on the integrity of the submissions made to it. A lawyer appearing before such a body must deal with it honestly and in conformity with applicable rules of procedure. See Rules 3.3(a) through (c), 3.4(a) through (c) and 3.5.

[2] Lawyers have no exclusive right to appear before nonadjudicative bodies, as they do before a court. The requirements of this Rule therefore may subject lawyers to regulations inapplicable to advocates who are not lawyers. However, legislatures and administrative agencies have a right to expect lawyers to deal with them as they deal with courts.

[3] This Rule only applies when a lawyer represents a client in connection with an official hearing or meeting of a governmental agency or a legislative body to

which the lawyer or the lawyer's client is presenting evidence or argument. It does not apply to representation of a client in a negotiation or other bilateral transaction with a governmental agency or in connection with an application for a license or other privilege or the client's compliance with generally applicable reporting requirements, such as the filing of income-tax returns. Nor does it apply to the representation of a client in connection with an investigation or examination of the client's affairs conducted by government investigators or examiners. Representation in such matters is governed by Rules 4.1 through 4.4.

ARTICLE 4.   TRANSACTIONS WITH PERSONS OTHER THAN CLIENTS

Rule 4.1   Truthfulness in Statements to Others   *(this does not change 1.6 "may" to shall)*

In the course of representing a client a lawyer shall not knowingly:

(a) make a false statement of material fact or law to a third person; or

(b) fail to disclose a material fact to a third person when disclosure is necessary to avoid assisting a criminal or fraudulent act by a client, unless disclosure is prohibited by Rule 1.6.

"criminal term" — can you be unethical before you're criminal? — yes. Bar can go after someone before any criminal activity

COMMENT

Misrepresentation

[1] A lawyer is required to be truthful when dealing with others on a client's behalf, but generally has no affirmative duty to inform an opposing party of relevant facts. A misrepresentation can occur if the lawyer incorporates or affirms a statement of another person that the lawyer knows is false. Misrepresentations can also occur by partially true but misleading statements or omissions that are the equivalent of affirmative false statements. For dishonest conduct that does not amount to a false statement or for misrepresentations by a lawyer other than in the course of representing a client, see Rule 8.4.

Statements of Fact

[2] This Rule refers to statements of fact. Whether a particular statement should be regarded as one of fact can depend on the circumstances. Under generally accepted conventions in negotiation, certain types of statements ordinarily are not taken as statements of material fact. Estimates of price or value placed on the subject of a transaction and a party's intentions as to an acceptable settlement of a claim are ordinarily in this category, and so is the existence of an undisclosed principal except where nondisclosure of the principal would constitute fraud. Lawyers should be mindful of their obligations under applicable law to avoid criminal and tortious misrepresentation.

Crime or Fraud by Client

[3] Under Rule 1.2(d), a lawyer is prohibited from counseling or assisting a client in conduct that the lawyer knows is criminal or fraudulent. Paragraph (b) states a specific application of the principle set forth in Rule 1.2(d) and addresses the situation where a client's crime or fraud takes the form of a lie or misrepresentation. Ordinarily, a lawyer can avoid assisting a client's crime or fraud by withdrawing from the representation. Sometimes it may be necessary for the lawyer to give notice of the fact of withdrawal and to disaffirm an opinion, document, affirmation or the like. In extreme cases, substantive law may require a lawyer to disclose information relating to the representation to avoid being deemed to have assisted the client's crime or fraud. If the lawyer can avoid assisting a client's crime or fraud only by disclosing this information, then under paragraph (b) the lawyer is required to do so, unless the disclosure is prohibited by Rule 1.6.

Rule 4.2   Communication with Person Represented by Counsel

In representing a client, a lawyer shall not communicate about the subject of the representation with a person the lawyer knows to be represented by another lawyer in the matter, unless the lawyer has the consent of the other lawyer or is authorized to do so by law or a court order.

COMMENT

[1] This Rule contributes to the proper functioning of the legal system by protecting a person who has chosen to be represented by a lawyer in a matter against possible overreaching by other lawyers who are participating in the matter, interference by those lawyers with the client-lawyer relationship and the uncounseled disclosure of information relating to the representation.

[2] This Rule applies to communications with any person who is represented by counsel concerning the matter to which the communication relates.

[3] The Rule applies even though the represented person initiates or consents to the communication. A lawyer must immediately terminate communication with a person if, after commencing communication, the lawyer learns that the person is one with whom communication is not permitted by this Rule.

[4] This Rule does not prohibit communication with a represented person, or an employee or agent of such a person, concerning matters outside the representation. For example, the existence of a controversy between a government agency and a private party, or between two organizations, does not prohibit a lawyer for either from communicating with nonlawyer representatives of the other regarding a separate matter. Nor does this Rule preclude communication with a represented person who is seeking advice from a lawyer who is not otherwise representing a client in the matter. A lawyer may not make a communication prohibited by this Rule through the acts of another. See Rule 8.4(a). Parties to a matter may communicate directly with each other, and a lawyer is not prohibited from advising a client concerning a communication that the client is legally entitled to make. Also, a lawyer

having independent justification or legal authorization for communicating with a represented person is permitted to do so.

[5] Communications authorized by law may include communications by a lawyer on behalf of a client who is exercising a constitutional or other legal right to communicate with the government. Communications authorized by law may also include investigative activities of lawyers representing governmental entities, directly or through investigative agents, prior to the commencement of criminal or civil enforcement proceedings. When communicating with the accused in a criminal matter, a government lawyer must comply with this Rule in addition to honoring the constitutional rights of the accused. The fact that a communication does not violate a state or federal constitutional right is insufficient to establish that the communication is permissible under this Rule.

[6] A lawyer who is uncertain whether a communication with a represented person is permissible may seek a court order. A lawyer may also seek a court order in exceptional circumstances to authorize a communication that would otherwise be prohibited by this Rule, for example, where communication with a person represented by counsel is necessary to avoid reasonably certain injury.

[7] In the case of a represented organization, this Rule prohibits communications with a constituent of the organization who supervises, directs or regularly consults with the organization's lawyer concerning the matter or has authority to obligate the organization with respect to the matter or whose act or omission in connection with the matter may be imputed to the organization for purposes of civil or criminal liability. Consent of the organization's lawyer is not required for communication with a former constituent. If a constituent of the organization is represented in the matter by his or her own counsel, the consent by that counsel to a communication will be sufficient for purposes of this Rule. Compare Rule 3.4(f). In communicating with a current or former constituent of an organization, a lawyer must not use methods of obtaining evidence that violate the legal rights of the organization. See Rule 4.4.

[8] The prohibition on communications with a represented person only applies in circumstances where the lawyer knows that the person is in fact represented in the matter to be discussed. This means that the lawyer has actual knowledge of the fact of the representation; but such actual knowledge may be inferred from the circumstances. See Rule 1.0(f). Thus, the lawyer cannot evade the requirement of obtaining the consent of counsel by closing eyes to the obvious.

[9] In the event the person with whom the lawyer communicates is not known to be represented by counsel in the matter, the lawyer's communications are subject to Rule 4.3.

Rule 4.3 Dealing with Unrepresented Person

In dealing on behalf of a client with a person who is not represented by counsel, a lawyer shall not state or imply that the lawyer is disinterested. When the lawyer knows or reasonably should know that the unrepresented person misunderstands the lawyer's role in the matter, the lawyer shall make reasonable efforts to correct the misunderstanding. The lawyer shall not give legal advice to an unrepresented person, other than the advice to secure counsel, if the lawyer knows or reasonably should know that the interests of

such a person are or have a reasonable possibility of being in conflict with the interests of the client.

COMMENT

[1] An unrepresented person, particularly one not experienced in dealing with legal matters, might assume that a lawyer is disinterested in loyalties or is a disinterested authority on the law even when the lawyer represents a client. In order to avoid a misunderstanding, a lawyer will typically need to identify the lawyer's client and, where necessary, explain that the client has interests opposed to those of the unrepresented person. For misunderstandings that sometimes arise when a lawyer for an organization deals with an unrepresented constituent, see Rule 1.13(f).

[2] The Rule distinguishes between situations involving unrepresented persons whose interests may be adverse to those of the lawyer's client and those in which the person's interests are not in conflict with the client's. In the former situation, the possibility that the lawyer will compromise the unrepresented person's interests is so great that the Rule prohibits the giving of any advice, apart from the advice to obtain counsel. Whether a lawyer is giving impermissible advice may depend on the experience and sophistication of the unrepresented person, as well as the setting in which the behavior and comments occur. This Rule does not prohibit a lawyer from negotiating the terms of a transaction or settling a dispute with an unrepresented person. So long as the lawyer has explained that the lawyer represents an adverse party and is not representing the person, the lawyer may inform the person of the terms on which the lawyer's client will enter into an agreement or settle a matter, prepare documents that require the person's signature and explain the lawyer's own view of the meaning of the document or the lawyer's view of the underlying legal obligations.

> **Editors' Note.** In August 2012, the ABA House of Delegates amended Rule 4.4(b) and the accompanying Comments. The ABA Commission on Ethics 20/20 proposed these changes in order to clarify that Rule 4.4(b) applies to electronically stored information, not just paper documents. The changes also clarify the meaning of the phrase "inadvertently sent." To alert readers to these changes, we underscore the new language and strike through deleted language. For more information regarding these changes, see the Legislative History for this Rule in the "Annotations on ABA Model Rules" section of this book.

Rule 4.4   Respect for Rights of Third Persons

(a) In representing a client, a lawyer shall not use means that have no substantial purpose other than to embarrass, delay, or burden a third person, or use methods of obtaining evidence that violate the legal rights of such a person.

(b) A lawyer who receives a document or electronically stored information relating to the representation of the lawyer's client and knows or reasonably should know that the document or electronically stored information was inadvertently sent shall promptly notify the sender.

COMMENT

[1] Responsibility to a client requires a lawyer to subordinate the interests of others to those of the client, but that responsibility does not imply that a lawyer may disregard the rights of third persons. It is impractical to catalogue all such rights, but they include legal restrictions on methods of obtaining evidence from third persons and unwarranted intrusions into privileged relationships, such as the client-lawyer relationship.

[2] Paragraph (b) recognizes that lawyers sometimes receive a documents or electronically stored information that were was mistakenly sent or produced by opposing parties or their lawyers. A document or electronically stored information is inadvertently sent when it is accidentally transmitted, such as when an email or letter is misaddressed or a document or electronically stored information is accidentally included with information that was intentionally transmitted. If a lawyer knows or reasonably should know that such a document or electronically stored information was sent inadvertently, then this Rule requires the lawyer to promptly notify the sender in order to permit that person to take protective measures. Whether the lawyer is required to take additional steps, such as returning the document or deleting the electronically stored information original document, is a matter of law beyond the scope of these Rules, as is the question of whether the privileged status of a document or electronically stored information has been waived. Similarly, this Rule does not address the legal duties of a lawyer who receives a document or electronically stored information that the lawyer knows or reasonably should know may have been wrongfully inappropriately obtained by the sending person. For purposes of this Rule, "document or electronically stored information" includes, in addition to paper documents, email and other forms of electronically stored information, including embedded data (commonly referred to as "metadata"), that is email or other electronic modes of transmission subject to being read or put into readable form. Metadata in electronic documents creates an obligation under this Rule only if the receiving lawyer knows or reasonably should know that the metadata was inadvertently sent to the receiving lawyer.

[3] Some lawyers may choose to return a document or delete electronically stored information unread, for example, when the lawyer learns before receiving it the document that it was inadvertently sent to the wrong address. Where a lawyer is not required by applicable law to do so, the decision to voluntarily return such a document or delete electronically stored information is a matter of professional judgment ordinarily reserved to the lawyer. See Rules 1.2 and 1.4.

ARTICLE 5.   LAW FIRMS AND ASSOCIATIONS

Rule 5.1   Responsibilities of Partners, Managers, and Supervisory Lawyers

(a) A partner in a law firm, and a lawyer who individually or together with other lawyers possesses comparable managerial authority in a law firm, shall make reasonable efforts to ensure that the firm has in effect measures giving reasonable assurance that all lawyers in the firm conform to the Rules of Professional Conduct.

(b) A lawyer having direct supervisory authority over another lawyer shall make reasonable efforts to ensure that the other lawyer conforms to the Rules of Professional Conduct.

(c) A lawyer shall be responsible for another lawyer's violation of the Rules of Professional Conduct if:

(1) the lawyer orders or, with knowledge of the specific conduct, ratifies the conduct involved; or

(2) the lawyer is a partner or has comparable managerial authority in the law firm in which the other lawyer practices, or has direct supervisory authority over the other lawyer, and knows of the conduct at a time when its consequences can be avoided or mitigated but fails to take reasonable remedial action.

COMMENT

[1] Paragraph (a) applies to lawyers who have managerial authority over the professional work of a firm. See Rule 1.0(c). This includes members of a partnership, the shareholders in a law firm organized as a professional corporation, and members of other associations authorized to practice law; lawyers having comparable managerial authority in a legal services organization or a law department of an enterprise or government agency; and lawyers who have intermediate managerial responsibilities in a firm. Paragraph (b) applies to lawyers who have supervisory authority over the work of other lawyers in a firm.

[2] Paragraph (a) requires lawyers with managerial authority within a firm to make reasonable efforts to establish internal policies and procedures designed to provide reasonable assurance that all lawyers in the firm will conform to the Rules of Professional Conduct. Such policies and procedures include those designed to detect and resolve conflicts of interest, identify dates by which actions must be taken in pending matters, account for client funds and property and ensure that inexperienced lawyers are properly supervised.

[3] Other measures that may be required to fulfill the responsibility prescribed in paragraph (a) can depend on the firm's structure and the nature of its practice. In a small firm of experienced lawyers, informal supervision and periodic review of compliance with the required systems ordinarily will suffice. In a large firm, or in practice situations in which difficult ethical problems frequently arise, more elaborate measures may be necessary. Some firms, for example, have a procedure whereby junior lawyers can make confidential referral of ethical problems directly to a designated senior partner or special committee. See Rule 5.2. Firms, whether large or small, may also rely on continuing legal education in professional ethics. In any event, the ethical atmosphere of a firm can influence the conduct of all its members and the partners may not assume that all lawyers associated with the firm will inevitably conform to the Rules.

[4] Paragraph (c) expresses a general principle of personal responsibility for acts of another. See also Rule 8.4(a).

[5] Paragraph (c)(2) defines the duty of a partner or other lawyer having comparable managerial authority in a law firm, as well as a lawyer who has direct

supervisory authority over performance of specific legal work by another lawyer. Whether a lawyer has supervisory authority in particular circumstances is a question of fact. Partners and lawyers with comparable authority have at least indirect responsibility for all work being done by the firm, while a partner or manager in charge of a particular matter ordinarily also has supervisory responsibility for the work of other firm lawyers engaged in the matter. Appropriate remedial action by a partner or managing lawyer would depend on the immediacy of that lawyer's involvement and the seriousness of the misconduct. A supervisor is required to intervene to prevent avoidable consequences of misconduct if the supervisor knows that the misconduct occurred. Thus, if a supervising lawyer knows that a subordinate misrepresented a matter to an opposing party in negotiation, the supervisor as well as the subordinate has a duty to correct the resulting misapprehension.

[6] Professional misconduct by a lawyer under supervision could reveal a violation of paragraph (b) on the part of the supervisory lawyer even though it does not entail a violation of paragraph (c) because there was no direction, ratification or knowledge of the violation.

[7] Apart from this Rule and Rule 8.4(a), a lawyer does not have disciplinary liability for the conduct of a partner, associate or subordinate. Whether a lawyer may be liable civilly or criminally for another lawyer's conduct is a question of law beyond the scope of these Rules.

[8] The duties imposed by this Rule on managing and supervising lawyers do not alter the personal duty of each lawyer in a firm to abide by the Rules of Professional Conduct. See Rule 5.2(a).

Rule 5.2   Responsibilities of a Subordinate Lawyer

(a) A lawyer is bound by the Rules of Professional Conduct notwithstanding that the lawyer acted at the direction of another person.

(b) A subordinate lawyer does not violate the Rules of Professional Conduct if that lawyer acts in accordance with a supervisory lawyer's reasonable resolution of an arguable question of professional duty.

COMMENT

[1] Although a lawyer is not relieved of responsibility for a violation by the fact that the lawyer acted at the direction of a supervisor, that fact may be relevant in determining whether a lawyer had the knowledge required to render conduct a violation of the Rules. For example, if a subordinate filed a frivolous pleading at the direction of a supervisor, the subordinate would not be guilty of a professional violation unless the subordinate knew of the document's frivolous character.

[2] When lawyers in a supervisor-subordinate relationship encounter a matter involving professional judgment as to ethical duty, the supervisor may assume responsibility for making the judgment. Otherwise a consistent course of action or position could not be taken. If the question can reasonably be answered only one way, the duty of both lawyers is clear and they are equally responsible for fulfilling it. However, if the question is reasonably arguable, someone has to decide upon

the course of action. That authority ordinarily reposes in the supervisor, and a subordinate may be guided accordingly. For example, if a question arises whether the interests of two clients conflict under Rule 1.7, the supervisor's reasonable resolution of the question should protect the subordinate professionally if the resolution is subsequently challenged.

> **Editors' Note.** In August 2012, the ABA House of Delegates amended the title of, and Comments to, Rule 5.3. The ABA Commission on Ethics 20/20 proposed these changes in order to give lawyers more guidance on the ethical considerations associated with the retention of nonlawyers outside the firm to work on client matters. To alert readers to these changes, we underscore the new language and strike through deleted language. For more information regarding these changes, see the Legislative History for this Rule in the "Annotations on ABA Model Rules" section of this book.

Rule 5.3   Responsibilities Regarding Nonlawyer Assistancets

With respect to a nonlawyer employed or retained by or associated with a lawyer:

(a) a partner, and a lawyer who individually or together with other lawyers possesses comparable managerial authority in a law firm shall make reasonable efforts to ensure that the firm has in effect measures giving reasonable assurance that the person's conduct is compatible with the professional obligations of the lawyer;

(b) a lawyer having direct supervisory authority over the nonlawyer shall make reasonable efforts to ensure that the person's conduct is compatible with the professional obligations of the lawyer; and

(c) a lawyer shall be responsible for conduct of such a person that would be a violation of the Rules of Professional Conduct if engaged in by a lawyer if:

(1) the lawyer orders or, with the knowledge of the specific conduct, ratifies the conduct involved; or

(2) the lawyer is a partner or has comparable managerial authority in the law firm in which the person is employed, or has direct supervisory authority over the person, and knows of the conduct at a time when its consequences can be avoided or mitigated but fails to take reasonable remedial action.

COMMENT

[21] Paragraph (a) requires lawyers with managerial authority within a law firm to make reasonable efforts to establish internal policies and procedures designed to provide to ensure that the firm has in effect measures giving reasonable assurance that nonlawyers in the firm and nonlawyers outside the firm who work on firm matters will act in a way compatible with the professional obligations of the lawyer. with

~~the Rules of Professional Conduct~~. See <u>Comment [6] to Rule 1.1 (retaining lawyers outside the firm) and</u> Comment [1] to Rule 5.1~~.~~ <u>(responsibilities with respect to lawyers within a firm)</u>. Paragraph (b) applies to lawyers who have supervisory authority over ~~the work of a nonlawyer.~~ <u>such nonlawyers within or outside the firm</u>. Paragraph (c) specifies the circumstances in which a lawyer is responsible for <u>the</u> conduct of ~~a nonlawyer~~ <u>such nonlawyers within or outside the firm</u> that would be a violation of the Rules of Professional Conduct if engaged in by a lawyer.

Nonlawyers Within the Firm

[~~1~~2] Lawyers generally employ assistants in their practice, including secretaries, investigators, law student interns, and paraprofessionals. Such assistants, whether employees or independent contractors, act for the lawyer in rendition of the lawyer's professional services. A lawyer must give such assistants appropriate instruction and supervision concerning the ethical aspects of their employment, particularly regarding the obligation not to disclose information relating to representation of the client, and should be responsible for their work product. The measures employed in supervising nonlawyers should take account of the fact that they do not have legal training and are not subject to professional discipline.

<u>Nonlawyers Outside the Firm</u>

<u>[3] A lawyer may use nonlawyers outside the firm to assist the lawyer in rendering legal services to the client. Examples include the retention of an investigative or paraprofessional service, hiring a document management company to create and maintain a database for complex litigation, sending client documents to a third party for printing or scanning, and using an Internet-based service to store client information. When using such services outside the firm, a lawyer must make reasonable efforts to ensure that the services are provided in a manner that is compatible with the lawyer's professional obligations. The extent of this obligation will depend upon the circumstances, including the education, experience and reputation of the nonlawyer; the nature of the services involved; the terms of any arrangements concerning the protection of client information; and the legal and ethical environments of the jurisdictions in which the services will be performed, particularly with regard to confidentiality. See also Rules 1.1 (competence), 1.2 (allocation of authority), 1.4 (communication with client), 1.6 (confidentiality), 5.4(a) (professional independence of the lawyer), and 5.5(a) (unauthorized practice of law). When retaining or directing a nonlawyer outside the firm, a lawyer should communicate directions appropriate under the circumstances to give reasonable assurance that the nonlawyer's conduct is compatible with the professional obligations of the lawyer.</u>

<u>[4] Where the client directs the selection of a particular nonlawyer service provider outside the firm, the lawyer ordinarily should agree with the client concerning the allocation of responsibility for monitoring as between the client and the lawyer. See Rule 1.2. When making such an allocation in a matter pending before a tribunal, lawyers and parties may have additional obligations that are a matter of law beyond the scope of these Rules.</u>

Rule 5.4   Professional Independence of a Lawyer

(a) A lawyer or law firm shall not share legal fees with a nonlawyer, except that:

(1) an agreement by a lawyer with the lawyer's firm, partner, or associate may provide for the payment of money, over a reasonable period of time after the lawyer's death, to the lawyer's estate or to one or more specified persons;

(2) a lawyer who purchases the practice of a deceased, disabled, or disappeared lawyer may, pursuant to the provisions of Rule 1.17, pay to the estate or other representative of that lawyer the agreed-upon purchase price;

(3) a lawyer or law firm may include nonlawyer employees in a compensation or retirement plan, even though the plan is based in whole or in part on a profit-sharing arrangement; and

(4) a lawyer may share court-awarded legal fees with a nonprofit organization that employed, retained or recommended employment of the lawyer in the matter.

(b) A lawyer shall not form a partnership with a nonlawyer if any of the activities of the partnership consist of the practice of law.

(c) A lawyer shall not permit a person who recommends, employs, or pays the lawyer to render legal services for another to direct or regulate the lawyer's professional judgment in rendering such legal services.

(d) A lawyer shall not practice with or in the form of a professional corporation or association authorized to practice law for a profit, if:

(1) a nonlawyer owns any interest therein, except that a fiduciary representative of the estate of a lawyer may hold the stock or interest of the lawyer for a reasonable time during administration;

(2) a nonlawyer is a corporate director or officer thereof or occupies the position of similar responsibility in any form of association other than a corporation; or

(3) a nonlawyer has the right to direct or control the professional judgment of a lawyer.

COMMENT

[1] The provisions of this Rule express traditional limitations on sharing fees. These limitations are to protect the lawyer's professional independence of judgment. Where someone other than the client pays the lawyer's fee or salary, or recommends employment of the lawyer, that arrangement does not modify the lawyer's obligation to the client. As stated in paragraph (c), such arrangements should not interfere with the lawyer's professional judgment.

[2] This Rule also expresses traditional limitations on permitting a third party to direct or regulate the lawyer's professional judgment in rendering legal services to another. See also Rule 1.8(f) (lawyer may accept compensation from a third party

as long as there is no interference with the lawyer's independent professional judgment and the client gives informed consent).

> **Editors' Note.** In August 2012, the ABA House of Delegates amended Rule 5.5(d) and several of the Rule's Comments. The ABA Commission on Ethics 20/20 proposed these changes to accomplish several unrelated goals. First, the amendments to Rule 5.5(d) clarify the paragraph's purpose: to explain the circumstances under which a lawyer is permitted to establish an office or other systematic and continuous presence for the practice of law in a jurisdiction without becoming admitted to the bar in that jurisdiction. Second, the amendments to Rule 5.5(d)(2) and Comment 18 are intended to remind lawyers of the practice authority afforded under the newly created Model Rule on Practice Pending Admission, which is described in more detail in the Related Materials for Rule 5.5 in the "Annotations on ABA Model Rules" section of this book. Comment 21 was amended to delete references to the phrase "prospective client," which is defined in Rule 1.18 and includes a narrower category of individuals than Comment 21 is intended to cover. Finally, the new language in Comment 1 offers a reminder that, when retaining or hiring a person outside the firm (either a nonlawyer or a lawyer) to work on a client's matter, the lawyer must not assist that person in the unauthorized practice of law. To alert readers to all of these changes, we underscore the new language and strike through deleted language. For more information regarding these changes, see the Legislative History for this Rule in the "Annotations on ABA Model Rules" section of this book.

Rule 5.5   Unauthorized Practice of Law; Multijurisdictional Practice of Law

(a) A lawyer shall not practice law in a jurisdiction in violation of the regulation of the legal profession in that jurisdiction, or assist another in doing so.

(b) A lawyer who is not admitted to practice in this jurisdiction shall not:

(1) except as authorized by these Rules or other law, establish an office or other systematic and continuous presence in this jurisdiction for the practice of law; or

(2) hold out to the public or otherwise represent that the lawyer is admitted to practice law in this jurisdiction.

(c) A lawyer admitted in another United States jurisdiction, and not disbarred or suspended from practice in any jurisdiction, may provide legal services on a temporary basis in this jurisdiction that:

(1) are undertaken in association with a lawyer who is admitted to practice in this jurisdiction and who actively participates in the matter;

(2) are in or reasonably related to a pending or potential proceeding before a tribunal in this or another jurisdiction, if the lawyer, or a person the lawyer is assisting, is authorized by law or order to appear in such proceeding or reasonably expects to be so authorized;

(3) are in or reasonably related to a pending or potential arbitration, mediation, or other alternative dispute resolution proceeding in this or another jurisdiction, if the services arise out of or are reasonably related to the lawyer's practice in a jurisdiction in which the lawyer is admitted to practice and are not services for which the forum requires pro hac vice admission; or

(4) are not within paragraphs (c)(2) or (c)(3) and arise out of or are reasonably related to the lawyer's practice in a jurisdiction in which the lawyer is admitted to practice.

(d) A lawyer admitted in another United States jurisdiction, and not disbarred or suspended from practice in any jurisdiction, may provide legal services <u>through an office or other systematic and continuous presence</u> in this jurisdiction that:

(1) are provided to the lawyer's employer or its organizational affiliates and are not services for which the forum requires pro hac vice admission; or

(2) are services that the lawyer is authorized by federal or other law <u>or rule</u> to provide in this jurisdiction.

COMMENT

[1] A lawyer may practice law only in a jurisdiction in which the lawyer is authorized to practice. A lawyer may be admitted to practice law in a jurisdiction on a regular basis or may be authorized by court rule or order or by law to practice for a limited purpose or on a restricted basis. Paragraph (a) applies to unauthorized practice of law by a lawyer, whether through the lawyer's direct action or by the lawyer assisting another person. <u>For example, a lawyer may not assist a person in practicing law in violation of the rules governing professional conduct in that person's jurisdiction.</u>

[2] The definition of the practice of law is established by law and varies from one jurisdiction to another. Whatever the definition, limiting the practice of law to members of the bar protects the public against rendition of legal services by unqualified persons. This Rule does not prohibit a lawyer from employing the services of paraprofessionals and delegating functions to them, so long as the lawyer supervises the delegated work and retains responsibility for their work. See Rule 5.3.

[3] A lawyer may provide professional advice and instruction to nonlawyers whose employment requires knowledge of the law; for example, claims adjusters, employees of financial or commercial institutions, social workers, accountants and persons employed in government agencies. Lawyers also may assist independent nonlawyers, such as paraprofessionals, who are authorized by the law of a jurisdiction to provide particular law-related services. In addition, a lawyer may counsel nonlawyers who wish to proceed pro se.

[4] Other than as authorized by law or this Rule, a lawyer who is not admitted to practice generally in this jurisdiction violates paragraph (b)<u>(1)</u> if the lawyer establishes an office or other systematic and continuous presence in this jurisdiction for the practice of law. Presence may be systematic and continuous even if the

lawyer is not physically present here. Such a lawyer must not hold out to the public or otherwise represent that the lawyer is admitted to practice law in this jurisdiction. See also Rules 7.1(a) and 7.5(b).

[5] There are occasions in which a lawyer admitted to practice in another United States jurisdiction, and not disbarred or suspended from practice in any jurisdiction, may provide legal services on a temporary basis in this jurisdiction under circumstances that do not create an unreasonable risk to the interests of their clients, the public or the courts. Paragraph (c) identifies four such circumstances. The fact that conduct is not so identified does not imply that the conduct is or is not authorized. With the exception of paragraphs (d)(1) and (d)(2), this Rule does not authorize a lawyer to establish an office or other systematic and continuous presence in this jurisdiction without being admitted to practice generally here.

[6] There is no single test to determine whether a lawyer's services are provided on a "temporary basis" in this jurisdiction, and may therefore be permissible under paragraph (c). Services may be "temporary" even though the lawyer provides services in this jurisdiction on a recurring basis, or for an extended period of time, as when the lawyer is representing a client in a single lengthy negotiation or litigation.

[7] Paragraphs (c) and (d) apply to lawyers who are admitted to practice law in any United States jurisdiction, which includes the District of Columbia and any state, territory or commonwealth of the United States. The word "admitted" in paragraph (c) contemplates that the lawyer is authorized to practice in the jurisdiction in which the lawyer is admitted and excludes a lawyer who while technically admitted is not authorized to practice, because, for example, the lawyer is on inactive status.

[8] Paragraph (c)(1) recognizes that the interests of clients and the public are protected if a lawyer admitted only in another jurisdiction associates with a lawyer licensed to practice in this jurisdiction. For this paragraph to apply, however, the lawyer admitted to practice in this jurisdiction must actively participate in and share responsibility for the representation of the client.

[9] Lawyers not admitted to practice generally in a jurisdiction may be authorized by law or order of a tribunal or an administrative agency to appear before the tribunal or agency. This authority may be granted pursuant to formal rules governing admission pro hac vice or pursuant to informal practice of the tribunal or agency. Under paragraph (c)(2), a lawyer does not violate this Rule when the lawyer appears before a tribunal or agency pursuant to such authority. To the extent that a court rule or other law of this jurisdiction requires a lawyer who is not admitted to practice in this jurisdiction to obtain admission pro hac vice before appearing before a tribunal or administrative agency, this Rule requires the lawyer to obtain that authority.

[10] Paragraph (c)(2) also provides that a lawyer rendering services in this jurisdiction on a temporary basis does not violate this Rule when the lawyer engages in conduct in anticipation of a proceeding or hearing in a jurisdiction in which the lawyer is authorized to practice law or in which the lawyer reasonably expects to be admitted pro hac vice. Examples of such conduct include meetings with the client, interviews of potential witnesses, and the review of documents. Similarly, a lawyer admitted only in another jurisdiction may engage in conduct temporarily in this jurisdiction in connection with pending litigation in another jurisdiction in which the lawyer is or reasonably expects to be authorized to appear, including taking depositions in this jurisdiction.

[11] When a lawyer has been or reasonably expects to be admitted to appear before a court or administrative agency, paragraph (c)(2) also permits conduct by lawyers who are associated with that lawyer in the matter, but who do not expect to appear before the court or administrative agency. For example, subordinate lawyers may conduct research, review documents, and attend meetings with witnesses in support of the lawyer responsible for the litigation.

[12] Paragraph (c)(3) permits a lawyer admitted to practice law in another jurisdiction to perform services on a temporary basis in this jurisdiction if those services are in or reasonably related to a pending or potential arbitration, mediation, or other alternative dispute resolution proceeding in this or another jurisdiction, if the services arise out of or are reasonably related to the lawyer's practice in a jurisdiction in which the lawyer is admitted to practice. The lawyer, however, must obtain admission pro hac vice in the case of a court-annexed arbitration or mediation or otherwise if court rules or law so require.

[13] Paragraph (c)(4) permits a lawyer admitted in another jurisdiction to provide certain legal services on a temporary basis in this jurisdiction that arise out of or are reasonably related to the lawyer's practice in a jurisdiction in which the lawyer is admitted but are not within paragraphs (c)(2) or (c)(3). These services include both legal services and services that nonlawyers may perform but that are considered the practice of law when performed by lawyers.

[14] Paragraphs (c)(3) and (c)(4) require that the services arise out of or be reasonably related to the lawyer's practice in a jurisdiction in which the lawyer is admitted. A variety of factors evidence such a relationship. The lawyer's client may have been previously represented by the lawyer, or may be resident in or have substantial contacts with the jurisdiction in which the lawyer is admitted. The matter, although involving other jurisdictions, may have a significant connection with that jurisdiction. In other cases, significant aspects of the lawyer's work might be conducted in that jurisdiction or a significant aspect of the matter may involve the law of that jurisdiction. The necessary relationship might arise when the client's activities or the legal issues involve multiple jurisdictions, such as when the officers of a multinational corporation survey potential business sites and seek the services of their lawyer in assessing the relative merits of each. In addition, the services may draw on the lawyer's recognized expertise developed through the regular practice of law on behalf of clients in matters involving a particular body of federal, nationally-uniform, foreign, or international law. Lawyers desiring to provide pro bono legal services on a temporary basis in a jurisdiction that has been affected by a major disaster, but in which they are not otherwise authorized to practice law, as well as lawyers from the affected jurisdiction who seek to practice law temporarily in another jurisdiction, but in which they are not otherwise authorized to practice law, should consult the Model Court Rule on Provision of Legal Services Following Determination of Major Disaster.

> **Editors' Note.** The ABA Model Court Rule on Provision of Legal Services Following Determination of Major Disaster referenced in Comment 14 is reprinted in the Related Materials for Rule 5.5 in the "Annotations on ABA Model Rules" section of this book.

[15] Paragraph (d) identifies two circumstances in which a lawyer who is admitted to practice in another United States jurisdiction, and is not disbarred or

suspended from practice in any jurisdiction, may establish an office or other systematic and continuous presence in this jurisdiction for the practice of law as well as provide legal services on a temporary basis. Except as provided in paragraphs (d)(1) and (d)(2), a lawyer who is admitted to practice law in another jurisdiction and who establishes an office or other systematic or continuous presence in this jurisdiction must become admitted to practice law generally in this jurisdiction.

[16] Paragraph (d)(1) applies to a lawyer who is employed by a client to provide legal services to the client or its organizational affiliates, i.e., entities that control, are controlled by, or are under common control with the employer. This paragraph does not authorize the provision of personal legal services to the employer's officers or employees. The paragraph applies to in-house corporate lawyers, government lawyers and others who are employed to render legal services to the employer. The lawyer's ability to represent the employer outside the jurisdiction in which the lawyer is licensed generally serves the interests of the employer and does not create an unreasonable risk to the client and others because the employer is well situated to assess the lawyer's qualifications and the quality of the lawyer's work.

[17] If an employed lawyer establishes an office or other systematic presence in this jurisdiction for the purpose of rendering legal services to the employer, the lawyer may be subject to registration or other requirements, including assessments for client protection funds and mandatory continuing legal education.

[18] Paragraph (d)(2) recognizes that a lawyer may provide legal services in a jurisdiction in which the lawyer is not licensed when authorized to do so by federal or other law, which includes statute, court rule, executive regulation or judicial precedent. See, e.g., The ABA Model Rule on Practice Pending Admission.

[19] A lawyer who practices law in this jurisdiction pursuant to paragraph (c) or (d) or otherwise is subject to the disciplinary authority of this jurisdiction. See Rule 8.5(a).

[20] In some circumstances, a lawyer who practices law in this jurisdiction pursuant to paragraph (c) or (d) may have to inform the client that the lawyer is not licensed to practice law in this jurisdiction. For example, that may be required when the representation occurs primarily in this jurisdiction and requires knowledge of the law of this jurisdiction. See Rule 1.4(b).

[21] Paragraphs (c) and (d) do not authorize communications advertising legal services to prospective clients in this jurisdiction by lawyers who are admitted to practice in other jurisdictions. Whether and how lawyers may communicate the availability of their services to prospective clients in this jurisdiction is governed by Rules 7.1 to 7.5.

Rule 5.6   Restrictions on Right to Practice

A lawyer shall not participate in offering or making:

(a) a partnership, shareholders, operating, employment, or other similar type of agreement that restricts the right of a lawyer to practice after termination of the relationship, except an agreement concerning benefits upon retirement; or

(b) an agreement in which a restriction on the lawyer's right to practice is part of the settlement of a client controversy.

COMMENT

[1] An agreement restricting the right of lawyers to practice after leaving a firm not only limits their professional autonomy but also limits the freedom of clients to choose a lawyer. Paragraph (a) prohibits such agreements except for restrictions incident to provisions concerning retirement benefits for service with the firm.

[2] Paragraph (b) prohibits a lawyer from agreeing not to represent other persons in connection with settling a claim on behalf of a client.

[3] This Rule does not apply to prohibit restrictions that may be included in the terms of the sale of a law practice pursuant to Rule 1.17.

Rule 5.7   Responsibilities Regarding Law-Related Services

(a) A lawyer shall be subject to the Rules of Professional Conduct with respect to the provision of law-related services, as defined in paragraph (b), if the law-related services are provided:

(1) by the lawyer in circumstances that are not distinct from the lawyer's provision of legal services to clients; or

(2) in other circumstances by an entity controlled by the lawyer individually or with others if the lawyer fails to take reasonable measures to assure that a person obtaining the law-related services knows that the services are not legal services and that the protections of the client-lawyer relationship do not exist.

(b) The term "law-related services" denotes services that might reasonably be performed in conjunction with and in substance are related to the provision of legal services, and that are not prohibited as unauthorized practice of law when provided by a nonlawyer.

COMMENT

[1] When a lawyer performs law-related services or controls an organization that does so, there exists the potential for ethical problems. Principal among these is the possibility that the person for whom the law-related services are performed fails to understand that the services may not carry with them the protections normally afforded as part of the client-lawyer relationship. The recipient of the law-related services may expect, for example, that the protection of client confidences, prohibitions against representation of persons with conflicting interests, and obligations of a lawyer to maintain professional independence apply to the provision of law-related services when that may not be the case.

[2] Rule 5.7 applies to the provision of law-related services by a lawyer even when the lawyer does not provide any legal services to the person for whom the law-related services are performed and whether the law-related services are performed through a law firm or a separate entity. The Rule identifies the circumstances in which all of the Rules of Professional Conduct apply to the provision of law-related services. Even when those circumstances do not exist, however, the conduct of a

lawyer involved in the provision of law-related services is subject to those Rules that apply generally to lawyer conduct, regardless of whether the conduct involves the provision of legal services. See, e.g., Rule 8.4.

[3] When law-related services are provided by a lawyer under circumstances that are not distinct from the lawyer's provision of legal services to clients, the lawyer in providing the law-related services must adhere to the requirements of the Rules of Professional Conduct as provided in paragraph (a)(1). Even when the law-related and legal services are provided in circumstances that are distinct from each other, for example through separate entities or different support staff within the law firm, the Rules of Professional Conduct apply to the lawyer as provided in paragraph (a)(2) unless the lawyer takes reasonable measures to assure that the recipient of the law-related services knows that the services are not legal services and that the protections of the client-lawyer relationship do not apply.

[4] Law-related services also may be provided through an entity that is distinct from that through which the lawyer provides legal services. If the lawyer individually or with others has control of such an entity's operations, the Rule requires the lawyer to take reasonable measures to assure that each person using the services of the entity knows that the services provided by the entity are not legal services and that the Rules of Professional Conduct that relate to the client-lawyer relationship do not apply. A lawyer's control of an entity extends to the ability to direct its operation. Whether a lawyer has such control will depend upon the circumstances of the particular case.

[5] When a client-lawyer relationship exists with a person who is referred by a lawyer to a separate law-related service entity controlled by the lawyer, individually or with others, the lawyer must comply with Rule 1.8(a).

[6] In taking the reasonable measures referred to in paragraph (a)(2) to assure that a person using law-related services understands the practical effect or significance of the inapplicability of the Rules of Professional Conduct, the lawyer should communicate to the person receiving the law-related services, in a manner sufficient to assure that the person understands the significance of the fact, that the relationship of the person to the business entity will not be a client-lawyer relationship. The communication should be made before entering into an agreement for provision of or providing law-related services, and preferably should be in writing.

[7] The burden is upon the lawyer to show that the lawyer has taken reasonable measures under the circumstances to communicate the desired understanding. For instance, a sophisticated user of law-related services, such as a publicly held corporation, may require a lesser explanation than someone unaccustomed to making distinctions between legal services and law-related services, such as an individual seeking tax advice from a lawyer-accountant or investigative services in connection with a lawsuit.

[8] Regardless of the sophistication of potential recipients of law-related services, a lawyer should take special care to keep separate the provision of law-related and legal services in order to minimize the risk that the recipient will assume that the law-related services are legal services. The risk of such confusion is especially acute when the lawyer renders both types of services with respect to the same matter. Under some circumstances the legal and law-related services may be so closely entwined that they cannot be distinguished from each other, and the requirement of disclosure and consultation imposed by paragraph (a)(2) of the Rule cannot be

met. In such a case a lawyer will be responsible for assuring that both the lawyer's conduct and, to the extent required by Rule 5.3, that of nonlawyer employees in the distinct entity that the lawyer controls complies in all respects with the Rules of Professional Conduct.

[9] A broad range of economic and other interests of clients may be served by lawyers' engaging in the delivery of law-related services. Examples of law-related services include providing title insurance, financial planning, accounting, trust services, real estate counseling, legislative lobbying, economic analysis, social work, psychological counseling, tax preparation, and patent, medical or environmental consulting.

[10] When a lawyer is obliged to accord the recipients of such services the protections of those Rules that apply to the client-lawyer relationship, the lawyer must take special care to heed the proscriptions of the Rules addressing conflict of interest (Rules 1.7 through 1.11, especially Rules 1.7(a)(2) and 1.8(a), (b) and (f)), and to scrupulously adhere to the requirements of Rule 1.6 relating to disclosure of confidential information. The promotion of the law-related services must also in all respects comply with Rules 7.1 through 7.3, dealing with advertising and solicitation. In that regard, lawyers should take special care to identify the obligations that may be imposed as a result of a jurisdiction's decisional law.

[11] When the full protections of all of the Rules of Professional Conduct do not apply to the provision of law-related services, principles of law external to the Rules, for example, the law of principal and agent, govern the legal duties owed to those receiving the services. Those other legal principles may establish a different degree of protection for the recipient with respect to confidentiality of information, conflicts of interest and permissible business relationships with clients. See also Rule 8.4 (Misconduct).

ARTICLE 6.   PUBLIC SERVICE

Rule 6.1   Voluntary Pro Bono Publico Service

Every lawyer has a professional responsibility to provide legal services to those unable to pay. A lawyer should aspire to render at least (50) hours of pro bono publico legal services per year. In fulfilling this responsibility, the lawyer should:

(a) provide a substantial majority of the (50) hours of legal services without fee or expectation of fee to:

(1) persons of limited means or

(2) charitable, religious, civic, community, governmental and educational organizations in matters that are designed primarily to address the needs of persons of limited means; and

(b) provide any additional services through:

(1) delivery of legal services at no fee or substantially reduced fee to individuals, groups or organizations seeking to secure or protect civil rights, civil liberties or public rights, or charitable, religious, civic, community, governmental and educational organizations in matters in

furtherance of their organizational purposes, where the payment of standard legal fees would significantly deplete the organization's economic resources or would be otherwise inappropriate;

(2) delivery of legal services at a substantially reduced fee to persons of limited means; or

(3) participation in activities for improving the law, the legal system or the legal profession.

In addition, a lawyer should voluntarily contribute financial support to organizations that provide legal services to persons of limited means.

COMMENT

[1] Every lawyer, regardless of professional prominence or professional work load, has a responsibility to provide legal services to those unable to pay, and personal involvement in the problems of the disadvantaged can be one of the most rewarding experiences in the life of a lawyer. The American Bar Association urges all lawyers to provide a minimum of 50 hours of pro bono services annually. States, however, may decide to choose a higher or lower number of hours of annual service (which may be expressed as a percentage of a lawyer's professional time) depending upon local needs and local conditions. It is recognized that in some years a lawyer may render greater or fewer hours than the annual standard specified, but during the course of his or her legal career, each lawyer should render on average per year, the number of hours set forth in this Rule. Services can be performed in civil matters or in criminal or quasi-criminal matters for which there is no government obligation to provide funds for legal representation, such as post-conviction death penalty appeal cases.

[2] Paragraphs (a)(1) and (2) recognize the critical need for legal services that exists among persons of limited means by providing that a substantial majority of the legal services rendered annually to the disadvantaged be furnished without fee or expectation of fee. Legal services under these paragraphs consist of a full range of activities, including individual and class representation, the provision of legal advice, legislative lobbying, administrative rule making and the provision of free training or mentoring to those who represent persons of limited means. The variety of these activities should facilitate participation by government lawyers, even when restrictions exist on their engaging in the outside practice of law.

[3] Persons eligible for legal services under paragraphs (a)(1) and (2) are those who qualify for participation in programs funded by the Legal Services Corporation and those whose incomes and financial resources are slightly above the guidelines utilized by such programs but, nevertheless, cannot afford counsel. Legal services can be rendered to individuals or to organizations such as homeless shelters, battered women's centers and food pantries that serve those of limited means. The term "governmental organizations" includes, but is not limited to, public protection programs and sections of governmental or public sector agencies.

[4] Because service must be provided without fee or expectation of fee, the intent of the lawyer to render free legal services is essential for the work performed to fall within the meaning of paragraphs (a)(1) and (2). Accordingly, services rendered cannot be considered pro bono if an anticipated fee is uncollected, but the award of statutory attorneys' fees in a case originally accepted as pro bono would not

disqualify such services from inclusion under this section. Lawyers who do receive fees in such cases are encouraged to contribute an appropriate portion of such fees to organizations or projects that benefit persons of limited means.

[5] While it is possible for a lawyer to fulfill the annual responsibility to perform pro bono services exclusively through activities described in paragraphs (a)(1) and (2), to the extent that any hours of service remained unfulfilled, the remaining commitment can be met in a variety of ways as set forth in paragraph (b). Constitutional, statutory or regulatory restrictions may prohibit or impede government and public sector lawyers and judges from performing the pro bono services outlined in paragraphs (a)(1) and (2). Accordingly, where those restrictions apply, government and public sector lawyers and judges may fulfill their pro bono responsibility by performing services outlined in paragraph (b).

[6] Paragraph (b)(1) includes the provision of certain types of legal services to those whose incomes and financial resources place them above limited means. It also permits the pro bono lawyer to accept a substantially reduced fee for services. Examples of the types of issues that may be addressed under this paragraph include First Amendment claims, Title VII claims and environmental protection claims. Additionally, a wide range of organizations may be represented, including social service, medical research, cultural and religious groups.

[7] Paragraph (b)(2) covers instances in which lawyers agree to and receive a modest fee for furnishing legal services to persons of limited means. Participation in judicare programs and acceptance of court appointments in which the fee is substantially below a lawyer's usual rate are encouraged under this section.

[8] Paragraph (b)(3) recognizes the value of lawyers engaging in activities that improve the law, the legal system or the legal profession. Serving on bar association committees, serving on boards of pro bono or legal services programs, taking part in Law Day activities, acting as a continuing legal education instructor, a mediator or an arbitrator and engaging in legislative lobbying to improve the law, the legal system or the profession are a few examples of the many activities that fall within this paragraph.

[9] Because the provision of pro bono services is a professional responsibility, it is the individual ethical commitment of each lawyer. Nevertheless, there may be times when it is not feasible for a lawyer to engage in pro bono services. At such times a lawyer may discharge the pro bono responsibility by providing financial support to organizations providing free legal services to persons of limited means. Such financial support should be reasonably equivalent to the value of the hours of service that would have otherwise been provided. In addition, at times it may be more feasible to satisfy the pro bono responsibility collectively, as by a firm's aggregate pro bono activities.

[10] Because the efforts of individual lawyers are not enough to meet the need for free legal services that exists among persons of limited means, the government and the profession have instituted additional programs to provide those services. Every lawyer should financially support such programs, in addition to either providing direct pro bono services or making financial contributions when pro bono service is not feasible.

[11] Law firms should act reasonably to enable and encourage all lawyers in the firm to provide the pro bono legal services called for by this Rule.

[12] The responsibility set forth in this Rule is not intended to be enforced through disciplinary process.

Rule 6.2   Accepting Appointments

A lawyer shall not seek to avoid appointment by a tribunal to represent a person except for good cause, such as:

(a) representing the client is likely to result in violation of the Rules of Professional Conduct or other law;

(b) representing the client is likely to result in an unreasonable financial burden on the lawyer; or

(c) the client or the cause is so repugnant to the lawyer as to be likely to impair the client-lawyer relationship or the lawyer's ability to represent the client.

COMMENT

[1] A lawyer ordinarily is not obliged to accept a client whose character or cause the lawyer regards as repugnant. The lawyer's freedom to select clients is, however, qualified. All lawyers have a responsibility to assist in providing pro bono publico service. See Rule 6.1. An individual lawyer fulfills this responsibility by accepting a fair share of unpopular matters or indigent or unpopular clients. A lawyer may also be subject to appointment by a court to serve unpopular clients or persons unable to afford legal services.

Appointed Counsel

[2] For good cause a lawyer may seek to decline an appointment to represent a person who cannot afford to retain counsel or whose cause is unpopular. Good cause exists if the lawyer could not handle the matter competently, see Rule 1.1, or if undertaking the representation would result in an improper conflict of interest, for example, when the client or the cause is so repugnant to the lawyer as to be likely to impair the client-lawyer relationship or the lawyer's ability to represent the client. A lawyer may also seek to decline an appointment if acceptance would be unreasonably burdensome, for example, when it would impose a financial sacrifice so great as to be unjust.

[3] An appointed lawyer has the same obligations to the client as retained counsel, including the obligations of loyalty and confidentiality, and is subject to the same limitations on the client-lawyer relationship, such as the obligation to refrain from assisting the client in violation of the Rules.

Rule 6.3   Membership in Legal Services Organization

A lawyer may serve as a director, officer or member of a legal services organization, apart from the law firm in which the lawyer practices, notwithstanding that the organization serves persons having interests adverse to a client of the lawyer. The lawyer shall not knowingly participate in a decision or action of the organization:

(a) if participating in the decision or action would be incompatible with the lawyer's obligations to a client under Rule 1.7; or

(b) where the decision or action could have a material adverse effect on the representation of a client of the organization whose interests are adverse to a client of the lawyer.

COMMENT

[1] Lawyers should be encouraged to support and participate in legal service organizations. A lawyer who is an officer or a member of such an organization does not thereby have a client-lawyer relationship with persons served by the organization. However, there is potential conflict between the interests of such persons and the interests of the lawyer's clients. If the possibility of such conflict disqualified a lawyer from serving on the board of a legal services organization, the profession's involvement in such organizations would be severely curtailed.

[2] It may be necessary in appropriate cases to reassure a client of the organization that the representation will not be affected by conflicting loyalties of a member of the board. Established, written policies in this respect can enhance the credibility of such assurances.

Rule 6.4   Law Reform Activities Affecting Client Interests

A lawyer may serve as a director, officer or member of an organization involved in reform of the law or its administration notwithstanding that the reform may affect the interests of a client of the lawyer. When the lawyer knows that the interests of a client may be materially benefitted by a decision in which the lawyer participates, the lawyer shall disclose that fact but need not identify the client.

COMMENT

[1] Lawyers involved in organizations seeking law reform generally do not have a client-lawyer relationship with the organization. Otherwise, it might follow that a lawyer could not be involved in a bar association law reform program that might indirectly affect a client. See also Rule 1.2(b). For example, a lawyer specializing in antitrust litigation might be regarded as disqualified from participating in drafting revisions of rules governing that subject. In determining the nature and scope of participation in such activities, a lawyer should be mindful of obligations to clients under other Rules, particularly Rule 1.7. A lawyer is professionally obligated to protect the integrity of the program by making an appropriate disclosure within the organization when the lawyer knows a private client might be materially benefitted.

Rule 6.5   Nonprofit and Court-Annexed Limited Legal Services Programs

(a) A lawyer who, under the auspices of a program sponsored by a non-profit organization or court, provides short-term limited legal services to a client without expectation by either the lawyer or the client that the lawyer will provide continuing representation in the matter:

(1) is subject to Rules 1.7 and 1.9(a) only if the lawyer knows that the representation of the client involves a conflict of interest; and

(2) is subject to Rule 1.10 only if the lawyer knows that another lawyer associated with the lawyer in a law firm is disqualified by Rule 1.7 or 1.9(a) with respect to the matter.

(b) Except as provided in paragraph (a)(2), Rule 1.10 is inapplicable to a representation governed by this Rule.

COMMENT

[1] Legal services organizations, courts and various nonprofit organizations have established programs through which lawyers provide short-term limited legal services—such as advice or the completion of legal forms—that will assist persons to address their legal problems without further representation by a lawyer. In these programs, such as legal advice hotlines, advice-only clinics or pro se counseling programs, a client-lawyer relationship is established, but there is no expectation that the lawyer's representation of the client will continue beyond the limited consultation. Such programs are normally operated under circumstances in which it is not feasible for a lawyer to systematically screen for conflicts of interest as is generally required before undertaking a representation. See, e.g., Rules 1.7, 1.9 and 1.10.

[2] A lawyer who provides short-term limited legal services pursuant to this Rule must secure the client's informed consent to the limited scope of the representation. See Rule 1.2(c). If a short-term limited representation would not be reasonable under the circumstances, the lawyer may offer advice to the client but must also advise the client of the need for further assistance of counsel. Except as provided in this Rule, the Rules of Professional Conduct, including Rules 1.6 and 1.9(c), are applicable to the limited representation.

[3] Because a lawyer who is representing a client in the circumstances addressed by this Rule ordinarily is not able to check systematically for conflicts of interest, paragraph (a) requires compliance with Rules 1.7 or 1.9(a) only if the lawyer knows that the representation presents a conflict of interest for the lawyer, and with Rule 1.10 only if the lawyer knows that another lawyer in the lawyer's firm is disqualified by Rules 1.7 or 1.9(a) in the matter.

[4] Because the limited nature of the services significantly reduces the risk of conflicts of interest with other matters being handled by the lawyer's firm, paragraph (b) provides that Rule 1.10 is inapplicable to a representation governed by this Rule except as provided by paragraph (a)(2). Paragraph (a)(2) requires the participating lawyer to comply with Rule 1.10 when the lawyer knows that the lawyer's firm is disqualified by Rule 1.7 or 1.9(a). By virtue of paragraph (b), however,

a lawyer's participation in a short-term limited legal services program will not preclude the lawyer's firm from undertaking or continuing the representation of a client with interests adverse to a client being represented under the program's auspices. Nor will the personal disqualification of a lawyer participating in the program be imputed to other lawyers participating in the program.

[5] If, after commencing a short-term limited representation in accordance with this Rule, a lawyer undertakes to represent the client in the matter on an ongoing basis, Rules 1.7, 1.9(a) and 1.10 become applicable.

ARTICLE 7.   INFORMATION ABOUT LEGAL SERVICES

Editors' Note. In August 2012, the ABA House of Delegates amended Comment 3 to Rule 7.1 by deleting the phrase "prospective client" and replacing it with the phrase "the public." The ABA Commission on Ethics 20/20 proposed this change because the phrase "prospective client" is defined in Rule 1.18 and includes a narrower category of individuals than Comment 3 is intended to cover. To alert readers to this change, we underscore the new language and strike through deleted language. For more information regarding this change, see the Legislative History for this Rule in the "Annotations on ABA Model Rules" section of this book.

Rule 7.1   Communications Concerning a Lawyer's Services

A lawyer shall not make a false or misleading communication about the lawyer or the lawyer's services. A communication is false or misleading if it contains a material misrepresentation of fact or law, or omits a fact necessary to make the statement considered as a whole not materially misleading.

COMMENT

[1] This Rule governs all communications about a lawyer's services, including advertising permitted by Rule 7.2. Whatever means are used to make known a lawyer's services, statements about them must be truthful.

[2] Truthful statements that are misleading are also prohibited by this Rule. A truthful statement is misleading if it omits a fact necessary to make the lawyer's communication considered as a whole not materially misleading. A truthful statement is also misleading if there is a substantial likelihood that it will lead a reasonable person to formulate a specific conclusion about the lawyer or the lawyer's services for which there is no reasonable factual foundation.

[3] An advertisement that truthfully reports a lawyer's achievements on behalf of clients or former clients may be misleading if presented so as to lead a reasonable person to form an unjustified expectation that the same results could be obtained for other clients in similar matters without reference to the specific factual and legal circumstances of each client's case. Similarly, an unsubstantiated comparison of the lawyer's services or fees with the services or fees of other lawyers may be misleading

if presented with such specificity as would lead a reasonable person to conclude that the comparison can be substantiated. The inclusion of an appropriate disclaimer or qualifying language may preclude a finding that a statement is likely to create unjustified expectations or otherwise mislead <u>the public.</u> ~~a prospective client.~~

[4] See also Rule 8.4(e) for the prohibition against stating or implying an ability to influence improperly a government agency or official or to achieve results by means that violate the Rules of Professional Conduct or other law.

> **Editors' Note.**   In August 2012, the ABA House of Delegates amended several Comments to Rule 7.2. The ABA Commission on Ethics 20/20 proposed the changes to provide lawyers with greater guidance on the use of various new forms of advertising, particularly Internet-based client development tools, such as pay-per-click and pay-per-lead advertising. To alert readers to the changes, we underscore the new language and strike through deleted language. For more information regarding these changes, see the Legislative History for this Rule in the "Annotations on ABA Model Rules" section of this book.

Rule 7.2   Advertising

(a) Subject to the requirements of Rules 7.1 and 7.3, a lawyer may advertise services through written, recorded or electronic communication, including public media.

(b) A lawyer shall not give anything of value to a person for recommending the lawyer's services except that a lawyer may

(1) pay the reasonable costs of advertisements or communications permitted by this Rule;

(2) pay the usual charges of a legal services plan or a not-for-profit or qualified lawyer referral service. A qualified lawyer referral service is a lawyer referral service that has been approved by an appropriate regulatory authority;

(3) pay for a law practice in accordance with Rule 1.17; and

(4) refer clients to another lawyer or a nonlawyer professional pursuant to an agreement not otherwise prohibited under these Rules that provides for the other person to refer clients or customers to the lawyer, if

(i) the reciprocal referral agreement is not exclusive, and

(ii) the client is informed of the existence and nature of the agreement.

(c) Any communication made pursuant to this rule shall include the name and office address of at least one lawyer or law firm responsible for its content.

COMMENT

[1] To assist the public in <u>learning about and</u> obtaining legal services, lawyers should be allowed to make known their services not only through reputation but also

through organized information campaigns in the form of advertising. Advertising involves an active quest for clients, contrary to the tradition that a lawyer should not seek clientele. However, the public's need to know about legal services can be fulfilled in part through advertising. This need is particularly acute in the case of persons of moderate means who have not made extensive use of legal services. The interest in expanding public information about legal services ought to prevail over tradition. Nevertheless, advertising by lawyers entails the risk of practices that are misleading or overreaching.

[2] This Rule permits public dissemination of information concerning a lawyer's name or firm name, address, email address, website, and telephone number; the kinds of services the lawyer will undertake; the basis on which the lawyer's fees are determined, including prices for specific services and payment and credit arrangements; a lawyer's foreign language ability; names of references and, with their consent, names of clients regularly represented; and other information that might invite the attention of those seeking legal assistance.

[3] Questions of effectiveness and taste in advertising are matters of speculation and subjective judgment. Some jurisdictions have had extensive prohibitions against television and other forms of advertising, against advertising going beyond specified facts about a lawyer, or against "undignified" advertising. Television, the Internet, and other forms of electronic communication are is now one of among the most powerful media for getting information to the public, particularly persons of low and moderate income; prohibiting television, Internet, and other forms of electronic advertising, therefore, would impede the flow of information about legal services to many sectors of the public. Limiting the information that may be advertised has a similar effect and assumes that the bar can accurately forecast the kind of information that the public would regard as relevant. Similarly, electronic media, such as the Internet, can be an important source of information about legal services, and lawful communication by electronic mail is permitted by this Rule. But see Rule 7.3(a) for the prohibition against the a solicitation of a prospective client through a real-time electronic exchange initiated by the lawyer. that is not initiated by the prospective client.

[4] Neither this Rule nor Rule 7.3 prohibits communications authorized by law, such as notice to members of a class in class action litigation.

Paying Others to Recommend a Lawyer

[5] Except as permitted under paragraphs (b)(1)-(b)(4), Llawyers are not permitted to pay others for channeling professional work recommending the lawyer's services or for channeling professional work in a manner that violates Rule 7.3. A communication contains a recommendation if it endorses or vouches for a lawyer's credentials, abilities, competence, character, or other professional qualities. Paragraph (b)(1), however, allows a lawyer to pay for advertising and communications permitted by this Rule, including the costs of print directory listings, on-line directory listings, newspaper ads, television and radio airtime, domain-name registrations, sponsorship fees, banner ads, Internet-based advertisements, and group advertising. A lawyer may compensate employees, agents and vendors who are engaged to provide marketing or client development services, such as publicists, public-relations personnel, business-development staff and website designers.

Moreover, a lawyer may pay others for generating client leads, such as Internet-based client leads, as long as the lead generator does not recommend the lawyer, any payment to the lead generator is consistent with Rules 1.5(e) (division of fees) and 5.4 (professional independence of the lawyer), and the lead generator's communications are consistent with Rule 7.1 (communications concerning a lawyer's services). To comply with Rule 7.1, a lawyer must not pay a lead generator that states, implies, or creates a reasonable impression that it is recommending the lawyer, is making the referral without payment from the lawyer, or has analyzed a person's legal problems when determining which lawyer should receive the referral. See also Rule 5.3 ~~for the~~ (duties of lawyers and law firms with respect to the conduct of nonlawyers); Rule 8.4(a) (duty to avoid violating the Rules through the acts of another). ~~who prepare marketing materials for them.~~

[6] A lawyer may pay the usual charges of a legal service plan or a not-for-profit or qualified lawyer referral service. A legal service plan is a prepaid or group legal service plan or a similar delivery system that assists people who seek ~~prospective clients~~ to secure legal representation. A lawyer referral service, on the other hand, is any organization that holds itself out to the public as a lawyer referral service. Such referral services are understood by ~~laypersons~~ the public to be consumer-oriented organizations that provide unbiased referrals to lawyers with appropriate experience in the subject matter of the representation and afford other client protections, such as complaint procedures or malpractice insurance requirements. Consequently, this Rule only permits a lawyer to pay the usual charges of a not-for-profit or qualified lawyer referral service. A qualified lawyer referral service is one that is approved by an appropriate regulatory authority as affording adequate protections for the public. ~~prospective clients.~~ See, e.g., the American Bar Association's Model Supreme Court Rules Governing Lawyer Referral Services and Model Lawyer Referral and Information Service Quality Assurance Act (requiring that organizations that are identified as lawyer referral services (i) permit the participation of all lawyers who are licensed and eligible to practice in the jurisdiction and who meet reasonable objective eligibility requirements as may be established by the referral service for the protection of the public ~~prospective clients~~; (ii) require each participating lawyer to carry reasonably adequate malpractice insurance; (iii) act reasonably to assess client satisfaction and address client complaints; and (iv) do not make referrals ~~prospective clients~~ to lawyers who own, operate or are employed by the referral service).

[7] A lawyer who accepts assignments or referrals from a legal service plan or referrals from a lawyer referral service must act reasonably to assure that the activities of the plan or service are compatible with the lawyer's professional obligations. See Rule 5.3. Legal service plans and lawyer referral services may communicate with ~~prospective clients~~ the public, but such communication must be in conformity with these Rules. Thus, advertising must not be false or misleading, as would be the case if the communications of a group advertising program or a group legal services plan would mislead the public ~~prospective clients~~ to think that it was a lawyer referral service sponsored by a state agency or bar association. Nor could the lawyer allow in-person, telephonic, or real-time contacts that would violate Rule 7.3.

[8] A lawyer also may agree to refer clients to another lawyer or a nonlawyer professional, in return for the undertaking of that person to refer clients or customers to the lawyer. Such reciprocal referral arrangements must not interfere with the lawyer's professional judgment as to making referrals or as to providing substantive

legal services. See Rules 2.1 and 5.4(c). Except as provided in Rule 1.5(e), a lawyer who receives referrals from a lawyer or nonlawyer professional must not pay anything solely for the referral, but the lawyer does not violate paragraph (b) of this Rule by agreeing to refer clients to the other lawyer or nonlawyer professional, so long as the reciprocal referral agreement is not exclusive and the client is informed of the referral agreement. Conflicts of interest created by such agreements are governed by Rule 1.7. Reciprocal referral agreements should not be of indefinite duration and should be reviewed periodically to determine whether they comply with these Rules. This Rule does not restrict referrals or divisions of revenues or net income among lawyers within firms comprised of multiple entities.

> **Editors' Note.** In August 2012, the ABA House of Delegates amended Rule 7.3 and several accompanying Comments. The ABA Commission on Ethics 20/20 proposed these changes to provide lawyers with greater guidance as to when advertising, particularly Internet-based advertising, constitutes a solicitation. The title of the Rule and the phrasing of several Comments were changed to avoid use of the phrase "prospective clients," because the Rule is intended to cover all possible future clients, not just those people who would qualify as "prospective clients" under Rule 1.18. To alert readers to the changes, we underscore the new language and strike through deleted language. For more information regarding these changes, see the Legislative History for this Rule in the "Annotations on ABA Model Rules" section of this book.

Rule 7.3 ~~Direct Contact with Prospective~~ <u>Solicitation of</u> Clients

(a) A lawyer shall not by in-person, live telephone or real-time electronic contact solicit professional employment ~~from a prospective client~~ when a significant motive for the lawyer's doing so is the lawyer's pecuniary gain, unless the person contacted:

(1) is a lawyer; or

(2) has a family, close personal, or prior professional relationship with the lawyer.

(b) A lawyer shall not solicit professional employment ~~from a prospective client~~ by written, recorded or electronic communication or by in-person, telephone or real-time electronic contact even when not otherwise prohibited by paragraph (a), if:

(1) the ~~prospective client~~ <u>target of the solicitation</u> has made known to the lawyer a desire not to be solicited by the lawyer; or

(2) the solicitation involves coercion, duress or harassment.

(c) Every written, recorded or electronic communication from a lawyer soliciting professional employment from <u>anyone</u> ~~a prospective client~~ known to be in need of legal services in a particular matter shall include the words "Advertising Material" on the outside envelope, if any, and at the beginning and ending of any recorded or electronic communication, unless the recipient of the communication is a person specified in paragraphs (a)(1) or (a)(2).

(d) Notwithstanding the prohibitions in paragraph (a), a lawyer may participate with a prepaid or group legal service plan operated by an organization not owned or directed by the lawyer that uses in-person or telephone contact to solicit memberships or subscriptions for the plan from persons who are not known to need legal services in a particular matter covered by the plan.

COMMENT

[1] A solicitation is a targeted communication initiated by the lawyer that is directed to a specific person and that offers to provide, or can reasonably be understood as offering to provide, legal services. In contrast, a lawyer's communication typically does not constitute a solicitation if it is directed to the general public, such as through a billboard, an Internet banner advertisement, a website or a television commercial, or if it is in response to a request for information or is automatically generated in response to Internet searches.

[~~1~~2] There is a potential for abuse when a solicitation involves ~~inherent in~~ direct in-person, live telephone or real-time electronic contact by a lawyer with someone ~~a prospective client~~ known to need legal services. These forms of contact ~~between a lawyer and a prospective client~~ subject ~~the layperson~~ a person to the private importuning of the trained advocate in a direct interpersonal encounter. The person ~~prospective client~~, who may already feel overwhelmed by the circumstances giving rise to the need for legal services, may find it difficult fully to evaluate all available alternatives with reasoned judgment and appropriate self-interest in the face of the lawyer's presence and insistence upon being retained immediately. The situation is fraught with the possibility of undue influence, intimidation, and overreaching.

[~~2~~3] This potential for abuse inherent in direct in-person, live telephone or real-time electronic solicitation ~~of prospective clients~~ justifies its prohibition, particularly since lawyers have ~~advertising and written and recorded communication permitted under Rule 7.2 offer~~ alternative means of conveying necessary information to those who may be in need of legal services. ~~Advertising and written and recorded~~ In particular, communications~~,~~ can ~~which may be~~ be mailed ~~or autodialed~~ or transmitted by email or other electronic means that do not involve real-time contact and do not violate other laws governing solicitations. These forms of communications and solicitations make it possible for the public ~~a prospective client~~ to be informed about the need for legal services, and about the qualifications of available lawyers and law firms, without subjecting ~~the prospective client~~ the public to direct in-person, telephone or real-time electronic persuasion that may overwhelm ~~the client's~~ a person's judgment.

[~~3~~4] The use of general advertising and written, recorded or electronic communications to transmit information from lawyer to the public ~~prospective client~~, rather than direct in-person, live telephone or real-time electronic contact, will help to assure that the information flows cleanly as well as freely. The contents of advertisements and communications permitted under Rule 7.2 can be permanently recorded so that they cannot be disputed and may be shared with others who know the lawyer. This potential for informal review is itself likely to help guard against statements and claims that might constitute false and misleading communications, in violation of Rule 7.1. The contents of direct-in-person, live telephone or real-time electronic ~~conversations between a lawyer and a prospective client~~ contact can be disputed and may not be subject to third-party scrutiny. Consequently, they are much more likely to approach (and occasionally cross) the dividing line between accurate representations and those that are false and misleading.

[4~~5~~] There is far less likelihood that a lawyer would engage in abusive practices against ~~an individual who is~~ a former client, or a person with whom the lawyer has close personal or family relationship, or in situations in which the lawyer is motivated by considerations other than the lawyer's pecuniary gain. Nor is there a serious potential for abuse when the person contacted is a lawyer. Consequently, the general prohibition in Rule 7.3(a) and the requirements of Rule 7.3(c) are not applicable in those situations. Also, paragraph (a) is not intended to prohibit a lawyer from participating in constitutionally protected activities of public or charitable legal-service organizations or bona fide political, social, civic, fraternal, employee or trade organizations whose purposes include providing or recommending legal services to ~~its~~ their members or beneficiaries.

[5~~6~~] But even permitted forms of solicitation can be abused. Thus, any solicitation which contains information which is false or misleading within the meaning of Rule 7.1, which involves coercion, duress or harassment within the meaning of Rule 7.3(b)(2), or which involves contact with ~~a prospective client~~ someone who has made known to the lawyer a desire not to be solicited by the lawyer within the meaning of Rule 7.3(b)(1) is prohibited. Moreover, if after sending a letter or other communication ~~to a client~~ as permitted by Rule 7.2 the lawyer receives no response, any further effort to communicate with the recipient of the communication ~~prospective client~~ may violate the provisions of Rule 7.3(b).

[6~~7~~] This Rule is not intended to prohibit a lawyer from contacting representatives of organizations or groups that may be interested in establishing a group or prepaid legal plan for their members, insureds, beneficiaries or other third parties for the purpose of informing such entities of the availability of and details concerning the plan or arrangement which the lawyer or lawyer's firm is willing to offer. This form of communication is not directed to people who are seeking legal services for themselves. ~~a prospective client~~. Rather, it is usually addressed to an individual acting in a fiduciary capacity seeking a supplier of legal services for others who may, if they choose, become prospective clients of the lawyer. Under these circumstances, the activity which the lawyer undertakes in communicating with such representatives and the type of information transmitted to the individual are functionally similar to and serve the same purpose as advertising permitted under Rule 7.2.

[7~~8~~] The requirement in Rule 7.3(c) that certain communications be marked "Advertising Material" does not apply to communications sent in response to requests of potential clients or their spokespersons or sponsors. General announcements by lawyers, including changes in personnel or office location, do not constitute communications soliciting professional employment from a client known to be in need of legal services within the meaning of this Rule.

[8~~9~~] Paragraph (d) of this Rule permits a lawyer to participate with an organization which uses personal contact to solicit members for its group or prepaid legal service plan, provided that the personal contact is not undertaken by any lawyer who would be a provider of legal services through the plan. The organization must not be owned by or directed (whether as manager or otherwise) by any lawyer or law firm that participates in the plan. For example, paragraph (d) would not permit a lawyer to create an organization controlled directly or indirectly by the lawyer and use the organization for the in-person or telephone solicitation of legal employment of the lawyer through memberships in the plan or otherwise. The communication permitted by these organizations also must not be directed to a person known to need legal services in a particular matter, but is to be designed to inform potential plan members generally of another means of affordable legal services. Lawyers who participate in a legal service plan must reasonably assure that the plan sponsors are in compliance with Rules 7.1, 7.2 and 7.3(b). See 8.4(a).

Rule 7.4 Communication of Fields of Practice and Specialization

(a) A lawyer may communicate the fact that the lawyer does or does not practice in particular fields of law.

(b) A lawyer admitted to engage in patent practice before the United States Patent and Trademark Office may use the designation "Patent Attorney" or a substantially similar designation.

(c) A lawyer engaged in Admiralty practice may use the designation "Admiralty," "Proctor in Admiralty" or a substantially similar designation.

(d) A lawyer shall not state or imply that a lawyer is certified as a specialist in a particular field of law, unless:

(1) the lawyer has been certified as a specialist by an organization that has been approved by an appropriate state authority or that has been accredited by the American Bar Association; and

(2) the name of the certifying organization is clearly identified in the communication.

COMMENT

[1] Paragraph (a) of this Rule permits a lawyer to indicate areas of practice in communications about the lawyer's services. If a lawyer practices only in certain fields, or will not accept matters except in a specified field or fields, the lawyer is permitted to so indicate. A lawyer is generally permitted to state that the lawyer "specialist," practices a "specialty," or "specializes in" particular fields, but such communications are subject to the "false and misleading" standard applied in Rule 7.1 to communications concerning a lawyer's services.

[2] Paragraph (b) recognizes the long-established policy of the Patent and Trademark Office for the designation of lawyers practicing before the Office. Paragraph (c) recognizes that designation of Admiralty practice has a long historical tradition associated with maritime commerce and the federal courts.

[3] Paragraph (d) permits a lawyer to state that the lawyer is certified as a specialist in a field of law if such certification is granted by an organization approved by an appropriate state authority or accredited by the American Bar Association or another organization, such as a state bar association, that has been approved

by the state authority to accredit organizations that certify lawyers as specialists. Certification signifies that an objective entity has recognized an advanced degree of knowledge and experience in the specialty area greater than is suggested by general licensure to practice law. Certifying organizations may be expected to apply standards of experience, knowledge and proficiency to insure that a lawyer's recognition as a specialist is meaningful and reliable. In order to insure that consumers can obtain access to useful information about an organization granting certification, the name of the certifying organization must be included in any communication regarding the certification.

Rule 7.5   Firm Names and Letterheads

(a) A lawyer shall not use a firm name, letterhead or other professional designation that violates Rule 7.1. A trade name may be used by a lawyer in private practice if it does not imply a connection with a government agency or with a public or charitable legal services organization and is not otherwise in violation of Rule 7.1.

(b) A law firm with offices in more than one jurisdiction may use the same name or other professional designation in each jurisdiction, but identification of the lawyers in an office of the firm shall indicate the jurisdictional limitations on those not licensed to practice in the jurisdiction where the office is located.

(c) The name of a lawyer holding a public office shall not be used in the name of a law firm, or in communications on its behalf, during any substantial period in which the lawyer is not actively and regularly practicing with the firm.

(d) Lawyers may state or imply that they practice in a partnership or other organization only when that is the fact.

COMMENT

[1] A firm may be designated by the names of all or some of its members, by the names of deceased members where there has been a continuing succession in the firm's identity or by a trade name such as the "ABC Legal Clinic." A lawyer or law firm may also be designated by a distinctive website address or comparable professional designation. Although the United States Supreme Court has held that legislation may prohibit the use of trade names in professional practice, use of such names in law practice is acceptable so long as it is not misleading. If a private firm uses a trade name that includes a geographical name such as "Springfield Legal Clinic," an express disclaimer that it is a public legal aid agency may be required to avoid a misleading implication. It may be observed that any firm name including the name of a deceased partner is, strictly speaking, a trade name. The use of such names to designate law firms has proven a useful means of identification. However, it is misleading to use the name of a lawyer not associated with the firm or a predecessor of the firm, or the name of a nonlawyer.

[2] With regard to paragraph (d), lawyers sharing office facilities, but who are not in fact associated with each other in a law firm, may not denominate themselves as, for example, "Smith and Jones," for that title suggests that they are practicing law together in a firm.

Rule 7.6   Political Contributions to Obtain Government Legal Engagements or Appointments by Judges

A lawyer or law firm shall not accept a government legal engagement or an appointment by a judge if the lawyer or law firm makes a political contribution or solicits political contributions for the purpose of obtaining or being considered for that type of legal engagement or appointment.

COMMENT

[1] Lawyers have a right to participate fully in the political process, which includes making and soliciting political contributions to candidates for judicial and other public office. Nevertheless, when lawyers make or solicit political contributions in order to obtain an engagement for legal work awarded by a government agency, or to obtain appointment by a judge, the public may legitimately question whether the lawyers engaged to perform the work are selected on the basis of competence and merit. In such a circumstance, the integrity of the profession is undermined.

[2] The term "political contribution" denotes any gift, subscription, loan, advance or deposit of anything of value made directly or indirectly to a candidate, incumbent, political party or campaign committee to influence or provide financial support for election to or retention in judicial or other government office. Political contributions in initiative and referendum elections are not included. For purposes of this Rule, the term "political contribution" does not include uncompensated services.

[3] Subject to the exceptions below, (i) the term "government legal engagement" denotes any engagement to provide legal services that a public official has the direct or indirect power to award; and (ii) the term "appointment by a judge" denotes an appointment to a position such as referee, commissioner, special master, receiver, guardian or other similar position that is made by a judge. Those terms do not, however, include (a) substantially uncompensated services; (b) engagements or appointments made on the basis of experience, expertise, professional qualifications and cost following a request for proposal or other process that is free from influence based upon political contributions; and (c) engagements or appointments made on a rotational basis from a list compiled without regard to political contributions.

[4] The term "lawyer or law firm" includes a political action committee or other entity owned or controlled by a lawyer or law firm.

[5] Political contributions are for the purpose of obtaining or being considered for a government legal engagement or appointment by a judge if, but for the desire to be considered for the legal engagement or appointment, the lawyer or law firm would not have made or solicited the contributions. The purpose may

be determined by an examination of the circumstances in which the contributions occur. For example, one or more contributions that in the aggregate are substantial in relation to other contributions by lawyers or law firms, made for the benefit of an official in a position to influence award of a government legal engagement, and followed by an award of the legal engagement to the contributing or soliciting lawyer or the lawyer's firm would support an inference that the purpose of the contributions was to obtain the engagement, absent other factors that weigh against existence of the proscribed purpose. Those factors may include among others that the contribution or solicitation was made to further a political, social, or economic interest or because of an existing personal, family, or professional relationship with a candidate.

[6] If a lawyer makes or solicits a political contribution under circumstances that constitute bribery or another crime, Rule 8.4(b) is implicated.

ARTICLE 8.   MAINTAINING THE INTEGRITY OF THE PROFESSION

Rule 8.1   Bar Admission and Disciplinary Matters

An applicant for admission to the bar, or a lawyer in connection with a bar admission application or in connection with a disciplinary matter, shall not:

(a) knowingly make a false statement of material fact; or

(b) fail to disclose a fact necessary to correct a misapprehension known by the person to have arisen in the matter, or knowingly fail to respond to a lawful demand for information from an admissions or disciplinary authority, except that this rule does not require disclosure of information otherwise protected by Rule 1.6.

COMMENT

[1] The duty imposed by this Rule extends to persons seeking admission to the bar as well as to lawyers. Hence, if a person makes a material false statement in connection with an application for admission, it may be the basis for subsequent disciplinary action if the person is admitted, and in any event may be relevant in a subsequent admission application. The duty imposed by this Rule applies to a lawyer's own admission or discipline as well as that of others. Thus, it is a separate professional offense for a lawyer to knowingly make a misrepresentation or omission in connection with a disciplinary investigation of the lawyer's own conduct. Paragraph (b) of this Rule also requires correction of any prior misstatement in the matter that the applicant or lawyer may have made and affirmative clarification of any misunderstanding on the part of the admissions or disciplinary authority of which the person involved becomes aware.

[2] This Rule is subject to the provisions of the Fifth Amendment of the United States Constitution and corresponding provisions of state constitutions. A

person relying on such a provision in response to a question, however, should do so openly and not use the right of nondisclosure as a justification for failure to comply with this Rule.

[3] A lawyer representing an applicant for admission to the bar, or representing a lawyer who is the subject of a disciplinary inquiry or proceeding, is governed by the rules applicable to the client-lawyer relationship, including Rule 1.6 and, in some cases, Rule 3.3.

Rule 8.2   Judicial and Legal Officials

(a) A lawyer shall not make a statement that the lawyer knows to be false or with reckless disregard as to its truth or falsity concerning the qualifications or integrity of a judge, adjudicatory officer or public legal officer, or of a candidate for election or appointment to judicial or legal office.

(b) A lawyer who is a candidate for judicial office shall comply with the applicable provisions of the Code of Judicial Conduct.

— No false statements about public officials

COMMENT

[1] Assessments by lawyers are relied on in evaluating the professional or personal fitness of persons being considered for election or appointment to judicial office and to public legal offices, such as attorney general, prosecuting attorney and public defender. Expressing honest and candid opinions on such matters contributes to improving the administration of justice. Conversely, false statements by a lawyer can unfairly undermine public confidence in the administration of justice.

[2] When a lawyer seeks judicial office, the lawyer should be bound by applicable limitations on political activity.

[3] To maintain the fair and independent administration of justice, lawyers are encouraged to continue traditional efforts to defend judges and courts unjustly criticized.

Rule 8.3   Reporting Professional Misconduct

(a) A lawyer who knows that another lawyer has committed a violation of the Rules of Professional Conduct that raises a substantial question as to that lawyer's honesty, trustworthiness or fitness as a lawyer in other respects, shall inform the appropriate professional authority.

(b) A lawyer who knows that a judge has committed a violation of applicable rules of judicial conduct that raises a substantial question as to the judge's fitness for office shall inform the appropriate authority.

(c) This Rule does not require disclosure of information otherwise protected by Rule 1.6 or information gained by a lawyer or judge while participating in an approved lawyers assistance program.

COMMENT

[1] Self-regulation of the legal profession requires that members of the profession initiate a disciplinary investigation when they know of a violation of the Rules of Professional Conduct. Lawyers have a similar obligation with respect to judicial misconduct. An apparently isolated violation may indicate a pattern of misconduct that only a disciplinary investigation can uncover. Reporting a violation is especially important where the victim is unlikely to discover the offense.

[2] A report about misconduct is not required where it would involve violation of Rule 1.6. However, a lawyer should encourage a client to consent to disclosure where prosecution would not substantially prejudice the client's interests.

[3] If a lawyer were obliged to report every violation of the Rules, the failure to report any violation would itself be a professional offense. Such a requirement existed in many jurisdictions but proved to be unenforceable. This Rule limits the reporting obligation to those offenses that a self-regulating profession must vigorously endeavor to prevent. A measure of judgment is, therefore, required in complying with the provisions of this Rule. The term "substantial" refers to the seriousness of the possible offense and not the quantum of evidence of which the lawyer is aware. A report should be made to the bar disciplinary agency unless some other agency, such as a peer review agency, is more appropriate in the circumstances. Similar considerations apply to the reporting of judicial misconduct.

[4] The duty to report professional misconduct does not apply to a lawyer retained to represent a lawyer whose professional conduct is in question. Such a situation is governed by the Rules applicable to the client-lawyer relationship.

[5] Information about a lawyer's or judge's misconduct or fitness may be received by a lawyer in the course of that lawyer's participation in an approved lawyers or judges assistance program. In that circumstance, providing for an exception to the reporting requirements of paragraphs (a) and (b) of this Rule encourages lawyers and judges to seek treatment through such a program. Conversely, without such an exception, lawyers and judges may hesitate to seek assistance from these programs, which may then result in additional harm to their professional careers and additional injury to the welfare of clients and the public. These Rules do not otherwise address the confidentiality of information received by a lawyer or judge participating in an approved lawyers assistance program; such an obligation, however, may be imposed by the rules of the program or other law.

Rule 8.4   Misconduct

It is professional misconduct for a lawyer to:

(a) violate or attempt to violate the Rules of Professional Conduct, knowingly assist or induce another to do so, or do so through the acts of another;

(b) commit a criminal act that reflects adversely on the lawyer's honesty, trustworthiness or fitness as a lawyer in other respects;

(c) engage in conduct involving dishonesty, fraud, deceit or misrepresentation;

(d) engage in conduct that is prejudicial to the administration of justice;

132

(e) state or imply an ability to influence improperly a government agency or official or to achieve results by means that violate the Rules of Professional Conduct or other law; or

(f) knowingly assist a judge or judicial officer in conduct that is a violation of applicable rules of judicial conduct or other law.

COMMENT

[1] Lawyers are subject to discipline when they violate or attempt to violate the Rules of Professional Conduct, knowingly assist or induce another to do so or do so through the acts of another, as when they request or instruct an agent to do so on the lawyer's behalf. Paragraph (a), however, does not prohibit a lawyer from advising a client concerning action the client is legally entitled to take.

[2] Many kinds of illegal conduct reflect adversely on fitness to practice law, such as offenses involving fraud and the offense of willful failure to file an income tax return. However, some kinds of offenses carry no such implication. Traditionally, the distinction was drawn in terms of offenses involving "moral turpitude." That concept can be construed to include offenses concerning some matters of personal morality, such as adultery and comparable offenses, that have no specific connection to fitness for the practice of law. Although a lawyer is personally answerable to the entire criminal law, a lawyer should be professionally answerable only for offenses that indicate lack of those characteristics relevant to law practice. Offenses involving violence, dishonesty, breach of trust, or serious interference with the administration of justice are in that category. A pattern of repeated offenses, even ones of minor significance when considered separately, can indicate indifference to legal obligation.

[3] A lawyer who, in the course of representing a client, knowingly manifests by words or conduct, bias or prejudice based upon race, sex, religion, national origin, disability, age, sexual orientation or socioeconomic status, violates paragraph (d) when such actions are prejudicial to the administration of justice. Legitimate advocacy respecting the foregoing factors does not violate paragraph (d). A trial judge's finding that peremptory challenges were exercised on a discriminatory basis does not alone establish a violation of this rule.

[4] A lawyer may refuse to comply with an obligation imposed by law upon a good faith belief that no valid obligation exists. The provisions of Rule 1.2(d) concerning a good faith challenge to the validity, scope, meaning or application of the law apply to challenges of legal regulation of the practice of law.

[5] Lawyers holding public office assume legal responsibilities going beyond those of other citizens. A lawyer's abuse of public office can suggest an inability to fulfill the professional role of lawyers. The same is true of abuse of positions of private trust such as trustee, executor, administrator, guardian, agent and officer, director or manager of a corporation or other organization.

Rule 8.5   Disciplinary Authority; Choice of Law

(a) Disciplinary Authority. A lawyer admitted to practice in this jurisdiction is subject to the disciplinary authority of this jurisdiction, regardless of where the lawyer's conduct occurs. A lawyer not admitted in this jurisdiction is also subject to the disciplinary authority of this jurisdiction if the lawyer provides or offers to provide any legal services in this jurisdiction. A lawyer may be subject to the disciplinary authority of both this jurisdiction and another jurisdiction for the same conduct.

(b) **Choice of Law.** In any exercise of the disciplinary authority of this jurisdiction, the rules of professional conduct to be applied shall be as follows:

(1) for conduct in connection with a matter pending before a tribunal, the rules of the jurisdiction in which the tribunal sits, unless the rules of the tribunal provide otherwise; and

(2) for any other conduct, the rules of the jurisdiction in which the lawyer's conduct occurred, or, if the predominant effect of the conduct is in a different jurisdiction, the rules of that jurisdiction shall be applied to the conduct. A lawyer shall not be subject to discipline if the lawyer's conduct conforms to the rules of a jurisdiction in which the lawyer reasonably believes the predominant effect of the lawyer's conduct will occur.

COMMENT

Disciplinary Authority

[1] It is longstanding law that the conduct of a lawyer admitted to practice in this jurisdiction is subject to the disciplinary authority of this jurisdiction. Extension of the disciplinary authority of this jurisdiction to other lawyers who provide or offer to provide legal services in this jurisdiction is for the protection of the citizens of this jurisdiction. Reciprocal enforcement of a jurisdiction's disciplinary findings and sanctions will further advance the purposes of this Rule. See Rules 6 and 22, ABA Model Rules for Lawyer Disciplinary Enforcement. A lawyer who is subject to the disciplinary authority of this jurisdiction under Rule 8.5(a) appoints an official to be designated by this Court to receive service of process in this jurisdiction. The fact that the lawyer is subject to the disciplinary authority of this jurisdiction may be a factor in determining whether personal jurisdiction may be asserted over the lawyer for civil matters.

Choice of Law

[2] A lawyer may be potentially subject to more than one set of rules of professional conduct which impose different obligations. The lawyer may be licensed to practice in more than one jurisdiction with differing rules, or may be admitted to practice before a particular court with rules that differ from those of the jurisdiction or jurisdictions in which the lawyer is licensed to practice. Additionally, the lawyer's conduct may involve significant contacts with more than one jurisdiction.

[3] Paragraph (b) seeks to resolve such potential conflicts. Its premise is that minimizing conflicts between rules, as well as uncertainty about which rules

are applicable, is in the best interest of both clients and the profession (as well as the bodies having authority to regulate the profession). Accordingly, it takes the approach of (i) providing that any particular conduct of a lawyer shall be subject to only one set of rules of professional conduct, (ii) making the determination of which set of rules applies to particular conduct as straightforward as possible, consistent with recognition of appropriate regulatory interests of relevant jurisdictions, and (iii) providing protection from discipline for lawyers who act reasonably in the face of uncertainty.

[4] Paragraph (b)(1) provides that as to a lawyer's conduct relating to a proceeding pending before a tribunal, the lawyer shall be subject only to the rules of the jurisdiction in which the tribunal sits unless the rules of the tribunal including its choice of law rule, provide otherwise. As to all other conduct, including conduct in anticipation of a proceeding not yet pending before a tribunal, paragraph (b)(2) provides that a lawyer shall be subject to the rules of the jurisdiction in which the lawyer's conduct occurred, or, if the predominant effect of the conduct is in another jurisdiction, the rules of that jurisdiction shall be applied to the conduct. In the case of conduct in anticipation of a proceeding that is likely to be before a tribunal, the predominant effect of such conduct could be where the conduct occurred, where the tribunal sits or in another jurisdiction.

[5] When a lawyer's conduct involves significant contacts with more than one jurisdiction, it may not be clear whether the predominant effect of the lawyer's conduct will occur in a jurisdiction other than the one in which the conduct occurred. So long as the lawyer's conduct conforms to the rules of a jurisdiction in which the lawyer reasonably believes the predominant effect will occur, the lawyer shall not be subject to discipline under this Rule.

[6] If two admitting jurisdictions were to proceed against a lawyer for the same conduct, they should, applying this rule, identify the same governing ethics rules. They should take all appropriate steps to see that they do apply the same rule to the same conduct, and in all events should avoid proceeding against a lawyer on the basis of two inconsistent rules.

[7] The choice of law provision applies to lawyers engaged in transnational practice, unless international law, treaties or other agreements between competent regulatory authorities in the affected jurisdictions provide otherwise.

INDEX TO THE ABA MODEL RULES OF PROFESSIONAL CONDUCT

Editors' Note. This index was originally prepared by the American Bar Association following the February 2002 Amendments to the ABA Model Rules of Professional Conduct and has been updated several times since then. The authors of this volume have further enhanced the ABA index by adding some additional terms. For example, the Comment to Rule 5.5 was amended in February 2007 to add a reference to the ABA Model Court Rule on Provision of Legal Services Following Determination of Major Disaster, and we have added new entries to the Index to reflect that amendment. For the 2009 edition, we added references to new provisions in Rule 3.8 that govern a prosecutor's duties upon discovering a wrongful conviction. Finally, for the 2010 edition, we added references to the new screening provisions in Rule 1.10. Finally, for the 2013 edition, we added references to recently adopted changes related to the lawyer's duty of competence, the detection of conflicts of interest, outsourcing, and technology. The index was up to date when we went to press in September 2012.

Funds of client
  handling of, Rule 1.15
  lawyer claims interest in, Rule 1.15(e)
  responsibility of firm, Rule 5.1
    (Comment)

G

Gift to lawyer by client, Rule 1.8(c)
Government agency
  appearance before, Rule 3.9
  communication with, Rule 4.2
    (Comment)
  conflict of interest, Rule 1.11
  constitutes firm, Rule 1.10 (Comment),
    Rule 5.1 (Comment)
  improper influence on, Rule 8.4(e)
  representation of, Rule 1.13 (Comment)
Government lawyer
  authority of, Scope
  communication with accused by, Rule 4.2
    (Comment)
  conflict of interest, Rule 1.11(d)
  duties of, Rule 1.13 (Comment)
  prosecutors, Rule 3.8
  representing multiple clients, Scope
  subject to Rules, Rule 1.11 (Comment)
  supervisory responsibilities, Rule 5.1
    (Comment)
Government legal engagements, Rule 7.6
Guardian of client with diminished capacity
  acting adversely to ward, Rule 1.14
    (Comment)
  appointment of, Rule 1.14(b)

H

Harass, law's procedures used to, Preamble
Harm, disclosure of information to prevent,
  serious bodily, Rule 1.6(b)(1)
Hearing officers. (*See* Adjudicative officers.)
Homicide, disclosure of information to
  prevent, Rule 1.6(b)(1)
Hotlines, Rule 6.5 (Comment)
Hypotheticals, Rule 1.6 (Comment)

I

Identity of client, conflicts of interest, Rule
  1.0 (Comment)
  explaining, Rule 1.13(d)
  government agency, Rule 1.11
    (Comment)
  organization, Rule 1.13 (Comment)

Impartiality and decorum of tribunal, Rule 3.5
Imperatives in rules, Scope
Imputed disqualification
  firm of former judge or other neutral,
    Rule 1.12(c)
  firm of political contributor, Rule 7.6
  former client, Rule 1.9 (Comment)
  general rule, Rule 1.10
  government lawyers, Rule 1.11(b)
  legal services program, Rule 6.5(a)(2),
    Rule 6.5(b)
  prospective client, Rule 1.18(c)
  types of conflicts, Rule 1.8(k)
  witness, when member of firm serves as,
    Rule 3.7(b)
Incompetent client
  appointment of guardian for, Rule
    1.14(b)
  representation of, Rule 1.14(a)
Independence of legal profession,
  Preamble, Rule 5.4
Independent professional judgment, duty to
  exercise, Rule 2.1, Rule 5.4(c), Rule
  5.4(d)(3)
Indigent client
  legal representation, Preamble, Rule 1.2
    (Comment), Rule 6.1
  paying court costs on behalf of, Rule
    1.8(e)(2)
Information
  used to disadvantage of client, Rule 1.8(b)
  withholding from client, Rule 1.4
    (Comment)
"Informed consent," defined, Rule 1.0(e)
Injury, client's intent to commit crime or
  fraud causing substantial financial or
  property, Rule 1.6(b)(1)
Injury, disclosure of information to prevent
  serious bodily, Rule 1.6(b)(1)
Interest, acquisition by lawyer adverse to
  client, Rule 1.8(a)
  in litigation, Rule 1.8(i)
Intimidation by lawyer, prohibitions on,
  Preamble, Rule 3.3 (Comment)
Investigation of client's affairs, Rule 2.1
  (Comment)

J

Judgment, exercise of, Preamble
Judges
  contributions to, Rule 7.6
  duty to show respect for, Preamble

Z

Annotations on
the ABA Model Rules
of Professional
Conduct

ANNOTATIONS ON PREAMBLE AND SCOPE

Canon and Code Antecedents

ABA Canons of Professional Ethics:* The Preamble to the ABA Canons (which had no separate Scope section) provided as follows:

> In America, where the stability of Courts and of all departments of government rests upon the approval of the people, it is peculiarly essential that the system for establishing and dispensing Justice be developed to a high point of efficiency and so maintained that the public shall have absolute confidence in the integrity and impartiality of its administration. The future of the Republic, to a great extent, depends upon our maintenance of Justice pure and unsullied. It cannot be so maintained unless the conduct and the motives of the members of our profession are such as to merit the approval of all just men.
>
> No code or set of rules can be framed, which will particularize all the duties of the lawyer in the varying phases of litigation or in all the relations of professional life. The following canons of ethics are adopted by the American Bar Association as a general guide, yet the enumeration of particular duties should not be construed as a denial of the existence of others equally imperative, though not specifically mentioned.

ABA Model Code of Professional Responsibility: Compare Preamble and Preliminary Statement (reprinted later in this volume).

---

* This and all other excerpts from the ABA Canons of Professional Ethics have been reprinted with permission of the American Bar Association. Copyright © 1956 by the American Bar Association. All rights reserved.

Cross-References in Other Rules

Scope ¶1; 21: "The Comment accompanying each Rule explains and illustrates the meaning and purpose of the Rule. The **Preamble** and this note on Scope provide general orientation. The Comments are intended as guides to interpretation, but the text of each Rule is authoritative."

Rule 1.6, Comment 3: "A lawyer may not disclose such information except as authorized or required by the Rules of Professional Conduct or other law. See also **Scope**."

Rule 1.7, Comment 3: "As to whether a client-lawyer relationship exists or, having once been established, is continuing, see Comment to Rule 1.3 and **Scope**."

Rule 1.13, Comment 9: "Defining precisely the identity of the client and prescribing the resulting obligations of such lawyers may be more difficult in the government context and is a matter beyond the scope of these Rules. See **Scope** [18]. . . . In addition, duties of lawyers employed by the government or lawyers in military service may be defined by statutes and regulation. This Rule does not limit that authority. See **Scope**."

Legislative History of Preamble and Scope

1980 Discussion Draft contained the following Preface:

> The decade past has witnessed an extraordinary concern with professional responsibility. Barely 10 years ago, the American Bar Association adopted its Model Code of Professional Responsibility, the product of a committee chaired by Edward L. Wright. . . . [I]n every sphere one finds searching inquiry into the meaning of professionally responsible conduct.
>
> That inquiry has led to reconsideration of the Model Code, the creation of the Commission on Evaluation of Professional Standards, and, finally, the development of this document — the Discussion Draft of the Model Rules of Professional Conduct.
>
> In reconsidering the concepts of professional standards, the Commission soon realized that more than a series of amendments or a general restatement of the Model Code of Professional Responsibility was in order. The Commission determined that a comprehensive reformulation was required. We have built on the Code's foundation, but we make no apology for having pushed beyond it.

1983 Rules: Most of the Preamble and Scope in the 1983 version were essentially the same as the 2002 version, but the 1983 version contained the following sentence regarding government lawyers near the end of what is now paragraph 18: "They also may have authority to represent the 'public interest' in circumstances where a private lawyer would not be authorized to do so." In addition, paragraph 20 (then paragraph 18) ended with the following sentence rather than the last sentence of the 2002 version: "Accordingly, nothing in the Rule should be deemed to augment any substantive legal duty of lawyers or the extra-disciplinary consequences of violating such a duty." Finally, the 1983 version contained the following two paragraphs that were entirely deleted in 2002:

> [19] Moreover, these Rules are not intended to govern or affect judicial application of either the attorney-client or work product privilege. Those privileges were developed to promote compliance with law and fairness in litigation. In reliance on the attorney-client privilege, clients are entitled to expect that communications within

the scope of the privilege will be protected against compelled disclosure. The attorney-client privilege is that of the client and not of the lawyer. The fact that in exceptional situations the lawyer under the rules has a limited discretion to disclose a client confidence does not vitiate the proposition that, as a general matter, the client has a reasonable expectation that information relating to the client will not be voluntarily disclosed and that disclosure of such information may be judicially compelled only in accordance with recognized exceptions to the attorney-client and work product privileges.

[20] The lawyer's exercise of discretion not to disclose information under Rule 1.6 should not be subject to reexamination. Permitting such reexamination would be incompatible with the general policy of promoting compliance with law through assurances that communications will be protected against disclosure.

2002 Amendments: At its February 2002 Mid-Year Meeting, the ABA House of Delegates adopted without change the ABA Ethics 2000 Commission proposal to amend the Preamble and Scope of the Model Rules of Professional Conduct. Most noteworthy were the addition of paragraph 3, the last sentence in paragraph 9, and the second and last sentences in paragraph 20, plus the deletion of paragraphs 19 and 20 of the former version of the Scope.

Selected State Variations

Arkansas adds the following paragraph to the Preamble:

[13A] A lawyer owes a solemn duty to uphold the integrity and honor of the profession; to encourage respect for the law and for the courts; to act as a member of a learned profession; to conduct affairs so as to reflect credit on the legal profession; and to inspire the confidence, respect and trust of clients and the public. To accomplish those objectives, the lawyer must strive to avoid not only professional impropriety, but also the appearance of impropriety. The duty to avoid the appearance of impropriety is not a mere phrase. It is part of the foundation upon which are built the rules that guide lawyers in their moral and ethical conduct. This obligation should be considered in any instance where a violation of the rules of professional conduct are at issue. The principle pervades these Rules and embodies their spirit.

Colorado: Paragraph 20 of the Scope section provides that, since the Rules establish standards of conduct by lawyers, "in appropriate cases" a lawyer's violation of a Rule may be evidence of breach of the applicable standard of conduct.

Connecticut omits several sentences of paragraph 6 of the Preamble but restores all of paragraphs 19 and 20 from the 1983 version of the Scope section (see Legislative History above).

Delaware, Kansas, North Carolina, Oklahoma, and *Virginia* omit the last sentence of paragraph 20 ("since the Rules do establish standards of conduct by lawyers, a lawyer's violation of a Rule may be evidence of breach of the applicable standard of conduct").

District of Columbia deletes the Preamble entirely and compresses the Scope. The D.C. equivalent to paragraph 20 provides as follows:

Nothing in these Rules, the Comments associated with them, or this Scope section is intended to enlarge or restrict existing law regarding the liability of lawyers to others or the requirements that the testimony of expert witnesses or other modes of proof must be employed in determining the scope of a lawyer's duty to others. Moreover, nothing in the Rules or associated Comments or this Scope section is intended to confer rights on an adversary of a lawyer to enforce the Rules in a proceeding other than a disciplinary proceeding. A tribunal presented with claims that the conduct of a lawyer appearing before that tribunal requires, for example, disqualification of the lawyer and/or the lawyer's firm may take such action as seems appropriate in the circumstances, which may or may not involve disqualification.

The next paragraph of the D.C. Scope section, which has no equivalent in the ABA Model Rules, states standards and principles for interpreting the Rules, including the following:

> In interpreting these Rules, the specific shall control the general in the sense that any rule that specifically addresses conduct shall control the disposition of matters and the outcome of such matters shall not turn upon the application of a more general rule that arguably also applies. [C]ompliance with one rule does not generally excuse compliance with other rules. Accordingly, once a lawyer has analyzed the ethical considerations under a given rule, the lawyer must generally extend the analysis to ensure compliance with all other applicable rules.

Florida omits paragraph 18 of the ABA Scope section, and replaces paragraphs 12 and 13 of the ABA Preamble with the following:

> Lawyers are officers of the court and they are responsible to the judiciary for the propriety of their professional activities. Within that context, the legal profession has been granted powers of self-government. Self-regulation helps maintain the legal profession's independence from undue government domination. An independent legal profession is an important force in preserving government under law, for abuse of legal authority is more readily challenged by a profession whose members are not dependent on the executive and legislative branches of government for the right to practice. Supervision by an independent judiciary, and conformity with the rules the judiciary adopts for the profession, assures both independence and responsibility.
>
> Thus, every lawyer is responsible for observance of the Rules of Professional Conduct. A lawyer should also aid in securing their observance by other lawyers. Neglect of these responsibilities compromises the independence of the profession and the public interest that it serves.

Georgia: In the rules effective November 3, 2011, Rule 1.0 includes definitions for the words "consult," "domestic lawyer," "foreign lawyer," "lawyer," and "nonlawyer."

Illinois deletes a portion of paragraph 6 and adds paragraphs 6A and 6B, which address a lawyer's responsibilities to perform pro bono work. Paragraph 6A specifically references Illinois Supreme Court Rule 756(f), which requires lawyers to disclose on their annual registration form the approximate amount of pro bono work that they performed in the past year. (See also the Illinois entry under Rule 6.1.)

Maryland replaces the last sentence of paragraph 20 by saying that "nothing in this Preamble and Scope is intended to detract from the holdings of the Court of Appeals in *Post v. Bregman*, 349 Md. 142 (1998), and *Son v. Margolius, Mallios, Davis, Rider & Tomar*, 349 Md. 441 (1998)."

Massachusetts: The Scope section, quoting case precedent, provides that "if a plaintiff can demonstrate that a disciplinary rule was intended to protect one in his position, a violation of that rule may be some evidence of the attorney's negligence."

Michigan: Rule 1.0(b), which is comparable to paragraph 20 of the Scope section in the ABA Model Rules, provides as follows:

Failure to comply with an obligation or prohibition imposed by a rule is a basis for invoking the disciplinary process. The rules do not, however, give rise to a cause of action for enforcement of a rule or for damages caused by failure to comply with an obligation or prohibition imposed by a rule. In a civil or criminal action, the admissibility of the Rules of Professional Conduct is governed by the Michigan Rules of Evidence and other provisions of law.

Missouri: Missouri replaces the last sentence of ABA paragraph 20 with the following sentence taken verbatim from the pre-2002 version of the ABA Scope section: "Accordingly, nothing in the Rules should be deemed to augment any substantive legal duty of lawyers or the extra-disciplinary consequences of violating such a duty."

Nevada: Nevada omits the ABA Preamble but adds a new Rule 1.0A entitled "Guidelines for Interpreting the Nevada Rules of Professional Conduct," which begins by saying, "The preamble and comments to the ABA Model Rules of Professional Conduct are not enacted by this Rule but may be consulted for guidance in interpreting and applying the Nevada Rules of Professional Conduct, unless there is a conflict between the Nevada Rules and the preamble or comments." Rule 1.0A then incorporates language from paragraphs 14, 17, 19, and 20 of the Scope section of the ABA Model Rules as guides for interpreting the Nevada Rules.

New Hampshire replaces the entire ABA Preamble and Scope with a "Statement of Purpose" that includes parts of ABA paragraphs 14 and 20 but is otherwise unique to New Hampshire. A special New Hampshire Comment explains that New Hampshire has rejected the ABA Preamble and Scope because of the following perceived "defects" in the ABA language:

> Much of the Preamble and Scope consists of imprecise restatements or summaries of the Rules, which are generally unnecessary, potentially confusing, or both. . . .
>
> Portions of the Preamble and Scope are aspirational in nature, which runs the risk of converting goals into mandates. The Rules will succeed better if the distinction between worthy aspirations and basic mandates is kept clear.
>
> The length and lack of clarity in the wording of the Preamble and Scope materially diminish their utility to their readers.

New York: The Preamble and Scope contain only ten paragraphs, omitting many paragraphs that appear in the Model Rules. Of particular note is a change to paragraph 2. Rather than urging lawyers to "zealously" assert a client's position, the paragraph provides as follows:

> The touchstone of the client-lawyer relationship is the lawyer's obligation to assert the client's position under the rules of the adversary system, to maintain the client's confidential information except in limited circumstances, and to act with loyalty during the period of the representation.

Ohio: In its Preamble, Ohio eliminates paragraphs 7 and 8, most of paragraphs 9 and 10, and all of paragraphs 12 and 13 of the ABA version of the Preamble.

Oklahoma: At the end of paragraph 20, Oklahoma restores all of former paragraphs 19 and 20 from the 1983 version of the ABA Scope section—see Legislative History above.

Pennsylvania adds the following sentences to its Scope section: "The Rules omit some provisions that appear in the ABA Model Rules of Professional Conduct. The omissions should not be interpreted as condoning behavior proscribed by the omitted provision."

Related Materials

ABA Formal Ethics Opinions: See ABA Formal Ethics Ops. 90-358 (1990), 92-365 (1992), 92-366 (1992), 92-368 (1992) (withdrawn), 95-390 (1995), 96-400 (1996), 96-403 (1996), 97-407 (1997), 98-411 n.10 (1998), 00-417 (2000), 02-425 (2002), 04-433 (2004), 06-440 (2006), and 08-453 (2008).

IRS Regulations: The regulations governing practice before the IRS are found at 31 C.F.R. Part 10 (often called "Circular 230"). Section 10.0, entitled "Scope of Part," begins as follows: "This part contains rules governing the recognition of attorneys ... and other persons representing taxpayers before the Internal Revenue Service." When the final regulations were published, see 69 Fed. Reg. 75839 (2004), the Federal Register included the following overall "Explanation of Provisions":

> Tax advisors play a critical role in the Federal tax system, which is founded on principles of compliance and voluntary self-assessment. The tax system is best served when the public has confidence in the honesty and integrity of the professionals providing tax advice. To restore, promote, and maintain the public's confidence in those individuals and firms, these final regulations set forth best practices applicable to all tax advisors. These regulations also provide mandatory requirements for practitioners who provide covered opinions. The scope of these regulations is limited to practice before the IRS. These regulations do not alter or supplant other ethical standards applicable to practitioners.

Restatement of the Law Governing Lawyers: The Restatement has no direct equivalent to the ABA Preamble or Scope, but it does contain a brief Introduction.

ANNOTATIONS ON ARTICLE 1.
CLIENT-LAWYER RELATIONSHIP

Rule 1.0   Terminology

Canon and Code Antecedents

ABA Canons of Professional Ethics: The Canons did not contain any equivalent to the Terminology section.

ABA Model Code of Professional Responsibility: Compare the Definitions following DR 9-102.

Cross-References in Other Rules

Rule 1.4(a): "A lawyer shall promptly inform the client of any decision or circumstance with respect to which the client's informed consent, as defined in **Rule 1.0(e)**, is required by these Rules."

Rule 1.4, Comment 5: "In certain circumstances ... the client must give informed consent, as defined in **Rule 1.0(e)**."

Rule 1.6, Comment 2: "See **Rule 1.0(e)** for the definition of informed consent."

Rule 1.6, Comment 7: "Paragraph (b)(2) is a limited exception to the rule of confidentiality that permits the lawyer to reveal information to the extent necessary to enable affected persons or appropriate authorities to prevent the client from committing a crime or fraud, as defined in **Rule 1.0(d)**. . . ."

Rule 1.7, Comment 1: "For definitions of 'informed consent' and 'confirmed in writing,' see **Rule 1.0(e) and (b)**."

Rule 1.7, Comment 17: "[M]ediation is not a proceeding before a 'tribunal' under **Rule 1.0(m)**."

Rule 1.7, Comment 18: "Informed consent requires that each affected client be aware of the relevant circumstances and of the material and reasonably foreseeable ways that the conflict could have adverse effects on the interests of that client. See **Rule 1.0(e)** (informed consent)."

Rule 1.7, Comment 20: "Paragraph (b) requires the lawyer to obtain the informed consent of the client, confirmed in writing. . . . See **Rule 1.0(b)**. See also **Rule 1.0(n)**. If it is not feasible to obtain or transmit the writing at the time the client gives informed consent, then the lawyer must obtain or transmit it within a reasonable time thereafter. See **Rule 1.0(b)**."

Rule 1.8, Comment 2: For a definition of informed consent, see **Rule 1.0(e)**.

Rule 1.8, Comment 13: See **Rule 1.0(e)** for a definition of informed consent.

Rule 1.9, Comment 9: "The provisions of this Rule are for the protection of former clients and can be waived if the client gives informed consent, which consent must be confirmed in writing under paragraphs (a) and (b). See **Rule 1.0(e)**."

Rule 1.10, Comment 1: "For purposes of the Rules of Professional Conduct, the term 'firm' denotes lawyers in a law partnership, professional corporation, sole proprietorship or other association authorized to practice law; or lawyers employed in a legal services organization or the legal department of a corporation or other organization. See **Rule 1.0** (c). Whether two or more lawyers constitute a firm within this definition can depend on the specific facts. . . . See **Rule 1.0**, Comments [2]-[4]."

Rule 1.10, Comment 4: Paragraph (a) does not "prohibit representation if the lawyer is prohibited from acting because of events before the person became a lawyer . . . Such persons, however, ordinarily must be screened from any personal participation in the matter to avoid communication to others in the firm of confidential information that both the nonlawyers and the firm have a legal duty to protect. See **Rules 1.0(k)** and 5.3."

Rule 1.10, Comment 6: "For a definition of informed consent, see **Rule 1.0(e)**."

Rule 1.10, Comment 7: "A description of effective screening mechanisms appears in **Rule 1.0(k)**."

Rule 1.11, Comment 1: "See **Rule 1.0(e)** for the definition of informed consent."

Rule 1.11, Comment 6: "Paragraphs (b) and (c) contemplate a screening arrangement. See **Rule 1.0(k)** (requirements for screening procedures)."

Rule 1.12, Comment 2: "This Rule forbids such representation unless all of the parties to the proceedings give their informed consent, confirmed in writing. See **Rule 1.0(e) and (b)**."

Rule 1.12, Comment 4: "Requirements for screening procedures are stated in **Rule 1.0(k)**."

Rule 1.13, Comment 3: "As defined in **Rule 1.0(f)**, knowledge can be inferred from circumstances. . . ."

Rule 1.17, Comment 11: A lawyer selling a law practice has an "obligation to avoid disqualifying conflicts, and to secure the client's informed consent for those conflicts that can be agreed to (see Rule 1.7 regarding conflicts and **Rule 1.0(e)** for the definition of informed consent)."

Rule 1.18, Comment 5: "See **Rule 1.0(e)** for the definition of informed consent."

Rule 1.18, Comment 7: "[I]mputation may be avoided if the conditions of paragraph (d)(2) are met and all disqualified lawyers are timely screened and written notice is promptly given to the prospective client. See **Rule 1.0(k)** (requirements for screening procedures)."

Rule 2.3, Comment 5: "Where, however, it is reasonably likely that providing the evaluation will affect the client's interests materially and adversely, the lawyer must first obtain the client's consent after the client has been adequately informed concerning the important possible effects on the client's interests. See Rules 1.6(a) and **1.0(e)**."

Rule 2.4, Comment 5: "When the dispute-resolution process takes place before a tribunal, as in binding arbitration (see **Rule 1.0(m)**), the lawyer's duty of candor is governed by Rule 3.3."

Rule 3.3, Comment 1: "See **Rule 1.0(m)** for the definition of tribunal."

Rule 3.3, Comment 8: "A lawyer's knowledge that evidence is false, however, can be inferred from the circumstances. See **Rule 1.0(f)**."

Rule 3.5, Comment 5: "The duty to refrain from disruptive conduct applies to any proceeding of a tribunal, including a deposition. See **Rule 1.0(m)**."

Rule 3.7, Comment 6: "See **Rule 1.0(b)** for the definition of 'confirmed in writing' and **Rule 1.0(e)** for the definition of 'informed consent.' "

Rule 4.2, Comment 8: "The prohibition on communications with a represented person only applies in circumstances where the lawyer knows that the person is in fact represented in the matter to be discussed. This means that the lawyer has actual knowledge of the fact of the representation; but such actual knowledge may be inferred from the circumstances. See **Rule 1.0(f)**."

Rule 5.1, Comment 1: "Paragraph (a) applies to lawyers who have managerial authority over the professional work of a firm. See **Rule 1.0(c)**."

Legislative History of Terminology

1983 Terminology: As originally adopted in 1983, Rule 1.0 was called "Terminology" but was not given a rule number and did not include any Comment.

The only terms originally defined were: "Belief" or "believes"; "Consult" or "consultation"; "Firm" or "law firm"; "fraud" or "fraudulent"; "Knowingly," "known," or "knows"; "Partner"; "Reasonable" or "reasonably"; "reasonable belief" or "reasonably believes"; "Reasonably should know"; and "Substantial." As defined in 1983, the terms "Consult" or "consultation," "Firm" or "law firm," "Fraud," and "Partner" had the following meanings:

> (b) "Consult" or "consultation" denotes communication of information reasonably sufficient to permit the client to appreciate the significance of the matter in question.
>
> (c) "Firm" or "law firm" denotes a lawyer or lawyers in a private firm, lawyers employed in the legal department of a corporation or other organization and lawyers employed in a legal services organization. See Comment, Rule 1.10.

(d) "Fraud" or "fraudulent" denotes conduct having a purpose to deceive and not merely negligent misrepresentation or failure to apprise another of relevant information.

(g) "Partner" denotes a member of a partnership and a shareholder in a law firm organized as a professional corporation.

2002 Amendments: At its February 2002 Mid-Year Meeting, the ABA House of Delegates adopted, with only minor changes, the ABA Ethics 2000 Commission proposals to add, delete, or amend various definitions in the Terminology section, to add the entire Comment to the Terminology section, and to designate the Terminology section as "Rule 1.0." The ABA made no changes to the definitions of "Belief" or "believes"; "Knowingly," "known," or "knows"; "Reasonable" or "reasonably"; "Reasonable belief" or "reasonably believes"; "Reasonably should know"; and "Substantial." But the definitions of "Firm" or "law firm," "Fraud," and "Partner" were amended; the definitions of "Confirmed in writing," "Informed consent," "Screened," "Tribunal," and "Writing" were added; and the definition of "Consult" or "consultation" was deleted.

2009 Amendments: In February 2009, the ABA House of Delegates adopted a minor amendment to Comment 8 to include a reference to the new screening provision in Model Rule 1.10. (For related information, see "2009 Amendments to Model Rule 1.10" in the Legislative History following Rule 1.10.)

2012 Amendments: In August 2012, the ABA House of Delegates adopted without change proposals by the ABA Commission on Ethics 20/20 to amend Rule 1.0(n) and Comment 9 to Rule 1.0. The definition of a "writing" in Rule 1.0(n) was updated to include all "electronic communications," not just "email." Comment 9 was amended to emphasize that, when employing a screen under Rule 1.0(k), lawyers need to take appropriate measures to deny access by the screened lawyer to firm files or other information — "including information in electronic form" — relating to the screened matter.

Selected State Variations

Alaska: Rule 9.1 (Alaska's terminology rule) adds an unusually detailed definition of "substantially related matters" to help guide lawyers in their assessment of conflicts of interest. The definition draws, in part, on Comment 3 to Model Rule 1.9.

Connecticut adds: " 'Client' or 'person' as used in these Rules includes an authorized representative unless otherwise stated."

District of Columbia defines "matter" as "any litigation, administrative proceeding, lobbying activity, application, claim, investigation, arrest, charge or accusation, the drafting of a contract, a negotiation, estate or family relationship practice issue, or any other representation, except as expressly limited in a particular Rule."

Massachusetts: Rule 9.1 retains the 1983 version of the ABA Terminology and adds a definition of "Qualified legal assistance organization." Amended Comment 3 to Rule 9.1 provides as follows: "The final category of qualified legal assistance organization requires that the organization 'receives no profit from the rendition of legal services.' That condition refers to the entire legal services operation of the organization; it does not prohibit the receipt of a court-awarded fee that would result in a 'profit' from that particular lawsuit."

New York adds definitions for the terms "advertisement," "computer-accessed communication," "differing interests," "domestic relations matters," "matter," "person," "reasonable lawyers," and "sexual relations." New York also includes a more detailed definition of "fraud," providing as follows:

> "Fraud" or "fraudulent" denotes conduct that is fraudulent under the substantive or procedural law of the applicable jurisdiction or has a purpose to deceive, provided that it does not include conduct that, although characterized as fraudulent by statute or administrative rule, lacks an element of scienter, deceit, intent to mislead, or knowing failure to correct misrepresentations that can be reasonably expected to induce detrimental reliance by another.

In addition, New York's definition of "confirmed in writing" includes "a statement by the person made on the record of any proceeding before a tribunal."

Ohio: Rule 1.0 defines "fraud" and "fraudulent" as denoting "conduct that has an intent to deceive and is either of the following:"

> (1) an actual or implied misrepresentation of a material fact that is made either with knowledge of its falsity or with such utter disregard and recklessness about its falsity that knowledge may be inferred; (2) a knowing concealment of a material fact where there is a duty to disclose the material fact.

Oregon adds or alters the meaning of a number of phrases, including "electronic communication," "informed consent," "law firm," "knowingly," and "matter."

Texas generally retains the 1983 version of the ABA Terminology, but modifies some of the 1983 definitions and adds others that are neither in the 1983 nor current versions of the ABA Terminology. Specifically, Texas includes the following definitions:

> "Adjudicatory Official" denotes a person who serves on a Tribunal.
> "Adjudicatory Proceeding" denotes the consideration of a matter by a Tribunal.
> "Competent" or "Competence" denotes possession or the ability to timely acquire the legal knowledge, skill, and training reasonably necessary for the representation of the client.
> "Firm" or "Law firm" denotes a lawyer or lawyers in a private firm; or a lawyer or lawyers employed in the legal department of a corporation, legal services organization, or other organization, or in a unit of government.
> "Fitness" denotes those qualities of physical, mental and psychological health that enable a person to discharge a lawyer's responsibilities to clients in conformity with the Texas Disciplinary Rules of Professional Conduct. Normally a lack of fitness is indicated most clearly by a persistent inability to discharge, or unreliability in carrying out, significant obligations.
> "Should know" when used in reference to a lawyer denotes that a reasonable lawyer under the same or similar circumstances would know the matter in question.
> "Substantial" when used in reference to degree or extent denotes a matter of meaningful significance or involvement.
> "Tribunal" denotes any governmental body or official or any other person engaged in a process of resolving a particular dispute or controversy. "Tribunal" includes such institutions as courts and administrative agencies when engaging in adjudicatory or licensing activities as defined by applicable law or rules of practice or procedure, as well as judges, magistrates, special masters, referees, arbitrators, mediators, hearing officers and comparable persons empowered to resolve or to recommend a resolution of a particular matter; but it does not include jurors, prospective jurors, legislative bodies or their committees, members or staffs, nor does

it include other governmental bodies when acting in a legislative or rule-making capacity.

Virginia retains the 1983 version of the Terminology section and adds: "'Should' when used in reference to a lawyer's action denotes an aspirational rather than a mandatory standard."

Wisconsin: Wisconsin adds or alters the meaning of a number of phrases, including "consultation," "firm," "misrepresentation," and "prosecutor."

Related Materials

ABA Formal Ethics Opinions: See, for example, ABA Formal Ethics Ops. 94-388 n.4 (1994), 95-390 (1995), 95-396 (1995), 98-411 (1998), 99-415 (1999), 04-433 (2004), 06-441 n.17 (2006), 11-460 (2011). (*Note: Opinions issued before 2002 refer to "Terminology," not to Rule 1.0. — Eds.*)

Model Rules of Professional Conduct for Federal Lawyers* add definitions of the terms "Federal Agency," "Federal lawyer," "Government lawyer," "Non-Government lawyer," and "Supervisory lawyer." The term "Government lawyer" is defined to mean "an individual who is a member of the bar . . . who represents persons before a Federal Agency," but the definition adds: "When a Government lawyer is engaged in the private practice of law or pro bono representation not related to the Government lawyer's official duties, the lawyer is considered a Non-Government lawyer."

Restatement of the Law Governing Lawyers: The Restatement does not have a separate Terminology section. Rather, the Restatement defines terms as needed within particular sections — see, for example, §87(1) (defining "work product") in our chapter on the Restatement later in this volume.

Rule 1.1   Competence

Canon and Code Antecedents

ABA Canons of Professional Ethics: No comparable Canon.
ABA Model Code of Professional Responsibility: Compare DR 6-101 (reprinted later in this volume).

Cross-References in Other Rules

Rule 1.2, Comment 7: Limited representation "is a factor to be considered when determining the legal knowledge, skill, thoroughness and preparation reasonably necessary for the representation (see **Rule 1.1**)."

---

* This and all other excerpts from the Model Rules of Professional Conduct for Federal Lawyers, copyright © 1990 Federal Bar Association, 1815 H Street, NW, Washington, D.C. 20006-3697, have been directly quoted here with the permission of the Federal Bar Association.

Rule 1.2, Comment 8: "All agreements concerning a lawyer's representation of a client must accord with the Rules of Professional Conduct and other law (see **Rules 1.1**, 1.8 and 5.6)."

Rule 1.5, Comment 7: "A lawyer should only refer a matter to a lawyer whom the referring lawyer reasonably believes is competent to handle the matter (see **Rule 1.1**)."

Rule 1.6, Comment 18: "A lawyer must act competently to safeguard information relating to the representation of a client against inadvertent or unauthorized disclosure by the lawyer or other persons who are participating in the representation of the client or who are subject to the lawyer's supervision (see **Rules 1.1**, 5.1 and 5.3)."

Rule 1.7, Comment 15: In the case of a conflict of interest, "representation is prohibited if in the circumstances the lawyer cannot reasonably conclude that the lawyer will be able to provide competent and diligent representation (see **Rules 1.1** and 1.3)."

Rule 1.17, Comment 11: A lawyer selling a law practice has an "obligation to exercise competence in identifying a purchaser qualified to assume the practice and the purchaser's obligation to undertake the representation competently (see **Rule 1.1**)."

Rule 1.18, Comment 9: "For the duty of competence of a lawyer who gives assistance on the merits of a matter to a prospective client, see **Rule 1.1**."

Rule 5.3, Comment 1: "Paragraph (a) requires lawyers with managerial authority within a law firm to make reasonable efforts to ensure that the firm has in effect measures giving reasonable assurance that nonlawyers in the firm and nonlawyers outside the firm who work on firm matters will act in a way compatible with the professional obligations of the lawyer. See Comment 6 to **Rule 1.1** (retaining lawyers outside the firm) and Comment 1 to Rule 5.1 (responsibilities with respect to lawyers within a firm)."

Rule 5.3, Comment 3: "The extent of this obligation will depend upon the circumstances, including the education, experience and reputation of the nonlawyer; the nature of the services involved; the terms of any arrangements concerning the protection of client information; and the legal and ethical environments of the jurisdictions in which the services will be performed, particularly with regard to confidentiality. See also **Rules 1.1** (competence), 1.2 (allocation of authority), 1.4 (communication with client), 1.6 (confidentiality), 5.4(a) (professional independence of the lawyer), and 5.5(a) (unauthorized practice of law)."

Rule 6.2, Comment 2: A lawyer has good cause to decline appointment by a court to represent a person "if the lawyer could not handle the matter competently, see **Rule 1.1**. . . ."

Legislative History of Model Rule 1.1

1979 Unofficial Pre-Circulation Draft:

. . . (b) A lawyer acts incompetently in a particular matter, if:

(i) He or she fails to use the knowledge, skill, preparation, and judgment that a reasonably competent lawyer would use in the circumstances; and

(ii) The result of the lawyer's act or failure to act is substantial expense, delay, harm, or risk of harm to a client or other person for whose benefit the advice or assistance is provided.

1980 Discussion Draft: "A lawyer shall undertake representation only in matters in which the lawyer can act with adequate competence. . . ."

1981 Draft defined competence to include "efficiency."

1982 Draft was adopted.

2002 Amendments: At its February 2002 Mid-Year Meeting, the ABA House of Delegates adopted without change the ABA Ethics 2000 Commission proposal to amend Comment 6 to Rule 1.1 to say that lawyers should "keep abreast of changes in the law and its practice" and comply with CLE requirements. (The Ethics 2000 Commission did not propose any changes to the text of Rule 1.1.)

2012 Amendments: At its August 2012 Annual Meeting, the ABA House of Delegates adopted without change proposals by the ABA Commission on Ethics 20/20 to add two new Comments to Rule 1.1 and to revise an existing Comment. The two new Comments — Comments 6 and 7 — were designed to give lawyers more guidance regarding their ethical obligations when outsourcing work to lawyers in other firms. The revision to former Comment 6 (now renumbered as Comment 8) was intended to remind lawyers that their duty of competence includes a duty to understand technology relevant to their particular practice areas.

Selected State Variations

Alabama: Effective March 26, 2012, Rule 1.1 explains that, when a lawyer and client agree to limit the scope of a lawyer's representation, the lawyer's duty of competence is limited to "the knowledge, skill, thoroughness, and preparation reasonably necessary for such limited representation."

California: Rule 3-110 (Failing to Act Competently) provides as follows:

(A) A member shall not intentionally, recklessly, or repeatedly fail to perform legal services with competence.

(B) For purposes of this rule, "competence" in any legal service shall mean to apply the 1) diligence, 2) learning and skill, and 3) mental, emotional, and physical ability reasonably necessary for the performance of such service.

(C) If a member does not have sufficient learning and skill when the legal service is undertaken, the member may nonetheless perform such services competently by 1) associating with or, where appropriate, professionally consulting another lawyer reasonably believed to be competent, or 2) by acquiring sufficient learning and skill before performance is required.

District of Columbia: Rule 1.1(a) is identical to ABA Model Rule 1.1, but D.C. adds Rule 1.1(b), which states: "A lawyer shall serve a client with skill and care commensurate with that generally afforded to clients by other lawyers in similar matters."

Michigan: Rule 1.1 retains some language from DR 6-101 of the ABA Model Code of Professional Responsibility.

New Hampshire: New Hampshire defines competence in detail, providing a long list of requirements that a lawyer must satisfy in order to achieve "legal competence."

New Jersey: Rule 1.1 provides that a lawyer shall not:

(a) Handle or neglect a matter entrusted to the lawyer in such manner that the lawyer's conduct constitutes gross negligence.

(b) Exhibit a pattern of negligence or neglect in the lawyer's handling of legal matters generally.

New York: New York substitutes the word "should" for "shall" and adds paragraphs (b) and (c), which are based on DR 6-101 and DR 7-101 of the old ABA Model Code.

Texas: Rule 1.01 provides as follows:

(a) A lawyer shall not accept or continue employment in a legal matter which the lawyer knows or should know is beyond the lawyer's competence, unless:

(1) another lawyer who is competent to handle the matter is, with the prior informed consent of the client, associated in the matter; or

(2) the advice or assistance of the lawyer is reasonably required in an emergency and the lawyer limits the advice and assistance to that which is reasonably necessary in the circumstances.

(b) In representing a client, a lawyer shall not:

(1) neglect a legal matter entrusted to the lawyer; or

(2) frequently fail to carry out completely the obligations that the lawyer owes to a client or clients.

(c) As used in this Rule, "neglect" signifies inattentiveness involving a conscious disregard for the responsibilities owed to a client or clients.

Related Materials

ABA Formal Ethics Opinions: See ABA Formal Ethics Ops. 87-354 (1987), 87-355 (1987), 92-362 (1992), 93-379 (1993), 96-399 (1996), 98-411 n.2 (1998), 03-431 (2003), 06-441 (2006), 07-448 (2007), 08-450 n.3 (2008), 08-451 (2008), 11-459 (2011), and 11-461 (2011).

ABA Guidelines for Appointment and Performance of Defense Counsel in Death Penalty Cases: Because capital cases are extraordinarily complex and demanding, defense counsel must possess a significantly greater degree of skill and experience than is required in most noncapital cases. To provide guidance for capital defense lawyers and capital defense programs, in 1989 the ABA House of Delegates adopted Guidelines for the Appointment and Performance of Defense Counsel in Death Penalty Cases. In 2003, the Guidelines were extensively amended. The Reporter for the amended Guidelines was Professor Eric Freedman of Hofstra University School of Law. Amended Guideline 1.1, entitled "Objective and Scope of Guidelines," provides as follows:

A. The objective of these Guidelines is to set forth a national standard of practice for the defense of capital cases in order to ensure high quality legal representation for all persons facing the possible imposition or execution of a death sentence by any jurisdiction.

B. These Guidelines apply from the moment the client is taken into custody and extend to all stages of every case in which the jurisdiction may be entitled to seek the death penalty, including initial and ongoing investigation, pretrial proceedings, trial, post-conviction review, clemency proceedings, and any connected litigation.

Guideline 2.1 urges each jurisdiction to "adopt and implement a plan formalizing the means by which high quality legal representation in death penalty cases is to be provided in accordance with these Guidelines." Remaining Guidelines establish (among other things) counsel's duties to be fully educated in the relevant fields of law, to conduct a complete investigation, to consider and thoroughly investigate all legal claims potentially available, to make full use of nonlawyer resources, and to cooperate with the legal strategies chosen by successor counsel, even if successor counsel seeks to prove that original counsel provided ineffective assistance.

Guidelines substantially similar to the ABA Guidelines have been adopted by the Alabama Circuit Court Judges Conference, the Georgia Public Defender Standards Council (except where the ABA Guidelines conflict with Georgia law), the State Bar of Texas (which adds two sections specific to Texas), the Nevada Supreme Court, and the Oregon Office of Public Defense Services. In Arizona, Rule 6.8(b)(1) of the Arizona Rules of Criminal Procedure provides that to be eligible for appointment as lead counsel in a capital case, an attorney must "be familiar with and guided by the performance standards in the 2003 American Bar Association Guidelines for the Appointment and Performance of Defense Counsel in Death Penalty Cases." The Guidelines have also been adopted by the National Association of Criminal Defense Lawyers (NACDL). The complete ABA Guidelines, together with extensive commentary and background, are available both in print at 31 Hofstra L. Rev. 913 (2003) and online at *www.probono.net/deathpenalty/*. A list showing which jurisdictions have implemented the Guidelines is available at *www.probono.net/deathpenalty/about/item.80-Guidelines_Implementation_Fact_Sheet.*

ABA Model Rule for Minimum Continuing Legal Education (MCLE): In 1986, the ABA House of Delegates approved a resolution declaring that the ABA supports mandatory continuing legal education for all active lawyers and urging states without mandatory MCLE to seriously consider its adoption. In 1987, the ABA House of Delegates approved a Model Rule for Minimum Continuing Legal Education.

Today, 44 states have adopted mandatory continuing legal education programs that require lawyers to take a minimum number of hours of CLE each year. (The most recent is New Jersey, where lawyers were first required to report CLE hours in 2011.) Nearly all of these states require that a portion of the MCLE hours be devoted to "ethics" or "professionalism." Many states adopted their MCLE programs after the ABA passed the 1986 resolution described above in support of MCLE. The only jurisdictions that have not adopted mandatory CLE are Connecticut, the District of Columbia, Hawaii, Maryland, Massachusetts, Michigan, and South Dakota. Michigan is the only state that has repealed an MCLE program; in 1994, after trying MCLE for a few years, the Michigan Supreme Court dropped the program as "ineffective."

Some states require mandatory CLE specifically regarding substance abuse and mental health. For example, California requires lawyers to take one hour of CLE every three years concerning the detection and prevention of substance abuse. Florida requires lawyers to take five hours of CLE every three years in ethics, professionalism, substance abuse, or mental health awareness. North Carolina requires one hour of CLE every three years relating to substance abuse or mental health. Ohio requires all law students to take a one-time, one-hour session on substance abuse in order to sit for the Ohio bar exam.

For a clickable map linking to each state's MCLE requirements, the full text of the ABA Model Rule for Minimum Continuing Legal Education, and other useful materials about CLE programs, see *http://www.americanbar.org/publications_cle/mandatory_cle.html.*

ABA Resolution on Legal Education: The ABA has expressed a strong interest in legal education for nearly a century. At its August 2011 Annual Meeting, for example, the House of Delegates adopted a resolution urging legal education providers to "implement curricular programs intended to develop practice ready lawyers including, but not limited to enhanced capstone and clinical courses that include client meetings and court appearances."

ABA Standards for Criminal Justice: The following Standard is related to ABA Model Rule 1.1:

Standard 4-6.1 Duty to Explore Disposition Without Trial

(a) Whenever the law, nature, and circumstances of the case permit, defense counsel should explore the possibility of an early diversion of the case from the criminal process through the use of other community agencies.

(b) Defense counsel may engage in plea discussions with the prosecutor. Under no circumstances should defense counsel recommend to a defendant acceptance of a plea unless appropriate investigation and study of the case has been completed, including an analysis of controlling law and the evidence likely to be introduced at trial.

*ABA Standards for Imposing Lawyer Sanctions:** The following ABA Standards for Imposing Lawyer Sanctions provide are relevant to Rule 1.1:

4.51. Disbarment is generally appropriate when a lawyer's course of conduct demonstrates that the lawyer does not understand the most fundamental legal doctrines or procedures, and the lawyer's conduct causes injury or potential injury to a client.

4.52. Suspension is generally appropriate when a lawyer engages in an area of practice in which the lawyer knows he or she is not competent, and causes injury or potential injury to a client.

ABA Standards for the Operation of a Telephone Hotline: In 2001, the ABA adopted Standards for the Operation of a Telephone Hotline Providing Legal Advice and Information. The Standards contain rules and extensive comments covering such topics as "Confidentiality and Expectations of Privacy," "Third Party Callers," "Prompt Service," "Managing Backlogs," "Referrals to Non-Legal Resources," "Identifying Callers," and "Emergency Matters."

ABA Task Force on the Future of Legal Education: In August 2012, the ABA appointed an 18-member Task Force on the Future of Legal Education. The Task Force plans to spend two years examining how well law schools are meeting the needs of the profession.

IRS Regulations: In the regulations governing practice before the Internal Revenue Service, 31 C.F.R. §10.33(a) provides that tax advisors should adhere to a series of "best practices," including these:

(2) Establishing the facts, determining which facts are relevant, evaluating the reasonableness of any assumptions or representations, relating the applicable law (including potentially applicable judicial doctrines) to the relevant facts, and arriving at a conclusion supported by the law and the facts.

* This and all subsequent ABA Standards for Imposing Lawyer Sanctions are copyright © 1986 by the American Bar Association. All rights reserved. Reprinted with permission of the American Bar Association.

(3) Advising the client regarding the import of the conclusions reached, including, for example, whether a taxpayer may avoid accuracy-related penalties under the Internal Revenue Code if a taxpayer acts in reliance on the advice.

Law School Accreditation: The ABA Section of Legal Education and Admissions to the Bar was established in 1879 as one of the ABA's first committees. The Section promulgates Standards and Rules of Procedure for Approval of Law Schools. The Preface to the Standards states: "Concern for improving the competence of those entering the legal profession was a major reason for creating the American Bar Association in 1878. The Standards for Approval of Law Schools are promulgated to serve that objective."

The Standards for approval of law schools are highly influential. In 1952, the United States Department of Education approved the Council of the ABA Section of Legal Education and Admissions to the Bar as the recognized national agency for accrediting law schools. Each state's bar admission authority decides whether to require graduation from an ABA-approved law school as a condition for taking the bar exam or gaining admission to the bar, but a majority of states rely upon ABA approval of a law school to determine whether a bar applicant has satisfied the state's legal education requirement. The Standards and related materials about law schools are available at *http://www.americanbar.org/groups/legal_education/resources/standards.html.*

Malpractice: A lawyer who violates Rule 1.1 by failing to provide "competent representation" may be committing legal malpractice. According to §48 of the Restatement of the Law Governing Lawyers (reprinted later in this book), a lawyer is liable to a person for legal malpractice (also called "professional negligence") if (i) the lawyer "owes a duty of care" to the person, and (ii) the lawyer "fails to exercise care," and (iii) the failure to exercise care is "a legal cause of injury" to the person. Restatement §§51, 50, 52, and 53 elaborate on these elements. For a prominent treatise on legal malpractice, see Ronald E. Mallen & Jeffrey M. Smith, Legal Malpractice (Thomson West 2012 ed.).

Malpractice Insurance: In 2004, the ABA House of Delegates narrowly adopted an ABA Model Court Rule on Insurance Disclosure. Where adopted, the rule requires lawyers in private practice to notify the jurisdiction's highest court annually whether the lawyer "is currently covered by professional liability insurance [and] . . . intends to maintain insurance. . . ." For more information about the Model Court Rule, see the Related Materials following ABA Model Rule 1.8 later in this book.

Restatement of the Law Governing Lawyers: See Restatement §§16(2), 29(2), 48, 49, 50, 52, 53, and 54(1) in our chapter on the Restatement later in this volume.

Sixth Amendment: The Sixth Amendment to the United States Constitution guarantees criminal defendants "the assistance of counsel" for their defense. This phrase has consistently been interpreted to guarantee the "effective" assistance of counsel, which means that lawyers for criminal defendants must perform at a certain minimum level of competence to satisfy the Sixth Amendment guarantee of effective assistance. If a convicted defendant believes that a lawyer was ineffective, the defendant can challenge the conviction. In *Strickland v. Washington,* 466 U.S. 668 (1984), the Supreme Court said that whether a lawyer was "ineffective" depended on "whether, in light of all the circumstances, the identified acts or omissions were outside the wide range of professionally competent assistance." ABA Model Rule 1.1 may help to determine the range of professionally "competent" assistance.

Rule 1.2   Scope of Representation and Allocation of Authority Between Client and Lawyer

Canon and Code Antecedents

ABA Canons of Professional Ethics: Canons 16, 24, and 32 provided as follows:

16.   Restraining Clients from Improprieties

A lawyer should use his best efforts to restrain and to prevent his clients from doing those things which the lawyer himself ought not to do, particularly with reference to their conduct towards Courts, judicial officers, jurors, witnesses and suitors. If a client persists in such wrongdoing the lawyer should terminate their relation.

24.   Right of Lawyer to Control the Incidents of the Trial

As to incidental matters pending the trial, not affecting the merits of the cause, or working substantial prejudice to the rights of the client, such as forcing the opposite lawyer to trial when he is under affliction or bereavement; forcing the trial on a particular day to the injury of the opposite lawyer when no harm will result from a trial at a different time; agreeing to an extension of time for signing a bill of exceptions, cross interrogatories and the like, the lawyer must be allowed to judge. In such matters no client has a right to demand that his counsel shall be illiberal, or that he do anything therein repugnant to his own sense of honor and propriety.

32.   The Lawyer's Duty in Its Last Analysis

No client, corporate or individual, however powerful, nor any cause, civil or political, however important, is entitled to receive nor should any lawyer render any service or advice involving disloyalty to the law whose ministers we are, or disrespect of the judicial office, which we are bound to uphold, or corruption of any person or persons exercising a public office or private trust, or deception or betrayal of the public. When rendering any such improper service or advice, the lawyer invites and merits stern and just condemnation. Correspondingly, he advances the honor of his profession and the best interests of his client when he renders service or gives advice tending to impress upon the client and his undertaking exact compliance with the strictest principles of moral law. He must also observe and advise his client to observe the statute law, though until a statute shall have been construed and interpreted by competent adjudication, he is free and is entitled to advise as to its validity and as to what he conscientiously believes to be its just meaning and extent. But above all a lawyer will find his highest honor in a deserved reputation for fidelity to private trust and to public duty, as an honest man and as a patriotic and loyal citizen.

ABA Model Code of Professional Responsibility: Compare DR 2-110(C)(1)(c), DR 7-101(A)(1), DR 7-101(B)(1), DR 7-102(A)(6)-(7), DR 7-106, and DR 9-101(C) (reprinted later in this volume).

Cross-References in Other Rules

Rule 1.0, Comment 6: "Many of the Rules of Professional Conduct require the lawyer to obtain the informed consent of a client or other person before accepting or continuing representation or pursuing a course of conduct (see **Rules 1.2(c)**, 1.6(a) and 1.7(b))."

Rule 1.1, Comment 5: "An agreement between the lawyer and the client regarding the scope of the representation may limit the matters for which the lawyer is responsible. See **Rule 1.2(c)**."

Rule 1.1, Comment 6: "Before a lawyer retains or contracts with other lawyers outside the lawyer's own firm to provide or assist in the provision of legal services to a client, the lawyer should ordinarily obtain informed consent from the client and must reasonably believe that the other lawyers' services will contribute to the competent and ethical representation of the client. See also **Rules 1.2** (allocation of authority), 1.4 (communication with client), 1.5(e) (fee sharing), 1.6 (confidentiality), and 5.5(a) (unauthorized practice of law)."

Rule 1.1, Comment 7: "When lawyers from more than one law firm are providing legal services to the client on a particular matter, the lawyers ordinarily should consult with each other and the client about the scope of their respective representations and the allocation of responsibility among them. See **Rule 1.2**."

Rule 1.3, Comment 1: "A lawyer may have authority to exercise professional discretion in determining the means by which a matter should be pursued. See **Rule 1.2**."

Rule 1.3, Comment 4: "Whether the lawyer is obligated to prosecute the appeal for the client depends on the scope of the representation the lawyer has agreed to provide to the client. See **Rule 1.2**."

Rule 1.4, Comment 2: "If these Rules require that a particular decision about the representation be made by the client, paragraph (a)(1) requires that the lawyer promptly consult with and secure the client's consent prior to taking action unless prior discussions with the client have resolved what action the client wants the lawyer to take. See **Rule 1.2(a)**."

Rule 1.6, Comment 7: "Although paragraph (b)(2) does not require the lawyer to reveal the client's misconduct, the lawyer may not counsel or assist the client in conduct the lawyer knows is criminal or fraudulent. See **Rule 1.2(d)**."

Rule 1.6, Comment 17: Some Rules require "disclosure of information relating to a client's representation to accomplish the purposes specified in paragraphs (b)(1) through (b)(6), only if such disclosure would be permitted by paragraph (b). See **Rules 1.2(d)**, 4.1(b), 8.1 and 8.3."

Rule 1.7, Comment 32: "Any limitations on the scope of the representation made necessary as a result of the common representation should be fully explained to the clients at the outset of the representation. See **Rule 1.2(c)**."

Rule 1.8, Comment 5: It is prohibited to partake in the "disadvantageous use of client information unless the client gives informed consent, except as permitted or required by these Rules. See **Rules 1.2(d)**, 1.6, 1.9(c), 3.3, 4.1(b), 8.1 and 8.3."

Rule 1.8, Comment 13: "**Rule 1.2(a)** protects each client's right to have the final say in deciding whether to accept or reject an offer of settlement and in deciding whether to enter a guilty or nolo contendere plea in a criminal case."

Rule 1.8, Comment 14: "An agreement in accordance with **Rule 1.2** that defines the scope of the representation" is not prohibited.

Rule 1.13, Comment 6: "If the lawyer's services are being used by an organization to further a crime or fraud by the organization. . . . **Rule 1.2(d)** may also be applicable," and withdrawal may be required.

Rule 1.14, Comment 4: "If the lawyer represents the guardian as distinct from the ward, and is aware that the guardian is acting adversely to the ward's interest, the lawyer may have an obligation to prevent or rectify the guardian's misconduct. See **Rule 1.2(d)**."

Rule 1.16, Comment 1: "Ordinarily, a representation in a matter is completed when the agreed-upon assistance has been concluded. See **Rules 1.2(c)** and 6.5."

Rule 2.3, Comment 1: "An evaluation may be performed at the client's direction or when impliedly authorized in order to carry out the representation. See **Rule 1.2**."

Rule 3.3, Comment 3: "The obligation prescribed in **Rule 1.2(d)** not to counsel a client to commit or assist the client in committing a fraud applies in litigation. Regarding compliance with **Rule 1.2(d)**, see the Comment to that Rule."

Rule 3.3, Comment 11: The alternative to disclosing a client's deception to the court or to the other party "is that the lawyer cooperate in deceiving the court, thereby subverting the truth-finding process which the adversary system is designed to implement. See **Rule 1.2(d)**."

Rule 4.1, Comment 3: "Under **Rule 1.2(d)**, a lawyer is prohibited from counseling or assisting a client in conduct that the lawyer knows is criminal or fraudulent. Paragraph (b) states a specific application of the principle set forth in **Rule 1.2(d)**. . . ."

Rule 4.4, Comment 3: "Where a lawyer is not required by applicable law to do so, the decision to voluntarily return such a document is a matter of professional judgment ordinarily reserved to the lawyer. See **Rules 1.2** and 1.4."

Rule 5.3, Comment 3: "The extent of this obligation will depend upon the circumstances, including the education, experience and reputation of the nonlawyer; the nature of the services involved; the terms of any arrangements concerning the protection of client information; and the legal and ethical environments of the jurisdictions in which the services will be performed, particularly with regard to confidentiality. See also **Rules** 1.1 (competence), **1.2** (allocation of authority), 1.4 (communication with client), 1.6 (confidentiality), 5.4(a) (professional independence of the lawyer), and 5.5(a) (unauthorized practice of law)."

Rule 5.3, Comment 4: "Where the client directs the selection of a particular nonlawyer service provider outside the firm, the lawyer ordinarily should agree with the client concerning the allocation of responsibility for monitoring as between the client and the lawyer. See **Rule 1.2**."

Rule 6.4, Comment 1: "Lawyers involved in organizations seeking law reform generally do not have a client–lawyer relationship with the organization. . . . See also **Rule 1.2(b)**."

Rule 6.5, Comment 2: "A lawyer who provides short-term limited legal services pursuant to this Rule must secure the client's informed consent to the limited scope of the representation. See **Rule 1.2(c)**."

Rule 8.4, Comment 4: "The provisions of **Rule 1.2(d)** concerning a good faith challenge to the validity, scope, meaning or application of the law apply to challenges of legal regulation of the practice of law."

Legislative History of Model Rule 1.2

1980 Discussion Draft (then called Rule 1.3):

(a) A lawyer shall accept a client's decisions concerning the objectives of the representation and the means by which they are to be pursued except as stated in paragraphs (b) and (c).

(b) A lawyer shall not pursue a course of action on behalf of a client in violation of law or the rules of professional conduct.

(c) The lawyer may decline to pursue a lawful course of action . . . and, if the client insists upon such course of action, the lawyer may withdraw from representation subject to the provisions of Rule 1.16.

The 1980 Draft also contained the following separate rules (then called Rules 2.3 and 2.4):

Advice Concerning Wrongful Conduct

(a) A lawyer shall not give advice which the lawyer can reasonably foresee will:

(1) Be used by the client to further an illegal course of conduct except as part of a good faith effort to determine the validity, scope, meaning, or application of the law; or

(2) Aid the client in contriving false testimony or making a legally wrongful misrepresentation.

(b) A lawyer may decline to give advice that might assist the client in any conduct that would violate the law or . . . that the lawyer considers repugnant.

Duty to Offer Advice

A lawyer who knows that a client contemplates a course of action which has a substantial likelihood of serious legal consequences shall warn the client of the legal implications of the conduct, unless a client has expressly or by implication asked not to receive such advice.

The 1980 Draft also contained the following rule (then called Rule 4.1) similar to the adopted version of Rule 1.2(a):

Disclosures to a Client

A lawyer conducting negotiations for a client shall:

(a) inform the client of facts relevant to the matter and of communications from another party that may significantly affect resolution of the matter;

(b) in connection with an offer, take reasonable steps to assure that the judgment of the client rather than that of the lawyer determines whether the offer will be accepted.

1981 Draft of Rule 1.2 (d) prohibited a lawyer from counseling or assisting a client "in the preparation of a written instrument containing terms the lawyer knows or reasonably should know are legally prohibited. . . ."

1982 Draft of Rule 1.2 was the same as adopted, except that Rule 1.2(d) also prohibited a lawyer from counseling or assisting "in the preparation of a written instrument containing terms the lawyer knows are expressly prohibited by law. . . ."

1983 Rule: From its original adoption in 1983 until its amendment in 2002, Rule 1.2 provided as follows:

Rule 1.2 Scope of Representation

(a) A lawyer shall abide by a client's decisions concerning the objectives of representation and shall consult with the client as to the means by which they are to be pursued. A lawyer shall abide by a client's decision whether to accept an offer of settlement of a matter. In a criminal case, the lawyer shall abide by the client's decision, after consultation with the lawyer, as to a plea to be entered, whether to waive jury trial and whether the client will testify.

(b) [Same as 2002 version of Rule 1.2(b).]

(c) A lawyer may limit the objectives of the representation if the client consents after consultation.

(d) [Same as 2002 version of Rule 1.2(d).]

(e) When a lawyer knows that a client expects assistance not permitted by the rules of professional conduct or other law, the lawyer shall consult with the client regarding the relevant limitations on the lawyer's conduct.

2002 Amendments: At its February 2002 Mid-Year Meeting, the ABA House of Delegates adopted with only minor changes the ABA Ethics 2000 Commission proposal to amend Rule 1.2 and its Comment. Before the amendment, Rule 1.2(a) did not contain the "impliedly authorized" sentence. The amendment also added "the limitation is reasonable under the circumstances and" to Rule 1.2(c). The amendment deleted paragraph (e) which provided: "When a lawyer knows that a client expects assistance not permitted by the rules of professional conduct or other law, the lawyer shall consult with the client regarding the relevant limitations on the lawyer's conduct." Comments 2, 3, and 7 were new.

Selected State Variations

Alabama: Effective March 26, 2012, Rule 1.2(c) requires consent to be confirmed in writing, unless the limitation fits within three exceptions.

Alaska: Rule 1.2(a) states as follows: "In a criminal case the lawyer shall abide by the client's decision . . . whether to take an appeal."

California: Rule 3-210 (Advising the Violation of Law) provides: "A member shall not advise the violation of any law, rule, or ruling of a tribunal unless the member believes in good faith that such law, rule, or ruling is invalid. A member may take appropriate steps in good faith to test the validity of any law, rule, or ruling of a tribunal." Business & Professions Code 6068(c) requires lawyers to "counsel or maintain those actions, proceedings, or defenses only as appear to him or her legal or just" except in defending a criminal case. In addition, §283 of the California Code of Civil Procedure gives a lawyer express statutory authority to bind a client in certain situations.

Colorado: Rule 1.2(a) and (c) and the Comment to Rule 1.2 encourage "limited representation" of pro se clients. Rule 1.2(c) provides that a lawyer may limit the scope or objectives, "or both," of the representation if the client consents after consultation, and a lawyer "may provide limited representation to pro se parties as permitted by C.R.C.P. 11(b) and C.R.C.P. 311(b)." The Comments to

Colorado Rules 4.2 and 4.3 provide that a pro se party who is receiving "limited representation" is considered "unrepresented" for purposes of Rules 4.2 and 4.3.

Connecticut adds the following sentence to the end of Rule 1.2(a):

> Subject to revocation by the client and to the terms of the contract, a client's decision to settle a matter shall be implied where the lawyer is retained to represent the client by a third party obligated under the terms of a contract to provide the client with a defense and indemnity for the loss, and the third party elects to settle a matter without contribution by the client.

In addition, Connecticut adds to Rule 1.2(c) that a client's informed consent to limit the scope of a representation "shall not be required when a client cannot be located despite reasonable efforts where the lawyer is retained to represent a client by a third party which is obligated by contract to provide the client with a defense." An "Amendment Note" explains that these revisions "address the situation where an insured/client cannot be located despite diligent and good faith efforts by both the lawyer and the insurer."

District of Columbia: D.C. Rule 1.2 generally tracks the ABA Model Rule, but adds a paragraph (d) providing that a "government lawyer's authority and control over decisions concerning the representation may, by statute or regulation, be expanded beyond the limits imposed by paragraphs (a) and (c)." D.C. Rule 1.2(f) — formerly 1.2(e) — retains language that the ABA deleted in 2002.

Florida adds the words "or reasonably should know" in Rule 1.2(d). In addition, Florida's Statement of Client's Rights, which must be provided to every contingent fee client (see Florida Rule 4-1.5(f)), provides that "[y]ou, the client, have the right to make the final decision regarding settlement of a case. . . ."

Illinois: Illinois adds Rule 1.2(e), which provides that, "[a]fter accepting employment on behalf of a client, a lawyer shall not thereafter delegate to another lawyer not in the lawyer's firm the responsibility for performing or completing that employment, without the client's informed consent." Comment 14 offers the following explanation:

> The prohibition stated in paragraph (e) has existed in Illinois ethics rules and in the prior Code since 1980. It is intended to curtail abuses that occasionally occur when a lawyer attempts to transfer complete or substantial responsibility for a matter to an unaffiliated lawyer without the client's awareness or consent. . . . The Rule is not intended to prohibit lawyers from hiring lawyers outside of their firm to perform certain services on the client's or the law firm's behalf. Nor is it intended to prevent lawyers from engaging lawyers outside of their firm to stand in for discrete events in situations such as personal emergencies, illness or schedule conflicts.

Massachusetts: Rule 1.2(a) provides that a lawyer "does not violate this rule . . . by acceding to reasonable requests of opposing counsel which do not prejudice the rights of his or her client, by being punctual in fulfilling all professional commitments, by avoiding offensive tactics, or by treating with courtesy and consideration all persons involved in the legal process."

Michigan deletes Rule 1.2(b) and adds the following sentence to Rule 1.2(a): "In representing a client, a lawyer may, where permissible, exercise professional judgment to waive or fail to assert a right or position of the client." Where the official ABA Comment to Rule 1.2 refers to "criminal or fraudulent conduct," the

Michigan Comment refers to "illegal or fraudulent conduct." Michigan places the substance of Rule 1.2(b) in the Comment to Rule 1.2.

Missouri: Rule 1.2(c) permits the unbundling of legal services, providing as follows:

> A lawyer may limit the scope of representation if the client gives informed consent in a writing signed by the client to the essential terms of the representation and the lawyer's limited role. Use of a written notice and consent form substantially similar to that contained in the comment to this Rule 4-1.2 creates the presumptions:
>
> (a) the representation is limited to the lawyer and the services described in the form, and (b) the lawyer does not represent the client generally or in any matters other than those identified in the form. . . ."

Missouri also retains Rule 1.2(e) from the 1983 version of ABA Model Rule 1.2 ("When a lawyer knows that a client expects assistance not permitted by the rules of professional conduct or other law, the lawyer shall consult with the client regarding the relevant limitations on the lawyer's conduct.").

New Hampshire: Rule 1.2(e) provides as follows:

> (e) It is not inconsistent with the lawyer's duty to seek the lawful objectives of a client through reasonably available means, for the lawyer to accede to reasonable requests of opposing counsel that do not prejudice the rights of the client, avoid the use of offensive or dilatory tactics, or treat opposing counsel or an opposing party with civility.

New Hampshire also adds Rule 1.2(f) to govern "limited representation to a client who is or may become involved in" litigation, and adds a detailed sample form for "Consent to Limited Representation" in a Rule 1.2(g).

New Mexico specifies in Rule 16-303(E) that a lawyer must disclose to a tribunal if the lawyer is representing the client in a "limited manner."

New York adds Rule 1.2(e)-(g), which are based on DR 7-101 of the old ABA Model Code. Comment 10 elaborates on what a lawyer must do when a client has undertaken an illegal or fraudulent course of action and "the representation will result in violation of the Rules of Professional Conduct or other law. . . ." Under these circumstances, "the lawyer must advise the client of any relevant limitation on the lawyer's conduct and remonstrate with the client. *See* Rules 1.4(a)(5) and 1.16(b)(1). Persuading a client to take necessary preventive or corrective action that will bring the client's conduct within the bounds of the law is a challenging but appropriate endeavor. If the client fails to take necessary corrective action and the lawyer's continued representation would assist client conduct that is illegal or fraudulent, the lawyer is required to withdraw."

North Carolina: Rule 1.2(a)(2) and (3) add language taken from DR 7-101(A)(1) and DR 7-101(B)(1) of the ABA Model Code of Professional Responsibility, and Rule 1.2(c) omits the ABA requirement that the client give informed consent.

Ohio: Rule 1.2(c) provides:

> A lawyer who undertakes representation of a client, other than by court appointment, shall confirm in writing, within a reasonable time, the nature and scope of the representation, unless the lawyer has regularly represented the client or the anticipated fee from the representation is $500.00 or less. A lawyer may limit the scope of a new or existing representation if the limitation is reasonable under the circumstances and communicated to the client in writing.

Texas omits ABA Model Rule 1.2(b). See also Texas Rule 1.05 and the annotations following Rule 1.6 below.

Virginia has moved the language of Rule 1.2(b) to Comment 3, and Virginia's Comment 1 requires lawyers to "advise the client about the advantages, disadvantages and availability of dispute resolution processes that might be appropriate in pursuing" the client's objectives. Virginia Rule 1.2(d) provides that a "lawyer may take such action on behalf of the client as is impliedly authorized to carry out the representation."

Wisconsin adds Rule 1.2(e) to clarify the obligations of counsel for an insurer.

Related Materials

ABA Formal Ethics Opinions: See ABA Formal Ethics Ops. 92-362 (1992), 92-366 (1992), 92-368 (1992), 93-371 (1993), 93-375 (1993), 93-379 (1993), 94-380 (1994), 94-387 (1994), 94-389 (1994), 96-399 (1996), 96-403 (1996), 97-405 (1997), 98-410 (1998), 01-421 (2001), 05-434 n.16 (2005), 06-438 (2006), 06-441 (2006), 07-446 (2007), 07-447 (2007), and 08-452 (2008).

ABA Handbook on Limited Scope Representation: In 2003, the Modest Means Task Force of the ABA Section of Litigation published a lengthy report (149 pages) entitled Handbook on Limited Scope Legal Assistance. The report is available online at *http://apps.americanbar.org/litigation/taskforces/modest/report.pdf.*

ABA Standards for Criminal Justice: The following Standard is related to ABA Model Rule 1.2:

Standard 4-5.2 Control and Direction of the Case

(a) Certain decisions relating to the conduct of the case are ultimately for the accused and others are ultimately for defense counsel. The decisions which are to be made by the accused after full consultation with counsel include:

what pleas to enter;

whether to accept a plea agreement;

whether to waive jury trial;

whether to testify in his or her own behalf; and

whether to appeal.

(b) Strategic and tactical decisions should be made by defense counsel after consultation with the client where feasible and appropriate. Such decisions include what witnesses to call, whether and how to conduct cross-examination, what jurors to accept or strike, what trial motions should be made, and what evidence should be introduced.

(c) If a disagreement on significant matters of tactics or strategy arises between defense counsel and the client, defense counsel should make a record of the circumstances, counsel's advice and reasons, and the conclusion reached. The record should be made in a manner which protects the confidentiality of the lawyer-client relationship.

Aiding and Abetting: In many jurisdictions, if a lawyer violates Rule 1.2(d) by counseling or assisting the client in criminal conduct, the lawyer would also be violating criminal laws prohibiting anyone from aiding or abetting the commission of a crime. For example, 18 U.S.C. §2(a) provides that whoever commits an offense against the United States "or aids, abets, counsels, commands, induces or procures its commission, is punishable as a principal." Similarly, California Penal Code, Title 2 §31, provides:

> All persons concerned in the commission of a crime, whether it be felony or misdemeanor, and whether they directly commit the act constituting the offense, or aid and abet in its commission, or, not being present, have advised and encouraged its commission . . . are principals in any crime so committed.

In *Stoneridge Investment Partners v. Scientific-Atlanta,* 552 U.S. 148 (2008), the Supreme Court held that §10(b) of the Securities Exchange Act of 1934 does not create a private right of action against aiders and abettors of securities law violations. The decision meant that private plaintiffs could not bring class actions based on §10(b) against lawyers who allegedly aided and abetted their clients in committing securities fraud. Under *Stoneridge,* only the government may sue aiders and abettors. In 2009, Senator Arlen Specter introduced a bill known as the Liability for Aiding and Abetting Securities Violations Act of 2009 (S. 1551). The bill was intended to override *Stoneridge* by authorizing private plaintiffs to bring civil suits against anyone who "knowingly or recklessly provides substantial assistance" to a person engaged in fraud, but the bill did not become law and has not been reintroduced.

However, in July 2011, pursuant to a mandate in the Dodd-Frank Wall Street Reform and Consumer Protection Act, the Government Accountability Office (GAO) sent a report to Congress analyzing the impact of creating a private right of action against lawyers and other "secondary actors" for aiding and abetting securities law violations. The GAO report, entitled "Securities Fraud Liability of Secondary Actors," examined the pros and cons of extending liability to aiders and abettors but did not make any recommendations. The report is available at *http://www.gao.gov/new.items/d11664.pdf.*

Collaborative Law: The collaborative dispute resolution process (commonly known as "collaborative law") is a form of limited-scope representation under Rule 1.2(c) in which the opposing parties agree to retain attorneys solely to negotiate a settlement, not to litigate. If either party ignores the agreement and goes to court, the attorneys must resign from the case. These terms are usually embodied in a "Participation Agreement" providing that if the parties are unable to reach a settlement, the lawyers will withdraw from the case and assist the clients in transitioning the case to trial attorneys. Practitioners of collaborative law generally believe that the agreement to collaborate and to withdraw if settlement cannot be achieved allows the parties and their lawyers to focus on problem-solving negotiations rather than tactical maneuvering. Collaborative law is most common in family law disputes, but its practice has spread to other areas of the law, including the settlement of contract and insurance disputes. For more information on collaborative law, visit the website of the Global Collaborative Law Council at *http://www.collaborativelaw.us.*

In 2009, the Uniform Law Commission (formerly the National Conference of Commissioners on Uniform State Laws, or NCCUSL) voted to approve a new Uniform Collaborative Law Act (UCLA). The aim was to increase consistency from state to state regarding (i) the enforceability of collaborative law agreements, (ii) the confidentiality of communications during the collaborative process, (iii) an automatic stay of any pending court proceedings that are also the subject of the collaborative law process, and (iv) the privilege against disclosure if the collaborative process does not lead to settlement. In 2010, the UCLA was amended to give states explicit options (a) to limit the UCLA to domestic relations matters and (b) to adopt the UCLA in full or in part by court rule.

The most recent version of the UCLA, as amended in 2010, is available at *http://www.uniformlaws.org/shared/docs/collaborative_law/uclranducla_amendments_ jul10.pdf.* The UCLA has been enacted in five jurisdictions (District of Columbia, Hawaii, Nevada, Texas, and Utah), and the UCLA was introduced in the legislature during 2012 in three jurisdictions (Maryland, Massachusetts, and Washington State). The ABA Section of Family Law has approved the UCLA and favors its adoption in the states. But at the ABA's August 2011 Annual Meeting, after a contentious debate, the ABA House of Delegates voted 298-154 against a resolution endorsing the UCLA. For legislative updates and other news regarding the UCLA, visit *http://www.uniformlaws.org/LegislativeFactSheet.aspx?title=Collaborative%20 Law%20Act.*

Medicaid Fraud Legislation: As part of the Balanced Budget Act of 1997, Congress enacted the so-called "Granny's Lawyer Goes to Jail" law, 42 U.S.C. §1320a-7b(a), which provided in part:

> Whoever ... (6) for a fee knowingly and willfully counsels or assists an individual to dispose of assets (including by any transfer in trust) in order for the individual to become eligible for medical assistance ... shall ... (ii) ... be guilty of a misdemeanor and upon conviction thereof fined not more than $10,000 or imprisoned for not more than one year, or both.

In *New York State Bar Ass'n v. Reno,* 999 F. Supp. 710 (N.D.N.Y. 1998), the court granted a preliminary injunction enjoining enforcement of the law. In *Magee v. United States,* 93 F. Supp. 2d 161 (D.R.I. 2000), however, a different court dismissed a suit challenging the law, even though the United States admitted that the law was "plainly unconstitutional," because in 1998 Attorney General Reno had informed Congress that the United States would not enforce the law, leaving no justiciable "case or controversy." For a history of the "Granny" statute, see *Rainey v. Guardianship of Mackey,* 773 So. 2d 118 (Fla. App. 4th Dist. 2000).

Restatement of the Law Governing Lawyers: See Restatement §§16, 21-23, 26, 51, 67, 82, 93, 94, and 120 in our chapter on the Restatement later in this volume. The Restatement has no provision comparable to ABA Model Rule 1.2(b).

Unbundled Legal Services: Some lawyers provide "unbundled" legal services, also called "discrete task representation," to clients otherwise acting pro se. Unbundled legal services are related to ABA Model Rule 1.2(c), which permits a lawyer to "limit the scope of the representation if the limitation is reasonable under the circumstances and the client gives informed consent." For example, if a person is conducting litigation pro se but wants some assistance from a lawyer, a lawyer who offers unbundled legal services might limit representation of the pro se litigant to drafting discovery requests, reviewing documents, or negotiating a settlement with the opposing lawyer. Some states, including California, Colorado, Florida, Maine, Missouri, Washington, Wisconsin, and Wyoming, have adopted rules expressly addressing unbundled legal services.

For extensive resources about unbundled legal services, including a 2005 white paper by the ABA Standing Committee on the Delivery of Legal Services entitled "An Analysis of Rules that Enable Lawyers to Serve Pro Se Litigants," visit the Pro Se/Unbundling Resource Center at *http://apps.americanbar.org/legalservices/delivery/ delunbund.html.* For a Handbook on Limited Scope Legal Assistance published by a task force of the ABA Section of Litigation, see *http://apps.americanbar.org/litigation/ taskforces/modest/report.pdf.*

Rule 1.3   Diligence

Canon and Code Antecedents

ABA Canons of Professional Ethics: Canon 21 provided as follows:

21. Punctuality and Expedition

It is the duty of the lawyer not only to his client, but also to the Courts and to the public to be punctual in attendance, and to be concise and direct in the trial and disposition of causes.

ABA Model Code of Professional Responsibility: Compare DR 6-101, DR 7-101(A), and DR 7-101(A)(3) (reprinted later in this volume).

Cross-References in Other Rules

Rule 1.7, Comment 3: "As to whether a client-lawyer relationship exists or, having once been established, is continuing, see Comment to **Rule 1.3** and Scope."

Rule 1.7, Comment 15: In the case of a conflict of interest, "representation is prohibited if in the circumstances the lawyer cannot reasonably conclude that the lawyer will be able to provide competent and diligent representation (see Rules 1.1 and **1.3**)."

Rule 1.16, Comment 1: "Ordinarily, a representation in a matter is completed when the agreed-upon assistance has been concluded. See Rules 1.2(c) and 6.5. See also **Rule 1.3**, Comment [4]."

Legislative History of Model Rule 1.3

1980 Discussion Draft: "A lawyer shall attend promptly to matters undertaken for a client and give them adequate attention until completed or until the lawyer has properly withdrawn from representing the client."

1981 and 1982 Drafts were the same as adopted.

1983 Rule: As originally adopted in 1983, Rule 1.3 was the same as the 2002 version.

2002 Amendments: At its February 2002 Mid-Year Meeting, the ABA House of Delegates adopted without change the ABA Ethics 2000 Commission proposal to amend the Comment to Rule 1.3 through additions and minor deletions. The amendments added Comments 2 and 5 and the final sentences in Comments 1, 3, and 4. The text of Rule 1.3 was not amended.

Selected State Variations

California: Rule 3-110(B) provides as follows:

(A) A member shall not intentionally, recklessly, or repeatedly fail to perform legal services with competence.

(B) For purposes of this rule, "competence" in any legal service shall mean to apply the 1) diligence, 2) learning and skill, and 3) mental, emotional, and physical ability reasonably necessary for the performance of such service.

(C) If a member does not have sufficient learning and skill when the legal service is undertaken, the member may nonetheless perform such services competently by 1) associating with or, where appropriate, professionally consulting another lawyer reasonably believed to be competent, or 2) by acquiring sufficient learning and skill before performance is required.

District of Columbia: D.C Rule 1.3(a) and (b) provide as follows:

(a) A lawyer shall represent a client zealously and diligently within the bounds of the law.

(b) A lawyer shall not intentionally:
   (1) Fail to seek the lawful objectives of a client through reasonably available means permitted by law and the disciplinary rules. . . .

Georgia: In the rules effective November 3, 2011, Georgia adds the following sentence to Rule 1.3: "Reasonable diligence as used in this Rule means that a lawyer shall not without just cause to the detriment of the client in effect wilfully abandon or wilfully disregard a legal matter entrusted to the lawyer."

Massachusetts: Rule 1.3 adds the following sentence: "The lawyer should represent a client zealously within the bounds of the law."

New York adds Rule 1.3(b)-(c), which is based on DR 6-101 of the old ABA Model Code. Moreover, rather than advising that reasonable diligence "does not require the use of offensive tactics," Comment 1 instructs lawyers that they "should not use offensive tactics."

Texas omits Rule 1.3.

Virginia adds the following subparagraphs (b) and (c) to Rule 1.3:

(b) A lawyer shall not intentionally fail to carry out a contract of employment entered into with a client for professional services, but may withdraw as permitted under Rule 1.16.

(c) A lawyer shall not intentionally prejudice or damage a client during the course of the professional relationship, except as required or permitted under Rule 1.6 and Rule 3.3.

Virginia also adds the following Comment to Rule 1.3:

[1a] Additionally, lawyers have long recognized that a more collaborative, problem-solving approach is often preferable to an adversarial strategy in pursuing the client's needs and interests. Consequently, diligence includes not only an adversarial strategy but also the vigorous pursuit of the client's interest in reaching a solution that satisfies the interests of all parties. The client can be represented zealously in either setting.

Related Materials

ABA Formal Ethics Opinions: See ABA Formal Ethics Ops. 92-367 (1992), 92-368 (1992) (withdrawn), 92-369 (1992), 94-387 (1994), 96-399 (1996), 96-400 (1996), 06-441 (2006), and 07-448 (2007).

ABA Standards for Imposing Lawyer Discipline: The following Standards for Imposing Lawyer Discipline are relevant to Rule 1.3:

4.41. Disbarment is generally appropriate when:
(a) a lawyer abandons the practice and causes serious or potentially serious injury to a client; or

(b) a lawyer knowingly fails to perform services for a client and causes serious or potentially serious injury to a client; or

(c) a lawyer engages in a pattern of neglect with respect to client matters and causes serious or potentially serious injury to a client.

4.42. Suspension is generally appropriate when:

(a) a lawyer knowingly fails to perform services for a client and causes injury or potential injury to a client; or

(b) a lawyer engages in a pattern of neglect and causes injury or potential injury to a client.

"Diligence" is defined in Black's Law Dictionary (9th ed. 2009) as: "1. A continual effort to accomplish something. 2. Care; caution; the attention and care required from a person in a given situation."

IRS Regulations: In the regulations governing practice before the Internal Revenue Service, 31 C.F.R. §10.22(a) requires each attorney to "exercise due diligence" in (i) preparing and filing tax returns, documents, affidavits, and other papers relating to Internal Revenue Service matters and in (ii) "determining the correctness of oral or written representations" to the Department of the Treasury or to clients in any matter administered by the Internal Revenue Service. Under §10.22(b), a practitioner will ordinarily be "presumed to have exercised due diligence . . . if the practitioner relies on the work product of another person and the practitioner used reasonable care in engaging, supervising, training, and evaluating the person, taking proper account of the nature of the relationship between the practitioner and the person."

Standards of Civility: In an effort to tamp down excessive zeal and "Rambo" litigation tactics, some bar associations have promulgated "standards of civility," and some tribunals have adopted these standards as guidelines. For example, on October 28, 2010, Chief Judge Carla Craig of the Bankruptcy Court for the Eastern District of New York issued an administrative order adopting guidelines for standards of civility for the legal profession. These guidelines were originally developed by the New York State Bar Association. Standards of civility vary from jurisdiction to jurisdiction and are invariably nonbinding.

Restatement of the Law Governing Lawyers: See Restatement §16(2) in our chapter on the Restatement later in this volume.

Rule 1.4   Communication

Canon and Code Antecedents

ABA Canons of Professional Ethics: Canon 8 provided as follows:

8. *Advising Upon the Merits of a Client's Cause*

A lawyer should endeavor to obtain full knowledge of his client's cause before advising thereon, and he is bound to give a candid opinion of the merits and probable result of pending or contemplated litigation. The miscarriages to which justice is subject, by reason of surprises and disappointments in evidence and witnesses, and through mistakes of juries and errors of Courts, even though only occasional, admonish lawyers to beware of bold and confident assurances to clients, especially where the employment may depend upon such assurance. Whenever the controversy will admit of fair adjustment, the client should be advised to avoid or to end the litigation.

ABA Model Code of Professional Responsibility: Compare DR 6-101(A)(3) and DR 9-102(B)(1) (reprinted later in this volume).

Cross-References in Other Rules

Rule 1.1, Comment 6: "Before a lawyer retains or contracts with other lawyers outside the lawyer's own firm to provide or assist in the provision of legal services to a client, the lawyer should ordinarily obtain informed consent from the client and must reasonably believe that the other lawyers' services will contribute to the competent and ethical representation of the client. See also **Rules** 1.2 (allocation of authority), **1.4** (communication with client), 1.5(e) (fee sharing), 1.6 (confidentiality), and 5.5(a) (unauthorized practice of law)."

Rule 1.2(a): "Subject to paragraphs (c) and (d), a lawyer shall abide by a client's decisions concerning the objectives of representation and, as required by **Rule 1.4**, shall consult with the client as to the means by which they are to be pursued."

Rule 1.2, Comment 1: "The decisions specified in paragraph (a) . . . must also be made by the client. See **Rule 1.4(a)(1)** for the lawyer's duty to communicate with the client about such decisions. With respect to the means by which the client's objectives are to be pursued, the lawyer shall consult with the client as required by **Rule 1.4 (a)(2)**. . . ."

Rule 1.2, Comment 3: "Absent a material change in circumstances and subject to **Rule 1.4**, a lawyer may rely on such an advance authorization."

Rule 1.2, Comment 13: "If a lawyer comes to know or reasonably should know that a client expects assistance not permitted by the Rules of Professional Conduct or other law or if the lawyer intends to act contrary to the client's instructions, the lawyer must consult with the client regarding the limitations on the lawyer's conduct. See **Rule 1.4(a)(5)**."

Rule 1.3, Comment 4: "Doubt about whether a client-lawyer relationship still exists should be clarified by the lawyer, preferably in writing, so that the client will not mistakenly suppose the lawyer is looking after the client's affairs when the lawyer has ceased to do so. See **Rule 1.4(a)(2)**."

Rule 1.6, Comment 12: "When disclosure of information relating to the representation appears to be required by other law, the lawyer must discuss the matter with the client to the extent required by **Rule 1.4**."

Rule 1.6, Comment 15: "In the event of an adverse ruling, the lawyer must consult with the client about the possibility of appeal to the extent required by **Rule 1.4**."

Rule 1.7, Comment 31: "As to the duty of confidentiality, continued common representation will almost certainly be inadequate if one client asks the lawyer not to disclose to the other client information relevant to the common representation. This is so because the lawyer has an equal duty of loyalty to each client, and each client has the right to be informed of anything bearing on the representation that might affect that client's interests and the right to expect that the lawyer will use that information to that client's benefit. See **Rule 1.4**."

Rule 2.1, Comment 5: "When a lawyer knows that a client proposes a course of action that is likely to result in substantial adverse legal consequences to the client, the lawyer's duty to the client under **Rule 1.4** may require that the lawyer offer advice if the client's course of action is related to the representation. Similarly, when a matter is likely to involve litigation, it may be necessary under **Rule 1.4** to inform the client of forms of dispute resolution that might constitute reasonable alternatives to litigation.''

Rule 4.4, Comment 3: ''Where a lawyer is not required by applicable law to do so, the decision to voluntarily return such a document is a matter of professional judgment ordinarily reserved to the lawyer. See Rules 1.2 and **1.4**.''

Rule 5.3, Comment 3: ''The extent of this obligation will depend upon the circumstances, including the education, experience and reputation of the nonlawyer; the nature of the services involved; the terms of any arrangements concerning the protection of client information; and the legal and ethical environments of the jurisdictions in which the services will be performed, particularly with regard to confidentiality. See also **Rules** 1.1 (competence), 1.2 (allocation of authority), **1.4** (communication with client), 1.6 (confidentiality), 5.4(a) (professional independence of the lawyer), and 5.5(a) (unauthorized practice of law).''

Rule 5.5, Comment 20: ''[A] lawyer who practices law in this jurisdiction pursuant to paragraphs (c) or (d) may have to inform the client that the lawyer is not licensed to practice law in this jurisdiction. For example, that may be required when the representation occurs primarily in this jurisdiction and requires knowledge of the law of this jurisdiction. See **Rule 1.4(b)**.''

Legislative History of Model Rule 1.4

1979 Unofficial Pre-Circulation Draft (then Rule 1.3):

(a) A lawyer shall keep a client informed about a matter in which the lawyer's services are being rendered. Informing the client includes:

(1) Periodically advising the client of the status and progress of the matter;

(2) Explaining the legal and practical aspects of the matter and foreseeable effects of alternative courses of action; and . . .

(c) A lawyer may withhold information to which a client is otherwise entitled only when doing so is necessary to protect the client's interest or some superior interest.

1980 Discussion Draft prohibited a lawyer from withholding information to which a client was entitled ''except when doing so is clearly necessary to protect the client's interest or to comply with the requirements of law or the rules of professional conduct.''

1981 Draft provided:

(b) A lawyer shall explain the legal and practical aspects of a matter and alternative courses of action to the extent reasonably necessary to permit the client to make informed decisions regarding the representation.

1982 Draft was adopted in 1983.

1983 Rule: As originally adopted in 1983, Rule 1.4(a) provided: ''A lawyer shall keep a client reasonably informed about the status of a matter and promptly comply with reasonable requests for information.'' Rule 1.4(b) was the same as the 2002 version.

2002 Amendments: At its February 2002 Mid-Year Meeting, the ABA House of Delegates adopted without change the ABA Ethics 2000 Commission proposal to amend Rule 1.4 and its Comment. Subparagraphs (a)(1)-(5) of Rule 1.4 replaced the 1983 version of Rule 1.4(a). Rule 1.4(b) was unchanged. Comments 1-4 and the final sentence in Comment 5 were added.

2012 Amendments: In August 2012, the ABA House of Delegates adopted without change proposals by the ABA Commission on Ethics 20/20 to amend Comment 4 to Rule 1.4. The change resulted in the replacement of the phrase "telephone calls" with the phrase "client communications," making clear that lawyers should respond promptly to all client communications, not just to telephone calls.

Selected State Variations

Arizona adds Rule 1.4(c), which provides: "In a criminal case, a lawyer shall promptly inform a client of all proffered plea agreements."

Arkansas adds the following Rule 1.4(c), which describes a lawyer's obligation to "promptly notify a client in writing of the actual or constructive receipt by the attorney of a check or other payment . . . of a settlement, judgment, or other monies to which the client is entitled.":

> A lawyer shall promptly notify a client in writing of the actual or constructive receipt by the attorney of a check or other payment received from an insurance company, an opposing party, or from any other source which constitutes the payment of a settlement, judgment, or other monies to which the client is entitled.

California: Rule 3-500 provides:

> A member shall keep a client reasonably informed about significant developments relating to the employment or representation, including promptly complying with reasonable requests for information and copies of significant documents when necessary to keep the client so informed.

Rule 3-510 provides:

> (A) A member shall promptly communicate to the member's client:
>   (1) All terms and conditions of any offer made to the client in a criminal matter; and
>   (2) All amounts, terms, and conditions of any written offer of settlement made to the client in all other matters.
>   (B) As used in this rule, "client" includes a person who possesses the authority to accept an offer of settlement or plea, or, in a class action, all the named representatives of the class.

California Business & Professions Code §6068(m) describes the same duties.

District of Columbia: D.C. adds Rule 1.4(c), which requires a lawyer "who receives an offer of settlement in a civil case or a proffered plea bargain in a criminal case" to "promptly" inform the client of its "substance."

Florida adds two rules relating to client communications that have no Model Rule counterpart. First, Rule 4-1.5(f)(4)(C) requires every lawyer who enters into a contingent fee agreement in a personal injury or property damage case to provide the client with a Statement of Client's Rights for Contingency Fees. The Statement must contain the following paragraph concerning the lawyer's obligation to communicate settlement offers:

> 10. . . . Your lawyer must notify you of all offers of settlement before and after the trial. Offers during the trial must be immediately communicated and you should consult with your lawyer regarding whether to accept a settlement. However, you must make the final decision to accept or reject a settlement.

Second, Rule 4-5.8 contains several provisions that restrict a lawyer's communications with clients when the lawyer decides to leave a law firm or when the law firm dissolves.

Louisiana: Rule 1.4(c) provides as follows:

> (c) A lawyer who provides any form of financial assistance to a client during the course of a representation shall, prior to providing such financial assistance, inform the client in writing of the terms and conditions under which such financial assistance is made, including but not limited to, repayment obligations, the imposition and rate of interest or other charges, and the scope and limitations imposed upon lawyers providing financial assistance as set forth in Rule 1.8(e).

Massachusetts: The Comment to Rule 1.4 states: "There will be circumstances in which a lawyer should advise a client concerning the advantages and disadvantages of available dispute resolution options. . . ."

Michigan adds to Rule 1.4(a): "A lawyer shall notify the client promptly of all settlement offers, mediation evaluations, and proposed plea bargains."

Missouri deletes subparagraphs (a)(1) and (a)(2) from ABA Model Rule 1.4.

Nevada has a Rule 1.4(c) entitled "Lawyer's Biographical Data Form." Among other details, it requires each lawyer or law firm to maintain a form containing "a factual statement detailing the background, training and experience of each lawyer or law firm." The form must list certain basic information and requires a lawyer or law firm to provide additional information upon request.

New York adds Rule 1.4(a)(1)(ii) and (iii), which provides that a lawyer should promptly inform a client of: "(ii) any information required by court rule or other law to be communicated to a client; and (iii) material developments in the matter including settlement or plea offers."

Ohio: Rule 1.4(c) provides:

> A lawyer shall inform a client at the time of the client's engagement of the lawyer or at any time subsequent to the engagement if the lawyer does not maintain professional liability insurance in the amounts of at least one hundred thousand dollars per occurrence and three hundred thousand dollars in the aggregate or if the lawyer's professional liability insurance is terminated. The notice shall be provided to the client on a separate form set forth following this rule and shall be signed by the client.

Rule 1.4(c) does not apply to government lawyers or to in-house counsel.

Virginia adds Rule 1.4(c), which requires a lawyer to "inform the client of facts pertinent to the matter and of communications from another party that may significantly affect settlement or resolution of the matter."

Related Materials

ABA Formal Ethics Opinions: See ABA Formal Ethics Ops. 92-362 (1992), 95-398 (1995), 96-399 (1996), 97-406 (1997), 99-414 (1999), 02-425 (2002), 02-426 (2002), 03-429 (2003), 06-441 (2006), 08-450 (2008), 08-453 n.14 (2008), 11-460 (2011).

ABA Standards for Imposing Lawyer Sanctions: The following ABA Standards for Imposing Lawyer Sanctions are relevant to Rule 1.4:

> 4.61. Disbarment is generally appropriate when a lawyer knowingly deceives a client with the intent to benefit the lawyer or another, and causes serious injury or potential serious injury to a client.
> 4.62. Suspension is generally appropriate when a lawyer knowingly deceives a client, and causes injury or potential injury to the client.

IRS Regulations: In the regulations governing practice before the Internal Revenue Service, 31 C.F.R. §10.33(a) provides that tax advisors should adhere to a series of "best practices," including:

> (1) Communicating clearly with the client regarding the terms of the engagement. For example, the advisor should determine the client's expected purpose for and use of the advice and should have a clear understanding with the client regarding the form and scope of the advice or assistance to be rendered. . . .
> (3) Advising the client regarding the import of the conclusions reached, including, for example, whether a taxpayer may avoid accuracy-related penalties under the Internal Revenue Code if a taxpayer acts in reliance on the advice. . . .

The explanatory material in 69 Fed. Reg. 75841 accompanying §10.33 says that these best practices are "aspirational" and that a practitioner who fails to comply with them "will not be subject to discipline under these regulations." Nevertheless, "tax professionals are expected to observe these practices to preserve public confidence in the tax system."

Restatement of the Law Governing Lawyers: See Restatement §20 in our chapter on the Restatement later in this volume.

Rule 1.5   Fees

Canon and Code Antecedents

ABA Canons of Professional Ethics: Canons 12, 13, 14, and 42 provided as follows:

12.   Fixing the Amount of the Fee

> In fixing fees, lawyers should avoid charges which overestimate their advice and services, as well as those which undervalue them. A client's ability to pay cannot justify a charge in excess of the value of the service, though his poverty may require a less charge, or even none at all. The reasonable requests of brother lawyers, and of their widows and orphans without ample means, should receive special and kindly consideration.
> In determining the amount of the fee, it is proper to consider: (1) the time and labor required, the novelty and difficulty of the questions involved and the skill requisite properly to conduct the cause; (2) whether the acceptance of employment in the particular case will preclude the lawyer's appearance for others in cases likely to arise out of the transaction, and in which there is a reasonable expectation that otherwise he would be employed, or will involve the loss of other employment while employed in the particular case or antagonisms with other clients; (3) the customary charges of the Bar for similar services; (4) the amount involved in the controversy and the benefits

resulting to the client from the services; (5) the contingency or the certainty of the compensation; and (6) the character of the employment, whether casual or for an established and constant client. No one of these considerations in itself is controlling. They are mere guides in ascertaining the real value of the service.

In determining the customary charges of the Bar for similar services, it is proper for a lawyer to consider a schedule of minimum fees adopted by a Bar Association, but no lawyer should permit himself to be controlled thereby or to follow it as his sole guide in determining the amount of his fee.

In fixing fees it should never be forgotten that the profession is a branch of the administration of justice and not a mere money-getting trade.

13.   *Contingent Fees*

A contract for a contingent fee, where sanctioned by law, should be reasonable under all the circumstances of the case, including the risk and uncertainty of the compensation, but should always be subject to the supervision of a court, as to its reasonableness.

14.   *Suing a Client for a Fee*

Controversies with clients concerning compensation are to be avoided by the lawyer so far as shall be compatible with his self-respect and with his right to receive reasonable recompense for his services; and lawsuits with clients should be resorted to only to prevent injustice, imposition or fraud.

42.   *Expenses of Litigation*

A lawyer may not properly agree with a client that the lawyer shall pay or bear the expenses of litigation; he may in good faith advance expenses as a matter of convenience, but subject to reimbursement.

ABA Model Code of Professional Responsibility: Compare DR 2-106(A), DR 2-106(B), DR 2-106(C), and DR 2-107(A) (reprinted later in this volume).

Cross-References in Other Rules

Rule 1.1, Comment 6: "Before a lawyer retains or contracts with other lawyers outside the lawyer's own firm to provide or assist in the provision of legal services to a client, the lawyer should ordinarily obtain informed consent from the client and must reasonably believe that the other lawyers' services will contribute to the competent and ethical representation of the client. See also **Rules** 1.2 (allocation of authority), 1.4 (communication with client), **1.5(e)** (fee sharing), 1.6 (confidentiality), and 5.5(a) (unauthorized practice of law)."

Rule 1.8, Comment 1: Rule 1.8 "does not apply to ordinary fee arrangements between client and lawyer, which are governed by **Rule 1.5**."

Rule 1.8, Comment 9: Rule 1.8(d) "does not prohibit a lawyer representing a client in a transaction concerning literary property from agreeing that the lawyer's fee shall consist of a share in ownership in the property, if the arrangement conforms to **Rule 1.5**. . . ."

Rule 1.8, Comment 16: Rule 1.8(i) "states the traditional general rule that lawyers are prohibited from acquiring a proprietary interest in litigation. . . . The Rule is subject to specific exceptions. . . . Contracts for contingent fees in civil cases are governed by **Rule 1.5**.''

Rule 1.17, Comment 5: ''If an area of practice is sold and the lawyer remains in the active practice of law, the lawyer must cease accepting any matters in the area of practice that has been sold, either as counsel or co-counsel or by assuming joint responsibility for a matter in connection with the division of a fee with another lawyer as would otherwise be permitted by **Rule 1.5(e)**.''

Rule 7.2, Comment 8: ''Except as provided in **Rule 1.5(e)**, a lawyer who receives referrals from a lawyer or nonlawyer professional must not pay anything solely for the referral. . . .''

Legislative History of Model Rule 1.5

1979 Unofficial Pre-Circulation Draft (then Rule 1.4):

(b) A fee agreement shall . . .
(2) State with reasonable definiteness, expressly or by implication, the nature and extent of the services to be provided; and . . .
(c) A fee agreement shall be expressed or confirmed in writing before the lawyer has rendered substantial services in the matter, except:
(1) Where an agreement as to the fee is implied by the fact that the lawyer's services are of the same general kind as previously rendered to and paid for by the client;
(2) For services rendered in an emergency where a written agreement or confirmation is impracticable. . . .

1980 Discussion Draft (then Rule 1.6):

(b) The basis or rate of a lawyer's fee shall be put in writing before the lawyer has rendered substantial services in the matter, except when:
(1) An agreement as to the fee is implied by the fact that the lawyer's services are of the same general kind as previously rendered to and paid for by the client; or
(2) The services are rendered in an emergency where a writing is impracticable.
(c) The form of a fee and the terms of a fee agreement shall involve no inducement for the lawyer to perform the services in a manner inconsistent with the best interests of the client. . . .
(e) A division of fee between lawyers who are not in the same firm may be made only if:
(1) The division is in proportion to the services performed by each lawyer, or both lawyers expressly assume responsibility as if they were partners;
(2) The terms of the division are disclosed to the client. . . .

1981 Draft of Rule 1.5(b) continued to require that the ''basis or rate of a lawyer's fee shall be communicated to the client in writing before the lawyer renders substantial services in a matter. . . .''

1982 Draft was substantially the same as adopted.

1983 Rule: From its original adoption in 1983 until its amendment in 2002, Rule 1.5 provided as follows:

Rule 1.5 Fees

(a) A lawyer's fee shall be reasonable. The factors to be considered in determining the reasonableness of a fee include the following:
(1)-(8) [Same as 2002 version of Rules 1.5(a)(1)-(8).]

(b) When the lawyer has not regularly represented the client, the basis or rate of the fee shall be communicated to the client, preferably in writing, before or within a reasonable time after commencing the representation.

(c) A fee may be contingent on the outcome of the matter for which the service is rendered, except in a matter in which a contingent fee is prohibited by paragraph (d) or other law. A contingent fee agreement shall be in a writing and shall state the method by which the fee is to be determined, including the percentage or percentages that shall accrue to the lawyer in the event of settlement, trial or appeal; litigation and other expenses to be deducted from the recovery; and whether such expenses are to be deducted before or after the contingent fee is calculated. Upon conclusion of a contingent fee matter, the lawyer shall provide the client with a written statement stating the outcome of the matter and, if there is a recovery, showing the remittance to the client and the method of its determination.

(d) [Same as 2002 version of Rule 1.5(d).]

(e) A division of a fee between lawyers who are not in the same firm may be made only if:

(1) the division is in proportion to the services performed by each lawyer or, by written agreement with the client, each lawyer assumes joint responsibility for the representation;

(2) the client is advised of and does not object to the participation of all lawyers involved; and

(3) the total fee is reasonable.

2002 Amendments: In 2001, the ABA House of Delegates adopted most of the ABA Ethics 2000 Commission's proposed amendments to Rule 1.5. Specifically, the ABA amended Rule 1.5(a) to forbid unreasonable expenses; amended Rule 1.5(c) to require that a contingent fee agreement be signed by the client and notify the client of expenses for which the client will be liable; and amended Rule 1.5(e)(2) to require that the client agree to "the share each lawyer will receive" and confirm the agreement "in writing." But regarding Rule 1.5(b), the House of Delegates rejected the Commission's proposal to delete the word "preferably" before the words "in writing" (which would have made written disclosure mandatory). In addition, the House substituted the words "to the client" for the words "in writing" at the end of Rule 1.5(b) (which requires lawyers to communicate any changes in the basis or rate of the fee or expenses). The amendments also added Comments 1, 3, 6, and 8 and amended various other Comments to reflect the changes in the text of the rule.

Selected State Variations

Alaska: Rule 1.5(b) requires all fee agreements to be in writing when the fee will exceed $1,000. Moreover, Rule 1.5(f) instructs lawyers that they "should seek to avoid controversies over fees with clients and should attempt to resolve amicably any differences on the subject."

Arizona: Rule 1.5(b) requires lawyers to enter written fee agreements "before or within a reasonable time after commencing the representation." Arizona adds Rule 1.5(d)(3), which provides that when a lawyer denominates a fee as "earned upon receipt" or "nonrefundable," the client must be informed "in writing that the client may nevertheless discharge the lawyer at any time and in that event may be entitled to a refund of all or part of the fee based upon the value of the representation pursuant to paragraph (a)." Finally, Comment 6 says that Rule 1.5(d) allows a contingent fee "for legal representation in connection with the recovery of post-judgment balances due under support, alimony or other financial orders because such contracts do not implicate the same policy concerns" as other domestic relations matters.

Arkansas: Rule 1.5(d)(1) adds that in a domestic relations matter, "after a final order or decree is entered a lawyer may enter into a contingent fee contract for collection of payments which are due pursuant to such decree or order."

California: Rule 4-200 forbids lawyers to "enter into an agreement for, charge, or collect an illegal or unconscionable fee." Unconscionability is determined based on facts "existing at the time the agreement is entered into except where the parties contemplate that the fee will be affected by later events." The rule contains 11 factors to weigh in determining conscionability, many of them derived from the Model Rules. In addition, see Business & Professions Code §§6147-6149 (governing contingency fee contracts and other fee arrangements), and Business & Professions Code §§6200-6206 (establishing a system and procedures for arbitrating fee disputes).

Colorado: Rule 1.5(b) requires a lawyer who has not regularly represented a client to communicate the basis or rate of the fee and expenses "in writing." Moreover, Rule 1.5(b) provides that "[a]ny changes in the basis or rate of the fee or expenses shall also be promptly communicated to the client, in writing." Rule 1.5(c) requires more elaborate disclosures in contingency fee cases than the Model Rule.

Delaware: Rule 1.5(e) does not require that the client know how lawyers in different firms are dividing a fee. Delaware adds Rule 1.5(f), which allows the lawyer to require the client to pay fees in advance, provided that the lawyer gives the client "a written statement" explaining, among other things, that "the fee is refundable if not earned."

District of Columbia: D.C. Rule 1.5(b) requires a written fee agreement where the lawyer has not "regularly represented" the client. Rule 1.5(d) forbids contingent fees in criminal cases but not in matrimonial cases. Rule 1.5(e) does not require that the client be told how much each lawyer is to receive when fees are divided between lawyers not in the same firm, but the client must be told "the effect of the association of lawyers outside the firm on the fee to be charged."

Florida: Rule 4-1.5(a) prohibits any fee "generated by employment that was obtained through advertising or solicitation not in compliance with the Rules Regulating The Florida Bar" or that is "clearly excessive." A clearly excessive fee includes (1) a fee that exceeds a reasonable fee by so much that it constitutes "clear overreaching or an unconscionable demand," or (2) a fee sought or secured "by means of intentional misrepresentation or fraud upon the client, a nonclient party, or any court, as to either entitlement to, or amount of, the fee." Florida also caps the percentage amount of any contingent fee.

Rule 4-1.5(e) provides that "a fee for legal services that is nonrefundable in any part shall be confirmed in writing and shall explain the intent of the parties as to the nature and amount of the nonrefundable fee. The test of reasonableness found in subdivision (b), above, applies to all fees for legal services without regard to their characterization by the parties."

Regarding fee sharing between lawyers in different firms, Rule 4-1.5(f)(2) requires that each participating lawyer "shall sign the contract with the client and shall agree to assume joint legal responsibility to the client for the performance of the services in question as if each were partners of the other lawyer or law firm involved." Florida also tightly controls the terms on which lawyers in different firms may share fees. Rule 4-1.5(f)(4)(D) provides that "the lawyer assuming primary responsibility for the legal services" must receive "a minimum of 75% of the total fee," and "the lawyer assuming secondary responsibility" can receive "a maximum of 25% of the total fee. Any fee in excess of 25% shall be presumed to be clearly excessive." But if two or more lawyers expect to "accept substantially equal active participation in the providing of legal services," then they may seek court authorization to divide the fee however they propose "based upon a sworn petition signed by all counsel that shall disclose in detail those services to be performed."

Florida Rule 4-1.5(g) provides that if lawyers in different firms share fees on a basis not in proportion to the amount of work done, then each lawyer must not only agree to assume "joint legal responsibility for the representation" but must also agree "to be available for consultation with the client."

The Florida Supreme Court may also order any lawyer found guilty of violating the fee rules "to forfeit the fee or any part thereof," either by returning the excessive part of any fee to the client or by forfeiting all or part of an otherwise improper fee to the Florida Bar Clients' Security Fund. See Florida Supreme Court Rule 3-5.1(h).

Finally, Rule 4-1.5(i) provides that, if a retainer agreement includes a mandatory arbitration clause, the agreement must include a verbatim, bolded recitation of the notice that appears at the end of Rule 1.5(i).

Georgia: In the rules effective November 3, 2011, Rule 1.5(c)(2) provides that, at the conclusion of a contingent fee matter, the lawyer must provide the client with a written statement that discloses, among other information, "if the attorney's fee is divided with another lawyer who is not a partner in or an associate of the lawyer's firm or law office, the amount of the fee received by each and the manner in which the division is determined." Georgia also adds to Rule 1.5(e)(2) that the client must be "advised of the share that each lawyer is to receive" when lawyers in different firms share a fee.

Illinois: Rule 1.5(e)(1) provides that a division of a fee with a lawyer in a different firm is permissible if it "is in proportion to the services performed by each lawyer, or if the primary service performed by one lawyer is the referral of the client to another lawyer and each lawyer assumes joint financial responsibility for the representation."

Maine includes two additional considerations in Rule 1.5(a): whether the client gave informed consent to the fee agreement and whether the fee agreement was in writing. In Rule 1.5(d)(3), Maine prohibits a lawyer from charging a fee based on "a percentage of the value of the estate" for administering an estate in probate.

Massachusetts: Rule 1.5(c) does not require a contingent fee to be in writing if it concerns "the collection of commercial accounts" or "insurance company subrogation claims," but all other contingent fee agreements must be in writing and must contain greater detail than Model Rule 1.5(c) requires. Rule 1.5(e) permits a lawyer to pay a fee to a referring lawyer even when the referring lawyer does not perform any services or take joint responsibility for the matter. Although client consent to such a referral fee must be in writing, a comment indicates that the lawyer does not have to disclose the size of the referral fee unless the client asks. Finally, Massachusetts Rule 1.5 appends two model form contingency fee agreements, and Rule 1.5(f), which has no Model Rule equivalent, identifies explanations that a lawyer must provide to clients when using the model form contingency fee agreements.

Michigan: Rule 1.5(d) forbids contingent fees in "a domestic relations matter" without qualification. In personal injury and wrongful death claims, Michigan Court Rule 8.121 sets a maximum contingent fee of "one-third of the amount recovered" and provides that receiving, retaining, or sharing a larger contingent fee "shall be deemed to be the charging of a 'clearly excessive fee' in violation of" Rule 1.5(a). Michigan omits ABA Model Rule 1.5(e)(1).

New Hampshire: Rule 1.5(e) permits fee sharing between lawyers in different firms if the division is made "either: (a) in reasonable proportion to the services performed or responsibility or risks assumed by each, or (b) based on an agreement with the referring lawyer," provided that in either case the lawyers obtain the client's signed written agreement to the division of fees and the total fee charged by all lawyers "is not increased by the division of fees and is reasonable."

New Jersey: Rule 1.5(b) requires a fee agreement to be in writing if the lawyer has not regularly represented the client. In addition, New Jersey has adopted various court rules that tightly control contingent fees, especially in tort cases.

New York: Rule 1.5 contains numerous significant variations. For example, 1.5(a) relies on the definition of an excessive fee found in DR 2-106(B) of the old Model Code. Moreover, Rule 1.5(d) prohibits:

> (2) a fee prohibited by law or rule of court;
> (3) a fee based on fraudulent billing;
> (4) a nonrefundable retainer fee; provided that a lawyer may enter into a retainer agreement with a client containing a reasonable minimum fee clause if it defines in plain language and sets forth the circumstances under which such fee may be incurred and how it will be calculated. . . .

Comments 1A and 1B explain the purpose of Rule 1.5(d)(3) as follows:

> [1A] A billing is fraudulent if it is knowingly and intentionally based on false or inaccurate information. Thus, under an hourly billing arrangement, it would be fraudulent to knowingly and intentionally charge a client for more than the actual number of hours spent by the lawyer on the client's matter; similarly, where the client has agreed to pay the lawyer's cost of in-house services, such as for photocopying or telephone calls, it would be fraudulent knowingly and intentionally to charge a client more than the actual costs incurred. Fraudulent billing requires an element of scienter and does not include inaccurate billing due to an innocent mistake.
> [1B] A supervising lawyer who submits a fraudulent bill for fees or expenses to a client based on submissions by a subordinate lawyer has not automatically violated this Rule. In this situation, whether the lawyer is responsible for a violation must be determined by reference to Rules 5.1, 5.2, and 5.3. . . .

Comment 5A explains that "New York Court Rules require every lawyer with an office located in New York to post in that office, in a manner visible to clients of the lawyer, a 'Statement of Client's Rights.' " Rule 1.5(e) provides that a copy of this Statement must be provided to all domestic relations clients.

Finally, New York Court Rules supplement Rule 1.5(b) and provide that most fee agreements must be in writing. 22 N.Y.C.R.R. Part 1215 provides as follows:

Part 1215 Written Letter of Engagement

§1215.1 Requirements

(a) Effective March 4, 2002, an attorney who undertakes to represent a client and enters into an arrangement for, charges or collects any fee from a client shall provide to the client a written letter of engagement before commencing the representation, or within a reasonable time thereafter (i) if otherwise impracticable or (ii) if the scope of services to be provided cannot be determined at the time of the commencement of representation. For purposes of this rule, where an entity (such as an insurance carrier) engages an attorney to represent a third party, the term "client" shall mean the entity that engages the attorney. Where there is a significant change in the scope of services or the fee to be charged, an updated letter of engagement shall be provided to the client.

(b) The letter of engagement shall address the following matters:

(1) explanation of the scope of the legal services to be provided;

(2) explanation of attorney's fees to be charged, expenses and billing practices; and,

(3) where applicable, shall provide that the client may have a right to arbitrate fee disputes under Part 137 of this Title.

(c) Instead of providing the client with a written letter of engagement, an attorney may comply with the provisions of subdivision (a) of this section by entering into a signed written retainer agreement with the client, before or within a reasonable time after commencing the representation, provided that the agreement addresses the matters set forth in subdivision (b) of this section.

§1215.2 Exceptions

This section shall not apply to

(a) representation of a client where the fee to be charged is expected to be less than $3000;

(b) representation where the attorney's services are of the same general kind as previously rendered to and paid for by the client;

(c) representation in domestic relations matters subject to Part 1400 of this Title; or

(d) representation where the attorney is admitted to practice in another jurisdiction and maintains no office in the State of New York, or where no material portion of the services are to be rendered in New York.

North Carolina: Rule 1.5(a) forbids a "clearly excessive fee" but otherwise substantially tracks ABA Model Rule 1.5(a). North Carolina adds Rule 1.5(f), which provides as follows:

(f) Any lawyer having a dispute with a client regarding a fee for legal services must:

(1) make reasonable efforts to advise his or her client of the existence of the North Carolina State Bar's program of fee dispute resolution at least 30 days prior to initiating legal proceedings to collect the disputed fee; and

(2) participate in good faith in the fee dispute resolution process if the client submits a proper request.

Ohio: Rule 1.5(b) requires fee agreements to be in writing unless the lawyer has "regularly represented" the client and is charging on the same basis or the fee is $500 or less. Any change in the basis of a fee previously communicated must be "promptly communicated to the client in writing." Rule 1.5(e), in permitting division of fees, does not require that the client be informed of the amount each lawyer is receiving.

Oregon: Among other variations, Rule 1.5(d) permits a division of fees between lawyers in different firms if "(1) the client gives informed consent to the fact that there will be a division of fees, and (2) the total fee of the lawyers for all legal services they rendered the client is not clearly excessive."

Pennsylvania: Rule 1.5(a) prohibits an "illegal or clearly excessive fee" (rather than an "unreasonable" one) and makes no reference to expenses. Rule 1.5(b) requires a fee agreement to be "in writing" if a lawyer has not "regularly" represented a client. Pennsylvania Rule 1.5(e) requires only that "(1) the client is advised of and does not object to the participation of all the lawyers involved, and (2) the total fee of the lawyers is not illegal or clearly excessive. . . ."

Rhode Island: Rule 1.5(b) provides that if a lawyer has not regularly represented a client, the basis or rate of the fee "shall be communicated to the client in writing." The same rule requires lawyers to send quarterly bills unless the client agrees to a different billing schedule or the fee is fixed or contingent.

South Carolina: Rule 1.5(d)(1) expressly permits a lawyer to charge a contingency fee "in collection of past due alimony or child support." Moreover, effective July 30, 2012, South Carolina adds Rule 1.5(f), which governs advance fees (*i.e.,* fees paid prior to the performance of the legal services for which the fee has been paid).

Texas: Rule 1.04(a) forbids "illegal" or "unconscionable" fees and lists the same considerations as in ABA Model Rule 1.5. The Texas Rules do not forbid contingent fees in family law matters but the Comment says they are "rarely justified." Rule 1.04(f), which governs the division of fees between lawyers in different firms, generally parallels ABA Model Rule 1.5(e) but requires client consent "in writing to the terms of the arrangement prior to the time of the association or referral proposed. . . ."

Tennessee adds two additional factors to Rule 1.5(b): "(9) prior advertisements or statements by the lawyer with respect to the fees the lawyer charges; and (10) whether the fee agreement is in writing." Moreover, Tennessee adds Rule 1.5(f), which allows lawyers to collect nonrefundable fees and retainers as long as the fee agreement is in writing, is signed by the client, and "explains the intent of the parties as to the nature and amount of the nonrefundable fee."

Virginia: Rule 1.5(b) provides in part: "The lawyer's fee shall be adequately explained to the client." Rule 1.5(d)(1) forbids contingent fees in "a domestic relations matter, except in rare instances." Comment 3a says that those rare instances include situations where "the parties are divorced and reconciliation is not a realistic prospect." Rule 1.5(e) requires full disclosure to the client when lawyers are dividing a fee. The "terms of the division of the fee" must be "disclosed to the client," the client must consent, the total fee must be reasonable, and the fee division and client consent must be "obtained in advance of the rendering of legal services." However, while a writing is said to be preferable, none is required.

Wisconsin: Rule 1.5(e) permits lawyers in different firms to divide a fee only if the total fee is reasonable and the lawyers satisfy several other specific requirements.

Related Materials

ABA Commission on Billable Hours: In 2001, the ABA appointed the Commission on the Billable Hour. In 2002, the commission issued its report, which is available (together with a lengthy appendix and other useful materials on the billable hour) at *http://www.judicialaccountability.org/articles/ABABillableHours2002.pdf.* The Commission's purpose is eloquently explained in the preface to the report, which provides, in pertinent part, as follows:

> It has become increasingly clear that many of the legal profession's contemporary woes intersect at the billable hour. The 1960s marked the coming of age of the billable hour. . . .
>
> Today, unintended consequences of the billable hours model have permeated the profession. A recent study by the ABA shows that many young attorneys are leaving the profession due to a lack of balance in their lives. The unending drive for billable hours has had a negative effect not only on family and personal relationships, but on the public service role that lawyers traditionally have played in society. The elimination of discretionary time has taken a toll on pro bono work and our profession's ability to be involved in our communities. At the same time, professional development, workplace stimulation, mentoring and lawyer/client relationships have all suffered as a result of billable hour pressures.
>
> The profession is paying the price. Disaffection with the practice of law is illustrated by a feeling of frustration and isolation on the part of newer lawyers who, due to time-billing pressures, are not being as well mentored as in the past. Time pressures also result in less willingness on the part of lawyers to be collegial, which only exacerbates work load since it necessitates that everything be put in writing. Not coincidentally, public respect for lawyers has been waning since the 1970s. All this at a time when lawyers are less interested in climbing the corporate ladder and more interested in life balance. Many lawyers indicate that they would gladly take a substantial pay cut in exchange for a decrease in billable hours. . . .
>
> . . . The billable hour is fundamentally about quantity over quality, repetition over creativity. With no gauge for intangibles such as productivity, creativity, knowledge or technological advancements, the billable hours model is a counter-intuitive measure of value. Alternatives that encourage efficiency and improve processes not only increase profits and provide early resolution of legal matters, but are less likely to garner ethical concerns.
>
> That said, the outright elimination of time billing is not a likely proposition. In fact, time billing as one aspect of price-setting for legal services is an appropriate and necessary tool in certain situations. Our profession's goal, however, should be to adopt innovative billing methods that provide an accurate measure of value to the client and, at the same time, make the practice of law more fulfilling and enjoyable.

ABA Formal Ethics Opinions: See ABA Formal Ethics Ops. 87-354 (1987), 93-373 (1993), 93-379 (1993), 94-389 (1994), 00-418 (2000), 00-420 (2000), 02-426 (2002), and 08-451 (2008).

ABA Model Rules for Fee Arbitration: In 1992, the ABA Commission on Evaluation of Disciplinary Enforcement (the McKay Commission) recommended that each state establish mandatory arbitration for fee disputes. In 1995, the ABA adopted Model Rules for Fee Arbitration, which mandate fee arbitration if the client requests it. Some states go further than the ABA Model by making fee arbitration binding as well as mandatory. (A few states do not mandate fee arbitration, but make it binding if the lawyer and client agree to arbitrate the dispute.) No state gives lawyers the option to require fee arbitration. The Model Rules for Fee Arbitration and the explanatory Comments were amended by the ABA House of Delegates at the ABA's Mid-Year Meeting. A redline version showing the amendments is available at *http://www.abanow.org/2012/01/2012mm105/.* The full set of the 2007 ABA Model Rules for Fee Arbitration is available online, together with other useful materials on client protection, at *http://www.americanbar.org/groups/professional_responsibility/resources/client_protection/contents.html.*

ABA TIPS Task Force on the Contingent Fee: In 2003, the Chair of the ABA Tort Trial & Insurance Practice Section (TIPS) appointed a Task Force on Contingent Fees. The Task Force is especially concerned about support by various state medical associations and other organizations for statutes and ethical rules severely limiting contingent fees. In 2004, the Task Force issued a lengthy Report on Contingent Fees in Medical Malpractice Litigation. The Report included the following conclusions:

> A. Limitations on fees … risk compromising access to justice by medical malpractice victims. Without the prospect of reasonable fees, competent counsel would be unwilling to assume the high cost burden associated with typically complex medical malpractice actions.
> B. The right of people who have suffered injury as a result of medical malpractice to seek redress for their injuries in the courts must be ensured. A fair and reasonable contingent fee is essential to preserve that right.

However, to help keep contingent fee rates down, the Task Force proposed standardized disclosures such as (a) details about how medical malpractice cases are typically handled; (b) predicted costs of litigation (expert fees, investigation, discovery, etc.); (c) alternative fee arrangements, including how fees are calculated; (d) urging clients to seek out experienced, perhaps specialized, law firms; and (e) noting that interviewing several firms and requesting written bids can lower litigation costs. More information about the Task Force, and the full text of its Report, is available at *http://apps.americanbar.org/tips/contingent/home.html.*

Bankruptcy Fee Guidelines: In 1996, pursuant to 28 U.S.C. §586, the United States Trustee Program (USTP) promulgated Guidelines for Reviewing Applications for Compensation and Reimbursement of Expenses filed under 11 U.S.C. §330 (the "1996 guidelines"). The fee guidelines are statements of policy that the USTP follows when reviewing applications for compensation. In an effort to control steep fee increases in bankruptcy cases, the USTP is revising the 1996 guidelines in phases.

On November 4, 2011, the USTP posted for public comment proposed guidelines for reviewing applications for attorney compensation in "larger" Chapter 11 cases (i.e., more than $50 million in combined assets and liabilities). The comment period on the proposed guidelines initially ended on January 31, 2012, but because of harsh comments, the USTP extended the comment period to May 21, 2012. When we went to press, the USTP was still considering the proposed guidelines. Until the USTP adopts superseding guidelines, the 1996 guidelines will continue in effect for the review of applications filed under 11 U.S.C. §330 in (1) larger Chapter 11 cases by non-attorneys seeking compensation, (2) all Chapter 11 cases below the $50 million threshold, and (3) cases under other chapters of the Bankruptcy Code. The 1996 guidelines are reprinted in an Appendix to 28 C.F.R. Part 58 and are available online at *http://www.justice.gov/ust/eo/rules_regulations/guidelines/docs/feeguide.htm.*

Caps on Contingent Fees: Various state and federal laws place upper limits on contingent fees, especially in medical malpractice cases, tort cases, and government benefit cases. At the federal level, for example, 42 U.S.C. §406(b) provides that attorneys who successfully represent Social Security benefits claimants may not charge more than 25 percent of the past-due benefits recovered. Another federal law, 28 U.S.C. §2678, imposes a strict 25 percent maximum on fees in suits brought under the Federal Tort Claims Act, and a violation is subject to criminal penalties ("Any attorney who charges, demands, receives, or collects . . . in excess of that allowed under this section . . . shall be fined not more than $2,000 or imprisoned not more than one year, or both").

At the state level, California's Medical Injury Compensation Reform Act (MICRA), Cal. Civ. Code §3333.2 ("Negligence of Health Care Provider; Noneconomic Losses; Limitation"), limits attorney fees in medical malpractice cases to 40 percent of the first $50,000 recovered, 33 percent of the second $50,000, 25 percent of a recovery between $100,000 and $600,000, and 15 percent of a recovery over $600,000. In New York, Judiciary Law §474-a ("Contingent Fees for Attorneys in Claims or Actions for Medical, Dental or Podiatric Malpractice") establishes a similar sliding scale. Outside the medical malpractice area, New York court rules such as 22 N.Y.C.R.R. §603.7(e) generally limit contingent fees to 33-⅓ percent in all personal injury and wrongful death cases.

In some states, ballot measures have limited contingent fees in medical malpractice cases. For example, in 2004, by a roughly 2-1 margin, Florida voters passed a constitutional amendment sponsored by Citizens for a Fair Share, a political action committee supported by the Florida Medical Association. The amendment, now codified as Article 1, §26 of the Florida Constitution, provides as follows:

> *Claimant's right to fair compensation.* In any medical liability claim involving a contingency fee, the claimant is entitled to receive no less than 70% of the first $250,000.00 in all damages received by the claimant, exclusive of reasonable and customary costs, whether received by judgment, settlement, or otherwise, and regardless of the number of defendants. The claimant is entitled to 90% of all damages in excess of $250,000.00, exclusive of reasonable and customary costs and regardless of the number of defendants. This provision is self-executing and does not require implementing legislation.

Also in 2004, in a referendum that won by a 59 percent to 41 percent margin, Nevada voters passed a law entitled "Keep Our Doctors in Nevada" that limits attorney fees in medical malpractice cases to 40 percent of the first $50,000 recovered, 33-⅓ percent of the next $50,000, 25 percent of the next $500,000, and 15 percent of any amount over $600,000.

FTC Mortgage Assistance Relief Services Rule: During the mortgage foreclosure crisis that began in 2008, many lawyers and nonlawyers went into the business of obtaining modifications to home mortgages. According to the Federal Trade Commission (FTC), many nonlawyer mortgage relief firms pretend to be affiliated with the government or with government housing assistance programs and routinely charge up-front fees for services, but often do not deliver the services. To combat these abuses, in 2010 the FTC issued a final Mortgage Assistance Relief Services Rule, 16 C.F.R. Part 322, that prohibits mortgage relief companies from accepting any payment for their services until they obtain a documented offer from a mortgage lender or servicer that satisfies any promises made to a borrower seeking assistance. The rule also requires mortgage relief companies to tell consumers that consumers have the right to reject an offer without any charge, and requires companies to make certain other disclosures.

However, lawyers who provide mortgage assistance relief services as part of the practice of law (such as when giving bankruptcy advice), and who are licensed in the state where the borrower is located, are generally exempt from all provisions of the final rule except the prohibition on advance fees—and lawyers are also exempt from that prohibition if they place any advance fees for loan mitigation services into a lawyer trust account and abide by state laws and regulations (including Rule 1.15) governing those accounts.

IRS Regulations: In the regulations governing practice before the Internal Revenue Service, 31 C.F.R. §10.27(a) prohibits an "unconscionable fee in connection with any matter before the Internal Revenue Service," and §10.27(b) generally prohibits a lawyer from charging a contingent fee for services rendered in connection with any matter before the Internal Revenue Service, but §10.27(b) states the following exceptions:

> (2) A practitioner may charge a contingent fee for services rendered in connection with the Service's examination of, or challenge to —
> (i) An original tax return; or
> (ii) An amended return or claim for refund or credit where the amended return or claim for refund or credit was filed within 120 days of the taxpayer receiving a written notice of the examination of, or a written challenge to the original tax return.
> (3) A practitioner may charge a contingent fee for services rendered in connection with a claim for credit or refund filed solely in connection with the determination of statutory interest or penalties assessed by the Internal Revenue Service.
> (4) A practitioner may charge a contingent fee for services rendered in connection with any judicial proceeding arising under the Internal Revenue Code.

Private Securities Litigation Reform Act: In 1995, over President Clinton's veto, Congress passed the Private Securities Litigation Reform Act, 15 U.S.C. §77z-1. Title I of the statute combats unreasonable fees by providing that total attorney fees and expenses awarded by a court "shall not exceed a reasonable percentage of the amount of any damages and prejudgment interest actually paid to the class." §77z-1(a)(6). According to the committee report, this provision is intended to replace the "lodestar" method of computing fees and to give courts flexibility to determine reasonable fees and expenses on a case-by-case basis.

Restatement of the Law Governing Lawyers: See Restatement §§17(1), 19(2), 34, 35, 37-43, and 47 in our chapter on the Restatement later in this volume.

Rule 1.6   Confidentiality of Information

Canon and Code Antecedents

ABA Canons of Professional Ethics: Canon 37 provided as follows:

37.   Confidences of a Client

> It is the duty of a lawyer to preserve his client's confidences. This duty outlasts the lawyer's employment, and extends as well to his employees; and neither of them should accept employment which involves or may involve the disclosure or use of these confidences, either for the private advantage of the lawyer or his employees or to the disadvantage of the client, without his knowledge and consent, and even though there

are other available sources of such information. A lawyer should not continue employment when he discovers that this obligation prevents the performance of his full duty to his former or to his new client.

 If a lawyer is accused by his client, he is not precluded from disclosing the truth in respect to the accusation. The announced intention of a client to commit a crime is not included within the confidences which he is bound to respect. He may properly make such disclosures as may be necessary to prevent the act or protect those against whom it is threatened.

ABA Model Code of Professional Responsibility: Compare DR 4-101(A)-(C) (reprinted later in this volume).

Cross-References in Other Rules

 Scope ¶17: "Most of the duties flowing from the client-lawyer relationship attach only after the client has requested the lawyer to render legal services and the lawyer has agreed to do so. But there are some duties, such as that of confidentiality under **Rule 1.6**, that attach when the lawyer agrees to consider whether a client-lawyer relationship shall be established."

 Rule 1.0, Comment 6: "Many of the Rules of Professional Conduct require the lawyer to obtain the informed consent of a client or other person before accepting or continuing representation or pursuing a course of conduct (see Rules 1.2(c), **1.6(a)** and 1.7(b))."

 Rule 1.1, Comment 6: "Before a lawyer retains or contracts with other lawyers outside the lawyer's own firm to provide or assist in the provision of legal services to a client, the lawyer should ordinarily obtain informed consent from the client and must reasonably believe that the other lawyers' services will contribute to the competent and ethical representation of the client. See also **Rules** 1.2 (allocation of authority), 1.4 (communication with client), 1.5(e) (fee sharing), **1.6** (confidentiality), and 5.5(a) (unauthorized practice of law)."

 Rule 1.8(f)(3): "A lawyer shall not accept compensation for representing a client from one other than the client unless information relating to representation of a client is protected as required by **Rule 1.6**."

 Rule 1.8, Comment 5: It is prohibited to partake in the "disadvantageous use of client information unless the client gives informed consent, except as permitted or required by these Rules. See Rules 1.2(d), **1.6**, 1.9(c), 3.3, 4.1(b), 8.1 and 8.3."

 Rule 1.8, Comment 12: "If, however, the fee arrangement creates a conflict of interest for the lawyer. . . . The lawyer must conform to the requirements of **Rule 1.6** concerning confidentiality."

 Rule 1.9(b): "A lawyer shall not knowingly represent a person in the same or a substantially related matter in which a firm with which the lawyer formerly was associated had previously represented a client whose interests are materially adverse to that person and about whom the lawyer had acquired information protected by **Rules 1.6** and 1.9(c) that is material to the matter. . . ."

 Rule 1.9, Comment 5: "Paragraph (b) operates to disqualify the lawyer only when the lawyer involved has actual knowledge of information protected by **Rules 1.6** and 1.9(c)."

 Rule 1.9, Comment 7: "Independent of the question of disqualification of a firm, a lawyer changing professional association has a continuing duty to preserve confidentiality of information about a client formerly represented. See **Rules 1.6** and 1.9(c)."

Rule 1.10(b)(2) restricts representation when "any lawyer remaining in the firm has information protected by **Rules 1.6** and 1.9(c) that is material to the matter."

Rule 1.10, Comment 5: When a lawyer who represents or formerly represented a client leaves a firm, the firm may not represent a person with interests adverse to that client where the matter is the same or substantially related and "any other lawyer currently in the firm has material information protected by **Rules 1.6** and 1.9 (c)."

Rule 1.12, Comment 3: "Although lawyers who serve as third-party neutrals do not have information concerning the parties that is protected under **Rule 1.6**, they typically owe the parties an obligation of confidentiality under law or codes of ethics governing third-party neutrals."

Rule 1.13, Comment 2: "When one of the constituents of an organizational client communicates with the organization's lawyer in that person's organizational capacity, the communication is protected by **Rule 1.6**. Thus, by way of example, if an organizational client requests its lawyer to investigate allegations of wrongdoing, interviews made in the course of that investigation between the lawyer and the client's employees or other constituents are covered by **Rule 1.6**. This does not mean, however, that constituents of an organizational client are the clients of the lawyer. The lawyer may not disclose to such constituents information relating to the representation except for disclosures explicitly or impliedly authorized by the organizational client in order to carry out the representation or as otherwise permitted by **Rule 1.6**."

Rule 1.13, Comment 6: Paragraph (c) of this Rule supplements **Rule 1.6(b)** by providing an additional basis upon which the lawyer may reveal information relating to the representation, but does not modify, restrict, or limit the provisions of **Rule 1.6(b)(1)-(6)**. . . . If the lawyer's services are being used by an organization to further a crime or fraud by the organization, **Rule 1.6(b)(2) and 1.6(b)(3)** may permit the lawyer to disclose confidential information.

Rule 1.14(c): "Information relating to the representation of a client with diminished capacity is protected by **Rule 1.6**. When taking protective action pursuant to paragraph (b), the lawyer is impliedly authorized under **Rule 1.6(a)** to reveal information about the client, but only to the extent reasonably necessary to protect the client's interests."

Rule 1.14, Comment 8: "Disclosure of the client's diminished capacity could adversely affect the client's interests. . . . Information relating to the representation is protected by **Rule 1.6**. Therefore, unless authorized to do so, the lawyer may not disclose such information."

Rule 1.16, Comment 3: "Lawyers should be mindful of their obligations to both clients and the court under **Rules 1.6** and 3.3."

Rule 1.17, Comment 7: "Negotiations between seller and prospective purchaser prior to disclosure of information relating to a specific representation of an identifiable client no more violate the confidentiality provisions of Model **Rule 1.6** than do preliminary discussions concerning the possible association of another lawyer or mergers between firms, with respect to which client consent is not required. See **Rule 1.6(b)(7)**. Providing the purchaser access to detailed information relating to the representation, such as the client's file, however, requires client consent."

Rule 1.17, Comment 11: A lawyer selling a law practice has "the obligation to protect information relating to the representation (see **Rules 1.6** and 1.9)."

Rule 2.3(c): "Except as disclosure is authorized in connection with a report of an evaluation, information relating to the evaluation is otherwise protected by **Rule 1.6**."

Rule 2.3, Comment 5: "Information relating to an evaluation is protected by **Rule 1.6**. In many situations, providing an evaluation to a third party poses no significant risk to the client; thus, the lawyer may be impliedly authorized to disclose information to carry out the representation. See **Rule 1.6(a)**. Where, however, it is reasonably likely that providing the evaluation will affect the client's interests materially and adversely, the lawyer must first obtain the client's consent after the client has been adequately informed concerning the important possible effects on the client's interests. See **Rules 1.6(a)** and 1.0(e)."

Rule 3.3(c): "The duties stated in paragraphs (a) and (b) continue to the conclusion of the proceeding, and apply even if compliance requires disclosure of information otherwise protected by **Rule 1.6**."

Rule 3.3, Comment 10: "If withdrawal from the representation is not permitted or will not undo the effect of the false evidence, the advocate must make such disclosure to the tribunal as is reasonably necessary to remedy the situation, even if doing so requires the lawyer to reveal information that otherwise would be protected by **Rule 1.6**."

Rule 3.3, Comment 15: "In connection with a request for permission to withdraw that is premised on a client's misconduct, a lawyer may reveal information relating to the representation only to the extent reasonably necessary to comply with this Rule or as otherwise permitted by **Rule 1.6**."

Rule 4.1(b): "In the course of representing a client a lawyer shall not knowingly fail to disclose a material fact when disclosure is necessary to avoid assisting a criminal or fraudulent act by a client, unless disclosure is prohibited by **Rule 1.6**."

Rule 4.1, Comment 3: "If the lawyer can avoid assisting a client's crime or fraud only by disclosing this information, then under paragraph (b) the lawyer is required to do so, unless the disclosure is prohibited by **Rule 1.6**."

Rule 5.3, Comment 3: "The extent of this obligation will depend upon the circumstances, including the education, experience and reputation of the nonlawyer; the nature of the services involved; the terms of any arrangements concerning the protection of client information; and the legal and ethical environments of the jurisdictions in which the services will be performed, particularly with regard to confidentiality. See also **Rules** 1.1 (competence), 1.2 (allocation of authority), 1.4 (communication with client), **1.6** (confidentiality), 5.4(a) (professional independence of the lawyer), and 5.5(a) (unauthorized practice of law)."

Rule 5.7, Comment 10: "When a lawyer is obliged to accord the recipients of such services the protections of those Rules that apply to the client-lawyer relationship, the lawyer must . . . scrupulously adhere to the requirements of **Rule 1.6** relating to disclosure of confidential information."

Rule 6.5, Comment 2: Regarding "a lawyer who provides short-term limited legal services pursuant to this Rule . . . [e]xcept as provided in this Rule, the Rules of Professional Conduct, including **Rules 1.6** and 1.9(c), are applicable to the limited representation."

Rule 8.1(b): "[T]his rule does not require disclosure of information otherwise protected by **Rule 1.6**."

Rule 8.1, Comment 3: "A lawyer representing an applicant for admission to the bar, or representing a lawyer who is the subject of a disciplinary inquiry or proceeding, is governed by the rules applicable to the client-lawyer relationship, including **Rule 1.6** and, in some cases, Rule 3.3."

Rule 8.3(c): "This Rule does not require disclosure of information otherwise protected by **Rule 1.6** or information gained by a lawyer or judge while participating in an approved lawyers assistance program."

Rule 8.3, Comment 2: "A report about misconduct is not required where it would involve violation of **Rule 1.6**."

Legislative History of Model Rule 1.6

1979 Unofficial Pre-Circulation Draft:

(a) In giving testimony or providing evidence concerning a client's affairs, a lawyer shall not disclose matter concerning the client except as permitted under the applicable law of evidentiary privilege. In other circumstances, a lawyer shall not disclose information about a client acquired in serving the client in a professional capacity except as stated in paragraphs (b), (c) and (d).

(b) A lawyer shall disclose information about a client when directed to do so by the client and may do so when disclosure is necessary in the representation.

(c) A lawyer shall disclose information about a client

(1) to the extent necessary to prevent the client from committing an act that would seriously endanger the life or safety of a person, result in wrongful detention or incarceration of a person or wrongful destruction of substantial property, or corrupt judicial or governmental procedure;

(2) when disclosure by the lawyer is required by law or the rules of professional conduct.

(d) A lawyer may disclose information about a client

(1) to the extent necessary to prevent or rectify the consequences of a deliberately wrongful act by the client in which the lawyer's services are or were involved, except when the lawyer has been employed after the commission of such an act to represent the client concerning the act or its consequences. . . .

1980 Discussion Draft:

(b) A lawyer shall disclose information about a client to the extent it appears necessary to prevent the client from committing an act that would result in death or serious bodily harm to another person, and to the extent required by law or the rules of professional conduct.

(c) A lawyer may disclose information about a client only:

(1) For the purposes of serving the client's interest, unless it is information the client has specifically requested not to be disclosed;

(2) To the extent it appears necessary to prevent or rectify the consequences of a deliberately wrongful act by the client, except when the lawyer has been employed after the commission of such an act to represent the client concerning the act or its consequences. . . .

1981 Draft:

(b) A lawyer may reveal such information to the extent the lawyer believes necessary:

(1) to serve the client's interests, unless it is information the client has specifically requested not to be disclosed;

(2) to prevent the client from committing a criminal or fraudulent act that the lawyer believes is likely to result in death or substantial bodily harm, or substantial injury to the financial interest or property of another;

(3) to rectify the consequences of a client's criminal or fraudulent act in the commission of which the lawyer's services had been used. . . .

1982 Draft:

(b) A lawyer may reveal such information to the extent the lawyer reasonably believes necessary:

(1) to prevent the client from committing a criminal or fraudulent act that the lawyer reasonably believes is likely to result in death or substantial bodily harm, or in substantial injury to the financial interests or property of another;

(2) to rectify the consequences of a client's criminal or fraudulent act in the furtherance of which the lawyer's services had been used. . . .

1983 Rule: From its original adoption in 1983 until it was first amended in 2002, Rule 1.6 provided as follows:

Rule 1.6 Confidentiality of Information

(a) A lawyer shall not reveal information relating to the representation of a client unless the client consents after consultation, except for disclosures that are impliedly authorized in order to carry out the representation and except as stated in paragraph (b).

(b) A lawyer may reveal such information to the extent the lawyer reasonably believes necessary:

(1) to prevent the client from committing a criminal act that the lawyer believes is likely to result in imminent death or substantial bodily harm;

(2) [Same as self-defense exception in 2003 version of Rule 1.6(b)(5).]

1991 Proposal: In 1991, the Standing Committee on Ethics and Professional Responsibility proposed amending Rule 1.6(b) to permit a lawyer to reveal information that the lawyer reasonably believed necessary to "rectify the consequences of a client's criminal or fraudulent act in the commission of which the lawyer's services had been used." The House of Delegates defeated this proposal by a vote of 251 to 158. The rejected amendment would have been accompanied by several new Comments to Rule 1.6, including one that said: "To the extent a lawyer is prohibited from making disclosure, the interests of the potential victim are sacrificed in favor of preserving the client's confidences even though the client's purpose is wrongful."

2002 Amendments: In 2002, the ABA House of Delegates adopted without change most of the ABA Ethics 2000 Commission proposals to amend Rule 1.6 and its Comment. But in 2001, the House of Delegates had voted against a proposed new paragraph in Rule 1.6(b) that was identical to the proposal adopted two years later (in 2003) as Rule 1.6(b)(2). After the House of Delegates defeated proposed subparagraph (b)(2), the Ethics 2000 Commission withdrew a proposed paragraph (b)(3) before any vote was taken, but the withdrawn paragraph was also adopted in 2003, as Rule 1.6(b)(3). The two proposed paragraphs would have been accompanied by two new proposed Comments to Rule 1.6, which were likewise adopted in 2003 as Comments 7 and 8 to Rule 1.6.

The unsuccessful proposals were eventually adopted with the support of the ABA Task Force on Corporate Responsibility, chaired by attorney James H. Cheek,

III, which recommended in April 2003 that the rejected paragraphs (b)(2) and (b)(3), and the accompanying Comments, be reconsidered and adopted. Until the 2002 amendments, ABA Model Rule 1.6 did not contain paragraphs (b)(4) and (b)(6) (relating to securing legal advice and complying with other laws or court orders). In addition, paragraph (b)(1) was originally much narrower, permitting revelation of client confidences only "to the extent the lawyer reasonably believes necessary . . . to prevent the *client* from committing a *criminal* act that the lawyer believes is likely to result in *imminent* death or substantial bodily harm." (Emphasis added.)

2003 Amendments: In 2003, by a vote of 218-201, the ABA House of Delegates added paragraphs (b)(2) and (b)(3) to Rule 1.6, added Comments 7 and 8, and deleted former Comment 14, which had provided, in relevant part, as follows:

> [14] If the lawyer's services will be used by the client in materially furthering a course of criminal or fraudulent conduct, the lawyer must withdraw. . . . Neither this Rule nor Rule 1.8(b) nor Rule 1.16(d) prevents the lawyer from giving notice of the fact of withdrawal, and the lawyer may also withdraw or disaffirm any opinion, document, affirmation, or the like. . . .

(Comment 14 was deleted because its substance was already separately addressed in the comments to Rules 1.2 and 4.1.) The ABA Ethics 2000 Commission had recommended the identical changes in 2001, but at that time the House had rejected (b)(2) by a significant margin, and (b)(3) was then withdrawn. The 2003 changes were part of a package of recommendations from the ABA Task Force on Corporate Responsibility. (For more information about the Task Force and for its full report, visit *http://www.americanbar.org/groups/business_law.html.*) In support of the 2003 amendments, the Task Force report states:*

> The Task Force believes that the interest of society, and the bar, in assuring that a lawyer's services are not used by a client in the furtherance of a crime or a fraud creates a demanding need for an exception to the important principle of confidentiality, as most states have recognized. The importance of protecting both society and the bar from the consequences of a client's misuse of the lawyer's services in the furtherance of a serious crime or fraud must be balanced against the importance to the client-lawyer relationship of the principle of confidentiality.
>
> The Model Rules leave no room for doubt as to whether a lawyer may permit his services to be used by a client for criminal or fraudulent activity. . . . But what if the client has misled the lawyer, leading the lawyer to believe that the client is pursuing a lawful and honest purpose while in fact using the lawyer's work product to perpetrate a crime or fraud? In such circumstances should the lawyer be prohibited from taking action to prevent or rectify such misuse of the lawyer's services?
>
> The Task Force believes, as did the Ethics 2000 Commission, that the use of the lawyer's services for such improper ends constitutes an abuse by the client of the client-lawyer relationship, forfeiting the client's absolute entitlement to the protection of Model Rule 1.6. In such circumstances, the Task Force believes that the lawyer must be permitted, where the crime or fraud has resulted or is reasonably certain to result in substantial injury to the financial interests or property of third parties, to reveal information relating to the representation as reasonably believed necessary to prevent the commission of, or to prevent or rectify the consequences of, the crime or fraud.

---

* Committee Reports do not represent official policy of the ABA. They are for information only, and the opinions are those of the authors of the report.

[T]here is a long-standing exception to Model Rule 1.6 that permits a lawyer to reveal information relating to a representation "to establish a claim or defense on behalf of the lawyer in a controversy between the lawyer and the client." We believe that it is at least as important to society, and to the integrity of the profession, to permit disclosure in order to prevent the lawyer's services from being used in the commission of a crime or fraud as it is to permit disclosure in order to collect the lawyer's fee or to protect the lawyer from a client's unmeritorious civil claim.

In opposition to the proposal to amend Model Rule 1.6, it has been suggested that the disclosure to third parties permitted under the laws of most states is "rarely if ever employed," and there is therefore no need to amend Rule 1.6. The Task Force is not persuaded by this suggestion. Even if the authorization to disclose afforded by most states' disciplinary rules is not often used, the existence of such authority gives lawyers the opportunity to use that power to encourage the client to remediate or refrain from unlawful conduct.

2012 Amendments: In August 2012, the ABA House of Delegates adopted proposals by the ABA Commission on Ethics 20/20 to add Rule 1.6(c), Rule 1.6(b)(7), and new Comment language. The proposals addressed two distinct issues. First, Rule 1.6(c) was added to emphasize that lawyers in a digital age have an obligation to protect their clients' confidential information from inadvertent or unauthorized disclosure and from unauthorized access. Comments 18 and 19 were added to elaborate on this obligation. Second, the Commission proposed to add Rule 1.6(b)(7) in order to address the following question: To what extent can lawyers in different firms disclose confidential information to each other to detect conflicts of interest that might arise when lawyers consider an association with another firm, when two or more firms consider a merger, or when lawyers consider the purchase of a law practice? Comments 13 and 14 were added to elaborate on the new guidance offered in Rule 1.6(b)(7).

Selected State Variations

Editors' Note. American jurisdictions have adopted many variations on Rule 1.6 and its exceptions. Under DR 4-101(C)(3) of the old ABA Model Code of Professional Responsibility, a lawyer was authorized to reveal "the intention of his client to commit a crime and the information necessary to prevent the crime." Under the original version of Rule 1.6(b)(1), however, a lawyer was authorized to reveal crimes by a client only if they were "likely to result in imminent death or substantial bodily harm." Among the questions addressed in state variations are the following:

- whether to continue the Code's authority to reveal any prospective crime, even if the crime will not cause death or substantial bodily harm;
- whether to extend the authority to reveal conduct other than criminal conduct, such as conduct that is reckless, fraudulent, or illegal, but not criminal;
- whether to keep the authority permissive or, instead, to mandate revelation of prospective criminal or harmful conduct;
- if revelation is mandatory, the prospective conduct that will be subject to the mandatory duty to reveal;
- whether to distinguish the right or obligation to disclose depending upon whether the lawyer's information is protected by the attorney-client privilege or only protected by the ethical duty of confidentiality.

Alaska, Arkansas, Connecticut, Illinois, Maine, Maryland, New Hampshire, New Mexico, North Dakota, Pennsylvania, and *Utah* permit a lawyer to reveal information necessary to prevent the client from committing a criminal act "likely to result in substantial injury to the financial interest or property of another" (or words to that effect). Of these, Alaska, Arkansas, Connecticut, Illinois, Maine, Maryland, New Mexico, North Dakota, and Utah also permit revelation when the client's act is only fraudulent, but not criminal. New Jersey, Vermont, and Wisconsin go one step further, imposing a duty to reveal the information under these circumstances.

Arizona, Arkansas, Colorado, Idaho, Illinois, Kansas, Michigan, North Carolina, Ohio, Oregon, South Carolina, Washington, and *Wyoming* essentially retain the formulation of DR 4-101(C)(3) of the ABA Model Code of Professional Responsibility — they all permit a lawyer to reveal "the intention of a client to commit a crime" (or words to that effect).

Arizona, Connecticut, Florida, Illinois, Nevada, New Jersey, North Dakota, Texas, Tennessee, Vermont, and Wisconsin mandate disclosure of information to prevent the client from committing serious violent crimes. However, mandatory disclosure applies in North Dakota only if the harm is "imminent," and Florida's provision applies to all crimes, not just violent ones.

Alaska: Alaska adds Rule 1.6(b)(1)(C), which permits disclosures in order to "prevent the wrongful execution or incarceration of another." Alaska also adds Rule 1.6(c), which requires a lawyer to take reasonable precautions to guard against the inadvertent or unauthorized disclosure of a client's confidential information.

Arizona: Rule 1.6(d)(5) applies only to "other law or a final order of a court or tribunal of competent jurisdiction directing the lawyer to disclose such information." Arizona also has an unusual statute governing the attorney-client privilege for corporations and other entities — see the Arizona entry in the Selected State Variations following ABA Model Rule 1.13.

Arkansas: Rule 1.6(c) contains a noisy withdrawal provision, which states as follows: "Neither this Rule nor Rule 1.8(b) nor Rule 1.16(d) prevents the lawyer from giving notice of the fact of withdrawal, and the lawyer may also withdraw or disaffirm any opinion, document, affirmation or the like."

California: California Business & Professions Code §6068(e)(1) provides that it is the duty of an attorney "[t]o maintain inviolate the confidence, and at every peril to himself or herself to preserve the secrets, of his or her client." However, §6068(e)(2) provides that an attorney "may, but is not required to, reveal confidential information relating to the representation of a client to the extent that the attorney reasonably believes the disclosure is necessary to prevent a criminal act that the attorney reasonably believes is likely to result in death of, or substantial bodily harm to, an individual." In addition, Rule 3-100 of the California Rules of Professional Conduct provides as follows:

> (A) A member shall not reveal information protected from disclosure by Business and Professions Code section 6068, subdivision (e)(1) without the informed consent of the client, or as provided in paragraph (B) of this rule.
> (B) A member may, but is not required to, reveal confidential information relating to the representation of a client to the extent that the member reasonably believes the disclosure is necessary to prevent a criminal act that the member reasonably believes is likely to result in death of, or substantial bodily harm to, an individual.
> (C) Before revealing confidential information to prevent a criminal act as provided in paragraph (B), a member shall, if reasonable under the circumstances:

(1) make a good faith effort to persuade the client: (i) not to commit or to continue the criminal act or (ii) to pursue a course of conduct that will prevent the threatened death or substantial bodily harm; or do both (i) and (ii); and

(2) inform the client, at an appropriate time, of the member's ability or decision to reveal information as provided in paragraph (B).

(D) In revealing confidential information as provided in paragraph (B), the member's disclosure must be no more than is necessary to prevent the criminal act, given the information known to the member at the time of the disclosure.

(E) A member who does not reveal information permitted by paragraph (B) does not violate this rule.

District of Columbia: Rule 1.6 combines language from the ABA Model Code and the ABA Model Rules plus other language unique to D.C. Rule 1.6(c)(2) permits a lawyer to reveal client confidences "to prevent the bribery or intimidation of witnesses, jurors, court officials, or other persons who are involved in proceedings before a tribunal if the lawyer reasonably believes" such acts will likely occur without revelation. Rule 1.6(d) is substantially the same as Model Rule 1.6(b)(2) and (3), although differently phrased. Rule 1.6(h) applies the obligations of the Rule "to confidences and secrets learned prior to becoming a lawyer in the course of providing assistance to another lawyer."

Florida: Rule 1.6 provides that a lawyer "shall reveal" information the lawyer believes "necessary (1) to prevent a client from committing a crime or (2) to prevent a death or substantial bodily harm to another." In addition, Florida Rule 1.6(c) permits a lawyer to reveal information necessary "(1) to serve the client's interest unless it is information the client specifically requires not to be disclosed . . . or (5) to comply with the Rules of Professional Conduct." Florida also adds Rule 1.6(d): "When required by a tribunal to reveal such information, a lawyer may first exhaust all appellate remedies." Finally, Florida adds Rule 1.6(e), which provides that "[w]hen disclosure is mandated or permitted, the lawyer shall disclose no more information than is required to meet the requirements or accomplish the purposes of this rule."

Georgia: In the rules effective November 3, 2011, Rule 1.6(a) combines language from ABA Model Rule 1.6 and DR 4-101(A) of the ABA Model Code of Professional Responsibility, as follows:

(a) A lawyer shall maintain in confidence all information gained in the professional relationship with a client, including information which the client has requested to be held inviolate or the disclosure of which would be embarrassing or would likely be detrimental to the client, unless the client gives informed consent, except for disclosures that are impliedly authorized in order to carry out the representation, or are required by these Rules or other law, or by order of the Court.

Georgia's Rule 1.6(b)(1) permits a lawyer to reveal protected information which the lawyer reasonably believes necessary "(i) to avoid or prevent harm or substantial financial loss to another as a result of client criminal conduct or third party criminal conduct clearly in violation of the law" or "(ii) to prevent serious injury or death not otherwise covered" by subparagraph (i). Georgia adds the following Rules 1.6(b)(2)-(3) and (c), (d), and (e):

(2) In a situation described in paragraph (b)(1), if the client has acted at the time the lawyer learns of the threat of harm or loss to a victim, use or disclosure is permissible only if the harm or loss has not yet occurred.

(3) Before using or disclosing information pursuant to paragraph (b)(1), if feasible, the lawyer must make a good faith effort to persuade the client either not to act or, if the client has already acted, to warn the victim.

(c) The lawyer may, where the law does not otherwise require, reveal information to which the duty of confidentiality does not apply under paragraph (b) without being subjected to disciplinary proceedings.

(d) The lawyer shall reveal information under paragraph (b) as the applicable law requires.

(e) The duty of confidentiality shall continue after the client-lawyer relationship has terminated.

Illinois adds Rule 1.6(c) and (d):

(c) A lawyer shall reveal information relating to the representation of a client to the extent the lawyer reasonably believes necessary to prevent reasonably certain death or substantial bodily harm.

(d) Information received by a lawyer participating in a meeting or proceeding with a trained intervener or panel of trained interveners of an approved lawyers' assistance program, or in an intermediary program approved by a circuit court in which nondisciplinary complaints against judges or lawyers can be referred, shall be considered information relating to the representation of a client for purposes of these Rules.

Maine: Before making a disclosure under Rule 1.6(b), lawyers must try to convince the client not to engage in the conduct that will produce the applicable harm. Moreover, Rule 1.6(d) and Comment 2 explain that the rule applies only to a client's confidences and secrets, not to the broader range of information (*i.e.,* "all information relating to the representation of the client") described in the Model Rule.

Massachusetts: Rule 1.6(b) provides as follows:

A lawyer may reveal, and to the extent required by Rule 3.3, Rule 4.1(b), or Rule 8.3 must reveal, such information:

(1) to prevent the commission of a criminal or fraudulent act that the lawyer reasonably believes is likely to result in death or substantial bodily harm, or in substantial injury to the financial interests or property of another, or to prevent the wrongful execution or incarceration of another; . . . or

(3) to the extent the lawyer reasonably believes necessary to rectify client fraud in which the lawyer's services have been used, subject to Rule 3.3 (e). . . .

(Massachusetts was the first state to adopt an exception for preventing the wrongful execution or incarceration of another.)

Michigan essentially retains the language of DR 4-101 of the ABA Model Code of Professional Responsibility but deletes the self-defense exception in DR 4-101(C)(4). Michigan also adds Rule 1.6(c)(3), which allows a lawyer to reveal "confidences and secrets to the extent reasonably necessary to rectify the consequences of a client's illegal or fraudulent act in the furtherance of which the lawyer's services have been used."

Minnesota: Rule 1.6(b) provides, in relevant part, as follows:

(b) A lawyer may reveal information relating to the representation of a client if:

(1) the client gives informed consent;

(2) the information is not protected by the attorney-client privilege under applicable law, the client has not requested that the information be held inviolate, and the lawyer reasonably believes the disclosure would not be embarrassing or likely detrimental to the client;

(3) the lawyer reasonably believes the disclosure is impliedly authorized in order to carry out the representation; . . .

(10) the lawyer reasonably believes the disclosure is necessary to inform the Office of Lawyers Professional Responsibility of knowledge of another lawyer's violation of the Rules of Professional Conduct that raises a substantial question as to that lawyer's honesty, trustworthiness, or fitness as a lawyer in other respects. See Rule 8.3.

Missouri: Missouri omits ABA Model Rules 1.6(b)(2) and (b)(3).

New Hampshire: Rule 1.6(b)(1) also permits disclosure to prevent the client from committing "a criminal act that the lawyer believes is likely to result in substantial injury to the financial interest or property of another," without any requirement that the client is using or has used the lawyer's services. New Hampshire omits ABA Model Rule 1.6(b)(3).

New Jersey: Rule 1.6(b) requires a lawyer to reveal confidential information "to the proper authorities . . . to prevent the client or another person (1) from committing a criminal, illegal or fraudulent act . . . likely to result in death or substantial bodily harm or substantial injury to the financial interest or property of another" or "(2) from committing a criminal, illegal or fraudulent act that the lawyer reasonably believes is likely to perpetrate a fraud upon a tribunal." Rule 1.6(c) permits a lawyer to reveal information as well "to the person threatened to the extent the lawyer reasonably believes is necessary to protect that person from death, substantial bodily harm, substantial financial injury, or substantial property loss."

New York: Rule 1.6 contains numerous variations as well as many new comments. For example, Rule 1.6(a) offers an elaborate definition of "confidential information," which provides as follows:

> "Confidential information" consists of information gained during or relating to the representation of a client, whatever its source, that is (a) protected by the attorney-client privilege, (b) likely to be embarrassing or detrimental to the client if disclosed, or (c) information that the client has requested be kept confidential. "Confidential information" does not ordinarily include (i) a lawyer's legal knowledge or legal research or (ii) information that is generally known in the local community or in the trade, field or profession to which the information relates.

Comment 4A, as amended in 2011, elaborates on this definition as follows:

> Information relates to the representation if it has any possible relevance to the representation or is received because of the representation. The accumulation of legal knowledge or legal research that a lawyer acquires through practice ordinarily is not client information protected by this Rule. However, in some circumstances, including where the client and the lawyer have so agreed, a client may have a proprietary interest in a particular product of the lawyer's research. Information that is generally known in the local community or in the trade, field or profession to which the information relates is also not protected, unless the client and the lawyer have otherwise agreed. Information is not "generally known" simply because it is in the public domain or available in a public file.

Drawing on DR 4-101(B) of the old Model Code, Rule 1.6(a) provides that a disclosure of confidential information violates the rule only when the disclosure occurs "knowingly."

Rule 1.6(b) does not permit disclosures to prevent or rectify financial injuries, but it adds to the Model Rule by permitting disclosures when the lawyer reasonably believes necessary:

(3) to withdraw a written or oral opinion or representation previously given by the lawyer and reasonably believed by the lawyer still to be relied upon by a third person, where the lawyer has discovered that the opinion or representation was based on materially inaccurate information or is being used to further a crime or fraud; . . .

Comment 6A offers a list of factors for lawyers to consider when deciding whether to disclose information under Rule 1.6(b), including:

> (i) the seriousness of the potential injury to others if the prospective harm or crime occurs, (ii) the likelihood that it will occur and its imminence, (iii) the apparent absence of any other feasible way to prevent the potential injury, (iv) the extent to which the client may be using the lawyer's services in bringing about the harm or crime, (v) the circumstances under which the lawyer acquired the information of the client's intent or prospective course of action, and (vi) any other aggravating or extenuating circumstances. In any case, disclosure adverse to the client's interest should be no greater than the lawyer reasonably believes necessary to prevent the threatened harm or crime. When a lawyer learns that a client intends to pursue or is pursuing a course of conduct that would permit disclosure under paragraphs (b)(1), (b)(2) or (b)(3), the lawyer's initial duty, where practicable, is to remonstrate with the client. In the rare situation in which the client is reluctant to accept the lawyer's advice, the lawyer's threat of disclosure is a measure of last resort that may persuade the client. When the lawyer reasonably believes that the client will carry out the threatened harm or crime, the lawyer may disclose confidential information when permitted by paragraphs (b)(1), (b)(2) or (b)(3). A lawyer's permissible disclosure under paragraph (b) does not waive the client's attorney-client privilege; neither the lawyer nor the client may be forced to testify about communications protected by the privilege, unless a tribunal or body with authority to compel testimony makes a determination that the crime-fraud exception to the privilege, or some other exception, has been satisfied by a party to the proceeding. For a lawyer's duties when representing an organizational client engaged in wrongdoing, *see* Rule 1.13(b).

New York Rule 1.6(c) is nearly identical to DR 4-101(D) of the old Model Code.

North Carolina combines modified language from ABA Model Rule 1.6 with language from DR 4-101 of the old ABA Model Code of Professional Responsibility. For example, North Carolina's equivalent to ABA Model Rules 1.6(b)(2) and (b)(3) provides simply that a lawyer may reveal confidential information to the extent the lawyer reasonably believes necessary "to prevent, mitigate, or rectify the consequences of a client's criminal or fraudulent act in the commission of which the lawyer's services were used." North Carolina also adds a Rule 1.6(c), which provides that the duty of confidentiality "encompasses information received by a lawyer then acting as an agent of a lawyers' or judges' assistance program approved by the North Carolina State Bar or the North Carolina Supreme Court regarding another lawyer or judge seeking assistance or to whom assistance is being offered."

Ohio: Rule 1.6(b) permits a lawyer "to reveal the intention of the client or other person to commit a crime and the information necessary to prevent the crime," or to reveal confidential information "to mitigate substantial injury to the financial interests or property of another that has resulted from the client's commission of an illegal or fraudulent act, in furtherance of which the client has used the lawyer's services." Ohio omits ABA Model Rule 1.6(b)(2).

Oklahoma: Rule 1.6(b)(2) permits revelation only if "the lawyer has first made reasonable efforts to contact the client so that the client can rectify such criminal or fraudulent act, but the lawyer has been unable to do so, or the lawyer has contacted the client and called upon the client to rectify such criminal or fraudulent act and the client has refused or has been unable to do so."

Oregon: Rule 1.0(f) defines "information relating to the representation" as denoting "both information protected by the attorney-client privilege under applicable law, and other information gained in a current or former professional relationship that the client has requested be held inviolate or the disclosure of which would be embarrassing or would be likely to be detrimental to the client." In addition, Oregon permits a lawyer to disclose "the intention of the lawyer's client to commit a crime and the information necessary to prevent the crime." Also, Oregon Rule 1.6(b)(6) permits disclosure of specified information in discussions preliminary to the sale of a law practice under Rule 1.17, but states: "A potential purchasing lawyer shall have the same responsibilities as the selling lawyer to preserve confidences and secrets of such clients whether or not the sale of the practice closes or the client ultimately consents to representation by the purchasing lawyer."

Pennsylvania adds a Rule 1.6(d) that states: "The duty not to reveal information relating to representation of a client continues after the client-lawyer relationship has terminated." In addition, a lawyer may reveal information relating to the representation of a client that the lawyer reasonably believes necessary to "effectuate the sale of a law practice consistent with Rule 1.17." Pennsylvania also has added a Rule 1.19, which provides that any disclosures that lawyer-lobbyists need to make in order to comply with other law are disclosures that are expressly authorized and thus do not violate Rule 1.6.

Tennessee: Rule 1.6(c) provides that a lawyer "shall" reveal information relating to the representation of a client to the extent the lawyer reasonably believes disclosure is necessary:

> (1) to prevent reasonably certain death or substantial bodily harm;
> (2) to comply with an order of a tribunal requiring disclosure, but only if ordered to do so by the tribunal after the lawyer has asserted on behalf of the client all non-frivolous claims that the information sought by the tribunal is protected against disclosure by the attorney-client privilege or other applicable law; or
> (3) to comply with RPC 3.3, 4.1, or other law.

Tennessee's version of Rule 4.1, which requires disclosure of confidential information in certain circumstances, is described in the state variations for that Rule.

Texas: Rule 1.02(d)-(e) provides:

> (d) When a lawyer has confidential information clearly establishing that a client is likely to commit a criminal or fraudulent act that is likely to result in substantial injury to the financial interests or property of another, the lawyer shall promptly make reasonable efforts under the circumstances to dissuade the client from committing the crime or fraud.
> (e) When a lawyer has confidential information clearly establishing that the lawyer's client has committed a criminal or fraudulent act in the commission of which the lawyer's services have been used, the lawyer shall make reasonable efforts under the circumstances to persuade the client to take corrective action.

Texas Rule 1.05 divides "confidential information" into two categories — "privileged information," which means information protected by the attorney-client privilege, and "unprivileged client information," which "means all information relating to a client or furnished by the client, other than privileged information, acquired by the lawyer in the course of or by reason of the representation of the client." A lawyer "may reveal confidential information" in eight instances, including when "the lawyer has reason to believe it is necessary to do so in order to prevent the client from committing a criminal or fraudulent act," and to "the extent revelation reasonably appears necessary to rectify the consequences of a client's criminal or fraudulent act in the commission of which the lawyer's services had been used." Rules 1.05(c)(7) and (8).

Vermont: Rule 1.6 imposes a duty to disclose confidential information "(1) to prevent the client or another person from committing a criminal act that the lawyer reasonably believes is likely to result in the death of, or substantial bodily harm to, a person other than the person committing the act; or (2) to prevent the client from committing a crime or fraud that is reasonably certain to result in substantial injury to the financial interests or property of another and in furtherance of which the client has used or is using the lawyer's services; or (3) to prevent, mitigate or rectify substantial injury to the financial interests or property of another that is reasonably certain to result or has resulted from the client's commission of a crime or fraud in furtherance of which the client has used the lawyer's services."

Virginia: Rule 1.6(a) contains the Code's definitions of "confidence" and "secret" without using these terms. A lawyer may reveal a client confidence "which clearly establishes that the client has, in the course of the representation, perpetrated upon a third party a fraud related to the subject matter of the representation." Rule 1.6(b)(3). The lawyer must "promptly" reveal "the intention of a client, as stated by the client, to commit a crime and the information necessary to prevent the crime," but if feasible must first give the client the opportunity to desist and must advise the client of the lawyer's obligation. If "the crime involves perjury by the client," the lawyer must advise the client that he or she "shall seek to withdraw as counsel." Rule 1.6(c)(1). Rule 1.6(c)(2) also requires the lawyer to promptly reveal "information which clearly establishes that the client has, in the course of the representation, perpetrated a fraud related to the subject matter of the representation upon a tribunal." Information is clearly established when "the client acknowledges to the attorney that the client has perpetrated a fraud."

Related Materials

ABA Formal Ethics Opinions: See ABA Formal Ethics Ops. 90-358 (1990), 92-365 (1992), 93-370 (1993), 94-380 (1994), 94-385 (1994), 95-393 (1995), 95-398 (1995), 98-411 (1998), 99-413 (1999), 03-431 (2003), 05-436 (2005), 06-440 (2006), 06-442 (2006), 07-449 (2007), 08-450 (2008), 08-451 (2008), 08-453 (2008), 09-455 (2009), 11-459 (2011), 11-460 (2011).

ABA Resolution on Inadvertent Disclosure: In 2006, the ABA House of Delegates approved a resolution regarding inadvertent disclosure of privileged materials. For details, see the Related Materials following ABA Model Rule 4.4.

ABA Standards for Imposing Lawyer Sanctions: The following ABA Standards for Imposing Lawyer Sanctions are relevant to Rule 1.6:

> 4.21. Disbarment is generally appropriate when a lawyer, with the intent to benefit the lawyer or another, knowingly reveals information relating to representation of a client not otherwise lawfully permitted to be disclosed, and this disclosure causes injury or potential injury to a client.

4.22. Suspension is generally appropriate when a lawyer knowingly reveals information relating to the representation of a client not otherwise lawfully permitted to be disclosed, and this disclosure causes injury or potential injury to a client.

4.23. Reprimand is generally appropriate when a lawyer negligently reveals information relating to representation of a client not otherwise lawfully permitted to be disclosed and this disclosure causes injury or potential injury to a client.

4.24. Admonition is generally appropriate when a lawyer negligently reveals information relating to representation of a client not otherwise lawfully permitted to be disclosed and this disclosure causes little or no actual or potential injury to a client.

ABA Task Force on the Attorney-Client Privilege: In 2004, the ABA appointed a Task Force on the Attorney-Client Privilege. The Task Force Chair was attorney William Ide, III, of Atlanta, its ABA staff director was R. Larson Frisby, and its Reporter was Professor Bruce Green of Fordham University School of Law. In 2005, the ABA House of Delegates adopted (with minor changes) the following Resolution recommended by the Task Force:

> RESOLVED, that the American Bar Association strongly supports the preservation of the attorney-client privilege and work product doctrine as essential to maintaining the confidential relationship between client and attorney required to encourage clients to discuss their legal matters fully and candidly with their counsel so as to (1) promote compliance with law through effective counseling, (2) ensure effective advocacy for the client, (3) ensure access to justice and (4) promote the proper and efficient functioning of the American adversary system of justice; and
>
> FURTHER RESOLVED, that the American Bar Association opposes policies, practices and procedures of governmental bodies that have the effect of eroding the attorney-client privilege and work-product doctrine and favors policies, practices and procedures that recognize the value of those protections.
>
> FURTHER RESOLVED, that the American Bar Association opposes the routine practice by government officials of seeking to obtain a waiver of the attorney-client privilege or work product doctrine through the granting or denial of any benefit or advantage.

The Task Force on the Attorney-Client Privilege was sunset in 2010, but by that time it had completed its primary mission of helping to reverse the United States Department of Justice policy on waiver of privilege. In addition, working with the ABA Governmental Affairs Office, the Task Force helped to persuade the Commodity Futures Trading Commission, the U.S. Sentencing Commission, the Government Services Administration, the Department of Defense, and NASA to reverse or modify their privilege waiver policies. For a wealth of resources about the attorney-client privilege, see the site maintained by the ABA Governmental Affairs Office at *http://www. americanbar.org/advocacy/governmental_legislative_work/priorities_policy/independence_ of_the_legal_profession/acprivilege.html.*

ABA Task Force on Corporate Responsibility: In 2003, a Task Force of the American Bar Association, chaired by Tennessee lawyer James H. Cheek, III, issued a report in satisfaction of its charge to ''examine systemic issues relating to corporate responsibility arising out of the unexpected and traumatic bankruptcy of Enron and other Enron-like situations.'' The report urged the ABA to adopt the exceptions to Rule 1.6 confidentiality that the ABA had rejected in 2002, and urged the ABA to modify Rule 1.13 to mandate ''reporting up'' and permit ''reporting out'' in specified circumstances. The ABA followed these recommendations. The Report and related events are discussed in the Special Section of the 2004 edition of this book.

Attorney-Client Privilege: Wigmore's famed treatise on the law of evidence defines the "attorney-client privilege" as follows:

> (1) Where legal advice of any kind is sought (2) from a professional legal advisor in his capacity as such, (3) the communications relating to that purpose, (4) made in confidence (5) by the client, (6) are at the client's instance permanently protected (7) from disclosure by himself or the legal advisor, (8) except the protection be waived.

See Arthur Best, Wigmore on Evidence §2292 (4th ed., Aspen Publishers 1988). For a selection of primary sources on the attorney-client privilege, see our chapter on Attorney-Client Privilege and Work Product Provisions later in this volume.

Cell Phone Calls: In 1999, the ABA House of Delegates passed a resolution encouraging courts and bar disciplinary authorities to recognize explicitly that cell phone communications are protected by the attorney-client privilege.

Federal Rules of Civil Procedure: Except in specified categories of proceedings or to the extent otherwise stipulated between the parties or ordered by the court, Rule 26(a) of the Federal Rules of Civil Procedure provides that each party to a civil suit "must, without awaiting a discovery request, provide to other parties" various categories of information, including: (A) the name, address, and telephone of each individual "likely to have discoverable information"; (B) a copy or description of "all documents, electrically stored information, and tangible things" in the party's "possession, custody or control" that the disclosing party "may use to support its claims or defenses"; (C) "a computation of each category of damages claimed by the disclosing party"; and (D) any "insurance agreement" that may cover the judgment or a corresponding indemnification obligation. These provisions relate to ABA Model Rule 1.6 because clients who take part in litigation in federal court may be deemed to have "impliedly authorized" the disclosures mandated by Rule 26(a).

Moreover, in 2006 a new Rule 26(b)(5)(B) took effect to address the problem of inadvertently produced privileged information. It provides that a party who receives notice that privileged information has been produced "must promptly return, sequester, or destroy the specified information" and "must not use or disclose the information until the claim is resolved" (but "may promptly present the information to the court under seal for a determination of the claim"). A companion 2006 amendment to Rule 16(b)(3)(B)(iv) provides that a district court's scheduling order may include "any agreements the parties reach for asserting claims of privilege or of protection as trial-preparation material after information is produced." For details, see the entry on the Federal Rules of Civil Procedure in the Related Materials following Rule 4.4.

Regarding expert witnesses, Rule 26(b)(4)(B) and (C) (as amended in 2010) provides heightened protection against discovery of communications between experts and counsel. Specifically, Rule 26(b)(4)(B) protects "drafts of any report or disclosure required under Rule 26(a)(2), regardless of the form in which the draft is recorded." Rule 26(b)(4)(C) protects communications between the party's attorney and any expert witness unless the communications (i) "relate to compensation for the expert's study or testimony"; or (ii) "identify facts or data that the party's attorney provided and that the expert considered in forming the opinions to be expressed"; or (iii) "identify assumptions that the party's attorney provided and that the expert relied on in forming the opinions to be expressed."

For updates on the Federal Rules of Civil Procedure, and for a wealth of information about recent and proposed amendments, visit *www.uscourts.gov/rulesandpolicies/rules.aspx.*

Federal Rules of Evidence: In federal courts, Rule 501 of the Federal Rules of Evidence controls the application of privileges, including the attorney-client privilege. As amended in 2011, Rule 501 provides as follows:

> The common law — as interpreted by United States courts in the light of reason and experience — governs a claim of privilege unless any of the following provides otherwise:
>
> • the United States Constitution;
> • a federal statute; or
> • rules prescribed by the Supreme Court.
>
> But in a civil case, state law governs privilege regarding a claim or defense for which state law supplies the rule of decision.

In addition, Rule 502 of the Federal Rules of Evidence clarifies and modifies common law rules relating to waiver of privilege and work product protection. For more information about the attorney-client privilege in federal courts, including the full text of Rule 502, see our chapter on Attorney-Client Privilege and Work Product Provisions later in this volume.

Financial Accounting Standards Board: The Financial Accounting Standards Board (FASB) is a private body whose accounting standards are officially recognized by the Securities and Exchange Commission. One set of FASB standards, Accounting Standards Codification 450, entitled "Disclosures of Certain Loss Contingencies" ("Topic 450"), requires public companies to determine whether losses that may be incurred in anticipated or pending litigation are "probable," "reasonably possible," or "remote." Since these classifications provide little information, in 2008 the FASB embarked on a project to expand the disclosures required in Topic 450 to assist users in assessing the likelihood, timing, and amount of future cashflows associated with loss contingencies, including litigation. However, vigorous opposition to the FASB's 2008 and 2010 "exposure drafts" — including strong criticism from the ABA based on confidentiality concerns — led the FASB to abandon the project in July 2012. For details, see *http://www.fasb.org/cs/ContentServer?site=FASB&c=FASBContent_C&pagename=FASB%2FFASBContent_C%2FProjectUpdatePage&cid=900000011071.*

Model Rules of Professional Conduct for Federal Lawyers: Rule 1.6(b) provides: "A Federal lawyer shall reveal such information to the extent the Federal lawyer reasonably believes necessary to prevent the client from committing a criminal act that the Federal lawyer believes is likely to result in imminent death or substantial bodily harm, or imminent and significant impairment of national security or defense." The Comment also cautions that government lawyers have confidentiality obligations under many federal statutes and regulations, so "it is always advisable for Government lawyers to review the applicable Federal law . . . and to consult with their supervisors."

Restatement of the Law Governing Lawyers: See Restatement §§14, 15, 41, and 59-93 in our chapter on the Restatement later in this volume.

SEC Statement on Corporate Cooperation ("Seaboard Report"): In the SEC's Securities and Exchange Act Release No. 44969 (October 23, 2001), often referred to as the "Seaboard Report," the SEC set forth some of the criteria the SEC considers in determining "whether, and how much, to credit self-policing, self-reporting, remediation and cooperation — from the extraordinary step of taking no enforcement action to bringing reduced charges, seeking lighter sanctions, or including mitigating language in documents we use to announce and resolve enforcement actions.'' The following examples of these criteria are particularly relevant to Rule 1.6:

> 10. Did the company commit to learn the truth, fully and expeditiously? Did it do a thorough review of the nature, extent, origins and consequences of the conduct and related behavior? . . .
>
> 11. Did the company promptly make available to our staff the results of its review and provide sufficient documentation reflecting its response to the situation? Did the company identify possible violative conduct and evidence with sufficient precision to facilitate prompt enforcement actions against those who violated the law? Did the company produce a thorough and probing written report detailing the findings of its review?
>
> Did the company voluntarily disclose information our staff did not directly request and otherwise might not have uncovered? Did the company ask its employees to cooperate with our staff and make all reasonable efforts to secure such cooperation?
>
> 12. . . . Did the company provide our staff with sufficient information for it to evaluate the company's measures to correct the situation and ensure that the conduct does not recur? . . .

United States Department of Justice Privilege Waiver Requests: Since 2003, the United States Department of Justice (DOJ) has adopted three different policies regarding DOJ requests that a corporation under federal investigation waive the attorney-client privilege or work product protection.

In 2003, the DOJ adopted Principles of Federal Prosecution of Business Organizations (the so-called "Thompson Memorandum," written by then-Deputy Attorney General Larry D. Thompson). The Thompson Memorandum contained the following comment:

> One factor the prosecutor may weigh in assessing the adequacy of a corporation's cooperation is the completeness of its disclosure including, if necessary, *a waiver of the attorney-client and work product protections*, both with respect to its internal investigation and with respect to communications between specific officers, directors and employees and counsel. Such waivers permit the government to obtain statements of possible witnesses, subjects, and targets, without having to negotiate individual cooperation or immunity agreements. In addition, they are often critical in enabling the government to evaluate the completeness of a corporation's voluntary disclosure and cooperation. Prosecutors may, therefore, request a waiver in appropriate circumstances. The Department does not, however, consider waiver of a corporation's attorney-client and work product protection an absolute requirement, and prosecutors should consider the willingness of a corporation to waive such protection when necessary to provide timely and complete information as one factor in evaluating the corporation's cooperation. [Emphasis added.]

The Thompson Memorandum's waiver policy generated substantial objections from the ABA and the business community, and the DOJ responded to these criticisms. In 2006, the Thompson Memorandum was replaced by the so-called McNulty Memorandum (written by then-Deputy Attorney General Paul J. McNulty). The revised business prosecution principles included the following Principle VII:

VII. Charging a Corporation: The Value of Cooperation

> *A. General Principle:* In determining whether to charge a corporation, that corporation's timely and voluntary disclosure of wrongdoing and its cooperation with the government's investigation may be relevant factors. In gauging the extent of the

corporation's cooperation, the prosecutor may consider, among other things, whether the corporation made a voluntary and timely disclosure, and the corporation's willingness to provide relevant evidence and to identify the culprits within the corporation, including senior executives.

Comment 2 to Principle VII explained the Department of Justice's revised policy:

> . . . Prosecutors may only request waiver of attorney-client or work product protections when there is a legitimate need for the privileged information to fulfill their law enforcement obligations. A legitimate need for the information is not established by concluding it is merely desirable or convenient to obtain privileged information.
>
> The test requires a careful balancing of important policy considerations underlying the attorney-client privilege and work product doctrine and the law enforcement needs of the government's investigation.
>
> Whether there is a legitimate need depends upon: (1) the likelihood and degree to which the privileged information will benefit the government's investigation; (2) whether the information sought can be obtained in a timely and complete fashion by using alternative means that do not require waiver; (3) the completeness of the voluntary disclosure already provided; and (4) the collateral consequences to a corporation of a waiver.
>
> If a legitimate need exists, prosecutors should seek the least intrusive waiver necessary to conduct a complete and thorough investigation, and should follow a step-by-step approach to requesting information. . . .

The McNulty Memorandum then divided information into two categories. Prosecutors should first seek Category I information, which consists of "purely factual information, which may or may not be privileged, relating to the underlying misconduct." Before requesting that a corporation waive the attorney-client or work product protections for Category I information, prosecutors must obtain written authorization from the United States Attorney, and only if the purely factual information provides an incomplete basis to conduct a thorough investigation may prosecutors ask the corporation to provide Category II information, which consists of "attorney-client communications or non-factual attorney work product" (*e.g.,* attorney notes, memoranda or reports containing counsel's mental impressions and conclusions, legal determinations reached as a result of an internal investigation, or legal advice given to the corporation). Prosecutors are cautioned to seek Category II information only in "rare circumstances," and must obtain written authorization from the Deputy Attorney General. But if a corporation declines to waive protection for Category II information, "prosecutors must not consider this declination against the corporation in making a charging decision."

Congressional critics of the McNulty Memorandum soon revived a bill called the Attorney-Client Privilege Protection Act. In August 2008, the DOJ responded to this pressure by adopting revised Principles of Federal Prosecution of Business Organizations. Regarding waiver of the attorney-client privilege, the revised Principles, which are contained in the United States Attorney's Manual (USAM), provide, in pertinent part, as follows:

> USAM 9-28.710 *Attorney-Client and Work Product Protections*
>
> The attorney-client privilege and the attorney work product protection serve an extremely important function in the American legal system. The attorney-client privilege is one of the oldest and most sacrosanct privileges under the law. See Upjohn v. United States, 449 U.S. 383, 389 (1981). . . .

For these reasons, waiving the attorney-client and work product protections has never been a prerequisite under the Department's prosecution guidelines for a corporation to be viewed as cooperative. Nonetheless, a wide range of commentators and members of the American legal community and criminal justice system have asserted that the Department's policies have been used, either wittingly or unwittingly, to coerce business entities into waiving attorney-client privilege and work-product protection. Everyone agrees that a corporation may freely waive its own privileges if it chooses to do so; indeed, such waivers occur routinely when corporations are victimized by their employees or others, conduct an internal investigation, and then disclose the details of the investigation to law enforcement officials in an effort to seek prosecution of the offenders. However, the contention, from a broad array of voices, is that the Department's position on attorney-client privilege and work product protection waivers has promoted an environment in which those protections are being unfairly eroded to the detriment of all.

The Department understands that the attorney-client privilege and attorney work product protection are essential and long-recognized components of the American legal system. What the government seeks and needs to advance its legitimate (indeed, essential) law enforcement mission is not waiver of those protections, but rather the facts known to the corporation about the putative criminal misconduct under review. In addition, while a corporation remains free to convey non-factual or "core" attorney-client communications or work product — if and only if the corporation voluntarily chooses to do so — prosecutors should not ask for such waivers and are directed not to do so. The critical factor is whether the corporation has provided the facts about the events, as explained further herein.

USAM 9-28.720 *Cooperation: Disclosing the Relevant Facts*

Eligibility for cooperation credit is not predicated upon the waiver of attorney-client privilege or work product protection. Instead, the sort of cooperation that is most valuable to resolving allegations of misconduct by a corporation and its officers, directors, employees, or agents is disclosure of the relevant *facts* concerning such misconduct. In this regard, the analysis parallels that for a non-corporate defendant, where cooperation typically requires disclosure of relevant factual knowledge and not of discussions between an individual and his attorneys.

Thus, when the government investigates potential corporate wrongdoing, it seeks the relevant facts. . . . The party under investigation may choose to cooperate by disclosing the facts, and the government may give credit for the party's disclosures. If a corporation wishes to receive credit for such cooperation, which then can be considered with all other cooperative efforts and circumstances in evaluating how fairly to proceed, then the corporation, like any person, must disclose the relevant facts of which it has knowledge.

The complete August 2008 Department of Justice business prosecution principles are available at *www.usdoj.gov/usao/eousa/foia_reading_room/usam/title9//28mcrm.htm.*

Rule 1.7　Conflict of Interest: Current Clients

Canon and Code Antecedents

ABA Canons of Professional Ethics: Canon 6 provided as follows:

6.　*Adverse Influences and Conflicting Interests*

It is the duty of a lawyer at the time of retainer to disclose to the client all the circumstances of his relations to the parties, and any interest in or connection with the controversy, which might influence the client in the selection of counsel.

It is unprofessional to represent conflicting interests, except by express consent of all concerned given after a full disclosure of the facts. Within the meaning of this canon, a lawyer represents conflicting interests when, in behalf of one client, it is his duty to contend for that which duty to another client requires him to oppose.

The obligation to represent the client with undivided fidelity and not to divulge his secrets or confidences forbids also the subsequent acceptance of retainers or employment from others in matters adversely affecting any interest of the client with respect to which confidence has been reposed.

ABA Model Code of Professional Responsibility: Compare DR 5-101(A), DR 5-105(A), DR 5-105(C), and DR 5-107(B) (reprinted later in this volume).

Cross-References in Other Rules

Rule 1.0, Comment 6: "Many of the Rules of Professional Conduct require the lawyer to obtain the informed consent of a client or other person before accepting or continuing representation or pursuing a course of conduct (see **Rules** 1.2(c), 1.6(a) and **1.7(b)**)."

Rule 1.0, Comment 7: "A number of Rules require that a person's consent be confirmed in writing. See **Rules 1.7(b)** and 1.9(a)."

Rule 1.8, Comment 3: "The risk to a client is greatest when the client expects the lawyer to represent the client in the transaction itself or when the lawyer's financial interest otherwise poses a significant risk that the lawyer's representation of the client will be materially limited by the lawyer's financial interest in the transaction. Here the lawyer's role requires that the lawyer must comply, not only with the requirements of paragraph (a), but also with the requirements of **Rule 1.7**. Under that Rule, the lawyer must disclose the risks associated with the lawyer's dual role as both legal adviser and participant in the transaction, such as the risk that the lawyer will structure the transaction or give legal advice in a way that favors the lawyer's interests at the expense of the client. Moreover, the lawyer must obtain the client's informed consent. In some cases, the lawyer's interest may be such that **Rule 1.7** will preclude the lawyer from seeking the client's consent to the transaction."

Rule 1.8, Comment 8: "This Rule does not prohibit a lawyer from seeking to have the lawyer or a partner or associate of the lawyer named as executor of the client's estate or to another potentially lucrative fiduciary position. Nevertheless, such appointments will be subject to the general conflict of interest provision in **Rule 1.7** when there is a significant risk that the lawyer's interest in obtaining the appointment will materially limit the lawyer's independent professional judgment in advising the client concerning the choice of an executor or other fiduciary."

Rule 1.8, Comment 12: "Sometimes, it will be sufficient for the lawyer to obtain the client's informed consent regarding the fact of the payment and the identity of the third-party payer. If, however, the fee arrangement creates a conflict of interest for the lawyer, then the lawyer must comply with **Rule 1.7**. . . .

Under **Rule 1.7(a)**, a conflict of interest exists if there is significant risk that the lawyer's representation of the client will be materially limited by the lawyers own interest in the fee arrangement or by the lawyer's responsibilities to the third-party payer. . . . Under **Rule 1.7(b)**, the lawyer may accept or continue the representation with the informed consent of each affected client, unless the conflict is nonconsentable under that paragraph. Under **Rule 1.7(b)**, the informed consent must be confirmed in writing."

Rule 1.8, Comment 13: "Differences in willingness to make or accept an offer of settlement are among the risks of common representation of multiple clients by a single lawyer. Under **Rule 1.7**, this is one of the risks that should be discussed before undertaking the representation. . . ."

Rule 1.8, Comment 18: In the situation of client-lawyer sexual relationships, "before proceeding with the representation . . . , the lawyer should consider whether the lawyer's ability to represent the client will be materially limited by the relationship. See **Rule 1.7(a)(2)**."

Rule 1.9, Comment 9: "With regard to the effectiveness of an advance waiver, see Comment [22] to **Rule 1.7**."

Rule 1.10(a): "While lawyers are associated in a firm, none of them shall knowingly represent a client when any one of them practicing alone would be prohibited from doing so by **Rules 1.7** or 1.9, unless the prohibition is based on a personal interest of the prohibited lawyer and does not present a significant risk of materially limiting the representation of the client by the remaining lawyers in the firm."

Rule 1.10(c): "A disqualification prescribed by this rule may be waived by the affected client under the conditions stated in **Rule 1.7**."

Rule 1.10, Comment 5: Despite Rule 1.10(b), a law firm "may not represent a person with interests adverse to those of a present client of the firm, which would violate **Rule 1.7**."

Rule 1.10, Comment 6: "Rule 1.10(c) removes imputation with the informed consent of the affected client or former client under the conditions stated in **Rule 1.7**. The conditions stated in **Rule 1.7** require the lawyer to determine that the representation is not prohibited by **Rule 1.7(b)**. . . . For a discussion of the effectiveness of client waivers of conflicts that might arise in the future, see **Rule 1.7**, Comment [22]."

Rule 1.11(d): "Except as law may otherwise expressly permit, a lawyer currently serving as a public officer or employee is subject to **Rules 1.7** and 1.9."

Rule 1.11, Comment 1: "A lawyer who has served or is currently serving as a public officer or employee is personally subject to the Rules of Professional Conduct, including the prohibition against concurrent conflicts of interest stated in **Rule 1.7**."

Rule 1.11, Comment 9: "Paragraphs (a) and (d) do not prohibit a lawyer from jointly representing a private party and a government agency when doing so is permitted by **Rule 1.7** and is not otherwise prohibited by law."

Rule 1.13(e): "A lawyer representing an organization may also represent any of its directors, officers, employees, members, shareholders or other constituents, subject to the provisions of **Rule 1.7**. If the organization's consent to the dual representation is required by **Rule 1.7**, the consent shall be given by an appropriate official of the organization other than the individual who is to be represented, or by the shareholders."

Rule 1.13, Comment 11: "[I]f the claim involves serious charges of wrongdoing by those in control of the organization, a conflict may arise between the lawyer's duty to the organization and the lawyer's relationship with the board. In those circumstances, **Rule 1.7** governs who should represent the directors and the organization."

Rule 1.17, Comment 11: A lawyer selling a law practice has an "obligation to avoid disqualifying conflicts, and to secure the client's informed consent for those conflicts that can be agreed to (see **Rule 1.7** regarding conflicts and Rule 1.0(e) for the definition of informed consent)."

Rule 1.18, Comment 4: "If the prospective client wishes to retain the lawyer, and if consent is possible under **Rule 1.7**, then consent from all affected present or former clients must be obtained before accepting the representation."

Rule 3.7(b): "A lawyer may act as advocate in a trial in which another lawyer in the lawyer's firm is likely to be called as a witness unless precluded from doing so by **Rule 1.7** or Rule 1.9."

Rule 3.7, Comment 4: In determining whether the lawyer should be disqualified, "[i]t is relevant that one or both parties could reasonably foresee that the lawyer would probably be a witness. The conflict of interest principles stated in **Rules 1.7**, 1.9 and 1.10 have no application to this aspect of the problem."

Rule 3.7, Comment 6: "In determining if it is permissible to act as advocate in a trial in which the lawyer will be a necessary witness, the lawyer must also consider that the dual role may give rise to a conflict of interest that will require compliance with **Rules 1.7** or 1.9. For example, if there is likely to be substantial conflict between the testimony of the client and that of the lawyer, the representation involves a conflict of interest that requires compliance with **Rule 1.7**. . . . If there is a conflict of interest, the lawyer must secure the client's informed consent, confirmed in writing. In some cases, the lawyer will be precluded from seeking the client's consent. See **Rule 1.7**."

Rule 3.7, Comment 7: "If, however, the testifying lawyer would also be disqualified by **Rule 1.7** or Rule 1.9 from representing the client in the matter, other lawyers in the firm will be precluded from representing the client by Rule 1.10 unless the client gives informed consent under the conditions stated in **Rule 1.7**."

Rule 5.2, Comment 2: "[I]f a question arises whether the interests of two clients conflict under **Rule 1.7**, the supervisor's reasonable resolution of the question should protect the subordinate professionally if the resolution is subsequently challenged."

Rule 5.7, Comment 10: "When a lawyer is obliged to accord the recipients of such services the protections of those Rules that apply to the client-lawyer relationship, the lawyer must take special care to heed the proscriptions of the Rules addressing conflict of interest (**Rules 1.7** through 1.11, especially **Rules 1.7** and 1.8(a), (b) and (f)). . . ."

Rule 6.3(a): "The lawyer shall not knowingly participate in a decision or action of the organization if participating in the decision or action would be incompatible with the lawyer's obligations to a client under **Rule 1.7**. . . ."

Rule 6.4, Comment 1: "In determining the nature and scope of participation in such activities, a lawyer should be mindful of obligations to clients under other Rules, particularly **Rule 1.7**."

Rule 6.5(a): "A lawyer who, under the auspices of a program sponsored by a nonprofit organization or court, provides short-term limited legal services to a client without expectation by either the lawyer or the client that the lawyer will provide continuing representation in the matter is subject to **Rules 1.7** and 1.9(a) only if the lawyer knows that the representation of the client involves a conflict of interest; and is subject to Rule 1.10 only if the lawyer knows that another lawyer associated with the lawyer in a law firm is disqualified by **Rule 1.7** or 1.9(a) with respect to the matter."

Rule 6.5, Comment 1: "Legal services organizations, courts and various nonprofit organizations have established programs through which lawyers provide short-term limited legal services. . . . Such programs are normally operated under circumstances in which it is not feasible for a lawyer to systematically screen for conflicts of interest as is generally required before undertaking a representation. See, e.g., **Rules 1.7**, 1.9 and 1.10.''

Rule 6.5, Comment 3: ''[P]aragraph (a) requires compliance with **Rules 1.7** or 1.9(a) only if the lawyer knows that the representation presents a conflict of interest for the lawyer, and with Rule 1.10 only if the lawyer knows that another lawyer in the lawyer's firm is disqualified by **Rules 1.7** or 1.9(a) in the matter.''

Rule 6.5, Comment 4: ''Paragraph (a)(2) requires the participating lawyer to comply with Rule 1.10 when the lawyer knows that the lawyer's firm is disqualified by **Rules 1.7** or 1.9(a).''

Rule 6.5, Comment 5: ''If, after commencing a short-term limited representation in accordance with this Rule, a lawyer undertakes to represent the client in the matter on an ongoing basis, **Rules 1.7**, 1.9(a) and 1.10 become applicable.''

Rule 7.2, Comment 8: ''Conflicts of interest created by such [reciprocal referral] arrangements are governed by **Rule 1.7**.''

Legislative History of Model Rule 1.7

1980 Discussion Draft (then Rule 1.8) provided as follows:

In circumstances in which a lawyer has interests, commitments, or responsibilities that may adversely affect the representation of a client, a lawyer shall not represent the client unless:

(a) the services contemplated in the representation can otherwise be performed in accordance with the rules of professional conduct; and

(b) the client consents after adequate disclosure of the circumstances.

1981 Draft:

(a) A lawyer shall not represent a client if the lawyer's ability to consider, recommend or carry out a course of action on behalf of the client will be adversely affected by the lawyer's responsibilities to another client or to a third person, or by the lawyer's own interests.

(b) When a lawyer's own interests or other responsibilities might adversely affect the representation of a client, the lawyer shall not represent the client unless:

(1) the lawyer reasonably believes the other responsibilities or interests involved will not adversely affect the best interest of the client. . . .

1982 Draft was adopted.

1983 Rule: From its initial adoption in 1983 until the text was first amended in 2002, ABA Model Rule 1.7 provided as follows:

Rule 1.7   Conflict of Interest: General Rule

(a) A lawyer shall not represent a client if the representation of that client will be directly adverse to another client, unless:

(1) the lawyer reasonably believes the representation will not adversely affect the relationship with the other client; and

(2) each client consents after consultation.

(b) A lawyer shall not represent a client if the representation of that client may be materially limited by the lawyer's responsibilities to another client or to a third person, or by the lawyer's own interests, unless:

(1) the lawyer reasonably believes the representation will not be adversely affected; and

(2) the client consents after consultation. When representation of multiple clients in a single matter is undertaken, the consultation shall include explanation of the implications of the common representation and the advantages and risks involved.

1987 Amendment: The ABA House of Delegates added the last sentence of what was then Comment 1 to Rule 1.7, and placed other parts of Comment 1 into a separate paragraph, which then became Comment 2.

2002 Amendments: At its February 2002 Mid-Year Meeting, the ABA House of Delegates adopted without change the ABA Ethics 2000 Commission's proposal to amend Rule 1.7 and its Comment extensively. This was the first time that the text of Rule 1.7 had been amended since the ABA originally adopted it in 1983.

Selected State Variations

California: Rule 3-310 (Avoiding the Representation of Adverse Interests) requires written informed consent to the conflicts it describes. This rule incorporates in one place principles spread across several rules in the ABA Model Rules, including current and former client conflicts and conflicts arising from the payment of a fee by a nonclient.

Section 2860 of the California Civil Code, adopted after the important decision in *San Diego Credit Union v. Cumis,* 208 Cal. Rptr. 494 (Ct. App. 1984), seeks to reconcile the multiple interests at stake when an insurance company has a duty to defend an insured whose interests might not be congruent with those of the insurer. The first paragraph of §2860 provides as follows:

> (a) If the provisions of a policy of insurance impose a duty to defend upon an insurer and a conflict of interest arises which creates a duty on the part of the insurer to provide independent counsel to the insured, the insurer shall provide independent counsel to represent the insured unless, at the time the insured is informed that a possible conflict may arise or does exist, the insured expressly waives, in writing, the right to independent counsel. An insurance contract may contain a provision which sets forth the method of selecting that counsel consistent with this section.

District of Columbia: Rule 1.7 differs significantly from the ABA Model Rule in its language but addresses the same current client conflicts. A unique provision is Rule 1.7(d), which in certain (but not all) instances allows a lawyer to continue with a conflicted representation when the conflict arises after the lawyer has begun work on a matter, but only if the conflict was "not reasonably foreseeable at the outset of a representation."

Florida adds Rule 1.7(d) (identical to the 1983 version of ABA Model Rule 1.8(i), now Comment 11 to ABA Model Rule 1.7), which provides:

> A lawyer related to another lawyer as parent, child, sibling, or spouse shall not represent a client in a representation directly adverse to a person who the lawyer knows is represented by the other lawyer except upon consent by the client after consultation regarding the relationship.

Florida also adds Rule 1.7(e), which requires a lawyer representing "an insured client at the expense of the insurer . . . to ascertain whether the lawyer will be representing both the insurer and the insured as clients, or only the insured, and to inform both the insured and the insurer regarding the scope of the representation.''

Georgia: In the rules effective November 3, 2011, George has a unique version of Rule 1.7 that draws heavily on the Restatement of the Law Governing Lawyers. Georgia Rule 1.7 provides, in full, as follows:

> (a) A lawyer shall not represent or continue to represent a client if there is a significant risk that the lawyer's own interests or the lawyer's duties to another client, a former client, or a third person will materially and adversely affect the representation of the client, except as permitted in (b).
>
> (b) If client informed consent is permissible a lawyer may represent a client notwithstanding a significant risk of material and adverse effect if each affected client or former client gives informed consent confirmed in writing to the representation after:
>
>> (1) consultation with the lawyer pursuant to Rule 1.0(c);
>>
>> (2) having received in writing reasonable and adequate information about the material risks of and reasonable available alternatives to the representation; and
>>
>> (3) having been given the opportunity to consult with independent counsel.
>
> (c) Client informed consent is not permissible if the representation:
>
>> (1) is prohibited by law or these Rules;
>>
>> (2) includes the assertion of a claim by one client against another client represented by the lawyer in the same or substantially related proceeding; or
>>
>> (3) involves circumstances rendering it reasonably unlikely that the lawyer will be able to provide adequate representation to one or more of the affected clients.

Illinois deletes the requirement that a client's consent to a conflict of interest be confirmed in writing.

Massachusetts retains the original 1983 version of ABA Model Rule 1.7, and the Comment to Massachusetts Rule 1.7 differs substantially from the Comment to ABA Model Rule 1.7. Among other things, the Massachusetts Comment addresses the situation of the lawyer who represents one member of a corporate family while opposing another member of the family, the issue of confidentiality and privilege in multiple representation, and the responsibilities of lawyers who represent classes. Comment 6 states that ''a lawyer should not accept referrals from a referral source . . . if the lawyer's desire to continue to receive referrals from that source or the lawyer's relationship to that source would or would reasonably be viewed as discouraging the lawyer from representing the client zealously.''

New Jersey: Rule 1.7(b)(1), the counterpart to ABA Model Rule 1.7(b)(4), contains a proviso to the effect ''that a public entity cannot consent to any such representation.'' In addition, New Jersey adds a sentence from the original 1983 version of ABA Model Rule 1.7 requiring the lawyer, when representing multiple clients in a single matter, to explain ''the advantages and risks involved'' in common representation.

With respect to mortgage transactions, New Jersey has an unusual conflict of interest statute, N.J.S.A. §46:10A-6(b), which provides as follows:

> If a lender makes a written offer to a borrower to make a loan secured by real property located in this State, the lender shall disclose, in writing, prominently and in bold type, to the borrower before the acceptance of the offer by the borrower, that the interests of the borrower and lender are or may be different and may conflict, and that

the lender's attorney represents only the lender and not the borrower and the borrower is, therefore, advised to employ an attorney of the borrower's choice licensed to practice law in this State to represent the interests of the borrower.

New York: Rule 1.7(a) draws, in part, on DR 5-101(A) and 5-105(A)-(B) of the old Model Code, providing as follows:

> (a) Except as provided in paragraph (b), a lawyer shall not represent a client if a reasonable lawyer would conclude that either:
>> (1) the representation will involve the lawyer in representing differing interests; or
>> (2) there is a significant risk that the lawyer's professional judgment on behalf of a client will be adversely affected by the lawyer's own financial, business, property or other personal interests.

The comments to the rule offer more detail than the Model Rule comments in several respects. For example, Comments 22 and 22A describe advance waivers of conflicts in detail, and Comments 34, 34A, and 34B all address conflicts involving a client's corporate affiliates.

Pennsylvania: Rule 1.7 tracks ABA Model Rule 1.7, except that Pennsylvania Rule 1.7(b)(4) does not require that client consent be "confirmed in writing."

Tennessee: Rule 1.7(c) expressly describes when a lawyer may represent two clients in the same criminal case.

Texas: Rule 1.06 provides as follows:

> (a) A lawyer shall not represent opposing parties to the same litigation.
> (b) In other situations and except to the extent permitted by paragraph (c), a lawyer shall not represent a person if the representation of that person:
>> (1) involves a substantially related matter in which that person's interests are materially and directly adverse to the interests of another client of the lawyer or the lawyer's firm; or
>> (2) reasonably appears to be or becomes adversely limited by the lawyer's or law firm's responsibilities to another client or to a third person or by the lawyer's or law firm's own interests.
> (c) A lawyer may represent a client in the circumstances described in (b) if:
>> (1) the lawyer reasonably believes the representation of each client will not be materially affected; and
>> (2) each affected or potentially affected client consents to such representation after full disclosure of the existence, nature, implications, and possible adverse consequences of the common representation and the advantages involved, if any.
> (d) A lawyer who has represented multiple parties in a matter shall not thereafter represent any of such parties in a dispute among the parties arising out of the matter, unless prior consent is obtained from all such parties to the dispute.
> (e) If a lawyer has accepted representation in violation of this Rule, or if multiple representation properly accepted becomes improper under this Rule, the lawyer shall promptly withdraw from one or more representations to the extent necessary for any remaining representation not to be in violation of these Rules.
> (f) If a lawyer would be prohibited by this Rule from engaging in particular conduct, no other lawyer while a member or associated with that lawyer's firm may engage in that conduct.

The Texas rule thus allows a lawyer to oppose a current client in a matter not "substantially related" to matters being handled for that client. However, in *In re Dresser Industries, Inc.,* 972 F.2d 540 (5th Cir. 1992), the Fifth Circuit refused to apply Texas Rule 1.06, stating that conflicts of interest in federal litigation are governed by "national standards," including ABA Model Rule 1.7 and the Restatement of the Law Governing Lawyers.

Washington: For consent to a conflict to be valid, Rule 1.7(b)(4) requires that each affected client gives informed consent, confirmed in writing "(following authorization from the other client to make any required disclosures)."

Related Materials

ABA Commission on Ethics 20/20: In 2009, the ABA created the ABA Commission on Ethics 20/20, which is comprehensively reviewing the ABA Model Rules of Professional Conduct in light of globalization and changes in technology. On July 11, 2012, the Commission sought comments on a third draft of a proposal regarding choice of law rules with respect to conflicts of interest. The new draft would offer lawyers and clients the freedom to agree, subject to certain limitations, that their relationship will be governed by a particular jurisdiction's conflict of interest rules. But whereas the two earlier drafts had proposed adding only a new Comment 23 to Rule 1.7, the third draft (as slightly revised in September 2012) proposes to amend the black letter text of Rule 1.7 by adding the following new paragraph (c):

> (c) A lawyer and client are permitted to agree that the lawyer's work on a matter will be governed by the conflict of interest rules of a specific jurisdiction, but only if:
>
> > (1) the client gives informed consent to the agreement, confirmed in writing;
> >
> > (2) the client has a reasonable opportunity to consult with independent legal counsel regarding the agreement;
> >
> > (3) the selected jurisdiction is one in which substantial work related to the matter, or the predominant effect of such work, is reasonably expected to occur; and
> >
> > (4) the agreement does not result in the application of a conflict rule that permits the lawyer to undertake a representation to which informed consent is not permissible under the rules of the jurisdiction whose rules would otherwise govern the lawyer's work on a matter under Rule 8.5(b).

A proposed new Comment 23 to Rule 1.7, under the heading "Choice of Rule Agreements," would explain Rule 1.7(c) as follows:

> [23] Paragraph (c) provides, with certain limitations, that a lawyer and client can agree that the conflict rules of a specific jurisdiction will govern the representation. Such an agreement can help lawyers and their clients to predict which jurisdiction's conflict rules will govern the lawyer's representation of a client. The agreement can be helpful, whether in addition to or instead of a consent to future conflicts now permitted under Comment [22], because it can incorporate by reference an entire body of law on conflicts of interests. Clients, however, may be less likely to understand the material risks of such an agreement than when they consent to a specific possible future conflict. For this reason, Rule 1.7(c) imposes a number of requirements and limitations. For example, paragraph (c)(3) requires the selected jurisdiction to be one in which substantial work related to the matter, or the predominant effect of such work, is reasonably expected to occur.

In addition, the Commission has proposed a new Comment 8 to Rule 8.5 that would cross-reference Rule 1.7(c)(4). The Ethics 20/20 Commission may place these proposals (or revised versions of them) before the ABA House of Delegates at the ABA's February 2013 Mid-Year Meeting. For updates, see the Ethics 20/20 Commission's website at *http://www.americanbar.org/Ethics2020.*

ABA Formal Ethics Opinions: See ABA Formal Ethics Ops. 92-365 (1992), 93-372 (1993), 95-390 (1995), 97-406 (1997), 97-407 (1997), 02-426 (2002), 02-428 (2002),

["

Defense counsel should not permit a person who recommends, employs, or pays defense counsel to render legal services for another to direct or regulate counsel's professional judgment in rendering such legal services.

(f) Defense counsel should not defend a criminal case in which counsel's partner or other professional associate is or has been the prosecutor in the same case.

(g) Defense counsel should not represent a criminal defendant in a jurisdiction in which he or she is also a prosecutor.

(h) Defense counsel who formerly participated personally and substantially in the prosecution of a defendant should not thereafter represent any person in the same or a substantially related matter. Defense counsel who was formerly a prosecutor should not use confidential information about a person acquired when defense counsel was a prosecutor in the representation of a client whose interests are adverse to that person in a matter.

(i) Defense counsel who is related to a prosecutor as parent, child, sibling or spouse should not represent a client in a criminal matter where defense counsel knows the government is represented in the matter by such prosecutor. Nor should defense counsel who has a significant personal or financial relationship with a prosecutor represent a client in a criminal matter where defense counsel knows the government is represented in the matter by such prosecutor, except upon consent by the client after consultation regarding the relationship.

(j) Defense counsel should not act as surety on a bond either for the accused represented by counsel or for any other accused in the same or a related case.

(k) Except as law may otherwise expressly permit, defense counsel should not negotiate to employ any person who is significantly involved as an attorney or employee of the government in a matter in which defense counsel is participating personally and substantially.

ABA Standards for Imposing Lawyer Sanctions: The following Standards for Imposing Lawyer Sanctions are relevant to ABA Model Rule 1.7:

Failure to Avoid Conflicts of Interest

4.31. Disbarment is generally appropriate when a lawyer, without the informed consent of client(s):

(a) engages in representation of a client knowing that the lawyer's interests are adverse to the client's with the intent to benefit the lawyer or another, and causes serious or potentially serious injury to the client; or

(b) simultaneously represents clients that the lawyer knows have adverse interests with the intent to benefit the lawyer or another, and causes serious or potentially serious injury to a client; or

(c) represents a client in a matter substantially related to a matter in which the interests of a present or former client are materially adverse, and knowingly uses information relating to the representation of a client with the intent to benefit the lawyer or another, and causes serious or potentially serious injury to a client.

4.32. Suspension is generally appropriate when a lawyer knows of a conflict of interest and does not fully disclose to a client the possible effect of that conflict, and causes injury or potential injury to a client.

4.33. Reprimand is generally appropriate when a lawyer is negligent in determining whether the representation of a client may be materially affected by the lawyer's own interests, or whether the representation will adversely affect another client, and causes injury or potential injury to a client.

4.34. Admonition is generally appropriate when a lawyer engages in an isolated instance of negligence in determining whether the representation of a client may be materially affected by the lawyer's own interests, or whether the representation will adversely affect another client, and causes little or no actual or potential injury to a client.

Bankruptcy Law: Lawyers handling federal bankruptcy matters are subject to stringent statutes prohibiting conflicts of interest. One of the most prominent bankruptcy statutes is 11 U.S.C. §327, which provides, in part:

> (a) Except as otherwise provided in this section, the trustee, with the court's approval, may employ one or more attorneys ... that do not hold or represent an interest adverse to the estate, and that are disinterested persons, to represent or assist the trustee in carrying out the trustee's duties under this title. . . .
>
> (c) In a case under chapter 7, 12, or 11 of this title, a person is not disqualified for employment under this section solely because of such person's employment by or representation of a creditor, unless there is objection by another creditor or the United States trustee, in which case the court shall disapprove such employment if there is an actual conflict of interest. . . .
>
> (e) The trustee, with the court's approval, may employ . . . an attorney that has represented the debtor, if in the best interest of the estate, and if such attorney does not represent or hold any interest adverse to the debtor or to the estate with respect to the matter on which such attorney is to be employed.

IRS Regulations: In the regulations governing practice before the Internal Revenue Service, 31 C.F.R. §10.29, entitled "Conflicting Interests," essentially adopts ABA Model Rule 1.7. In pertinent part, §10.29 provides that "a practitioner shall not represent a client in his or her practice before the Internal Revenue Service if the representation involves a conflict of interest" unless:

> (1) The practitioner reasonably believes that the practitioner will be able to provide competent and diligent representation to each affected client;
>
> (2) The representation is not prohibited by law;
>
> (3) Each affected client waives the conflict of interest and gives informed consent, confirmed in writing by each affected client, at the time the existence of the conflict of interest is known by the practitioner. . . .

Section 10.29(c) requires lawyers to keep copies of the written consents for at least 36 months after the representation of the affected clients concludes, and lawyers must provide the written consents to any officer or employee of the Internal Revenue Service on request.

Paralegal Conflicts: Paralegals and other nonlawyer members can sometimes cause conflicts of interest for the lawyers and law firms who employ them, and some authorities seek to regulate conflicts caused by nonlawyers. For example, Nebraska addresses "support person" conflicts in Rule 1.9(d), and Guideline 7 of the ABA Model Guidelines for the Utilization of Paralegal Services provides as follows: "A lawyer should take reasonable measures to prevent conflicts of interest resulting from a paralegal's other employment or interests."

Private Securities Litigation Reform Act: The Federal Private Securities Litigation Reform Act provides, in 15 U.S.C.A. §77z-1(a)(8), that if a plaintiff class is represented by an attorney who directly owns or has a beneficial interest in the securities that are the subject of the litigation, "the court shall make a determination of whether such ownership or other interest constitutes a conflict of interest sufficient to disqualify the attorney from representing the plaintiff class."

Restatement of the Law Governing Lawyers: See Restatement §§108, 121, 122, 125, 128-130, and 135 in our chapter on the Restatement later in this volume.

Sixth Amendment: The Sixth Amendment to the United States Constitution, which guarantees effective assistance of counsel, imposes certain obligations on courts regarding conflicts of interest. In *Holloway v. Arkansas,* 435 U.S. 475 (1978), the Court held that the Sixth Amendment requires automatic reversal when a trial court fails to conduct an inquiry either after a timely conflict objection, or after the court knows or reasonably should know that a particular conflict exists. In *Cuyler v. Sullivan,* 446 U.S. 335 (1980), the Court ruled that this "automatic reversal" rule does not apply when the trial court is not informed of a conflict and is not on notice of the conflict. If a conflict is later alleged, the Sixth Amendment requires a defendant to establish that "an actual conflict of interest adversely affected his lawyer's performance." In *Mickens v. Taylor,* 535 U.S. 162 (2002), the Court held that, to demonstrate a Sixth Amendment violation due to the trial court's failure to inquire into a potential conflict of interest about which it knew or reasonably should have known, defendant must establish that this conflict of interest adversely affected counsel's performance.

Rule 1.8   Conflict of Interest: Current Clients: Specific Rules

Canon and Code Antecedents

ABA Canons of Professional Ethics: Canons 10, 11, and 38 provided as follows:

10.   Acquiring Interest in Litigation

The lawyer should not purchase any interest in the subject matter of the litigation which he is conducting.

11.   Dealing with Trust Property

The lawyer should refrain from any action whereby for his personal benefit or gain he abuses or takes advantage of the confidence reposed in him by his client.

Money of the client or collected for the client or other trust property coming into the possession of the lawyer should be reported and accounted for promptly, and should not under any circumstances be commingled with his own or be used by him.

38.   Compensation, Commissions and Rebates

A lawyer should accept no compensation, commissions, rebates or other advantages from others without the knowledge and consent of his client after full disclosure.

ABA Model Code of Professional Responsibility: Compare DR 4-101(B)(3), DR 5-103(A), DR 5-103(B), DR 5-104(A), DR 5-104(B), DR 5-106, DR 5-107(A)(1), and DR 6-102(A) (reprinted later in this volume).

Cross-References in Other Rules

Rule 1.0, Comment 7: Certain "Rules require that a client's consent be obtained in a writing signed by the client. See, e.g., **Rules 1.8(a)** and **(g)**."

Rule 1.2, Comment 8: "All agreements concerning a lawyer's representation of a client must accord with the Rules of Professional Conduct and other law. See, e.g., **Rules** 1.1, **1.8** and 5.6."

Rule 1.5, Comment 4: "A lawyer may accept property in payment for services, such as an ownership interest in an enterprise, providing this does not involve acquisition of a proprietary interest in the cause of action or subject matter of the litigation contrary to **Rule 1.8(i)**. However, a fee paid in property instead of money may be subject to the requirements of **Rule 1.8 (a)**. . . ."

Rule 1.6, Comment 1: See "**Rules 1.8(b)** and 1.9(c)(1) for the lawyer's duties with respect to the use of such information to the disadvantage of clients and former clients."

Rule 1.7, Comment 1: "For specific Rules regarding certain concurrent conflicts of interest, see **Rule 1.8**."

Rule 1.7, Comment 10: "See **Rule 1.8** for specific Rules pertaining to a number of personal interest conflicts, including business transactions with clients."

Rule 1.7, Comment 12: "A lawyer is prohibited from engaging in sexual relationships with a client unless the sexual relationship predates the formation of the client-lawyer relationship. See **Rule 1.8(j)**."

Rule 1.7, Comment 13: "A lawyer may be paid from a source other than the client, including a co-client, if the client is informed of that fact and consents and the arrangement does not compromise the lawyer's duty of loyalty or independent judgment to the client. See **Rule 1.8(f)**."

Rule 1.10, Comment 8: "Where a lawyer is prohibited from engaging in certain transactions under **Rule 1.8**, paragraph (**k**) of that Rule, and not this Rule, determines whether that prohibition also applies to other lawyers associated in a firm with the personally prohibited lawyer."

Rule 1.13, Comment 6: "[T]his Rule does not limit or expand the lawyer's responsibility under **Rule 1.8**, 1.16, 3.3 or 4.1."

Rule 5.4, Comment 2: Rule 5.4 "expresses traditional limitations on permitting a third party to direct or regulate the lawyer's professional judgment in rendering legal services to another. See also **Rule 1.8(f)**. . . ."

Rule 5.7, Comment 5: "When a client-lawyer relationship exists with a person who is referred by a lawyer to a separate law-related service entity controlled by the lawyer, individually or with others, the lawyer must comply with **Rule 1.8(a)**."

Rule 5.7, Comment 10: "When a lawyer is obliged to accord the recipients of such services the protections of those Rules that apply to the client-lawyer relationship, the lawyer must take special care to heed the proscriptions of the Rules addressing conflict of interest (Rules 1.7 through 1.11, especially Rules 1.7 and **1.8(a)**, **(b)**, and **(f)**). . . ."

Legislative History of Model Rule 1.8

1979 Unofficial Pre-Circulation Draft:

(e) A lawyer shall not provide financial assistance to a client in connection with pending or contemplated litigation, except that a lawyer may advance expenses, including:

Alternative (1): Court costs, expenses of investigation, medical and other experts, and obtaining and presenting evidence.

Alternative (2): Court costs, expenses of litigation, and living expenses.

1980 Discussion Draft (then called Rule 1.9):

> (f) A lawyer may serve as general counsel to a corporation or other organization of which the lawyer is a director only if:
>> (1) There is adequate disclosure to and consent by all persons having an investment interest in the organization; or
>> (2) When doing so would not involve serious risk of conflict between the lawyer's responsibilities as general counsel and those as director.

1981 and *1982 Drafts* were substantially the same as adopted, except that Rule 1.8(f) contained no restrictions other than the client's consent "after consultation."

1983 Rule: From 1983 until its extensive amendment in 2002, Rule 1.8 provided:

> (a) [Same as the 2002 version of Rule 1.8(a).]
>> (1) [Same as the 2002 version of Rule 1.8(a)(1).]
>> (2) the client is given a reasonable opportunity to seek the advice of independent counsel in the transaction; and
>> (3) the client consents in writing thereto.
> (b) [Same as the 2002 version of Rule 1.8(b), but requiring that the client "consent after consultation" instead of "gives informed consent."]
> (c) A lawyer shall not prepare an instrument giving the lawyer or a person related to the lawyer as parent, child, sibling, or spouse any substantial gift from a client, including a testamentary gift, except where the client is related to the donee.
> (d) [Same as the 2002 version of Rule 1.8(d).]
> (e) [Same as the 2002 version of Rule 1.8(e).]
> (f) [Same as the 2002 version of Rule 1.8(f), but requiring that the client "consent after consultation" instead of "gives informed consent."]
> (g) A lawyer who represents two or more clients shall not participate in making an aggregate settlement of the claims of or against the clients, or in a criminal case an aggregated agreement as to guilty or nolo contendere pleas, unless each client consents after consultation, including disclosure of the existence and nature of all the claims or pleas involved and of the participation of each person in the settlement.
> (h) A lawyer shall not make an agreement prospectively limiting the lawyer's liability to a client for malpractice unless permitted by law and the client is independently represented in making the agreement, or settle a claim for such liability with an unrepresented client or former client without first advising that person in writing that independent representation is appropriate in connection therewith.
> (i) A lawyer related to another lawyer as parent, child, sibling or spouse shall not represent a client in a representation directly adverse to a person whom the lawyer knows is represented by the other lawyer except upon consent by the client after consultation regarding the relationship.
> (j) [Same as the 2002 version of Rule 1.8(i).]

2002 Amendments: At its February 2002 Mid-Year Meeting, the ABA House of Delegates adopted without change the ABA Ethics 2000 Commission's extensive proposal to amend Rule 1.8 and its Comment. Among other things, the amendment created the writing requirement in paragraph (a)(2) and added the description of the writing required in paragraph (a)(3). The amendment also added the writing requirement to paragraph (g). Paragraphs (j) and (k) were completely new. In addition, the Comment was extensively revised.

Also, former Rule 1.8(i) was deleted. Before 2002, Rule 1.8(i) prohibited lawyers in certain familial relationships (parent, child, sibling, or spouse) from representing adverse clients without consent after consultation. This provision was deleted in 2002 and replaced by a new Comment 11 to Rule 1.7. The Reporter explained that the deleted Rule 1.8(i) was both overinclusive and underinclusive. It was underinclusive "because it does not address personal-interest conflicts arising from close family or family-like relationships other than those enumerated in the Rules, such as couples who live together in a relationship approximating marriage." The rule was deemed overinclusive because it would permit client consent even of conflicts that would "be deemed nonconsentable under Rule 1.7." For these and other reasons, the Commission deleted the rule in favor of Rule 1.7 Comment 11.

Selected State Variations

Alabama: Alabama's Rule 1.8(e)(3) provides as follows:

> (3) a lawyer may advance or guarantee emergency financial assistance to the client, the repayment of which may not be contingent on the outcome of the matter, provided that no promise or assurance of financial assistance was made to the client by the lawyer, or on the lawyer's behalf, prior to the employment of the lawyer.

Alabama also adds Rule 1.8(k), which identifies when a lawyer can represent both parties to an uncontested divorce or domestic relations proceeding. Relating to Rule 1.8(h), the Alabama Legal Services Liability Act, Ala. Code §§6-5-570 et seq., provides as follows: "There shall be only one form and cause of action against legal service providers in courts in the State of Alabama and it shall be known as the legal service liability action." Finally, Rules 1.8(*l*) and (m) describe prohibitions on sexual relations between lawyers and clients. Notably, Rule 1.8(m) states that "except for a spousal relationship or a relationship that existed at the commencement of the lawyer-client relationship, sexual relations between the lawyer and the client shall be presumed to be exploitative [and thus violate Rule 1.8(*l*)]. This presumption is rebuttable."

Arizona: Rule 1.8(h)(2) adds a clause forbidding a lawyer to "make an agreement prospectively limiting the client's right to report the lawyer to appropriate professional authorities." Rule 1.8(*l*), which retains the 1983 version of ABA Model Rule 1.8(i), provides: "A lawyer related to another lawyer as parent, child, sibling, spouse or cohabitant shall not represent a client in a representation directly adverse to a person who the lawyer knows is represented by the other lawyer except upon consent by the client after consultation regarding the relationship."

California: California's rules are generally equivalent to Model Rule 1.8, but two exceptions deserve attention. Rule 3-320 provides as follows:

> A member shall not represent a client in a matter in which another party's lawyer is a spouse, parent, child, or sibling of the member, lives with the member, is a client of the member, or has an intimate personal relationship with the member, unless the member informs the client in writing of the relationship.

And Rule 4-210 provides in part as follows:

> (A) A member shall not directly or indirectly pay or agree to pay, guarantee, represent, or sanction a representation that the member or member's law firm will pay

the personal or business expenses of a prospective or existing client, except that this rule shall not prohibit a member: . . . (2) After employment, from lending money to the client upon the client's promise in writing to repay such loan.

Connecticut adds the following language to Rule 1.8(a), providing that lawyers can enter into business transactions with clients under the following circumstances:

(4) With regard to a business transaction, the lawyer advises the client or former client in writing either (A) that the lawyer will provide legal services to the client or former client concerning the transaction, or (B) that the lawyer will not provide legal services to the client or former client and that the lawyer is involved as a business person only and not as a lawyer representing the client or former client and that the lawyer is not one to whom the client or former client can turn for legal advice concerning the transaction.

(5) With regard to the providing of investment services, the lawyer advises the client or former client in writing (A) whether such services are covered by legal liability insurance or other insurance, and [makes either disclosure set out in paragraph (a)(4)]. Investment services shall only apply where the lawyer has either a direct or indirect control over the invested funds and a direct or indirect interest in the underlying investment.

For purposes of subsection (a)(1) through (a)(5), the phrase "former client" shall mean a client for whom the two year period starting from the conclusion of representation has not expired.

District of Columbia: D.C. Rule 1.8(d) permits lawyers to advance "financial assistance which is reasonably necessary to permit the client to institute or maintain the litigation or administrative proceeding." Rule 1.8(i) provides as follows:

A lawyer may acquire and enforce a lien granted by law to secure the lawyer's fees or expenses, but a lawyer shall not impose a lien upon any part of a client's files, except upon the lawyer's own work product, and then only to the extent that the work product has not been paid for. This work product exception shall not apply when the client has become unable to pay, or when withholding the lawyer's work product would present a significant risk to the client of irreparable harm.

Florida: Rule 4-8.4(i) provides that a lawyer shall not engage in sexual conduct with a client "or a representative of a client that exploits or adversely affects the interests of the client or the lawyer-client relationship."

Georgia: In the rules effective November 3, 2011, Rule 1.8(a), drawing on DR 5-104 of the ABA Code of Professional Responsibility, applies "if the client expects the lawyer to exercise the lawyer's professional judgment therein for the protection of the client." Georgia retains the language of deleted ABA Model Rule 1.8(i) but adds that the disqualification of a lawyer due to a parent, grandparent, child, grandchild, sibling, or spousal relationship "is personal and is not imputed to members of firms with whom the lawyers are associated."

Illinois: Rule 1.8(a)(2) omits the phrase "desirability of seeking."

Louisiana: Rule 1.8(g) permits an aggregate settlement if "a court approves the settlement in a certified class action." Rule 1.8(e) permits a lawyer to "provide financial assistance to a client who is in necessitous circumstances" subject to strict controls, including:

(ii) The advance or loan guarantee, or the offer thereof, shall not be used as an inducement by the lawyer, or anyone acting on the lawyer's behalf, to secure employment.

(iii) Neither the lawyer nor anyone acting on the lawyer's behalf may offer to make advances or loan guarantees prior to being hired by a client, and the lawyer shall not publicize nor advertise a willingness to make advances or loan guarantees to clients.

Massachusetts: Rule 1.8(b) forbids a lawyer to use confidential information "for the lawyer's advantage or the advantage of a third person" without consent.

Michigan: Rules 1.8(a)(2) and 1.8(h)(2) (regarding business transactions with clients and settlement of legal malpractice claims) both require that the client be given a reasonable opportunity to seek the advice of independent counsel but lack the ABA requirement that the client be "advised in writing of the desirability of seeking" independent counsel. Michigan Rule 1.8(g), regarding aggregate settlements, lacks the ABA requirement that the client's consent be "in a writing signed by the client." Michigan retains the language of deleted ABA Model Rule 1.8(i) verbatim.

Minnesota: Rule 1.8(e)(3) allows a lawyer to guarantee a loan necessary for a client to withstand litigation delay. Rule 1.8(k)'s provision on sexual relationships with clients prohibits a lawyer from having sexual relations with a client unless a consensual relationship existed between the lawyer and client when the client-lawyer relationship commenced. The rule also defines "sexual relations" and adds the following Rules 1.8(k)(2)-(3) to explain the meaning of sex with a "client" when a lawyer represents an organization:

> (2) if the client is an organization, any individual who oversees the representation and gives instructions to the lawyer on behalf of the organization shall be deemed to be the client. . . .
>
> (3) this paragraph does not prohibit a lawyer from engaging in sexual relations with a client of the lawyer's firm provided that the lawyer has no involvement in the performance of the legal work for the client. . . .

Mississippi: Rule 1.8(e)(2) permits a lawyer to advance medical and living expenses to a client under certain narrowly defined circumstances.

New Hampshire: The New Hampshire rules include a Rule 1.19 (Disclosure of Information to the Client), which requires a lawyer (other than a government or in-house lawyer) to inform a client at the time of engagement if "the lawyer does not maintain professional liability insurance" of at least $100,000 per occurrence and $300,000 in the aggregate "or if the lawyer's professional liability insurance ceases to be in effect."

New Jersey: Rule 1.8(e)(3) creates an exception allowing financial assistance by a "non-profit organization authorized under [other law]" if the organization is representing the indigent client without a fee. Rule 1.8(h)(1), while forbidding agreements prospectively limiting liability to a client, contains an exception if "the client fails to act in accordance with the lawyer's advice and the lawyer nevertheless continues to represent the client at the client's request." New Jersey Rule 1.8(k) and (*l*) provide as follows:

> (k) A lawyer employed by a public entity, either as a lawyer or in some other role, shall not undertake the representation of another client if the representation presents a substantial risk that the lawyer's responsibilities to the public entity would limit the lawyer's ability to provide independent advice or diligent and competent representation to either the public entity or the client.
>
> (*l*) A public entity cannot consent to a representation otherwise prohibited by this Rule.

New York: Rule 1.8(a) deletes the language "knowingly acquire an owner-ship, possessory, security or other pecuniary interest adverse to a client" and adds language from DR 5-104(A) of the old Model Code: "if they have differing inter-ests therein and if the client expects the lawyer to exercise professional judgment therein for the protection of the client. . . . " Comments 3A and 4A-4F, which have no Model Rule equivalents, describe in detail the problem of business transactions with clients, including (in Comments 4D-4F) issues related to a lawyer's receipt of a client's securities. New York omits Comment 5.

Rule 1.8(d) draws, in part, on DR 5-104(B) of the old Model Code, and Comment 9 provides more guidance than the equivalent Model Rule provisions concerning a lawyer's acquisition of media or literary rights that relate to a client matter.

Finally, Rule 1.8(j) and (k) as well as Comments 17, 17A, 17B, and 18-20, all address sexual relationships with clients and provide significantly more guidance in this regard than the equivalent Model Rule provision. Comment 17B concludes that "[a] law firm's failure to educate lawyers about the restrictions on sexual rela-tions — or a firm's failure to enforce those restrictions against lawyers who violate them — may constitute a violation of Rule 5.1, which obligates a law firm to make reasonable efforts to ensure that all lawyers in the firm conform to these Rules."

North Dakota: Rule 1.8(g), regarding aggregate settlements, applies "other than in class actions." North Dakota adds Rule 1.8(k), which restricts the practice of law by a part-time prosecutor or judge in certain circumstances.

Ohio: Rule 1.8(c) forbids a lawyer to solicit "any substantial gift from a client" and forbids a lawyer to "prepare on behalf of a client an instrument giving the lawyer, the lawyer's partner, associate, paralegal, law clerk or other employee of the lawyer's firm, a lawyer acting 'of counsel' in the lawyer's firm, or a person related to the lawyer any gift unless the lawyer or other recipient of the gift is related to the cli-ent." "Gift" is defined to include "a testamentary gift." Ohio Rule 1.8(f)(4) provides a detailed "statement of insured client's rights" that a lawyer "selected and paid by an insurer to represent an insured" must give to the client.

An Ohio statute (R.C. §1349.55) regulates companies that make cash advances to plaintiffs in pending civil cases in exchange for the right to receive part of the pro-ceeds of any settlement, award, or judgment. Paragraph (C) of the statute provides that if a plaintiff gets into a dispute concerning the contract for the cash advance, "the responsibilities of the attorney representing the consumer [the plaintiff] in the civil action or claim shall be no greater than the attorney's responsibilities under the Ohio Rules of Professional Conduct."

Oregon: Rule 1.8(b) permits a lawyer to use confidential information to a cli-ent's disadvantage only if the client's consent is "confirmed in writing" (except as otherwise permitted or required by the Rules). Rule 1.8(e) permits a lawyer to advance litigation expenses only if "the client remains ultimately liable for such expenses to the extent of the client's ability to pay." Finally, Oregon's rule gov-erning sexual relations with clients contains a detailed description of "sexual rela-tions," providing that it includes "sexual intercourse or any touching of the sexual or other intimate parts of a person or causing such person to touch the sexual or other intimate parts of the lawyer for the purpose of arousing or gratifying the sexual desire of either party."

Pennsylvania: Rule 1.8(g) does not require that client consent be "confirmed in writing."

Texas: Rule 1.08(c) provides that prior to the conclusion of "all aspects of the matter giving rise to the lawyer's employment," a lawyer shall not make or negotiate an agreement "with a client, prospective client, or former client" giving the lawyer literary or media rights to a portrayal or account based in substantial part on information relating to the representation. Rule 1.08(d) provides as follows:

> (d) A lawyer shall not provide financial assistance to a client in connection with pending or contemplated litigation or administrative proceedings, except that:
> (1) a lawyer may advance or guarantee court costs, expenses of litigation or administrative proceedings, and reasonably necessary medical and living expenses, the repayment of which may be contingent on the outcome of the matter; and
> (2) a lawyer representing an indigent client may pay court costs and expenses of litigation on behalf of the client.

Virginia: Rule 1.8(b) forbids the use of information "for the advantage of the lawyer or of a third person or to the disadvantage of the client." Rule 1.8(e)(1) requires a client ultimately to be liable for court costs and expenses. Rule 1.8(h) contains an exception where the lawyer is "an employee" of the client "as long as the client is independently represented in making the agreement" prospectively limiting the lawyer's liability for malpractice.

Washington: Rule 1.8(e) permits a lawyer to (1) advance or guarantee the expenses of litigation "provided the client remains ultimately liable for such expenses; and (2) in matters maintained as class actions only, repayment of expenses of litigation may be contingent on the outcome of the matter." Washington deletes ABA Model Rule 1.8(e)(2) (permitting lawyers to pay litigation costs for indigent clients).

Wisconsin: Rule 1.8(c) creates an exception to testamentary gifts where:

> (1) the client is related to the donee, (2) the donee is a natural object of the bounty of the client, (3) there is no reasonable ground to anticipate a contest, or a claim of undue influence or for the public to lose confidence in the integrity of the bar, and (4) the amount of the gift or bequest is reasonable and natural under the circumstances.

Related Materials

ABA Formal Ethics Opinions: See ABA Formal Ethics Ops. 90-358 (1990), 92-364 (1992), 96-401 (1996), 00-416 (2000), 00-418 (2000), 01-421 (2001), 02-425 (2002), 02-426 (2002), 02-427 (2002), 02-428 (2002), 03-430 (2003), 04-432 (2004), 04-433 (2004), 05-435 (2005), 06-438 (2006), 08-448 (2008), and 08-450 (2008).

ABA Model Court Rule on Insurance Disclosure: The ABA has extensively explored problems relating to legal malpractice insurance and has developed a Model Court Rule on Insurance Disclosure, which was approved by the House of Delegates at the ABA's August 2004 Annual Meeting by the slender vote of 213-203. As approved, the rule provides as follows:

ABA Model Court Rule on Insurance Disclosure

> A. Each lawyer admitted to the active practice of law shall certify to the [highest court of the jurisdiction] on or before [December 31 of each year]: 1) whether the lawyer is engaged in the private practice of law; 2) if engaged in the private practice of law, whether the lawyer is currently covered by professional liability insurance; 3)

whether the lawyer intends to maintain insurance during the period of time the lawyer is engaged in the private practice of law; and 4) whether the lawyer is exempt from the provisions of this Rule because the lawyer is engaged in the practice of law as a full-time government lawyer or is counsel employed by an organizational client and does not represent clients outside that capacity. Each lawyer admitted to the active practice of law in this jurisdiction who reports being covered by professional liability insurance shall notify [the highest court in the jurisdiction] in writing within 30 days if the insurance policy providing coverage lapses, is no longer in effect or terminates for any reason.

B. The foregoing shall be certified by each lawyer admitted to the active practice of law in this jurisdiction in such form as may be prescribed by the [highest court of the jurisdiction]. The information submitted pursuant to this Rule will be made available to the public by such means as may be designated by the [highest court of the jurisdiction].

C. Any lawyer admitted to the active practice of law who fails to comply with this Rule in a timely fashion, as defined by the [highest court in the jurisdiction], may be suspended from the practice of law until such time as the lawyer complies. Supplying false information in response to this Rule shall subject the lawyer to appropriate disciplinary action.

The brackets throughout the rule indicate that each jurisdiction should adopt or modify the bracketed language to suit its own circumstances. The Report submitted in support of the ABA Model Court Rule on Insurance Disclosure is available online at *http://www.americanbar.org/content/dam/aba/migrated/cpr/clientpro/malprac_disc_report.authcheckdam.pdf.* For information on state malpractice insurance disclosure rules, see the entry below entitled "Malpractice Insurance Disclosure Requirements."

ABA Resolution on Fee Payment for Corporate Employees: In 2006, the ABA House of Delegates approved a resolution opposing various government "policies, practices and procedures that have the effect of eroding the constitutional and other legal rights of current or former employees, officers, directors, or agents." The ABA especially criticized the government's consideration of "whether an organization provided counsel to an employee or agreed to pay an employee's legal fees and expenses" in evaluating corporate cooperation with its investigations. For more information, see *http://apps.americanbar.org/buslaw/attorneyclient/materials/hod/emprights_recommendation_adopted.pdf.*

ABA Tort Trial and Insurance Practice Section Guidelines: In 1991, the ABA's Section of Tort Trial and Insurance Practice (then called the Tort and Insurance Practice Section, or TIPS) approved Guidelines for the Selection and Performance of Retained Counsel. The following provisions relate to Rule 1.8(f):

c. *Relationships Involving Three Parties — Attorney, Insured, and Insurer — Must Be Balanced with Legal and Contractual Obligations*

. . . When counsel is retained by an insurer to represent an insured, counsel's duty is owed to both clients to the extent that the interests of each party are aligned. When the interests of the insurer and the insured conflict, counsel's primary duty is to the insured.

When counsel is retained by an insurer to represent an insured and a conflict exists between insured and insurer, counsel for the insured may not provide counsel to the insurer. All potential conflicts between insurer and insured must be identified and disclosed in detail to the insured by the insurer.

If the insurer agrees to retain counsel to defend an insured (a) under a reservation of rights to deny coverage or (b) while contending that some of the allegations asserted against the insured are not covered by the insurance policy, counsel's primary duty is to the insured. In such a case, counsel should defend the action so as to avoid prejudice to, or impairment of, the rights of the insured.

Where there are matters within the policy coverage and matters potentially outside the policy coverage, the insurer should advise the insured of the excess exposure and inform the insured of the right to retain personal counsel.

Litigation Finance Companies: Because Rule 1.8(e) generally prohibits lawyers from providing financial assistance to clients in connection with contemplated or pending litigation, nonlawyer companies have sprung up that give cash advances to plaintiffs in civil litigation in exchange for a share of the proceeds of any settlement or judgment. Litigation finance companies usually charge a plaintiff a high rate of interest (typically from 3 to 6 percent per month, but sometimes higher). However, such a cash advance is not usually considered a ''loan'' for purposes of usury laws because the advance is ''nonrecourse,'' meaning that if the plaintiff loses the case, then the plaintiff does not have to repay the advance (*i.e.*, the litigation finance company has no recourse to the plaintiff's personal assets).

Because some litigation finance companies have allegedly engaged in abusive practices, various methods have been used or suggested to regulate or reform the litigation finance industry. For example, in 2009 an Ohio statute (R.C. §1349.55) imposed strict requirements on litigation finance companies. In December 2012, the 20/20 Commission released a 39-page "Information Report to the House of Delegates" (a "White Paper") regarding alternative litigation financing. The White Paper is available at *http://www.americanbar.org/content/dam/aba/administrative/ ethics_2020/20111212_ethics_20_20_alf_white_paper_final_hod_informational_report. authcheckdam.pdf.* For an industry view of litigation financing, see the website of the American Litigation Finance Association (ALFA) at *www.americanlegalfin.com.*

Malpractice Insurance and Uninsured Lawyers: Although Model Rule 1.8(h) generally prohibits lawyers from prospectively limiting their liability to clients for legal malpractice, clients who successfully sue their lawyers for malpractice are not assured of any recovery. Only one jurisdiction (Oregon) requires its lawyers to maintain legal malpractice insurance, and a surprising number of lawyers in other states do not carry malpractice insurance. In Massachusetts, for example, a survey published in 1997 revealed that about 25 percent of the lawyers who responded said they did not carry professional liability insurance. The lawyers most likely to be insured were partners in private law firms (97.4 percent) and their associates (94.7 percent). Solo practitioners fell in the middle (75 percent). The lawyers least likely to be insured were lawyers employed by corporations (28.6 percent) and public service lawyers (17.4 percent). A 2002 survey by the Illinois Attorney Registration and Disciplinary Commission revealed that only 60 percent of the Illinois solo practitioners who responded had professional liability insurance, but 96 percent of lawyers in firms of two to ten lawyers were covered, and over 99 percent of lawyers in firms of 11 or more lawyers maintained professional liability insurance. For a detailed treatment of legal malpractice insurance, see Ronald E. Mallen, Legal Malpractice: The Law Office Guide to Purchasing Legal Malpractice Insurance (West 2012 ed.).

Malpractice Insurance Disclosure Requirements: Many lawyers do not carry legal malpractice insurance. States have responded to the problem of uninsured lawyers

236

in various ways. In Illinois, for example, Supreme Court Rule 756(e) requires all lawyers to disclose on the annual attorney registration form whether they carry malpractice insurance, and allows the state to "conduct random audits to assure the accuracy of the information reported." New Hampshire Rule 1.19(a) requires a lawyer to inform a client, both at the outset of an engagement and during an engagement, if the lawyer does not maintain professional liability insurance of at least $100,000 per occurrence and $300,000 in the aggregate, or if the lawyer's insurance ceases to be in effect. In Massachusetts, to qualify for the State Bar's Lawyer Referral Service, a lawyer must carry a policy of at least $250,000 per occurrence and $500,000 in the aggregate. In 2004, the ABA adopted an ABA Model Court Rule on Insurance Disclosure, set out above in these Related Materials.

At our press deadline in September 2012, 24 states require some form of malpractice insurance disclosure. Of these, 17 states require disclosure in connection with bar registration, while only 8 states require disclosure directly to clients. (Those numbers add up to 25 because New Mexico requires both.) At least 5 states (Maine, New York, South Carolina, Utah, and Vermont) are listed by the ABA as still considering some form of legal malpractice insurance disclosure rule, while 5 states (Arkansas, Connecticut, Florida, Kentucky, and Texas) have formally rejected a proposed mandatory insurance disclosure rule, and North Carolina withdrew its insurance disclosure rule in 2010. Oregon is the only state that requires lawyers to carry malpractice insurance. For a state-by-state chart regarding malpractice insurance disclosure, see *http://www.americanbar.org/content/dam/aba/migrated/2011_build/ professional_responsibility/malprac_disc_chart.authcheckdam.pdf*.

Restatement of the Law Governing Lawyers: See Restatement §§18, 36, 43, 54, 62, 126, 127, and 134 in our chapter on the Restatement later in this volume.

Rule 1.9   Duties to Former Clients

Canon and Code Antecedents

ABA Canons of Professional Ethics: Canon 37 provided as follows:

37.   Confidences of a Client

It is the duty of a lawyer to preserve his client's confidences. This duty outlasts the lawyer's employment, and extends as well to his employees; and neither of them should accept employment which involves or may involve the disclosure or use of these confidences, either for the private advantage of the lawyer or his employees or to the disadvantage of the client, without his knowledge and consent, and even though there are other available sources of such information. A lawyer should not continue employment when he discovers that this obligation prevents the performance of his full duty to his former or to his new client.

If a lawyer is accused by his client, he is not precluded from disclosing the truth in respect to the accusation. The announced intention of a client to commit a crime is not included within the confidences which he is bound to respect. He may properly make such disclosures as may be necessary to prevent the act or protect those against whom it is threatened.

ABA Model Code of Professional Responsibility: Compare DR 5-105(C) (reprinted later in this volume).

Cross-References in Other Rules

Rule 1.0, Comment 7: "A number of Rules require that a person's consent be confirmed in writing. See **Rules** 1.7(b) and **1.9(a)**."

Rule 1.6, Comment 1: See "**Rules** 1.8(b) and **1.9(c)(1)** for the lawyer's duties with respect to the use of such information to the disadvantage of clients and former clients."

Rule 1.6, Comment 20: "The duty of confidentiality continues after the client-lawyer relationship has terminated. See **Rule 1.9(c)(2)**. See **Rule 1.9(c)(1)** for the prohibition against using such information to the disadvantage of the former client."

Rule 1.7, Comment 1: "For former client conflicts of interest, see **Rule 1.9**."

Rule 1.7, Comment 4: "Where more than one client is involved, whether the lawyer may continue to represent any of the clients is determined both by the lawyer's ability to comply with duties owed to the former client and by the lawyer's ability to represent adequately the remaining client or clients, given the lawyer's duties to the former client. See **Rule 1.9**."

Rule 1.7, Comment 5: "The lawyer must continue to protect the confidences of the client from whose representation the lawyer has withdrawn. See **Rule 1.9(c)**."

Rule 1.7, Comment 9: "In addition to conflicts with other current clients, a lawyer's duties of loyalty and independence may be materially limited by responsibilities to former clients under **Rule 1.9**. . . ."

Rule 1.7, Comment 33: "Subject to the above limitations, each client in the common representation has the right to loyal and diligent representation and the protection of **Rule 1.9** concerning the obligations to a former client."

Rule 1.8, Comment 5: It is prohibited to partake in the "disadvantageous use of client information unless the client gives informed consent, except as permitted or required by these Rules. See **Rules** 1.2(d), 1.6, **1.9(c)**, 3.3, 4.1(b), 8.1 and 8.3."

Rule 1.10(a): "While lawyers are associated in a firm, none of them shall knowingly represent a client when any one of them practicing alone would be prohibited from doing so by **Rules** 1.7 or **1.9**, unless the prohibition is based on a personal interest of the prohibited lawyer and does not present a significant risk of materially limiting the representation of the client by the remaining lawyers in the firm."

Rule 1.10(b)(2) restricts representation when "any lawyer remaining in the firm has information protected by **Rules** 1.6 and **1.9(c)** that is material to the matter."

Rule 1.10, Comment 2: "When a lawyer moves from one firm to another, the situation is governed by **Rules 1.9(b)** and 1.10(b)."

Rule 1.10, Comment 5: When a lawyer who represents or formerly represented a client leaves a firm, the firm may not represent a person with interests adverse to that client where the matter is the same or substantially related and "any other lawyer currently in the firm has material information protected by **Rules** 1.6 and **1.9(c)**."

Rule 1.11(a): "Except as law may otherwise expressly permit, a lawyer who has formerly served as a public officer or employee of the government is subject to **Rule 1.9(c)**. . . ."

Rule 1.11(d): "Except as law may otherwise expressly permit, a lawyer currently serving as a public officer or employee is subject to **Rules** 1.7 and **1.9**."

Rule 1.17, Comment 11: A lawyer selling a law practice has an "obligation to protect information relating to the representation (see **Rules** 1.6 and **1.9**)."

Rule 1.18(b): "Even when no client-lawyer relationship ensues, a lawyer who has had discussions with a prospective client shall not use or reveal information learned in the consultation, except as **Rule 1.9** would permit with respect to information of a former client."

Rule 1.18, Comment 3: When a prospective client reveals information, "Paragraph (b) prohibits the lawyer from using or revealing that information, except as permitted by **Rule 1.9**, even if the client or lawyer decides not to proceed with the representation."

Rule 3.7(b): "A lawyer may act as advocate in a trial in which another lawyer in the lawyer's firm is likely to be called as a witness unless precluded from doing so by Rule 1.7 or **Rule 1.9**."

Rule 3.7, Comment 4: "It is relevant that one or both parties could reasonably foresee that the lawyer would probably be a witness. The conflict of interest principles stated in **Rules** 1.7, **1.9** and 1.10 have no application to this aspect of the problem."

Rule 3.7, Comment 6: "In determining if it is permissible to act as advocate in a trial in which the lawyer will be a necessary witness, the lawyer must also consider that the dual role may give rise to a conflict of interest that will require compliance with **Rules** 1.7 or **1.9**. . . . [A] lawyer who might be permitted to simultaneously serve as an advocate and a witness by paragraph (a)(3) might be precluded from doing so by **Rule 1.9**."

Rule 3.7, Comment 7: "If, however, the testifying lawyer would also be disqualified by Rule 1.7 or **Rule 1.9** from representing the client in the matter, other lawyers in the firm will be precluded from representing the client by Rule 1.10 unless the client gives informed consent under the conditions stated in Rule 1.7."

Rule 5.7, Comment 10: "When a lawyer is obliged to accord the recipients of such services the protections of those Rules that apply to the client-lawyer relationship, the lawyer must take special care to heed the proscriptions of the Rules addressing conflict of interest (**Rules 1.7 through 1.11**, especially Rules 1.7 and 1.8(a), (b) and (f)). . . . "

Rule 6.5(a): "A lawyer who, under the auspices of a program sponsored by a nonprofit organization or court, provides short-term limited legal services to a client without expectation by either the lawyer or the client that the lawyer will provide continuing representation in the matter is subject to **Rules** 1.7 and **1.9(a)** only if the lawyer knows that the representation of the client involves a conflict of interest; and is subject to Rule 1.10 only if the lawyer knows that another lawyer associated with the lawyer in a law firm is disqualified by **Rule** 1.7 or **1.9(a)** with respect to the matter."

Rule 6.5, Comment 1: "Legal services organizations, courts and various nonprofit organizations have established programs through which lawyers provide short-term limited legal services. . . . Such programs are normally operated under circumstances in which it is not feasible for a lawyer to systematically screen for conflicts of interest as is generally required before undertaking a representation. See, e.g., **Rules** 1.7, 1.9 and 1.10."

Rule 6.5, Comment 2: Regarding "a lawyer who provides short-term limited legal services pursuant to this Rule . . . [e]xcept as provided in this Rule, the Rules of Professional Conduct, including **Rules** 1.6 and **1.9(c)**, are applicable to the limited representation."

Rule 6.5, Comment 3: "[P]aragraph (a) requires compliance with **Rules** 1.7 or **1.9(a)** only if the lawyer knows that the representation presents a conflict of interest for the lawyer, and with Rule 1.10 only if the lawyer knows that another lawyer in the lawyer's firm is disqualified by **Rules** 1.7 or **1.9(a)** in the matter."

Rule 6.5, Comment 4: "Paragraph (a)(2) requires the participating lawyer to comply with Rule 1.10 when the lawyer knows that the lawyer's firm is disqualified by **Rules** 1.7 or **1.9(a)**."

Rule 6.5, Comment 5: "If, after commencing a short-term limited representation in accordance with this Rule, a lawyer undertakes to represent the client in the matter on an ongoing basis, **Rules** 1.7, **1.9(a)** and 1.10 become applicable."

Legislative History of Model Rule 1.9

1980 Discussion Draft: Rule 1.9(c) (then Rule 1.10(a)(2)) provided that a lawyer who has represented a client in a matter shall not thereafter "make use of information acquired in service to the client in a manner disadvantageous to the client . . . unless the information has become generally known or *accessible.*"

1981 Draft was substantially the same as adopted.

1982 Draft was adopted.

1983 Rule: From its original adoption in 1983 until its first amendment in 1989, Rule 1.9 provided as follows:

> A lawyer who has formerly represented a client in a matter shall not thereafter:
> (a) represent another person in the same or a substantially related matter in which that person's interests are materially adverse to the interests of the former client unless the former client consents after consultation; or
> (b) [Same as 2002 version of Rule 1.9(c)(2).]

1989 Amendments: In 1989, the ABA House of Delegates moved former Rule 1.10(b) to Rule 1.9(b), amended Rule 1.9(b) and redesignated it as Rule 1.9(c), amended the balance of Rule 1.9 in minor ways, and changed the Comments to Rules 1.9 and 1.10 to match the amendments. The most significant amendments were to add the phrase "or whose present or former firm has formerly represented a client in a matter" to the introductory language in Rule 1.9(c), which restricts a lawyer's use of confidential client information, and to add a new Rule 1.9(c)(2) providing that a lawyer shall not "reveal information relating to the representation except as these Rules would permit or require with respect to a client." The Committee Report to the House of Delegates explained the amendments to Rule 1.9(c) as follows:*

> The addition of explanatory language to . . . paragraph (c), is intended to eliminate another oversight in the drafting of Rule 1.9. The added language makes clear that a lawyer's duty of confidentiality with respect to former clients applies to clients who were personally represented by the lawyer and to clients who, although not personally represented by the lawyer, were represented by the lawyer's firm. In addition, a prohibition on the "revelation" of confidential information is added to Rule 1.9. As originally drafted, Rule 1.9 prohibited only the "use" of such information to the disadvantage of the former client. . . . The Comments to Rules 1.9 and 1.10 are amended in conformity with the amendments to the black letter Rules.

* Committee Reports do not represent official policy of the ABA. They are for information only, and the opinions are those of the authors of the report.

2002 Amendments: In 2002, the ABA House of Delegates adopted without change the ABA Ethics 2000 Commission proposal to amend Rule 1.9 and its Comment. The amendments added the requirement that the consent be "confirmed in writing" in Rules 1.9(a) and (b). In addition, Comments 1, 6, and 9 were significantly revised; Comment 3 was added; and former Comments 4, 5, 7, and 10 were deleted.

Selected State Variations

California: Rule 3-310(E) forbids representation adverse to a client or former client if a lawyer "by reason of the representation of the client or former client . . . has obtained confidential information material to the employment."

District of Columbia: Rule 1.9 contains only the language of ABA Model Rule 1.9(a), but does not require that consent be in writing or confirmed in writing. D.C.'s version of Rule 1.9(b), which appears in Rule 1.10(b), is substantially similar to 1.9(b) but provides an exception when "the lawyer participated in a previous representation or acquired information under the circumstances covered by Rule 1.6(h) or Rule 1.18."

Illinois deletes the requirement that a client's consent to a conflict of interest be confirmed in writing.

Massachusetts: Rule 1.9(c), which draws on DR 4-101(B)(3) of the ABA Model Code of Professional Responsibility, adds that a lawyer may not use confidential information "to the lawyer's advantage, or to the advantage of a third person" unless permitted or required by other rules, without the client's consent.

Nebraska adds Rules 1.9(d)-(f) to govern conflicts arising from the past work of law clerks, paralegals, secretaries, messengers, and any other "support person." Notably, Rule 1.9(d) parallels ABA Model Rule 1.9(b), but Nebraska Rule 1.9(e) does not impute support person conflicts to other lawyers at the firm if the former client consents or the conflicted support person is screened to protect the former client's confidential information.

New York: Rule 1.9 is substantially similar to the Model Rule, except that New York uses the term "confidential" information in Rule 1.9(c) instead of the phrase "information related to the representation." New York moves Comments 4-6 to the Comments following Rule 1.10.

Pennsylvania: Rule 1.9 tracks ABA Model Rule 1.9, except Pennsylvania Rule 1.9(a) and Rule 1.9(b)(2) do not require that client consent be "confirmed in writing."

Texas: Rule 1.09(a) provides that without prior consent, a lawyer who "personally" has formerly represented a client in a matter shall not thereafter represent another person in a matter adverse to the former client:

> (1) in which such other person questions the validity of the lawyer's services or work product for the former client;
> (2) if the representation in reasonable probability will involve a violation of Rule 1.05 [the Texas confidentiality rule]; or
> (3) if it is the same or a substantially related matter.

Virginia: Rule 1.9(b) requires the consent of both the present and former client.

Related Materials

ABA Formal Ethics Opinions: See ABA Formal Ethics Ops. 84-351 (1984), 88-356 (1988), 94-381 (1994), 95-395 (1995), 96-400 (1996), 96-403 (1996), 97-407 (1997), 97-409 (1997), 99-415 (1999), 00-417 (2000), 05-436 (2005), and 08-453 (2008).

ABA Standards for Imposing Lawyer Sanctions: See Standard 4.3 in the Related Materials following Model Rule 1.7.

Restatement of the Law Governing Lawyers: See Restatement §§33(2)(a), 77, and 132 in our chapter on the Restatement later in this volume.

Sixth Amendment: The Sixth Amendment to the United States Constitution, which guarantees effective assistance of counsel, imposes certain obligations on courts regarding conflicts of interest, but those obligations are less stringent for successive conflicts than for concurrent conflicts. In *Holloway v. Arkansas,* 435 U.S. 475 (1978), which involved a concurrent conflict, the Court held that the Sixth Amendment requires automatic reversal when a trial court fails to conduct an inquiry either after a timely conflict objection, or after the court knows or reasonably should know that a particular conflict exists. In *Cuyler v. Sullivan,* 446 U.S. 335 (1980), also a concurrent conflict case, the Court ruled that this "automatic reversal" rule did not apply when the trial court is not informed or is not on notice of a conflict. If a conflict is later alleged, the Sixth Amendment requires a defendant to establish that "an actual conflict of interest adversely affected his lawyer's performance."

Mickens v. Taylor, 535 U.S. 162 (2002), involved a successive conflict. A murder defendant was represented by a lawyer who, until a week before his appointment as defendant's counsel, had been representing the victim of the defendant's alleged homicide on an unrelated criminal matter. The judge dismissed the criminal charges against the now-deceased murder victim, but a week later the same judge appointed the victim's lawyer to represent the alleged murderer. The Supreme Court held that these facts did not require "automatic reversal" as in *Holloway.* "Since this was not a case in which (as in *Holloway*) counsel protested his inability simultaneously to represent multiple defendants . . . it was at least necessary, to void the conviction, for petitioner to establish that the conflict of interest adversely affected his counsel's performance." The Court left open the possibility that a defendant who alleged only a successive conflict might not even enjoy *Cuyler v. Sullivan*'s test for establishing ineffectiveness, but might instead be required to satisfy the stricter Sixth Amendment effectiveness test set out in *Strickland v. Washington,* 466 U.S. 668 (1984).

Rule 1.10   Imputation of Conflicts of Interest: General Rule

Canon and Code Antecedents

ABA Canons of Professional Ethics: No comparable Canon.
ABA Model Code of Professional Responsibility: Compare DR 5-105(D) (reprinted later in this volume).

Cross-References in Other Rules

Rule 1.0, Comment 8: "This definition applies to situations where screening of a personally disqualified lawyer is permitted to remove imputation of a conflict of interest under **Rules 1.10**, 1.11, 1.12 or 1.18."

Rule 1.7, Comment 10: "See Rule 1.8 for specific Rules pertaining to a number of personal interest conflicts, including business transactions with clients. See also **Rule 1.10** (personal interest conflicts under Rule 1.7 ordinarily are not imputed to other lawyers in a law firm)."

Rule 1.7, Comment 11: "The disqualification arising from a close family relationship is personal and ordinarily is not imputed to members of firms with whom the lawyers are associated. See **Rule 1.10**."

Rule 1.9, Comment 5: "See **Rule 1.10(b)** for the restrictions on a firm once a lawyer has terminated association with the firm."

Rule 1.9, Comment 9: "With regard to disqualification of a firm with which a lawyer is or was formerly associated, see **Rule 1.10**."

Rule 1.11, Comment 2: "**Rule 1.10** is not applicable to the conflicts of interest addressed by this Rule."

Rule 1.11, Comment 3: "As with paragraphs (a)(1) and (d)(1), **Rule 1.10** is not applicable to the conflicts of interest addressed by these paragraphs."

Rule 1.18, Comment 7: "Under paragraph (c), the prohibition in this Rule is imputed to other lawyers as provided in **Rule 1.10**. . . ."

Rule 3.7, Comment 4: "It is relevant that one or both parties could reasonably foresee that the lawyer would probably be a witness. The conflict of interest principles stated in **Rules** 1.7, 1.9 and **1.10** have no application to this aspect of the problem."

Rule 3.7, Comment 7: "If, however, the testifying lawyer would also be disqualified by Rule 1.7 or Rule 1.9 from representing the client in the matter, other lawyers in the firm will be precluded from representing the client by **Rule 1.10** unless the client gives informed consent under the conditions stated in Rule 1.7."

Rule 5.7, Comment 10: "When a lawyer is obliged to accord the recipients of such services the protections of those Rules that apply to the client-lawyer relationship, the lawyer must take special care to heed the proscriptions of the Rules addressing conflict of interest (**Rules 1.7 through 1.11**, especially Rules 1.7 and 1.8(a), (b) and (f)). . . ."

Rule 6.5(a): "A lawyer who, under the auspices of a program sponsored by a non-profit organization or court, provides short-term limited legal services to a client without expectation by either the lawyer or the client that the lawyer will provide continuing representation in the matter is subject to Rules 1.7 and 1.9(a) only if the lawyer knows that the representation of the client involves a conflict of interest; and is subject to **Rule 1.10** only if the lawyer knows that another lawyer associated with the lawyer in a law firm is disqualified by Rule 1.7 or 1.9(a) with respect to the matter."

Rule 6.5(b): "Except as provided in paragraph (a)(2), **Rule 1.10** is inapplicable to a representation governed by this Rule."

Rule 6.5, Comment 1: "Legal services organizations, courts and various non-profit organizations have established programs through which lawyers provide short-term limited legal services. . . . Such programs are normally operated under circumstances in which it is not feasible for a lawyer to systematically screen for conflicts of interest as is generally required before undertaking a representation. See, e.g., **Rules** 1.7, 1.9 and **1.10.**''

Rule 6.5, Comment 3: "[P]aragraph (a) requires compliance with Rules 1.7 or 1.9(a) only if the lawyer knows that the representation presents a conflict of interest for the lawyer . . . and with **Rule 1.10** only if the lawyer knows that another lawyer in the lawyer's firm is disqualified by Rules 1.7 or 1.9(a) in the matter.''

Rule 6.5, Comment 4: "[P]aragraph (b) provides that **Rule 1.10** is inapplicable to a representation governed by this Rule except as provided by paragraph (a)(2). Paragraph (a)(2) requires the participating lawyer to comply with Rule 1.10 when the lawyer knows that the lawyer's firm is disqualified by Rules 1.7 or 1.9(a).''

Rule 6.5, Comment 5: "If, after commencing a short-term limited representation in accordance with this Rule, a lawyer undertakes to represent the client in the matter on an ongoing basis, **Rules** 1.7, 1.9(a) and **1.10** become applicable.''

Legislative History of Model Rule 1.10

1980 Discussion Draft had no comparable provision on imputed disqualification.

1981 Draft:

(b) When lawyers terminate an association in a firm, none of them, nor any other lawyer with whom any of them subsequently become associated, shall undertake or continue representation that involves a material risk of revealing information relating to representation of a client in violation of Rule 1.6, or of making use of information to the disadvantage of a former client in violation of Rule 1.9.

1982 Draft:

(b) When lawyers terminate an association in a firm, none of them, nor any other lawyer with whom any of them subsequently becomes associated, shall knowingly represent a client when doing so involves a material risk of violating Rule 1.6 or Rule 1.9.

1983 Rule: From its original adoption in 1983 until its amendment in 1989, Rule 1.10 provided as follows:

(a) While lawyers are associated in a firm, none of them shall knowingly represent a client when any one of them practicing alone would be prohibited from doing so by Rules 1.7, 1.8(c), 1.9 or 2.2.

(b) When a lawyer becomes associated with a firm, the firm may not knowingly represent a person in the same or a substantially related matter in which that lawyer, or a firm with which the lawyer was associated, had previously represented a client whose interests are materially adverse to that person and about whom the lawyer had acquired information protected by Rules 1.6 and 1.9(b) that is material to the matter.

(c) [Same as 2002 version of Rule 1.10(b) except that the 1983 version did not include the phrase "and not currently represented by the firm" at the end of the introductory clause.]

(d) [Same as 2002 version of Rule 1.10(c).]

1989 Amendments: At its 1989 Mid-Year Meeting, the House of Delegates amended Rule 1.10 by moving former Rule 1.10(b) to its current position as Rule

1.9(b), by moving the corresponding Comment paragraphs to Rule 1.9's Comment, by redesignating former Rule 1.10(c) as Rule 1.10(b), by adding the phrase "and not currently represented by the firm" at the end of the introductory phrase in new Rule 1.10(b), and by redesignating former Rule 1.10(d) as Rule 1.10(c). An excerpt from the Committee Report explaining the changes is reprinted in the Legislative History following Rule 1.9. The Committee's explanation regarding the amendment to former Rule 1.10(c) states:

> Paragraph (c) (now paragraph (b)) of Rule 1.10 was never intended to permit the representation of a client whose interests are directly adverse to the interests of a present client of a firm. Such representation would violate Rule 1.7. In order to make it clear that when a lawyer leaves a law firm, this paragraph does not override the proscription in Rule 1.7, the limiting words "and not currently represented by the firm" are proposed to be added to Rule 1.10(b).

2002 Amendments: In 2001, the ABA House of Delegates adopted the ABA Ethics 2000 Commission proposal to amend Rules 1.10(a) and (d) without change, but rejected the Ethics 2000 Commission proposal to amend Rule 1.10(c). (The Ethics 2000 Commission did not propose any changes to Rule 1.10(b).) As amended, Rule 1.10 adds the language following "unless" in paragraph (a) (regarding conflicts based on a lawyer's personal interests) and adds paragraph (d) (regarding current or former government lawyers). In the Comment, new paragraphs 3, 4, 6, portions of 7, and 8 were added.

The rejected proposals would have permitted a law firm to use timely "screens" and related measures to overcome a former client's objections to an adverse representation. The rejected provisions of Rule 1.10(c) provided as follows:

> (c) When a lawyer becomes associated with a firm, no lawyer associated in the firm shall knowingly represent a person in a matter in which that lawyer is disqualified under Rule 1.9 unless:
> > (1) the personally disqualified lawyer is timely screened from any participation in the matter and is apportioned no part of the fee therefrom; and
> > (2) written notice is promptly given to any affected former client to enable it to ascertain compliance with the provisions of this Rule.

By rejecting the proposed text of Rule 1.10(c), the ABA also rejected three proposed Comments that would have explained the proposed language. The three rejected Comments provided as follows:

> [6] Where the conditions of paragraph (c) are met, imputation is removed, and consent to the new representation is not required. Lawyers should be aware, however, that courts may impose more stringent obligations in ruling upon motions to disqualify a lawyer from pending litigation.
> [7] Requirements for screening procedures are stated in Rule 1.0(k). Paragraph (c)(2) does not prohibit the screened lawyer from receiving a salary or partnership share established by prior independent agreement, but that lawyer may not receive compensation directly related to the matter in which the lawyer is disqualified.
> [8] Notice, including a description of the screened lawyer's prior representation and of the screening procedures employed, generally should be given as soon as practicable after the need for screening becomes apparent.

The Reporter's Explanation Memo regarding the rejected screening language provided, in relevant part, as follows:

Model Rule 1.10 — Reporter's Explanation of Changes*

A number of jurisdictions now provide that former-client conflicts of lawyers who have moved laterally are not imputed to the new law firm if the personally disqualified lawyer has been timely screened from participation in the matter and the former client is notified of the screen. The Commission is recommending that current Rule 1.10 be amended to permit nonconsensual screening of lawyers who have joined a law firm.

The Commission is persuaded that nonconsensual screening in these cases adequately balances the interests of the former client in confidentiality of information, the interests of current clients in hiring the counsel of their choice (including a law firm that may have represented the client in similar matters for many years) and the interests of lawyers in mobility, particularly when they are moving involuntarily because their former law firms have downsized, dissolved or drifted into bankruptcy. There are presently seven jurisdictions that permit screening of laterals by Rule. The testimony the Commission has heard indicates that there have not been any significant numbers of complaints regarding lawyers' conduct under these Rules.

In addition, in 2002, the ABA House of Delegates adopted with little change the Ethics 2000 Commission proposals to add two new rules to the Model Rules (Rules 1.18 and 6.5) to govern imputed conflicts of interest regarding two special categories of clients — prospective clients who ultimately did not retain a lawyer, and clients consulting a lawyer who (under the auspices of a program sponsored by a nonprofit organization or court) is providing "short-term limited legal services to a client without expectation by either the lawyer or the client that the lawyer will provide continuing representation in the matter." For more information about these rules, see the Legislative History following Rules 1.18 and 6.5 below.

2008 Proposed Amendment: At its August 2008 Annual Meeting, the ABA House of Delegates had been scheduled to debate a proposal by the ABA Standing Committee on Ethics and Professional Responsibility that would have permitted screening of laterally hired attorneys under certain circumstances. That proposal would have amended Rule 1.10(e) as follows:

> (e) notwithstanding paragraph (a), and in the absence of a waiver under paragraph (c), when a lawyer becomes associated with a firm, no lawyer associated in the firm shall knowingly represent a person in a matter in which that lawyer is disqualified under Rule 1.9 unless:
>
> > (1) the personally disqualified lawyer is timely screened from any participation in the matter and is apportioned no part of the fee therefrom; and
> >
> > (2) written notice is promptly given to any affected former client to enable it to ascertain compliance with the provisions of this Rule.

The proposal also would have amended the Comment to Rule 1.10 as follows:

> [9] When the conditions of paragraph (e) are met, no imputation of a lawyer's disqualification occurs, and consent to the new representation is therefore not required. Lawyers should be aware, however, that courts may impose more stringent obligations in ruling upon motions to disqualify a lawyer from pending litigation.
>
> [10] Requirements for screening procedures are stated in Rule 1.0(k). Paragraph (e)(1) does not prohibit the screened lawyer from receiving a salary or partnership share established by prior independent agreement, but that lawyer may not receive compensation directly related to the matter in which the lawyer is disqualified.

* Committee Reports, and the Reporter's Explanation of Changes contained therein, do not represent official policy of the ABA. They are for information only, and the opinions are those of the authors of the report.

[11] Notice, including a description of the screened lawyer's prior representation and of the screening procedures employed, generally should be given as soon as practicable after the need for screening becomes apparent.

Before the House of Delegates voted on the Standing Committee's proposal, an opponent of screening moved to postpone "indefinitely" any further consideration of the topic. Reflecting how closely divided the profession is on this issue, the motion carried by a single vote, 192-191. (For a more detailed discussion of that debate, including the text of several amendments to the proposal that had been offered on the House floor, see the 2008 Proposed Amendments in the 2009 edition of this book.)

2009 Amendments: Undaunted by the August 2008 setback, the ABA Standing Committee on Ethics and Professional Responsibility submitted a revised screening proposal at the February 2009 House of Delegates meeting. This time it passed by a vote of 226-191. The House of Delegates also approved four new paragraphs in the Comment to Rule 1.10 (numbered 7 through 10) and renumbered former Comments 7 and 8 as Comments 11 and 12 (leaving the text of those comments unchanged). For the Report and Recommendation submitted to the ABA House of Delegates in support of the amendments, see *http://www.americanbar.org/groups/ professional_responsibility/publications/model_rules_of_professional_conduct/background_ resources.html.*

The ABA's Section of Litigation had submitted a competing proposal, which would have permitted screening only when the lateral attorney had no substantial involvement in the matter and had not acquired any material confidential information about it. For details about that proposal, which the House of Delegates rejected by a vote of 182-267, see *http://www.americanbar.org/content/dam/aba/migrated/ leadership/2009/midyear/recommendations/110.authcheckdam.pdf.*

The screening provision as adopted in February 2009 did not explicitly limit screening to laterally hired attorneys. As a result, the new Rule 1.10 appeared to allow a firm to sue its own former client in a substantially related matter, without obtaining client consent, as long as the firm screened off the lawyers who worked on the former client's matter. This was not intended. At the August 2009 House of Delegates meeting, therefore, the ABA Standing Committee on Ethics and Professional Responsibility proposed a modest amendment to clarify that the screening provision should apply only to laterally hired attorneys. Specifically, the proposal sought to amend Rule 1.10(a)(2) by adding the phrase "arises out of the disqualified lawyer's association with a prior firm." It also sought to replace the word "prohibited" with the word "disqualified" in Rule 1.10(a)(1). Both changes were uncontroversial and were adopted as part of the meeting's consent calendar.

Selected State Variations

Editors' Note. As of September 2012, approximately two dozen states provide that a timely and effective screen around a laterally hired attorney will prevent the imputation of certain types of conflicts. Some of these provisions differ from the Model Rule, often by permitting screening to avoid imputed conflicts only in more narrowly defined circumstances than Model Rule 1.10 allows.

Arizona: Rule 1.10(d) permits screening of a personally disqualified lateral lawyer if the "matter does not involve a proceeding before a tribunal in which the personally disqualified lawyer had a substantial role," the lawyer gets no part of the fee, and "written notice is promptly given to any affected former client to enable it to ascertain compliance with the provisions of this Rule."

California has no provision comparable to ABA Model Rule 1.10.

District of Columbia adds Rule 1.10(a)(2), which notes that imputation does not apply "if the representation is permitted by Rules 1.11, 1.12, or 1.18." The D.C. rule also contains a Rule 1.10(e) that creates a partial exception to imputation when a lawyer assists "the Office of the Attorney General of the District of Columbia in providing legal services to that agency."

Illinois: The screening provision in Rule 1.10 is substantially similar to the Model Rule, except that Illinois has not adopted the additional requirements contained in Model Rule 1.10(a)(2)(ii) and (iii).

Maine: Rule 1.10(e) provides that "[i]f a lawyer or law student affiliated both with a law school legal clinic and with one or more lawyers outside the clinic is required to decline representation of any client solely by virtue of this Rule 1.10, this rule imposes no disqualification on any other lawyer or law student who would otherwise be disqualified solely by reason of an affiliation with that individual, provided that the originally disqualified individual is screened from all participation in the matter at and outside the clinic."

Massachusetts: Rule 1.10(d) provides for screening a "personally disqualified lawyer" if he or she "had neither substantial involvement nor substantial material information relating to the matter . . . and is apportioned no part of the fee therefrom." Rule 1.10(e) describes an appropriate screening process, including a requirement in Rule 1.10(e)(4) that the former client receives an affidavit of the personally disqualified lawyer and the firm describing the screening procedures and attesting that:

> (i) the personally disqualified lawyer will not participate in the matter and will not discuss the matter or the representation with any other lawyer or employee of his or her current firm; (ii) no material information was transmitted by the personally disqualified lawyer before implementation of the screening procedures and notice to the former client; and (iii) during the period of the lawyer's personal disqualification those lawyers or employees who do participate in the matter will be apprised that the personally disqualified lawyer is screened from participating in or discussing the matter. . . .

In any matter not before a tribunal, "the firm, the personally disqualified lawyer, or the former client may seek judicial review in a court of general jurisdiction of the screening procedures used, or may seek court supervision to ensure that implementation of the screening procedures has occurred and that effective actual compliance has been achieved."

Michigan: The screening provision in Rule 1.10(b) is substantially similar to the Model Rule, except that Michigan has fewer disclosure requirements than Model Rule 1.10(a)(2)(ii) and omits all of the requirements contained in Model Rule 1.10(a)(2)(iii).

Minnesota includes the following screening provision in its version of Rule 1.10. It is based largely on §124 of the Restatement of the Law Governing Lawyers:

(b) When a lawyer becomes associated with a firm, and the lawyer is prohibited from representing a client pursuant to Rule 1.9(b), other lawyers in the firm may represent that client if there is no reasonably apparent risk that confidential information of the previously represented client will be used with material adverse effect on that client because:

(1) any confidential information communicated to the lawyer is unlikely to be significant in the subsequent matter;

(2) the lawyer is subject to screening measures adequate to prevent disclosure of the confidential information and to prevent involvement by that lawyer in the representation; and

(3) timely and adequate notice of the screening has been provided to all affected clients.

Nebraska adds Rules 1.9(d)-(f) to govern conflicts arising from the past work of law clerks, paralegals, secretaries, messengers, and any other "support person," but Rule 1.9(e) does not impute support person conflicts to other lawyers at the firm if the former client consents or if the conflicted support person is screened to protect the former client's confidential information.

New Jersey adds Rule 1.10(c), which permits screening of a conflicted lawyer who becomes associated with a firm unless that lawyer had "primary responsibility" for the matter. Rule 1.10(f) provides as follows:

Any law firm that enters a screening arrangement, as provided by this Rule, shall establish appropriate written procedures to insure that: (1) all attorneys and other personnel in the law firm screen the personally disqualified attorney from any participation in the matter, (2) the screened attorney acknowledges the obligation to remain screened and takes action to insure the same, and (3) the screened attorney is apportioned no part of the fee therefrom.

Pursuant to Rule 1.7, public entities may not waive conflicts or agree to screening. And New Jersey Rule 1.9(c) reinforces Rule 1.10(c) by providing that "neither consent shall be sought from the client nor screening pursuant to RPC 1.10 permitted in any matter in which the attorney had sole or primary responsibility for the matter in the previous firm."

New York: Rule 1.10(c), which is simply the logical extension of Rule 1.9(b), specifies that a newly hired attorney does not create an imputed conflict of interest as long as that attorney had not acquired "any information protected by Rule 1.6 or Rule 1.9(c) that is material to the current matter." In effect, then, the New York rules do not permit non-consensual screening of lateral lawyers from private practice (*i.e.*, screening to avoid imputation without need for consent from the lateral lawyer's former client). The former New York Code did not do so either, but the New York Court of Appeals, in *Kassis v. TIAA,* 717 N.E.2d 674 (N.Y. 1999), ruled that screening would be allowed if the lateral lawyer's information with regard to the matter is "unlikely to be significant or material." It remains to be seen whether the new rules were intended to "overrule" *Kassis* and whether, if they were, they can.

New York adds Rule 1.10(e)-(g), which contains detailed recordkeeping requirements for new engagements. These additional requirements are described in more depth in Comments 9 and 9A-9G.

Finally, New York adds Rule 1.10(h), which provides as follows: "A lawyer related to another lawyer as parent, child, sibling or spouse shall not represent in any matter a client whose interests differ from those of another party to the matter who the lawyer knows is represented by the other lawyer unless the client consents to the representation after full disclosure and the lawyer concludes that the lawyer can adequately represent the interests of the client.''

North Carolina: The screening provision in Rule 1.10(c) is substantially similar to the Model Rule, except that North Carolina omits the requirements contained in Model Rule 1.10(a)(2)(iii) and has fewer disclosure requirements than Model Rule 1.10(a)(2)(ii).

Ohio: Rule 1.10 permits screening of a lateral lawyer, but only if the lawyer did not have a ''substantial role'' in the matter.

Oregon has a screening procedure in Rule 1.10(c) that requires lawyers to submit affidavits confirming compliance with the screen.

Pennsylvania: The screening provision in Rule 1.10(b) is substantially similar to the Model Rule, except that Pennsylvania omits the requirements contained in Model Rule 1.10(a)(2)(iii) and has fewer disclosure requirements than Model Rule 1.10(a)(2)(ii).

South Carolina: Rule 1.10 tracks ABA Model Rule 1.10 verbatim but adds the following limited screening provision in Rule 1.10(e):

> (e) A lawyer representing a client of a public defender office, legal services association, or similar program serving indigent clients shall not be disqualified under this Rule because of the program's representation of another client in the same or a substantially related matter if:
> (1) the lawyer is screened in a timely manner from access to confidential information relating to and from any participation in the representation of the other client; and
> (2) the lawyer retains authority over the objectives of the representation pursuant to Rule 5.4(c).

Texas: Rule 1.09 provides:

> (a) Without prior consent, a lawyer who personally has formerly represented a client in a matter shall not thereafter represent another person in a matter adverse to the former client:
> (1) in which such other person questions the validity of the lawyer's services or work product for the former client;
> (2) if the representation in reasonable probability will involve a violation of Rule 1.05; or
> (3) if it is the same or a substantially related matter.
> (b) Except to the extent authorized by Rule 1.10 [concerning government lawyers], when lawyers are or have become members of or associated with a firm, none of them shall knowingly represent a client if any one of them practicing alone would be prohibited from doing so by paragraph (a).
> (c) When the association of a lawyer with a firm has terminated, the lawyers who were then associated with that lawyer shall not knowingly represent a client if the lawyer whose association with that firm has terminated would be prohibited from doing so by paragraph (a)(1) or if the representation in reasonable probability will involve a violation of Rule 1.05.

Wisconsin: Rule 1.10(a)(2) permits law firms to avoid imputation of a lateral lawyer's Rule 1.9 conflict if ''(i) the personally disqualified lawyer performed no more than minor and isolated services in the disqualifying representation and did so only at a firm with which the lawyer is no longer associated''; (ii) the personally disqualified lawyer is timely screened and is apportioned no part of the fee from the matter; and (iii) written notice is promptly given to any affected former client to enable the former client to ascertain compliance with this rule.

Related Materials

ABA Commission on Ethics 20/20: In 2009, the ABA created the Commission on Ethics 20/20, which is comprehensively reviewing the ABA Model Rules of Professional Conduct and other regulations of the American legal profession in the context of globalization and changes in technology. On July 11, 2012, the Commission sought comments on a draft proposal to add a new Rule 1.7(c) that would permit lawyers and clients to agree, subject to certain limitations, that their relationship will be governed by a particular jurisdiction's conflict of interest rules. The Commission's report explained the relevance of the proposal to Rule 1.10 as follows:

> Conflicts-related choice of law problems can arise in many situations. For example, a lawyer may work on a transaction that involves parties and commitments in several U.S. or foreign jurisdictions. The lawyer (or the lawyer's firm) may then be asked to handle an unrelated matter that is adverse to a party the lawyer is representing in the business deal. Although the new matter would give rise to a conflict of interest under Rule 1.7 of the Model Rules of Professional Conduct, the new matter may not be a conflict of interest under the rules of other jurisdictions. The problem is that, if it is not clear which jurisdiction's conflicts rules apply, the lawyer (or the lawyer's firm) cannot be certain whether a conflict of interest would arise if the new matter is accepted. *Similar issues arise, for example, because of inconsistencies among jurisdictions with regard to the permissibility of conflicts screens for laterally-hired lawyers under Rule 1.10.* [Emphasis added.]

For additional details, see our entry on "ABA Commission on Ethics 20/20" in the Related Materials after Rule 1.7. The draft proposal to add Rule 1.7(c), and the 20/20 Commission's accompanying report, are available on the Ethics 20/20 Commission's website at *http://www.americanbar.org/Ethics2020.*

ABA Formal Ethics Opinions: See ABA Formal Ethics Ops. 84-351 (1984), 88-356 (1988), 90-357 (1990), 92-367 (1992), 96-400 (1996), 97-406 (1997), 97-407 (1997), 97-409 (1997), 98-410 (1998), 99-415 (1999), and 03-430 nn.38 & 39 (2003).

Model Rules of Professional Conduct for Federal Lawyers: Rule 1.10(a) provides that "Government lawyers working in the same Federal Agency are not automatically disqualified from representing a client because any of them practicing alone would be prohibited from doing so by Rules 1.7, 1.8(c), 1.9 or 2.2." The Comment states:

> The circumstances of Government service may require representation of opposing sides by Government lawyers working in the same Federal Agency. Such representation is permissible so long as conflicts of interest are avoided and independent judgment, zealous representation, and protection of client confidences are not compromised. Thus, the principle of imputed disqualification is not automatically controlling for Government lawyers. The knowledge, action, and conflicts of interest of one Government lawyer are not to be imputed to another simply because they operate from the same office. . . .

Restatement of the Law Governing Lawyers: See Restatement §§15(2), 123, 124, and 132 in our chapter on the Restatement later in this volume.

Rule 1.11   Special Conflicts of Interest for Former and Current Government Officers and Employees

Canon and Code Antecedents

ABA Canons of Professional Ethics: No comparable Canon.
ABA Model Code of Professional Responsibility: Compare DR 9-101(B) (reprinted later in this volume).

Cross-References in Other Rules

Rule 1.0, Comment 8: "Screened" applies to "situations where screening of a personally disqualified lawyer is permitted to remove imputation of a conflict of interest under **Rules 1.11**, 1.12 or 1.18."

Rule 1.9, Comment 1: "Current and former government lawyers must comply with this Rule to the extent required by **Rule 1.11**."

Rule 1.10(d): "The disqualification of lawyers associated in a firm with former or current government lawyers is governed by **Rule 1.11**."

Rule 1.10, Comment 7: "Where a lawyer has joined a private firm after having represented the government, imputation is governed by **Rule 1.11(b)** and **(c)**. . . .

Under **Rule 1.11(d)**, where a lawyer represents the government after having served clients in private practice, nongovernmental employment, or in another government agency, former-client conflicts are not imputed to government lawyers associated with the individually disqualified lawyer."

Rule 1.12, Comment 1: "This Rule generally parallels **Rule 1.11**. . . . Compare the Comment to **Rule 1.11**."

Rule 5.7, Comment 10: "When a lawyer is obliged to accord the recipients of such services the protections of those Rules that apply to the client-lawyer relationship, the lawyer must take special care to heed the proscriptions of the Rules addressing conflict of interest (**Rules** 1.7 through **1.11**, especially Rules 1.7 and 1.8(a), (b) and (f)). . . ."

Legislative History of Model Rule 1.11

1980 Discussion Draft:

. . . (e) If a lawyer is required by this rule to decline representation on account of personal and substantial participation in a matter, except where the participation was as a judicial law clerk, no lawyer in a firm with the disqualified lawyer may accept such employment. . . .

1981 and *1982 Drafts* were substantially the same as adopted.
1983 Rule: From its original adoption in 1983 until its amendment in 2002, Rule 1.11 provided as follows:

Rule 1.11　Successive Government and Private Employment

(a) Except as law may otherwise expressly permit, a lawyer shall not represent a private client in connection with a matter in which the lawyer participated personally and substantially as a public officer or employee, unless the appropriate government agency consents after consultation. No lawyer in a firm with which that lawyer is associated may knowingly undertake or continue representation in such a matter unless:

(1) [Same as 2002 version of Rule 1.11 except that the word "timely" did not modify "screened."]

(2) [Same as 2002 version of Rule 1.11(b)(2).]

(b) [Same as 2002 version of Rule 1.11 except that the word "timely" did not modify "screened" in the last sentence, and the definition of the term "confidential government information" was then in a separate Rule 1.11(e).]

(c) Except as law may otherwise expressly permit, a lawyer serving as a public officer or employee shall not:

(1) participate in a matter in which the lawyer participated personally and substantially while in private practice or nongovernmental employment, unless under applicable law no one is, or by lawful delegation may be, authorized to act in the lawyer's stead in the matter; or

(2) [Same as Rule 1.11(d)(ii) in 2002 version.]

(d) [Same definition of "matter" as in 2002 version of Rule 1.11(e).]

(e) [Same definition of "confidential government information" as in 2002 version of Rule 1.11(c).]

2002 Amendments: In its May 2001 report to the ABA House of Delegates, the Ethics 2000 Commission proposed several changes to Rule 1.11, including a proposed new subparagraph (a)(1) to make clear that a lawyer who has formerly served as a public officer or governmental employee "is subject to Rules 1.9(a) and (b), except that 'matter' is defined as in paragraph (e) of this Rule." Before the House of Delegates debated the proposal, however, the Commission revised its proposal by deleting the quoted paragraph.

In 2002, the House of Delegates adopted without change the revised ABA Ethics 2000 Commission proposal to amend Rule 1.11 and its Comment. As a result of the amendments to Rule 1.11, the successive conflicts of former government lawyers are determined solely by the terms of Rule 1.11. (In 1997, ABA Formal Ethics Op. 97-409 had reached the same conclusion.) Consequently, former government lawyers are exempt from the strictures of Rule 1.9(a) and (b), but are subject to the limitations in Rule 1.9(c) because that provision is incorporated by reference in Rule 1.11(a)(1).

Selected State Variations

Arizona, Connecticut, and Florida omit the law clerk exception to ABA Model Rule 1.11(d)(2).

California has no provision comparable to ABA Model Rule 1.11.

Colorado: Rule 1.11(b)(2) requires the written notice to contain "a general description of the personally disqualified lawyer's prior participation in the matter and the screening procedures to be employed." Colorado also adds a subparagraph (b)(3) prohibiting other lawyers in the firm from undertaking or continuing representation unless the personally disqualified lawyer and the partners of the firm "reasonably believe that the steps taken to accomplish the screening of material information are likely to be effective in preventing material information from being disclosed to the firm and its client."

District of Columbia: Rule 1.11 tracks the basic provisions of ABA Model Rule 1.11, but D.C. requires a personally disqualified former government lawyer and another lawyer in the firm to file certain documents with the disqualified lawyer's former agency or department. As an alternative, the rule permits the former government lawyer to file those documents with bar counsel under seal if the firm's client requests it.

Georgia has adopted a Rule 9.5 that provides as follows:

Rule 9.5   Lawyer as a Public Official

(a) A lawyer who is a public official and represents the State, a municipal corporation in the State, the United States government, their agencies or officials, is bound by the provisions of these Rules.

(b) No provision of these Rules shall be construed to prohibit such a lawyer from taking a legal position adverse to the State, a municipal corporation in the State, the United States government, their agencies or officials, when such action is authorized or required by the U.S. Constitution, the Georgia Constitution or statutes of the United States or Georgia.

Illinois: Rule 1.11(a) does not require consent to be confirmed in writing.

Iowa adds the following paragraph to Rule 1.11 relating to part-time prosecutors serving as criminal defense counsel:

(f) Prosecutors for the state or county shall not engage in the defense of an accused in any criminal matter during the time they are engaged in such public responsibilities. However, this paragraph does not apply to a lawyer not regularly employed as a prosecutor for the state or county who serves as a special prosecutor for a specific criminal case, provided that the employment does not create a conflict of interest or the lawyer complies with the requirements of rule 32:1.7(b).

Massachusetts: The law clerk exception in Model Rule 1.11(d)(2)(ii) is extended to law clerks working for mediators.

Missouri: Rule 1.11(e) provides as follows:

(1) A lawyer who also holds public office, whether full or part-time, shall not engage in activities in which his or her personal or professional interests are or foreseeably could be in conflict with his or her official duties or responsibilities. . . .

(2) No lawyer in a firm in which a lawyer holding a public office is associated may undertake or continue representation in a matter in which the lawyer who holds public office would be disqualified, unless the lawyer holding public office is screened in the manner set forth in Rule 4-1.11(a).

New Hampshire adds a detailed provision regarding the responsibilities of "lawyer-officials," who are defined as lawyers who are "actively engaged in the practice of law" and who are members of a "governmental body."

New Jersey: Rules 1.11(a), (b), and (d) deviate from the Model Rules as follows:

(a) Except as law may otherwise expressly permit, and subject to RPC 1.9, a lawyer who formerly has served as a government lawyer or public officer or employee of the government shall not represent a private client in connection with a matter:

(1) in which the lawyer participated personally and substantially as a public officer or employee; or

(2) for which the lawyer had substantial responsibility as a public officer or employee; or

(3) when the interests of the private party are materially adverse to the appropriate government agency, provided, however, that the application of this provision shall be limited to a period of six months immediately following the termination of the attorney's service as a government lawyer or public officer.

(b) Except as law may otherwise expressly permit, a lawyer who formerly has served as a government lawyer or public officer or employee of the government:

(1) shall be subject to RPC 1.9(c)(2) in respect of information relating to a private party or information that the lawyer knows is confidential government information about a person acquired by the lawyer while serving as a government lawyer or public officer or employee of the government, and

(2) shall not represent a private person whose interests are adverse to that private party in a matter in which the information could be used to the material disadvantage of that party. . . .

(d) Except as law may otherwise expressly permit, a lawyer serving as a government lawyer or public officer or employee of the government:

(1) shall be subject to RPC 1.9(c)(2) in respect of information relating to a private party acquired by the lawyer while in private practice or nongovernmental employment.

(2) shall not participate in a matter (i) in which the lawyer participated personally and substantially while in private practice or nongovernmental employment, or (ii) for which the lawyer had substantial responsibility while in private practice or nongovernmental employment, or (iii) with respect to which the interests of the appropriate government agency are materially adverse to the interests of a private party represented by the lawyer while in private practice or nongovernmental employment, unless under applicable law no one is, or by lawful delegation may be, authorized to act in the lawyer's stead in the matter or unless the private party gives its informed consent, confirmed in writing, and

(3) shall not negotiate for private employment with any person who is involved as a party or as attorney for a party in a matter in which the lawyer is participating personally and substantially or for which the lawyer has substantial responsibility, except that a lawyer serving as a law clerk shall be subject to RPC 1.12(c). . . .

New York: Rule 1.11(b) amplifies the procedures necessary to avoid the imputation of a conflict, including that a law firm must "notify, as appropriate, lawyers and nonlawyer personnel within the firm that the personally disqualified lawyer is prohibited from participating in the representation of the current client," and that "there are no other circumstances in the particular representation that create an appearance of impropriety." Several new comments offer further guidance regarding these procedures. Rule 1.11(e) specifies that the term "matter" does "not include or apply to agency rulemaking functions." Rule 1.11(f) is a nearly verbatim adoption of DR 8-101 of the old Model Code.

Oregon expands the "law clerk" exception to include a lawyer who is a "staff lawyer to or otherwise assisting in the official duties of" a judge, other adjudicative officer or arbitrator. Oregon Rule 1.11(d) adds language drawn partly from DR 8-101 of the ABA Model Code of Professional Responsibility providing that, except as law otherwise expressly permits, a lawyer shall not:

(i) use the lawyer's public position to obtain, or attempt to obtain, special advantage in legislative matters for the lawyer or for a client.

(ii) use the lawyer's public position to influence, or attempt to influence, a tribunal to act in favor of the lawyer or of a client.

(iii) accept anything of value from any person when the lawyer knows or it is obvious that the offer is for the purpose of influencing the lawyer's action as a public official.

(iv) either while in office or after leaving office use information the lawyer knows is confidential government information obtained while a public official to represent a private client.

Oregon also deletes ABA Model Rule 1.11(e) and adds these paragraphs to Rule 1.11:

(e) Notwithstanding any Rule of Professional Conduct, and consistent with the "debate" clause, Article IV, section 9, of the Oregon Constitution, or the "speech or debate" clause, Article I, section 6, of the United States Constitution, a lawyer-legislator shall not be subject to discipline for words uttered in debate in either house of the Oregon Legislative Assembly or for any speech or debate in either house of the United States Congress.

(f) A member of a lawyer-legislator's firm shall not be subject to discipline for representing a client in any claim against the State of Oregon provided:

(1) the lawyer-legislator is screened from participation or representation in the matter in accordance with the procedure set forth in Rule 1.10(c) (the required affidavits shall be served on the Attorney General); and

(2) the lawyer-legislator shall not directly or indirectly receive a fee for such representation.

Pennsylvania: Rule 1.11(a)(2) does not require that client consent be "confirmed in writing."

Texas: Rule 1.10(f) specifically excludes "regulation-making" and "rule-making" from the definition of "matter."

Virginia: Rule 1.11 is similar to the original 1983 version of ABA Model Rule 1.11, though Rule 1.11(b) requires consent from the private client in addition to consent from the appropriate government agency. Rule 1.11(e) adds that, when a lawyer who is serving as a public officer or employee is disqualified, the disqualification "does not disqualify other lawyers in the disqualified lawyer's agency." Rule 1.11(a) draws on the following language from DR 8-101 of the ABA Model Code of Professional Responsibility:

(a) A lawyer who holds public office shall not:

(1) use the public position to obtain, or attempt to obtain, a special advantage in legislative matters for the lawyer or for a client under circumstances where the lawyer knows or it is obvious that such action is not in the public interest;

(2) use the public position to influence, or attempt to influence, a tribunal to act in favor of the lawyer or of a client; or

(3) accept anything of value from any person when the lawyer knows or it is obvious that the offer is for the purpose of influencing the lawyer's action as a public official.

Related Materials

ABA Formal Ethics Opinions: See ABA Formal Ethics Ops. 97-409 (1997) and 99-415 n.8 (1999).

"Confidential Government Information": Model Rule 1.11(c) defines "confidential government information" to include information the government is *"prohibited by law* from disclosing to the public" or "has a *legal privilege* not to disclose," and (if the information satisfies one of those two criteria) is "not otherwise *available to the public"* (emphasis added).

As to disclosures "prohibited by law," prohibitions on public disclosure are contained in various federal statutes, including, for example, the Privacy Act of 1974, 5 U.S.C. §552a, and the Trade Secrets Act, 18 U.S.C. §1905.

As to "legal privilege not to disclose," the government has successfully claimed various privileges under Federal Rule of Evidence 501, including the executive privilege, the deliberative privilege, the national security privilege, and the attorney-client privilege.

As to whether information is "available to the public," the Freedom of Information Act (FOIA), 5 U.S.C. §552, makes a broad range of government information available to the public on demand but exempts specified categories of information from disclosure.

IRS Regulations: In the regulations governing practice before the Internal Revenue Service, 31 C.F.R. §10.25, entitled "Practice by Former Government Employees, Their Partners and Their Associates," sets forth elaborate restrictions on the practice of law before the IRS by former government attorneys and their law firms.

Restatement of the Law Governing Lawyers: See Restatement §§74, 97, 124, and 133 in our chapter on the Restatement later in this volume.

Revolving Door Provisions: Rule 1.11(e)(2) refers to "the conflict of interest rules of the appropriate government agency." All former lawyers for the executive branch of the federal government, as well as former employees of Congress and various federal agencies, are covered by the "revolving door" provisions in 18 U.S.C. §207. Those provisions generally prohibit former government lawyers from opposing the government, either directly or in matters in which the government has "a direct and substantial interest," for two years after leaving government, if the lawyer was involved in the matter while in federal government service. For regulations generally implementing 18 U.S.C. §207, see 73 Fed. Reg. 36168 (June 25, 2008). In addition, several agencies of the federal government have their own "revolving door" provisions. *See, e.g.,* 45 C.F.R. Part 680 (National Science Foundation) and 22 C.F.R. Part 18 (Foreign Service). Many states have enacted parallel provisions.

Rule 1.12   Former Judge, Arbitrator, Mediator or Other Third-Party Neutral

Canon and Code Antecedents

ABA Canons of Professional Ethics: Canon 36 provided as follows:

36.   Retirement from Judicial Position or Public Employment

A lawyer should not accept employment as an advocate in any matter upon the merits of which he has previously acted in a judicial capacity.

A lawyer, having once held public office or having been in the public employ, should not after his retirement accept employment in connection with any matter which he has investigated or passed upon while in such office or employ.

ABA Model Code of Professional Responsibility: Compare DR 5-105(C) and DR 9-101(A) (reprinted later in this volume).

Cross-References in Other Rules

Preamble, ¶ 3: "Some of these Rules apply directly to lawyers who are or have served as third-party neutrals. See, *e.g.,* **Rules 1.12** and 2.4."

Rule 1.0, Comment 8: "Screened" "applies to situations where screening of a personally disqualified lawyer is permitted to remove imputation of a conflict of interest under **Rules** 1.11, **1.12** or 1.18."

Rule 1.11(d): "[A] lawyer serving as a law clerk to a judge, other adjudicative officer or arbitrator may negotiate for private employment as permitted by **Rule 1.12(b)** and subject to the conditions stated in **Rule 1.12(b)**."

Rule 2.4, Comment 4: "A lawyer who serves as a third-party neutral subsequently may be asked to serve as a lawyer representing a client in the same matter. The conflicts of interest that arise for both the individual lawyer and the lawyer's law firm are addressed in **Rule 1.12**."

Legislative History of Model Rule 1.12

1980 Discussion Draft (then Rules 1.11(d), 1.11(e), and 1.11(f)):

(d) A lawyer who has served as a judge in an adjudicatory proceeding shall not thereafter represent anyone in connection with the subject matter of the proceeding.

(e) If a lawyer is required by this rule to decline representation on account of personal and substantial participation in a matter, except where the participation was as a judicial law clerk, no lawyer in a firm with the disqualified lawyer may accept such employment.

(f) . . . The disqualification stated in paragraph (d) may be waived by the consent of all parties to the adjudication.

1981 and *1982 Drafts:* Substantially the same as adopted.

1983 Rule: From its original adoption in 1983 until its amendment in 2002, Rule 1.12 provided as follows:

Rule 1.12　Former Judge or Arbitrator

(a) Except as stated in paragraph (d), a lawyer shall not represent anyone in connection with a matter in which the lawyer participated personally and substantially as a judge or other adjudicative officer, arbitrator or law clerk to such a person, unless all parties to the proceeding consent after consultation.

(b) A lawyer shall not negotiate for employment with any person who is involved as a party or as attorney for a party in a matter in which the lawyer is participating personally and substantially as a judge or other adjudicative officer or arbitrator. A lawyer serving as a law clerk to a judge, other adjudicative officer or arbitrator may negotiate for employment with a party or lawyer involved in a matter in which the clerk is participating personally and substantially, but only after the lawyer has notified the judge, other adjudicative officer or arbitrator.

(c) [Same as 2002 version of Rule 1.12.]
(d) [Same as 2002 version of Rule 1.12.]

2002 Amendments: At its February 2002 Mid-Year Meeting, the ABA House of Delegates adopted with only minor changes the ABA Ethics 2000 Commission proposal to amend Rule 1.12 and its Comment. The amendments added Comments 2-5. The reference to "an arbitrator, mediator, or other third-party neutral" in Rule 1.12(a) and (b) is new, as is the requirement in Rule 1.12(a) that consent be informed and confirmed in writing.

Selected State Variations

California has no direct counterpart to Rule 1.12.

District of Columbia: Rule 1.12 does not include former judges.

Georgia: Rule 1.12(b) adds that a law clerk who accepts employment with a party or lawyer involved in a matter in which the clerk is participating personally and substantively "shall promptly provide written notice of acceptance of employment to all counsel of record in all such matters in which the prospective employee is involved."

Illinois: Rule 1.12(a) does not require consent to be confirmed in writing.

Massachusetts extends the law clerk exception in Rule 1.12(b) to law clerks working for mediators.

New York: Rule 1.12(a) is a nearly verbatim adoption of DR 9-101(A) of the old Model Code. Rule 1.12(d) describes in more detail the procedures necessary to avoid the imputation of a conflict, and several additional comments offer further guidance regarding these procedures.

Pennsylvania: Rule 1.12 tracks ABA Model Rule 1.12 except Pennsylvania Rule 1.12(a) does not require that client consent be "confirmed in writing."

Texas has no equivalent to Rule 1.12(d).

Related Materials

ABA Formal Ethics Opinions: No formal ethics opinions have construed Rule 1.12.

Code of Conduct for Law Clerks: In an article entitled *Some Ethical Considerations for Judicial Clerks,* 4 Geo. J. Legal Ethics 771, 786-790 (1991), Professor John Paul Jones of the University of Richmond School of Law proposed a Code of Conduct for Law Clerks. Proposed Canon 3(D) of this Code, which relates to Model Rule 1.12(b), provides:

> A law clerk should inform the appointing judge of any circumstance or activity of the law clerk that might serve as a basis for disqualification of the judge, *e.g.,* a prospective employment relation with a law firm, association of the law clerk's spouse with a law firm or litigant, etc.

Restatement of the Law Governing Lawyers: See Restatement §124 in our chapter on the Restatement later in this volume.

Rule 1.13   Organization as Client

Canon and Code Antecedents

ABA Canons of Professional Ethics: No comparable Canon.
ABA Model Code of Professional Responsibility: Compare DR 5-107(B) (reprinted later in this volume).

Cross-References in Other Rules

Rule 1.4, Comment 6: "When the client is an organization or group, it is often impossible or inappropriate to inform every one of its members about its legal affairs; ordinarily, the lawyer should address communications to the appropriate officials of the organization. See **Rule 1.13**."

Rule 1.6, Comment 7: "See . . . **Rule 1.13(c)**, which permits the lawyer, where the client is an organization, to reveal information relating to the representation in limited circumstances."

Rule 1.7, Comment 34: "A lawyer who represents a corporation or other organization does not, by virtue of that representation, necessarily represent any constituent or affiliated organization, such as a parent or subsidiary. See **Rule 1.13(a)**."

Rule 1.11, Comment 5: "The question of whether two government agencies should be regarded as the same or different clients for conflict of interest purposes is beyond the scope of these Rules. See **Rule 1.13** Comment [6]."

Rule 4.3, Comment 1: "For misunderstandings that sometimes arise when a lawyer for an organization deals with an unrepresented constituent, see **Rule 1.13(d)**."

Legislative History of Model Rule 1.13

1980 Discussion Draft:

An Organization as the Client

(a) A lawyer employed or retained by an organization represents the organization as distinct from its directors, officers, employees, members, shareholders, or other constituents.

(b) If a lawyer for an organization knows that an officer, employee, or other person associated with the organization is engaged in or intends action, or a refusal to act, that is a violation of law and is likely to result in significant harm to the organization, the lawyer shall use reasonable efforts to prevent the harm. [The rest of subparagraph (b) was substantially the same as adopted.]

(c) If, despite the lawyer's efforts in accordance with paragraph (b), the highest authority that can act on behalf of the organization insists upon action, or a refusal to act, that is clearly a violation of law and is likely to result in substantial injury to the organization, the lawyer may take further remedial action, including disclosure of client confidences to the extent necessary, if the lawyer reasonably believes such action to be in the best interest of the organization.

(d) A lawyer representing an organization may also represent any of its directors, officers, members, or shareholders subject to the provisions of Rule 1.7. A lawyer undertaking such dual representation shall disclose that fact to an appropriate official of the organization other than the person so represented.

(e) When a shareholder or member of an organization brings a derivative action, the lawyer for the organization may act as its advocate only as permitted by Rule 1.7.

(f) In dealing with an organization's officials and employees, a lawyer shall explain the identity of the client when necessary to avoid embarrassment or unfairness to them.

1981 Draft: Rule 1.13(a) was the same as 1980 Draft. In Rule 1.13(b), a lawyer discovering conduct likely to result in "material" injury (rather than "significant" injury) to the corporation was to "proceed as is reasonably necessary in the best interest of the organization." Rule 1.13(c), describing remedial action, provided:

> Such action may include revealing information relating to the representation of the organization only if the lawyer reasonably believes that:
> (1) the highest authority in the organization has acted to further the personal or financial interests of members of that authority which are in conflict with the interests of the organization; and
> (2) revealing the information is necessary in the best interest of the organization.

1982 Draft: Substantially the same as 1981 Draft.

1983 Rule: From its original adoption in 1983 until its amendment in 2002, Rule 1.13 provided, in relevant part, as follows:

Rule 1.13   Organization as Client

(a) [Same as 2003 version of Rule 1.13(a).]

(b) If a lawyer for an organization knows that an officer, employee or other person associated with the organization is engaged in action, intends to act or refuses to act in a matter related to the representation that is a violation of a legal obligation to the organization, or a violation of law which reasonably might be imputed to the organization, and is likely to result in substantial injury to the organization, the lawyer shall proceed as is reasonably necessary in the best interest of the organization. In determining how to proceed, the lawyer shall give due consideration to the seriousness of the violation and its consequences, the scope and nature of the lawyer's representation, the responsibility in the organization and the apparent motivation of the person involved, the policies of the organization concerning such matters and any other relevant considerations. Any measures taken shall be designed to minimize disruption of the organization and the risk of revealing information relating to the representation to persons outside the organization. Such measures may include among others:

(1) asking for reconsideration of the matter;

(2) advising that a separate legal opinion on the matter be sought for presentation to appropriate authority in the organization; and

(3) referring the matter to higher authority in the organization, including, if warranted by the seriousness of the matter, referral to the highest authority that can act in behalf of the organization as determined by applicable law.

(c) If, despite the lawyer's efforts in accordance with paragraph (b), the highest authority that can act on behalf of the organization insists upon action, or a refusal to act, that is clearly a violation of law and is likely to result in substantial injury to the organization, the lawyer may resign in accordance with Rule 1.16.

(d) [Same as 2003 version of Rule 1.13(f).]

(e) [Same as 2003 version of Rule 1.13(g).]

2002 Amendments: At its February 2002 Mid-Year Meeting, the ABA House of Delegates adopted without change the ABA Ethics 2000 Commission proposal to amend Rule 1.13 and its Comment. The only substantive change in the Rule was to substitute "the lawyer knows or reasonably should know" for "it is apparent" in paragraph (d).

2003 Amendments: At its August 2003 Annual Meeting, by a margin of 239-147, the ABA House of Delegates voted to amend paragraphs (b) and (c) of Rule 1.13 significantly, and to add new paragraphs (d) and (e). (Former paragraphs (d) and (e) were redesignated paragraphs (f) and (g).) The amendment to Rule 1.13(b) had the effect of underscoring the lawyer's obligation to report the described misconduct to higher authority, including the highest authority of the organization. Lawyers must now do this unless they reasonably believe it is not necessary. The amendment to Rule 1.13(c) permits lawyers, when the preconditions are satisfied, to reveal the confidential information of the organizational client to outsiders, which in effect creates another exception to Rule 1.6. The ABA also added or substantially amended Comments 3-8. The changes were part of a package of recommendations from the ABA Presidential Task Force on Corporate Responsibility. (For more information about the Task Force and its work, including a copy of its full report, visit *http://www.americanbar.org/groups/business_law.html.*) In support of the changes, the Task Force report stated:[*]

> The key provision, in current Rule 1.13(b), is that the lawyer must take appropriate action in the best interest of the client, namely the organization. While this obligation is a mandate, the Rule cannot and does not prescribe precisely what action is appropriate; the lawyer is obligated to exercise informed professional judgment in determining what steps are "reasonably necessary in the best interest of the organization." That can be determined, in specific detail, only in the context of the circumstances in which the problem arises. The current rule suggests, very generally, a few kinds of action open to the lawyer, but mandates none of them. The Task Force has concluded that these provisions confuse rather than clarify the mandatory nature of the lawyer's obligations under the rule, and accordingly recommends that they be deleted.
>
> In lieu of those open-ended provisions, the Task Force recommends two substantive revisions to Rule 1.13(b). The first is a refinement of the definition of the circumstances that trigger the lawyer's duty to take action within the organization.

> **Editors' Note.** The above recommendation was deleted through a friendly amendment during the debate in the ABA House of Delegates. The original Task Force recommendation would have added the words "facts from which a reasonable lawyer, under the circumstances, would conclude" after the word "knows" in the first sentence of Rule 1.13(b). The result of the friendly amendment deleting these proposed words was to leave the first sentence of Rule 1.13(b) unchanged from the 2002 version. The Task Force report continued as follows:

> The second substantive change to Rule 1.13(b) recommended by the Task Force addresses the lawyer's obligation to report wrongdoing to higher authority in

---

[*] Task Force Reports do not represent official policy of the ABA. They are for information only, and the opinions are those of the authors of the Report.

the organizational client. Currently, that rule identifies "reporting up" as a potential course of action when the lawyer has discerned an actual or threatened violation of law or violation of legal obligation to the organization, but the Rule imposes no clear obligation to pursue that course of action. The Task Force believes, however, that the Rule should more actively encourage such action, by requiring that the lawyer refer the matter to higher authority in the organization — including, if warranted, the organization's highest authority — unless the lawyer reasonably believes that it is not necessary to do so.

In its deliberations, the Task Force considered whether the lawyer's duties under the Rule should continue to be triggered only by matters that are "related to the representation." The Task Force's Preliminary Report recommended that the Rule require the lawyer to act with respect to any known violation, even if not related to the representation. Others pointed out, however, that it would be unfair to hold responsible a lawyer working in one field of the law to understand that facts of which he was aware should have led to a conclusion of law violation in a field with which he was unfamiliar. The Task Force is persuaded by this analysis and recommends that this qualification be retained in the Rule. . . .

The Task Force also recommends that Rule 1.13 be amended to include a new provision to assure that the organization's highest authority is made aware that a lawyer for the organization has withdrawn or is discharged in circumstances addressed by the Rule. In some instances, the actions of the lawyer within the organization, pursuant to Rule 1.13(b), may fail to prevent or avoid action that seriously threatens the interest of the organization. Current Rule 1.13(c) provides that a lawyer, in this circumstance, may choose to withdraw. In that event, or if the organizational client discharges the lawyer because of the lawyer's actions under Rule 1.13(b) in reporting to higher authority, the lawyer's professional obligations to act in the best interest of the organization should require the lawyer to take reasonable steps to assure that the organization's highest authority is aware of the withdrawal or discharge, and the lawyer's understanding of the circumstances that brought it about. . . .

In proposing amendments to Model Rule 1.6, the Task Force has reviewed confidentiality considerations that reflect a balance between the policy of preserving the confidentiality of client information and countervailing policy that a client may not abuse the client-lawyer relationship by using the lawyer's services to commit a crime or fraud. That balance of policy considerations applies to both individual and organizational clients. The Task Force has focused, however, on two additional aspects of the duty of confidentiality with respect to organizational clients. The first such aspect is the uncontroversial but perhaps not universally understood proposition that a lawyer does not violate Model Rule 1.6 by disclosing to an organizational constituent, acting as such, information relating to the representation that was imparted to the lawyer by another organizational constituent (e.g., by sharing with a corporation's general counsel or its board of directors facts learned from a corporate officer). Organizational constituents thus cannot legitimately expect that the lawyer will not reveal to others within the organization information they have imparted to the lawyer.

The second aspect on which the Task Force has focused arises because, just as with individual clients, full and frank communication with the organization's lawyer is encouraged if organizational constituents expect that information they communicate to the organization's lawyer will not be revealed outside the organization (except as the organization may decide). That expectation is undoubtedly valuable to an organizational client as a general proposition. The organization may have a countervailing interest, however, when a lawyer's actions within the organization, including advice to the organization's highest authority, are unavailing to protect the organization against substantial injury arising from a constituent's clear violation of law. In such a circumstance, the Task Force believes that [the] organization's interest in having the lawyer proceed "as is reasonably necessary in the best interest of the organization" outweighs the organization's general interest in preserving confidentiality.

The Task Force agrees with the Reporter to the ALI Restatement that Model Rule 1.6 ". . . should not be understood to preclude controlled disclosure beyond the organization in the limited circumstances where the wrongdoing is clear, the injury to the client organization is substantial, and disclosure would clearly be in the interest of the entity client." The Task Force considers this especially important in the circumstance in which the board of directors or other highest authority of the organizational client is disabled from acting in the best interest of the organization, e.g., because of self-interest or personal involvement in the violation.

Because such disclosure may reveal client information otherwise protected under Rule 1.6(a), the proposed addition to Rule 1.13 contains strict conditions that must exist before any "reporting out" is allowed. The lawyer must have a heightened level of certainty as to the violation of law, and the actual or threatened violation must be "clear." Moreover, there is no permission to "report out" when the organizational governance failure involves a violation of legal duty to the organization but is not otherwise a violation of law. As under Rule 1.6, communication of client information outside the organization must be limited to information reasonably believed to be necessary to prevent substantial injury to the organization that is reasonably certain to occur. In most circumstances, this limitation would permit communication only with persons outside the organization who have authority and responsibility to take appropriate preventive action.

Finally, although the following language was adopted at the ABA's 2003 Annual Meeting, it was subsequently deleted as an administrative matter (i.e., not by the House of Delegates) to ensure conformity with the friendly amendments described above:

The lawyer's obligation to proceed as is reasonably necessary in the best interest of the organization is determined by the conclusions that a reasonable lawyer would, under the circumstances, draw from the facts known. The terms "reasonable" and "reasonably" imply a range within which the lawyer's conduct will satisfy the requirements of Rule 1.13. In determining what is reasonable in the best interest of the organization the circumstances at the time of determination are relevant. Such circumstances may include, among others, the lawyer's area of expertise, the time constraints under which the lawyer is acting, and the lawyer's previous experience and familiarity with the client. For example, the facts suggesting a violation may be part of a large volume of information that the lawyer has insufficient time fully to comprehend. Or the facts known to the lawyer may be sufficient to signal the likely existence of a violation to an expert in a particular field of law but not to a lawyer who works in another specialty. Under such circumstances the lawyer would not have an obligation to proceed under Paragraph (b).

Selected State Variations

Arizona has adopted the 2003 version of ABA Model Rule 1.13 verbatim. Regarding entity clients, the Arizona Legislature has also enacted the following statute, A.R.S. §12-2234, to codify the attorney-client privilege for corporations and other entities in civil cases:

(B) . . . [A]ny communication is privileged between an attorney for a corporation, governmental entity, partnership, business, association or other similar entity or an employer and any employee, agent or member of the entity or employer regarding acts or omissions of or information obtained from the employee, agent or member if the communication is either:

    1. For the purpose of providing legal advice to the entity or employer or to the employee, agent or member.

    2. For the purpose of obtaining information in order to provide legal advice to the entity or employer or to the employee, agent or member.

    (C) The privilege defined in this section shall not be construed to allow the employee to be relieved of a duty to disclose the facts solely because they have been communicated to an attorney.

The statute was passed in reaction to the Arizona Supreme Court's decision in *Samaritan Foundation v. Goodfarb*, 862 P.2d 870 (Ariz. 1993), which rejected the federal courts' broad view of the attorney-client privilege for corporations announced in *Upjohn Co. v. United States*, 449 U.S. 383 (1981). The *Samaritan* court instead adopted a "functional" test for the attorney-client privilege and required a defendant hospital to disclose information that the defendant contended was privileged. The following year, after intense lobbying by corporate interests, the Arizona Legislature enacted §12-2234, which effectively overruled the *Samaritan* opinion and adopted *Upjohn*. However, in *Roman Catholic Diocese of Phoenix v. Superior Court*, 62 P.3d 970 (Ariz. App. 2003), an intermediate appellate court held that §12-2334 applies only in civil proceedings and that *Samaritan* remains good law in criminal cases.

    California: Rule 3-600 substantially follows the positions in Rule 1.13 as originally adopted. Among other things, it does not create an exception to confidentiality when conditions like those in Model Rule 1.13(c) are present but says only that the lawyer may, or must, resign.

    District of Columbia omits paragraphs (c), (d), and (e) of ABA Model Rule 1.13.

    Maryland, Michigan, and *New Jersey* all retain verbatim the Kutak Commission's 1981 draft of Rule 1.13(c), which provides that "remedial action" may, if necessary, include "revealing information otherwise protected by Rule 1.6" — but "only if the lawyer reasonably believes that: (1) the highest authority in the organization has acted to further the personal or financial interests of members of the authority which are in conflict with the interests of the organization; and (2) revealing the information is necessary in the best interest of the organization."

    Michigan: Rule 1.13(a) tracks the Kutak Commission's 1980 draft by providing that a lawyer for an organization represents the organization "as distinct from" its directors, officers, employees, members, shareholders, or other constituents. Moreover, Michigan Rule 1.13(f) provides as follows:

> For purposes of this rule "organization" includes any corporation, partnership, association, joint stock company, union, trust, pension fund, unincorporated association, proprietorship or other business entity, state or local government or political subdivision thereof, or non-profit organization.

    Minnesota effectively deletes the requirement in ABA Rule 1.13(c)(2) that the lawyer "reasonably believes that the violation is reasonably certain to result in substantial injury to the organization." Minnesota also deletes ABA Model Rule 1.13(d).

    Missouri: Missouri retains the 2002 version of ABA Model Rule 1.13 verbatim and thus has no equivalent to paragraphs (d) and (e) of the current version of ABA Model Rule 1.13.

New Jersey: Rule 1.13(a), which borrows from the Kutak Commission's 1980 draft, states that a lawyer employed or retained to represent an organization represents the organization "as distinct from" its directors, officers, employees, members, shareholders, or other constituents. In addition, New Jersey adds that for purposes of Rules 4.2 and 4.3 "the organization's lawyer shall be deemed to represent not only the organizational entity but also the members of its litigation control group," which is defined as follows:

> Members of the litigation control group shall be deemed to include current agents and employees responsible for, or significantly involved in, the determination of the organization's legal position in the matter whether or not in litigation, provided, however, that "significant involvement" requires involvement greater, and other than, the supplying of factual information or data respecting the matter. Former agents and employees who were members of the litigation control group shall presumptively be deemed to be represented in the matter by the organization's lawyer but may at any time disavow said representation.

New Jersey Rule 1.13(b) retains verbatim the 1983 version of ABA Model Rule 1.13(b). New Jersey Rule 1.13(c) retains verbatim the Kutak Commission's 1981 draft — see Maryland entry above. New Jersey has not adopted ABA Model Rules 1.13(d) and (e), and New Jersey's equivalent to ABA Model Rule 1.13(f) provides that in dealing with an organization's directors, officers, employees, members, shareholders or other constituents, a lawyer shall explain the identity of the client when the lawyer "believes that such explanation is necessary to avoid misunderstanding on their part." Finally, New Jersey also adds a subparagraph (f) that defines the term "organization" in Rule 1.13 to include "any corporation, partnership, association, joint stock company, union, trust, pension fund, unincorporated association, proprietorship or other business entity, state or local government or political subdivision thereof, or nonprofit organization."

New York: Rule 1.13 is substantially similar to the pre-2003 version of Model Rule 1.13.

Ohio: Rule 1.13(b) adds "or reasonably should know" after "knows" in the first sentence. Ohio omits ABA Model Rules 1.13(c), (d), and (e). Ohio Rule 1.13(c) provides: "The discretion or duty of the lawyer for an organization to reveal information relating to the representation outside the organization is governed by Rule 1.6(b) and (c)."

Pennsylvania retains the 1983 version of ABA Model Rule 1.13(b) essentially verbatim, and retains the 2002 version of ABA Model Rule 1.13(c).

Texas: Rule 1.12(a) says that a lawyer retained or employed by an organization "represents the entity." Texas Rule 1.12(d) relieves the lawyer of responsibilities to the entity when the lawyer properly withdraws from the representation. Texas Rule 1.12(e) (equivalent to ABA Model Rule 1.13(f)) requires a lawyer to explain the identity of the client "when explanation appears reasonably necessary to avoid misunderstanding. . . ."

Related Materials

ABA Formal Ethics Opinions: See ABA Formal Ethics Ops. 91-361 (1991), 92-364 (1992), 92-365 (1992), 92-366 (1992), 95-390 (1995), 99-415 (1999), 06-441 (2006), and 08-453 (2008).

ABA Task Force on Corporate Responsibility: In 2002, the President of the American Bar Association appointed a Task Force on Corporate Responsibility whose charge was to "examine systemic issues relating to corporate responsibility arising out of the unexpected and traumatic bankruptcy of Enron and other Enron-like situations." The Task Force Chair was Tennessee lawyer James H. Cheek, III, and its Reporter was Professor Lawrence Hamermesh of Widener University School of Law. In March 2003, the Task Force issued an influential final report recommending (among other things) that the ABA (1) adopt the exceptions to Rule 1.6 confidentiality that the ABA had rejected in 2002, and (2) modify Rule 1.13 to permit lawyers to reveal confidential information outside the organization in certain circumstances. At the ABA's August 2003 Annual Meeting, the ABA House of Delegates approved the substance of the Task Force's recommendations regarding Rules 1.6 and 1.13. (See "2003 Amendments" in the Legislative History following both Rule 1.6 and this Rule.) The Task Force's final report and related events are discussed in the Special Section at the end of the 2004 edition of this book.

Model Rules of Professional Conduct for Federal Lawyers: Rule 1.13 provides (with emphasis added):

(a) Except when representing another client pursuant to paragraphs (e), (f) and (g), *a Government lawyer represents the Federal Agency that employs the Government lawyer.* Government lawyers are often formally employed by a Federal Agency but assigned to an organizational element within the Federal Agency. Unless otherwise specifically provided, the Federal Agency, not the organizational element, is ordinarily considered the client. The Federal Agency acts through its authorized officials. These officials include the heads of organizational elements within the Federal Agency. When a Government lawyer is assigned to an organizational element and designated to provide legal services and advice to the head of that organization, the client-lawyer relationship exists between the Government lawyer and the Federal Agency, as represented by the head of the organization. *The head of the organization may only invoke the attorney-client privilege or the rule of confidentiality for the benefit of the Federal Agency.* In so invoking either the attorney-client privilege or attorney-client confidentiality on behalf of the Federal Agency, the head of the organization is subject to being overruled by higher agency authority.

(b) . . . [The measures a Government lawyer may take] may include, among others: . . .

(3) Advising the person that the lawyer is ethically obligated to preserve the interests of the Federal agency and, as a result, must consider discussing the matter with supervisory lawyers within the Government lawyer's office or at a higher level within the Federal Agency.

(c) If, despite the Government lawyer's efforts in accordance with paragraph (b), the highest authority that can act concerning the matter insists upon action, or refusal to act, that is clearly a violation of law, the Government lawyer shall terminate representation with respect to the matter in question. In no event may the Government lawyer participate or assist in the illegal activity. . . .

(e) A Government lawyer shall not form a client-lawyer relationship or represent a client other than the Federal Agency unless specifically authorized or authorized by competent authority. . . .

(g) A Government lawyer who has been duly assigned or authorized to represent an individual who is subject to disciplinary action or administrative proceedings, or to provide civil legal assistance to an individual, has, for those purposes, a lawyer-client relationship with that individual.

The Comment to these Rules states, in part, as follows:

> Except when a Government lawyer is assigned to represent the interest of another client, the Federal Agency that employs the Government lawyer is the client. This principle is critical to the application of these Rules, since the identity of the client affects significant confidentiality and conflict issues.
>
> . . . Although arguments have been made that the Government lawyer's ultimate obligation is to serve the public interest or the "government as a whole," for practical purposes, these may be unworkable ethical guidelines, particularly with regard to client control and confidentiality.
>
> A Federal Agency may, of course, establish different client-lawyer obligations by Executive or court order, regulation, or statute. *See, e.g.,* 5 U.S.C. §2302 (defining "prohibited personnel practice" and assigning responsibility for preventing them).

Partnerships: Entities or Aggregates? A "partnership" is a form of business organization that exists whenever two or more people associate, without incorporating, for the purpose of doing business for profit. For purposes of identifying the client under Rule 1.13(a), does a lawyer for a partnership represent only the entity itself and not the partners (the "entity" theory), or does the lawyer for a partnership represent an aggregation of partners so that each partner is a client of the lawyer for the partnership (the "aggregate" theory)? In the original Uniform Partnership Act (UPA), which was approved by the National Conference of Commissioners on Uniform State Laws (NCCUSL) in 1914, a partnership was viewed not as a distinct entity but rather as an aggregation of individuals. The original UPA thus generally embraced the "aggregate" theory of partnerships. In contrast, §201 of the Revised Uniform Partnership Act (RUPA), provides that a partnership "is an entity distinct from its partners," thus embracing the "entity" theory of partnerships. (The UPA had no specific section comparable to §201 of the RUPA.)

The RUPA was approved in 1994 by the National Conference of Commissioners on Uniform State Laws — now called the Uniform Law Commission — and has been adopted by 37 states and the District of Columbia. For more information, including a link to the full text of the RUPA, see the website of the Uniform Law Commission at *http://uniformlaws.org/LegislativeFactSheet.aspx?title=Partnership%20Act*.

Restatement of the Law Governing Lawyers: See Restatement §§67, 73, 82, 85, 96, 97, and 131 in our chapter on the Restatement later in this volume.

Sarbanes-Oxley Act and SEC Regulations: In 2002, in the wake of massive corporate scandals at Enron, WorldCom, and other corporations, Congress enacted the Sarbanes-Oxley Act of 2002. A provision of the Act directly aimed at attorneys is §307 (codified at 15 U.S.C. §7245), which provides as follows:

§7245. Rules of Professional Responsibility for Attorneys

> Not later than 180 days after July 30, 2002, the [Securities and Exchange] Commission shall issue rules, in the public interest and for the protection of investors, setting forth minimum standards of professional conduct for attorneys appearing and practicing before the Commission in any way in the representation of issuers, including a rule —
>
> (1) requiring an attorney to report evidence of a material violation of securities law or breach of fiduciary duty or similar violation by the company or any agent thereof, to the chief legal counsel or the chief executive officer of the company (or the equivalent thereof); and
>
> (2) if the counsel or officer does not appropriately respond to the evidence (adopting, as necessary, appropriate remedial measures or sanctions with respect to

the violation), requiring the attorney to report the evidence to the audit committee of the board of directors of the issuer or to another committee of the board of directors comprised solely of directors not employed directly or indirectly by the issuer, or to the board of directors.

To carry out the mandate of the Act, in 2003 the SEC adopted detailed rules codified at 17 C.F.R. Part 205, which are reprinted below in our selection of Federal Statutes and Regulations. Additional context surrounding the Sarbanes-Oxley Act and the SEC regulations can be found in the Special Section at the end of the 2004 edition of this book.

SEC Statement on Corporate Cooperation ("Seaboard Report"): In the SEC's Securities and Exchange Act Release No. 44969 (October 23, 2001), often referred to as the "Seaboard Report," the SEC set forth some of the criteria the SEC considers in determining "whether, and how much, to credit self-policing, self-reporting, remediation and cooperation — from the extraordinary step of taking no enforcement action to bringing reduced charges, seeking lighter sanctions, or including mitigating language in documents we use to announce and resolve enforcement actions." The following examples of these criteria are particularly relevant to Rule 1.13:

1. What is the nature of the misconduct involved? Did it result from inadvertence, honest mistake, simple negligence, reckless or deliberate indifference to indicia of wrongful conduct, willful misconduct or unadorned venality? Were the company's auditors misled?

2. How did the misconduct arise? Is it the result of pressure placed on employees to achieve specific results, or a tone of lawlessness set by those in control of the company? What compliance procedures were in place to prevent the misconduct now uncovered? Why did those procedures fail to stop or inhibit the wrongful conduct?

5. How much harm has the misconduct inflicted upon investors and other corporate constituencies? Did the share price of the company's stock drop significantly upon its discovery and disclosure?

6. How was the misconduct detected and who uncovered it? . . .

8. What steps did the company take upon learning of the misconduct? Did the company immediately stop the misconduct? Are persons responsible for any misconduct still with the company? If so, are they still in the same positions? Did the company promptly, completely and effectively disclose the existence of the misconduct to the public, to regulators and to self-regulators? Did the company cooperate completely with appropriate regulatory and law enforcement bodies? Did the company identify what additional related misconduct is likely to have occurred? Did the company take steps to identify the extent of damage to investors and other corporate constituencies? Did the company appropriately recompense those adversely affected by the conduct?

9. What processes did the company follow to resolve many of these issues and ferret out necessary information? Were the Audit Committee and the Board of Directors fully informed? If so, when? . . .

In 2010, the SEC announced a series of measures to strengthen its enforcement program by encouraging greater cooperation from individuals and companies in the agency's investigations and enforcement actions. Among other things, the SEC set out, for the first time, the way in which it will evaluate whether, how much, and in what manner to credit cooperation by individuals to ensure that potential cooperation arrangements maximize the SEC's law enforcement interests. The 2010 pronouncement, which is similar to the Seaboard Report, identifies four general considerations in assessing the value of cooperation: (1) "The assistance provided by the cooperating individual''; (2) ''The importance of the underlying matter in which the individual cooperated''; (3) ''The societal interest in ensuring the individual is held accountable for his or her misconduct''; and (4) ''The appropriateness of cooperation credit based upon the risk profile of the cooperating individual.'' For more information, see *www.sec.gov/news/press/2010/2010-6.htm.*

Sentencing Guidelines: The U.S. Sentencing Guidelines set forth factors intended to guide courts in imposing criminal sentences. When a corporation is convicted of a crime, one factor militating toward a reduced sentence is cooperation. Following §8C2.5 of the Sentencing Guidelines, entitled ''Culpability Score,'' the official Application Note explains ''cooperation'' as follows:

> 12. To qualify for a reduction . . . cooperation must be both timely and thorough. To be timely, the cooperation must begin essentially at the same time as the organization is officially notified of a criminal investigation. To be thorough, the cooperation should include the disclosure of all pertinent information known by the organization. A prime test of whether the organization has disclosed all pertinent information is whether the information is sufficient for law enforcement personnel to identify the nature and extent of the offense and the individual(s) responsible for the criminal conduct. However, the cooperation to be measured is the cooperation of the organization itself, not the cooperation of individuals within the organization. If, because of the lack of cooperation of particular individual(s), neither the organization nor law enforcement personnel are able to identify the culpable individual(s) within the organization despite the organization's efforts to cooperate fully, the organization may still be given credit for full cooperation.

Until 2006, the U.S. Sentencing Commission maintained a policy authorizing and encouraging prosecutors to require corporations and other business entities to waive the attorney-client privilege and constitutional protections in order to receive ''credit'' for ''cooperating'' in government investigations. In 2006, the Commission voted unanimously to rescind this policy and to delete the final sentence of the Application Note to §8C2.5, which had stated: ''Waiver of attorney-client privilege and of work product protections is not a prerequisite to a reduction in culpability score . . . unless such waiver is necessary in order to provide timely and thorough disclosure of all pertinent information known to the organization.''

Rule 1.14　　Client with Diminished Capacity

Canon and Code Antecedents

ABA Canons of Professional Ethics: No comparable Canon.
ABA Model Code of Professional Responsibility: No comparable Disciplinary Rule.

Cross-References in Other Rules

Rule 1.2, Comment 4: ''In a case in which the client appears to be suffering diminished capacity, the lawyer's duty to abide by the client's decisions is to be guided by reference to **Rule 1.14**.''

Rule 1.4, Comment 6: A client is to be provided with information appropriate for a ''comprehending and responsible adult. However, . . . this standard may be impracticable, for example, where the client is a child or suffers from diminished capacity. See **Rule 1.14**.''

Rule 1.16, Comment 6: ''If the client has severely diminished capacity, the client may lack the legal capacity to discharge the lawyer, and in any event the discharge may be seriously adverse to the client's interests. The lawyer should make special effort to help the client consider the consequences and may take reasonably necessary protective action as provided in **Rule 1.14**.''

Legislative History of Model Rule 1.14

1980 Discussion Draft:

. . . (b) A lawyer shall secure the appointment of a guardian or other legal representative, or seek a protective order with respect to a client, when doing so is necessary in the client's best interests.

1981 Draft: Rule 1.14(a) was the same as the version finally adopted. Rule 1.14(b) required a lawyer to seek appointment of a guardian or a protective order ''only when the lawyer reasonably believes that the client cannot adequately communicate or exercise judgment in the client-lawyer relationship.''

1982 Draft was adopted.

1983 Rule: From its adoption in 1983 until its text was first amended in 2002, Rule 1.14 provided as follows:

Rule 1.14. Client Under a Disability

(a) When a client's ability to make adequately considered decisions in connection with the representation is impaired, whether because of minority, mental disability or for some other reason, the lawyer shall, as far as reasonably possible, maintain a normal client-lawyer relationship with the client.

(b) A lawyer may seek the appointment of a guardian or take other protective action with respect to a client, only when the lawyer reasonably believes that the client cannot adequately act in the client's own interest.

1995 Proposal: In May 1995, the ABA Commission on Legal Problems of the Elderly filed a proposal to amend Rule 1.14. However, the proposal was withdrawn during the ABA's August 1995 Annual Meeting. The proposal would have revised Rule 1.14(b) and added new sections 1.14(c), (d), and (e) so that those sections would have provided as follows:

(b) A lawyer may take protective action or seek the appointment of a guardian only when the lawyer reasonably believes the client cannot adequately act in the client's own interest.

(c) While it might be necessary to disclose information, the disclosure should be strictly limited to that which is necessary to accomplish the protective purpose.

(d)(1) A lawyer is an agent who acts upon the authority of a principal. In many cases, the lawyer will have a pre-existing relationship with a person or that person's family. In the absence of such a pre-existing relationship or a contractual agreement, express or implied, a lawyer generally may not act on behalf of a client.

(2) In certain circumstances, a lawyer may act as lawyer for a purported client even without express or limited agreement from the purported client, and may take those actions necessary to maintain the status quo or to avoid irreversible harm, if

(i) An emergency situation exists in which the purported client's substantial health, safety, financial, or liability interests would be irreparably damaged;

(ii) The purported client, in the lawyer's good faith judgment, lacks the ability to make or express considered judgments about action required to be taken because of an impairment of decision-making capacity;

(iii) Time is of the essence; and

(iv) The lawyer reasonably believes in good faith that no other lawyer who has an established relationship with the purported client is available or willing to act on behalf of the purported client.

(3) A "purported client" is a person who has contact with a lawyer and who would be a client but for the inability to enter into an express agreement.

(e) The lawyer should not be subject to professional discipline for invoking or failing to invoke the permissive conduct authorized by 1.14(b) if the lawyer has a reasonable basis for his or her action or inaction.

The proposal was accompanied by an 11-page report, which explained that the genesis of the proposal was a conference on Ethical Issues in Representing Older Clients held at Fordham University Law School in December 1993. Much of the report quoted or cited papers from that conference, which are published in 62 Fordham L. Rev. (March 1994).

1997 Amendment: In 1997, the ABA House of Delegates voted to add two new paragraphs to the Comment to Rule 1.14. (The amendment did not alter the text of Rule 1.14 or the existing Comment.) The new Comment paragraphs, co-sponsored by the ABA Standing Committee on Ethics and Professional Responsibility and the ABA Commission on Legal Problems of the Elderly, grew out of amendments to Rule 1.14 that the Commission proposed in 1995. The new Comment paragraphs explain what a lawyer should do when an "emergency" threatens the health, safety or financial interest of a disabled person who is not yet a client. The new paragraphs should be read in conjunction with ABA Ethics Op. 96-404 (1996), which addressed ethical issues that arise when existing clients are no longer mentally capable of handling their own affairs. The House of Delegates approved the new paragraphs exactly as proposed, by an overwhelming voice vote. We reprint here excerpts from the ABA Committee Report submitted in support of the 1997 amendment.

ABA Report Explaining 1997 Amendment to Comment*

[A] lawyer may reasonably conclude that an elderly person who has not been judged incompetent is in need of emergency legal assistance, but is, or appears to be, unable to make decisions on his or her own behalf — including a decision to retain a lawyer. Such situations fall most naturally within the spirit of Model Rule 1.14 ("Client Under a Disability"). The question is whether it is ethically permissible for a lawyer to take legal action on behalf of a disabled person who cannot, in the first instance, form a client-lawyer relationship.

The question whether and under what circumstances a lawyer may take emergency legal action on behalf of a disabled person who is not a client is not, of course, unique to the representation of the elderly. It may arise in a variety of practice settings where individuals appear to be in need of immediate legal assistance but are unable to make adequately considered decisions in connection with initiating legal representation.

* Committee Reports do not represent official policy of the ABA. They are for information only, and the opinions are those of the authors of the report.

Most of the duties arising under the Model Rules (the most notable exception being that of confidentiality) attach only after the formation of a client-lawyer relationship, and the Rules are silent with respect to any forms of representation that do not arise from such relationship. . . .

However, the Committee believes that such emergency action is permissible under the Model Rules, if properly limited. . . .

2002 Amendments: At its February 2002 Mid-Year Meeting, the ABA House of Delegates adopted without change the ABA Ethics 2000 Commission proposal to amend Rule 1.14 and its Comment. The amendments substantially revised paragraph (b) and added paragraph (c) and all or most of Comments 3, 5, 6, 7, and 8.

Selected State Variations

California has no rule comparable to ABA Model Rule 1.14.

Indiana adds Rule 1.14(d), which states: "This Rule is not violated if the lawyer acts in good faith to comply with the Rule."

Massachusetts: Rule 1.14(b) adds that a lawyer may take reasonably necessary measures to protect a client with diminished capacity, but only in "connection with the representation" and only when the client's diminished capacity "prevents the client from making an adequately considered decision regarding a specific issue that is part of the representation. . . ." Comment 7 explains that

"[i]f a client is unable to make an adequately considered decision regarding an issue, and [when] achieving the client's expressed preferences would place the client at risk of a substantial harm, the attorney has four options. The attorney may: i. advocate the client's expressed preferences regarding the issue; ii. advocate the client's expressed preferences and request the appointment of a guardian ad litem or investigator to make an independent recommendation to the court; iii. request the appointment of a guardian ad litem or next friend to direct counsel in the representation; or iv. determine what the client's preferences would be if he or she were able to make an adequately considered decision regarding the issue and represent the client in accordance with that determination. . . ."

New York: Rule 1.14 is substantially similar to the Model Rule equivalent, but New York adds Comment 7A, which states as follows: "Prior to withdrawing from the representation of a client whose capacity is in question, the lawyer should consider taking reasonable protective action."

Texas: Rule 1.02(g) provides: "A lawyer shall take reasonable action to secure the appointment of a guardian or other legal representative for, or seek other protective orders with respect to, a client whenever the lawyer reasonably believes that the client lacks legal competence and that such action should be taken to protect the client."

Related Materials

ABA Formal Ethics Opinions: See ABA Formal Ethics Ops. 92-364 (1992), 96-404 (1996), and 07-448 (2007).

Americans with Disabilities Act: Lawyers in private practice should be mindful of Title III of the Americans with Disabilities Act, which took effect in 1992. Section 302(a) of Title III, 42 U.S.C. §12182(a), states the general rule:

> No individual shall be discriminated against on the basis of disability in the full and equal enjoyment of the goods, services, facilities, privileges, advantages, or accommodations of any place of public accommodation by any person who owns, leases (or leases to), or operates a place of public accommodation.

The term "public accommodation" is defined in 42 U.S.C. §12181(7)(F) to include the "office of an accountant or lawyer" if the firm's operations affect commerce.

Restatement of the Law Governing Lawyers: See Restatement §24 in our chapter on the Restatement later in this volume.

Rule 1.15 Safekeeping Property

Canon and Code Antecedents

ABA Canons of Professional Ethics: Canon 11 provided as follows:

11. Dealing with Trust Property

> The lawyer should refrain from any action whereby for his personal benefit or gain he abuses or takes advantage of the confidence reposed in him by his client.
>
> Money of the client or collected for the client or other trust property coming into the possession of the lawyer should be reported and accounted for promptly, and should not under any circumstances be commingled with his own or be used by him.

ABA Model Code of Professional Responsibility: Compare DR 9-102(A) and DR 9-102(B) (reprinted later in this volume).

Cross-References in Other Rules

Rule 1.16, Comment 9: "Even if the lawyer has been unfairly discharged by the client, a lawyer must take all reasonable steps to mitigate the consequences to the client. The lawyer may retain papers as security for a fee only to the extent permitted by law. See **Rule 1.15**."

Rule 1.18, Comment 9: "For a lawyer's duties when a prospective client entrusts valuables or papers to the lawyer's care, see **Rule 1.15**."

Legislative History of Model Rule 1.15

1980 Discussion Draft (then Rule 1.12) provided in (a) that funds "shall be kept in a trust account." Subparagraph (d) provided:

> (d) When a lawyer and another person both have interests in property, the property shall be treated by the lawyer as trust property until an accounting and severance of their interests. If a dispute arises concerning their respective interests, the portion in dispute shall be treated as trust property until the dispute is resolved.

1981 and 1982 Drafts were substantially the same as adopted.

1983 Rule: As originally adopted in 1983, Rule 1.15 consisted of only three paragraphs, which are today designated (a), (d), and (e). (Paragraphs (b) and (c) were not added until 2002.) Paragraphs (a) and (d) remain in their original form. The 1983 version of today's Rule 1.15(e) provided as follows:

> When in the course of representation a lawyer is in the possession of property in which both the lawyer and another person claim interests, the property shall be kept separate by the lawyer until there is an accounting and severance of their interests. If a dispute arises concerning their respective interest, the portion in dispute shall be kept separate by the lawyer until the dispute is resolved.

2002 Amendments: In 2002, the ABA House of Delegates adopted without change the ABA Ethics 2000 Commission proposal to amend Rule 1.15 and its Comment. The amendments added Rule 1.15(b) and (c), significantly revised Rule 1.15(e), added Comment 2, and amended the remaining Comments in relatively minor ways.

Selected State Variations

Editors' Note. Many state versions of Rule 1.15 diverge substantially from ABA Model Rule 1.15. The state variations tend to be lengthy (often several pages), highly detailed, and idiosyncratic. We reprint below only a small selection of the state variations on Rule 1.15.

Arizona permits lawyers to accept credit card payments to cover advance fees, costs, and expenses.

Colorado: Rule 1.15(l) contains a special provision governing the handling of records and files when a lawyer departs from a firm. Rule 1.16(a) describes record retention obligations in elaborate detail.

District of Columbia: The language of D.C. Rule 1.15 differs significantly from the ABA Model Rule, though the basic requirements are the same.

Florida: Chapter 5 of Florida's Supreme Court Rules regulates lawyer trust accounts.

Georgia: In the rules effective November 3, 2011, Rule 1.15(I) generally tracks the 1983 version of ABA Model Rule 1.15, but Georgia adds Rule 1.15(II) to govern trust accounts and IOLTA accounts, and Rule 1.15(III) to govern trust account recordkeeping, overdraft notification, and auditing by disciplinary authorities. Rule 1.15(III) requires that lawyers deposit trust funds in a financial institution that agrees "to report to the State Disciplinary Board whenever any properly payable instrument is presented against a lawyer trust account containing insufficient funds, and the instrument is not honored."

Illinois: Rule 1.15(c) provides that an "agreement for an advance payment retainer" must be in writing, signed by the client, and include a number of disclosures regarding how the lawyer intends to handle the advance payment. Comment 3B instructs lawyers to read the provision in conjunction with *Dowling v. Chicago Options Associates, Inc.*, 226 Ill. 2d 277 (2007), which distinguishes different types of retainers. According to the Comment, an "advance payment retainer" is "a present payment to the lawyer in exchange for the commitment to provide legal services in the future. Ownership of this retainer passes to the lawyer immediately upon payment.''

Rule 1.15(j) contains a highly unusual provision, originally adopted in 1998 at the urging of the real estate bar, which under certain circumstances permits lawyers to hold funds that have been ''deposited but not collected' in a separate Real Estate Funds Account (REFA).

Massachusetts: Rule 1.15 has extensive provisions for deposit of client funds in IOLTA accounts, and contains provisions to ensure that disciplinary authorities are notified in the event a lawyer's check is dishonored.

Michigan provides for IOLTA accounts in Rule 1.15(d) and for Trust Account Overdraft Notification in Rule 1.15(A).

Minnesota: Rule 1.15 differs significantly in structure and substance from ABA Model Rule 1.15.

New Jersey: Under Rule 1.15(a), funds must be deposited in New Jersey institutions, without exception. Rule 1.15(a) also incorporates the substance of ABA Model Rule 1.15(b), and requires lawyers to keep trust account records for seven years. New Jersey deletes ABA Model Rule 1.15(c), and New Jersey Rule 1.15(b) deletes the requirement in ABA Model Rule 1.15(d) that a lawyer promptly render a full accounting of property upon request. New Jersey adds 1.15(d), which refers lawyers to section 1:21-6 of the Court Rules on recordkeeping.

New York: Rule 1.15 addresses the same issues as the Model Rule, but in more detail. For example, New York imposes a seven-year recordkeeping requirement for eight specified categories of documents, such as ''records of all deposits in and withdrawals from'' trust accounts, and copies of ''all retainer and compensation agreements with clients,'' ''all bills rendered to clients,'' and ''all records showing payments to lawyers, investigators or other persons, not in the lawyer's regular employ, for services rendered or performed.''

Ohio: Rule 1.15 differs significantly from ABA Model Rule 1.15. Among other things, Rule 1.15(f) provides as follows: ''Upon dissolution of any law firm, the former partners, managing partners, or supervisory lawyers shall promptly account for all client funds and shall make appropriate arrangements for one of them to maintain all records. . . .'' Rule 1.15(h) imposes strict requirements on every lawyer or law firm that ''owns an interest in a business that provides a law-related service. . . .''

Pennsylvania: The Pennsylvania rules include requirements and definitions that are far more detailed and nuanced than the Model Rule.

Vermont: Rule 1.15B requires lawyers to "maintain a pooled interest-bearing trust account for deposit of client funds that are not reasonably expected to earn a substantial amount of interest for the client, individually or in combination with other client funds held by the lawyer or law firm." The interest from the fund must be paid to the Vermont Bar Foundation, which uses most of the funds to support "legal services for the disadvantaged" and the remainder "for public education relating to the courts and legal matters."

Virginia: Rule 1.15 differs significantly from the Model Rule and includes requirements that were carried forward from Virginia's former Code of Professional Responsibility.

Washington: Rule 1.15A(e) provides that a lawyer ''must promptly provide a written accounting to a client or third person after distribution of property or upon request. A lawyer must provide at least annually a written accounting to a client or third person for whom the lawyer is holding funds.''

Wisconsin: Rule 1.15 is so highly detailed and so long (about 16 pages) that it has its own table of contents. Rule 1.15(a) defines 10 separate terms (such as "Demand account," "Fiduciary property," and "Financial institution"). Rule 1.15(b)(4) provides: "Unearned fees and advanced payments of fees shall be held in trust until earned by the lawyer. . . . Funds advanced by a client or 3rd party for payment of costs shall be held in trust until the costs are incurred." Particularly interesting is Rule 1.15(e)(4), which elaborates on a series of "Prohibited transactions," including:

a. **Cash.** No disbursement of cash shall be made from a trust account or from a deposit to a trust account, and no check shall be made payable to "Cash."

b. **Telephone transfers.** No deposits or disbursements shall be made to or from a pooled trust account by a telephone transfer of funds. This section does not prohibit any of the following: (1) wire transfers, and (2) telephone transfers between separate, non-pooled demand and separate, non-pooled, non-demand trust accounts that a lawyer maintains for a particular client.

c. **Internet transactions.** A lawyer shall not make deposits to or disbursements from a trust account by way of an Internet transaction.

d. **Electronic transfers by 3rd parties.** A lawyer shall not authorize a 3rd party to electronically withdraw funds from a trust account. A lawyer shall not authorize a 3rd party to deposit funds into the lawyer's trust account through a form of electronic deposit that allows the 3rd party making the deposit to withdraw the funds without the permission of the lawyer.

e. **Credit card transactions.** A lawyer shall not authorize transactions by way of credit card to or from a trust account. However, earned fees may be deposited by way of credit card to a lawyer's business account. . . .

Related Materials

ABA Commission on Interest on Lawyers' Trust Accounts: In 1986, to support the initiation and operation of IOLTA programs (see our entry on "IOLTA Programs" below), the ABA created a nine-member ABA Commission on IOLTA, which engages in the following activities: (1) collects, maintains, analyzes, and disseminates information on programs involving the use of interest on lawyers' trust accounts for the support of law-related public service activities; (2) recommends ABA policies for creating and operating IOLTA programs; (3) maintains liaisons with state IOLTA programs; (4) oversees the IOLTA Clearing-house, which provides information, materials, and technical assistance on IOLTA program design and operation; and (5) monitors developments in areas that may affect IOLTA operations, such as banking law, grant-making law, tax law, and constitutional law. For additional information about IOLTA, visit *http://www.americanbar.org/groups/interest_lawyers_trust_accounts. html.*

ABA Financial Recordkeeping Rule: In 1993, to provide guidance for complying with Model Rule 1.15, the ABA approved a Model Financial Recordkeeping Rule. It required lawyers to maintain nine categories of records and to retain them for five years after a representation ended. The rule also provided guidelines for deposits, withdrawals, and bookkeeping, and for handling lawyer trust accounts upon dissolution of a law firm or sale of a law practice. In 2010, the ABA replaced the Financial Recordkeeping Rule with the ABA Model Rules for Client Trust Accounts (see entry below).

ABA Formal Ethics Opinions: See ABA Formal Ethics Ops. 92-369 (1992), 02-427 (2002), 11-460 n.9 (2011).

ABA Model Rules for Client Trust Account Records: In 2010, the ABA approved Model Rules for Client Trust Account Records (which replace the ABA Financial Recordkeeping Rule—see entry above). The new Model Rules, which expressly refer to ABA Model Rule 1.15, consist of five separate rules (with explanatory comments) entitled "Recordkeeping Generally," "Trust Account Safeguards," "Availability of Funds," "Dissolution of Law Firm," and "Sale of Law Practice." The Model Rules for Client Trust Account Records are available online at *http://www.americanbar.org/content/dam/aba/migrated/2011_build/professional_responsibility/adopted_8_10_10.auth-checkdam.pdf.*

ABA Model Rules for Lawyers' Funds for Client Protection: Some lawyers steal from their clients, and lawyers who steal from clients often lack sufficient financial resources to make restitution to their victims. The organized bar has responded by creating Client Protection Funds in each state to provide necessary reimbursement. (For more information, see our entry below on "Client Protection Funds.") The ABA Model Rules for Lawyers' Funds for Client Protection seek to establish standards for effective financing and efficient administration of such funds to achieve meaningful, prompt, and cost-free reimbursement to clients who have been injured by a lawyer's dishonest conduct. The ABA originally adopted these rules in 1981 under the name Model Rules for Clients' Security Funds. In 1989, the ABA amended the rules and renamed them the Model Rules for Lawyers' Funds for Client Protection to avoid confusion about the word "security" (which could mean a stock or bond).

In 2006, the ABA House of Delegates amended Rules 1 and 10 of the Model Rules for Lawyers' Funds for Client Protection to respond to the 2002 amendments to ABA Model Rules 5.5 and 8.5 (both of which relate to multijurisdictional practice). The amended Model Rules for Lawyers' Funds for Client Protection are available online at *http://www.americanbar.org/groups/professional_responsibility/resources/client_protection/rule1.html.*

ABA Random Audit Rule: In 1993, by the narrow vote of 110 to 105, the ABA House of Delegates approved a Model Rule for the Random Audit of Lawyer Trust Accounts. The rule was opposed by the ABA Section on General Practice, which is composed mainly of sole practitioners and small firms. The Random Audit Rule and its Comment, which are available at *http://www.americanbar.org/groups/professional_responsibility/resources/client_protection/apreface.html,* provide in pertinent part as follows:

Random Audits of Lawyer Trust Accounts

[R]andom audits are a proven deterrent to the misuse of money and property in the practice of law. The examination of trust accounts by court-paid auditors also provides practitioners with expert and practical assistance in maintaining necessary records and supporting books of account.

1. The [highest court of the jurisdiction] shall approve procedures to randomly select lawyer or law firm trust accounts for audit.

2. An audit of a lawyer or law firm trust account conducted pursuant to this rule shall be commenced by the issuance of an investigative subpoena to compel the production of records relating to a lawyer's or law firm's trust accounts. . . .

5. In the event that the audit report asserts deficiencies in the audited lawyer's or law firm's records or procedures, the lawyer or law firm shall, within [10] business days

after receipt of the report, provide evidence that the alleged deficiencies are incorrect, or that they have been corrected. . . .

6. All records produced for an audit conducted pursuant to this rule shall remain confidential, and their contents shall not be disclosed in violation of the attorney-client privilege.

7. Records produced for an audit conducted pursuant to this rule may be disclosed to:

(1) the lawyer disciplinary agency or to a court to the extent disclosure is necessary for the purposes of the particular audit;

(2) the lawyer disciplinary agency for the purposes of a disciplinary proceeding; and

(3) any other person, including a law enforcement agency, with the permission of the [highest court of the jurisdiction]. . . .

COMMENT

The Model Rule [for the Random Audit of Lawyer Trust Accounts] proposes a basic structure and system for a random audit program, including such procedural safeguards as adequate prior notice before the commencement of an audit; written audit reports; the opportunity for an audited lawyer or law firm to respond to an examiner's report; the preservation of confidentiality for law client records; and the frequency of audits conducted by random selection. . . .

ABA Standards for Imposing Lawyer Sanctions: The following ABA Standards for Imposing Lawyer Sanctions are relevant to Rule 1.15:

4.11. Disbarment is generally appropriate when a lawyer knowingly converts client property and causes injury or potential injury to a client.

4.12. Suspension is generally appropriate when a lawyer knows or should know that he is dealing improperly with client property and causes injury or potential injury to a client.

4.13. Reprimand is generally appropriate when a lawyer is negligent in dealing with client property and causes injury or potential injury to a client.

4.14. Admonition is generally appropriate when a lawyer is negligent in dealing with client property and causes little or no actual or potential injury to a client.

ABA Standing Committee on Client Protection: The ABA Standing Committee on Client Protection was established in 1984 by merging the ABA Standing Committee on Unauthorized Practice of Law with the ABA Standing Committee on Clients' Security Funds. The Committee's mission is to develop and strengthen mechanisms to protect clients from lawyers who misappropriate client funds. The Standing Committee has been influential in persuading states to establish lawyers' funds for client protection. (See "Client Protection Funds" entry below for more information.) The Standing Committee also promotes consumer and governmental interests in prohibiting or regulating nonlawyers who engage in law-related activities, which raises issues such as the interstate practice of law, the provision of legal services by nonlawyers, and the investment in law firms by nonlawyers. Finally, the Standing Committee on Client Protection sponsors educational programs, provides on-site consultations, develops model rules, and conducts surveys. For more information, see *http://www.americanbar.org/groups/professional_responsibility/resources/client_protection/client.html.*

Client Protection Funds: In keeping with Comment 6 to Rule 1.15, every jurisdiction has established a client protection fund (once called a "client security fund"). The purpose of client protection funds is to reimburse clients who have lost money or property as a result of dishonest conduct by lawyers. For example, Chapter 7 of Rules Regulating the Florida Bar authorizes establishment of a Clients' Security Fund "to provide monetary relief to persons who suffer reimbursable losses as a result of misappropriation, embezzlement, or other wrongful taking or conversion" by a Florida lawyer. For further information about client protection funds, see *http://www.americanbar.org/groups/professional_responsibility/resources/client_protection/client.html.*

IOLTA Programs: ABA Model Rule 1.15(a) requires lawyers to hold funds belonging to clients or others in a special separate account, often referred to as a "lawyer trust account." (Common examples of such funds include a down payment on a house, an advance payment of attorney fees, or a settlement check.) Every state has a rule equivalent to Rule 1.15(a). However, since some client and third-party funds are too small or are held for too short a time to justify opening a separate bank account, lawyers usually pool these small or short-term funds into a single trust account. For many years, lawyers deposited these pooled funds into non-interest-bearing accounts because it was difficult to allocate small amounts of interest to the individual clients or third parties who owned the funds.

In the late 1970s, however, states began requiring lawyers to deposit these small or short-term funds into interest-bearing accounts at banks that agreed to remit the interest directly to a special state-administered fund. (The first such program was created by Florida in 1978.) The programs establishing and administering these special state funds are typically referred to as "IOLTA" programs, which stands for "interest on lawyer trust accounts" (or in some states simply as "IOLA" programs). IOLTA funds are often governed by detailed statutes, court rules, and/or administrative regulations. For an example, see the IOLTA rules of the Ohio Legal Assistance Foundation (OLAF) at *http://www.olaf.org/iolta-and-iota/rules/*, and see Ohio Stat. §§4705.09 and 4705.10.

By 1995, every state had adopted some form of IOLTA program. About forty-four (44) of these IOLTA programs are mandatory (meaning every attorney must maintain an IOLTA account absent a specific exemption in the governing statute or rules); six (6) are "opt-out" (meaning every lawyer must participate unless a lawyer affirmatively opts out); and one (1) is "opt-in" or "voluntary" (meaning that a lawyer participates only if the lawyer voluntarily and affirmatively opts in). The most recent state to convert to a mandatory program is Idaho, which changed from opt-out to mandatory effective July 1, 2012. A chart showing the status of IOLTA programs in all U.S. jurisdictions is available at *http://www.americanbar.org/groups/interest_lawyers_trust_accounts/resources/status_of_iolta_programs.html.*

Many state IOLTA programs generate millions of dollars per year, though the amounts have declined in recent years due to plunging interest rates. In Illinois, for example, the IOLTA program awarded $12.5 million in grants in fiscal 2009, but that amount dropped to $7.7 million in fiscal 2010, $7.5 million in fiscal 2011, $7.2 million in fiscal 2012, and $8 million in fiscal 2013—see *www.ltf.org* (click on "Grant Information"). New Jersey's IOLTA Fund disbursed $14.3 million in grants in 2004 and $50.8 million in grants in 2007, but only $13.7 million in 2010 and $12.4 million in 2011—see *www.ioltanj.org/grnt_home.html.* Since the inception of New Jersey's

IOLTA Fund in 1988, it has distributed over $375 million in total grants. Nationwide, total IOLTA grants from all jurisdictions were $240 million in 2007 and $263.4 million in 2008, but fell to only $124.7 million in 2009 (the most recent year for which statistics are available). Funds are generally distributed to legal services offices, law school clinics, and other programs that provide legal services to the poor. For more information about IOLTA programs, see the website of IOLTA.org at *http://www.iolta.org/* and the website of the ABA Commission on Interest on Lawyers Trust Accounts at *http://www.americanbar.org/groups/interest_lawyers_trust_accounts.html.*

In the mid-1990s, the Washington Legal Foundation challenged mandatory IOLTA programs, arguing that such programs constituted an unconstitutional "taking" of client property (the interest) without compensation, thus violating the Fifth Amendment. Two cases reached the United States Supreme Court. In *Phillips v. Washington Legal Foundation,* 524 U.S. 156 (1998), the Court held (by a 5-4 decision) that the interest on lawyer trust accounts was "property" for purposes of the Takings Clause, but the Court remanded the case for a determination of whether there had been a "taking" (and, if so, what constituted just compensation). In *Brown v. Legal Foundation of Washington,* 538 U.S. 216 (2003) (also a 5-4 decision), the Court held that Washington's mandatory IOLTA plan constituted a "public use," was not a "taking," and did not entitle clients to any compensation for the interest earned on IOLTA accounts. Since that decision, which made clear that mandatory IOLTA programs did not violate the Takings Clause, about 40 states have converted their IOLTA programs from "opt-out" or "opt-in" programs to mandatory programs.

In 2008, the Federal Deposit Insurance Corporation (FDIC) extended unlimited deposit insurance coverage to client funds deposited in IOLTA accounts at participating financial institutions. The FDIC extended this unlimited coverage until December 31, 2010. Congress then amended the Federal Deposit Insurance Act, extending this unlimited coverage through December 31, 2012. Until then, all IOLTA accounts in all insured depository institutions will be insured in full by the FDIC and will be backed by the full faith and credit of the United States government. For more information about unlimited coverage and its history, see *www.fdic.gov/regulations/resources/TLGP.*

Model Rules of Professional Conduct for Federal Lawyers add a new paragraph (d) to Rule 1.15 that provides: "When property of a client or third party is admitted into evidence or otherwise included in the record of a proceeding, the Federal lawyer should take reasonable action to ensure its prompt return."

Money Laundering and Terrorist Financing: At its August 2010 Annual Meeting, the ABA House of Delegates approved a resolution adopting Voluntary Good Practices Guidance for Lawyers to Detect and Combat Money Laundering and Terrorist Financing, and encouraging state, local, and specialty bar associations "to embrace the Good Practices Guidance and to educate legal professionals and law students regarding the risks addressed by the Guidance." The Guidelines were accompanied by a lengthy report that explains the background of money laundering and terrorist financing and provides practice pointers to lawyers. Some of the Good Practices Guidelines concern lawyer trust accounts. The resolution is available at *http://www.abanow.org/2010/07/am-2010-116/.*

National Client Protection Organization (NCPO): The National Client Protection Organization, Inc. (NCPO) is a not-for-profit membership corporation that was organized in 1998. NCPO is primarily an educational resource facilitating the exchange of information among lawyers' funds for client protection throughout the United States and Canada. NCPO's purposes include providing help and support to client protection funds and developing and implementing programs to protect legal consumers from dishonest conduct by lawyers and their employees. In 2006, NCPO adopted Standards for Evaluating Lawyers' Funds for Client Protection. For more information, including the Standards and a map of client protection funds in the United States, visit NCPO's website at *www.ncpo.org.*

Restatement of the Law Governing Lawyers: See Restatement §§43-46 in our chapter on the Restatement later in this volume.

Rule 1.16   Declining or Terminating Representation

Canon and Code Antecedents

ABA Canons of Professional Ethics: Canons 7 and 44 provided as follows:

7.   *Professional Colleagues and Conflicts of Opinion*

A client's proffer of assistance of additional counsel should not be regarded as evidence of want of confidence, but the matter should be left to the determination of the client. A lawyer should decline association as colleague if it is objectionable to the original counsel, but if the lawyer first retained is relieved, another may come into the case.

When lawyers jointly associated in a cause cannot agree as to any matter vital to the interest of the client, the conflict of opinion should be frankly stated to him for his final determination. His decision should be accepted unless the nature of the difference makes it impracticable for the lawyer whose judgment has been overruled to co-operate effectively. In this event it is his duty to ask the client to relieve him.

Efforts, direct or indirect, in any way to encroach upon the professional employment of another lawyer, are unworthy of those who should be brethren at the Bar; but, nevertheless, it is the right of any lawyer, without fear or favor, to give proper advice to those seeking relief against unfaithful or neglectful counsel, generally after communication with the lawyer of whom the complaint is made.

44.   *Withdrawal from Employment as Attorney or Counsel*

The right of an attorney or counsel to withdraw from employment, once assumed, arises only from good cause. Even the desire or consent of the client is not always sufficient. The lawyer should not throw up the unfinished task to the detriment of his client except for reasons of honor or self-respect. If the client insists upon an unjust or immoral course in the conduct of his case, or if he persists over the attorney's remonstrance in presenting frivolous defenses, or if he deliberately disregards an agreement or obligation as to fees or expenses, the lawyer may be warranted in withdrawing on due notice to the client, allowing him time to employ another lawyer. So also when a lawyer discovers that his client has no case and the client is determined to continue it; or even if the lawyer finds himself incapable of conducting the case effectively. Sundry other instances may arise in which withdrawal is to be justified. Upon withdrawing from a case after a retainer has been paid, the attorney should refund such part of the retainer as has not been clearly earned.

ABA Model Code of Professional Responsibility: Compare DR 2-109(A), DR 2-110(A), DR 2-110(B), and DR 2-110(C) (reprinted later in this volume).

Cross-References in Other Rules

Rule 1.2, Comment 2: When a lawyer and client disagree, the "lawyer should also consult with the client and seek a mutually acceptable resolution of the disagreement. If such efforts are unavailing and the lawyer has a fundamental disagreement with the client, the lawyer may withdraw from the representation. See **Rule 1.16(b)(4)**. Conversely, the client may resolve the disagreement by discharging the lawyer. See **Rule 1.16(a)(3)**."

Rule 1.2, Comment 10: "A lawyer may not continue assisting a client in conduct that the lawyer originally supposed was legally proper but then discovers is criminal or fraudulent. The lawyer must, therefore, withdraw from the representation of the client in the matter. See **Rule 1.16(a)**."

Rule 1.3, Comment 4: "Unless the relationship is terminated as provided in **Rule 1.16,** a lawyer should carry through to conclusion all matters undertaken for a client."

Rule 1.5, Comment 4: "A lawyer may require advance payment of a fee, but is obliged to return any unearned portion. See **Rule 1.16(d)**."

Rule 1.6, Comment 7: "See also **Rule 1.16** with respect to the lawyer's obligation or right to withdraw from the representation of the client in such circumstances. . . ."

Rule 1.7, Comment 4: "If a conflict arises after representation has been undertaken, the lawyer ordinarily must withdraw from the representation, unless the lawyer has obtained the informed consent of the client under the conditions of paragraph (b). See **Rule 1.16**."

Rule 1.7, Comment 5: When unforeseeable circumstances create conflicts the "lawyer must seek court approval where necessary and take steps to minimize harm to the clients. See **Rule 1.16**."

Rule 1.7, Comment 33: Each client in the common representation "has the right to discharge the lawyer as stated in **Rule 1.16**."

Rule 1.13, Comment 6: When a lawyer's services are being used to further a crime or fraud, Rule 1.6 may permit the lawyer to reveal confidential information and Rule 1.2(d) may also be applicable, "in which event, withdrawal from the representation under **Rule 1.16(a)(1)** may be required."

Rule 1.13, Comment 6: "[T]his Rule does not limit or expand the lawyer's responsibility under Rule 1.8, **1.16**, 3.3 or 4.1."

Rule 1.17, Comment 12: "If approval of the substitution of the purchasing lawyer for the selling lawyer is required by the rules of any tribunal in which a matter is pending, such approval must be obtained before the matter can be included in the sale (see **Rule 1.16**)."

Rule 3.3, Comment 15: "The lawyer may . . . be required by **Rule 1.16(a)** to seek permission of the tribunal to withdraw if the lawyer's compliance with this Rule's duty of candor results in such an extreme deterioration of the client-lawyer relationship that the lawyer can no longer competently represent the client. Also see **Rule 1.16(b)** for the circumstances in which a lawyer will be permitted to seek a tribunal's permission to withdraw."

Legislative History of Model Rule 1.16

1980 Discussion Draft: Rule 1.16(b) provided:

> (b) Except as stated in paragraph (c), a lawyer may withdraw from representing a client if:
>> (1) Withdrawal can be effected without material prejudice to the client;
>> (2) The client persists in a course of conduct that is illegal or unjust; or
>> (3) The client fails to fulfill an obligation to the lawyer regarding the lawyer's services.

1981 and *1982 Drafts* were substantially the same as adopted.

1983 Rule: From its original adoption in 1983 until its amendment in 2002, Rule 1.16 was nearly the same as the 2002 version. Only two provisions differed in any substantive way from the 2002 version. The 1983 counterpart to the 2002 version of Rule 1.16(b)(4) permitted withdrawal if "a client insists upon pursuing an objective that the lawyer considers repugnant or imprudent," and the 1983 version of Rule 1.16(c) provided simply: "When ordered to do so by a tribunal, a lawyer shall continue representation notwithstanding good cause for terminating the representation," which is identical to the second sentence of the 2002 version.

2002 Amendments: At its February 2002 Mid-Year Meeting, the ABA House of Delegates adopted without change the ABA Ethics 2000 Commission proposal to amend Rule 1.16 and its Comment. The most significant change was the deletion in Rule 1.16(b)(4) of the word "imprudent." A lawyer may no longer withdraw or seek permission to withdraw because the client wishes to pursue a course of action the lawyer considers merely "imprudent."

Selected State Variations

Arizona: Rule 1.16(d) adds that "upon the client's request, the lawyer shall provide the client with all of the client's documents, and all documents reflecting work performed for the client. The lawyer may retain documents reflecting work performed for the client to the extent permitted by other law only if retaining them would not prejudice the client's rights."

California: Rule 3-700 allows a lawyer to withdraw if a client "by other conduct renders it unreasonably difficult for the member to carry out the employment effectively" or if the client "breaches an agreement or obligation to the member as to expenses or fees." A lawyer may also withdraw if the "inability to work with co-counsel indicates that the best interests of the client likely will be served by withdrawal."

Connecticut: Connecticut adds the following sentence at the end of Rule 1.16(d): "If the representation of the client is terminated either by the lawyer withdrawing from representation or by the client discharging the lawyer, the lawyer shall confirm the termination in writing to the client before or within a reasonable time after the termination of the representation."

Florida: In Rule 1.16(a), Florida also requires withdrawal if:

> (4) the client persists in a course of action involving the lawyer's services that the lawyer reasonably believes is criminal or fraudulent, unless the client agrees to disclose and rectify the crime or fraud; or
> (5) the client has used the lawyer's services to perpetrate a crime or fraud, unless the client agrees to disclose and rectify the crime or fraud.

Florida Rule 1.16(b)(2) adds that a lawyer may withdraw if the client insists upon taking action that the lawyer considers "imprudent." Rule 1.16(d) provides that, upon termination, a lawyer may retain papers "and other property relating to or belonging to the client" to the extent permitted by law.

Florida also adds Rule 4-5.8, which has no Model Rule counterpart. The rule governs a lawyer's communications to clients when the lawyer ceases to represent a client as a result of the lawyer's departure from a law firm.

Louisiana: Rule 1.16(d) adds the following:

> Upon written request by the client, the lawyer shall promptly release to the client or the client's new lawyer the entire file relating to the matter. The lawyer may retain a copy of the file but shall not condition release over issues relating to the expense of copying the file or for any other reason. The responsibility for the cost of copying shall be determined in an appropriate proceeding.

Maryland: Rule 1.16(b)(4) permits withdrawal if the client insists upon taking action "or inaction" that the lawyer considers repugnant.

Massachusetts: Rule 1.16(e) provides as follows:

> A lawyer must make available to a former client, within a reasonable time following the client's request for his or her file, the following:
>
> all papers, documents, and other materials the client supplied to the lawyer. The lawyer may at his or her own expense retain copies of any such materials.
>
> all pleadings and other papers filed with or by the court or served by or upon any party. The client may be required to pay any copying charge consistent with the lawyer's actual cost for these materials, unless the client has already paid for such materials.
>
> all investigatory or discovery documents for which the client has paid the lawyer's out-of-pocket costs, including but not limited to medical records, photographs, tapes, disks, investigative reports, expert reports, depositions, and demonstrative evidence. The lawyer may at his or her own expense retain copies of any such materials.
>
> if the lawyer and the client have not entered into a contingent fee agreement, the client is entitled only to that portion of the lawyer's work product (as defined in subparagraph (6) below) for which the client has paid.
>
> if the lawyer and the client have entered into a contingent fee agreement, the lawyer must provide copies of the lawyer's work product (as defined in subparagraph (6) below). The client may be required to pay any copying charge consistent with the lawyer's actual cost for the copying of these materials.
>
> for purposes of this paragraph (e), work product shall consist of documents and tangible things prepared in the course of the representation of the client by the lawyer or at the lawyer's direction by his or her employee, agent, or consultant, and not described in paragraphs (2) or (3) above. Examples of work product include without limitation legal research, records of witness interviews, reports of negotiations, and correspondence.
>
> notwithstanding anything in this paragraph (e) to the contrary, a lawyer may not refuse, on grounds of nonpayment, to make available materials in the client's file when retention would prejudice the client unfairly.

Minnesota deletes the last sentence of Rule 1.16(d) ("The lawyer may retain papers relating to the client to the extent permitted by other law") and adds a detailed set of rules regarding a client's right to documents.

Missouri: Rule 1.16(c) provides that, when a lawyer has filed a limited appearance pursuant to Missouri's version of Rule 1.2(c), the lawyer is not subject to the usual rule regarding termination of representation. Rule 1.16(c) provides as follows:

> A lawyer must comply with applicable law requiring notice to or permission of a tribunal when terminating a representation unless the lawyer has filed a notice of termination of limited appearance. Except when such notice is filed, a lawyer shall continue representation when ordered to do so by a tribunal notwithstanding good cause for terminating the representation.

New Hampshire: New Hampshire makes the protective steps in Rule 1.16(d) a "condition" to terminating a representation.

New York: Rule 1.16(a) and (b) is substantially similar to DR 2-109 and 2-110(B) of the old Model Code, respectively. Rule 1.16(c) adds numerous bases for discretionary withdrawals, which are drawn nearly verbatim from DR 2-110(C) of the old Model Code. Finally, Rule 1.16(d) specifies that, "if permission for withdrawal from employment is required by the rules of a tribunal, a lawyer shall not withdraw from employment in a matter before that tribunal without its permission."

North Carolina: Rule 1.16(b)(4) retains the word "imprudent" and permits withdrawal if the client insists upon taking action "contrary to the advice and judgment of the lawyer. . . ." North Carolina also adds Rule 1.16(b)(8), which permits withdrawal if "the client insists upon presenting a claim or defense that is not warranted under existing law and cannot be supported by good faith argument for an extension, modification, or reversal of existing law."

Texas: Rule 1.15(d) permits a lawyer to retain papers relating to the client to the extent permitted by other law "only if such retention will not prejudice the client in the subject matter of the representation."

Virginia: Rule 1.16(b)(1) replaces "criminal or fraudulent" with "illegal or unjust." Rule 1.16(e) specifies in detail the papers to which a client is entitled after a lawyer withdraws and whether the client or the lawyer must bear the cost of duplication. The client's entitlement does not depend upon "whether or not the client has paid the fees and costs owed a lawyer."

Related Materials

ABA Formal Ethics Opinions: See ABA Formal Ethics Ops. 92-366 (1992), 93-376 (1993), 94-380 (1994), 94-384 (1994), 96-399 (1996), 96-400 (1996), 96-404 (1996), 99-414 (1999), 00-418 n.33 (2000), 03-429 (2003), 03-431 (2003), 06-441 (2006), 07-448 (2007), and 08-450 (2008).

Collaborative Law: The collaborative dispute resolution process (commonly known as "collaborative law") is a voluntary, non-adversarial dispute resolution process for parties represented by counsel. In the collaborative law process, the parties and their attorneys agree in advance to retain attorneys solely to negotiate a settlement, not to litigate. If either party ignores the agreement and goes to court, the attorneys must resign from the case. These terms are usually embodied in a "Participation Agreement" providing that if the parties are unable to reach a settlement, the lawyers will withdraw from the case and assist the clients in transitioning the case to trial attorneys. For more information, see the website of the Global Collaborative Law Council at *http://www.collaborativelaw.us/process.html.*

Model Rules of Professional Conduct for Federal Lawyers: Rule 1.16(c) provides: "When properly ordered to do so by a tribunal or other competent authority, a Federal lawyer shall continue representation notwithstanding good cause for terminating the representation."

Restatement of the Law Governing Lawyers: See Restatement §§31-33, 40, and 46 in our chapter on the Restatement later in this volume.

Rule 1.17   Sale of Law Practice

Canon and Code Antecedents

ABA Canons of Professional Ethics: No comparable Canon.

ABA Model Code of Professional Responsibility: No comparable Disciplinary Rule, but EC 4-6 provided that "a lawyer should not attempt to sell a law practice as a going business because . . . to do so would involve the disclosure of confidences and secrets."

Cross-References in Other Rules

Rule 1.6, Comment 13: "Paragraph (b)(7) recognizes that lawyers in different firms may need to disclose limited information to each other to detect and resolve conflicts of interest, such as when a lawyer is considering an association with another firm, two or more firms are considering a merger, or a lawyer is considering the purchase of a law practice. See **Rule 1.17**, Comment 7."

Rule 5.4(a)(2) provides that "a lawyer who purchases the practice of a deceased, disabled, or disappeared lawyer may, pursuant to the provisions of **Rule 1.17**, pay to the estate or other representative of that lawyer the agreed-upon purchase price."

Rule 5.6, Comment 3: "This Rule does not apply to prohibit restrictions that may be included in the terms of the sale of a law practice pursuant to **Rule 1.17**."

Rule 7.2(b)(3) permits a lawyer to "pay for a law practice in accordance with **Rule 1.17**."

Legislative History of Model Rule 1.17

1990 Adoption: Rule 1.17 was adopted by the ABA House of Delegates in 1990. It was not proposed in any form in Kutak Commission drafts and was not part of the ABA Model Rules until 1990. As originally adopted, the unnumbered introductory language at the beginning of Rule 1.17 permitted the purchase or sale only of "a law practice," meaning that only an entire law practice could be bought or sold. In addition, Rule 1.17(d) as originally adopted provided that the purchaser may "refuse to undertake the representation unless the client consents to pay the purchaser fees at a rate not exceeding the fees charged by the purchaser for rendering substantially similar services prior to the initiation of the purchase negotiations."

The proposal to add Rule 1.17 to the Model Rules was initiated by the State Bar of California, based on California Rule 2-300, and was joined by the ABA Section of General Practice and the ABA Section of Law Practice Management. The

Committee Report submitted to the House of Delegates in support of Rule 1.17 explained the Rule as follows:*

Impetus for Formulation of the Rule

Protection of Clients

[California] Rule of Professional Conduct 2-300 and proposed Model Rule 1.17 are consumer protection measures designed to address the disparity between the treatment of the clients of sole practitioners and the clients of law firms when the attorney handling the client matter leaves the practice, by ensuring that the client matters handled by sole practitioners are attended to when the sole practitioner leaves the practice.

If the attorney leaving the practice is or was part of a law firm, in most cases, the firm continues to handle the matter. In the majority of situations, the transition for the client is very smooth. However, if the attorney was in sole practice, the transition is not so smooth because there is no law firm standing ready to continue to handle the client matter. The clients of sole practitioners who leave the practice of law are relatively unprotected because there are no regulations in place to protect them during the transition.

Sole Practitioners in Unfair Financial Position

In addition to the issues of the client protection, sole practitioners are in an unfair financial position concerning the "good will" of their law practice. The "good will" of a business is "the expectation of continued public patronage." . . . Attorneys, like other business persons, may sell the physical assets of their law practice, such as equipment, the library or the furniture. However, case authority and ethics opinions held that the sale of "good will" of a law practice is unethical and against public policy. . . .

Treatment of "good will" in other contexts presents a mixed picture. For example, attorneys who are members of firms with two or more members may ethically enter into retirement agreements which may require lump sum payments that implicitly include sums for the attorney's share of the firm's "good will."

The estate of a deceased attorney may receive payments from the attorney who completes the unfinished client matters of the deceased attorney. However, in the absence of a rule like that which is being proposed, the payments are limited to the "proportion of the total compensation which fairly represents the services rendered by the deceased member" and thus do not permit an allowance for "good will." . . .

In marital dissolution proceedings, the "good will" of the attorney-spouse's share in his or her law practice may be valued for the purpose of determining the community or other divisible assets.

This inconsistent treatment of "good will" resulted in a series of awkward results: the estate of a sole practitioner could not receive payment for the "good will" of the law practice, while the estate of an attorney who was a member of a law firm could; upon retirement, an attorney who was a member of a law firm could receive compensation including "good will", while the compensation received by a sole practitioner could not include "good will"; the "good will" of a sole practice may be considered an asset of the marital community for purposes of a dissolution, but could not be sold.

2002 Amendments: In 2002, the ABA House of Delegates adopted with some changes the ABA Ethics 2000 Commission proposal to amend Rule 1.17 and its

---

* Committee Reports do not represent official policy of the ABA. They are for information only, and the opinions are those of the authors of the report.

Comment. The proposal as drafted would have allowed the sale only of an "entire practice," but the House of Delegates voted also to allow the sale of "an area of practice." However, the House of Delegates approved the Ethics 2000 Commission proposal to delete language from subparagraph (d) that had permitted a purchaser to refuse to undertake a representation "unless the client consents to pay the purchaser fees at a rate not exceeding the fees charged by the purchaser for rendering substantially similar services prior to the initiation of the purchase negotiations." The amendments also added Comment 5 and amended Comments 1, 2, 4, 6, 9, and 15 to reflect the new right to sell "an area of practice," and deleted most of former Comment 9 and all of former Comment 10, which had provided as follows:

> [9] . . . The purchaser may, however, advise the client that the purchaser will not undertake the representation unless the client consents to pay the higher fees the purchaser usually charges. To prevent client financing of the sale, the higher fee the purchaser may charge must not exceed the fees charged by the purchaser for substantially similar service rendered prior to the initiation of the purchase negotiations.
>
> [10] The purchaser may not intentionally fragment the practice which is the subject of the sale by charging significantly different fees in substantially similar matters. Doing so would make it possible for the purchaser to avoid the obligation to take over the entire practice by charging arbitrarily higher fees for less lucrative matters, thereby increasing the likelihood that those clients would not consent to the new representation.

2012 Amendments: In August 2012, the ABA House of Delegates adopted without change a proposal by the ABA Commission on Ethics 20/20 to amend Comment 7 to Rule 1.17. The change ensured that the Comment was consistent with the approach to conflicts detection set out in newly created Rule 1.6(b)(7). (For more information, see the Legislative History after Rule 1.6 above.)

Selected State Variations

Arkansas adds Rule 1.17(e), which requires the seller to file a detailed and timely affidavit with the Committee on Professional Conduct showing that the seller has complied with the notice provisions of Rule 1.17.

California: Rule 2-300, using different language, addresses the same policy issues as Rule 1.17 and provides that "fees shall not be increased solely by reason of" the sale. "All or substantially all" of a practice may be sold.

Colorado: Rule 1.17(a) is satisfied only if the seller ceases to engage in the private practice of law "in Colorado," or in the area of practice "in Colorado" that has been sold.

Florida omits the requirement in ABA Model Rule 1.17(a) that the seller cease practicing law, and adds or modifies several provisions, including the following:

> (c) *Court Approval Required.* If a representation involves pending litigation, there shall be no substitution of counsel or termination of representation unless authorized by the court. . . .
>
> (d) *Client Objections.* If a client objects to the proposed substitution of counsel, the seller shall comply with the requirements of rule 4-1.16(d) [which governs withdrawal]. . . .
>
> (e) *Existing Fee Contracts Controlling.* The purchaser shall honor the fee agreements that were entered into between the seller and the seller's clients. The fees charged clients shall not be increased by reason of the sale.

Florida's Comment to subparagraph (f) provides as follows:

> The sale may not be financed by increases in fees charged the clients of the practice. Existing agreements between the seller and the client as to fees and the scope of the work must be honored by the purchaser. This obligation of the purchaser is a factor that can be taken into account by seller and purchaser when negotiating the sale price of the practice.

Georgia: Rule 1.17 tracks the 1990 version of ABA Model Rule 1.17 verbatim except that Georgia deletes paragraph (a) (requiring that the seller stop practicing law).

Illinois: Rule 1.17 also applies to "the estate of a deceased lawyer or the guardian or authorized representative of a disabled lawyer. . . ."

Kansas: Kansas omits ABA Model Rule 1.17 entirely.

Maryland: Rule 1.17 differs significantly from ABA Model Rule 1.17. Maryland Rule 1.17(a)(1) permits the sale of a law practice, upon appropriate notice, if "(1) Except in the case of death, disability, or appointment of the seller to judicial office, the entire practice that is the subject of the sale has been in existence at least five years prior to the date of sale" and "(2) The practice is sold as an entirety to another lawyer or law firm."

Michigan: Rule 1.17(a) provides that a "lawyer or a law firm may sell or purchase a private law practice, including good will, according to this rule." Michigan adds Rule 1.17(e), which permits the "sale of the good will of a law practice . . . conditioned upon the seller ceasing to engage in the private practice of law for a reasonable period of time within the geographical area in which the practice has been conducted."

Minnesota: Rule 1.17(b), which is based on the 1990 version of ABA Model Rule 1.17, provides as follows:

> (b) The buying lawyer or firm of lawyers shall not increase the fees charged to clients by reason of the sale for a period of at least one year from the date of the sale. The buying lawyer or firm of lawyers shall honor all existing fee agreements for at least one year from the date of the sale and shall continue to completion, on the same terms agreed to by the selling lawyer and the client, any matters that the selling lawyer has agreed to do on a pro bono publico basis or for a reduced fee.

Rule 1.17(d) provides that the notice to clients must include a "summary of the buying lawyer's or law firm's professional background, including education and experience and the length of time that the buyer lawyer or members of the buying law firm has been in practice." Minnesota also adds four paragraphs, including Rule 1.17(f), which permits the selling lawyer to promise that he or she "will not engage in the practice of law for a reasonable period of time within a reasonable geographic area and will not advertise for or solicit clients within that area for that time," and Rule 1.17(g), which provides that the selling lawyer "shall retain responsibility for the proper management and disposition of all inactive files that are not transferred as part of the sale of the law practice."

Missouri: Rule 1.17(d) adopts the ABA mandate that fees charged to clients shall not be increased by reason of the sale of the practice, but adds that the purchaser may "refuse to undertake the representation unless the client consents to pay the purchaser fees at a rate not exceeding the fees charged by the purchaser for rendering substantially similar services prior to the initiation of the purchase negotiations."

New Jersey: Rule 1.17 permits a lawyer or firm to sell or purchase a law practice, including goodwill, if the seller is ceasing to engage in private law practice in New Jersey, the practice is sold as an entirety and certain notices are given to the clients of the seller and by publication in the New Jersey Law Journal and the New Jersey Lawyer at least 30 days in advance of the sale.

New York: Rule 1.17 allows for the sale of a "law practice, including goodwill, to one or more lawyers or law firms." The parties may agree "on reasonable restrictions on the seller's private practice of law." Provisions are made for protecting confidential information and checking for conflicts.

North Carolina: Rule 1.17(d) provides that if a conflict of interest disqualifies the purchaser from representing a client, then "the seller's notice to the client shall advise the client to retain substitute counsel." In addition, Rule 1.17(g) permits the purchaser to pay the seller in installments — but the seller "shall have no say regarding the purchaser's conduct of the law practice."

Ohio: Rule 1.17 incorporates most of the substantive provisions of the Model Rule, but uses different language and adds many different provisions. For example, Ohio Rule 1.17(a) requires that a law practice must be sold "in its entirety, except where a conflict of interest is present that prevents the transfer of representation of a client or class of clients." In addition, Rule 1.17(a) prohibits the sale or purchase of a law practice "where the purchasing lawyer is buying the practice for the sole or primary purpose of reselling the practice to another lawyer or law firm," and Rule 1.17(d)(1) requires the sale agreement to include a statement that "the purchasing lawyer is purchasing the law practice in good faith and with the intention of delivering legal services to clients of the selling lawyer and others in need of legal services."

Ohio Rule 1.17(d)(2) requires the sale agreement to provide that "the purchasing lawyer will honor any fee agreements between the selling lawyer and the clients of the selling lawyer relative to legal representation that is ongoing at the time of the sale," but the purchasing lawyer "may negotiate fees with clients of the selling lawyer for legal representation that is commenced after the date of the sale." Rule 1.17(d)(3) generally permits the sale agreement to include terms that "reasonably limit the ability of the selling lawyer to reenter the practice of law," but prohibits such limitations "if the selling lawyer is selling his or her law practice to enter academic, government, or public service or to serve as in-house counsel to a business."

Ohio Rule 1.17(e) specifies in considerable detail what the notice to clients must contain, and a Rule 1.17(g) allows the selling lawyer and purchasing lawyer to give notice of the sale to a missing client by publishing notice of the sale in a newspaper. A Rule 1.17(i) provides as follows:

> (i) Neither the selling lawyer nor the purchasing lawyer shall attempt to exonerate the lawyer or law firm from or limit liability to the former or prospective client for any malpractice or other professional negligence. The provisions of Rule 1.8(h) shall be incorporated in all agreements for the sale or purchase of a law practice. The selling lawyer or the purchasing lawyer, or both, may agree to provide for the indemnification or other contribution arising from any claim or action in malpractice or other professional negligence.

Oklahoma: Rule 1.17(a) requires the selling lawyer to cease practice only "in the geographic area in Oklahoma in which the practice has been conducted," not in the entire state. Rule 1.17(b)(2) provides that matters shall not be transferred to a purchaser "unless the seller has reasonable basis to believe that the purchaser has the requisite knowledge and skill to handle such matters, or reasonable assurances are obtained that such purchaser will either acquire such knowledge and skill or associate with another lawyer having such competence." Rule 1.17(c) requires the "signed written consent of each client whose representation is proposed to be transferred" unless the client takes no action within 90 days of the notice. Rule 1.17(d) permits the purchaser to "refuse to undertake the representation unless the client consents to pay the purchaser fees at a rate not exceeding the fees charged by the purchaser for rendering substantially similar services prior to the initiation of the purchase negotiations."

Pennsylvania: Rule 1.17 differs significantly from ABA Model Rule 1.17. For example, Pennsylvania Rule 1.17(b) requires that the seller must sell the practice "as an entirety to a single lawyer," and explains that a practice is sold as an entirety "if the purchasing lawyer assumes responsibility for all of the active files" except those specified in Rule 1.17(g). Rule 1.17(d) adds the following: "Existing agreements between the seller and the client concerning fees and the scope of work must be honored by the purchaser, unless the client gives informed consent confirmed in writing." Pennsylvania also adds Rules 1.17(e) and (g), which provide as follows:

> (e) The agreement of sale shall include a clear statement of the respective responsibilities of the parties to maintain and preserve the records and files of the seller's practice, including client files.
> (g) The sale shall not be effective as to any client for whom the proposed sale would create a conflict of interest for the purchaser or who cannot be represented by the purchaser because of other requirements of the Pennsylvania Rules of Professional Conduct or rules of the Pennsylvania Supreme Court governing the practice of law in Pennsylvania, unless such conflict, requirement or rule can be waived by the client and the client gives informed consent.

Virginia requires the selling lawyer, when notifying clients about the proposed sale, to disclose "any proposed change in the terms of the future representation including the fee arrangement."

ABA Formal Ethics Opinions: No formal ethics opinions have construed Rule 1.17.

Restatement of the Law Governing Lawyers: The Restatement has no provision comparable to ABA Model Rule 1.17.

Rule 1.18   Duties to Prospective Client

Cross-References in Other Rules

Scope, ¶17: "Most of the duties flowing from the client-lawyer relationship attach only after the client has requested the lawyer to render legal services and the lawyer has agreed to do so. But there are some duties, such as that of confidentiality under Rule 1.6, that attach when the lawyer agrees to consider whether a client-lawyer relationship shall be established. See **Rule 1.18**."

Rule 1.0, Comment 8: The definition of "screened" "applies to situations where screening of a personally disqualified lawyer is permitted to remove imputation of a conflict of interest under Rules 1.11, 1.12 or **1.18**."

Rule 1.6, Comment 1: Regarding disclosure: "See **Rule 1.18** for the lawyer's duties with respect to information provided to the lawyer by a prospective client."

Rule 1.7, Comment 1: "For conflicts of interest involving prospective clients, see **Rule 1.18.**"

Legislative History of Model Rule 1.18

2002 Adoption: Rule 1.18 was added to the Model Rules in February 2002. No equivalent rule was proposed in the Kutak Commission drafts or contained in the Model Rules before 2002. The new rule and its Comment were based on a proposal by the ABA Ethics 2000 Commission, which the ABA House of Delegates adopted without change. The Reporter's Explanation Memo that accompanied the Ethics 2000 Commission proposal provided, in relevant part, as follows:

Model Rule 1.18 — Reporter's Explanation of Changes*

Rule 1.18 is a proposed new Rule in response to the Commission's concern that important events occur in the period during which a lawyer and prospective client are considering whether to form a client-lawyer relationship. For the most part, the current Model Rules do not address that pre-retention period.

Paragraph (a) defines the limited circumstances to which this Rule applies by defining who qualifies as a "prospective client."

Paragraph (b) identifies the duty to treat all communications with a prospective client as confidential. This obligation is a well-settled matter under the law of attorney-client privilege, and the fact that Model Rule 1.9 does not now technically cover these communications is an omission that this proposal corrects.

Paragraph (c) extends the application of Rule 1.9 to prohibit representation adverse to the prospective client in the same or a substantially related matter. Unlike Rule 1.9, however, this Rule does so only if the lawyer received information from the prospective client that could be "significantly harmful" to that person in the later representation.

The prospective client situation justifies that different treatment because, prior to the representation decision, there is an inevitable period in which it is in the interest of the prospective client to share enough information with the lawyer to determine whether there is a conflict of interest or simple incompatibility. The lawyer may learn very early in the consultation, for example, that the party adverse to the prospective client is a client of the lawyer's firm. If the discussion stops before "significantly harmful" information is shared, it seems that the law firm's regular client should not be denied counsel of its choice if a substantially related matter arises. . . .

Paragraph (d) makes clear that the prohibition imposed by this Rule can be waived with the informed consent, confirmed in writing, of both the former prospective client and the client on whose behalf the lawyer later plans to take action adverse to the former prospective client. The expression of this requirement is parallel to that in Rules 1.7 and 1.9.

In the event that "significantly harmful" information is revealed, paragraph (d) provides that the lawyer who received the information may be screened from any involvement in the subsequent matter but others in the law firm may represent the adverse party.

2012 Amendments: In August 2012, the ABA House of Delegates adopted without change proposals by the ABA Commission on Ethics 20/20 that provided lawyers

---

* Committee Reports, and the Reporter's Explanation of Changes contained therein, do not represent official policy of the ABA. They are for information only, and the opinions are those of the authors of the report.

with greater guidance regarding when a prospective client relationship arises as a result of electronic communications with the public. The changes included replacing the word "discusses" in Rule 1.18(a) with the word "consults" and adding substantial new clarifying language in Comment 2.

Selected State Variations

Connecticut: Rule 1.18(a) defines a "prospective client" as a person who discusses "or communicates" with a lawyer concerning the possibility of forming a client-lawyer relationship with respect to a matter.

District of Columbia adopts the essence of Rule 1.18 except that it omits Model Rule 1.18(d)(2) and (2)(ii) while retaining the language in (2)(i).

Florida omits the words "significantly harmful" from paragraph (c), so a lawyer is personally disqualified if he or she received information "that could be used to the disadvantage" of the prospective client.

Illinois: Rule 1.18(d) does not require that a prospective client receive notice when a firm employs a screen to avoid a conflict of interest.

Maryland deletes the introductory language in ABA Model Rule 1.18(d)(2) and all of Rule 1.18(d)(2)(ii). Thus, Maryland Rule 1.18(d) is a single sentence permitting representation if either "both the affected client and the prospective client have given informed consent, confirmed in writing, or the disqualified lawyer is timely screened from any participation in the matter and is apportioned no part of the fee therefrom."

Missouri: Rule 1.18(d)(2) deletes the ABA Model Rule requirements that the lawyer who received the disqualifying information be apportioned no part of the fee and that written notice be promptly given to the prospective client.

Nevada: Nevada adds the following new paragraphs to Rule 1.18:

> (e) A person who communicates information to a lawyer without any reasonable expectation that the lawyer is willing to discuss the possibility of forming a client-lawyer relationship, or for purposes which do not include a good faith intention to retain the lawyer in the subject matter of the consultation, is not a "prospective client" within the meaning of this Rule.

> (f) A lawyer may condition conversations with a prospective client on the person's informed consent that no information disclosed during the consultation will prohibit the lawyer from representing a different client in the matter. If the agreement expressly so provides, the prospective client may also consent to the lawyer's subsequent use of information received from the prospective client.

> (g) Whenever a prospective client shall request information regarding a lawyer or law firm for the purpose of making a decision regarding employment of the lawyer or law firm:

>> (1) The lawyer or law firm shall promptly furnish (by mail if requested) the written information described in Rule 1.4(c).

>> (2) The lawyer or law firm may furnish such additional factual information regarding the lawyer or law firm deemed valuable to assist the client.

>> (3) If the information furnished to the client includes a fee contract, the top of each page of the contract shall be marked "SAMPLE" in red ink in a type size one size larger than the largest type used in the contract and the words "DO NOT SIGN" shall appear on the client signature line.

New York: Rule 1.18(d) describes in more detail the procedures necessary to avoid a conflict as a result of consultations with prospective clients. Comments 7A-7C offer further guidance regarding these procedures. New York adds Rule 1.18(e), which provides (in language copied partly from Comment 2 to Model Rule 1.18) that a "prospective client" does not include a person who "(1) communicates information unilaterally to a lawyer, without any reasonable expectation that the lawyer is willing to discuss the possibility of forming a client-lawyer relationship" or "(2) communicates with a lawyer for the purpose of disqualifying the lawyer. . . ."

North Carolina omits the language in Rule 1.18(d)(2) requiring "reasonable measures to avoid exposure" to unnecessary confidential information. North Carolina does not require that a disqualified lawyer be denied part of the fee.

Oregon omits the language in Rule 1.18(d)(2) requiring "reasonable measures to avoid exposure" to unnecessary confidential information.

South Carolina: Rule 1.18(a) provides that a person with whom a lawyer discusses the possibility of forming a client-lawyer relationship with respect to a matter is a prospective client "only when there is a reasonable expectation that the lawyer is likely to form the relationship."

Vermont: Rule 1.18(a) extends prospective client status only to those people who are "in good faith" seeking to hire that attorney.

Virginia: Virginia includes two additional requirements in Rule 1.18(d). First, the disqualified lawyer must reasonably believe "that the screen would be effective to sufficiently protect information that could be significantly harmful to the prospective client." And second, the written notice to the prospective client must include "a general description of the subject matter about which the lawyer was consulted and the screening procedures employed. . . ."

Related Materials

ABA Formal Ethics Opinions: See ABA Formal Ethics Op. 10-457 (2010).

Restatement of the Law Governing Lawyers: See Restatement §15 in our chapter on the Restatement later in this volume.

ANNOTATIONS ON ARTICLE 2. COUNSELOR

Rule 2.1   Advisor

Canon and Code Antecedents

ABA Canons of Professional Ethics: No comparable Canon.

ABA Model Code of Professional Responsibility: Compare DR 5-107(B) (reprinted later in this volume).

Cross-References in Other Rules

Rule 7.2, Comment 8: "[R]eciprocal referral arrangements must not interfere with the lawyer's professional judgment as to making referrals or as to providing substantive legal services. See Rules 2.1 and 5.4(c)."

Legislative History of Model Rule 2.1

1980 Discussion Draft: The Introduction to the section entitled "Attorney as Advisor" contained the following paragraph:

> The lawyer's professional function historically originated as attorney and advocate, that is, appearing on behalf of a party to litigation. Giving legal advice evolved from giving advice about how to proceed in litigation. Today, serving as advisor is the lawyer's predominant role.

Rule 2.1 provided:

Independence and Candor

> In advising a client a lawyer shall exercise independent and candid professional judgment, uncontrolled by the interests or wishes of a third person, or by the lawyer's own interests or wishes.

In addition, Rule 2.2 (now incorporated into Rule 2.1) provided:

Scope of Advice

> In rendering advice a lawyer may refer to all relevant considerations unless in the circumstances it is evident that the client desires advice confined to strictly legal considerations.

1981 and ***1982 Drafts*** were the same as adopted.

1983 Rule: As originally adopted in 1983, Rule 2.1 was the same as the 2002 version.

2002 Amendments: At its February 2002 Mid-Year Meeting, the ABA House of Delegates adopted with only minor changes the ABA Ethics 2000 Commission proposal to amend the Comment to Rule 2.1. (The Ethics 2000 Commission did not propose any changes to the text of Rule 2.1.) The amendment added a sentence to Comment 5 to the effect that Rule 1.4 may require a lawyer representing a client in litigation to inform the client of other forms of dispute resolution.

Selected State Variations

California has no direct counterpart to Rule 2.1.

Colorado adds the following sentence at the end of Rule 2.1: "In a matter involving or expected to involve litigation, a lawyer should advise the client of alternative forms of dispute resolution that might reasonably be pursued to attempt to resolve the legal dispute or to reach the legal objective sought."

Georgia moves the second sentence of the ABA rule to a Comment, and adds the following sentence to the text of the rule in its place: "A lawyer should not be deterred from giving candid advice by the prospect that the advice will be unpalatable to the client."

New York: Rule 2.1 adds the word "psychological," after "moral, economic, social" but is otherwise the same as the Model Rule.

Texas: Rule 2.01 begins, "In advising or otherwise representing a client . . . ," and deletes the second sentence of ABA Model Rule 2.1.

Related Materials

ABA Formal Ethics Opinions: See ABA Formal Ethics Op. 92-364 (1992), 94-389 (1994), and 00-418 (2000).

Restatement of the Law Governing Lawyers: See Restatement §94(3) in our chapter on the Restatement later in this volume.

<h1>Rule 2.2   Intermediary</h1>

Editors' Note.   Rule 2.2 was deleted from the ABA Model Rules of Professional Conduct in 2002—see Legislative History below.

<h3>Canon and Code Antecedents</h3>

ABA Canons of Professional Ethics: No comparable Canon.

ABA Model Code of Professional Responsibility: Compare DR 5-105(B) and DR 5-105(C) (reprinted later in this volume).

<h3>Cross-References in Other Rules</h3>

None.

<h3>Legislative History of Model Rule 2.2</h3>

1980 Discussion Draft (then Rules 5.1 and 5.2) began with the following Introduction:

> A lawyer acts as intermediary in seeking to establish or adjust a relationship between clients on an amicable and mutually advantageous basis. . . .
>
> . . . In some nonlitigation situations, the stakes involved may be so modest that separate representation of the parties is financially impractical. Given these factors, all the clients may prefer that the lawyer act as intermediary. . . .
>
> This Rule does not deal with a lawyer acting as mediator or arbitrator between parties with whom the lawyer does not have a client-lawyer relationship, nor does it govern a situation where a lawyer represents a party in negotiation with a party who is unrepresented. A lawyer acts as intermediary under this Rule when the lawyer represents both parties. A key factor in defining the relationship is whether the parties share responsibility for paying the lawyer's fee, but the existence of a joint or common representation can be inferred from other circumstances. Because confusion can arise as to the lawyer's role and responsibility where each party is not separately represented, it is important that the lawyer make clear whom he represents in such situations.

Rules 5.1 and 5.2 of the 1980 Discussion Draft provided:

Conditions for Acting as an Intermediary

> (a) A lawyer may act as an intermediary between clients if:
>
> (1) the possibility of adjusting the clients' interests is strong; and
>
> (2) each client will be able to make adequately informed decisions in the matter, and there is little likelihood that any of the clients will be significantly prejudiced if the contemplated adjustment of interests is unsuccessful; and
>
> (3) the lawyer can act impartially and without improper effect on other services the lawyer is performing for any of the clients; and
>
> (4) the lawyer fully explains to each client the implications of the common representation, including the advantages and risks involved, and obtains each client's consent to the common representation.
>
> (b) Before serving as intermediary a lawyer shall explain fully to each client the decisions to be made and the considerations relevant to making them, so that each client can make adequately informed decisions.

Withdrawal as an Intermediary

A lawyer shall withdraw as intermediary if any of the clients so requests, if the conditions stated in Rule 5.1 cannot be met, or if it becomes apparent that a mutually advantageous adjustment of interests cannot be made. Upon withdrawal, the lawyer may continue to represent any of the clients only to the extent compatible with the lawyer's responsibilities to the other client or clients.

1981 Draft: Rule 2.2(c) required a lawyer to withdraw if the conditions in (a) could not be met "or if in the light of subsequent events the lawyer reasonably should know that a mutually advantageous resolution cannot be achieved."

1982 Draft: Rule 2.2(a)(1) was substantially the same as adopted except that it did not require the lawyer to explain "the effect on the attorney-client privileges." Rule 2.2(c)'s second sentence provided: "Upon withdrawal, the lawyer shall not continue to represent any of the clients unless doing so is clearly compatible with the lawyer's responsibilities to the other client or clients." The remainder of Rule 2.2 was substantially the same as adopted.

1983 Rule: From the original adoption of the ABA Model Rules of Professional Conduct in 1983 until Rule 2.2 was deleted in 2002, Rule 2.2 provided as follows:

Rule 2.2   Intermediary

(a) A lawyer may act as an intermediary between clients if:

(1) the lawyer consults with each client concerning the implications of the common representation, including the advantages and risks involved, and the effect on the attorney-client privileges, and obtains each client's consent to the common representation;

(2) the lawyer reasonably believes that the matter can be resolved on terms compatible with the clients' best interests, that each client will be able to make adequately informed decisions in the matter and that there is little risk of material prejudice to the interests of any of the clients if the contemplated resolution is unsuccessful; and

(3) the lawyer reasonably believes that the common representation can be undertaken impartially and without improper effect on other responsibilities the lawyer has to any of the clients.

(b) While acting as intermediary, the lawyer shall consult with each client concerning the decisions to be made and the considerations relevant in making them, so that each client can make adequately informed decisions.

(c) A lawyer shall withdraw as intermediary if any of the clients so requests, or if any of the conditions stated in paragraph (a) is no longer satisfied. Upon withdrawal, the lawyer shall not continue to represent any of the clients in the matter that was the subject of the intermediation.

2002 Deletion: At its February 2002 Mid-Year Meeting, the ABA House of Delegates adopted without change the ABA Ethics 2000 Commission proposal to delete Rule 2.2 and its Comment and to move discussion of common representation to Rule 1.7's Comment. The Reporter's explanation for these changes stated:

[T]he Commission believes that the ideas expressed therein are better dealt with in the Comment to Rule 1.7. There is much in Rule 2.2 and its Comment that applies to all examples of common representation and ought to appear in Rule 1.7. Moreover, there is less resistance to common representation today than there was in 1983; thus, there is no longer any particular need to establish the propriety of common representation through a separate Rule.

Selected State Variations

California has no direct counterpart to ABA Model Rule 2.2.

Georgia: Rule 2.2 differs significantly from former ABA Model Rule 2.2. Essentially, Georgia has adopted only Rule 2.2(c), moving the substance of Rules 2.2(a)(2) and (3) to Comment 6 and deleting ABA Model Rules 2.2(a)(1) and 2.2(b) entirely.

Massachusetts has no equivalent to ABA Model Rule 2.2, but Comments 12 through 12F to Rule 1.7 provide guidance concerning joint representation.

New York omits Model Rule 2.2.

Related Materials

Restatement of the Law Governing Lawyers: The Restatement has no black letter provision directly comparable to former ABA Model Rule 2.2.

Rule 2.3   Evaluation for Use by Third Persons

Canon and Code Antecedents

ABA Canons of Professional Ethics: No comparable Canon.

ABA Model Code of Professional Responsibility: No comparable Disciplinary Rule.

Cross-References in Other Rules

None.

Legislative History of Model Rule 2.3

1980 Discussion Draft (then Rules 6.1 through 6.3):

Confidential Evaluation (Rule 6.1)

A lawyer undertakes a confidential evaluation of a matter affecting a client when a report of the evaluation is to be given to the client alone and to be disclosed to others only at the direction of the client.

Independent Evaluation (Rule 6.2)

(a) A lawyer undertakes an independent evaluation of a matter affecting a client when a report of the evaluation is to be given to someone other than the client. A lawyer may make an independent evaluation if:

(1) Making the evaluation is compatible with other aspects of the lawyer's relationship with the client; and

(2) The terms upon which the evaluation is made are clearly described, particularly the lawyer's access to information and the persons to whom the report of the evaluation is to be made; and

(3) The client agrees that the lawyer may, within the terms upon which the evaluation is made, disclose information about the client, including matter otherwise confidential or privileged, that the lawyer determines ought to be disclosed in making a fair and accurate evaluation; and

(4) After adequate disclosure of the terms upon which the evaluation is to be made and their implications for the client, the client requests the lawyer to make the evaluation.

(b) In reporting the evaluation, the lawyer shall indicate any limitations on the scope of the inquiry that are reasonably necessary to a proper interpretation of the report.

(c) If, after a lawyer has commenced an independent evaluation, the client refuses to comply with the terms upon which it is to be made, the lawyer shall give to the person for whom the evaluation is intended the fullest report that can be made in the circumstances.

(d) Except as disclosure is required in connection with a report of the evaluation, information relating to an independent evaluation is confidential under Rule 1.7.

Financial Auditors' Requests for Information (Rule 6.3)

When a question concerning the legal situation of a client arises at the instance of the client's financial auditor and the question is referred to the lawyer, the lawyer's response shall be made in accordance with procedures recognized in the legal profession unless some other procedure is established after consent by the client upon adequate disclosure.

1981 Draft: Rule 2.3(a)(2) provided:

the terms upon which the evaluation is to be made are stated in writing, particularly the terms relating to the lawyer's access to information, the contemplated disclosure of otherwise confidential information and the persons to whom report of the evaluation is to be made. . . .

Rule 2.3(b) provided: "In reporting the evaluation, the lawyer shall indicate any material limitations that were imposed on the scope of the inquiry or on the disclosure of information."

1982 Draft: Rule 2.3(a)(2) required that "the conditions of the evaluation [be] described to the client in writing, including contemplated disclosure of information otherwise protected by Rule 1.6. . . ."

1983 Rule: As originally adopted in 1983, Rule 2.3 provided as follows:

(a) A lawyer may undertake an evaluation of a matter affecting a client for the use of someone other than the client if:

(1) the lawyer reasonably believes that making the evaluation is compatible with other aspects of the lawyer's relationship with the client; and

(2) the client consents after consultation.

(b) Except as disclosure is required in connection with a report of an evaluation, information relating to the evaluation is otherwise protected by Rule 1.6.

2002 Amendments: At its February 2002 Mid-Year Meeting, the ABA House of Delegates adopted without change the ABA Ethics 2000 Commission proposal to amend Rule 2.3 and its Comment. The amendments added Rule 2.3(b), deleted former Comment 2, added Comment 5, and made minor changes elsewhere in the Rule and Comment.

Selected State Variations

California has no direct counterpart to ABA Model Rule 2.3.

Florida adds the following subparagraph: "*Limitation on Scope of Evaluation.* In reporting the evaluation, the lawyer shall indicate any material limitations that were imposed on the scope of the inquiry or on the disclosure of information."

Georgia: In the rules effective November 3, 2011, Rule 2.3(a) requires a lawyer to obtain the client's informed consent before undertaking an evaluation for someone other than the client, even if the lawyer has no reason to believe that the evaluation will adversely affect the client.

Missouri: Missouri replaces ABA Model Rule 2.3(b) with Rule 2.3(a)(2), which permits a lawyer to undertake an evaluation "if the client consents after consultation."

New Jersey's version of Rule 2.3(b) and (d) provide as follows:

> (b) When the lawyer knows or reasonably should know that the evaluation is likely to affect the client's interests materially and adversely, the lawyer shall not provide the evaluation unless:
> (1) the lawyer describes the conditions of the evaluation to the client, in writing, including disclosure of information otherwise protected by RPC 1.6;
> (2) the lawyer consults with the client; and
> (3) the client gives informed consent. . . .
> (d) In reporting an evaluation, the lawyer shall indicate any material limitations that were imposed on the scope of the inquiry or on the disclosure of information.

Virginia: Rule 2.3(a) provides as follows: "(a) A lawyer acts as evaluator by examining a client's legal affairs and reporting about them to the client or to others." Rule 2.3(b) is substantially the same as ABA Model Rule 2.3(a) but requires client consent after consultation.

Related Materials

ABA Formal Ethics Opinions: See ABA Formal Ethics Op. 00-418 n.30 (2000).

Audit Inquiry Responses: In 1976, the ABA House of Delegates approved a Statement of Policy Regarding Lawyers' Responses to Auditors' Requests for Information (often referred to as the "Treaty" because it resolved a battle between accountants and lawyers). The Statement was drafted by the ABA Section on Business Law's Committee on Audit Inquiry Responses and is available online at *http://apps. americanbar.org/buslaw/attorneyclient/policies/aicpa.pdf.*

Financial Accounting Standards Board (FASB): The Financial Accounting Standards Board (FASB) is a private body whose standards are officially recognized by the Securities and Exchange Commission. FASB standards are important to lawyers who assist companies in preparing financial reports for the benefit of investors and other third parties. In 2007, in response to investor complaints that corporate financial statements do not adequately disclose loss contingencies from pending and potential lawsuits, FASB began a project to improve the rules regarding disclosures of loss contingencies. FASB circulated several proposed new rules, including one requiring companies to disclose management's estimate of the maximum exposure to loss from litigation, but the change was opposed by ABA, the Association of Corporate Counsel, and others, who argued that the new rule would erode the attorney-client privilege. In July of 2012, FASB voted to abandon the project to revise the standards and instead to focus on strengthening enforcement of existing standards.

IRS Regulations: A lawyer issuing an opinion evaluating a tax-shelter transaction must abide by strict IRS regulations, especially 31 C.F.R. §10.35. In that rule, §10.35(b) defines several types of tax opinions. For example, a lawyer's written advice constitutes a "reliance opinion" if the lawyer "concludes at a confidence level of at least more likely than not (a greater than 50 percent likelihood) that one or more significant Federal tax issues would be resolved in the taxpayer's favor."

Written advice is not treated as a "reliance opinion," however, if the lawyer "prominently discloses in the written advice that it was not intended or written by the practitioner to be used, and that it cannot be used by the taxpayer, for the purpose of avoiding penalties that may be imposed on the taxpayer." A "marketed opinion" results if a practitioner "knows or has reason to know that the written advice will be used or referred to by a person other than the practitioner . . . in promoting, marketing or recommending a partnership or other entity, investment plan or arrangement to one or more taxpayer(s)." Section 10.35(d)(1) requires a lawyer who renders certain tax opinions and relies in any way upon the opinion of another lawyer to "identify the other opinion and set forth the conclusions reached."

Legal Opinion Letters: A major area governed by Rule 2.3 is the "legal opinion letter" — a letter issued by a lawyer to a third party (typically a buyer or lender) assuring that the lawyer believes the transaction is legal, the seller is authorized to sell, etc. Banks, opposing parties, and others often rely upon such legal opinion letters, and a satisfactory legal opinion letter from the seller's or borrower's lawyer is often a condition of completing a deal.

The ABA Section of Business Law has developed a Legal Opinion Accord that addresses numerous issues raised by legal opinion letters issued to third parties. The Legal Opinion Accord (sometimes called the "Silverado Accord") is reprinted with commentary in *Third-Party Legal Opinion Report, Including the Legal Opinion Accord, of the Section of Business Law, American Bar Association*, 47 Bus. Law. 167 (1991).

In addition, a group called the TriBar Opinion Committee was formed in 1977 to provide "guidelines and/or forms respecting lawyers' opinions in commercial transactions." (The TriBar Opinion Committee originally consisted of representatives from the New York City Bar, the New York County Lawyers' Association, and the New York State Bar Association. Today, the TriBar Opinion Committee has expanded to include lawyers from Boston, Delaware, Chicago, Ontario, and elsewhere.) TriBar reports have covered third-party "closing" opinions generally, as well as opinion letters in particular areas of practice, such as remedies opinions and opinions on preferred stock. Many TriBar and ABA reports on opinion letters are reprinted in Collected ABA and Tri-Bar Opinion Reports 2009 (ABA Section of Business Law 2009).

For more information about opinion letters, see M. John Sterba, Jr., Editor, Legal Opinion Letters: A Comprehensive Guide to Opinion Letter Practice (3d ed., Aspen Publishers 2003), and Scott T. Fitzgibbon, Donald W. Glazer, & Steven O. Weise, Glazer and Fitzgibbon on Legal Opinions: Drafting, Interpreting, and Supporting Closing Opinions in Business Transactions (3d ed., Aspen Publishers 2008). An excellent online site is the Legal Opinion Resource Center, *http://apps. americanbar.org/buslaw/tribar/*, which features more than a dozen reports on opinion letters from the ABA Business Law Section and the TriBar Committee.

Restatement of the Law Governing Lawyers: See Restatement §§51, 79, 95, and 98 in our chapter on the Restatement later in this volume.

Rule 2.4　Lawyer Serving as Third-Party Neutral

Canon and Code Antecedents

ABA Canons of Professional Ethics: No comparable Canon.
ABA Model Code of Professional Responsibility: No comparable Disciplinary Rule.

Cross-References in Other Rules

Preamble, ¶3: "Some of these Rules apply directly to lawyers who are or have served as third-party neutrals. See, *e.g.*, **Rules** 1.12 and **2.4**."

Rule 1.12, Comment 2: "Other law or codes of ethics governing third-party neutrals may impose more stringent standards of personal or imputed disqualification. See **Rule 2.4**."

Legislative History of Model Rule 2.4

1983 Rule: As originally adopted in 1983, the ABA Model Rules did not contain Rule 2.4.

2002 Amendments: Rule 2.4 was added to the Model Rules in February 2002. The new rule and its Comment were based on a proposal by the ABA Ethics 2000 Commission, which the ABA House of Delegates adopted without change. The Reporter's Explanation Memo that accompanied the Ethics 2000 Commission proposal provided, in relevant part, as follows:

Model Rule 2.4 — Reporter's Explanation of Changes*

The role of third-party neutral is not unique to lawyers, but the Commission recognizes that lawyers are increasingly serving in these roles. Unlike nonlawyers who serve as neutrals, lawyers may experience unique ethical problems, for example, those arising from possible confusion about the nature of the lawyer's role. The Commission notes that there have been a number of attempts by various organizations to promulgate codes of ethics for neutrals (e.g., aspirational codes for arbitrators or mediators or court enacted rules governing court-sponsored mediators), but such codes do not typically address the special problems of lawyers. The Commission's proposed approach is designed to promote dispute resolution parties' understanding of the lawyer-neutral's role.

Paragraph (a) defines the term "third-party neutral" and emphasizes assistance at the request of the parties who participate in the resolution of disputes and other matters.

Paragraph (b) requires the lawyer serving as a third-party neutral to inform unrepresented parties in all cases that the lawyer does not represent them. The potential for confusion is sufficiently great to mandate this requirement in all cases involving unrepresented parties. Consistent with the standard of Rule 4.3, paragraph (b) requires the lawyer to explain the differences in a lawyer's role as a third-party neutral and the role of a lawyer representing a party in situations where the lawyer knows or reasonably should know that the unrepresented party does not understand the lawyer's role as a third-party neutral.

Selected State Variations

Georgia: In the rules effective November 3, 2011, Rule 2.4(c) provides that, "when one or more of the parties in a mediation is a current or former client of the neutral lawyer or the neutral's law firm, a lawyer may serve as a third-party neutral only if the matter in which the lawyer serves as a third-party neutral is not the same matter in which the lawyer or law firm represents or represented the party and all parties give informed consent, confirmed in writing."

* Committee Reports, and the Reporter's Explanation of Changes contained therein, do not represent official policy of the ABA. They are for information only, and the opinions are those of the authors of the report.

Illinois: Rule 2.4(b) requires third-party neutrals to explain to unrepresented parties "the difference between the lawyer's role as a third-party neutral and a lawyer's role as one who represents a client" regardless of whether the lawyer believes the unrepresented parties misunderstand the lawyer's role.

New York: Rule 2.4 is substantially the same as Model Rule 2.4.

South Carolina: Rule 2.4 adds a new subparagraph (c) that permits a lawyer to serve as a neutral only if the lawyer or law firm does not represent (and has not previously represented) any party in the matter.

Tennessee: Rule 2.4 defines the circumstances under which a lawyer may act as a "dispute resolution neutral," the limitations on a lawyer who assumes that position, the circumstances under which the lawyer must withdraw from the position, and the lawyer's responsibilities following withdrawal. The rule and its comment are much more extensive than Model Rule 2.4.

Virginia: Long before the ABA adopted Model Rule 2.4 in 2002, Virginia adopted its own Rule 2.10 (Third Party Neutral) and Rule 2.11 (Mediator), which provide as follows:

Virginia Rule 2.10 Third Party Neutral

(a) A third party neutral assists parties in reaching a voluntary settlement of a dispute through a structured process known as a dispute resolution proceeding. The third party neutral does not represent any party.

(b) A lawyer who serves as a third party neutral

(1) shall inform the parties of the difference between the lawyer's role as third party neutral and the lawyer's role as one who represents a client;

(2) shall encourage unrepresented parties to seek legal counsel before an agreement is executed; and

(3) may encourage and assist the parties in reaching a resolution of their dispute; but

(4) may not compel or coerce the parties to make an agreement.

(c) A lawyer may serve as a third party neutral only if the lawyer has not previously represented and is not currently representing one of the parties in connection with the subject matter of the dispute resolution proceeding. . . .

(g) A lawyer who serves as a third party neutral shall not charge a fee contingent on the outcome of the resolution proceeding.

(h) This Rule does not apply to joint representation, which is covered by Rule 1.7.

Virginia Rule 2.11 Mediator

(a) A lawyer-mediator is a third party neutral (see Rule 2.10) who facilitates communication between the parties and, without deciding the issues or imposing a solution on the parties, enables them to understand and resolve their dispute.

(b) Prior to agreeing to mediate and throughout the mediation process a lawyer-mediator should reasonably determine that:

(1) mediation is an appropriate process for the parties;

(2) each party is able to participate effectively within the context of the mediation process; and

(3) each party is willing to enter and participate in the process in good faith.

(c) A lawyer-mediator may offer legal information if all parties are present or separately to the parties if they consent. The lawyer-mediator shall inform unrepresented parties or those parties who are not accompanied by legal counsel about the importance of reviewing the lawyer-mediator's legal information with legal counsel.

(d) A lawyer-mediator may offer evaluation of, for example, strengths and weaknesses of positions, assess the value and cost of alternatives to settlement or assess the barriers to settlement (collectively referred to as evaluation) only if such evaluation is incidental to the facilitative role and does not interfere with the lawyer-mediator's impartiality or the self-determination of the parties. . . .

Related Materials

Editors' Note. Comment 2 to Rule 2.4 notes that lawyer neutrals "may also be subject to various codes of ethics. . . ." The Related Materials below include some examples.

ABA Formal Ethics Opinions: See ABA Formal Ethics Op. 06-439 n.2 (2006).

Alternative Dispute Resolution (ADR) refers to a variety of techniques or procedures for resolving disputes without going to a court, or (if litigation has commenced) without holding a trial. Examples of ADR techniques include mediation, arbitration, conciliation, early neutral evaluation, summary jury trials, mini-trials, neutral fact finding, and nonjudicial settlement conferences.

American Arbitration Association (AAA): The American Arbitration Association, a nonprofit organization founded in 1926, is (according to its Mission Statement) "dedicated to the development and widespread use of prompt, effective and economical methods of dispute resolution." The AAA once concentrated on arbitration, but today it offers a broad range of alternative dispute resolution (ADR) services, including mediation, arbitration, fact finding, mini-trials, elections, and other out-of-court settlement procedures. The AAA typically administers over 200,000 cases per year, using a roster of over 7,000 neutral experts around the world to hear and resolve cases. Many of the neutral experts are lawyers, and are thus governed by Rule 2.4 in jurisdictions that have adopted it. The AAA also helps to develop legislation (such as the Uniform Arbitration Act, or UAA), and has helped develop arbitration procedures to govern many different specific types of disputes (*e.g.,* Construction Industry Arbitration Rules, Employment Dispute Arbitration Rules, Commercial Mediation Rules, and Securities Arbitration Rules). For more information about the AAA, visit *www.adr.org.*

Association for Conflict Resolution: The Association for Conflict Resolution (ACR) describes itself as "a professional organization dedicated to enhancing the practice and public understanding of conflict resolution." ACR serves an international audience that includes more than 6,000 mediators, arbitrators, facilitators, educators, and others involved in conflict resolution and collaborative decision-making. The organization was created through the merger of three other organizations active in the ADR field: the Academy of Family Mediators, the Conflict Resolution Education Network, and the Society of Professionals in Dispute Resolution (SPIDR). In 2011, ACR approved Model Standards for Mediation Certification Programs, which are available at *www.acrnet.org/uploadedFiles/Practitioner/ModelStandardsCertification.pdf.* For more information about ACR generally, visit *www.acrnet.org.*

Code of Ethics for Arbitrators in Commercial Disputes: A Joint Committee of the ABA and the American Arbitration Association (AAA) has prepared a code of ethics for commercial arbitrators. It is expressly mentioned in Comment 2 to Rule 2.4. The Code seeks to provide ethical guidelines and standards of conduct for arbitrators and others involved in alternative dispute resolution. It was first promulgated in 1977, and was extensively amended in 2004 based on the work of another joint ABA-AAA working group. The 1977 Code is available online at *www.lectlaw.com/files/adr12.htm.* The 2004 Code is available online at *www.abanet.org/dispute/commercial_disputes.pdf.*

FINRA Codes for Arbitration and Mediation: The Financial Industry Regulatory Authority (FINRA) is the largest independent regulator for securities firms doing business in the United States. FINRA has developed a Code of Arbitration Procedure for Customer Disputes that applies to any dispute between a customer and a FINRA member (or a person associated with a FINRA member) if the dispute is submitted to arbitration under certain FINRA rules. FINRA has also developed a Code of Mediation Procedure that applies to any matter submitted to mediation at FINRA. FINRA handles about 5,000 arbitration cases annually and conducts about 700 mediations annually. For the complete FINRA Code of Mediation Procedure, see *http://finra.complinet.com/en/display/display_main.html?rbid=2403&element_id=4293.*

"Lawyer for the Situation": During the Senate hearings on the nomination of Louis Brandeis to the Supreme Court in 1916, Brandeis was criticized for alleged conflicts of interest in a complex bankruptcy where he said he was "counsel for the situation." The phrase "lawyer for the situation" has since mystified and intrigued legal scholars, but usually suggests that lawyers should facilitate common goals among multiple parties instead of adhering to the interests of any one client. A thorough recounting of the origin of the phrase is found in several sources, including Alden L. Todd, Justice on Trial: The Case of Louis D. Brandeis (1964); John Frank, *The Legal Ethics of Louis D. Brandeis,* 17 Stan. L. Rev. 683, 699-702 (1965); and John Dzienkowski, *Lawyers as Intermediaries: The Representation of Multiple Clients in the Modern Legal Profession,* 1992 U. Ill. L. Rev. 741 (1992).

Model Rules of Professional Conduct for Federal Lawyers: Federal lawyers are permitted to act as intermediaries only between two individuals. After withdrawal as an intermediary, a federal lawyer may continue to represent some of the clients in the same matter if each client consents.

Model Standards of Conduct for Mediators: In 1994, a joint task force of the ABA, the American Arbitration Association (AAA), and the Society of Professionals in Dispute Resolution (SPIDR) published Model Standards of Conduct for Mediators, which are expressly mentioned in Comment 2 to ABA Model Rule 2.4. The Model Standards are intended to govern all mediators, including lawyers serving as mediators. The Model Standards, as amended in 2005, are available at *www.abanet.org/dispute/documents/model_standards_conduct_april2007.pdf.*

Model Standards of Practice for Family and Divorce Mediation: In 2000, the Association of Family Conciliation Courts (AFCC) adopted the Model Standards of Practice for Family and Divorce Mediation. (The Model Standards replaced the 1984 ABA Standards of Practice for Lawyer Mediators in Family Disputes.) The 2000 Standards are, according to the Reporter's Foreword, "the latest milestone in a nearly twenty-year-old effort by the family mediation community to create standards of practice that will increase public confidence in an evolving profession and provide guidance for its practitioners." The Standards were spearheaded by the ABA Family Law Section and the ABA Mediation Committee, a broad-based committee whose members included several nonlawyer mediator groups, and were approved by the ABA in 2001. The Reporter for the ABA Mediation Committee was Professor Andrew Schepard of Hofstra University School of Law. The Model Standards, as approved by the ABA in 2001, are available at *http://www.mediate.com/articles/afccstds.cfm.*

Restatement of the Law Governing Lawyers: See Restatement §§103 and 130 in our chapter on the Restatement later in this volume.

ANNOTATIONS ON ARTICLE 3. ADVOCATE

Rule 3.1   Meritorious Claims and Contentions

Canon and Code Antecedents

ABA Canons of Professional Ethics: Canons 5, 15, 30, and 31 provided as follows:

5.   *The Defense or Prosecution of Those Accused of Crime*

It is the right of the lawyer to undertake the defense of a person accused of crime, regardless of his personal opinion as to the guilt of the accused; otherwise innocent persons, victims only of suspicious circumstances, might be denied proper defense. Having undertaken such defense, the lawyer is bound, by all fair and honorable means, to present every defense that the law of the land permits, to the end that no person may be deprived of life or liberty, but by due process of law.

The primary duty of a lawyer engaged in public prosecution is not to convict, but to see that justice is done. The suppression of facts or the secreting of witnesses capable of establishing the innocence of the accused is highly reprehensible.

15.   *How Far a Lawyer May Go in Supporting a Client's Cause*

Nothing operates more certainly to create or to foster popular prejudice against lawyers as a class, and to deprive the profession of that full measure of public esteem and confidence which belongs to the proper discharge of its duties than does the false claim, often set up by the unscrupulous in defense of questionable transactions, that it is the duty of the lawyer to do whatever may enable him to succeed in winning his client's cause.

It is improper for a lawyer to assert in argument his personal belief in his client's innocence or in the justice of his cause.

The lawyer owes "entire devotion to the interest of the client, warm zeal in the maintenance and defense of his rights and the exertion of his utmost learning and ability," to the end that nothing be taken or be withheld from him, save by the rules of law, legally applied. No fear of judicial disfavor or public unpopularity should restrain him from the full discharge of his duty. In the judicial forum the client is entitled to the benefit of any and every remedy and defense that is authorized by the law of the land, and he may expect his lawyer to assert every such remedy or defense. But it is steadfastly to be borne in mind that the great trust of the lawyer is to be performed within and not without the bounds of the law. The office of attorney does not permit, much less does it demand of him for any client, violation of law or any manner of fraud or chicane. He must obey his own conscience and not that of his client.

30.   *Justifiable and Unjustifiable Litigations*

The lawyer must decline to conduct a civil cause or to make a defense when convinced that it is intended merely to harass or to injure the opposite party or to work oppression or wrong. But otherwise it is his right, and, having accepted retainer, it becomes his duty to insist upon the judgment of the Court as to the legal merits of his client's claim. His appearance in Court should be deemed equivalent to an assertion on his honor that in his opinion his client's case is one proper for judicial determination.

31. Responsibility for Litigation

No lawyer is obliged to act either as adviser or advocate for every person who may wish to become his client. He has the right to decline employment. Every lawyer upon his own responsibility must decide what employment he will accept as counsel, what causes he will bring into Court for plaintiffs, what cases he will contest in Court for defendants. The responsibility for advising as to questionable transactions, for bringing questionable suits, for urging questionable defenses, is the lawyer's responsibility. He cannot escape it by urging as an excuse that he is only following his client's instructions.

ABA Model Code of Professional Responsibility: Compare DR 7-102(A)(1) and DR 7-102(A)(2) (reprinted later in this volume).

Cross-References in Other Rules

Rule 3.3, Comment 3: "An advocate is responsible for pleadings and other documents prepared for litigation, but is usually not required to have personal knowledge of matters asserted therein, for litigation documents ordinarily present assertions by the client, or by someone on the client's behalf, and not assertions by the lawyer. Compare **Rule 3.1.**"

Legislative History of Model Rule 3.1

1980 Discussion Draft contained the following Introduction to Article 3:

As advocate, a lawyer presents evidence and argument before a tribunal in behalf of a client. The advocate's duty in the adversary system is to present the client's case as persuasively as possible, leaving presentation of the opposing case to the other party. An advocate may not present a claim or defense lacking serious merit for the purpose of delay, although an advocate for the defendant in a criminal case may insist on proof of the offense charged. An advocate does not vouch for the justness of a client's cause but only its legal merit.

In addition, Rule 3.1 provided that

(A) lawyer shall not:
(1) file a complaint, motion, or pleading other than one that puts the prosecution to its proof in a criminal case, unless according to the lawyer's belief there is good ground to support it; . . .

1981 and *1982 Drafts* were substantially the same as adopted.

1983 Rule: As originally adopted in 1983, the first sentence of Rule 3.1 provided that a lawyer shall not bring or defend a proceeding, or assert or controvert an issue therein, unless there is "a basis for doing so" that is not frivolous, which includes a good faith argument for an extension, modification, or reversal of existing law. The second sentence of Rule 3.1 was the same as the 2002 version.

2002 Amendments: At its February 2002 Mid-Year Meeting, the ABA House of Delegates adopted without change the ABA Ethics 2000 Commission proposal to amend Rule 3.1 and its Comment. The amendment added the phrase "in law and fact" after the word "basis" in the first sentence, modified Comment 2, and added Comment 3. The second sentence of Rule 3.1 was not changed.

Selected State Variations

Arizona generally tracks ABA Model Rule 3.1, but the "unless" clause in the first sentence applies if there is a "good faith" basis in law and fact, which "may include" a good faith "and nonfrivolous" argument for an extension, modification, or reversal of existing law.

California: Rule 3-200 provides:

> A member shall not seek, accept, or continue employment if the member knows or should know that the objective of such employment is:
>> (A) To bring an action, conduct a defense, assert a position in litigation, or take an appeal, without probable cause and for the purpose of harassing or maliciously injuring any person; or
>> (B) To present a claim or defense in litigation that is not warranted under existing law, unless it can be supported by a good faith argument for an extension, modification, or reversal of such existing law.

Also, California Business & Professions Code §6068(c) states that an attorney has a duty to "counsel or maintain those actions, proceedings, or defenses only as appear to him or her legal or just, except the defense of a person charged with a public offense." In addition, California Civil Code §§128.5, 128.6, and 128.7 provide sanctions for bad faith lawsuits and for frivolous litigation tactics.

Colorado: Rule 1.2(c) permits a lawyer to "provide limited representation to pro se parties . . . ," but Rule 11(b) of the Colorado Rules of Civil Procedure provides as follows:

> *Limited Representation*
>
> . . . Pleadings or papers filed by the pro se party that were prepared with the drafting assistance of the attorney shall include the attorney's name, address, telephone number and registration number. . . . The attorney in providing such drafting assistance may rely on the pro se party's representation of facts, unless the attorney has reason to believe that such representations are false or materially insufficient, in which instance the attorney shall make an independent reasonable inquiry into the facts. . . .

Merely "helping to draft the pleading or paper filed by the pro se party" constitutes a certification by the attorney that the pro se client's document is "(1) well-grounded in fact based upon a reasonable inquiry of the pro se party by the attorney . . . and (3) is not interposed for any improper purpose, such as to harass or to cause unnecessary delay or needless increase in the cost of litigation."

District of Columbia: The second sentence of Rule 3.1 provides that a lawyer for the defendant in a criminal proceeding, or for the respondent in a proceeding that could result in "involuntary institutionalization, shall, if the client elects to go to trial or to a contested factfinding hearing, nevertheless so defend the proceeding as to require that the government carry its burden of proof."

Georgia rejects ABA Model Rule 3.1 and instead retains the language of DR 7-102(A)(1) and (A)(2) from the ABA Model Code of Professional Responsibility.

New Jersey adds the phrase "the lawyer knows or reasonably believes" after "unless" in the first sentence and adds "or the establishment of new law" at the end of the first sentence.

New Mexico creates a Rule 3.0 (Rule 16-300), which specifies as follows:

> In the course of any judicial or quasi-judicial proceeding before a tribunal, a lawyer shall refrain from intentionally manifesting, by words or conduct, bias or prejudice based on race, gender, religion, national origin, disability, age or sexual orientation against the judge, court personnel, parties, witnesses, counsel or others. This rule does not preclude legitimate advocacy when race, gender, religion, national origin, disability, age or sexual orientation is material to the issues in the proceeding.

New York adds Rule 3.1(b), which has no Model Rule equivalent. It defines conduct as "frivolous" if "(1) the lawyer knowingly advances a claim or defense that is unwarranted under existing law, except that the lawyer may advance such claim or defense if it can be supported by good faith argument for an extension, modification, or reversal of existing law; (2) the conduct has no reasonable purpose other than to delay or prolong the resolution of litigation, in violation of Rule 3.2, or serves merely to harass or maliciously injure another; or (3) the lawyer knowingly asserts material factual statements that are false."

Texas: Rule 3.01 ends after the word "frivolous" in the first sentence.

Related Materials

ABA Formal Ethics Opinions: See ABA Formal Ethics Ops. 92-363 (1992), 94-383 (1994), and 94-387 (1994).

Asbestos and Silica Legislation: Since 2004, in response to allegedly frivolous product liability suits in which plaintiffs claim injuries arising from exposure to asbestos or silica (or both), at least seven states have enacted statutes making it more difficult to file such suits. (The seven states are Florida, Georgia, Kansas, Ohio, South Carolina, Tennessee, and Texas.) The statutes establish medical criteria and place other restrictions on plaintiffs. For example, the Silica and Asbestos Claims Act signed by Kansas Governor Kathleen Sebelius in May 2006 requires a plaintiff to (a) meet certain statutorily established medical standards before filing a lawsuit, (b) describe his or her work and medical history, (c) obtain a diagnosis by a qualified physician, (d) undergo recognized diagnostic tests, and (e) prove physical impairment as an essential element in any civil action asserting a silica or asbestos claim.

Congress has also considered bills relating to asbestos litigation. In 2005, the House of Representatives considered a bill that would have established a series of medical criteria for claimants seeking to prove that they suffer from eligible diseases or conditions caused by asbestos exposure. In 2006, the Senate considered the Fairness in Asbestos Injury Resolution (FAIR) Act of 2006. Neither the House bill nor the Senate bill became law. Each bill is related to ABA Model Rule 3.1 because the law is designed to combat allegedly frivolous lawsuits.

Federal Rules of Appellate Procedure: Rule 38, entitled "Frivolous Appeal — Damages and Costs," provides: "If a court of appeals determines that an appeal is frivolous, it may, after a separately filed motion or notice from the court and reasonable opportunity to respond, award just damages and single or double costs to the appellee."

Federal Rules of Civil Procedure: Rule 11(b)(1)-(2) provides that a lawyer's signature on a pleading, written motion, or other paper certifies, among other things, that to the best of the lawyer's "knowledge, information, and belief, formed after an inquiry reasonable under the circumstances":

> (1) it is not being presented for any improper purpose, such as to harass, cause unnecessary delay, or needlessly increase the cost of litigation;
>
> (2) the claims, defenses, and other legal contentions are warranted by existing law or by a nonfrivolous argument for extending, modifying, or reversing existing law or for establishing new law; . . .

Rule 11(c) gives courts discretion to impose various monetary and other sanctions on those who violate the rule.

Fee Award Statutes: Dozens of state and federal statutes permit courts to award attorney fees to a prevailing party in litigation if the opposing party's position is frivolous or unjustified. In federal criminal prosecutions, for example, 18 U.S.C. §3006A provides that a court "may" award reasonable attorney fees and other litigation expenses to a federal criminal defendant (other than one represented by assigned counsel paid for by the public) "where the court finds that the position of the United States was vexatious, frivolous, or in bad faith, unless the court finds that special circumstances make such an award unjust." Similarly, in federal civil cases to which the United States is a party, the Equal Access to Justice Act, 28 U.S.C. §2412(d)(1), provides that a court "shall" award attorney fees to the prevailing party if the government's position in the litigation was not "substantially justified" unless "special circumstances make an award unjust."

IRS Regulations: In the regulations governing practice before the Internal Revenue Service, 31 C.F.R. §10.34(b) provides as follows:

> (b) *Documents, affidavits, and other papers*
>
> (1) A practitioner may not advise a client to take a position on a document, affidavit or other paper submitted to the Internal Revenue Service unless the position is not frivolous.
>
> (2) A practitioner may not advise a client to submit a document, affidavit or other paper to the Internal Revenue Service
>
> > (i) The purpose of which is to delay or impede the administration of the Federal tax laws;
> >
> > (ii) That is frivolous; or
> >
> > (iii) That contains or omits information in a manner that demonstrates an intentional disregard of a rule or regulation unless the practitioner also advises the client to submit a document that evidences a good faith challenge to the rule or regulation.

Lawsuit Abuse Reduction Act: In March 2011, Rep. Lamar Smith (R-Texas) introduced and held hearings on a bill (H.R. 966) called the Lawsuit Abuse Reduction Act (LARA). Senator Charles Grassley (R-Iowa) introduced a companion bill (S. 533) in the Senate. The bill, which never made it to a floor vote, proposed to (a) reinstate the pre-1993 requirement of mandatory sanctions for a violation of Rule 11 of the Federal Rules of Civil Procedure, (b) require that judges impose monetary sanctions, including the opposing party's costs and attorney's fees, against lawyers who file frivolous lawsuits, and (c) reverse the 1993 amendments to Rule 11 that allow parties and their attorneys to avoid sanctions for making frivolous claims by withdrawing the claims within 21 days after a motion for sanctions has been served.

Private Securities Litigation Reform Act: The Private Securities Litigation Reform Act (PSLRA), 15 U.S.C. §77z-1, Title I (entitled "Reduction of Abusive Litigation"), requires a court, upon "final adjudication" of a securities fraud action, to make "specific findings" as to whether each attorney in the action complied with Rule 11(b) of the Federal Rules of Civil Procedure with respect to any complaint, responsive pleading, or dispositive motion. The law also establishes a rebuttable presumption that a party who has violated Rule 11 should pay the opposing party's reasonable attorney fees and expenses as an appropriate sanction.

Restatement of the Law Governing Lawyers: See Restatement §§57(2) and 110(1) and (2) in our chapter on the Restatement later in this volume.

Rule 3.2   Expediting Litigation

Canon and Code Antecedents

ABA Canons of Professional Ethics: No comparable Canon.

ABA Model Code of Professional Responsibility: Compare DR 7-101(A)(1) and DR 7-102(A)(1) (reprinted later in this volume).

Cross-References in Other Rules

None.

Legislative History of Model Rule 3.2

1980 Discussion Draft (then Rule 3.3(a)) provided:

> A lawyer shall make every effort consistent with the legitimate interests of the client to expedite litigation. Realizing financial or other benefit from otherwise improper delay in litigation is not a legitimate interest of the client. A lawyer shall not engage in any procedure or tactic having no substantial purpose other than delay or increasing the cost of litigation to another party.

1981 Draft: "A lawyer shall make reasonable effort consistent with the *legitimate* interests of the client to expedite litigation."

1982 Draft was adopted.

1983 Rule: As originally adopted in 1983, Rule 3.2 was the same as the 2002 version.

2002 Amendments: At its February 2002 Mid-Year Meeting, the ABA House of Delegates adopted without change the ABA Ethics 2000 Commission proposal to amend the Comment to Rule 3.2. (The Ethics 2000 Commission did not propose any changes to the text of Rule 3.2.) The amendment to the Comment deleted the clause, "Delay should not be indulged merely for the convenience of the advocates," and replaced it with the entire second sentence and the beginning of the third sentence ("Although there will be occasions when a lawyer may properly seek a postponement for personal reasons, it is not proper for a lawyer to routinely fail to expedite litigation solely for the convenience of the advocates. Nor will a failure to expedite be reasonable if done . . .").

Selected State Variations

California: The California Rules of Professional Conduct have no comparable provision. California Business & Professions Code §6128(b) provides that an attorney is "guilty of a misdemeanor," punishable by six months in jail and/or a $2,500 fine, if the attorney "[w]illfully delays his client's suit with a view to his own gain."

District of Columbia adds Rule 3.2(a), which provides: "In representing a client, a lawyer shall not delay a proceeding when the lawyer knows or when it is obvious that such action would serve solely to harass or maliciously injure another." Rule 3.2(b) is identical to ABA Model Rule 3.2.

Nevada: Rule 3.2(a) is identical to ABA Model Rule 3.2, but Nevada adds a new Rule 3.2(b) providing that paragraph (a) "does not preclude a lawyer from granting a reasonable request from opposing counsel for an accommodation, such as an extension of time, or from disagreeing with a client's wishes on administrative and tactical matters, such as scheduling depositions, the number of depositions to be taken, and the frequency and use of written discovery requests."

New Jersey adds "and shall treat with courtesy and consideration all persons involved in the legal process" at the end of Rule 3.2.

New York: Rule 3.2 provides that "a lawyer shall not use means that have no substantial purpose other than to delay or prolong the proceeding or to cause needless expense."

Ohio omits ABA Model Rule 3.2. A Note following the rule explains that the "substance" of ABA Model Rule 3.2 "is addressed by other provisions," including Rules 1.3, 3.1, and 4.4(a).

Texas: Rule 3.02 provides that during litigation a lawyer "shall not take a position that unreasonably increases the costs or other burdens of the case or that unreasonably delays resolution of the matter."

Virginia omits Rule 3.2.

Related Materials

ABA Formal Ethics Opinions: See ABA Formal Ethics Ops. 93-370 (1993), 93-379 (1993), and 96-400 (1996).

Abusive Litigation Tactics: 28 U.S.C. §1927 gives federal courts the authority to penalize litigants who engage in abusive litigation tactics. It provides as follows:

> Any attorney . . . who so multiplies the proceedings in any case unreasonably and vexatiously may be required by the court to satisfy personally the excess costs, expenses, and attorneys' fees reasonably incurred because of such conduct.

Alternative Dispute Resolution (ADR): Some lawyers believe that the obligation in Rule 3.2 to "expedite litigation" includes the obligation to inform a client about the availability of alternatives to litigation. For example, The Texas Lawyer's Creed, promulgated in 1989 by the Supreme Court of Texas and the Texas Court of Criminal Appeals, states: "I will advise my client regarding the availability of mediation, arbitration, and other alternative methods of resolving and settling disputes. . . ." The Colorado and Hawaii versions of Rule 2.1 state that a lawyer "should advise a client of alternative forms of dispute resolution which might reasonably be pursued to attempt to resolve the legal dispute or to reach the legal objective sought," and numerous state and federal courts have adopted mandatory ADR to move litigation along more quickly and inexpensively.

Federal Rules of Civil Procedure: Fed. R. Civ. P. 1 provides that the Federal Rules of Civil Procedure shall be construed "to secure the just, speedy, and inexpensive determination of every action." Fed. R. Civ. P. 11, the broadest and most frequently invoked sanctions rule, requires attorneys to sign every pleading, motion, or other paper to certify that (among other things) the paper is not being presented for any improper purpose, such as to "cause unnecessary delay" in the litigation. Fed. R. Civ. P. 26(g)(1)(B)(ii) requires a similar certification for discovery requests, responses, and objections. Fed. R. Civ. P. 56(h) provides for sanctions whenever the court finds that any affidavit supporting or opposing a motion for summary judgment has been presented in bad faith "or solely for delay."

Federal Rules of Evidence: Rule 102 of the Federal Rules of Evidence provides that the Rules shall be construed to secure "elimination of unjustifiable expense and delay. . . ."

Model Rules of Professional Conduct for Federal Lawyers: Rule 3.2 provides: "A Federal lawyer shall make reasonable efforts to expedite litigation and other proceedings consistent with the interests of the client and the lawyer's responsibilities to the tribunal to avoid unwarranted delay."

Restatement of the Law Governing Lawyers: The Restatement has no comparable provision.

Rule 3.3   Candor Toward the Tribunal

Canon and Code Antecedents

ABA Canons of Professional Ethics: Canons 5, 15, 22, and 41 provided, in pertinent part, as follows:

5.   *The Defense or Prosecution of Those Accused of Crime*

It is the right of the lawyer to undertake the defense of a person accused of crime, regardless of his personal opinion as to the guilt of the accused; otherwise innocent persons, victims only of suspicious circumstances, might be denied proper defense. Having undertaken such defense, the lawyer is bound, by all fair and honorable means, to present every defense that the law of the land permits, to the end that no person may be deprived of life or liberty, but by due process of law.

15.   *How Far a Lawyer May Go in Supporting a Client's Cause*

Nothing operates more certainly to create or to foster popular prejudice against lawyers as a class, and to deprive the profession of that full measure of public esteem and confidence which belongs to the proper discharge of its duties than does the false claim, often set up by the unscrupulous in defense of questionable transactions, that it is the duty of the lawyer to do whatever may enable him to succeed in winning his client's cause. . . .

The lawyer owes "entire devotion to the interest of the client, warm zeal in the maintenance and defense of his rights and the exertion of his utmost learning and ability," to the end that nothing be taken or be withheld from him, save by the rules of law, legally applied. No fear of judicial disfavor or public unpopularity should restrain him from the full discharge of his duty. In the judicial forum the client is entitled to the benefit of any and every remedy and defense that is authorized by the law of the land, and he may expect his lawyer to assert every such remedy or defense. But it is steadfastly to be borne in mind that the great trust of the lawyer is to be performed within and not without the bounds of the law. The office of attorney does not permit, much less does it demand of him for any client, violation of law or any manner of fraud or chicane. He must obey his own conscience and not that of his client.

22. *Candor and Fairness*

The conduct of the lawyer before the Court and with other lawyers should be characterized by candor and fairness.

It is not candid or fair for the lawyer knowingly to misquote the contents of a paper, the testimony of a witness, the language or the argument of opposing counsel, or the language of a decision or a textbook; or with knowledge of its invalidity, to cite as authority a decision that has been overruled, or a statute that has been repealed; or in argument to assert as a fact that which has not been proved, or in those jurisdictions where a side has the opening and closing arguments to mislead his opponent by concealing or withholding positions in his opening argument upon which his side then intends to rely.

It is unprofessional and dishonorable to deal other than candidly with the facts in taking the statements of witnesses, in drawing affidavits and other documents, and in the presentation of causes.

A lawyer should not offer evidence which he knows the Court should reject, in order to get the same before the jury by argument for its admissibility, nor should he address to the Judge arguments upon any point not properly calling for determination by him. Neither should he introduce into an argument, addressed to the court, remarks or statements intended to influence the jury or bystanders.

These and all kindred practices are unprofessional and unworthy of an officer of the law charged, as is the lawyer, with the duty of aiding in the administration of justice.

41. *Discovery of Imposition and Deception*

When a lawyer discovers that some fraud or deception has been practiced, which has unjustly imposed upon the court or a party, he should endeavor to rectify it; at first by advising his client, and if his client refuses to forego the advantage thus unjustly gained, he should promptly inform the injured person or his counsel, so that they may take appropriate steps.

ABA Model Code of Professional Responsibility: Compare DR 7-102(A)(3), DR 7-102(A)(4), DR 7-102(A)(5), DR 7-102(B)(1), and DR 7-106(B)(1) (reprinted later in this volume).

Cross-References in Other Rules

Rule 1.6, Comment 17: "Rule 3.3 . . . requires disclosure in some circumstances regardless of whether such disclosure is permitted by this Rule. See **Rule 3.3(c)**."

Rule 1.8, Comment 5: It is prohibited to partake in the "disadvantageous use of client information unless the client gives informed consent, except as permitted or required by these Rules. See Rules 1.2(d), 1.6, 1.9(c), **3.3**, 4.1(b), 8.1 and 8.3."

Rule 1.13, Comment 6: "[T]his Rule does not limit or expand the lawyer's responsibility under Rule 1.8, 1.16, **3.3** or 4.1."

Rule 1.16, Comment 3: "Lawyers should be mindful of their obligations to both clients and the court under Rules 1.6 and **3.3**."

Rule 2.4, Comment 5: "When the dispute-resolution process takes place before a tribunal, as in binding arbitration (see Rule 1.0(m)), the lawyer's duty of candor is governed by **Rule 3.3**."

Rule 3.9: "A lawyer representing a client before a legislative body or adminis-trative agency in a nonadjudicative proceeding shall disclose that the appearance is in a representative capacity and shall conform to the provisions of **Rules 3.3(a)** through **(c)**, 3.4(a) through (c), and 3.5."

Rule 3.9, Comment 1: "In representation before bodies such as legislatures, municipal councils, and executive and administrative agencies acting in a rule-making or policy-making capacity" lawyers must deal "honestly and in conformity with appli-cable rules of procedure. See **Rules 3.3(a)** through **(c)**, 3.4(a) through (c) and 3.5."

Rule 8.1, Comment 3: "A lawyer representing an applicant for admission to the bar, or representing a lawyer who is the subject of a disciplinary inquiry or proceed-ing, is governed by the rules applicable to the client-lawyer relationship, including Rule 1.6 and, in some cases, **Rule 3.3**."

Legislative History of Model Rule 3.3

1980 Discussion Draft (then Rule 3.1) provided:

(a) A lawyer shall not: . . .

(3) except as provided in paragraph (f), offer evidence that the lawyer is con-vinced beyond a reasonable doubt is false, or offer without suitable explanation evidence that the lawyer knows is substantially misleading; or

(4) make a representation about existing legal authority that the lawyer knows to be inaccurate or so incomplete as to be substantially misleading.

(b) Except as provided in paragraph (f), if a lawyer discovers that evidence or testimony presented by the lawyer is false, the lawyer shall disclose that fact and take suitable measures to rectify the consequences, even if doing so requires disclosure of a confidence of the client or disclosure that the client is implicated in the falsification.

(c) If a lawyer discovers that the tribunal has not been apprised of legal authority known to the lawyer that would probably have a substantial effect on the determination of a material issue, the lawyer shall advise the tribunal of that authority.

(d) Except as provided in paragraph (f), a lawyer shall disclose a fact known to the lawyer, even if the fact is adverse, when disclosure:

(1) is required by law or the Rules of Professional Conduct; or

(2) is necessary to correct a manifest misapprehension resulting from a previ-ous representation the lawyer has made to the tribunal.

(e) Except as provided in paragraph (f), a lawyer may apprise another party of evidence favorable to that party and may refuse to offer evidence that the lawyer believes with substantial reason to be false.

(f) A lawyer for a defendant in a criminal case:

(1) is not required to apprise the prosecutor or the tribunal of evidence adverse to the accused, except as law may otherwise provide;

(2) may not disclose facts as required by paragraph (d) if doing so is prohib-ited by applicable law;

(3) shall offer evidence regardless of belief as to whether it is false if the client so demands and applicable law requires that the lawyer comply with such a demand.

(g) A prosecutor has the further duty of disclosure stated in Rule 3.10.

1981 Draft was substantially the same as adopted in 1983 except that subparagraph (a) provided that a lawyer shall not knowingly:

(1) make a false statement of fact or law to a tribunal, or fail to disclose a fact in circumstances where the failure to make the disclosure is the equivalent of the lawyer's making a material misrepresentation;

(2) fail to make a disclosure of fact necessary to prevent a fraud on the tribunal. . . .

1982 Draft was adopted.

1983 Rule: As originally adopted in 1983, Rule 3.3 provided as follows:

(a) A lawyer shall not knowingly:

(1) make a false statement of material fact or law to a tribunal;

(2) fail to disclose a material fact to a tribunal when disclosure is necessary to avoid assisting a criminal or fraudulent act by the client;

(3) [Same as 2002 version of Rule 3.3(a)(2).]

(4) offer evidence that the lawyer knows to be false. If a lawyer has offered material evidence and comes to know of its falsity, the lawyer shall take reasonable remedial measures.

(b) The duties stated in paragraph (a) continue [remainder is same as in the 2002 version of Rule 3.3(c).]

(c) A lawyer may refuse to offer evidence that the lawyer reasonably believes is false.

(d) [Same as 2002 version of Rule 3.3(d).]

2002 Amendments: At its February 2002 Mid-Year Meeting, the ABA House of Delegates adopted without change the ABA Ethics 2000 Commission proposal to amend Rule 3.3 and its Comment. The amendments revised Rule 3.3(a)(1), deleted (a)(2), revised (a)(3), added (b), deleted (c) (moving its substance to (a)(3)), added Comments 1, 5-7, 12 and 15, and amended or deleted most other Comments. The pre-2002 version of Rule 3.3, which continues to influence the rules of many states, provided as follows:

(a) A lawyer shall not knowingly:

(1) make a false statement of material fact or law to a tribunal;

(2) fail to disclose a material fact to a tribunal when disclosure is necessary to avoid assisting a criminal or fraudulent act by the client;

(3) fail to disclose to the tribunal legal authority in the controlling jurisdiction known to the lawyer to be directly adverse to the position of the client and not disclosed by opposing counsel; or

(4) offer evidence that the lawyer knows to be false. If a lawyer has offered material evidence and comes to know of its falsity, the lawyer shall take reasonable remedial measures.

(b) The duties stated in paragraph (a) continue to the conclusion of the proceeding, and apply even if compliance requires disclosure of information otherwise protected by Rule 1.6.

(c) A lawyer may refuse to offer evidence that the lawyer reasonably believes is false.

(d) In an ex parte proceeding, a lawyer shall inform the tribunal of all material facts known to the lawyer that will enable the tribunal to make an informed decision, whether or not the facts are adverse.

Selected State Variations

California: Rule 5-200 provides as follows:

> In presenting a matter to a tribunal, a member:
>   (A) Shall employ, for the purpose of maintaining the causes confided to the member such means only as are consistent with truth;
>   (B) Shall not seek to mislead the judge, judicial officer, or jury by an artifice or false statement of fact or law;
>   (C) Shall not intentionally misquote to a tribunal the language of a book, statute, or decision;
>   (D) Shall not, knowing its invalidity, cite as authority a decision that has been overruled or a statute that has been repealed or declared unconstitutional; and
>   (E) Shall not assert personal knowledge of the facts at issue, except when testifying as a witness.

In addition, California Business & Professions Code §6068(d) provides that it is the duty of an attorney to employ "those means only as are consistent with truth, and never to seek to mislead the judge or any judicial officer by an artifice or false statement of fact or law." And §6128(a) makes an attorney guilty of a misdemeanor if the attorney engages in "any deceit or collusion, or consents to any deceit or collusion, with intent to deceive the court or any party."

District of Columbia: Rule 3.3(a)(1) provides that a lawyer shall not knowingly make a false statement of fact or law to a tribunal or fail to correct a false statement of material fact or law previously made to the tribunal by the lawyer, "unless correction would require disclosure of information that is prohibited by Rule 1.6." Rule 3.3(a)(2) is nearly identical to ABA Model Rule 1.2(d). D.C.'s equivalent to ABA Model Rule 3.3(a)(2) applies to undisclosed, directly adverse legal authority in the controlling jurisdiction not disclosed by opposing counsel and known to be "dispositive of a question at issue."

D.C. Rule 3.3(a)(4) provides that a lawyer shall not knowingly offer evidence that the lawyer knows to be false, "except as provided in paragraph (b)." D.C. Rule 3.3(b) adopts the so-called "narrative method" for presenting false testimony by providing as follows:

> When the witness who intends to give evidence that the lawyer knows to be false is the lawyer's client and is the accused in a criminal case, the lawyer shall first make a good-faith effort to dissuade the client from presenting the false evidence; if the lawyer is unable to dissuade the client, the lawyer shall seek leave of the tribunal to withdraw.
> If the lawyer is unable to dissuade the client or to withdraw without seriously harming the client, the lawyer may put the client on the stand to testify in a narrative fashion, but the lawyer shall not examine the client in such manner as to elicit testimony which the lawyer knows to be false, and shall not argue the probative value of the client's testimony in closing argument.

Rule 3.3(c) provides simply: "The duties stated in paragraph (a) continue to the conclusion of the proceeding." D.C. omits both the second sentence of ABA Model Rule 3.3(a)(3) ("If a lawyer . . . has offered material evidence and the lawyer comes to know of its falsity . . . "), and all of ABA Model Rule 3.3(b) ("A lawyer . . . who knows that a person . . . has engaged in criminal or fraudulent conduct relating to the proceeding . . . ") but covers both situations by adding Rule 3.3(d), which provides as follows: "(d) A lawyer who receives information clearly establishing that a fraud has been perpetrated upon the tribunal shall promptly take reasonable remedial measures, including disclosure to the tribunal to the extent disclosure is permitted by Rule 1.6(d)." (The relevant part of D.C. Rule 1.6(d)(2) provides that when a client has used or is using a lawyer's services to further a crime or fraud, the lawyer may reveal client confidences and secrets to the extent reasonably necessary to "prevent, mitigate or rectify substantial injury to the financial interests or property of another that is reasonably certain to result or has resulted from the client's commission of the crime or fraud.") Finally, D.C. omits ABA Model Rule 3.3(d) (regarding ex parte proceedings).

Florida: Rule 3.3(d) provides that "the duties stated in Rule 3.3(a) continue beyond the conclusion of the proceeding. . . ."

Georgia: In the rules effective November 3, 2011, Rule 3.3(a)(1) is limited to false statements of "material" fact or law. Rule 3.3(a)(2) requires the disclosure of material facts to a tribunal only when doing so is necessary to avoid assisting a criminal or fraudulent act by the client. In Rule 3.3(d), Georgia adds an exception for grand jury proceedings.

Maryland adds the following Rule 3.3(e): "[A] lawyer for an accused in a criminal case need not disclose that the accused intends to testify falsely or has testified falsely if the lawyer reasonably believes that the disclosure would jeopardize any constitutional right of the accused."

Massachusetts: Rule 3.3(b) states that the conclusion of the proceedings includes "all appeals." Rule 3.3(e) permits a lawyer representing a criminal defendant to elicit false testimony in narrative fashion if withdrawal is not otherwise possible without prejudicing the defendant. However, "the lawyer shall not argue the probative value of the false testimony in closing argument or in any other proceedings, including appeals." A lawyer who is unable to withdraw when he or she knows that a criminal defendant will testify falsely "may not prevent the client from testifying" but must not "examine the client in such a manner as to elicit any testimony from the client the lawyer knows to be false."

Michigan: Michigan omits the last sentence of Model Rule 3.3(a)(3) concerning a lawyer's ethical obligations when the lawyer reasonably believes, but does not know, that testimony the lawyer plans to offer will be false. Michigan also adds Rule 3.3(e), which describes in detail the procedures that a lawyer should follow upon discovering that testimony the lawyer previously offered is false.

New Jersey adheres closely to the pre-2002 version of ABA Model Rule 3.3 but adds, in a new Rule 3.3(a)(5), that a lawyer shall not fail to disclose to the tribunal a material fact "knowing that the omission is reasonably certain to mislead the tribunal." Also, New Jersey Rule 1.6(b)(2) requires a lawyer to reveal confidences to prevent a client from committing "a criminal, illegal or fraudulent act that the lawyer reasonably believes is likely to perpetrate a fraud upon a tribunal."

New Mexico specifies in Rule 16-303(E) that a lawyer must disclose to a tribunal whether the lawyer is representing the client in a "limited manner."

New York: Rule 3.3(c) omits the phrase "continue to the conclusion of the proceeding" (and thus has no express time limit). New York also adds Rule 3.3(e), which is substantially similar to 7-106(B)(2) of the old Model Code. Rule 3.3(f), which also has no Model Rule equivalent, is substantially similar to 7-106(C)(5)-(7) of the old Model Code, but it also prohibits "conduct intended to disrupt the tribunal." New York adds Comment 6A, which addresses the rule's application to prosecutors, and omits Comment 13 concerning the duration of the Rule 3.3 obligation.

North Dakota: Rule 3.3(a)(3) provides that if a lawyer, the lawyer's client, or a witness called by the lawyer has offered material evidence and the lawyer comes to know of its falsity, then:

> the lawyer shall take reasonable remedial measures, including, if necessary, disclosure to the tribunal unless the evidence was contained in testimony of the lawyer's client. If the evidence was contained in testimony of the lawyer's client, the lawyer shall make reasonable efforts to convince the client to consent to disclosure. If the client refuses to consent to disclosure, the lawyer shall seek to withdraw from the representation without disclosure. If withdrawal is not permitted, the lawyer may continue the representation and such continuation alone is not a violation of these rules. The lawyer may not use or argue the client's false testimony.

Ohio: Rule 3.3(c) provides that the duties stated in Rules 3.3(a) and (b) continue "until the issue to which the duty relates is determined by the highest tribunal that may consider the issue, or the time has expired for such determination. . . ."

Oregon provides that the duties in Rule 3.3(a) and (b) are suspended if "compliance requires disclosure of information otherwise protected by Rule 1.6."

Pennsylvania adds that it applies if a lawyer, the lawyer's client, or a witness called by the lawyer has offered material evidence "before a tribunal or in an ancillary proceeding conducted pursuant to a tribunal's adjudicative authority, such as a deposition. . . ."

Texas: Rule 3.03(b) and (c) provides:

> (b) If a lawyer has offered material evidence and comes to know of its falsity, the lawyer shall make a good faith effort to persuade the client to authorize the lawyer to correct or withdraw the false evidence. If such efforts are unsuccessful, the lawyer shall take reasonable remedial measures, including disclosure of the true facts.
>
> (c) The duties stated in paragraphs (a) and (b) continue until remedial legal measures are no longer reasonably possible.

Virginia: Rule 3.3(a)(2) provides that a lawyer shall not knowingly "fail to disclose a fact to a tribunal when disclosure is necessary to avoid assisting a criminal or fraudulent act by the client, subject to Rule 1.6." Virginia Rule 3.3(a)(3) requires disclosure only of "controlling" legal authority and omits the word "directly" before "adverse." (The Comment explains that "directly" was deleted because "the limiting effect of that term could seriously dilute the paragraph's meaning.") Virginia Rule 3.3(a)(4) and Rule 3.3(b) are identical to the pre-2002 version of ABA Model Rule 3.3(a)(4) and Rule 3.3(c). Virginia omits ABA Model Rules 3.3(b) and (c) and adds a new paragraph taken verbatim from DR 7-102(B)(2) of the ABA Model Code of Professional Responsibility that provides: "A lawyer who receives information clearly establishing that a person other than a client has perpetrated a fraud upon a tribunal shall promptly reveal the fraud to the tribunal."

Related Materials

ABA Formal Ethics Opinions: See ABA Formal Ethics Ops. 87-353 (1987), 92-366 (1992), 93-370 (1993), 93-376 (1993), and 98-412 (1998).

ABA Standards for Criminal Justice: Defense Function Standard 4-7.5 (Presentation of Evidence) states: "(a) Defense counsel should not knowingly offer false evidence, whether by documents, tangible evidence, or the testimony of witnesses, or fail to take reasonable remedial measures upon discovery of its falsity."

The original draft of The Defense Function, which was drafted in the early 1970s, contained the following version of Standard 4-7.7, sometimes called the "narrative" method:

> If the defendant has admitted to defense counsel facts which establish guilt and counsel's independent investigation established that the admissions are true but the defendant insists on the right to trial, counsel must strongly discourage the defendant against taking the witness stand to testify perjuriously.
>
> If, in advance of trial, the defendant insists that he or she will take the stand to testify perjuriously, the lawyer may withdraw from the case, if that is feasible, seeking leave of the court if necessary, but the court should not be advised of the lawyer's reason for seeking to do so.
>
> If withdrawal from the case is not feasible or is not permitted by the court, or if the situation arises immediately preceding trial or during the trial and the defendant insists upon testifying perjuriously in his or her own behalf, it is unprofessional conduct for the lawyer to lend aid to the perjury or use the perjured testimony. Before the defendant takes the stand in these circumstances, the lawyer should make a record of the fact that the defendant is taking the stand against the advice of counsel in some appropriate manner without revealing the fact to the court. The lawyer may identify the witness as the defendant and may ask appropriate questions of the defendant when it is believed that the defendant's answers will not be perjurious. As to matters for which it is believed the defendant will offer perjurious testimony, the lawyer should seek to avoid direct examination of the defendant in the conventional manner; instead, the lawyer should ask the defendant if he or she wishes to make any additional statement concerning the case to the trier or triers of the facts. A lawyer may not later argue the defendant's known false version of facts to the jury as worthy of belief, and may not recite or rely upon the false testimony in his or her closing argument.

When Standard 4-7.7 was published, it was accompanied by the following official Editorial Note written by the ABA:

> This proposed standard was approved by the ABA Standing Committee on Association Standards for Criminal Justice but was withdrawn prior to submission of this chapter to the ABA House of Delegates. Instead, the question of what should be done in situations dealt with by the standard has been deferred until the ABA Special Commission on Evaluation of Professional Standards [the Kutak Commission] reports its final recommendations.

The final recommendation of the Kutak Commission is found in the original version of ABA Model Rule 3.3 and its Comment. In particular, the original Comment 9 to Rule 3.3 (deleted in 2002) expressly referred to the "narrative" approach suggested in Standard 4-7.7, but both Rule 3.3 and its Comment appeared to reject the narrative method, and ABA Formal Ethics Op. 87-353 (1987) rejected the narrative method explicitly. *See also Nix v. Whiteside,* 475 U.S. 157 (1986). Nevertheless, some courts continue to approve the narrative method, and at least three jurisdictions (D.C., Florida, and Massachusetts) expressly permit a narrative in certain circumstances.

ABA Standards for Imposing Lawyer Sanctions:

6.11. Disbarment is generally appropriate when a lawyer, with the intent to deceive the court, makes a false statement, submits a false document, or improperly withholds material information, and causes serious or potentially serious injury to a party, or causes a significant or potentially significant adverse effect on the legal proceeding.

6.12. Suspension is generally appropriate when a lawyer knows that false statements or documents are being submitted to the court or that material information is improperly being withheld, and takes no remedial action, and causes injury or potential injury to a party to the legal proceeding, or causes an adverse or potentially adverse effect on the legal proceeding.

6.13. Reprimand is generally appropriate when a lawyer is negligent either in determining whether statements or documents are false or in taking remedial action when material information is being withheld, and causes injury or potential injury to a party to the legal proceeding, or causes an adverse or potentially adverse effect on the legal proceeding.

6.14. Admonition is generally appropriate when a lawyer engages in an isolated instance of neglect in determining whether submitted statements or documents are false or in failing to disclose material information upon learning of its falsity, and causes little or no actual or potential injury to a party, or causes little or no adverse or potentially adverse effect on the legal proceeding. . . .

6.31. Disbarment is generally appropriate when a lawyer:

. . . (b) makes an ex parte communication with a judge or juror with intent to affect the outcome of the proceeding, and causes serious or potentially serious injury to a party, or causes significant or potentially significant interference with the outcome of the legal proceeding. . . .

Federal Rules of Civil Procedure: Under Fed. R. Civ. P. 26(e)(1)(A), parties have a duty to supplement or correct all discovery information given to the other side (whether the information was given under the automatic initial disclosure provisions of Rule 26(a)(1) or in response to a party's specific request). The duty arises both when additional disclosure is ordered by a court and when the disclosing party "learns that in some material respect the information disclosed is incomplete or incorrect" and "the additional or corrective information has not otherwise been made known to the other parties during the discovery process or in writing."

IRS Regulations: In the regulations governing practice before the Internal Revenue Service, 31 C.F.R. §10.21 provides as follows:

§10.21.   Knowledge of Client's Omission

A practitioner who, having been retained by a client with respect to a matter administered by the Internal Revenue Service, knows that the client has not complied with the revenue laws of the United States or has made an error in or omission from any return, document, affidavit, or other paper which the client submitted or executed under the revenue laws of the United States, must advise the client promptly of the fact of such noncompliance, error, or omission. The practitioner must advise the client of the consequences as provided under the Code and regulations of such noncompliance, error, or omission.

Restatement of the Law Governing Lawyers: See Restatement §§111, 112, 118(1), and 120 in our chapter on the Restatement later in this volume.

Rule 3.4   Fairness to Opposing Party and Counsel

Canon and Code Antecedents

ABA Canons of Professional Ethics: Canons 15, 17, 25, and 39 provided, in pertinent part, as follows:

15.   How Far a Lawyer May Go in Supporting a Client's Cause

Nothing operates more certainly to create or to foster popular prejudice against lawyers as a class, and to deprive the profession of that full measure of public esteem and confidence which belongs to the proper discharge of its duties than does the false claim, often set up by the unscrupulous in defense of questionable transactions, that it is the duty of the lawyer to do whatever may enable him to succeed in winning his client's cause.

It is improper for a lawyer to assert in argument his personal belief in his client's innocence or in the justice of his cause. . . .

17.   Ill-Feeling and Personalities Between Advocates

Clients, not lawyers, are the litigants. Whatever may be the ill-feeling existing between clients, it should not be allowed to influence counsel in their conduct and demeanor toward each other or toward suitors in the case. All personalities between counsel should be scrupulously avoided. In the trial of a cause it is indecent to allude to the personal history or the personal peculiarities and idiosyncrasies of counsel on the other side. Personal colloquies between counsel which cause delay and promote unseemly wrangling should also be carefully avoided.

25.   Taking Technical Advantage of Opposite Counsel; Agreements with Him

A lawyer should not ignore known customs or practice of the Bar or of a particular Court, even when the law permits, without giving timely notice to the opposing counsel. As far as possible, important agreements, affecting the rights of clients, should be reduced to writing; but it is dishonorable to avoid performance of an agreement fairly made because it is not reduced to writing, as required by rules of Court.

39.   Witnesses

A lawyer may properly interview any witness or prospective witness for the opposing side in any civil or criminal action without the consent of opposing counsel or party. In doing so, however, he should scrupulously avoid any suggestion calculated to induce the witness to suppress or deviate from the truth, or in any degree to affect his free and untrammeled conduct when appearing at the trial or on the witness stand.

ABA Model Code of Professional Responsibility: Compare DR 7-102(A)(6), DR 7-104(A)(2), DR 7-106(A), DR 7-106(C)(1), DR 7-106(C)(2), DR 7-106(C)(3), DR 7-106(C)(4), DR 7-106(C)(5), DR 7-106(C)(7), DR 7-109(A), and DR 7-109(C) (reprinted later in this volume).

Rule 1.4, Comment 7: "Rules or court orders governing litigation may provide that information supplied to a lawyer may not be disclosed to the client. **Rule 3.4(c)** directs compliance with such rules or orders."

Rule 3.6, Comment 2: "Special rules of confidentiality may validly govern proceedings in juvenile, domestic relations and mental disability proceedings, and perhaps other types of litigation. **Rule 3.4(c)** requires compliance with such rules."

Rule 3.9: "A lawyer representing a client before a legislative body or administrative agency in a nonadjudicative proceeding shall disclose that the appearance is in a representative capacity and shall conform to the provisions of **Rules** 3.3(a) through (c), **3.4(a)** through (c), and 3.5."

Rule 3.9, Comment 1: "In representation before bodies such as legislatures, municipal councils, and executive and administrative agencies acting in a rule-making or policy-making capacity" lawyers must deal "honestly and in conformity with applicable rules of procedure. See **Rules** 3.3(a) through (c), **3.4(a)** through (c) and 3.5."

Rule 4.2, Comment 7: "If a constituent of the organization is represented in the matter by his or her own counsel, the consent by that counsel to a communication will be sufficient for purposes of this Rule. Compare **Rule 3.4(f)**."

Legislative History of Model Rule 3.4

1980 Discussion Draft (then Rule 3.2):

(a) A lawyer shall be fair to other parties and their counsel, accord them their procedural rights, and fulfill obligations under the procedural law and established practices of the tribunal.

(b) A lawyer shall not:

(1) improperly obstruct another party's access to evidence, destroy, falsify or conceal evidence, or use illegal methods of obtaining evidence;

(2) disobey an obligation under procedural law, except for an open refusal based on a good faith belief that no valid obligation exists;

(3) refer in a proceeding to a matter that the lawyer has no reasonable basis to believe is relevant thereto, or does not reasonably expect will be supported by admissible evidence;

(4) make a knowing misrepresentation of fact or law to an opposing party or counsel;

(5) interview or otherwise communicate with a party who the lawyer knows is represented by other counsel concerning the subject matter of the representation, except with the consent of that party's counsel or as authorized by law.

In addition, the 1980 Discussion Draft contained the following Rule 2.5:

Alteration or Destruction of Evidence

A lawyer shall not advise a client to alter or destroy a document or other material when the lawyer reasonably should know that the material is relevant to a pending proceeding or one that is clearly foreseeable.

1981 Draft: Substantially the same as finally adopted, except subparagraph (a), which provided:

> A lawyer shall not:
> (a) unlawfully obstruct another party's access to evidence or alter, destroy or conceal a document or other material that the lawyer knows or reasonably should know is relevant to a pending proceeding or one that is reasonably foreseeable. A lawyer shall not counsel or assist another person to do any such act.

1982 Draft was adopted.

1983 Rule: As originally adopted in 1983, Rule 3.4 was the same as the 2002 version.

2002 Amendments: At its February 2002 Mid-Year Meeting, the ABA House of Delegates adopted with only minor changes the ABA Ethics 2000 Commission proposal to amend Comment 2 to Rule 3.4 by adding the last two sentences. (The Ethics 2000 Commission did not propose any changes to the text of Rule 3.4 or to the remaining Comments.)

Selected State Variations

Alabama adds two exceptions that allow a lawyer to ask a non-client not to give information to another party if: "(2) the person may be required by law to refrain from disclosing the information; or (3) the information pertains to covert law enforcement investigations in process, such as the use of undercover law enforcement agents."

California: Compare Rule 5-200 (reprinted in the Selected State Variations following ABA Model Rule 3.3 above) and Rule 5-220, which provides that a lawyer "shall not suppress any evidence that the member or the member's client has a legal obligation to reveal or to produce." Also, Rule 5-310 provides that a member shall not:

> (A) Advise or directly or indirectly cause a person to secrete himself or herself or to leave the jurisdiction of a tribunal for the purpose of making that person unavailable as a witness therein.
> (B) Directly or indirectly pay, offer to pay, or acquiesce in the payment of compensation to a witness contingent upon the content of the witness's testimony or the outcome of the case. Except where prohibited by law, a member may advance, guarantee, or acquiesce in the payment of:
> (1) Expenses reasonably incurred by a witness in attending or testifying.
> (2) Reasonable compensation to a witness for loss of time in attending or testifying.
> (3) A reasonable fee for the professional services of an expert witness.

In addition, California Penal Code §135, which was enacted in 1872, provides as follows:

> *Destroying evidence.* Every person who, knowing that any book, paper, record, instrument in writing, or other matter or thing, is about to be produced in evidence upon any trial, inquiry, or investigation whatever, authorized by law, willfully destroys or conceals the same, with intent thereby to prevent it from being produced, is guilty of a misdemeanor.

District of Columbia: Rule 3.4 provides that a lawyer shall not:

> (a) Obstruct another party's access to evidence or alter, destroy, or conceal evidence, or counsel or assist another person to do so, if the lawyer reasonably should know that the evidence is or may be the subject of discovery or subpoena in any pending or imminent proceeding. Unless prohibited by law, a lawyer may receive physical evidence of any kind from the client or from another person. If the evidence received by the lawyer belongs to anyone other than the client, the lawyer shall make a good-faith effort to preserve it and to return it to the owner, subject to Rule 1.6; . . .
>
> (g) Peremptorily strike jurors for any reason prohibited by law.

Florida: Rule 3.4(a) replaces the ABA phrase "having potential evidentiary value" with the phrase "that the lawyer knows or reasonably should know is relevant to a pending or a reasonably foreseeable proceeding. . . ." Rule 3.4(b) provides that a lawyer shall not "fabricate" evidence, and provides that a lawyer shall not

> offer an inducement to a witness, except a lawyer may pay a witness reasonable expenses incurred by the witness in attending or testifying at proceedings; a reasonable, noncontingent fee for professional services of an expert witness; and reasonable compensation to reimburse a witness for the loss of compensation incurred by reason of preparing for, attending, or testifying at proceedings.

Florida Rule 3.4(d) deletes the phrase "to make a reasonably diligent effort," instead providing that a lawyer shall not "intentionally" fail to comply with a legally proper discovery request by an opposing party. Florida Rules 3.4(g) and (h) expand upon DR 7-105 of the ABA Model Code of Professional Responsibility by providing that a lawyer must not present, participate in presenting, or threaten to present either criminal charges or "disciplinary charges under these rules" solely to obtain an advantage in a civil matter.

Georgia: In the rules effective November 3, 2011, Rule 3.4(b)(3) provides a more detailed explanation of the kinds of payments that may be made to witnesses. Georgia omits ABA Model Rules 3.4(c), (d), and (e) entirely. Georgia Rule 3.4(f) adds that a lawyer may request a person not to volunteer information to another party "if the information is subject to the assertion of a privilege by the client."

Georgia also adds a new Rule 3.4(g), based on ABA Model Rule 4.4, which provides that a lawyer shall not "use methods of obtaining evidence that violate the legal rights of the opposing party or counsel," and a new Rule 3.4(h), taken verbatim from DR 7-105 of the ABA Model Code, which provides that a lawyer shall not "present, participate in presenting or threaten to present criminal charges solely to obtain an advantage in a civil matter." Georgia similarly adds Rule 9.2, which prohibits a lawyer from entering "into an agreement containing a condition that prohibits or restricts a person from filing a disciplinary complaint, or that requires the person to request dismissal of a pending disciplinary complaint."

Illinois expands on ABA Model Rule 3.4(b)'s command not to "offer an inducement to a witness that is prohibited by law." Comment 3 elaborates on this restriction in even more detail.

Massachusetts: Rule 3.4(g) tracks DR 7-109(C) of the ABA Model Code of Professional Responsibility. Rule 3.4(h) retains the language of DR 7-105. Rule 3.4(i) says that a lawyer shall not, "in appearing in a professional capacity before a tribunal, engage in conduct manifesting bias or prejudice based on race, sex, religion, national origin, disability, age, or sexual orientation against a party, witness, counsel, or other person," but the paragraph expressly does not preclude "legitimate advocacy" when the same factors or similar ones are "an issue in the proceeding."

New Jersey adds Rule 3.4(g), which provides, based on DR 7-105 of the ABA Model Code of Professional Responsibility, that a lawyer shall not "present, participate in presenting, or threaten to present criminal charges to obtain an improper advantage in a civil matter."

New York: Rule 3.4 draws almost exclusively on the old Model Code. Rule 3.4(a)(1)-(2) is substantially the same as DR 7-109(A)-(B). Rule 3.4(a)(3)-(6) is substantially the same as DR 7-102(A)(3), (4), (6), and (8). Rule 3.4(b) is substantially similar to DR 7-109(C). Rule 3.4(c) is substantially the same as DR 7-106(A), and Rule 3.4(d) is substantially the same as DR 7-106(C)(1)-(4). New York adds several comments, including Comment 5, which describes the use of threats:

> The use of threats in negotiation may constitute the crime of extortion. However, not all threats are improper. For example, if a lawyer represents a client who has been criminally harmed by a third person (for example, a theft of property), the lawyer's threat to report the crime does not constitute extortion when honestly claimed in an effort to obtain restitution or indemnification for the harm done. But extortion is committed if the threat involves conduct of the third person unrelated to the criminal harm (for example, a threat to report tax evasion by the third person that is unrelated to the civil dispute).

North Carolina: Rule 3.4(b) adds that a lawyer shall not "counsel or assist a witness to hide or leave the jurisdiction for the purpose of being unavailable as a witness." Rule 3.4(c) provides that a lawyer shall not "advise a client to disobey" an obligation under the rules of a tribunal, except that "a lawyer acting in good faith may take appropriate steps to test the validity of such an obligation." Rule 3.4(f)(1) limits the "employee" exception to a "managerial employee."

Ohio: The exception clause in Ohio Rule 3.4(c) applies to an open refusal based on a "good faith" assertion that no valid obligation exists. Rule 3.4(d) provides that a lawyer engaged in pretrial procedure shall not "intentionally or habitually" make a frivolous "motion or" discovery request. Ohio omits Rule 3.4(f) because it is inconsistent with a lawyer's obligations under Ohio law, and Ohio adds a new Rule 3.4(g) that provides that a lawyer shall not "advise or cause a person to hide or to leave the jurisdiction of a tribunal for the purpose of becoming unavailable as a witness."

Oklahoma omits the clause "other than the testimony of a defendant in a criminal matter" in the last sentence of Rule 3.4(a)(3). In addition, Oklahoma adds a new Rule 3.4(a)(4), which provides that a lawyer "shall not knowingly . . . fail to disclose a fact to a tribunal when disclosure is necessary to avoid assisting a criminal or fraudulent act by the client."

Oregon: Rules 3.4(b) and (g) provide that a lawyer shall not:

> (b) falsify evidence; counsel or assist a witness to testify falsely; offer an inducement to a witness that is prohibited by law; or pay, offer to pay, or acquiesce in payment of compensation to a witness contingent upon the content of the witness's testimony or the outcome of the case; except that a lawyer may advance, guarantee or acquiesce in the payment of: (1) expenses reasonably incurred by a witness in attending or testifying; (2) reasonable compensation to a witness for the witness's loss of time in attending or testifying; or (3) a reasonable fee for the professional services of an expert witness. . . .

(g) threaten to present criminal charges to obtain an advantage in a civil matter unless the lawyer reasonably believes the charge to be true and if the purpose of the lawyer is to compel or induce the person threatened to take reasonable action to make good the wrong which is the subject of the charge.

Pennsylvania: Rule 3.4(b) deletes the ABA phrase "or offer an inducement to a witness that is prohibited by law" and substitutes language nearly identical to DR 7-109(C) of the ABA Model Code of Professional Responsibility. Pennsylvania deletes ABA Model Rule 3.4(c) and substitutes the language of DR 7-106(C)(4). Pennsylvania deletes subparagraphs (d) and (e) of ABA Model Rule 3.4, and adds "and such conduct is not prohibited by Rule 4.2" at the end of Pennsylvania Rule 3.4(d), which is equivalent to ABA Model Rule 3.4(f).

Texas: Rule 3.04(a)'s prohibition on unlawfully altering, destroying, or concealing evidence applies "in anticipation of a dispute." (Regarding "unlawfully," Texas Penal Law §37.09 makes it a felony if a person "knowing that an investigation or official proceeding is pending or in progress . . . alters, destroys, or conceals any record, document, or thing with intent to impair its verity, legibility, or availability as evidence," but §37.09 does not apply to items that are "privileged" or "work product.") Texas Rule 3.04(b) retains the substance of DR 7-109(C) of the ABA Model Code of Professional Responsibility. Rule 3.04(c) retains language from DR 7-106(C), and Rule 3.04(c)(5) provides that a lawyer shall not "engage in conduct intended to disrupt the proceedings." Rule 3.04(d) provides that a lawyer shall not knowingly disobey "or advise the client to disobey" an obligation under the tribunal's "standing rules" or under a "ruling" by the tribunal, except for an open refusal based *either* on an assertion that no valid obligation exists "or on the client's willingness to accept any sanctions arising from such disobedience."

Virginia eliminates the word "unlawfully" from Rule 3.4(a), and provides that a lawyer shall not alter, destroy or conceal material having potential evidentiary value "for the purpose of obstructing a party's access to evidence." Rule 3.4 (b) and (c) incorporates language from DR 7-109(B) and (C) of the ABA Model Code of Professional Responsibility. Rule 3.4(i), which expands on DR 7-105 of the Model Code, provides that a lawyer shall not present or threaten to present criminal "or disciplinary" charges solely to obtain an advantage in a civil matter, and Rule 3.4(j) is taken verbatim from DR 7-102(A)(1) of the Model Code but adds "or initiate criminal charges" to the list of forbidden conduct.

Related Materials

ABA Civil Discovery Standards: In 1999, the ABA approved Civil Discovery Standards developed by the ABA Section of Litigation to help courts and lawyers deal with discovery issues that frequently occur in civil litigation but that often fall outside the scope of the statutes and court rules governing civil discovery. The Standards, which relate to ABA Model Rule 3.4(d), were updated in 2004. They are available online at *www.maestro.abanet.org/leadership/2004/annual/dailyjournal/103B.doc.*

ABA Formal Ethics Opinions: See ABA Formal Ethics Ops. 93-378 (1993), 96-402 (1996), and 09-454 (2009).

ABA Standards for Criminal Justice: See Prosecution Function Standards 3-5.2 (Courtroom Professionalism) and 3-5.6 (Presentation of Evidence) and Defense

Function Standards 4-1.2 (The Function of Defense Counsel), 4-4.3 (Relations with Prospective Witnesses), 4-4.5 (Compliance with Discovery Procedure), 4-4.6 (Physical Evidence), and 4-7.1 (Courtroom Professionalism). Standard 4-4.6 is especially important because it concerns a criminal defense lawyer's obligations upon the receipt of physical evidence. It provides:

Standard 4-4.6. Physical Evidence

(a) Defense counsel who receives a physical item under circumstances implicating a client in criminal conduct should disclose the location of or should deliver that item to law enforcement authorities only: (1) if required by law or court order, or (2) as provided in paragraph (d).

(b) Unless required to disclose, defense counsel should return the item to the source from whom defense counsel received it, except as provided in paragraphs (c) and (d). In returning the item to the source, defense counsel should advise the source of the legal consequences pertaining to possession or destruction of the item. Defense counsel should also prepare a written record of these events for his or her file, but should not give the source a copy of such record.

(c) Defense counsel may receive the item for a reasonable period of time during which defense counsel: (1) intends to return it to the owner; (2) reasonably fears that return of the item to the source will result in destruction of the item; (3) reasonably fears that return of the item to the source will result in physical harm to anyone; (4) intends to test, examine, inspect, or use the item in any way as part of defense counsel's representation of the client; or (5) cannot return it to the source. If defense counsel tests or examines the item, he or she should thereafter return it to the source unless there is reason to believe that the evidence might be altered or destroyed or used to harm another or return is otherwise impossible. If defense counsel retains the item, he or she should retain it in his or her law office in a manner that does not impede the lawful ability of law enforcement authorities to obtain the item.

(d) If the item received is contraband, i.e. an item, possession of which is in and of itself a crime, such as narcotics, defense counsel may suggest that the client destroy it where there is no pending case or investigation relating to this evidence and where such destruction is clearly not in violation of any criminal statute. If such destruction is not permitted by law or if in defense counsel's judgment he or she cannot retain the item, whether or not it is contraband, in a way that does not pose an unreasonable risk of physical harm to anyone, defense counsel should disclose the location of or should deliver the item to law enforcement authorities.

(e) If defense counsel discloses the location of or delivers the item to law enforcement authorities under paragraphs (a) or (d), or to a third party under paragraph (c)(1), he or she should do so in the way best designed to protect the client's interests.

In the chapter of the ABA Standards for Criminal Justice entitled "Discovery," Standard 11-3.2 (Preservation of Evidence and Testing or Evaluation by Experts) provides: "(a) If either party intends to destroy or transfer out of its possession any objects or information otherwise discoverable under the standards, the party should give notice to the other party sufficiently in advance to afford that party an opportunity to object or take other appropriate action." In addition, Standard 11-6.3 (Investigations Not to Be Impeded) provides:

Neither the counsel for the parties nor other prosecution or defense personnel should advise persons (other than the defendant) who have relevant material or information to refrain from discussing the case with opposing counsel or showing opposing counsel any relevant material, nor should they otherwise impede opposing counsel's investigation of the case.

ABA Standards for Imposing Lawyer Sanctions:

6.2. Abuse of the Legal Process

6.21. Disbarment is generally appropriate when a lawyer knowingly violates a court order or rule with the intent to obtain a benefit for the lawyer or another, and causes serious injury or potentially serious injury to a party or causes serious or potentially serious interference with a legal proceeding.

6.22. Suspension is generally appropriate when a lawyer knows that he or she is violating a court order or rule, and causes injury or potential injury to a client or a party, or causes interference or potential interference with a legal proceeding.

See also Standard 6.3, reprinted in the Related Materials following Model Rule 4.2.

Administrative Procedure: 49 C.F.R. §1103.20(h), which is a provision in the Rules of Procedure governing lawyers who appear before the federal Surface Transportation Board, provides: "Compensation of a witness is not to be made contingent on the success of a case in which the witness is called." The provision is related to Rule 3.4(b).

Bribing Witnesses: 18 U.S.C. §201, which is related to Rule 3.4(b), is entitled "Bribery of Public Officials and Witnesses." Paragraph (c)(2) provides that whoever "directly or indirectly, gives, offers, or promises anything of value to any person, for or because of the testimony . . . given or to be given by such person as a witness upon a trial, hearing, or other proceeding," shall be imprisoned for up to two years, or fined, or both. However, 18 U.S.C. §201(d) makes clear that the statute does not prohibit paying an ordinary witness "the reasonable cost of travel and subsistence incurred and the reasonable value of time lost in attendance at any such trial, hearing, or proceeding" and does not prohibit paying an expert witness "a reasonable fee for time spent" in preparing an expert opinion and in "appearing and testifying."

Contempt of Court: Various statutes and court rules make it a civil or criminal offense to disobey the rules of a tribunal, and give judges power to punish such contempt of court with fines or imprisonment. For example, 18 U.S.C. §401 (Power of Court) gives a federal court the power to punish, by fine, imprisonment, or both, "(1) Misbehavior of any person in its presence or so near thereto as to obstruct the administration of justice; (2) Misbehavior of any of its officers in their official transactions; [and] (3) Disobedience or resistance to its lawful writ, process, order, rule, decree, or command." Similarly, Rule 42(b) of the Federal Rules of Criminal Procedure provides that a federal judge "may summarily punish a person who commits criminal contempt in its presence if the judge saw or heard the contemptuous conduct and so certifies." For a state statute specifying numerous categories of conduct that constitute contempt of court, see §1209 of the California Code of Civil Procedure.

Cooperation Proclamation: In 2008, The Sedona Conference—a nonprofit group that includes judges, lawyers, and experts—issued The Sedona Conference Cooperation Proclamation to "promote open and forthright information sharing, dialogue (internal and external), training, and the development of practical tools to facilitate cooperative, collaborative, transparent discovery." The Cooperation Proclamation, which relates to ABA Model Rule 3.4(d), "calls on trial lawyers, in-house counsel, and judges to rethink the contentious practices that have grown up around civil discovery and refocus litigation toward the substantive resolution of legal disputes." It has been endorsed by more than 100 federal and state judges and has been cited in dozens of court opinions addressing discovery disputes. The Cooperation Proclamation is available online at *https://thesedonaconference.org/ cooperation-proclamation.*

Electronic Evidence: The exponential growth in the use of e-mail and other electronic methods to create and preserve documents has raised many new issues in discovery, and the intentional or negligent failure to preserve electronic evidence has sometimes led to civil sanctions or criminal prosecution. For an extended treatment of these issues, see Paul Rice, Electronic Evidence: Law and Practice (ABA 2d ed., 2008).

Federal Rules of Appellate Procedure: Fed. R. App. P. 46(c) provides that a federal court of appeals, after reasonable notice and a hearing if requested, may discipline an attorney who practices before it for "conduct unbecoming a member of the bar or for failure to comply with any court rule."

Federal Rules of Civil Procedure: Various provisions of the Federal Rules of Civil Procedure penalize the kinds of behavior condemned in Rule 3.4. With respect to Rule 3.4(c), Fed. R. Civ. P. 41(b) provides: "If the plaintiff fails to prosecute or to comply with these rules or a court order, a defendant may move to dismiss the action or any claim against it," and such a dismissal ordinarily "operates as an adjudication on the merits." Fed. R. Civ. P. 45(e) provides that the court many hold any person in contempt who "fails without adequate excuse to obey a subpoena." With respect to Rule 3.4(d), Fed. R. Civ. P. 26(g) provides sanctions for improper or bad faith conduct in discovery, and Fed. R. Civ. P. 37 authorizes courts to compel a party to respond to discovery requests and authorizes courts to sanction a party's unjustified failure to respond to discovery.

Model Rules of Professional Conduct for Federal Lawyers clarify that Rule 3.4 applies to an obligation "to an opposing party and counsel." The Rules for Federal Lawyers address obligations to a tribunal in a new Rule 3.3(a)(5), quoted after Rule 3.3 above.

Restatement of the Law Governing Lawyers: See Restatement §§105, 107, 110(3), and 116-119 in our chapter on the Restatement later in this volume.

Spoliation of Evidence: "Spoliation" is a term often used by courts to describe the intentional or negligent loss or destruction of evidence. Spoliation is thus related to ABA Model Rule 3.4(a), which provides that a lawyer shall not unlawfully "destroy" material evidence. In some jurisdictions, spoliation of evidence is an independent tort, and a party who has been damaged by spoliation may sue the spoliator for damages. In virtually all jurisdictions, courts have authority to punish spoliation with sanctions, such as adverse inferences, preclusion of testimony about the destroyed item, or even dismissal of claims or defenses. For an extended treatment of spoliation, see Margaret M. Koesel, Tracey L. Turnbull, & Daniel F. Gourash, Spoliation of Evidence: Sanctions and Remedies for Destruction of Evidence in Civil Litigation (2d ed., ABA 2006).

Witness Tampering: Federal law makes it a crime to kill, intimidate, or harass a witness, victim, or informant in an official proceeding, and many states have parallel laws. The main federal statute on witness tampering is 18 U.S.C. §1512 (entitled "Tampering with a Witness, Victim, or an Informant"). A typical example of a parallel state statute is Missouri Revised Statutes §575.270, which provides that "a person commits the crime of tampering with a witness if, with purpose to induce a witness or a prospective witness to disobey a subpoena or other legal process, or to absent himself or avoid subpoena or other legal process, or to withhold evidence, information or documents, or to testify falsely, he: (1) Threatens or causes harm to any person or property; or (2) Uses force, threats or deception; or (3) Offers, confers or agrees to confer any benefit, direct or indirect, upon such witness; or (4) Conveys any of the foregoing to another in furtherance of a conspiracy."

Rule 3.5   Impartiality and Decorum of the Tribunal

Canon and Code Antecedents

ABA Canons of Professional Ethics: Canons 3 and 23 provided as follows:

3.   Attempts to Exert Personal Influence on the Court

Marked attention and unusual hospitality on the part of a lawyer to a Judge, uncalled for by the personal relations of the parties, subject both the Judge and the lawyer to misconstructions of motive and should be avoided. A lawyer should not communicate or argue privately with the Judge as to the merits of a pending cause, and he deserves rebuke and denunciation for any device or attempt to gain from a Judge special personal consideration or favor. A self-respecting independence in the discharge of professional duty, without denial or diminution of the courtesy and respect due the Judge's station, is the only proper foundation for cordial personal and official relations between Bench and Bar.

23.   Attitude Toward Jury

All attempts to curry favor with juries by fawning, flattery or pretended solicitude for their personal comfort are unprofessional. Suggestions of counsel, looking to the comfort or convenience of jurors, and propositions to dispense with argument, should be made to the Court out of the jury's hearing. A lawyer must never converse privately with jurors about the case; and both before and during the trial he should avoid communicating with them, even as to matters foreign to the cause.

ABA Model Code of Professional Responsibility: Compare DR 7-106(C)(6), DR 7-108(A), DR 7-108(B), and DR 7-110(B) (reprinted later in this volume).

Cross-References in Other Rules

Rule 3.9: "A lawyer representing a client before a legislative body or administrative agency in a nonadjudicative proceeding shall disclose that the appearance is in a representative capacity and shall conform to the provisions of **Rules** 3.3(a) through (c), 3.4(a) through (c), and **3.5**."

Rule 3.9, Comment 1: "In representation before bodies such as legislatures, municipal councils, and executive and administrative agencies acting in a rule-making or policy-making capacity" lawyers must deal "honestly and in conformity with applicable rules of procedure. See **Rules** 3.3(a) through (c), 3.4(a) through (c) and **3.5**."

Legislative History of Model Rule 3.5

1980 Discussion Draft (then called **Rule 3.7**) provided as follows:

(a) A lawyer shall assist a tribunal in maintaining impartiality and conducting the proceedings with decorum.

(b) A lawyer shall not:

(1) seek improperly to influence a judge, juror, or other decision-maker, or, except as permitted by law, communicate ex parte with such a person;

(2) seek improperly to influence a witness;

(3) be abusive or obstreperous;

(4) refuse to comply with an obligation of procedural law or an order of the tribunal, except for an open refusal based on a good faith belief that compliance is not legally required.

1981 Draft was substantially the same as adopted, except that subparagraph (a) used the phrase "other decision-maker" instead of "other official."

1982 Draft was adopted.

1983 Rule: As originally adopted in 1983, Rule 3.5 had only three paragraphs. It provided that a lawyer shall not:

(a) [Same as 2002 version of Rule 3.5(a).]

(b) communicate ex parte with such a person except as permitted by law; or

(c) [Same as 2002 version of Rule 3.5(d).]

2002 Amendments: At its February 2002 Mid-Year Meeting, the ABA House of Delegates adopted without change the ABA Ethics 2000 Commission proposal to amend Rule 3.5 and its Comment. The amendments slightly changed Rule 3.5(a), added all of Rule 3.5(c), re-lettered the old paragraph (c) as paragraph (d), and added Comments 2, 3, and 5.

Selected State Variations

Arizona clarifies that Rule 3.5(a) applies only to an official "of a tribunal," and substitutes "likely" for "intended" in Rule 3.5(d).

California: Rule 5-300 provides as follows:

(A) A member shall not directly or indirectly give or lend anything of value to a judge, official, or employee of a tribunal unless the personal or family relationship between the member and the judge, official, or employee is such that gifts are customarily given and exchanged. Nothing contained in this rule shall prohibit a member from contributing to the campaign fund of a judge running for election or confirmation pursuant to applicable law pertaining to such contributions.

(B) A member shall not directly or indirectly communicate with or argue to a judge or judicial officer upon the merits of a contested matter pending before such judge or judicial officer, except:

(1) In open court; or

(2) With the consent of all other counsel in such matter; or

(3) In the presence of all other counsel in such matter; or

(4) In writing with a copy thereof furnished to such other counsel; or

(5) In ex parte matters.

(C) As used in this rule, "judge" and "judicial officer" shall include law clerks, research attorneys, or other court personnel who participate in the decision-making process.

Florida: Rule 3.5(a) provides that a lawyer shall not seek to influence a judge, juror, prospective juror, or other decision maker "except as permitted by law or the rules of court." Rule 3.5(d), governing communications with jurors, former jurors, and prospective jurors, generally tracks DR 7-108 of the ABA Model Code of Professional Responsibility, but adds that a lawyer shall not:

> (4) after dismissal of the jury in a case with which the lawyer is connected, initiate communication with or cause another to initiate communication with any juror regarding the trial except to determine whether the verdict may be subject to legal challenge; provided, a lawyer may not interview jurors for this purpose unless the lawyer has reason to believe that grounds for such challenge may exist; and provided further, before conducting any such interview the lawyer must file in the cause a notice of intention to interview setting forth the name of the juror or jurors to be interviewed. A copy of the notice must be delivered to the trial judge and opposing counsel a reasonable time before such interview. . . .

Georgia: Rule 3.5 adopts most of the pre-2002 version of ABA Model Rule 3.5 verbatim, but alters the introductory phrase to make clear that the prohibitions apply "without regard to whether the lawyer represents a client in the matter."

Maryland: Rule 3.5 includes several sui generis provisions, including a prohibition against discussing employment of a judge before whom the lawyer's firm has a matter, a limitation on contacts with discharged jurors, and a requirement to report knowledge of improper contacts with jurors or prospective jurors.

Massachusetts: Rule 3.5(d) restricts the ability of lawyers connected to a case to initiate a communication with a member of the jury after discharge without leave of the court.

Nevada adds Rule 3.5(e):

> (e) Before the jury is sworn to try the cause, a lawyer may investigate the prospective jurors to ascertain any basis for challenge, provided that a lawyer or the lawyer's employees or independent contractors may not, at any time before the commencement of the trial, conduct or authorize any investigation of the prospective jurors, through any means which are calculated or likely to lead to communication with prospective jurors of any allegations or factual circumstances relating to the case at issue. Conduct prohibited by this Rule includes, but is not limited to, any direct or indirect communication with a prospective juror, a member of the juror's family, any employer, or any other person that may lead to direct or indirect communication with a prospective juror.

New Jersey: Rule 3.5(b) provides only that a lawyer shall not communicate ex parte with anyone specified in subparagraph (a) "except as permitted by law," and New Jersey Rule 3.5(c) says only that a lawyer shall not "engage in conduct intended to disrupt a tribunal." New Jersey deletes ABA Model Rules 3.5(c)(1)-(3) and Rule 3.5(d).

New York: Rule 3.5 draws heavily on the old Model Code. Rule 3.5(a)(1)-(2) is similar to 7-110(A) and (B), respectively. Rule 3.5(a)(4) is similar to DR 7-108(A) and (B)(1), and Rule 3.5(a)(6) is similar to DR 7-108(E). Rule 3.5(b)-(d) is nearly identical to DR 7-108(B)(2), 7-108(F), and 7-108(G), respectively.

North Carolina: Rule 3.5 adds language from DR 7-106(C)(5)-(7), DR 7-108(D),(F), and (G), and DR 7-110(B) of the ABA Model Code of Professional Responsibility.

Ohio replaces the term "judge" with the term "judicial officer" throughout Rule 3.5. Ohio adds Rule 3.5(a)(2), which provides that a lawyer shall not "lend anything of value or give anything of more than *de minimis* value to a judicial officer, official, or employee of a tribunal." Ohio Rule 3.5(a)(3) provides that a lawyer shall not communicate ex parte with "(i) a judicial officer or other official as to the merits of the case during the proceeding unless authorized to do so by law or court order" or "(ii) a juror or prospective juror during the proceeding unless otherwise authorized to do so by law or court order." Ohio also adds a new Rule 3.5(b), which provides that a lawyer "shall reveal promptly to the tribunal improper conduct by a juror or prospective juror, or by another toward a juror, prospective juror, or family member of a juror or prospective juror, of which the lawyer has knowledge."

Texas: Rule 3.05 is substantially the same as DR 7-110(B) of the ABA Model Code of Professional Responsibility. Rule 3.06 borrows heavily from DR 7-108, but rearranges the order somewhat, adds references to an "alternate juror," and provides in Rule 3.06(A)(2) that a lawyer shall not "seek to influence a venireman or juror concerning the merits of a pending matter by means prohibited by law or applicable rules of practice or procedure."

Virginia: Rule 3.5(a)(2) generally tracks DR 7-108(D) of the ABA Model Code of Professional Responsibility but adds that a lawyer shall not "after discharge of the jury from further consideration of a case: (i) ask questions of or make comments to a member of that jury that are calculated merely to harass or embarrass the juror or to influence the juror's actions in future jury service." A new Rule 3.5(e) adds exceptions to the rule against ex parte communications with a judge.

Related Materials

ABA Formal Ethics Opinions: See ABA Formal Ethics Op. 07-449 n.7 (2007).

ABA Model Code of Judicial Conduct: The ABA Model Code of Judicial Conduct, which is cited in Rule 3.5, Comment 1, is reprinted in full later in this volume.

ABA Standards for Criminal Justice: See Prosecution Function Standard 3-2.8 (Relations with the Courts and Bar), Standard 3-5.2 (Courtroom Professionalism), Standard 3-5.4 (Relations with Jury), and Defense Function Standard 4-7.1 (Courtroom Professionalism) and Standard 4-7.3 (Relations with Jury). See also ABA Standards for Special Functions of the Trial Judge.

ABA Standards for Imposing Lawyer Sanctions: See Standard 6.3, which is reprinted in the Related Materials following ABA Model Rule 4.2.

Federal Rules of Civil Procedure: Rule 65(b)(1) permits ex parte communications by attorneys for parties seeking temporary restraining orders under the following circumstances:

> *Issuing Without Notice.* The court may issue a temporary restraining order without written or oral notice to the adverse party or its attorney only if:
>> (A) specific facts in an affidavit or a verified complaint clearly show that immediate and irreparable injury, loss, or damage will result to the movant before the adverse party can be heard in opposition; and
>> (B) the movant's attorney certifies in writing any efforts made to give notice and the reasons why it should not be required.

Model Rules of Professional Conduct for Federal Lawyers: Rule 3.5(a) prohibits a federal lawyer from seeking to influence "a tribunal, a member of a tribunal, a prospective member of a tribunal, or other official by means prohibited by law."

Obstruction of Justice: Various federal and state statutes make it a crime to obstruct justice. For example, 18 U.S.C. §1503, entitled "Influencing or Injuring Officer or Juror Generally," makes it illegal to use "threats or force . . . to influence, intimidate, or impede any grand or petit juror, or officer in or of any court of the United States . . . in the discharge of his duty"; and 18 U.S.C. §1512, entitled "Tampering with a Witness, Victim or an Informant," makes it a crime to kill, intimidate, harass, or threaten a witness, victim, or informant in connection with an official proceeding. (We reprint §§1503 and 1512 below in our chapter of Federal Provisions on Conflicts, Confidentiality, and Crimes.)

Restatement of the Law Governing Lawyers: See Restatement §§112, 113, and 115 in our chapter on the Restatement later in this volume.

Rule 3.6   Trial Publicity

Canon and Code Antecedents

ABA Canons of Professional Ethics: Canon 20 provided as follows:

20. *Newspaper Discussion of Pending Litigation*

Newspaper publications by a lawyer as to pending or anticipated litigation may interfere with a fair trial in the Courts and otherwise prejudice the due administration of justice. Generally they are to be condemned. If the extreme circumstances of a particular case justify a statement to the public, it is unprofessional to make it anonymously. An *ex parte* reference to the facts should not go beyond quotation from the records and papers on file in the court; but even in extreme cases it is better to avoid any *ex parte* statement.

ABA Model Code of Professional Responsibility: Compare DR 7-107 (reprinted later in this volume).

Cross-References in Other Rules

Rule 3.8(f) provides that the prosecutor of a criminal case shall "exercise reasonable care to prevent investigators . . . or other persons . . . from making an extrajudicial statement that the prosecutor would be prohibited from making under **Rule 3.6** or this Rule."

Rule 3.8, Comment 5: "Paragraph (f) supplements **Rule 3.6**, which prohibits extrajudicial statements that have a substantial likelihood of prejudicing an adjudicatory proceeding. . . . Nothing in this Comment is intended to restrict the statements which a prosecutor may make which comply with **Rule 3.6(b)** or **3.6(c)**."

Legislative History of Model Rule 3.6

1980 Discussion Draft (then Rule 3.8) was essentially an amalgam and reorganization of DR 7-107, except that paragraphs (F), (I), and (J) of DR 7-107 were deleted, and the following new provisions were added:

(a) To ensure a fair trial, a lawyer involved in the investigation of a criminal matter or in criminal or civil litigation shall not, except as provided in paragraph (b), make an extrajudicial statement: . . .

(2) when the matter under investigation or in litigation is a criminal case or a civil case triable to a jury and the statement relates to: . . .

(v) information the lawyer knows or reasonably should know would be inadmissible as evidence in a trial;

(vi) any other matter that similarly creates a serious and imminent risk of prejudicing an impartial trial.

(b) A lawyer involved in the investigation or litigation of a matter may state without elaboration . . .

(6) in a criminal case: . . .

(vi) that the accused denies the charges.

(c) When evidence or information received in or relating to a proceeding is by law or order of a tribunal to be kept confidential, the lawyer shall not unlawfully disclose the evidence or information.

1981 Draft was the same as adopted, except (b)(7)(iii), which provided: "the fact, time, and place of arrest, resistance, pursuit and use of weapons."

1982 Draft was adopted.

1983 Rule: From its original adoption in 1983 until its amendment in 1994, Rule 3.6 provided as follows:

(a) A lawyer shall not make an extrajudicial statement that a reasonable person would expect to be disseminated by means of public communication if the lawyer knows or reasonably should know that it will have a substantial likelihood of materially prejudicing an adjudicative proceeding.

(b) A statement referred to in paragraph (a) ordinarily is likely to have such an effect when it refers to a civil matter triable to a jury, a criminal matter, or any other proceeding that could result in incarceration, and the proceeding relates to:

(1)-(6) [Same as items (1) through (6) in Comment 5 to 2002 version of Rule 3.6.]

(c) Notwithstanding paragraph (a) and (b)(1-5), a lawyer involved in the investigation or litigation of a matter may state without elaboration:

(1) the general nature of the claim or defense;

(2) [Same as (b)(2) in 2002 version of Rule 3.6.]

(3) that an investigation of the matter is in progress, including the general scope of the investigation, the offense or claim or defense involved and, except when prohibited by law, the identity of the persons involved;

(4)-(6) [Same as (b)(4)-(6) in 2002 version of Rule 3.6.]

(7) In a criminal case:

(i)-(iv) [Same as (b)(7)(i)-(iv) in 2002 version of Rule 3.6.]

1994 Amendment: At its August 1994 Annual Meeting, by a voice vote, the ABA House of Delegates significantly amended Rule 3.6. The amendment was spurred by the Supreme Court's decision in *Gentile v. Nevada State Bar,* 501 U.S. 1030 (1991), which cast doubt on the constitutionality of some parts of Rule 3.6. (Companion amendments to Rule 3.8 were approved at the same time, also in response to *Gentile.*)

The 1994 amendment to Rule 3.6 had three purposes: (1) to list various types of information that a lawyer may disclose in out-of-court statements despite the general ban on extrajudicial statements substantially likely to prejudice a court proceeding; (2) to create a "safe harbor" that allows a lawyer to protect clients against undue prejudice resulting from recent publicity not initiated by the lawyer or client; and (3) to make clear that all lawyers in a firm or government agency are governed by Rule 3.6. For a legislative-style version of the Rule showing what was added and deleted by the 1994 amendment, see our 1995 edition.

The 1994 amendment also substantially rewrote the Comment and Code Comparison, deleting former paragraph 2 of the Comment and adding paragraphs 3 through 7. The deleted paragraph of the Comment had stated as follows:

> [2] No body of rules can simultaneously satisfy all interests of fair trial and all those of free expression. The formula in this Rule is based upon the ABA Model Code of Professional Responsibility and the ABA Standards Relating to Fair Trial and Free Press, as amended in 1978.

The amendment was co-sponsored by the ABA Standing Committee on Ethics and Professional Responsibility and the ABA Criminal Justice Section. Below are excerpts from the joint ABA report explaining the amendments.

Excerpts from ABA Report Explaining 1994 Amendments*

> In *Gentile*, a criminal defense lawyer challenged disciplinary action taken against him by the State Bar of Nevada under its version of Rule 3.6, because of certain remarks made by him at a press conference relating to his client's anticipated defense. The lawyer challenged the state's action on grounds that his extrajudicial statements were protected by the First Amendment, and that in any event his remarks were within the Rule's "safe harbor" provision.
>
> The Supreme Court unanimously upheld the Rule's "substantial likelihood of material prejudice" test. However, a majority of five Justices held the Rule void for vagueness as interpreted and applied by the Nevada State Bar in the circumstances of the case. . . . The five members of the Court who reversed the state's disciplinary action noted that the safe harbor provision of Rule 3.6 allows a criminal lawyer to explain the "general" nature of his client's defense "without elaboration," and pointed out that the terms "general" and "elaboration" have "no settled usage or tradition of interpretation in law." As worded, they said, the provision gives a lawyer "no principle for determining when his remarks pass from the safe harbor of the general to the forbidden sea of the elaborated," and creates "a trap for the wary as well as the unwary."
>
> The Standing Committee on Ethics and Professional Responsibility . . . proposes to revise the Rule's safe harbor provision by deleting the qualifying terms which the Supreme Court held unconstitutionally vague. . . .
>
> The Committee adopted . . . a provision entitling a lawyer to respond where adverse publicity has been initiated by an opposing party or third persons, in order to avoid substantial undue prejudice to the lawyer's client. The Committee felt that in this situation, the danger of the second statement prejudicing the proceeding is minimized, and the rights of the client can be protected.
>
> [F]or completeness, the Rule must also extend to lawyers associated with those participating in a matter, and those who formerly participated in a matter. The need for lawyers outside a proceeding to interpret those proceedings to the public is so great,

---

* Committee Reports do not represent official policy of the ABA. They are for information only, and the opinions are those of the authors of the report.

and the right of comment on government process so fundamental that the Committee felt that the lawyers affected by speech restrictions of Rule 3.6 should be clearly and narrowly defined.

The Committee also considered whether Rule 3.6 should be limited to criminal cases, or to cases involving jury trials. While . . . there is less chance of prejudice from statements made in the course of a civil proceeding than in the context of a criminal matter, and in a bench trial than in a jury trial, it is the Committee's view that the nature of the proceeding and the identity of the trier of fact are relevant to but not dispositive of the issue of likelihood of prejudice. . . .

2002 Amendments: At its February 2002 Mid-Year Meeting, the ABA House of Delegates adopted without change the ABA Ethics 2000 Commission proposal to amend Rule 3.6(a) and to add Comment 8. The rest of Rule 3.6 and its Comment were unchanged. The former version of Rule 3.6(a) applied to an extrajudicial statement that "a reasonable person would expect" to be disseminated by means of public communication, instead of "if the lawyer knows or reasonably should know" as provided in the current rule.

Selected State Variations

Alabama: Rule 3.8(a) provides as follows:

(a) A lawyer shall not make an extrajudicial statement that a reasonable person would expect to be disseminated by means of public communication if the lawyer knows or reasonably should know that it will have a substantial likelihood of materially prejudicing an adjudicative proceeding in the matter.

Alabama Rule 3.8(b) provides that a statement referred to in Rule 3.8(a) ordinarily is likely to have a materially prejudicial effect if it refers to "a civil matter triable to a jury, a criminal matter, or any other proceeding that could result in incarceration" and the statement relates to one of the subjects listed in Comment 5 to ABA Model Rule 3.6 (which Alabama moves to the text of the rule). Alabama omits Rule 3.6(d).

California: Rule 5-120 tracks the pre-2002 version of ABA Model Rule 3.6 nearly verbatim, except that California omits subparagraph (d).

District of Columbia: Rule 3.6 consists of only one sentence: "A lawyer engaged in a case being tried to a judge or jury shall not make an extrajudicial statement that the lawyer knows or reasonably should know will be disseminated by means of mass public communication and will create a serious and imminent threat of material prejudice to the proceeding."

Florida: Rule 3.6(a) omits the ABA phrase "who is participating or has participated in the investigation or litigation of a matter" and provides that a lawyer shall not make an extrajudicial statement that a "reasonable person" would expect to be disseminated by means of public communication if the lawyer knows or reasonably should know that it will have a substantial likelihood of materially prejudicing an adjudicative proceeding "due to its creation of an imminent and substantial detrimental effect on that proceeding." Florida deletes ABA Model Rule 3.6(b), (c), and (d), and substitutes the following Rule 3.6(b):

Statements of Third Parties. A lawyer shall not counsel or assist another person to make such a statement. Counsel shall exercise reasonable care to prevent investigators, employees, or other persons assisting in or associated with a case from making extrajudicial statements that are prohibited under this rule.

Georgia: Rule 3.6(a), (c), and (d) tracks the pre-2002 version of ABA Model Rule 3.6 verbatim, but Georgia has relegated Rule 3.6(b) to a new paragraph 5B of the Comment, which notes that there are "certain subjects which are more likely than not to have no material prejudicial effect on a proceeding." The Comment then lists all of the items in ABA Model Rule 3.6(b) as examples of things that a lawyer may "usually" state.

Illinois: Rule 3.6(a) prohibits an extrajudicial statement if the lawyer "knows or reasonably should know" that the statement would "pose a serious and imminent threat to the fairness of an adjudicative proceeding in the matter."

Iowa: In Rule 3.6, Iowa adds a paragraph (e) that provides: "Any communication made under paragraph (b) that includes information that a defendant will be or has been charged with a crime must also include a statement explaining that a criminal charge is merely an accusation and the defendant is presumed innocent until and unless proven guilty."

Michigan: Rule 3.6(a) includes a lengthy explanation of when "a statement is likely to have a substantial likelihood of materially prejudicing an adjudicative proceeding," drawing nearly verbatim from a description of such statements contained in Comment 5 to Model Rule 3.6.

New Jersey deletes ABA Model Rule 3.6(d).

New York moves Rule 3.6(b)-(d) to Rule 3.6(c)-(e) and uses 3.6(b) for a list of subjects that are likely to "prejudice materially an adjudicative proceeding." The list is drawn nearly verbatim from Comment 5 of the Model Rules.

North Carolina adds Rule 3.6(e), which provides that Rule 3.6 does not "preclude a lawyer from replying to charges of misconduct publicly made against the lawyer or from participating in the proceedings of legislative, administrative, or other investigative bodies."

Ohio: Rule 3.6(b) makes clear that a lawyer may not engage in trial publicity if doing so would violate a duty of confidentiality under Rule 1.6.

Texas: Rule 3.07(a) begins "[i]n the course of representing a client" in place of the ABA phrase "[a] lawyer who is participating or has participated in the investigation or litigation of a matter," then tracks ABA Model Rule 3.6(a) verbatim, but Texas, at the end of Rule 3.07(a), adds that a lawyer "shall not counsel or assist another person to make such a statement."

Texas Rule 3.07(b) provides that a lawyer "ordinarily will violate paragraph (a), and the likelihood of a violation increases if the adjudication is ongoing or imminent," by making an extrajudicial statement described in Rule 3.07(a) if the statement refers to five specified categories of information, which track verbatim the items listed in Comment 5 to ABA Model Rule 3.6 — except that Texas omits from this list "(6) the fact that a defendant has been charged with a crime, unless there is included therein a statement explaining that the charge is merely an accusation and that the defendant is presumed innocent until and unless proven guilty."

Texas Rule 3.07(c) generally tracks ABA Model Rule 3.6(b), with slight variations. Texas omits ABA Model Rule 3.6(c) and (d).

Virginia: Rule 3.6 provides as follows:

> (a) A lawyer participating in or associated with the investigation or the prosecution or the defense of a criminal matter that may be tried by a jury shall not make

or participate in making an extrajudicial statement that a reasonable person would expect to be disseminated by means of public communication that the lawyer knows, or should know, will have a substantial likelihood of interfering with the fairness of the trial by a jury.

(b) A lawyer shall exercise reasonable care to prevent employees and associates from making an extrajudicial statement that the lawyer would be prohibited from making under this Rule.

Related Materials

ABA Formal Ethics Opinions: No ABA formal ethics opinion has discussed ABA Model Rule 3.6.

ABA Standards of Criminal Justice: See Prosecution Function Standard 3-1.4 (Public Statements). In 1991 the ABA House of Delegates approved a section of the ABA Standards for Criminal Justice entitled "Fair Trial and Free Press." Standard 8-1.1 (Extrajudicial Statements by Attorneys) parallels an earlier version of ABA Model Rule 3.6. The Standards governing Fair Trial and Free Press are available online at *http://www.americanbar.org/publications/criminal_justice_section_archive/ crimjust_standards_fairtrial_blk.html.*

Department of Justice Guidelines: To help strike "a fair balance between the protection of individuals accused of crime or involved in civil proceedings with the Government," on the one hand, and "public understandings of the problems of controlling crime and administering government," on the other hand, the United States Department of Justice has adopted 28 C.F.R. §50.2 (Release of Information by Personnel of the Department of Justice Relating to Criminal and Civil Proceedings), which we reprint in our chapter on Federal Provisions on Conflicts, Confidentiality, and Crimes.

Model Rules of Professional Conduct for Federal Lawyers: Rule 3.6(a) prohibits extrajudicial statements likely to prejudice an adjudicative proceeding "or an official review process thereof." Rule 3.6(b)(4) states that Rule 3.6 applies to any proceeding that could result in incarceration "or other adverse action." The Rules for Federal Lawyers also add Rule 3.6(d), which provides: "The protection and release of information in matters pertaining to the Government shall be consistent with law."

Restatement of the Law Governing Lawyers: See Restatement §109 in our chapter on the Restatement later in this volume.

United States Attorney's Manual: The United States Attorney's Manual, which is designed to be "a quick and ready reference" for U.S. Attorneys, Assistant U.S. Attorneys, and Department of Justice attorneys responsible for prosecuting violations of federal law, contains a series of rules at §§1-7.000 *et seq.* entitled "Media Relations." Section 1-7.112 (Need for Free Press and Public Trial) states:

> [C]areful weight must be given in each case to the constitutional requirements of a free press and public trials as well as the right of the people in a constitutional democracy to have access to information about the conduct of law enforcement officers, prosecutors and courts, consistent with the individual rights of the accused. Further, recognition should be given to the needs of public safety, the apprehension of fugitives, and the rights of the public to be informed on matters that can affect enactment or enforcement of public laws or the development or change of public policy.

These principles must be evaluated in each case and must involve a fair degree of discretion and the exercise of sound judgment, as every possibility cannot be predicted and covered by written policy statement.

Section 1-7.210 vests final responsibility for "all matters involving the news media and the Department of Justice" in the Director of the DOJ's Office of Public Affairs (OPA). Other sections require prosecutors to consult with the Director of OPA before commenting in the public media about a criminal case. To read United States Attorney's Manual sections on media relations, see *http://www.justice.gov/ usao/eousa/foia_reading_room/usam/*.

Rule 3.7   Lawyer as Witness

Canon and Code Antecedents

ABA Canons of Professional Ethics: Canons 18 and 19 provided as follows:

18.   Treatment of Witnesses and Litigants

A lawyer should always treat adverse witnesses and suitors with fairness and due consideration, and he should never minister to the malevolence or prejudices of a client in the trial or conduct of a cause. The client cannot be made the keeper of the lawyer's conscience in professional matters. He has no right to demand that his counsel shall abuse the opposite party or indulge in offensive personalities. Improper speech is not excusable on the ground that it is what the client would say if speaking in his own behalf.

19.   Appearance of Lawyer as Witness for His Client

When a lawyer is a witness for his client, except as to merely formal matters, such as the attestation or custody of an instrument and the like, he should leave the trial of the case to other counsel. Except when essential to the ends of justice, a lawyer should avoid testifying in court in behalf of his client.

ABA Model Code of Professional Responsibility: Compare DR 5-101(B), DR 5-102(A), and DR 5-102(B) (reprinted later in this volume).

Cross-References in Other Rules

None.

Legislative History of Model Rule 3.7

1980 Discussion Draft (then Rule 3.9) prohibited a lawyer from acting as an advocate, "except on the lawyer's own behalf, in litigation in which the lawyer's own conduct is a material issue or in which the lawyer is likely to be a witness," unless the lawyer satisfied exceptions that were substantially the same as finally adopted.

1981 Draft was substantially the same as adopted.

1982 Draft was adopted.

1983 Rule: As originally adopted in 1983, Rule 3.7 was essentially the same as the 2002 version.

2002 Amendments: At its February 2002 Mid-Year Meeting, the ABA House of Delegates adopted without change the ABA Ethics 2000 Commission proposal to amend Rule 3.7 and its Comment. The amendments changed "except where" to "unless" in the text of Rule 3.7(a), made minor changes to Comments 1 through 4, added Comment 5, significantly amended Comment 6, and added Comment 7.

Selected State Variations

California: Rule 5-210 provides as follows:

> A member shall not act as an advocate before a jury which will hear testimony from the member unless:
> (A) The testimony relates to an uncontested matter; or
> (B) The testimony relates to the nature and value of legal services rendered in the case; or
> (C) The member has the informed written consent of the client. If the member represents the People or a governmental entity, the consent shall be obtained from the head of the office or a designee of the head of the office by which the member is employed and shall be consistent with principles of recusal.

District of Columbia: Rule 3.7(b) provides that a lawyer may not act as advocate in a trial in which another lawyer in the lawyer's firm is likely to be called as a witness "if the other lawyer would be precluded from acting as advocate in the trial by Rule 1.7 or Rule 1.9." D.C. also adds that the provisions of Rule 3.7(b) "do not apply if the lawyer who is appearing as an advocate is employed by, and appears on behalf of, a government agency."

Florida: Rule 3.7(a) applies when a lawyer is likely to be a necessary witness "on behalf of the client," and creates an exception when "the testimony will relate solely to a matter of formality and there is no reason to believe that substantial evidence will be offered in opposition to the testimony." Florida adopts ABA Model Rule 3.7(b) verbatim.

New York: Rule 3.7(a) applies only when a lawyer is likely to be a necessary witness "on a significant issue of fact." Rule 3.7(a) also adds two additional exceptions: "(4) the testimony will relate solely to a matter of formality, and there is no reason to believe that substantial evidence will be offered in opposition to the testimony; or (5) the testimony is authorized by the tribunal."

Ohio adds a new Rule 3.7(c), which provides as follows: "A government lawyer participating in a case shall not testify or offer the testimony of another lawyer in the same government agency, except where division (a) applies or where permitted by law."

Texas: Rule 3.08(a) disqualifies a lawyer if the lawyer knows or believes that the lawyer is or may be a witness "necessary to establish an essential fact on behalf of the lawyer's client," unless specified exceptions apply. The exceptions are substantially identical to DR 5-101(B)(1)-(3) of the ABA Model Code of Professional Responsibility, but Texas adds an exception if "(4) the lawyer is a party to the action and is appearing pro se," and Texas applies the "substantial hardship" exception only if "the lawyer has promptly notified opposing counsel that the lawyer expects to testify in the matter. . . ." Texas Rules 3.08(b) and (c) provide as follows:

(b) A lawyer shall not continue as an advocate in a pending adjudicatory proceeding if the lawyer believes that the lawyer will be compelled to furnish testimony that will be substantially adverse to the lawyer's client, unless the client consents after full disclosure.

(c) Without the client's informed consent, a lawyer may not act as advocate in an adjudicatory proceeding in which another lawyer in the lawyer's firm is prohibited by paragraphs (a) or (b) from serving as advocate. If the lawyer to be called as a witness could not also serve as an advocate under this Rule, that lawyer shall not take an active role before the tribunal in the presentation of the matter.

Virginia: In Rule 3.7(a), Virginia substitutes "adversarial proceeding" for "trial." In Rule 3.7(b), Virginia incorporates language from DR 5-102(B) of the ABA Model Code of Professional Responsibility to deal with situations in which a lawyer learns that he or she may be called as a witness "other than on behalf of the client" after accepting the representation.

Related Materials

ABA Formal Ethics Opinions: See ABA Formal Ethics Ops. 90-357 (1990), 97-407 (1997), and 98-410 n.26 (1998).

Model Rules of Professional Conduct for Federal Lawyers: Rule 3.7(a)(2) permits a lawyer to testify to the nature, value, "and quality" of legal services rendered in the case.

Restatement of the Law Governing Lawyers: See Restatement §108 in our chapter on the Restatement later in this volume.

Rule 3.8   Special Responsibilities of a Prosecutor

Canon and Code Antecedents

ABA Canons of Professional Ethics: Canon 5 provided, in relevant part, as follows:

5.   The Defense or Prosecution of Those Accused of Crime

. . . The primary duty of a lawyer engaged in public prosecution is not to convict, but to see that justice is done. The suppression of facts or the secreting of witnesses capable of establishing the innocence of the accused is highly reprehensible.

ABA Model Code of Professional Responsibility: Compare DR 7-103(A) and DR 7-103(B) (reprinted later in this volume).

Cross-References in Other Rules

Rule 3.6, Comment 8: "See **Rule 3.8(f)** for additional duties of prosecutors in connection with extrajudicial statements about criminal proceedings."

Legislative History of Model Rule 3.8

1980 Discussion Draft (then Rule 3.10) provided that the prosecutor in a criminal case shall:

> (a) refrain from prosecuting a charge that the prosecutor knows is not supported by probable cause;
> (b) advise the defendant of the right to counsel and provide assistance in obtaining counsel;
> (c) not induce an unrepresented defendant to surrender important procedural rights, such as the right to a preliminary hearing;
> (d) seek all evidence, whether or not favorable to the accused, and make timely disclosure to the defense of all evidence supporting innocence or mitigating the offense;
> (e) not discourage a person from giving relevant information to the defense;
> (f) in connection with sentencing, disclose to the defendant and to the court all unprivileged information known to the prosecution that is relevant thereto.

The 1980 Discussion Draft also contained a separate rule, with no direct counterpart in the Rules as adopted, that read as follows:

Special Responsibilities of Defense Counsel in a Criminal Case

> A lawyer for the accused in a criminal case, shall not:
> (a) agree to represent a person proposing to commit a crime, except as part of a good faith effort to determine the validity, scope, meaning, or application of the law;
> (b) act in a case in which the lawyer's partner or other professional associate is or has been the prosecutor;
> (c) accept payment of fees by one person for the defense of another except with the consent of the accused after adequate disclosure; or
> (d) charge a contingent fee.

1981 Draft: Substantially the same as adopted, except subparagraph (d), which included an obligation to "make reasonable efforts to seek all evidence, whether or not favorable to the defendant," but did not refer to protective orders. Also, the 1981 Draft did not include subparagraph (e) of the rule as adopted.

1982 Draft: Same as adopted, except that the 1982 Draft did not include subparagraph (e) of the rule as adopted.

1983 Rule: As originally adopted in 1983, Rule 3.8(a)-(d) was the same as the 2002 version of ABA Model Rule 3.8, but the original version did not contain any equivalent to the 2002 version of Rule 3.8(e). In addition, Rule 3.8(e) of the original rule provided that a prosecutor shall:

> (e) exercise reasonable care to prevent investigators, law enforcement personnel, employees or other persons assisting or associated with the prosecutor in a criminal case from making an extrajudicial statement that the prosecutor would be prohibited from making under Rule 3.6.

1990 Amendment: At its 1990 Mid-Year Meeting, the ABA House of Delegates added paragraph (f) (now (e)) to Rule 3.8 to govern subpoenas to lawyers, and added paragraph 4 to the Comment. The ABA's Standing Committee on Ethics and Professional Responsibility explained the amendment as follows:

Excerpt from ABA Report Explaining 1990 Amendment*

Any rule regulating subpoenas to lawyers must, at a minimum, provide for full protection of the privilege.

A subpoena rule which does no more than recognize the attorney-client privilege, however, will ignore other important aspects of the relationship between a client and his attorney. . . . Because information protected by the attorney-client privilege is not coterminous with information which an ethical attorney is supposed to hold confidential, there is much information in the hands of an attorney which remains exposed to the subpoena power, even if that power is limited by the privilege. For example, the prevailing judicial position is that, absent special circumstances, an attorney may be compelled by subpoena to reveal information about the identity of the client and the size and source of the fee-information frequently sought by government attorneys. Similarly, an attorney in possession of documents received from a client in the course of a case may be compelled by subpoena to produce those documents, assuming that the client personally could be compelled to produce the documents were they in the client's hands.

Since a subpoena may compel production of information which, though unprivileged, is certainly confidential under Rule 1.6 and DR 4-101, the mere issuance of the subpoena undermines the client's confidence and trust. . . .

. . . Confronted by a powerful adversary and by a seemingly bewildering array of procedures, with their liberty at stake, clients rightfully expect that their lawyer will, within the constraints of the law and the profession's code of ethics, zealously argue their case at every turn. There could be few things more destructive of this expectation than the spectacle of their own attorney forced by their adversary to supply information detrimental to their interest.

1994 Amendment: At its August 1994 Annual Meeting, by a voice vote, the ABA House of Delegates amended Rule 3.8 by adding a new paragraph (g) (now (f)) that permits prosecutors to make statements "necessary to inform the public of the nature and extent of the prosecutor's action and that serve a legitimate law enforcement purpose," even if these statements may heighten "public condemnation of the accused." The amendment added a corresponding paragraph to the Comment. The amendment supplements the 1994 amendment to Rule 3.6, which generally governs extrajudicial statements by lawyers.

The amendment was co-sponsored by the ABA Standing Committee on Ethics and Professional Responsibility and the ABA Criminal Justice Section, which submitted a joint report in support of the 1994 amendment to Rule 3.6 and Rule 3.8. We reprint below the small portion of the joint ABA report explaining the amendment to Rule 3.8. (Excerpts from the remainder of the report, which provides further background and context for the amendment, are found in the Legislative History section following Rule 3.6.)

Excerpts from ABA Report Explaining 1994 Amendment*

In connection with its proposed revision of Rule 3.6, the Committee also proposes to add a new section (g) to Rule 3.8, prohibiting gratuitous comments by a prosecutor which have a substantial likelihood of increasing public opprobrium toward the accused. Not only can pretrial publicity taint the fairness of a trial, but it can also subject the accused to unfair and unnecessary condemnation before the trial takes place.

---

* Committee Reports do not represent official policy of the ABA. They are for information only, and the opinions are those of the authors of the report.

Because of a prosecutor's special power and visibility, a prosecutor should use special care to avoid such publicity.

1995 Amendment: At its August 1995 Annual Meeting, the ABA House of Delegates voted 187-113 to amend Rule 3.8 by deleting subparagraph (f)(2), which had required prosecutors to obtain "prior judicial approval after an opportunity for an adversarial hearing" before serving a subpoena on a lawyer in a grand jury or other criminal proceeding to seek evidence about the lawyer's past or present clients. The ABA also removed the last sentence of Comment 4, which had explained the need for judicial approval. The amendment was jointly sponsored by the ABA's Standing Committee on Ethics and Professional Responsibility and the ABA Criminal Justice Section. Below are excerpts from the joint Committee Report explaining the amendment.

Excerpts from ABA Report Explaining 1995 Amendment

Subparagraph (2) of Rule 3.8(f) is an anomaly in the Model Rules. Rather than stating a substantive ethical precept, it sets out a type of implementing requirement that is properly established by rules of criminal procedure rather than established as an ethical norm. Moreover, while nominally addressed to the conduct of prosecutors, subparagraph (2) affects the operation of courts and grand juries by "requir[ing] the erection of novel court procedures and interject[ing] an additional layer of judicial supervision over the grand jury subpoena process." Baylson v. Disciplinary Board, 764 F. Supp. 328, 337 (E.D. Pa. 1991). The procedural obligations it seeks to impose as a matter of professional ethics have no parallel in any other enforceable provision of the Model Rules.

We therefore recommend deletion of subparagraph (2) of Rule 3.8(f). . . . The limiting description of the circumstances in which a prosecutor could ethically issue such a subpoena, set forth in subparagraph (1), would remain unchanged. The proposed amendment would remove the feature of the rule that courts have found objectionable. . . .

2002 Amendments: At its February 2002 Mid-Year Meeting, the ABA House of Delegates adopted without change the ABA Ethics 2000 Commission proposal to amend Rule 3.8 and its Comment. The amendment to the text redesignated former Rule 3.8(f) as Rule 3.8(e), redesignated former Rule 3.8(g) as Rule 3.8(f) and moved all of the language in former Rule 3.8(e) to its current position at the end of Rule 3.8(f) (beginning with "exercise reasonable care"). The amendment to the Comment moderately changed Comments 1, 2, 4, and 5, and added all of Comment 6.

2008 Amendments: At its February 2008 Mid-Year Meeting, by voice vote (signifying overwhelming approval), the ABA House of Delegates amended Rule 3.8 by adding new paragraphs (g) and (h), which impose certain post-conviction responsibilities on prosecutors. At the same time, the ABA amended Comment 1 to Rule 3.8 to reflect the new obligations and added new Comments 7, 8, and 9 to explain the new paragraphs.

The amendments were spearheaded by the ABA Criminal Justice Section (chaired by Professor Stephen J. Saltzburg of The George Washington University Law School) and were co-sponsored by the ABA Standing Committee on Ethics and Professional Responsibility, the ABA Death Penalty Representation Project, the ABA Section of Individual Rights and Responsibilities, the ABA Section of Litigation, the ABA Section of State and Local Government Law, the ABA Government and

Public Sector Lawyers Division, the ABA Commission on Domestic Violence, the New York State Bar Association, the Association of the Bar of the City of New York, and the National Organization of Bar Counsel. The full Report submitted by the ABA Section of Criminal Justice to explain the history and purpose of the amendments is available online at *www.abanet.org/cpr/mrpc/ model_rules.html* (look for "Most Recent Changes to the Model Rules"). Here are extensive excerpts from that Report (with most footnotes omitted):

Excerpts from ABA Report Explaining 2008 Amendments*

In Achieving Justice: Freeing the Innocent, Convicting the Guilty, the ABA's Section of Criminal Justice explored the systemic causes for wrongful convictions in our criminal justice system. Its report made numerous recommendations for systemic remedies to better ensure that individuals will not be convicted of crimes that they did not commit and that the innocent will be exonerated. That report did not address the well established ethical obligations of a prosecutor toward innocent persons.

The United States Supreme Court recognized in *Imbler v. Pachtman*, 424 U.S. 409, 427 n. 25 (1976), that prosecutors are "bound by the ethics of [their] office to inform the appropriate authority of after-acquired or other information that casts doubt upon the correctness of the conviction." Further, when a prosecutor concludes upon investigation of such evidence that an innocent person was convicted, it is well recognized that the prosecutor has an obligation to endeavor to rectify the injustice. These obligations have not, however, been codified in Rule 3.8 of the ABA Model Rules of Professional Conduct, which identifies the "Special Responsibilities of a Prosecutor." Proposed Rules 3.8(g) and (h), and the accompanying Comments would rectify this omission.

Proposed Rules 3.8(g) and (h) and the accompanying Comments are based on provisions adopted by the House of Delegates of the New York State Bar Association on November 4, 2006 in the course of its comprehensive review of the state's disciplinary code. The rules had their genesis in a 2006 Report of the Association of the Bar of the City of New York ("ABCNY"), which considered various aspects of prosecutors' duties. Among other provisions, against the background of recent knowledge about the fallibility of the criminal justice process, the Report proposed a rule regarding the prosecutor's obligation when a convicted defendant may be innocent. The report stated: "In light of the large number of cases in which defendants have been exonerated . . . it is appropriate to obligate prosecutors' offices to" . . . consider "credible post-conviction claims of innocence." The premise of the proposal was that prosecutors have ethical responsibilities upon learning of new and material evidence that shows that it is likely that a convicted person was innocent. These responsibilities include a duty to disclose the evidence, to conduct an appropriate investigation, and, upon becoming convinced that a miscarriage of justice occurred, to take steps to remedy it.

The ABCNY proposal was presented to the state bar's Committee on Standards of Attorney Conduct ("COSAC"), which agreed with the premise of the ABCNY proposal and drafted provisions that captured the substance of the proposal, and circulated them for a lengthy period of public comment. COSAC's original proposed Rules 3.8(g) and (h) received comment from a wide range of state and federal prosecutors and district attorneys' organizations, defense organizations and bar associations, and revised its proposals in light of suggestions received from around the state.

The version adopted by the New York State Bar Association was closely examined and refined by the ABA Section of Criminal Justice, which drew on the experience and

* Committee Reports do not represent official policy of the ABA. They are for information only, and the opinions are those of the authors of the report.

expertise of prosecutors, criminal defense lawyers and legal academics in its leadership, including those who serve as representatives of other national organizations such as the National District Attorneys Association. It was then further refined in collaboration with the ABA Standing Committee on Ethics and Professional Responsibility, to ensure its general consistency with the philosophy, purposes, structure and style of the ABA Model Rules of Professional Conduct.

As the proposed provisions reflect, it is important to codify prosecutorial duties upon learning of possible false convictions. The obligations in the proposed rule are triggered when a prosecutor either "knows" of new, credible and material evidence creating a reasonable likelihood of a convicted defendant's innocence or "knows" of clear and convincing evidence establishing the convicted defendant's innocence. The ABA Model Rules define "knows" to "denote[] actual knowledge of the fact in question"; therefore, indirect or imputed knowledge will not suffice.

The obligation to avoid and rectify convictions of innocent people, to which the proposed provisions give expression, is the most fundamental professional obligation of criminal prosecutors. The inclusion of these provisions in the rules of professional conduct, rather than only in the provisions of the ABA Standards Relating to the Administration of Justice, which are not intended to be enforced, will express the vital importance that the profession places on this obligation. Further, it is important not simply to educate prosecutors but to hold out the possibility of professional discipline for lawyers who intentionally ignore persuasive evidence of an unjust conviction. Prosecutors' offices have institutional disincentives to comport with these obligations and, as courts have recognized, their failures are not self-correcting by the criminal justice process. Codification of these obligations, which are meant to express prosecutors' minimum responsibilities, will help counter these institutional disincentives. . . .

The Rule and Comments are designed to provide clear guidance to prosecutors concerning their minimum disciplinary responsibilities,[1] with the expectation that, as ministers of justice, prosecutors routinely will and should go beyond the disciplinary minimum. In many instances, a prosecutor will receive information about a defendant that does not trigger the rule's disclosure obligation and will be called upon to decide whether that information is nevertheless sufficient to require some investigation. The quality and specificity of the information received by a prosecutor often will vary dramatically, and it is expected that a prosecutor will decide whether and how to investigate based upon a good faith assessment of the information received. In some cases, the prosecutor may recognize the need to reinvestigate the underlying case; in others, it may be appropriate to await development of the record in collateral proceedings initiated by the defendant.

With the understanding that prosecutors should be presumed to take their ethical and professional obligations seriously, the Comment specifically notes that

---

1. Prosecutors and their representative organizations involved in the drafting process generally agreed on the need to identify specific measures to be taken upon learning of new evidence of a convicted defendant's innocence. Accordingly, the proposed provisions specifically identify when a prosecutor's disciplinary obligations are implicated regarding disclosure, investigation, and remedial measures. Recognizing, however, that individual cases and jurisdictions differ, the rule does not prescribe particular investigative steps and remedial measures that must be pursued. Although the proposed Comments identify steps that might be taken when necessary to remedy a wrongful conviction, the list is not exclusive. Sometimes disclosure to the defendant or the court, or making or joining in an application to the court, will suffice, whereas in jurisdictions where courts lack jurisdiction to release an innocent individual, the appropriate step may be to make, or join in, an application for executive clemency. [*Footnote by the ABA Committee—Eds.*]

good faith exercises of judgment are not disciplinary violations under the proposed provisions. A convicted defendant might easily complain that a prosecutor "knows" that the defendant is innocent. Indeed, the defendant may support a complaint by relying on much the same evidence that might have been presented at trial. We are confident, however, that disciplinary authorities will not assume that prosecutors ignore substantial evidence of innocence and will not burden prosecutors with the need to respond to and defend ethics charges that are not supported by specific and particular credible evidence that the prosecutor violated his or her disciplinary responsibilities.

The provisions build upon the ABA's historic commitment to developing policies and standards designed to give concrete meaning to the "duty of prosecutors to seek justice, not merely to convict," and, in particular, to prevent and rectify the conviction of innocent defendants. For example, the ABA has endorsed draft legislation that would generally ensure the preservation of material evidence for post-conviction review, and that would require the preservation of DNA evidence in particular until the convicted defendant has completed his sentence. These prior resolutions implicitly recognized the need to reexamine convictions in light of newly discovered, material exculpatory evidence. The proposed additions to the ABA Model Rules will codify public prosecutors' obligations to conduct such reexaminations.

Selected State Variations

Editors' Note. When this book went to press in September 2012, only seven states — Colorado, Delaware, Idaho, New York, North Dakota, Tennessee, and Wisconsin — had adopted the 2008 amendments to ABA Model Rule 3.8 in substantially equivalent form, and Washington State has adopted Rule 3.8(g) but not (h). For up-to-date state-by-state information on adoptions of the 2008 amendments to Model Rule 3.8, see *http://www.americanbar.org/content/dam/ aba/administrative/professional_responsibility/3_8_g_h.authcheckdam.pdf.*

California: Rule 5-110 provides as follows:

A member in government service shall not institute or cause to be instituted criminal charges when the member knows or should know that the charges are not supported by probable cause. If, after the institution of criminal charges, the member in government service having responsibility for prosecuting the charges becomes aware that those charges are not supported by probable cause, the member shall promptly so advise the court in which the criminal matter is pending.

In addition, Rule 5-220 provides that a lawyer "shall not suppress any evidence that the member or the member's client has a legal obligation to reveal or to produce."

Connecticut omits paragraphs (e) and (f).

District of Columbia: Every paragraph of Rule 3.8 differs from the Model Rule. The D.C. version of Rule 3.8 provides that the prosecutor in a criminal case shall not:

(a) In exercising discretion to investigate or to prosecute, improperly favor or invidiously discriminate against any person;

(b) File in court or maintain a charge that the prosecutor knows is not supported by probable cause;

(c) Prosecute to trial a charge that the prosecutor knows is not supported by evidence sufficient to establish a *prima facie* showing of guilt;

(d) Intentionally avoid pursuit of evidence or information because it may damage the prosecution's case or aid the defense;

(e) Intentionally fail to disclose to the defense, upon request and at a time when use by the defense is reasonably feasible, any evidence or information that the prosecutor knows or reasonably should know tends to negate the guilt of the accused or to mitigate the offense, or in connection with sentencing, intentionally fail to disclose to the defense upon request any unprivileged mitigating information known to the prosecutor and not reasonably available to the defense, except when the prosecutor is relieved of this responsibility by a protective order of the tribunal;

(f) Except for statements which are necessary to inform the public of the nature and extent of the prosecutor's action and which serve a legitimate law enforcement purpose, make extrajudicial comments which serve to heighten condemnation of the accused; or

(g) In presenting a case to a grand jury, intentionally interfere with the independence of the grand jury, preempt a function of the grand jury, abuse the processes of the grand jury, or fail to bring to the attention of the grand jury material facts tending substantially to negate the existence of probable cause.

Florida omits paragraphs (b), (e), and (f) of ABA Model Rule 3.8.

Georgia: In place of Rule 3.8(b) and (c), Georgia substitutes the simple caution that a prosecutor shall "refrain from making any effort to prevent the accused from exercising a reasonable effort to obtain counsel." Georgia also shortens Rule 3.8(d) by eliminating the part that begins "in connection with sentencing." Georgia also limits the application of Rule 3.8(e) to statements the prosecutor would be prohibited from making only under Rule 3.6(g) (as opposed to the entire rule).

Illinois: Rule 3.8 adds the following sentence: "The duty of a public prosecutor or other government lawyer is to seek justice, not merely to convict." Comment 1A elaborates on this sentence, quoting cases concerning a prosecutor's duties.

Massachusetts: Rule 3.8(c) prohibits prosecutors from seeking waivers of important pretrial rights from unrepresented defendants unless "a court has first obtained from the accused a knowing and intelligent written waiver of counsel." Massachusetts Rule 3.8(f) tracks ABA Model Rule 3.8(e), but adds that the prosecutor must obtain "prior judicial approval after an opportunity for an adversarial proceeding."

Massachusetts also adds paragraphs (h) and (i), which track DR 7-106(C)(3) and (4), and adds a new paragraph (j) providing that a prosecutor in a criminal case shall "not intentionally avoid pursuit of evidence because the prosecutor believes it will damage the prosecution's case or aid the accused."

The Massachusetts federal court version of Rule 3.8(e) — Local Rule 3.8(f) — was declared invalid in *Stern v. United States District Court for the District of Massachusetts*, 16 F. Supp. 2d 88 (1st Cir.), *reh'g and reh'g en banc denied*, 214 F.3d 4 (1st Cir. 2000) (concluding that "the adoption of Local Rule 3.8(f) exceeded the district court's lawful authority to regulate both grand jury and trial subpoenas" in federal courts).

Michigan omits paragraphs (e) and (f).

New Jersey: Rule 3.8(c) prohibits a prosecutor from seeking to obtain from an unrepresented accused a waiver only of important "post-indictment" pretrial rights, and New Jersey Rule 3.8(d) requires timely disclosure to the defense only of all "evidence," not "information."

New York: Rule 3.8(a)-(b) is substantially similar to DR 7-103(A) of the old Model Code. Effective July 1, 2012, Rule 3.8(c)-(e) provides as follows:

> (c) When a prosecutor knows of new, credible and material evidence creating a reasonable likelihood that a convicted defendant did not commit an offense of which the defendant was convicted, the prosecutor shall within a reasonable time:
>> (1) disclose that evidence to an appropriate court or prosecutor's office; or
>> (2) if the conviction was obtained by that prosecutor's office,
>>> (A) notify the appropriate court and the defendant that the prosecutor's office possesses such evidence unless a court authorizes delay for good cause shown;
>>> (B) disclose that evidence to the defendant unless the disclosure would interfere with an ongoing investigation or endanger the safety of a witness or other person, and a court authorizes delay for good cause shown; and
>>> (C) undertake or make reasonable efforts to cause to be undertaken such further inquiry or investigation as may be necessary to provide a reasonable belief that the conviction should or should not be set aside.
>
> (d) When a prosecutor knows of clear and convincing evidence establishing that a defendant was convicted, in a prosecution by the prosecutor's office, of an offense that the defendant did not commit, the prosecutor shall seek a remedy consistent with justice, applicable law, and the circumstances of the case.
>
> (e) A prosecutor's independent judgment, made in good faith, that the new evidence is not of such nature as to trigger the obligations of sections (c) and (d), though subsequently determined to have been erroneous, does not constitute a violation of this rule.

North Carolina: Rule 3.8(e) adds that the prosecutor shall not "participate in the application for the issuance of a search warrant to a lawyer for the seizure of information of a past or present client in connection with an investigation of someone other than the lawyer," unless the conditions stated in ABA Model Rule 3.8(e) are satisfied.

Ohio: Rule 3.8(a) provides that a prosecutor shall not "pursue or" prosecute a charge that the prosecutor knows is not supported by probable cause. (A note by the drafters says the rule is thus expanded to prohibit either the pursuit or prosecution of unsupported charges and thus is broad enough to include grand jury proceedings.) Ohio omits Rule 3.8(b) because (according to a Model Rules Comparison) ensuring that the defendant is advised about the right to counsel is a police and judicial function, and because Rule 4.3 already sets forth duties applicable to all lawyers in dealing with unrepresented persons. Ohio also omits Rule 3.8(c) because that rule has a potential adverse impact on defendants who seek continuances or seek to participate in diversion programs. Rule 3.8(d) deletes the words "and to the tribunal" in connection with sentencing disclosures. Ohio omits Rule 3.8(f) because prosecutors, like all lawyers, are already subject to Rule 3.6.

Pennsylvania deletes Rule 3.8(e) (governing subpoenas to lawyers) and instead adopts a separate rule, Pennsylvania Rule 3.10, which forbids a prosecutor or other governmental lawyer, absent judicial approval, to subpoena a lawyer before a grand jury or other tribunal investigating criminal conduct if the prosecutor seeks to compel evidence concerning a current or former client of the lawyer.

Texas: Rule 3.09(a) provides that a prosecutor shall refrain from prosecuting "or threatening to prosecute" a charge that the prosecutor knows is not supported by probable cause. Texas Rule 3.09(b) and (c) provides that a prosecutor shall:

(b) refrain from conducting or assisting in a custodial interrogation of an accused unless the prosecutor has made reasonable efforts to be assured that the accused has been advised of any right to, and the procedure for obtaining, counsel and has been given reasonable opportunity to obtain counsel;

(c) not initiate or encourage efforts to obtain from an unrepresented accused a waiver of important pre-trial, trial or post-trial rights.

Texas omits paragraph (e) and the first half of ABA Model Rule 3.8(f) but retains in Rule 3.07 the obligation to exercise reasonable care to prevent "persons employed or controlled by the prosecutor" in a criminal case from making an extrajudicial statement that the prosecutor would be prohibited from making.

Utah: Rule 3.8(d) eliminates the obligation to disclose unprivileged mitigating information "to the tribunal" in connection with sentencing; Utah omits ABA Model Rule 3.8(e) (regarding subpoenas to lawyers); and Utah's equivalent to ABA Model Rule 3.8(f) deletes everything up to the phrase "exercise reasonable care."

Virginia: Rule 3.8, which Virginia calls "Additional Responsibilities of a Prosecutor," states that a prosecutor shall:

(b) not knowingly take advantage of an unrepresented defendant.

(c) not instruct or encourage a person to withhold information from the defense after a party has been charged with an offense.

(d) make timely disclosure to counsel for the defendant, or to the defendant if he has no counsel, of the existence of evidence which the prosecutor knows tends to negate the guilt of the accused, mitigate the degree of the offense, or reduce the punishment, except when disclosure is precluded or modified by order of a court; . . .

Virginia omits paragraph (e) and the first half of paragraph (f) of ABA Model Rule 3.8 and replaces the duty to "exercise reasonable care to prevent" in the second half of Rule 3.8(f) with a mandate that a prosecutor not "direct or encourage" others to make statements that Rule 3.6 would prohibit the prosecutor from making.

Wisconsin: Rule 3.8(b) requires a prosecutor who is "communicating with an unrepresented person in the context of an investigation or proceeding" to "inform the person of the prosecutor's role and interest in the matter."

Related Materials

ABA Formal Ethics Opinions: See ABA Formal Ethics Ops. 92-363 n.5 (1992) and 09-454 n.12 (2009).

ABA Resolution on Timely Disclosure by Prosecutors: At its August 2011 Annual Meeting, the ABA House of Delegates adopted the following resolution related to Rule 3.8(d):

RESOLVED, That the American Bar Association urges federal, state, territorial and tribal governments to adopt disclosure rules requiring the prosecution to seek from its agents and to timely disclose to the defense before the commencement of trial all information known to the prosecution that tends to negate the guilt of the accused, mitigate the offense charged or sentence, or impeach the prosecution's witnesses or evidence, except when relieved of this responsibility by a protective order.

FURTHER RESOLVED, That the American Bar Association urges federal, state, territorial and tribal governments to adopt disclosure rules requiring the prosecution to make timely disclosure to the defense before a guilty plea of all information, which may include impeachment evidence, known to the prosecution that tends to negate the guilt of the accused or mitigate the offense charged or sentence, except when relieved of this responsibility by a protective order.

ABA Standards for Criminal Justice: The following ABA Standards for Criminal Justice are related to ABA Model Rule 3.8:

Standard 3-2.5 Prosecutor's Handbook; Policy Guidelines and Procedures

(a) Each prosecutor's office should develop a statement of (i) general policies to guide the exercise of prosecutorial discretion and (ii) procedures of the office. The objectives of these policies as to discretion and procedures should be to achieve a fair, efficient, and effective enforcement of the criminal law.

(b) In the interest of continuity and clarity, such statement of policies and procedures should be maintained in an office handbook. This handbook should be available to the public, except for subject matters declared "confidential," when it is reasonably believed that public access to their contents would adversely affect the prosecution function.

Standard 3-3.9   Discretion in the Charging Decision

(a) A prosecutor should not institute, or cause to be instituted, or permit the continued pendency of criminal charges when the prosecutor knows that the charges are not supported by probable cause. A prosecutor should not institute, cause to be instituted, or permit the continued pendency of criminal charges in the absence of sufficient admissible evidence to support a conviction.

(b) The prosecutor is not obliged to present all charges which the evidence might support. The prosecutor may in some circumstances and for good cause consistent with the public interest decline to prosecute, notwithstanding that sufficient evidence may exist which would support a conviction. Illustrative of the factors which the prosecutor may properly consider in exercising his or her discretion are:

(i) the prosecutor's reasonable doubt that the accused is in fact guilty;

(ii) the extent of the harm caused by the offense;

(iii) the disproportion of the authorized punishment in relation to the particular offense or the offender;

(iv) possible improper motives of a complainant;

(v) reluctance of the victim to testify;

(vi) cooperation of the accused in the apprehension or conviction of others; and

(vii) availability and likelihood of prosecution by another jurisdiction.

(c) A prosecutor should not be compelled by his or her supervisor to prosecute a case in which he or she has a reasonable doubt about the guilt of the accused.

(d) In making the decision to prosecute, the prosecutor should give no weight to the personal or political advantages or disadvantages which might be involved or to a desire to enhance his or her record of convictions.

(e) In cases which involve a serious threat to the community, the prosecutor should not be deterred from prosecution by the fact that in the jurisdiction juries have tended to acquit persons accused of the particular kind of criminal act in question.

(f) The prosecutor should not bring or seek charges greater in number or degree than can reasonably be supported with evidence at trial or than are necessary to fairly reflect the gravity of the offense.

(g) The prosecutor should not condition a dismissal of charges, nolle prosequi, or similar action on the accused's relinquishment of the right to seek civil redress unless the accused has agreed to the action knowingly and intelligently, freely and voluntarily, and where such waiver is approved by the court.

Standard 3-3.11   Disclosure of Evidence by the Prosecutor

(a) A prosecutor should not intentionally fail to make timely disclosure to the defense, at the earliest feasible opportunity, of the existence of all evidence or information which tends to negate the guilt of the accused or mitigate the offense charged or which would tend to reduce the punishment of the accused.

(b) A prosecutor should not fail to make a reasonably diligent effort to comply with a legally proper discovery request.

(c) A prosecutor should not intentionally avoid pursuit of evidence because he or she believes it will damage the prosecution's case or aid the accused.

Standard 3-4.1   Availability for Plea Discussions

(a) The prosecutor should have and make known a general policy or willingness to consult with defense counsel concerning disposition of charges by plea.

(b) A prosecutor should not engage in plea discussions directly with an accused who is represented by defense counsel, except with defense counsel's approval. Where the defendant has properly waived counsel, the prosecuting attorney may engage in plea discussions with the defendant, although, where feasible, a record of such discussions should be made and preserved.

(c) A prosecutor should not knowingly make false statements or representations as to fact or law in the course of plea discussions with defense counsel or the accused.

ABA Standards for Imposing Lawyer Sanctions: See Standard 5.2, which is reprinted in the Related Materials following Model Rule 8.4.

American Lawyer's Code of Conduct: Chapter 9 of the American Lawyer's Code of Conduct, entitled ''Responsibilities of Government Lawyers,'' contains the following provisions:

9.3. A lawyer serving as public prosecutor shall not seek or sign formal charges, or proceed to trial, unless a fair-minded juror could conclude beyond a reasonable doubt that the accused is guilty, on the basis of all of the facts that are known to the prosecutor and likely to be admissible into evidence. . . .

9.5. A lawyer serving as public prosecutor shall not use unconscionable pressures in plea bargaining, such as charging the accused in several counts for what is essentially a single offense, or charging the accused with a more serious offense than is warranted under Rule 9.3. . . .

9.7. A lawyer serving as public prosecutor shall promptly make available to defense counsel, without request for it, any information that the prosecutor knows is likely to be useful to the defense. . . .

9.9. A lawyer serving as public prosecutor, who knows that a defendant is not receiving or has not received effective assistance of counsel, shall promptly advise the court, on the record when possible.

Attorney Fee Forfeiture: Prosecutors sometimes seize an attorney's fees when the government is confident it can prove that the money used to pay the fees is the fruit of federal drug crimes or RICO violations. In 1989, the Supreme Court decided two cases on fee forfeiture, *Caplin & Drysdale v. United States,* 491 U.S. 617 (1989), and *United States v. Monsanto,* 491 U.S. 600 (1989).

Brady Material: The constitutional basis for the disclosure obligations in Rule 3.8(d) is found in *Brady v. Maryland,* 373 U.S. 83, 87 (1963), which held that ''the suppression by the prosecution of evidence favorable to an accused upon request violates due process where the evidence is material. . . .'' In 2012, Senator

Lisa Murkowski (D-Alaska) introduced a bill (S. 2197) entitled the "Fairness in Disclosure of Evidence Act" that would require the attorney for the government to disclose favorable information to the defendant in criminal prosecutions brought by the United States. In effect, the bill would codify and strengthen *Brady* in federal criminal prosecutions. The Senate Judiciary Committee held hearings on the bill in June 2012 but took no further action.

Federal Rules of Criminal Procedure: Rules 16 and 26.2 of the Federal Rules of Criminal Procedure impose disclosure obligations on both sides in criminal cases. Before trial, Rule 16(a)(1) provides that federal prosecutors must allow a criminal defendant to inspect seven categories of information, including: (A) defendant's oral statement; (B) defendant's written or recorded statement; (C) in the case of an organizational defendant, any oral, written, or recorded statement by a person who "(i) was legally able to bind the defendant regarding the subject of the statement because of that person's position as the defendant's director, officer, employee, or agent; or (ii) was personally involved in the alleged conduct constituting the offense and was legally able to bind the defendant regarding that conduct because of that person's position as the defendant's director, officer, employee, or agent"; (D) the defendant's prior criminal record; (E) books, papers, documents, photographs, tangible objects, buildings or places that are material to the preparation of the defense, or are intended for use by the government as evidence in chief at trial, or were obtained from or belong to the defendant; (F) results or reports of physical or mental examinations, and scientific tests or experiments, which are material to the preparation of the defense or which the government intends to use as evidence in chief at trial; and (G) a written summary of any expert testimony that the government intends to use during its case-in-chief at trial.

However, Rules 16(a)(2) and (3) provide that the government's duty to disclose does not apply to the prosecutor's work product ("reports, memoranda, or other internal government documents made by the attorney for the government or other government agents in connection with the investigation or prosecution of the case"), or to statements made by the government's prospective witnesses "except as provided by 18 U.S.C. §3500," or to most grand jury transcripts.

Conversely, Rule 16(b)(1) provides that if the government complies with a defendant's request for documents and tangible objects, or scientific tests and reports, or expert witness disclosures, then the defendant must give the government the same categories of materials in the control of the defendant. However, Rule 16(b)(2) protects the defense attorney's work product. Rule 16(c) imposes a continuing duty to disclose on both sides, and Rule 16(d)(2)(C) provides for protective orders or sanctions, including an order to "prohibit a party from introducing the undisclosed evidence."

At trial, Rule 26.2(a) of the Federal Rules of Criminal Procedure provides that after any witness other than the defendant has testified on direct examination, the court, on motion of a party who did not call the witness, shall order whichever side called the witness to produce "any statement of the witness that is in their possession and that relates to the subject matter of the witness's testimony."

Model Rules of Professional Conduct for Federal Lawyers: Rule 3.8(a) mandates that a prosecutor shall "[r]efrain from prosecuting a charge that the prosecutor knows is not supported by probable cause, or if not authorized to decline the prosecution of a charge to recommend to the appropriate authority that any charge not warranted by the evidence be withdrawn." Rule 3.8(d) requires timely disclosure only to the defense, not to the tribunal. Rule 3.8(f) obligates a prosecutor to "[r]espect the attorney-client privilege of defendants and not diminish the privilege through investigative or judicial processes."

Restatement of the Law Governing Lawyers: See Restatement §§97 and 109(2) in our chapter on the Restatement later in this volume.

United States Attorney's Manual: The United States Attorney's Manual (USAM) is a set of guidelines designed to be "a quick and ready reference" for U.S. Attorneys, Assistant U.S. Attorneys, and Department of Justice attorneys responsible for prosecuting violations of federal law. Title 9 of the USAM, entitled "Criminal Division," sets forth Department of Justice policies on a wide range of subjects related to criminal prosecution. The entire USAM is available at *www.usdoj.gov/usao/eousa/foia_reading_room/usam/index.html.*

Witness Statements (Jencks Act): In federal criminal trials, a prosecutor's "timely disclosure" of witness statements is governed by 18 U.S.C. §3500 (often called the Jencks Act), which provides, in pertinent part:

§3500. Demands for Production of Statements and Reports of Witnesses

(b) After a witness called by the United States has testified on direct examination, the court shall, on motion of the defendant, order the United States to produce any statement (as hereinafter defined) of the witness in the possession of the United States which relates to the subject matter as to which the witness has testified. If the entire contents of any such statement relate to the subject matter of the testimony of the witness, the court shall order it to be delivered directly to the defendant for his examination and use.

Rule 3.9   Advocate in Nonadjudicative Proceedings

Canon and Code Antecedents

ABA Canons of Professional Ethics: Canon 26 provided as follows:

26.   Professional Advocacy Other Than Before Courts

A lawyer openly, and in his true character may render professional services before legislative or other bodies, regarding proposed legislation and in advocacy of claims before departments of government, upon the same principles of ethics which justify his appearance before the Courts; but it is unprofessional for a lawyer so engaged to conceal his attorneyship, or to employ secret personal solicitations, or to use means other than those addressed to the reason and understanding, to influence action.

ABA Model Code of Professional Responsibility: Compare DR 7-106(B)(1) (reprinted later in this volume).

Cross-References in Other Rules

None.

Legislative History of Model Rule 3.9

1980 Draft (then Rule 3.12) provided as follows:

(a) A lawyer representing a client before a legislative or administrative tribunal in a nonadjudicative proceeding shall deal fairly with the body conducting the proceeding and with other persons making presentations therein and their counsel.

(b) A lawyer in such a proceeding shall:

(1) identify the client on whose behalf the lawyer appears, unless the identity of the client is privileged;

(2) conform to the provisions of Rules 3.1 and 3.4.

1981 and *1982 Drafts* were the same as adopted.

1983 Rule: As originally adopted in 1983, Rule 3.9 provided:

A lawyer representing a client before a legislature or administrative tribunal in a nonadjudicative proceeding shall disclose that the appearance is in a representative capacity and shall conform to the provisions of Rules 3.3(a) through (c), 3.4(a) through (c), and 3.5.

2002 Amendments: At its February 2002 Mid-Year Meeting, the ABA House of Delegates adopted without change the ABA Ethics 2000 Commission proposal to amend Rule 3.9 and its Comment. The amendments substituted the current phrase "legislative body or administrative agency" for the former phrase "legislative body or tribunal" in the text of the rule, added the cross-references at the end of Comment 1, and expanded Comment 3, which previously said only, "This Rule does not apply to representation of a client in a negotiation or other bilateral transaction with a government agency; such a transaction is governed by Rules 4.1 through 4.4."

Selected State Variations

California has no direct counterpart to ABA Model Rule 3.9.

Colorado adds the following in lieu of the second sentence of ABA Model Rule 3.9:

Further, in such a representation, the lawyer:

(a) shall conform to the provisions of Rules 3.3(a)(1), 3.3(a)(3), 3.3(b), 3.3(c), and 3.4(a) and (b);

(b) shall not engage in conduct intended to disrupt such proceeding unless such conduct is protected by law; and

(c) may engage in ex parte communications, except as prohibited by law.

District of Columbia: Rule 3.9 applies to a lawyer representing a client before a "legislative or administrative body" (rather than "legislative body or administrative agency").

Florida omits the reference to Rule 3.5.

New Jersey: Rule 3.9 tracks ABA Model Rule 3.9 essentially verbatim, but New Jersey's cross-references to Rules 3.3, 3.4, and 3.5 differ slightly due to differences in New Jersey's versions of those rules.

New York: Rule 3.9 is reworded as follows: "A lawyer communicating in a representative capacity with a legislative body or administrative agency in connection with a pending non-adjudicative matter or proceeding shall disclose that the appearance is in a representative capacity, except when the lawyer seeks information from an agency that is available to the public." Comment 1A emphasizes that "Rule 3.9 does not apply to adjudicative proceedings before a tribunal."

North Carolina omits Rule 3.9.

Pennsylvania: In addition to Rule 3.9, Pennsylvania has a Rule 1.19, which provides that any disclosures that lawyer-lobbyists need to make in order to comply with other law are disclosures that are expressly authorized and thus do not violate Rule 1.6.

Virginia omits Rule 3.9.

Related Materials

ABA Formal Ethics Opinions: No ABA formal ethics opinion has discussed ABA Model Rule 3.9.

Lobbying Laws: The federal government and all states have laws regulating lobbyists, including lobbyists who are lawyers. On the federal level, the most prominent statute is the Lobbying Disclosure Act of 1995, 2 U.S.C. §§1601-1614, which requires registration of federal lobbyists and regulates their conduct. Lawyer-lobbyists are also regulated by a host of other federal statutes and regulations, such as the Foreign Agents Registration Act of 1938 (22 U.S.C. §§611 *et seq.* and 28 C.F.R. Part 5), the HUD Reform Act of 1989 (42 U.S.C. §3545), Federal Acquisition Regulations, and Office of Management and Budget Regulations. These statutes and regulations are thoroughly explained in William V. Luneburg, Thomas M. Susman, & Rebecca H. Gordon eds., The Lobbying Manual: A Complete Guide to Federal Law Governing Lawyers and Lobbyists (4th ed., ABA 2009), published by the ABA Section of Administrative Law and Regulatory Practice.

On the state level, an example of a lobbying law is 25 Illinois Compiled Statutes 170/1 through 170/12 (the Lobbyist Registration Act), which requires registration of any person who "undertakes to influence executive, legislative or administrative action" (or employs another for that purpose). State and federal lobbying laws and regulations are discussed in detail in Abner Mikva & Eric Lane, The Legislative Process (3d ed., Aspen 2009).

Restatement of the Law Governing Lawyers: See Restatement §104 in our chapter on the Restatement later in this volume.

ANNOTATIONS ON ARTICLE 4. TRANSACTIONS WITH PERSONS OTHER THAN CLIENTS

Rule 4.1   Truthfulness in Statements to Others

Canon and Code Antecedents

ABA Canons of Professional Ethics: No comparable Canon.

ABA Model Code of Professional Responsibility: Compare DR 7-102(A)(3) and DR 7-102(A)(5) (reprinted later in this volume).

Cross-References in Other Rules

Rule 1.2, Comment 10: "A lawyer may not continue assisting a client in conduct that the lawyer originally supposed was legally proper but then discovers is criminal or fraudulent. The lawyer must, therefore, withdraw from the representation. . . . In some cases, withdrawal alone might be insufficient. It may be necessary for the lawyer to give notice of the fact of withdrawal and to disaffirm any opinion, document, affirmation or the like. See **Rule 4.1**."

Rule 1.6, Comment 15: Some Rules require "disclosure of information relating to a client's representation to accomplish the purposes specified in paragraphs (b)(1) through (b)(6)," only if such disclosure would be permitted by paragraph (b). See **Rules** 1.2(d), **4.1(b)**, 8.1 and 8.3.

Rule 1.8, Comment 5: It is prohibited to partake in the "disadvantageous use of client information unless the client gives informed consent, except as permitted or required by these Rules. See **Rules** 1.2(d), 1.6, 1.9(c), 3.3, **4.1(b)**, 8.1 and 8.3."

Rule 1.13, Comment 6: "[T]his Rule does not limit or expand the lawyer's responsibility under **Rule** 1.8, 1.16, 3.3 or **4.1**."

Rule 2.3, Comment 4: "In no circumstances is the lawyer permitted to knowingly make a false statement of material fact or law in providing an evaluation under this Rule. See **Rule 4.1**."

Rule 2.4, Comment 5: "When the dispute-resolution process takes place before a tribunal, as in binding arbitration (see Rule 1.0(m)), the lawyer's duty of candor is governed by Rule 3.3. Otherwise, the lawyer's duty of candor toward both the third-party neutral and other parties is governed by **Rule 4.1**."

Rule 3.9, Comment 3: This Rule "does not apply to representation of a client in a negotiation or other bilateral transaction with a governmental agency. . . . Representation in such matters is governed by **Rules 4.1** through 4.4."

Legislative History of Model Rule 4.1

1980 Discussion Draft contained the following Introduction:

Negotiator

. . . A negotiator should seek the most advantageous result for the client that is consistent with the requirements of law and the lawyer's responsibilities under the Rules of Professional Conduct. As negotiator, a lawyer should consider not only the client's short-run advantage but also his or her long-run interests, such as the state of future relations between the parties. The lawyer should help the client appreciate the interests and position of the other party and should encourage concessions that will effectuate the client's larger objectives. A lawyer should not transform a bargaining situation into a demonstration of toughness or hypertechnicality or forget that the purely legal aspects of an agreement are often subordinate to its practical aspects. When the alternative to reaching agreement is likely to be litigation, the lawyer should be aware that, although litigation is wholly legitimate as a means of resolving controversy, a fairly negotiated settlement generally yields a better conclusion. A lawyer should also recognize that the lawyer's own interest in resorting to litigation may be different from a client's interest in doing so.

. . . [I]n negotiations a lawyer is the agent for the client and not an arbitrator or mediator. Negotiation is in part a competition for advantage between parties who have the legal competence to settle their own affairs. A lawyer as negotiator should not impose an agreement on the client, even if the lawyer believes the agreement is in the client's best interests. By the same token, a lawyer does not necessarily endorse the substance of an agreement arrived at through his or her efforts.

The 1980 Discussion Draft of Rule 4.1 (then called Rule 4.2) provided as follows:

Fairness to Other Participants

(a) In conducting negotiations a lawyer shall be fair in dealing with other participants.

(b) A lawyer shall not make a knowing misrepresentation of fact or law, or fail to disclose a material fact known to the lawyer, even if adverse, when disclosure is:

(1) required by law or the Rules of Professional Conduct; or

(2) necessary to correct a manifest misapprehension of fact or law resulting from a previous representation made by the lawyer or known by the lawyer to have been made by the client. . . .

1980 Discussion Draft also contained the following provision (then called Rule 4.3) that has no equivalent in the Rules as adopted:

Illegal, Fraudulent, or Unconscionable Transactions

A lawyer shall not conclude an agreement, or assist a client in concluding an agreement, that the lawyer knows or reasonably should know is illegal, contains legally prohibited terms, would work a fraud, or would be held to be unconscionable as a matter of law.

1981 Draft: Subparagraph (a) was substantially the same as adopted. Subparagraph (b) provided that a lawyer must not:

(b) knowingly fail to disclose a fact to a third person when:

(1) in the circumstances failure to make the disclosure is equivalent to making a material misrepresentation;

(2) disclosure is necessary to prevent assisting a criminal or fraudulent act, as required by Rule 1.2(d); or

(3) disclosure is necessary to comply with other law.

1982 Draft: Substantially the same as adopted, except that Rule 4.1(b) provided: "The duties stated in this Rule apply even if compliance requires disclosure of information otherwise protected by Rule 1.6."

1983 Rule: As originally adopted in 1983, Rule 4.1 was the same as the 2002 version.

2002 Amendments: At its February 2002 Mid-Year Meeting, the ABA House of Delegates adopted without change the ABA Ethics 2000 Commission proposal to amend Comments 1, 2, and 3 to Rule 4.1. (The Ethics 2000 Commission did not propose any changes to the text of Rule 4.1.) The amendments added the language of Comment 1 beginning with "partially true but misleading" in place of the former phrase "failure to act," added the last sentence of Comment 2, and significantly expanded Comment 3, which formerly consisted of only the following two sentences: "Paragraph (b) recognizes that substantive law may require a lawyer to disclose certain information to avoid being deemed to have assisted the client's crime or fraud. The requirement of disclosure created by this paragraph is, however, subject to the obligations created by Rule 1.6."

Selected State Variations

California: Business & Professions Code §6128(a) provides that an attorney commits a misdemeanor if the attorney is "guilty of any deceit or collusion, or consents to any deceit or collusion, with intent to deceive the court or any party."

District of Columbia: Rule 4.1 is identical to ABA Model Rule 4.1.

Illinois: Rule 4.1 is the same as the ABA rule.

Kansas: The disclosure obligation under Rule 4.1(b) applies unless disclosure is prohibited by "or made discretionary under" Rule 1.6.

Maryland adds a separate paragraph (b) providing: "The duties stated in this Rule apply even if compliance requires disclosure of information otherwise protected by Rule 1.6."

Massachusetts: Comment 3 to Massachusetts Rule 4.1 defines "assisting" to refer "to that level of assistance which would render a third party liable for another's crime or fraud, i.e., assistance sufficient to render one liable as an aider or abettor under criminal law or as a joint tortfeasor under principles of tort and agency law." The comment also cross-references "the special meaning of 'assistance' in the context of a lawyer's appearance before a tribunal in Comment 2A to Rule 3.3."

Michigan: Rule 4.1 says only: "In the course of representing a client, a lawyer shall not knowingly make a false statement of material fact or law to a third person."

Mississippi: Rule 4.1(b) omits the phrase "unless disclosure is prohibited by Rule 1.6."

New Jersey adds a separate paragraph (b) stating: "The duties stated in this Rule apply even if compliance requires disclosure of information otherwise protected by RPC 1.6."

New York omits Model Rule 4.1(b).

North Carolina omits Rule 4.1(b).

North Dakota: Rule 4.1 provides only that "[i]n the course of representing a client a lawyer shall not make a statement to a third person of fact or law that the lawyer knows to be false."

Ohio: Rule 4.1(b) prohibits lawyers from assisting "illegal" and fraudulent acts of clients, (rather than "criminal" and fraudulent acts), and omits the phrase "unless disclosure is prohibited by Rule 1.6."

Pennsylvania: Rule 4.1(b) replaces the ABA word "assisting" with the phrase "aiding and abetting."

Tennessee adopts Rule 4.1(a). Rule 4.1(b) provides:

(b) If, in the course of representing a client in a nonadjudicative matter, a lawyer knows that the client intends to perpetrate a crime or fraud, the lawyer shall promptly advise the client to refrain from doing so and shall discuss with the client the consequences of the client's conduct. If after such discussion, the lawyer knows that the client still intends to engage in the wrongful conduct, the lawyer shall:

(1) withdraw from the representation of the client in the matter; and

(2) give notice of the withdrawal to any person who the lawyer knows is aware of the lawyer's representation of the client in the matter and whose financial or property interests are likely to be injured by the client's criminal or fraudulent

conduct. The lawyer shall also give notice to any such person of the lawyer's disaffirmance of any written statements, opinions, or other material prepared by the lawyer on behalf of the client and which the lawyer reasonably believes may be used by the client in furtherance of the crime or fraud.

(c) If a lawyer who is representing or has represented a client in a nonadjudicative matter comes to know, prior to the conclusion of the matter, that the client has, during the course of the lawyer's representation of the client, perpetrated a crime or fraud, the lawyer shall promptly advise the client to rectify the crime or fraud and discuss with the client the consequences of the client's failure to do so. If the client refuses or is unable to rectify the crime or fraud, the lawyer shall:

(1) if currently representing the client in the matter, withdraw from the representation and give notice of the withdrawal to any person whom the lawyer knows is aware of the lawyer's representation of the client in the matter and whose financial or property interests are likely to be injured by the client's criminal or fraudulent conduct; and

(2) give notice to any such person of the lawyer's disaffirmance of any written statements, opinions, or other material prepared by the lawyer on behalf of the client and that the lawyer reasonably believes may be used by the client in furtherance of the crime or fraud.

Texas: Rule 4.01(b) provides that a lawyer shall not fail to disclose a material fact to a third person when disclosure is necessary to "avoid making the lawyer a party to a criminal act or knowingly assisting a fraudulent act perpetrated by a client."

Virginia: In both subparagraphs of Rule 4.1, Virginia deletes the words "material" and "to a third person." At the end of Rule 4.1(b), Virginia deletes the phrase "unless disclosure is prohibited by Rule 1.6."

Wisconsin: Rule 4.1(c) states that notwithstanding Wisconsin Rules 5.3(c)(1) and 8.4, which address supervision of non-legal personnel and the duty not to violate a rule through another respectively, "a lawyer may advise or supervise others with respect to lawful investigative activities."

Related Materials

ABA Formal Ethics Opinions: See ABA Formal Ethics Ops. 92-363 (1992), 93-370 (1993), 93-375 (1993), 93-378 (1993), 94-383 (1994), 94-387 (1994), 95-397 (1995), 01-422 (2001), 06-439 (2006), 07-446 (2007), and 10-457 (2010).

Ethical Guidelines for Settlement Negotiations: In 2002, the ABA Section of Litigation issued Ethical Guidelines for Settlement Negotiations. They are organized into three sections: "Settlement Negotiations Generally," "Issues Relating to Lawyers and Their Clients," and "Issues Relating to a Lawyer's Negotiations with Opposing Parties." They are available online at *http://www.aspenlawschool.com/books/folberg_resolvingdisputes/egsn.pdf.*

Restatement of the Law Governing Lawyers: See Restatement §§51, 56 and 98 in our chapter on the Restatement later in this volume.

Rule 4.2   Communication with Person Represented by Counsel

Canon and Code Antecedents

ABA Canons of Professional Ethics: Canon 9 provided as follows:

9.   *Negotiations with Opposite Party*

A lawyer should not in any way communicate upon the subject of controversy with a party represented by counsel; much less should he undertake to negotiate or compromise the matter with him, but should deal only with his counsel. It is incumbent upon the lawyer most particularly to avoid everything that may tend to mislead a party not represented by counsel, and he should not undertake to advise him as to the law.

ABA Model Code of Professional Responsibility: Compare DR 7-104(A)(1) (reprinted later in this volume).

Cross-References in Other Rules

Rule 3.4, Comment 4: "Paragraph (f) permits a lawyer to advise employees of a client to refrain from giving information to another party, for the employees may identify their interests with those of the client. See also **Rule 4.2**."

Rule 3.9, Comment 3: This Rule "does not apply to representation of a client in a negotiation or other bilateral transaction with a governmental agency. . . . Representation in such matters is governed by **Rules 4.1** through **4.4**."

Legislative History of Model Rule 4.2

1980 Discussion Draft (then Rule 3.2(b)(5)) provided that a lawyer shall not "interview or otherwise communicate with a party who the lawyer knows is represented by other counsel concerning the subject matter of the representation, except with the consent of that party's counsel or as authorized by law."

1981 Draft was substantially the same as adopted.

1982 Draft was adopted.

1983 Rule: As originally adopted in 1983, Rule 4.2 provided: "In representing a client, a lawyer shall not communicate about the subject of the representation with a *party* the lawyer knows to be represented by another lawyer in the matter, unless the lawyer has the consent of the other lawyer or is authorized by law to do so." (Emphasis added.)

1994 Proposal: In May of 1994, the ABA's Standing Committee on Ethics and Professional Responsibility submitted a proposed amendment to Rule 4.2. In June of 1994, however, after receiving criticism of the proposal, the Standing Committee withdrew the proposal to circulate it for public comment. The withdrawn proposal would have substituted the word "person" for "party" and added the phrase "or reasonably should know" to the text of the rule. Had the proposed amendments been adopted, Rule 4.2 would have provided:

In representing a client, a lawyer shall not communicate about the subject of the representation with a *person* the lawyer knows *or reasonably should know* to be represented by another lawyer in the matter, unless the lawyer has the consent of the other lawyer or is authorized by law to do so. (Emphasis added.)

A proposed addition to the Comment stated:

> Because of the interest in ensuring that persons have the assistance of counsel who represent them in a matter, a lawyer has an affirmative obligation to act as would a lawyer of reasonable prudence and competence to ascertain whether a person is represented in a matter before undertaking further communication on that matter with that person; and if the person is so represented, to communicate only as the Rule allows.

The Standing Committee's report in support of the proposed amendment explained:*

> The situation presented by the current language of the Rule permits a lawyer who believes or suspects that a person is represented in the matter by another lawyer to subvert the purpose and spirit of the Rule by avoiding learning whether that belief or suspicion is correct. The protection of represented persons the Rule is designed to foster . . . would be enhanced by an amendment to Model Rule 4.2 requiring a lawyer contemplating communicating with other persons . . . to *ascertain* whether the person with whom communication is sought is represented in the matter by another lawyer.
>
> The Standing Committee has also taken the occasion presented by this amendment to clarify the fact that the Rule protects represented *persons* whether or not they are, in a formal sense, actual or prospective *"parties"* to a proceeding or transaction. . . . (Emphasis added.)

1995 Amendment: At the ABA's 1995 Annual Meeting, the House of Delegates voted to amend Rule 4.2 by changing the word "party" to "person" in Rule 4.2. (Unlike the withdrawn 1994 proposal, the 1995 proposal omitted the phrase "or reasonably should know.") The House of Delegates also added three new paragraphs to the Comment and revised the three original paragraphs. The amendment was overwhelmingly approved on a voice vote. For a legislative-style version of the Rule and Comment, see our 1996 edition.

The sole sponsor of the 1995 amendment was the ABA Standing Committee on Ethics and Professional Responsibility. The United States Department of Justice, which followed its own rules on communications with represented parties and persons (reprinted in the Special Section at the end of our 1996 edition), officially opposed the amendment and spoke against it during the House of Delegates debate. The ABA Section on Criminal Justice also voted against the amendment. The Standing Committee's report in support of the amendment provided, in part, as follows (with all citations omitted).

*Excerpt from ABA Report Explaining 1995 Amendment***

[II] C.   SUBSTITUTION OF THE WORD "PERSON" FOR "PARTY"

> In choosing whether "party" or "person" better describes the proper scope of the Rule, the Standing Committee . . . has addressed the question of what the meaning of the Rule *should* be, in light of the purposes the Rule is designed to serve.
> . . . [T]he appropriate operative term is "person," and not "party," for neither the need to protect uncounselled persons against being taken advantage of by

---

* Committee Reports do not represent official policy of the ABA. They are for information only, and represent only the opinions of the authors.
** Committee Reports do not represent official policy of the ABA. They are for information only, and the opinions are those of the authors of the report.

opposing counsel nor the importance of preserving the client-attorney relationship is limited to those circumstances where the represented person is a party to an adjudicative or other formal proceeding. The interests sought to be protected by the Rule may equally well be involved when litigation is merely under consideration, even though it has not actually been instituted, and the persons who are potentially parties to the litigation have retained counsel with respect to the matter in dispute.

Concerns regarding the need to protect uncounselled persons against the wiles of opposing counsel and preserving the attorney-client relationship may also be involved where a person is a target of a criminal investigation, knows this, and has retained counsel to advise him with respect to the investigation. The same concerns may be involved where a "third-party" witness furnishes testimony in an investigation or proceeding and, even though not a formal party, has seen fit to retain counsel to advise him with respect thereto. Such concerns are equally applicable in a non-adjudicatory context, such as a commercial transaction involving a sale, a lease or some other form of contract.

E.   OBJECTIONS TO THE PROPOSED CHANGE IN THE RULE

. . . The Rule now applies, and as amended would continue to apply, only where the person to be contacted is known to be represented with respect to the particular matter that is the subject of the prospective communication. The fact that a particular entity or person has retained a lawyer for one matter does not mean that the representation extends to any other matter; and even a general representation for all purposes, such as might be asserted by inside counsel for a corporation, does not, for purposes of the Rule, necessarily imply a representation with respect to a matter that has not in fact been brought to the attention of such counsel. . . .

III.   The Proposed Change to Clarify That an Attorney's Knowledge Regarding Representation May Be Inferred from the Circumstances

C.   REASONS FOR THE PROPOSED CHANGE

It would not . . . be reasonable to require a lawyer in all circumstances where the lawyer wishes to speak to a third person in the course of his representation of a client first to inquire whether the person is represented by counsel: among other things, such a routine inquiry would unnecessarily complicate perfectly routine fact-finding, and might well unnecessarily obstruct such fact-finding by conveying a suggestion that there was a need for counsel in circumstances where there was none, and thus discouraging witnesses from talking. In consequence, the Rule's requirement of securing permission of counsel is reasonably limited to those circumstances where the inquiring lawyer *knows* that the person to whom he wants to speak is represented by counsel with respect to the subject of the communication.

However, a lawyer should not be able to ignore the obvious and then claim lack of certain knowledge, thus excusing a failure to secure consent of counsel whose likely involvement should have been obvious. . . . [A] lawyer may not avoid Rule 4.2 by closing eyes to what is plainly to be seen.

1999 Proposal (withdrawn): In 1999, in an effort to resolve years of stalemated negotiations between the United States Department of Justice (representing all federal government lawyers) and the Conference of Chief Justices (representing the high courts of the fifty states and the District of Columbia), the ABA's Standing Committee on Ethics and Professional Responsibility proposed to add the following new paragraphs (b) and (c) to Rule 4.2:

(b) A government lawyer supervising a criminal or civil law enforcement investigation may authorize an investigative agent to communicate with a person represented in the matter prior to the arrest of or the filing of a formal criminal charge or civil complaint against that person in the matter, if the lawyer makes reasonable efforts to ensure that the agent's conduct is compatible with paragraph (c).

(c) Unless permitted to do otherwise by the consent of the represented person's lawyer, a lawyer communicating with a represented person pursuant to this Rule shall not

(1) seek information protected by the attorney-client privilege or as attorney work product;

(2) attempt to induce the represented person to forego representation by or disregard the advice of his or her lawyer; or

(3) initiate or engage in negotiation of an agreement, settlement or plea with respect to the matter in which the person is represented by a lawyer, except as authorized by law or court order.

The Standing Committee also proposed extensively amending the Comment to Rule 4.2. One of the proposed new paragraphs provided as follows:

Ordinarily a lawyer may not direct an investigative agent to communicate with a represented person in circumstances where the lawyer would be prohibited from doing so by this Rule. . . . This prohibition is qualified by paragraph (b) of this Rule to permit government lawyers to supervise criminal and civil law enforcement investigations. The lawyer representing the government in the matter must not directly and personally communicate with the represented person unless otherwise permitted to do so by paragraph (a) of this Rule. In addition, the lawyer must make reasonable efforts to ensure that investigative agents comply with paragraph (c). . . .

The Committee Report explaining the proposed changes noted that Department of Justice lawyers have for years "expressed concerns that Rule 4.2 imposes undue restrictions on law enforcement investigations directly or by creating ambiguities as to the allowable parameters of investigative methods." The ABA negotiated with the Department of Justice in an effort to address those concerns, but the Department of Justice did not endorse the proposal, so the ABA withdrew it from consideration shortly before the ABA's 1999 Annual Meeting. Discussions between the ABA and the Department of Justice continued, however, and the ABA Ethics 2000 Commission proposals reflected some of the Department of Justice's concerns. For information about other historical developments pertaining to Rule 4.2, see the Related Materials following Rule 4.2.

2002 Amendments: At its February 2002 Mid-Year Meeting, the ABA House of Delegates adopted with only minor changes the ABA Ethics 2000 Commission proposal to amend Rule 4.2 and its Comment. The amendments added "or a court order" to the text, added Comments 1, 3, and 6, and extensively amended Comments 2, 4, 5, 7, and 8.

Selected State Variations

Alabama: Effective March 26, 2012, Alabama recognizes "limited-scope representation" in its civil procedure rules. Specifically, Rule 11(b) provides:

(b) *Limited-scope representation.* An attorney may draft or help to draft a pleading, motion, or other paper filed by an otherwise self-represented person. The attorney need not sign that pleading, motion, or other paper but shall include a notation at the end stating: "This document was prepared with the assistance of a licensed Alabama lawyer pursuant to Rule 1.2(c), Alabama Rules of Professional Conduct." In providing such drafting assistance, the attorney may rely on the otherwise self-represented person's representation of the facts, unless the attorney has reason to believe that such representation is false or materially insufficient.

Rule 4.2 of the Alabama Rules of Professional Conduct then provides:

(b) A person to whom limited-scope representation is being provided or has been provided in accordance with Rule 1.2(c) is considered to be unrepresented for purposes of this rule unless the opposing lawyer has been provided with a written notice of the limited-scope representation. If such notice is provided, the opposing lawyer shall not communicate with the person regarding matters designated in the notice of limited-scope representation without consent or authorization as provided by Rule 4.2(a).

Arizona: Rule 4.2 restricts communication with a "party" rather than a "person" and omits the phrase "or a court order."

California: Rule 2-100 (Communication with a Represented Party), provides as follows:

(A) While representing a client, a member shall not communicate directly or indirectly about the subject of the representation with a party the member knows to be represented by another lawyer in the matter, unless the member has the consent of the other lawyer.

(B) For purposes of this rule, a "party" includes:

(1) An officer, director, or managing agent of a corporation or association, and a partner or managing agent of a partnership; or

(2) An association member or an employee of an association, corporation, or partnership, if the subject of the communication is any act or omission of such person in connection with the matter which may be binding upon or imputed to the organization for purposes of civil or criminal liability or whose statement may constitute an admission on the part of the organization.

(C) This rule shall not prohibit:

(1) Communications with a public officer, board, committee, or body; or

(2) Communications initiated by a party seeking advice or representation from an independent lawyer of the party's choice; or

(3) Communications otherwise authorized by law.

District of Columbia adds the following three paragraphs to Rule 4.2:

(b) During the course of representing a client, a lawyer may communicate about the subject of the representation with a nonparty employee of an organization without obtaining the consent of that organization's lawyer. If the organization is an adverse party, however, prior to communicating with any such nonparty employee, a lawyer must disclose to such employee both the lawyer's identity and the fact that the lawyer represents a party that is adverse to the employee's employer.

(c) For purposes of this rule, the term "party" or "person" includes any person or organization, including an employee of an organization, who has the authority to bind an organization as to the representation to which the communication relates.

(d) This rule does not prohibit communication by a lawyer with government officials who have the authority to redress the grievances of the lawyer's client, whether or not those grievances or the lawyer's communications relate to matters that are the subject of the representation, provided that in the event of such communications the disclosures specified in (b) are made to the government official to whom the communication is made.

Florida: Rule 4.2 deletes the phrase "or is authorized to do so by law or a court order" and substitutes the following new language:

> [A]n attorney may, without such prior consent, communicate with another's client in order to meet the requirements of any statute, court rule, or contract requiring notice or service of process directly on an adverse party, in which event the communication shall be strictly restricted to that required by the court rule, statute or contract, and a copy shall be provided to the adverse party's attorney.

In addition, Florida adds a new paragraph (b) stating as follows:

> (b) An otherwise unrepresented person to whom limited representation is being provided or has been provided in accordance with Rule Regulating the Florida Bar 4-1.2 is considered to be unrepresented for purposes of this rule unless the opposing lawyer knows of, or has been provided with, a written notice of appearance under which, or a written notice of time period during which, the opposing lawyer is to communicate with the limited representation lawyer as to the subject matter within the limited scope of the representation.

Georgia replaces the phrase "authorized to do so by law" with the phrase "authorized to do so by constitutional law or statute." Georgia also adds a new paragraph (b) that provides: "Attorneys for the State and Federal Government shall be subject to this Rule in the same manner as other attorneys in this State." Georgia also adds the following unusual Comment 4B:

> In administering this Rule it should be anticipated that in many instances, prior to the beginning of the interview, the interviewing lawyer will not possess sufficient information to determine whether the relationship of the interviewee to the entity is sufficiently close to place the person in the "represented" category. In those situations the good faith of the lawyer in undertaking the interview should be considered. Evidence of good faith includes an immediate and candid statement of the interest of the person on whose behalf the interview is being taken, a full explanation of why that person's position is adverse to the interests of the entity with which the interviewee is associated, the exploration of the relationship issue at the outset of the interview and the cessation of the interview immediately upon determination that the interview is improper.

Illinois adopts ABA Model Rule 4.2 in substance.

Louisiana adds a new paragraph (b) that prohibits communication with:

> a person the lawyer knows is presently a director, officer, employee, member, shareholder, or other constituent of a represented organization and
> (1) Who supervises, directs or regularly consults with the organization's lawyer concerning the matter;
> (2) Who has the authority to obligate the organization with respect to the matter; or
> (3) Whose act or omission in connection with the matter may be imputed to the organization for purpose of civil or criminal liability.

Maryland adds the following paragraphs to Rule 4.2 and limits the reach of paragraph (a), which is the same as ABA Model Rule 4.2, by reference to paragraph (c):

> (b) If the person represented by another lawyer is an organization, the prohibition extends to each of the organization's (1) current officers, directors, and managing agents and (2) current agents or employees who supervise, direct, or regularly communicate with the organization's lawyers concerning the matter or whose acts or

omissions in the matter may bind the organization for civil or criminal liability. The lawyer may not communicate with a current agent or employee of the organization unless the lawyer first has made inquiry to ensure that the agent or employee is not an individual with whom communication is prohibited by this paragraph and has disclosed to the individual the lawyer's identity and the fact that the lawyer represents a client who has an interest adverse to the organization.

(c) A lawyer may communicate with a government official about matters that are the subject of the representation if the government official has the authority to redress the grievances of the lawyer's client and the lawyer first makes the disclosures specified in paragraph (b).

Michigan currently retains the pre-2002 version of ABA Model Rule 4.2 (which lacks an express "court order" exception).

New Jersey: Rule 4.2 provides as follows:

> In representing a client, a lawyer shall not communicate about the subject of the representation with a person the lawyer knows, or by the exercise of reasonable diligence should know, to be represented by another lawyer in the matter, including members of an organization's litigation control group as defined by RPC 1.13, unless the lawyer has the consent of the other lawyer, or is authorized by law or court order to do so, or unless the sole purpose of the communication is to ascertain whether the person is in fact represented. Reasonable diligence shall include, but not be limited to, a specific inquiry of the person as to whether that person is represented by counsel. Nothing in this rule shall, however, preclude a lawyer from counseling or representing a member or former member of an organization's litigation control group who seeks independent legal advice.

Rule 4.2 must be read in conjunction with New Jersey's Rule 1.13, which defines the phrase "litigation control group" as follows:

> For the purposes of RPC 4.2 and 4.3 . . . the organization's lawyer shall be deemed to represent not only the organizational entity but also the members of its litigation control group. Members of the litigation control group shall be deemed to include current agents and employees responsible for, or significantly involved in, the determination of the organization's legal position in the matter whether or not in litigation, provided, however, that "significant involvement" requires involvement greater, and other than, the supplying of factual information or data respecting the matter. Former agents and employees who were members of the litigation control group shall presumptively be deemed to be represented in the matter by the organization's lawyer but may at any time disavow said representation.

New Mexico adds the following sentence to Rule 4.2: "Except for persons having a managerial responsibility on behalf of the organization, an attorney is not prohibited from communicating directly with employees of a corporation, partnership or other entity about the subject matter of the representation even though the corporation, partnership or entity itself is represented by counsel."

New York: New York Rule 4.2(a) is the same as Model Rule 4.2 except that New York substitutes "party" for "person," adds "or cause another to communicate" before "about," and deletes "or a court order." New York adds Rule 4.2(b), which uses "person," not "party," as follows:

> Notwithstanding the prohibitions of paragraph (a), and unless otherwise prohibited by law, a lawyer may cause a client to communicate with a represented person unless the represented person is not legally competent, and may counsel the client

with respect to those communications, provided the lawyer gives reasonable advance notice to the represented person's counsel that such communications will be taking place.

North Carolina: Rule 4.2(a) adds: "It is not a violation of this rule for a lawyer to encourage his or her client to discuss the subject of the representation with the opposing party in a good-faith attempt to resolve the controversy." North Carolina also adds a new Rule 4.2(b) that provides as follows:

(b) Notwithstanding section (a) above, in representing a client who has a dispute with a government agency or body, a lawyer may communicate about the subject of the representation with the elected officials who have authority over such government agency or body, even if the lawyer knows that the government agency or body is represented by another lawyer in the matter, but such communications may only occur under the following circumstances:

(1) in writing, if a copy of the writing is promptly delivered to opposing counsel;

(2) orally, upon adequate notice to opposing counsel; or

(3) in the course of official proceedings.

Oregon: Rule 4.2 provides as follows:

In representing a client or the lawyer's own interests, a lawyer shall not communicate or cause another to communicate on the subject of the representation with a person the lawyer knows to be represented by a lawyer on that subject unless:

(a) the lawyer has the prior consent of a lawyer representing such other person;

(b) the lawyer is authorized by law or by court order to do so; or

(c) a written agreement requires a written notice or demand to be sent to such other person, in which case a copy of such notice or demand shall also be sent to such other person's lawyer.

Texas: Rule 4.02 provides:

(a) In representing a client, a lawyer shall not communicate or cause or encourage another to communicate about the subject of the representation with a person, organization or entity of government the lawyer knows to be represented by another lawyer regarding that subject, unless the lawyer has the consent of the other lawyer or is authorized by law to do so.

(b) In representing a client a lawyer shall not communicate or cause another to communicate about the subject of representation with a person or organization a lawyer knows to be employed or retained for the purpose of conferring with or advising another lawyer about the subject of the representation, unless the lawyer has the consent of the other lawyer or is authorized by law to do so.

(c) For the purpose of this rule, "organization or entity of government" includes: (1) those persons presently having a managerial responsibility with an organization or entity of government that relates to the subject of the representation, or (2) those persons presently employed by such organization or entity and whose act or omission in connection with the subject of representation may make the organization or entity of government vicariously liable for such act or omission.

(d) When a person, organization, or entity of government that is represented by a lawyer in a matter seeks advice regarding that matter from another lawyer, the second lawyer is not prohibited by paragraph (a) from giving such advice without notifying or seeking consent of the first lawyer.

Utah: Rule 4.2 contains 17 separate paragraphs and subparagraphs. Rule 4.2(a) begins by tracking ABA Model Rule 4.2, but omits "or is authorized to do so by law or court order" and adds that an attorney may, without prior consent, communicate with another lawyer's client "if authorized to do so by any law, rule, or court order . . . or as authorized by paragraph (b), (c), (d) or (e) of this Rule." Paragraphs (b) and (d) cover "Rules Relating to Unbundling of Legal Services" and "Organizations as Represented Persons." Paragraph (c), which is highly unusual, provides as follows:

(c) *Rules Relating to Government Lawyers Engaged in Civil or Criminal Law Enforcement.* A government lawyer engaged in a criminal or civil law enforcement matter, or a person acting under the lawyer's direction in the matter, may communicate with a person known to be represented by a lawyer if:

(1) the communication is in the course of, and limited to, an investigation of a different matter unrelated to the representation or any ongoing, unlawful conduct; or

(2) the communication is made to protect against an imminent risk of death or serious bodily harm or substantial property damage that the government lawyer reasonably believes may occur and the communication is limited to those matters necessary to protect against the imminent risk; or

(3) the communication is made at the time of the arrest of the represented person and after that person is advised of the right to remain silent and the right to counsel and voluntarily and knowingly waives these rights; or

(4) the communication is initiated by the represented person, directly or through an intermediary, if prior to the communication the represented person has given a written or recorded voluntary and informed waiver of counsel, including the right to have substitute counsel, for that communication.

Paragraph (e), which covers "Limitations on Communications," provides that when communicating with a represented person pursuant to this Rule, no lawyer may:

(e)(1) inquire about privileged communications between the person and counsel or about information regarding litigation strategy or legal arguments of counsel or seek to induce the person to forgo representation or disregard the advice of the person's counsel; or

(2) engage in negotiations of a plea agreement, settlement, statutory or non-statutory immunity agreement or other disposition of actual or potential criminal charges or civil enforcement claims or sentences or penalties with respect to the matter in which the person is represented by counsel unless such negotiations are permitted by law, rule or court order.

Wyoming makes clear that Rule 4.2 applies to communications with a person "or entity" represented by another lawyer. Effective October 1, 2011, Wyoming Comment 7 states that "Consent of the organization's lawyer is not required for communication with a former constituent."

Related Materials

ABA Formal Ethics Opinions: See ABA Formal Ethics Ops. 91-359 (1991), 93-378 (1993), 95-396 (1995), 96-400 (1996), 97-408 (1997), 06-443 (2006), and 07-445 (2007).

ABA Standards for Criminal Justice: See Prosecution Function Standard 3-4.1(b) (Availability for Plea Discussions).

ABA Standards for Imposing Lawyer Sanctions:

6.3. Improper Communications with Individuals in the Legal System

6.31. Disbarment is generally appropriate when a lawyer:

(a) intentionally tampers with a witness and causes serious or potentially serious injury to a party, or causes significant or potentially significant interference with the outcome of the legal proceeding; or

(b) makes an ex parte communication with a judge or juror with intent to affect the outcome of the proceeding, and causes serious or potentially serious injury to a party, or causes significant or potentially significant interference with the outcome of the legal proceeding; or

(c) improperly communicates with someone in the legal system other than a witness, judge, or juror with the intent to influence or affect the outcome of the proceeding, and causes significant or potentially significant interference with the outcome of the legal proceeding.

6.32. Suspension is generally appropriate when a lawyer engages in communication with an individual in the legal system when the lawyer knows that such communication is improper, and causes injury or potential injury to a party or causes interference or potential interference with the outcome of the legal proceeding.

6.33. Reprimand is generally appropriate when a lawyer is negligent in determining whether it is proper to engage in communication with an individual in the legal system, and causes injury or potential injury to a party or interference or potential interference with the outcome of the legal proceeding.

American Lawyer's Code of Conduct: Rule 3.9 provides: "[A] lawyer may send a written offer of settlement directly to an adverse party, seven days or more after that party's attorney has received the same offer of settlement in writing."

Department of Justice Rules: In 1989, U.S. Attorney General Richard Thornburgh issued a memorandum, widely known as the "Thornburgh Memorandum," arguing that Rule 4.2 did not prohibit Department of Justice employees and their agents and investigators from communicating with a represented person before indictment. Thornburgh also argued that (1) the Supremacy Clause prohibited state ethics rules from controlling federal employees, and (2) federal undercover investigations, including undercover contacts with suspects or unindicted grand jury targets known to be represented by counsel, were "authorized by law" within the meaning of Rule 4.2. In 1991, however, a federal court held that the Thornburgh Memorandum did not have the force of law, and the court dismissed an indictment on grounds that a prosecutor had contacted a defendant represented by counsel without being "authorized by law." *United States v. Lopez,* 765 F. Supp. 1433 (N.D. Cal. 1991), *vacated on other grounds,* 989 F.2d 1032 (9th Cir. 1993).

President George H. W. Bush sought to remedy this problem by publishing proposed regulations resembling the Thornburgh Memorandum in the Federal Register for public comment in late 1992. (*See* 57 Fed. Reg. 54737.) Criminal defense lawyers harshly criticized these proposed regulations, but the proposals would have become law automatically if the Clinton administration had not withdrawn the proposals two days after taking office. Later in 1993, under Attorney General Janet Reno, the Department of Justice republished the original proposed regulations with only minor changes for 30 days of public comment. (*See* 58 Fed. Reg. 39976.) Criticism was again harsh.

In 1994, the Department of Justice circulated a third set of proposed regulations for public comment. (*See* 59 Fed. Reg. 10086.) Finally, effective September 6, 1994, the Department of Justice issued a "final rule" on the subject, sometimes called the "Reno Rules." (*See* 59 Fed. Reg. 39910, formally codified at 28 C.F.R. Part 77.) The final rule was expressly intended "to preempt the entire field of rules concerning" contacts by government attorneys with represented parties. (We reprinted the full text of the Reno Rules in our Special Section at the end of our 1996 edition.)

In *O'Keefe v. McDonnell Douglas Corp.*, 132 F.3d 1252 (8th Cir. 1998), however, the court held that the Department of Justice had lacked authority to promulgate the Reno Rules. Congress then enacted 28 U.S.C. §530B, entitled "Ethical Standards for Attorneys for the Government," which provides that federal government attorneys are subject to the same ethical standards as other attorneys practicing in the same state. Section 530B also commanded the Attorney General to amend the Department of Justice's rules "to assure compliance with this section." (The full text of §530B is reprinted below in these Related Materials under the heading "Ethical Standards for Attorneys for the Government.") Pursuant to the statutory directive, the Attorney General then amended 28 C.F.R. Part 77.

Ethical Standards for Attorneys for the Government: In 1998, Congress enacted a new statute, 28 U.S.C. §530B (often called the "McDade Amendment," after its main sponsor in the House of Representatives), which provides as follows:

§530B.   Ethical Standards for Attorneys for the Government

(a) An attorney for the Government shall be subject to State laws and rules, and local Federal court rules, governing attorneys in each State where such attorney engages in that attorney's duties, to the same extent and in the same manner as other attorneys in that State.

(b) The Attorney General shall make and amend rules of the Department of Justice to assure compliance with this section.

(c) As used in this section, the term "attorney for the Government" includes any attorney described in section 77.2(a) of part 77 of title 28 of the Code of Federal Regulations and also includes any independent counsel, or employee of such a counsel, appointed under chapter 40.

Federal Rules of Civil Procedure: Rule 5(b)(1) provides: "If a party is represented by an attorney, service under this rule must be made on the attorney unless the court orders service on the party."

Federal Rules of Evidence: Rule 801(d)(2)(D), often cited in opinions regarding Rule 4.2, provides:

(d) *Statements which are not hearsay.* A statement that meets the following conditions is not hearsay:

(2) *An Opposing Party's Statement.* The statement is offered against an opposing party and:

(D) was made by the party's agent or employee on a matter within the scope of that relationship and while it existed. . . .

Joint Proposal by U.S. Department of Justice and Conference of Chief Justices: In 1997, the Conference of Chief Justices (the Conference), representing all state courts,, and the United States Department of Justice (the DOJ), representing all federal government lawyers, circulated a joint proposal to amend ABA Model Rule 4.2. The proposal, which took more than two years to negotiate, represented a compromise between the DOJ's position that the so-called "Reno Rules" (28 C.F.R. Part 77) govern all federal lawyers, on the one hand, and the Conference's position that state ethics rules govern all federal lawyers, on the other hand. The tentative plan was that the DOJ would withdraw the Reno Rules in states that adopted the proposed amendment to Rule 4.2.

After soliciting public comments on the joint proposal, the Conference of Chief Justices determined that there was "a decided lack of consensus in the national legal community as to both the principles underlying the draft and the specific language of the proposal." The Conference also noted that the ABA and various other groups were then "actively considering" proposals to amend Rule 4.2. Therefore, in 1998 the Conference passed a resolution stating that it was "premature for the Conference to take action on the draft at this time." The Conference never acted on the draft proposal. The full text of the joint proposal to amend Rule 4.2 and the Conference's 1998 resolution regarding the joint proposal are reprinted in the Special Section at the end of our 1999 edition.

Model Rules of Professional Conduct for Federal Lawyers: In a criminal matter, Rule 4.2(a) creates an exception to the no-contact rule "if the individual initiates the communication with the Government lawyer and voluntarily and knowingly waives the right to counsel for the purposes of that communication. . . ." The Comment explains:

> In a criminal case there may be times when communications between a defendant and a Federal Agency without notice to defense counsel are in the interest of the defendant. Some communications will serve to protect the defendant and to identify sham representations. For example, in certain criminal enterprises, such as organized crime or drug rings, a defendant may wish to cooperate with a Federal Agency, but the counsel may also be the counsel of others involved in the enterprise. To insure that in such instances there is no abuse, this rule would permit communications by the defendant with the Government lawyer, as long as the defendant voluntarily and knowingly waives the right to counsel.

In addition, Rule 4.2(b) of the Model Rules of Professional Conduct for Federal Lawyers provides:

> (b) This Rule does not prohibit communications by a Non-Government lawyer with Federal Agency officials who have the authority to resolve a matter affecting the lawyer's client, whether or not the lawyer's communications relate to matters that are the subject of the representation, provided that the lawyer discloses the lawyer's identity; the fact that the lawyer represents a client in a matter involving the official's Federal Agency; and that the matter is being handled for the Federal Agency by a Government lawyer.

Restatement of the Law Governing Lawyers: See Restatement §§99-102 in our chapter on the Restatement later in this volume.

Rule 4.3   Dealing with Unrepresented Person

Canon and Code Antecedents

ABA Canons of Professional Ethics: Canon 9 provided as follows:

9.   *Negotiations with Opposite Party*

A lawyer should not in any way communicate upon the subject of controversy with a party represented by counsel; much less should he undertake to negotiate or compromise the matter with him, but should deal only with his counsel. It is incumbent upon the lawyer most particularly to avoid everything that may tend to mislead a party not represented by counsel, and he should not undertake to advise him as to the law.

ABA Model Code of Professional Responsibility: Compare DR 7-104(A)(2) (reprinted later in this volume).

Cross-References in Other Rules

Rule 3.9, Comment 3: This Rule "does not apply to representation of a client in a negotiation or other bilateral transaction with a governmental agency. . . . Representation in such matters is governed by **Rules 4.1** through **4.4**."

Rule 4.2, Comment 9: "In the event the person with whom the lawyer communicates is not known to be represented by counsel in the matter, the lawyer's communications are subject to **Rule 4.3**."

Legislative History of Model Rule 4.3

1980 Discussion Draft (then Rule 3.6) provided as follows:

Appearing Against an Unrepresented Party

When an opposing party is unrepresented, a lawyer shall refrain from unfairly exploiting that party's ignorance of the law or the practices of the tribunal.

1981 Draft was substantially the same as adopted.

1982 Draft was adopted.

1983 Rule: As originally adopted in 1983, Rule 4.3 was the same as the first two sentences of the 2002 version of Rule 4.3, but did not contain the third sentence.

2002 Amendments: At its February 2002 Mid-Year Meeting, the ABA House of Delegates adopted without change the ABA Ethics 2000 Commission proposal to amend Rule 4.3 and its Comment. The amendments changed the text of Rule 4.3 by adding the last sentence (the substance of which had previously been in Comment 1) and amended the Comment by adding the last two sentences of Comment 1 and all of Comment 2.

Selected State Variations

Alabama: Effective March 26, 2011, Alabama adds the following paragraph (b) to Rule 4.3:

> A person to whom limited-scope representation is being provided or has been provided in accordance with Rule 1.2(c) is considered to be unrepresented for purposes of this rule unless the opposing lawyer has been provided with a written notice of the limited-scope representation. If such notice is provided, the person is considered to be unrepresented regarding matters not designated in the notice of limited-scope representation.

For the definition of "limited-scope representation" within the meaning of Rule 4.3(b), see the entry for Alabama in the Selected State Variations after Rule 4.2.

California has no comparable provision.

District of Columbia: Rule 4.3 contains the same words as ABA Model Rule 4.3, but D.C. divides the rule into paragraphs and subparagraphs.

Florida: The last sentence of Rule 4.3 provides only that a lawyer "shall not give legal advice to an unrepresented person, other than the advice to secure counsel." Florida also adds a new Rule 4.3(b) that provides as follows:

> (b) An otherwise unrepresented person to whom limited representation is being provided or has been provided in accordance with Rule Regulating the Florida Bar 4-1.2 is considered to be unrepresented for purposes of this rule unless the opposing lawyer knows of, or has been provided with, a written notice of appearance under which, or a written notice of time period during which, the opposing lawyer is to communicate with the limited representation lawyer as to the subject matter within the limited scope of the representation.

(Florida's version of Rule 1.2(c) provides, in part, that "a lawyer and client may agree to limit the objectives or scope of the representation if the limitation is reasonable under the circumstances and the client consents in writing after consultation.")

Georgia adds that a lawyer shall not:

> (c) initiate any contact with a potentially adverse party in a matter concerning personal injury or wrongful death or otherwise related to an accident or disaster involving the person to whom the contact is addressed or a relative of that person, unless the accident or disaster occurred more than 30 days prior to the contact.

Kansas, Maryland, and ***Michigan*** retain the pre-2002 version of Rule 4.3.

New Jersey: Rule 4.3 deletes the last sentence of ABA Model Rule 4.3 and adds the following new sentence:

> If the person is a director, officer, employee, member, shareholder or other constituent of an organization concerned with the subject of the lawyer's representation but not a person defined by RPC 1.13(a), the lawyer shall also ascertain by reasonable diligence whether the person is actually represented by the organization's attorney pursuant to RPC 1.13(e) or who has a right to such representation on request, and, if the person is not so represented or entitled to representation, the lawyer shall make known to the person that insofar as the lawyer understands, the person is not being represented by the organization's attorney.

New Jersey Rule 4.3 must be read in conjunction with New Jersey Rule 1.13(a). See Selected State Variations under Rule 4.2.

New York: Rule 4.3 tracks the ABA Model Rule except that it substitutes "communicating" for "dealing" as the second word of the rule.

North Carolina and *Pennsylvania:* Rule 4.3 tracks the substance of ABA Model Rule 4.3, but reorders the language and divides the rule into subparagraphs.

Utah adds Rule 4.3(b), which provides that if a person's counsel does not represent the person in all aspects of a particular matter, a lawyer may consider the person to be entirely "unrepresented" for purposes of this Rule and Rule 4.2, "unless that person's counsel has provided written notice to the lawyer of those aspects of the matter or the time limitation for which the person is represented. Only as to such aspects and time is the person considered to be represented by counsel."

Washington: Washington adds the following Comments to Rule 4.3:

"An otherwise unrepresented person to whom limited representation is being provided or has been provided in accordance with Rule 1.2(c) is considered to be unrepresented for purposes of this Rule unless the opposing lawyer knows of, or has been provided with, a written notice of appearance under which, or a written notice of time period during which, he or she is to communicate only with the limited representation lawyer as to the subject matter within the limited scope of the representation."

"Government lawyers are frequently called upon by unrepresented persons, and in some instances by the courts, to provide general information on laws and procedures relating to claims against the government. The provision of such general information by government lawyers is not a violation of this Rule."

Wisconsin: The first sentence of Rule 4.3 provides that in dealings on behalf of a client with a person who is not represented by counsel, "a lawyer shall inform such person of the lawyer's role in the matter."

Related Materials

ABA Formal Ethics Opinions: See ABA Formal Ethics Ops. 91-359 (1991), 93-378 (1993), 95-396 (1995), and 07-445 (2007).

ABA Standards for Criminal Justice: See Prosecution Function Standards 3-3.2(b) (Relations with Victims and Prospective Witnesses) and 3-3.10(c) (Role in First Appearance and Preliminary Hearing).

American Academy of Matrimonial Lawyers: In the Bounds of Advocacy, Rule 3.2 provides that an attorney "should not advise an unrepresented party," and the AAML Comment to Rule 3.2 provides as follows:

Once it becomes apparent that another party intends to proceed without a lawyer, the attorney should, at the earliest opportunity, inform the opposing party in writing as follows:

1. I am your spouse's lawyer.
2. I do not and will not represent you.
3. I will at all times look out for your spouse's interests, not yours.
4. Any statements I make to you about this case should be taken by you as negotiation or argument on behalf of your spouse and not as advice to you as to your best interest.
5. I urge you to obtain your own lawyer.

Restatement of the Law Governing Lawyers: See Restatement §103 in our chapter on the Restatement later in this volume.

Rule 4.4   Respect for Rights of Third Persons

Canon and Code Antecedents

ABA Canons of Professional Ethics: Canon 18 provided as follows:

18.   Treatment of Witnesses and Litigants

A lawyer should always treat adverse witnesses and suitors with fairness and due consideration, and he should never minister to the malevolence or prejudices of a client in the trial or conduct of a cause. The client cannot be made the keeper of the lawyer's conscience in professional matters. He has no right to demand that his counsel shall abuse the opposite party or indulge in offensive personalities. Improper speech is not excusable on the ground that it is what the client would say if speaking in his own behalf.

ABA Model Code of Professional Responsibility: Compare DR 7-102(A)(1), DR 7-106(C)(2), DR 7-108(D), and DR 7-108(E) (reprinted later in this volume).

Cross-References in Other Rules

Rule 3.9, Comment 3: This transaction "does not apply to representation of a client in a negotiation or other bilateral transaction with a governmental agency. . . . Representation in such matters is governed by **Rules** 4.1 through **4.4.**"

Rule 4.2, Comment 7: "In communicating with a current or former constituent of an organization, a lawyer must not use methods of obtaining evidence that violate the legal rights of the organization. See **Rule 4.4.**"

Legislative History of Model Rule 4.4

1980 Discussion Draft (then Rule 3.4) provided as follows:

(a) In preparing and presenting a cause, a lawyer shall respect the interests of third persons, including witnesses, jurors, and persons incidentally concerned with the proceeding. . . .

1981 and 1982 Drafts were the same as adopted.

1983 Rule: As originally adopted in 1983, Rule 4.4 contained only one sentence, which was identical to the 2002 version of Rule 4.4(a). There was no Rule 4.4(b) in the 1983 rule.

2002 Amendments: Before the ABA's February 2002 Mid-Year Meeting the ABA Ethics 2000 Commission revised its May 2001 proposal to amend Rule 4.4 by adding "relating to the representation of the lawyer's client" to Rule 4.4(b) and revising the Comment to Rule 4.4 accordingly. At its February 2002 Mid-Year Meeting, the ABA House of Delegates adopted without change the ABA Ethics 2000 Commission's revised proposal to amend Rule 4.4 and its Comment. The amendments added Rule 4.4(b), added the last clause of Comment 1 ("and unwarranted intrusions . . ."), and added all of Comments 2 and 3.

2012 Amendments: In August 2012, Rule 4.4(b) was amended to add the words "or electronically stored information" after both instances of the word "document."

Comment 2 was amended to include "electronically stored information" and "metadata" and was expanded to provide more guidance on the meaning of "inadvertently sent." Comment 3 was amended to include electronically stored information.

Selected State Variations

Alabama: Alabama Rule 4.4(b) provides:

> (b) A lawyer who receives a document that on its face appears to be subject to the attorney-client privilege or otherwise confidential, and who knows or reasonably should know that the document was inadvertently sent, should promptly notify the sender and
>> (1) abide by the reasonable instructions of the sender regarding the disposition of the document; or
>> (2) submit the issue to an appropriate tribunal for a determination of the disposition of the document.

Arizona has adopted ABA Model Rule 4.4(b) but, in addition to requiring the lawyer who receives an inadvertently transmitted document to notify the sender, Arizona Rule 4.4(b) requires the lawyer to "preserve the status quo for a reasonable period of time in order to permit the sender to take protective measures."

California: Rule 3-200(A) provides that a member "shall not seek, accept, or continue employment if the member knows or should know that the objective of such employment is: (A) To bring an action, conduct a defense, assert a position in litigation, or take an appeal, without probable cause and for the purpose of harassing or maliciously injuring any person." Rule 5-100 provides:

> (A) A member shall not threaten to present criminal, administrative, or disciplinary charges to obtain an advantage in a civil dispute.
> (B) As used in paragraph (A) of this rule, the term "administrative charges" means the filing or lodging of a complaint with a federal, state, or local governmental entity which may order or recommend the loss or suspension of a license, or may impose or recommend the imposition of a fine, pecuniary sanction, or other sanction of a quasi-criminal nature but does not include filing charges with an administrative entity required by law as a condition precedent to maintaining a civil action.
> (C) As used in paragraph (A) of this rule, the term "civil dispute" means a controversy or potential controversy over the rights and duties of two or more parties under civil law, whether or not an action has been commenced, and includes an administrative proceeding of a quasi-civil nature pending before a federal, state, or local governmental entity.

California Business & Professions Code §§6068(c), 6068(f), and 6068(g) provide that it is the "duty" of an attorney to do all of the following:

> (c) To counsel or maintain those actions, proceedings, or defenses only as appear to him or her legal or just, except the defense of a person charged with a public offense. . . .
> (f) To advance no fact prejudicial to the honor or reputation of a party or witness, unless required by the justice of the cause with which he or she is charged.
> (g) Not to encourage either the commencement or the continuance of an action or proceeding from any corrupt motive of passion or interest.
> Section 6128(b) provides that an attorney is guilty of a misdemeanor who "[w]illfully delays his client's suit with a view to his own gain."

Colorado adds the following additional paragraph to Rule 4.4:

> (c) Unless otherwise permitted by court order, a lawyer who receives a document relating to the representation of the lawyer's client and who, before reviewing the document, receives notice from the sender that the document was inadvertently sent, shall not examine the document and shall abide by the sender's instructions as to its disposition.

Colorado has also adopted the following Rule 4.5:

> (a) A lawyer shall not threaten criminal, administrative or disciplinary charges to obtain an advantage in a civil matter nor shall a lawyer present or participate in presenting criminal, administrative or disciplinary charges solely to obtain an advantage in a civil matter.
>
> (b) It shall not be a violation of Rule 4.5 for a lawyer to notify another person in a civil matter that the lawyer reasonably believes that the other's conduct may violate criminal, administrative or disciplinary rules or statutes.

(A version of Rule 4.5(a) is in the ABA Code of Professional Responsibility as DR 7-105 but is limited to criminal conduct.)

District of Columbia: Rule 4.4(b) provides that a lawyer who receives a "writing" relating to the representation of a client and "knows, before examining the writing, that it has been inadvertently sent, shall not examine the writing, but shall notify the sending party and abide by the instructions of the sending party regarding the return or destruction of the writing."

Florida: Rule 4.4(a) provides that a lawyer shall not "knowingly" use methods of obtaining evidence that violate the legal rights of a third person. Florida has adopted ABA Model Rule 4.4(b) verbatim.

Idaho: Rule 4.4 provides that a lawyer, in representing a client, shall not use means that have no substantial purpose other than to embarrass, delay, or burden a third person, "including conduct intended to appeal to or engender bias against a person on account of that person's gender, race, religion, national origin, or sexual preference, whether that bias is directed to other counsel, court personnel, witnesses, parties, jurors, judges, judicial officers, or any other participants." In subparagraphs (a)(3) and (a)(4), Idaho retains the substance of DR 7-105 of the ABA Model Code of Professional Responsibility. Idaho Rule 4.4(b) deletes the phrase "relating to the representation of the lawyer's client."

Kentucky: Kentucky Rule 4.4(b) provides as follows:

> (b) A lawyer who receives a document relating to the representation of the lawyer's client and knows or reasonably should know that the document was inadvertently sent shall:
>> (1) refrain from reading the document,
>> (2) promptly notify the sender, and
>> (3) abide by the instructions of the sender regarding its disposition.

Louisiana adopts ABA Model Rule 4.4(a) verbatim but modifies Rule 4.4(b) to provide as follows:

> (b) A lawyer who receives a writing that, on its face, appears to be subject to the attorney-client privilege or otherwise confidential, under circumstances where it is clear that the writing was not intended for the receiving lawyer, shall refrain from examining the writing, promptly notify the sending lawyer, and return the writing.

Maryland adds the following paragraph (b) to Rule 4.4:

> (b) In communicating with third persons, a lawyer representing a client in a matter shall not seek information relating to the matter that the lawyer knows or reasonably should know is protected from disclosure by statute or by an established evidentiary privilege, unless the protection has been waived. The lawyer who receives information that is protected from disclosure shall (1) terminate the communication immediately and (2) give notice of the disclosure to any tribunal in which the matter is pending and to the person entitled to enforce the protection against disclosure.

Michigan omits Rule 4.4(b).

New Jersey adopts ABA Model Rule 4.4(a) verbatim but modifies Rule 4.4(b) to provide as follows:

> (b) A lawyer who receives a document and has reasonable cause to believe that the document was inadvertently sent shall not read the document or, if he or she has begun to do so, shall stop reading the document, promptly notify the sender, and return the document to the sender.

New York: Rule 4.4(a) substitutes "embarrass or harm" for "embarrass, delay, or burden" a third person. Rule 4.4(b) is the same as the Model Rule.

North Carolina: Rule 4.4(b) replaces the ABA word "document" with "writing."

North Dakota adds a new Rule 4.5(a) that is identical to ABA Model Rule 4.4(b), and adds a new Rule 4.5(b) providing that a lawyer who receives a document under the circumstances specified in Rule 4.5(a) "does not violate Rule 1.2 or Rule 1.4 by not communicating to or consulting with the client regarding the receipt or the return of the document."

Ohio: Rule 4.4(a) adds the word "harass" to the list of forbidden purposes.

South Carolina adds a new Rule 4.5, which says a lawyer "shall not present, participate in presenting, or threaten to present criminal or professional disciplinary charges solely to obtain an advantage in a civil matter."

Tennessee: Rule 4.4(b) forbids a lawyer to threaten to present a criminal charge or lawyer disciplinary charge, or to offer or to agree to refrain from filing such a charge, for the purpose of obtaining an advantage in a civil matter. Rule 4.4(b) provides:

> (b) A lawyer who receives information relating to the representation of the lawyer's client that the lawyer knows or reasonably should know is protected by RPC 1.6 (including information protected by the attorney-client privilege or the work-product rule) and has been disclosed to the lawyer inadvertently or by a person not authorized to disclose such information to the lawyer, shall:
>
> (1) immediately terminate review or use of the information;
>
> (2) notify the person, or the person's lawyer if communication with the person is prohibited by RPC 4.2, of the inadvertent or unauthorized disclosure; and
>
> (3) abide by that person's or lawyer's instructions with respect to disposition of written information or refrain from using the written information until obtaining a definitive ruling on the proper disposition from a court with appropriate jurisdiction.

Texas: Rule 4.04(b) forbids lawyers to present or threaten disciplinary or criminal charges "solely to gain an advantage in a civil matter" or civil, criminal, or disciplinary charges "solely" to prevent participation by a complainant or witness in a disciplinary matter.

Virginia: Rule 4.4(a) deletes the word "substantial" before the word "purpose." Virginia has not adopted Rule 4.4(b).

Wyoming adds Rule 4.4(c), which provides that a lawyer "shall not present, participate in presenting, or threaten to present criminal charges solely to obtain an advantage in a civil matter."

Related Materials

ABA Formal Ethics Opinions: See ABA Formal Ethics Ops. 92-363 (1992), 92-368 (1992) (withdrawn), 94-382 (1994) (withdrawn), 95-396 (1995), 01-422 (2001), 05-437 (2005), 06-440 (2006), 06-442 (2006), 11-460 (2011). (*Note: The ABA adopted Rule 4.4(b) in 2002. Opinions on this list that were issued before 2002 may be relevant to Rule 4.4(b) but do not cite it — Eds.*)

ABA Standards for Criminal Justice: See Prosecution Function Standards 3-2.9(b) (Prompt Disposition of Criminal Charges), 3-3.1(c) (Investigative Function of Prosecutor), and 3-5.7(a) (Examination of Witnesses); and Defense Function Standards 4-4.2 (Illegal Investigation), 4-7.1(a) (Courtroom Professionalism), and 4-7.6(a) (Examination of Witnesses).

Federal Rules of Civil Procedure: In 2006, the Federal Rules of Civil Procedure were amended to address inadvertent production of documents and waiver of attorney-client privilege during discovery. The amendment added a new Rule 26(b)(5)(B) — which is more demanding than ABA Model Rule 4.4(b) — that provides as follows:

> *(B) Information Produced.* If information produced in discovery is subject to a claim of privilege or of protection as trial-preparation material, the party making the claim may notify any party that received the information of the claim and the basis for it. After being notified, a party must promptly return, sequester, or destroy the specified information and any copies it has; must not use or disclose the information until the claim is resolved; must take reasonable steps to retrieve the information if the party disclosed it before being notified; and may promptly present the information to the court under seal for a determination of the claim. The producing party must preserve the information until the claim is resolved.

The Advisory Committee Note to Subdivision 26(b)(5) explains the quoted provision as follows:

> The Committee has repeatedly been advised that the risk of privilege waiver, and the work necessary to avoid it, add to the costs and delay of discovery. When the review is of electronically stored information, the risk of waiver, and the time and effort required to avoid it, can increase substantially because of the volume of electronically stored information and the difficulty in ensuring that all information to be produced has in fact been reviewed. Rule 26(b)(5)(A) provides a procedure for a party that has withheld information on the basis of privilege or protection as trial-preparation material to make the claim so that the requesting party can decide whether to contest the claim and the court can resolve the dispute. Rule 26(b)(5)(B) is added to provide a procedure for a party to assert a claim of privilege or trial-preparation material protection after information is produced in discovery in the action and, if the claim is contested, permit any party that received the information to present the matter to the court for resolution.

Rule 26(b)(5)(B) does not address whether the privilege or protection that is asserted after production was waived by the production. The courts have developed principles to determine whether, and under what circumstances, waiver results from inadvertent production of privileged or protected information. Rule 26(b)(5)(B) provides a procedure for presenting and addressing these issues. . . .

A party asserting a claim of privilege or protection after production must give notice to the receiving party. That notice should be in writing unless the circumstances preclude it. Such circumstances could include the assertion of the claim during a deposition. The notice should be as specific as possible in identifying the information and stating the basis for the claim. . . . Courts will continue to examine whether a claim of privilege or protection was made at a reasonable time when delay is part of the waiver determination under the governing law.

After receiving notice, each party that received the information must promptly return, sequester, or destroy the information and any copies it has. . . . No receiving party may use or disclose the information pending resolution of the privilege claim. The receiving party may present to the court the questions whether the information is privileged or protected as trial-preparation material, and whether the privilege or protection has been waived. . . . In presenting the question, the party may use the content of the information only to the extent permitted by the applicable law of privilege, protection for trial-preparation material, and professional responsibility.

If a party disclosed the information to nonparties before receiving notice of a claim of privilege or protection as trial-preparation material, it must take reasonable steps to retrieve the information and to return it, sequester it until the claim is resolved, or destroy it.

Whether the information is returned or not, the producing party must preserve the information pending the court's ruling on whether the claim of privilege or of protection is properly asserted and whether it was waived. As with claims made under Rule 26(b)(5)(A), there may be no ruling if the other parties do not contest the claim.

A companion 2006 amendment to Rule 26(f) provides that in most cases, before a scheduling conference is held or a scheduling order is due, the parties must confer to develop a proposed discovery plan that indicates the parties' views and proposals concerning "(4) any issues relating to claims of privilege or of protection as trial-preparation material, including—if the parties agree on a procedure to assert such claims after production—whether to ask the court to include their agreement in an order." The Advisory Committee Note explaining the amendment to Rule 26(f)(4) says:

Rule 26(f) is also amended to provide that the parties should discuss any issues relating to assertions of privilege or of protection as trial-preparation materials, including whether the parties can facilitate discovery by agreeing on procedures for asserting claims of privilege or protection after production and whether to ask the court to enter an order that includes any agreement the parties reach. The Committee has repeatedly been advised about the discovery difficulties that can result from efforts to guard against waiver of privilege and work-product protection. Frequently parties find it necessary to spend large amounts of time reviewing materials requested through discovery to avoid waiving privilege. These efforts are necessary because materials subject to a claim of privilege or protection are often difficult to identify. A failure to withhold even one such item may result in an argument that there has been a waiver of privilege as to all other privileged materials on that subject matter. Efforts to avoid the risk of waiver can impose substantial costs on the party producing the material and the time required for the privilege review can substantially delay access for the party seeking discovery. . . .

Parties may attempt to minimize these costs and delays by agreeing to protocols that minimize the risk of waiver. They may agree that the responding party will provide certain requested materials for initial examination without waiving any privilege or protection — sometimes known as a "quick peek." The requesting party then designates the documents it wishes to have actually produced. This designation is the Rule 34 request. The responding party then responds in the usual course, screening only those documents actually requested for formal production and asserting privilege claims as provided in Rule 26(b)(5)(A). On other occasions, parties enter agreements — sometimes called "clawback agreements" — that production without intent to waive privilege or protection should not be a waiver so long as the responding party identifies the documents mistakenly produced, and that the documents should be returned under those circumstances. Other voluntary arrangements may be appropriate depending on the circumstances of each litigation. In most circumstances, a party who receives information under such an arrangement cannot assert that production of the information waived a claim of privilege or of protection as trial-preparation material. . . .

Rule 26(b)(5)(B) is added to establish a parallel procedure to assert privilege or protection as trial-preparation material after production, leaving the question of waiver to later determination by the court.

A related 2006 amendment to Rule 16(b)(3)(B)(iv) provides that a district court's scheduling order may include "any agreements the parties reach for asserting claims of privilege or of protection as trial preparation material after information is produced." The Advisory Committee Note explains that this amendment "recognizes the propriety of including such agreements in the court's order. The rule does not provide the court with authority to enter such a case-management or other order without party agreement, or limit the court's authority to act on motion."

For updates on the Federal Rules of Civil Procedure, visit the official website of the United States Courts at *www.uscourts.gov*. For more information about the attorney-client privilege and work product generally, see our chapter on Attorney-Client Privilege and Work Product Provisions.

Federal Rules of Evidence: In 2008, President George W. Bush signed into law a new Rule 502 of the Federal Rules of Evidence. The new rule, based on a proposal by the Judicial Conference of the United States, was enacted as a statute by Congress because it concerns privilege. Rule 502 is related to Rule 4.4(b) because it includes the following section on inadvertent disclosure:

(b) *Inadvertent disclosure.* When made in a federal proceeding or to a federal office or agency, the disclosure [of a communication or information covered by the attorney-client privilege or work product protection] does not operate as a waiver in a federal or state proceeding if:

(1) the disclosure is inadvertent;

(2) the holder of the privilege or protection took reasonable steps to prevent disclosure; and

(3) the holder promptly took reasonable steps to rectify the error, including (if applicable) following Fed. R. Civ. P. 26(b)(5)(B).

For further background and for the full text Rule 502, see our chapter on Attorney-Client Privilege and Work Product Provisions below.

Restatement of the Law Governing Lawyers: See Restatement §§30, 51, 56, 102, and 106 in our chapter on the Restatement later in this volume.

ANNOTATIONS ON ARTICLE 5.
LAW FIRMS AND ASSOCIATIONS

Rule 5.1   Responsibilities of Partners, Managers, and Supervisory Lawyers

Canon and Code Antecedents

ABA Canons of Professional Ethics: No comparable Canon.

ABA Model Code of Professional Responsibility: Compare DR 1-102 and DR 1-103(A) (reprinted later in this volume).

Cross-References in Other Rules

Rule 1.6, Comment 16: "A lawyer must act competently to safeguard information relating to the representation of a client against inadvertent or unauthorized disclosure by the lawyer or other persons who are participating in the representation of the client or who are subject to the lawyer's supervision. See **Rules** 1.1, **5.1** and 5.3."

Rule 1.7, Comment 3: "To determine whether a conflict of interest exists, a lawyer should adopt reasonable procedures, appropriate for the size and type of firm and practice, to determine in both litigation and non-litigation matters the persons and issues involved. See also Comment to **Rule 5.1**."

Rule 3.8, Comment 6: "Like other lawyers, prosecutors are subject to **Rules 5.1** and 5.3, which relate to responsibilities regarding lawyers and nonlawyers who work for or are associated with the lawyer's office."

Rule 5.3, Comment 2: "Paragraph (a) requires lawyers with managerial authority within a law firm to make reasonable efforts to establish internal policies and procedures designed to provide reasonable assurance that nonlawyers in the firm will act in a way compatible with the Rules of Professional Conduct. See Comment [1] to **Rule 5.1**."

Legislative History of Model Rule 5.1

1980 Discussion Draft of Rule 5.1 (then Rule 7.2) provided as follows:

Responsibilities of a Supervisory Lawyer

(a) A lawyer having supervisory authority over another lawyer shall make a reasonable effort to see that the conduct of the lawyer under supervision conforms to the Rules of Professional Conduct.

(b) A lawyer is chargeable with another lawyer's violation of the Rules of Professional Conduct if:

(1) the lawyer orders or ratifies the conduct involved; or

(2) the lawyer has supervisory responsibility over the other lawyer and has knowledge of the conduct at a time when its consequences can be avoided or mitigated but fails to take appropriate remedial action.

1981 Draft was substantially the same as adopted, except that Rule 5.2(a) applied to "all lawyers in the firm, including other partners. . . ."

1982 Draft was adopted.

1983 Rule: As originally adopted in 1983, Rule 5.1 provided as follows:

> (a) A partner in a law firm shall make reasonable efforts to ensure that the firm has in effect measures giving reasonable assurance that all lawyers in the firm conform to the Rules of Professional Conduct.
> (b) [Same as 2002 version of Rule 5.1(b).]
> (c) [Same as 2002 version of Rule 5.1(c).]
>   (1) [Same as 2002 version of Rule 5.1(c)(1).]
>   (2) [Same as 2002 version of Rule 5.1(c)(2), except that the 1983 rule did not include the phrase "or comparable managerial authority" after "partner" in the first line.]

2002 Amendments: In 2002, the ABA House of Delegates adopted without change the ABA Ethics 2000 Commission proposal to amend Rule 5.1 and its Comment. The amendments added the clause following the first six words of paragraph (a) (beginning "and a lawyer who"), added the reference to "comparable managerial authority" in paragraph (c)(2), added Comments 2 and 8, and made other minor changes.

Selected State Variations

California has no counterpart to Rule 5.1.

District of Columbia: Rule 5.1 substantially tracks the Model Rule.

New Hampshire: Rules 5.1(a) and (b) impose duties on "each" partner in a firm, "each" lawyer with comparable managerial authority, and "each" lawyer with direct supervisory authority. A New Hampshire Comment explains that the change "is intended to emphasize that the obligations created by the rule are shared by all of the managers of a law firm and cannot be delegated to one manager by the others."

New Jersey begins Rule 5.1(a) with: "Every law firm and organization authorized by the Court Rules to practice law in this jurisdiction . . ." instead of "A partner in a law firm." Rule 5.1(c)(2) applies only to lawyers having "direct supervisory authority"; it deletes "is a partner or has comparable managerial authority in the law firm in which the other lawyer practices."

New York: Rule 5.1 provides:

> (a) A law firm shall make reasonable efforts to ensure that all lawyers in the firm conform to these Rules.
> (b)(1) A lawyer with management responsibility in a law firm shall make reasonable efforts to ensure that other lawyers in the law firm conform to these Rules.
>   (2) A lawyer with direct supervisory authority over another lawyer shall make reasonable efforts to ensure that the supervised lawyer conforms to these Rules.
> (c) A law firm shall ensure that the work of partners and associates is adequately supervised, as appropriate. A lawyer with direct supervisory authority over another lawyer shall adequately supervise the work of the other lawyer, as appropriate. In either case, the degree of supervision required is that which is reasonable under the

circumstances, taking into account factors such as the experience of the person whose work is being supervised, the amount of work involved in a particular matter, and the likelihood that ethical problems might arise in the course of working on the matter.

(d) A lawyer shall be responsible for a violation of these Rules by another lawyer if:

(1) the lawyer orders or directs the specific conduct or, with knowledge of the specific conduct, ratifies it; or

(2) the lawyer is a partner in a law firm or is a lawyer who individually or together with other lawyers possesses comparable managerial responsibility in a law firm in which the other lawyer practices or is a lawyer who has supervisory authority over the other lawyer; and

(i) knows of such conduct at a time when it could be prevented or its consequences avoided or mitigated but fails to take reasonable remedial action; or

(ii) in the exercise of reasonable management or supervisory authority should have known of the conduct so that reasonable remedial action could have been taken at a time when the consequences of the conduct could have been avoided or mitigated.

Oregon: Rule 5.1 deletes the language of ABA Model Rules 5.1(a) and (b), but adopts ABA Model Rule 5.1(c) verbatim.

Texas: The text of Texas Rule 5.01 has no equivalent to ABA Model Rules 5.1(a) and (b), but Comment 6 to Texas Rule 5.01 provides:

> Wholly aside from the dictates of these rules for discipline, a lawyer in a position of authority in a firm or government agency or over another lawyer should feel a moral compunction to make reasonable efforts to ensure that the office, firm, or agency has in effect appropriate procedural measures giving reasonable assurance that all lawyers in the office conform to these rules. This moral obligation, although not required by these rules, should fall also upon lawyers who have intermediate managerial responsibilities in the law department of an organization or government agency.

Texas Rule 5.01(b), which is similar to ABA Model Rule 5.1(c)(2), also applies to "the general counsel of a government agency's legal department."

Related Materials

ABA Formal Ethics Opinions: See ABA Formal Ethics Ops. 94-388 (1994), 96-401 (1996), 01-423 (2001), 03-429 (2003), 06-441 (2006), 08-451 (2008), 08-453 (2009), and 09-454 (2009).

IRS Regulations: In the regulations governing practice before the Internal Revenue Service, 31 C.F.R. §10.33(b) provides:

> *(b) Procedures to ensure best practices for tax advisors.* Tax advisors with responsibility for overseeing a firm's practice of providing advice concerning Federal tax issues or of preparing or assisting in the preparation of submissions to the Internal Revenue Service should take reasonable steps to ensure that the firm's procedures for all members, associates, and employees are consistent with the best practices set forth in paragraph (a) of this section.

The best practices set forth in §10.33(a) are excerpted in the entry entitled "IRS Regulations" in the Related Materials following ABA Model Rule 1.4 above.

Model Rules of Professional Conduct for Federal Lawyers add the following new subparagraphs to Rule 5.1:

(c) A Federal lawyer, who is a supervisory lawyer, is responsible for ensuring that the subordinate lawyer is properly trained and is competent to perform the duties to which the subordinate lawyer is assigned.

(d) A Government lawyer, who is a supervisory lawyer, should encourage subordinate lawyers to participate in pro bono publico service activities and the activities of bar associations and law reform organizations.

Partnership Law: Model Rule 5.1 roughly parallels partnership law provisions concerning the financial liability and tort liability of general partners for the wrongful acts or omissions of other partners in the ordinary course of business. Section 305 of the Revised Uniform Partnership Act (RUPA), which has been adopted in more than 30 states, provides:

§305. Partnership Liable for Partner's Actionable Conduct.

(a) A partnership is liable for loss or injury caused to a person, or for a penalty incurred, as a result of a wrongful act or omission, or other actionable conduct, of a partner acting in the ordinary course of business of the partnership or with authority of the partnership.

(b) If, in the course of the partnership's business or while acting with authority of the partnership, a partner receives or causes the partnership to receive money or property of a person not a partner, and the money or property is misapplied by a partner, the partnership is liable for the loss.

Restatement of the Law Governing Lawyers: See Restatement §§11(1)-(3) and 58 in our chapter on the Restatement later in this volume.

Rule 5.2   Responsibilities of a Subordinate Lawyer

Canon and Code Antecedents

ABA Canons of Professional Ethics: No comparable Canon.
ABA Model Code of Professional Responsibility: No comparable Disciplinary Rule.

Cross-References in Other Rules

Rule 5.1, Comment 3: "Some firms . . . have a procedure whereby junior lawyers can make confidential referral of ethical problems directly to a designated senior partner or special committee. See **Rule 5.2**."

Rule 5.1, Comment 8: "The duties imposed by this Rule on managing and supervising lawyers do not alter the personal duty of each lawyer in a firm to abide by the Rules of Professional Conduct. See **Rule 5.2(a)**."

Legislative History of Model Rule 5.2

1980 Discussion Draft (then Rule 7.3) provided as follows:

(a) A lawyer acting under the supervisory authority of another person is bound by the Rules of Professional Conduct notwithstanding the fact that the lawyer's conduct was ordered by the supervisor.

1981 Draft was substantially the same as adopted.

1982 Draft was adopted.

1983 Rule: As originally adopted in 1983, Rule 5.2 was the same as the 2002 version.

2002 Amendments: The ABA Ethics 2000 Commission did not propose any changes to the text or Comment of Rule 5.2.

Selected State Variations

California has no provision comparable to ABA Model Rule 5.2.

Connecticut deletes ABA Model Rule 5.2(b).

Ohio: Rule 5.2(b) omits the word "arguable" before "question of professional duty."

Virginia omits Rule 5.2.

Related Materials

ABA Formal Ethics Opinions: See ABA Formal Ethics Ops. 88-356 n.9 (1988) and 06-441 (2006).

Insubordination: Rule 5.2 is related to the employment law concept of "insubordination," which typically refers to an employee's willful disregard of an express or implied direction from the employer. Insubordination is ordinarily grounds for an employee's discharge unless the direction was not reasonable.

Restatement of the Law Governing Lawyers: See Restatement §12 in our chapter on the Restatement later in this volume.

Rule 5.3   Responsibilities Regarding Nonlawyer Assistants

Canon and Code Antecedents

ABA Canons of Professional Ethics: No comparable Canon.

ABA Model Code of Professional Responsibility: Compare DR 4-101(D) (reprinted later in this volume).

Cross-References in Other Rules

Rule 1.6, Comment 16: "A lawyer must act competently to safeguard information relating to the representation of a client against inadvertent or unauthorized disclosure by the lawyer or other persons who are participating in the representation of the client or who are subject to the lawyer's supervision (see **Rules** 1.1, 5.1 and **5.3**)."

Rule 1.6, Comment 16: "For a lawyer's duties when sharing information with nonlawyers outside the lawyer's own firm, see **Rule 5.3**, Comments [3]-[4]."

Rule 1.10, Comment 4: Paragraph (a) does not "prohibit representation if the lawyer is prohibited from acting because of events before the person became a lawyer. . . . Such persons, however, ordinarily must be screened from any personal participation in the matter to avoid communication to others in the firm of confidential information that both the nonlawyers and the firm have a legal duty to protect. See **Rules** 1.0(k) and **5.3**.''

Rule 3.8, Comment 6: ''Like other lawyers, prosecutors are subject to **Rules** 5.1 and **5.3**, which relate to responsibilities regarding lawyers and nonlawyers who work for or are associated with the lawyer's office.''

Rule 5.5, Comment 2: ''This Rule does not prohibit a lawyer from employing the services of paraprofessionals and delegating functions to them, so long as the lawyer supervises the delegated work and retains responsibility for their work. See **Rule 5.3**.''

Rule 5.7, Comment 8: When rendering both legal and law-related services in the same matter, ''a lawyer will be responsible for assuring that both the lawyer's conduct and, to the extent required by **Rule 5.3**, that of nonlawyer employees in the distinct entity that the lawyer controls complies in all respects with the Rules of Professional Conduct.''

Rule 7.2, Comment 5: ''See **Rule 5.3** for the duties of lawyers and law firms with respect to the conduct of nonlawyers who prepare marketing materials for them.''

Rule 7.2, Comment 7: ''A lawyer who accepts assignments or referrals from a legal service plan or referrals from a lawyer referral service must act reasonably to assure that the activities of the plan or service are compatible with the lawyer's professional obligations. See **Rule 5.3**.''

Legislative History of Model Rule 5.3

1980 Discussion Draft (then Rule 7.4) provided:

Supervision of Nonlawyer Assistants

A lawyer shall use reasonable effort to ensure that nonlawyers employed or retained by the lawyer conduct themselves in a manner compatible with the professional obligations of the lawyer.

1981 Draft was substantially the same as adopted.

1982 Draft was adopted.

1983 Rule: As originally adopted in 1983, Rule 5.3 was the same as the 2002 version of Rule 5.3, except that the 1983 version of Rule 5.3(a) did not include the phrase ''and a lawyer who individually or together with other lawyers possesses comparable managerial authority,'' and Rule 5.3(c)(2) did not contain the phrase ''or has comparable managerial authority.''

2002 Amendments: In 2002, the ABA House of Delegates adopted without change the ABA Ethics 2000 Commission proposal to amend Rule 5.3 and its Comment. The amendments insert the same references to ''managerial authority'' in the text of paragraphs (a) and (c)(2) as were inserted by the amendments to Rule 5.1. Comment 2 was added.

2012 Amendments: In August 2012, the ABA amended Comment 2 and reversed it with Comment 1, which was not amended. As amended, Comment 1 (formerly Comment 2) provides more guidance for a lawyer's supervisory duties when work is assigned to nonlawyers, whether inside or outside the firm. Comments 3 and 4 are new and deal specifically with situations in which lawyers are assisted by nonlawyers outside the firm.

Selected State Variations

California has no provision comparable to ABA Model Rule 5.3.

Georgia adds a new Rule 5.3(d) that indirectly restricts the activities of suspended or disbarred lawyers who work in a law office.

New Hampshire: Rules 5.3(a) and (b) impose duties on "each" partner in a firm, "each" lawyer with comparable managerial authority, and "each" lawyer with direct supervisory authority. Separately, New Hampshire Supreme Court Rule 35 (Guidelines for the Utilization by Lawyers of the Services of Legal Assistants under the New Hampshire Rules of Professional Conduct) contains nine rules for using the services of legal assistants in compliance with Rule 5.3. For example, Rule 1 provides:

> It is the responsibility of the lawyer to take all steps reasonably necessary to ensure that a legal assistant for whose work the lawyer is responsible does not provide legal advice or otherwise engage in the unauthorized practice of law; provided, however, that with adequate lawyer supervision the legal assistant may provide information concerning legal matters and otherwise act as permitted under these rules.

New Jersey: Rule 5.3(a) provides that "every lawyer or organization authorized by the Court Rules to practice law in this jurisdiction shall adopt and maintain reasonable efforts to ensure that the conduct of nonlawyers retained or employed by the lawyer, law firm or organization is compatible with the professional obligations of the lawyer." In addition, New Jersey has added Rule 5.3(c)(3), which provides that a lawyer is responsible for the conduct of a nonlawyer employee if "the lawyer has failed to make reasonable investigation of circumstances that would disclose past instances of conduct by the nonlawyer incompatible with the professional obligations of a lawyer, which evidence a propensity for such conduct."

New York: Rule 5.3 provides:

> (a) A law firm shall ensure that the work of nonlawyers who work for the firm is adequately supervised, as appropriate. A lawyer with direct supervisory authority over a nonlawyer shall adequately supervise the work of the nonlawyer, as appropriate. In either case, the degree of supervision required is that which is reasonable under the circumstances, taking into account factors such as the experience of the person whose work is being supervised, the amount of work involved in a particular matter and the likelihood that ethical problems might arise in the course of working on the matter.
>
> (b) A lawyer shall be responsible for conduct of a nonlawyer employed or retained by or associated with the lawyer that would be a violation of these Rules if engaged in by a lawyer, if:
>
>> (1) the lawyer orders or directs the specific conduct or, with knowledge of the specific conduct, ratifies it; or
>>
>> (2) the lawyer is a partner in a law firm or is a lawyer who individually or together with other lawyers possesses comparable managerial responsibility in a law firm in which the nonlawyer is employed or is a lawyer who has supervisory authority over the nonlawyer; and
>>
>>> (i) knows of such conduct at a time when it could be prevented or its consequences avoided or mitigated but fails to take reasonable remedial action; or
>>>
>>> (ii) in the exercise of reasonable management or supervisory authority should have known of the conduct so that reasonable remedial action could have been taken at a time when the consequences of the conduct could have been avoided or mitigated.

Oregon: Rule 5.3(b) begins: "except as provided by Rule 8.4(b). . . ." Under Oregon Rule 8.4(b), it is generally not professional misconduct for a lawyer to give advice about or to supervise "lawful covert activity in the investigation of violations of civil or criminal law or constitutional rights" provided the lawyer otherwise abides by the Rules of Professional Conduct. Rule 8.4(b) continues:

> "Covert activity," as used in this rule, means an effort to obtain information on unlawful activity through the use of misrepresentations or other subterfuge. "Covert activity" may be commenced by a lawyer or involve a lawyer as an advisor or supervisor only when the lawyer in good faith believes there is a reasonable possibility that unlawful activity has taken place, is taking place or will take place in the foreseeable future.

Rhode Island: Immediately after the Comment to Rule 5.3, Rhode Island includes a lengthy set of "Guidelines" for the use of legal assistants. These Guidelines are a heavily modified version of the ABA Model Guidelines for the Utilization of Paralegal Services (see Related Materials below). For example, Rhode Island's Guideline 3, which is closely related to Rule 5.3, provides as follows:

> 3. A lawyer shall direct a legal assistant to avoid any conduct which if engaged in by a lawyer would violate the Rules of Professional Conduct. In particular, the lawyer shall instruct the legal assistant regarding the confidential nature of the attorney/client relationship, and shall direct the legal assistant to refrain from disclosing any confidential information obtained from a client or in connection with representation of a client.

Texas relegates ABA Model Rule 5.3(a) to Comment 2 after Texas Rule 5.03. The Comment applies to "[e]ach lawyer in a position of authority in a law firm or in a government agency," including lawyers having supervisory authority or "intermediate managerial responsibilities in the law department of any enterprise or government agency." Texas Rule 5.03(b), which is equivalent to ABA Model Rule 5.3(c), subjects a lawyer to discipline for a nonlawyer's misconduct if (1) the lawyer orders, "encourages, or permits" the conduct involved; or (2) the lawyer:

> (i) is a partner in the law firm in which the person is employed, retained by, or associated with; or is the general counsel of a government agency's legal department in which the person is employed, retained by or associated with; or has direct supervisory authority over such person; and
> (ii) with knowledge of such misconduct by the nonlawyer knowingly fails to take reasonable remedial action to avoid or mitigate the consequences of that person's misconduct.

Virginia: Rule 5.3(c)(2) applies if a lawyer knows "or should have known" of the conduct in question.

Related Materials

ABA Definition of "Legal Assistant": In 1997, the ABA Board of Governors adopted the following definition of the phrase "legal assistant," a phrase used interchangeably with the term "paralegal":

> A legal assistant or paralegal is a person qualified by education, training or work experience who is employed or retained by a lawyer, law office, corporation,

governmental agency or other entity who performs specifically delegated substantive legal work for which a lawyer is responsible.

In 2001, the National Association of Legal Assistants adopted the ABA definition. To see how this definition has evolved over the years, visit *www.nala.org/terms.aspx.*

ABA Formal Ethics Opinions: See ABA Formal Ethics Ops. 94-388 (1994), 95-396 (1995), 95-398 (1995), 08-451 (2008), and 10-457 (2010).

ABA Guidelines for Approval of Paralegal Education Programs: In 1973, the ABA adopted Guidelines for the Approval of Paralegal Education Programs. These Guidelines, which were amended in 2006, 2007, and 2008, are enforced by an ABA Approval Commission that examines and approves paralegal education programs. Like the accreditation process for law schools, the approval process for paralegal programs consists of several stages, including (a) the preparation of a self-evaluation report and supporting documents, (b) review by educational consultants, (c) an onsite evaluation of all program operations to verify that they operate in compliance with the ABA Guidelines, and (d) consideration by the Standing Committee on Paralegals & Approval Commission. The approval process is voluntary, since it is not required by any governmental agency. The Guidelines for Approval of Paralegal Education Programs and other materials on paralegals and paralegal education are available at *http://www.americanbar.org/groups/paralegals.html.* The ABA works closely with the American Association for Paralegal Education (see entry below).

ABA Model Guidelines for the Utilization of Paralegal Services: In 1991, the ABA Standing Committee on Paralegals drafted the ABA Model Guidelines for the Utilization of Legal Assistant Services and the ABA House of Delegates adopted them. In 2004, the ABA amended the Guidelines, substituting the term "paralegal" for the old term "legal assistant." The Guidelines are aimed at lawyers rather than paralegals, and are intended to encourage lawyers to use paralegal services effectively. Guidelines 1 and 6 are closely related to ABA Model Rule 5.3. They provide as follows:

> *Guideline 1.* A lawyer is responsible for all of the professional actions of a paralegal performing services at the lawyer's direction and should take reasonable measures to ensure that the paralegal's conduct is consistent with the lawyer's obligations under the rules of professional conduct of the jurisdiction in which the lawyer practices.
> *Guideline 6.* A lawyer is responsible for taking reasonable measures to ensure that all client confidences are preserved by a paralegal.

Some states have adopted paralegal guidelines based on the ABA Guidelines. The complete ABA Guidelines for the Utilization of Paralegal Services are available, with ABA Comments, at *http://apps.americanbar.org/legalservices/paralegals/downloads/modelguidelines.pdf.*

ABA Standards for Criminal Justice: See Prosecution Function Standards 3-3.1(a) and (c) (Investigative Function of the Prosecutor) and Defense Function Standard 4-4.2 (Illegal Investigations).

ABA Standing Committee on Paralegals: The mission of the ABA Standing Committee on Paralegals, according to the Committee's home page, "is to improve the American system of justice by establishing ABA standards for the education of paralegals and by promoting attorneys' professional, effective and ethical utilization of paralegals." For more information, and for resources concerning paralegals, visit *http://www.americanbar.org/groups/paralegals.html.*

American Association for Paralegal Education: The American Association for Paralegal Education (AAfPE) is an organization for those who educate paralegals. According to its mission statement, the AAfPE "promotes quality paralegal education, develops educational standards and encourages professional growth, in order to prepare graduates to perform a significant role in the delivery of legal services." A central focus of the AAfPE has been establishing standards by which to measure paralegal education. The AAfPE works closely with the ABA Approval Commission to ensure that paralegal programs are providing quality education. For more information, see *www.aafpe.org.*

Independent Paralegals: Some states allow "independent paralegals" (also called "freelance paralegals") who are retained by lawyers on an "as needed" basis but are not employees of any lawyer or law firm. Because Rule 5.3 covers nonlawyers who are "retained by or associated with" a lawyer, the rule apparently reaches independent paralegals.

International Paralegal Management Association: The International Paralegal Management Association "promotes the development, professional standing and visibility of paralegal management professionals." For more information about IPMA, visit *www.paralegalmanagement.org.*

National Association of Legal Assistants: The National Association of Legal Assistants, Inc. (NALA), an organization representing more than 18,000 legal assistants, publishes Model Standards and Guidelines for Utilization of Legal Assistants. The NALA Guidelines, most recently amended in 2007, may help lawyers understand their supervisory responsibilities under Model Rule 5.3. Excerpts from the Guidelines are reprinted in the Related Materials following Rule 5.5 (Unauthorized Practice of Law) and are available with Comments at *www.nala.org/model.aspx.*

NALA has also adopted a very brief Code of Ethics and Professional Responsibility for legal assistants. Canon 9 of this Code, which is the reciprocal of ABA Model Rule 5.3, provides: "A legal assistant must do all other things incidental, necessary, or expedient for the attainment of the ethics and responsibilities as defined by statute or rule of court." The code is available at *www.nala.org/code.aspx.*

Respondeat Superior: The doctrine of "respondeat superior" (a Latin phrase meaning "let the master answer") provides, in essence, that employers (principals) are responsible for the wrongful acts or omissions of their employees (agents) during the course of employment.

Restatement of the Law Governing Lawyers: See Restatement §§11(4) and 58 in our chapter on the Restatement later in this volume.

Student Practice Rules: All states have student practice rules that permit law students to represent clients under certain conditions. These provisions, which are codified in state statutes, court rules, and state bar rules, typically require lawyers to supervise the law students. For example, Florida Rule 11-1.2(b) provides as follows:

> **Appearance in Court or Administrative Proceedings.** An eligible law student may appear in any court or before any administrative tribunal in this state on behalf of any indigent person if the person on whose behalf the student is appearing has indicated in writing consent to that appearance and the supervising lawyer has also indicated in writing approval of that appearance. In those cases in which an indigent has a right to appointed counsel, the supervising attorney shall be personally present at all critical stages of the proceeding. In all cases, the supervising attorney shall be personally present when required by the court or administrative tribunal who shall determine the extent of the eligible law student's participation in the proceeding.

For links to student practice rules and forms adopted by both federal and state courts, visit *www.ll.georgetown.edu/guides/StudentPractice.cfm.*

    Unauthorized Practice of Law: A lawyer who authorizes or permits a paralegal to perform law-related tasks but fails to supervise the paralegal adequately may be assisting the paralegal in the unauthorized practice of law, in violation of Rule 5.5. (For examples of statutes governing the unauthorized practice of law, see the Related Materials following ABA Model Rule 5.5 below.)

Rule 5.4   Professional Independence of a Lawyer

Canon and Code Antecedents

ABA Canons of Professional Ethics: Canons 33, 34, and 35 provided as follows:

33. Partnerships — Names

    Partnerships among lawyers for the practice of their profession are very common and are not to be condemned. In the formation of partnerships and the use of partnership names care should be taken not to violate any law, custom, or rule of court locally applicable. Where partnerships are formed between lawyers who are not all admitted to practice in the courts of the state, care should be taken to avoid any misleading name or representation which would create a false impression as to the professional position or privileges of the member not locally admitted. In the formation of partnerships for the practice of law, no person should be admitted or held out as a practitioner or member who is not a member of the legal profession duly authorized to practice, and amenable to professional discipline. In the selection and use of a firm name, no false, misleading, assumed or trade name should be used. The continued use of the name of a deceased or former partner, when permissible by local custom, is not unethical, but care should be taken that no imposition or deception is practiced through this use. When a member of the firm, on becoming a judge, is precluded from practicing law, his name should not be continued in the firm name.

    Partnerships between lawyers and members of other professions or nonprofessional persons should not be formed or permitted where any part of the partnership's employment consists of the practice of law.

34. Division of Fees

    No division of fees for legal services is proper, except with another lawyer, based upon a division of service or responsibility.

35. Intermediaries

    The professional services of a lawyer should not be controlled or exploited by any lay agency, personal or corporate, which intervenes between client and lawyer. A lawyer's responsibilities and qualifications are individual. He should avoid all relations which direct the performance of his duties by or in the interest of such intermediary. A lawyer's relation to his client should be personal, and the responsibility should be direct to the client. Charitable societies rendering aid to the indigents are not deemed such intermediaries.

    A lawyer may accept employment from any organization, such as an association, club or trade organization, to render legal services in any matter in which the organization, as an entity, is interested, but this employment should not include the rendering of legal services to the members of such an organization in respect to their individual affairs.

ABA Model Code of Professional Responsibility: Compare DR 3-102(A), DR 3-103(B), DR 5-107(B), and DR 5-107(C) (reprinted later in this volume).

Cross-References in Other Rules

Rule 1.8, Comment 11: "See also **Rule 5.4(c)** (prohibiting interference with a lawyer's professional judgment by one who recommends, employs or pays the lawyer to render legal services for another)."

Rule 1.17, Comment 1: "[W]hen a lawyer or an entire firm ceases to practice, or ceases to practice in an area of law, and other lawyers or firms take over the representation, the selling lawyer or firm may obtain compensation for the reasonable value of the practice as may withdrawing partners of law firms. See **Rules 5.4** and 5.6."

Rule 5.3, Comment 3: "A lawyer may use nonlawyers outside the firm to assist the lawyer in rendering legal services to the client. ... When using such services outside the firm, a lawyer must make reasonable efforts to ensure that the services are provided in a manner that is compatible with the lawyer's professional obligations. ... See also **Rules** 1.1 (competence), 1.2 (allocation of authority), 1.4 (communication with client), 1.6 (confidentiality), **5.4(a)** (professional independence of the lawyer), and 5.5(a) (unauthorized practice of law)."

Rule 7.2, Comment 5: "[A] lawyer may pay others for generating client leads, such as Internet-based client leads, as long as ... any payment to the lead generator is consistent with **Rules** 1.5(e) (division of fees) and **5.4** (professional independence of the lawyer), and the lead generator's communications are consistent with Rule 7.1 (communications concerning a lawyer's services)."

Rule 7.2, Comment 8: "[R]eciprocal referral arrangements must not interfere with the lawyer's professional judgment as to making referrals or as to providing substantive legal services. See **Rules** 2.1 and **5.4(c)**."

Legislative History of Model Rule 5.4

1980 Discussion Draft (then Rule 7.5) provided as follows:

Professional Independence of a Firm

A lawyer shall not practice with a firm in which an interest is owned or managerial authority is exercised by a nonlawyer, unless services can be rendered in conformity with the Rules of Professional Conduct. The terms of the relationship shall expressly provide that:

(a) there is no interference with the lawyer's independence of professional judgment or with the client-lawyer relationship; and

(b) the confidences of clients are protected as required by Rule 1.7; and

(c) the arrangement does not involve advertising or solicitation prohibited by Rules 9.2 and 9.3; and

(d) the arrangement does not result in charging a client a fee which violates Rule 1.6.

1981 Draft:

Professional Independence of a Firm

A lawyer may be employed by an organization in which a financial interest is held or managerial authority is exercised by a non-lawyer, or by a lawyer acting in a capacity other than that of representing clients, such as a business corporation, insurance company, legal services organization or government agency, but only if the terms of the relationship provide in writing that:

(a) there is no interference with the lawyer's independence of professional judgment or with the client-lawyer relationship;

(b) information relating to representation of a client is protected as required by Rule 1.6;

(c) the arrangement does not involve advertising or personal contract with prospective clients prohibited by Rules 7.2 and 7.3; and

(d) the arrangement does not result in charging a fee that violates Rule 1.5.

1982 Draft was substantially the same as the 1981 Draft.

1983 Rule: The version of Rule 5.4 finally adopted in 1983 was proposed by the ABA's General Practice Section as a substitute for the Kutak Commission's draft. (Rule 5.4 was the only rule from the 1982 Draft that was completely rejected and rewritten by the House of Delegates in 1983.) As adopted in 1983, Rule 5.4 was the same as the 2002 version of Rule 5.4, except that Rule 5.4(a)(4) was not yet in the rule, and Rules 5.4(a)(2) and (d)(2) provided:

(a)(2) a lawyer who undertakes to complete unfinished legal business of a deceased lawyer may pay to the estate of the deceased lawyer that proportion of the total compensation which fairly represents the services rendered by the deceased lawyer.

(d)(2) a nonlawyer is a corporate director or officer thereof.

1990 Amendment: In 1990, the ABA House of Delegates amended Rule 5.4(a)(2) to conform to Rule 1.17 (permitting the sale of a law practice), which was added to the Rules at the same meeting. (There was no Committee Report to explain the change, but the reason for the change is obvious.) Before the amendment, Rule 5.4(a)(2) had provided that "a lawyer who undertakes to complete unfinished legal business of a deceased lawyer may pay to the estate of the deceased lawyer that proportion of the total compensation which fairly represents the services rendered by the deceased lawyer."

2002 Amendments: In 2002, the ABA House of Delegates adopted without change the ABA Ethics 2000 Commission proposal to amend Rule 5.4 and its Comment. The amendments added (a)(4) to the text of the rule, added the language following "thereof" in paragraph (d)(2) of the text, and added all of Comment 2.

Selected State Variations

California: Rule 1-310 forbids lawyers to form partnerships with nonlawyers if "any of the activities of that partnership consist of the practice of law." Rule 1-320 forbids sharing legal fees with nonlawyers with exceptions, including those described in Rules 5.4(1) and (3).

Connecticut: Connecticut omits ABA Model Rule 5.4(a)(4) (relating to fee sharing with nonprofit organizations).

District of Columbia: D.C. Rules 5.4(a)(4) and (b), which are unique in the United States, permit fee sharing between lawyers and nonlawyers "in a partnership or other form of organization which meets the requirements of paragraph (b)." Paragraph (b) provides:

(b) A lawyer may practice law in a partnership or other form of organization in which a financial interest is held or managerial authority is exercised by an individual nonlawyer who performs professional services which assist the organization in providing legal services to clients, but only if:

(1) The partnership or organization has as its sole purpose providing legal services to clients;

(2) All persons having such managerial authority or holding a financial interest undertake to abide by these Rules of Professional Conduct;

(3) The lawyers who have a financial interest or managerial authority in the partnership or organization undertake to be responsible for the nonlawyer participants to the same extent as if nonlawyer participants were lawyers under Rule 5.1;

(4) The foregoing conditions are set forth in writing.

In addition, D.C. Rule 5.4(a)(5) permits a lawyer to "share legal fees, whether awarded by a tribunal or received in settlement of a matter, with a nonprofit organization that employed, retained, or recommended employment of the lawyer in the matter and that qualifies under Section 501(c)(3) of the Internal Revenue Code."

Florida: In place of ABA Model Rule 5.4(a)(2), Florida retains the language from the 1983 Model Rule providing that "a lawyer who undertakes to complete unfinished legal business of a deceased lawyer may pay to the estate of the deceased lawyer that proportion of the total compensation which fairly represents the services rendered by the deceased lawyer."

Florida Rule 4-8.6 describes the business entities through which lawyers may practice law and forbids practice other than through "officers, directors, partners, agents, or employees who are qualified to render legal services in this state." Further, only persons who are so qualified may serve as "a partner, manager, director, or executive officer" of such an entity. Florida has substantially adopted Rule 5.4(a)(4).

Illinois tracks the Model Rule. Illinois Rule 5.4(d)(2) permits a nonlawyer to serve as secretary for a professional corporation or for-profit association authorized to practice law "if such secretary performs only ministerial duties."

Indiana deletes ABA Model Rule 5.4(a)(4).

Iowa deletes ABA Model Rule 5.4(a)(4).

Kansas: Kansas replaces ABA Model Rule 5.4(a)(2) with language from the 1983 version of ABA Model Rule 5.4 providing that "a lawyer who undertakes to complete unfinished legal business of a deceased lawyer may pay to the estate of the deceased lawyer that proportion of the total compensation which fairly represents the services rendered by the deceased lawyer." Kansas makes no reference to the purchase of a law practice or to Rule 1.17, which Kansas has not adopted.

Maryland restores language from the 1983 version of ABA Model Rule 5.4 providing that "a lawyer who undertakes to complete unfinished legal business of a deceased, retired, disabled, or suspended lawyer may pay to that lawyer or that lawyer's estate the proportion of the total compensation which fairly represents the services rendered by the former lawyer."

Massachusetts: Rule 5.4(a) allows a lawyer or law firm to share "a statutory or tribunal-approved" legal fee with "a qualified legal assistance organization that referred the matter to the lawyer or law firm" if the organization is not for profit and tax-exempt, the fee is made in connection with a proceeding to advance the organization's purposes, and the client consents. The Comment to this rule explains that the "financial needs of these organizations, which serve important public ends, justify a limited exception to the prohibition against fee-sharing with nonlawyers.'' The Comment also explains that the exception does not extend to fees generated in connection with proceedings unrelated to the organization's tax-exempt purpose, ''such as generating business income for the organization.'' Massachusetts Rule 5.4(b) prohibits a lawyer from forming a partnership ''or other business entity'' with a nonlawyer if any of the activities of the ''entity'' consist of the practice of law.

Minnesota: Rule 5.4(a)(4) permits a lawyer to share court-awarded fees with a nonprofit organization only ''subject to full disclosure and court approval,'' and Rule 5.4(a)(5) restores language from the 1983 version of ABA Model Rule 5.4 providing that ''a lawyer who undertakes to complete unfinished legal business of a deceased lawyer may pay to the estate of the deceased lawyer the proportion of the total compensation that fairly represents the services rendered by the deceased lawyer.''

Missouri restores language from the 1983 version of ABA Model Rule 5.4(a) permitting a lawyer who completes unfinished legal business of a deceased lawyer to pay the deceased lawyer's estate ''that proportion of the total compensation that fairly represents the services rendered by the deceased lawyer.''

New Hampshire: Rule 5.4(a)(4) permits a lawyer to ''share legal fees with a nonprofit organization that employed, retained or recommended employment of the lawyer in the matter,'' whether or not the fees are ''court-awarded.''

New Jersey Rule 5.4(a)(5) provides that ''a lawyer may share court-awarded legal fees with a nonprofit organization that employed, retained, or recommended employment of the lawyer in the matter.''

New York: Rule 5.4 is substantially the same as the Model Rule except New York omits Rule 5.4(a)(4).

North Carolina omits ABA Model Rule 5.4(d)(2) and adds Rule 5.4(a)(3), which permits a lawyer who undertakes to complete unfinished legal business of a deceased lawyer ''or a disbarred lawyer'' may pay to the estate of the deceased lawyer ''or to the disbarred lawyer'' that proportion of the total compensation which fairly represents the services rendered by the deceased lawyer ''or the disbarred lawyer.''

Ohio: Rule 5.4(a)(4) omits the words ''or recommended employment of'' and inserts ''or'' between ''employed'' and ''retained.'' Rule 5.4(a)(5) permits a lawyer to ''share legal fees with a non-profit organization that recommended employment of the lawyer in the matter,'' whether or not the fees are court-awarded, provided that the nonprofit organization complies with Ohio's Supreme Court Rules governing lawyer referral and information services.

Oklahoma: Rule 5.4(2A) adds language from the 1983 version of ABA Model Rule 5.4 providing that ''a lawyer who undertakes to complete unfinished legal business of a deceased lawyer may pay to the estate of the deceased lawyer that proportion of the total compensation which fairly represents the services rendered by the deceased lawyer.'' Oklahoma Rule 5.4(a)(4) says, in brackets: ''The concept of this subsection of the ABA Model Rule is addressed in the Comment.'' Oklahoma's Comment says that Rule 5.4(a) ''does not prohibit a lawyer from *voluntarily* sharing court-awarded legal fees with a nonprofit organization that employed, retained or recommended employment of the lawyer in the matter. This shall not be deemed a sharing of attorneys fees.'' (Emphasis added.)

Oregon adds a new Rule 5.4(e) providing that a lawyer ''shall not refer a client to a nonlawyer with the understanding that the lawyer will receive a fee, commission or anything of value in exchange for the referral, but a lawyer may accept gifts in the ordinary course of social or business hospitality."

Pennsylvania adds Rule 5.4(d)(4), which provides that "in the case of any form of association other than a professional corporation, the organic law governing the internal affairs of the association provides the equity owners of the association with greater liability protection than is available to the shareholders of a professional corporation." Rule 5.4(d) concludes by stating that subparagraphs (d)(1), (2), and (4) "shall not apply to a lawyer employed in the legal department of a corporation or other organization." The provision that does apply, Rule 5.4(d)(3), is the same as Model Rule 5.4(d)(3).

Rhode Island: After some uncertainty over whether Rhode Island would sub-scribe to the position in Rule 5.4(a)(4), as described in Selected State Variations for our 2008 edition, Rhode Island has adopted the following version of ABA Model Rule 5.4(a)(4):

> (4) a lawyer or law firm may agree to share a statutory or tribunal-approved fee award, or a settlement in a matter eligible for such an award, with an organization that referred the matter to the lawyer or law firm if: (i) the organization is one that is not for profit; (ii) the organization is tax-exempt under federal law; (iii) the fee award or settlement is made in connection with a proceeding to advance one or more of the pur-poses by virtue of which the organization is tax-exempt; and (iv) the tribunal approves the fee-sharing arrangement.

Tennessee: Rule 5.4(a) provides, in pertinent part:

> (4) a lawyer may share a court-awarded fee with a client represented in the matter or with a non-profit organization that employed, retained, or recommended employ-ment of the lawyer in the matter;
> (5) a lawyer who is a full-time employee of a client may share a legal fee with the client to the extent necessary to reimburse the client for the actual cost to the client of permitting the lawyer to represent another client while continuing in the full-time employ of the client with whom the fee will be shared; and
> (6) a lawyer may pay to a registered non-profit intermediary organization a refer-ral fee calculated by reference to a reasonable percentage of the fee paid to the lawyer by the client referred to the lawyer by the intermediary organization.

Texas: Under Texas Rule 5.04(a)(1), either a lawyer's agreement or a lawful court order may provide for the payment of money over time to the lawyer's estate "to or for the benefit of the lawyer's heirs or personal representatives, beneficiaries, or former spouse, after the lawyer's death or as otherwise provided by law or court order."

Virginia omits Rule 5.4(a)(4) and substitutes "a lawyer may accept discounted payment of his fee from a credit card company on behalf of a client."

Related Materials

ABA Commission on Ethics 20/20: In 2009, the ABA created the ABA Commission on Ethics 20/20, which is comprehensively reviewing the ABA Model Rules of Professional Conduct in light of globalization and changes in technology. From its inception, the Commission studied possible alternative law practice structures, such as structures that would allow some form of nonlawyer ownership, which is currently prohibited by ABA Model Rule 5.4(d). By June 2011, the Commission had publicly rejected certain forms of nonlawyer ownership that some other countries currently permit, including multidisciplinary practices, publicly traded law firms, and passive, outside nonlawyer investment or ownership in law firms.

On December 2, 2011, the Commission released for comment a Discussion Draft describing a limited form of court-regulated, nonlawyer ownership of law firms. The structure described in the draft would have allowed nonlawyers to have a minority financial interest in the firm, and share in its profits, provided the non-lawyers who obtained an ownership interest were both (i) employed by the law firm, and (ii) assisted the firm's lawyers in the provision of legal services. The Discussion Draft reflected an approach that was similar to (but more restrictive than) the structure that has been permitted by District of Columbia Rule 5.4(b) for more than 20 years. However, after holding hearings and studying the comments on the Discussion Draft, the Commission decided at its April 2012 meeting not to propose changes to ABA policy prohibiting nonlawyer ownership of law firms. Ethics 20/20 Commission Co-Chairs Jamie Gorelick and Michael Traynor said, "Based on the Commission's extensive outreach, research, consultation, and the response of the profession, there does not appear to be a sufficient basis for recommending a change to ABA policy on nonlawyer ownership of law firms."

Although it will not propose any changes to ABA policy on nonlawyer ownership of law firms, the Commission will continue to consider how to provide practical guidance about choice of law questions, such as: (i) may a law firm divide fees with a different law firm that has nonlawyer owners in a jurisdiction (such as D.C.) that allows nonlawyer ownership (*i.e.*, inter-firm fee division)? and (ii) under what circumstances (if any) may one office of a law firm divide fees with another office of the same firm that has nonlawyer owners in a jurisdiction that allows nonlawyer ownership (*i.e.*, intra-firm fee sharing)? These questions arise because some juris-dictions, including the District of Columbia and a growing number of foreign juris-dictions, permit nonlawyer ownership of law firms. The Commission had already released draft proposals on choice of law issues before abandoning its exploration of nonlawyer ownership of law firms, and the Commission was scheduled to decide at its October 2012 meeting whether to submit formal proposals on choice of law to the ABA House of Delegates for consideration in February 2013. For more informa-tion on the Commission's work on choice of law proposals and alternative business structures, see the Ethics 20/20 Commission's website at *http://www.americanbar.org/Ethics2020*.

ABA Commission on Multidisciplinary Practice: In 1998, the ABA appointed a Commission on Multidisciplinary Practice (MDP Commission) to study and report on efforts by accounting firms and other nonlawyer professional service firms to provide legal services to the public. (Unauthorized practice of law statutes and eth-ics rules like Rule 5.4 prohibited lawyers from offering legal services to the public through nonlegal entities such as accounting firms, but lawyers in some professional service firms owned by nonlawyers allegedly did so anyway.) The MDP Commission's Reporter was the late Mary Daly, who was then a professor at Fordham University School of Law.

During 1998 and 1999, the MDP Commission held public hearings, received written comments, and issued a "Background Paper" and some "Hypotheticals and Models" to focus public discussion. The MDP Commission's first report, issued in

June 1999, recommended amendments to the ABA Model Rules of Professional Conduct that would have permitted nonlawyers to become partners with lawyers if the nonlawyers agreed to be bound by the ethics rules that govern lawyers. Specifically, the MDP Commission recommended that the ABA amend Model Rule 5.4 to permit fee sharing between lawyers and nonlawyers within a new type of multidisciplinary practice entity called an "MDP," which was defined as:

> a partnership, professional corporation, or other association or entity that includes lawyers and nonlawyers and has as one, but not all, of its purposes the delivery of legal services to a client(s) other than the MDP itself or that holds itself out to the public as providing nonlegal, as well as legal, services. It includes an arrangement by which a law firm joins with one or more other professional firms to provide services, and there is a direct or indirect sharing of profits as part of the arrangement.

At the ABA's August 1999 Annual Meeting, however, the House of Delegates voted overwhelmingly (304 to 98) to reject the MDP Commission's recommendations. Instead, the ABA adopted a resolution not to change the ABA Model Rules to permit multidisciplinary practice "unless and until additional study demonstrates that such changes will further the public interest without sacrificing or compromising lawyer independence and the legal profession's tradition of loyalty to clients."

In July 2000, after holding additional public hearings, the MDP Commission issued a new report to the House of Delegates with more modest proposals, but the House of Delegates voted 314-106 to reject the MDP Commission's report. Instead, the House adopted a recommendation that the ABA continue to prohibit partnerships with nonlawyers and continue to prohibit nonlawyer equity interests in law firms. In the Special Section at the end of our 2001 edition, we reprinted the MDP Commission's July 2000 report and the ABA's July 2000 recommendation. For additional information, including copies of public comments and all of the MDP Commission's reports, visit the MDP Commission's website at *http://www.americanbar.org/groups/professional_responsibility/commission_multidisciplinary_practice.html*.

ABA Formal Ethics Opinions: See ABA Formal Ethics Ops. 87-355 (1987), 88-356 (1988), 91-360 (1991), 93-374 (1993), 95-392 (1995), 96-401 (1996), 01-423 (2001), 02-428 (2002), and 03-430 (2003).

ABA Model Guidelines for the Utilization of Paralegal Services: Guideline 9 of the ABA Model Guidelines for the Utilization of Paralegal Services parallels ABA Model Rule 5.4(a) by providing as follows:

> A lawyer may not split legal fees with a paralegal nor pay a paralegal for the referral of legal business. A lawyer may compensate a paralegal based on the quantity and quality of the paralegal's work and the value of that work to a law practice, but the paralegal's compensation may not be contingent, by advance agreement, upon the outcome of a particular case or class of cases.

The ABA Guidelines for the Utilization of Paralegal Services, with ABA Comments, are at *http://apps.americanbar.org/legalservices/paralegals/downloads/modelguidelines.pdf*.

American Lawyer's Code of Conduct: Rule 4.7 provides:

> If a lawyer forms a partnership with a nonlawyer for the purpose of more effectively serving clients' interests, the terms of the partnership shall be consistent with the lawyer's obligations under this Code, with particular reference to Rule 2.1, requiring undivided fidelity to the client.

Limited Liability Companies: Rule 5.4(d) governs lawyers who practice with or in the form of "a professional corporation or association authorized to practice law for a profit" if certain circumstances apply. Some states expressly extend coverage of Rule 5.4(d) to limited liability companies (LLCs), which combine the benefits of partnership taxation rules with the benefits of limited liability for corporations. Since Wyoming passed the first Limited Liability Company Act in the United States in 1977, all states have enacted statutes permitting LLCs, or their close cousins limited liability partnerships (LLPs), or both.

Model Rules of Professional Conduct for Federal Lawyers insert a substantially different version of Rule 5.4, the most interesting parts of which provide as follows:

> (d) A Government lawyer shall obey the lawful orders of superiors when representing the United States and individual clients, but a Government lawyer shall not permit a nonlawyer to direct or regulate the Government lawyer's professional judgment in rendering legal services.

> (e) A Non-Government lawyer shall not permit a nonlawyer who recommends, employs, or pays the Non-Government lawyer to render legal services for another to direct or regulate the Non-Government lawyer's professional judgment in rendering legal services.

> (f) A Non-Government lawyer shall comply with the Rules of Professional Conduct or other applicable laws of the jurisdiction in which the Non-Government lawyer is licensed or is practicing law concerning the limitations on sharing fees and the organizational form of their practice.

Restatement of the Law Governing Lawyers: See Restatement §§10 and 134 in our chapter on the Restatement later in this volume.

Strategic Alliances: Rule 5.4 prohibits law firms from forming partnerships with nonlawyers, so some law firms have instead formed "strategic alliances" with nonlegal entities. A strategic alliance typically provides for non-exclusive reciprocal referrals between the law firm and the nonlegal entity, and sometimes provides for shared offices, shared overhead expenses, and joint marketing.

Rule 5.5   Unauthorized Practice of Law; Multijurisdictional Practice of Law

Canon and Code Antecedents

ABA Canons of Professional Ethics: Canon 47 provided as follows:

47.   Aiding the Unauthorized Practice of Law

No lawyer shall permit his professional services, or his name, to be used in aid of, or to make possible, the unauthorized practice of law by any lay agency, personal or corporate.

ABA Model Code of Professional Responsibility: Compare DR 3-101(A) and DR 3-101(B) (reprinted later in this volume).

None.

Legislative History of Model Rule 5.5

1980 Discussion Draft (then Rule 10.4(d) and (e)) provided that it was "professional misconduct" for a lawyer to "(d) practice law in a jurisdiction in violation of the regulation of the legal profession in that jurisdiction; or (e) aid a person who is not a member of the bar in the performance of activity that constitutes the practice of law."

1981 and 1982 Drafts (then Rule 8.4(d) and (e)) were the same as adopted.

1983 Rule: From 1983 to 2002, Rule 5.5 provided, in full, as follows:

Rule 5.5   Unauthorized Practice of Law

A lawyer shall not:

(a) practice law in a jurisdiction where doing so violates the regulation of the legal profession in that jurisdiction; or

(b) assist a person who is not a member of the bar in the performance of activity that constitutes the unauthorized practice of law.

2002 Amendments: In 2002, by voice vote (meaning the vote was overwhelming), the ABA House of Delegates approved significant amendments to ABA Model Rule 5.5. These amendments were proposed by the ABA Commission on Multijurisdictional Practice, which was formed in 2000 to consider a host of issues pertaining to the practice of law by lawyers in jurisdictions where they are not admitted to practice, either permanently or pro hac vice. The amendments substantially changed the Rule. Paragraph (b) was entirely rewritten and paragraphs (c) and (d) were new. All comments were new except for portions of Comments 2 and 3. (The ABA Ethics 2000 Commission had also considered amendments to Rule 5.5 but eventually deferred to the Commission on Multijurisdictional Practice, which was studying the issues more comprehensively.)

The full report of the ABA Commission on Multijurisdictional Practice regarding Rule 5.5 and related multijurisdictional practice issues may be found at *http://www.americanbar.org/groups/professional_responsibility/committees_commissions/commission_on_multijurisditional_practice.html* (scroll down to "Final Reports, as adopted August 12, 2002").

2007 Amendment: At its February 2007 Mid-Year Meeting, the ABA House of Delegates adopted the ABA Model Court Rule on Provision of Legal Services Following Determination of Major Disaster (often called the "Katrina Rule"). At the same time, the House of Delegates added the last sentence of Comment 14 to Rule 5.5 to reflect the adoption of the Model Court Rule. (The text of the ABA Model Court Rule is reprinted below in the Related Materials following Rule 5.5.)

2012 Amendment: In August 2012, the ABA amended paragraph (d) to insert the words from "through" to "presence in" to clarify the scope of the prohibition absent an exception. It also added the final sentence to Comment 1, added a cross-reference to Comment 18, and made technical changes to Comment 21.

Selected State Variations

> **Editors' Note.** At least 44 jurisdictions have adopted multijurisdictional practice rules similar or identical to ABA Model Rule 5.5 as amended in 2002. Three states are still studying those amendments, and one state has recommended adoption of a rule similar to Rule 5.5. New York and Kansas have amended their rules since the ABA's adoption of Rule 5.5 in its current form but did not include the 2002 amendments to Rule 5.5. For up-to-date charts showing how all American jurisdictions have responded to the recommendations of the ABA Commission on Multijurisdictional Practice, go to *http://www.americanbar.org/content/dam/aba/administrative/professional_responsibility/recommendations.authcheckdam.pdf.*

Alabama: Alabama Rule 5.5(b) is similar to ABA Model Rule 5.5(c), but Alabama limits the activities of out-of-state lawyers to services that

> (1) are performed on a temporary basis by a lawyer admitted and in good standing in another United States jurisdiction, including transactional, counseling, or other nonlitigation services that arise out of or are reasonably related to the lawyer's practice in a jurisdiction in which the lawyer is admitted to practice;
>
> (2) are in or reasonably related to a pending or potential arbitration, mediation, or other alternative dispute resolution proceeding held or to be held in this or in another jurisdiction; or
>
> (3) are performed by an attorney admitted as an authorized house counsel under Rule IX of the Rules Governing Admission to the Alabama State Bar and who is performing only those services defined in that rule.

Arizona augments ABA Model Rule 5.5 by adding these paragraphs:

> (e) Any attorney who engages in the authorized multijurisdictional practice of law in the State of Arizona under this rule must advise the lawyer's client that the lawyer is not admitted to practice in Arizona, and must obtain the client's informed consent to such representation.
>
> (f) Attorneys not admitted to practice in the State of Arizona, who are admitted to practice law in any other jurisdiction in the United States and who appear in any court of record or before any administrative hearing officer in the State of Arizona, must also comply with Rules of the Supreme Court of Arizona governing pro hac vice admission.
>
> (g) Any attorney who engages in the multijurisdictional practice of law in the State of Arizona, whether authorized in accordance with these Rules or not, shall be subject to the Rules of Professional Conduct and the Rules of the Supreme Court regarding attorney discipline in the State of Arizona.

In addition, Arizona's lead-in language to Rule 5.5(d) requires the lawyer who relies on that paragraph to have "registered pursuant to Rule 38(i) of these rules." That rule recognizes limited admission status for "an attorney who is employed within the State of Arizona as in-house counsel or a related position for a for-profit or a non-profit corporation, association, or other organizational entity, which can include its parents, subsidiaries and/or affiliates, the business of which is lawful and is other than the practice of law or the provision of legal services."

California: California Supreme Court Rules 9.45, 9.46, 9.47, and 9.48 give lawyers admitted in other American jurisdictions limited authority to provide legal services in California. The four rules deal with in-house counsel, legal services lawyers, lawyers involved in dispute resolution, and lawyers providing other legal services in California. The California rules are less expansive than ABA Model Rule 5.5(c). In addition, two other rules — 9.43 and 9.44 — provide authority for lawyers who enter California to participate in arbitrations and for lawyers admitted in foreign countries to register as foreign legal consultants.

Colorado: Rule 5.5(a)(1) provides that a lawyer shall not "practice law in this jurisdiction without a license to practice law issued by the Colorado Supreme Court unless specifically authorized by C.R.C.P. 220, C.R.C.P. 221, C.R.C.P. 221.1, C.R.C.P. 222 or federal or tribal law. . . ."

Colorado Rule of Civil Procedure 220, entitled "Out-of-State Attorney-Conditions of Practice," permits an out-of-state attorney who is not domiciled in Colorado and has not established a place for the regular practice of law in Colorado to "practice law in the state of Colorado except that an out-of-state attorney who wishes to appear in any state court of record must comply with [rules] concerning pro hac vice admission." Unlike ABA Model Rule 5.5, Colorado's Rule 220 does not restrict out-of-state lawyers to "temporary" law practice. However, Rule 220 permits an out-of-state lawyer to practice in Colorado only if the lawyer "has not established domicile in Colorado" and "has not established a place for the regular practice of law in Colorado from which such attorney holds himself or herself out to the public as practicing Colorado law or solicits or accepts Colorado clients." Rule 222 provides for admission of single-client lawyers (effectively a house counsel rule): "An attorney who is not licensed to practice law in the state of Colorado may be certified to act as counsel for a single-client upon application to and approval by the Colorado Supreme Court" under conditions and with limitations specified.

Connecticut adopts most of ABA Model Rule 5.5 verbatim, with some additions and modifications. Rule 5.5(a) adds that the "practice of law" in Connecticut "is defined in Practice Book Section 2-44A," a lengthy and detailed court rule. Rule 5.5(a) also adds that conduct described in Rules 5.5(c) and (d) in another jurisdiction "shall not be deemed the unauthorized practice of law for purposes of this paragraph (a)."

Most significantly, Connecticut Rule 5.5(c) extends temporary practice privileges only to a lawyer admitted in another United States jurisdiction "which accords similar privileges to Connecticut lawyers in its jurisdiction." Connecticut Rule 5.5(d)(1) applies only if the lawyer "is an authorized house counsel as provided in Practice Book Section 2-15A." Section 2-15A(c)(1) authorizes an in-house lawyer to engage in the following activities in Connecticut:

> (A) the giving of legal advice to the directors, officers, employees, and agents of the organization with respect to its business and affairs;
> (B) negotiating and documenting all matters for the organization; and
> (C) representation of the organization in its dealings with any administrative agency, tribunal or commission having jurisdiction; provided, however, authorized house counsel shall not be permitted to make appearances as counsel before any state or municipal administrative tribunal, agency, or commission, and shall not be permitted to make appearances in any court of this state, unless the attorney is specially admitted to appear in a case before such tribunal, agency, commission or court.

However, §2-15(A)(c)(4) provides that an authorized house counsel "shall not express or render a legal judgment or opinion to be relied upon by any third person or party other than legal opinions rendered in connection with commercial, financial or other business transactions to which the authorized house counsel's employer organization is a party and in which the legal opinions have been requested from the authorized house counsel by another party to the transaction."

A lawyer licensed in a "foreign jurisdiction" may qualify as an authorized house counsel.

Drawing on ABA Model Rule 8.5(a), Connecticut adds a new Rule 5.5(e), which provides: "A lawyer not admitted to practice in this jurisdiction and authorized by the provisions of this Rule to engage in providing legal services on a temporary basis in this jurisdiction is thereby subject to the disciplinary rules of this jurisdiction with respect to the activities in this jurisdiction." Finally, Connecticut adds an unusual new Rule 5.5(f), which provides:

> A lawyer desirous of obtaining the privileges set forth in subparagraphs (c)(3) or (4), (1) shall notify the Statewide Bar Counsel as to each separate matter prior to any such representation in Connecticut, (2) shall notify the Statewide Bar Counsel upon termination of each such representation in Connecticut, and (3) shall pay such fees as may be prescribed by the Judicial Branch.

Delaware has adopted Rule 5.5 and adds lawyers "admitted . . . in a foreign jurisdiction" to the authority granted in Rule 5.5(c) and 5.5(d). Delaware Supreme Court Rule 55.1 implements the authority of Rule 5.5(d)(1).

District of Columbia retains the pre-2002 version of ABA Model Rule 5.5. In addition, D.C. has developed one of the most detailed unauthorized practice rules in the country (D.C. Rule 49). The rule contains many exceptions to the general prohibition against unauthorized practice. These include exceptions for lawyers providing legal services to the United States while employed by the United States; lawyers appearing before a "special court, department or agency of the United States" where authorized by statute; employees of the District of Columbia and lawyers practicing before "a department or agency of the District of Columbia" pursuant to statutory authorization; employed lawyers where the employer "does not reasonably expect that it is receiving advice from a person" admitted in the District; lawyers who have moved to the District for a period of 360 days while applying for admission in the District and so long as they are under "the direct supervision of an enrolled, active member" of the D.C. Bar; up to five appearances per year for lawyers coming into the district for an ADR proceeding; up to five pro hac vice applications per year; and lawyers providing pro bono services under limited circumstances. Foreign lawyers are also exempt from the UPL prohibition for "incidental and temporary" work in the District.

Florida: Rule 5.5 is based on ABA Model Rule 5.5 but has many significant differences. For example, Florida Rule 5.5(c) permits temporary practice only by lawyers who have neither been disbarred from practice in any jurisdiction "nor disciplined or held in contempt in Florida by reason of misconduct committed while engaged in the practice of law permitted pursuant to this rule." Rule 5.5(b) adds a provision forbidding an outside lawyer to "(3) appear in court, before an administrative agency, or before any other tribunal unless authorized to do so by the court, administrative agency, or tribunal pursuant to the applicable rules of the court, administrative agency, or tribunal." Florida Rule 5.5(c)(3) adds that a lawyer may provide temporary legal services related to an alternative dispute resolution proceeding or non-litigation services "if the services are performed for a client who resides in or has an office in the lawyer's home state" or the services arise out of or are reasonably related to the lawyer's [home state] practice." The same language describes the scope of other (transactional) services. Florida also adds a subparagraph entitled "Authorized Temporary Practice by Lawyer Admitted in a Non-United States Jurisdiction," which largely parallels the portions of Rule 5.5 governing temporary practice by lawyers admitted in other U.S. jurisdictions.

Georgia: Rule 5.5 generally tracks ABA Model Rule 5.5, but Georgia distinguishes between a "Domestic Lawyer" (defined in Georgia's Terminology section as, essentially, a lawyer admitted elsewhere in the United States or its territories but not in Georgia) and a "Foreign Lawyer" (defined as "a person authorized to practice law by the duly constituted and authorized governmental body of any foreign nation" but not by Georgia). Georgia adds Rule 5.5(e) to permit temporary practice in Georgia by Foreign Lawyers on terms roughly equivalent to those that govern Domestic Lawyers, provided the foreign lawyer is "a member in good standing of a recognized legal profession in a foreign jurisdiction, the members of which are admitted to practice as lawyers or counselors at law or the equivalent and subject to effective regulation and discipline by a duly constituted professional body or a public authority."

Illinois: Illinois Rule 5.5 tracks ABA Model Rule 5.5. In addition, Supreme Court Rule 716, entitled "Limited Admission of House Counsel," permits an out-of-state lawyer to receive a limited license to perform legal services in Illinois when the lawyer is "employed in Illinois as house counsel exclusively for a single . . . legal entity (as well as any parent, subsidiary or affiliate thereof). . . ." The legal services must be limited to (a) advising the directors, officers, employees and agents of the employer regarding its business and affairs, and (b) negotiating, documenting and consummating transactions to which the employer is a party. An in-house lawyer may not appear as counsel before any court, administrative tribunal, agency or commission in Illinois unless (a) that body's rules authorize the appearance or (b) the body specially admits the lawyer for the particular matter. Lawyers licensed under the house counsel rule "shall not offer legal services or advice to the public or in any manner hold themselves out to be so engaged or authorized."

Illinois Supreme Court Rule 717, entitled "Limited Admission of Legal Service Program Lawyers," permits an out-of-state lawyer to receive a limited license to practice law in Illinois, for a maximum of 18 months, when the lawyer is "employed in Illinois for an organized legal service, public defender or law school clinical program providing legal assistance to indigent persons." A lawyer holding this limited license may perform legal services "solely on behalf of such employer and the indigent clients represented by such employer," and in felony cases the lawyer may participate in the proceedings only as "an assistant of a supervising member of the bar who shall be present and responsible for the conduct of the proceedings."

Kansas: Kansas retains the original 1983 version of ABA Model Rule 5.5 verbatim.

Louisiana adopts Model Rule 5.5(a)-(d) with minor modifications.

Maine, Michigan, and *Nebraska* adopt Model Rule 5.5.

Minnesota: Rule 5.5(a) adds an "immunity clause" for Minnesota lawyers by providing that a Minnesota lawyer "does not violate this rule by conduct in another jurisdiction" that an out-of-state lawyer may do in Minnesota pursuant to Rules 5.5(c) and (d). Minnesota also deletes Rule 5.5(d)(1) (which governs legal services provided to a lawyer's employer).

Missouri renumbers paragraph (c)(4) as (c)(5) and adds as Rule 5.5(c)(4) permission for temporary legal services that "are provided to the lawyer's employer or its organizational affiliates and are not services for which the forum requires pro hac vice admission." In addition, Missouri Rule 5.5(d) omits paragraph (d)(2) and substantially adopts paragraph (d)(1) but requires that the lawyer have "obtained a limited license pursuant to Rule 8.105" (quoted below). Finally, Missouri adds a new Rule 5.5(e), which prohibits the practice of law by a lawyer who has been reported to the authorities for failure to comply with Missouri's Continuing Legal Education requirements.

Missouri Supreme Court Rule 8.105 provides:

> A lawyer admitted to the practice of law in another state or territory of the United States may receive a limited license to practice law in this state if the lawyer:
>
> (1) Is employed in Missouri as a lawyer exclusively for: a corporation, its subsidiaries or affiliates; an association; a business; or a governmental entity and the employer's lawful business consists of activities other than the practice of law or the provision of legal services;
>
> (2) Was conferred a professional degree in law (J.D. or L.L.B) by a law school that at the time of the lawyer's graduation was approved by the American Bar Association;
>
> (3) Has filed such application forms as prescribed by the board and paid the prescribed fee, which is non-refundable; and
>
> (4) Receives the approval of the board.

New Jersey: Effective, September 1, 2010, Rule 5.5(b) provides:

> A lawyer not admitted to the Bar of this State who is admitted to practice law before the highest court of any other state, territory of the United States, Puerto Rico, or the District of Columbia (hereinafter a United States jurisdiction) may engage in the lawful practice of law in New Jersey only if:
>
> (1) the lawyer is admitted to practice *pro hac vice* pursuant to R. 1:21-2 or is preparing for a proceeding in which the lawyer reasonably expects to be so admitted and is associated in that preparation with a lawyer admitted to practice in this jurisdiction; or
>
> (2) the lawyer is an in-house counsel and complies with R. 1:27-2; or
>
> (3) under any of the following circumstances:
>
> (i) the lawyer engages in the negotiation of the terms of a transaction in furtherance of the lawyer's representation on behalf of an existing client in a jurisdiction in which the lawyer is admitted to practice and the transaction originates in or is otherwise related to a jurisdiction in which the lawyer is admitted to practice;
>
> (ii) the lawyer engages in representation of a party to a dispute by participating in arbitration, mediation or other alternate or complementary dispute resolution program and the services arise out of or are reasonably related to the lawyer's practice in a jurisdiction in which the lawyer is admitted to practice and are not services for which pro hac vice admission pursuant to R. 1:21-2 is required;
>
> (iii) the lawyer investigates, engages in discovery, interviews witnesses or deposes witnesses in this jurisdiction for a proceeding pending or anticipated to be instituted in a jurisdiction in which the lawyer is admitted to practice;
>
> (iv) the lawyer associates in a matter with a lawyer admitted to the Bar of this State who shall be held responsible for the conduct of the out-of-State lawyer in the matter; or

(v) the lawyer practices under circumstances other than (i) through (iii) above, with respect to a matter where the practice activity arises directly out of the lawyer's representation on behalf of an existing client in a jurisdiction in which the lawyer is admitted to practice, provided that such practice in this jurisdiction is occasional and is undertaken only when the lawyer's disengagement would result in substantial inefficiency, impracticality or detriment to the client.

(c) A lawyer admitted to practice in another jurisdiction who acts in this jurisdiction pursuant to paragraph (b) above shall:

(1) be licensed and in good standing in all jurisdictions of admission and not be the subject of any pending disciplinary proceedings, nor a current or pending license suspension or disbarment;

(2) be subject to the Rules of Professional Conduct and the disciplinary authority of the Supreme Court of this jurisdiction;

(3) consent in writing on a form approved by the Supreme Court to the appointment of the Clerk of the Supreme Court as agent upon whom service of process may be made for all actions against the lawyer or the lawyer's firm that may arise out of the lawyer's participation in legal matters in this jurisdiction, except that a lawyer who acts in this jurisdiction pursuant to subparagraph (b)(3)(ii) or (b)(3)(iii) above shall be deemed to have consented to such appointment without completing the form;

(4) not hold himself or herself out as being admitted to practice in this jurisdiction;

(5) maintain a bona fide office in conformance with R. 1:21-1(a), except that, when admitted pro hac vice, the lawyer may maintain the bona fide office within the bona fide law office of the associated New Jersey attorney pursuant to R. 1:21- 2(a)(1)(B); and

(6) except for a lawyer who acts in this jurisdiction pursuant to subparagraph (b)(3)(ii) or (b)(3)(iii) above, annually register with the New Jersey Lawyers' Fund for Client Protection and comply with R. 1:20-1(b) and (c), R. 1:28-2, and R. 1:28B-1(e) during the period of practice.

New Jersey Rule 1:27-2(a) defines in-house counsel for purposes of its Rule 5.5(b)(2) as follows:

In-House Counsel is a lawyer who is employed in New Jersey for a corporation, a partnership, association, or other legal entity (taken together with its respective parents, subsidiaries, and affiliates) authorized to transact business in this State that is not itself engaged in the practice of law or the rendering of legal services outside such organization, whether for a fee or otherwise, and does not charge or collect a fee for the representation or advice other than to entities comprising such organization.

New Jersey Rule 1:27-2(b)(iii) permits the in-house lawyer to provide legal services "solely for the identified employer and its constituents (employees, directors, officers, members, partners, shareholders) in respect of the same proceeding or claim as the employer, provided that the performance of such services is consistent with RPC 1.13 and RPC 1.7."

New Jersey Rule 1:21-1(e) provides:

(e) *Legal Services Organizations.* Nonprofit organizations incorporated in this or any other state for the purpose of providing legal services to the poor or functioning as a public interest law firm, and other federally tax exempt legal services organizations or trusts . . . which provide legal services to a defined and limited class of clients, may practice law in their own names through staff attorneys who are members of the bar of the State of New Jersey, provided that: (1) the legal work serves the intended beneficiaries of the organizational purpose, (2) the staff attorney responsible for the matter signs all papers prepared by the organization, and (3) the relationship between staff attorney and client meets the attorney's professional responsibilities to the client and is not subject to interference, control, or direction by the organization's board or employees except for a supervising attorney who is a member of the New Jersey bar.

New Jersey Rule 1:21-1(a) requires that every attorney practicing law in New Jersey maintain "a bona fide office for the practice of law" in any United States jurisdiction, not necessarily New Jersey. The rule continues as follows:

> For the purpose of this section, a bona fide office is a place where clients are met, files are kept, the telephone is answered, mail is received and the attorney or a responsible person acting on the attorney's behalf can be reached in person and by telephone during normal business hours to answer questions posed by the courts, clients or adversaries and to ensure that competent advice from the attorney can be obtained within a reasonable period of time.

New Jersey Rule 1-21-10 substantially adopts the ABA's rule permitting temporary practice of out-of-state lawyers in the event of a "major disaster" ("the Katrina Rule").

New York: New York Rule 5.5 adopts the language of former DR 3-101 with minor variations. In 2011, New York adopted a heavily modified version of the ABA Model Rule on Registration of In-House Counsel, See 22 NYCRR Part 522.

North Carolina: Rule 5.5 does not use the word "temporary" as it appears in ABA Model Rule 5.5(c), but Rule 5.5(b)(1) forbids a "systematic and continuous presence" in the jurisdiction for the practice of law. North Carolina Rule 5.5(c)(2)(E) adds an additional category that permits a lawyer admitted in another jurisdiction to practice in North Carolina if "the lawyer is providing services limited to federal law, international law, the law of a foreign jurisdiction, or the law of the jurisdiction in which the lawyer is admitted to practice."

Ohio: Rule 5.5(c)(4) permits a lawyer to "provide legal services on a temporary basis" in Ohio if "the lawyer engages in negotiations, investigations, or other non-litigation activities that arise out of or are reasonably related to the lawyer's practice in a jurisdiction in which the lawyer is admitted to practice." Otherwise, the Ohio rule is substantially the same as the Model Rule.

Oregon moves Rule 5.5(d)(1) (which permits temporary legal services that are provided to the lawyer's employer or its affiliates) to Rule 5.5(c)(5), meaning that these services may be performed only on a "temporary" basis.

Pennsylvania changes the lead-in language to Rule 5.5(c) to apply to a lawyer admitted in another United States jurisdiction "or in a foreign jurisdiction."

Tennessee has adopted the 2003 amendments to ABA Model Rule 5.5, except that Tennessee Rule 5.5(c)(3) and (c)(4) require that the work "arise out of or [be] reasonably related to the lawyer's representation of an existing client in a jurisdiction in which the lawyer is admitted to practice." In addition, Tennessee adds the following paragraphs:

> (e) A lawyer authorized to provide legal services in this jurisdiction pursuant to paragraph (d)(1) of this Rule may also provide pro bono legal services in this jurisdiction, provided that these services are offered through an established not-for-profit bar association, pro bono program or legal services program or through such organization(s) specifically authorized in this jurisdiction and provided that these are services for which the forum does not require pro hac vice admission.

(f) A lawyer providing legal services in Tennessee pursuant to paragraph (c) or (d) shall advise the lawyer's client that the lawyer is not admitted to practice in Tennessee and shall obtain the client's informed consent to such representation.

(g) A lawyer providing legal services in Tennessee pursuant to paragraph (c) or (d) shall be deemed to have submitted himself or herself to personal jurisdiction in Tennessee for claims arising out of the lawyer's actions in providing such services in this state.

Virginia Rule 5.5(d)(4) substantially tracks the temporary practice authority granted in ABA Rule 5.5(c) and extends that authority to "foreign lawyers," defined to include a "person authorized to practice law by the duly constituted and authorized governmental body of any State or Territory of the United States or the District of Columbia, or a foreign nation, but is neither licensed by the Supreme Court of Virginia or authorized under its rules to practice law generally in the Commonwealth of Virginia, nor disbarred or suspended from practice in any jurisdiction."

Washington: Rule 5.5(e) permits lawyers practicing in the state under the equivalent to Rule 5.5(d)(1) also to provide pro bono services to clients through a "qualified legal services provider."

Wisconsin: Wisconsin adopts ABA Rule 5.5 but adds a clause to the effect that the Clerk of the Wisconsin Supreme Court may accept service of process "for all actions against the lawyer or the lawyer's firm that may arise out of the lawyer's participation in legal matters in this jurisdiction."

Related Materials

ABA Commission on Ethics 20/20: In 2009, the ABA created the Commission on Ethics 20/20, which is comprehensively reviewing the ABA Model Rules of Professional Conduct and other professional regulations in light of globalization and changes in technology. On June 19, 2012, the 20/20 Commission's Working Group on Uniformity, Choice of Law, and Conflicts of Interest released an "Issues Paper" concerning ABA Model Rule 5.5 and "the Limits on Virtual Presence in a Jurisdiction." That paper provides, in part, as follows:

> Traditionally, a U.S.-licensed lawyer who established a physical presence in another U.S. jurisdiction had to obtain a license to practice there. Model Rule 5.5(b)(1) largely reflects this view, requiring a lawyer to obtain a license in a jurisdiction if the lawyer has an office or a "systematic and continuous" presence there, unless the lawyer's work falls within one of the exceptions identified in Rule 5.5(d). . . .
>
> [S]ince 2002, the proliferation of lawyers' use of technology has raised new questions about the meaning of the phrase "systematic and continuous presence" in Rule 5.5(b). In particular, technology now enables lawyers to be physically present in one jurisdiction, yet have a substantial virtual practice in another. The problem is that it is not always clear when this virtual practice in a jurisdiction is sufficiently "systematic and continuous" to require a license in that jurisdiction.
>
> Currently, Comment 4 to Model Rule 5.5 identifies the issue, but provides limited guidance as to how to resolve it. The Comment states that a lawyer's "[p]resence may be systematic and continuous even if the lawyer is not physically present" in the jurisdiction.
>
> Neither the Rule nor the Comment provides any clarity as to when a lawyer who is "not physically present" in a jurisdiction nevertheless has a systematic and continuous presence there. . . . The Working Group has identified several possible approaches.

Possible Approaches

One possible approach is to identify the factors that lawyers and disciplinary authorities should consider when deciding whether a lawyer's presence has become sufficiently systematic and continuous to trigger Rule 5.5(b)'s requirement that the lawyer become licensed. For example, those factors might include:

- the nature and volume of communications directed to potential clients in the jurisdiction;
- whether the purpose of the communications is to obtain new clients in the jurisdiction;
- the number of the lawyer's clients in the jurisdiction;
- the proportion of the lawyer's clients in the jurisdiction;
- the frequency of representing clients in the jurisdiction;
- the extent to which the legal services have their predominant effect in the jurisdiction; and
- the extent to which the representation of clients in the jurisdiction arises out of, or is reasonably related to, the lawyer's practice in a jurisdiction in which the lawyer is admitted to practice.

A second possibility is for the Commission to make no proposal in this area and to refer the issue to the Standing Committee on Ethics and Professional Responsibility for an opinion on the meaning of "systematic and continuous presence" in the context of virtual law practice.

A third possibility is for the Commission to make no proposal in this area, but identify the relevant issues in an informational report that the Commission could file with the ABA House of Delegates to help educate the profession about this issue.

In September 2012, after considering the feedback on these possible approaches, the Commission decided not to proceed with a proposal for augmenting the ambiguous guidance currently provided by Comment 4 to Rule 5.5 regarding the meaning of the phrase "systematic and continuous." For updates on the work of the ABA Ethics 20/20 Commission, visit *http://www.americanbar.org/Ethics2020*.

ABA Commission on Multidisciplinary Practice: Lawyers who provide legal services to the public through accounting firms or other professional service firms controlled by nonlawyers may be violating Rule 5.5(a) (among other rules) by assisting nonlawyers in the unauthorized practice of law. In 1998, the ABA appointed a Commission on Multidisciplinary Practice (MDP Commission) to study and report on efforts by accounting firms and other nonlawyer professional service firms to provide legal services to the public. The MDP Commission sought to persuade the ABA to liberalize the rules governing relationships between lawyers and nonlawyers, but the ABA House of Delegates overwhelmingly defeated the MDP Commission's proposals to amend the rules. For further information, see the entry on "ABA Commission on Multidisciplinary Practice" in the Related Materials after Rule 5.4 and visit the website of the former ABA Commission on Multidisciplinary Practice at *http://www.americanbar.org/groups/professional_responsibility/commission_multidisciplinary_practice.html*.

ABA Commission on Multijurisdictional Practice: In 2000, the ABA created a Commission on Multijurisdictional Practice (the MJP Commission — not to be confused with the MDP Commission). The mission of the MJP Commission was to research, study, and report on how ethics and bar admission rules applied to lawyers who practiced law both in jurisdictions where they were admitted and in jurisdictions where they were not admitted. Professor Bruce Green of Fordham was the MJP Commission's Reporter, and Professor Stephen Gillers (a co-author of this book) was a member of the MJP Commission.

The MJP Commission held public hearings and solicited public comments to enable it to analyze the impact of ethics and bar admission rules on in-house counsel, transactional lawyers, litigators, and arbitrators, and on lawyers and law firms that maintain offices and practice in multiple state and federal jurisdictions. In June 2002, the MJP Commission submitted its Final Report to the ABA House of Delegates recommending that the ABA amend Model Rules 5.5 and 8.5 to their present form and that the ABA take seven other measures to facilitate and regulate the multijurisdictional practice of law. In 2002, the House of Delegates approved all nine of the MJP Commission's recommendations. The MJP Commission's Final Report and many other useful materials are available on the MJP Commission's website at *http://www.americanbar.org/groups/professional_responsibility/committees_com-missions/commission_on_multijurisditional_practice.html.*

ABA Commission on Nonlawyer Practice: In 1992, the ABA appointed a 17-member Commission on Nonlawyer Practice, composed of both lawyers and nonlawyers, to examine all aspects of work done by nonlawyers. The Commission held hearings in nine cities, heard 337 witnesses, and reviewed more than 12,000 pages of statements, studies, statutes, reports, and scholarly articles. In 1995, the Commission issued a final report entitled "NonLawyer Activity in Law-Related Situations," which concluded that "[w]hen adequate protections for the public are in place, nonlawyers have important roles to perform in providing the public with access to justice." The Commission reported that as many as 70 percent of people with low and moderate incomes do not hire lawyers to meet their law-related needs, but instead go without any help, represent themselves, or turn to nonprofit agencies or nonlawyers.

The ABA Board of Governors did not reappoint the Commission on Nonlawyer Practice, which therefore automatically ceased to exist on August 31, 1995. Moreover, the Commission's report was never transmitted to the ABA House of Delegates for approval. Nevertheless, the report is available online at *http://www.americanbar.org/content/dam/aba/migrated/2011_build/professional_responsibility/non_lawyer_activity.authcheckdam.pdf.*

ABA Formal Ethics Opinions: See ABA Formal Ethics Ops. 87-355 (1987), 01-423 (2001), and 08-451 (2008).

ABA Model Court Rule on Provision of Legal Services Following Determination of Major Disaster: In 2007, the ABA House of Delegates adopted a Model Court Rule on the Provision of Legal Services Following Determination of Major Disaster, commonly called the "Katrina Rule" (after Hurricane Katrina, which spurred the ABA to adopt the rule) or the "Major Disaster Rule" (to reflect that the rule applies after all types of disasters). Under the Major Disaster Rule, lawyers from states that have suffered a major disaster may carry on their practices temporarily in other states that have adopted the Major Disaster Rule, and lawyers licensed in other states may perform pro bono work both in states that have suffered the disaster and in states to which persons displaced by the disaster have temporarily relocated. The Major Disaster Rule provides, in full, as follows:

(a) *Determination of existence of major disaster.* Solely for purposes of this Rule, this Court shall determine when an emergency affecting the justice system, as a result of a natural or other major disaster has occurred in:

(1) this jurisdiction and whether the emergency caused by the major disaster affects the entirety or only a part of this jurisdiction, or

(2) another jurisdiction but only after such a determination and its geographical scope have been made by the highest court of that jurisdiction. The authority to engage in the temporary practice of law in this jurisdiction pursuant to paragraph (c) shall extend only to lawyers who principally practice in the area of such other jurisdiction determined to have suffered a major disaster causing an emergency affecting the justice system and the provision of legal services.

(b) *Temporary practice in this jurisdiction following major disaster.* Following the determination of an emergency affecting the justice system in this jurisdiction pursuant to paragraph (a) of this Rule, or a determination that persons displaced by a major disaster in another jurisdiction and residing in this jurisdiction are in need of pro bono services and the assistance of lawyers from outside of this jurisdiction is required to help provide such assistance, a lawyer authorized to practice law in another United States jurisdiction, and not disbarred, suspended from practice or otherwise restricted from practice in any jurisdiction, may provide legal services in this jurisdiction on a temporary basis. Such legal services must be provided on a pro bono basis without compensation, expectation of compensation or other direct or indirect pecuniary gain to the lawyer. Such legal services shall be assigned and supervised through an established not-for-profit bar association, pro bono program or legal services program or through such organization(s) specifically designated by this Court.

(c) *Temporary practice in this jurisdiction following major disaster in another jurisdiction.* Following the determination of a major disaster in another United States jurisdiction, a lawyer who is authorized to practice law and who principally practices in that affected jurisdiction, and who is not disbarred, suspended from practice or otherwise restricted from practice in any jurisdiction, may provide legal services in this jurisdiction on a temporary basis. Those legal services must arise out of and be reasonably related to that lawyer's practice of law in the jurisdiction, or area of such other jurisdiction, where the major disaster occurred.

(d) *Duration of authority for temporary practice.* The authority to practice law in this jurisdiction granted by paragraph (b) of this Rule shall end when this Court determines that the conditions caused by the major disaster in this jurisdiction have ended except that a lawyer then representing clients in this jurisdiction pursuant to paragraph (b) is authorized to continue the provision of legal services for such time as is reasonably necessary to complete the representation, but the lawyer shall not thereafter accept new clients. The authority to practice law in this jurisdiction granted by paragraph (c) of this Rule shall end [60] days after this Court declares that the conditions caused by the major disaster in the affected jurisdiction have ended.

(e) *Court appearances.* The authority granted by this Rule does not include appearances in court except:

(1) pursuant to that court's pro hac vice admission rule and, if such authority is granted, any fees for such admission shall be waived; or

(2) if this Court, in any determination made under paragraph (a), grants blanket permission to appear in all or designated courts of this jurisdiction to lawyers providing legal services pursuant to paragraph (b). If such an authorization is included, any pro hac vice admission fees shall be waived.

(f) *Disciplinary authority and registration requirement.* Lawyers providing legal services in this jurisdiction pursuant to paragraphs (b) or (c) are subject to this Court's disciplinary authority and the Rules of Professional Conduct of this jurisdiction as provided in Rule 8.5 of the Rules of Professional Conduct. Lawyers providing legal services in this jurisdiction under paragraphs (b) or (c) shall, within 30 days from the commencement of the provision of legal services, file a registration statement with the Clerk of this Court. The registration statement shall be in a form prescribed by this

Court. Any lawyer who provides legal services pursuant to this Rule shall not be considered to be engaged in the unlawful practice of law in this jurisdiction.

(g) *Notification to clients.* Lawyers authorized to practice law in another United States jurisdiction who provide legal services pursuant to this Rule shall inform clients in this jurisdiction of the jurisdiction in which they are authorized to practice law, any limits of that authorization, and that they are not authorized to practice law in this jurisdiction except as permitted by this Rule. They shall not state or imply to any person that they are otherwise authorized to practice law in this jurisdiction.

Professor Stephen Gillers (a co-author of this book) was instrumental in drafting the Major Disaster Rule. When we went to press in September 2012, 13 jurisdictions had adopted the Major Disaster Rule; 16 were considering adoption; and 6 had decided not to adopt the rule. A chart tracking state-by-state implementation of the Major Disaster Rule is available at *http://www.americanbar.org/content/dam/aba/ migrated/cpr/clientpro/katrina_chart.authcheckdam.pdf.*

ABA Model Guidelines for the Utilization of Paralegal Services: Guidelines 2, 3, and 4 of the ABA Model Guidelines for the Utilization of Paralegal Services, which relate closely to Rule 5.5(a), provide as follows:

Guideline 2: Provided the lawyer maintains responsibility for the work product, a lawyer may delegate to a paralegal any task normally performed by the lawyer except those tasks proscribed to a nonlawyer by statute, court rule, [etc.].

Guideline 3: A lawyer may not delegate to a paralegal:

(a) Responsibility for establishing an attorney-client relationship.

(b) Responsibility for establishing the amount of a fee to be charged for a legal service.

(c) Responsibility for a legal opinion rendered to a client.

Guideline 4: A lawyer is responsible for taking reasonable measures to ensure that clients, courts, and other lawyers are aware that a paralegal, whose services are utilized by the lawyer in performing legal services, is not licensed to practice law.

The ABA Model Guidelines for the Utilization of Paralegal Services are available online at *http://apps.americanbar.org/legalservices/paralegals/downloads/modelguidelines. pdf.*

ABA Model Rule for the Licensing and Practice of Foreign Legal Consultants: In 1993, the ABA House of Delegates approved a Model Rule for the Licensing of Foreign Legal Consultants. A registered Foreign Legal Consultant is an attorney or counselor at law (or equivalent) who is licensed in another country and has received a Certificate of Registration from a U.S. State as a Foreign Legal Consultant. The rule allowing Foreign Legal Consultants to practice was motivated by concern that foreign countries might not allow American lawyers to practice abroad if the United States does not allow foreign lawyers to practice in America. Section 1 of the Model Rule allows a state to license a "legal consultant" without requiring an examination if the applicant:

(a) is, and for at least five years has been, a member in good standing of a recognized legal profession in a foreign country, the members of which are admitted to practice as lawyers or counselors at law or the equivalent and are subject to effective regulation and discipline by a duly constituted professional body or a public authority;

(b) for at least five years preceding his or her application, has been a member in good standing of such legal profession and has been lawfully engaged in the practice of law in the foreign country or elsewhere substantially involving or relating to the rendering of advice or the provision of legal services concerning the law of the foreign country;

(c) possesses the good moral character and general fitness requisite for a member of the bar of this jurisdiction; and

(d) intends to practice as a foreign legal consultant in this jurisdiction and to maintain an office in this jurisdiction for that purpose.

Other sections of the Model Rule for the Licensing of Foreign Legal Consultants set forth application procedures, limit the scope of the practice by foreign legal consultants, and govern discipline, bar admission, and other subjects. Foreign legal consultants are not "admitted to the bar" in the U.S. licensing state but are "subject to professional discipline in the same manner and to the same extent as members of the bar" of the U.S. licensing jurisdiction.

When we went to press in September 2012, about 31 states had adopted a foreign legal consultant rule, and various other states were actively considering a foreign legal consultant rule or reviewing their existing temporary practice rules. The full text of the ABA Model Rule for the Licensing and Practice of Foreign Legal Consultants and a chart showing which states have adopted the rule are available online at *http://www.americanbar.org/groups/professional_responsibility/committees_commissions/commission_on_multijurisditional_practice.html.* A state-by-state chart showing the number of foreign legal consultants admitted to practice each year in recent years is online at *http://www.ncbex.org/assets/media_files/Statistics/2011Statistics.pdf.* (The numbers are small — between 2007 and 2011, between 64 and 99 foreign legal consultants were admitted nationally each year.)

ABA Model Rule on Admission by Motion: In 2002, by a vote of 257-150, the ABA adopted a Model Rule on Admission by Motion, which was part of the package proposed by the ABA Commission on Multijurisdictional Practice. This Model Rule describes the procedures by which lawyers admitted in one jurisdiction may gain admission in another jurisdiction without taking the other jurisdiction's bar examination. Currently, more than 40 jurisdictions have an admission by motion procedure, but many of those jurisdictions impose requirements that do not exist in the Model Rule.

At its February 2011 Mid-Year Meeting, pursuant to a proposal by the ABA Section on Legal Education and Admission to the Bar an the ABA Standing Committee on Client Protection, the ABA amended the Model Rule on Admission by Motion. At its August 2012 Annual Meeting, on the recommendation of the ABA Commission on Ethics 20/20, the ABA amended the Rule even further. The rule, with the August 2012 amendments indicated in legislative style, provides as follows:

ABA Model Rule on Admission by Motion

1. An applicant who meets the requirements of (a) through (g) of this Rule may, upon motion, be admitted to the practice of law in this jurisdiction.

The applicant shall:

(a) have been admitted to practice law in another state, territory, or the District of Columbia;

(b) hold a J.D. or LL.B degree from a law school approved by the Council of the Section of Legal Education and Admission to the Bar of the American Bar Association at the time the applicant matriculated or graduated;

(c) have been primarily engaged in the active practice of law in one or more states, territories or the District of Columbia for three ~~five~~ of the five ~~seven~~ years immediately preceding the date upon which the application is filed;

(d) establish that the applicant is currently a member in good standing in all jurisdictions where admitted;

(e) establish that the applicant is not currently subject to lawyer discipline or the subject of a pending disciplinary matter in any ~~other~~ jurisdiction;

(f) establish that the applicant possesses the character and fitness to practice law in this jurisdiction; and

(g) designate the Clerk of the jurisdiction's highest court for service of process.

2. For the purposes of this ~~r~~Rule, the "active practice of law" shall include the following activities, if performed in a jurisdiction in which the applicant is admitted and authorized to practice, or if performed in a jurisdiction that affirmatively permits such activity by a lawyer not admitted to practice in that jurisdiction; however, in no event shall any activities that were performed <u>pursuant to the Model Rule on Practice Pending Admission or</u> in advance of bar admission in some state, territory, or the District of Columbia be accepted toward the durational requirement:

(a) Representation of one or more clients in the practice of law;

(b) Service as a lawyer with a local, state, territorial or federal agency, including military service;

(c) Teaching law at a law school approved by the Council of the Section of Legal Education and Admissions to the Bar of the American Bar Association;

(d) Service as a judge in a federal, state, territorial or local court of record;

(e) Service as a judicial law clerk; or

(f) Service as provided to the lawyer's employer or its organizational affiliates.

3. For the purposes of this ~~r~~Rule, the active practice of law shall not include work that, as undertaken, constituted the unauthorized practice of law in the jurisdiction in which it was performed or in the jurisdiction in which the clients receiving the unauthorized services were located.

4. An applicant who has failed a bar examination administered in this jurisdiction within five years of the date of filing an application under this ~~r~~Rule shall not be eligible for admission on motion.

The resolution accompanying the 2012 amendments "urges jurisdictions that have not adopted the Model Rule on Admission by Motion to do so, and urges jurisdictions that have adopted admission by motion procedures to eliminate any restrictions that do not appear in the Model Rule on Admission by Motion." The Model Rule (as amended in 2012) and the proposed resolution and report that led to the 2012 amendments are available online at *http://www.abanow.org/2012/06/2012am105e/*.

ABA Model Rule on Practice Pending Admission: At its August 2012 Annual Meeting, on the recommendation of the ABA Commission on Ethics 20/20, the ABA adopted a Model Rule on Practice Pending Admission. The rule provides, in part, as follows:

ABA Model Rule on Practice Pending Admission

A lawyer currently holding an active license to practice law in another U.S. jurisdiction and who has been engaged in the active practice of law for three of the last five years, may provide legal services in this jurisdiction through an office or other systematic and continuous presence for no more than [365] days, provided that the lawyer:

a. is not disbarred or suspended from practice in any jurisdiction and is not currently subject to discipline or a pending disciplinary matter in any jurisdiction;

b. has not previously been denied admission to practice in this jurisdiction or failed this jurisdiction's bar examination;

c. notifies Disciplinary Counsel and the Admissions Authority in writing prior to initiating practice in this jurisdiction that the lawyer will be doing so pursuant to the authority in this Rule;

d. submits within [45] days of first establishing an office or other systematic and continuous presence for the practice of law in this jurisdiction a complete application for admission by motion or by examination;

e. reasonably expects to fulfill all of this jurisdiction's requirements for that form of admission;

f. associates with a lawyer who is admitted to practice in this jurisdiction;

g. complies with Rules 7.1 and 7.5 of the Model Rules of Professional Conduct [or jurisdictional equivalent] in all communications with the public and clients regarding the nature and scope of the lawyer's practice authority in this jurisdiction; and

h. pays any annual client protection fund assessment.

3. Prior to admission by motion, through examination, or as a foreign legal consultant, the lawyer may not appear before a tribunal in this jurisdiction that requires pro hac vice admission unless the lawyer is granted such admission.

4. The lawyer must immediately notify Disciplinary Counsel and the Admissions Authority in this jurisdiction if the lawyer becomes subject to a disciplinary matter or disciplinary sanctions in any other jurisdiction at any time during the [365] days of practice authorized by this Rule. The Admissions Authority shall take into account such information in determining whether to grant the lawyer's application for admission to this jurisdiction. ...

8. The Court, in its discretion, may extend the time limits set forth in this Rule for good cause shown.

The Comment to the Model Rule on Practice Pending Admission says, in part:

[1] This Rule recognizes that a lawyer admitted in another jurisdiction may need to relocate to or commence practice in this jurisdiction, sometimes on short notice. The admissions process can take considerable time, thus placing a lawyer at risk of engaging in the unauthorized practice of law and leaving the lawyer's clients without the benefit of their chosen counsel. This Rule closes this gap by authorizing the lawyer to practice in this jurisdiction for a limited period of time, up to 365 days, subject to restrictions, while the lawyer diligently seeks admission. The practice authority provided pursuant to this Rule commences immediately upon the lawyer's establishment of an office or other systematic and continuous presence for the practice of law.

The full text of the Model Rule on Practice Pending Admission and the report submitted in support of the rule are available online at *http://www.abanow. org/2012/06/2012am105d/*. The report also recommended amendments to Rule 5.5 and its Comment, which the House of Delegates approved. Those changes, which affected Rule 5.5(d), are shown in legislative style in the text of and Comment to Rule 5.5 above.

ABA Model Rule on Pro Hac Vice Admission: Litigators who are not licensed to practice permanently in a certain jurisdiction may nevertheless seek admission "pro hac vice" (meaning "for this turn") to allow them to participate in a particular case in that jurisdiction. In 2002, to foster greater national uniformity, the ABA adopted a lengthy and detailed Model Rule on Pro Hac Vice Admission. The Model Rule on Pro Hac Vice Admission can be found at *www.americanbar.org/content/dam/aba/ migrated/cpr/mjp/rule_prohac.authcheckdam.pdf.* For more information, see the entry below entitled "Pro Hac Vice Admission" in these Related Materials. In May 2011, the Ethics 20/20 Commission issued for public comment a draft proposal to add foreign (*i.e.*, non-U.S.) lawyers to the ABA Model Rule for Pro Hac Vice Admission, subject to specific limitations. The Commission may present that proposal (or a revised version of it) to the ABA House of Delegates in 2013.

ABA Model Rule on Registration of In-House Counsel: In 2008, the ABA House of Delegates overwhelmingly approved, by voice vote, a Model Rule on Registration of In-House Counsel. The Model Rule provides, in part, as follows:

GENERAL PROVISIONS:

A. A lawyer admitted to the practice of law in another United States jurisdiction who has a continuous presence in this jurisdiction and is employed as a lawyer by an organization as permitted pursuant to Rule 5.5(d)(1) of the Model Rules of Professional Conduct, the business of which is lawful and consists of activities other than the practice of law or the provision of legal services, shall register as in-house counsel within [180] days of the commencement of employment as a lawyer or if currently so employed then within [180] days of the effective date of this rule ...

SCOPE OF AUTHORITY OF REGISTERED LAWYER:

B. A lawyer registered under this section shall have the rights and privileges otherwise applicable to members of the bar of this jurisdiction with the following restrictions:
1. The registered lawyer is authorized to provide legal services to the entity client or its organizational affiliates ...

PRO BONO PRACTICE:

C. [A] lawyer registered under this section is authorized to provide pro bono legal services through an established not-for-profit bar association, pro bono program or legal services program or through such organization(s) specifically authorized in this jurisdiction.

OBLIGATIONS:

D. A lawyer registered under this section shall:
1. Pay an annual fee in the amount of $_____;
2. Fulfill the continuing legal education requirements that are required of active members of the bar in this jurisdiction;
3. Report within [_____] days to the jurisdiction the following:
   a. Termination of the lawyer's employment as described in paragraph A.4.;
   b. Whether or not public, any change in the lawyer's license status in another jurisdiction, including by the lawyer's resignation;
   c. Whether or not public, any disciplinary charge, finding, or sanction concerning the lawyer by any disciplinary authority, court, or other tribunal in any jurisdiction.

LOCAL DISCIPLINE:

E. A registered lawyer under this section shall be subject to the [jurisdiction's Rules of Professional Conduct] and all other laws and rules governing lawyers admitted to the active practice of law in this jurisdiction. The [jurisdiction's disciplinary counsel] has and shall retain jurisdiction over the registered lawyer with respect to the conduct of the lawyer in this or another jurisdiction to the same extent as it has over lawyers generally admitted in this jurisdiction.

AUTOMATIC TERMINATION:

F. A registered lawyer's rights and privileges under this section automatically terminate when:
    1. The lawyer's employment terminates;
    2. The lawyer is suspended or disbarred from practice in any jurisdiction or any court or agency before which the lawyer is admitted; or
    3. The lawyer fails to maintain active status in at least one jurisdiction. . . .

SANCTIONS:

H. A lawyer under this rule who fails to register shall be:
    1. Subject to professional discipline in this jurisdiction;
    2. Ineligible for admission on motion in this jurisdiction;
    3. Referred by the [registration authority] to the [jurisdiction's bar admission authority]; and
    4. Referred by the [registration authority] to the disciplinary authority of the jurisdictions of licensure.

The report submitted in 2006 in support of the Model Rule on Registration of In-House Counsel explains the connection to Rule 5.5(d) as follows:*

The Council of the Section of Legal Education and Admissions to the Bar . . . approved the Model Rule for Registration of House Counsel (Rule) for use by jurisdictions adopting or intending to adopt amended Model Rule 5.5(d) of the Model Rules of Professional Conduct. Rule 5.5(d) now excludes from the definition of unauthorized practice of law the provision of legal services by in-house counsel admitted in one jurisdiction and practicing in another jurisdiction, when the lawyer is providing legal services solely to the lawyer's employer. Rule 5.5(d) states:

A lawyer admitted in another United States jurisdiction, and not disbarred or suspended from practice in any jurisdiction, may provide legal services in this jurisdiction that:
    (1) are provided to the lawyer's employer or its organizational affiliates and are not services for which the forum requires pro hac vice admission.

Rule 5.5(d) applies to lawyers who are in-house corporate lawyers, government lawyers, and others who are employed to render legal services to the employer. The provision assumes that the in-house lawyer can establish an office or other "systematic presence" in the jurisdiction and forgo local licensure without unreasonable risk to the client or others because the employer is able to assess the lawyer's qualifications and the quality of the lawyer's work.

* Committee Reports do not represent official policy of the ABA. They are for information only, and the opinions are those of the authors of the report.

Model Rule 5.5, Comment [17], states that lawyers who establish an office or continuous presence in the state "may be subject to registration or other requirements, including assessments for client protection funds and mandatory continuing legal education." In an effort to create a regulatory model useful to states that might wish to follow the registration approach, the Bar Admission Committee drafted, and the Council of the Section has approved for submission to the House, this Rule.

The Model Rule for Registration of In-House Counsel is available online at *http://www.americanbar.org/content/dam/aba/migrated/cpr/mjp/in_house_registration.auth-checkdam.pdf*. A chart describing each state's in-house counsel regulations is available at *http://www.americanbar.org/content/dam/aba/migrated/cpr/mjp/in_house_comp.auth-checkdam.pdf*. In May 2011, the Ethics 20/20 Commission issued for public comment a draft proposal to add foreign (*i.e.,* non-U.S.) lawyers to the ABA Model Rule for Registration of In-House Counsel, subject to specific limitations. The Commission may present that proposal (or a revised version of it) to the ABA House of Delegates in 2013.

ABA Model Rule for Temporary Practice by Foreign Lawyers: In 2002, the ABA adopted a Model Rule for Temporary Practice by Foreign Lawyers, which was part of the package proposed by the ABA Commission on Multijurisdictional Practice. As of our press deadline in September 2012, six U.S. jurisdictions (Delaware, Florida, Georgia, New Hampshire, Pennsylvania, and Virginia) had adopted a rule explicitly referring to foreign lawyer temporary practice, and three other jurisdictions (D.C. Illinois, and North Carolina) appeared to permit foreign lawyer temporary practice through other rules. The Model Rule for Temporary Practice by Foreign Lawyers provides as follows:

(a) A lawyer who is admitted only in a non-United States jurisdiction shall not, except as authorized by this Rule or other law, establish an office or other systematic and continuous presence in this jurisdiction for the practice of law, or hold out to the public or otherwise represent that the lawyer is admitted to practice law in this jurisdiction. Such a lawyer does not engage in the unauthorized practice of law in this jurisdiction when on a temporary basis the lawyer performs services in this jurisdiction that:

(1) are undertaken in association with a lawyer who is admitted to practice in this jurisdiction and who actively participates in the matter;

(2) are in or reasonably related to a pending or potential proceeding before a tribunal held or to be held in a jurisdiction outside the United States if the lawyer, or a person the lawyer is assisting, is authorized by law or by order of the tribunal to appear in such proceeding or reasonably expects to be so authorized;

(3) are in or reasonably related to a pending or potential arbitration, mediation or other alternative dispute resolution proceeding held or to be held in this or another jurisdiction, if the services arise out of or are reasonably related to the lawyer's practice in a jurisdiction in which the lawyer is admitted to practice;

(4) are not within paragraphs (2) or (3) and

(i) are performed for a client who resides or has an office in a jurisdiction in which the lawyer is authorized to practice to the extent of that authorization; or

(ii) arise out of or are reasonably related to a matter that has a substantial connection to a jurisdiction in which the lawyer is authorized to practice to the extent of that authorization; or

(5) are governed primarily by international law or the law of a non-United States jurisdiction.

(b) For purposes of this grant of authority, the lawyer must be a member in good standing of a recognized legal profession in a foreign jurisdiction, the members of which are admitted to practice as lawyers or counselors at law or the equivalent and subject to effective regulation and discipline by a duly constituted professional body or a public authority.

The ABA Model Rule for Temporary Practice by Foreign Lawyers and the report explaining the rule and recommending its adoption are available online at *http://www.americanbar.org/content/dam/aba/administrative/ethics_2020/20110919_ ethics_20_20_foreign_lawyers_and_model_rule_5_5_resolution_report.authcheckdam.pdf.*

ABA Model Rules for Advisory Opinions on Unauthorized Practice of Law: In 1984, the ABA House of Delegates adopted Model Rules for Advisory Opinions on Unauthorized Practice of Law, which set forth model procedures for committees and courts to follow in issuing opinions on unauthorized practice. These rules, according to their Preamble, recognize "the need to prevent harm to the public from the unauthorized practice of law and to make public a clear and timely understanding of what is the unauthorized practice of law." The Model Rules for Advisory Opinions on Unauthorized Practice of Law are available at *http://www.americanbar. org/content/dam/aba/migrated/cpr/clientpro/upl_op_rules.authcheckdam.pdf.*

ABA Resolution on Unauthorized Practice: In 1999, by a vote of 305-118, the ABA House of Delegates passed a resolution urging every jurisdiction to "establish and implement effective procedures for the discovery and investigation of any apparent violation of its laws prohibiting the unauthorized practice of law and to pursue active enforcement of those laws." The resolution also required the ABA to "establish and support a mechanism for identifying and reporting to state, local, and territorial bar associations and designated authorities instances of persons or organizations engaging in the unauthorized practice of law in more than one jurisdiction." The report submitted in support of the resolution noted that statutes prohibiting the unauthorized practice of law (which are in force in virtually every state) have not been enforced aggressively or effectively. The report added: "It is becoming more apparent that unlicensed and unsupervised persons are peddling legal services to the public and that adequate protection to the public is not being provided."

ABA Task Force on the Model Definition of the Practice of Law: In August 2002, the ABA House of Delegates created a seven-member Task Force on the Model Definition of the Practice of Law. The Task Force worked with the ABA Standing Committee on Client Protection to develop a model definition of the practice of law. In September 2002, the task force sought public comments on the following preliminary draft definition:

Definition of the Practice of Law

(a) The practice of law shall be performed only by those authorized by the highest court of this jurisdiction.

(b) Definitions:

(1) The "practice of law" is the application of legal principles and judgment with regard to the circumstances or objectives of a person that require the knowledge and skill of a person trained in the law.

(2) "Person" includes the plural as well as the singular and denotes an individual or any legal or commercial entity.

(3) "Adjudicative body" includes a court, a mediator, an arbitrator or a legislative body, administrative agency or other body acting in an adjudicative capacity.

A legislative body, administrative agency or other body acts in an adjudicative capacity when a neutral official, after the presentation of evidence or legal argument by a party or parties, will render a binding legal judgment directly affecting a party's interests in a particular matter.

(c) A person is presumed to be practicing law when engaging in any of the following conduct on behalf of another:

(1) Giving advice or counsel to persons as to their legal rights or responsibilities or to those of others;

(2) Selecting, drafting, or completing legal documents or agreements that affect the legal rights of a person;

(3) Representing a person before an adjudicative body, including, but not limited to, preparing or filing documents or conducting discovery; or

(4) Negotiating legal rights or responsibilities on behalf of a person.

(d) Exceptions and exclusions: Whether or not they constitute the practice of law, the following are permitted:

(1) Practicing law authorized by a limited license to practice;

(2) Pro se representation;

(3) Serving as a mediator, arbitrator, conciliator or facilitator; and

(4) Providing services under the supervision of a lawyer in compliance with the Rules of Professional Conduct.

(e) Any person engaged in the practice of law shall be held to the same standard of care and duty of loyalty to the client independent of whether the person is authorized to practice law in this jurisdiction. With regard to the exceptions and exclusions listed in paragraph (d), if the person providing the services is a nonlawyer, the person shall disclose that fact in writing. In the case of an entity engaged in the practice of law, the liability of the entity is unlimited and the liability of its constituent members is limited to those persons participating in such conduct and those persons who had knowledge of the conduct and failed to take remedial action immediately upon discovery of same.

(f) If a person who is not authorized to practice law is engaged in the practice of law, that person shall be subject to the civil and criminal penalties of this jurisdiction.

The Task Force received many comments on the proposed definition. Of particular interest was a letter dated December 20, 2002, jointly sent by the Federal Trade Commission (FTC) and the U.S. Department of Justice's Antitrust Division. The joint letter harshly criticized the draft proposal, saying it was so broad that it could prevent nonlawyers from offering many services they already offer, leading to higher prices for legal services and fewer choices for consumers. For example, the joint letter said, the proposed definition could be interpreted to prohibit real estate agents from explaining smoke detector ordinances and termite inspection laws, to prohibit tax preparers from interpreting tax code provisions, and to prohibit software makers from selling software to write wills and other legal documents.

In April 2003, after holding a hearing on the proposed definition, the Task Force decided not to attempt a single uniform nationwide definition of the practice of law, but instead recommended that every jurisdiction adopt its own definition of the practice of law. The ABA acted on this recommendation by adopting the following resolution in August 2003:

> RESOLVED, That the American Bar Association recommends that every state and territory adopt a definition of the practice of law.
>
> FURTHER RESOLVED, That each state's and territory's definition should include the basic premise that the practice of law is the application of legal principles and judgment to the circumstances or objectives of another person or entity.

FURTHER RESOLVED, That each state and territory should determine who may provide services that are included within the state's or territory's definition of the practice of law and under what circumstances, based upon the potential harm and benefit to the public. The determination should include consideration of minimum qualifications, competence and accountability.

Admission to the Bar by Motion: Nearly every U.S. jurisdiction allows some form of admission to the bar "by motion" or "on motion," meaning admission without taking and passing the state's bar examination. However, a majority of jurisdictions allow admission by motion only to lawyers admitted in states that would allow reciprocal rights of admission on motion to lawyers admitted in the first jurisdiction. Oregon Attorney Admission Rule 15.05, entitled "Admission of Attorneys Licensed to Practice Law in Other Jurisdictions," is a good example of admission by motion restricted to applicants from states that grant reciprocity. As amended effective January 1, 2010, that rule provides as follows:

(1) Attorneys who have taken and passed the bar examination in another qualifying jurisdiction, who are active members of the bar in that qualifying jurisdiction, and who have lawfully engaged in the active, substantial and continuous practice of law for no less than five of the seven years immediately preceding their application for admission under this rule may be admitted to the practice of law in Oregon without having to take and pass the Oregon bar examination, subject to the requirements of this rule.

(2) For purposes of this rule, a "qualifying jurisdiction" means any other United States jurisdiction which allows attorneys licensed in Oregon to become regular members of the bar in that jurisdiction without passage of that jurisdiction's bar examination. . . .

Admission by motion rules typically require applicants to demonstrate good moral character, pay substantial fees, and meet various other requirements. For a chart summarizing the rules and policies for admission on motion in every U.S. jurisdiction and comparing them to the ABA Model Rule for Admission on Motion (reprinted above), visit *http://www.americanbar.org/content/dam/aba/migrated/cpr/ mjp/admission_motion_comp.authcheckdam.pdf.*

European Community Law on Multijurisdictional Practice: The member states of the European Community (EC) are much more permissive of cross-border practice than are American jurisdictions, even though the members of the EC are different nations, not just different states within a single nation. The EC's approach to multijurisdictional practice is explained in depth in an online interview with Professor Laurel Terry of Penn State Dickinson School of Law, which we reprinted in the Special Section of our 2002 edition (see pp. 1052-1056). For more background information about the EC, see Laurel S. Terry, *A Case Study of the Hybrid Model for Facilitating Cross-Border Legal Practice: The Agreement Between the American Bar Association and the Brussels Bars,* 21 Fordham Intl. L.J. 1382 (1998); Florence R. Liu, *The Establishment of a Cross-Border Legal Practice in the European Union,* 20 B.C. Intl. & Comp. L. Rev. 369 (1997); and Diane M. Venezia, *EU Lawyer's Right to Practice Throughout the European Union,* 3 Cardozo J. Intl. & Comp. L. 427 (1995).

Foreign Countries and U.S. Lawyers: As would be expected, foreign countries have widely varying policies regarding the activities of U.S. lawyers. For example, the Bombay High Court in India ruled in December of 2009, in *Lawyers Collective v. Bar Council of India,* that "practising non-litigious matters amounts to 'practising the profession of law' under section 29 of the Advocates Act, 1961," which is India's unauthorized practice of law statute. More recently, the India Supreme Court issued an interim order in *Bar Council of India v. Balaji,* No. 17150-17154/2012 (July 4, 2012), declaring that foreign-licensed lawyers are permitted to "fly in and fly out" of India to advise clients on foreign or international law on a case-to-case basis, but may not open liaison offices in India or practice litigation or nonlitigation law without becoming members of the Indian bar. The effect of these rulings is to prohibit all U.S. lawyers (and other foreign lawyers) from practicing law in India except in narrow circumstances. In Israel, however, U.S. lawyers are permitted to establish an office to advise Israeli clients about U.S. law (but not Israeli law). For materials summarizing the policies of various countries regarding law practice by U.S. lawyers, visit *www.personal.psu.edu/faculty/l/s/lst3/publications%20by%20topic.htm#1.*

Foreign-Educated Bar Applicants: Lawyers who received their legal education outside the United States are sometimes eligible to take the bar exam without attending law school in the United States. The rules on the eligibility of foreign-educated lawyers to sit for the bar exam vary from state to state. From 2000 through 2005, the number of foreign-educated lawyers sitting for a bar exam somewhere in the United States increased by 28 percent, to 3,571. In 2005, all but 234 of the foreign-educated lawyers who took a U.S. bar exam sat for the bar exam in New York, which has relatively liberal policies on eligibility to take the bar exam. In contrast, no foreign-educated lawyer took the bar exam in 2005 in Florida, which requires foreign-educated lawyers to have 10 years of experience in a U.S. jurisdiction before taking Florida's bar exam.

General Agreement on Trade in Services (GATS): In 1993, the so-called Uruguay Round of international trade negotiations produced a revised multilateral trade system based upon the 1994 document known as the Agreement Establishing the World Trade Organization (WTO). The General Agreement on Trade in Services, referred to as "GATS," is an "Annex" to the Agreement Establishing the World Trade Organization and is thus binding on countries that belong to the WTO, including the United States. The GATS is the first multilateral trade agreement that applies to services, including legal services.

The current round of GATS negotiations is commonly called the "Doha Round." WTO member countries are negotiating more liberal access to the service markets covered by the GATS. The Office of the United States Trade Representative (USTR), a Cabinet-level position, conducts the GATS negotiations on behalf of all service sectors in the United States, including legal services. The USTR is seeking to make it easier for U.S. lawyers to practice law in foreign countries. But any agreement regarding the ability of American lawyers to offer legal services abroad will also make it easier for foreign (non-U.S.) lawyers to offer legal services in the United States. The GATS agreements could also affect American legal education standards, bar admissions criteria, licensing requirements, rules of professional conduct, disciplinary enforcement rules, and other regulations of the legal profession that have historically been adopted and enforced in the United States by states in U.S. jurisdictions.

In December 2005, WTO members agreed that they would try to conclude the GATS negotiations by the end of 2006. That did not happen, however, and when we went to press in September 2012 the Doha Round was stalled and perhaps near collapse. On July 26, 2011, WTO members acknowledged that a package of issues selected from the Doha Round agenda for the December 2011 Ministerial

Conference "is not taking shape." The members accepted Director-General Pascal Lamy's call to focus on how to proceed afterwards in order to end the "paralysis" in the organization's ability to negotiate. The negotiations continue, however, and in July 2012 Director-General Lamy told WTO members in the General Council that they should "change gears" after the summer break and engage seriously to produce results. For a wealth of material on GATS and its potential impact on the U.S. legal profession, see the website about GATS maintained by Professor Laurel Terry of Penn State Dickinson School of Law at *www.personal.psu.edu/faculty/l/s/lst3/gats3.htm.*

In-House Lawyers: A lawyer who regularly practices law in a jurisdiction in which the lawyer is not licensed to practice is generally engaged in the unauthorized practice of law. However, the majority of U.S. jurisdictions have statutes or court rules that permit an in-house lawyer who is licensed and in good standing in at least one U.S. jurisdiction to provide legal services to an employer (such as a corporation) even though the lawyer is not licensed to practice law in the jurisdiction where the services are performed, provided the in-house lawyer registers with the appropriate authority in that jurisdiction. ABA Model Rule 5.5(d)(1) reflects this policy. Some states have issued court decisions, policy statements, or ethics opinions stating that in-house lawyers who serve only their employer are not engaged in unauthorized practice despite lack of admission to the bar in the state where the services are performed.

In 2008, the ABA responded to the proliferation of state in-house registration rules by approving the ABA Model Rule on Registration of In-House Counsel (see entry above in this section), and the ABA Commission on Ethics 20/20 may recommend amendments to the in-house registration rule in 2013. A chart describing each state's rules and regulations regarding the practice of law by in-house lawyers is available at *http://www.americanbar.org/content/dam/aba/migrated/cpr/mjp/in_house_comp.authcheckdam.pdf.*

IRS Regulations: In the regulations governing practice before the Internal Revenue Service, 31 C.F.R. §10.3(c) is in essence the opposite of an unauthorized practice law statute — it expressly authorizes certain categories of nonlawyers to appear before the IRS as "enrolled agents" on the same terms (or nearly the same terms) as attorneys. According to §10.4(a), the IRS may grant "enrolled agent" status to an applicant "who demonstrates special competence in tax matters by written examination . . . and who has not engaged in any conduct that would justify the censure, suspension, or disbarment. . . ." Under §10.4(d), former IRS employees may become enrolled agents without examination. However, §10.24(a) provides that a practitioner may not knowingly, directly or indirectly, "[a]ccept assistance from or assist any person who is under disbarment or suspension from practice before the Internal Revenue Service if the assistance relates to a matter or matters constituting practice before the Internal Revenue Service." Moreover, §10.32 provides that "[n]othing in the regulations in this part shall be construed as authorizing persons not members of the bar to practice law."

Limited Practice Rules for Nonlawyers: For many years, various people have suggested that the supply of legal services to the poor and middle class could be increased by granting nonlawyers limited rights to provide legal assistance. Effective September 1, 2012, a divided Washington Supreme Court approved a new rule, Admission to Practice Rule 28 (Limited Practice Rule for Limited License Legal Technicians), that made Washington State the first U.S. jurisdiction to create a category of nonlawyers who are allowed to provide certain types of legal services in civil matters without the supervision of a lawyer. But the rule does not allow legal technicians to represent clients in court or to negotiate with opposing parties. The rule is posted online at *http://www.courts.wa.gov/content/publicUpload/Press%20 Releases/25700-A-1005.pdf.*

Model Rules of Professional Conduct for Federal Lawyers: Rule 5.5(a) provides that "[e]xcept as authorized by law," a federal lawyer shall not practice in a jurisdiction where doing so violates the regulation of the legal profession in that jurisdiction.

National Association of Legal Assistants: The National Association of Legal Assistants, an organization comprised of more than 18,000 paralegals, publishes the NALA Code of Ethics and Professional Responsibility. Canon 3 of the NALA Code, which complements Rule 5.5(a) of the ABA Model Rules of Professional Conduct, provides:

> A legal assistant must not: (a) engage in, encourage, or contribute to any act which could constitute the unauthorized practice of law; and (b) establish attorney-client relationships, set fees, give legal opinions or advice or represent a client before a court or agency unless so authorized by that court or agency; and (c) engage in conduct or take any action which would assist or involve the attorney in a violation of professional ethics or give the appearance of professional impropriety.

NALA also publishes the NALA Model Standards and Guidelines for Utilization of Paralegals, which is more detailed than the NALA Code of Ethics. Guideline 3 provides that legal assistants may "perform services for an attorney in the representation of a client" if the following conditions are met:

> 1. The services performed by the legal assistant do not require the exercise of independent professional legal judgment;
> 2. The attorney maintains a direct relationship with the client and maintains control of all client matters;
> 3. The attorney supervises the legal assistant;
> 4. The attorney remains professionally responsible for all work on behalf of the client, including any actions taken or not taken by the legal assistant in connection therewith; and
> 5. The services performed supplement, merge with and become the attorney's work product.

Guideline 5 generally permits a legal assistant to perform "any function delegated by an attorney, including but not limited to the following":

> 1. Conduct client interviews and maintain general contact with the client after the establishment of the attorney-client relationship, so long as the client is aware of the status and function of the legal assistant, and the client contact is under the supervision of the attorney.
> 2. Locate and interview witnesses, so long as the witnesses are aware of the status and function of the legal assistant.
> 3. Conduct investigations and statistical and documentary research for review by the attorney.
> 4. Conduct legal research for review by the attorney.
> 5. Draft legal documents for review by the attorney.
> 6. Draft correspondence and pleadings for review by and signature of the attorney.
> 7. Summarize depositions, interrogatories, and testimony for review by the attorney.

8. Attend executions of wills, real estate closings, depositions, court or administrative hearings and trials with the attorney.

9. Author and sign letters provided the legal assistant's status is clearly indicated and the correspondence does not contain independent legal opinions or legal advice.

The Guidelines are available with Comments at *www.nala.org* (hover over "About Paralegals," then scroll down to "Model Standards and Guidelines for Utilization of Legal Assistants").

National Federation of Paralegal Associations: The National Federation of Paralegal Associations, Inc. (NFPA), founded in 1974, is a nonprofit federation comprised of more than 50 member associations representing over 11,000 individual members. The NFPA's "core purpose" is to "advance the paralegal profession." In 1993, the NFPA adopted a Model Code of Ethics and Professional Responsibility. Section 1 of the Code contains Rules and Ethical Considerations governing topics such as competence, confidentiality, and conflicts. Section 2 establishes a Disciplinary Committee and disciplinary procedures for paralegals who violate the Code. The Code is available at *www.paralegals.org* (click on the top menu on "Positions & Issues," then on the drop-down menu click on either "Model Code of Ethics" or "Ethics").

Patent "Agents" and Patent "Attorneys": The United States Patent and Trademark Office (USPTO) registers both people who are attorneys at law (referred to as "patent attorneys") and people who are not attorneys at law (referred to as "patent agents") to practice before the USPTO. Under USPTO rules, both patent attorneys and patent agents may prepare patent applications and prosecute patents in the USPTO. Patent agents, however, cannot conduct patent litigation in the courts or perform services that a state considers to be the practice of law (other than preparing patent applications and prosecuting patents). For example, a patent agent could not draw up a contract relating to a patent, such as an assignment or a license, if the state in which the patent agent resides considers drafting contracts to be the practice of law. For more information, see *www.uspto.gov.*

Pro Hac Vice Admission: In all states, courts have authority to admit out-of-state lawyers to practice before the court "pro hac vice," meaning for a particular matter ("for this turn"). Most states allow pro hac vice admission only to lawyers from other U.S. jurisdictions, but at least 13 states also extend pro hac vice admission to foreign (non-U.S.) lawyers. An example of a pro hac vice admission provision is Michigan Court Rule 8.126 (Temporary Admission to the Bar). As amended in 2011, Rule 8.126 begins as follows:

(A) *Temporary Admission.* Any person who is licensed to practice law in another state . . . *or in any foreign country,* and who is not disbarred or suspended in any jurisdiction, and who is eligible to practice in at least one jurisdiction, may be permitted to appear and practice in a specific case in a court, before an administrative tribunal or agency, or in a specific arbitration proceeding in this state when associated with and on motion of an active member of the State Bar of Michigan who appears of record in the case. An out-of-state attorney may appear and practice under this rule in no more than five cases in a 365-day period. Permission to appear and practice is within the discretion of the court or administrative tribunal or agency, and may be revoked at any time for misconduct. Permission to appear and practice is within the discretion of the court, or administrative tribunal or agency, or arbitrator and may be revoked at any time for misconduct. For purposes of this rule, an out-of-state attorney is one who is licensed to practice law in another state or territory, or in the District of Columbia, of the United

States of America, *or in a foreign country* and who is not a member of the State Bar of Michigan. . . . [Emphasis added.]

A more detailed and complex pro hac vice rule is District of Columbia Rule 49(c)(7)(ii). In addition to prohibiting a lawyer from applying for admission pro hac vice in more than five cases pending in D.C. courts per calendar year absent "exceptional cause," the D.C. rule requires each applicant for admission pro hac vice to file a sworn statement meeting all of the following criteria:

> . . . (3) certifying that there are no disciplinary complaints pending against the applicant for violation of the rules of any jurisdiction or court, or describing all pending complaints, (4) certifying that the applicant has not been suspended or disbarred for disciplinary reasons or resigned with charges pending in any jurisdiction or court, or describing the circumstances of all suspensions, disbarments, or resignations, (5) certifying that the person has not had an application for admission to the D.C. Bar denied, or describing the circumstances of all such denials, (6) agreeing promptly to notify the Court if, during the course of the proceeding, the person is suspended or disbarred for disciplinary reasons or resigns with charges pending in any jurisdiction or court, . . . (8) certifying that the applicant does not practice or hold out to practice law in the District of Columbia or that the applicant qualifies under an identified exception in Rule 49(c), . . . (10) explaining the reasons for the application, (11) acknowledging the power and jurisdiction of the courts of the District of Columbia over the applicant's professional conduct in or related to the proceeding, and (12) agreeing to be bound by the District of Columbia Court of Appeals Rules of Professional Conduct in the matter, if the applicant is admitted pro hac vice.

In California, Utah, and perhaps in other jurisdictions, a lawyer may also be admitted pro hac vice in arbitration proceedings—see California Code of Civil Procedure §1282.4 (effective January 1, 2013), which says: "Notwithstanding any other provision of law . . . an attorney admitted to the bar of any other state may represent the parties in . . . an arbitration proceeding in this state," provided that attorneys not admitted in California satisfy various conditions.

More than 25 states charge a fee to out-of-state attorneys who appear pro hac vice in state courts. (Federal courts do not charge any similar fee.) In Texas, for example, Government Code §82.0361 (Nonresident Attorney Fee) requires an out-of-state lawyer to pay the Texas Board of Law Examiners a $250 fee for each case in which the attorney is asking to participate pro hac vice. In Arizona, Supreme Court Rule 38(a), as amended effective January 1, 2012, requires applicants for admission pro hac vice to pay a non-refundable application fee equal to the current annual dues paid by active members of the State Bar of Arizona (currently $460). For a state-by-state chart of pro hac vice admission rules in every U.S. jurisdiction, see *http://www.americanbar.org/content/dam/aba/migrated/cpr/mjp/prohac_admin_rules.authcheckdam.pdf.*

Restatement of the Law Governing Lawyers: See Restatement §§2-4 in our chapter on the Restatement later in this volume.

Retired Attorneys: Some jurisdictions permit retired attorneys to represent pro bono clients or legal services clients under certain circumstances. For example, New Mexico Supreme Court Rule 15-301.2 (Legal Services Provider Limited Law License for Emeritus and Non-Admitted Attorneys), as amended effective January 1, 2012, permits inactive members of the State Bar of New Mexico to apply for a limited law license that will authorize them to "represent legal services clients through a qualified legal services provider. . . ."

Tax Consequences of Multijurisdictional Practice: Lawyers who take advantage of temporary practice rules similar to ABA Model Rule 5.5(b) may be required to comply with tax laws and pay income taxes based on their work in states where they are not licensed. For example, West Virginia State Tax Department Publication TSD-423 (revised August 2007), entitled "Nonresident Lawyers—Tax Reporting and Filing Requirements," advises out-of-state lawyers about many tax obligations arising out of law practice in West Virginia. To learn more, visit *http://www.state.wv.us/taxrev/publications/tsd/tsd423.pdf.*

Tax Court Rules of Practice: The Tax Court Rules of Practice (which are completely separate from IRS regulations) permit qualified nonlawyers to practice before the Tax Court. For example, Tax Court Rule 200(a)(3) allows nonlawyers to practice before the Tax Court if they pay a fee and pass a written examination (and, in the court's discretion, an oral examination as well).

Unauthorized Practice Laws: Most states have enacted statutes making it a crime to engage in the unauthorized practice of law. A typical unauthorized practice of law statute is California Business and Professions Code §6126 (Unauthorized Practice or Attempted Practice; Advertising or Holding Out; Penalties), which provides, in part, as follows:

> Any person advertising or holding himself or herself out as practicing or entitled to practice law or otherwise practicing law who is not an active member of the State Bar, or otherwise authorized pursuant to statute or court rule to practice law in this state at the time of doing so, is guilty of a misdemeanor punishable by up to one year in a county jail or by a fine of up to one thousand dollars ($1,000) or by both that fine and imprisonment. . . .

A similar but harsher statute is found in Florida, where the legislature amended Florida's unauthorized practice statute in 2004 to make the unauthorized practice of law a felony. The amended statute, F.S.A. §454.23 (Penalties), provides as follows:

> Any person not licensed or otherwise authorized to practice law in this state who practices law in this state or holds himself or herself out to the public as qualified to practice law in this state, or who willfully pretends to be, or willfully takes or uses any name, title, addition, or description implying that he or she is qualified, or recognized by law as qualified, to practice law in this state, commits a felony of the third degree. . . .

(A felony in the third degree in Florida is punishable by a term of imprisonment not exceeding five years and a fine not exceeding $5,000.)

A more detailed definition of the unauthorized practice of law is contained in Georgia Statutes Annotated §15-19-50 (Practice of Law Defined), which provides:

> The practice of law in this state is defined as: (1) Representing litigants in court and preparing pleadings and other papers incident to any action or special proceedings in any court or other judicial body; (2) Conveyancing; (3) The preparation of legal instruments of all kinds whereby a legal right is secured; (4) The rendering of opinions as to the validity or invalidity of titles to real or personal property; (5) The giving of any legal advice; and (6) Any action taken for others in any matter connected with the law.

Regarding electronic media, some have claimed that providing legal advice through computer programs, disks, and the Internet constitutes the unauthorized practice of law. In 1999, the Texas Legislature responded to these claims by enacting

Texas Government Code §81.101(c) to govern websites, CD-ROMs, and other electronic media. The statute provides:

> In this chapter, the ''practice of law'' does not include the design, creation, publication, distribution, display or sale, including publication, distribution, display, or sale by means of an Internet web site, of written materials, books, forms, computer software, or similar products if the products clearly and conspicuously state that the products are not a substitute for the advice of an attorney. . . .

For a highly detailed court rule governing unauthorized practice, see D.C. Court of Appeals Rule 49, available at *http://www.dccourts.gov/internet/appellate/unauthcommittee/main.jsf.*

In many states, the state bar has authority to enforce unauthorized practice laws. In Florida, for example, Rule 1-8.2 of the Rules Regulating the Florida Bar provides: ''The board of governors shall act as an arm of the Supreme Court of Florida for the purpose of seeking to prohibit the unlicensed practice of law by investigating, prosecuting, and reporting to this court and to appropriate authorities incidents involving the unlicensed practice of law. . . .''

Some jurisdictions issue advisory opinions as to whether a specific activity constitutes the unauthorized practice of law. For example, in 2010 the Virginia Supreme Court approved the State Bar's petition to amend Virginia's Rules of Court (Part Six, ¶10) to establish detailed procedures for lawyers to request unauthorized practice of law opinions. However, mindful of the possible antitrust implications of enforcing unauthorized practice laws, §10-2(E) of the amended rule provides that whenever a bar committee concludes that the conduct in question constitutes or would constitute the unauthorized practice of law, ''the Bar shall seek comment from the Attorney General's office analyzing any restraint on competition that might result from the promulgation and implementation of the opinion.''

Rule 5.6   Restrictions on Right to Practice

Canon and Code Antecedents

ABA Canons of Professional Ethics: No comparable Canon.
ABA Model Code of Professional Responsibility: Compare DR 2-108 (reprinted later in this volume).

Cross-References in Other Rules

Rule 1.2, Comment 8: ''All agreements concerning a lawyer's representation of a client must accord with the Rules of Professional Conduct and other law. See, e.g., **Rules** 1.1, 1.8 and **5.6**.''

Rule 1.17, Comment 1 provides that ''when a lawyer or an entire firm ceases to practice, or ceases to practice in an area of law, and other lawyers or firms take over the representation, the selling lawyer or firm may obtain compensation for the reasonable value of the practice as may withdrawing partners of law firms. See **Rules** 5.4 and **5.6**.''

Legislative History of Model Rule 5.6

1980 and 1981 Drafts had no equivalent to Rule 5.6.

1982 Draft was adopted.

1983 Rule: As originally adopted in 1983, ABA Model Rule 5.6 provided:

> A lawyer shall not participate in offering or making:
>   (a) a partnership or employment agreement that restricts the rights of a law-
> yer to practice after termination of the relationship, except an agreement concern-
> ing benefits upon retirement; or
>   (b) [Same as 2002 version of Rule 5.6(b).]

2002 Amendments: The ABA Ethics 2000 Commission recommended replacing
the phrase "controversy between private parties" with the phrase "client controversy" at the end of Rule 5.6(b), thus making clear that the Rule applies to settlements between private parties and the government, not just to settlements between
private parties. The proposal also expanded the phrase "partnership or employment agreement" in Rule 5.6(a) to include a "partnership, shareholders, operating, employment, or other similar type of agreement." In 2002, the ABA House of
Delegates adopted without change the Ethics 2000 proposal to amend Rule 5.6 and
its Comment. The changes to the Comment were minor (replacing "partners or
associates" with "lawyers" in Comment 1).

Selected State Variations

Arkansas: Rule 5.6(a) deletes references to a shareholder, operating, or other
similar type of agreement, but adds a reference to "an agreement pursuant to the
provisions of Rule 1.17" (which governs the sale of a law practice).

California: Rule 1-500 is essentially the same as Rule 5.6, but adds references to
certain statutory exceptions.

Florida: Without amending the text of Rule 5.6, Florida added the following
new paragraph to the Comment to its version of Rule 5.6:

> This rule is not a per se prohibition against severance agreements between law-
> yers and law firms. Severance agreements containing reasonable and fair compensation
> provisions designed to avoid disputes required by time-consuming quantum meruit
> analysis are not prohibited by this rule. Severance agreements, on the other hand, that
> contain punitive clauses, the effect of which are to restrict competition or encroach
> upon a client's inherent right to select counsel, are prohibited. . . .

In addition, a new Florida Rule 4-5.8 prohibits a lawyer who is leaving a law firm
from unilaterally notifying clients of the anticipated departure, or soliciting representation of the firm's clients, unless bona fide negotiations between the lawyer
and the law firm to draft a joint communication have failed. Similarly, a lawyer in
a law firm undergoing dissolution must not unilaterally contact the firm's clients
unless bona fide negotiations among authorized members of the firm have failed
to produce an agreement on a method for notifying clients of the dissolution. If
there is no agreement on notice to client, the rule provides: "When a joint response
has not been successfully negotiated, unilateral contact by individual members or
the law firm shall give notice to clients that the lawyer is leaving the law firm and

provide options to the clients to choose to remain a client of the law firm, to choose representation by the departing lawyer, or to choose representation by other lawyers or law firms.''

Georgia has adopted the pre-2002 version of ABA Model Rule 5.6 and its Comment essentially verbatim. (Georgia's previous DR 2-108(B) permitted a lawyer to agree in a settlement not to ''accept any other representation arising out of a transaction or event embraced in the subject matter of the controversy or suit thus settled.'')

New York: New York follows Model Rule 5.6 except New York adds that the rule ''does not prohibit restrictions that may be included in the terms of the sale of a law practice pursuant to Rule 1.17.''

Oregon: Rule 5.6(b) applies to a ''direct or indirect'' restriction on a lawyer's right to practice.

Pennsylvania: Rule 5.6(a) permits an agreement that restricts the rights of a lawyer to practice as part of ''an agreement for the sale of a law practice consistent with Rule 1.17.''

Texas: Rule 5.06(b) adds that ''as part of the settlement of a disciplinary proceeding against a lawyer an agreement may be made placing restrictions on the right of that lawyer to practice.''

Virginia: Rule 5.6(b) forbids an agreement in which a restriction of the lawyer's right to practice is part of the settlement of a controversy, ''except where such a restriction is approved by a tribunal or a governmental entity.''

Related Materials

ABA Formal Ethics Opinions: See ABA Formal Ethics Ops. 93-371 (1993), 94-381 (1994), 95-394 (1995), 00-417 (2000), 06-444 (2006), 07-447 n.7 (2007), and 09-455 (2009).

Arbitration Provisions: To reduce the expense of litigating disputes that often arise when partners leave their law firms, many partnership agreements contain mediation or arbitration clauses. These clauses are encouraged by legal malpractice insurers. In Pennsylvania, for example, Bertholon-Rowland Agencies has sometimes given a 5 percent ''quality of management credit'' on professional liability policies that contain the following paragraph:

> Any controversy or claim arising out of or relating to the dissolution of the partnership, or relating to a partner's withdrawal from the partnership, shall be settled through mediation conducted in accordance with the then-existing rules of the Pennsylvania Bar Association Lawyer Dispute Resolution Program (the ''PBA Program''). Any issues that are not resolved through such mediation shall be submitted for arbitration conducted in accordance with the then-existing rules of the PBA Program. . . .

Non-Compete Provisions: A non-compete clause is a restrictive covenant that bars an ex-employee from going to work for a competitor. Outside of the legal profession, non-compete clauses in employment and partnership agreements are common, and are generally valid if they are reasonable in temporal duration, geographic scope, and the nature of the restricted activities. In the legal profession, however, non-compete clauses for lawyers (whether partners, associates, or of counsel) are barred in most jurisdictions by Rule 5.6(a).

Nevertheless, some law firm partnership agreements provide greater benefits or pay greater severance payments to departing lawyers who do not compete with the firm than to those who do compete. In a variation, severance payments to departing partners may be based on a sliding scale so that partners who earn more than a specified amount after they leave (such as those who join competing law firms) will receive less than partners who earn less than the specified amount (such as partners who leave to enter government service or to take a public interest job). Such provisions have met with mixed results when challenged.

No-Sue Promises: For an argument that Rule 5.6(b) should be amended, see Stephen Gillers & Richard W. Painter, *Free the Lawyers: A Proposal to Permit No-Sue Promises in Settlement Agreements,* 18 Geo. J. Legal Ethics 291 (2005).

Restatement of the Law Governing Lawyers: See Restatement §§9 and 13 in our chapter on the Restatement later in this volume.

Rule 5.7 Responsibilities Regarding Law-Related Services

Canon and Code Antecedents

ABA Canons of Professional Ethics: No comparable Canon.
ABA Model Code of Professional Responsibility: No comparable Disciplinary Rule.

Cross-References in Other Rules

Rule 1.8, Comment 1: "The Rule applies to lawyers engaged in the sale of goods or services related to the practice of law. . . . See **Rule 5.7.**"

Legislative History of Model Rule 5.7

1980, 1981, and 1982 Drafts: None of the Kutak Commission drafts had any provision equivalent to Rule 5.7.

1983 Rule: As originally adopted in 1983, the ABA Model Rules had no provision equivalent to Rule 5.7.

1991 Adoption: Rule 5.7 was originally added to the Model Rules in 1991. The rule adopted in 1991 was proposed by the ABA's Litigation Section, which had been studying ancillary businesses for several years. Before the House of Delegates voted on the Litigation Section's proposal, it rejected by voice vote an alternative version of Rule 5.7 proposed by the ABA's Standing Committee on Ethics and Professional Responsibility. After rejecting the Standing Committee's proposal, the House of Delegates voted 197-186 to adopt the Litigation Section's version of Rule 5.7. The original version of Rule 5.7 provided as follows:

Provision of Ancillary Services

(a) A lawyer shall not practice law in a law firm which owns a controlling interest in, or operates, an entity which provides non-legal services which are ancillary to the practice of law, or otherwise provides such ancillary non-legal services, except as provided in paragraph (b).

(b) A lawyer may practice law in a law firm which provides non-legal services which are ancillary to the practice of law if:

(1) The ancillary services are provided solely to clients of the law firm and are incidental to, in connection with and concurrent to, the provision of legal services by the law firm to such clients;

(2) Such ancillary services are provided solely by employees of the law firm itself and not by a subsidiary or other affiliate of the law firm;

(3) The law firm makes appropriate disclosure in writing to its clients; and

(4) The law firm does not hold itself out as engaging in any non-legal activities except in conjunction with the provision of legal services, as provided in this rule.

(c) One or more lawyers who engage in the practice of law in a law firm shall neither own a controlling interest in, nor operate, an entity which provides non-legal services which are ancillary to the practice of law, nor otherwise provide such ancillary non-legal services, except that their firms may provide such services as provided in paragraph (b).

(d) Two or more lawyers who engage in the practice of law in separate law firms shall neither own a controlling interest in, nor operate, an entity which provides non-legal services which are ancillary to the practice of law, nor otherwise provide such ancillary non-legal services.

The Comment to the 1991 version of Rule 5.7 was nineteen paragraphs, making it one of the longest comments in the Model Rules. The following excerpt from the original Comment explains the origin and purpose of the 1991 version of Rule 5.7:

Excerpt from Comment to 1991 Version of Rule 5.7

[1] For many years, lawyers have provided to their clients non-legal services which are ancillary to the practice of law. Such services included title insurance, trust services and patent consulting. In most instances, these ancillary non-legal services were provided to law firm clients in connection with, and concurrent to, the provision of legal services by the lawyer or law firm. The provision of such services afforded benefits to clients, including making available a greater range of services from one source and maintaining technical expertise in various fields within a law firm. However, the provision of both legal and ancillary non-legal services raises ethical concerns, including conflicts of interest, confusion on the part of clients and possible loss (or inapplicability) of the attorney-client privilege, which may not have been addressed adequately by the other Model Rules of Professional Conduct.

[2] Eventually, law firms began to form affiliates, largely staffed by non-lawyers, to provide ancillary non-legal services to both clients and customers who were not clients for legal services. In addition to exacerbating the ethical problems of conflicts of interest, confusion and threats to confidentiality, the large-scale movement of law firms into ancillary non-legal businesses raised serious professionalism concerns, including compromising lawyers' independent judgment, the loss of the bar's right to self-regulation and the provision of legal services by entities controlled by non-lawyers.

[3] Rule 5.7 addresses both the ethical and professionalism concerns implicated by the provision of ancillary non-legal services by lawyers and law firms. It preserves the ability of lawyers to provide additional services to their clients and maintain within the law firm a broad range of technical expertise. However, Rule 5.7 restricts the ability of law firms to provide ancillary non-legal services through affiliates to non-client customers and clients alike, the rendition of which raises serious ethical and professionalism concerns.

1992 Deletion: The 1991 version of Rule 5.7 was deleted from the ABA Model Rules in its entirety at the ABA's 1992 Annual Meeting, just one year after its adoption. The report urging deletion of the rule was jointly submitted by the Illinois State Bar Association, the ABA Standing Committee on Lawyers Title Guaranty Funds, and six ABA sections. The House of Delegates voted 190-183 to delete the rule. Rule 5.7 was the first rule ever to be deleted from the Model Rules. From August 1992 (when the original version of Rule 5.7 was deleted) until February 1994 (when a new version was adopted), the Model Rules did not contain any version of Rule 5.7.

1994 Version: In 1994, by a margin of 237-183, the ABA House of Delegates adopted a new and radically different version of Rule 5.7. The new version was the work of a Special Committee on Ancillary Business Services that was appointed by the Chair of the House of Delegates after the ABA voted in 1992 to delete the original version of Rule 5.7. The Special Committee recommended that the ABA adopt the 1994 version of Rule 5.7. The House of Delegates did so, and the 1994 version stayed in effect until 2002. Here are excerpts from the Special Committee's Report in support of the 1994 version of Rule 5.7:

Excerpt from Report of the Special House of Delegates Committee on Ancillary Business in Support of the 1994 Version of Rule 5.7*

[T]he Committee is satisfied that law-related services are being provided wherever lawyers practice, that law-related services are often provided by separate entities, and that there has been no reported disciplinary infraction or malpractice claim resulting from the provision of law-related services. . . . Several respondents expressed concern about potential confusion on the part of recipients of law-related services regarding the nature of their relationship with the lawyer, although no instances of actual confusion were reported to the Committee. Responses also indicated a profusion of law-related services, some traditional in the jurisdiction, and others of more recent origin. These include not only the provision of trust services, title insurance, accounting and escrow services, but also the furnishing of insurance investigation, psychological counseling, lobbying, arbitration and mediation, registered corporate agent representation, and environmental consulting services. The Committee believes that the list of law-related services is not only long, but growing longer.

The Committee concluded that law-related services should not be prohibited. Instead, the Committee proposes adoption of a rule that specifically treats lawyers' dealings with recipients of law-related services. The proposed rule supplements existing Rules that apply to such relationships. . . .

Examples of law-related services are provided in the Comment to the proposed Rule, but these are by no means exhaustive. The Committee found that the types of law-related services are virtually unlimited, and that new types continue to be developed. Accordingly, the definition is intended to encompass a wide range of services whether or not the services are of a type currently being provided. . . .

Even when the recipient of law-related services is not a client of the lawyer, the law of principal and agent affords the recipient significant protections against disclosure or use of confidence, conflicts of interest, and self-dealing. The Committee notes, in this context, that it found no justification for affording recipients of law-related services through separate entities greater protection than that to which they would otherwise be entitled solely because lawyers control the separate entity.

---

* Committee Reports do not represent official policy of the ABA. They are for information only, and the opinions are those of the author of the report.

2002 Amendments: In its May 2001 report to the ABA House of Delegates, the ABA Ethics 2000 Commission proposed to amend the Comment, but not the text, of Rule 5.7. Before the House of Delegates acted on the proposal, however, the Commission revised its proposal to broaden the text of Rule 5.7(a)(2) so that it would apply to law-related services provided directly by a lawyer or the lawyer's law firm. In 2002, the ABA House of Delegates adopted without change a revised ABA Ethics 2000 Commission proposal to amend Rule 5.7 and its Comment. The amendments deleted references to a "separate" entity in the 1994 version of Rule 5.7(a)(2), inserted the phrase "and whether the law-related services are performed through a law firm or a separate entity" in Comment 2, and added the second sentence of Comment 3.

Selected State Variations

Arkansas retains the 1994 version of Rule 5.7(a)(2), which applies if law-related services are provided by a "separate" entity controlled by the lawyer and if the lawyer fails to take reasonable measures to assure that a person obtaining the law-related services knows that the services "of the separate entity" are not legal services.

California has no equivalent provision in its Rules of Professional Conduct.

Connecticut omits Rule 5.7.

Georgia adopts the pre-2002 version of ABA Model Rule 5.7 and its Comment essentially verbatim.

Illinois omits Rule 5.7.

New York: New York incorporates the substance of Model Rule 5.7 in a longer version of the rule that, among other things, gives lawyers a duty to ensure that non-lawyers at an affiliated entity who are providing nonlegal services do not give legal advice or compromise client confidential information. The New York rule also creates a presumption when nonlegal services are "distinct" from legal services provided by the law firm, or when a separate entity affiliated with the law firm is providing nonlegal services. Under Rule 5.7(a)(4), the presumption in either situation is as follows:

> It will be presumed that the person receiving nonlegal services believes the services to be the subject of a client-lawyer relationship unless the lawyer or law firm has advised the person receiving the services in writing that the services are not legal services and that the protection of a client-lawyer relationship does not exist with respect to the nonlegal services, or if the interest of the lawyer or law firm in the entity providing nonlegal services is de minimis.

Ohio: Rule 5.7(a) generally tracks ABA Model Rule 5.7(a), with minor changes, and Ohio Rule 5.7(e) is nearly the same as ABA Model Rule 5.7(b), but Ohio Rules 5.7(b), (c), and (d) differ significantly from the ABA Model Rule. They provide as follows:

> (b) A lawyer who controls or owns an interest in a business that provides a law-related service shall not require any customer of that business to agree to legal representation by the lawyer as a condition of the engagement of that business. A lawyer who controls or owns an interest in a business that provides law-related services shall disclose the interest to a customer of that business, and the fact that the customer may obtain legal services elsewhere, before performing legal services for the customer.
>
> (c) A lawyer who controls or owns an interest in a business that provides a law-related service shall not require the lawyer's client to agree to use that business as

a condition of the engagement for legal services. A lawyer who controls or owns an interest in a business that provides a law-related service shall disclose the interest to the client, and the fact that the client may obtain the law-related services elsewhere, before providing the law-related services to the client.

(d) Limitations or obligations imposed by this rule on a lawyer shall apply to all lawyers in that lawyer's firm and every lawyer in a firm that controls or owns an interest in a business that provides a law-related service.

Oregon omits Rule 5.7.

Pennsylvania adopted a version of Rule 5.7 in 1996, becoming the first state to do so. The Pennsylvania rule, which differs significantly from ABA Model Rule 5.7, provides:

Rule 5.7   Responsibilities Regarding Nonlegal Services

(a) A lawyer who provides nonlegal services to a recipient that are not distinct from legal services provided to that recipient is subject to the Rules of Professional Conduct with respect to the provision of both legal and nonlegal services.

(b) A lawyer who provides nonlegal services to a recipient that are distinct from any legal services provided to the recipient is subject to the Rules of Professional Conduct with respect to the nonlegal services if the lawyer knows or reasonably should know that the recipient might believe that the recipient is receiving the protection of a client-lawyer relationship.

(c) A lawyer who is an owner, controlling party, employee, agent, or is otherwise affiliated with an entity providing nonlegal services to a recipient is subject to the Rules of Professional Conduct with respect to the nonlegal services if the lawyer knows or reasonably should know that the recipient might believe that the recipient is receiving the protection of a client-lawyer relationship.

(d) Paragraph (b) or (c) does not apply if the lawyer makes reasonable efforts to avoid any misunderstanding by the recipient receiving nonlegal services. Those efforts must include advising the recipient that the services are not legal services and that the protection of a client-lawyer relationship does not exist with respect to the provision of nonlegal services to the recipient.

(e) The term "nonlegal services" denotes services that might reasonably be performed in conjunction with and in substance are related to the provision of legal services, and that are not prohibited as unauthorized practice of law when provided by a nonlawyer.

Texas omits Rule 5.7.

Virginia omits Rule 5.7.

Wisconsin omits Rule 5.7. (Wisconsin SCR 20:5.7 governs lawyers practicing in limited liability organizations. A Wisconsin Committee Comment to that rule says expressly that "Model Rule 5.7, concerning law-related services, is not part of these rules.")

Related Materials

ABA Formal Ethics Opinions: See ABA Formal Ethics Ops. 97-407 (1997) and 01-423 n.18 (2001).

Ancillary Businesses: Many law firms own, operate, or otherwise affiliate with ancillary non-legal businesses. In 2003, the law firm consulting company Hildebrandt International (now the Hildebrandt Institute) published a survey entitled Beyond

Legal Practice: Organizing and Managing Ancillary Businesses. The survey indicated that law firms were offering more than 70 separate lines of law-related businesses. The most common ancillary businesses at that time, according to the survey, were (a) lobbying or government relations services; (b) financial counseling and planning; (c) client asset management through registered investment companies; (d) human resources or benefits consulting or training; (e) international trade or finance services; and (f) educational, environmental, or health care consulting.

Professionalism Report: The ABA's Stanley Commission Report on Professionalism, 112 F.R.D. 243 (1986), called the trend toward law firm involvement in nonlegal services "disturbing" and urged the ABA to "initiate a study to see what, if any, controls or prohibitions should be imposed." The ultimate result of the study was ABA Model Rule 5.7.

Restatement of the Law Governing Lawyers: The Restatement has no provision comparable to ABA Model Rule 5.7.

ANNOTATIONS ON ARTICLE 6. PUBLIC SERVICE

Rule 6.1   Voluntary Pro Bono Publico Service

Canon and Code Antecedents

ABA Canons of Professional Ethics: No comparable Canon.
ABA Model Code of Professional Responsibility: No comparable Disciplinary Rule.

Cross-References in Other Rules

Rule 6.2, Comment 1: "All lawyers have a responsibility to assist in providing pro bono publico service. See Rule 6.1."

Legislative History of Model Rule 6.1

1980 Discussion Draft of Rule 6.1 (then Rule 8.1) provided as follows: "A lawyer shall render unpaid public interest legal services. . . . A lawyer shall make an annual report concerning such service to appropriate regulatory authority."

1981 and 1982 Drafts were the same as adopted in 1983, except that neither draft contained the final clause, "by financial support for organizations that provide legal services to persons of limited means."

1983 Rule: The version of Rule 6.1 originally adopted by the ABA in 1983 (which remained in effect until its amendment in 1993) provided as follows:

> A lawyer should render public interest legal service. A lawyer may discharge this responsibility by providing professional services at no fee or a reduced fee to persons of limited means or to public service or charitable groups or organizations, by service in activities for improving the law, the legal system or the legal profession, and by financial support for organizations that provide legal services to persons of limited means.

1993 Amendment: In 1993, the ABA amended Rule 6.1 substantially and rewrote its Comment entirely. As amended in 1993, the rule was substantially longer and more detailed than the 1983 rule, but was identical to the version of the rule in force since 2002, except that the opening sentence ("Every lawyer has a professional responsibility to provide legal services to those unable to pay.") and Comment 11 were not added until 2002. The 1993 amendment was highly controversial and passed by the close vote of 228-215.

The principal sponsor and author of the amended rule was the ABA's Standing Committee on Lawyers' Public Service Responsibility (SCLPSR). SCLPSR attempted to develop a joint proposal with the ABA's Standing Committee on Ethics and Professional Responsibility, which usually drafts proposed amendments to the Model Rules, but the joint effort failed because the Standing Committee on Ethics and Professional Responsibility (1) opposed setting a specific target number of 50 hours of pro bono service per year (preferring a word like "substantial" instead of a number); (2) opposed urging lawyers to allocate a substantial majority of their pro bono hours to serving the poor (out of concern that pro bono work for civil rights, the environment, and other important areas would diminish); and (3) favored adding a "buy-out" provision allowing lawyers to substitute financial support for personal service.

We reprint below excerpts from the Committee Report issued by SCLPSR and its five co-sponsors in support of the 1993 amendment to Rule 6.1:

Excerpts from ABA Committee Report Supporting 1993 Amendment to Rule 6.1*

THE CURRENT CRISIS IN THE DELIVERY OF LEGAL
SERVICES TO THE POOR

[B]ecause the legal problems of the economically disadvantaged often involve areas of basic need such as minimum levels of income and entitlements, shelter, utilities and child support, their inability to obtain legal services can have dire consequences. For example, the failure of a poor person to have effective legal counsel in an eviction proceeding may well result in homelessness; the failure to have legal counsel present at a public aid hearing may result in the denial of essential food or medical benefits.

The inability of the poor to obtain needed legal services has been well documented: since 1983, when Rule 6.1 was adopted, at least one national and 13 statewide studies assessing the legal needs of the poor have been conducted. Of those studies reporting unmet legal need, there has been a consistent finding that only about 15%-20% of the legal needs of the poor are being addressed. The legal need studies also confirmed that unmet need exists in critical areas such as public benefits, utilities, shelter, medical benefits and family matters. . . .

The Committee firmly believes that the private bar alone cannot be expected to fill the gap for service that exists among the poor. Rather, the federal government, through adequate funding of the Legal Services Corporation (LSC), should bear the major responsibility for addressing the problem. . . .

The Association . . . must again turn to members of the private bar and call upon them to help ease the crisis that exists in the provision of legal services to the poor. The Committee believes that one effective means of doing this is by revising Model Rule 6.1 to reflect a new emphasis on service to the disadvantaged. . . .

---

* Committee Reports do not represent official policy of the ABA. They are for information only, and the opinions are those of the authors of the report.

. . . To address the crisis in the delivery of legal services to the poor, the proposed revision provides that a substantial majority of the annual hours of pro bono legal services should be rendered at no cost to persons of limited means or to organizations in matters which are designed primarily to address the needs of persons of limited means. The Committee purposely chose the words "substantial majority" to make clear that a simple majority of the hours would not suffice. While the Committee recognizes the value and importance of other types of pro bono activity, it strongly believes that due to the enormity of the unmet need for legal services that exists among the disadvantaged, the provision of legal services to that group must be given priority over all other types of pro bono service. . . .

In addition to voluntarily rendering pro bono service, the revised Rule 6.1 calls upon every lawyer to voluntarily make financial contributions to organizations providing legal services to persons of limited means. In those cases in which a lawyer determines that it is not feasible to render legal services and makes a financial contribution instead, he or she is expected to make an additional contribution pursuant to the last sentence of the new Rule. . . .

It is the Committee's intent that the ethical responsibilities set forth in Rule 6.1 apply to all lawyers and not just those currently engaged in the practice of law. . . .

Although neither the Rule nor the Comment explicitly so states, it should be self evident that every lawyer is expected to provide the same quality of legal services to pro bono clients as he or she would provide to paying clients. . . . Therefore, to the extent that an attorney is unfamiliar with a given area of the law, he or she is expected to seek advice or training in that area before advising a client, either for a fee or on a pro bono basis. Many pro bono programs provide free training on a wide range of topics to assist their volunteer attorneys in attaining competency to handle the cases referred to them. The Committee strongly endorses the provision of these training events and urges pro bono attorneys to take advantage of them whenever possible.

[T]he Comment to the revised Rule explicitly states that the pro bono responsibility is not intended to be enforced through the disciplinary process. Thus as drafted, revised Rule 6.1 does not mandate pro bono. Although the Committee recognizes that since 1988, mandatory pro bono proposals have been considered in many states and remain under active consideration in several of them, it nevertheless believes that it is not practical nor feasible at this time to address the issue of mandatory pro bono on a national level. Rather, the Committee views the question of mandatory pro bono as an issue that needs to be examined by state and local bar associations.

2002 Amendments: At its February 2002 Mid-Year Meeting, the ABA House of Delegates adopted with only minor changes the ABA Ethics 2000 Commission proposal to amend Rule 6.1 and its Comment. The amendments added the first sentence of the rule and a new Comment 11. (Comment 11 was not in the Ethics 2000 Commission's proposal but rather was added by the House of Delegates.)

Selected State Variations

Editors' Note. No state yet requires lawyers to perform pro bono work. Some states, however, require lawyers to report their pro bono hours, and other states encourage lawyers to do so. When we went to press in September 2012, a state-by-state chart of pro bono reporting rules and policies found at *http://apps.americanbar.org/legalservices/probono/reporting.html* indicated that 7 states have mandatory pro bono reporting (Florida, Hawaii, Illinois, Maryland, Mississippi, Nevada, and New Mexico); 8 states have formally rejected mandatory pro bono reporting (Colorado, Indiana, Massachusetts, Minnesota, New York, Pennsylvania,

Tennessee, and Utah); 11 states encourage voluntary pro bono reporting (Arizona, Georgia, Kentucky, Louisiana, Missouri, Montana, New Mexico, Oregon, Texas, Utah, and Washington); and 2 states were actively considering voluntary pro bono reporting (Michigan and Vermont). Moreover, as of January 1, 2015, New York will require all applicants to the New York State Bar (except those applying for admission by motion) to show that they have completed at least 50 hours of law-related pro bono service as a condition of bar admission.

Alabama: See the Alabama entry following Rule 6.5.

Arizona: Rule 6.1 contains the following key provisions:

> (a) A lawyer should voluntarily render public interest legal service. A lawyer may discharge this responsibility by rendering a minimum of fifty hours of service per calendar year. . . .
>
> (c) A law firm or other group of lawyers may satisfy their responsibility under this Rule, if they desire, collectively. For example, the designation of one or more lawyers to work on pro bono publico matters may be attributed to other lawyers within the firm or group who support the representation. . . .
>
> (d) The efforts of individual lawyers are not enough to meet the needs of the poor. The profession and government have instituted programs to provide direct delivery of legal services to the poor. The direct support of such programs is an alternative expression of support to provide law in the public interest, and a lawyer is encouraged to provide financial support for organizations that provide legal services to persons of limited means or to the Arizona Bar Foundation for the direct delivery of legal services to the poor.

California: California has no rule of professional conduct comparable to ABA Model Rule 6.1, but California Business and Professions Code §6068(h) makes it the duty of a lawyer "[n]ever to reject, for any consideration personal to himself or herself, the cause of the defenseless or the oppressed." In addition, the California State Bar's Board of Governors has adopted a Pro Bono Resolution that echoes the substance of ABA Model Rule 6.1. It provides as follows:

> (3) Urges all law schools to promote and encourage the participation of law students in pro bono activities, including requiring any law firm wishing to recruit on campus to provide a written statement of its policy, if any, concerning the involvement of its attorneys in public service and pro bono activities. . . .

Colorado: Colorado adds the following paragraph at the end of the rule:

> Where constitutional, statutory or regulatory restrictions prohibit government and public sector lawyers or judges from performing the pro bono services outlined in paragraphs (a)(1) and (2), those individuals should fulfill their pro bono responsibility by performing services or participating in activities outlined in paragraph (b).

In 1999, the Colorado Supreme Court rejected a recommendation by the state's Judicial Advisory Council to institute mandatory pro bono reporting. The court said that mandatory reporting was a step toward mandatory pro bono, and "[s]ince we are unwilling to arrive at that destination, we are also unwilling to take the first step." However, the Colorado Supreme Court has adopted a detailed "recommended Model Pro Bono Policy" for law firms, which is reprinted in the Colorado Rules of Professional Conduct immediately after Rule 6.1. Among other things, the Model Pro Bono Policy urges firms to include "a statement that the firm will value at least 50 hours of such pro bono service per year by each Colorado licensed attorney in the firm, for all purposes of attorney evaluation, advancement, and compensation in the firm as the firm values compensated client representation." In addition, the Colorado Supreme Court will annually recognize Colorado law firms that "voluntarily advise the Court . . . that their attorneys, on average, during the previous calendar year, performed 50 hours of pro bono legal service, primarily for persons of limited means or organizations serving persons of limited means. . . ."

Connecticut, Georgia, Indiana, Kansas, Michigan, Missouri, Pennsylvania, and *South Carolina* have retained the 1983 version of ABA Model Rule 6.1, which provides as follows:

> A lawyer should render public interest service. A lawyer may discharge this responsibility by providing professional services at no fee or a reduced fee to persons of limited means or to public service or charitable groups or organizations, by service in activities for improving the law, the legal system or the legal profession, and by financial support for organizations that provide legal services to persons of limited means.

District of Columbia: D.C. Rule 6.1 provides as follows:

> A lawyer should participate in serving those persons, or groups of persons, who are unable to pay all or a portion of reasonable attorneys' fees or who are otherwise unable to obtain counsel. A lawyer may discharge this responsibility by providing professional services at no fee, or at a substantially reduced fee, to persons and groups who are unable to afford or obtain counsel, or by active participation in the work of organizations that provide legal services to them. When personal representation is not feasible, a lawyer may discharge this responsibility by providing financial support for organizations that provide legal representation to those unable to obtain counsel.

Florida: In 1993, in a divided opinion, the Florida Supreme Court adopted an elaborate pro bono rule requiring lawyers to report their pro bono hours. See 630 So. 2d 501 (Fla. 1993). The Florida Bar subsequently sought to eliminate mandatory reporting, but the Florida Supreme Court refused to do so at 696 So. 2d 734 (1997). In *Schwarz v. Kogan,* 132 F.3d 1387 (11th Cir. 1998), the court upheld Florida's mandatory reporting provisions against a federal constitutional challenge. The full rule provides as follows:

4-6.1 Pro Bono Public Service

> (a) *Professional Responsibility.* Each member of the Florida Bar in good standing, as part of that member's professional responsibility, should (1) render pro bono legal services to the poor or (2) participate, to the extent possible, in other pro bono service activities that directly relate to the legal needs of the poor. This professional responsibility does not apply to members of the judiciary or their staffs or to government lawyers who are prohibited from performing legal services by constitutional, statutory, rule, or regulatory prohibitions. Neither does this professional responsibility apply to those members of The Bar who are retired, inactive, or suspended, or who have been placed on the inactive list for incapacity not related to discipline.
>
> (b) *Discharge of the Professional Responsibility to Provide Pro Bono Legal Service to the Poor.* The professional responsibility to provide pro bono legal services as established under this rule is aspirational rather than mandatory in nature. The failure to fulfill one's professional responsibility under this rule will not subject a lawyer to discipline. The professional responsibility to provide pro bono legal service to the poor may be discharged by:
>
> > (1) annually providing at least 20 hours of pro bono legal service to the poor; or
> >
> > (2) making an annual contribution of at least $350 to a legal aid organization.

(c) *Collective Discharge of the Professional Responsibility to Provide Pro Bono Legal Service to the Poor.* Each member of the bar should strive to individually satisfy the member's professional responsibility to provide pro bono legal service to the poor. Collective satisfaction of this professional responsibility is permitted by law firms only under a collective satisfaction plan that has been filed previously with the circuit pro bono committee and only when providing pro bono legal service to the poor:

(1) in a major case or matter involving a substantial expenditure of time and resources; or

(2) through a full-time community or public service staff; or

(3) in any other manner that has been approved by the circuit pro bono committee in the circuit in which the firm practices.

(d) *Reporting Requirement.* Each member of the bar shall annually report whether the member has satisfied the member's professional responsibility to provide pro bono legal services to the poor. Each member shall report this information through a simplified reporting form that is made a part of the member's annual dues statement . . . . The failure to report this information shall constitute a disciplinary offense under these rules. . . .

Florida also adds a lengthy Rule 6.5 (Voluntary Pro Bono Plan). Rule 6.5(c)(2) instructs every judicial circuit to "(a) prepare in written form a circuit pro bono plan after evaluating the needs of the circuit and making a determination of present available pro bono services; (b) implement the plan and monitor its results; [and] (c) submit an annual report to The Florida Bar standing committee. . . ." Rule 6.5(d) provides as follows:

The following are suggested pro bono service opportunities that should be included in each circuit plan:

(1) representation of clients through case referral;

(2) interviewing of prospective clients;

(3) participation in pro se clinics and other clinics in which lawyers provide advice and counsel;

(4) acting as co-counsel on cases or matters with legal assistance providers and other pro bono lawyers;

(5) providing consultation services to legal assistance providers for case reviews and evaluations;

(6) participation in policy advocacy;

(7) providing training to the staff of legal assistance providers and other volunteer pro bono attorneys;

(8) making presentations to groups of poor persons regarding their rights and obligations under the law;

(9) providing legal research;

(10) providing guardian ad litem services;

(11) providing assistance in the formation and operation of legal entities for groups of poor persons; and

(12) serving as a mediator or arbitrator at no fee to the client-eligible party.

Georgia: Rule 6.1 tracks the pre-2002 version of ABA Model Rule 6.1, but Georgia adds the following: "No reporting rules or requirements may be imposed without specific permission of the Supreme Court granted through amendments to these Rules. There is no disciplinary penalty for a violation of this Rule."

Illinois: Illinois omits Rule 6.1. Comment 6B of the Preamble explains the omission as follows:

The absence from the Illinois Rules of a counterpart to ABA Model Rule 6.1 regarding *pro bono* and public service should not be interpreted as limiting the responsibility of lawyers to render uncompensated service in the public interest. Rather, the rationale is that this responsibility is not appropriate for disciplinary rules because it is not possible to articulate an appropriate disciplinary standard regarding *pro bono* and public service.

However, Illinois encourages *pro bono* obligations through court rules. The Preamble's Comment 6A refers to Illinois Supreme Court Rule 756(f), which provides as follows:

> (f) *Disclosure of Voluntary Pro Bono Service.* As part of registering under this rule, each lawyer shall report the approximate amount of his or her pro bono legal service and the amount of qualified monetary contributions made during the preceding 12 months. . . .

Rule 756(f) then defines the term "*Pro bono* legal service," stating explicitly that legal services for which payment "was expected, but is uncollectible, do not qualify as *pro bono* legal service." The rule also sets out the precise contents of the form for reporting such service on the annual registration statement. Information provided pursuant to Rule 756(f) is considered "confidential," but the information may be reported "in the aggregate." Rule 756(g) instructs the Bar's Administrator to "remove from the master roll" any attorney who has failed to provide the information on voluntary pro bono service required by Rule 756(f). A person whose name is not on the master roll and who practices law in Illinois "is engaged in the unauthorized practice of law and may also be held in contempt of the court."

Finally, Rule 756(j) permits retired and inactive attorneys, as well as in-house attorneys who have a more limited registration status, to provide pro bono legal services under certain circumstances that are described in the Rule.

Kentucky: Rule 6.1, entitled "Donated Legal Services," encourages lawyers to render voluntary public interest legal service and permits lawyers to report donated legal services on the Bar's annual dues statement. "Lawyers rendering a minimum of fifty (50) hours of donated legal service shall receive a recognition award for such service from the Kentucky Bar Association."

Maryland adds that a lawyer "in part-time practice" should aspire to render at least "a pro rata number of hours." Maryland also makes an exception for lawyers who are "prohibited by law" from rendering certain types of pro bono legal services. Maryland allows a substantial majority of pro bono services to be rendered to "individuals, groups, or organizations seeking to secure or protect civil rights, civil liberties, or public rights. . . ." Maryland Rule 6.1 concludes: "This Rule is aspirational, not mandatory. Noncompliance with this Rule shall not be grounds for disciplinary action or other sanctions."

Massachusetts: Rule 6.1 states that a lawyer "should provide annually at least 25 hours of pro bono publico legal services for the benefit of persons of limited means." Alternatively, the lawyer should "contribute from $250 to 1 percent of the lawyer's annual taxable, professional income to one or more organizations that provide or support legal services to persons of limited means."

Michigan essentially retains the 1983 version of ABA Model Rule 6.1.

New Jersey: Rule 6.1 tracks the original (1983) version of ABA Model Rule 6.1 except that the first sentence reads: "Every lawyer has a professional responsibility to render public interest legal service."

New York: Rule 6.1 provides as follows:

Lawyers are strongly encouraged to provide pro bono legal services to benefit poor persons.

(a) Every lawyer should aspire to: (1) provide at least 20 hours of pro bono legal services each year to poor persons; and (2) contribute financially to organizations that provide legal services to poor persons.

(b) Pro bono legal services that meet this goal are: (1) professional services rendered in civil matters, and in those criminal matters for which the government is not obliged to provide funds for legal representation, to persons who are financially unable to compensate counsel; (2) activities related to improving the administration of justice by simplifying the legal process for, or increasing the availability and quality of legal services to, poor persons; and (3) professional services to charitable, religious, civic and educational organizations in matters designed predominantly to address the needs of poor persons.

(c) Appropriate organizations for financial contributions are: (1) organizations primarily engaged in the provision of legal services to the poor; and (2) organizations substantially engaged in the provision of legal services to the poor, provided that the donated funds are to be used for the provision of such legal services.

(d) This Rule is not intended to be enforced through the disciplinary process, and the failure to fulfill the aspirational goals contained herein should be without legal consequence.

In addition, beginning January 1, 2015 New York will require all applicants for the New York Bar (other than those seeking admission by motion) to show that they have completed at least 50 hours of law-related pro bono service as a condition of bar admission.

North Carolina omits Rule 6.1, but Paragraph 6 of North Carolina's Preamble states that "all lawyers should devote professional time and resources and use civic influence to ensure equal access to our system of justice for all those who because of economic or social barriers cannot afford or secure adequate legal counsel," and Paragraph 7 of the Preamble contains language almost identical to the 1983 version of ABA Model Rule 6.1.

Ohio omits ABA Model Rule 6.1. The Supreme Court of Ohio explains that it "deferred consideration of Model Rule 6.1 in light of recommendations contained in the final report of the Supreme Court Task Force on Pro Se & Indigent Representation and recommendations from the Ohio Legal Assistance Foundation." (The Task Force on Pro Se & Indigent Representation, which was appointed by the Supreme Court of Ohio in 2004, recommended in its April 2006 final report that Ohio attorneys be required to report their pro bono activities. The report is available at *www.sconet.state.oh.us/publications/prose/report_april06.pdf.*)

Texas omits Rule 6.1, but Paragraph 6 of the Texas Preamble addresses pro bono services by stating, among other things: "The provision of free legal services to those unable to pay reasonable fees is a moral obligation of each lawyer as well as the profession generally."

Virginia: Rule 6.1 says that a lawyer "should render at least 2 percent per year of the lawyer's professional time to pro bono publico legal services." The Rule also defines pro bono services and allows a law firm or group of lawyers to satisfy their responsibility under the Rule collectively. Further, "direct financial support of programs that provide direct delivery of legal services to meet the need described" in the Rule "is an alternative method for fulfilling a lawyer's responsibility."

AALS Commission on Pro Bono and Public Service Opportunities: In 1999, the Association of American Law Schools (AALS) issued a report entitled "Learning to Serve" (*see www.aals.org/probono/report.html*), which then—AALS President Deborah Rhode identified as "the first systematic effort by the Association of American Law Schools to address the role of pro bono and public service in legal education." The report recommended that law schools "make available to all law students at least once during their law school careers a well-supervised law-related pro bono opportunity and either require participation or find ways to attract the great majority of students to volunteer."

The report also urged law schools to adopt a policy (a) stating an annual pro bono expectation for all faculty members, (b) going beyond teaching and institutional service, (c) extending institutional support similar to research support, (d) granting autonomy, and (e) requiring annual reporting. For details on faculty pro bono, see *www.abanet.org/legalservices/probono/lawschools/pb_faculty.html*.

ABA Formal Ethics Opinions: No formal ethics opinions have construed Rule 6.1, but ABA Formal Ethics Op. 96-399 (1996) mentioned Rule 6.1.

ABA Model Guidelines for the Utilization of Paralegal Services: The ABA has approved Model Guidelines for the Utilization of Paralegal Services. Guideline 10 provides: "A lawyer who employs a paralegal should facilitate the paralegal's participation in appropriate continuing education and pro bono publico activities." The Model Guidelines are at *http://apps.americanbar.org/legalservices/paralegals/downloads/modelguidelines.pdf*.

ABA Pro Bono Disclosure Requirements for Law School Recruiters: In 2006, the ABA adopted a resolution urging law schools (a) to "require legal employers that recruit on campus to disclose, and to make available to each school's students and alumni, specific information regarding the employer's pro bono policies, practices and activities," and (b) to adopt an August 2006 document entitled "Pro Bono Disclosure Requirements for Law School Recruiters" that requires on-campus recruiters to disclose information such as "(a) stated goals regarding the number of pro bono hours to be contributed by the employer each year; (b) the number of actual pro bono hours contributed by the employer in the prior calendar year; (c) the average number of pro bono hours contributed by junior associates, midlevel associates, senior associates, and partners at the firm in the prior calendar year; [and] (d) whether and to what extent pro bono hours are counted as billable hours (if attorneys are expected to meet billable hours targets). . . ." The resolution and the report submitted in support of the resolution are available at *www.abanet.org/leadership/2006/annual/dailyjournal/hundredtwentyoneb.doc*.

ABA Resolution on Encouraging Pro Bono Work: In 2006, the ABA adopted a resolution urging larger law firms, corporate legal departments, and government and military law offices to adopt specific policies and procedures designed to increase the willingness of lawyers to perform pro bono work. Specific policies are recommended for each type of law office. The resolution is available at *www.abanet.org/leadership/2006/annual/dailyjournal/hundredtwentyonea.doc*. An accompanying report recommended various specific procedures, including:

> **Count pro bono hours as billable hours.** It is essential that pro bono hours be counted as billable hours and that they also count, like hours spent on client work,

toward annual billable hours targets, requirements or expectations. The failure to treat pro bono hours as billable hours sends a signal that the firm does not truly value and support this work.

Consider attorneys' commitment to pro bono activity as a favorable factor in advancement and compensation decisions. If a pro bono culture is to flourish, the attorneys who engage in pro bono work need to know that their efforts will be viewed favorably by the firm when the time comes to make advancement and compensation decisions.

Set annual goals regarding the number of hours contributed through firm pro bono programs and the number of attorneys who participate. By setting goals, firms can continually monitor participation while demonstrating their commitment to pro bono and public service to their lawyers, clients and prospective recruits.

ABA Standards for Approval of Law Schools: The ABA has adopted Standards for the Approval of Law Schools, as well as formal interpretations of the Standards, to determine whether law schools merit ABA accreditation. The Standards are available in full at *www.abanet.org/legaled/standards/standards.html.* Some of the Standards relate to pro bono work. For example, Standard 302(b)(2) requires every law school to offer "substantial opportunities for . . . student participation in pro bono activities." Interpretation 302-10 states as follows:

> *Interpretation 302-10.* Each law school is encouraged to be creative in developing substantial opportunities for student participation in pro bono activities. Pro bono opportunities should at a minimum involve the rendering of meaningful law-related service to persons of limited means or to organizations that serve such persons; however volunteer programs that involve meaningful services that are not law-related also may be included within the law school's overall program. . . . While most existing law school pro bono programs include only activities for which students do not receive academic credit, Standard 302(b)(2) does not preclude the inclusion of credit-granting activities within a law school's overall program of pro bono opportunities so long as law-related non-credit bearing initiatives are also part of that program.

ABA Standards for Programs Providing Civil Pro Bono Legal Services to Persons of Limited Means: In 1996, the ABA approved Standards for Programs Providing Civil Pro Bono Legal Services to Persons of Limited Means. The Standards cover such things as fundraising (Standard 1.1-4), conflicts of interest (Standard 1.1-7), communication with clients (Standard 3.4-4), training of volunteers (Standard 3.5-3), and case acceptance policy (Standard 4.1). The complete Standards are available online at *www.americanbar.org/groups/probono_public_service/policy/standards.html.*

ABA Standing Committee on Pro Bono and Public Service: The ABA Standing Committee on Pro Bono and Public Service is the lead ABA committee for developing and promoting pro bono policies and initiatives. The Pro Bono Committee's mission includes "fostering the development of pro bono programs and activities by law firms, bar associations, corporate legal departments, law schools, government attorney offices and others; analyzing the scope and function of pro bono programs; and proposing and reviewing legislation that affects lawyers' ability to provide pro bono legal services." For example, the Pro Bono Committee took the lead in drafting the 1993 amendments to ABA Model Rule 6.1. For more information about the Pro Bono Committee, and for a wealth of news, charts, and other resources about pro bono, visit *http://www.americanbar.org/groups/probono_public_service.html.*

Bar Admission Pro Bono Requirements: In 2012, New York became the first jurisdiction in the nation to require a minimum amount of pro bono work as a condition of bar admission. Starting January 1, 2015, applicants for admission to the New York Bar (other than applicants seeking admission by motion), no matter where they attend law school, will be required to perform at least 50 hours of law-related pro bono service before being admitted. It remains to be seen whether other states will follow New York's lead.

Federal Statutes on Pro Bono: Certain federal statutes or other regulations may preclude federal government lawyers from doing any pro bono work adverse to any federal agency or department. As Comment 5 to Rule 6.1 notes, "Constitutional, statutory or regulatory restrictions may prohibit or impede government and public sector lawyers and judges from performing the pro bono services outlined in paragraphs (a)(1) and (2)." For example, 18 U.S.C. §205 makes it a criminal offense for a federal government lawyer, "other than in the proper discharge of his official duties," to act as an attorney for anyone "before any department, agency, court, court-martial, officer, or civil, military, or naval commission in connection with any covered matter in which the United States is a party or has a direct and substantial interest. . . ."

Law School Pro Bono Requirements: More than 30 law schools require law students to complete a specified amount of pro bono work as a condition of graduation. Columbia Law School, for example, requires all students to perform 40 hours of uncompensated public interest service between the end of the first year and graduation. Students who do not complete the 40 hours cannot graduate. Harvard Law School also requires 40 hours of pro bono work before graduation. The ABA Standing Committee on Pro Bono and Public Service maintains a Directory of Law School Public Interest and Pro Bono Programs available at *http://apps.americanbar.org/legalservices/probono/lawschools/pb_programs_chart. html#graduation_requirement.*

Legal Services Corporation's "Justice Gap" Study: In 2007, the Legal Services Corporation updated and re-issued a report (originally issued in 2005) entitled "Documenting the Justice Gap in America: The Current Unmet Civil Legal Needs of Low-Income Americans." The report concluded that at least 80 percent of the civil legal needs of low-income Americans are not being met and that programs funded by Legal Services Corporation turn away half of their potential clients (about one million cases per year) because the programs lack sufficient resources. The full "Justice Gap" study is available online at *www.lsc.gov/JusticeGap.pdf.*

Model Rules of Professional Conduct for Federal Lawyers adds a new paragraph to Rule 6.1 providing that government lawyers "should provide pro bono legal services consistent with applicable law." In addition, Rule 5.1(d) provides that a supervisory government lawyer "should encourage subordinate lawyers to participate in pro bono publico service activities and the activities of bar associations and law reform organizations." However, the Comment by the Federal Lawyers to Rule 6.1 explains that "18 U.S.C. §205 and §209 and other laws . . . may regulate a Government lawyer's ability to provide legal services on a pro bono basis outside the scope of the Government lawyer's official duties."

Restatement of the Law Governing Lawyers: The Restatement has no provision comparable to ABA Model Rule 6.1.

Rule 6.2   Accepting Appointments

Canon and Code Antecedents

ABA Canons of Professional Ethics: Canon 4 provided as follows:

4.   When Counsel for an Indigent Prisoner

A lawyer assigned as counsel for an indigent prisoner ought not to ask to be excused for any trivial reason, and should always exert his best efforts in his behalf.

ABA Model Code of Professional Responsibility: No comparable Disciplinary Rule.

Cross-References in Other Rules

Rule 1.1, Comment 4: "A lawyer may accept representation where the requisite level of competence can be achieved by reasonable preparation. This applies as well to a lawyer who is appointed as counsel for an unrepresented person. See also *Rule 6.2.*"

Rule 1.16, Comment 3: "When a lawyer has been appointed to represent a client, withdrawal ordinarily requires approval of the appointing authority. See also *Rule 6.2.*"

Legislative History of Model Rule 6.2

1980 Discussion Draft and ***1981 Draft*** were substantially the same as adopted, with only minor changes in phrasing.

1982 Draft was the same as adopted *except* that it completely omitted subparagraph (c).

1983 Rule: As originally adopted in 1983, Rule 6.2 was the same as the 2002 version.

2002 Amendments: The ABA Ethics 2000 Commission did not propose any changes to the text or Comment of Rule 6.2.

Selected State Variations

California has no comparable provision in its Rules of Professional Conduct.

Georgia shortens ABA Model Rule 6.2 to a single sentence: "For good cause a lawyer may seek to avoid appointment by a tribunal to represent a person."

New York: omits Rule 6.2.

North Carolina omits Rule 6.2.

Ohio substitutes the word "court" for "tribunal" in the first line of the rule to reflect the Ohio Supreme Court's view that "the inherent authority to make appointments is limited to courts and does not extend to other bodies" included within the definition of "tribunal." Ohio also omits ABA Model Rule 6.2(c) because "the substance . . . is addressed in Rule 1.1, which mandates that a lawyer shall provide competent representation to a client."

Related Materials

ABA Formal Ethics Opinions: See ABA Formal Ethics Op. 06-441 n.16 (2006).

In Forma Pauperis Status: In forma pauperis status for prisoners who file civil suits in federal court is governed by 28 U.S.C. §1915. The language most relevant to ABA Model Rule 6.2 is found in §1915(e)(1), which provides: "The court may *request* an attorney to represent any person unable to afford counsel." (Emphasis added.) In *Mallard v. United States District Court,* 490 U.S. 296 (1989), the Supreme Court held 5-4 that the word "request" does not give federal courts the power to compel lawyers to represent indigent prisoners. However, the *Mallard* Court declined to rule on whether federal statutes that permit courts to "assign" or "appoint" counsel, such as 18 U.S.C. §3006A and 42 U.S.C. §2000e-5(f)(1), empower courts to compel unwilling attorneys to represent indigents. The court also did not reach the question whether federal courts have "inherent authority to require lawyers to serve" because this issue had not been raised below. Justice Brennan's majority opinion concluded by saying:

> We do not mean to question, let alone denigrate, lawyers' ethical obligation to assist those who are too poor to afford counsel, or to suggest that requests made pursuant to [§1915] may be lightly declined because they give rise to no ethical claim. On the contrary, in a time when the need for legal services among the poor is growing and public funding for such services has not kept pace, lawyers' ethical obligation to volunteer their time and skills pro bono publico is manifest. . . .

Restatement of the Law Governing Lawyers: See Restatement §§9 and 13 in our chapter on the Restatement later in this volume.

Rule 6.3   Membership in Legal Services Organization

Canon and Code Antecedents

ABA Canons of Professional Ethics: No comparable Canon.

ABA Model Code of Professional Responsibility: No comparable Disciplinary Rule.

Cross-References in Other Rules

None.

Legislative History of Model Rule 6.3

1980 Discussion Draft (then Rule 8.2(c)) provided as follows:

> (c) A lawyer may serve as a director, member or officer of an organization involved in reform of the law or its administration notwithstanding the fact that the reform may affect interests of a client of the lawyer if:
> (1) when the interests of the client could be affected, the fact is disclosed in the course of deliberations on the matter, but the identity of the client need not be disclosed;

(2) when the client could be adversely affected, the lawyer complies with Rule 1.8 with respect to the client; and

(3) the lawyer takes no part in any decision that could result in a direct material benefit or detriment to the client.

1981 Draft was similar to the adopted version of Rule 6.3, except that it contained an additional requirement that "the organization complies with Rule 5.4 concerning the professional independence of its legal staff."

1982 Draft was adopted.

1983 Rule: As originally adopted in 1983, Rule 6.3 was the same as the 2002 version.

2002 Amendments: The ABA Ethics 2000 Commission did not propose any changes to the text or Comment of Rule 6.3.

Selected State Variations

California has no equivalent provision in its Rules of Professional Conduct.

Georgia adds that there is "no disciplinary penalty for a violation of this Rule."

Illinois: Rule 6.3 applies to a "not-for-profit" legal services organization.

Michigan: Rule 6.3 adds extensive rules governing lawyer participation in "not-for-profit referral service[s] that recommend legal services to the public."

New Jersey: Rule 6.3(a) requires that the organization comply with Rule 5.4 "concerning the professional independence of its legal staff," and Rule 6.3(b) includes adverse effect on the interest of a client "or class of clients of the organization or upon the independence of professional judgment of a lawyer representing such a client."

New York: Rule 6.3(a) extends the restriction to any conflict that would arise "under Rule 1.7 through Rule 1.13."

Ohio omits ABA Model Rule 6.3 because the Supreme Court of Ohio believes the substance of Rule 6.3 is addressed by other rules governing conflicts of interest, including Rule 1.7(a).

Texas: Rule 1.13 (entitled "Conflicts: Public Interest Activities") is similar to ABA Model Rule 6.3, but the Texas rule also governs a lawyer's activities in a "civic, charitable or law reform organization." Texas Rule1.13 omits the clause "notwithstanding that the organization serves persons having interests adverse to a client of the lawyer."

Related Materials

ABA Formal Ethics Opinions: No formal ethics opinions have construed Rule 6.3.

Restatement of the Law Governing Lawyers: See Restatement §135 in our chapter on the Restatement later in this volume.

Rule 6.4   Law Reform Activities Affecting Client Interests

Canon and Code Antecedents

ABA Canons of Professional Ethics: No comparable Canon.

ABA Model Code of Professional Responsibility: No comparable Disciplinary Rule.

Cross-References in Other Rules

None.

Legislative History of Model Rule 6.4

1980 Discussion Draft (then Rule 8.2(a) and (b)) provided as follows:

Conflict of Interest in Pro Bono Publico Service

(a) A lawyer engaged in service pro bono publico shall avoid improper conflicts of interest therein.

(b) A lawyer may serve as a director, officer, or member of an organization providing legal services to persons of limited means notwithstanding that such services are provided to persons having interests adverse to a client of the lawyer if:

(1) the organization complies with Rule 7.5 [now Rule 5.4(c)] concerning the professional independence of its legal staff;

(2) when the interests of a client of the lawyer could be affected, the lawyer takes no part in any decision by the organization that could have a material adverse effect on the interest of a client of the organization or upon the independence of professional judgment of a lawyer representing such a client; and

(3) the lawyer otherwise complies with Rule 1.8 with respect to the lawyer's client.

1981 Draft provided as follows:

A lawyer may serve as a director, officer or member of an organization involved in reform of the law or its administration notwithstanding the fact that the reform may affect the interests of a client of the lawyer if the lawyer takes no part in any decision that could have a direct material effect on the client.

1982 Draft was adopted.

1983 Rule: As originally adopted in 1983, Rule 6.4 was the same as the 2002 version.

2002 Amendments: The ABA Ethics 2000 Commission did not propose any changes to the text or Comment of Rule 6.4.

Selected State Variations

California has no comparable provision.

District of Columbia: Rule 6.4 adds the following paragraph (a): "A lawyer should assist in improving the administration of justice. A lawyer may discharge this requirement by rendering services in activities for improving the law, the legal system, or the legal profession."

Florida replaces "materially benefited" with "materially affected" in the second sentence of Rule 6.4.

Georgia adds that "[t]here is no disciplinary penalty for a violation of this Rule."

New Hampshire: New Hampshire substitutes the word "affected" for the word "benefitted" in the second sentence of Rule 6.4. A special New Hampshire Comment explains the reasoning: "Since situations may arise in which law reform activities may materially impinge on a client's interest in an adverse, as well as beneficial manner, the change was made to reflect that possibility."

New York: Rule 6.4 adds a third sentence stating: "In determining the nature and scope of participation in such activities, a lawyer should be mindful of obligations to clients under other Rules, particularly Rule 1.7."

Ohio omits ABA Model Rule 6.4 because the Supreme Court of Ohio believes that the "substance of Model Rule 6.4 is addressed by other provisions of the Ohio Rules of Professional Conduct that address conflicts of interest."

Related Materials

ABA Formal Ethics Opinions: No formal ethics opinions have construed Rule 6.4.

Model Rules of Professional Conduct for Federal Lawyers: Rule 6.4 adds a sentence providing that a federal lawyer "shall not knowingly participate in a decision or action of the organization if participating in the decision would be incompatible with the Federal lawyer's obligations to the client under Rule 1.7."

Restatement of the Law Governing Lawyers: The Restatement has no comparable provision.

Rule 6.5   Nonprofit and Court-Annexed Limited Legal Services Programs

Cross-References in Other Rules

Rule 1.16, Comment 1: "Ordinarily, a representation in a matter is completed when the agreed-upon assistance has been concluded. See Rules 1.2(c) and 6.5. See also Rule 1.3, Comment [4]."

Canon and Code Antecedents

ABA Canons of Professional Ethics: No comparable Canon.

ABA Model Code of Professional Responsibility: No comparable Disciplinary Rule.

Legislative History of Model Rule 6.5

2002 Amendments: Rule 6.5 was added to the Model Rules in February 2002. The new rule and its Comment were based on a proposal by the ABA Ethics 2000 Commission, which the ABA House of Delegates adopted without change. The Reporter's Explanation that accompanied the Ethics 2000 Commission proposal provided, in relevant part, as follows:

Model Rule 6.5—Reporter's Explanation of Changes*

Rule 6.5 is a new Rule in response to the Commission's concern that a strict application of the conflict-of-interest rules may be deterring lawyers from serving as volunteers in programs in which clients are provided short-term limited legal services under the auspices of a nonprofit organization or a court-annexed program. The paradigm is the legal-advice hotline or pro se clinic, the purpose of which is to provide short-term limited legal assistance to persons of limited means who otherwise would go unrepresented.

Paragraph (a) limits Rule 6.5 to situations in which lawyers provide clients short-term limited legal services under the auspices of a program sponsored by a nonprofit organization or court. The Commission believes that the proposed relaxation of the conflict rules does not pose a significant risk to clients when the lawyer is working in a program sponsored by a nonprofit organization or a court and will eliminate an impediment to lawyer participation in such programs. See Comment [1].

Paragraph (a)(1) provides that the lawyer is subject to the requirements of Rules 1.7 and 1.9(a) only if the lawyer knows that the representation involves a conflict of interest. The purpose is to make it unnecessary for the lawyer to do a comprehensive conflicts check in a practice setting in which it normally is not feasible to do so. See Comment [3]. In cases in which the lawyer knows of a conflict of interest, however, compliance with Rules 1.7 and 1.9(a) is required.

Paragraph (a)(2) provides that a lawyer participating in a short-term legal services program must comply with Rule 1.10 if the lawyer knows that a lawyer with whom the lawyer is associated in a firm would be disqualified from handling the matter by Rules 1.7 or 1.9(a). By otherwise exempting a representation governed by this Rule from Rule 1.10, however, paragraph (b) protects lawyers associated with the participating lawyer from a vicarious disqualification that might otherwise be required. Thus, as explained in Comment [4], a lawyer's participation in a short-term limited legal services program will not preclude the lawyer's firm from undertaking or continuing the representation of a client with interests adverse to a client being represented under the program's auspices. Nor will a personal disqualification of a lawyer participating in the program be imputed to other lawyers participating in the program. Given the limited nature of the representation provided in nonprofit short-term limited legal services programs, the Commission thinks that the protections afforded clients by Rule 1.10 are not necessary except in the circumstances specified in paragraph (a)(2).

The remainder of the Reporter's Explanation of Changes tracks each paragraph of the Comment to Rule 6.5. To view the full Reporter's Explanation, visit *www.abanet. org/cpr/e2k-rule65rem.html.*

Selected State Variations

Alabama: Rule 6.5 is based on Model Rule 6.5, but Alabama also has a Rule 6.6, which has no Model Rule equivalent. Rule 6.6 states that any inactive member of the Alabama State Bar may render pro bono services by paying special membership dues and becoming a special member of the Alabama State Bar for the year in which the pro bono services are rendered.

California has adopted Rule 1-650 that is substantially similar to Model Rule 6.5, but Rule 1-650(A) also refers to programs sponsored by a "government agency,

---

* Committee Reports do not represent official policy of the ABA. They are for information only, and the opinions are those of the authors of the report.

bar association, [or] law school,'' and California adds a new Rule 1-650(C) that states as follows: ''The personal disqualification of a lawyer participating in the program will not be imputed to other lawyers participating in the program.''

Connecticut adds the following paragraph that is identical to Comment 2 to ABA Rule 6.5:

> (b) A lawyer who provides short-term limited legal services pursuant to this Rule must secure the client's informed consent to the limited scope of the representation. See Rule 1.2 (c). If a short-term limited representation would not be reasonable under the circumstances, the lawyer may offer advice to the client but must also advise the client of the need for further assistance of counsel. Except as provided in this Rule, the Rules of Professional Conduct, including Rules 1.6 and 1.9(c), are applicable to the limited representation.

New Hampshire: Rule 6.5(a) applies only to a ''one time consultation with a client'' instead of the ABA's version ''short-term limited legal services to a client.'' Also, echoing ABA Comment 2 to Rule 6.5, New Hampshire's Rule 6.5(c) provides that ''Rules 1.6 and 1.9(c) are applicable to a representation governed by this Rule.'' Finally, a special New Hampshire Comment states as follows:

> Should a lawyer participating in a one-time consultation under this Rule later discover that the lawyer's firm was representing or later undertook the representation of an adverse client, the prior participation of the attorney will not preclude the lawyer's firm from continuing or undertaking representation of such adverse client. But the participating lawyer will be disqualified and must be screened from any involvement with the firm's adverse client. See ABA Comment [4].

New York: Rule 6.5(a) covers programs sponsored by government agencies and bar associations. The Rule also specifies that a conflict arises only if a lawyer ''has actual knowledge [of the conflict] at the time of commencement of representation.'' New York also adds Rule 6.5(c)-(e), which provides as follows:

> (c) Short-term limited legal services are services providing legal advice or representation free of charge as part of a program described in paragraph (a) with no expectation that the assistance will continue beyond what is necessary to complete an initial consultation, representation or court appearance.
> (d) The lawyer providing short-term limited legal services must secure the client's informed consent to the limited scope of the representation, and such representation shall be subject to the provisions of Rule 1.6.
> (e) This Rule shall not apply where the court before which the matter is pending determines that a conflict of interest exists or, if during the course of the representation, the lawyer providing the services becomes aware of the existence of a conflict of interest precluding continued representation.

Wisconsin: Rule 6.5(a) also applies to a program sponsored by ''a bar association'' or ''an accredited law school.''

Related Materials

ABA Formal Ethics Opinions: No formal ethics opinions have construed Rule 6.5.

Restatement of the Law Governing Lawyers: See Restatement §§121 and 123 in our chapter on the Restatement later in this volume.

ANNOTATIONS ON ARTICLE 7.
INFORMATION ABOUT LEGAL SERVICES

Rule 7.1 Communications Concerning a Lawyer's Services

Canon and Code Antecedents

ABA Canons of Professional Ethics: Canons 27 and 43 provided as follows:

27. Advertising, Direct or Indirect

It is unprofessional to solicit professional employment by circulars, advertisements, through touters or by personal communications or interviews not warranted by personal relations. Indirect advertisements for professional employment such as furnishing or inspiring newspaper comments, or procuring his photograph to be published in connection with causes in which the lawyer has been or is engaged or concerning the manner of their conduct, the magnitude of the interest involved, the importance of the lawyer's position, and all other like self-laudation, offend the traditions and lower the tone of our profession and are reprehensible; but the customary use of simple professional cards is not improper.

Publication in reputable law lists in a manner consistent with the standards of conduct imposed by these canons of brief biographical and informative data is permissible. Such data must not be misleading and may include only a statement of the lawyer's name and the names of his professional associates; addresses, telephone numbers, cable addresses; branches of the profession practiced; date and place of birth and admission to the bar; schools attended; with dates of graduation, degrees and other educational distinctions; public or quasi-public offices; posts of honor; legal authorships; legal teaching positions; memberships and offices in bar associations and committees thereof, in legal and scientific societies and legal fraternities; foreign language ability; the fact of listings in other reputable law lists; the names and addresses of references; and, with their written consent, the names of clients regularly represented. A certificate of compliance with the Rules and Standards issued by the Standing Committee on Law Lists may be treated as evidence that such list is reputable.

It is not improper for a lawyer who is admitted to practice as a proctor in admiralty to use that designation on his letterhead or shingle or for a lawyer who has complied with the statutory requirements of admission to practice before the patent office, to so use the designation "patent attorney" or "patent lawyer" or "trademark attorney" or "trademark lawyer" or any combination of those terms.

43. Approved Law Lists

It shall be improper for a lawyer to permit his name to be published in a law list the conduct, management or contents of which are calculated or likely to deceive or injure the public or the profession, or to lower the dignity or standing of the profession.

ABA Model Code of Professional Responsibility: Compare DR 2-101 and DR 9-101(C) (reprinted later in this volume).

Cross-References in Other Rules

Rule 5.5, Comment 21: "Whether and how lawyers may communicate the availability of their services to prospective clients in this jurisdiction is governed by **Rules 7.1** to 7.5."

Rule 5.7, Comment 10: "The promotion of the law-related services must also in all respects comply with **Rules 7.1** through 7.3, dealing with advertising and solicitation."

Rule 7.2(a): "Subject to the requirements of **Rules 7.1** and 7.3, a lawyer may advertise services through written, recorded or electronic communication, including public media."

Rule 7.2, Comment 5: "Moreover, a lawyer may pay others for generating client leads, such as Internet-based client leads, as long as the lead generator does not recommend the lawyer, any payment to the lead generator is consistent with Rules 1.5(e) (division of fees) and 5.4 (professional independence of the lawyer), and the lead generator's communications are consistent with **Rule 7.1** (communications concerning a lawyer's services). To comply with **Rule 7.1**, a lawyer must not pay a lead generator that states, implies, or creates a reasonable impression that it is recommending the lawyer, is making the referral without payment from the lawyer, or has analyzed a person's legal problems when determining which lawyer should receive the referral."

Rule 7.3, Comment 4: The "potential for informal review is itself likely to help guard against statements and claims that might constitute false and misleading communications, in violation of **Rule 7.1**."

Rule 7.3, Comment 6: "[A]ny solicitation which contains information which is false or misleading within the meaning of **Rule 7.1** . . . is prohibited."

Rule 7.3, Comment 9: "Lawyers who participate in a legal service plan must reasonably assure that the plan sponsors are in compliance with **Rules 7.1**, 7.2 and 7.3(b). See 8.4(a)."

Rule 7.4, Comment 1: Communications claiming specialization "are subject to the 'false and misleading' standard applied in **Rule 7.1** to communications concerning a lawyer's services."

Rule 7.5(a): "A lawyer shall not use a firm name, letterhead or other professional designation that violates **Rule 7.1**. A trade name may be used by a lawyer in private practice if it does not imply a connection with a government agency or with a public or charitable legal services organization and is not otherwise in violation of **Rule 7.1**."

Legislative History of Model Rule 7.1

1980 Discussion Draft of Rule 7.1 (then Rule 9.1) was substantially the same as adopted, except that the first sentence prohibited a lawyer from making any "false, fraudulent, or misleading statement. . . ."

1981 and 1982 Drafts were the same as adopted.

1983 Rule: From 1983 until its amendment in 2002, Rule 7.1 provided as follows:

> A lawyer shall not make a false or misleading communication about the lawyer or the lawyer's services. A communication is false or misleading if it:
>> (a) contains a material misrepresentation of fact or law, or omits a fact necessary to make the statement considered as a whole not materially misleading;
>> (b) is likely to create an unjustified expectation about results the lawyer can achieve, or states or implies that the lawyer can achieve results by means that violate the Rules of Professional Conduct or other law; or

(c) compares the lawyer's services with other lawyers' services, unless the comparison can be factually substantiated.

2002 Amendments: In 2002, the ABA House of Delegates adopted with only minor changes the ABA Ethics 2000 Commission proposal to amend Rule 7.1 and its Comment. The amendments deleted paragraphs (b) and (c) from the former rule, deleted language in Comment 1 relating to "unjustified expectations," and added Comments 2, 3, and 4 to address subjects previously covered in the language deleted from the text and Comment of Rule 7.1.

2012 Amendments: In August 2012, the ABA House of Delegates adopted without change a proposal by the ABA Commission on Ethics 20/20 to amend Comment 3 to Rule 7.1. The amendment deleted the phrase "prospective client" and replaced it with the phrase "the public." The reason for the change was that the phrase "prospective client" had become a defined term in Rule 1.18 and included a narrower category of individuals than Comment 3 was intended to cover.

Selected State Variations

California: Rule 1-400 provides, in pertinent part, as follows:

(A) For purposes of this rule, "communication" means any message or offer made by or on behalf of a member concerning the availability for professional employment of a member or a law firm directed to any former, present, or prospective client, including but not limited to the following:

(1) Any use of firm name, trade name, fictitious name, or other professional designation of such member or law firm; or

(2) Any stationery, letterhead, business card, sign, brochure, or other comparable written material describing such member, law firm, or lawyers; or

(3) Any advertisement (regardless of medium) of such member or law firm directed to the general public or any substantial portion thereof; or

(4) Any unsolicited correspondence from a member or law firm directed to any person or entity. . . .

(C) A communication or a solicitation (as defined herein) shall not:

(1) Contain any untrue statement; or

(2) Contain any matter, or present or arrange any matter in a manner or format which is false, deceptive, or which tends to confuse, deceive, or mislead the public; or

(3) Omit to state any fact necessary to make the statements made, in the light of circumstances under which they are made, not misleading to the public; or

(4) Fail to indicate clearly, expressly, or by context, that it is a communication or solicitation, as the case may be; or

(5) Be transmitted in any manner which involves intrusion, coercion, duress, compulsion, intimidation, threats, or vexatious or harassing conduct. . . .

(E) The Board of Governors of the State Bar shall formulate and adopt standards as to communications which will be presumed to violate this rule 1-400. The standards shall only be used as presumptions affecting the burden of proof in disciplinary proceedings involving alleged violations of these rules. . . . Such standards . . . shall be effective and binding on all members.

The Standards adopted by the State Bar's Board of Governors pursuant to rule 1-400(E) are long and detailed. For example, Standards 1 and 2 provide that the following forms of communication "are presumed to be in violation of rule 1-400":

(1) A "communication" which contains guarantees, warranties, or predictions regarding the result of the representation.

(2) A "communication" which contains testimonials about or endorsements of a member unless such communication also contains an express disclaimer such as "this testimonial or endorsement does not constitute a guarantee, warranty, or prediction regarding the outcome of your legal matter."

See also Business & Professions Code §§6157-6159.2 (generally prohibiting "any false, misleading, or deceptive statement" in a lawyer advertisement; imposing detailed restrictions on advertisements containing dramatizations, impersonations, and spokespersons; and prohibiting various specific claims and techniques); California Labor Code §139.45 ("the Industrial Medical Council and the administrative director shall take particular care to preclude any advertisements with respect to industrial injuries or illnesses that are false or mislead the public with respect to workers' compensation. In promulgating rules with respect to advertising, the State Bar . . . shall also take particular care to achieve the same goal"); and California Labor Code §5432 (requiring every advertisement soliciting workers' compensation clients to state conspicuously: "Making a false or fraudulent workers' compensation claim is a felony subject to up to 5 years in prison or a fine of up to $50,000 or double the value of the fraud, whichever is greater, or by both imprisonment and fine").

Colorado: Colorado retains the pre-2002 version of ABA Model Rule 7.1(a) and adds the following paragraphs:

(b) No lawyer shall, directly or indirectly, pay all or a part of the cost of communications concerning a lawyer's services by a lawyer not in the same firm unless the communication discloses the name and address of the non-advertising lawyer, the relationship between the advertising lawyer and the non-advertising lawyer, and whether the advertising lawyer may refer any case received through the advertisement to the non-advertising lawyer.

(c) Unsolicited communications concerning a lawyer's services mailed to prospective clients shall be sent only by regular U.S. mail, not by registered mail or other forms of restricted delivery, and shall not resemble legal pleadings or other legal documents.

(d) Any communication that states or implies the client does not have to pay a fee if there is no recovery shall also disclose that the client may be liable for costs. This provision does not apply to communications that only state that contingent or percentage fee arrangements are available, or that only state the initial consultation is free.

District of Columbia: Rule 7.1(a) adds that a communication is false or misleading if it "[c]ontains an assertion about the lawyer or the lawyer's services that cannot be substantiated."

Florida: Florida's lawyer advertising rules are more comprehensive and detailed than the ABA Model Rules of Professional Conduct or those in any other American jurisdiction. They are often revised and defy easy summary or comparison with the ABA rules. (Indeed, in July 2011, just before this book went to press, the Florida Bar submitted to the Florida Supreme Court substantial proposed revisions to the advertising rules.) The rules address in depth the content of advertisements, electronic and computer advertising, referral services, and filing requirements. Some of the more noteworthy Florida advertising and solicitation provisions appear in Selected State Variations under other rules in Article 7.

Georgia: In the rules effective November 3, 2011, Georgia generally tracks the pre-2002 version of ABA Model Rule 7.1, but adds special subparagraphs requiring that all advertisements mentioning contingent fees or stating "no fee unless you win or collect" or any similar phrase must also conspicuously present a disclaimer stating: "Court costs and other additional expenses of legal action usually must be paid by the client. Contingent fees are not permitted in all types of cases."

Indiana: Comment 2 to Rule 7.1 identifies ten types of statements that are presumptively misleading, such as a statement that "appeals primarily to a lay person's fear, greed, or desire for revenge" or "contains a dramatization or re-creation of events unless the advertising clearly and conspicuously discloses that a dramatization or re-creation is being presented."

Iowa has many rules on lawyer advertising. Its version of Rule 7.1 adds the following:

> (b) A lawyer shall not communicate with the public using statements that are unverifiable. In addition, advertising permitted under these rules shall not rely on emotional appeal or contain any statement or claim relating to the quality of the lawyer's legal services.

Louisiana: Rule 7.1(a) identifies a non-exclusive list of advertising methods that lawyers may use. Among other variations, Rule 7.1(c) explicitly exempts from the rules any advertising that is not "motivated by pecuniary gain."

Michigan adds restrictions to the black letter of Rule 7.1 that appear only in Comments to the Model Rule, including limitations on statements that might create unjustified expectations and statements that involve comparisons with other lawyers.

Mississippi: Rule 7.5(a) requires that a copy or recording of any lawyer advertisement to be published must be submitted to the Office of the General Counsel of the Mississippi Bar "prior to its first dissemination" unless exempted under an extensive list in Rule 7.5(b). If a lawyer submits a proposed advertisement 45 days before its dissemination, the lawyer may request an "advisory opinion." If the Office of the General Counsel does not respond within 45 days, the advertisement will be "deemed approved," but if the Office of General Counsel determines within the 45-day period that there is "reasonable doubt" that the advertisement complies with the rules, it may extend the 45-day period.

Missouri: Rule 7.1 adds that a communication is false or misleading if it:

> (b) is likely to create an unjustified expectation about results the lawyer can achieve;
>
> (c) proclaims results obtained on behalf of clients, such as the amount of a damage award or the lawyer's record in obtaining favorable verdicts or settlements, without stating that past results afford no guarantee of future results and that every case is different and must be judged on its own merits;
>
> (d) states or implies that the lawyer can achieve results by means that violate the Rules of Professional Conduct or other law;
>
> (e) compares the quality of a lawyer's or a law firm's services with other lawyers' services, unless the comparison can be factually substantiated;
>
> (f) advertises for a specific type of case concerning which the lawyer has neither experience nor competence;
>
> (g) indicates an area of practice in which the lawyer routinely refers matters to other lawyers, without conspicuous identification of such fact;

(h) contains any paid testimonial about or endorsement of the lawyer, without conspicuous identification of the fact that payment has been made for the testimonial or endorsement;

(i) contains any simulated portrayal of a lawyer, client, victim, scene, or event without conspicuous identification of the fact that it is a simulation. . . .

(j) provides an office address for an office staffed only part-time or by appointment only, without conspicuous identification of such fact; or

(k) states that legal services are available on a contingent or no-recovery-no-fee basis without stating conspicuously that the client may be responsible for costs or expenses, if that is the case.

The presumptions that statements are misleading contained in Rule 4-7.1(c), (g), (h), and (k) shall not apply to a not-for-profit organization funded in whole or in part by the Legal Services Corporation . . . or to pro bono services provided free of charge by a not-for-profit organization, a court-annexed program, a bar association, or an accredited law school.

Nevada: Among many other variations, Rule 7.1(d) adds that a communication is false or misleading if it "contains a testimonial or endorsement which violates any portion of this Rule."

In addition, Rule 1.4(c) requires every lawyer or law firm to "have available" a "Lawyer's Biographical Data Form" that must "be provided upon request of the State Bar or a client or prospective client. . . ." Rule 1.4(c) also specifies information that must be included in the form and included with every written advertisement, and it specifies other detailed information that must be provided to a client or prospective client upon request (such as a "good faith estimate of the number of jury trials tried to a verdict by the lawyer to the present date, identifying the court or courts"). These requirements are also reinforced in Rule 1.18(g) (relating to prospective clients).

New Jersey: Rule 7.1 prohibits a lawyer from making a false or misleading communication about the lawyer, the lawyer's services, or "any matter in which the lawyer has or seeks professional involvement." A communication is false or misleading under New Jersey Rule 7.1(a) if (among other things) it "(2) is likely to create an unjustified expectation about results the lawyer can achieve," or "(3) compares the lawyer's services with other lawyers' services, unless (i) the name of the comparing organization is stated, (ii) the basis for the comparison can be substantiated, and (iii) the communication includes the following disclaimer in a readily discernable manner: 'No aspect of this advertisement has been approved by the Supreme Court of New Jersey'" or "(4) relates to legal fees other than" a specified list of permitted statements, including "the fee for an initial consultation," "fees for specifically described legal services, provided there is a reasonable disclosure of all relevant variables and considerations so that the statement would not be misunderstood or deceptive," and "specified hourly rates, provided the statement makes clear that the total charge will vary according to the number of hours devoted to the matter, and in relation to the varying hourly rates charged for the services of different individuals who may be assigned to the matter. . . ." Rule 7.1(b) makes it "unethical" for a lawyer to use an advertisement "known to have been disapproved by the Committee on Attorney Advertising, or one substantially the same as the one disapproved, until or unless modified or reversed by the Advertising Committee. . . ."

New York: New York adds the following definitions to Rule 1.0 (terminology):

> (a) "Advertisement" means any public or private communication made by or on behalf of a lawyer or law firm about that lawyer or law firm's services, the primary purpose of which is for the retention of the lawyer or law firm. It does not include communications to existing clients or other lawyers.
>
> (c) "Computer-accessed communication" means any communication made by or on behalf of a lawyer or law firm that is disseminated through the use of a computer or related electronic device, including, but not limited to, web sites, weblogs, search engines, electronic mail, banner advertisements, pop-up and pop-under advertisements, chat rooms, list servers, instant messaging, or other internet presences, and any attachments or links related thereto.

Rule 7.1 varies considerably from the Model Rule and contains many unique prohibitions, requirements, and comments. For example, Rule 7.1(b) lists numerous items (*e.g.*, "legal and nonlegal education," "foreign language fluency," "fees for initial consultation," and "bona fide professional ratings") that may be included in an advertisement. Rule 7.1(e)-(f) mandates various disclosures and disclaimers.

Rule 7.1(c) was amended to remove or revise several advertising provisions restrictions that were held to be unconstitutional in *Alexander v. Cahill*, 598 F.3d 79 (2d Cir. 2010), including restrictions on endorsements by current clients, a ban on the portrayal of a judge, and a ban on the use of a "nickname, moniker, motto or trade name that implies an ability to obtain results in a matter." Other restrictions remain intact, however, including mandatory disclosures when using actors or depicting fictionalized events.

North Carolina retains the subparagraphs that were deleted from the pre-2002 version of ABA Model Rule 7.1. North Carolina also adds a Rule 7.1(b) providing that a "dramatization depicting a fictional situation is misleading unless it . . . contains a conspicuous written or oral statement at the beginning and end of the communication, explaining that the communication contains a dramatization and does not depict actual events or real persons."

Ohio: Rule 7.1 also prohibits a lawyer from making or using a "nonverifiable" communication about the lawyer or the lawyer's services.

Oregon: Rule 7.1(a) contains a list of 12 specific items that may not appear in advertisements or may only appear under particular circumstances. Actors may be used if the communication "clearly and conspicuously discloses" that status.

Pennsylvania: Rule 7.1 tracks ABA Model Rule 7.1 verbatim — but Pennsylvania Rule 7.2 contains numerous restrictions designed to prevent false or misleading communications. For example, Rule 7.2 prohibits endorsements by any celebrity or public figure; prohibits lawyers from stating or implying that they are associated together in a law firm if that is not the case; prohibits any portrayal of a client by a non-client; and prohibits the use of "pictures, or persons, which are not actual or authentic, without a disclosure that such depiction is a dramatization." An unusual Rule 7.2(k) provides that "[i]f a lawyer or law firm advertises for a particular type of case that the lawyer or law firm ordinarily does not handle from intake through trial, that fact must be disclosed. A lawyer or law firm shall not advertise as a pretext to refer cases obtained from advertising to other lawyers."

Virginia In the Rules effective December 1, 2012, Virginia adds Rule 7.1(b)-(d) as follows:

(b) A communication violates this rule if it advertises specific or cumulative case results, without a disclaimer that (i) puts the case results in a context that is not misleading; (ii) states that case results depend upon a variety of factors unique to each case; and (iii) further states that case results do not guarantee or predict a similar result in any future case undertaken by the lawyer. The disclaimer shall precede the communication of the case results. When the communication is in writing, the disclaimer shall be in bold type face and uppercase letters in a font size that is at least as large as the largest text used to advertise the specific or cumulative case results and in the same color and against the same colored background as the text used to advertise the specific or cumulative case results.

(c) Any advertising pursuant to this Rule shall include the name and office address of at least one lawyer responsible for its content or, in the alternative, a law firm may file with the Virginia State Bar a current written statement identifying the lawyer responsible for the law firm's advertising and its office address. The law firm shall promptly update the written statement if there is any change in status.

(d) A lawyer shall timely respond to and fully cooperate with any requests for information by Ethics Counsel regarding the lawyer's advertising.

Related Materials

ABA Aspirational Goals for Lawyer Advertising: In 1988, the ABA's House of Delegates endorsed a series of nonbinding "aspirational" goals written by the ABA's Commission on Advertising. These Aspirational Goals are intended to permit lawyers to advertise "effectively yet with dignity." They are available in full online at *http://www.americanbar.org/groups/professional_responsibility/resources/professionalism/ professionalism_ethics_in_lawyer_advertising/abaaspirationalgoals.html.* Here are some significant excerpts:*

Preamble

[E]mpirical evidence suggests that undignified advertising can detract from the public's confidence in the legal profession and respect for the justice system.

Under present case law, the matter of dignity is widely believed to be so subjective as to be beyond the scope of constitutionally permitted regulation. Nevertheless, it seems entirely proper for the organized bar to suggest non-binding aspirational goals urging lawyers who wish to advertise to do so in a dignified manner. . . .

Aspirational Goals

6. Lawyers should consider that the use of inappropriately dramatic music, unseemly slogans, hawkish spokespersons, premium offers, slapstick routines or outlandish settings in advertising does not instill confidence in the lawyer or the legal profession and undermines the serious purpose of legal services and the judicial system. . . .

9. Lawyers should design their advertising to attract legal matters which they are competent to handle.

10. Lawyers should be concerned with making legal services more affordable to the public. Lawyer advertising may be designed to build up client bases so that efficiencies of scale may be achieved that will translate into more affordable legal services.

ABA Best Practice Guidelines for Legal Information Web Site Providers: In 2003, the ABA adopted a set of Best Practice Guidelines for Legal Information Web Site Providers. The goal of the Guidelines is "to promote the development of quality legal web sites and to provide guidance to legal web site developers." The Guidelines are available online at *http://meetings.abanet.org/webupload/commupload/EP024500/relatedresources/best_practice_presentation.pdf.*

ABA Commission on Ethics 20/20: In 2009, the ABA created the ABA Commission on Ethics 20/20, which is comprehensively reviewing the ABA Model Rules of Professional Conduct and other lawyer regulatory sources in light of globalization and changes in technology. In 2010, the ABA House of Delegates approved a resolution stating: "Resolved, that the American Bar Association examine any efforts to publish national, state, territorial, and local rankings of law firms and law schools." ABA President Carolyn Lamm then asked the Commission on Ethics 20/20 to examine the issue of lawyer and law firm ratings and rankings. (A special committee of the ABA Section of Legal Education and Admissions to the Bar was created to study law school rankings, which are a separate subject.) The Ethics 20/20 Commission, in turn, formed a Working Group on Lawyer and Law Firm Ratings and Rankings and asked former ABA President Roberta Cooper Ramo and Donald B. Hilliker to co-chair it.

In August 2011, the Commission finalized its Informational Report. The Report identified various issues associated with rankings and ratings, but concluded that "no change is currently required to the black letter text of or Comment to Model Rule 7.1." However, the Commission recommended that the ABA Standing Committee on Ethics and Professional Responsibility draft a Formal Opinion that discusses related issues, including (i) the extent to which lawyers can respond to requests for information from rankings and ratings providers in a manner that is consistent with lawyers' duty to protect confidential information and (ii) the extent to which lawyers can communicate to the public the results of various rankings and ratings while ensuring that those communications are truthful and not misleading. A copy of the Informational Report, as well as more information about the Ethics 20/20 Commission, is available on the website of the Commission on Ethics 20/20 at *www.americanbar.org/Ethics2020.*

ABA Commission on Responsibility in Client Development (formerly the ABA Commission on Advertising) and ABA Standing Committee on Professionalism: In 1977, the year that the United States Supreme Court extended First Amendment protection to lawyer advertising, the ABA appointed a Commission on Advertising. In 1994, the Commission on Advertising held public hearings to explore whether advertising by lawyers was contributing to a perceived decline in the public's opinion of lawyers, and whether advertising by lawyers was helping a significant number of people, especially the poor, to locate lawyers. In 1995, the Commission issued a final report entitled Lawyer Advertising at the Crossroads (ISBN No. 1-57073-142-X). The Executive Summary of the report included the following observations:

> While many find some forms of advertising offensive, regulations which violate the right of lawyers to communicate their services do nothing more than create stopgap measures that forestall true solutions. . . .

Public opinion research recurrently shows that the principal factors contributing to a decline in the public image of lawyers involve perceptions of honesty, caring and value. Those who dislike lawyers believe they are dishonest, selfish and too expensive. While the legal profession strongly believes that advertising contributes to the decline of the profession's image, the public rarely mentions advertising as a factor. Dominant influences in forming opinions about lawyers are personal contacts, media reports and fictional representations on television, in movies and in books.

Research specifically on lawyer advertising indicates the public considers it a source of information, but tends to find it objectionable when it becomes increasingly invasive. Therefore, people tend to object to television commercials, billboards, and direct mail more so than ads in the Yellow Pages and in newspapers. . . .

[I]t is clear that advertising is a major factor in the delivery of legal services, especially to the poor. While 70 to 80 percent of those who have used a lawyer found the lawyer through some form of personal referral, an increasing number of people find their lawyers through impersonal methods such as lawyer referral services, prepaid services and group legal plans and advertising. Advertising, including the use of the Yellow Pages, is consistently the most frequently used of the impersonal methods of finding a lawyer. . . .

In 1999, to reflect its expanding mission, the Commission on Advertising changed its name to the Commission on Responsibility in Client Development. In 2002, however, the ABA "sunset" the Commission because its work duplicated the work of the ABA Standing Committee on Professionalism. Questions on lawyer advertising should now be directed to the ABA Standing Committee on Professionalism. For more information, visit *http://www.americanbar.org/groups/professional_responsibility/resources/professionalism/professionalism_ethics_in_lawyer_advertising.html.*

ABA Formal Ethics Opinions: See ABA Formal Ethics Ops. 87-355 (1987), 90-357 (1990), 93-379 (1993), 94-388 (1994), 95-391 (1995), 99-414 (1999), 03-430 (2003), 08-451 (2008), and 10-457 (2010).

FTC Guides Concerning the Use of Endorsements and Testimonials in Advertising: The Federal Trade Commission (FTC) has issued Guides to address endorsements by consumers, experts, organizations, and celebrities, as well as the disclosure of important connections between advertisers and endorsers. In 2009, the FTC amended the Guides (the first amendments since 1980). Among other changes, the 2009 Guides contain examples to illustrate the principle that advertisers must disclose "material connections" (such as cash payments or free services) between advertisers and endorsers. Of particular interest to the legal profession, the examples address what constitutes an "endorsement" when a message is conveyed by bloggers or other "word-of-mouth" marketers. The revised Guides specify that if a blogger receives cash or in-kind payment to post a review, the post is considered an endorsement.

The revised Guides also address celebrity endorsers. The Guides state that both advertisers and endorsers may be liable either for making false or unsubstantiated claims in an endorsement, or for failing to disclose material connections between the advertiser and an endorser. The revised Guides also make clear that celebrities have a duty to disclose their relationships with advertisers when making endorsements outside the context of traditional ads, such as on talk shows or in social media.

The revised Guides are available at 16 C.F.R. Part 255, and are available with historical analysis and commentary by the FTC at 74 Fed. Reg. 53124 (Oct. 15, 2009).

IRS Regulations: In the regulations governing practice before the Internal Revenue Service, 31 C.F.R. §10.30(a)(1) provides that a lawyer admitted to practice before the IRS "may not, with respect to any Internal Revenue Service matter, in any way use or participate in the use of any form of public communication or private solicitation containing a false, fraudulent, ... misleading or deceptive statement or claim."

Lanham Act: False advertising by a lawyer may violate §1125(a)(1)(B) of the Lanham Act, 15 U.S.C. §1125(a)(1)(B), which imposes potential civil liability on any person who "uses in commerce any . . . false or misleading description of fact, or false or misleading representation of fact, which . . . in commercial advertising or promotion, misrepresents the nature, characteristics, qualities, or geographic origin of his or her . . . services, or commercial activities. . . ." In *Haymond v. Lundy*, 2001 WL 15956 (E.D. Pa. 2001), the court held that advertising by a lawyer, if false or misleading, would be actionable under §1125(a) of the Lanham Act.

National Federation of Paralegal Associations: The National Federation of Paralegal Associations, Inc. (NFPA) is an organization comprised of paralegal associations and individual paralegals throughout the United States and Canada. In 1993, the NFPA adopted a Model Code of Ethics and Professional Responsibility to "delineate the principles for ethics and conduct to which every paralegal should aspire." The Code, last updated in 2006, contains the following language related to ABA Model Rule 7.1:

Rule 1.7 A Paralegal's Title Shall be Fully Disclosed

EC-1.7(a) A paralegal's title shall clearly indicate the individual's status and shall be disclosed in all business and professional communications to avoid misunderstandings and misconceptions about the paralegal's role and responsibilities.

EC-1.7(b) A paralegal's title shall be included if the paralegal's name appears on business cards, letterhead, brochures, directories, and advertisements.

EC-1.7(c) A paralegal shall not use letterhead, business cards or other promotional materials to create a fraudulent impression of his/her status or ability to practice in the jurisdiction in which the paralegal practices.

The full NFPA Model Code of Ethics and Professional Responsibility and other ethics resources regarding paralegals are available at *www.paralegals.org* (click on the top menu on "Positions & Issues," then on "Ethics," then on "Model Code of Ethics and Professional Responsibility and Guidelines for Enforcement").

Restatement of the Law Governing Lawyers: The Restatement has no provision comparable to ABA Model Rule 7.1.

Rule 7.2   Advertising

Canon and Code Antecedents

ABA Canons of Professional Ethics: Canons 40 and 46 provided as follows:

40. Newspapers

A lawyer may with propriety write articles for publications in which he gives information upon the law; but he should not accept employment from such publications to advise inquirers in respect to their individual rights.

46. Notice to Local Lawyers

A lawyer available to act as an associate of other lawyers in a particular branch of the law or legal service may send to local lawyers only and publish in his local legal journal, a brief and dignified announcement of his availability to serve other lawyers in connection therewith. The announcement should be in a form which does not constitute a statement or representation of special experience or expertness.

ABA Model Code of Professional Responsibility: Compare DR 2-101(B), DR 2-101(D), DR 2-101(I), DR 2-103(B), and DR 2-103(D) (reprinted later in this volume).

Cross-References in Other Rules

Rule 5.5, Comment 21: "Whether and how lawyers may communicate the availability of their services to prospective clients in this jurisdiction is governed by **Rules 7.1 to 7.5**."

Rule 5.7, Comment 10: "The promotion of the law-related services must also in all respects comply with **Rules 7.1 through 7.3**, dealing with advertising and solicitation."

Rule 7.1, Comment 1: "This Rule governs all communications about a lawyer's services, including advertising permitted by **Rule 7.2**."

Rule 7.3, Comment 4: "The contents of advertisements and communications permitted under **Rule 7.2** can be permanently recorded so that they cannot be disputed and may be shared with others who know the lawyer."

Rule 7.3, Comment 6: "[I]f after sending a letter or other communication to a client as permitted by **Rule 7.2** the lawyer receives no response, any further effort to communicate with the prospective client may violate the provisions of Rule 7.3(b)."

Rule 7.3, Comment 7: Rule 7.3 does not prohibit lawyers from communicating with representatives of organizations or groups regarding group or prepaid legal service plans because such communications "are functionally similar to and serve the same purpose as advertising permitted under **Rule 7.2**."

Rule 7.3, Comment 9: "Lawyers who participate in a legal service plan must reasonably assure that the plan sponsors are in compliance with **Rules** 7.1, **7.2** and 7.3(b). See 8.4(a)."

Legislative History of Model Rule 7.2

1980 Discussion Draft (then Rule 9.2) provided as follows:

(b) A copy or record of an advertisement in its entirety shall be kept for one year after its dissemination.

(c) A lawyer shall not give anything of value to a person for recommending the lawyer's services, except that a lawyer may pay the reasonable cost of advertising permitted by this rule.

1981 and 1982 Drafts were substantially the same as adopted, except that subparagraph (a) permitted any "written communication not involving personal contact."

1983 Rule: As originally adopted in 1983, Rule 7.2 provided as follows:

(a) Subject to the requirements of Rule 7.1, a lawyer may advertise services through public media, such as a telephone directory, legal directory, newspaper or other periodical, outdoor, radio or television, or through written communications not involving solicitation as defined in Rule 7.3.

(b) A copy or recording of an advertisement or written communication shall be kept for two years after its last dissemination along with a record of when and where it was used.

(c) A lawyer shall not give anything of value to a person for recommending the lawyer's services, except that a lawyer may pay the reasonable cost of advertising or written communication permitted by this rule, and may pay the usual charges of a not-for-profit lawyer referral service or other legal service organization.

(d) Any communication made pursuant to this rule shall include the name of at least one lawyer responsible for its content.

1989 Amendments: In 1989, the ABA House of Delegates made minor amendments to Rule 7.2(a) and (c), but did not amend the Comment in any way.

1990 Amendment: At its 1990 Mid-Year Meeting, the ABA House of Delegates added subparagraph 7.2(b)(3) to reflect the addition of Rule 1.17 (Sale of Law Practice).

2002 Amendments: In 2002, the ABA House of Delegates adopted with minor changes the ABA Ethics 2000 Commission proposal to amend Rule 7.2 and its Comment. The amendments simplified Rule 7.2(a), deleted former Rule 7.2(b), added the last sentence of current Rule 7.2(b)(2), expanded Comment 3, deleted former Comment 5, revised current Comment 5, and added Comments 6 and 7.

In addition, the ABA added Rule 7.2(b)(4) based on a proposal by the ABA Standing Committee on Ethics and Professional Responsibility. (The ABA simultaneously added a new sentence to the Comment to Rule 7.5 — see the Legislative History following that rule.) We reprint the following excerpts from the Report that the Standing Committee submitted in support of its proposal to add Rule 7.2(b)(4):

*ABA Committee Report in Support of August 2002 Amendment**

In July 2000 the House of Delegates adopted Resolution 10F relating to the issue of multi-disciplinary practice. By that resolution, the Standing Committee on Ethics and Professional Responsibility was directed to review the Model Rules of Professional

---

* Committee Reports do not represent official policy of the ABA. They are for information only, and the opinions are those of the authors of the report.

Conduct . . . and to recommend any changes the Committee believed necessary "to assure that there are safeguards in the [Model Rules of Professional Conduct] relating to strategic alliances and other contractual relationships with non-legal professional services providers consistent with the statement of principles in [Resolution 10F]."

The Committee reviewed the Model Rules and Resolution 10F as directed by the House of Delegates. It considered the "strategic alliance" or "contractual relationship" arrangements identified in Resolution 10F to be arrangements by professional services providers and lawyers to steer business to each other on a systematic and regular basis. Such arrangements may range from a simple understanding generally to refer business to each other to an agreement that includes sharing space, computer systems, and the like to reduce costs by obtaining economies of scale or other efficiencies.

The Committee took into account the "core values" of the profession as described in paragraph 1 of Resolution 10F: the duty of loyalty, the duty to exercise independent professional judgment for the benefit of the client, the duty to protect client confidences, and the traditional prohibitions against sharing legal fees with nonlawyers and against ownership and control of the practice of law by nonlawyers. . . .

[W]hen lawyers enter into cross-referral agreements with other lawyers and nonlawyer professionals, clients need to be informed of those agreements in order to decide whether to accept the lawyer's suggestions to use the other professionals' services. A per se prohibition against exclusive referral arrangements also is required, to ensure that a lawyer is free to exercise independent professional judgment when counseling clients to consult with other professionals. Each of these concepts is therefore embodied in the Committee's proposed changes to the black-letter of Rule 7.2(b).

The . . . Comment to Rule 7.2(b) should be amplified to address lawyers' participation in referral arrangements in the context of related Model Rules. For example, the independent professional judgment required of a lawyer who is making referrals to other professionals is set out in Rules 2.1 and 5.4(c), which are therefore included in the Comment. Similarly, the Comment notes that actual payment by a lawyer to a referring nonlawyer professional for the referral itself is prohibited, except in the narrow lawyer-to-lawyer referral situation that is permitted under Rule 1.5(e)'s exception to the prohibition against fee-sharing. Finally, reference is made in the Comment to Rule 1.7 ("Conflict of Interest"), to remind lawyers that they must not allow their contractual relationships for reciprocal referrals, which might be considered "related business interests," to adversely affect the representation of their clients.

The Committee believes that these proposed amendments to Model Rule 7.2 and its Comment, addressing reciprocal referral agreements between lawyers and other lawyers or nonlawyer professionals, and its amendment to Model Rule 7.5's Comment, will provide necessary and helpful safeguards to the ethical practice of law, . . . and therefore urges their adoption.

2012 Amendments: In August 2012, the ABA House of Delegates adopted without change a proposal by the ABA Commission on Ethics 20/20 to amend several Comments to Rule 7.2, particularly Comment 5. The changes provided lawyers with greater guidance on the use of new forms of advertising, particularly Internet-based client development tools.

Selected State Variations

Arizona: Rule 7.2(b)(2) explicitly permits a lawyer to pay a not-for-profit or qualified lawyer referral service "a fee calculated as a percentage of legal fees earned by the lawyer to whom the service or organization has referred a matter, provided that any such percentage fee shall not exceed ten percent, and shall be used only to help defray the reasonable operating expenses of the service or organization and to fund public service activities, including the delivery of pro bono legal services. The fees paid by a client referred by such service shall not exceed the total charges that the client would have paid had no such service been involved." Arizona omits Rule 7.2(b)(4) (governing reciprocal referral agreements), but adds Rule 7.2(d) (setting forth detailed requirements for all advertisements containing information about legal fees). Arizona also adds Rule 7.2(e), which provides:

> (e) . . . If a law firm advertises on electronic media and a person appears purporting to be a lawyer, such person shall in fact be a lawyer employed full-time at the advertising law firm. If a law firm advertises a particular legal service on electronic media, and a lawyer appears as the person purporting to render the service, the lawyer appearing shall be the lawyer who will actually perform the service advertised unless the advertisement discloses that the service may be performed by other lawyers in the firm.

Finally, Arizona adds Rule 7.2(f), which requires that certain information be presented to potential clients in a manner that is "clear and conspicuous."

Arkansas permits actors to be used in advertisements so long as they are identified by name and relationship to the advertising lawyer. Dramatizations are forbidden. Clients and former clients "shall not be used in any manner whatsoever in advertisements."

California: Rule 1-320 provides, in pertinent part, as follows:

> (A) Neither a member nor a law firm shall directly or indirectly share legal fees with a person who is not a lawyer, except that . . .
>
> (4) A member may pay a prescribed registration, referral, or participation fee to a lawyer referral service established, sponsored, and operated in accordance with the State Bar of California's Minimum Standards for a Lawyer Referral Service in California.
>
> (B) A member shall not compensate, give, or promise anything of value to any person or entity for the purpose of recommending or securing employment of the member or the member's law firm by a client, or as a reward for having made a recommendation resulting in employment of the member or the member's law firm by a client. A member's offering of or giving a gift or gratuity to any person or entity having made a recommendation resulting in the employment of the member or the member's law firm shall not of itself violate this rule, provided that the gift or gratuity was not offered or given in consideration of any promise, agreement, or understanding that such a gift or gratuity would be forthcoming or that referrals would be made or encouraged in the future.
>
> (C) A member shall not compensate, give, or promise anything of value to any representative of the press, radio, television, or other communication medium in anticipation of or in return for publicity of the member, the law firm, or any other member as such in a news item, but the incidental provision of food or beverage shall not of itself violate this rule.

Rule 1-400(F) provides:

> (D) A member shall retain for two years a true and correct copy or recording of any communication made by written or electronic media. Upon written request, the member shall make any such copy or recording available to the State Bar, and, if requested, shall provide to the State Bar evidence to support any factual or objective claim contained in the communication.

The Standards adopted by the State Bar pursuant to Rule 1-400 provide that a communication is "presumed to be in violation of rule 1-400" if it "implies that the member or law firm is participating in a lawyer referral service which has been certified by the State Bar of California or as having satisfied the Minimum Standards for Lawyer Referral Services in California, when that is not the case." Rule 1-600(B) provides that the State Bar's Board of Governors "shall formulate and adopt Minimum Standards for Lawyer Referral Services, which . . . shall be binding on members." Those standards are found after California Business & Professions Code §6155, which governs lawyer referral services.

Also relevant to ABA Model Rule 7.2 are Business & Professions Code §6129 (prohibiting lawyers from purchasing claims) and §§6157.1-6159.2 (governing lawyer advertising, especially in the electronic media).

Connecticut adds many paragraphs with no counterpart in ABA Model Rule 7.2 but omits ABA Model Rule 7.2(b)(4) (regarding reciprocal referral agreements).

District of Columbia omits ABA Model Rule 7.2, but D.C. Rule 7.1(c) provides that a lawyer "shall not knowingly assist an organization that furnishes or pays for legal services to others to promote the use of the lawyer's services . . . as a private practitioner, if the promotional activity involves the use of coercion, duress, compulsion, intimidation, threats, or vexatious or harassing conduct."

Florida: Rule 4-7.1(e), (g) expressly exempts from the advertising rules any communications to other lawyers as well as to existing or former clients. Rule 4-7.4(b)(2) provides that "[e]very written communication disseminated by a lawyer referral service shall be accompanied by a written statement detailing the background, training, and experience of each lawyer to whom the recipient may be referred." Rule 4-7.10 sets forth elaborate requirements for lawyer referral services. In addition, Chapter 8 of the Rules Regulating the Florida Bar sets forth extensive requirements for the operation of lawyer referral services by local bar associations, and no local bar association may operate a referral service absent express approval from the state bar.

Georgia: In the rules effective November 3, 2011, Georgia moves Rule 7.2(b) and its Comment to Rule 7.3(c), and modifies and expands the exceptions in ABA Model Rule 7.2(c) regarding lawyer referral services.

Indiana: Rule 7.2(b) defines "advertising" as "any manner of public communication partly or entirely intended or expected to promote the purchase or use of the professional services of a lawyer, law firm, or any employee of either involving the practice of law or law-related services." Comment 2 identifies 20 different permissible subjects for advertising, such as the lawyer's "date and place of birth," "names and addresses of bank references," and "whether credit cards . . . are accepted."

Iowa: Rule 7.2 does not govern communications between lawyers, but prohibits any "visual display" on television unless the same display would be "allowed in print"; prohibits "background sound" in electronic media; and expressly permits lawyers to communicate 14 items to the public provided if it is done "in a dignified style." Rule 7.2 also imposes extensive limitations on advertising fee information; and requires any communication advising the institution of litigation to "disclose that the filing of a claim or suit solely to coerce a settlement or to harass another could be illegal and could render the person so filing liable for malicious prosecution or abuse of process." In addition, borrowing from the ABA Model Code of Professional Responsibility, Iowa has a detailed rule (Rule 7.7) called "Recommendation of

Professional Employment'' and another (Rule 7.8) on "Suggestion of Need of Legal Services."

Louisiana: Some portions of Rule 7.2(c) were struck down as unconstitutional in *Public Citizen, Inc. v. Louisiana Attorney Disciplinary Board,* 632 F.3d 212 (5th Cir. 2011). Rule 7.2(c) nevertheless contains many other detailed restrictions that survived the constitutional challenge, including provisions related to how long a lawyer must honor an advertised fee and a provision concerning the use of dual language advertisements. Finally, subject to some exceptions in Rule 7.8, Rule 7.7 requires lawyers to file their advertising with the Louisiana State Bar Association, which is charged with ensuring that advertising complies with the advertising rules.

Maine: Maine Rule 7.2-A offers a variety of aspirational goals for lawyer advertising, including that lawyers use "dignified" advertisements and avoid "crass" marketing that "undermines the serious purpose of legal services and the judicial system."

Maryland: Among other variations, Maryland adds Rule 7.2(e), which provides that "[a]n advertisement or communication indicating that no fee will be charged in the absence of a recovery shall also disclose whether the client will be liable for any expenses," and Rule 7.2(f), which requires lawyers, including those participating in an advertising group or lawyer referral service, to be "personally responsible for compliance with the provisions of Rules 7.1, 7.2, 7.3, 7.4, and 7.5."

Massachusetts: Rule 7.2(a) adds that lawyers may advertise in "an electronic or computer accessed directory." Comment 3A provides, in part, as follows:

> The advertising and solicitation rules can generally be applied to computer-accessed or other similar types of communications by analogizing the communication to its hard-copy form. Thus, because it is not a communication directed to a specific recipient, a web site or home page would generally be considered advertising subject to this rule, rather than solicitation subject to Rule 7.3. . . .

Michigan: Rule 7.2 omits ABA Model Rule 7.2(b)(4) and 7.2(c). Rule 7.2(b) adds a recordkeeping requirement for advertisements. Finally, Rule 6.3(b) permits a lawyer to "participate in and pay the usual charges of a not-for-profit lawyer referral service that recommends legal services to the public" only if the referral service meets detailed requirements, including that the service:

> (3) is open to all lawyers licensed and eligible to practice in this state who maintain an office within the geographical area served, and who:
>> (i) meet reasonable and objective requirements of experience . . . ;
>> (ii) pay reasonable registration and membership fees not to exceed an amount established by the State Bar to encourage widespread lawyer participation; and
>> (iii) maintain a policy of errors and omissions insurance, or provide proof of financial responsibility, in an amount at least equal to the minimum established by the State Bar.
> (4) ensures that the combined fees and expenses charged a prospective client by a qualified service and a lawyer to whom the client is referred not exceed the total charges the client would have incurred had no referral service been involved. . . .

Under Rule 6.3(d), the State Bar or "any aggrieved person" may seek an injunction against violations of Rule 6.3(b), and if the injunction is granted, the petitioner shall be entitled to reasonable costs and attorney fees.

Missouri: Rule 7.2(a) adds permission to advertise "through direct mail advertising distributed generally to persons not known to need legal services of the kind provided by the lawyer in a particular matter.'' Missouri omits ABA Model Rule 7.2(b)(4). Rule 7.2(d) provides that a lawyer may not "pay all or a part of the cost of an advertisement in the public media unless such advertisement discloses the name and address of the financing lawyer, the relationship between the advertising lawyer and the financing lawyer, and whether the advertising lawyer is likely to refer cases received through the advertisement to the financing lawyer.'' In addition, Rules 7.2(f) and (g) require all advertisements (except targeted letters and emails and advertisements limited to specified basic information such as name, address, and fields of practice) to state the following: "The choice of a lawyer is an important decision and should not be based solely upon advertisements.'' Rule 7.2(h) governs advertisements that use more than one language, and Rule 7.2(i) explains that the Rule does not apply to "services provided by a not-for-profit organization funded in whole or in part by the Legal Services Corporation . . . or to pro bono services provided free of charge by a not-for-profit organization, a court-annexed program, a bar association, or an accredited law school.'' The Rule also does not apply to "law firms or lawyers who promote, support or publicize through advertising that substantially and predominantly features any of the following: legal services corporation; community or other non-profit organization; recognized community events or celebrations; institutions; entities; or individuals other than themselves.''

Nevada: Rule 7.2(b) provides, in part, as follows:

> If a person appears as a lawyer in an advertisement for legal services . . . such person must be a member of the State Bar of Nevada . . . and must be the lawyer who will actually perform the service advertised or a lawyer associated with the law firm that is advertising. If a person appears in an advertisement as an employee of a lawyer or law firm, such person must be an actual employee of the lawyer or law firm whose services are advertised unless the advertisement discloses that such person is an actor. If an actor appears in any other role not prohibited by these Rules, the advertisement must disclose that such person is an actor.

Among other variations, Nevada Rule 7.2A requires lawyers to file all advertisements with the State Bar "within 15 days of first dissemination. . . .'' Rule 7.2B(a) commands the State Bar to create "Standing Lawyer Advertising Advisory Committees . . . to review filings submitted under Rule 7.2A and to respond to written requests from an advertising lawyer or law firm voluntarily seeking an advance opinion regarding that lawyer's compliance with the advertising rules.'' Rule 7.2B(c) permits a lawyer or law firm to "file a written request with the state bar seeking an advance opinion on whether a proposed advertisement complies with these Rules.''

New Hampshire: Rule 7.2(b)(2) permits payment only to "an organization that is recognized by the Internal Revenue Service as exempt from taxation pursuant to Section 501(c)(3) of the Internal Revenue Code.'' New Hampshire omits ABA Model Rule 7.2(b)(4) (governing reciprocal referral agreements).

New Jersey: Rule 7.3(c) adds that a lawyer in private practice "shall not knowingly assist an organization that furnishes or pays for legal services to others to promote the use of the lawyer's services" if the organization's promotional activity (1) uses false or misleading statements or claims, or (2) uses "coercion, duress, compulsion, intimidation, threats, unwarranted promises of benefits, over-reaching, or vexatious or harassing conduct.'' New Jersey regulates lawyer referral services in a lengthy Rule 7.3(e). New Jersey omits ABA Model Rule 7.2(b)(4) (governing reciprocal referral agreements).

To regulate broadcast advertising, New Jersey Rule 7.2(a) incorporates the following language taken verbatim from the New Jersey Supreme Court's opinion in *Felmeister & Isaacs,* 518 A.2d 188, 208 (1986):

> . . . All advertisements shall be predominantly informational. No drawings, animations, dramatizations, music, or lyrics shall be used in connection with televised advertising. No advertisement shall rely in any way on techniques to obtain attention that depend upon absurdity and that demonstrate a clear and intentional lack of relevance to the selection of counsel; included in this category are all advertisements that contain any extreme portrayal of counsel exhibiting characteristics clearly unrelated to legal competence.

New York: Rule 7.2(a) is substantially similar to DR 2-103(B) of the old Model Code, but it adds an exception that permits lawyers to refer clients to a nonlegal professional pursuant to a contractual agreement under New York Rule 5.8, which has no Model Rule equivalent. Rule 5.8 provides that a lawyer or law firm "may enter into and maintain a contractual relationship with a nonlegal professional or nonlegal professional service firm for the purpose of offering to the public, on a systematic and continuing basis, legal services performed by the lawyer or law firm as well as other nonlegal professional services, notwithstanding the provisions of Rule 1.7(a)," when certain requirements are satisfied.

New York Rule 7.2(b) is substantially similar to DR 2-103(D) of the old Model Code. Notably, rather than adopting ABA Model Rule 7.6 (prohibiting pay-to-play arrangements), New York has added two new Comments to Rule 7.2 explaining the pay-to-play prohibition as a logical consequence of Rule 7.2(b) — see the New York entry in the Selected State Variations following Rule 7.6 below.

North Carolina omits ABA Model Rule 7.2(b)(4) and adds an unusual Rule 7.2(d) that permits a lawyer to participate in a lawyer referral service only if the lawyer and the referral service satisfy seven specific conditions.

Ohio: Rule 7.2(b) deletes the ABA reference to a "qualified lawyer referral service" and substitutes a reference to the Ohio Supreme Court Rules governing lawyer referral services. Ohio also deletes ABA Model Rule 7.2(b)(4), thus effectively prohibiting reciprocal referral agreements between two lawyers or between a lawyer and a nonlawyer professional. Ohio adds Rule 7.2(d), which prohibits a lawyer from soliciting employment if the lawyer does not intend to participate in the matter but instead will refer the matter to other counsel.

Pennsylvania: Rule 7.2 differs significantly from ABA Model Rule 7.2. For example, Pennsylvania omits ABA Model Rule 7.2(b)(4) (governing reciprocal referral agreements). Pennsylvania Rule 7.2(j) provides that a lawyer shall not pay "any part of the costs of an advertisement by a lawyer not in the same firm" unless the advertisement discloses the name and principal office address of each lawyer paying for the advertisement and, "if any lawyer or law firm will receive referrals from the advertisement, the circumstances under which referrals will be made and the basis and criteria on which the referral system operates."

Pennsylvania also adds Rule 7.7, which forbids lawyers to accept referrals from a "lawyer referral service" (a defined term) "if the service engaged in communication with the public or direct contact with prospective clients in a manner that would violate the Rules of Professional Conduct if the communication or contact were made by the lawyer."

Rhode Island: Among other variations, Rhode Island has adopted Rule 7.2(f), which provides as follows:

> (f) Any lawyer or law firm who advertises that his or her practice includes or concentrates in particular fields of law and then refers the majority of cases in those fields of law or of that type to another lawyer, law firm or group of lawyers shall clearly state the following disclaimer:
>
> (1) "Most cases of this type are not handled by this firm, but are referred to other attorneys," or if applicable:
>
> (2) "While this firm maintains joint responsibility, most cases of this type are referred to other attorneys for principal responsibility."

Tennessee adds Rule 7.6 (Intermediary Organizations), which provides that a lawyer shall not seek or accept a referral of a client or compensation for representing a client from an "intermediary organization" (a defined term) if the lawyer "knows or reasonably should know that: (1) the organization: (i) is owned or controlled by the lawyer, a law firm with which the lawyer is associated, or a lawyer with whom the lawyer is associated in a firm; or (ii) is engaged in the unauthorized practice of law; or (iii) engages in marketing activities that are false or misleading or are otherwise prohibited by the Board of Professional Responsibility; or (iv) has not registered with the Board of Professional Responsibility and complied with all requirements imposed by the Board." In addition, Supreme Court Rule 44, entitled "Regulation of Lawyer Intermediary Organizations," sets forth the requirements that lawyer intermediary organizations must meet in order to do business in Tennessee under Rule 7.6.

Texas: Rule 7.02 forbids "false or misleading communication about the qualifications or the services of any lawyer or firm." In addition, Texas has adopted guidelines for advertising on the Internet, including a requirement that "homepages" be submitted for review.

Virginia: In the Rules effective December 1, 2012, Virginia omits Rule 7.2. Virginia addresses issues relating to Model Rule 7.2 in Rules 7.1 and 7.3.

Wisconsin: Rule 7.2(b)(4) permits referrals pursuant to a nonexclusive reciprocal referral agreement between a lawyer and another lawyer or nonlawyer professional if "(ii) the client gives informed consent; (iii) there is no interference with the lawyer's independence of professional judgment or with the client-lawyer relationship; and (iv) information relating to representation of a client is protected. . . . "

Related Materials

ABA Formal Ethics Opinions: See ABA Formal Ethics Ops. 87-355 (1987), 88-356 (1988), 93-374 (1993), 94-388 (1994), 99-414 (1999).

ABA Model Supreme Court Rules Governing Lawyer Referral and Information Services: In 1989, the ABA House of Delegates adopted Model Supreme Court Rules Governing Lawyer Referral and Information Services (LRIS), as well as model legislation to implement the rules. (Because many referral services are run by nonlawyers, referral services cannot be regulated solely through rules governing lawyers. Since courts do not possess inherent jurisdiction over nonlawyers, legislation is typically needed to govern nonlawyers.)

The Model Supreme Court Rules Governing Lawyer Referral and Information Services are summarized in ABA Model Rule 7.2, Comment 6. The Model Supreme Court Rules reflect concern over sham referral services operated by lawyers who refer cases only to themselves or their partners. The Model Supreme Court Rules are available online at *http://apps.americanbar.org/legalservices/lris/modelrules.html.*

Criminal Statutes: Some states make it a crime for a nonlawyer to accept anything of value for referring a matter to a lawyer. For example, California Labor Code §3215 makes it a crime for anyone to receive money or any non-monetary thing "as compensation or inducement for referring clients. . . ." Similarly, New York Judiciary Law §479 makes it a crime for any person to "make it a business" to solicit business for an attorney.

Pay-to-Play: The term "pay-to-play" refers to an informal system in which law firms allegedly are not eligible to be retained to perform government legal work unless the lawyers have made or solicited campaign contributions to the government officials who retain (or influence the selection of) outside counsel. In 1997, the ABA adopted a resolution condemning so-called pay-to-play practices and directing the ABA President to appoint a Task Force to study and report on the pay-to-play issue. In 1998, the ABA received a report from the Task Force and passed a resolution directing the ABA's Standing Committee on Ethics and Professional Responsibility to draft a new Model Rule 7.6 to govern pay-to-play. In 1999, the ABA House of Delegates rejected the Standing Committee's proposed rule, but in 2000, the House of Delegates approved an identical proposal, thus incorporating restrictions on pay-to-play into the ABA Model Rules.

Prepaid and Group Legal Services: Comment 6 to Rule 7.2 notes that a lawyer, pursuant to Rule 7.2(b)(2), may pay the reasonable charges of a legal service plan, including a "prepaid" or "group" legal service plan that assists people who seek prospective clients to secure legal representation. Generally speaking, a "prepaid legal plan" is any type of arrangement in which a participant (or an employer on behalf of employees) pays in advance for legal services that participants may require in the future. Prepaid legal plans resemble medical benefit plans: A consumer pays a fixed amount each year or month in exchange for certain service benefits to be used when and if needed. A "group legal plan" may be a "prepaid" plan if employers offer the plan via a payroll deduction, but may instead resemble a group discount service that buys legal services. Group legal plan benefits are usually available without charge to members of an association, union, coop, or other group. They typically feature telephone legal advice at no charge and other services at discounted rates from participating lawyers. For extensive information about prepaid and group legal services plans, see the website of the American Prepaid Legal Services Institute at *www.aplsi.org.*

Restatement of the Law Governing Lawyers: The Restatement has no provision comparable to ABA Model Rule 7.2.

Rule 7.3   Direct Contact with Prospective Clients

Canon and Code Antecedents

ABA Canons of Professional Ethics: Canon 28 provided as follows:

28.   *Stirring Up Litigation, Directly or Through Agents*

It is unprofessional for a lawyer to volunteer advice to bring a lawsuit, except in rare cases where ties of blood, relationship or trust make it his duty to do so. Stirring up strife and litigation is not only unprofessional, but it is indictable at common law. It is disreputable to hunt up defects in titles or other causes of action and inform thereof in order to be employed to bring suit or collect judgment, or to breed litigation by seeking out those with claims for personal injuries or those having any other grounds of action in order to secure them as clients, or to employ agents or runners for like purposes, or to pay or reward, directly or indirectly, those who bring or influence the bringing of such cases to his office, or to remunerate policemen, court or prison officials, physicians, hospital *attachés* or others who may succeed, under the guise of giving disinterested friendly advice, in influencing the criminal, the sick and the injured, the ignorant or others, to seek his professional services. A duty to the public and to the profession devolves upon every member of the Bar having knowledge of such practices upon the part of any practitioner immediately to inform thereof, to the end that the offender may be disbarred.

ABA Model Code of Professional Responsibility: Compare DR 2-104(A) (reprinted later in this volume).

Cross-References in Other Rules

Rule 5.5, Comment 21: "Whether and how lawyers may communicate the availability of their services to prospective clients in this jurisdiction is governed by **Rules 7.1 to 7.5**."

Rule 5.7, Comment 10: "The promotion of the law-related services must also in all respects comply with **Rules** 7.1 through **7.3**, dealing with advertising and solicitation."

Rule 7.2(a): "Subject to the requirements of **Rules** 7.1 and **7.3**, a lawyer may advertise services through written, recorded or electronic communication, including public media."

Rule 7.2, Comment 3: "[S]ee **Rule 7.3(a)** for the prohibition against the solicitation of a prospective client through a real-time electronic exchange that is not initiated by the prospective client."

Rule 7.2, Comment 4: "Neither this Rule nor **Rule 7.3** prohibits communications authorized by law, such as notice to members of a class in class action litigation."

Rule 7.2, Comment 5: "Except as permitted under paragraphs (b)(1)-(b)(4), lawyers are not permitted to pay others for recommending the lawyer's services or for channeling professional work in a manner that violates **Rule 7.3**."

Rule 7.2, Comment 7: A lawyer accepting assignments or referrals from a legal service plan or referrals from a lawyer referral service is not permitted to "allow in-person, telephonic, or real-time contacts that would violate **Rule 7.3**."

Legislative History of Model Rule 7.3

1980 Discussion Draft (then Rule 9.3) provided as follows:

Solicitation

> (a) A lawyer shall not initiate contact with a prospective client if:
> (1) the lawyer reasonably should know that the physical, emotional, or mental state of the person solicited is such that the person could not exercise reasonable judgment in employing a lawyer;

(2) the person solicited has made known a desire not to receive communications from the lawyer; or

(3) the solicitation involves coercion, duress, or harassment.

(b) subject to the requirements of paragraph (a), a lawyer may initiate contact with a prospective client in the following circumstances:

(1) if the prospective client is a close friend or relative of the lawyer;

(2) by a letter concerning a specific event or transaction if the letter is followed up only upon positive response from the addressee;

(3) under the auspices of a public or charitable legal services organization or a bona fide political, social, civic, fraternal, employee, or trade organization whose purposes include but are not limited to providing or recommending legal services.

(c) A lawyer shall not give another person anything of value to initiate contact with a prospective client on behalf of the lawyer.

1981 and 1982 Drafts both provided as follows:

Personal Contact with Prospective Clients

(a) A lawyer may initiate personal contact with a prospective client for the purpose of obtaining professional employment only in the following circumstances and subject to the requirements of paragraph (b):

(1) if the prospective client is a close friend, relative, former client or one whom the lawyer reasonably believes to be a client;

(2) under the auspices of a public or charitable legal services organization; or

(3) under the auspices of a bona fide political, social, civic, fraternal, employee or trade organization whose purposes include but are not limited to providing or recommending legal services, if the legal services are related to the principal purposes of the organization.

(b) A lawyer shall not contact, or send a written communication to, a prospective client for the purpose of obtaining professional employment if:

(1) the lawyer knows or reasonably should know that the physical, emotional or mental state of the person is such that the person could not exercise reasonable judgment in employing a lawyer;

(2) the person has made known to the lawyer a desire not to receive communications from the lawyer; or

(3) the communication involves coercion, duress or harassment.

1983 Rule: As originally adopted in 1983, Rule 7.3 provided as follows:

A lawyer may not solicit professional employment from a prospective client with whom the lawyer has no family or prior professional relationship by mail, in-person or otherwise, when a significant motive for the lawyer's doing so is the lawyer's pecuniary gain. The term "solicit" includes contact in person, by telephone or telegraph, by letter or other writing or by other communications directed to a specific recipient, but does not include letters addressed or advertising circulars distributed generally to persons not known to need legal services of the kind provided by the lawyer in a particular matter but who are so situated that they might in general find such services useful.

1989 Amendments: In 1989, the ABA House of Delegates substantially amended Rule 7.3 and its Comment. The 1989 version of Rule 7.3 provided as follows:

(a) A lawyer shall not by in-person or live telephone contact solicit professional employment from a prospective client with whom the lawyer has no family or prior professional relationship when a significant motive for the lawyer's doing so is the lawyer's pecuniary gain.

(b) A lawyer shall not solicit professional employment from a prospective client by written or recorded communication or by in-person or telephone contact even when not otherwise prohibited by paragraph (a), if:

(1) [Same as 2002 version of Rule 7.3(b)(1).]

(2) [Same as 2002 version of Rule 7.3(b)(2).]

(c) Every written or recorded communication from a lawyer soliciting professional employment from a prospective client known to be in need of legal services in a particular matter, and with whom the lawyer has no family or prior professional relationship, shall include the words "Advertising Material" on the outside envelope, if any, and at the beginning and ending of any recorded or electronic communication.

(d) [Same as 2002 version of Rule 7.3(d).]

The 1989 amendments also deleted the following paragraphs from the Comment to Rule 7.3:

These dangers [of false and misleading representations] attend direct solicitation whether in-person or by mail. Direct mail solicitation cannot be effectively regulated by means less drastic than outright prohibition. One proposed safeguard is to require that the designation "Advertising" be stamped on any envelope containing a solicitation letter. This would do nothing to assure the accuracy and reliability of the contents. Another suggestion is that solicitation letters be filed with a state regulatory agency. This would be ineffective as a practical matter. State lawyer discipline agencies struggle for resources to investigate specific complaints, much less for those necessary to screen lawyers' mail solicitation material. Even if they could examine such materials, agency staff members are unlikely to know anything about the lawyer or about the prospective client's underlying problem. Without such knowledge they cannot determine whether the lawyer's representations are misleading. In any event, such review would be after the fact, potentially too late to avert the undesirable consequences of disseminating false and misleading material.

General mailings not speaking to a specific matter do not pose the same danger of abuse as targeted mailings, and therefore are not prohibited by this Rule. The representations made in such mailings are necessarily general rather than tailored, less importuning than informative. They are addressed to recipients unlikely to be specially vulnerable at the time, hence who are likely to be more skeptical about unsubstantiated claims. General mailings not addressed to recipients involved in a specific legal matter or incident, therefore, more closely resemble permissible advertising rather than prohibited solicitation.

The amendments to Rules 7.2 and 7.3 were explained by the ABA's Standing Committee on Ethics and Professional Responsibility as follows:

ABA Committee Report Explaining 1989 Amendments to Rule 7.3 *

The Supreme Court of the United States, in *Shapero v. Kentucky Bar Association,* 486 U.S. 466 (1988), ruled that the First Amendment does not allow states to impose blanket bans on targeted mail solicitation by lawyers of prospective clients. Held unconstitutional was a Kentucky Supreme Court rule identical to Model Rule 7.3. The

---

* Committee Reports do not represent official policy of the ABA. They are for information only, and the opinions are those of the authors of the report.

principal purpose of the amendments proposed here is to bring the Model Rules into compliance with the *Shapero* decision. . . .

2002 Amendments: In 2002, the ABA House of Delegates adopted with only minor changes the ABA Ethics 2000 Commission proposal to amend Rule 7.3 and its Comment. The main changes were to add express prohibitions on "real-time electronic" contact in Rules 7.3(a) and (b) and in Comments 1, 2, and 3, and to amend Comment 4 by adding the second sentence ("Nor is there . . .") and the last sentence ("Also, paragraph (a) is not intended . . .").

2012 Amendments: In August 2012, the ABA House of Delegates adopted without change a proposal by the ABA Commission on Ethics 20/20 to amend Rule 7.3 and several accompanying Comments, particularly Comment 1. The changes provided lawyers with greater guidance as to when advertising — especially Internet-based advertising — constitutes a solicitation. The title of the Rule and the phrasing of several Comments were also changed to avoid use of the phrase "prospective clients." The reason for the change was that the phrase "prospective client" had become a defined term in Rule 1.18 and included a narrower category of individuals than Rule 7.1 and its Comments were intended to cover.

Selected State Variations

Arizona adds a subparagraph (b)(3) prohibiting solicitation relating to a personal injury or wrongful death within 30 days after the occurrence, and Arizona adds detailed requirements regarding targeted mail.

California: Rule 1-400 provides, in pertinent part, as follows:

> (B) For purposes of this rule, a "solicitation" means any communication:
>> (1) Concerning the availability for professional employment of a member or a law firm in which a significant motive is pecuniary gain; and
>> (2) Which is . . . .
>>> (b) delivered in person or by telephone, or
>>> (c) directed by any means to a person known to the sender to be represented by counsel in a matter which is a subject of the communication.
>
> (C) A solicitation shall not be made by or on behalf of a member or law firm to a prospective client with whom the member or law firm has no family or prior professional relationship, unless the solicitation is protected from abridgment by the Constitution of the United States or by the Constitution of the State of California. A solicitation to a former or present client in the discharge of a member's or law firm's professional duties is not prohibited. . . .

In addition, California Business & Professions Code §6152(a)(1) provides, in part, that it is unlawful for any person "to act as a runner or capper for any attorneys or to solicit any business for any attorneys in and about the state prisons, county jails, city jails, city prisons, or other places of detention of persons, city receiving hospitals, city and county receiving hospitals, county hospitals, superior courts, or in any public institution or in any public place or upon any public street or highway or in and about private hospitals, sanitariums or in and about any private institution or upon private property of any character whatsoever. . . ."

Colorado: Rule 7.3(c) imposes a waiting period of 30 days after an event causing personal injury or death before a lawyer may solicit professional employment in connection with the event unless the lawyer has "a family or prior professional relationship with the prospective client." The rule also prohibits solicitation if the sending lawyer "knows or reasonably should know" that the recipient is represented by a lawyer in the matter, and requires the sending lawyer to say whether that lawyer will "actually handle the case or matter" or if it "will be referred to another lawyer or firm." Rule 7.3(d) prohibits the envelope from revealing "the nature of the prospective client's legal problem."

Connecticut: Rule 7.3 differs significantly from ABA Model Rule 7.3. For example, Rule 7.3(a)(4) does not prohibit personal, live telephone, or real-time electronic contact with a prospective client that is "a business organization, a not-for-profit organization or governmental body and the lawyer seeks to provide services related to the organization." Rule 7.3(b)(b) forbids a lawyer to "contact, or send, a written or electronic communication to, a prospective client" if:

> (1) The lawyer knows or reasonably should know that the physical, emotional or mental state of the person makes it unlikely that the person would exercise reasonable judgment in employing a lawyer; . . .
> (3) The communication involves coercion, duress, fraud, overreaching, harassment, intimidation or undue influence; [or]
> (4) The written communication concerns a specific matter and the lawyer knows or reasonably should know that the person to whom the communication is directed is represented by a lawyer in the matter. . . .

Connecticut Rule 7.3(b)(5) prohibits written solicitation in personal injury or wrongful death matters for 40 days after an accident or disaster. Rule 7.3(c) requires every written communication used by a lawyer "for the purpose of obtaining professional employment from a prospective client known to be in need of legal services in a particular matter" to say "Advertising Material" on the envelope and first page "in red ink." Rule 7.3(d) requires the first sentence of a written communication about a specific matter to say: "If you have already retained a lawyer for this matter, please disregard this letter."

District of Columbia omits Rule 7.3, but D.C. Rule 7.1(b) generally permits in-person solicitation by providing as follows:

> (1) A lawyer shall not seek by in-person contact, employment (or employment of a partner or associate) by a nonlawyer who has not sought the lawyer's advice regarding employment of a lawyer, if:
> (A) The solicitation involves use of a statement or claim that is false or misleading . . . ;
> (B) The solicitation involves the use of coercion, duress or harassment; or
> (C) The potential client is apparently in a physical or mental condition which would make it unlikely that the potential client could exercise reasonable, considered judgment as to the selection of a lawyer.
> (2) A lawyer shall not give anything of value to a person (other than the lawyer's partner or employee) for recommending the lawyer's services through in-person contact.

D.C. also has adopted an unusual Rule 7.1(e) that provides, in part, as follows:

> Any lawyer . . . who solicits . . . any person incarcerated at the District of Columbia Jail . . . for the purpose of representing that person for a fee paid by or on behalf of that person . . . in any then-pending criminal case in which that person is represented, must provide timely and adequate notice to the person's then-current lawyer prior to accepting any fee from or on behalf of the incarcerated person.

Florida: Rule 4-7.4(a) defines the term "solicit" to include (among other things) contact by fax. Rule 4-7.4(b)(1), which is essentially the rule upheld in *Florida Bar v. Went for It, Inc.,* 515 U.S. 618 (1995), prohibits a lawyer from soliciting prospective clients in writing if:

> (A) the written communication concerns an action for personal injury or wrongful death or otherwise relates to an accident or disaster involving the person to whom the communication is addressed or a relative of that person, unless the accident or disaster occurred more than 30 days prior to the mailing of the communication;
>
> (B) the written communication concerns a specific matter and the lawyer knows or reasonably should know that the person to whom the communication is directed is represented by a lawyer in the matter. . . .

Rule 4-7.4(b)(2) imposes stringent, detailed requirements on all written communications to prospective clients, including that the first sentence of every written communication prompted by a specific occurrence must be: "If you have already retained a lawyer for this matter, please disregard this letter."

Florida Rule 4-7.6, entitled "Computer-Accessed Communications," provides that all websites controlled or sponsored by a lawyer or law firm and that contain information concerning the lawyer's or law firm's services "shall disclose all jurisdictions in which the lawyer or members of the law firm are licensed to practice law." A lawyer shall not send an "unsolicited electronic mail communication directly or indirectly to a prospective client for the purpose of obtaining professional employment" unless it complies with a host of requirements, including that the subject line of the communication must begin with "LEGAL ADVERTISEMENT."

Georgia: In the rules effective November 3, 2011, Rule 7.3(a)(3) prohibits a written communication relating to an accident or disaster involving the person to whom the communication is sent for 30 days after the accident or disaster. Georgia omits ABA Model Rule 7.3(c), but adds Rule 7.3(e), which provides that a lawyer "shall not accept employment when the lawyer knows or it is obvious that the person who seeks to employ the lawyer does so as a result of conduct by any person or organization prohibited under" these rules. Georgia's rule also adds detailed provisions regarding a lawyer's participation in referral services.

Kentucky: An elaborate Rule 7.60 (Kentucky Disaster Response Plan) addresses problems that occur when lawyers and nonlawyers who are not subject to disciplinary jurisdiction in Kentucky "engage in the provision of legal services, legal advice, and outright solicitation of persons and their families affected by a disastrous event." The policy of Rule 7.60 is to "[m]onitor the conduct of all attorneys, both members and non-members of the Kentucky Bar Association, and thereby deter violations of the rules of ethical conduct. . . ."

Kentucky has also enacted a criminal statute, Ky. Rev. Stat. §21A.300, providing that for 30 days after "the filing of a criminal or civil action, or claim for damages, or a traffic citation, injury, accident, or disaster," an attorney "shall not directly solicit . . . a victim of the accident or disaster, or a relative of the victim, for the purpose of obtaining professional employment," and "shall not knowingly accept a referral from an attorney referral service" if the referral service has violated that prohibition. Ky. Rev. Stat. §21A.310 makes violation of the 30-day blackout law a Class A misdemeanor, and may subject an attorney to professional discipline in addition to any criminal penalty. Kentucky Supreme Court Rule 3.130 provides:

If a lawyer illegally or unethically solicited a client for which compensation is paid or payable, all fees arising from such transaction shall be deemed waived and forfeited and shall be returned to the client. A civil action for recovery of such fees may be brought in a court of competent jurisdiction.

Louisiana deletes Rule 7.3 and addresses solicitation in Rule 7.4. Among other variations, Rule 7.4(b)(1)(A) contains a provision that prohibits any solicitation (including letters) that concern "an action for personal injury or wrongful death . . . unless the accident or disaster occurred more than thirty days prior to the mailing of the communication." Rule 7.4(b)(2) also requires lawyers to include a variety of information in letters to potential clients.

Maine: The restrictions on in-person solicitation apply only to "non-commercial" clients. Moreover, the Rule provides that a variety of factors are relevant when determining the permissibility of a solicitation, including "the prospective client's sophistication regarding legal matters; the physical, emotional state of the prospective non-commercial client; and the circumstances in which the solicitation is made. . . ."

Massachusetts: Rule 7.3(b)(1) prohibits solicitation if "the lawyer knows or reasonably should know that the physical, mental, or emotional state of the prospective client is such that there is a substantial potential that the person cannot exercise reasonable judgment in employing a lawyer," unless the solicitation is "not for a fee." Rule 7.3(d) prohibits solicitation in person "or by personal communication by telephone, electronic device, or otherwise," but Rule 7.3(e) exempts: (1) communications with "members of the bar of any state or jurisdiction"; (2)(A) "grandparents of the lawyer or the lawyer's spouse, (B) descendants of the grandparents of the lawyer or the lawyer's spouse, or (C) the spouse of any of the foregoing persons"; (3) "prospective clients with whom the lawyer had a prior attorney-client relationship"; (4)(i) "non-profit and governmental entities" regarding their activities, and (ii) "persons engaged in trade or commerce" in connection with their trade or commerce.

Michigan includes the following definition of a "solicitation" in Rule 7.3(a):

> The term "solicit" includes contact in person, by telephone or telegraph, by letter or other writing, or by other communication directed to a specific recipient, but does not include letters addressed or advertising circulars distributed generally to persons not known to need legal services of the kind provided by the lawyer in a particular matter, but who are so situated that they might in general find such services useful, nor does the term "solicit" include "sending truthful and nondeceptive letters to potential clients known to face particular legal problems" as elucidated in *Shapero v. Kentucky Bar Ass'n,* 486 U.S. 466, 468; 108 S. Ct. 1916; 100 L. Ed. 2d 475 (1988).

Michigan also omits ABA Model Rule 7.3(c)-(d).

Mississippi: Rule 7.2(a) defines an "advertisement" as "an active quest for clients involving a public or non-public communication." Rule 7.5(a) requires a lawyer to submit a "copy or recording of any advertisement" to the Office of the General Counsel of the Mississippi Bar (OGCMB) "prior to its first dissemination," but Rule 7.5(b) exempts 13 categories of advertisements from the filing requirement, such as telephone directory advertisements, business cards, web pages, and "scholarly writings." Under Rule 7.5(d), a lawyer may request an "advisory opinion concerning the compliance of a contemplated advertisement or communication with these Rules in advance of disseminating the advertisement or communication," provided the advertisement is submitted at least 45 days in advance. The OGCMB must "render its advisory opinion within forty-five days of receipt of a request unless the OGCMB determines that there is reasonable doubt that the advertisement or communication is in compliance with the Rules and that further examination is warranted but such evaluation cannot be completed within the forty-five day time period. . . ." In that event, "the OGCMB shall complete its review as promptly as the circumstances reasonably allow. If the OGCMB does not send any correspondence or notice to the lawyer within forty-five days, the advertisement or communication will be deemed approved." Under Rule 7.5(d)(2), a "finding by the OGCMB of either compliance or non-compliance shall not be binding in disciplinary proceedings, but may be offered as evidence."

Missouri: Rule 7.3(a) provides that a lawyer may not "initiate" in-person, telephone, or real-time electronic solicitation of legal business "under any circumstance, other than with an existing or former client, lawyer, close friend or relative." Regarding written communications to "others," Rules 7.3(b) and (c) provide as follows:

> (b)(3) each written solicitation must include the following:
>
> "Disregard this solicitation if you have already engaged a lawyer in connection with the legal matter referred to in this solicitation. You may wish to consult your lawyer or another lawyer instead of me (us). The exact nature of your legal situation will depend on many facts not known to me (us) at this time. You should understand that the advice and information in this solicitation is general and that your own situation may vary. This statement is required by rule of the Supreme Court of Missouri." . . .
>
> (8) if a lawyer knows that a lawyer other than the lawyer whose name or signature appears on the solicitation will actually handle the case or matter or that the case or matter will be referred to another lawyer or law firm, any written solicitation concerning a specific matter shall include a statement so advising the potential client; and
>
> (9) a lawyer shall not send a written solicitation regarding a specific matter if the lawyer knows or reasonably should know that the person to whom the solicitation is directed is represented by a lawyer in the matter.
>
> (c) A lawyer shall not send, nor knowingly permit to be sent . . . a written solicitation to any prospective client . . . if: . . .
>
> (4) the written solicitation concerns an action for personal injury or wrongful death or otherwise relates to an accident or disaster involving the person solicited or a relative of that person if the accident or disaster occurred less than 30 days prior to the solicitation . . . ; or
>
> (5) the written solicitation vilifies, denounces or disparages any other potential party.

Montana: Rule 7.3(b)(4) prohibits a lawyer from contacting a prospective client if "the lawyer reasonably should know that the person is already represented by another lawyer."

Nevada: Rule 7.3(d) provides, in part: "Written communication directed to a specific prospective client who may need legal services due to a particular transaction or occurrence is prohibited in Nevada within 45 days of the transaction or occurrence giving rise to the communication."

New Hampshire: Rule 7.3(a) does not use the words "solicit" or "pecuniary gain" but provides that a lawyer "shall not initiate, by in-person, live voice, recorded or other real-time means, contact with a prospective client for the purpose of obtaining professional employment,'' unless the person contacted fits the exemptions in ABA Model Rule 7.3(a)(1)-(2) or:

> (3) is an employee, agent, or representative of a business, non-profit or governmental organization not known to be in need of legal services in a particular matter, and the lawyer seeks to provide services on behalf of the organization; or
> (4) is an individual who regularly requires legal services in a commercial context and is not known to be in need of legal services in a particular matter.

New Hampshire Rule 7.3(d)(iii) exempts contact with ''those the lawyer is permitted under applicable law to seek to join in litigation in the nature of a class action, if success in asserting rights or defenses of the litigation is dependent upon the joinder of others.''

New Jersey omits Rule 7.3(c) and Rule 7.3(d). In addition, to control solicitation after mass disasters, New Jersey adds Rule 7.3(b)(4), which provides that a lawyer shall not contact, or send a written communication to, a prospective client for the purpose of obtaining professional employment if ''the communication involves unsolicited direct contact with a prospective client within thirty days after a specific mass-disaster event, when such contact concerns potential compensation arising from the event.'' To prevent out-of-state attorneys from improperly soliciting New Jersey victims and their families after mass disasters, the Court's Clerk has issued a statement saying that it ''has jurisdiction over out-of-state attorneys who make such solicitations to prospective claimants in New Jersey.''

Regarding events other than mass disasters, New Jersey adds Rule 7.3(b)(5)(iii), which generally permits targeted mail if (among other things) it contains an additional notice that ''the recipient may, if the letter is inaccurate or misleading, report same to the Committee on Attorney Advertising, Hughes Justice Complex, P.O. Box 037, Trenton, New Jersey 08625.''

New York: Rule 7.3(b) defines ''solicitation'' to mean ''any advertisement initiated by or on behalf of a lawyer or law firm that is directed to, or targeted at, a specific recipient or group of recipients, or their family members or legal representatives, the primary purpose of which is the retention of the lawyer or law firm, and a significant motive for which is pecuniary gain. It does not include a proposal or other writing prepared and delivered in response to a specific request of a prospective client.''

Rule 7.3(a) provides as follows: ''A lawyer shall not engage in solicitation . . . by in-person or telephone contact, or by real-time or interactive computer-accessed communication unless the recipient is a close friend, relative, former client or existing client. . . .'' Solicitation by any means is forbidden if (among other things) ''the lawyer intends or expects, but does not disclose, that the legal services necessary to handle the matter competently will be performed primarily by another lawyer who is not affiliated with the soliciting lawyer as a partner, associate or of counsel.'' Rule 7.3(c) imposes detailed filing requirements for most solicitations, including ''a transcript of the audio portion of any radio or television solicitation'' and ''if the solicitation is in a language other than English, an accurate English-language translation.''

Rule 7.3(e) restricts solicitation in personal injury and wrongful death cases as follows: ''No solicitation relating to a specific incident involving potential claims for personal injury or wrongful death shall be disseminated before the 30th day after the date of the incident, unless a filing must be made within 30 days of the incident as a legal prerequisite to the particular claim, in which case no unsolicited communication shall be made before the 15th day after the date of the incident." New York addresses a similar issue in Rule 4.5, which has no Model Rule equivalent. That Rule restricts defense lawyers from engaging in unsolicited communications with prospective claimants in personal injury or wrongful death cases during the same time period described in Rule 7.3(e), unless the communication is with the claimant's counsel.

Rule 7.3(i) provides that New York's solicitation rules apply to lawyers from out of state who solicit clients in New York.

Also, under 22 NYCRR §130-1.1a, an attorney filing an "initiating pleading" must certify that "(i) the matter was not obtained through illegal conduct, or that if it was, the attorney or other persons responsible for the illegal conduct are not participating in the matter or sharing in any fee earned therefrom" and "(ii) the matter was not obtained in violation of [the rules of professional conduct]."

North Carolina: Rule 7.3(d)(1) defines the phrase "prepaid or group legal services plan," and Rule 7.3(d)(2) sets forth detailed conditions that a lawyer must satisfy before participating in such a plan.

Ohio: Rule 7.3(c) requires targeted direct mail solicitation to: "(1) Disclose accurately and fully the manner in which the lawyer or law firm became aware of the identity and specific legal need of the addressee" and "(2) Disclaim or refrain from expressing any predetermined evaluation of the merits of the addressee's case." Rule 7.3(d) provides that before soliciting professional employment from a defendant in a civil action, a lawyer "shall verify that the party has been served with notice of the action filed against that party." Service shall be verified by "consulting the docket of the court in which the action was filed. . . ."

Ohio Rule 7.3(e) provides that if a communication solicits professional employment in a potential claim for personal injury or wrongful death within 30 days of an accident or disaster, the communication must include a lengthy text headed "Understanding Your Rights," which provides, in relevant part, as follows:

> 2. *You do not have to sign anything* — You may not want to give an interview or recorded statement without first consulting with an attorney, because the statement can be used against you. If you may be at fault or have been charged with a traffic or other offense, it may be advisable to consult an attorney right away. However, if you have insurance, your insurance policy probably requires you to cooperate with your insurance company and to provide a statement to the company. If you fail to cooperate with your insurance company, it may void your coverage.
>
> 3. *Your interests versus interests of insurance company* — Your interests and those of the other person's insurance company are in conflict. Your interests may also be in conflict with your own insurance company. Even if you are not sure who is at fault, you should contact your own insurance company and advise the company of the incident to protect your insurance coverage. . . .
>
> 8. *Check a lawyer's qualifications* — Before hiring any lawyer, you have the right to know the lawyer's background, training, and experience in dealing with cases similar to yours.
>
> 9. *How much will it cost?* — In deciding whether to hire a particular lawyer, you should discuss, and the lawyer's written fee agreement should reflect:
>
> a. How is the lawyer to be paid? If you already have a settlement offer, how will that affect a contingent fee arrangement?
>
> b. How are the expenses involved in your case, such as telephone calls, deposition costs, and fees for expert witnesses, to be paid? Will these costs be advanced by

the lawyer or charged to you as they are incurred? Since you are obligated to pay all expenses even if you lose your case, how will payment be arranged?

     c. Who will handle your case? If the case goes to trial, who will be the trial attorney?

Furthermore, a footnote to "Understanding Your Rights" says, in part: "THE SUPREME COURT OF OHIO . . . NEITHER PROMOTES NOR PROHIBITS THE DIRECT SOLICITATION OF PERSONAL INJURY VICTIMS."

    Pennsylvania omits Rules 7.3(c) and (d).

    Rhode Island: Rule 7.3(a)(3) permits "in-person, live telephone or real-time electronic contact" solicitation for profit if the prospective client is "a business organization, a not-for-profit organization, or governmental body and the lawyer seeks to provide services related to the organization."

    South Carolina: Rule 7.3(d) provides:

    (2) Each solicitation must include the following statements:

    (A) "You may wish to consult your lawyer or another lawyer instead of me (us). You may obtain information about other lawyers by consulting directories, seeking the advice of other, or calling the South Carolina Bar Lawyer Referral Service at 799-7100 in Columbia or toll free at 1-800-868-2284. If you have already engaged a lawyer in connection with the legal matter referred to in this communication, you should direct any questions you have to that lawyer" and

    (B) "The exact nature of your legal situation will depend on many facts not known to me (us) at this time. You should understand that the advice and information in this communication is general and that your own situation may vary."

Where the solicitation is written, the above statements must be in a type no smaller than that used in the body of the communication.

    (3) Each solicitation must include the following statement:

    "ANY COMPLAINTS ABOUT THIS COMMUNICATION OR THE REPRESENTATIONS OF ANY LAWYER MAY BE DIRECTED TO THE COMMISSION ON LAWYER CONDUCT, 1015 SUMTER STREET, SUITE 305, COLUMBIA, SOUTH CAROLINA 29201 TELEPHONE NUMBER 803-734-2037." Where the solicitation is written, this statement must be printed in capital letters and in a size no smaller than that used in the body of the communication.

See more discussion of South Carolina Rule 418 in Selected State Variations under Rule 8.5.

    Texas: Rule 7.06 provides that a lawyer "shall not accept or continue employment when the lawyer knows or reasonably should know that the person who seeks the lawyer's services does so as a result of conduct prohibited by these Rules." In addition, under §38.12 of the Texas Penal Code it is a crime if a lawyer, "with intent to obtain an economic benefit . . . (2) solicits employment, either in person or by telephone, for himself or for another." Section 38.01(11) of the Texas Penal Code defines the phrase "solicit employment" as follows:

    (11) "Solicit employment" means to communicate in person or by telephone with a prospective client or a member of the prospective client's family concerning professional employment . . . arising out of a particular occurrence or event, or series of occurrences or events, or concerning an existing problem of the prospective client . . . for the purpose of providing professional services to the prospective client, when neither the person receiving the communication nor anyone acting on that person's

behalf has requested the communication. The term does not include a communication initiated by a family member of the person receiving a communication. . . .

Virginia: In the Rules effective December 1, 2012, Rule 7.3(a) provides as follows:

> (a) A lawyer shall not solicit professional employment from a potential client if:
> (1) the potential client has made known to the lawyer a desire not to be solicited by the lawyer; or
> (2) the solicitation involves harassment, undue influence, coercion, duress, compulsion, intimidation, threats or unwarranted promises of benefits.

Rule 7.3(b) is substantially similar to Model Rule 7.2(b), which regulates payments for recommending the lawyer's services, except that Virginia Rule 7.3(b)(4) does not reference non-exclusive reciprocal referral agreements. Rather, Rule 7.3(b)(4) allows for "nominal gifts of gratitude that are neither intended nor reasonably expected to be a form of compensation for recommending a lawyer's services." Virginia also omits Model Rule 7.2(d), but addresses similar issues in Comments.

Wisconsin: Rule 7.3(b)(1) adds that solicitation is prohibited if "(1) the lawyer knows or reasonably should know that the physical, emotional or mental state of the person makes it unlikely that the person would exercise reasonable judgment in employing a lawyer." Rule 7.3(e) (e) provides that ordinarily a lawyer "shall not draft legal documents, such as wills, trust instruments or contracts, which require or imply that the lawyer's services be used in relation to that document."

Related Materials

ABA Formal Ethics Opinions: See ABA Formal Ethics Ops. 99-414 (1999), 04-432 n.7 (2004), and 07-445 (2007).

American Prepaid Legal Services Institute: In certain circumstances, ABA Model Rule 7.3(d) permits lawyers to participate with "a prepaid or group legal service plan operated by an organization not owned or directed by the lawyer that uses in-person or telephone contact to solicit memberships or subscriptions for the plan . . .". For more information about prepaid legal services, visit the website maintained by the American Prepaid Legal Services Institute (API) at *www.aplsi.org*. The API is a professional trade organization representing the legal services plan industry. It is affiliated with the American Bar Association and is headquartered in Chicago, Illinois.

Aviation Disaster Family Assistance Act: In 1996, amidst allegations that lawyers had improperly solicited relatives of the victims of the crashes of ValueJet Flight 109 in the Florida Everglades and TWA Flight 800 off Long Island, Congress passed the Aviation Disaster Family Assistance Act, 49 U.S.C. §1136(g)(2). As amended in 2000, that statute restricts solicitation of air crash victims and their relatives as follows:

> *Unsolicited communications.* In the event of an accident involving an air carrier . . .
> no unsolicited communication concerning a potential action for personal injury or
> wrongful death may be made by an attorney (including any associate, agent, employee,
> or other representative of an attorney) or any potential party to the litigation to an

individual injured in the accident, or to a relative of an individual involved in the accident, before the 45th day following the date of the accident.

IRS Regulations: In the regulations governing practice before the Internal Revenue Service, 31 C.F.R. §10.30(a)(2) provides:

> A practitioner may not make, directly or indirectly, an uninvited written or oral solicitation of employment in matters related to the Internal Revenue Service if the solicitation violates Federal or State law or other applicable rule, *e.g.*, attorneys are precluded from making a solicitation that is prohibited by conduct rules applicable to all attorneys in their State(s) of licensure. Any lawful solicitation made by or on behalf of a practitioner eligible to practice before the Internal Revenue Service must, nevertheless, clearly identify the solicitation as such and, if applicable, identify the source of the information used in choosing the recipient.

In addition, 31 C.F.R. §10.30(d) provides that a practitioner may not "assist, or accept assistance from, any person or entity who, to the knowledge of the practitioner, obtains clients or otherwise practices in a manner forbidden under this section."

"Jail Mail": In 1996, to make it more difficult for private criminal defense attorneys to send targeted mail to potential clients who had recently been arrested (so-called "jail mail"), California amended Government Code §6254(f)(3) to require any person requesting an arrestee's address to declare under penalty of perjury that the information "shall not be used directly or indirectly to sell a product or service. . . ." In *Los Angeles Police Dep't v. United Reporting Publishing Corp.*, 528 U.S. 32 (1999), the United States Supreme Court held that this statute was not *facially* invalid, but left open the possibility that it might be invalid as applied. The Court therefore remanded for further proceedings. (No decision on the merits is reported on remand.)

Prepaid and Group Legal Services Plans: ABA Model Rule 7.3(d) refers to but does not define a "prepaid or group legal services plan." A helpful definition is found in North Carolina Rule 7.3(d)(1), which provides as follows:

> (1) *Definition.* A prepaid legal services plan or a group legal services plan ("a plan") is any arrangement by which a person, firm, or corporation, not otherwise authorized to engage in the practice of law, in exchange for any valuable consideration, offers to provide or arranges the provision of legal services that are paid for in advance of the need for the service ("covered services"). In addition to covered services, a plan may provide specified legal services at fees that are less than what a non-member of the plan would normally pay. The legal services offered by a plan must be provided by a licensed lawyer who is not an employee, director or owner of the plan. A plan does not include the sale of an identified, limited legal service, such as drafting a will, for a fixed, one-time fee.

According to the American Prepaid Legal Services Institute (APLSI):

> Almost every legal plan provides legal advice and consultation by telephone as a basic service and may also include brief office consultations, review of simple legal documents, preparation of a simple will, and short letters written or phone calls made by a lawyer. Other plans offer more comprehensive coverage for trials, marital problems, bankruptcy, real estate matters and the like. In addition to the member, most plans include or offer coverage for his or her spouse and dependent children.

For more information about prepaid and group legal services plans, see *www.aplsi. org* (click on ''Legal Plans'').

Restatement of the Law Governing Lawyers: The Restatement has no provision comparable to ABA Model Rule 7.3.

Rule 7.4   Communication of Fields of Practice and Specialization

Canon and Code Antecedents

ABA Canons of Professional Ethics: Canons 45 and 46 provided as follows:

45. Specialists

The canons of the American Bar Association apply to all branches of the legal profession; specialists in particular branches are not to be considered as exempt from the application of these principles.

46. Notice to Local Lawyers

A lawyer available to act as an associate of other lawyers in a particular branch of the law or legal service may send to local lawyers only and publish in his local legal journal, a brief and dignified announcement of his availability to serve other lawyers in connection therewith. The announcement should be in a form which does not constitute a statement or representation of special experience or expertness.

ABA Model Code of Professional Responsibility: Compare DR 2-105(A) (reprinted later in this volume).

Cross-References in Other Rules

Rule 5.5, Comment 21: ''Whether and how lawyers may communicate the availability of their services to prospective clients in this jurisdiction is governed by **Rules 7.1 to 7.5**.''

Legislative History of Model Rule 7.4

1979 Unofficial Pre-Circulation Draft (then Rule 9.3) provided, in pertinent part, as follows:

(a) A lawyer whose practice is limited to specified types of legal matters may communicate that fact except as otherwise provided by regulations governing specialization. A lawyer may indicate that he or she is a specialist only as permitted by paragraphs (b) and (c) and as follows: [Insert applicable provisions on designation of specialization.]

The remainder of the 1979 Draft was substantially the same as adopted.
1980 Discussion Draft was substantially the same as adopted.

1981 and 1982 Drafts were the same as adopted.

1983 Rule: As originally adopted in 1983, Rule 7.4 provided as follows:

A lawyer may communicate the fact that the lawyer does or does not practice in particular fields of law. A lawyer shall not state or imply that the lawyer is a specialist except as follows:

(a) [Same as 2002 version of Rule 7.4(a)(1).]

(b) [Same as 2002 version of Rule 7.4(a)(2).]

(c) (Provisions on designation of specialization of the particular state)

1989 Amendments: In 1989, the ABA House of Delegates substantially amended the Comment (but not the text) to Rule 7.4. The changes were explained in the following report:

ABA Committee Report Explaining 1989 Amendment to Rule 7.4*

Rule 7.4 prohibits a lawyer from stating or implying that he or she is a "specialist," with certain limited exceptions. The Rule further provides for designation of specialty in accordance with the rules of the particular jurisdiction. Rule 7.4(c). This rule operates only to prohibit factually inaccurate or misleading information. . . .

As presently written, however, the Comment to Rule 7.4 *also* prohibits statements that the lawyer's practice is "limited to" or "concentrated in" certain fields, under the theory that these terms also connote formal recognition of the lawyer as a "specialist." . . . The use of the words "limited to" or "concentrated in" in denoting areas of practice do not clearly imply *formal* recognition as a "specialist" and simply do not pose sufficient danger of misleading to warrant a proscription of their use. . . .

Therefore, the Comment to Rule 7.4 should not prohibit statements that a lawyer's practice is "limited to" or "concentrated in" a particular field.

1992 Amendments: In 1992, the ABA House of Delegates substantially amended Rule 7.4 and its Comment to conform the rule to the holding of *Peel v. Attorney Registration and Disciplinary Commission*, 496 U.S. 91 (1990). The amendments are explained in the following committee report:

ABA Committee Report Explaining 1992 Amendment to Rule 7.4*

Background

The findings in a recent survey conducted by the ABA Young Lawyers Division . . . revealed that 64 percent of all lawyers in private practice spend at least 50 percent of their time in one substantive field of law. Further, this phenomenon is not limited to large firms. Fifty five percent of sole practitioners responding to the survey were found to spend half or more of their time in just one field. . . .

The Peel Decision

In 1990 the legal specialization issue was addressed again by the Supreme Court in *Peel v. Attorney Registration and Disciplinary Commission*. . . .

The *Peel* decision invalidated the broad prohibition of ABA Model Rule 7.4 on lawyers' communications about their specialties, holding that states may not categorically

---

* Committee Reports do not represent official policy of the ABA. They are for information only, and the opinions are those of the authors of the report.

ban a truthful communication by a lawyer that he or she is certified as a specialist by a bona fide private certifying organization. . . .

The proposed amendment of Model Rule 7.4 would bring the ABA Model Rules of Professional Conduct into compliance with the *Peel* decision. . . . Amending Model Rule 7.4 as we have proposed will help to insure protection of the users of legal services while authorizing legitimate, truthful advertising claims of lawyer specialists.

1994 Amendments: In 1994, the ABA House of Delegates amended Rule 7.4 by adding a single new sentence to the text of the existing rule (and an identical sentence to the end of the Comment) to bring Rule 7.4 into line with the ABA's new system for accrediting organizations that certify lawyers as specialists. (The ABA Standing Committee on Specialization began approving such organizations in 1993.) In essence, the amendment made it unnecessary for lawyers in states without certifying procedures to use a disclaimer when claiming certification by an organization accredited by the American Bar Association.

Below are excerpts from the joint report and recommendation submitted by the two co-sponsors in support of the amendment.

ABA Committee Report Explaining 1994 Amendment to Rule 7.4*

The purpose of this recommendation is to harmonize Model Rule 7.4 with the Association's newly enacted procedure for accrediting organizations that certify specialists in particular areas of the law. . . .

In August, 1993 the Standing Committee on Specialization reported to the House that six specialty certification programs . . . had met the Standards. The Standing Committee on Specialization therefore recommended that those programs be accredited, which recommendation was approved by the House.

However, under the 1992 amendments, a lawyer who is certified by one of those accredited programs, and who practices in a State that has not yet adopted a procedure for approving certifying organizations, would have to add, to any communication setting forth his or her certification, a statement to the effect that there is no procedure in that particular jurisdiction for approving certifying organizations. Many lawyers believe that such a disclaimer would dilute the positive fact of certification; therefore, those lawyers would end up refraining from publicizing their certification rather than adding the required statement, even though the certifying organization had been fully accredited by the ABA. As a consequence, the value of the ABA accreditation would be considerably diminished.

The Standing Committee on Specialization and the Standing Committee on Ethics and Professional Responsibility believe that Rule 7.4 should now be further amended to permit any accreditations authorized by the House to have their intended effect and be given recognition in those states which have not yet created a mechanism for approving organizations that grant certification.

2002 Amendments: At its February 2002 Mid-Year Meeting, the ABA House of Delegates adopted without change the ABA Ethics 2000 Commission proposal to amend Rule 7.4 and its Comment. The amendments substituted Rule 7.4(d) in place of several longer subparagraphs covering essentially the same ground in greater detail, including an alternative paragraph for jurisdictions lacking any procedures for certifying specialties or for approving organizations that grant specialty certifications. Comments 1, 2, and 3 were amended, and Comments 4 and 5 were deleted.

Selected State Variations

> **Editors' Note.** For a state-by-state chart of rules governing lawyer specialty certification, see the ABA Standing Committee on Specialization's website at *http://www.americanbar.org/groups/professional_responsibility/committees_commissions/specialization.html.*

Arizona: The equivalent to Rule 7.4(d) permits lawyers to state or imply that they are specialists only if they are "certified by the Arizona Board of Legal Specialization" or by a "national entity" that the Board has recognized as having standards substantially the same as the Board's standards.

California has no rule comparable to ABA Model Rule 7.4 in the California Rules of Professional Conduct, but California has developed an extensive program of specialty certification. To be eligible for certification, an attorney must be a member of the California State Bar in good standing and must (1) have spent at least 25 percent of his or her occupational time during the previous five years working in the area of law in which certification is sought, (2) pass a written exam tailored to the particular specialty field, (3) demonstrate a high level of experience in the specialty field by meeting specific task and experience requirements, (4) complete at least 45 hours of continuing legal education in the specialty field, and (5) be favorably evaluated by other attorneys and judges familiar with the attorney's work. California offers specialty certification in eight areas of practice, including Appellate Law, Bankruptcy Law (both Personal and Small Business), Criminal Law, Estate Planning, Trust and Probate Law, Family Law, Immigration and Nationality Law, Taxation Law, and Workers' Compensation Law. Each field has its own particular requirements. For more information, including links to the Rules Governing the State Bar of California Program for Certifying Legal Specialists (most recently amended effective November 1, 2003) and the requirements for each specialty field, visit the California State Bar's website at *www.calbar.org* and enter "Legal Specialization" in the site's search box.

Connecticut: Rule 7.4A(d) describes in some detail 27 different fields of law in which lawyers may be certified as specialists. Rule 7.4B concerns the appointment, powers, and duties of a Legal Specialization Screening Committee that evaluates certifying entities, and Rule 7.4C concerns applications for approval as a certifying entity.

District of Columbia omits ABA Model Rule 7.4.

Florida: Rule 4-7.2(c)(6) divides the rules regulating claims and disclaimers for specialty certification into three categories, depending on whether a lawyer is certified as a specialist by (A) the Florida Bar, (B) another state bar, or (C) an entity not connected with any state bar.

Georgia: In the rules effective November 3, 2011, Georgia tracks the first sentence of ABA Model Rule 7.4 verbatim, but eliminates the rest of the ABA rule and instead states the following: "A lawyer who is a specialist in a particular field of law by experience, specialized training or education, or is certified by a recognized and bona fide professional entity, may communicate such specialty or certification so long as the statement is not false or misleading."

Illinois: Rule 7.4(c) requires that if a lawyer's advertisement uses the terms "certified," "specialist," or "expert," then the terms (1) must be "truthful and verifiable and may not be misleading," and (2) must state that "the Supreme Court of Illinois does not recognize certifications of specialties in the practice of law and that the certificate, award or recognition is not a requirement to practice law in Illinois."

Iowa: Rule 7.4 contains a list of 71 distinct fields of practice that a lawyer may identify or describe in communications.

Louisiana addresses this issue in Rule 7.2(c)(5) and specifies that lawyers generally cannot state or imply that they are specialists or experts unless they fit within certain narrow exceptions identified in the rule.

Massachusetts: Rule 7.4(a) permits lawyers to hold themselves out as "specialists" if the holding out does not include a false or misleading communication. The rule defines "holding out" to include "(1) a statement that the lawyer concentrates in, specializes in, is certified in, has expertise in, or limits practice to a particular service, field, or area of law, (2) directory listings, including electronic, computer-accessed or other similar types of directory listings, by particular service, field, or area of law, and (3) any other association of the lawyer's name with a particular service, field, or area of law." Comment 3A to Rule 7.2 provides, in part, as follows:

> Depending upon the topic or purpose of the newsgroup, bulletin board, or chat group, the posting might also constitute an association of the lawyer or law firm's name with a particular service, field, or area of law amounting to a claim of specialization under Rule 7.4 and would therefore be subject to the restrictions of that rule.

Michigan: Rule 7.4 omits ABA Model Rule 7.4(b)-(d).

Missouri: Rule 7.4 provides that a lawyer other than an admiralty or patent attorney shall not state or imply that the lawyer is a specialist "unless the communication contains a disclaimer that neither the Supreme Court of Missouri nor The Missouri Bar reviews or approves certifying organizations or specialist designations."

Nevada: Rule 7.4(d)(2)(iii) requires that any lawyer claiming to be a specialist "shall carry a minimum of $500,000 in professional liability insurance, with the exception of lawyers who practice exclusively in public law." Nevada also adds a Rule 7.4A to establish procedures for the State Bar Board of Governors to approve organizations that certify lawyers as specialists.

New Jersey: Rule 7.4(d) permits a lawyer to communicate that the lawyer has been certified as a specialist only if the lawyer states (among other things) that "the certification has been granted by the Supreme Court of New Jersey or by an organization that has been approved by the American Bar Association." If the certification has been granted by an organization that has not been approved, or has been denied approval, by either the Supreme Court of New Jersey or the American Bar Association, "the absence or denial of such approval shall be clearly identified in each such communication by the lawyer."

New York: Rule 7.4(c)(1) provides that a lawyer who is "certified as a specialist in a particular area of law or law practice by a private organization approved for that purpose by the American Bar Association" may advertise the certification only if the lawyer identifies the certifying organization and "prominently" makes the following disclaimer: "The [name of the private certifying organization] is not affiliated with any governmental authority." If the lawyer is certified as a specialist by an "authority having jurisdiction over specialization under the laws of another state" (rather than by an ABA-approved private organization), Rule 7.4(c)(2) requires a slightly different disclaimer.

New York also previously required lawyers advertising specialization to state: "Certification is not a requirement for the practice of law in the State of New York and does not necessarily indicate greater competence than other attorneys experienced in this field of law," but that disclaimer was struck down as unconstitutional in *Hayes v. New York Attorney Grievance Committee of the Eighth Judicial District*, 672 F.3d 158 (2d Cir. 2012). The State did not seek review in the United States Supreme Court.

North Carolina relegates the substance of ABA Model Rule 7.4(b) (regarding patent and trademark practice) to a Comment and deletes Rule 7.4(c) (regarding admiralty practice).

Ohio: Rule 7.4(a) expressly adds that a lawyer may state that the lawyer "limits his or her practice to or concentrates in particular fields of law." Rule 7.4(c) provides that a lawyer engaged in "trademark practice" may use the designation "Trademarks," "Trademark Attorney," or a substantially similar designation. "Ohio's equivalent to ABA Model Rule 7.4(d)(1) applies if the lawyer has been certified as a specialist by an organization approved by the Supreme Court Commission on Certification of Attorneys as Specialists."

Pennsylvania: Rule 7.4 permits lawyers to advertise that they are certified by organizations approved by the Supreme Court. The Supreme Court may approve an organization upon recommendation of the State Bar Association if the court finds that advertising certification by the organization "will provide meaningful information, which is not false, misleading or deceptive, for use of the public in selecting or retaining a lawyer." Certification must be available to all lawyers "who meet objective and consistently applied standards relevant to practice in the area of law to which the certification relates."

Texas: Rule 7.04(b)(2) permits lawyers to advertise that they have been certified as specialists by the Texas Board of Legal Specialization or by an organization that has been:

> accredited by the Texas Board of Legal Specialization as a bona fide organization that admits to membership or grants certification only on the basis of objective, exacting, publicly available standards (including high standards of individual character, conduct, and reputation) that are reasonably relevant to the special training or special competence that is implied and that are in excess of the level of training and competence generally required for admission to the Bar. . . .

Virginia: In the Rules effective December 1, 2012, Rule 7.4(c) is similar to Model Rule 7.4(d), except that it does not permit a lawyer to use the designation "specialist" simply because the lawyer has received such a designation from an organization that has been accredited by the American Bar Association. Rather, the lawyer may use the designation of "certified" only if the lawyer is "certified by the Supreme Court of Virginia as a specialist in some capacity."

Related Materials

ABA Formal Ethics Opinions: See ABA Formal Ethics Op. 90-357 n.8 (1990).

ABA Standards for Accreditation of Specialty Certification Programs for Lawyers: In 1992, the ABA amended Rule 7.4 to allow lawyers to advertise that they were "certified" by private organizations as specialists. In 1993, the ABA adopted Standards for Accreditation of Specialty Certification Programs for Lawyers. The ABA Standards are strict — accredited certifying organizations must be made up primarily of lawyers and must only certify lawyers who (1) have been involved in the specialty area for at least the past three years; (2) devote at least 25 percent of their practice to the specialty area; (3) have passed a written examination of "suitable length and complexity"; (4) have been favorably recommended by five or more lawyers or judges knowledgeable in the specialty area; and (5) have taken at least 36 hours of CLE in the specialty area during the three years before applying for specialty certification. The Standards for Accreditation of Specialty Certification Programs are available at *http://www.americanbar.org/groups/professional_responsibility/committees_commissions/ specialization/resources/resources_for_programs/accreditation_standards.html.*

Since 1993, the ABA has accredited more than a dozen specialty certification programs offered by seven private certifying organizations. The private certifying organizations are: the American Board of Certification (Business Bankruptcy, Consumer Bankruptcy, Creditors Rights); the American Board of Professional Liability Attorneys (Accounting Professional Liability, Legal Professional Liability, Medical Professional Liability); the National Association of Counsel for Children (Juvenile Law-Child Welfare); the National Association of Estate Planners & Councils Estate Law Specialist Board, Inc. (Estate Planning Law); the National Board of Trial Advocacy (Civil Trial Advocacy, Criminal Trial Advocacy, Family Law Trial Advocacy, Social Security Disability Law); the National College for DUI Defense, Inc. (DUI Defense Law); and the National Elder Law Foundation (Elder Law).

The Standing Committee on Specialization continues to help private groups develop new certification programs that meet the ABA Standards. For an up-to-date list of certification programs accredited by the ABA and by various state authorities (including a state-by-state chart of available certifications), visit the Standing Committee's website at *http://www.americanbar.org/groups/professional_responsibility/ committees_commissions/specialization.html.*

ABA Standing Committee on Specialization: The ABA maintains a Standing Committee on Specialization. The Standing Committee (a) publishes a quarterly newsletter, "Certification Link," that reports legal specialization news from around the country; (b) holds an annual National Roundtable on Lawyer Specialty Certification; (c) assists certifying organizations in developing additional certification programs; and (d) maintains a state-by-state summary of specialty advertising regulations on its website. For more information, visit *http://www.americanbar.org/ groups/professional_responsibility/committees_commissions/specialization.html.*

Paralegal Certification: Since 1976, the National Association of Legal Assistants (NALA) has administered a certifying examination for paralegals. Passing the exam entitles a paralegal to the designation "Certified Legal Assistant" (CLA) or "Certified Paralegal" (CP). The NALA may revoke the CLA or CP designation for a variety of reasons, including "[v]iolation of the NALA Code of Ethics and Professional Responsibility."

Paralegals who hold the CLA credential are eligible to take four-hour specialty certification examinations in more than a dozen areas of law, including Alternative Dispute Resolution, Bankruptcy, Contracts, Civil Litigation, Corporations/Business Law, Criminal Law and Procedure, Discovery, Intellectual Property, Estate Planning and Probate, and Real Estate. Those who pass a specialty certification exam earn the designation "APC" (standing for "Advanced Paralegal Certification") and a specialty (*e.g.,* "APC-Civil Litigation" or "APC-Bankruptcy"). Since 1976, more than 15,000 people have become Certified Legal Assistants. For more information, check *www.nala.org* (click "Certification" at top of screen).

Restatement of the Law Governing Lawyers: The Restatement has no provision comparable to ABA Model Rule 7.4.

Rule 7.5   Firm Names and Letterheads

Canon and Code Antecedents

ABA Canons of Professional Ethics: Canon 33 provided as follows:

33.   Partnerships-Names

Partnerships among lawyers for the practice of their profession are very common and are not to be condemned. In the formation of partnerships and the use of partnership names care should be taken not to violate any law, custom, or rule of court locally applicable. Where partnerships are formed between lawyers who are not all admitted to practice in the courts of the state, care should be taken to avoid any misleading name or representation which would create a false impression as to the professional position or privileges of the member not locally admitted. In the formation of partnerships for the practice of law, no person should be admitted or held out as a practitioner or member who is not a member of the legal profession duly authorized to practice, and amenable to professional discipline. In the selection and use of a firm name, no false, misleading, assumed or trade name should be used. The continued use of the name of a deceased or former partner, when permissible by local custom, is not unethical, but care should be taken that no imposition or deception is practiced through this use. When a member of the firm, on becoming a judge, is precluded from practicing law, his name should not be continued in the firm name.

Partnerships between lawyers and members of other professions or nonprofessional persons should not be formed or permitted where any part of the partnership's employment consists of the practice of law.

ABA Model Code of Professional Responsibility: Compare DR 2-102(A), DR 2-102(B), DR 2-102(C), and DR 2-102(D) (reprinted later in this volume).

Cross-References in Other Rules

Rule 5.5, Comment 21: "Whether and how lawyers may communicate the availability of their services to prospective clients in this jurisdiction is governed by **Rules 7.1 to 7.5**."

Legislative History of Model Rule 7.5

1980 Discussion Draft (then Rule 9.5) did not include the clause in subparagraph (b) requiring lawyers to indicate their jurisdictional limitations, and did not contain subparagraph (d).

1981 Draft was generally the same as adopted, except that Rule 7.5(d) provided: "Lawyers shall not hold themselves out as practicing in a law firm unless the association is in fact a firm."

1982 Draft was adopted.

1983 Rule: As originally adopted in 1983, Rules 7.5(a), (c), and (d) were identical to the 2002 version, and Rule 7.5(b) was nearly identical to the 2002 version but did not contain the phrase "or other professional designation."

2002 Amendments: In 2002, the ABA House of Delegates adopted without change the ABA Ethics 2000 Commission proposal to amend Rule 7.5 and its

Comment. The amendments added "or other professional designation" to Rule 7.5(b), added the second sentence (regarding web addresses) to Comment 1, and made minor changes to Comment 2.

In addition, in 2002, the House of Delegates approved a proposal by the ABA Standing Committee on Ethics and Professional Responsibility to add the final clause ("or the name of a nonlawyer") to Comment 1 of Rule 7.5. The Report submitted by the Standing Committee in support of this proposal (and a companion proposal to amend Rule 7.2) noted that the Standing Committee had consulted with the New York State Bar Association, which recommended amending Rule 7.5 to address "its concern that law firms engaged in offering certain services jointly with other nonlawyer professionals not create confusion by adding names of nonlawyer professionals to their law firm names." The Standing Committee agreed with this recommendation, and therefore recommended adding the final clause of Comment 1 to Model Rule 7.5. The House of Delegates approved the recommendation.

Selected State Variations

Alaska adds the following paragraph (e): "The term 'of counsel' shall be used only to refer to a lawyer who has a close continuing relationship with the firm."

California: Compare Standards 6 through 9 following Rule 1-400. In addition, §16952 of the California Corporations Law, entitled "Requirements for Name," provides that the name of a registered limited liability partnership must contain the words "Registered Limited Liability Partnership" or "Limited Liability Partnership" or one of the abbreviations "L.L.P.," "LLP," "R.L.L.P.," or "RLLP" as the last words or letters of its name.

Florida: Rule 4-7.9(b) permits a lawyer to practice under a trade name if the name is "not deceptive" and "does not imply that the firm is something other than a private law firm." The same rule permits a lawyer to use the term "legal clinic" or "legal services" in conjunction with the lawyer's own name "if the lawyer's practice is devoted to providing routine legal services for fees that are lower than the prevailing rate in the community for those services."

Under Rule 4-7.9(c) a lawyer may not advertise under a trade or fictitious name "unless the same name is the law firm name that appears on the lawyer's letterhead, business cards, office sign, and fee contracts, and appears with the lawyer's signature on pleadings and other legal documents." The Comment to Rule 4-7.9 notes that a lawyer may not advertise under "a nonsense name designed to obtain an advantageous position for the lawyer in alphabetical directory listings unless the lawyer actually practices under that nonsense name."

Georgia: In the rules effective November 3, 2011, Georgia adds Rule 7.5(e) (1), which permits a lawyer in private practice to use a trade name if it "includes the name of at least one of the lawyers practicing under said name. A law firm name consisting solely of the name or names of deceased or retired members of the firm does not have to include the name of an active member of the firm."

Iowa: Rule 7.5 provides in paragraph (f) that a "lawyer who is engaged both in the practice of law and in another profession or business shall not so indicate on the lawyer's letterhead, office sign, or professional card, and shall not be identified as a lawyer in any publication in connection with the lawyer's other profession or business."

Massachusetts adds to ABA Comment 2 that the term "associates" implies practice in either a partnership or sole proprietorship form and "may not be used by a group in which the individual members disclaim the joint or vicarious responsibility inherent in such forms of business in the absence of an effective disclaimer of such responsibility."

Nevada: Rule 7.5(b) provides that a law firm with offices in more than one jurisdiction "that has registered with the State Bar of Nevada under Rule 7.5A" may use the same name in each jurisdiction. Rule 7.5A(a) provides: "All law firms having an office in Nevada and in one or more other jurisdictions shall register with the State Bar of Nevada and shall pay an annual fee of $500 for such registration." The remainder of the rule sets out lengthy, detailed disclosure requirements such as: "(1) The names and addresses of all lawyers employed by the firm, the jurisdictions in which each lawyer is licensed, and verification that each lawyer is in good standing in the jurisdictions in which each lawyer is licensed; (2) Any pending disciplinary action or investigation against a lawyer employed by the firm;" and (5) a certification that:

> (i) The firm will maintain a permanent office in Nevada with a resident member of the firm who is also an active member in good standing of the State Bar of Nevada at all times the firm is practicing in Nevada . . . [and]
> (ii) The firm agrees to disclose in writing to its Nevada clients whether all of its lawyers are licensed to practice in Nevada and, if any of its lawyers are not so licensed, to disclose what legal work will be performed by lawyers not admitted to practice in this state. Upon request of the State Bar of Nevada, the firm shall provide documentation evidencing its compliance with these disclosure requirements. . . .

New Jersey: Rule 7.5(b) permits a law firm with offices in more than one jurisdiction to use the same name in each jurisdiction, but all advertisements, letterheads or "anywhere else that the firm name is used," must indicate the jurisdictional limitations on those not licensed to practice in New Jersey. If a firm name includes the name of any lawyer not licensed in New Jersey, then any advertisement, letterhead or other communication containing the firm name "must include the name of at least one licensed New Jersey attorney who is responsible for the firm's New Jersey practice or the local office thereof. . . ." Rule 7.5(d) permits lawyers to state or imply that they practice in a partnership "only if the persons designated in the firm name and the principal members of the firm share in the responsibility and liability for the firm's performance of legal services." Rule 7.5(e) provides as follows:

> (e) A law firm name may include additional identifying language such as "& Associates" only when such language is accurate and descriptive of the firm. Any firm name including additional identifying language such as "Legal Services" or other similar phrases shall inform all prospective clients in the retainer agreement or other writing that the law firm is not affiliated or associated with a public, quasi-public or charitable organization. However, no firm shall use the phrase "legal aid" in its name or in any additional identifying language.

However, in *In the Matter of the Decision on CAA 47-2007*, 2009 WL 468292 (N.J. 2009), the New Jersey Supreme Court ordered its Committee on Attorney Advertising to consider and make recommendations on "any additional information, or change in format, that this Court should allow in respect of law firm names, including specifically any additional or changed language that the Committee recommends for insertion into the present *RPC* 7.5," and "to consider (among other things) "whether special rules should be established for attorney practices that include the performance of activities that may be performed by non-attorneys.'' When we went to press in September 2011, the Committee had submitted its recommendations to the New Jersey Supreme Court, and the Supreme Court had released proposed amendments for comment. The proposed amendments are available online at *http://www.judiciary.state.nj.us/notices/2011/n110408a.pdf.*

New York sets forth detailed regulations in Rule 7.5(a) regarding ''internet web sites, professional cards, professional announcements, office signs, letterheads or similar professional notices or devices.'' Rule 7.5(b), which is based on DR 2-102(B) of the old ABA Model Code, provides as follows:

> A lawyer in private practice shall not practice under a trade name, a name that is misleading as to the identity of the lawyer or lawyers practicing under such name, or a firm name containing names other than those of one or more of the lawyers in the firm, except that . . . a firm may use as, or continue to include in its name, the name or names of one or more deceased or retired members of the firm or of a predecessor firm in a continuing line of succession. . . . A lawyer or law firm may not include the name of a nonlawyer in its firm name. . . .

New York adds Rule 7.5(e)-(f), which addresses domain names and firm names as follows:

> (e) A lawyer or law firm may utilize a domain name for an internet web site that does not include the name of the lawyer or law firm provided:
> (1) all pages of the web site clearly and conspicuously include the actual name of the lawyer or law firm;
> (2) the lawyer or law firm in no way attempts to engage in the practice of law using the domain name;
> (3) the domain name does not imply an ability to obtain results in a matter; and
> (4) the domain name does not otherwise violate these Rules.
> (f) A lawyer or law firm may utilize a telephone number which contains a domain name, nickname, moniker or motto that does not otherwise violate a disciplinary rule.

North Carolina: Rule 7.5(a) adds the following: ''Every trade name used by a law firm shall be registered with the North Carolina State Bar for a determination of whether the name is misleading.'' Rule 7.5(d) ends with the words ''whether or not the lawyer is precluded from practicing law.''

Ohio: Rule 7.5(a) expressly provides that a lawyer in private practice ''shall not practice under a trade name,'' and generally permits a law firm to ''use as, or continue to include in, its name the name or names of one or more deceased or retired members of the firm or of a predecessor firm in a continuing line of succession.'' Rule 7.5(b) provides that a law firm with offices in more than one jurisdiction that lists attorneys associated with the firm ''shall indicate the jurisdictional limitations on those not licensed to practice in Ohio.''

Oregon: Rule 7.5(d) forbids a lawyer to ''permit his or her name to remain in the name of a law firm or to be used by the firm during the time the lawyer is not actively and regularly practicing law as a member of the firm'' and forbids members of the firm to use the lawyer's name. The rule does not apply for absences of one year or less during which the lawyer is not actively practicing law if the lawyer plans to return to the firm. The rule also does not apply to the names of ''retiring, deceased, or retired members of the firm or a predecessor law firm in a continuing line of succession.''

Related Materials

ABA Formal Ethics Opinions: See ABA Formal Ethics Op. 84-351 (1984), 88-356 (1988), 90-357 (1990), 94-388 (1994), 95-391 (1995), 01-423 (2001), 03-430 (2003), and 08-451 (2008).

Partnership Law: ABA Model Rule 7.5(d) provides that lawyers may state or imply that they practice in a partnership "only when that is the fact." In the Revised Uniform Partnership Act, §202(a) (Formation of Partnership) provides that "the association of two or more persons to carry on as co-owners a business for profit forms a partnership, whether or not the persons intend to form a partnership." Section 202(c)(3) elaborates on this general rule by stating: "A person who receives a share of the profits of a business is presumed to be a partner in the business, unless [among other exceptions] the profits were received in payment . . . (ii) for services as an independent contractor or of wages or other compensation to an employee."

Restatement of the Law Governing Lawyers: The Restatement has no provision comparable to ABA Model Rule 7.5.

Rule 7.6   Political Contributions to Obtain Government Legal Engagements or Appointments by Judges

Canon and Code Antecedents

ABA Canons of Professional Ethics: No comparable Canon.

ABA Model Code of Professional Responsibility: No comparable Disciplinary Rule.

Cross-References in Other Rules

None.

Legislative History of Model Rule 7.6

1983 Rule: As originally adopted in 1983, the ABA Model Rules did not contain Rule 7.6 or any close equivalent.

1997 Proposal and Resolution: At the ABA's August 1997 Annual Meeting, the Association of the Bar of the City of New York proposed that the ABA adopt a detailed and highly restrictive "pay-to-play" rule. As described in a later ABA report:

> The practice commonly known as "pay-to-play" . . . is a system whereby lawyers and law firms are considered for or awarded either government legal engagements or appointments by a judge only upon their making or soliciting contributions for the political campaigns of officials who are in a position to "steer" such business their way. . . .

The heart of the 1997 proposal provided as follows:

3. Prohibitions on Certain Government Finance Engagements

(a) No lawyer shall undertake a Government Finance Engagement awarded by an Official of an Issuer within two years after making either a Political Contribution or a Political Solicitation; provided, however, that this Rule shall not prohibit a lawyer from undertaking a Government Finance Engagement with a particular Official of an Issuer if:

(i)(A) the only Political Contribution made by the lawyer to that Official of an Issuer within the previous two years was (I) for a position for which the lawyer was entitled to vote and (II) not in excess of $250 for each stage of the electoral campaign (i.e., primary and general election) and (B) the lawyer did not make any political contribution in excess of $1,000 to any political party or committee of the State or of any political subdivision, agency or instrumentality thereof; or

(ii) the only Political Solicitation made by the lawyer on behalf of that Official of an Issuer or any political party or committee of the State or of any political subdivision, agency or instrumentality thereof, was for Political Contributions made within the previous two years for an Official of an Issuer for whom the lawyer was entitled to vote, no Political Contribution solicited was in excess of $100 to the Official of an Issuer for each complete electoral campaign (primary and general election combined), and the aggregate of all Political Contributions solicited in any such campaign within the previous two years did not exceed $2,500. . . .

(b) Notwithstanding subsection (a), any lawyer who is personally involved in the undertaking of Government Finance Engagements who solicits Political Contributions in any amount at the request of an Official of an Issuer or one of the Official's subordinates, is prohibited from undertaking a Government Finance Engagement awarded by that Official of an Issuer for a period of two years. . . .

(c) To the extent that a lawyer is prohibited from undertaking a Government Finance Engagement by operation of this Rule, the law firm employing such lawyer (whether or not that lawyer is admitted to practice in New York) shall also be prohibited from undertaking a Government Finance Engagement. . . .

(d) If a law firm or a political action committee controlled by a law firm itself makes a Political Contribution or a Political Solicitation that would operate to prohibit a lawyer from undertaking certain Government Finance Engagements, the law firm is likewise prohibited from undertaking such Government Finance Engagements for the same two year period that would be applicable to a lawyer prohibited through operation of the Rule.

The ABA House of Delegates did not approve the New York City Bar's proposal. Instead, the House of Delegates approved a resolution (a) condemning pay-to-play practices wherever they existed, and (b) calling for the creation of a Task Force that would study the problems created by a pay-to-play system, develop appropriate professional standards or rules on the subject, and report to the House of Delegates within a year.

The next month, in keeping with this resolution, the ABA President appointed a Task Force on Lawyer's Political Contributions. The twelve-member Task Force was chaired by John W. Martin, Jr., Vice-President and General Counsel of Ford Motor Company, and included such distinguished members as former CIA and FBI Director William H. Webster, former United States Senator Howard H. Baker Jr., and SEC General Counsel Harvey J. Goldschmid. The Task Force collected and reviewed empirical data and media reporting on pay-to-play practices and considered possible ways to discourage or prevent such practices.

1998 Resolution: Shortly before the ABA's 1998 Annual Meeting, the ABA Task Force on Lawyer's Political Contributions issued a report unanimously condemning pay-to-play practices, urging the ABA to adopt a new Model Rule making pay-to-play practices unethical, and recommending broader disclosure of campaign contributions. However, the Task Force was sharply divided as to whether a new Model Rule alone would be sufficient, and what the new Model Rule should say. Six of the 12 Task Force members favored a strict rule that would

(a) disqualify both lawyers who made political contributions and their law firms,

(b) require lawyers to publicly disclose their political contributions, and

(c) require lawyers facing disciplinary charges to show that their political contributions were not made to obtain government legal work.

Five other Task Force members believed that requiring lawyers to disclose their contributions and to prove that the contributions were not made to obtain government work would be ineffective and would have an undue chilling effect on the First Amendment rights of lawyers to take part in the political process. In the face of this split, the House of Delegates did not adopt a new Model Rule but adopted the following resolution:

RESOLVED, That the American Bar Association urges the following actions be taken to address any conduct by lawyers making or soliciting campaign contributions to public officials for the purpose of being considered or retained for government legal engagements.

(1) All state, territorial and local bar associations should unequivocally condemn any arrangement under which the selection or consideration of lawyers to be retained for government legal engagements depends, in whole or in part, on whether the lawyer has made or solicited campaign contributions.

(2) State, territorial and local government entities should create, establish and maintain full and effective systems for the reporting and disclosure of campaign contributions to candidates for elective public office so that the public may have reasonable notice of contributions made by lawyers or law firms, and where they have not, bar and disciplinary authorities should adopt rules that require disclosure of campaign contributions by lawyers and law firms to government officials in a position to influence the award of legal engagements to the contributor.

(3) Merit procurement processes should be adopted for the selection of lawyers performing legal services for government agencies as a means of ensuring that no political contribution or solicitation has influenced the selection.

(4) The Standing Committee on Ethics and Professional Responsibility is directed to report to the House of Delegates by its 1999 Annual Meeting a proposed Model Rule that declares that a lawyer or law firm shall not make a political contribution or solicitation for the purpose of obtaining or being considered for a legal engagement. . . .

Regarding paragraph (4) of the resolution, a motion was made to give the Standing Committee "discretion" to address the problem of pay-to-play either by amending the comment to an existing rule, by issuing a formal ethics opinion, or by proposing a new model rule. That motion failed by a vote of 158-151.

1999 Proposal: At the ABA's August 1999 Annual Meeting, the ABA Standing Committee on Ethics and Professional Responsibility proposed a new Rule 7.6, but the ABA House of Delegates voted 164 to 146 to reject the proposed rule. We reprint below substantial excerpts from the report submitted by the ABA Standing Committee on Ethics and Professional Responsibility in support of the proposal that the House of Delegates rejected.

ABA Committee Report Submitted in Support of Rejected Rule 7.6*

[A]lthough lawyers and their political contributions are an important component of the pay-to-play system, lawyers are not the most important players in such a system. The primary actor in any pay-to-play situation is the public official who . . . may be acting in dereliction of official duties. For this reason, the rules of professional conduct governing lawyer behavior should not be relied upon as the primary method of preventing the practice of pay-to-play. Rather, consistent and diligent enforcement of statutory provisions governing fair campaign finance practices and the conduct of public officials is the most fundamental method of addressing the problem of pay-to-play. The fundamental harm done by a pay-to-play system is the harm that befalls the public when a government official, motivated by campaign contributions, chooses lawyers or law firms that may not be the best qualified to perform legal services on the public's behalf. Thus it is the integrity of a basic governmental process, and not just the integrity of the legal profession, that is undermined when such action by a public official is tolerated.

[A] second method of protecting against the evils of a pay-to-play system exists, and it also lies outside the scope of rules governing lawyer conduct: the use of uniform procurement or acquisition procedures for the placement of legal services engagements by government entities and the granting of appointments by judges. The Association has strongly supported . . . fundamental principles of competition in public acquisitions. . . .

The Standing Committee therefore notes emphatically that where there is aggressive enforcement of prohibitions against pay-to-play conduct by public officials, and where there is reliance on uniform procurement codes and procedures in the placement of legal engagements and in appointments by judges, the need to focus on lawyer conduct will be diminished. . . .

BACKGROUND FOR DEVELOPING A MODEL RULE

. . . In carrying out its charge, the Task Force expanded the scope of its investigation in two important ways. Initial concerns had focused on the existence of the phenomenon in the area of municipal finance engagements. The Task Force's review revealed at least some evidence that the practice occurs in a wider range of practice areas. Early proposals for a Model Rule limited in application to lawyers engaged in municipal finance work were therefore put aside and the Task Force focused on developing a Rule of wider application.

The Task Force also discovered that a similar system was sometimes in evidence as well in the context of appointments of lawyers made by judges following the making or soliciting of substantial contributions to the judges' election campaigns.

DEVELOPMENT OF THE PROPOSED RULE

The Committee . . . develop[ed] two possible "trial" rules addressing lawyers' roles in the pay-to-play system. One was . . . prohibiting political contributions when the purpose of such contributions was the obtaining of legal business. Because the

---

* Committee Reports do not represent official policy of the ABA. They are for information only, and the opinions are those of the authors of the report.

Committee questioned the wisdom of basing the restriction solely on a lawyer's purpose for making political contributions, and recognized the difficulty of proving "purpose," it developed a second rule . . . prohibiting lawyers from accepting legal engagements where the awarding of the engagements was based upon lawyer's political contributions. Each draft rule was accompanied by extensive commentary that was intended, among other things, to establish criteria whereby a contributing lawyer's "purpose" could be proven.

. . . The following summary . . . explains the Committee's ultimate decision to advance the proposed Model Rule presented here, which represents a combination of its two initial alternative proposals with refinements.

CONSTITUTIONAL ISSUES

. . . The Committee undertook a review of recent First Amendment jurisprudence treating legislatively-enacted campaign contribution limits. It found, not surprisingly, that limitations on the making and solicitation of political contributions must be predicated on the need to protect a valid state interest; that they must be narrowly drawn; and that their language must be sufficiently clear as to provide fair notice of when and how they operate, thereby satisfying the requirements of due process. . . .

ENACTED OR PROPOSED REGULATIONS

The Committee examined numerous regulations that have been either adopted or proposed in different forums to regulate lawyers' contributions to political campaigns in connection with "pay-to-play" type problems. They ranged from federal criminal statutes (18 U.S.C. Sec. 201) relating to the most egregious violations (bribery or the giving of illegal gratuities) to a considerably more narrowly-drawn Association of the Bar of the City of New York proposal which, like Municipal Securities Rulemaking Board Rule GS-37, applicable to municipal finance professionals, would prohibit a lawyer or law firm from undertaking a municipal finance engagement within a certain period of time after having made a contribution in excess of a de minimis amount to a public official capable of influencing the public finance engagement.

[I]n some circumstances, the Model Rules of Professional Conduct already apply to lawyers' participation in pay-to-play. For example, the prophylactic effect of criminal statutes potentially applicable to pay-to-play participation by lawyers already has a parallel in the Model Rules of Professional Conduct: a lawyer whose style of participation in pay-to-play is so egregious as to result in conviction of bribery or a similar serious crime would also violate Model Rule 8.4 ("Misconduct"). Model Rule 7.2(c), which prohibits a lawyer from giving anything of value to another for recommending the lawyer for employment, may in some pay-to-play circumstances also be applicable. . . .

The House has, however, adopted the Task Force's position that the Association should adopt more stringent restrictions on pay-to-play than these Model Rules would afford. The Rule submitted herewith accords with that position.

ENFORCEMENT ISSUES

. . . A common and understandable concern of the bar counsel was the number of elements that would need to be proven in order to find that a lawyer's conduct in making political contributions constituted a violation of either draft rule. In this regard, bar counsel comment echoed that of other commentators, both proponents and opponents of either draft rule.

The successful enforcement of each of the draft proposals was considered to depend on the ability of disciplinary counsel to prove an element of purpose, whether it were the purpose of the lawyer making the contribution, or the purpose of the official or judge in giving the engagement or appointment to reward the lawyer's contribution. . . .

The lawyer's purpose in making or soliciting political contributions was deemed by many commentators to be the most significant test in determining if a Rule violation exists. Hence, it has been retained in the submitted Rule along with carefully crafted standards in the Comments designed to explain how "purpose" will be identified.

Disciplinary counsel . . . also appeared generally unpersuaded that pay-to-play exists as a significant problem. Hence self-enforcement of this Rule to stem pay-to-play practices by lawyers and law firms is an even more important consideration than it is in enforcement of certain other Model Rules.

2000 Amendment: In 2000, the House of Delegates voted 266-157 to adopt the very same version of Rule 7.6 and its Comment that the delegates had rejected in 1999. In 2000, however, the proposed rule was sponsored not only by the ABA Standing Committee on Ethics and Professional Responsibility (which had been the sole sponsor in 1999), but also by the ABA Section of Business Law, the ABA Section of State and Local Government Law, and the Association of the Bar of the City of New York. (The New York City Bar had sponsored the original proposal to add a pay-to-play rule back in 1997.) The report submitted in support of the new rule was nearly identical to the report submitted in 1999, but it began with the following passages explaining the 1999 proposal and why it failed:

*ABA Committee Report Submitted in Support of Rule 7.6 as Adopted**

. . . At the 1999 Annual Meeting, the House of Delegates, by a vote of 164 to 146, rejected the Standing Committee's proposal.

The Sponsors believe that the very important issue of pay-to-play should be reconsidered by the House. The [1999] vote was taken very late in the session after a substantial number of delegates had departed (only 310 of the 530 members of the House were present and voting) and without adequate opportunity for balanced debate (only one "pro" speaker, other than the moving sponsor, was recognized before a tired House called the question). Accordingly, the Sponsors resubmit the proposed Model Rule 7.6 governing lawyers' political contributions to the House of Delegates at the 2000 Midwinter Meeting.

2002 Amendments: The ABA Ethics 2000 Commission did not propose any changes to Rule 7.6 or its Comment.

Selected State Variations

Arizona, California, the District of Columbia, Illinois, Michigan, New Jersey, Ohio, Pennsylvania, Texas, and *Virginia* (among others) have no rule equivalent to ABA Model Rule 7.6.

---

* Committee Reports do not represent official policy of the ABA. They are for information only, and the opinions are those of the authors of the report.

New York omits Rule 7.6. However, Comment 5 to New York Rule 7.2 provides as follows:

> Campaign contributions by lawyers to government officials or candidates for public office who are, or may be, in a position to influence the award of a legal engagement may threaten governmental integrity by subjecting the recipient to a conflict of interest. Correspondingly, when a lawyer makes a significant contribution to a public official or an election campaign for a candidate for public office and is later engaged by the official to perform legal services for the official's agency, it may appear that the official has been improperly influenced in selecting the lawyer, whether or not this is so. This appearance of influence reflects poorly on the integrity of the legal profession and government as a whole. For these reasons, just as the Code prohibits a lawyer from compensating or giving anything of value to a person or organization to recommend or obtain employment by a client, the Code prohibits a lawyer from making or soliciting a political contribution to any candidate for government office, government official, political campaign committee or political party, if a disinterested person would conclude that the contribution is being made or solicited for the purpose of obtaining or being considered eligible to obtain a government legal engagement. This would be true even in the absence of an understanding between the lawyer and any government official or candidate that special consideration will be given in return for the political contribution or solicitation.

> [J]ust as the Code prohibits a lawyer from compensating or giving anything of value to a person or organization to recommend or obtain employment by a client, the Code prohibits a lawyer from making or soliciting a political contribution to any candidate for government office, government official, political campaign committee or political party, if a disinterested person would conclude that the contribution is being made or solicited for the purpose of obtaining or being considered eligible to obtain a government legal engagement. This would be true even in the absence of an understanding between the lawyer and any government official or candidate that special consideration will be given in return for the political contribution or solicitation.

Comment 6 complements Comment 5 by setting forth seven factors to consider in determining "whether a disinterested person would conclude that a contribution to a candidate for government office, government official, political campaign committee or political party is or has been made for the purpose of obtaining or being considered eligible to obtain a government legal engagement. . . ." For example, the factors include "(a) whether legal work awarded to the contributor or solicitor, if any, was awarded pursuant to a process that was insulated from political influence, such as a 'Request for Proposal' process" and "(c) whether the contributor or any law firm with which the lawyer is associated has sought or plans to seek government legal work from the official or candidate." (The Comments have been adopted only by the New York State Bar Association, not by the courts, but Comments 5 and 6 have special status. In an extraordinary press release in March of 2000 explaining why the courts were rejecting a proposed pay-to-play Disciplinary Rule, the courts expressly endorsed the language of old Ethical Considerations 2-37 and 2-38, and these ECs have been incorporated verbatim into Comments 5 and 6 to Rule 7.2.)

Ohio omits ABA Model Rule 7.6, explaining as follows: "The substance of Model Rule 7.6 is addressed by provisions of the Ohio Ethics Law . . . and other criminal prohibitions relative to bribery and attempts to influence the conduct of elected officials. A lawyer or law firm that violates these statutory prohibitions would be in violation of other provisions of the Ohio Rules of Professional Conduct, such as Rule 8.4.''

Related Materials

Judicial Assignment Restrictions: In 2011, the New York courts adopted 22 N.Y.C.R.R. §151.1, entitled "Assignments in Cases Involving Contributors to Judicial Campaigns." It provides that no case shall be assigned to a judge, other than in an emergency or as dictated by the rule of necessity, where an individual attorney, law firm, or party in the case contributed $2,500 or more to the judge's election campaign in the previous two years, or where the appearing attorneys, their law firms, and their clients collectively contributed $3,500 or more to the judge's election campaign. A press release announcing the new rule said that New York's courts were "the first in the country to systemically address the issue of money in judicial elections by administrative action." (New York's rule does not specifically concern contributions to judicial campaigns for the purpose of being considered for government legal engagements or appointments by a judge, but it is related to ABA Model Rule 7.6 because it regulates political contributions to judges.)

Municipal Securities Rulemaking Board Rule G-37: MSRB Rule G-37, entitled "Political Contributions and Prohibitions on Municipal Securities Business," was cited in the 1999 and 2000 ABA Committee Reports submitted in support of Rule 7.6. Rule G-37(b) provides as follows:

> *(b) Ban on Municipal Securities Business.*
>   (i) No broker, dealer or municipal securities dealer shall engage in municipal securities business with an issuer within two years after any contribution [exceeding $250] to an official of such issuer made by:
>   (A) the broker, dealer or municipal securities dealer;
>   (B) any municipal finance professional associated with such broker, dealer or municipal securities dealer; or
>   (C) any political action committee controlled by the broker, dealer or municipal securities dealer or by any municipal finance professional. ...

The rule does not apply if the contributions to the issuer do not exceed $250. The full text of Rule G-37 is available online at *www.msrb.org/Rules-and-Interpretations/MSRB-Rules/General/Rule-G-37.aspx.*

Proposed Rule on Contributions to Judicial Candidates: In 2011, in the wake of the United States Supreme Court's decisions in *Caperton v. A.T. Massey Coal Co.*, 556 U.S. 868 (2009), and *Citizens United v. Federal Election Comm'n*, 130 S. Ct. 876 (2010), both of which concerned campaign contributions, the ABA House of Delegates approved Resolution 107, which stated that "the Standing Committee on Ethics and Professional Responsibility and the Standing Committee on Professional Discipline should proceed on an expedited basis to consider what amendments, if any, should be made to the ABA Model Code of Judicial Conduct or to the ABA Model Rules of Professional Conduct to provide necessary additional guidance to the states on disclosure requirements and standards for judicial disqualification." In early 2012, the ABA Ethics and Discipline Committees circulated for comment proposed amendments to the ABA Model Code of Judicial Conduct and proposed the following new Rule 5.1A of the ABA Model Rules of Professional Conduct:

Proposed Rule 5.1A   Responsibility of Partners, Managers, and Supervisory Lawyers Regarding Contributions to Judicial Campaigns

A lawyer who individually or together with other lawyers possesses managerial authority in a law firm shall institute procedures pursuant to which all lawyers and other employees in the firm report to the firm all financial and other support provided, directly or indirectly to any judge or judicial candidate running for election. Records of such reports shall be retained for at least [number] years.

(1) The aggregate information compiled by the firm shall be reported to the agency, if any, designated by Court Rule.

The drafters also included an alternative version of subparagraph (1), as follows:

(1) When a lawyer appears before an elected judge, the lawyer shall inform the judge of the aggregate financial or other support the lawyer, the lawyer's firm, or other lawyers or employees in the firm have provided to the [most recent] election campaign of the judge.

A public hearing was held on the package of proposals at the ABA's February 2012 Mid-Year Meeting. After the hearing, the Ethics and Discipline Committee jointly decided not to pursue the proposed new Rule 5.1A. (However, they are continuing to explore amendments to Rule 2.11 of the Code of Judicial Conduct.) The report submitted in favor of the proposals is available at *http://www.americanbar.org/content/ dam/aba/migrated/cpr/ethics/20111228_scepr_draft_proposed_amendments_and_hearing_notice_dec_2011.authcheckdam.pdf.*

Restatement of the Law Governing Lawyers: The Restatement has no provision comparable to ABA Model Rule 7.6.

ANNOTATIONS ON ARTICLE 8. MAINTAINING THE INTEGRITY OF THE PROFESSION

Rule 8.1   Bar Admission and Disciplinary Matters

Canon and Code Antecedents

ABA Canons of Professional Ethics: Canon 29 provided in pertinent part:

29.   Upholding the Honor of the Profession

. . . The lawyer should aid in guarding the Bar against the admission to the profession of candidates unfit or unqualified because deficient in either moral character or education. He should strive at all times to uphold the honor and to maintain the dignity of the profession and to improve not only the law but the administration of justice.

ABA Model Code of Professional Responsibility: Compare DR 1-101(A), DR 1-101(B), and DR 1-102(A)(5) (reprinted later in this volume).

Cross-References in Other Rules

Rule 1.6, Comment 17: Some Rules require "disclosure of information relating to a client's representation to accomplish the purposes specified in paragraphs (b)

(1) through (b)(6)," only if such disclosure would be permitted by paragraph (b). See **Rules** 1.2(d), 4.1(b), **8.1** and 8.3.

Rule 1.8, Comment 5: It is prohibited to partake in the "disadvantageous use of client information unless the client gives informed consent, except as permitted or required by these Rules. See **Rules** 1.2(d), 1.6, 1.9(c), 3.3, 4.1(b), **8.1** and 8.3."

Legislative History of Model Rule 8.1

1980 Discussion Draft of Rule 8.1 was substantially the same as adopted, except that subparagraph (a) prohibited a lawyer from making "a knowing misrepresentation of fact," and subparagraph (b) did not include the clause beginning "or knowingly fail to respond. . . ."

1981 and 1982 Drafts were substantially the same as adopted.

1983 Rule: As originally adopted in 1983, the text of Rule 8.1 was identical to the 2002 version of Rule 8.1.

2002 Amendments: At its February 2002 Mid-Year Meeting, the ABA House of Delegates adopted without change the ABA Ethics 2000 Commission proposal to amend Comments 1 and 3 to Rule 8.1 in relatively minor ways. (The Ethics 2000 Commission did not propose any changes to the text of Rule 8.1.)

Selected State Variations

California: Rule 1-200 provides as follows:

> (A) A member shall not knowingly make a false statement regarding a material fact or knowingly fail to disclose a material fact in connection with an application for admission to the State Bar.
>
> (B) A member shall not further an application for admission to the State Bar of a person whom the member knows to be unqualified in respect to character, education, or other relevant attributes.
>
> (C) This rule shall not prevent a member from serving as counsel of record for an applicant for admission to practice in proceedings related to such admission.

Colorado: Rule 8.1(a) also applies to "readmission" and "reinstatement."

Georgia: In the rules effective November 3, 2011, Georgia has adopted a Rule 9.3, entitled "Cooperation with Disciplinary Authority," which provides as follows: "During the investigation of a grievance filed under these Rules, the lawyer complained against shall respond to disciplinary authorities in accordance with State Bar Rules." Comment 2 to this provision states: "Nothing in this Rule prohibits a lawyer from responding by making a Fifth Amendment objection, if appropriate. However, disciplinary proceedings are civil in nature and the use of a Fifth Amendment objection will give rise to a presumption against the lawyer."

Michigan adds the following new language to its version of ABA Model Rule 8.1:

> (b) An applicant for admission to the bar
> (1) shall not engage in the unauthorized practice of law (this does not apply to activities permitted under MCR 8.120), and

(2) has a continuing obligation, until the date of admission, to inform the standing committee on character and fitness, in writing, if any answers in the applicant's affidavit of personal history change or cease to be true.

New York: Rule 8.1(a) provides as follows:

(a) A lawyer shall be subject to discipline if, in connection with the lawyer's own application for admission to the bar previously filed in this state or in any other jurisdiction, or in connection with the application of another person for admission to the bar, the lawyer knowingly:
(1) has made or failed to correct a false statement of material fact; or
(2) has failed to disclose a material fact requested in connection with a lawful demand for information from an admissions authority.

Ohio: Rule 8.1(a) deletes the opening phrase "[a]n applicant for admission to the bar." According to the Ohio Supreme Court's note, Rule 8.1(b) clarifies the "unwieldy" language of the ABA Model Rule but does not lower the standard of candor expected of a lawyer in bar admission or disciplinary matters.

Virginia: Rule 8.1 adds language to cover certifications required to be filed as a condition of maintaining or renewing a law license. Virginia also moves the second clause of Rule 8.1(b) to a separate subparagraph (c), and adds Rule 8.1(d), which makes it a separate violation to "obstruct a lawful investigation by an admissions or disciplinary authority."

Related Materials

ABA Formal Ethics Opinions: No ABA formal ethics opinion has discussed ABA Model Rule 8.1.

ABA Model Federal Rules of Disciplinary Enforcement: To provide guidance for federal courts to operate independent disciplinary systems, in 1978 the ABA approved the Model Federal Rules of Disciplinary Enforcement. These rules, which were amended in 1991 and have been adopted by a number of federal district courts, can be found at *www.americanbar.org/content/dam/aba/migrated/cpr/discipline/mfrde.pdf.* Separate federal rules of disciplinary enforcement are needed because in *Theard v. United States,* 354 U.S. 278 (1957), the Supreme Court held that a state court disbarment was entitled to "high respect" but was "not conclusively binding on the federal courts." Consequently "disbarment by federal courts does not automatically flow from disbarment by state courts."

ABA Model Rules for Judicial Disciplinary Enforcement: In 1994, to assist jurisdictions in reviewing the procedures of their judicial discipline systems and in drafting fair and efficient procedures for enforcing the Code of Judicial Conduct, the ABA developed Model Rules for Judicial Disciplinary Enforcement. These replaced the ABA Standards Relating to Judicial Discipline and Disability Retirement, which had been adopted in 1979. The Model Rules for Judicial Disciplinary Enforcement, with the official ABA commentary, are available online at *http://www.americanbar.org/groups/professional_responsibility/model_rules_judicial_disciplinary_enforcement/contents.html.*

ABA Model Rules for Lawyer Disciplinary Enforcement: The ABA Model Rules for Lawyer Disciplinary Enforcement provide a blueprint for the structure, procedures, and standards of a comprehensive system of lawyer regulation. Rule 1, entitled

"Comprehensive Lawyer Regulatory System," provides that such a system should include, at a minimum: (a) a discipline and disability system, (b) a client protection fund, (c) mandatory arbitration of fee disputes, (d) voluntary arbitration of lawyer malpractice claims and other disputes, (e) mediation, (f) lawyer practice assistance, and (g) lawyer substance abuse counseling.

The Model Rules for Lawyer Disciplinary Enforcement have a long history. In the late 1960s, the ABA appointed a Special Committee on Evaluation of Disciplinary Enforcement (the "Clark Committee"), which conducted the first nationwide examination of lawyer disciplinary procedures in the United States. In 1970, the Clark Committee published a report warning of a "scandalous situation" in professional discipline. The ABA responded by creating a Standing Committee on Professional Discipline in 1973 and by developing the ABA Standards for Lawyer Discipline, which the ABA approved in 1979. In 1985, the ABA amended those Standards and renamed them the ABA Model Rules for Lawyer Disciplinary Enforcement. The Rules, which have been amended four times (most recently in 2002), are available online at *http://www.americanbar.org/groups/professional_responsibility/resources/lawyer_ethics_regulation/model_rules_for_lawyer_disciplinary_enforcement.html*. For more information on the history of lawyer disciplinary enforcement, see the law review article by Mary Devlin entitled "The Development of Lawyer Disciplinary Procedures in the United States," available online at *http://www.americanbar.org/content/dam/aba/migrated/cpr/pubs/devlin.authcheckdam.pdf*.

ABA Standards for Lawyer Discipline and Disability Proceedings: In 1979, the ABA published Standards for Lawyer Discipline and Disability Proceedings. Standard 7.1 stated that the discipline imposed should depend upon the facts and circumstances of the case, should be fashioned in light of the purpose of lawyer discipline, and could take into account aggravating or mitigating circumstances. (In 1994, the ABA replaced the Discipline and Disability Standards with the ABA Model Rules for Judicial Disciplinary Enforcement—see entry above.)

ABA Standing Committee on Professional Discipline: The ABA is not a disciplinary agency and has no authority to investigate or act upon complaints filed against lawyers or judges, but in 1973 the ABA created a Standing Committee on Professional Discipline. The Standing Committee's mission is to assist the judiciary and the Bar in every jurisdiction in developing, coordinating, and strengthening disciplinary enforcement. For example, if invited by a jurisdiction's highest court, the Standing Committee sends a team to consult regarding the structure, operation, practice, and procedures of the jurisdiction's disciplinary system. Since 1980, the Standing Committee has reviewed the disciplinary systems in more than 40 jurisdictions (at least five of them twice). After a review, the Standing Committee files a confidential report with the jurisdiction's highest court, which determines whether to make the report public. For more information, visit *http://www.americanbar.org/groups/professional_responsibility/committees_commissions/standing_committee_on_professional_discipline.html*.

ABA Survey on Lawyer Discipline Systems: Since 1999, the ABA Standing Committee on Professional Discipline and the ABA Center for Professional Responsibility have annually conducted a comprehensive survey of lawyer discipline in more than 50 lawyer disciplinary agencies around the United States. The survey includes eight separate charts showing data on such things as Lawyer Population and Agency Caseload Volume, Sanctions Imposed, and Reinstatement and Readmission

Statistics. The most recent available annual survey is online at *http://www.americanbar. org/groups/professional_responsibility/resources/survey_lawyer_discipline_systems_2010. html.*

Association of Professional Responsibility Lawyers (APRL): The Association of Professional Responsibility Lawyers (APRL) is an independent national organization of lawyers concentrating in the fields of professional responsibility and legal ethics. The organization includes law professors, bar association counsel, counsel for respondents in disciplinary hearings, expert witnesses, legal malpractice litigators, disciplinary counsel, and in-house law firm ethics counsel. APRL provides a national clearinghouse of information regarding recent developments and emerging issues in the areas of admission to practice law, professional ethics, disciplinary standards and procedures, and professional liability. For more information, including a nationwide directory of APRL members, visit *www.aprl.net.*

Character and Fitness: Nearly every state requires bar applicants to demonstrate good moral character and fitness. In New York, for example, 22 N.Y.C.R.R. §602.1(b) provides: "Every completed application shall be referred for investigation of the applicant's character and fitness to a committee on character and fitness. . . ." In Illinois, §2 of the Illinois Attorney Act provides that no person shall be entitled to receive a law license "until he shall have obtained a certificate of his good moral character from a circuit court."

About 33 states have adopted written standards for character and fitness. An example of these rules is Rule IV of the Texas Board of Law Examiners, which provides, in pertinent part, as follows:

Good Moral Character and Fitness Requirement

> (b) Good moral character is a functional assessment of character and fitness of a prospective lawyer. The purpose of requiring an Applicant to possess present good moral character is to exclude from the practice of law those persons possessing character traits that are likely to result in injury to future clients, in the obstruction of the administration of justice, or in a violation of the Texas Disciplinary Rules of Professional Conduct. These character traits usually involve either dishonesty or lack of trustworthiness in carrying out responsibilities. There may be other character traits that are relevant in the admission process, but such traits must have a rational connection with the Applicant's present fitness or capacity to practice law and accordingly must relate to the legitimate interests of Texas in protecting prospective clients and in safeguarding the system of justice within Texas.

> (c) Fitness, as used in these Rules, is the assessment of mental and emotional health as it affects the competence of a prospective lawyer. The purpose of requiring an Applicant to possess this fitness is to exclude from the practice of law any person having a mental or emotional illness or condition which would be likely to prevent the person from carrying out duties to clients, courts or the profession. A person may be of good moral character, but may be incapacitated from proper discharge of his or her duties as a lawyer by such illness or condition. The fitness required is a present fitness, and prior mental or emotional illness or conditions are relevant only so far as they indicate the existence of a present lack of fitness. . . .

Under Rule IV(e)(2) of the Texas Board of Law Examiners, an individual who has been disciplined in another jurisdiction is "deemed not to have present good moral character and fitness and is therefore ineligible to file an Application for Admission to the Texas Bar during the period of such discipline. . . .'' But Rule IV(e)(3) allows such a person to file an Application for Admission if:

> (A) The procedure followed in the disciplining jurisdiction was so lacking in notice or opportunity to be heard as to constitute a deprivation of due process.
>
> (B) There was such an infirmity of proof establishing the misconduct in the other jurisdiction as to give rise to the clear conviction that the Board, consistent with its duty, should not accept as final the conclusion on the evidence reached in the disciplining jurisdiction.
>
> (C) The deeming of lack of present good moral character and fitness by the Board during the period required under the provisions of section (e) would result in grave injustice.
>
> (D) The misconduct for which the individual was disciplined does not constitute professional misconduct in Texas.
>
> (4) If the Board determines that one or more of the foregoing defenses has been established, it shall render such orders as it deems necessary and appropriate.

Rule IV(f) of the Texas Board of Law Examiners provides that an individual who applies for admission to practice law in Texas after completing a period of professional discipline must prove, by a preponderance of the evidence:

> (1) that the best interest of the public and the profession, as well as the ends of justice, would be served by his or her admission to practice law;
>
> (2) that (s)he is of present good moral character and fitness; and
>
> (3) that during the five years immediately preceding the present action, (s)he has been living a life of exemplary conduct.

Finally, Rule IV(g) provides that if an applicant receives a negative determination of character and fitness based on a felony conviction, felony probation, professional misconduct, or resignation in lieu of disciplinary action, the applicant is not eligible to petition for redetermination for three years.

Model Rules of Professional Conduct for Federal Lawyers: Rule 8.1 also applies to an ''applicant for admission to a bar or employment as a lawyer with a Federal Agency, [and] a Federal lawyer seeking the right to practice before a Federal Agency. . . .''

National Lawyer Regulatory Data Bank: In 1968, the ABA established a National Lawyer Regulatory Data Bank, the only national repository of information concerning public disciplinary sanctions imposed against lawyers throughout the United States. Today the Data Bank operates under the aegis of the ABA Standing Committee on Professional Discipline. The courts of all states and the District of Columbia, as well as many federal courts and some federal agencies, now voluntarily provide disciplinary information to the Data Bank. The Data Bank is particularly useful to bar admissions agencies evaluating applications from out-of-state lawyers and to disciplinary agencies considering reciprocal discipline on lawyers who have been disbarred or suspended elsewhere. For more information, visit *http://www.americanbar.org/groups/professional_responsibility/services/databank.html.*

National Organization of Bar Counsel (NOBC): The National Organization of Bar Counsel (NOBC) is a nonprofit organization of legal professionals whose members enforce ethics rules that regulate the professional conduct of lawyers in the United States, Canada, and Australia. Among its purposes are (1) protecting the public and the courts against unethical conduct; (2) protecting attorneys against unfounded complaints; (3) taking joint, coordinated action to promote solutions to nationwide problems relating to the legal profession; and (4) providing mutual assistance in gathering evidence and testimony at the request of fellow bar counsel. For more information, visit the NOBC's website at *www.nobc.org*.

Restatement of the Law Governing Lawyers: See Restatement §2 in our chapter on the Restatement later in this volume.

Rule 8.2   Judicial and Legal Officials

Canon and Code Antecedents

ABA Canons of Professional Ethics: Canons 1 and 2 provided as follows:

1.   The Duty of the Lawyer to the Courts

It is the duty of the lawyer to maintain towards the Courts a respectful attitude, not for the sake of the temporary incumbent of the judicial office, but for the maintenance of its supreme importance. Judges, not being wholly free to defend themselves, are peculiarly entitled to receive the support of the Bar against unjust criticism and clamor. Whenever there is proper ground for serious complaint of a judicial officer, it is the right and duty of the lawyer to submit his grievances to the proper authorities. In such cases, but not otherwise, such charges should be encouraged and the person making them should be protected.

2.   The Selection of Judges

It is the duty of the Bar to endeavor to prevent political considerations from outweighing judicial fitness in the selections of Judges. It should protest earnestly and actively against the appointment or election of those who are unsuitable for the Bench; and it should strive to have elevated thereto only those willing to forego other employments, whether of a business, political or other character, which may embarrass their free and fair consideration of questions before them for decision. The aspiration of lawyers for judicial position should be governed by an impartial estimate of their ability to add honor to the office and not by a desire for the distinction the position may bring to themselves.

ABA Model Code of Professional Responsibility: Compare DR 8-102(A), DR 8-102(B), and DR 8-103 (reprinted later in this volume).

Cross-References in Other Rules

None.

Legislative History of Model Rule 8.2

1980 Discussion Draft (then Rule 10.2): Subparagraph (a) provided: "A lawyer who is a candidate for judicial office shall comply with the applicable provisions of the code of judicial conduct." Subparagraph (b) was the same as adopted.

1981 and 1982 Drafts were substantially the same as adopted.

1983 Rule: As originally adopted in 1983, the text of Rule 8.2 was identical to the 2002 version of Rule 8.2.

2002 Amendments: The ABA Ethics 2000 Commission did not propose any changes to the text or Comment of Rule 8.2.

Selected State Variations

California: The California Rules of Professional Conduct have no comparable provision, but California Business & Professions Code §6068(b) provides that it is the duty of an attorney to "maintain the respect due to the courts of justice and judicial officers."

District of Columbia omits ABA Model Rule 8.2.

Florida: Rule 8.2(a) also applies to statements about a mediator, arbitrator, juror or member of the venire.

Georgia: In the rules effective November 3, 2011, Georgia omits ABA Model Rule 8.2(a) but adopts Rule 8.2(b) verbatim.

Maryland: Rule 8.2(b)(2) provides that a lawyer who is a candidate for judicial office "with respect to a case, controversy or issue that is likely to come before the court, shall not make a commitment, pledge, or promise that is inconsistent with the impartial performance of the adjudicative duties of the office."

New Jersey: Rule 8.2(b) provides that a lawyer who "has been confirmed for judicial office" shall comply with the applicable provisions of the Code of Judicial Conduct. The rule does not apply to lawyers who are only candidates for judicial office.

New York: Rule 8.2 provides as follows: "(a) A lawyer shall not knowingly make a false statement of fact concerning the qualifications, conduct or integrity of a judge or other adjudicatory officer or of a candidate for election or appointment to judicial office. (b) A lawyer who is a candidate for judicial office shall comply with the applicable provisions of Part 100 of the Rules of the Chief Administrator of the Courts."

Ohio: Rule 8.2(a) omits the ABA reference to an "adjudicatory officer or public legal officer."

Pennsylvania: Rule 8.2 replaces all of ABA Model Rule 8.2(a) with language taken verbatim from DR 8-102(A) and (B) and 8-103(A) of the ABA Model Code of Professional Responsibility.

Virginia: Rule 8.2 provides, in its entirety, as follows: "A lawyer shall not make a statement that the lawyer knows to be false or with reckless disregard as to its truth or falsity concerning the qualifications or integrity of a judge or other judicial officer."

Related Materials

ABA Formal Ethics Opinions: No ABA formal ethics opinions have discussed ABA Model Rule 8.2.

ABA Model Code of Judicial Conduct: Rule 8.2(b) requires candidates for judicial office to "comply with the applicable provisions of the code of judicial conduct." The applicable provisions vary from state to state, but in the ABA Model Code of Judicial Conduct as amended in 2007, which is reprinted later in this book, the applicable provisions governing judicial candidates are found in Canon 4. (In the ABA's 1990 Code of Judicial Conduct, the applicable provisions were found in Canon 5.)

Restatement of the Law Governing Lawyers: See Restatement §114 in our chapter on the Restatement later in this volume.

Rule 8.3   Reporting Professional Misconduct

Canon and Code Antecedents

ABA Canons of Professional Ethics: Canon 29 provided as follows:

29.   *Upholding the Honor of the Profession*

Lawyers should expose without fear or favor before the proper tribunals corrupt or dishonest conduct in the profession, and should accept without hesitation employment against a member of the Bar who has wronged his client. The counsel upon the trial of a cause in which perjury has been committed owe it to the profession and to the public to bring the matter to the knowledge of the prosecuting authorities. The lawyer should aid in guarding the Bar against the admission to the profession of candidates unfit or unqualified because deficient in either moral character or education. He should strive at all times to uphold the honor and to maintain the dignity of the profession and to improve not only the law but the administration of justice.

ABA Model Code of Professional Responsibility: Compare DR 1-103(A) (reprinted later in this volume).

Cross-References in Other Rules

Rule 1.6, Comment 17: Some Rules require "disclosure of information relating to a client's representation to accomplish the purposes specified in paragraphs (b)(1) through (b)(6)," only if such disclosure would be permitted by paragraph (b). See **Rules** 1.2(d), 4.1(b), 8.1 and **8.3**.

Rule 1.8, Comment 5: It is prohibited to partake in the "disadvantageous use of client information unless the client gives informed consent, except as permitted or required by these Rules. See **Rules** 1.2(d), 1.6, 1.9(c), 3.3, 4.1(b), 8.1 and **8.3**."

Legislative History of Model Rule 8.3

1980 Discussion Draft (then Rule 10.3) provided:

A lawyer having information indicating that another lawyer has committed a substantial violation of the Rules of Professional Conduct shall report the information to the appropriate disciplinary authority.

1981 Draft was substantially the same as adopted, except that it did not include any equivalent to Rule 8.3(b).

1982 Draft was adopted.

1983 Rule: As originally adopted in 1983, Rules 8.3(a) and (b) were identical to the 2002 version of those rules, except that the word "knows" in the 2002 version was originally "having knowledge" in both paragraphs. The 1983 version of Rule 8.3(c) provided simply: "This rule does not require the disclosure of information otherwise protected by Rule 1.6."

1991 Amendments: At its August 1991 Annual Meeting, the ABA House of Delegates added the clause beginning "or information gained . . ." to Rule 8.3(c). The following excerpts from the Report of the ABA Standing Committee on Ethics and Professional Responsibility explain the rationale and scope of the amendments:

16.   *ABA Committee Report Explaining 1991 Amendments to Rule 8.3**

   The serious concerns that have arisen recently as a result of "lawyer impairment" have led to the creation of special programs throughout the nation to assist lawyers and judges who face alcohol or drug addiction or other serious problems which threaten to affect or have already affected the performance of their professional responsibilities.

   . . . The Committee believes that it is in the interest of the legal profession and the public that the ABA Model Rules be amended to provide for the confidentiality of information that is furnished by the impaired lawyer or judge.

   Under the amendment to Model Rule 8.3, the protection of information obtained in the circumstances of a lawyer's or judge's participation in an assistance program is similar to the protection ordinarily provided by the attorney-client privilege. Where the attorney-client privilege would not apply because the information relates to the intention to commit a crime, for example where a lawyer indicates the intention to continue to convert client funds to his or her own use, such information may be disclosed to the appropriate authority, permitting the recipient of the information to comply with the obligation imposed upon him or her by paragraphs (a) or (b). In such situations concerns other than the recovery of the impaired lawyer or judge necessarily outweigh the impaired lawyer's or judge's right to confidentiality. . . . Although the Committee recognizes that disclosure of such information by one member of the profession to the detriment of a professional colleague is painful and difficult, it considers such a situation indistinguishable from other situations in which important public policy considerations require disclosure of confidential information. To extend the confidentiality protection to a lawyer's or judge's intention to commit a crime likely to result in significant harm to others, moreover, would lend support to claims that the profession is unable or unwilling to live up to its obligation to regulate itself in the public interest.

2002 Amendments: At its February 2002 Mid-Year Meeting, the ABA House of Delegates adopted without change the ABA Ethics 2000 Commission proposal to amend Rule 8.3 and its Comment. The main changes were to modify Rule 8.3(c) by substituting the phrase "while participating in an approved lawyers assistance program" for the phrase "while serving as a member of an approved lawyers assistance program to the extent that such information would be confidential if it were communicated subject to the attorney-client privilege," and to rewrite much of Comment 5.

Selected State Variations

Alaska exempts a lawyer from making a report under Rule 8.3(a) or (b) if "the lawyer reasonably believes that the misconduct has been or will otherwise be reported."

---

   * Committee Reports do not represent official policy of the ABA. They are for information only, and the opinions are those of the authors of the report.

Arizona: Rule 8.3(c) retains language similar to the pre-2002 version of the ABA Model Rule, protecting information gained while serving in a lawyer assistance program that "would be confidential if it related to the representation of a client" and if confidentiality has not otherwise been waived.

Arkansas: Rule 8.3(d) generally exempts lawyers working with the Arkansas Lawyer Assistance Program from mandatory reporting obligations "unless it appears . . . that the attorney in question, after entry into the ALAP, is failing to desist from said violation, or is failing to cooperate with a program of assistance to which said attorney has agreed, or is engaged in the sale of a controlled substance or theft of property constituting a felony under Arkansas law, or the equivalent thereof if the offense is not within the State's jurisdiction."

California: The California Rules of Professional Conduct have no comparable provision.

Connecticut adds the following sentence to Rule 8.3(a): "A lawyer may not condition settlement of a civil dispute involving allegations of improprieties on the part of a lawyer on an agreement that the subject misconduct not be reported to the appropriate disciplinary authority." Rule 8.3(c) tracks the pre-2002 version of ABA Model Rule 8.3(c), but Connecticut's version also refers to Connecticut General Statutes §51-81d(f), which governs crisis intervention assistance to attorneys.

District of Columbia: Rule 8.3(c) omits the phrase "or information gained by a lawyer or judge while participating in an approved lawyers assistance program." The phrase is unnecessary because D.C. Rule 1.6(i) provides as follows:

> [A] lawyer who serves as a member of the D.C. Bar Lawyer Counseling Committee, or as a trained intervenor for that committee, shall be deemed to have a lawyer-client relationship with respect to any lawyer-counselee being counseled under programs conducted by or on behalf of the committee. Information obtained from another lawyer being counseled under the auspices of the committee . . . shall be treated as a confidence or secret within the terms of paragraph (b) [of Rule 1.6]. Such information may be disclosed only to the extent permitted by this rule.

D.C. Rule 1.6(j) contains parallel language regarding information that a lawyer receives in connection with service on the D.C. Bar Practice Management Service Committee (formerly known as the Lawyer Practice Assistance Committee).

Florida: Rule 8.3(c)(2) exempts from disclosure information "gained by a lawyer while serving as a mediator or mediation participant if the information is privileged or confidential under applicable law." Moreover, Rule 8.3(c)(3) provides that information obtained pursuant to a "lawyers assistance program" is not exempted if the lawyer's participation in the program "is part of a disciplinary sanction." Finally, Florida adds Rule 8.3(d), which provides as follows:

> *Limited Exception for LOMAS Counsel.* A lawyer employed by or acting on behalf of the Law Office Management Assistance Service (LOMAS) shall not have an obligation to disclose knowledge of the conduct of another member . . . if the lawyer employed by or acting on behalf of LOMAS acquired the knowledge while engaged in a LOMAS review of the other lawyer's practice. *Provided further,* however, that if the LOMAS review is conducted as a part of a disciplinary sanction this limitation shall not be applicable and a report shall be made to the appropriate disciplinary agency.

Georgia: In the rules effective November 3, 2011, Georgia changes "shall" to "should" in Rule 8.3(a) and (b), and replaces ABA Model Rule 8.3(c) by stating:

"There is no disciplinary penalty for a violation of this Rule." Georgia also adds a special self-reporting provision, Rule 9.1(a), which requires members of the Georgia Bar to notify the State Bar of Georgia within 60 days of (1) becoming admitted to another jurisdiction and the date of admission; (2) the conviction "of any felony or of a misdemeanor involving moral turpitude where the underlying conduct relates to the lawyer's fitness to practice law"; and (3) "the imposition of discipline by any jurisdiction other than the Supreme Court of Georgia." Rule 9.1(b) defines what constitutes "discipline" for purposes of the Rule. Finally, Georgia adds a special Rule 9.2, regarding agreements not to report, which provides as follows:

> A lawyer shall not enter into an agreement containing a condition that prohibits or restricts a person from filing a disciplinary complaint, or that requires the person to request dismissal of a pending disciplinary complaint.

Illinois: Rule 8.3(a) deletes the reference to "honesty, trustworthiness or fitness as a lawyer" and simply imposes a duty to report when "another lawyer has committed a violation of Rule 8.4(b) or 8.4(c). . . ." Moreover, Rule 8.3(c) excludes from the reporting obligation any information that is "protected by the attorney-client privilege." This provision is narrower than the Model Rule's exception, which applies to all information protected by Rule 1.6. Illinois also adds Rule 8.3(d), which requires lawyers to report to the Illinois Disciplinary Commission any discipline that has been imposed on them by a body other than the Illinois Commission.

Kansas: Rule 8.3(c) adds that lawyers are "not required to disclose information" learned through participation in a variety of self-help organizations, such as Alcoholics Anonymous.

Also, Rule 223 of the Kansas Rules Relating to Discipline of Attorneys, entitled "Immunity," provides as follows: "Complaints, reports, or testimony in the course of disciplinary proceedings under these Rules shall be deemed to be made in the course of judicial proceedings. All participants shall be entitled to judicial immunity and all rights, privileges and immunities afforded public officials and other participants in actions filed in the courts of this state."

Massachusetts: The Comment to Rule 8.3 provides as follows:

> [3] While a measure of judgment is required in complying with the provisions of the Rule, a lawyer must report misconduct that, if proven and without regard to mitigation, would likely result in an order of suspension or disbarment, including misconduct that would constitute a "serious crime." . . . Section 12(3) of Rule 4:01 provides that a serious crime is "any felony, and . . . any lesser crime a necessary element of which . . . includes interference with the administration of justice, false swearing, misrepresentation, fraud, willful failure to file income tax returns, deceit, bribery, extortion, misappropriation, theft, or an attempt or a conspiracy, or solicitation of another, to commit [such a crime]." In addition to conviction of a felony, misappropriation of client funds or perjury before a tribunal are common examples of reportable conduct. . . .
>
> [3A] In most situations, a lawyer may defer making a report under this Rule until the matter has been concluded, but the report should be made as soon as practicable thereafter. An immediate report is ethically compelled, however, when a client or third person will likely be injured by a delay in reporting, such as where the lawyer has knowledge that another lawyer has embezzled client or fiduciary funds and delay may impair the ability to recover the funds.

Michigan adds the word "significant" before "violation" in Rules 8.3(a) and (b). The duty to report is suspended if the lawyer gained the information "while serving as an employee or volunteer of the substance abuse counseling program of the State Bar of Michigan, to the extent that the information would be protected under Rule 1.6 from disclosure if it were a communication between lawyer and client." Rule 8.3(c)(2).

New Jersey cuts off Rule 8.3(c) after "Rule 1.6" and adds Rule 8.3(d), which provides as follows:

> Paragraph (a) of this Rule shall not apply to knowledge obtained as a result of participation in a Lawyers Assistance Program established by the Supreme Court and administered by the New Jersey State Bar Association, except as follows:
> (i) if the effect of discovered ethics infractions on the practice of an impaired attorney is irremediable or poses a substantial and imminent threat to the interests of clients, then attorney volunteers, peer counselors, or program staff have a duty to disclose the infractions to the disciplinary authorities, and attorney volunteers have the obligation to apply immediately for the appointment of a conservator, who also has the obligation to report ethics infractions to disciplinary authorities; and
> (ii) attorney volunteers or peer counselors assisting the impaired attorney in conjunction with his or her practice have the same responsibility as any other lawyer to deal candidly with clients, but that responsibility does not include the duty to disclose voluntarily, without inquiry by the client, information of past violations or present violations that did not or do not pose a serious danger to clients.

New York: Rule 8.3(b) provides as follows: "A lawyer who possesses knowledge or evidence concerning another lawyer or a judge shall not fail to respond to a lawful demand for information from a tribunal or other authority empowered to investigate or act upon such conduct."

North Carolina: Rule 8.3(c) provides only that Rule 8.3 "does not require disclosure of information otherwise protected by Rule 1.6," omitting the ABA reference to a lawyers' assistance program, but North Carolina accomplishes the same result by providing in Rule 1.6(c) that the duty of confidentiality under Rule 1.6 "encompasses information received by a lawyer then acting as an agent of a lawyers' or judges' assistance program . . . regarding another lawyer or judge seeking assistance or to whom assistance is being offered." (Rule 1.6 also defines the term "client" to include lawyers seeking assistance from approved lawyers' or judges' assistance programs.)

North Carolina also adds a Rule 8.3(d), which provides that a lawyer who has been disciplined in any state or federal court for violating that court's Rules of Professional Conduct must "inform the . . . State Bar of such action in writing no later than 30 days after entry of the order of discipline." Finally, North Carolina Rule 1.15-2(o), entitled "Duty to Report Misappropriation," provides that a lawyer who "discovers or reasonably believes that entrusted property has been misappropriated or misapplied shall promptly inform the North Carolina State Bar."

Ohio: Rule 8.3 provides as follows:

> (a) A lawyer who possesses unprivileged knowledge of a violation of the Ohio Rules of Professional Conduct that raises a question as to any lawyer's honesty, trustworthiness, or fitness as a lawyer in other respects, shall inform a disciplinary authority empowered to investigate or act upon such a violation.

(b) A lawyer who possesses unprivileged knowledge that a judge has committed a violation of the Ohio Rules of Professional Conduct or applicable rules of judicial conduct shall inform the appropriate authority.

(c) Any information obtained by a member of a committee . . . of a bar association . . . designed to assist lawyers with substance abuse or mental health problems . . . shall be privileged for all purposes under this rule.

South Carolina: Rule 8.3(a) requires that a "lawyer who is arrested for or has been charged by way of indictment, information or complaint with a serious crime shall inform the Commission on Lawyer Conduct in writing within fifteen days of being arrested or being charged by way of indictment, information or complaint."

Texas alters Rule 8.3(c) as follows:

(c) A lawyer having knowledge or suspecting that another lawyer or judge whose conduct the lawyer is required to report pursuant to paragraphs (a) or (b) of this Rule is impaired by chemical dependency on alcohol or drugs or by mental illness may report that person to an approved peer assistance program rather than to an appropriate disciplinary authority. If a lawyer elects that option, the lawyer's report to the approved peer assistance program shall disclose any disciplinary violations that the reporting lawyer would otherwise have to disclose to the authorities referred to in paragraphs (a) and (b).

Texas also adds a Rule 8.3(d), which makes clear that Rule 8.3 does not require disclosure of knowledge or information otherwise protected as confidential information by Texas Rule 1.05 (the Texas equivalent to ABA Model Rule 1.6) or by "any statutory or regulatory provisions applicable to the counseling activities of the approved peer assistance program."

Virginia: Rule 8.3(b) replaces the phrase "who knows" with the phrase "having reliable information." Virginia Rule 8.3(c) provides that if a lawyer serving as a third-party neutral receives "reliable information" in that capacity about another lawyer's misconduct that would otherwise have to be reported, the lawyer/neutral "shall attempt to obtain the parties' written agreement to waive confidentiality and permit disclosure of such information to the appropriate professional authority." Rule 8.3(d) — equivalent to ABA Model Rule 8.3(c) — also exempts disclosure by a lawyer who is a "trained intervenor or volunteer" for an approved lawyers' assistance committee, or who is "cooperating in a particular assistance effort," when the information is obtained "for the purposes of fulfilling the recognized objectives of the program."

Virginia also adds Rule 8.3(e), which requires a lawyer to inform the Virginia State Bar if (1) the lawyer has been disciplined by a state or federal disciplinary authority, agency or court in any jurisdiction for violating that jurisdiction's rules of professional conduct, or (2) the lawyer has been convicted of a felony in any United States jurisdiction, or (3) the lawyer has been convicted of either "a crime involving theft, fraud, extortion, bribery or perjury," or "an attempt, solicitation or conspiracy to commit any of the foregoing offenses" in any United States jurisdiction.

Related Materials

ABA Commission on Lawyer Assistance Programs (CoLAP): The ABA Commission on Lawyer Assistance Programs educates the legal profession concerning alcoholism, chemical dependencies, stress, depression and other emotional health issues. The ABA originally formed a Commission on Impaired Attorneys in 1988 to assist state and local bar associations in establishing programs to help addicted lawyers and judges. In 1995, the ABA House of Delegates adopted the Commission's Model Lawyer Assistance Program, which assists state and local bar associations in developing and maintaining effective lawyer assistance programs and identifying lawyers, judges, and law students impaired by alcoholism, drugs, or mental health problems. In 1996, the ABA changed the name of the Commission on Impaired Attorneys to the Commission on Lawyer Assistance Programs (CoLAP). CoLAP reviews lawyer assistance programs, makes recommendations for expanding and improving them, holds an annual National Workshop for Lawyer Assistance Programs, and circulates guidelines and policies.

In 2002, after a Special Committee of the Association of American Law Schools (AALS) issued a disturbing report entitled "Substance Abuse in the Law Schools," CoLAP appointed a new committee in an effort to assist law students and law schools. The Law School Assistance Committee encourages law schools to (1) develop close working relationships with local lawyers assistance programs, and (2) "have ongoing programs in place to educate law students and faculty about stress-related issues (depression, substance abuse, eating disorders, gambling addictions, etc.) and a procedure for identifying and assisting law students and faculty who may be affected by these issues."

For further information about CoLAP and its programs, visit CoLAP's website at *http://apps.americanbar.org/legalservices/colap/resourcelib.html.*

ABA Formal Ethics Opinions: See ABA Formal Ethics Ops. 92-363 (1992), 94-383 (1994), 03-429 (2003), 03-431 (2003), 04-433 (2004), 07-449 (2007), and 08-453 (2008).

Lawyer Assistance Programs: Since 1991, ABA Model Rule 8.3(c) has referred to information gained by a lawyer or judge while participating in "an approved lawyers assistance program." Lawyer assistance programs, or LAPs, are operated by the bar to help lawyers who have problems with alcoholism, drug addiction, mental health, or stress. To assist lawyers and judges in the recovery process, LAPs use techniques such as intervention, peer counseling, and referral to 12-Step Programs. In 1980, lawyer assistance programs operated in only 26 states, but today lawyer assistance programs operate in every state. For a state-by-state directory of LAPs, see *www.americanbar.org/groups/lawyer_assistance/resources/lap_programs_by_state.html.*

Oath of Office: All states require new attorneys to take an oath upon being admitted to the bar. In Illinois, for example, §4 of the Attorney Act requires every new attorney to take the following oath:

> I do solemnly swear (or affirm, as the case may be), that I will support the constitution of the United States and the constitution of the state of Illinois, and that I will faithfully discharge the duties of the office of attorney and counselor at law to the best of my ability.

Reporting Obligations by Courts and Nonlawyers: Certain judges and nonlawyers may be obligated to report lawyer misconduct. For example, California Business & Professions Code §6086.7 requires a court to notify the State Bar whenever the court holds an attorney in contempt, imposes sanctions of $1,000 or more, or the attorney commits other specified wrongs, and California Insurance Code §1872.83 requires the Insurance Department's Fraud Division to send lawyer disciplinary authorities "the names, along with all supporting evidence," of all lawyers "who are suspected of actively engaging in fraudulent activity."

Restatement of the Law Governing Lawyers: See Restatement §5(3) in our chapter on the Restatement later in this volume.

Rule 8.4　Misconduct

Canon and Code Antecedents

ABA Canons of Professional Ethics: No comparable Canon.

ABA Model Code of Professional Responsibility: Compare DR 1-102(A) and DR 9-101(C) (reprinted later in this volume).

Cross-References in Other Rules

Preamble, 3: "[T]here are Rules that apply to lawyers who are not active in the practice of law or to practicing lawyers even when they are acting in a non-professional capacity. . . . See **Rule 8.4**."

Rule 3.3, Comment 3: "Regarding compliance with Rule 1.2(d), see the Comment to that Rule. See also the Comment to **Rule 8.4(b)**."

Rule 3.8, Comment 1: "Applicable law may require other measures by the prosecutor and knowing disregard of those obligations or a systematic abuse of prosecutorial discretion could constitute a violation of **Rule 8.4**."

Rule 4.1, Comment 1: "For dishonest conduct that does not amount to a false statement or for misrepresentations by a lawyer other than in the course of representing a client, see **Rule 8.4**."

Rule 4.2, Comment 4: "A lawyer may not make a communication prohibited by this Rule through the acts of another. See **Rule 8.4(a)**."

Rule 5.1, Comment 4: "Paragraph (c) expresses a general principle of personal responsibility for acts of another. See also **Rule 8.4(a)**."

Rule 5.1, Comment 7: "Apart from this Rule and **Rule 8.4(a)**, a lawyer does not have disciplinary liability for the conduct of a partner, associate or subordinate."

Rule 5.7, Comment 2: "[T]he conduct of a lawyer involved in the provision of law-related services is subject to those Rules that apply generally to lawyer conduct, regardless of whether the conduct involves the provision of legal services. See, e.g., **Rule 8.4**."

Rule 5.7, Comment 11: "When the full protections of all of the Rules of Professional Conduct do not apply to the provision of law-related services, principles of law external to the Rules, for example, the law of principal and agent, govern the legal duties owed to those receiving the services. . . . See also **Rule 8.4** (Misconduct)."

Rule 7.1, Comment 4: "See also **Rule 8.4(e)** for the prohibition against stating or implying an ability to influence improperly a government agency or official or to achieve results by means that violate the Rules of Professional Conduct or other law."

Rule 7.2, Comment 5: "To comply with Rule 7.1, a lawyer must not pay a lead generator that states, implies, or creates a reasonable impression that it is recommending the lawyer, is making the referral without payment from the lawyer, or has analyzed a person's legal problems when determining which lawyer should receive the referral. See also Rule 5.3 for the (duties of lawyers and law firms with respect to the conduct of nonlawyers); **Rule 8.4(a)** (duty to avoid violating the Rules through the acts of another)."

Rule 7.3, Comment 9: "Lawyers who participate in a legal service plan must reasonably assure that the plan sponsors are in compliance with Rules 7.1, 7.2 and 7.3(b). See **Rule 8.4(a)**."

Rule 7.6, Comment 6: "If a lawyer makes or solicits a political contribution under circumstances that constitute bribery or another crime, **Rule 8.4(b)** is implicated."

Legislative History of Model Rule 8.4

1980 Discussion Draft (then Rule 10.4) provided:

> It is professional misconduct for a lawyer to:
> (a) violate the Rules of Professional Conduct or knowingly aid another to do so;
> (b) commit a crime or other deliberately wrongful act that reflects adversely on the lawyer's honesty, trustworthiness, or fitness in other respects to practice law. . . .

1981 and 1982 Drafts: Subparagraph (b) of both drafts provided that it was misconduct for a lawyer to "commit a criminal or *fraudulent* act that reflects adversely . . . ," and neither draft included subparagraphs (c) and (d) of the rule as adopted (relating to conduct involving "dishonesty, fraud, deceit or misrepresentation" and to conduct "prejudicial to the administration of justice").

1983 Rule: As originally adopted in 1983, Rules 8.4(a)-(d) and (f) were identical to the 2002 versions of those rules, but the original version of Rule 8.4(e) provided simply that a lawyer shall not "state or imply an ability to influence improperly a government agency or official."

1994 Proposals: Two competing "anti-discrimination" proposals, each in the form of a proposed new paragraph (g) to Rule 8.4, were on the agenda at the ABA's February 1994 Mid-Year Meeting. However, at the last minute both proposals were withdrawn, and the competing sponsors announced their intention to work together to develop a single proposal. The two proposals withdrawn in 1994 differed mainly in their scope. The narrower proposal was submitted by the ABA Standing Committee on Ethics and Professional Responsibility. It provided that it would be professional misconduct for a lawyer to:

> (g) knowingly manifest by words or conduct, in the course of representing a client, bias or prejudice based upon race, sex, religion, national origin, disability, age, sexual orientation or socio-economic status. This paragraph does not apply to a lawyer's confidential communications to a client or preclude legitimate advocacy with respect to the foregoing factors.

The Report submitted in support of the Standing Committee's 1994 proposal explained that the Committee's proposed amendment has three essential aspects:*

---

* Committee Reports do not represent official policy of the ABA. They are for information only, and the opinions are those of the authors of the report.

The first is its limitation to situations in which the lawyer is representing a client in a legal matter. . . .

The second aspect is the Rule's identification of particular types of bias or prejudice that are to be prohibited. . . . The proposed amendment establishes a standard of conduct broader than that mandated by statutory enactments; this standard enables the profession to set an example of fairness and impartiality that is at the core of its commitment to the public interest. . . .

The third aspect of the rule comprises its exceptions. In order to avoid inquiry into a lawyer's confidential communications to a client, the rule excepts those communications from its ambit. The rule, as well, does not preclude legitimate advocacy by the lawyer with respect to the specified factors. An example of this would be when the national origin of a party is a factor in selecting a jury for a particular case. . . .

A broader proposal was submitted by the ABA Young Lawyers Division. It provided that it would be professional misconduct for a lawyer to:

(g) commit a discriminatory act prohibited by law or to harass a person on the basis of sex, race, age, creed, religion, color, national origin, disability, sexual orientation or marital status, where the act of discrimination or harassment is committed in connection with a lawyer's professional activities.

The Report submitted in support of the Young Lawyers Division's 1994 proposal explained the proposed language as follows:

The amendment is designed to regulate conduct in all manifestations of a lawyer's professional activities, and thereby avoid the inexplicable nuances of a rule which would allow reprehensible behavior to go unchecked merely because it is calculatedly inflicted outside the courtroom or after a case is concluded. . . . [T]he proposed rule will reach also to each situation where a lawyer is engaged in endeavors associated with professional activities.

The proposed amendment will apply to professional activities regardless of whether the lawyer is representing a client. Implicit therein is the notion that the administration of justice must be protected from offensive conduct committed by officers of the court in all instances where a lawyer is called upon by virtue of the distinction of being a member of our profession. To do otherwise makes a mockery of the concept of fair and impartial administration of justice for all, and enhances the perception that lawyers are somehow outside or above the law. . . .

The proposal must regulate a lawyer's conduct both inside and outside the courtroom because all lawyers represent the judicial system each time they act within their professional capacity. . . .

1995 Resolution: After the Young Lawyers Division and the Standing Committee on Ethics and Professional Responsibility withdrew their competing 1994 proposals to add a new paragraph 8.4(g), the Young Lawyers Division worked with the Standing Committee in an attempt to produce a unified proposal. That attempt failed, partly because of concerns that a rule prohibiting bias and prejudice could infringe First Amendment rights. The Young Lawyers Division therefore decided to recommend the following policy statement, which the House of Delegates approved:

RESOLVED, That the American Bar Association:
(a) condemns the manifestation by lawyers in the course of their professional activities, by words or conduct, of bias or prejudice against clients, opposing parties

and their counsel, other litigants, witnesses, judges and court personnel, jurors and others, based upon race, sex, religion, national origin, disability, age, sexual orientation or socio-economic status, unless such words or conduct are otherwise permissible as legitimate advocacy on behalf of a client or a cause;

(b) opposes unlawful discrimination by lawyers in the management or operation of a law practice in hiring, promoting, discharging or otherwise determining the conditions of employment, or accepting or terminating representation of a client;

(c) condemns any conduct by lawyers that would threaten, harass, intimidate or denigrate any other person on the basis of the aforementioned categories and characteristics;

(d) discourages members from belonging to any organization that practices invidious discrimination on the basis of the aforementioned categories and characteristics;

(e) encourages affirmative steps such as continuing education, studies, and conferences to discourage the speech and conduct described above.

1998 Mid-Year Proposals: As in 1994 and 1995, proposals condemning bias and prejudice were withdrawn on the eve of the ABA meeting. A withdrawn proposal to amend the text of Rule 8.4, sponsored by the ABA's Criminal Justice Section, would have made it professional misconduct to:

(1) commit, in the course of representing a client, any verbal or physical discriminatory act, on account of race, ethnicity, or gender, if intended to abuse litigants, jurors, witnesses, court personnel, opposing counsel or other lawyers, or to gain a tactical advantage; or

(2) engage, in the course of representing a client, in any continuing course of verbal or physical discriminatory conduct, on account of race, ethnicity or gender, in dealings with litigants, jurors, witnesses, court personnel, opposing counsel or other lawyers, if such conduct constitutes harassment.

A competing withdrawn proposal, sponsored by the ABA's Standing Committee on Ethics and Professional Responsibility, would not have amended the text of Rule 8.4 but would have added the following new paragraph to the comment:

A lawyer who, in the course of representing a client, knowingly manifests by words or conduct, bias or prejudice based on race, sex, religion, national origin, disability, age, sexual orientation or socioeconomic status, violates paragraph (d) [of Rule 8.4] when such actions are prejudicial to the administration of justice. Legitimate advocacy respecting the foregoing factors does not violate paragraph (d).

1998 Amendment: After the 1998 Mid-Year Meeting proposals to amend the text of Rule 8.4 were withdrawn, the sponsors realized that the House of Delegates would not support an amendment to the text of Rule 8.4 but might support an amendment to the Comment. Eventually, the ABA's Standing Committee on Ethics and Professional Responsibility (later joined by the ABA Section on Criminal Justice and the ABA Commission on Minorities in the Profession) proposed adding a new paragraph 2 to the Comment to make clear that words and conduct manifesting bias or prejudice in the course of representing a client violate Rule 8.4(d) when such actions are prejudicial to the administration of justice. The proposal to amend the Comment passed by a voice vote. We reprint the following excerpts (with most citations omitted) from the report of the ABA Standing Committee on Ethics and Professional Responsibility in support of the amendment:

Excerpts from ABA Report Explaining 1998 Amendment to Comment to Rule 8.4*

. . . For a lawyer to display bias or discrimination in the course of representing a client, whether in the courtroom or a conference room, discredits the fundamental principles that all people are equal before the law, and that controversies should be resolved according to their merits under the law. . . .

Formulation of a black-letter rule barring unacceptable conduct while preserving legitimate advocacy and First Amendment freedoms is a difficult task because manifestations of bias and prejudice may include protected speech and because race, gender and other factors are sometimes legitimate subjects of consideration and comment in the legal process. At the heart of the First Amendment is the right to free speech regarding matters relating to the functioning of government, including the judicial process. . . .

When a personal attack is made upon a judge, witness, or court official for the sole purpose of ridicule or harassment, however, such speech does not enjoy First Amendment protection. . . .

The . . . Comment to the existing model rule prohibiting conduct prejudicial to the administration of justice should be amended to make explicit that expressions of bias and prejudice are among the actions of a lawyer that can prejudice the administration of justice and subject a lawyer to disciplinary action.

. . . Three important issues are addressed in the proposed new Comment: (1) the context in which expressions of bias or prejudice will be subject to possible discipline; (2) the specific characteristics that must not be the basis for bias or prejudice; and (3) a guarantee that the rule is not intended and will be ineffective to diminish a lawyer's advocacy where a listed characteristic is at issue in a matter. This report addresses these three issues.

The amended Comment identifies as conduct subject to scrutiny that which occurs "in the course of representing a client." . . . Conduct and communications by a lawyer other than in the course of representing a client are not intended to be made subject to review under the revised Comment. . . .

We have included language in the Comment to address a concern of the criminal bar, namely whether a finding by a trial judge that a lawyer exercised a peremptory challenge in a discriminatory manner could be considered a per se violation of this Rule. We think that it should not. A trial court may find that a lawyer has exercised a peremptory challenge with impermissible, discriminatory intent if it disbelieves the lawyer's neutral explanation for striking the juror. See, Batson v. Kentucky, 476 U.S. 79, 98 (1986). Although . . . some reasons for striking a juror . . . are easily verifiable, neutral grounds for striking the juror, more subjective reasons such as body language, eye contact, or tone of voice are less subject to verification. . . .

The Comment, reasonably interpreted, is meant only to reach conduct of such a nature or frequency that it is prejudicial to the administration of justice. Single incidents that suggest or imply bias or prejudice, or expressions of so slight a nature that they do not give serious offense, are not necessarily prejudicial to the administration of justice and therefore violative of Rule 8.4(d). The determination of when this threshold is met is left to the disciplinary process, which will properly be informed by a variety of considerations that may differ from one situation or jurisdiction to another.

---

* Committee Reports do not represent official policy of the ABA. They are for information only, and the opinions are those of the authors of the report.

2002 Amendments: At its February 2002 Mid-Year Meeting, the ABA House of Delegates adopted with only minor changes the ABA Ethics 2000 Commission proposal to amend Rule 8.4 and its Comment. The only significant changes were to add the phrase "or achieve results by means that violate the Rules of Professional Conduct or other law" at the end of Rule 8.4(e), to add all of Comment 1, and to renumber all subsequent comments.

Selected State Variations

Alabama adds Rule 3.10, which provides that a lawyer "shall not present, participate in presenting, or threaten to present criminal charges solely to obtain an advantage in a civil matter."

Arizona adds Rule 8.4(g), which makes it professional misconduct for a lawyer to "file a notice of change of judge under Rule 10.2, Arizona Rules of Criminal Procedure, for an improper purpose, such as obtaining a trial delay. . . ."

California: Rule 2-400 provides, in part, as follows:

(B) In the management or operation of a law practice, a member shall not unlawfully discriminate or knowingly permit unlawful discrimination on the basis of race, national origin, sex, sexual orientation, religion, age or disability in:

(1) hiring, promoting, discharging or otherwise determining the conditions of employment of any person; or

(2) accepting or terminating representation of any client.

(C) No disciplinary investigation or proceeding may be initiated by the State Bar against a member under this rule unless and until a tribunal of competent jurisdiction, other than a disciplinary tribunal, shall have first adjudicated a complaint of alleged discrimination and found that unlawful conduct occurred. Upon such adjudication, the tribunal finding or verdict shall then be admissible evidence of the occurrence or non-occurrence of the alleged discrimination in any disciplinary proceeding initiated under this rule. In order for discipline to be imposed under this rule, however, the finding of unlawfulness must be upheld and final after appeal, the time for filing an appeal must have expired, or the appeal must have been dismissed.

In addition, California Business & Professions Code §125.6 (Discrimination in the Performance of Licensed Activity) subjects a lawyer to professional discipline if, because of a prospective client's "race, color, sex, religion, ancestry, disability, marital status, or national origin," the lawyer "refuses to perform the licensed activity" (i.e., the practice of law) or "makes any discrimination or restriction in the performance of the licensed activity."

Also, Business & Professions Code §490.5 permits the State to suspend a lawyer's license if the lawyer "is not in compliance with a child support order or judgment." Finally, Rule 290(a) of the Rules of Procedure of the California State Bar provides that (unless otherwise ordered by the Supreme Court) a member of the bar "shall be required to satisfactorily complete the State Bar Ethics School in all dispositions or decisions involving the imposition of discipline, unless the member previously completed the course within the prior two years."

Colorado: In addition to Rule 8.4(g), which forbids bias in various forms, Colorado adds Rule 4.5, which addresses threats of "criminal, administrative or disciplinary charges" to gain a civil case advantage. See Selected State Variations under Rule 4.4.

District of Columbia: Rule 8.4(d) prohibits conduct that "seriously interferes with" the administration of justice. Rule 8.4(e) omits the ABA phrase "or to achieve results by means that violate the Rules of Professional Conduct or other law." D.C. adds Rule 8.4(g), which makes it misconduct to "[s]eek or threaten to seek criminal charges or disciplinary charges solely to obtain an advantage in a civil matter."

In addition, D.C. adds Rule 9.1, which provides that a lawyer "shall not discriminate against any individual in conditions of employment because of the individual's race, color, religion, national origin, sex, age, marital status, sexual orientation, family responsibility, or physical handicap."

Florida expands Rule 8.4(d) to provide that a lawyer shall not:

> (d) engage in conduct in connection with the practice of law that is prejudicial to the administration of justice, including to knowingly, or through callous indifference, disparage, humiliate, or discriminate against litigants, jurors, witnesses, court personnel, or other lawyers on any basis, including, but not limited to, on account of race, ethnicity, gender, religion, national origin, disability, marital status, sexual orientation, age, socioeconomic status, employment, or physical characteristic.

Florida also adds Rule 8.4(g), which provides that a lawyer shall not "fail to respond, in writing, to any official inquiry by bar counsel or a disciplinary agency . . . when bar counsel or the agency is conducting an investigation into the lawyer's conduct."

In addition, Florida adds Rule 8.4(h) that makes it professional misconduct for a lawyer to "willfully refuse, as determined by a court of competent jurisdiction, to timely pay a child support obligation." The Comment explains that subparagraph (h) was added to make the treatment of lawyers who fail to pay child support consistent with the treatment of other professionals in Florida who fail to pay child support. Those other professionals are governed by §61.13015 of the Florida Statutes, which provides for the suspension or denial of a professional license due to delinquent child support payments after all other available remedies for the collection of child support have been exhausted.

Florida also adds Rule 4-8.4(i), which relates to sexual conduct with a client and provides that a lawyer shall not engage in sexual conduct with a client "or a representative of a client." See the Selected Variations following Rule 1.8 for more detail.

Finally, the Florida Supreme Court has promulgated Rule 3-4.7, which provides:

> Violation of the oath taken by an attorney to support the constitutions of the United States and the State of Florida is ground for disciplinary action. Membership in, alliance with, or support of any organization, group, or party advocating or dedicated to the overthrow of the government by violence or by any means in violation of the Constitution of the United States or constitution of this state shall be a violation of the oath.

Georgia: In the rules effective November 3, 2011, Georgia deletes ABA Model Rule 8.4(b) in favor of two subparagraphs making it a violation to be "convicted of a felony" or to be "convicted of a misdemeanor involving moral turpitude where the underlying conduct relates to the lawyer's fitness to practice law." Rule 8.4(a)(4) prohibits the commission of a "criminal act that relates to the lawyer's fitness to practice law or reflects adversely on the lawyer's honesty, trustworthiness or fitness

as a lawyer, where the lawyer has admitted in judicio the commission of such act."
Rule 8.4(a)(5) — Georgia's equivalent to ABA Model Rule 8.4(c) — makes it
improper to engage in "professional" conduct involving dishonesty, fraud, deceit
or misrepresentation. Georgia adds a Rule 8.4(a)(6) that makes it improper for a
lawyer to "fail to pay any final judgment or rule absolute rendered against such lawyer for money collected by him or her as a lawyer within ten (10) days after the time
appointed in the order or judgment." Rule 8.4(a)(7) not only prohibits the same
conduct as Model Rule 8.4(e), but it also prohibits a lawyer from stating "an ability
to achieve results by means that violate the Rules of Professional Conduct or other
law" or achieving "results by means that violate the Rules of Professional Conduct
or other law." Rule 8.4(b) describes what constitutes a "conviction" for purposes of
the Rule. Rule 8.4(d) provides that Rule 8.4(a)(1) "does not apply to Part Six of
the Georgia Rules of Professional Conduct" (which covers pro bono work, court
appointments, legal service organizations, and law reform organizations). Georgia
deletes ABA Model Rules 8.4(d)-(f).

Illinois expands Rule 8.4(f) and adds paragraphs (g)-(k), some of which are
taken directly from the old ABA Model Code of Professional Responsibility. They
provide that it is professional misconduct for a lawyer to:

> (f) . . . give or lend anything of value to a judge, official, or employee of a tri-
> bunal, except those gifts or loans that a judge or a member of the judge's family may
> receive under Rule 65(C)(4) of the Illinois Code of Judicial Conduct. Permissible cam-
> paign contributions to a judge or candidate for judicial office may be made only by
> check, draft, or other instrument payable to or to the order of an entity that the lawyer
> reasonably believes to be a political committee supporting such judge or candidate.
> Provision of volunteer services by a lawyer to a political committee shall not be deemed
> to violate this paragraph.

> (g) present, participate in presenting, or threaten to present criminal or profes-
> sional disciplinary charges to obtain an advantage in a civil matter.

> (h) enter into an agreement with a client or former client limiting or purporting
> to limit the right of the client or former client to file or pursue any complaint before
> the Illinois Attorney Registration and Disciplinary Commission.

> (i) avoid in bad faith the repayment of an education loan guaranteed by the
> Illinois Student Assistance Commission or other governmental entity. The lawful dis-
> charge of an education loan in a bankruptcy proceeding shall not constitute bad faith
> under this paragraph, but the discharge shall not preclude a review of the lawyer's
> conduct to determine if it constitutes bad faith.

> (j) violate a federal, state or local statute or ordinance that prohibits discrimi-
> nation based on race, sex, religion, national origin, disability, age, sexual orientation
> or socioeconomic status by conduct that reflects adversely on the lawyer's fitness as a
> lawyer. Whether a discriminatory act reflects adversely on a lawyer's fitness as a law-
> yer shall be determined after consideration of all the circumstances, including: the
> seriousness of the act; whether the lawyer knew that the act was prohibited by stat-
> ute or ordinance; whether the act was part of a pattern of prohibited conduct; and
> whether the act was committed in connection with the lawyer's professional activities.
> No charge of professional misconduct may be brought pursuant to this paragraph
> until a court or administrative agency of competent jurisdiction has found that the
> lawyer has engaged in an unlawful discriminatory act, and the finding of the court
> or administrative agency has become final and enforceable and any right of judicial
> review has been exhausted.

> (k) if the lawyer holds public office:

(1) use that office to obtain, or attempt to obtain, a special advantage in a legislative matter for a client under circumstances where the lawyer knows or reasonably should know that such action is not in the public interest;

(2) use that office to influence, or attempt to influence, a tribunal to act in favor of a client; or

(3) represent any client, including a municipal corporation or other public body, in the promotion or defeat of legislative or other proposals pending before the public body of which such lawyer is a member or by which such lawyer is employed.

Iowa: Rule 8.4(g) forbids lawyers to "engage in sexual harassment or other unlawful discrimination in the practice of law or knowingly permit staff or agents subject to the lawyer's direction and control to do so."

Louisiana: Among other variations, Louisiana adds a Rule 8.4(g), which makes it professional misconduct for a lawyer to "[t]hreaten to present criminal or disciplinary charges solely to obtain an advantage in a civil matter."

Maryland: Rule 8.4(e) provides that a lawyer may not "manifest by words or conduct" various kinds of bias or prejudice when such action is prejudicial to the administration of justice.

Massachusetts: Rule 8.4(h) forbids a lawyer to "engage in any other conduct that adversely reflects on his or her fitness to practice law." Comment 5 states that such conduct is subject to discipline even if it "does not constitute a criminal, dishonest, or fraudulent or other act specifically described in the other paragraphs of this rule."

Michigan: Rule 6.5, entitled "Professional Conduct," provides as follows:

(a) A lawyer shall treat with courtesy and respect all persons involved in the legal process. A lawyer shall take particular care to avoid treating such a person discourteously or disrespectfully because of the person's race, gender, or other protected personal characteristic. To the extent possible, a lawyer shall require subordinate lawyers and nonlawyer assistants to provide such courteous and respectful treatment.

(b) A lawyer serving as an adjudicative officer shall, without regard to a person's race, gender, or other protected personal characteristic, treat every person fairly, with courtesy and respect. To the extent possible, the lawyer shall require staff and others who are subject to the adjudicative officer's direction and control to provide such fair, courteous, and respectful treatment to persons who have contact with the adjudicative tribunal.

In addition, the Michigan Court Rules include the following Rule 9.104:

(A) The following acts or omissions by an attorney, individually or in concert with another person, are misconduct and grounds for discipline, whether or not occurring in the course of an attorney-client relationship:

(1) conduct prejudicial to the proper administration of justice;

(2) conduct that exposes the legal profession or the courts to obloquy, contempt, censure, or reproach;

(3) conduct that is contrary to justice, ethics, honesty, or good morals;

(4) conduct that violates the standards or rules of professional responsibility adopted by the Supreme Court;

(5) conduct that violates a criminal law of a state or of the United States;

(6) knowing misrepresentation of any facts or circumstances surrounding a request for investigation or complaint;

(7) failure to answer a request for investigation or complaint in conformity with MCR 9.113 and 9.115(D);

(8) contempt of the board or a hearing panel; or

(9) violation of an order of discipline.

(B) Proof of an adjudication of misconduct in a disciplinary proceeding by another state or a United States court is conclusive proof of misconduct in a disciplinary proceeding in Michigan. The only issues to be addressed in the Michigan proceeding are whether the respondent was afforded due process of law in the course of the original proceedings and whether imposition of identical discipline in Michigan would be clearly inappropriate.

Minnesota adds Rule 8.4(g)-(h), which prohibits various kinds of harassment and discrimination.

Missouri adds the following to Rule 8.4(c):

> It shall not be professional misconduct for a lawyer for a criminal law enforcement agency, regulatory agency, or state attorney general to advise others about or to supervise another in an undercover investigation if the entity is authorized by law to conduct undercover investigations, and it shall not be professional misconduct for a lawyer employed in a capacity other than as a lawyer by a criminal law enforcement agency, regulatory agency, or state attorney general to participate in an undercover investigation, if the entity is authorized by law to conduct undercover investigations.

Moreover, Rule 8.4(g) forbids a lawyer to "manifest by words or conduct, in representing a client, bias or prejudice based upon race, sex, religion, national origin, disability, age, or sexual orientation." However, the rule "does not preclude legitimate advocacy when race, sex, religion, national origin, disability, age, sexual orientation, or other similar factors, are issues."

New Jersey: Rule 8.4(g) makes it professional misconduct for a lawyer to "engage, in a professional capacity, in conduct involving discrimination (except employment discrimination unless resulting in a final agency or judicial determination) because of race, color, religion, age, sex, sexual orientation, national origin, language, marital status, socio-economic status, or handicap, where the conduct is intended or likely to cause harm." The Supreme Court's comment states that the rule

> would, for example, cover activities in the court house, such as a lawyer's treatment of court support staff, as well as conduct more directly related to litigation; activities related to practice outside of the court house, whether or not related to litigation, such as treatment of other attorneys and their staff; bar association and similar activities; and activities in the lawyer's office and firm. Except to the extent that they are closely related to the foregoing, purely private activities are not intended to be covered by this rule amendment, although they may possibly constitute a violation of some other ethical rule. Nor is employment discrimination in hiring, firing, promotion, or partnership status intended to be covered unless it has resulted in either an agency or judicial determination of discriminatory conduct.

New Mexico creates a Rule 3.0 (Rule 16-300), which specifies as follows:

> In the course of any judicial or quasi-judicial proceeding before a tribunal, a lawyer shall refrain from intentionally manifesting, by words or conduct, bias or prejudice based on race, gender, religion, national origin, disability, age or sexual orientation against the judge, court personnel, parties, witnesses, counsel or others. This rule

does not preclude legitimate advocacy when race, gender, religion, national origin, disability, age or sexual orientation is material to the issues in the proceeding.

New York adds Rule 8.4(g) and (h), which provides that a lawyer or law firm shall not:

> (g) unlawfully discriminate in the practice of law, including in hiring, promoting or otherwise determining conditions of employment on the basis of age, race, creed, color, national origin, sex, disability, marital status or sexual orientation. Where there is a tribunal with jurisdiction to hear a complaint, if timely brought, other than a Departmental Disciplinary Committee, a complaint based on unlawful discrimination shall be brought before such tribunal in the first instance. A certified copy of a determination by such a tribunal, which has become final and enforceable and as to which the right to judicial or appellate review has been exhausted, finding that the lawyer has engaged in an unlawful discriminatory practice shall constitute prima facie evidence of professional misconduct in a disciplinary proceeding; or
> (h) engage in any other conduct that adversely reflects on the lawyer's fitness as a lawyer.

North Carolina: Rule 8.4(e) omits the clause "or to achieve results by means that violate the Rules of Professional Conduct or other law," and a Rule 8.4(g) makes it professional misconduct for a lawyer to "intentionally prejudice or damage his or her client during the course of the professional relationship, except as may be required by Rule 3.3." North Carolina also adds a Rule 6.6, which prohibits lawyers who hold "public office" from abusing their public positions.

Ohio adds Rule 8.4(g)-(h), which makes it professional misconduct for a lawyer to:

> (g) engage, in a professional capacity, in conduct involving discrimination prohibited by law because of race, color, religion, age, gender, sexual orientation, national origin, marital status, or disability;
> (h) engage in any other conduct that adversely reflects on the lawyer's fitness to practice law.

Ohio also adds an unusual Comment 2A, which provides that Rule 8.4(c) "does not prohibit a lawyer from supervising or advising about lawful covert activity in the investigation of criminal activity or violations of constitutional or civil rights when authorized by law."

Oregon: Rule 8.4(b) is the result of a decision of the Oregon Supreme Court, *In re Gatti,* 8 P.3d 966 (Or. 2000). It provides that, notwithstanding Rules 8.4(a)(1), (3), and (4) and Rule 3.3(a)(1), "it shall not be professional misconduct for a lawyer to advise clients or others about or to supervise lawful covert activity in the investigation of violations of civil or criminal law or constitutional rights," provided the lawyer's conduct otherwise complies with the Rules of Professional Conduct. "Covert activity" is defined in Rule 8.4(b) to mean "an effort to obtain information on unlawful activity through the use of misrepresentations or other subterfuge." The rule permits covert activity to "be commenced by a lawyer or involve the lawyer as an advisor or supervisor only when the lawyer in good faith believes there is a reasonable possibility that unlawful activity has taken place, is taking place, or will take place in the foreseeable future."

Rhode Island adds Rule 9.1, which establishes an ethics advisory panel to be appointed by the Supreme Court and provides that "[a]ny lawyer who acts in accordance with an opinion given by the panel shall be conclusively presumed to have abided by the Rules of Professional Conduct.''

Texas: Rule 5.08, entitled ''Prohibited Discriminatory Activities,'' provides as follows:

> (a) A lawyer shall not willfully, in connection with an adjudicatory proceeding, except as provided in paragraph (b), manifest, by words or conduct, bias or prejudice based on race, color, national origin, religion, disability, age, sex, or sexual orientation towards any person involved in that proceeding in any capacity.
>
> (b) Paragraph (a) does not apply to a lawyer's decision whether to represent a particular person in connection with an adjudicatory proceeding, nor to the process of jury selection, nor to communications protected as ''confidential information'' under these Rules. See Rule 1.05(a), (b). It also does not preclude advocacy in connection with an adjudicatory proceeding involving any of the factors set out in paragraph (a) if that advocacy:
>
> > (i) is necessary in order to address any substantive or procedural issues raised by the proceeding; and
> >
> > (ii) is conducted in conformity with applicable rulings and orders of a tribunal and applicable rules of practice and procedure.

Texas Rule 8.04(a)(9) forbids a lawyer to ''engage in conduct that constitutes barratry as defined by the laws of this state.'' Rule 8.04(a)(2) forbids a lawyer to ''commit a serious crime or commit any other criminal act that reflects adversely on the lawyer's honesty, trustworthiness or fitness as a lawyer in other respects.'' Rule 8.04(b) defines ''serious crime'' to include ''barratry; any felony involving moral turpitude; any misdemeanor involving theft, embezzlement, or fraudulent or reckless misappropriation of money or other property; or any attempt, conspiracy, or solicitation of another to commit any of the foregoing crimes.''

Virginia: Rule 8.4(b) applies to a criminal ''or deliberately wrongful act,'' and Rule 8.4(c) applies to conduct involving dishonesty, fraud, deceit or misrepresentation ''which reflects adversely on the lawyer's fitness to practice law.'' Virginia omits Rule 8.4(d) (which forbids ''conduct that is prejudicial to the administration of justice''), and retains the pre-2002 version of ABA Model Rule 8.4(e), which made it professional misconduct for a lawyer to ''state or imply an ability to influence improperly or upon irrelevant grounds any tribunal, legislative body or public official,'' without any reference to ''means that violate the Rules of Professional Conduct or other law.''

Wisconsin: Among other variations, Wisconsin omits paragraph (d) and adds several additional paragraphs, including one relating to harassment.

Related Materials

ABA Formal Ethics Opinions: See ABA Formal Ethics Ops. 92-362 (1992), 92-363 (1992), 94-383 (1994), 94-387 (1994) (dissent only), 95-391 (1995), 95-394 (1995), 01-422 (2001), 04-433 (2004), 06-439 (2006), 06-442 nn.3 & 10 (2006), 07-446 (2007), 07-449 (2007), 08-451 (2008), and 10-457 (2010).

ABA Model Rule for Minimum Continuing Legal Education (MCLE): In 1987, the ABA House of Delegates approved a Model Rule for Minimum Continuing Legal Education (MCLE). The Comment to §2 of the ABA Model MCLE Rule, which relates to ABA Model Rule 8.4 and Comment 3 to Rule 8.4, provides as follows:

> Regulatory systems should require that lawyers . . . complete programs related to the promotion of racial and ethnic diversity in the legal profession, the promotion of full and equal participation in the profession of women and persons with disabilities, and the elimination of all forms of bias in the profession. Lawyers who practice in states and territories that do not require mandatory continuing legal education are encouraged to complete such programs as part of their continuing legal education.

For extensive information about MCLE, including a state-by-state directory of MCLE requirements, see *http://www.americanbar.org/publications_cle/mandatory_cle.html.*

ABA Model Rules for Lawyer Disciplinary Enforcement: In 1989, the ABA adopted Model Rules for Lawyer Disciplinary Enforcement, which set forth model procedures for state disciplinary agencies to follow. The ABA amended these rules in 1993, 1999, and 2002. Rule 19 provides for immediate interim suspension of a lawyer who is found guilty of a serious crime. Rule 25 provides that a lawyer who is disbarred may not apply for reinstatement for five years and must pass the bar examination as a condition of reinstatement. (In 2002, the ABA rejected a proposal to prohibit disbarred lawyers from applying for reinstatement for at least eight years after disbarment.) The Model Rules for Lawyer Disciplinary Enforcement are available at *http://www.americanbar.org/groups/professional_responsibility/resources/lawyer_ethics_regulation/model_rules_for_lawyer_disciplinary_enforcement.html.*

ABA Resolution Against Bias and Prejudice: In 1995, after various ABA committees could not agree on the text of a new Model Rule prohibiting bias and prejudice, the House of Delegates passed a resolution recommended by the ABA Young Lawyers Division to condemn bias and prejudice by lawyers in their professional activities and to encourage affirmative steps to reduce bias and prejudice among lawyers. The full resolution is set out in the Legislative History following Rule 8.4 under the heading "1995 Resolution."

ABA Resolution on Increasing Diversity in the Legal Profession: In 2006, the ABA approved a resolution urging all bar associations to take four steps to increase diversity in the legal profession: (1) collaborate with the bar examiner to "ensure that the bar examination does not result in a disparate impact on bar passage rates of minority candidates"; (2) "collaborate with accredited law schools to combat high rates of minority student attrition and to ensure that admission policies do not result in a disparate impact on acceptance rates of minority applicants"; (3) "collaborate with colleges and universities to develop and support prelaw programs that will increase minority applications to law schools and will increase the readiness of minority applicants for law school"; and (4) "collaborate with elementary and secondary schools to develop and support programs that will increase minority applications to college and will increase the readiness of minority applicants for college." The resolution (No. 113) and a background report are at *www.abanet.org/leadership/2006/annual/onehundredthirteen.doc.*

ABA Standards for Approval of Law Schools: In 1921 the ABA began promulgating Standards for Approval of Law Schools. Today, a majority of the states rely upon the ABA to determine whether a law school satisfies the state's legal education requirement for admission to the bar. The Standards have been amended periodically. In 2006, the ABA amended Standards 211 through 213, which address discrimination by law schools and thus relate to ABA Model Rule 8.4(d) and Comment 3 to Rule 8.4. The amended Standards provide:

Standard 211. Non-discrimination and Equality of Opportunity.

(a) A law school shall foster and maintain equality of opportunity in legal education, including employment of faculty and staff, without discrimination or segregation on the basis of race, color, religion, national origin, gender, sexual orientation, age or disability.

(b) A law school shall not use admission policies or take other action to preclude admission of applicants or retention of students on the basis of race, color, religion, national origin, gender, sexual orientation, age or disability.

(c) This Standard does not prevent a law school from having a religious affiliation or purpose and adopting and applying policies of admission of students and employment of faculty and staff that directly relate to this affiliation or purpose so long as (i) notice of these policies has been given to applicants, students, faculty, and staff before their affiliation with the law school, and (ii) the religious affiliation, purpose, or policies do not contravene any other Standard, including Standard 405(b) concerning academic freedom. These policies may provide a preference for persons adhering to the religious affiliation or purpose of the law school, but shall not be applied to use admission policies or take other action to preclude admission of applicants or retention of students on the basis of race, color, religion, national origin, gender, sexual orientation, age or disability. This Standard permits religious affiliation or purpose policies as to admission, retention, and employment only to the extent that these policies are protected by the United States Constitution. It is administered as though the First Amendment of the United States Constitution governs its application.

(d) Non-discrimination and equality of opportunity in legal education includes equal opportunity to obtain employment. A law school shall communicate to every employer to whom it furnishes assistance and facilities for interviewing and other placement functions the school's firm expectation that the employer will observe the principles of non-discrimination and equality of opportunity on the basis of race, color, religion, national origin, gender, sexual orientation, age and disability in regard to hiring, promotion, retention and conditions of employment.

Standard 212. Equal Opportunity and Diversity.

(a) Consistent with sound legal education policy and the Standards, a law school shall demonstrate by concrete action a commitment to providing full opportunities for the study of law and entry into the profession by members of underrepresented groups, particularly racial and ethnic minorities, and a commitment to having a student body that is diverse with respect to gender, race, and ethnicity.

(b) Consistent with sound educational policy and the Standards, a law school shall demonstrate by concrete action a commitment to having a faculty and staff that are diverse with respect to gender, race and ethnicity.

Standard 213. Reasonable Accommodation for Qualified Individuals with Disabilities.

Assuring equality of opportunity for qualified individuals with disabilities, as required by Standard 211, may require a law school to provide such students, faculty and staff with reasonable accommodations.

More information on the ABA Standards for Approval of Law Schools can be found at *http://www.americanbar.org/groups/legal_education/resources/standards.html.*

ABA Standards for Imposing Lawyer Sanctions:

5.1. Failure to Maintain Personal Integrity

5.11. Disbarment is generally appropriate when:

(a) a lawyer engages in serious criminal conduct a necessary element of which includes intentional interference with the administration of justice, false swearing, misrepresentation, fraud, extortion, misappropriation, or theft; or the sale, distribution or importation of controlled substances; or the intentional killing of another; or an attempt or conspiracy or solicitation of another to commit any of these offenses; or

(b) a lawyer engages in any other intentional conduct involving dishonesty, fraud, deceit, or misrepresentation that seriously adversely reflects on the lawyer's fitness to practice.

5.12. Suspension is generally appropriate when a lawyer knowingly engages in criminal conduct which does not contain the elements listed in Standard 5.11 and that seriously adversely reflects on the lawyer's fitness to practice.

5.13. Reprimand is generally appropriate when a lawyer knowingly engages in any other conduct that involves dishonesty, fraud, deceit, or misrepresentation and that adversely reflects on the lawyer's fitness to practice law.

5.14. Admonition is generally appropriate when a lawyer engages in any other conduct that reflects adversely on the lawyer's fitness to practice law.

5.2. Failure to Maintain the Public Trust

5.21. Disbarment is generally appropriate when a lawyer in an official or governmental position knowingly misuses the position with the intent to obtain a significant benefit or advantage for himself or another, or with the intent to cause serious or potentially serious injury to a party or to the integrity of the legal process.

5.22. Suspension is generally appropriate when a lawyer in an official or governmental position knowingly fails to follow proper procedures or rules and causes injury or potential injury to a party or to the integrity of the legal process.

8.0. Prior Discipline Orders

8.1. Disbarment is generally appropriate when a lawyer:

(a) intentionally or knowingly violates the terms of a prior disciplinary order and such violation causes injury or potential injury to a client, the public, the legal system, or the profession; or

(b) has been suspended for the same or similar misconduct, and intentionally or knowingly engages in further similar acts of misconduct that cause injury or potential injury to a client, the public, the legal system, or the profession.

8.2. Suspension is generally appropriate when a lawyer has been reprimanded for the same or similar misconduct and engages in further similar acts of misconduct that cause injury or potential injury to a client, the public, the legal system, or the profession.

The ABA Standards for Imposing Lawyer Sanctions, are available online at *www.americanbar.org/content/dam/aba/migrated/cpr/regulation/standards_sanctions.pdf.*

ABA Study of Women of Color in Law Firms: In 2006, with help from the University of Chicago's National Opinion Research Center, the ABA Commission on Women in the Profession released a study entitled "Visible Invisibility: Women of Color in Law Firms." The 141-page study, part of the ABA's Women of Color Research Initiative, explores the experiences of women of color who formerly worked in law firms of at least 25 attorneys. It attempts to answers such critical questions as: "What attracts women of color to the legal profession? Do their work experiences surpass or fall short of expectations? How do legal employers hinder or increase job satisfaction? Why do women attorneys of color change practice areas and organizations, or leave the profession at an alarming rate?" The study, which is available for purchase online, concludes that discrimination is causing growing numbers of minority women to leave large law firms.

In 2008, the ABA Commission on Women in the Profession released a follow-up study entitled "From Visible Invisibility to Visibly Successful: Success Strategies for Law Firms and Women of Color in Law Firms." And in 2012, the Commission released a study entitled "Visible Invisibility: Women of Color in Fortune 500 Legal Depts." The Executive Summary of the 2006 study, and the full text of the 2008 and 2012 studies, may be downloaded at no cost from *http://www.americanbar.org/groups/ women/initiatives_awards/women_of_color_research_initiative.html.*

Discipline: Professional discipline for engaging in misconduct of the kinds described in ABA Model Rule 8.4 (and sometimes for other types of misconduct) can take many varieties. Some of the varieties of discipline are set out in rules or regulations. At the state level, for example, Illinois Supreme Court Rule 770 provides as follows:

> Conduct of attorneys which violates the Rules of Professional Conduct . . . or which tends to defeat the administration of justice or to bring the courts or the legal profession into disrepute shall be grounds for discipline by the court. Discipline may be:
> (a) disbarment;
> (b) disbarment on consent;
> (c) suspension for a specified period and until further order of court;
> (d) suspension for a specified period of time;
> (e) suspension until further order of the court;
> (f) suspension for a specified period of time or until further order of the court with probation;
> (g) censure; or
> (h) reprimand by the court, the Review Board or a hearing panel.

At the federal level, a regulation of the United States Patent and Trademark Office (USPTO) provides as follows:

> (a) *Types of discipline.* The USPTO Director, after notice and opportunity for a hearing, and where grounds for discipline exist, may impose on a practitioner the following types of discipline:
> (1) Exclusion from practice before the Office;
> (2) Suspension from practice before the Office for an appropriate period of time;
> (3) Reprimand or censure; or
> (4) Probation. Probation may be imposed in lieu of or in addition to any other disciplinary sanction. Any conditions of probation shall be stated in writing in the order imposing probation. . . .

See 37 C.F.R. §11.20.

Discrimination Statutes: Comment 3 to Rule 8.4 discusses bias or prejudice that is "prejudicial to the administration of justice," but some state ethics rules, such as New York's Rule 8.4(g) and California's Rule 2-400(B), prohibit bias and discrimination only to the extent that the conduct would violate federal or state laws prohibiting discrimination. Under federal law, three major statutes prohibit discrimination in employment: Title VII of the Civil Rights Act of 1964, 42 U.S.C §§2000 *et seq.*; the Americans with Disabilities Act (ADA), 42 U.S.C. §§12101 *et seq.*; and the Age Discrimination in Employment Act (ADEA), 29 U.S.C. §§621 *et seq.* Most states have parallel laws, and some state and local laws reach further than the federal statutes, prohibiting employment discrimination based on such factors as sexual orientation, color, and marital status in addition to the federal criteria.

Federal Rules of Appellate Procedure: Fed. R. App. P. 46(c) gives a federal court of appeals power to discipline any attorney who practices before it for "conduct unbecoming a member of the bar or for failure to comply with any court rule."

IRS Regulations: In the regulations governing practice before the Internal Revenue Service, 31 C.F.R. §10.50(a) authorizes the Secretary of the Treasury to "censure, suspend or disbar" any practitioner from practice before the IRS who is shown to be "incompetent or disreputable . . . , fails to comply with any regulation in this part . . . , or with intent to defraud, willfully and knowingly misleads or threatens a client or prospective client."

Section 10.51 defines "incompetence and disreputable conduct" to encompass a long list of misdeeds, including conviction of any crime under federal tax laws; conviction of any crime involving "dishonesty, or breach of trust"; knowingly giving false or misleading information to any employee of the Treasury Department or to "any tribunal authorized to pass upon Federal tax matters . . ."; misappropriating client funds; engaging in "[c]ontemptuous conduct in connection with practice before the Internal Revenue Service, including the use of abusive language, making false accusations and statements, knowing them to be false, or circulating or publishing malicious or libelous matter" or "[g]iving a false opinion, knowingly, recklessly, or through gross incompetence, including an opinion which is intentionally or recklessly misleading, or engaging in a pattern of providing incompetent opinions on questions arising under the Federal tax laws."

Misconduct: Many states define "misconduct" in a statute or court rule. In Washington, D.C., for example, Rule XI §2(b) of the Rules Governing the District of Columbia Bar provides, *inter alia:* "Acts or omissions by an attorney . . . which violate the attorney's oath of office or the rules or code of professional conduct currently in effect in the District of Columbia shall constitute misconduct and shall be grounds for discipline, whether or not the act or omission occurred in the course of an attorney-client relationship."

Readmission: When a lawyer is suspended or disbarred, readmission generally is not automatic. An example of a state readmission rule is Florida Supreme Court Rule 2-13.1 (Disbarred or Resigned Pending Disciplinary Proceedings). Rule 2-13.1 provides as follows:

> A person who has been disbarred from the practice of law, or who has resigned pending disciplinary proceedings . . . based on conduct that occurred in Florida for the disbarment or resignation, will not be eligible to apply for readmission for a period of 5 years from the date of disbarment, or 3 years from the date of resignation . . . or longer period set for readmission by the Supreme Court of Florida. If the person's disbarment or disciplinary resignation is based on conduct that occurred in a foreign

jurisdiction, then the person will not be eligible to apply for admission or readmission to The Florida Bar until the person is readmitted in the foreign jurisdiction in which the conduct that resulted in discipline occurred. . . .

Restatement of the Law Governing Lawyers: See Restatement §§1, 5, and 113 in our chapter on the Restatement later in this volume.

Securities and Exchange Commission Rules: The Securities and Exchange Commission (the SEC or the Commission) has power to discipline attorneys who appear or practice before the SEC. The main regulatory provision for imposing discipline is Rule 102(e), 17 C.F.R. §201.102(e) (at one time numbered Rule 2(e)), which provides as follows:

> (e) *Suspension and disbarment.*
>
> (1) *Generally.* The Commission may censure a person or deny, temporarily or permanently, the privilege of appearing or practicing before it in any way to any person who is found by the Commission after notice and opportunity for hearing in the matter:
>
> (i) Not to possess the requisite qualifications to represent others; or
>
> (ii) To be lacking in character or integrity or to have engaged in unethical or improper professional conduct; or
>
> (iii) To have willfully violated, or willfully aided and abetted the violation of any provision of the Federal securities laws or the rules and regulations thereunder. . . .

In addition, in 2003 the SEC adopted a new regulation, 17 C.F.R. §205.6, which is part of the Standards of Professional Conduct for Attorneys that the SEC promulgated to implement §307 of the Sarbanes-Oxley Act of 2002, 15 U.S.C. §7245. Section 205.6 provides as follows:

> *§205.6.   Sanctions and Discipline.*
>
> (a) A violation of this part by any attorney appearing and practicing before the Commission in the representation of an issuer shall subject such attorney to the civil penalties and remedies for a violation of the federal securities laws available to the Commission in an action brought by the Commission thereunder.
>
> (b) An attorney appearing and practicing before the Commission who violates any provision of this part is subject to the disciplinary authority of the Commission, regardless of whether the attorney may also be subject to discipline for the same conduct in a jurisdiction where the attorney is admitted or practices. An administrative disciplinary proceeding initiated by the Commission for violation of this part may result in an attorney being censured, or being temporarily or permanently denied the privilege of appearing or practicing before the Commission.
>
> (c) An attorney who complies in good faith with the provisions of this part shall not be subject to discipline or otherwise liable under inconsistent standards imposed by any state or other United States jurisdiction where the attorney is admitted or practices.
>
> (d) An attorney practicing outside the United States shall not be required to comply with the requirements of this part to the extent that such compliance is prohibited by applicable foreign law.

Statutes of Limitations: Some states and federal agencies have adopted statutes of limitations for disciplinary matters. At the state level, for example, the Florida Supreme Court adopted the following statute of limitations provision in 1995:

Rule 3-7.16.   Limitation on Time to Bring Complaint

(a) *Time for Inquiries, Complaints and Reopened Cases.* Inquiries raised or complaints presented by or to The Florida Bar under these rules shall be commenced within 6 years from the time the matter giving rise to the inquiry or complaint is discovered or, with due diligence, should have been discovered. . . .

(b) *Exception for Theft or Conviction of a Felony Criminal Offense.* There shall be no limit on the time in which to present or bring a matter alleging theft or conviction of a felony criminal offense by a member of The Florida Bar.

(c) *Tolling Based on Fraud, Concealment or Misrepresentation.* In matters covered by this rule where it can be shown that fraud, concealment, or intentional misrepresentation of fact prevented the discovery of the matter giving rise to the inquiry or complaint, the limitation of time in which to bring an inquiry or complaint within this rule shall be tolled. . . .

At the federal level, the America Invents Act, which was signed into law by President Obama on September 16, 2011, requires that disciplinary proceedings relating to misconduct by lawyers who practice before the United States Patent and Trademark Office (USPTO) be commenced not later than the earlier of (i) 10 years after the date on which the misconduct occurred, or (ii) one year from the date on which the misconduct was made known to an officer or employee of the USPTO. To implement the America Invents Act, the USPTO adopted a new paragraph of 37 C.F.R. Part 11 that provides as follows:

(d) *Time for filing a complaint.* A complaint shall be filed within one year after the date on which the OED [Office of Enrollment and Discipline] Director receives a grievance forming the basis of the complaint. No complaint shall be filed more than ten years after the date on which the misconduct forming the basis for the proceeding occurred.

See 37 C.F.R. §11.34(d) (effective August 30, 2012).

Rule 8.5   Disciplinary Authority; Choice of Law

Canon and Code Antecedents

ABA Canons of Professional Ethics: No comparable Canon.
ABA Model Code of Professional Responsibility: No comparable Disciplinary Rule.

Cross-References in Other Rules

Rule 5.5, Comment 19: "A lawyer who practices law in this jurisdiction pursuant to paragraph (c) or (d) or otherwise is subject to the disciplinary authority of this jurisdiction. See **Rule 8.5(a)**."

Legislative History of Model Rule 8.5

1980 Discussion Draft had no comparable provision.
1981 Draft was substantially the same as the 1982 draft (see next entry).

1982 Draft was adopted.

1983 Rule: As originally adopted in 1983, Rule 8.5 consisted of a single sentence: "A lawyer admitted to practice in this jurisdiction is subject to the disciplinary authority of this jurisdiction although engaged in practice elsewhere."

1993 Amendment: At its August 1993 Annual Meeting, the ABA House of Delegates voted to amend Rule 8.5 by (i) rephrasing the first sentence of paragraph (a) (which had been the only sentence in the entire rule), (ii) adding a second sentence to paragraph (a), and (iii) adding an entirely new paragraph (b). The purpose of the new paragraph (b) was to provide guidelines for deciding which jurisdiction's disciplinary rules apply to lawyers who are licensed (either generally or pro hac vice) to practice in more than one jurisdiction. The amendment also included a wholesale revision of the Comment, replacing the three existing paragraphs with six completely new paragraphs, five of which explained the new choice of law rules contained in paragraph (b). The text of the Rule 8.5 as amended in 1993 thus provided as follows:

> (a) *Disciplinary Authority.* [First sentence was same as 2002 version of Rule 8.5(a). Second sentence of 2002 version had not yet been added.] A lawyer may be subject to the disciplinary authority of both this jurisdiction and another jurisdiction where the lawyer is admitted for the same conduct.
>
> (b) *Choice of Law.* In any exercise of the disciplinary authority of this jurisdiction, the rules of professional conduct to be applied shall be as follows:
>
> > (1) for conduct in connection with a proceeding in a court before which a lawyer has been admitted to practice (either generally or for purposes of that proceeding), the rules to be applied shall be the rules of the jurisdiction in which the court sits, unless the rules of the court provide otherwise; and
> >
> > (2) for any other conduct,
> >
> > > (i) if the lawyer is licensed to practice only in this jurisdiction, the rules to be applied shall be the rules of this jurisdiction, and
> > >
> > > (ii) if the lawyer is licensed to practice in this and another jurisdiction, the rules to be applied shall be the rules of the admitting jurisdiction in which the lawyer principally practices; provided, however, that if particular conduct clearly has its predominant effect in another jurisdiction in which the lawyer is licensed to practice, the rules of that jurisdiction shall be applied to that conduct.

The 1993 amendment was proposed by the ABA's Standing Committee on Ethics and Professional Responsibility. We reprint here excerpts from the committee report submitted in support of the amendment (with most citations omitted):

ABA Committee Report Explaining 1993 Amendment to Rule 8.5*

The objective of this proposed change in Rule 8.5 is to bring some measure of certainty and clarity to the frequently encountered, and often difficult, decisions a lawyer must make when encountering a situation in which the lawyer is potentially subject to differing ethical requirements of more than one jurisdiction. It is generally the case that such decisions cannot await an authoritative ruling or advisory opinion from an independent source.

---

* Committee Reports do not represent official policy of the ABA. They are for information only, and the opinions are those of the authors of the report.

The most compelling circumstance of a lawyer caught between conflicting ethical obligations in all likelihood is that where a lawyer has become aware of a client's fraud committed in the course of the lawyer's representation, and the rule of one jurisdiction with authority over the lawyer would require disclosure of the fraud and that of another jurisdiction with authority would forbid it. But this is by no means the only circumstance in which the problem arises. . . .

[E]xisting authority as to choice of law in the area of ethics rules is unclear and inconsistent. Some authorities suggest that particular conduct should be subject to only one set of rules, while others suggest that more than one set of rules can apply simultaneously to the same conduct. Widely differing approaches to how to identify the applicable rules have been taken. . . .

The proposed amendment to Rule 8.5 seeks to provide clear answers to these problems in nearly all cases. In litigation, the ethical rules of the tribunal, and only those rules, would apply. In other matters, the multiply admitted lawyer would be subject only to the rules of the jurisdiction where he or she principally practices, except when the particular conduct clearly has its predominant effect in another admitting jurisdiction. . . .

[I]t might be argued that, because of the exception for particular conduct that clearly has its predominant effect in another jurisdiction, the proposal falls short of achieving perfect clarity and certainty. This is indeed true, and there may be instances in which it is difficult to define the "particular conduct" and to decide whether it has its "predominant effect" in one jurisdiction or another. However, to provide for no exception would allow substantial conduct to occur in a second admitting jurisdiction without being subject to that jurisdiction's rules. . . .

2002 Amendments: At its August 2002 Annual Meeting, by voice vote, the ABA House of Delegates approved significant amendments to ABA Model Rule 8.5. The main changes were (i) to add the second sentence of Rule 8.5(a) (regarding a lawyer not admitted in the jurisdiction), (ii) to delete the phrase "where the lawyer is admitted" in the last sentence of Rule 8.5(a), and (iii) to replace the pre-2002 version of Rules 8.5(b)(1) and (2) (see "1993 Amendment" above).

The Comment was extensively amended as well in 2002, and Comment 5 was added. Most of the amendments were proposed by the ABA Commission on Multijurisdictional Practice, which was formed in July 2000 to study issues pertaining to the practice of law by lawyers in jurisdictions where they are not admitted to practice, either permanently or pro hac vice. However, the last two sentences of Comment 1 (regarding service of process and personal jurisdiction) were added based on negotiations between the MJP Commission and lawyers from the Ohio State Bar Association. The Ohio lawyers wanted to ensure that lawyers who harmed clients in states where they were not admitted would be amenable to disciplinary and civil jurisdiction in those states.

The Final Reports of the ABA Commission on Multijurisdictional Practice regarding Rule 8.5 and related issues are available online at the MJP Commission's website at *http://www.americanbar.org/groups/professional_responsibility/committees_commissions/commission_on_multijurisditional_practice.html* (look for "Final Reports, as adopted August 12, 2002"). We excerpt here (with footnotes omitted) the portions of Report 201C that relate directly to the 2002 Amendments to Rule 8.5:

Excerpts from Final Report of the ABA Commission on Multijurisdictional Practice in Support of Amendments to Rule 8.5*

It is important that state regulatory authorities acknowledge the increasing prevalence of cross-border law practice and respond appropriately. Allowances must be made for effectively regulating lawyers who practice law outside the states in which they are licensed. Sanctions must be available both against lawyers who do unauthorized work outside their home states and against those who violate rules of professional conduct when they engage in otherwise permissible multijurisdictional law practice.

The Ethics 2000 Commission proposed amending Rule 8.5(a) (Disciplinary Authority) to make clear that a jurisdiction in which a lawyer engages in disciplinary misconduct may sanction the lawyer regardless of whether the lawyer is licensed to practice law in that jurisdiction. Most significantly, a sentence would be added to provide that: "A lawyer not admitted in this jurisdiction is also subject to the disciplinary authority of this jurisdiction if the lawyer provides or offers to provide any legal services in this jurisdiction." . . . As the Ethics 2000 Commission noted, "this is an appropriate Rule to adopt in the *Model Rules of Professional Conduct,* given that a jurisdiction in which a lawyer is not admitted may be the one most interested in disciplining the lawyer for improper conduct." As a further enhancement to this Rule, the MJP Commission recommends that the following statement be added to the end of Comment [1]: "Reciprocal enforcement of a jurisdiction's disciplinary findings and sanctions will further advance the purposes of this Rule. See Rules 6 and 22, *ABA Model Rules for Lawyer Disciplinary Enforcement.*"

Additionally, the Ethics 2000 Commission proposed amending Rule 8.5(b) (Choice of Law) in two principal respects. First, a number of changes would clarify the choice of law rule applicable to lawyers participating in adjudications. It would provide that a lawyer who participates in a formal adjudication before any "tribunal" — and not only a "court" — is bound by the rules of professional conduct of the jurisdiction in which the tribunal sits or by the rules of the tribunal itself if they provide otherwise.

Second, the Ethics 2000 Commission proposed changing the choice of law rule applicable to legal work outside the context of adjudications. . . . Under the proposed amendment, the applicable rules would be those of the jurisdiction in which the lawyer's conduct had its predominant effect or, where the conduct did not have its predominant effect in a single jurisdiction, the rules of the jurisdiction in which the conduct occurred. However, a lawyer who acts reasonably in the face of uncertainty about which jurisdiction's rules apply would not be subject to discipline.

Selected State Variations

California: Rule 1-100(D), headed "Geographic Scope of Rules," provides as follows:

(1) As to members: These rules shall govern the activities of members in and outside this state, except as members lawfully practicing outside this state may be specifically required by a jurisdiction in which they are practicing to follow rules of professional conduct different from these rules.

(2) As to lawyers from other jurisdictions who are not members: These rules shall also govern the activities of lawyers while engaged in the performance of lawyer functions in this state; but nothing contained in these rules shall be deemed to authorize

---

* Committee Reports do not represent official policy of the ABA. They are for information only, and the opinions are those of the authors of the report.

the performance of such functions by such persons in this state except as otherwise permitted by law.

In addition, in 2004 California Supreme Court adopted Rules 964 and 965, which permit "Registered Legal Services Attorneys" and "Registered In-House Counsel" to practice law in California without being members of the California Bar. Each requires that qualifying attorneys "[a]bide by all of the laws and rules that govern members of the State Bar of California, including the Minimum Continuing Legal Education (MCLE) requirements." Rules 966 and 967, respectively entitled "Attorneys Practicing Law Temporarily in California as Part of Litigation" and "Non-Litigating Attorneys Temporarily in California to Provide Legal Services," each contain the following language:

> [*Conditions*] By practicing law in California pursuant to this rule, an attorney agrees that he or she is providing legal services in California subject to:
> 　　(1) The jurisdiction of the State Bar of California;
> 　　(2) The jurisdiction of the courts of this state to the same extent as is a member of the State Bar of California; and
> 　　(3) The laws of the State of California relating to the practice of law, the State Bar of Professional Conduct, the rules and regulations of the State Bar of California, and these rules.

Substantial excerpts from Rules 964 through 967 are reprinted below in our chapter on California Materials following Rule 1-300 of the California Rules of Professional Conduct.

District of Columbia: Rule 8.5(a) omits the second sentence of ABA Model Rule 8.5(a) ("A lawyer not admitted in this jurisdiction is also subject to the disciplinary authority of this jurisdiction if the lawyer provides or offers to provide any legal services in this jurisdiction.") Rule 8.5(b)(2) provides as follows:

> (2) For any other conduct,
> 　　(i) If the lawyer is licensed to practice only in this jurisdiction, the rules to be applied shall be the rules of this jurisdiction, and
> 　　(ii) If the lawyer is licensed to practice in this and another jurisdiction, the rules to be applied shall be the rules of the admitting jurisdiction in which the lawyer principally practices; provided, however, that if particular conduct clearly has its predominant effect in another jurisdiction in which the lawyer is licensed to practice, the rules of that jurisdiction shall be applied to that conduct.

Florida: In Supreme Court Rule 3-4.6, Florida has adopted the language of Rule 8.5(b) except for the second sentence of paragraph (b)(2). In addition, Florida Rule 3-4.1 provides as follows:

> Every member of The Florida Bar and every attorney of another state or foreign country who provides or offers to provide any legal services in this state is within the jurisdiction and subject to the disciplinary authority of this court and its agencies under this rule and is charged with notice and held to know the provisions of this rule and the standards of ethical and professional conduct prescribed by this court. Jurisdiction over an attorney of another state who is not a member of The Florida Bar shall be limited to conduct as an attorney in relation to the business for which the attorney was permitted to practice in this state and the privilege in the future to practice law in the state of Florida.

When the Florida Supreme Court rejected a proposal to amend this rule in 1999, it said: "Out-of-state lawyers are not lawyers who are subject to the Rules Regulating the Florida Bar; rather, they are 'nonlawyers' subject to chapter 10 unlicensed practice of law charges if they . . . engage in improper solicitation or advertising in Florida." See Amendments to Rules Regulating the Florida Bar — Advertising Rules, 762 So. 2d 392, 393-395 (Fla. 1999).

Georgia: In the rules effective November 3, 2011, Rules 8.5(a) and (b) both use the phrase "Domestic and Foreign Lawyer" in place of the phrase "lawyer." Georgia defines those terms as follows:

> "Domestic Lawyer" denotes a person authorized to practice law by the duly constituted and authorized government body of any State or Territory of the United States or the District of Columbia but not authorized by the Supreme Court of Georgia or its rules to practice law in the State of Georgia.
>
> "Foreign Lawyer" denotes a person authorized to practice law by the duly constituted and authorized government body of any foreign nation but not authorized by the Supreme Court of Georgia or its Rules to practice law in the State of Georgia.

In addition, Georgia Rule 9.4 generally tracks Rules 6 and 22 of the ABA Model Rules of Lawyer Disciplinary Enforcement (reprinted below in the Related Materials for ABA Model Rule 8.5), which govern jurisdiction and reciprocal discipline.

Illinois: Illinois Supreme Court Rules 716 and 717 (summarized above in the Related Materials following ABA Model Rule 5.5) permit in-house and legal services lawyers to engage in limited law practice in Illinois. Rules 716 and 717 both provide that all lawyers licensed under the rules "shall be subject to the jurisdiction of the Court for disciplinary purposes to the same extent as all other lawyers licensed to practice law in this state."

Maryland: Rule 8.5(a) explicitly extends disciplinary jurisdiction to any lawyer who "holds himself or herself out as practicing law in this State," or who "has an obligation to supervise or control another lawyer practicing law in this State whose conduct constitutes a violation of these Rules."

Massachusetts: Rule 8.5(b)(2) refers to the "jurisdiction in which the lawyer's principal office is located" instead of where "the predominant effect of the conduct" occurred. The rule also adds several comments that clarify how the choice of law provisions are supposed to operate.

Nevada: Rule 8.5 consists of only one sentence: "A lawyer admitted to practice in this jurisdiction is subject to the disciplinary authority of this jurisdiction although engaged in practice elsewhere." Also relevant is Nevada Rule 7.2(a), which states as follows: "These Rules shall not apply to any advertisement broadcast or disseminated in another jurisdiction in which the advertising lawyer is admitted if such advertisement complies with the rules governing lawyer advertising in that jurisdiction and the advertisement is not intended primarily for broadcast or dissemination within the State of Nevada."

New Jersey deletes the last sentence of Rule 8.5(b) ("A lawyer shall not be subject to discipline. . . .").

New York: Rule 8.5 provides as follows:

> (a) A lawyer admitted to practice in this state is subject to the disciplinary authority of this state, regardless of where the lawyer's conduct occurs. A lawyer may be subject to the disciplinary authority of both this state and another jurisdiction where the lawyer is admitted for the same conduct.
>
> (b) In any exercise of the disciplinary authority of this state, the Rules of Professional Conduct to be applied shall be as follows:

(1) For conduct in connection with a proceeding in a court before which a lawyer has been admitted to practice (either generally or for purposes of that proceeding), the rules to be applied shall be the rules of the jurisdiction in which the court sits, unless the rules of the court provide otherwise; and

(2) For any other conduct:

(i) If the lawyer is licensed to practice only in this state, the rules to be applied shall be the rules of this state, and

(ii) If the lawyer is licensed to practice in this state and another jurisdiction, the rules to be applied shall be the rules of the admitting jurisdiction in which the lawyer principally practices; provided, however, that if particular conduct clearly has its predominant effect in another jurisdiction in which the lawyer is licensed to practice, the rules of that jurisdiction shall be applied to that conduct.

Oregon: Rule 8.6 designates certain entities authorized to issue advisory ethics opinions and provides that in any disciplinary matter, the tribunal "may consider any lawyer's good faith effort to comply with an opinion" in evaluating the lawyer's conduct or in mitigation of sanction.

South Carolina: S.C. Appellate Court Rule 418 requires any "unlicensed lawyer" (defined as "any person who is admitted to practice law in another jurisdiction but who is not admitted to practice law in South Carolina") to comply with South Carolina's lawyer advertising rules (Rules 7.1 through 7.5) if the unlicensed lawyer engages in any of six specified forms of advertising or solicitation.

Texas: Rule 8.05(b) provides as follows:

(b) A lawyer admitted to practice in this state is also subject to the disciplinary authority of this state for:

(1) an advertisement in the public media that does not comply with these rules and that is broadcast or disseminated in another jurisdiction, even if the advertisement complies with the rules governing lawyer advertisements in that jurisdiction, if the broadcast or dissemination of the advertisement is intended to be received by prospective clients in this state and is intended to secure employment to be performed in this state; and

(2) a written solicitation communication that does not comply with these rules and that is mailed in another jurisdiction, even if the communication complies with the rules governing written solicitation communications by lawyers in that jurisdiction, if the communication is mailed to an addressee in this state or is intended to secure employment to be performed in this state.

Virginia rejects the "predominant effect" test used in Rule 8.5(b)(2), favoring instead the rules from the jurisdiction where the lawyer's conduct occurred. The Virginia rule also contains specific provisions regarding lawyers who hold themselves out as Virginia attorneys. Virginia also explicitly rejects Comments 2 through 7 of the Model Rule and adopts its own explanations for how to resolve conflicts between different choice of law rules.

Related Materials

ABA Commission on Ethics 20/20: In 2009, the ABA created the Commission on Ethics 20/20, which is comprehensively reviewing the ABA Model Rules of Professional Conduct and other regulatory sources in the context of globalization and changes in technology. In September 2011, the Commission released for public comment a proposed new Comment 23 to Rule 1.7 that was intended to "provide more predictability to clients and their lawyers by permitting them to agree in advance to be bound by the conflict rules of a particular jurisdiction."

In July 2012, after studying public comments on the 2011 proposal, the 20/20 Commission issued "a possible proposal that is designed to address inconsistencies among jurisdictions' conflict of interest rules." As slightly refined in September 2012, the proposal would add a new Rule 1.7(c) to the black letter text that would permit a lawyer and client to agree that "the lawyer's work on a matter will be governed by the conflict of interest rules of a specific jurisdiction"—but only if the lawyer meets several specified conditions, including the following two conditions closely related to Rule 8.5:

> (3) the selected jurisdiction is one in which substantial work related to the matter, or the predominant effect of such work, is reasonably expected to occur; and
>
> (4) the agreement does not result in the application of a conflict rule that permits the lawyer to undertake a representation to which informed consent is not permissible under the rules of the jurisdiction whose rules would otherwise govern the lawyer's work on a matter under Rule 8.5(b).

To explain Rule 1.7(c), the 20/20 Commission proposed to add the following new paragraph to the Comment to Rule 1.7, under the heading "Choice of Rule Agreements":

> [23] Paragraph (c) provides, with certain limitations, that a lawyer and client can agree that the conflict rules of a specific jurisdiction will govern the representation. Such an agreement can help lawyers and their clients to predict which jurisdiction's conflict rules will govern the lawyer's representation of a client. The agreement can be helpful, whether in addition to or instead of a consent to future conflicts now permitted under Comment [22], because it can incorporate by reference an entire body of law on conflicts of interests. Clients, however, may be less likely to understand the material risks of such an agreement than when they consent to a specific possible future conflict. For this reason, Rule 1.7(c) imposes a number of requirements and limitations. For example, paragraph (c)(3) requires the selected jurisdiction to be one in which substantial work related to the matter, or the predominant effect of such work, is reasonably expected to occur.

The 20/20 Commission's reasons for locating a choice of law provision in Rule 1.7 instead of Rule 8.5 were briefly explained in a July 11, 2012 cover letter from Ethics 20/20 Commission Co-Chairs Jamie Gorelick and Michael Traynor, which said:

> Several commenters had suggested that the express authority for choice of rule agreements should appear in Model Rule 8.5 instead of Model Rule 1.7. The Commission felt, however, that any proposal in this area should only authorize choice of rule agreements to address inconsistencies among jurisdictions' conflict of interest rules and not other kinds of choice of law problems (*e.g.*, inconsistencies among jurisdictions with regard to the duty of confidentiality). For this reason, the Commission believes this authority should be located in Model Rule 1.7, which relates to conflicts of interest, rather than in Model Rule 8.5, which concerns choice of law issues more generally.

Nevertheless, because Rule 8.5 ordinarily governs choice of law questions, in September 2012 the Commission proposed a new Comment [8] to Rule 8.5 that would cross-reference the new Rule 1.7(c). Specifically, the new Comment to Rule 8.5 would provide as follows:

> [8] A lawyer and client may agree, pursuant to Rule 1.7(c), to be bound by the conflict of interest rules of a specified jurisdiction. Such an agreement, however, must not result in the application of a conflict rule that would permit the lawyer to undertake

a representation to which informed consent is not permissible under the rules of the jurisdiction that would otherwise govern the lawyer's work on the matter under Rule 8.5(b). See Rule 1.7(c)(4).

For additional information about the 20/20 Commission's work in the choice of law areas, see our entry entitled "ABA Commission on Ethics 20/20" in the Related Materials after Rule 1.7.

ABA Formal Ethics Opinions: See ABA Formal Ethics Ops. 91-360 (1991) and 01-423 n.21 (2001).

ABA Model Rules of Lawyer Disciplinary Enforcement: Comment 1 to ABA Model Rule 8.5 expressly mentions Rules 6 and 22 of the ABA Model Rules for Lawyer Disciplinary Enforcement. Those rules provide, in relevant part, as follows:

Rule 6. Jurisdiction

1. *Lawyers Admitted to Practice.* Any lawyer admitted to practice law in this jurisdiction, including any formerly admitted lawyer with respect to acts committed prior to resignation, suspension, disbarment, or transfer to inactive status . . . and any lawyer specially admitted by a court of this jurisdiction for a particular proceeding and any lawyer not admitted in this jurisdiction who practices law or renders or offers to render any legal services in this jurisdiction, is subject to the disciplinary jurisdiction of this court and the board.

Rule 22. Reciprocal Discipline and Reciprocal Disability Inactive Status

1. *Disciplinary Counsel Duty to Obtain Order of Discipline or Disability Inactive Status from Other Jurisdiction.* Upon being disciplined or transferred to disability inactive status in another jurisdiction, a lawyer admitted to practice in [this jurisdiction] shall promptly inform disciplinary counsel of the discipline or transfer. . . .

4. *Discipline to be Imposed.* . . . [T]his court shall impose the identical discipline or disability inactive status unless disciplinary counsel or the lawyer demonstrates, or this court finds that it clearly appears upon the face of the record from which the discipline is predicated, that:

(1) The procedure was so lacking in notice or opportunity to be heard as to constitute a deprivation of due process; or

(2) There was such infirmity of proof establishing the misconduct as to give rise to the clear conviction that the court could not, consistent with its duty, accept as final the conclusion on that subject; or

(3) The discipline imposed would result in grave injustice or be offensive to the public policy of the jurisdiction; or

(4) The reason for the original transfer to disability inactive status no longer exists.

If this court determines that any of those elements exists, this court shall enter such other order as it deems appropriate. The burden is on the party seeking different discipline in this jurisdiction to demonstrate that the imposition of the same discipline is not appropriate.

5. *Conclusiveness of Adjudication in Other Jurisdictions.* In all other aspects, a final adjudication in another jurisdiction that a lawyer, whether or not admitted in that jurisdiction, has been guilty of misconduct or should be transferred to disability inactive status shall establish conclusively the misconduct or the disability for purposes of a disciplinary or disability proceeding in this jurisdiction.

For more information concerning the ABA Model Rules of Disciplinary Enforcement, go to *http://www.americanbar.org/groups/professional_responsibility/resources/lawyer_ethics_regulation/model_rules_for_lawyer_disciplinary_enforcement.html.*

Federal Government Attorneys: In 1998, Congress passed 28 U.S.C. §530B, enti-tled "Ethical Standards for Attorneys for the Government" (commonly called the McDade Act), which provides, in pertinent part, as follows:

> (a) An attorney for the Government shall be subject to State laws and rules, and local Federal court rules, governing attorneys in each State where such attorney engages in that attorney's duties, to the same extent and in the same manner as other attorneys in that State.

When the McDade Act became law, all federal government lawyers were for the first time formally required to comply with the rules of professional conduct of the states in which they practiced. The long and winding history leading up to §530B is recounted in the Related Materials following Rule 4.2 in the entry entitled "Department of Justice Rules."

Federal Rules of Appellate Procedure: Fed. R. App. P. 46(b)(1) provides that a federal court of appeals may suspend or disbar a member of the court's bar if the member "(A) has been suspended or disbarred from practice in any other court; or (B) is guilty of conduct unbecoming a member of the court's bar."

Jurisdiction Over Out-of-State Lawyers: A state's willingness to exercise jurisdic-tion over an unethical lawyer licensed only in other states may depend on whether the alleged misconduct in the non-licensing state is related to the practice of law. For example, Rule 3-4.1 of the Rules Regulating the Florida Bar provides that "every attorney of another state or foreign country who provides or offers to provide any legal services in this state is within the jurisdiction and subject to the disciplinary authority of this court and its agencies. . . . Jurisdiction over an attorney of another state who is not a member of The Florida Bar shall be limited to conduct as an attorney in relation to the business for which the attorney was permitted to practice in this state and the privilege in the future to practice law in the state of Florida." In South Carolina, S.C. Appellate Court Rule 418 requires any "unlicensed lawyer" (defined as "any person who is admitted to practice law in another jurisdiction but who is not admitted to practice law in South Carolina") to comply with South Carolina's lawyer advertising rules (Rules 7.1 through 7.5) if the unlicensed lawyer engages in any of six specified forms of advertising or solicitation.

Model Rules of Professional Conduct for Federal Lawyers: Rule 8.5 provides:

> (a) A Federal lawyer shall comply with the rules of professional conduct applica-ble to the Federal Agency that employs the Government lawyer or the Federal Agency before which the Federal lawyer practices.
> (b) If the Federal Agency has not adopted or promulgated rules of professional conduct, the Federal lawyer shall comply with the rules of professional conduct of the state bars in which the Federal lawyer is admitted to practice.

The Comment to this rule states:

> While the Federal lawyer may remain subject to the governing authority of their licensing jurisdiction, the Federal lawyer is also subject to these Rules. However, when a Government lawyer is engaged in the conduct of Federal Agency legal functions, whether servicing the Federal Agency as a client or serving an individual client in the course of official duties, these Rules are regarded as superseding any conflicting rules applicable in the jurisdictions in which the Government lawyer may be licensed.

Restatement of the Law Governing Lawyers: See Restatement §§1 and 5 in our chapter on the Restatement later in this volume.

Restatement of the Law Governing Lawyers*

Editors' Introduction. The Restatement of the Law Governing Lawyers is published by the American Law Institute (ALI), an organization established in 1923 "to promote the clarification and simplification of the law and its better adaptation to social needs." The ALI drafts restatements of the law in many fields (*e.g.,* contracts, agency, and torts).

In 1986, realizing that the regulation of lawyers had become a specialized and highly developed field of law, the ALI began organizing the massive project of drafting a restatement of the law governing lawyers. The ALI appointed Professor Charles Wolfram as the Reporter, and named Professors John Leubsdorf, Thomas Morgan, and Linda Mullenix as Associate Reporters. From 1988 through 1997, the ALI annually published proposed drafts of various sections of the Restatement, accompanying each section with Comments, Illustrations, and a Reporter's Note. In 1998, the full membership of the ALI approved the entire draft Restatement and sent it on to the Reporters to make final changes (in consultation with the various groups within the ALI) to reflect amendments and discussions over the years.

In 2000, the ALI published the final version of the Restatement of the Law Governing Lawyers. With all of the Comments, Illustrations, and Reporter's Notes, it is over 1,000 pages. We reprint below only the black letter sections from the Restatement, without any of the Comments, Illustrations, or Reporter's Notes. Our version of the Restatement is based on the final version of the Restatement as published in 2000, which has not been amended in any way since then. The full Restatement of the Law Governing Lawyers (and pocket parts) can be ordered from the ALI's website at *www.ali.org* (click on "Publications Catalog").

In the Related Materials in the Annotations on the ABA Model Rules of Professional Conduct above, we have cross-referenced the Restatement sections most relevant to the ABA Model Rule at hand. However, some ABA Model Rules have no counterpart in the Restatement, and some Restatement sections have no counterpart in the ABA Model Rules.

CHAPTER 1   REGULATION OF THE LEGAL PROFESSION

CHAPTER 2   THE CLIENT-LAWYER RELATIONSHIP

TOPIC 3. THE LAWYER WORK-PRODUCT IMMUNITY

CHAPTER 6   REPRESENTING CLIENTS—IN GENERAL

TOPIC 1. LAWYER FUNCTIONS IN REPRESENTING CLIENTS—IN GENERAL

TOPIC 2. REPRESENTING ORGANIZATIONAL CLIENTS

TOPIC 3. LAWYER DEALINGS WITH A NONCLIENT

CHAPTER 1   REGULATION OF THE LEGAL PROFESSION

TOPIC 1.   REGULATION OF LAWYERS—IN GENERAL

§1.   Regulation of Lawyers—In General

Upon admission to the bar of any jurisdiction, a person becomes a lawyer and is subject to applicable law governing such matters as professional discipline, procedure and evidence, civil remedies, and criminal sanctions.

TOPIC 2.   PROCESS OF PROFESSIONAL REGULATION

Title A.   Admission to Practice Law

§2.   Admission to Practice Law

In order to become a lawyer and qualify to practice law in a jurisdiction of admission, a prospective lawyer must comply with requirements of the jurisdiction relating to such matters as education, other demonstration of competence such as success in a bar examination, and character.

Title B.   Authorized and Unauthorized Practice

§3.   Jurisdictional Scope of the Practice of Law by a Lawyer

A lawyer currently admitted to practice in a jurisdiction may provide legal services to a client:

(1) at any place within the admitting jurisdiction;

(2) before a tribunal or administrative agency of another jurisdiction or the federal government in compliance with requirements for temporary or regular admission to practice before that tribunal or agency; and

(3) at a place within a jurisdiction in which the lawyer is not admitted to the extent that the lawyer's activities arise out of or are otherwise reasonably related to the lawyer's practice under Subsection (1) or (2).

§4.   Unauthorized Practice by a Nonlawyer

A person not admitted to practice as a lawyer (see §2) may not engage in the unauthorized practice of law, and a lawyer may not assist a person to do so.

Title C.   Professional Discipline

§5.   Professional Discipline

(1) A lawyer is subject to professional discipline for violating any provision of an applicable lawyer code.

(2) A lawyer is also subject to professional discipline under Subsection (1) for attempting to commit a violation, knowingly assisting or inducing another to do so, or knowingly doing so through the acts of another.

(3) A lawyer who knows of another lawyer's violation of applicable rules of professional conduct raising a substantial question of the lawyer's honesty or trustworthiness or the lawyer's fitness as a lawyer in some other respect must report that information to appropriate disciplinary authorities.

TOPIC 3.   CIVIL JUDICIAL REMEDIES IN GENERAL

§6.   Judicial Remedies Available to a Client or Nonclient for Lawyer Wrongs

For a lawyer's breach of a duty owed to the lawyer's client or to a nonclient, judicial remedies may be available through judgment or order entered in accordance with the standards applicable to the remedy awarded, including standards concerning limitation of remedies. Judicial remedies include the following:

(1) awarding a sum of money as damages;

(2) providing injunctive relief, including requiring specific performance of a contract or enjoining its nonperformance;

(3) requiring restoration of a specific thing or awarding a sum of money to prevent unjust enrichment;

(4) ordering cancellation or reformation of a contract, deed, or similar instrument;

(5) declaring the rights of the parties, such as determining that an obligation claimed by the lawyer to be owed to the lawyer is not enforceable;

(6) punishing the lawyer for contempt;

(7) enforcing an arbitration award;

(8) disqualifying a lawyer from a representation;

(9) forfeiting a lawyer's fee (see §37);

(10) denying the admission of evidence wrongfully obtained;

(11) dismissing the claim or defense of a litigant represented by the lawyer;

(12) granting a new trial; and

(13) entering a procedural or other sanction.

§7. Judicial Remedies Available to a Lawyer for Client Wrongs

A lawyer may obtain a remedy based on a present or former client's breach of a duty to the lawyer if the remedy:

(1) is appropriate under applicable law governing the remedy; and

(2) does not put the lawyer in a position prohibited by an applicable lawyer code.

TOPIC 4.   LAWYER CRIMINAL OFFENSES

§8.   Lawyer Criminal Offenses

The traditional and appropriate activities of a lawyer in representing a client in accordance with the requirements of the applicable lawyer code are relevant factors for the tribunal in assessing the propriety of the lawyer's conduct under the criminal law. In other respects, a lawyer is guilty of an offense for an act committed in the course of representing a client to the same extent and on the same basis as would a nonlawyer acting similarly.

TOPIC 5. LAW-FIRM STRUCTURE AND OPERATION

Title A.   Association of Lawyers in Law Organizations

§9. Law-Practice Organizations—In General

(1) A lawyer may practice as a solo practitioner, as an employee of another lawyer or law firm, or as a member of a law firm constituted as a partnership, professional corporation, or similar entity.

(2) A lawyer employed by an entity described in Subsection (1) is subject to applicable law governing the creation, operation, management, and dissolution of the entity.

(3) Absent an agreement with the firm providing a more permissive rule, a lawyer leaving a law firm may solicit firm clients:

(a) prior to leaving the firm:

(i) only with respect to firm clients on whose matters the lawyer is actively and substantially working; and

(ii) only after the lawyer has adequately and timely informed the firm of the lawyer's intent to contact firm clients for that purpose; and

(b) after ceasing employment in the firm, to the same extent as any other nonfirm lawyer.

Title B.   Limitations on Nonlawyer Involvement in a Law Firm

§10. Limitations on Nonlawyer Involvement in a Law Firm

(1) A nonlawyer may not own any interest in a law firm, and a nonlawyer may not be empowered to or actually direct or control the professional activities of a lawyer in the firm.

(2) A lawyer may not form a partnership or other business enterprise with a nonlawyer if any of the activities of the enterprise consist of the practice of law.

(3) A lawyer or law firm may not share legal fees with a person not admitted to practice as a lawyer, except that:

(a) an agreement by a lawyer with the lawyer's firm or another lawyer in the firm may provide for payment, over a reasonable period of time after the lawyer's death, to the lawyer's estate or to one or more specified persons;

(b) a lawyer who undertakes to complete unfinished legal business of a deceased lawyer may pay to the estate of the deceased lawyer a portion of the total compensation that fairly represents services rendered by the deceased lawyer; and

(c) a lawyer or law firm may include nonlawyer employees in a compensation or retirement plan, even though the plan is based in whole or in part on a profit-sharing arrangement.

Title C.   Supervision of Lawyers and Nonlawyers Within an Organization

§11.   A Lawyer's Duty of Supervision

(1) A lawyer who is a partner in a law-firm partnership or a principal in a law firm organized as a corporation or similar entity is subject to professional discipline for failing to make reasonable efforts to ensure that the firm has in effect measures giving reasonable assurance that all lawyers in the firm conform to applicable lawyer-code requirements.

(2) A lawyer who has direct supervisory authority over another lawyer is subject to professional discipline for failing to make reasonable efforts to ensure that the other lawyer conforms to applicable lawyer-code requirements.

(3) A lawyer is subject to professional discipline for another lawyer's violation of the rules of professional conduct if:

(a) the lawyer orders or, with knowledge of the specific conduct, ratifies the conduct involved; or

(b) the lawyer is a partner or principal in the law firm, or has direct supervisory authority over the other lawyer, and knows of the conduct at a time when its consequences can be avoided or mitigated but fails to take reasonable remedial measures.

(4) With respect to a nonlawyer employee of a law firm, the lawyer is subject to professional discipline if either:

(a) the lawyer fails to make reasonable efforts to ensure:

(i) that the firm in which the lawyer practices has in effect measures giving reasonable assurance that the nonlawyer's conduct is compatible with the professional obligations of the lawyer; and

(ii) that conduct of a nonlawyer over whom the lawyer has direct supervisory authority is compatible with the professional obligations of the lawyer; or

(b) the nonlawyer's conduct would be a violation of the applicable lawyer code if engaged in by a lawyer, and

(i) the lawyer orders or, with knowledge of the specific conduct, ratifies the conduct; or

(ii) the lawyer is a partner or principal in the law firm, or has direct supervisory authority over the nonlawyer, and knows of the conduct at a time when its consequences can be avoided or mitigated but fails to take reasonable remedial measures.

§12.   Duty of a Lawyer Subject to Supervision

(1) For purposes of professional discipline, a lawyer must conform to the requirements of an applicable lawyer code even if the lawyer acted at the direction of another lawyer or other person.

(2) For purposes of professional discipline, a lawyer under the direct supervisory authority of another lawyer does not violate an applicable lawyer code by acting in accordance with the supervisory lawyer's direction based on a reasonable resolution of an arguable question of professional duty.

Title D.   Restrictions on the Right to Practice Law

§13.   Restrictions on the Right to Practice Law

(1) A lawyer may not offer or enter into a law-firm agreement that restricts the right of the lawyer to practice law after terminating the relationship, except for a restriction incident to the lawyer's retirement from the practice of law.

(2) In settling a client claim, a lawyer may not offer or enter into an agreement that restricts the right of the lawyer to practice law, including the right to represent or take particular action on behalf of other clients.

CHAPTER 2   THE CLIENT-LAWYER RELATIONSHIP

TOPIC 1.   CREATING A CLIENT-LAWYER RELATIONSHIP

§14.   Formation of a Client-Lawyer Relationship

A relationship of client and lawyer arises when:

(1) a person manifests to a lawyer the person's intent that the lawyer provide legal services for the person; and either

(a) the lawyer manifests to the person consent to do so; or

(b) the lawyer fails to manifest lack of consent to do so, and the lawyer knows or reasonably should know that the person reasonably relies on the lawyer to provide the services; or

(2) a tribunal with power to do so appoints the lawyer to provide the services.

§15.   A Lawyer's Duties to a Prospective Client

(1) When a person discusses with a lawyer the possibility of their forming a client-lawyer relationship for a matter and no such relationship ensues, the lawyer must:

(a) not subsequently use or disclose confidential information learned in the consultation, except to the extent permitted with respect to confidential information of a client or former client as stated in §§61-67;

(b) protect the person's property in the lawyer's custody as stated in §§44-46; and

(c) use reasonable care to the extent the lawyer provides the person legal services.

(2) A lawyer subject to Subsection (1) may not represent a client whose interests are materially adverse to those of a former prospective client in the same or a substantially related matter when the lawyer or another lawyer whose disqualification is imputed to the lawyer under §§123 and 124 has received from the prospective client confidential information that could be significantly harmful to the prospective client in the matter, except that such a representation is permissible if:

(a)(i) any personally prohibited lawyer takes reasonable steps to avoid exposure to confidential information other than information appropriate to determine whether to represent the prospective client, and (ii) such lawyer is screened as stated in §124(2)(b) and (c); or

(b) both the affected client and the prospective client give informed consent to the representation under the limitations and conditions provided in §122.

TOPIC 2. SUMMARY OF THE DUTIES UNDER A CLIENT-LAWYER RELATIONSHIP

§16. A Lawyer's Duties to a Client—In General

To the extent consistent with the lawyer's other legal duties and subject to the other provisions of this Restatement, a lawyer must, in matters within the scope of the representation:

(1) proceed in a manner reasonably calculated to advance a client's lawful objectives, as defined by the client after consultation;

(2) act with reasonable competence and diligence;

(3) comply with obligations concerning the client's confidences and property, avoid impermissible conflicting interests, deal honestly with the client, and not employ advantages arising from the client-lawyer relationship in a manner adverse to the client; and

(4) fulfill valid contractual obligations to the client.

§17. A Client's Duties to a Lawyer

Subject to the other provisions of this Restatement, in matters covered by the representation a client must:

(1) compensate a lawyer for services and expenses as stated in Chapter 3;

(2) indemnify the lawyer for liability to which the client has exposed the lawyer without the lawyer's fault; and

(3) fulfill any valid contractual obligations to the lawyer.

§18.   Client-Lawyer Contracts

(1) A contract between a lawyer and client concerning the client-lawyer relationship, including a contract modifying an existing contract, may be enforced by either party if the contract meets other applicable requirements, except that:

(a) if the contract or modification is made beyond a reasonable time after the lawyer has begun to represent the client in the matter (see §38(1)), the client may avoid it unless the lawyer shows that the contract and the circumstances of its formation were fair and reasonable to the client; and

(b) if the contract is made after the lawyer has finished providing services, the client may avoid it if the client was not informed of facts needed to evaluate the appropriateness of the lawyer's compensation or other benefits conferred on the lawyer by the contract.

(2) A tribunal should construe a contract between client and lawyer as a reasonable person in the circumstances of the client would have construed it.

§19.   Agreements Limiting Client or Lawyer Duties

(1) Subject to other requirements stated in this Restatement, a client and lawyer may agree to limit a duty that a lawyer would otherwise owe to the client if:

(a) the client is adequately informed and consents; and

(b) the terms of the limitation are reasonable in the circumstances.

(2) A lawyer may agree to waive a client's duty to pay or other duty owed to the lawyer.

TOPIC 3.   AUTHORITY TO MAKE DECISIONS

§20.   Lawyer's Duty to Inform and Consult with a Client

(1) A lawyer must keep a client reasonably informed about the matter and must consult with a client to a reasonable extent concerning decisions to be made by the lawyer under §§21-23.

(2) A lawyer must promptly comply with a client's reasonable requests for information.

(3) A lawyer must notify a client of decisions to be made by the client under §§21-23 and must explain a matter to the extent reasonably necessary to permit the client to make informed decisions regarding the representation.

§21. **Allocating the Authority to Decide Between a Client and a Lawyer**

As between client and lawyer:

(1) A client and lawyer may agree which of them will make specified decisions, subject to the requirements stated in §§18, 19, 22, 23, and other provisions of this Restatement. The agreement may be superseded by another valid agreement.

(2) A client may instruct a lawyer during the representation, subject to the requirements stated in §§22, 23, and other provisions of this Restatement.

(3) Subject to Subsections (1) and (2) a lawyer may take any lawful measure within the scope of representation that is reasonably calculated to advance a client's objectives as defined by the client, consulting with the client as required by §20.

(4) A client may ratify an act of a lawyer that was not previously authorized.

§22. **Authority Reserved to a Client**

(1) As between client and lawyer, subject to Subsection (2) and §23, the following and comparable decisions are reserved to the client except when the client has validly authorized the lawyer to make the particular decision: whether and on what terms to settle a claim; how a criminal defendant should plead; whether a criminal defendant should waive jury trial; whether a criminal defendant should testify; and whether to appeal in a civil proceeding or criminal prosecution.

(2) A client may not validly authorize a lawyer to make the decisions described in Subsection (1) when other law (such as criminal procedure rules governing pleas, jury-trial waiver, and defendant testimony) requires the client's personal participation or approval.

(3) Regardless of any contrary contract with a lawyer, a client may revoke a lawyer's authority to make the decisions described in Subsection (1).

§23. **Authority Reserved to a Lawyer**

As between client and lawyer, a lawyer retains authority that may not be overridden by a contract with or an instruction from the client:

(1) to refuse to perform, counsel, or assist future or ongoing acts in the representation that the lawyer reasonably believes to be unlawful;

(2) to make decisions or take actions in the representation that the lawyer reasonably believes to be required by law or an order of a tribunal.

§24. A Client with Diminished Capacity

(1) When a client's capacity to make adequately considered decisions in connection with the representation is diminished, whether because of minority, physical illness, mental disability, or other cause, the lawyer must, as far as reasonably possible, maintain a normal client-lawyer relationship with the client and act in the best interests of the client as stated in Subsection (2).

(2) A lawyer representing a client with diminished capacity as described in Subsection (1) and for whom no guardian or other representative is available to act, must, with respect to a matter within the scope of the representation, pursue the lawyer's reasonable view of the client's objectives or interests as the client would define them if able to make adequately considered decisions on the matter, even if the client expresses no wishes or gives contrary instructions.

(3) If a client with diminished capacity as described in Subsection (1) has a guardian or other person legally entitled to act for the client, the client's lawyer must treat that person as entitled to act with respect to the client's interests in the matter, unless:

(a) the lawyer represents the client in a matter against the interests of that person; or

(b) that person instructs the lawyer to act in a manner that the lawyer knows will violate the person's legal duties toward the client.

(4) A lawyer representing a client with diminished capacity as described in Subsection (1) may seek the appointment of a guardian or take other protective action within the scope of the representation when doing so is practical and will advance the client's objectives or interests, determined as stated in Subsection (2).

TOPIC 4.   A LAWYER'S AUTHORITY TO ACT FOR A CLIENT

§25. Appearance Before a Tribunal

A lawyer who enters an appearance before a tribunal on behalf of a person is presumed to represent that person as a client. The presumption may be rebutted.

§26. A Lawyer's Actual Authority

A lawyer's act is considered to be that of a client in proceedings before a tribunal or in dealings with third persons when:

(1) the client has expressly or impliedly authorized the act;

(2) authority concerning the act is reserved to the lawyer as stated in §23; or

(3) the client ratifies the act.

§27. A Lawyer's Apparent Authority

A lawyer's act is considered to be that of the client in proceedings before a tribunal or in dealings with a third person if the tribunal or third person reasonably assumes that the lawyer is authorized to do the act on the basis of the client's (and not the lawyer's) manifestations of such authorization.

§28. A Lawyer's Knowledge; Notification to a Lawyer; and Statements of a Lawyer

(1) Information imparted to a lawyer during and relating to the representation of a client is attributed to the client for the purpose of determining the client's rights and liabilities in matters in which the lawyer represents the client, unless those rights or liabilities require proof of the client's personal knowledge or intentions or the lawyer's legal duties preclude disclosure of the information to the client.

(2) Unless applicable law otherwise provides, a third person may give notification to a client, in a matter in which the client is represented by a lawyer, by giving notification to the client's lawyer, unless the third person knows of circumstances reasonably indicating that the lawyer's authority to receive notification has been abrogated.

(3) A lawyer's unprivileged statement is admissible in evidence against a client as if it were the client's statement if either:

(a) the client authorized the lawyer to make a statement concerning the subject; or

(b) the statement concerns a matter within the scope of the representation and was made by the lawyer during it.

§29. A Lawyer's Act or Advice as Mitigating or Avoiding a Client's Responsibility

(1) When a client's intent or mental state is in issue, a tribunal may consider otherwise admissible evidence of a lawyer's advice to the client.

(2) In deciding whether to impose a sanction on a person or to relieve a person from a criminal or civil ruling, default, or judgment, a tribunal may consider otherwise admissible evidence to prove or disprove that the lawyer who represented the person did so inadequately or contrary to the client's instructions.

§30. A Lawyer's Liability to a Third Person for Conduct on Behalf of a Client

(1) For improper conduct while representing a client, a lawyer is subject to professional discipline as stated in §5, to civil liability as stated in Chapter 4, and to prosecution as provided in the criminal law (see §7).

(2) Unless at the time of contracting the lawyer or third person disclaimed such liability, a lawyer is subject to liability to third persons on contracts the lawyer entered into on behalf of a client if:

(a) the client's existence or identity was not disclosed to the third person; or

(b) the contract is between the lawyer and a third person who provides goods or services used by lawyers and who, as the lawyer knows or reasonably should know, relies on the lawyer's credit.

(3) A lawyer is subject to liability to a third person for damages for loss proximately caused by the lawyer's acting without authority from a client under §26 if:

(a) the lawyer tortiously misrepresents to the third person that the lawyer has authority to make a contract, conveyance, or affirmation on behalf of the client and the third person reasonably relies on the misrepresentation; or

(b) the lawyer purports to make a contract, conveyance, or affirmation on behalf of the client, unless the lawyer manifests that the lawyer does not warrant that the lawyer is authorized to act or the other party knows that the lawyer is not authorized to act.

TOPIC 5. ENDING A CLIENT-LAWYER RELATIONSHIP

§31. Termination of a Lawyer's Authority

(1) A lawyer must comply with applicable law requiring notice to or permission of a tribunal when terminating a representation and with an order of a tribunal requiring the representation to continue.

(2) Subject to Subsection (1) and §33, a lawyer's actual authority to represent a client ends when:

(a) the client discharges the lawyer;

(b) the client dies or, in the case of a corporation or similar organization, loses its capacity to function as such;

(c) the lawyer withdraws;

(d) the lawyer dies or becomes physically or mentally incapable of providing representation, is disbarred or suspended from practicing law, or is ordered by a tribunal to cease representing a client; or

(e) the representation ends as provided by contract or because the lawyer has completed the contemplated services.

(3) A lawyer's apparent authority to act for a client with respect to another person ends when the other person knows or should know of facts from which it can be reasonably inferred that the lawyer lacks actual authority, including knowledge of any event described in Subsection (2).

§32.   Discharge by a Client and Withdrawal by a Lawyer

(1) Subject to Subsection (5), a client may discharge a lawyer at any time.

(2) Subject to Subsection (5), a lawyer may not represent a client or, where representation has commenced, must withdraw from the representation of a client if:

(a) the representation will result in the lawyer's violating rules of professional conduct or other law;

(b) the lawyer's physical or mental condition materially impairs the lawyer's ability to represent the client; or

(c) the client discharges the lawyer.

(3) Subject to Subsections (4) and (5), a lawyer may withdraw from representing a client if:

(a) withdrawal can be accomplished without material adverse effect on the interests of the client;

(b) the lawyer reasonably believes withdrawal is required in circumstances stated in Subsection (2);

(c) the client gives informed consent;

(d) the client persists in a course of action involving the lawyer's services that the lawyer reasonably believes is criminal, fraudulent, or in breach of the client's fiduciary duty;

(e) the lawyer reasonably believes the client has used or threatens to use the lawyer's services to perpetrate a crime or fraud;

(f) the client insists on taking action that the lawyer considers repugnant or imprudent;

(g) the client fails to fulfill a substantial financial or other obligation to the lawyer regarding the lawyer's services and the lawyer has given the client reasonable warning that the lawyer will withdraw unless the client fulfills the obligation;

(h) the representation has been rendered unreasonably difficult by the client or by the irreparable breakdown of the client-lawyer relationship; or

(i) other good cause for withdrawal exists.

(4) In the case of permissive withdrawal under Subsections (3)(f)-(i), a lawyer may not withdraw if the harm that withdrawal would cause significantly exceeds the harm to the lawyer or others in not withdrawing.

(5) Notwithstanding Subsections (1)-(4), a lawyer must comply with applicable law requiring notice to or permission of a tribunal when terminating a representation and with a valid order of a tribunal requiring the representation to continue.

§33.   A Lawyer's Duties When a Representation Terminates

(1) In terminating a representation, a lawyer must take steps to the extent reasonably practicable to protect the client's interests, such as

giving notice to the client of the termination, allowing time for employ-ment of other counsel, surrendering papers and property to which the client is entitled, and refunding any advance payment of fee the lawyer has not earned.

(2) Following termination of a representation, a lawyer must:

(a) observe obligations to a former client such as those deal-ing with client confidences (see Chapter 5), conflicts of interest (see Chapter 8), client property and documents (see §§44-46), and fee col-lection (see §41);

(b) take no action on behalf of a former client without new autho-rization and give reasonable notice, to those who might otherwise be misled, that the lawyer lacks authority to act for the client;

(c) take reasonable steps to convey to the former client any mate-rial communication the lawyer receives relating to the matter involved in the representation; and

(d) take no unfair advantage of a former client by abusing knowl-edge or trust acquired by means of the representation.

CHAPTER 3   CLIENT AND LAWYER: THE FINANCIAL AND PROPERTY RELATIONSHIP

TOPIC 1.   LEGAL CONTROLS ON ATTORNEY FEES

§34.   Reasonable and Lawful Fees

A lawyer may not charge a fee larger than is reasonable in the cir-cumstances or that is prohibited by law.

§35.   Contingent-Fee Arrangements

(1) A lawyer may contract with a client for a fee the size or payment of which is contingent on the outcome of a matter, unless the contract violates §34 or another provision of this Restatement or the size or pay-ment of the fee is:

(a) contingent on success in prosecuting or defending a criminal proceeding; or

(b) contingent on a specified result in a divorce proceeding or a proceeding concerning custody of a child.

(2) Unless the contract construed in the circumstances indicates otherwise, when a lawyer has contracted for a contingent fee, the lawyer is entitled to receive the specified fee only when and to the extent the client receives payment.

§36. Forbidden Client-Lawyer Financial Arrangements

(1) A lawyer may not acquire a proprietary interest in the cause of action or subject matter of litigation that the lawyer is conducting for a client, except that the lawyer may:

(a) acquire a lien as provided by §43 to secure the lawyer's fee or expenses; and

(b) contract with a client for a contingent fee in a civil case except when prohibited as stated in §35.

(2) A lawyer may not make or guarantee a loan to a client in connection with pending or contemplated litigation that the lawyer is conducting for the client, except that the lawyer may make or guarantee a loan covering court costs and expenses of litigation, the repayment of which to the lawyer may be contingent on the outcome of the matter.

(3) A lawyer may not, before the lawyer ceases to represent a client, make an agreement giving the lawyer literary or media rights to a portrayal or account based in substantial part on information relating to the representation.

§37. Partial or Complete Forfeiture of a Lawyer's Compensation

A lawyer engaging in clear and serious violation of duty to a client may be required to forfeit some or all of the lawyer's compensation for the matter. Considerations relevant to the question of forfeiture include the gravity and timing of the violation, its willfulness, its effect on the value of the lawyer's work for the client, any other threatened or actual harm to the client, and the adequacy of other remedies.

TOPIC 2.   A LAWYER'S CLAIM TO COMPENSATION

§38. Client-Lawyer Fee Contracts

(1) Before or within a reasonable time after beginning to represent a client in a matter, a lawyer must communicate to the client, in writing when applicable rules so provide, the basis or rate of the fee, unless the communication is unnecessary for the client because the lawyer has previously represented that client on the same basis or at the same rate.

(2) The validity and construction of a contract between a client and a lawyer concerning the lawyer's fees are governed by §18.

(3) Unless a contract construed in the circumstances indicates otherwise:

(a) a lawyer may not charge separately for the lawyer's general office and overhead expenses;

(b) payments that the law requires an opposing party or that party's lawyer to pay as attorney-fee awards or sanctions are credited to the client, not the client's lawyer, absent a contrary statute or court order; and

(c) when a lawyer requests and receives a fee payment that is not for services already rendered, that payment is to be credited against whatever fee the lawyer is entitled to collect.

§39. A Lawyer's Fee in the Absence of a Contract

If a client and lawyer have not made a valid contract providing for another measure of compensation, a client owes a lawyer who has performed legal services for the client the fair value of the lawyer's services.

§40. Fees on Termination

If a client-lawyer relationship ends before the lawyer has completed the services due for a matter and the lawyer's fee has not been forfeited under §37:

(1) a lawyer who has been discharged or withdraws may recover the lesser of the fair value of the lawyer's services as determined under §39 and the ratable proportion of the compensation provided by any otherwise enforceable contract between lawyer and client for the services performed; except that

(2) the tribunal may allow such a lawyer to recover the ratable proportion of the compensation provided by such a contract if:

(a) the discharge or withdrawal is not attributable to misconduct of the lawyer;

(b) the lawyer has performed severable services; and

(c) allowing contractual compensation would not burden the client's choice of counsel or the client's ability to replace counsel.

TOPIC 3.   FEE-COLLECTION PROCEDURES

§41. Fee-Collection Methods

In seeking compensation claimed from a client or former client, a lawyer may not employ collection methods forbidden by law, use confidential information (as defined in Chapter 5) when not permitted under §65, or harass the client.

§42. Remedies and the Burden of Persuasion

(1) A fee dispute between a lawyer and a client may be adjudicated in any appropriate proceeding, including a suit by the lawyer to recover

an unpaid fee, a suit for a refund by a client, an arbitration to which both parties consent unless applicable law renders the lawyer's consent unnecessary, or in the court's discretion a proceeding ancillary to a pending suit in which the lawyer performed the services in question.

(2) In any such proceeding the lawyer has the burden of persuading the trier of fact, when relevant, of the existence and terms of any fee contract, the making of any disclosures to the client required to render a contract enforceable, and the extent and value of the lawyer's services.

§43. Lawyer Liens

(1) Except as provided in Subsection (2) or by statute or rule, a lawyer does not acquire a lien entitling the lawyer to retain the client's property in the lawyer's possession in order to secure payment of the lawyer's fees and disbursements. A lawyer may decline to deliver to a client or former client an original or copy of any document prepared by the lawyer or at the lawyer's expense if the client or former client has not paid all fees and disbursements due for the lawyer's work in preparing the document and nondelivery would not unreasonably harm the client or former client.

(2) Unless otherwise provided by statute or rule, client and lawyer may agree that the lawyer shall have a security interest in property of the client recovered for the client through the lawyer's efforts, as follows:

(a) the lawyer may contract in writing with the client for a lien on the proceeds of the representation to secure payment for the lawyer's services and disbursements in that matter;

(b) the lien becomes binding on a third party when the party has notice of the lien;

(c) the lien applies only to the amount of fees and disbursements claimed reasonably and in good faith for the lawyer's services performed in the representation; and

(d) the lawyer may not unreasonably impede the speedy and inexpensive resolution of any dispute concerning those fees and disbursements or the lien.

(3) A tribunal where an action is pending may in its discretion adjudicate any fee or other dispute concerning a lien asserted by a lawyer on property of a party to the action, provide for custody of the property, release all or part of the property to the client or lawyer, and grant such other relief as justice may require.

(4) With respect to property neither in the lawyer's possession nor recovered by the client through the lawyer's efforts, the lawyer may obtain a security interest on property of a client only as provided by other law and consistent with §§18 and 126. Acquisition of such a security interest is a business or financial transaction with a client within the meaning of §126.

TOPIC 4. PROPERTY AND DOCUMENTS OF CLIENTS AND OTHERS

§44. Safeguarding and Segregating Property

(1) A lawyer holding funds or other property of a client in connection with a representation, or such funds or other property in which a client claims an interest, must take reasonable steps to safeguard the funds or property. A similar obligation may be imposed by law on funds or other property so held and owned or claimed by a third person. In particular, the lawyer must hold such property separate from the lawyer's property, keep records of it, deposit funds in an account separate from the lawyer's own funds, identify tangible objects, and comply with related requirements imposed by regulatory authorities.

(2) Upon receiving funds or other property in a professional capacity and in which a client or third person owns or claims an interest, a lawyer must promptly notify the client or third person. The lawyer must promptly render a full accounting regarding such property upon request by the client or third person.

§45. Surrendering Possession of Property

(1) Except as provided in Subsection (2), a lawyer must promptly deliver, to the client or nonclient so entitled, funds or other property in the lawyer's possession belonging to a client or nonclient.

(2) A lawyer may retain possession of funds or other property of a client or non-client if:

(a) the client or non-client consents;

(b) the lawyer's client is entitled to the property, the lawyer appropriately possesses the property for purposes of the representation, and the client has not asked for delivery of the property;

(c) the lawyer has a valid lien on the property (see §43);

(d) there are substantial grounds for dispute as to the person entitled to the property; or

(e) delivering the property to the client or non-client would violate a court order or other legal obligation of the lawyer.

§46. Documents Relating to a Representation

(1) A lawyer must take reasonable steps to safeguard documents in the lawyer's possession relating to the representation of a client or former client.

(2) On request, a lawyer must allow a client or former client to inspect and copy any document possessed by the lawyer relating to the representation, unless substantial grounds exist to refuse.

(3) Unless a client or former client consents to non-delivery or substantial grounds exist for refusing to make delivery, a lawyer must deliver to the client or former client, at an appropriate time and in any event promptly after the representation ends, such originals and copies of other documents possessed by the lawyer relating to the representation as the client or former client reasonably needs.

(4) Notwithstanding Subsections (2) and (3), a lawyer may decline to deliver to a client or former client an original or copy of any document under circumstances permitted by §43(1).

TOPIC 5. FEE-SPLITTING WITH A LAWYER NOT IN THE SAME FIRM

§47. Fee-Splitting Between Lawyers Not in the Same Firm

A division of fees between lawyers who are not in the same firm may be made only if:

(1)(a) the division is in proportion to the services performed by each lawyer or (b) by agreement with the client, the lawyers assume joint responsibility for the representation;

(2) the client is informed of and does not object to the fact of division, the terms of the division, and the participation of the lawyers involved; and

(3) the total fee is reasonable (see §34).

CHAPTER 4 LAWYER CIVIL LIABILITY

TOPIC 1. LIABILITY FOR PROFESSIONAL NEGLIGENCE AND BREACH OF FIDUCIARY DUTY

§48. Professional Negligence — Elements and Defenses Generally

In addition to the other possible bases of civil liability described in §§49, 55, and 56, a lawyer is civilly liable for professional negligence to a person to whom the lawyer owes a duty of care within the meaning of §50 or §51, if the lawyer fails to exercise care within the meaning of §52 and if that failure is a legal cause of injury within the meaning of §53, unless the lawyer has a defense within the meaning of §54.

§49. Breach of Fiduciary Duty — Generally

In addition to the other possible bases of civil liability described in §§48, 55, and 56, a lawyer is civilly liable to a client if the lawyer breaches a fiduciary duty to the client set forth in §16(3) and if that failure is a legal cause of injury within the meaning of §53, unless the lawyer has a defense within the meaning of §54.

§50. Duty of Care to a Client

For purposes of liability under §48, a lawyer owes a client the duty to exercise care within the meaning of §52 in pursuing the client's lawful objectives in matters covered by the representation.

§51. Duty of Care to Certain Nonclients

For purposes of liability under §48, a lawyer owes a duty to use care within the meaning of §52 in each of the following circumstances:

(1) to a prospective client, as stated in §15;

(2) to a nonclient when and to the extent that:

(a) the lawyer or (with the lawyer's acquiescence) the lawyer's client invites the nonclient to rely on the lawyer's opinion or provision of other legal services, and the nonclient so relies; and

(b) the nonclient is not, under applicable tort law, too remote from the lawyer to be entitled to protection;

(3) to a nonclient when and to the extent that:

(a) the lawyer knows that a client intends as one of the primary objectives of the representation that the lawyer's services benefit the nonclient;

(b) such a duty would not significantly impair the lawyer's performance of obligations to the client; and

(c) the absence of such a duty would make enforcement of those obligations to the client unlikely; and

(4) to a nonclient when and to the extent that:

(a) the lawyer's client is a trustee, guardian, executor, or fiduciary acting primarily to perform similar functions for the nonclient;

(b) the lawyer knows that appropriate action by the lawyer is necessary with respect to a matter within the scope of the representation to prevent or rectify the breach of a fiduciary duty owed by the client to the nonclient, where (i) the breach is a crime or fraud or (ii) the lawyer has assisted or is assisting the breach;

(c) the nonclient is not reasonably able to protect its rights; and

(d) such a duty would not significantly impair the performance of the lawyer's obligations to the client.

§52. The Standard of Care

(1) For purposes of liability under §§48 and 49, a lawyer who owes a duty of care must exercise the competence and diligence normally exercised by lawyers in similar circumstances.

(2) Proof of a violation of a rule or statute regulating the conduct of lawyers:

(a) does not give rise to an implied cause of action for professional negligence or breach of fiduciary duty;

(b) does not preclude other proof concerning the duty of care in Subsection (1) or the fiduciary duty; and

(c) may be considered by a trier of fact as an aid in understanding and applying the standard of Subsection (1) or §49 to the extent that (i) the rule or statute was designed for the protection of persons in the position of the claimant and (ii) proof of the content and construction of such a rule or statute is relevant to the claimant's claim.

§53. Causation and Damages

A lawyer is liable under §48 or §49 only if the lawyer's breach of a duty of care or breach of fiduciary duty was a legal cause of injury, as determined under generally applicable principles of causation and damages.

§54. Defenses; Prospective Liability Waiver; Settlement with a Client

(1) Except as otherwise provided in this Section, liability under §§48 and 49 is subject to the defenses available under generally applicable principles of law governing respectively actions for professional negligence and breach of fiduciary duty. A lawyer is not liable under §48 or §49 for any action or inaction the lawyer reasonably believed to be required by law, including a professional rule.

(2) An agreement prospectively limiting a lawyer's liability to a client for malpractice is unenforceable.

(3) The client or former client may rescind an agreement settling a claim by the client or former client against the person's lawyer if:

(a) the client or former client was subjected to improper pressure by the lawyer in reaching the settlement; or

(b)(i) the client or former client was not independently represented in negotiating the settlement, and (ii) the settlement was not fair and reasonable to the client or former client.

(4) For purposes of professional discipline, a lawyer may not:

(a) make an agreement prospectively limiting the lawyer's liability to a client for malpractice; or

(b) settle a claim for such liability with an unrepresented client or former client without first advising that person in writing that independent representation is appropriate in connection therewith.

TOPIC 2.   OTHER CIVIL LIABILITY

§55.   Civil Remedies of a Client Other Than for Malpractice

(1) A lawyer is subject to liability to a client for injury caused by breach of contract in the circumstances and to the extent provided by contract law.

(2) A client is entitled to restitutionary, injunctive, or declaratory remedies against a lawyer in the circumstances and to the extent provided by generally applicable law governing such remedies.

§56.   Liability to a Client or Nonclient Under General Law

Except as provided in §57 and in addition to liability under §§48-55, a lawyer is subject to liability to a client or nonclient when a nonlawyer would be in similar circumstances.

§57.   Nonclient Claims — Certain Defenses and Exceptions to Liability

(1) In addition to other absolute or conditional privileges, a lawyer is absolutely privileged to publish matter concerning a nonclient if:

(a) the publication occurs in communications preliminary to a reasonably anticipated proceeding before a tribunal or in the institution or during the course and as a part of such a proceeding;

(b) the lawyer participates as counsel in that proceeding; and

(c) the matter is published to a person who may be involved in the proceeding, and the publication has some relation to the proceeding.

(2) A lawyer representing a client in a civil proceeding or procuring the institution of criminal proceedings by a client is not liable to a nonclient for wrongful use of civil proceedings or for malicious prosecution if the lawyer has probable cause for acting, or if the lawyer acts primarily to help the client obtain a proper adjudication of the client's claim in that proceeding.

(3) A lawyer who advises or assists a client to make or break a contract, to enter or dissolve a legal relationship, or to enter or not enter a contractual relation, is not liable to a nonclient for interference with contract or with prospective contractual relations or with a legal relationship, if the lawyer acts to advance the client's objectives without using wrongful means.

TOPIC 3.   VICARIOUS LIABILITY

§58.   Vicarious Liability

(1) A law firm is subject to civil liability for injury legally caused to a person by any wrongful act or omission of any principal or employee

of the firm who was acting in the ordinary course of the firm's business or with actual or apparent authority.

(2) Each of the principals of a law firm organized as a general partnership without limited liability is liable jointly and severally with the firm.

(3) A principal of a law firm organized other than as a general partnership without limited liability as authorized by law is vicariously liable for the acts of another principal or employee of the firm to the extent provided by law.

CHAPTER 5   CONFIDENTIAL CLIENT INFORMATION

TOPIC 1.   CONFIDENTIALITY RESPONSIBILITIES OF LAWYERS

Title A.   Lawyer's Confidentiality Duties

§59.   Definition of "Confidential Client Information"

Confidential client information consists of information relating to representation of a client, other than information that is generally known.

§60.   A Lawyer's Duty to Safeguard Confidential Client Information

(1) Except as provided in §§61-67, during and after representation of a client:

(a) the lawyer may not use or disclose confidential client information as defined in §59 if there is a reasonable prospect that doing so will adversely affect a material interest of the client or if the client has instructed the lawyer not to use or disclose such information;

(b) the lawyer must take steps reasonable in the circumstances to protect confidential client information against impermissible use or disclosure by the lawyer's associates or agents that may adversely affect a material interest of the client or otherwise than as instructed by the client.

(2) Except as stated in §62, a lawyer who uses confidential information of a client for the lawyer's pecuniary gain other than in the practice of law must account to the client for any profits made.

Title B.   Using or Disclosing Confidential Client Information

§61.   Using or Disclosing Information to Advance Client Interests

A lawyer may use or disclose confidential client information when the lawyer reasonably believes that doing so will advance the interests of the client in the representation.

§62. Using or Disclosing Information with Client Consent

A lawyer may use or disclose confidential client information when the client consents after being adequately informed concerning the use or disclosure.

§63. Using or Disclosing Information When Required by Law

A lawyer may use or disclose confidential client information when required by law, after the lawyer takes reasonably appropriate steps to assert that the information is privileged or otherwise protected against disclosure.

§64. Using or Disclosing Information in a Lawyer's Self-Defense

A lawyer may use or disclose confidential client information when and to the extent that the lawyer reasonably believes necessary to defend the lawyer or the lawyer's associate or agent against a charge or threatened charge by any person that the lawyer or such associate or agent acted wrongfully in the course of representing a client.

§65. Using or Disclosing Information in a Compensation Dispute

A lawyer may use or disclose confidential client information when and to the extent that the lawyer reasonably believes necessary to permit the lawyer to resolve a dispute with the client concerning compensation or reimbursement that the lawyer reasonably claims the client owes the lawyer.

§66. Using or Disclosing Information to Prevent Death or Serious Bodily Harm

(1) A lawyer may use or disclose confidential client information when the lawyer reasonably believes that its use or disclosure is necessary to prevent reasonably certain death or serious bodily harm to a person.

(2) Before using or disclosing information under this Section, the lawyer must, if feasible, make a good-faith effort to persuade the client not to act. If the client or another person has already acted, the lawyer must, if feasible, advise the client to warn the victim or to take other action to prevent the harm and advise the client of the lawyer's ability to use or disclose information as provided in this Section and the consequences thereof.

(3) A lawyer who takes action or decides not to take action permitted under this Section is not, solely by reason of such action or inaction, subject

to professional discipline, liable for damages to the lawyer's client or any third person, or barred from recovery against a client or third person.

§67. Using or Disclosing Information to Prevent, Rectify, or Mitigate Substantial Financial Loss

(1) A lawyer may use or disclose confidential client information when the lawyer reasonably believes that its use or disclosure is necessary to prevent a crime or fraud, and:
    (a) the crime or fraud threatens substantial financial loss;
    (b) the loss has not yet occurred;
    (c) the lawyer's client intends to commit the crime or fraud either personally or through a third person; and
    (d) the client has employed or is employing the lawyer's services in the matter in which the crime or fraud is committed.
(2) If a crime or fraud described in Subsection (1) has already occurred, a lawyer may use or disclose confidential client information when the lawyer reasonably believes its use or disclosure is necessary to prevent, rectify, or mitigate the loss.
(3) Before using or disclosing information under this Section, the lawyer must, if feasible, make a good-faith effort to persuade the client not to act. If the client or another person has already acted, the lawyer must, if feasible, advise the client to warn the victim or to take other action to prevent, rectify, or mitigate the loss. The lawyer must, if feasible, also advise the client of the lawyer's ability to use or disclose information as provided in this Section and the consequences thereof.
(4) A lawyer who takes action or decides not to take action permitted under this Section is not, solely by reason of such action or inaction, subject to professional discipline, liable for damages to the lawyer's client or any third person, or barred from recovery against a client or third person.

TOPIC 2.   THE ATTORNEY-CLIENT PRIVILEGE

Title A.   The Scope of the Privilege

§68.   Attorney-Client Privilege

Except as otherwise provided in this Restatement, the attorney-client privilege may be invoked as provided in §86 with respect to:
    (1) a communication
    (2) made between privileged persons
    (3) in confidence
    (4) for the purpose of obtaining or providing legal assistance for the client.

§69. Attorney-Client Privilege — "Communication"

A communication within the meaning of §68 is any expression through which a privileged person, as defined in §70, undertakes to convey information to another privileged person and any document or other record revealing such an expression.

§70. Attorney-Client Privilege — "Privileged Persons"

Privileged persons within the meaning of §68 are the client (including a prospective client), the client's lawyer, agents of either who facilitate communications between them, and agents of the lawyer who facilitate the representation.

§71. Attorney-Client Privilege — "In Confidence"

A communication is in confidence within the meaning of §68 if, at the time and in the circumstances of the communication, the communicating person reasonably believes that no one will learn the contents of the communication except a privileged person as defined in §70 or another person with whom communications are protected under a similar privilege.

§72. Attorney-Client Privilege — Legal Assistance as the Object of a Privileged Communication

A communication is made for the purpose of obtaining or providing legal assistance within the meaning of §68 if it is made to or to assist a person:

(1) who is a lawyer or who the client or prospective client reasonably believes to be a lawyer; and

(2) whom the client or prospective client consults for the purpose of obtaining legal assistance.

Title B.   The Attorney-Client Privilege for Organizational and Multiple Clients

§73. The Privilege for an Organizational Client

When a client is a corporation, unincorporated association, partnership, trust, estate, sole proprietorship, or other for-profit or not-for-profit organization, the attorney-client privilege extends to a communication that:

(1) otherwise qualifies as privileged under §§68-72;

(2) is between an agent of the organization and a privileged person as defined in §70;

(3) concerns a legal matter of interest to the organization; and

(4) is disclosed only to:

    (a) privileged persons as defined in §70; and

    (b) other agents of the organization who reasonably need to know of the communication in order to act for the organization.

§74. The Privilege for a Governmental Client

Unless applicable law otherwise provides, the attorney-client privilege extends to a communication of a governmental organization as stated in §73 and of an individual employee or other agent of a governmental organization as a client with respect to his or her personal interest as stated in §§68-72.

§75. The Privilege of Co-Clients

(1) If two or more persons are jointly represented by the same lawyer in a matter, a communication of either co-client that otherwise qualifies as privileged under §§68-72 and relates to matters of common interest is privileged as against third persons, and any co-client may invoke the privilege, unless it has been waived by the client who made the communication.

(2) Unless the co-clients have agreed otherwise, a communication described in Subsection (1) is not privileged as between the co-clients in a subsequent adverse proceeding between them.

§76. The Privilege in Common-Interest Arrangements

(1) If two or more clients with a common interest in a litigated or nonlitigated matter are represented by separate lawyers and they agree to exchange information concerning the matter, a communication of any such client that otherwise qualifies as privileged under §§68-72 that relates to the matter is privileged as against third persons. Any such client may invoke the privilege, unless it has been waived by the client who made the communication.

(2) Unless the clients have agreed otherwise, a communication described in Subsection (1) is not privileged as between clients described in Subsection (1) in a subsequent adverse proceeding between them.

Title C. *Duration of the Attorney-Client Privilege; Waivers and Exceptions*

§77. Duration of the Privilege

Unless waived (see §§78-80) or subject to exception (see §§81-85), the attorney-client privilege may be invoked as provided in §86 at any time during or after termination of the relationship between client or prospective client and lawyer.

§78. Agreement, Disclaimer, or Failure to Object

The attorney-client privilege is waived if the client, the client's lawyer, or another authorized agent of the client:

(1) agrees to waive the privilege;

(2) disclaims protection of the privilege and

    (a) another person reasonably relies on the disclaimer to that person's detriment; or

    (b) reasons of judicial administration require that the client not be permitted to revoke the disclaimer; or

(3) in a proceeding before a tribunal, fails to object properly to an attempt by another person to give or exact testimony or other evidence of a privileged communication.

§79. Subsequent Disclosure

The attorney-client privilege is waived if the client, the client's lawyer, or another authorized agent of the client voluntarily discloses the communication in a non-privileged communication.

§80. Putting Assistance or a Communication in Issue

(1) The attorney-client privilege is waived for any relevant communication if the client asserts as to a material issue in a proceeding that:

    (a) the client acted upon the advice of a lawyer or that the advice was otherwise relevant to the legal significance of the client's conduct; or

    (b) a lawyer's assistance was ineffective, negligent, or otherwise wrongful.

(2) The attorney-client privilege is waived for a recorded communication if a witness:

    (a) employs the communication to aid the witness while testifying; or

    (b) employed the communication in preparing to testify, and the tribunal finds that disclosure is required in the interests of justice.

§81. Dispute Concerning a Decedent's Disposition of Property

The attorney-client privilege does not apply to a communication from or to a decedent relevant to an issue between parties who claim an interest through the same deceased client, either by testate or intestate succession or by an inter vivos transaction.

§82. Client Crime or Fraud

The attorney-client privilege does not apply to a communication occurring when a client:

(a) consults a lawyer for the purpose, later accomplished, of obtaining assistance to engage in a crime or fraud or aiding a third person to do so, or

(b) regardless of the client's purpose at the time of consultation, uses the lawyer's advice or other services to engage in or assist a crime or fraud.

§83. Lawyer Self-Protection

The attorney-client privilege does not apply to a communication that is relevant and reasonably necessary for a lawyer to employ in a proceeding:

(1) to resolve a dispute with a client concerning compensation or reimbursement that the lawyer reasonably claims the client owes the lawyer; or

(2) to defend the lawyer or the lawyer's associate or agent against a charge by any person that the lawyer, associate, or agent acted wrongfully during the course of representing a client.

§84. Fiduciary-Lawyer Communications

In a proceeding in which a trustee of an express trust or similar fiduciary is charged with breach of fiduciary duties by a beneficiary, a communication otherwise within §68 is nonetheless not privileged if the communication:

(a) is relevant to the claimed breach; and

(b) was between the trustee and a lawyer (or other privileged person within the meaning of §70) who was retained to advise the trustee concerning the administration of the trust.

§85. Communications Involving a Fiduciary Within an Organization

In a proceeding involving a dispute between an organizational client and shareholders, members, or other constituents of the organization toward whom the directors, officers, or similar persons managing the organization bear fiduciary responsibilities, the attorney-client privilege of the organization may be withheld from a communication otherwise within §68 if the tribunal finds that:

(a) those managing the organization are charged with breach of their obligations toward the shareholders, members, or other constituents or toward the organization itself;

(b) the communication occurred prior to the assertion of the charges and relates directly to those charges; and

(c) the need of the requesting party to discover or introduce the communication is sufficiently compelling and the threat to confidentiality sufficiently confined to justify setting the privilege aside.

Title D. Invoking the Privilege and Its Exceptions

§86. Invoking the Privilege and Its Exceptions

(1) When an attempt is made to introduce in evidence or obtain discovery of a communication privileged under §68:

(a) A client, a personal representative of an incompetent or deceased client, or a person succeeding to the interest of a client may invoke or waive the privilege, either personally or through counsel or another authorized agent.

(b) A lawyer, an agent of the lawyer, or an agent of a client from whom a privileged communication is sought must invoke the privilege when doing so appears reasonably appropriate, unless the client:

(i) has waived the privilege; or

(ii) has authorized the lawyer or agent to waive it.

(c) Notwithstanding failure to invoke the privilege as specified in Subsections (1)(a) and (1)(b), the tribunal has discretion to invoke the privilege.

(2) A person invoking the privilege must ordinarily object contemporaneously to an attempt to disclose the communication and, if the objection is contested, demonstrate each element of the privilege under §68.

(3) A person invoking a waiver of or exception to the privilege (§§78-85) must assert it and, if the assertion is contested, demonstrate each element of the waiver or exception.

TOPIC 3.   THE LAWYER WORK-PRODUCT IMMUNITY

Title A.   The Scope of the Lawyer Work-Product Immunity

§87. Lawyer Work-Product Immunity

(1) Work product consists of tangible material or its intangible equivalent in unwritten or oral form, other than underlying facts, prepared by a lawyer for litigation then in progress or in reasonable anticipation of future litigation.

(2) Opinion work product consists of the opinions or mental impressions of a lawyer; all other work product is ordinary work product.

(3) Except for material which by applicable law is not so protected, work product is immune from discovery or other compelled disclosure to the extent stated in §§88 (ordinary work product) and 89 (opinion work product) when the immunity is invoked as described in §90.

§88. Ordinary Work Product

When work product protection is invoked as described in §90, ordinary work product (§87(2)) is immune from discovery or other compelled disclosure unless either an exception recognized in §§91-93 applies or the inquiring party:

(1) has a substantial need for the material in order to prepare for trial; and

(2) is unable without undue hardship to obtain the substantial equivalent of the material by other means.

§89. Opinion Work Product

When work product protection is invoked as described in §90, opinion work product (§87(2)) is immune from discovery or other compelled disclosure unless either the immunity is waived or an exception applies (§§91-93) or extraordinary circumstances justify disclosure.

Title B. Procedural Administration of the Lawyer Work-Product Immunity

§90. Invoking the Lawyer Work-Product Immunity and Its Exceptions

(1) Work-product immunity may be invoked by or for a person on whose behalf the work product was prepared.

(2) The person invoking work-product immunity must object and, if the objection is contested, demonstrate each element of the immunity.

(3) Once a claim of work product has been adequately supported, a person entitled to invoke a waiver or exception must assert it and, if the assertion is contested, demonstrate each element of the waiver or exception.

Title C. Waivers and Exceptions to the Work-Product Immunity

§91. Voluntary Acts

Work-product immunity is waived if the client, the client's lawyer, or another authorized agent of the client:

(1) agrees to waive the immunity;

(2) disclaims protection of the immunity and:

(a) another person reasonably relies on the disclaimer to that person's detriment; or

(b) reasons of judicial administration require that the client not be permitted to revoke the disclaimer; or

(3) in a proceeding before a tribunal, fails to object properly to an attempt by another person to give or exact testimony or other evidence of work product; or

(4) discloses the material to third persons in circumstances in which there is a significant likelihood that an adversary or potential adversary in anticipated litigation will obtain it.

§92. Use of Lawyer Work Product in Litigation

(1) Work-product immunity is waived for any relevant material if the client asserts as to a material issue in a proceeding that:

(a) the client acted upon the advice of a lawyer or that the advice was otherwise relevant to the legal significance of the client's conduct; or

(b) a lawyer's assistance was ineffective, negligent, or otherwise wrongful.

(2) The work-product immunity is waived for recorded material if a witness

(a) employs the material to aid the witness while testifying, or

(b) employed the material in preparing to testify, and the tribunal finds that disclosure is required in the interests of justice.

§93. Client Crime or Fraud

Work-product immunity does not apply to materials prepared when a client consults a lawyer for the purpose, later accomplished, of obtaining assistance to engage in a crime or fraud or to aid a third person to do so or uses the materials for such a purpose.

CHAPTER 6   REPRESENTING CLIENTS—IN GENERAL

TOPIC 1.   LAWYER FUNCTIONS IN REPRESENTING CLIENTS—IN GENERAL

§94. Advising and Assisting a Client — In General

(1) A lawyer who counsels or assists a client to engage in conduct that violates the rights of a third person is subject to liability:

(a) to the third person to the extent stated in §§51 and 56-57; and

(b) to the client to the extent stated in §§50, 55, and 56.

(2) For purposes of professional discipline, a lawyer may not counsel or assist a client in conduct that the lawyer knows to be criminal or fraudulent or in violation of a court order with the intent of facilitating or encouraging the conduct, but the lawyer may counsel or assist a client in conduct when the lawyer reasonably believes:

(a) that the client's conduct constitutes a good-faith effort to determine the validity, scope, meaning, or application of a law or court order; or

(b) that the client can assert a nonfrivolous argument that the client's conduct will not constitute a crime or fraud or violate a court order.

(3) In counseling a client, a lawyer may address non-legal aspects of a proposed course of conduct, including moral, reputational, economic, social, political, and business aspects.

§95. An Evaluation Undertaken for a Third Person

(1) In furtherance of the objectives of a client in a representation, a lawyer may provide to a nonclient the results of the lawyer's investigation and analysis of facts or the lawyer's professional evaluation or opinion on the matter.

(2) When providing the information, evaluation, or opinion under Subsection (1) is reasonably likely to affect the client's interests materially and adversely, the lawyer must first obtain the client's consent after the client is adequately informed concerning important possible effects on the client's interests.

(3) In providing the information, evaluation, or opinion under Subsection (1), the lawyer must exercise care with respect to the nonclient to the extent stated in §51(2) and not make false statements prohibited under §98.

TOPIC 2. REPRESENTING ORGANIZATIONAL CLIENTS

§96. Representing an Organization as Client

(1) When a lawyer is employed or retained to represent an organization:

(a) the lawyer represents the interests of the organization as defined by its responsible agents acting pursuant to the organization's decision-making procedures; and

(b) subject to Subsection (2), the lawyer must follow instructions in the representation, as stated in §21(2), given by persons authorized so to act on behalf of the organization.

(2) If a lawyer representing an organization knows of circumstances indicating that a constituent of the organization has engaged in action or intends to act in a way that violates a legal obligation to the organization that will likely cause substantial injury to it, or that reasonably can be foreseen to be imputable to the organization and likely to result in substantial injury to it, the lawyer must proceed in what the lawyer reasonably believes to be the best interests of the organization.

(3) In the circumstances described in Subsection (2), the lawyer may, in circumstances warranting such steps, ask the constituent to reconsider the matter, recommend that a second legal opinion be sought, and seek review by appropriate supervisory authority within the organization, including referring the matter to the highest authority that can act in behalf of the organization.

§97. Representing a Governmental Client

A lawyer representing a governmental client must proceed in the representation as stated in §96, except that the lawyer:

(1) possesses such rights and responsibilities as may be defined by law to make decisions on behalf of the governmental client that are within the authority of a client under §§22 and 21(2);

(2) except as otherwise provided by law, must proceed as stated in §§96(2) and 96(3) with respect to an act of a constituent of the governmental client that violates a legal obligation that will likely cause substantial public or private injury or that reasonably can be foreseen to be imputable to and thus likely result in substantial injury to the client;

(3) if a prosecutor or similar lawyer determining whether to file criminal proceedings or take other steps in such proceedings, must do so only when based on probable cause and the lawyer's belief, formed after due investigation, that there are good factual and legal grounds to support the step taken; and

(4) must observe other applicable restrictions imposed by law on those similarly functioning for the governmental client.

TOPIC 3.   LAWYER DEALINGS WITH A NONCLIENT

Title A.   Dealings with a Nonclient—Generally

§98.   Statements to a Nonclient

A lawyer communicating on behalf of a client with a nonclient may not:

(1) knowingly make a false statement of material fact or law to the nonclient;

(2) make other statements prohibited by law; or

(3) fail to make a disclosure of information required by law.

Title B.   Contact with a Represented Nonclient

§99.   A Represented Nonclient — The General Anti-Contact Rule

(1) A lawyer representing a client in a matter may not communicate about the subject of the representation with a nonclient whom the lawyer knows to be represented in the matter by another lawyer or with a representative of an organizational nonclient so represented as defined in §100, unless:

(a) the communication is with a public officer or agency to the extent stated in §101;

(b) the lawyer is a party and represents no other client in the matter;

(c) the communication is authorized by law;

(d) the communication reasonably responds to an emergency; or

(e) the other lawyer consents.

(2) Subsection (1) does not prohibit the lawyer from assisting the client in otherwise proper communication by the lawyer's client with a represented nonclient.

§100.   Definition of a Represented Nonclient

Within the meaning of §99, a represented nonclient includes:

(1) a natural person represented by a lawyer; and:

(2) a current employee or other agent of an organization represented by a lawyer:

(a) if the employee or other agent supervises, directs, or regularly consults with the lawyer concerning the matter or if the agent has power to compromise or settle the matter;

(b) if the acts or omissions of the employee or other agent may be imputed to the organization for purposes of civil or criminal liability in the matter; or

(c) if a statement of the employee or other agent, under applicable rules of evidence, would have the effect of binding the organization with respect to proof of the matter.

§101.   A Represented Governmental Agency or Officer

(1) Unless otherwise provided by law (see §99(1)(c)) and except as provided in Subsection (2), the prohibition stated in §99 against contact with a represented nonclient does not apply to communications with employees of a represented governmental agency or with a governmental officer being represented in the officer's official capacity.

(2) In negotiation or litigation by a lawyer of a specific claim of a client against a governmental agency or against a governmental officer in

the officer's official capacity, the prohibition stated in §99 applies, except that the lawyer may contact any officer of the government if permitted by the agency or with respect to an issue of general policy.

§102. Information of a Nonclient Known to Be Legally Protected

A lawyer communicating with a nonclient in a situation permitted under §99 may not seek to obtain information that the lawyer reasonably should know the nonclient may not reveal without violating a duty of confidentiality to another imposed by law.

Title C.   Dealings with an Unrepresented Nonclient

§103. Dealings with an Unrepresented Nonclient

In the course of representing a client and dealing with a nonclient who is not represented by a lawyer:

(1) the lawyer may not mislead the nonclient, to the prejudice of the nonclient, concerning the identity and interests of the person the lawyer represents; and

(2) when the lawyer knows or reasonably should know that the unrepresented nonclient misunderstands the lawyer's role in the matter, the lawyer must make reasonable efforts to correct the misunderstanding when failure to do so would materially prejudice the nonclient.

TOPIC 4. LEGISLATIVE AND ADMINISTRATIVE MATTERS

§104. Representing a Client in Legislative and Administrative Matters

A lawyer representing a client before a legislature or administrative agency:

(1) must disclose that the appearance is in a representative capacity and not misrepresent the capacity in which the lawyer appears;

(2) must comply with applicable law and regulations governing such representations; and

(3) except as applicable law otherwise provides:

(a) in an adjudicative proceeding before a government agency or involving such an agency as a participant, has the legal rights and responsibilities of an advocate in a proceeding before a judicial tribunal; and

(b) in other types of proceedings and matters, has the legal rights and responsibilities applicable in the lawyer's dealings with a private person.

CHAPTER 7   REPRESENTING CLIENTS IN LITIGATION

TOPIC 1.   ADVOCACY IN GENERAL

§105.   Complying with Law and Tribunal Rulings

In representing a client in a matter before a tribunal, a lawyer must comply with applicable law, including rules of procedure and evidence and specific tribunal rulings.

§106.   Dealing with Other Participants in Proceedings

In representing a client in a matter before a tribunal, a lawyer may not use means that have no substantial purpose other than to embarrass, delay, or burden a third person or use methods of obtaining evidence that are prohibited by law.

§107.   Prohibited Forensic Tactics

In representing a client in a matter before a tribunal, a lawyer may not, in the presence of the trier of fact:

(1) state a personal opinion about the justness of a cause, the credibility of a witness, the culpability of a civil litigant, or the guilt or innocence of an accused, but the lawyer may argue any position or conclusion adequately supported by the lawyer's analysis of the evidence; or

(2) allude to any matter that the lawyer does not reasonably believe is relevant or that will not be supported by admissible evidence.

§108.   An Advocate as a Witness

(1) Except as provided in Subsection (2), a lawyer may not represent a client in a contested hearing or trial of a matter in which:

(a) the lawyer is expected to testify for the lawyer's client; or

(b) the lawyer does not intend to testify but (i) the lawyer's testimony would be material to establishing a claim or defense of the client, and (ii) the client has not consented as stated in §122 to the lawyer's intention not to testify.

(2) A lawyer may represent a client when the lawyer will testify as stated in Subsection (1)(a) if:

(a) the lawyer's testimony relates to an issue that the lawyer reasonably believes will not be contested or to the nature and value of legal services rendered in the proceeding;

(b) deprivation of the lawyer's services as advocate would work a substantial hardship on the client; or

(c) consent has been given by

(i) opposing parties who would be adversely affected by the lawyer's testimony and,

(ii) if relevant, the lawyer's client, as stated in §122 with respect to any conflict of interest between lawyer and client (see §125) that the lawyer's testimony would create.

(3) A lawyer may not represent a client in a litigated matter pending before a tribunal when the lawyer or a lawyer in the lawyer's firm will give testimony materially adverse to the position of the lawyer's client or materially adverse to a former client of any such lawyer with respect to a matter substantially related to the earlier representation, unless the affected client has consented as stated in §122 with respect to any conflict of interest between lawyer and client (see §125) that the testimony would create.

(4) A tribunal should not permit a lawyer to call opposing trial counsel as a witness unless there is a compelling need for the lawyer's testimony.

§109. An Advocate's Public Comment on Pending Litigation

(1) In representing a client in a matter before a tribunal, a lawyer may not make a statement outside the proceeding that a reasonable person would expect to be disseminated by means of public communication when the lawyer knows or reasonably should know that the statement will have a substantial likelihood of materially prejudicing a juror or influencing or intimidating a prospective witness in the proceeding. However, a lawyer may in any event make a statement that is reasonably necessary to mitigate the impact on the lawyer's client of substantial, undue, and prejudicial publicity recently initiated by one other than the lawyer or the lawyer's client.

(2) A prosecutor must, except for statements necessary to inform the public of the nature and extent of the prosecutor's action and that serve a legitimate law-enforcement purpose, refrain from making extrajudicial comments that have a substantial likelihood of heightening public condemnation of the accused.

TOPIC 2. LIMITS ON ADVOCACY

§110. Frivolous Advocacy

(1) A lawyer may not bring or defend a proceeding or assert or controvert an issue therein, unless there is a basis for doing so that is not frivolous, which includes a good-faith argument for an extension, modification, or reversal of existing law.

(2) Notwithstanding Subsection (1), a lawyer for the defendant in a criminal proceeding or the respondent in a proceeding that could result in incarceration may so defend the proceeding as to require that the prosecutor establish every necessary element.

(3) A lawyer may not make a frivolous discovery request, fail to make a reasonably diligent effort to comply with a proper discovery request of another party, or intentionally fail otherwise to comply with applicable procedural requirements concerning discovery.

§111. Disclosure of Legal Authority

In representing a client in a matter before a tribunal, a lawyer may not knowingly:

(1) make a false statement of a material proposition of law to the tribunal; or

(2) fail to disclose to the tribunal legal authority in the controlling jurisdiction known to the lawyer to be directly adverse to the position asserted by the client and not disclosed by opposing counsel.

§112. Advocacy in Ex Parte and Other Proceedings

In representing a client in a matter before a tribunal, a lawyer applying for ex parte relief or appearing in another proceeding in which similar special requirements of candor apply must comply with the requirements of §110 and §§118-120 and further:

(1) must not present evidence the lawyer reasonably believes is false;

(2) must disclose all material and relevant facts known to the lawyer that will enable the tribunal to reach an informed decision; and

(3) must comply with any other applicable special requirements of candor imposed by law.

TOPIC 3. ADVOCATES AND TRIBUNALS

§113. Improperly Influencing a Judicial Officer

(1) A lawyer may not knowingly communicate ex parte with a judicial officer before whom a proceeding is pending concerning the matter, except as authorized by law.

(2) A lawyer may not make a gift or loan prohibited by law to a judicial officer, attempt to influence the officer otherwise than by legally proper procedures, or state or imply an ability so to influence a judicial officer.

§114.   A Lawyer's Statements Concerning a Judicial Officer

A lawyer may not knowingly or recklessly make publicly a false statement of fact concerning the qualifications or integrity of an incumbent of a judicial office or a candidate for election to such an office.

§115.   Lawyer Contact with a Juror

A lawyer may not:

(1) except as allowed by law, communicate with or seek to influence a person known by the lawyer to be a member of a jury pool from which the jury will be drawn;

(2) except as allowed by law, communicate with or seek to influence a member of a jury; or

(3) communicate with a juror who has been excused from further service:

(a) when that would harass the juror or constitute an attempt to influence the juror's actions as a juror in future cases; or

(b) when otherwise prohibited by law.

TOPIC 4.   ADVOCATES AND EVIDENCE

§116.   Interviewing and Preparing a Prospective Witness

(1) A lawyer may interview a witness for the purpose of preparing the witness to testify.

(2) A lawyer may not unlawfully obstruct another party's access to a witness.

(3) A lawyer may not unlawfully induce or assist a prospective witness to evade or ignore process obliging the witness to appear to testify.

(4) A lawyer may not request a person to refrain from voluntarily giving relevant testimony or information to another party, unless:

(a) the person is the lawyer's client in the matter; or

(b)(i) the person is not the lawyer's client but is a relative or employee or other agent of the lawyer or the lawyer's client, and (ii) the lawyer reasonably believes compliance will not materially and adversely affect the person's interests.

§117.   Compensating a Witness

A lawyer may not offer or pay to a witness any consideration:

(1) in excess of the reasonable expenses of the witness incurred and the reasonable value of the witness's time spent in providing evidence,

except that an expert witness may be offered and paid a noncontingent fee;

(2) contingent on the content of the witness's testimony or the outcome of the litigation; or

(3) otherwise prohibited by law.

§118. Falsifying or Destroying Evidence

(1) A lawyer may not falsify documentary or other evidence.

(2) A lawyer may not destroy or obstruct another party's access to documentary or other evidence when doing so would violate a court order or other legal requirements, or counsel or assist a client to do so.

§119. Physical Evidence of a Client Crime

With respect to physical evidence of a client crime, a lawyer:

(1) may, when reasonably necessary for purposes of the representation, take possession of the evidence and retain it for the time reasonably necessary to examine it and subject it to tests that do not alter or destroy material characteristics of the evidence; but

(2) following possession under Subsection (1), the lawyer must notify prosecuting authorities of the lawyer's possession of the evidence or turn the evidence over to them.

§120. False Testimony or Evidence

(1) A lawyer may not:

(a) knowingly counsel or assist a witness to testify falsely or otherwise to offer false evidence;

(b) knowingly make a false statement of fact to the tribunal;

(c) offer testimony or other evidence as to an issue of fact known by the lawyer to be false.

(2) If a lawyer has offered testimony or other evidence as to a material issue of fact and comes to know of its falsity, the lawyer must take reasonable remedial measures and may disclose confidential client information when necessary to take such a measure.

(3) A lawyer may refuse to offer testimony or other evidence that the lawyer reasonably believes is false, even if the lawyer does not know it to be false.

CHAPTER 8   CONFLICTS OF INTEREST

TOPIC 1.   CONFLICTS OF INTEREST—IN GENERAL

§121.   The Basic Prohibition of Conflicts of Interest

Unless all affected clients and other necessary persons consent to the representation under the limitations and conditions provided in §122, a lawyer may not represent a client if the representation would involve a conflict of interest. A conflict of interest is involved if there is a substantial risk that the lawyer's representation of the client would be materially and adversely affected by the lawyer's own interests or by the lawyer's duties to another current client, a former client, or a third person.

§122.   Client Consent to a Conflict of Interest

(1) A lawyer may represent a client notwithstanding a conflict of interest prohibited by §121 if each affected client or former client gives informed consent to the lawyer's representation. Informed consent requires that the client or former client have reasonably adequate information about the material risks of such representation to that client or former client.

(2) Notwithstanding the informed consent of each affected client or former client, a lawyer may not represent a client if:

(a) the representation is prohibited by law;

(b) one client will assert a claim against the other in the same litigation; or

(c) in the circumstances, it is not reasonably likely that the lawyer will be able to provide adequate representation to one or more of the clients.

§123.   Imputation of a Conflict of Interest to an Affiliated Lawyer

Unless all affected clients consent to the representation under the limitations and conditions provided in §122 or unless imputation hereunder is removed as provided in §124, the restrictions upon a lawyer imposed by §§125-135 also restrict other affiliated lawyers who:

(1) are associated with that lawyer in rendering legal services to others through a law partnership, professional corporation, sole proprietorship, or similar association;

(2) are employed with that lawyer by an organization to render legal services either to that organization or to others to advance the interests or objectives of the organization; or

(3) share office facilities without reasonably adequate measures to protect confidential client information so that it will not be available to other lawyers in the shared office.

§124. Removing Imputation

(1) Imputation specified in §123 does not restrict an affiliated lawyer when the affiliation between the affiliated lawyer and the personally prohibited lawyer that required the imputation has been terminated, and no material confidential information of the client, relevant to the matter, has been communicated by the personally prohibited lawyer to the affiliated lawyer or that lawyer's firm.

(2) Imputation specified in §123 does not restrict an affiliated lawyer with respect to a former-client conflict under §132, when there is no substantial risk that confidential information of the former client will be used with material adverse effect on the former client because:

(a) any confidential client information communicated to the personally prohibited lawyer is unlikely to be significant in the subsequent matter;

(b) the personally prohibited lawyer is subject to screening measures adequate to eliminate participation by that lawyer in the representation; and

(c) timely and adequate notice of the screening has been provided to all affected clients.

(3) Imputation specified in §123 does not restrict a lawyer affiliated with a former government lawyer with respect to a conflict under §133 if:

(a) the personally prohibited lawyer is subject to screening measures adequate to eliminate involvement by that lawyer in the representation; and

(b) timely and adequate notice of the screening has been provided to the appropriate government agency and to affected clients.

TOPIC 2. CONFLICTS OF INTEREST BETWEEN A LAWYER AND A CLIENT

§125. A Lawyer's Personal Interest Affecting the Representation of a Client

Unless the affected client consents to the representation under the limitations and conditions provided in §122, a lawyer may not represent a client if there is a substantial risk that the lawyer's representation of the client would be materially and adversely affected by the lawyer's financial or other personal interests.

§126. Business Transactions Between a Lawyer and a Client

A lawyer may not participate in a business or financial transaction with a client, except a standard commercial transaction in which the lawyer does not render legal services, unless:

(1) the client has adequate information about the terms of the transaction and the risks presented by the lawyer's involvement in it;

(2) the terms and circumstances of the transaction are fair and reasonable to the client; and

(3) the client consents to the lawyer's role in the transaction under the limitations and conditions provided in §122 after being encouraged, and given a reasonable opportunity, to seek independent legal advice concerning the transaction.

§127. A Client Gift to a Lawyer

(1) A lawyer may not prepare any instrument effecting any gift from a client to the lawyer, including a testamentary gift, unless the lawyer is a relative or other natural object of the client's generosity and the gift is not significantly disproportionate to those given other donees similarly related to the donor.

(2) A lawyer may not accept a gift from a client, including a testamentary gift, unless:

(a) the lawyer is a relative or other natural object of the client's generosity;

(b) the value conferred by the client and the benefit to the lawyer are insubstantial in amount; or

(c) the client, before making the gift, has received independent advice or has been encouraged, and given a reasonable opportunity, to seek such advice.

TOPIC 3.   CONFLICTS OF INTEREST AMONG CURRENT CLIENTS

§128.   Representing Clients with Conflicting Interests in Civil Litigation

Unless all affected clients consent to the representation under the limitations and conditions provided in §122, a lawyer in civil litigation may not:

(1) represent two or more clients in a matter if there is a substantial risk that the lawyer's representation of one client would be materially and adversely affected by the lawyer's duties to another client in the matter; or

(2) represent one client to assert or defend a claim against or brought by another client currently represented by the lawyer, even if the matters are not related.

§129. Conflicts of Interest in Criminal Litigation

Unless all affected clients consent to the representation under the limitations and conditions provided in §122, a lawyer in a criminal matter may not represent:

(1) two or more defendants or potential defendants in the same matter; or

(2) a single defendant, if the representation would involve a conflict of interest as defined in §121.

§130. Multiple Representation in a Nonlitigated Matter

Unless all affected clients consent to the representation under the limitations and conditions provided in §122, a lawyer may not represent two or more clients in a matter not involving litigation if there is a substantial risk that the lawyer's representation of one or more of the clients would be materially and adversely affected by the lawyer's duties to one or more of the other clients.

§131. Conflicts of Interest in Representing an Organization

Unless all affected clients consent to the representation under the limitations and conditions provided in §122, a lawyer may not represent both an organization and a director, officer, employee, shareholder, owner, partner, member, or other individual or organization associated with the organization if there is a substantial risk that the lawyer's representation of either would be materially and adversely affected by the lawyer's duties to the other.

TOPIC 4. CONFLICTS OF INTEREST WITH A FORMER CLIENT

§132. A Representation Adverse to the Interests of a Former Client

Unless both the affected present and former clients consent to the representation under the limitations and conditions provided in §122, a lawyer who has represented a client in a matter may not thereafter represent another client in the same or a substantially related matter in which the interests of the former client are materially adverse. The current matter is substantially related to the earlier matter if:

(1) the current matter involves the work the lawyer performed for the former client; or

(2) there is a substantial risk that representation of the present client will involve the use of information acquired in the course of representing the former client, unless that information has become generally known.

§133. A Former Government Lawyer or Officer

(1) A lawyer may not act on behalf of a client with respect to a matter in which the lawyer participated personally and substantially while acting as a government lawyer or officer unless both the government and the client consent to the representation under the limitations and conditions provided in §122.

(2) A lawyer who acquires confidential information while acting as a government lawyer or officer may not:

(a) if the information concerns a person, represent a client whose interests are materially adverse to that person in a matter in which the information could be used to the material disadvantage of that person; or

(b) if the information concerns the governmental client or employer, represent another public or private client in circumstances described in §132(2).

TOPIC 5. CONFLICTS OF INTEREST DUE TO A LAWYER'S OBLIGATION TO A THIRD PERSON

§134. Compensation or Direction of a Lawyer by a Third Person

(1) A lawyer may not represent a client if someone other than the client will wholly or partly compensate the lawyer for the representation, unless the client consents under the limitations and conditions provided in §122 and knows of the circumstances and conditions of the payment.

(2) A lawyer's professional conduct on behalf of a client may be directed by someone other than the client if:

(a) the direction does not interfere with the lawyer's independence of professional judgment;

(b) the direction is reasonable in scope and character, such as by reflecting obligations borne by the person directing the lawyer; and

(c) the client consents to the direction under the limitations and conditions provided in §122.

§135. A Lawyer with a Fiduciary or Other Legal Obligation to a Nonclient

Unless the affected client consents to the representation under the limitations and conditions provided in §122, a lawyer may not represent a client in any matter with respect to which the lawyer has a fiduciary or other legal obligation to another if there is a substantial risk that the lawyer's representation of the client would be materially and adversely affected by the lawyer's obligation.

ABA Model Code of
Professional Responsibility*
(In effect from
August 1969 until August 1983)

Editors' Introduction. From 1908 to 1969, the ABA's formal position on matters of legal ethics was embodied in the ABA's Canons of Professional Ethics. In 1964, however, amidst growing dissatisfaction with the Canons, the ABA appointed a Special Committee on the Evaluation of Ethical Standards (the "Wright Committee") to study the Canons. The Wright Committee drafted a proposed Code of Professional Responsibility, which was ultimately approved by the ABA House of Delegates in August 1969.

By 1980, nearly every state had adopted a Code of Professional Responsibility modeled on the ABA Code. The Code of Professional Responsibility consists of a Preamble, a Preliminary Statement, nine "Canons" (which essentially divide the rules into chapters, much like the Article headings do in the ABA Model Rules of Professional Conduct), and a set of Definitions. Each Canon consists of three parts: (i) an overarching heading (a "Canon") stating one of the "axiomatic norms" of the profession; (ii) a non-binding series of "aspirational" Ethical Considerations (ECs); and (iii) a binding set of "mandatory" Disciplinary Rules (DRs). The "Preliminary Statement" immediately following the Preamble to the Code explains the three parts this way:

> The Canons are statements of axiomatic norms, expressing in general terms the standards of professional conduct expected of lawyers in their relationships with the public, with the legal system, and with the legal profession. They embody the general concepts from which the Ethical Considerations and the Disciplinary Rules are derived.
>
> The Ethical Considerations are aspirational in character and represent the objectives toward which every member of the profession should strive. They constitute

a body of principles upon which the lawyer can rely for guidance in many specific situations.

The Disciplinary Rules, unlike the Ethical Considerations, are mandatory in character. The Disciplinary Rules state the minimum level of conduct below which no lawyer can fall without being subject to disciplinary action. . . .

In 1983, the ABA replaced the Model Code with the Model Rules of Professional Conduct. Since then, every U.S. jurisdiction has revised its ethical rules to conform, in some degree, to the ABA Model Rules. Today, no state uses the Model Code's format or numbering system. Many of the Model Rules, however, closely parallel their counterparts in the Model Code. To relate the Disciplinary Rules in the Model Code to comparable provisions in the ABA Model Rules, we have included a "Model Rules Comparison" table after each Canon of the ABA Model Code of Professional Responsibility. (Readers who want to go in the other direction, locating the Disciplinary Rules comparable to each Model Rule of Professional Conduct, should see our "Canon and Code Antecedents" in our Annotations on the ABA Model Rules of Professional Conduct earlier in this book.)

The Model Code was amended seven times during the 1970s, principally in response to landmark Supreme Court opinions holding that lawyers had the constitutional right to advertise and to participate in group legal services. The version of the Model Code reprinted below is the 1980 version of the Code, which remained in effect until the ABA adopted the Model Rules of Professional Conduct in August 1983. Because the ABA has not amended the Model Code in more than three decades, and because no state still uses the Code format, we reprint only the Preamble, the Preliminary Statement, the Canons, the Disciplinary Rules, and the Definitions. We omit all footnotes (whose main purpose was to relate the Code to the old ABA Canons of Professional Ethics), and we omit all Ethical Considerations (which are lengthy and non-binding). The full ABA Model Code of Professional Responsibility is available online at *http://www.americanbar.org/content/dam/aba/migrated/cpr/mrpc/mcpr.authcheckdam.pdf.*

Contents

PREAMBLE

The continued existence of a free and democratic society depends upon recognition of the concept that justice is based upon the rule of law grounded in respect for the dignity of the individual and his capacity through reason for enlightened self-government. Law so grounded makes justice possible, for only through such law does the dignity of the individual attain respect and protection. Without it, individual rights become subject to unrestrained power, respect for law is destroyed, and rational self-government is impossible.

Lawyers, as guardians of the law, play a vital role in the preservation of society. The fulfillment of this role requires an understanding by lawyers of their relationship with and function in our legal system. A consequent obligation of lawyers is to maintain the highest standards of ethical conduct.

In fulfilling his professional responsibilities, a lawyer necessarily assumes various roles that require the performance of many difficult tasks. Not every situation which he may encounter can be foreseen, but fundamental ethical principles are always present to guide him. Within the framework of these principles, a lawyer must with courage and foresight be able and ready to shape the body of the law to the ever-changing relationships of society.

The Model Code of Professional Responsibility points the way to the aspiring and provides standards by which to judge the transgressor. Each lawyer must find within his own conscience the touchstone against which to test the extent to which his actions should rise above minimum standards. But in the last analysis it is the desire for the respect and confidence of the members of his profession and of the society which he serves that should provide to a lawyer the incentive for the highest possible degree of ethical conduct. The possible loss of that respect and confidence is the ultimate sanction. So long as its practitioners are guided by these principles, the law will continue to be a noble profession. This is its greatness and its strength, which permit of no compromise.

PRELIMINARY STATEMENT

In furtherance of the principles stated in the Preamble, the American Bar Association has promulgated this Model Code of Professional Responsibility, consisting of three separate but interrelated parts: Canons, Ethical Considerations, and Disciplinary Rules. The Model Code is designed to be adopted by appropriate agencies both as an inspirational guide to the members of the profession and as a basis for disciplinary action when the conduct of a lawyer falls below the required minimum standards stated in the Disciplinary Rules.

Obviously the Canons, Ethical Considerations, and Disciplinary Rules cannot apply to non-lawyers; however, they do define the type of ethical conduct that the public has a right to expect not only of lawyers but also of their non-professional employees and associates in all matters pertaining to professional employment. A lawyer should ultimately be responsible for the conduct of his employees and associates in the course of the professional representation of the client.

The Canons are statements of axiomatic norms, expressing in general terms the standards of professional conduct expected of lawyers in their relationships with the public, with the legal system, and with the legal profession. They embody the general concepts from which the Ethical Considerations and the Disciplinary Rules are derived.

The Ethical Considerations are aspirational in character and represent the objectives toward which every member of the profession should strive. They constitute a body of principles upon which the lawyer can rely for guidance in many specific situations.

The Disciplinary Rules, unlike the Ethical Considerations, are mandatory in character. The Disciplinary Rules state the minimum level of conduct below which no lawyer can fall without being subject to disciplinary action. Within the framework of fair trial, the Disciplinary Rules should be uniformly applied to all lawyers, regardless of the nature of their professional activities. The Model Code makes no attempt to prescribe either disciplinary procedures or penalties for violation of a Disciplinary Rule, nor does it undertake to define standards for civil liability of lawyers for professional conduct. The severity of judgment against one found guilty of violating a Disciplinary Rule should be determined by the character of the offense and the attendant circumstances. An enforcing agency, in applying the Disciplinary Rules, may find interpretive guidance in the basic principles embodied in the Canons and in the objectives reflected in the Ethical Considerations.

CANON 1.   A LAWYER SHOULD ASSIST IN MAINTAINING THE INTEGRITY AND COMPETENCE OF THE LEGAL PROFESSION

DR 1-101   Maintaining Integrity and Competence of the Legal Profession

(A) A lawyer is subject to discipline if he has made a materially false statement in, or if he has deliberately failed to disclose a material fact requested in connection with, his application for admission to the bar.

613

(B) A lawyer shall not further the application for admission to the bar of another person known by him to be unqualified in respect to character, education, or other relevant attribute.

DR 1-102   Misconduct

(A) A lawyer shall not:

(1) Violate a Disciplinary Rule.

(2) Circumvent a Disciplinary Rule through actions of another.

(3) Engage in illegal conduct involving moral turpitude.

(4) Engage in conduct involving dishonesty, fraud, deceit, or misrepresentation.

(5) Engage in conduct that is prejudicial to the administration of justice.

(6) Engage in any other conduct that adversely reflects on his fitness to practice law.

DR 1-103   Disclosure of Information to Authorities

(A) A lawyer possessing unprivileged knowledge of a violation of DR 1-102 shall report such knowledge to a tribunal or other authority empowered to investigate or act upon such violation.

(B) A lawyer possessing unprivileged knowledge or evidence concerning another lawyer or a judge shall reveal fully such knowledge or evidence upon proper request of a tribunal or other authority empowered to investigate or act upon the conduct of lawyers or judges.

Model Rules Comparison

Model Code	ABA Model Rules	Model Code	ABA Model Rules
DR 1-101	8.1(a)	DR 1-102(A)(5)	3.1 through 3.9,
DR 1-102(A)(1)	8.4(a)		8.1, 8.4(d) & (f)
DR 1-102(A)(2)	5.1(c), 5.3(b), 8.4(a)	DR 1-102(A)(6)	3.4(b), 8.4
DR 1-102(A)(3)	8.4(b), (f)	DR 1-103(A)	5.1, 8.3
DR 1-102(A)(4)	3.3(a), 3.4(a) &(b), 4.1, 8.4(c)	DR 1-103(B)	8.1(b)

CANON 2.   A LAWYER SHOULD ASSIST THE LEGAL PROFESSION IN FULFILLING ITS DUTY TO MAKE LEGAL COUNSEL AVAILABLE

DR 2-101   Publicity

(A) lawyer shall not, on behalf of himself, his partner, associate or any other lawyer affiliated with him or his firm, use or participate in the use of any form of public communication containing a false, fraudulent, misleading, deceptive, self-laudatory or unfair statement or claim.

(B) In order to facilitate the process of informed selection of a lawyer by potential consumers of legal services, a lawyer may publish or broadcast, subject to DR 2-103, the following information in print media distributed or over television or radio broadcast in the geographic area or areas in which the lawyer resides or maintains offices or in which a significant part of the lawyer's clientele resides, provided that the information disclosed by the lawyer in such publication or broadcast complies with DR 2-101(A), and is presented in a dignified manner:

(1) Name, including name of law firm and names of professional associates; addresses and telephone numbers;

(2) One or more fields of law in which the lawyer or law firm practices, a statement that practice is limited to one or more fields of law, or a statement that the lawyer or law firm specializes in a particular field of law practice, to the extent authorized under DR 2-105;

(3) Date and place of birth;

(4) Date and place of admission to the bar of state and federal courts;

(5) Schools attended, with dates of graduation, degrees and other scholastic distinctions;

(6) Public or quasi-public offices;

(7) Military service;

(8) Legal authorships;

(9) Legal teaching positions;

(10) Memberships, offices, and committee assignments, in bar associations;

(11) Membership and offices in legal fraternities and legal societies;

(12) Technical and professional licenses;

(13) Memberships in scientific, technical and professional associations and societies;

(14) Foreign language ability;

(15) Names and addresses of bank references;

(16) With their written consent, names of clients regularly represented;

(17) Prepaid or group legal services programs in which the lawyer participates;

(18) Whether credit cards or other credit arrangements are accepted;

(19) Office and telephone answering service hours;

(20) Fee for an initial consultation;

(21) Availability upon request of a written schedule of fees and/or an estimate of the fee to be charged for specific services;

(22) Contingent fee rates subject to DR 2-106(C), provided that the statement discloses whether percentages are computed before or after deduction of costs;

(23) Range of fees for services, provided that the statement discloses that the specific fee within the range which will be charged will vary depending upon the particular matter to be handled for each client and the client is entitled without obligation to an estimate of the fee within the range likely to be charged, in print size equivalent to the largest print used in setting forth the fee information;

(24) Hourly rate, provided that the statement discloses that the total fee charged will depend upon the number of hours which must be devoted to the particular matter to be handled for each client and the client is entitled to without obligation an estimate of the fee likely to be charged, in print size at least equivalent to the largest print used in setting forth the fee information;

(25) Fixed fees for specific legal services, the description of which would not be misunderstood or be deceptive, provided that the statement discloses that the quoted fee will be available only to clients whose matters fall into the services described and that the client is entitled without obligation to a specific estimate of the fee likely to be charged in print size at least equivalent to the largest print used in setting forth the fee information.

(C) Any person desiring to expand the information authorized for disclosure in DR 2-101(B), or to provide for its dissemination through other forums may apply to [the agency having jurisdiction under state law]. Any such application shall be served upon [the agencies having jurisdiction under state law over the regulation of the legal profession and consumer matters] who shall be heard, together with the applicant, on the issue of whether the proposal is necessary in light of the existing provisions of the Code, accords with standards of accuracy, reliability and truthfulness, and would facilitate the process of informed selection of lawyers by potential consumers of legal services. The relief granted in response to any such application shall be promulgated as an amendment to DR 2-101(B), universally applicable to all lawyers.

(D) If the advertisement is communicated to the public over television or radio, it shall be prerecorded, approved for broadcast by the lawyer, and a recording of the actual transmission shall be retained by the lawyer.

(E) If a lawyer advertises a fee for a service, the lawyer must render that service for no more than the fee advertised.

(F) Unless otherwise specified in the advertisement if a lawyer publishes any fee information authorized under DR 2-101(B) in a publication that is published more frequently than one time per month, the lawyer shall be bound by any representation made therein for a period of not less than 30 days after such publication. If a lawyer publishes any fee information authorized under DR 2-101(B) in a publication that is published once a month or less frequently, he shall be bound by any representation made therein until the publication of the succeeding issue. If a lawyer publishes any fee information authorized under DR 2-101(B) in a publication which has no fixed date for publication of a succeeding issue, the lawyer shall be bound by any representation made therein for a reasonable period of time after publication but in no event less than one year.

(G) Unless otherwise specified, if a lawyer broadcasts any fee information authorized under DR 2-101(B), the lawyer shall be bound by any representation made therein for a period of not less than 30 days after such broadcast.

(H) This rule does not prohibit limited and dignified identification of a lawyer as a lawyer as well as by name:

(1) In political advertisements when his professional status is germane to the political campaign or to a political issue.

(2) In public notices when the name and profession of a lawyer are required or authorized by law or are reasonably pertinent for a purpose other than the attraction of potential clients.

(3) In routine reports and announcements of a bona fide business, civic, professional, or political organization in which he serves as a director or officer.

(4) In and on legal documents prepared by him.

(5) In and on legal textbooks, treatises, and other legal publications, and in dignified advertisements thereof.

(I) A lawyer shall not compensate or give any thing of value to representatives of the press, radio, television, or other communication medium in anticipation of or in return for professional publicity in a news item.

DR 2-102   Professional Notices, Letterheads and Offices

(A) A lawyer or law firm shall not use or participate in the use of professional cards, professional announcement cards, office signs, letterheads, or similar professional notices or devices, except that the following may be used if they are in dignified form:

(1) A professional card of a lawyer identifying him by name and as a lawyer, and giving his addresses, telephone numbers, the name of his law firm, and any information permitted under DR 2-105. A professional card of a law firm may also give the names of members and associates. Such cards may be used for identification.

(2) A brief professional announcement card stating new or changed associations or addresses, change of firm name, or similar matters pertaining to the professional offices of a lawyer or law firm,

which may be mailed to lawyers, clients, former clients, personal friends, and relatives. It shall not state biographical data except to the extent reasonably necessary to identify the lawyer or to explain the change in his association, but it may state the immediate past position of the lawyer. It may give the names and dates of predecessor firms in a continuing line of succession. It shall not state the nature of the practice except as permitted under DR 2-105.

(3) A sign on or near the door of the office and in the building directory identifying the law office. The sign shall not state the nature of the practice, except as permitted under DR 2-105.

(4) A letterhead of a lawyer identifying him by name and as a lawyer, and giving his addresses, telephone numbers, the name of his law firm, associates and any information permitted under DR 2-105. A letterhead of a law firm may also give the names of members and associates, and names and dates relating to deceased and retired members. A lawyer may be designated "Of Counsel" on a letterhead if he has a continuing relationship with a lawyer or law firm, other than as a partner or associate. A lawyer or law firm may be designated as "General Counsel" or by similar professional reference on stationery of a client if he or the firm devotes a substantial amount of professional time in the representation of that client. The letterhead of a law firm may give the names and dates of predecessor firms in a continuing line of succession.

(B) A lawyer in private practice shall not practice under a trade name, a name that is misleading as to the identity of the lawyer or lawyers practicing under such name, or a firm name containing names other than those of one or more of the lawyers in the firm, except that the name of a professional corporation or professional association may contain "P.C." or "P.A." or similar symbols indicating the nature of the organization, and if otherwise lawful a firm may use as, or continue to include in, its name the name or names of one or more deceased or retired members of the firm or of a predecessor firm in a continuing line of succession. A lawyer who assumes a judicial, legislative, or public executive or administrative post or office shall not permit his name to remain in the name of a law firm or to be used in professional notices of the firm during any significant period in which he is not actively and regularly practicing law as a member of the firm, and during such period other members of the firm shall not use his name in the firm name or in professional notices of the firm.

(C) A lawyer shall not hold himself out as having a partnership with one or more other lawyers or professional corporations unless they are in fact partners.

(D) A partnership shall not be formed or continued between or among lawyers licensed in different jurisdictions unless all enumerations of the members and associates of the firm on its letterhead and in other permissible listings make clear the jurisdictional limitations on those members and associates of the firm not licensed to practice in all listed jurisdictions; however, the same firm name may be used in each jurisdiction.

(E) Nothing contained herein shall prohibit a lawyer from using or permitting the use of, in connection with his name, an earned degree or title derived therefrom indicating his training in the law.

DR 2-103   Recommendation of Professional Employment

(A) A lawyer shall not, except as authorized in DR 2-101(B), recommend employment as a private practitioner, of himself, his partner, or associate to a layperson who has not sought his advice regarding employment of a lawyer.

(B) A lawyer shall not compensate or give anything of value to a person or organization to recommend or secure his employment by a client, or as a reward for having made a recommendation resulting in his employment by a client, except that he may pay the usual and reasonable fees or dues charged by any of the organizations listed in DR 2-103(D).

(C) A lawyer shall not request a person or organization to recommend or promote the use of his services or those of his partner or associate, or any other lawyer affiliated with him or his firm, as a private practitioner, except as authorized in DR 2-101, and except that

(1) He may request referrals from a lawyer referral service operated, sponsored, or approved by a bar association and may pay its fees incident thereto.

(2) He may cooperate with the legal service activities of any of the offices or organizations enumerated in DR 2-103(D)(1) through (4) and may perform legal services for those to whom he was recommended by it to do such work if:

(a) The person to whom the recommendation is made is a member or beneficiary of such office or organization; and

(b) The lawyer remains free to exercise his independent professional judgment on behalf of his client.

(D) A lawyer or his partner or associate or any other lawyer affiliated with him or his firm may be recommended, employed or paid by, or may cooperate with, one of the following offices or organizations that promote the use of his services or those of his partner or associate or any other lawyer affiliated with him or his firm if there is no interference with the exercise of independent professional judgment in behalf of his client:

(1) A legal aid office or public defender office:

(a) Operated or sponsored by a duly accredited law school.

(b) Operated or sponsored by a bona fide nonprofit community organization.

(c) Operated or sponsored by a governmental agency.

(d) Operated, sponsored, or approved by a bar association.

(2) A military legal assistance office.

(3) A lawyer referral service operated, sponsored, or approved by a bar association.

(4) Any bona fide organization that recommends, furnishes or pays for legal services to its members or beneficiaries provided the following conditions are satisfied:

(a) Such organization, including any affiliate, is so organized and operated that no profit is derived by it from the rendition of legal services by lawyers, and that, if the organization is organized for profit, the legal services are not rendered by lawyers employed, directed, supervised or selected by it except in connection with matters where such organization bears ultimate liability of its member or beneficiary.

(b) Neither the lawyer, nor his partner, nor associate, nor any other lawyer affiliated with him or his firm, nor any non-lawyer, shall have initiated or promoted such organization for the primary purpose of providing financial or other benefit to such lawyer, partner, associate or affiliated lawyer.

(c) Such organization is not operated for the purpose of procuring legal work or financial benefit for any lawyer as a private practitioner outside of the legal services program of the organization.

(d) The member or beneficiary to whom the legal services are furnished, and not such organization, is recognized as the client of the lawyer in the matter.

(e) Any member or beneficiary who is entitled to have legal services furnished or paid for by the organization may, if such member or beneficiary so desires, select counsel other than that furnished, selected or approved by the organization for the particular matter involved; and the legal service plan of such organization provides appropriate relief for any member or beneficiary who asserts a claim that representation by counsel furnished, selected or approved would be unethical, improper or inadequate under the circumstances of the matter involved and the plan provides an appropriate procedure for seeking such relief.

(f) The lawyer does not know or have cause to know that such organization is in violation of applicable laws, rules of court and other legal requirements that govern its legal service operations.

(g) Such organization has filed with the appropriate disciplinary authority at least annually a report with respect to its legal service plan, if any, showing its terms, its schedule of benefits, its subscription charges, agreements with counsel, and financial results of its legal service activities or, if it has failed to do so, the lawyer does not know or have cause to know of such failure.

(E) A lawyer shall not accept employment when he knows or it is obvious that the person who seeks his services does so as a result of conduct prohibited under this Disciplinary Rule.

DR 2-104   Suggestion of Need of Legal Services

(A) A lawyer who has given in-person unsolicited advice to a layperson that he should obtain counsel or take legal action shall not accept employment resulting from that advice, except that:

(1) A lawyer may accept employment by a close friend, relative, former client (if the advice is germane to the former employment), or one whom the lawyer reasonably believes to be a client.

(2) A lawyer may accept employment that results from his participation in activities designed to educate laypersons to recognize legal problems, to make intelligent selection of counsel, or to utilize available legal services if such activities are conducted or sponsored by a qualified legal assistance organization.

(3) A lawyer who is recommended, furnished or paid by a qualified legal assistance organization enumerated in DR 2-103(D)(1) through (4) may represent a member or beneficiary thereof, to the extent and under the conditions prescribed therein.

(4) Without affecting his right to accept employment, a lawyer may speak publicly or write for publication on legal topics so long as he does not emphasize his own professional experience or reputation and does not undertake to give individual advice.

(5) If success in asserting rights or defenses of his client in litigation in the nature of a class action is dependent upon the joinder of others, a lawyer may accept, but shall not seek, employment from those contacted for the purpose of obtaining their joinder.

DR 2-105   Limitation of Practice

(A) A lawyer shall not hold himself out publicly as a specialist, as practicing in certain areas of law or as limiting his practice permitted under DR 2-101(B), except as follows:

(1) A lawyer admitted to practice before the United States Patent and Trademark Office may use the designation "Patents," "Patent Attorney," "Patent Lawyer," or "Registered Patent Attorney" or any combination of those terms, on his letterhead and office sign.

(2) A lawyer who publicly discloses fields of law in which the lawyer or the law firm practices or states that his practice is limited to

one or more fields of law shall do so by using designations and definitions authorized and approved by [the agency having jurisdiction of the subject under state law].

(3) A lawyer who is certified as a specialist in a particular field of law or law practice by [the authority having jurisdiction under state law over the subject of specialization by lawyers] may hold himself out as such, but only in accordance with the rules prescribed by that authority.

DR 2-106   Fees for Legal Services

(A) A lawyer shall not enter into an agreement for, charge, or collect an illegal or clearly excessive fee.

(B) A fee is clearly excessive when, after a review of the facts, a lawyer of ordinary prudence would be left with a definite and firm conviction that the fee is in excess of a reasonable fee. Factors to be considered as guides in determining the reasonableness of a fee include the following:

(1) The time and labor required, the novelty and difficulty of the questions involved, and the skill requisite to perform the legal service properly.

(2) The likelihood, if apparent to the client, that the acceptance of the particular employment will preclude other employment by the lawyer.

(3) The fee customarily charged in the locality for similar legal services.

(4) The amount involved and the results obtained.

(5) The time limitations imposed by the client or by the circumstances.

(6) The nature and length of the professional relationship with the client.

(7) The experience, reputation, and ability of the lawyer or lawyers performing the services.

(8) Whether the fee is fixed or contingent.

(C) A lawyer shall not enter into an arrangement for, charge, or collect a contingent fee for representing a defendant in a criminal case.

DR 2-107   Division of Fees Among Lawyers

(A) A lawyer shall not divide a fee for legal services with another lawyer who is not a partner in or associate of his law firm or law office, unless:

(1) The client consents to employment of the other lawyer after a full disclosure that a division of fees will be made.

(2) The division is made in proportion to the services performed and responsibility assumed by each.

(3) The total fee of the lawyers does not clearly exceed reasonable compensation for all legal services they rendered the client.

(B) This Disciplinary Rule does not prohibit payment to a former partner or associate pursuant to a separation or retirement agreement.

DR 2-108   Agreements Restricting the Practice of a Lawyer

(A) A lawyer shall not be a party to or participate in a partnership or employment agreement with another lawyer that restricts the right of a lawyer to practice law after the termination of a relationship created by the agreement, except as a condition to payment of retirement benefits.

(B) In connection with the settlement of a controversy or suit, a lawyer shall not enter into an agreement that restricts his right to practice law.

DR 2-109   Acceptance of Employment

(A) A lawyer shall not accept employment on behalf of a person if he knows or it is obvious that such person wishes to:

(1) Bring a legal action, conduct a defense, or assert a position in litigation, or otherwise have steps taken for him, merely for the purpose of harassing or maliciously injuring any person.

(2) Present a claim or defense in litigation that is not warranted under existing law, unless it can be supported by good faith argument for an extension, modification, or reversal of existing law.

DR 2-110   Withdrawal from Employment

(A) *In general.*

(1) If permission for withdrawal from employment is required by the rules of a tribunal, a lawyer shall not withdraw from employment in a proceeding before that tribunal without its permission.

(2) In any event, a lawyer shall not withdraw from employment until he has taken reasonable steps to avoid foreseeable prejudice to the rights of his client, including giving due notice to his client, allowing time for employment of other counsel, delivering to the client all papers and property to which the client is entitled, and complying with applicable laws and rules.

(3) A lawyer who withdraws from employment shall refund promptly any part of a fee paid in advance that has not been earned.

(B) *Mandatory withdrawal.*

A lawyer representing a client before a tribunal, with its permission if required by its rules, shall withdraw from employment, and a lawyer representing a client in other matters shall withdraw from employment, if:

(1) He knows or it is obvious that his client is bringing the legal action, conducting the defense, or asserting a position in the litigation, or is otherwise having steps taken for him, merely for the purpose of harassing or maliciously injuring any person.

(2) He knows or it is obvious that his continued employment will result in violation of a Disciplinary Rule.

(3) His mental or physical condition renders it unreasonably difficult for him to carry out the employment effectively.

(4) He is discharged by his client.

(C) *Permissive withdrawal.*

If DR 2-110(B) is not applicable, a lawyer may not request permission to withdraw in matters pending before a tribunal, and may not withdraw in other matters, unless such request or such withdrawal is because:

(1) His client:

(a) Insists upon presenting a claim or defense that is not warranted under existing law and cannot be supported by good faith argument for an extension, modification, or reversal of existing law.

(b) Personally seeks to pursue an illegal course of conduct.

(c) Insists that the lawyer pursue a course of conduct that is illegal or that is prohibited under the Disciplinary Rules.

(d) By other conduct renders it unreasonably difficult for the lawyer to carry out his employment effectively.

(e) Insists, in a matter not pending before a tribunal, that the lawyer engage in conduct that is contrary to the judgment and advice of the lawyer but not prohibited under the Disciplinary Rules.

(f) Deliberately disregards an agreement or obligation to the lawyer as to expenses or fees.

(2) His continued employment is likely to result in a violation of a Disciplinary Rule.

(3) His inability to work with co-counsel indicates that the best interests of the client likely will be served by withdrawal.

(4) His mental or physical condition renders it difficult for him to carry out the employment effectively.

(5) His client knowingly and freely assents to termination of his employment.

(6) He believes in good faith, in a proceeding pending before a tribunal, that the tribunal will find the existence of other good cause for withdrawal.

Model Rules Comparison

Model Code	ABA Model Rules	Model Code	ABA Model Rules
DR 2-101(A)	7.1	DR 2-103(C)	5.4(c), 7.2(b), 7.3
DR 2-101(B)	7.1, 7.2(a)	DR 2-103(D)	5.4(c), 7.2(b), 7.3
DR 2-101(C)	No comparable Rule	DR 2-103(E)	1.16(a), 8.4(a)
DR 2-101(D)	No comparable Rule	DR 2-104	1.16(a), 7.3
DR 2-101(E)	7.1	DR 2-105	7.4
DR 2-101(F)	7.1	DR 2-106(A)	1.5(a)
DR 2-101(G)	7.1	DR 2-106(B)	1.5(a)
DR 2-101(H)	7.2(a)	DR 2-106(C)	1.5(d)
DR 2-101(I)	7.2(b)	DR 2-107(A)	1.5(e)
DR 2-102(A)	7.2(a), 7.5	DR 2-107(B)	5.4(a)
DR 2-102(B)	7.1, 7.5(a), (c)	DR 2-108(A)	5.6(a)
DR 2-102(C)	7.5(d)	DR 2-108(B)	5.6(b)
DR 2-102(D)	7.5(b)	DR 2-109(A)	1.16(a), 3.1, 3.2
DR 2-102(E)	7.1(a), 7.4	DR 2-110(A)	1.16(c), (d)
DR 2-103(A)	7.3	DR 2-110(B)	1.16(a), 3.1, 4.4(a)
DR 2-103(B)	5.4(c), 7.2(b), 7.6	DR 2-110(C)	1.16(b)

CANON 3.   A LAWYER SHOULD ASSIST IN PREVENTING THE UNAUTHORIZED PRACTICE OF LAW

DR 3-101   Aiding Unauthorized Practice of Law

(A) A lawyer shall not aid a non-lawyer in the unauthorized practice of law.

(B) A lawyer shall not practice law in a jurisdiction where to do so would be in violation of regulations of the profession in that jurisdiction.

DR 3-102   Dividing Legal Fees with a Non-Lawyer

(A) A lawyer or law firm shall not share legal fees with a non-lawyer, except that:

(1) An agreement by a lawyer with his firm, partner, or associate may provide for the payment of money, over a reasonable period of time after his death, to his estate or to one or more specified persons.

(2) A lawyer who undertakes to complete unfinished legal business of a deceased lawyer may pay to the estate of the deceased lawyer that proportion of the total compensation which fairly represents the services rendered by the deceased lawyer.

(3) A lawyer or law firm may include non-lawyer employees in a compensation or retirement plan, even though the plan is based in whole or in part on a profit-sharing arrangement, providing such plan does not circumvent another Disciplinary Rule.

DR 3-103   Forming a Partnership with a Non-Lawyer

(A) A lawyer shall not form a partnership with a non-lawyer if any of the activities of the partnership consist of the practice of law.

Model Rules Comparison

Model Code	ABA Model Rules
DR 3-101(A)	5.5(a)
DR 3-101(B)	5.5(a)
DR 3-102	5.4(a)
DR 3-103	5.4(b)

CANON 4.   A LAWYER SHOULD PRESERVE THE CONFIDENCES AND SECRETS OF A CLIENT

DR 4-101   Preservation of Confidences and Secrets of a Client

(A) "Confidence" refers to information protected by the attorney- client privilege under applicable law, and "secret" refers to other information gained in the professional relationship that the client has requested be held inviolate or the disclosure of which would be embarrassing or would be likely to be detrimental to the client.

(B) Except when permitted under DR 4-101(C), a lawyer shall not knowingly:

(1) Reveal a confidence or secret of his client.

(2) Use a confidence or secret of his client to the disadvantage of the client.

(3) Use a confidence or secret of his client for the advantage of himself or of a third person, unless the client consents after full disclosure.

(C) A lawyer may reveal:

(1) Confidences or secrets with the consent of the client or clients affected, but only after a full disclosure to them.

(2) Confidences or secrets when permitted under Disciplinary Rules or required by law or court order.

(3) The intention of his client to commit a crime and the information necessary to prevent the crime.

(4) Confidences or secrets necessary to establish or collect his fee or to defend himself or his employees or associates against an accusation of wrongful conduct.

(D) A lawyer shall exercise reasonable care to prevent his employees, associates, and others whose services are utilized by him from disclosing or using confidences or secrets of a client, except that a lawyer may reveal the information allowed by DR 4-101(C) through an employee.

Model Rules Comparison

Model Code	ABA Model Rules
DR 4-101(A)	1.6(a)
DR 4-101(B)	1.6(a), 1.8(b), 1.9(c), 1.18(b)
DR 4-101(C)	1.6(a), (b), 1.9(c), 1.13(c)
DR 4-101(D)	5.1(a), (b), 5.3(a), (b)

CANON 5. A LAWYER SHOULD EXERCISE INDEPENDENT PROFESSIONAL JUDGMENT ON BEHALF OF A CLIENT

DR 5-101 Refusing Employment When the Interests of the Lawyer May Impair His Independent Professional Judgment

(A) Except with the consent of his client after full disclosure, a lawyer shall not accept employment if the exercise of his professional judgment on behalf of his client will be or reasonably may be affected by his own financial, business, property, or personal interests.

(B) A lawyer shall not accept employment in contemplated or pending litigation if he knows or it is obvious that he or a lawyer in his firm ought to be called as a witness, except that he may undertake the employment and he or a lawyer in his firm may testify:

(1) If the testimony will relate solely to an uncontested matter.

(2) If the testimony will relate solely to a matter of formality and there is no reason to believe that substantial evidence will be offered in opposition to the testimony.

(3) If the testimony will relate solely to the nature and value of legal services rendered in the case by the lawyer or his firm to the client.

(4) As to any matter, if refusal would work a substantial hardship on the client because of the distinctive value of the lawyer or his firm as counsel in the particular case.

DR 5-102 Withdrawal as Counsel When the Lawyer Becomes a Witness

(A) If, after undertaking employment in contemplated or pending litigation, a lawyer learns or it is obvious that he or a lawyer in his firm ought to be called as a witness on behalf of his client, he shall withdraw from the conduct of the trial and his firm, if any, shall not continue representation in the trial, except that he may continue the representation and he or a lawyer in his firm may testify in the circumstances enumerated in DR 5-101(B)(1) through (4).

(B) If, after undertaking employment in contemplated or pending litigation, a lawyer learns or it is obvious that he or a lawyer in his firm may be called as a witness other than on behalf of his client, he may continue the representation until it is apparent that his testimony is or may be prejudicial to his client.

DR 5-103   Avoiding Acquisition of Interest in Litigation

(A) A lawyer shall not acquire a proprietary interest in the cause of action or subject matter of litigation he is conducting for a client, except that he may:

(1) Acquire a lien granted by law to secure his fee or expenses.

(2) Contract with a client for a reasonable contingent fee in a civil case.

(B) While representing a client in connection with contemplated or pending litigation, a lawyer shall not advance or guarantee financial assistance to his client, except that a lawyer may advance or guarantee the expenses of litigation, including court costs, expenses of investigation, expenses of medical examination, and costs of obtaining and presenting evidence, provided the client remains ultimately liable for such expenses.

DR 5-104   Limiting Business Relations with a Client

(A) A lawyer shall not enter into a business transaction with a client if they have differing interests therein and if the client expects the lawyer to exercise his professional judgment therein for the protection of the client, unless the client has consented after full disclosure.

(B) Prior to conclusion of all aspects of the matter giving rise to his employment, a lawyer shall not enter into any arrangement or understanding with a client or a prospective client by which he acquires an interest in publication rights with respect to the subject matter of his employment or proposed employment.

DR 5-105   Refusing to Accept or Continue Employment If the Interests of Another Client May Impair the Independent Professional Judgment of the Lawyer

(A) A lawyer shall decline proffered employment if the exercise of his independent professional judgment in behalf of a client will be or is likely to be adversely affected by the acceptance of the proffered employment, or if it would be likely to involve him in representing differing interests, except to the extent permitted under DR 5-105(C).

(B) A lawyer shall not continue multiple employment if the exercise of his independent professional judgment in behalf of a client will be or is likely to be adversely affected by his representation of another client, or if it would be likely to involve him in representing differing interests, except to the extent permitted under DR 5-105(C).

(C) In the situations covered by DR 5-105(A) and (B), a lawyer may represent multiple clients if it is obvious that he can adequately represent the interest of each and if each consents to the representation after full disclosure of the possible effect of such representation on the exercise of his independent professional judgment on behalf of each.

(D) If a lawyer is required to decline employment or to withdraw from employment under a Disciplinary Rule, no partner, or associate, or any other lawyer affiliated with him or his firm, may accept or continue such employment.

DR 5-106   Settling Similar Claims of Clients

(A) A lawyer who represents two or more clients shall not make or participate in the making of an aggregate settlement of the claims of or against his clients, unless each client has consented to the settlement after being advised of the existence and nature of all the claims involved in the proposed settlement, of the total amount of the settlement, and of the participation of each person in the settlement.

DR 5-107   Avoiding Influence by Others Than the Client

(A) Except with the consent of his client after full disclosure, a lawyer shall not:

(1) Accept compensation for his legal services from one other than his client.

(2) Accept from one other than his client any thing of value related to his representation of or his employment by his client.

(B) A lawyer shall not permit a person who recommends, employs, or pays him to render legal services for another to direct or regulate his professional judgment in rendering such legal services.

(C) A lawyer shall not practice with or in the form of a professional corporation or association authorized to practice law for a profit, if:

(1) A non-lawyer owns any interest therein, except that a fiduciary representative of the estate of a lawyer may hold the stock or interest of the lawyer for a reasonable time during administration;

(2) A non-lawyer is a corporate director or officer thereof; or

(3) A non-lawyer has the right to direct or control the professional judgment of a lawyer.

629

Model Rules Comparison

Model Code	ABA Model Rules	Model Code	ABA Model Rules
DR 5-101(A)	1.7, 1.8(a)-(j), 6.3, 6.4	DR 5-105(A)	1.7, 1.13(e)
DR 5-101(B)	1.7, 3.7	DR 5-105(B)	1.7, 1.13(e)
DR 5-102(A)	1.7, 3.7	DR 5-105(C)	1.7, 1.9, 1.13(e)
DR 5-102(B)	1.7, 3.7	DR 5-105(D)	1.10(a), 1.12(c), 1.18(c), (d), 6.5
DR 5-103(A)	1.5(c), 1.8(c), (i), 1.15(e)	DR 5-106	1.8(g)
DR 5-103(B)	1.8(e)	DR 5-107(A)	1.7, 1.8(f)
DR 5-104(A)	1.7, 1.8(a)	DR 5-107(B)	1.7, 1.8(f), 1.13(b), 2.1, 5.4(c)
DR 5-104(B)	1.8(d)	DR 5-107(C)	5.4(d)

CANON 6.   A LAWYER SHOULD REPRESENT A CLIENT COMPETENTLY

DR 6-101   Failing to Act Competently

(A) A lawyer shall not:

(1) Handle a legal matter which he knows or should know that he is not competent to handle, without associating with him a lawyer who is competent to handle it.

(2) Handle a legal matter without preparation adequate in the circumstances.

(3) Neglect a legal matter entrusted to him.

DR 6-102   Limiting Liability to Client

(A) A lawyer shall not attempt to exonerate himself from or limit his liability to his client for his personal malpractice.

Model Rules Comparison

Model Code	ABA Model Rules
DR 6-101	1.1, 1.3, 1.4
DR 6-102	1.8(h)

CANON 7.   A LAWYER SHOULD REPRESENT A CLIENT ZEALOUSLY WITHIN THE BOUNDS OF THE LAW

DR 7-101   Representing a Client Zealously

(A) A lawyer shall not intentionally:

(1) Fail to seek the lawful objectives of his client through reasonably available means permitted by law and the Disciplinary Rules, except as provided by DR 7-101(B). A lawyer does not violate this

Disciplinary Rule, however, by acceding to reasonable requests of opposing counsel which do not prejudice the rights of his client, by being punctual in fulfilling all professional commitments, by avoiding offensive tactics, or by treating with courtesy and consideration all persons involved in the legal process.

(2) Fail to carry out a contract of employment entered into with a client for professional services, but he may withdraw as permitted under DR 2-110, DR 5-102, and DR 5-105.

(3) Prejudice or damage his client during the course of the professional relationship, except as required under DR 7-102(B).

(B) In his representation of a client, a lawyer may:

(1) Where permissible, exercise his professional judgment to waive or fail to assert a right or position of his client.

(2) Refuse to aid or participate in conduct that he believes to be unlawful, even though there is some support for an argument that the conduct is legal.

DR 7-102   Representing a Client Within the Bounds of the Law

(A) In his representation of a client, a lawyer shall not:

(1) File a suit, assert a position, conduct a defense, delay a trial, or take other action on behalf of his client when he knows or when it is obvious that such action would serve merely to harass or maliciously injure another.

(2) Knowingly advance a claim or defense that is unwarranted under existing law, except that he may advance such claim or defense if it can be supported by good faith argument for an extension, modification, or reversal of existing law.

(3) Conceal or knowingly fail to disclose that which he is required by law to reveal.

(4) Knowingly use perjured testimony or false evidence.

(5) Knowingly make a false statement of law or fact.

(6) Participate in the creation or preservation of evidence when he knows or it is obvious that the evidence is false.

(7) Counsel or assist his client in conduct that the lawyer knows to be illegal or fraudulent.

(8) Knowingly engage in other illegal conduct or conduct contrary to a Disciplinary Rule.

(B) A lawyer who receives information clearly establishing that:

(1) His client has, in the course of the representation, perpetrated a fraud upon a person or tribunal shall promptly call upon his client to rectify the same, and if his client refuses or is unable to do so, he shall reveal the fraud to the affected person or tribunal, except when the information is protected as a privileged communication.

631

(2) A person other than his client has perpetrated a fraud upon a tribunal shall promptly reveal the fraud to the tribunal.

DR 7-103   Performing the Duty of Public Prosecutor or Other Government Lawyer

(A) A public prosecutor or other government lawyer shall not institute or cause to be instituted criminal charges when he knows or it is obvious that the charges are not supported by probable cause.

(B) A public prosecutor or other government lawyer in criminal litigation shall make timely disclosure to counsel for the defendant, or to the defendant if he has no counsel, of the existence of evidence, known to the prosecutor or other government lawyer, that tends to negate the guilt of the accused, mitigate the degree of the offense, or reduce the punishment.

DR 7-104   Communicating with One of Adverse Interest

(A) During the course of his representation of a client a lawyer shall not:

(1) Communicate or cause another to communicate on the subject of the representation with a party he knows to be represented by a lawyer in that matter unless he has the prior consent of the lawyer representing such other party or is authorized by law to do so.

(2) Give advice to a person who is not represented by a lawyer, other than the advice to secure counsel, if the interests of such person are or have a reasonable possibility of being in conflict with the interests of his client.

DR 7-105   Threatening Criminal Prosecution

(A) A lawyer shall not present, participate in presenting, or threaten to present criminal charges solely to obtain an advantage in a civil matter.

DR 7-106   Trial Conduct

(A) A lawyer shall not disregard or advise his client to disregard a standing rule of a tribunal or a ruling of a tribunal made in the course of a proceeding, but he may take appropriate steps in good faith to test the validity of such rule or ruling.

(B) In presenting a matter to a tribunal, a lawyer shall disclose:

(1) Legal authority in the controlling jurisdiction known to him to be directly adverse to the position of his client and which is not disclosed by opposing counsel.

(2) Unless privileged or irrelevant, the identities of the clients he represents and of the persons who employed him.

(C) In appearing in his professional capacity before a tribunal, a lawyer shall not:

(1) State or allude to any matter that he has no reasonable basis to believe is relevant to the case or that will not be supported by admissible evidence.

(2) Ask any question that he has no reasonable basis to believe is relevant to the case and that is intended to degrade a witness or other person.

(3) Assert his personal knowledge of the facts in issue, except when testifying as a witness.

(4) Assert his personal opinion as to the justness of a cause, as to the credibility of a witness, as to the culpability of a civil litigant, or as to the guilt or innocence of an accused; but he may argue, on his analysis of the evidence, for any position or conclusion with respect to the matters stated herein.

(5) Fail to comply with known local customs of courtesy or practice of the bar or a particular tribunal without giving to opposing counsel timely notice of his intent not to comply.

(6) Engage in undignified or discourteous conduct which is degrading to a tribunal.

(7) Intentionally or habitually violate any established rule of procedure or of evidence.

DR 7-107   Trial Publicity

(A) A lawyer participating in or associated with the investigation of a criminal matter shall not make or participate in making an extrajudicial statement that a reasonable person would expect to be disseminated by means of public communication and that does more than state without elaboration:

(1) Information contained in a public record.

(2) That the investigation is in progress.

(3) The general scope of the investigation including a description of the offense and, if permitted by law, the identity of the victim.

(4) A request for assistance in apprehending a suspect or assistance in other matters and the information necessary thereto.

(5) A warning to the public of any dangers.

(B) A lawyer or law firm associated with the prosecution or defense of a criminal matter shall not, from the time of the filing of a complaint, information, or indictment, the issuance of an arrest warrant, or arrest until the commencement of the trial or disposition without trial, make or participate in making an extrajudicial statement that a reasonable person would expect to be disseminated by means of public communication and that relates to:

(1) The character, reputation, or prior criminal record (including arrests, indictments, or other charges of crime) of the accused.

(2) The possibility of a plea of guilty to the offense charged or to a lesser offense.

(3) The existence or contents of any confession, admission, or statement given by the accused or his refusal or failure to make a statement.

(4) The performance or results of any examinations or tests or the refusal or failure of the accused to submit to examinations or tests.

(5) The identity, testimony, or credibility of a prospective witness.

(6) Any opinion as to the guilt or innocence of the accused, the evidence, or the merits of the case.

(C) DR 7-107(B) does not preclude a lawyer during such period from announcing:

(1) The name, age, residence, occupation, and family status of the accused.

(2) If the accused has not been apprehended, any information necessary to aid in his apprehension or to warn the public of any dangers he may present.

(3) A request for assistance in obtaining evidence.

(4) The identity of the victim of the crime.

(5) The fact, time, and place of arrest, resistance, pursuit, and use of weapons.

(6) The identity of investigating and arresting officers or agencies and the length of the investigation.

(7) At the time of seizure, a description of the physical evidence seized, other than a confession, admission, or statement.

(8) The nature, substance, or text of the charge.

(9) Quotations from or references to public records of the court in the case.

(10) The scheduling or result of any step in the judicial proceedings.

(11) That the accused denies the charges made against him.

(D) During the selection of a jury or the trial of a criminal matter, a lawyer or law firm associated with the prosecution or defense of a criminal matter shall not make or participate in making an extrajudicial statement that a reasonable person would expect to be disseminated by means of public communication and that relates to the trial, parties, or issues in the trial or other matters that are reasonably likely to interfere with a fair trial, except that he may quote from or refer without comment to public records of the court in the case.

(E) After the completion of a trial or disposition without trial of a criminal matter and prior to the imposition of sentence, a lawyer or law firm associated with the prosecution or defense shall not make or participate in making an extrajudicial statement that a reasonable person would expect to be disseminated by public communication and that is reasonably likely to affect the imposition of sentence.

(F) The foregoing provisions of DR 7-107 also apply to professional disciplinary proceedings and juvenile disciplinary proceedings when pertinent and consistent with other law applicable to such proceedings.

(G) A lawyer or law firm associated with a civil action shall not during its investigation or litigation make or participate in making an extrajudicial statement, other than a quotation from or reference to public records, that a reasonable person would expect to be disseminated by means of public communication and that relates to:

(1) Evidence regarding the occurrence or transaction involved.

(2) The character, credibility, or criminal record of a party, witness, or prospective witness.

(3) The performance or results of any examinations or tests or the refusal or failure of a party to submit to such.

(4) His opinion as to the merits of the claims or defenses of a party, except as required by law or administrative rule.

(5) Any other matter reasonably likely to interfere with a fair trial of the action.

(H) During the pendency of an administrative proceeding, a lawyer or law firm associated therewith shall not make or participate in making a statement, other than a quotation from or reference to public records, that a reasonable person would expect to be disseminated by means of public communication if it is made outside the official course of the proceeding and relates to:

(1) Evidence regarding the occurrence or transaction involved.

(2) The character, credibility, or criminal record of a party, witness, or prospective witness.

(3) Physical evidence or the performance or results of any examinations or tests or the refusal or failure of a party to submit to such.

(4) His opinion as to the merits of the claims, defenses, or positions of an interested person.

(5) Any other matter reasonably likely to interfere with a fair hearing.

(I) The foregoing provisions of DR 7-107 do not preclude a lawyer from replying to charges of misconduct publicly made against him or from participating in the proceedings of legislative, administrative, or other investigative bodies.

(J) A lawyer shall exercise reasonable care to prevent his employees and associates from making an extrajudicial statement that he would be prohibited from making under DR 7-107.

DR 7-108   Communication with or Investigation of Jurors

(A) Before the trial of a case a lawyer connected therewith shall not communicate with or cause another to communicate with anyone he knows to be a member of the venire from which the jury will be selected for the trial of the case.

(B) During the trial of a case:

(1) A lawyer connected therewith shall not communicate with or cause another to communicate with any member of the jury.

(2) A lawyer who is not connected therewith shall not communicate with or cause another to communicate with a juror concerning the case.

(C) DR 7-108(A) and (B) do not prohibit a lawyer from communicating with veniremen or jurors in the course of official proceedings.

(D) After discharge of the jury from further consideration of a case with which the lawyer was connected, the lawyer shall not ask questions of or make comments to a member of that jury that are calculated merely to harass or embarrass the juror or to influence his actions in future jury service.

(E) A lawyer shall not conduct or cause, by financial support or otherwise, another to conduct a vexatious or harassing investigation of either a venireman or a juror.

(F) All restrictions imposed by DR 7-108 upon a lawyer also apply to communications with or investigations of members of a family of a venireman or a juror.

(G) A lawyer shall reveal promptly to the court improper conduct by a venireman or a juror, or by another toward a venireman or a juror or a member of his family, of which the lawyer has knowledge.

DR 7-109   Contact with Witnesses

(A) A lawyer shall not suppress any evidence that he or his client has a legal obligation to reveal or produce.

(B) A lawyer shall not advise or cause a person to secrete himself or to leave the jurisdiction of a tribunal for the purpose of making him unavailable as a witness therein.

(C) A lawyer shall not pay, offer to pay, or acquiesce in the payment of compensation to a witness contingent upon the content of his testimony or the outcome of the case. But a lawyer may advance, guarantee, or acquiesce in the payment of:

(1) Expenses reasonably incurred by a witness in attending or testifying.

(2) Reasonable compensation to a witness for his loss of time in attending or testifying.

(3) A reasonable fee for the professional services of an expert witness.

DR 7-110 Contact with Officials

(A) A lawyer shall not give or lend any thing of value to a judge, official, or employee of a tribunal except as permitted by Section C(4) of Canon 5 of the Code of Judicial Conduct, but a lawyer may make a contribution to the campaign fund of a candidate for judicial office in conformity with Section B(2) under Canon 7 of the Code of Judicial Conduct.

(B) In an adversary proceeding, a lawyer shall not communicate, or cause another to communicate, as to the merits of the cause with a judge or an official before whom the proceeding is pending, except:

(1) In the course of official proceedings in the cause.

(2) In writing if he promptly delivers a copy of the writing to opposing counsel or to the adverse party if he is not represented by a lawyer.

(3) Orally upon adequate notice to opposing counsel or to the adverse party if he is not represented by a lawyer.

(4) As otherwise authorized by law, or by Section A(4) under Canon 3 of the Code of Judicial Conduct.

Model Rules Comparison

Model Code	ABA Model Rules	Model Code	ABA Model Rules
DR 7-101(A)	1.2(a), (d), 1.3, 3.2, 3.5, 4.4	DR 7-106(C)	3.4(a), (c), (d), (e), 3.5, 4.4
DR 7-101(B)	1.2(a), (c), (d), 1.16(b)	DR 7-107(A)-(H)	3.6
DR 7-102(A)(1)	3.1, 3.2, 4.4	DR 7-107(I)	1.6(b), 3.9
DR 7-102(A)(2)	3.1	DR 7-107(J)	3.8(f), 5.1(a), (b), 5.3(a), (b)
DR 7-102(A)(3)	3.3(a), 3.4(a), 4.1	DR 7-108(A)	3.5(a), (b), 8.4(a)
DR 7-102(A)(4)	3.3(a), (b)	DR 7-108(B)	3.5(a), (b), 5.1(c), 5.3(a), (b), 8.4(a)
DR 7-102(A)(5)	3.3(a), 4.1	DR 7-108(C)	3.5(a), (b)
DR 7-102(A)(6)	1.2(d), 3.3(a), (b), 3.4(b)	DR 7-108(D)	3.5(c), 4.4
DR 7-102(A)(7)	1.2(d), 3.3(a), 4.1	DR 7-108(E)	3.5(b), 4.4, 5.1(c), 5.3(a), (b), 8.4(a)
DR 7-102(A)(8)	1.2(d), 8.4(a), (b)	DR 7-108(F)	4.4
DR 7-102(B)	1.6(b), 3.3(a), (b), 4.1(b)	DR 7-108(G)	3.3(b), (c)
DR 7-103(A)	3.8(a)	DR 7-109(A)	3.3(a), (b), 3.4(a)
DR 7-103(B)	3.8(d)	DR 7-109(B)	3.4(a), (f)
DR 7-104(A)(1)	4.2, 8.4(a)	DR 7-109(C)	3.4(b)
DR 7-104(A)(2)	3.4(f), 4.3	DR 7-110(A)	3.5(a), 8.4(f)
DR 7-105	No comparable Rule	DR 7-110(B)	3.5(a), (b), 8.4(a)
DR 7-106(A)	1.2(d), 3.4(c), (d)		
DR 7-106(B)	3.3(a), 3.9		

CANON 8.   A LAWYER SHOULD ASSIST IN IMPROVING THE LEGAL SYSTEM

DR 8-101   Action as a Public Official

(A) A lawyer who holds public office shall not:

(1) Use his public position to obtain, or attempt to obtain, a special advantage in legislative matters for himself or for a client under circumstances where he knows or it is obvious that such action is not in the public interest.

(2) Use his public position to influence, or attempt to influence, a tribunal to act in favor of himself or of a client.

(3) Accept any thing of value from any person when the lawyer knows or it is obvious that the offer is for the purpose of influencing his action as a public official.

DR 8-102   Statements Concerning Judges and Other Adjudicatory Officers

(A) A lawyer shall not knowingly make false statements of fact concerning the qualifications of a candidate for election or appointment to a judicial office.

(B) A lawyer shall not knowingly make false accusations against a judge or other adjudicatory officer.

DR 8-103   Lawyer Candidate for Judicial Office

(A) A lawyer who is a candidate for judicial office shall comply with the applicable provisions of Canon 7 of the Code of Judicial Conduct.

Model Rules Comparison

Model Code	ABA Model Rules
DR 8-101	1.11(d), 3.5(a), 8.4(b), (c), (e)
DR 8-102	8.2(a), 8.4(c), (d)
DR 8-103	8.2(b)

CANON 9.   A LAWYER SHOULD AVOID EVEN THE APPEARANCE OF PROFESSIONAL IMPROPRIETY

DR 9-101   Avoiding Even the Appearance of Impropriety

(A) A lawyer shall not accept private employment in a matter upon the merits of which he has acted in a judicial capacity.

(B) A lawyer shall not accept private employment in a matter in which he had substantial responsibility while he was a public employee.

(C) A lawyer shall not state or imply that he is able to influence improperly or upon irrelevant grounds any tribunal, legislative body, or public official.

DR 9-102   Preserving Identity of Funds and Property of a Client

(A) All funds of clients paid to a lawyer or law firm, other than advances for costs and expenses, shall be deposited in one or more identifiable bank accounts maintained in the state in which the law office is situated and no funds belonging to the lawyer or law firm shall be deposited therein except as follows:

(1) Funds reasonably sufficient to pay bank charges may be deposited therein.

(2) Funds belonging in part to a client and in part presently or potentially to the lawyer or law firm must be deposited therein, but the portion belonging to the lawyer or law firm may be withdrawn when due unless the right of the lawyer or law firm to receive it is disputed by the client, in which event the disputed portion shall not be withdrawn until the dispute is finally resolved.

(B) A lawyer shall:

(1) Promptly notify a client of the receipt of his funds, securities, or other properties.

(2) Identify and label securities and properties of a client promptly upon receipt and place them in a safe deposit box or other place of safekeeping as soon as practicable.

(3) Maintain complete records of all funds, securities, and other properties of a client coming into the possession of the lawyer and render appropriate accounts to his client regarding them.

(4) Promptly pay or deliver to the client as requested by a client the funds, securities, or other properties in the possession of the lawyer which the client is entitled to receive.

Model Rules Comparison

Model Code	ABA Model Rules
DR 9-101(A)	1.12(a), (b)
DR 9-101(B)	1.11(a), 1.12(a), (b)
DR 9-101(C)	1.2(d), 7.1, 8.4(e)
DR 9-102	1.4(a), 1.15

DEFINITIONS*

As used in the Disciplinary Rules of the Model Code of Professional Responsibility:

(1) "Differing interests" include every interest that will adversely affect either the judgment or the loyalty of a lawyer to a client, whether it be a conflicting, inconsistent, diverse, or other interest.

(2) "Law firm" includes a professional legal corporation.

(3) "Person" includes a corporation, an association, a trust, a partnership, and any other organization or legal entity.

(4) "Professional legal corporation" means a corporation, or an association treated as a corporation, authorized by law to practice law for profit.

(5) "State" includes the District of Columbia, Puerto Rico, and other federal territories and possessions.

(6) "Tribunal" includes all courts and all other adjudicatory bodies.

(7) "A Bar association" includes a bar association of specialists as referred to in DR 2-105(A)(1) or (3).

(8) "Qualified legal assistance organization" means an office or organization of one of the four types listed in DR 2-103(D)(1)-(4), inclusive, that meets all the requirements thereof.

Model Rules Comparison

Model Code	ABA Model Rules
Definitions	Rule 1.0 (Terminology)

*"Confidence" and "secret" are defined in DR 4-101(A).

Federal Materials

Federal Provisions on Conflicts, Confidentiality, and Crimes

Editors' Introduction. This chapter reprints a number of federal statutes and regulations that govern lawyers. Many of the provisions also govern nonlawyers, including lawyers' clients. These federal statutes and regulations amplify, reinforce, and sometimes supersede the obligations imposed by state rules of professional conduct. For example, lawyers who work for the federal government (or who have previously worked for the federal government) are governed not only by state rules of professional conduct on conflicts and confidentiality equivalent to ABA Model Rules 1.6, 1.9 and 1.11, but also by stringent federal statutes such as 18 U.S.C. §207. Lawyers who appear and practice before the federal Securities and Exchange Commission in the representation of securities issuers are governed by rules found at 17 C.F.R. Part 205.

Since our last edition went to press in October 2011, the statutes and regulations reprinted below have not been amended.

Contents

SELECTED PROVISIONS FROM 28 U.S.C.

SELECTED PROVISIONS FROM 28 C.F.R. PART 77

SELECTED PROVISIONS FROM 28 C.F.R. PART 50

SELECTED PROVISIONS FROM 15 U.S.C.

Editors' Note.   Title 15 of the United States Code is entitled "Commerce and Trade." On July 30, 2002, in the wake of the massive corporate scandals at Enron, WorldCom, and other companies, President George W. Bush signed into law the Sarbanes-Oxley Act of 2002. Section 307 of that law (later codified at 15 U.S.C. §7245) commanded the Securities and Exchange Commission (the "SEC" or the "Commission") to adopt rules to govern the responsibilities of attorneys who appear and practice before the SEC in the representation of issuers (*i.e.,* companies that issue stock). We reprint §307 below, followed by the regulations that the SEC adopted in 2003 pursuant to the mandate of §307. For additional background information about §307 of the Sarbanes-Oxley Act, see the Special Section at the back of the 2004 edition of this book. Rules adopted in the wake of the Dodd-Frank law contemplate rewards for whistleblowers, including lawyers and persons who work for lawyers, if their information "would otherwise be permitted by an attorney pursuant §205.3(d)(2) of this chapter [see below], the applicable state attorney conduct rules, or otherwise." *See* 17 C.F.R. §240.21F-4(i) and (ii), which is not printed below.

§7245 Rules of Professional Responsibility for Attorneys

Not later than 180 days after the date of enactment of this Act, the Commission shall issue rules, in the public interest and for the protection of investors, setting forth minimum standards of professional conduct for attorneys appearing and practicing before the Commission in any way in the representation of issuers, including a rule—

(1) requiring an attorney to report evidence of a material violation of securities law or breach of fiduciary duty or similar violation by the company or any agent thereof, to the chief legal counsel or the chief executive officer of the company (or the equivalent thereof); and

(2) if the counsel or officer does not appropriately respond to the evidence (adopting, as necessary, appropriate remedial measures or sanctions with respect to the violation), requiring the attorney to report the evidence to the audit committee of the board of directors of the issuer or to another committee of the board of directors comprised solely of directors not employed directly or indirectly by the issuer, or to the board of directors.

SELECTED PROVISIONS FROM 17 C.F.R. PART 205

Editors' Note. The regulations that follow were promulgated pursuant to the mandate of Congress contained in §307 of the Sarbanes-Oxley Act of 2002, 15 U.S.C. §7245 (reprinted above), and took effect on August 5, 2003. For background information about the regulations and proposed regulations, see the Special Section at the back of the 2004 edition of this book.

STANDARDS OF PROFESSIONAL CONDUCT FOR ATTORNEYS APPEARING AND PRACTICING BEFORE THE COMMISSION IN THE REPRESENTATION OF AN ISSUER

§205.1 Purpose and Scope

This part sets forth minimum standards of professional conduct for attorneys appearing and practicing before the Commission in the representation of an issuer. These standards supplement applicable standards of any jurisdiction where an attorney is admitted or practices and are not intended to limit the ability of any jurisdiction to impose additional obligations on an attorney not inconsistent with the application of this part. Where the standards of a state or other United States jurisdiction where an attorney is admitted or practices conflict with this part, this part shall govern.

§205.2   Definitions

For purposes of this part, the following definitions apply:

(a) *Appearing and practicing* before the Commission:

(1) Means:

(i) Transacting any business with the Commission, including communications in any form;

(ii) Representing an issuer in a Commission administrative proceeding or in connection with any Commission investigation, inquiry, information request, or subpoena;

(iii) Providing advice in respect of the United States securities laws or the Commission's rules or regulations thereunder regarding any document that the attorney has notice will be filed with or submitted to, or incorporated into any document that will be filed with or submitted to, the Commission, including the provision of such advice in the context of preparing, or participating in the preparation of, any such document; or

(iv) Advising an issuer as to whether information or a statement, opinion, or other writing is required under the United States securities laws or the Commission's rules or regulations thereunder to be filed with or submitted to, or incorporated into any document that will be filed with or submitted to, the Commission; but

(2) Does not include an attorney who:

(i) Conducts the activities in paragraphs (a)(1)(i) through (a)(1)(iv) of this section other than in the context of providing legal services to an issuer with whom the attorney has an attorney-client relationship; or

(ii) Is a non-appearing foreign attorney.

(b) *Appropriate response* means a response to an attorney regarding reported evidence of a material violation as a result of which the attorney reasonably believes:

(1) That no material violation, as defined in paragraph (i) of this section, has occurred, is ongoing, or is about to occur;

(2) That the issuer has, as necessary, adopted appropriate remedial measures, including appropriate steps or sanctions to stop any material violations that are ongoing, to prevent any material violation

that has yet to occur, and to remedy or otherwise appropriately address any material violation that has already occurred and to minimize the likelihood of its recurrence; or

(3) That the issuer, with the consent of the issuer s board of directors, a committee thereof to whom a report could be made pursuant to §205.3(b)(3), or a qualified legal compliance committee, has retained or directed an attorney to review the reported evidence of a material violation and either:

(i) Has substantially implemented any remedial recommendations made by such attorney after a reasonable investigation and evaluation of the reported evidence; or

(ii) Has been advised that such attorney may, consistent with his or her professional obligations, assert a colorable defense on behalf of the issuer (or the issuer's officer, director, employee, or agent, as the case may be) in any investigation or judicial or administrative proceeding relating to the reported evidence of a material violation.

(c) *Attorney* means any person who is admitted, licensed, or otherwise qualified to practice law in any *jurisdiction*, domestic or foreign, or who holds himself or herself out as admitted, licensed, or otherwise qualified to practice law.

(d) *Breach of fiduciary duty* refers to any breach of fiduciary or similar duty to the issuer recognized under an applicable Federal or State statute or at common law, including but not limited to misfeasance, nonfeasance, abdication of duty, abuse of trust, and approval of unlawful transactions.

(e) *Evidence of a material violation* means credible evidence, based upon which it *would* be unreasonable, *under* the circumstances, for a prudent and competent attorney not to conclude that it is reasonably likely that a material violation has occurred, is ongoing, or is about to occur. . . .

(f) *Foreign government issuer* . . .

(g) *In the representation of an issuer* means providing legal services as an *attorney* for an issuer, regardless of whether the attorney is employed or retained by the issuer.

(h) *Issuer* . . . does not include a foreign government issuer. For purposes of paragraphs (a) and (g) of this section, the term "issuer" includes any person controlled by an issuer, where an attorney provides legal services to such person on behalf of, or at the behest, or for the benefit of the issuer, regardless of whether the attorney is employed or retained by the issuer.

(i) *Material violation* means a material violation of an applicable United States federal or state securities law, a *material* breach of fiduciary duty arising under United States federal or state law, or a similar material violation of any United States federal or state law.

(j) *Non-appearing foreign attorney* . . .

(k) *Qualified legal compliance committee* . . .

(l) *Reasonable* or *reasonably* denotes, with respect to the actions of an attorney, conduct that would not be unreasonable for a prudent and competent attorney.

(m) *Reasonably believes* means that an attorney believes the matter in question and that the circumstances are such that the belief is not unreasonable.

(n) *Report* means to make known to directly, either in person, by telephone, by e-mail, electronically, or in writing.

§205.3   Issuer as Client

(a) *Representing an issuer.* An attorney appearing and practicing before the Commission in the representation of an issuer owes his or her professional and ethical duties to the issuer as an organization. That the attorney may work with and advise the issuer's officers, directors, or employees in the course of representing the issuer does not make such individuals the attorney's clients.

(b) *Duty to report evidence of a material violation.*

(1) If an attorney, appearing and practicing before the Commission in the representation of an issuer, becomes aware of evidence of a material violation by the issuer or by any officer, director, employee, or agent of the issuer, the attorney shall report such evidence to the issuer's chief legal officer (or the equivalent thereof) or to both the issuer's chief legal officer and its chief executive officer (or the equivalents thereof) forthwith. By communicating such information to the issuer's officers or directors, an attorney does not reveal client confidences or secrets or privileged or otherwise protected information related to the attorney's representation of an issuer.

(2) The chief legal officer (or the equivalent thereof) shall cause such inquiry into the evidence of a material violation as he or she reasonably believes is appropriate to determine whether the material violation described in the report has occurred, is ongoing, or is about to occur. If the chief legal officer (or the equivalent thereof) determines no material violation has occurred, is ongoing, or is about to occur, he or she shall notify the reporting attorney and advise the reporting attorney of the basis for such determination. Unless the chief legal officer (or the equivalent thereof) reasonably believes that no material violation has occurred, is ongoing, or is about to occur, he or she shall take all reasonable steps to cause the issuer to adopt an appropriate response, and shall advise the reporting attorney thereof. . . .

(3) Unless an attorney who has made a report under paragraph (b)(1) of this section reasonably believes that the chief legal officer or

the chief executive officer of the issuer (or the equivalent thereof) has provided an appropriate response within a reasonable time, the attorney shall report the evidence of a material violation to:

(i) The audit committee of the issuer's board of directors;

(ii) Another committee of the issuer's board of directors consisting solely of directors who are not employed, directly or indirectly, by the issuer . . . ; or

(iii) The issuer's board of directors (if the issuer's board of directors has no committee consisting solely of directors who are not employed, directly or indirectly, by the issuer . . .).

(4) If an attorney reasonably believes that it would be futile to report evidence of a material violation to the issuer's chief legal officer and chief executive officer (or the equivalents thereof) under paragraph (b)(1) of this section, the attorney may report such evidence as provided under paragraph (b)(3) of this section.

(5) An attorney retained or directed by an issuer to investigate evidence of a material violation reported under paragraph (b)(1), (b)(3), or (b)(4) of this section shall be deemed to be appearing and practicing before the Commission. Directing or retaining an attorney to investigate reported evidence of a material violation does not relieve an officer or director of the issuer to whom such evidence has been reported under paragraph (b)(1), (b)(3), or (b)(4) of this section from a duty to respond to the reporting attorney.

(6) An attorney shall not have any obligation to report evidence of a material violation under this paragraph (b) if:

(i) The attorney was retained or directed by the issuer's chief legal officer (or the equivalent thereof) to investigate such evidence of a material violation and:

(A) The attorney reports the results of such investigation to the chief legal officer (or the equivalent thereof); and

(B) Except where the attorney and the chief legal officer (or the equivalent thereof) each reasonably believes that no material violation has occurred, is ongoing, or is about to occur, the chief legal officer (or the equivalent thereof) reports the results of the investigation to the issuer's board of directors, a committee thereof to whom a report could be made pursuant to paragraph (b)(3) of this section, or a qualified legal compliance committee; or

(ii) The attorney was retained or directed by the chief legal officer (or the equivalent thereof) to assert, consistent with his or her professional obligations, a colorable defense on behalf of the issuer (or the issuer's officer, director, employee, or agent, as the case may be) in any investigation or judicial or administrative proceeding relating to such evidence of a material violation, and the chief legal officer (or the equivalent thereof) provides reasonable and timely reports on the progress and outcome of such proceeding to the issuer's board of directors, a committee thereof to whom a report could be made pursuant to paragraph (b)(3) of this section, or a qualified legal compliance committee. . . .

(8) An attorney who receives what he or she reasonably believes is an appropriate and timely response to a report he or she has made pursuant to paragraph (b)(1), (b)(3), or (b)(4) of this section need do nothing more under this section with respect to his or her report.

(9) An attorney who does not reasonably believe that the issuer has made an appropriate response within a reasonable time to the report or reports made pursuant to paragraph (b)(1), (b)(3), or (b)(4) of this section shall explain his or her reasons therefor to the chief legal officer (or the equivalent thereof), the chief executive officer (or the equivalent thereof), and directors to whom the attorney reported the evidence of a material violation pursuant to paragraph (b)(1), (b)(3), or (b)(4) of this section.

(10) An attorney formerly employed or retained by an issuer who has reported evidence of a material violation under this part and reasonably believes that he or she has been discharged for so doing may notify the issuer's board of directors or any committee thereof that he or she believes that he or she has been discharged for reporting evidence of a material violation under this section. . . .

(d) *Issuer confidences.*

(1) Any report under this section (or the contemporaneous record thereof) or any response thereto (or the contemporaneous record thereof) may be used by an attorney in connection with any investigation, proceeding, or litigation in which the attorney's compliance with this part is in issue.

(2) An attorney appearing and practicing before the Commission in the representation of an issuer may reveal to the Commission, without the issuer's consent, confidential information related to the representation to the extent the attorney reasonably believes necessary:

(i) To prevent the issuer from committing a material violation that is likely to cause substantial injury to the financial interest or property of the issuer or investors;

(ii) To prevent the issuer, in a Commission investigation or administrative proceeding from committing perjury, proscribed in 18 U.S.C. 1621; suborning perjury, proscribed in 18 U.S.C. 1622; or committing any act proscribed in 18 U.S.C. 1001 that is likely to perpetrate a fraud upon the Commission; or

(iii) To rectify the consequences of a material violation by the issuer that caused, or may cause, substantial injury to the financial interest or property of the issuer or investors in the furtherance of which the attorney's services were used.

§205.4   Responsibilities of Supervisory Attorneys

(a) An attorney supervising or directing another attorney who is appearing and practicing before the Commission in the representation of an issuer is a supervisory attorney. An issuer's chief legal officer (or the equivalent thereof) is a supervisory attorney under this section.

(b) A supervisory attorney shall make reasonable efforts to ensure that a subordinate attorney, as defined in §205.5(a), that he or she supervises or directs conforms to this part. To the extent a subordinate attorney appears and practices before the Commission in the representation of an issuer, that subordinate attorney's supervisory attorneys also appear and practice before the Commission.

(c) A supervisory attorney is responsible for complying with the reporting requirements in §205.3 when a subordinate attorney has reported to the supervisory attorney evidence of a material violation. . . .

§205.5   Responsibilities of a Subordinate Attorney

(a) An attorney who appears and practices before the Commission in the representation of an issuer on a matter under the supervision or direction of another attorney (other than under the direct supervision or direction of the issuer's chief legal officer (or the equivalent thereof)) is a subordinate attorney.

(b) A subordinate attorney shall comply with this part notwithstanding that the subordinate attorney acted at the direction of or under the supervision of another person.

(c) A subordinate attorney complies with §205.3 if the subordinate attorney reports to his or her supervising attorney under §205.3(b) evidence of a material violation of which the subordinate attorney has become aware in appearing and practicing before the Commission.

(d) A subordinate attorney may take the steps permitted or required by §205.3(b) or (c) if the subordinate attorney reasonably believes that a supervisory attorney to whom he or she has reported evidence of a material violation under §205.3(b) has failed to comply with §205.3.

§205.6   Sanctions and Discipline

(a) A violation of this part by any attorney appearing and practicing before the Commission in the representation of an issuer shall subject such attorney to the civil penalties and remedies for a violation of the federal securities laws available to the Commission in an action brought by the Commission thereunder.

(b) An attorney appearing and practicing before the Commission who violates any provision of this part is subject to the disciplinary authority of the Commission, regardless of whether the attorney may also be subject to discipline for the same conduct in a jurisdiction where the attorney is admitted or practices. An administrative disciplinary proceeding initiated by the Commission for violation of this part may result in an attorney being censured, or being temporarily or permanently denied the privilege of appearing or practicing before the Commission.

(c) An attorney who complies in good faith with the provisions of this part shall not be subject to discipline or otherwise liable under inconsistent standards imposed by any state or other United States jurisdiction where the attorney is admitted or practices.

(d) An attorney practicing outside the United States shall not be required to comply with the requirements of this part to the extent that such compliance is prohibited by applicable foreign law.

§205.7　No Private Right of Action

(a) Nothing in this part is intended to, or does, create a private right of action against any attorney, law firm, or issuer based upon compliance or noncompliance with its provisions.

(b) Authority to enforce compliance with this part is vested exclusively in the Commission.

SELECTED PROVISIONS FROM 18 U.S.C.

Editors' Note.　Title 18 of the United States Code is entitled "Crimes and Criminal Procedure." A violation of any of the provisions reprinted below from Title 18 is a crime.

§201.　Bribery of Public Official and Witnesses . . .

(c) Whoever— . . .

(2) directly or indirectly, gives, offers or promises anything of value to any person, for or because of the testimony under oath or affirmation given or to be given by such person as a witness upon a trial, hearing, or other proceeding, before any court, any committee of either House or both Houses of Congress, or any agency, commission, or officer authorized by the laws of the United States to hear evidence or take testimony, or for or because of such person's absence therefrom;

(3) directly or indirectly, demands, seeks, receives, accepts, or agrees to receive or accept anything of value personally for or because

of the testimony under oath or affirmation given or to be given by such person as a witness upon any such trial, hearing, or other proceeding, or for or because of such person's absence therefrom; shall be fined under this title or imprisoned for not more than two years, or both.

(d) Paragraphs (3) and (4) of subsection (b) and paragraphs (2) and (3) of subsection (c) shall not be construed to prohibit the payment or receipt of witness fees provided by law, or the payment, by the party upon whose behalf a witness is called and receipt by a witness, of the reasonable cost of travel and subsistence incurred and the reasonable value of time lost in attendance at any such trial, hearing, or proceeding, or in the case of expert witnesses, a reasonable fee for time spent in the preparation of such opinion, and in appearing and testifying.

§202. Definitions

(b) For the purposes of sections 205 and 207 of this title, the term "official responsibility" means the direct administrative or operating authority, whether intermediate or final, and either exercisable alone or with others, and either personally or through subordinates, to approve, disapprove, or otherwise direct Government action. . . .

§207. Restrictions on Former Officers, Employees, and Elected Officials of the Executive and Legislative Branches

(a) Restrictions on all officers and employees of the executive branch and certain other agencies.—

(1) *Permanent restrictions on representation on particular matters.*— Any person who is an officer or employee (including any special Government employee) of the executive branch of the United States (including any independent agency of the United States), or of the District of Columbia, and who, after the termination of his or her service or employment with the United States or the District of Columbia, knowingly makes, with the intent to influence, any communication to or appearance before any officer or employee of any department, agency, court, or court-martial of the United States or the District of Columbia, on behalf of any other person (except the United States or the District of Columbia) in connection with a particular matter—

(A) in which the United States or the District of Columbia is a party or has a direct and substantial interest,

(B) in which the person participated personally and substantially as such officer or employee, and

(C) which involved a specific party or specific parties at the time of such participation, shall be punished as provided in section 216 of this title.

(2) *Two-year restrictions concerning particular matters under official responsibility.*—Any person subject to the restrictions contained in paragraph (1) who, within 2 years after the termination of his or her service or employment with the United States or the District of Columbia, knowingly makes, with the intent to influence, any communication to or appearance before any officer or employee of any department, agency, court, or court-martial of the United States or the District of Columbia, on behalf of any other person (except the United States or the District of Columbia), in connection with a particular matter—

(A) in which the United States or the District of Columbia is a party or has a direct and substantial interest,

(B) which such person knows or reasonably should know was actually pending under his or her official responsibility as such officer or employee within a period of 1 year before the termination of his or her service or employment with the United States or the District of Columbia, and

(C) which involved a specific party or specific parties at the time it was so pending, shall be punished as provided in section 216 of this title.

(3) *Clarification of restrictions.*— The restrictions contained in paragraphs (1) and (2) shall apply—

(A) in the case of an officer or employee of the executive branch of the United States (including any independent agency), only with respect to communications to or appearances before any officer or employee of any department, agency, court, or court-martial of the United States on behalf of any other person (except the United States), and only with respect to a matter in which the United States is a party or has a direct and substantial interest. . . .

Editors' Note. Violations of these provisions carry sentences of up to five years if willful, one year if not willful. Further, the Attorney General is authorized to seek civil penalties and injunctive relief. *See* 18 U.S.C. §216. The remainder of §207, which is lengthy and detailed, imposes restrictions on various categories of former government officers and employees, including (among others) trade negotiators and treaty negotiators; certain "senior personnel" and "very senior personnel" of the executive branch and independent agencies; and former Members of Congress and their "personal staff," "committee staff," and "leadership staff."

---

§1503.   Influencing or Injuring Officer or Juror Generally

(a) Whoever corruptly, or by threats or force, or by any threatening letter or communication, endeavors to influence, intimidate, or impede any grand or petit juror, or officer in or of any court of the United States, or officer who may be serving at any examination or other proceeding before any United States magistrate judge or other committing magistrate, in the discharge of his duty, or injures any such grand or petit juror in his person or property on account of any verdict or indictment assented to by him, or on account of his being or having been such juror, or injures any such officer, magistrate judge, or other committing magistrate in his person or property on account of the performance of his official duties, or corruptly or by threats or force, or by any threatening letter or communication, influences, obstructs, or impedes, or endeavors to influence, obstruct, or impede, the due administration of justice, shall be punished as provided in subsection (b). If the offense under this section occurs in connection with a trial of a criminal case, and the act in violation of this section involves the threat of physical force or physical force, the maximum term of imprisonment which may be imposed for the offense shall be the higher of that otherwise provided by law or the maximum term that could have been imposed for any offense charged in such case.

(b) The punishment for an offense under this section is—

(1) in the case of a killing, the punishment provided in sections 1111 and 1112;

(2) in the case of an attempted killing, or a case in which the offense was committed against a petit juror and in which a class A or B felony was charged, imprisonment for not more than 20 years, a fine under this title, or both; and

(3) in any other case, imprisonment for not more than 10 years, a fine under this title, or both.

§1505.   Obstruction of Proceedings Before Departments, Agencies, and Committees

Whoever, with intent to avoid, evade, prevent, or obstruct compliance, in whole or in part, with any civil investigative demand duly and properly made under the Antitrust Civil Process Act, willfully withholds, misrepresents, removes from any place, conceals, covers up, destroys, mutilates, alters, or by other means falsifies any documentary material, answers to written interrogatories, or oral testimony, which is the subject of such demand; or attempts to do so or solicits another to do so; or

Whoever corruptly, or by threats or force, or by any threatening letter or communication influences, obstructs, or impedes or endeavors to influence, obstruct, or impede the due and proper administration of the law under which any pending proceeding is being had before any department or agency of the United States, or the due and proper exercise of the power of inquiry under which any inquiry or investigation is being had by either House, or any committee of either House or any joint committee of the Congress—Shall be fined under this title, imprisoned not more than 5 years or, if the offense involves international or domestic terrorism (as defined in section 2331), imprisoned not more than 8 years, or both.

§1510.   Obstruction of Criminal Investigations

(a) Whoever willfully endeavors by means of bribery to obstruct, delay, or prevent the communication of information relating to a violation of any criminal statute of the United States by any person to a criminal investigator shall be fined under this title, or imprisoned not more than five years, or both. . . .

§1512.   Tampering with a Witness, Victim, or an Informant . . .

Editors' Note.   Section 1512(c) was added by the Sarbanes-Oxley Act of 2002, Pub. L. No. 107-204, which was signed into law by President Bush on July 30, 2002.

(b) Whoever knowingly uses intimidation, threatens, or corruptly persuades another person, or attempts to do so, or engages in misleading conduct toward another person, with intent to—
   (1) influence, delay, or prevent the testimony of any person in an official proceeding;
   (2) cause or induce any person to—
      (A) withhold testimony, or withhold a record, document, or other object, from an official proceeding;
      (B) alter, destroy, mutilate, or conceal an object with intent to impair the object's integrity or availability for use in an official proceeding;
      (C) evade legal process summoning that person to appear as a witness, or to produce a record, document, or other object, in an official proceeding; or
      (D) be absent from an official proceeding to which such person has been summoned by legal process; or
   (3) hinder, delay, or prevent the communication to a law enforcement officer or judge of the United States of information relating to the commission or possible commission of a Federal offense or a violation of conditions of probation, parole, or release pending judicial proceedings; shall be fined under this title or imprisoned not more than 20 years, or both.
   (c) Whoever corruptly—

(1) alters, destroys, mutilates, or conceals a record, document, or other object, or attempts to do so, with the intent to impair the object's integrity or availability for use in an official proceeding; or

(2) otherwise obstructs, influences, or impedes any official proceeding, or attempts to do so, shall be fined under this title or imprisoned not more than 20 years, or both.

(d) Whoever intentionally harasses another person and thereby hinders, delays, prevents, or dissuades any person from—

(1) attending or testifying in an official proceeding;

(2) reporting to a law enforcement officer or judge of the United States the commission or possible commission of a Federal offense or a violation of conditions of probation, supervised release, parole, or release pending judicial proceedings;

(3) arresting or seeking the arrest of another person in connection with a Federal offense; or

(4) causing a criminal prosecution, or a parole or probation revocation proceeding, to be sought or instituted, or assisting in such prosecution or proceeding; or attempts to do so, shall be fined under this title or imprisoned not more than 3 years, or both.

(e) In a prosecution for an offense under this section, it is an affirmative defense, as to which the defendant has the burden of proof by a preponderance of the evidence, that the conduct consisted solely of lawful conduct and that the defendant's sole intention was to encourage, induce, or cause the other person to testify truthfully.

(f) For the purposes of this section—

(1) an official proceeding need not be pending or about to be instituted at the time of the offense; and

(2) the testimony, or the record, document, or other object need not be admissible in evidence or free of a claim of privilege. . . .

(j) If the offense under this section occurs in connection with a trial of a criminal case, the maximum term of imprisonment which may be imposed for the offense shall be the higher of that otherwise provided by law or the maximum term that could have been imposed for any offense charged in such case.

(k) Whoever conspires to commit any offense under this section shall be subject to the same penalties as those prescribed or the offense the commission of which was the object of the conspiracy.

§1513. Retaliating Against a Witness, Victim, or an Informant . . .

Editors' Note. Section 1513(e) was added by the Sarbanes-Oxley Act of 2002, Pub. L. 107-204, which was signed into law by President Bush on July 30, 2002.

(e) Whoever knowingly, with the intent to retaliate, takes any action harmful to any person, including interference with the lawful employment or livelihood of any person, for providing to a law enforcement officer any truthful information relating to the commission or possible commission of any Federal offense, shall be fined under this title or imprisoned not more than 10 years, or both.

§1515.   Definitions for Certain Provisions; General Provisions

(a) As used in sections 1512 and 1513 of this title and in this section . . .

     (1) the term "official proceeding" means—

         (A) a proceeding before a judge or court of the United States . . . ;

         (B) a proceeding before the Congress;

         (C) a proceeding before a Federal Government agency which is authorized by law; or

         (D) a proceeding involving the business of insurance whose activities affect interstate commerce before any insurance regulatory official or agency . . . ;

     (2) the term "physical force" means physical action against another, and includes confinement;

     (3) the term "misleading conduct" means—

         (A) knowingly making a false statement;

         (B) intentionally omitting information from a statement and thereby causing a portion of such statement to be misleading, or intentionally concealing a material fact, and thereby creating a false impression by such statement;

         (C) with intent to mislead, knowingly submitting or inviting reliance on a writing or recording that is false, forged, altered, or otherwise lacking in authenticity;

         (D) with intent to mislead, knowingly submitting or inviting reliance on a sample, specimen, map, photograph, boundary mark, or other object that is misleading in a material respect; or

         (E) knowingly using a trick, scheme, or device with intent to mislead; . . . and

     (6) the term "corruptly persuades" does not include conduct which would be misleading conduct but for a lack of a state of mind.

(b) As used in section 1505, the term "corruptly" means acting with an improper purpose, personally or by influencing another, including making a false or misleading statement, or withholding, concealing, altering, or destroying a document or other information.

(c) This chapter does not prohibit or punish the providing of lawful, bona fide, legal representation services in connection with or anticipation of an official proceeding.

§1519.   Destruction, Alteration, or Falsification of Records in Federal Investigations and Bankruptcy

> **Editors' Note.**   Section 1519 was added by the Sarbanes-Oxley Act of 2002, Pub. L. No. 107-204, which was signed into law by President Bush on July 30, 2002.

Whoever knowingly alters, destroys, mutilates, conceals, covers up, falsifies, or makes a false entry in any record, document, or tangible object with the intent to impede, obstruct, or influence the investigation or proper administration of any matter within the jurisdiction of any department or agency of the United States or any case filed under title 11, or in relation to or contemplation of any such matter or case, shall be fined under this title, imprisoned not more than 20 years, or both.

§1621.   Perjury Generally

Whoever—

(1) having taken an oath before a competent tribunal, officer, or person, in any case in which a law of the United States authorizes an oath to be administered, that he will testify, declare, depose, or certify truly, or that any written testimony, declaration, deposition, or certificate by him subscribed, is true, willfully and contrary to such oath states or subscribes any material matter which he does not believe to be true; or

(2) in any declaration, certificate, verification, or statement under penalty of perjury as permitted under section 1746 of title 28, United States Code, willfully subscribes as true any material matter which he does not believe to be true;

is guilty of perjury and shall, except as otherwise expressly provided by law, be fined under this title or imprisoned not more than five years, or both. This section is applicable whether the statement or subscription is made within or without the United States.

> **Editors' Note.**   28 U.S.C. §1746, which is mentioned in 18 U.S.C. §1621, provides, in essence, that whenever federal law permits or requires a person to support any matter with an affidavit or other sworn declaration, then "such matter may, with like force and effect, be supported . . . by the unsworn declaration . . . in writing of such person which is subscribed by him, as true under penalty of perjury . . . in substantially the following form: . . . 'I declare . . . under penalty of perjury under the laws of the United States of America that the foregoing is true and correct.' "

§1622.   Subornation of Perjury

Whoever procures another to commit any perjury is guilty of subornation of perjury, and shall be fined under this title or imprisoned not more than five years, or both.

§1905.   Disclosure of Confidential Information Generally

Whoever, being an officer or employee of the United States or of any department or agency thereof, . . . publishes, divulges, discloses, or makes known in any manner or to any extent not authorized by law any information coming to him in the course of his employment or official duties or by reason of any examination or investigation made by, or return, report or record made to or filed with, such department or agency or officer or employee thereof, which information concerns or relates to the trade secrets, processes, operations, style of work, or apparatus, or to the identity, confidential statistical data, amount or source of any income, profits, losses, or expenditures of any person, firm, partnership, corporation, or association; or permits any income return or copy thereof or any book containing any abstract or particulars thereof to be seen or examined by any person except as provided by law; shall be fined under this title, or imprisoned not more than one year, or both; and shall be removed from office or employment.

§3500.   Demands for Production of Statements and Reports of Witnesses ["Jencks Act"]

(a) In any criminal prosecution brought by the United States, no statement or report in the possession of the United States which was made by a Government witness or prospective Government witness (other than the defendant) shall be the subject of subpoena, discovery, or inspection until said witness has testified on direct examination in the trial of the case.

(b) After a witness called by the United States has testified on direct examination, the court shall, on motion of the defendant, order the United States to produce any statement (as hereinafter defined) of the witness in the possession of the United States which relates to the subject matter as to which the witness has testified. If the entire contents of any such statement relate to the subject matter of the testimony of the witness, the court shall order it to be delivered directly to the defendant for his examination and use.

(c) If the United States claims that any statement ordered to be produced under this section contains matter which does not relate to the subject matter of the testimony of the witness, the court shall order the United States to deliver such statement for the inspection of the court in camera. Upon such delivery the court shall excise the portions of such statement which do not relate to the subject matter of the testimony of the witness. With such material excised, the court shall then direct delivery of such statement to the defendant for his use. . . .

(d) If the United States elects not to comply with an order of the court under subsection (b) or (c) hereof to deliver to the defendant any such statement, or such portion thereof as the court may direct, the court shall strike from the record the testimony of the witness, and the trial shall proceed unless the court in its discretion shall determine that the interests of justice require that a mistrial be declared.

(e) The term "statement", as used in subsections (b), (c), and (d) of this section in relation to any witness called by the United States, means —

(1) a written statement made by said witness and signed or otherwise adopted or approved by him;

(2) a stenographic, mechanical, electrical, or other recording, or a transcription thereof, which is a substantially verbatim recital of an oral statement made by said witness and recorded contemporaneously with the making of such oral statement; or

(3) a statement, however taken or recorded, or a transcription thereof, if any, made by said witness to a grand jury.

SELECTED PROVISIONS FROM 28 U.S.C.

Editors' Note. The section reprinted here, 28 U.S.C. §530B, resolved a disagreement between courts and the U.S. Department of Justice over whether the so-called no-contact rule applied to lawyers working for the federal government. (The no-contact rule, which is set forth in Rule 4.2 of the ABA Model Rules of Professional Conduct, generally prohibits a lawyer who represents a client from communicating about the subject of the representation with a person the lawyer knows to be represented by counsel in the matter.) For more information about the history of 28 U.S.C. §530B, see the entry entitled "Department of Justice Rules" in the Related Materials following ABA Model Rule 4.2 above.

§530B. Ethical Standards for Attorneys for the Government

(a) An attorney for the Government shall be subject to State laws and rules, and local Federal court rules, governing attorneys in each State where such attorney engages in that attorney's duties, to the same extent and in the same manner as other attorneys in that State.

(b) **The Attorney General shall make and amend rules of the Department of Justice to assure compliance with this section.**

(c) **As used in this section, the term "attorney for the Government" includes any attorney described in section 77.2(a) of part 77 of title 28 of the Code of Federal Regulations and also includes any independent counsel, or employee of such a counsel, appointed under chapter 40.**

SELECTED PROVISIONS FROM 28 C.F.R. PART 77

Editors' Note.   The Department of Justice has issued the following regulations implementing 28 U.S.C. §530B.

§77.1.   Purpose and Authority

(a) **The Department of Justice is committed to ensuring that its attorneys perform their duties in accordance with the highest ethical standards. The purpose of this part is to implement 28 U.S.C. 530B and to provide guidance to attorneys concerning the requirements imposed on Department attorneys by 28 U.S.C. 530B.**

(b) **Section 530B requires Department attorneys to comply with state and local federal court rules of professional responsibility, but should not be construed in any way to alter federal substantive, procedural, or evidentiary law or to interfere with the Attorney General's authority to send Department attorneys into any court in the United States.**

(c) **Section 530B imposes on Department attorneys the same rules of professional responsibility that apply to non-Department attorneys, but should not be construed to impose greater burdens on Department attorneys than those on non-Department attorneys or to alter rules of professional responsibility that expressly exempt government attorneys from their application.**

(d) **The regulations set forth in this part seek to provide guidance to Department attorneys in determining the rules with which such attorneys should comply.**

§77.2.   Definitions

As used in this part, the following terms shall have the following meanings, unless the context indicates otherwise: . . .

(b) **The term** *case* **means any proceeding over which a state or federal court has jurisdiction, including criminal prosecutions and civil actions. This term also includes grand jury investigations and related proceedings (such as motions to quash grand jury subpoenas** and motions to compel testimony), applications for search warrants, and applications for electronic surveillance.

(c) The phrase *civil law enforcement investigation* means an investigation of possible civil violations of, or claims under, federal law that may form the basis for a civil law enforcement proceeding.

(d) The phrase *civil law enforcement proceeding* means a civil action or proceeding before any court or other tribunal brought by the Department of Justice under the authority of the United States to enforce federal laws or regulations, and includes proceedings related to the enforcement of an administrative subpoena or summons or civil investigative demand.

(e) The terms *conduct* and *activity* mean any act performed by a Department attorney that implicates a rule governing attorneys, as that term is defined in paragraph (h) of this section. . . .

(g) The term *person* means any individual or organization.

(h) The phrase *state laws and rules and local federal court rules governing attorneys* means rules enacted or adopted by any State or Territory of the United States or the District of Columbia or by any federal court, that prescribe ethical conduct for attorneys and that would subject an attorney, whether or not a Department attorney, to professional discipline, such as a code of professional responsibility. The phrase does not include:

(1) Any statute, rule, or regulation which does not govern ethical conduct, such as rules of procedure, evidence, or substantive law, whether or not such rule is included in a code of professional responsibility for attorneys;

(2) Any statute, rule, or regulation that purports to govern the conduct of any class of persons other than attorneys, such as rules that govern the conduct of all litigants and judges, as well as attorneys; or

(3) A statute, rule, or regulation requiring licensure or membership in a particular state bar.

(i) The phrase *state of licensure* means the District of Columbia or any State or Territory where a Department attorney is duly licensed and authorized to practice as an attorney. . . .

(j)(1) The phrase *where such attorney engages in that attorney's duties* identifies which rules of ethical conduct a Department attorney should comply with, and means, with respect to particular conduct:

(i) If there is a case pending, the rules of ethical conduct adopted by the local federal court or state court before which the case is pending; or

(ii) If there is no case pending, the rules of ethical conduct that would be applied by the attorney's state of licensure.

(2) A Department attorney does not "engage[] in that attorney's duties" in any states in which the attorney's conduct is not

substantial and continuous, such as a jurisdiction in which an attorney takes a deposition (related to a case pending in another court) or directs a contact to be made by an investigative agent, or responds to an inquiry by an investigative agent. Nor does the phrase include any jurisdiction that would not ordinarily apply its rules of ethical conduct to particular conduct or activity by the attorney.

(k) The phrase *to the same extent and in the same manner as other attorneys* means that Department attorneys shall only be subject to laws and rules of ethical conduct governing attorneys in the same manner as such rules apply to non-Department attorneys. The phrase does not, however, purport to eliminate or otherwise alter state or federal laws and rules and federal court rules that expressly exclude some or all government attorneys from particular limitations or prohibitions.

§77.3.   Application of 28 U.S.C. 530B

In all criminal investigations and prosecutions, in all civil investigations and litigation (affirmative and defensive), and in all civil law enforcement investigations and proceedings, attorneys for the government shall conform their conduct and activities to the state rules and laws, and federal local court rules, governing attorneys in each State where such attorney engages in that attorney s duties, to the same extent and in the same manner as other attorneys in that State, as these terms are defined in §77.2 of this part.

§77.4.   Guidance

(a) *Rules of the court before which a case is pending.* A government attorney shall, in all cases, comply with the rules of ethical conduct of the court before which a particular case is pending.

(b) *Inconsistent rules where there is a pending case.*

(1) If the rule of the attorney's state of licensure would prohibit an action that is permissible under the rules of the court before which a case is pending, the attorney should consider:

(i) Whether the attorney's state of licensure would apply the rule of the court before which the case is pending, rather than the rule of the state of licensure;

(ii) Whether the local federal court rule preempts contrary state rules; and

(iii) Whether application of traditional choice-of-law principles directs the attorney to comply with a particular rule.

(2) In the process of considering the factors described in paragraph (b)(1) of this section, the attorney is encouraged to consult with

a supervisor or Professional Responsibility Officer to determine the best course of conduct.

(c) *Choice of rules where there is no pending case.*

(1) Where no case is pending, the attorney should generally comply with the ethical rules of the attorney's state of licensure, unless application of traditional choice-of-law principles directs the attorney to comply with the ethical rule of another jurisdiction or court, such as the ethical rule adopted by the court in which the case is likely to be brought.

(2) In the process of considering the factors described in paragraph (c)(1) of this section, the attorney is encouraged to consult with a supervisor or Professional Responsibility Officer to determine the best course of conduct.

(d) *Rules that impose an irreconcilable conflict.* If, after consideration of traditional choice-of-law principles, the attorney concludes that multiple rules may apply to particular conduct and that such rules impose irreconcilable obligations on the attorney, the attorney should consult with a supervisor or Professional Responsibility Officer to determine the best course of conduct.

(e) *Supervisory attorneys.* Each attorney, including supervisory attorneys, must assess his or her ethical obligations with respect to particular conduct. Department attorneys shall not direct any attorney to engage in conduct that violates section 530B. A supervisor or other Department attorney who, in good faith, gives advice or guidance to another Department attorney about the other attorney's ethical obligations should not be deemed to violate these rules.

(f) *Investigative Agents.* A Department attorney shall not direct an investigative agent acting under the attorney's supervision to engage in conduct under circumstances that would violate the attorney's obligations under section 530B. A Department attorney who in good faith provides legal advice or guidance upon request to an investigative agent should not be deemed to violate these rules.

§77.5. No Private Remedies

The principles set forth herein, and internal office procedures adopted pursuant hereto, are intended solely for the guidance of attorneys for the government. They are not intended to, do not, and may not be relied upon to create a right or benefit, substantive or procedural, enforceable at law by a party to litigation with the United States, including criminal defendants, targets or subjects of criminal investigations, witnesses in criminal or civil cases (including civil law enforcement proceedings), or plaintiffs or defendants in civil investigations or litigation; or any other person, whether or not a party to litigation with the United

States, or their counsel; and shall not be a basis for dismissing criminal or civil charges or proceedings or for excluding relevant evidence in any judicial or administrative proceeding. Nor are any limitations placed on otherwise lawful litigative prerogatives of the Department of Justice as a result of this part.

SELECTED PROVISIONS FROM 28 C.F.R. PART 50

Editors' Note. Employees of the U.S. Department of Justice (including lawyers) must abide by various guidelines set out in 28 C.F.R. Part 50. We reprint here 28 C.F.R. §50.2, which establishes guidelines regarding extrajudicial statements and the release of information to the press.

§50.2   Release of Information by Personnel of the Department of Justice Relating to Criminal and Civil Proceedings

(a) *General.*

(1) The availability to news media of information in criminal and civil cases is a matter which has become increasingly a subject of concern in the administration of justice. The purpose of this statement is to formulate specific guidelines for the release of such information by personnel of the Department of Justice.

(2) While the release of information for the purpose of influencing a trial is, of course, always improper, there are valid reasons for making available to the public information about the administration of the law. The task of striking a fair balance between the protection of individuals accused of crime or involved in civil proceedings with the Government and public understandings of the problems of controlling crime and administering government depends largely on the exercise of sound judgment by those responsible for administering the law and by representatives of the press and other media.

(3) Inasmuch as the Department of Justice has generally fulfilled its responsibilities with awareness and understanding of the competing needs in this area, this statement, to a considerable extent, reflects and formalizes the standards to which representatives of the Department have adhered in the past. Nonetheless, it will be helpful in ensuring uniformity of practice to set forth the following guidelines for all personnel of the Department of Justice.

(4) Because of the difficulty and importance of the questions they raise, it is felt that some portions of the matters covered by this statement, such as the authorization to make available Federal conviction

records and a description of items seized at the time of arrest, should be the subject of continuing review and consideration by the Department on the basis of experience and suggestions from those within and outside the Department.

(b) *Guidelines to criminal actions.*

(1) These guidelines shall apply to the release of information to news media from the time a person is the subject of a criminal investigation until any proceeding resulting from such an investigation has been terminated by trial or otherwise.

(2) At no time shall personnel of the Department of Justice furnish any statement or information for the purpose of influencing the outcome of a defendant's trial, nor shall personnel of the Department furnish any statement or information, which could reasonably be expected to be disseminated by means of public communication, if such a statement or information may reasonably be expected to influence the outcome of a pending or future trial.

(3) Personnel of the Department of Justice, subject to specific limitations imposed by law or court rule or order, may make public the following information:

(i) The defendant's name, age, residence, employment, marital status, and similar background information.

(ii) The substance or text of the charge, such as a complaint, indictment, or information.

(iii) The identity of the investigating and/or arresting agency and the length or scope of an investigation.

(iv) The circumstances immediately surrounding an arrest, including the time and place of arrest, resistance, pursuit, possession and use of weapons, and a description of physical items seized at the time of arrest.

Disclosures should include only incontrovertible, factual matters, and should not include subjective observations. In addition, where background information or information relating to the circumstances of an arrest or investigation would be highly prejudicial or where the release thereof would serve no law enforcement function, such information should not be made public.

(4) Personnel of the Department shall not disseminate any information concerning a defendant's prior criminal record.

(5) Because of the particular danger of prejudice resulting from statements in the period approaching and during trial, they ought strenuously to be avoided during that period. Any such statement or release shall be made only on the infrequent occasion when circumstances absolutely demand a disclosure of information and shall include only information which is clearly not prejudicial.

(6) The release of certain types of information generally tends to create dangers of prejudice without serving a significant law enforcement function. Therefore, personnel of the Department should refrain from making available the following:

(i) Observations about a defendant's character.

(ii) Statements, admissions, confessions, or alibis attributable to a defendant, or the refusal or failure of the accused to make a statement

(iii) Reference to investigative procedures such as fingerprints, polygraph examinations, ballistic tests, or laboratory tests, or to the refusal by the defendant to submit to such tests or examinations.

(iv) Statements concerning the identity, testimony, or credibility of prospective witnesses.

(v) Statements concerning evidence or argument in the case, whether or not it is anticipated that such evidence or argument will be used at trial.

(vi) Any opinion as to the accused's guilt, or the possibility of a plea of guilty to the offense charged, or the possibility of a plea to a lesser offense.

(7) Personnel of the Department of Justice should take no action to encourage or assist news media in photographing or televising a defendant or accused person being held or transported in Federal custody. Departmental representatives should not make available photographs of a defendant unless a law enforcement function is served thereby.

(8) This statement of policy is not intended to restrict the release of information concerning a defendant who is a fugitive from justice.

(9) Since the purpose of this statement is to set forth generally applicable guidelines, there will, of course, be situations in which it will limit the release of information which would not be prejudicial under the particular circumstances. If a representative of the Department believes that in the interest of the fair administration of justice and the law enforcement process information beyond these guidelines should be released, in a particular case, he shall request the permission of the Attorney General or the Deputy Attorney General to do so.

(c) *Guidelines to civil actions.* Personnel of the Department of Justice associated with a civil action shall not during its investigation or litigation make or participate in making an extrajudicial statement, other than a quotation from or reference to public records, which a reasonable person would expect to be disseminated by means of public communication if there is a reasonable likelihood that such dissemination will interfere with a fair trial and which relates to:

(1) Evidence regarding the occurrence or transaction involved.

(2) The character, credibility, or criminal records of a party, witness, or prospective witness.

(3) The performance or results of any examinations or tests or the refusal or failure of a party to submit to such.

(4) An opinion as to the merits of the claims or defenses of a party, except as required by law or administrative rule.

(5) Any other matter reasonably likely to interfere with a fair trial of the action.

Attorney-Client Privilege and Work Product Provisions

Editors' Introduction.   The ethical obligation of confidentiality addressed in Rule 1.6 of the ABA Model Rules of Professional Conduct is closely related to the evidentiary rules governing the attorney-client privilege and the procedural rules protecting attorney work product. The materials in this chapter show how the attorney-client privilege and the work product doctrine are codified in the Federal Rules of Evidence and the Federal Rules of Civil Procedure.

Additional privilege and work product provisions are found in this book in the Restatement (Third) of the Law Governing Lawyers (see the attorney-client privilege and work product provisions in §§59-93). Those editions of the book that contain the California or New York materials (or both) have privilege and work product provisions from those states in their respective chapters.

Rule 26 of the Federal Rules of Civil Procedure was last amended effective December 1, 2010. Specifically, amendments to Rule 26(b)(4)(B) and (C) provide heightened protection against discovery of communications between experts and counsel. Amended Rule 26(b)(4)(B) protects "drafts of any report or disclosure required under Rule 26(a)(2), regardless of the form in which the draft is recorded." Amended Rule 26(b)(4)(C) protects "communications between the party's attorney and any witness required to provide a report under Rule 26(a)(2)(B)" unless the communications: (i) relate to the expert's compensation; or (ii) "identify facts or data that the party's attorney provided and that the expert considered in forming the opinions to be expressed"; or (iii) "identify assumptions that the party's attorney provided and that the expert relied on in forming the opinions to be expressed."

For updates on future rule amendments, and for a wealth of information about recent and proposed amendments to the Federal Rules of Civil Procedure, the Federal Rules of Evidence, and other federal court rules that may affect privilege or work product, visit the official website of the United States Courts at *www.uscourts.gov* or call John Rabiej, Chief of the Rules Committee Support Office, at (202) 502-1820.

Contents

FEDERAL RULES OF EVIDENCE

Rule 501.   General Rule

Except as otherwise required by the Constitution of the United States or provided by Act of Congress or in rules prescribed by the Supreme Court pursuant to statutory authority, the privilege of a witness, person, government, State, or political subdivision thereof shall be governed by the principles of the common law as they may be interpreted by the courts of the United States in the light of reason and experience. However, in civil actions and proceedings, with respect to an element of a claim or defense as to which State law supplies the rule of decision, the privilege of a witness, person, government, State, or political subdivision thereof shall be determined in accordance with State law.

Rule 502.   Attorney-Client Privilege and Work Product; Limitations on Waiver

The following provisions apply, in the circumstances set out, to disclosure of a communication or information covered by the attorney-client privilege or work-product protection.

    (a) *Disclosure made in a federal proceeding or to a federal office or agency; scope of a waiver.* — **When the disclosure is made in a federal proceeding or to a federal office or agency and waives the attorney-client privilege or work-product protection, the waiver extends to an undisclosed communication or information in a federal or state proceeding only if:**

(1) the waiver is intentional;

(2) the disclosed and undisclosed communications or information concern the same subject matter; and

(3) they ought in fairness to be considered together.

(b) *Inadvertent disclosure.* — When made in a federal proceeding or to a federal office or agency, the disclosure does not operate as a waiver in a federal or state proceeding if:

(1) the disclosure is inadvertent;

(2) the holder of the privilege or protection took reasonable steps to prevent disclosure; and

(3) the holder promptly took reasonable steps to rectify the error, including (if applicable) following Fed. R. Civ. P. 26(b)(5)(B).

(c) *Disclosure made in a state proceeding.* — When the disclosure is made in a state proceeding and is not the subject of a state-court order concerning waiver, the disclosure does not operate as a waiver in a federal proceeding if the disclosure:

(1) would not be a waiver under this rule if it had been made in a federal proceeding; or

(2) is not a waiver under the law of the state where the disclosure occurred.

(d) *Controlling effect of a court order.* — A federal court may order that the privilege or protection is not waived by disclosure connected with the litigation pending before the court — in which event the disclosure is also not a waiver in any other federal or state proceeding.

(e) *Controlling effect of a party agreement.* — An agreement on the effect of disclosure in a federal proceeding is binding only on the parties to the agreement, unless it is incorporated into a court order.

(f) *Controlling effect of this rule.* — Notwithstanding Rules 101 and 1101, this rule applies to state proceedings and to federal court-annexed and federal court-mandated arbitration proceedings, in the circumstances set out in the rule. And notwithstanding Rule 501, this rule applies even if state law provides the rule of decision.

(g) *Definitions.* — In this rule:

(1) "attorney-client privilege" means the protection that applicable law provides for confidential attorney-client communications; and

(2) "work-product protection" means the protection that applicable law provides for tangible material (or its intangible equivalent) prepared in anticipation of litigation or for trial.

Proposed Rule 503.   Lawyer-Client Privilege (not enacted)

Editors' Note. When the Supreme Court transmitted the proposed Federal Rules of Evidence to Congress in 1973, the proposals contained 13 separate rules on privileges, ranging from Rule 501 through Rule 513. The proposed privilege rules were extremely controversial, however. Congress substantially altered proposed Rule 501, and completely rejected proposed Rules 502 through 513. We reprint Rule 503 here because, despite its rejection, it is an accurate general statement of the law governing the attorney-client privilege in many jurisdictions and has been adopted nearly verbatim in the evidence codes of some states (*see, e.g.,* Rule 503 of the Texas Rules of Criminal Evidence). To indicate that it did not become law, we reprint it in ordinary type rather than in bold.

(a) *Definitions.* As used in this rule:

(1) A "client" is a person, public officer, or corporation, association, or other organization or entity, either public or private, who is rendered professional legal services by a lawyer, or who consults a lawyer with a view to obtaining professional legal services from him.

(2) A "lawyer" is a person authorized, or reasonably believed by the client to be authorized, to practice law in any state or nation.

(3) A "representative of the lawyer" is one employed to assist the lawyer in the rendition of professional legal services.

(4) A communication is "confidential" if not intended to be disclosed to third persons other than those to whom disclosure is in furtherance of the rendition of professional legal services to the client or those reasonably necessary for the transmission of the communication.

(b) *General rule of privilege.* A client has a privilege to refuse to disclose and to prevent any other person from disclosing confidential communications made for the purpose of facilitating the rendition of professional legal services to the client, (1) between himself or his representative and his lawyer or his lawyer's representative, or (2) between his lawyer and the lawyer's representative, or (3) by him or his lawyer to a lawyer representing another in a matter of common interest, or (4) between representatives of the client or between the client and a representative of the client, or (5) between lawyers representing the client.

(c) *Who may claim the privilege?* The privilege may be claimed by the client, his guardian or conservator, the personal representative of a deceased client, or the successor, trustee, or similar representative of a corporation, association, or other organization, whether or not in existence. The person who was the lawyer at the time of the communication may claim the privilege but only on behalf of the client. His authority to do so is presumed in the absence of evidence to the contrary.

(d) *Exceptions.* There is no privilege under this rule:

(1) *Furtherance of crime or fraud.* If the services of the lawyer were sought or obtained to enable or aid anyone to commit or plan to commit what the client knew or reasonably should have known to be a crime or fraud; or

(2) *Claimants through same deceased client.* As to a communication relevant to an issue between parties who claim through the same deceased

client, regardless of whether the claims are by testate or intestate succession or by inter vivos transaction; or

(3) *Breach of duty by lawyer or client.* As to a communication relevant to an issue of breach of duty by the lawyer to his client or by the client to his lawyer; or

(4) *Document attested by lawyer.* As to a communication relevant to an issue concerning an attested document to which the lawyer is an attesting witness; or

(5) *Joint clients.* As to a communication relevant to a matter of common interest between two or more clients if the communication was made by any of them to a lawyer retained or consulted in common, when offered in an action between any of the clients.

FEDERAL RULES OF CIVIL PROCEDURE

Editors' Note. In federal courts, the work product doctrine is codified in Rules 26(b)(3)-(4) of the Federal Rules of Civil Procedure. These provisions were added to the rules in 1970 to resolve confusion and disagreement over the scope of the judicially created work product doctrine stemming from *Hickman v. Taylor,* 329 U.S. 495 (1947). Rule 26(b)(3) governs work product generally, including the mental opinions and impressions of lawyers, and Rule 26(b)(4) governs work product relating to experts. Rule 26(b)(5) was added in 1993 to enable parties to assess the applicability of privilege and work product protection to items withheld during discovery.

The Federal Rules of Criminal Procedure, in Rules 16(a)(2) and (b)(2) (which are not reprinted in this book), contain a form of work product protection, but the criminal work product protection is subject to many exceptions. For example, Rule 26.2 requires lawyers in criminal cases to turn over upon request any relevant statement made by a witness who has completed a direct examination at trial.

In addition, the Federal Rules, as interpreted by cases such as *Zubulake v. UBS Warburg LLC,* 229 F.R.D 422 (S.D.N.Y. 2004) and 220 F.R.D. 212 (S.D.N.Y. 2003), impose significant duties on lawyers with regard to a client's electronically stored information (ESI). See especially Rules 26(a)(1)(A)(ii); 26(b)(2)(B); 26(f)(3); and 37(f).

**Rule 26.   Duty to Disclose; General Provisions Governing
              Discovery . . .**

(b) Discovery Scope and Limits . . .

(3) *Trial Preparation: Materials.*

(A) *Documents and Tangible Things.* **Ordinarily, a party may not discover documents and tangible things that are prepared in anticipation of litigation or for trial by or for another party or its**

representative (including the other party's attorney, consultant, surety, indemnitor, insurer, or agent). But, subject to Rule 26(b)(4), those materials may be discovered if:

(i) they are otherwise discoverable under Rule 26(b)(1); and

(ii) the party shows that it has substantial need for the materials to prepare its case and cannot, without undue hardship, obtain their substantial equivalent by other means.

(B) *Protection Against Disclosure.* If the court orders discovery of those materials, it must protect against disclosure of the mental impressions, conclusions, opinions, or legal theories of a party's attorney or other representative concerning the litigation.

(C) *Previous Statement.* Any party or other person may, on request and without the required showing, obtain the person's own previous statement about the action or its subject matter. If the request is refused, the person may move for a court order, and Rule 37(a)(5) applies to the award of expenses. A previous statement is either:

(i) a written statement that the person has signed or otherwise adopted or approved; or

(ii) a contemporaneous stenographic, mechanical, electrical, or other recording — or a transcription of it — that recites substantially verbatim the person's oral statement.

(4) *Trial Preparation: Experts.*

(A) *Expert Who May Testify.* A party may depose any person who has been identified as an expert whose opinions may be presented at trial. If Rule 26(a)(2)(B) requires a report from the expert, the deposition may be conducted only after the report is provided.

(B) *Trial-Preparation Protection for Draft Reports or Disclosures.* Rule 26(b)(3)(A) and (B) protect drafts of any report or disclosure required under Rule 26(a)(2), regardless of the form in which the draft is recorded.

(C) *Trial-Preparation Protection for Communications Between a Party's Attorney and Expert Witnesses.* Rule 26(b)(3)(A) and (B) protect communications between the party's attorney and any witness required to provide a report under Rule 26(a)(2)(B) regardless of the form of the communications, except to the extent that the communications:

(i) relate to compensation for the expert's study or testimony;

(ii) identify facts or data that the party's attorney provided and that the expert considered in forming the opinions to be expressed; or

(iii) identify assumptions that the party's attorney provided and that the expert relied on in forming the opinions to be expressed.

(D) *Expert Employed Only for Trial Preparation.* Ordinarily, a party may not, by interrogatories or deposition, discover facts known or opinions held by an expert who has been retained or specially employed by another party in anticipation of litigation or to prepare for trial and who is not expected to be called as a witness at trial. But a party may do so only:

   (i) as provided in Rule 35(b); or

   (ii) on showing exceptional circumstances under which it is impracticable for the party to obtain facts or opinions on the same subject by other means.

   (E) *Payment*. Unless manifest injustice would result, the court must require that the party seeking discovery:

   (i) pay the expert a reasonable fee for time spent in responding to discovery under Rule 26(b)(4)(A) or (B); and

   (ii) for discovery under (B), also pay the other party a fair portion of the fees and expenses it reasonably incurred in obtaining the expert's facts and opinions.

   (5) *Claiming Privilege or Protecting Trial-Preparation Materials.*

   (A) *Information Withheld*. When a party withholds information otherwise discoverable by claiming that the information is privileged or subject to protection as trial-preparation material, the party must:

   (i) expressly make the claim; and

   (ii) describe the nature of the documents, communications, or tangible things not produced or disclosed — and do so in a manner that, without revealing information itself privileged or protected, will enable other parties to assess the claim.

   (B) *Information Produced*. If information produced in discovery is subject to a claim of privilege or of protection as trial-preparation material, the party making the claim may notify any party that received the information of the claim and the basis for it. After being notified, a party must promptly return, sequester, or destroy the specified information and any copies it has; must not use or disclose the information until the claim is resolved; must take reasonable steps to retrieve the information if the party disclosed it before being notified; and may promptly present the information to the court under seal for a determination of the claim. The producing party must preserve the information until the claim is resolved.

Judicial Conduct Materials

ABA Model Code of
Judicial Conduct*

Editors' Introduction. The ABA House of Delegates approved extensive revisions to the ABA Code of Judicial Conduct at its February 2007 meeting. The major changes in the 2007 Code are discussed below, following discussion of the evolution of ABA judicial conduct codes from 1924-2006. (In addition, on November 1, 1993, in an unusual press release, seven Justices of the Supreme Court issued an announcement, entitled "Statement of Recusal Policy." The Statement is closely related to the recusal and disqualification provisions of Rule 2.11 of the Code of Judicial Conduct, but it primarily construes 28 U.S.C. §455. We therefore reprint the Statement following 28 U.S.C. §455 in our chapter entitled "Statutes on Disqualification and Discipline of Federal Judges.")

Historical background: The first three ABA codes. The ABA first adopted a code of judicial conduct, originally called the Canons of Judicial Ethics, in 1924. (The original spur for judicial canons came from Judge Kennesaw Mountain Landis, a federal judge who was appointed as the first Commissioner of Baseball after the infamous "Black Sox" scandal of 1919. Despite demands that he resign his federal judgeship after he began serving as Commissioner, he refused to step down. The ABA promptly began drafting Canons of Judicial Ethics.) With occasional amendments, the Canons of Judicial Ethics served the profession well for nearly 50 years and were adopted by most states.

In 1969, however, the ABA created a Special Committee on Standards of Judicial Conduct, chaired by California Supreme Court Justice Roger Traynor, "to draw up modern standards and to replace the Canons of Judicial Ethics."

In August 1972, the ABA House of Delegates formally adopted the ABA Model Code of Judicial Conduct to replace the Canons. The ABA made minor changes in 1982 and 1984. The 1972 ABA Model Code of Judicial Conduct proved widely influential. Nearly all states (plus the District of Columbia) eventually adopted codes of judicial conduct closely modeled on the 1972 ABA Code.

In August 1990, the ABA revised the Model Code of Judicial Conduct. Although the 1990 Code (as it came to be called) is like the 1972 Code in many regards, it also contains many differences, affecting such issues as judicial membership in exclusionary clubs and judicial responsibility to prohibit racial and sex discrimination and other kinds of bias in the courtroom. For a legislative history of the 1990 Code, see L. Milord, The Development of the ABA Judicial Code (1992).

The problem of political contributions. At the ABA's 1997 Annual Meeting, the House of Delegates voted to amend the 1990 Judicial Code for the first time since its adoption. The amendment substantially changed the Commentary to (but not the text of) Canon 5C(2), a provision that governed the solicitation and acceptance of campaign contributions by judges and judicial candidates who are "subject to public election" (as distinct from appointed judges). The amendment to the Commentary addressed widespread concern about "the appearance of impropriety that may arise when parties whose interests may come before a judge or the lawyers who represent such parties have made contributions to the election campaigns of judicial candidates."

Shortly before the ABA's 1998 Annual Meeting, the ABA's elite Task Force on Lawyers' Political Contributions (which was appointed in 1997 to study so-called "pay-to-play" issues) issued a report recommending various amendments to the Code of Judicial Conduct intended "to protect the integrity and independence of judges and candidates for judicial office." The Task Force noted that judges in 42 states were then required to stand for election in some fashion and that their need to raise campaign funds created an appearance of impropriety. The Task Force therefore recommended amendments to Canon 5 of the Code of Judicial Conduct that would (a) require judicial candidates and/or their campaign committees to publicly disclose all campaign contributions from lawyers; (b) limit the amount of money a judicial candidate may accept from any one lawyer, law firm, political action committee, or political party; (c) require judges, upon motion, to recuse themselves from hearing any case in which a litigant or lawyer has contributed more than a specified amount to the judge's campaign; (d) prohibit judges from appointing a lawyer as a guardian, executor, special master, or other paid position if the lawyer, the lawyer's firm, or any employee of the firm has contributed more than a specified limit to the judge's campaign; and (e) require unopposed judicial candidates and judicial candidates who have campaign funds remaining after an election to return the surplus funds to contributors pro rata and/or give the funds to an entity to be determined by the jurisdiction.

In 1999, the ABA adopted a definition of the word "aggregate" in computing the value of a person's or entity's contributions and new provisions in Canons 3 and 5 as part of the Association's continuing efforts to address "concern about the relationship between lawyers making political contributions and the award of engagements to perform legal services in a variety of contexts." (These provisions survive in somewhat different language in Rules 2.11 and 4.4 of the 2007 Code.)

First Amendment concerns. In June 2002, in a 5-4 opinion by Justice Scalia, the Supreme Court held that a Minnesota rule limiting judicial campaign speech violated the First Amendment. *Republican Party of Minnesota v. White*, 536 U.S. 765 (2002). The Minnesota state rule, which had been derived from the 1972 ABA Code of Judicial Conduct, prohibited a judicial candidate from "announc[ing] his or her views on disputed legal or political issues." Lower federal courts and the Minnesota Supreme Court had interpreted this language to encompass only those disputed issues likely to come before the candidate if elected and not to forbid general discussion of case law and judicial philosophy. (Another Minnesota provision, not before the Court, prohibited judicial candidates from making "pledges or promises of conduct in office." This prohibition also appeared in Canon 5A(3)(d)(i) of the ABA Code.) Justices O'Connor and Kennedy concurred in the Court's opinion and also wrote separate opinions. Justices Stevens, Souter, Ginsburg, and Breyer dissented in opinions by Justices Stevens and Ginsburg.

At the ABA's August 2003 Annual Meeting, the House of Delegates amended the Code of Judicial Conduct to bring it into conformity with *White*. The amendments added a definition of "impartiality" and "impartial." They also prohibited judges, with respect to cases, controversies or issues that are likely to come before the court, from making "pledges, promises or commitments that are inconsistent with the impartial performance of the adjudicative duties of the office;" required a judge to disqualify himself or herself if, while either serving as a judge or running for judicial office, the judge has made a public statement that "commits, or appears to commit," the judge with respect to either "(i) an issue in the proceeding; or (ii) the controversy in the proceeding;" and deleted a subparagraph that had prohibited judicial candidates from making statements that committed or appeared to commit them on issues that were likely to come before their courts.

Also at the ABA's 2003 Annual Meeting, the House of Delegates adopted a series of recommendations by the ABA Commission on the 21st Century Judiciary that set forth "principles" intended to preserve judicial independence, accountability and efficiency. The principles affirm that the ABA prefers merit selection rather than elections to select state court judges. Under the system of judicial selection that the ABA Commission recommended to the states, governors would appoint judges from a pool of aspirants reviewed and approved by a neutral commission. Judges would be appointed to serve a single lengthy term, and they would not be subject to reselection. The Commission also developed alternative recommendations for states in which judges are elected or subject to reselection. Specifically, the Commission recommended nonpartisan elections for judges, both initially and for reselection. Where elections remained partisan, however, the Commission recommended that election campaigns should be funded with public financing.

The 2007 Code of Judicial Conduct. As the historical account above shows, the ABA has twice before amended the Code of Judicial Conduct comprehensively since its original promulgation in 1924 — once in 1970, and again in 1990. In September 2003, ABA President Dennis W. Archer, Jr., appointed a Joint Commission to Evaluate the Model Code of Judicial Conduct. The Commission's charge was to review the Code of Judicial Conduct and to recommend revisions. The Chair of the Commission was attorney Mark I. Harrison of Phoenix, and its Reporters were Professor Charles G. Geyh of Indiana University School of Law and attorney W. William Hodes of Indianapolis, formerly a professor at Indiana University School of Law.

The Commission held hearings in 2004, 2005, and 2006 and made extensive recommendations for revision. The House of Delegates adopted the revisions in February 2007. Aside from the substantive changes, summarized below, the Commission recommended that the Code follow the same format as the Model Rules of Professional Conduct — i.e., with numbered rules and comments. For more information about the Commission's work, including various drafts, testimony at hearings, and reports, visit its website at *http://www.american-bar.org/groups/professional_responsibility/publications/model_code_of_judicial_conduct.html.* The site also contains tables comparing the new Code with the 1990 Code, the Reporters' notes, and other legislative history. For a critique of the Code from the American Judicature Society, which submitted many suggestions (not all adopted), see Cynthia Gray, The 2007 ABA Model Code: Taking Judicial Ethics to the Next Level, 90 Judicature 284 (May-June 2007). It can also be found at *www.ajs.org/ethics/pdfs/Judicaturemodelcodearticle.pdf.*

In August 2010, the ABA amended the Code mainly to revise the section marked APPLICATION. It also amended Comment 2 to Rule 2.10. These changes are shown in legislative format.

Following are some significant new and carryover provisions in the 2007 ABA Model Code of Judicial Conduct:

- The "appearance of impropriety" standard as an independent basis for discipline appears in Rule 1.2. The Commission's final draft deleted this standard as an independent basis for discipline, but the Conference of Chief Justices objected and the Commission agreed to reinstate it.
- In Rule 1.3, the new Code forbids judges to "abuse the prestige of judicial office to advance the personal or economic interests of the judge or others," whereas the 1990 Code said a judge "shall not lend the prestige of office" to such interests.
- Rule 2.2 cmt. 4, which is new, allows judges "to make reasonable accommodations to ensure pro se litigants the opportunity to have their matters fairly heard." Rule 2.2 itself requires that judges perform all duties "fairly and impartially."
- Rule 2.3(B) adds "or engage in harassment" to the prohibition against a judge manifesting bias based on a list of categories and adds "gender, ethnicity, marital status, and political affiliation" to that list. Rule 2.3(C), which states that judges "shall require lawyers . . . to refrain from manifesting bias or prejudice," also adds "harassment" and adds the same categories to the list.
- Rule 2.6(B) continues to permit judges to "encourage parties . . . and their lawyers to settle" but directs that the judge "not act in a manner that coerces any party into settlement." New commentary identifies six factors a judge may consider in deciding the judge's "settlement practice" and raises the possibility that in some instances participation in settlement talks may lead to disqualification.

- Rule 2.8 cmt. 3, which is new, permits a judge, if not legally prohibited, to "meet with jurors who choose to remain after trial but should be careful not to discuss the merits of the case."

- Rule 2.9(A)(2) continues to permit a judge to consult with an independent expert but the rule now requires "advance notice to the parties" and "a reasonable opportunity to object and respond to the notice and to the advice received."

- Rule 2.9(B) is new and requires notification to the parties if a judge "inadvertently receives an unauthorized ex parte communication bearing upon the substance of a matter." The Reporter explains that this rule responds to the risk of such things as a misdirected fax.

- For some specialized courts, Rule 2.9 cmt. 4 contains a new exception to the prohibition against ex parte contacts as follows:

    A judge may initiate, permit, or consider ex parte communications expressly authorized by law, such as when serving on therapeutic or problem-solving courts, mental health courts, or drug courts. In this capacity, judges may assume a more interactive role with parties, treatment providers, probation officers, social workers, and others.

- Rule 2.9 cmt. 6, which is new, makes it clear that the prohibition against independently investigating the facts extends to doing so by electronic research.

- Rule 2.9 cmt. 7 is new and allows a judge to "consult ethics advisory committees, outside counsel, or legal experts concerning the judge's compliance with this Code."

- Rule 2.10(E) is new. It permits a judge "to respond directly or through a third party to allegations in the media or elsewhere concerning the judge's conduct in a matter." This new authority is subject to Rule 2.10(A), which is present in the 1990 Code and which forbids public comment "that might reasonably be expected to affect the outcome or impair the fairness of a matter pending or impending in any court. . . ."

- Disqualification based on the interests of family members in Rule 2.11 now extends to a "domestic partner," which the Terminology now defines as "a person with whom another person maintains a household and an intimate relationship, other than a person to whom he or she is legally married."

- Comment 2 to Rule 2.11, on disqualification, is new. It provides that "a judge's obligation not to hear or decide matters in which disqualification is required applies regardless of whether a motion to disqualify is filed."

- Rule 2.14 newly provides that a judge who has "a reasonable belief" that a judge's or lawyer's performance "is impaired" by mental or physical illness or alcohol or substance abuse must "take appropriate action, which may include a confidential referral to a lawyer or judicial assistance program."

- Rule 3.2(B), which is new, allows a judge to make a voluntary appearance at a public hearing convened by an executive or legislative body "in connection with matters about which the judge acquired knowledge or expertise in the course of the judge's judicial duties."

- The prior Code prohibited a judge from belonging to an organization that discriminated based on race, sex, religion, or national origin. Rule 3.6 adds gender, ethnicity, and sexual orientation to the list. Comment 3 now requires a judge to "resign immediately" from any such organization, whereas previously judges were allowed to remain members for a year during which time they could work to change the rules of the organization. As before, there are exceptions for organizations identified in cmts. 2, 4, and 5 of the rule, including religious organizations, and for "national or state military service."

- A new set of rules (Rules 3.7(A)(3-5)) permits judges to solicit members for an organization even though membership dues help support the organization; to appear, speak, and be honored at fundraising events of an organization; and to make recommendations to a grant-making organization, *but in each case* only if the particular organization is "concerned with the law, the legal system, or the administration of justice." Also, Rule 3.7(A)(4) allows a judge to be featured and receive an award at events sponsored by educational, charitable, and like organizations that are not "concerned with" the law, but only if the event is not a fundraiser. (The Rule 3.7 authority is subordinate to Rule 3.1, which, among other things, forbids conduct "that would appear to a reasonable person to undermine the judge's independence, integrity, or impartiality.")
- Rule 3.7 cmt. 4 continues to allow a judge's name to appear on fundraising and membership solicitation letters of organizations identified in Rule 3.7. The judge's title or office may also be listed "if comparable designations" are used for others.
- Rule 3.14, which is new, addresses expenses to travel to and at seminars. It permits a judge to "accept reimbursement of necessary and reasonable expenses for travel, food, lodging, and other incidental expenses" associated with participation in "extrajudicial activities permitted by this Code." The rule also permits reimbursement of these expenses "when appropriate to the occasion, by the judge's spouse, domestic partner, or guest." The fact of reimbursement for expenses at these events must be made known "within 30 days following the conclusion of the event or program." Posting on the court's website is required "when technically feasible." Comment 3 to Rule 3.14 lists eight separate factors a judge should consider "when deciding whether to accept reimbursement or a fee waiver for attendance at a particular activity." These factors bear on whether or not reimbursement would "appear to a reasonable person to undermine the judge's independence, integrity, or impartiality."
- Rule 4.1, whose subject is political activity of judges and judicial candidates (via election or appointment), is mostly unchanged except for three additional prohibitions in paragraphs (A)(6, 7, 10). Most notable, though, are new cmts. 11-15, which describe what judges and non-judge candidates may ethically say and not say consistent with the ABA's reading of *Republican Party of Minnesota v. White.*

To monitor the progress of the adoption of the Code nationwide, go to the interactive map at *http://www.americanbar.org/groups/professional_responsibility/resources/judicial_ethics_regulation/mcjc.html.*

Code of Conduct for U.S. Judge. The Committee on Codes of Conduct of the Judicial Conference of the United States adopts ethical rules for all federal judges, including magistrate judges and bankruptcy judges, but excluding the Justices of the Supreme Court. The latest version of this code, which is based on but different from, the ABA Code, was effective July 1, 2009, and can be found at the following website or by Googling "Code of Conduct for U.S. Judges": *http://www.uscourts.gov/rulesandpolicies/codesofconduct/codeconductunitedstatesjudges.aspx.* In addition, the Judicial Conference has adopted rules governing a judge's attendance at privately funded educational programs, which critics have called "judicial junkets." These can be found at *www.uscourts.gov/uscourts/RulesAndPolicies/SeminarDisclosure/judbrappc906c.pdf.*

A committee of the U.S. Judicial Conference will answer questions from judges about the application of the Code to proposed conduct. Many of these answers are published and they can be found at *www.uscourts.gov/uscourts/RulesAndPolicies/conduct/Vol02B-Ch02-OGC-Post2USCOURTS-PublAdvisoryOps.pdf.*

Caperton v. A.T. Massey Coal Co., 556 U.S. 868 (2009). On June 8, 2009, the Supreme Court issued its opinion in this much-watched case. The question before the Court was whether, on the facts of the case, the plaintiff's due process rights were violated. The plaintiff had won a $50 million judgment in the state trial court. While the defendant's appeal to the West Virginia Supreme Court of Appeals was pending, its chief executive officer contributed $3 million to the campaign effort of a candidate for the state high court, amounting to 60 percent of the candidate's campaign funds. That candidate was elected, and he then cast a deciding vote that overturned the plaintiff's victory. The Court held, 5-4, in a decision by Justice Kennedy, that the Due Process Clause was violated on these facts. The decision rested on the Due Process Clause, not an ethical rule. The Supreme Court has no power to enforce a state's ethical rules. During 2011, ABA committees were reviewing the Code of Judicial Conduct to determine what if any amendments might be appropriate in light of the *Caperton* decision. At the 2011 ABA Annual Meeting, the House of Delegates adopted the following resolution:

RESOLVED, That the American Bar Association urges states to establish clearly articulated procedures for:

A. Judicial disqualification determinations; and

B. Prompt review by another judge or tribunal, or as otherwise provided by law or rule of court, of denials of requests to disqualify a judge.

FURTHER RESOLVED, That the American Bar Association urges states in which judges are subject to elections of any kind to adopt:

A. Disclosure requirements for litigants and lawyers who have provided, directly or indirectly, campaign support in an election involving a judge before whom they are appearing.

B. Guidelines for judges concerning disclosure and disqualification obligations regarding campaign contributions.

FURTHER RESOLVED, That the Standing Committee on Ethics and Professional Responsibility and the Standing Committee on Professional

Discipline should proceed on an expedited basis to consider what amendments, if any, should be made to the ABA Model Code of Judicial Conduct or to the ABA Model Rules of Professional Conduct to provide necessary additional guidance to the states on disclosure requirements and standards for judicial disqualification.

Two ABA committees are now reviewing the disqualification provisions of the Code but have made no recommendations as of May 2012. Their work can be reviewed at *http://www.americanbar.org/content/dam/aba/migrated/ cpr/ethics/20111228_scepr_draft_ proposed_amendments_and_hearing_notice_ dec_2011.authcheckdam.pdf.*

Contents

ABA MODEL CODE OF JUDICIAL CONDUCT (2007)

CANON 3

A JUDGE SHALL CONDUCT THE JUDGE'S PERSONAL AND EXTRAJUDICIAL ACTIVITIES TO MINIMIZE THE RISK OF CONFLICT WITH THE OBLIGATIONS OF JUDICIAL OFFICE.

CANON 4

A JUDGE OR CANDIDATE FOR JUDICIAL OFFICE SHALL NOT ENGAGE IN POLITICAL OR CAMPAIGN ACTIVITY THAT IS INCONSISTENT WITH THE INDEPENDENCE, INTEGRITY, OR IMPARTIALITY OF THE JUDICIARY.

ABA MODEL CODE OF JUDICIAL CONDUCT

February 2007

PREAMBLE

[1] An independent, fair and impartial judiciary is indispensable to our system of justice. The United States legal system is based upon the principle that an

independent, impartial, and competent judiciary, composed of men and women of integrity, will interpret and apply the law that governs our society. Thus, the judiciary plays a central role in preserving the principles of justice and the rule of law. Inherent in all the Rules contained in this Code are the precepts that judges, individually and collectively, must respect and honor the judicial office as a public trust and strive to maintain and enhance confidence in the legal system.

[2] Judges should maintain the dignity of judicial office at all times, and avoid both impropriety and the appearance of impropriety in their professional and personal lives. They should aspire at all times to conduct that ensures the greatest possible public confidence in their independence, impartiality, integrity, and competence.

[3] The Model Code of Judicial Conduct establishes standards for the ethical conduct of judges and judicial candidates. It is not intended as an exhaustive guide for the conduct of judges and judicial candidates, who are governed in their judicial and personal conduct by general ethical standards as well as by the Code. The Code is intended, however, to provide guidance and assist judges in maintaining the highest standards of judicial and personal conduct, and to provide a basis for regulating their conduct through disciplinary agencies.

SCOPE

[1] The Model Code of Judicial Conduct consists of four Canons, numbered Rules under each Canon, and Comments that generally follow and explain each Rule. Scope and Terminology sections provide additional guidance in interpreting and applying the Code. An Application section establishes when the various Rules apply to a judge or judicial candidate.

[2] The Canons state overarching principles of judicial ethics that all judges must observe. Although a judge may be disciplined only for violating a Rule, the Canons provide important guidance in interpreting the Rules. Where a Rule contains a permissive term, such as "may" or "should," the conduct being addressed is committed to the personal and professional discretion of the judge or candidate in question, and no disciplinary action should be taken for action or inaction within the bounds of such discretion.

[3] The Comments that accompany the Rules serve two functions. First, they provide guidance regarding the purpose, meaning, and proper application of the Rules. They contain explanatory material and, in some instances, provide examples of permitted or prohibited conduct. Comments neither add to nor subtract from the binding obligations set forth in the Rules. Therefore, when a Comment contains the term "must," it does not mean that the Comment itself is binding or enforceable; it signifies that the Rule in question, properly understood, is obligatory as to the conduct at issue.

[4] Second, the Comments identify aspirational goals for judges. To implement fully the principles of this Code as articulated in the Canons, judges should strive to exceed the standards of conduct established by the Rules, holding themselves to the highest ethical standards and seeking to achieve those aspirational goals, thereby enhancing the dignity of the judicial office.

[5] The Rules of the Model Code of Judicial Conduct are rules of reason that should be applied consistent with constitutional requirements, statutes, other court

rules, and decisional law, and with due regard for all relevant circumstances. The Rules should not be interpreted to impinge upon the essential independence of judges in making judicial decisions.

[6] Although the black letter of the Rules is binding and enforceable, it is not contemplated that every transgression will result in the imposition of discipline. Whether discipline should be imposed should be determined through a reasonable and reasoned application of the Rules, and should depend upon factors such as the seriousness of the transgression, the facts and circumstances that existed at the time of the transgression, the extent of any pattern of improper activity, whether there have been previous violations, and the effect of the improper activity upon the judicial system or others.

[7] The Code is not designed or intended as a basis for civil or criminal liability. Neither is it intended to be the basis for litigants to seek collateral remedies against each other or to obtain tactical advantages in proceedings before a court.

TERMINOLOGY

The first time any term listed below is used in a Rule in its defined sense, it is followed by an asterisk (*).

"**Aggregate,**" in relation to contributions for a candidate, means not only contributions in cash or in kind made directly to a candidate's campaign committee, but also all contributions made indirectly with the understanding that they will be used to support the election of a candidate or to oppose the election of the candidate's opponent. See Rules 2.11 and 4.4.

"**Appropriate authority**" means the authority having responsibility for initiation of disciplinary process in connection with the violation to be reported. See Rules 2.14 and 2.15.

"**Contribution**" means both financial and in-kind contributions, such as goods, professional or volunteer services, advertising, and other types of assistance, which, if obtained by the recipient otherwise, would require a financial expenditure. See Rules 2.11, 2.13, 3.7, 4.1, and 4.4.

"**De minimis,**" in the context of interests pertaining to disqualification of a judge, means an insignificant interest that could not raise a reasonable question regarding the judge's impartiality. See Rule 2.11.

"**Domestic partner**" means a person with whom another person maintains a household and an intimate relationship, other than a person to whom he or she is legally married. See Rules 2.11, 2.13, 3.13, and 3.14.

"**Economic interest**" means ownership of more than a de minimis legal or equitable interest. Except for situations in which the judge participates in the management of such a legal or equitable interest, or the interest could be substantially affected by the outcome of a proceeding before a judge, it does not include:

(1) an interest in the individual holdings within a mutual or common investment fund;

(2) an interest in securities held by an educational, religious, charitable, fraternal, or civic organization in which the judge or the judge's spouse, domestic partner, parent, or child serves as a director, an officer, an advisor, or other participant;

(3) a deposit in a financial institution or deposits or proprietary interests the judge may maintain as a member of a mutual savings association or credit union, or similar proprietary interests; or

(4) an interest in the issuer of government securities held by the judge.

See Rules 1.3 and 2.11.

"Fiduciary" includes relationships such as executor, administrator, trustee, or guardian. See Rules 2.11, 3.2, and 3.8.

"Impartial," "impartiality," and **"impartially"** mean absence of bias or prejudice in favor of, or against, particular parties or classes of parties, as well as maintenance of an open mind in considering issues that may come before a judge. See Canons 1, 2, and 4, and Rules 1.2, 2.2, 2.10, 2.11, 2.13, 3.1, 3.12, 3.13, 4.1, and 4.2.

"Impending matter" is a matter that is imminent or expected to occur in the near future. See Rules 2.9, 2.10, 3.13, and 4.1.

"Impropriety" includes conduct that violates the law, court rules, or provisions of this Code, and conduct that undermines a judge's independence, integrity, or impartiality. See Canon 1 and Rule 1.2.

"Independence" means a judge's freedom from influence or controls other than those established by law. See Canons 1 and 4, and Rules 1.2, 3.1, 3.12, 3.13, and 4.2.

"Integrity" means probity, fairness, honesty, uprightness, and soundness of character. See Canon 1 and Rule 1.2.

"Judicial candidate" means any person, including a sitting judge, who is seeking selection for or retention in judicial office by election or appointment. A person becomes a candidate for judicial office as soon as he or she makes a public announcement of candidacy, declares or files as a candidate with the election or appointment authority, authorizes or, where permitted, engages in solicitation or acceptance of contributions or support, or is nominated for election or appointment to office. See Rules 2.11, 4.1, 4.2, and 4.4.

"Knowingly," "knowledge," "known," and **"knows"** mean actual knowledge of the fact in question. A person's knowledge may be inferred from circumstances. See Rules 2.11, 2.13, 2.15, 2.16, 3.6, and 4.1.

"Law" encompasses court rules as well as statutes, constitutional provisions, and decisional law. See Rules 1.1, 2.1, 2.2, 2.6, 2.7, 2.9, 3.1, 3.4, 3.9, 3.12, 3.13, 3.14, 3.15, 4.1, 4.2, 4.4, and 4.5.

"Member of the candidate's family" means a spouse, domestic partner, child, grandchild, parent, grandparent, or other relative or person with whom the candidate maintains a close familial relationship.

"**Member of the judge's family**" means a spouse, domestic partner, child, grandchild, parent, grandparent, or other relative or person with whom the judge maintains a close familial relationship. See Rules 3.7, 3.8, 3.10, and 3.11.

"**Member of a judge's family residing in the judge's household**" means any relative of a judge by blood or marriage, or a person treated by a judge as a member of the judge's family, who resides in the judge's household. See Rules 2.11 and 3.13.

"**Nonpublic information**" means information that is not available to the public. Nonpublic information may include, but is not limited to, information that is sealed by statute or court order or impounded or communicated in camera, and information offered in grand jury proceedings, presentencing reports, dependency cases, or psychiatric reports. See Rule 3.5.

"**Pending matter**" is a matter that has commenced. A matter continues to be pending through any appellate process until final disposition. See Rules 2.9, 2.10, 3.13, and 4.1.

"**Personally solicit**" means a direct request made by a judge or a judicial candidate for financial support or in-kind services, whether made by letter, telephone, or any other means of communication. See Rule 4.1.

"**Political organization**" means a political party or other group sponsored by or affiliated with a political party or candidate, the principal purpose of which is to further the election or appointment of candidates for political office. For purposes of this Code, the term does not include a judicial candidate's campaign committee created as authorized by Rule 4.4. See Rules 4.1 and 4.2.

"**Public election**" includes primary and general elections, partisan elections, nonpartisan elections, and retention elections. See Rules 4.2 and 4.4.

"**Third degree of relationship**" includes the following persons: great-grandparent, grandparent, parent, uncle, aunt, brother, sister, child, grandchild, great-grandchild, nephew, and niece. See Rule 2.11.

APPLICATION

The Application section establishes when the various Rules apply to a judge or judicial candidate.

I. Applicability of This Code

(A) The provisions of the Code apply to all full-time judges. Parts II through V of this section identify provisions that apply to four categories

of part-time judges only while they are serving as judges, and provisions that do not apply to part-time judges at any time. All other Rules are therefore applicable to part-time judges at all times. The four categories of judicial service in other than a full-time capacity are necessarily defined in general terms because of the widely varying forms of judicial service. Canon 4 applies to judicial candidates.

(B) A judge, within the meaning of this Code, is anyone who is authorized to perform judicial functions, including an officer such as a justice of the peace, magistrate, court commissioner, special master, referee, or member of the administrative law judiciary.[1]

COMMENT

[1] The Rules in this Code have been formulated to address the ethical obligations of any person who serves a judicial function, and are premised upon the supposition that a uniform system of ethical principles should apply to all those authorized to perform judicial functions.

[2] The determination of which category and, accordingly, which specific Rules apply to an individual judicial officer, depends upon the facts of the particular judicial service.

[3] In recent years many jurisdictions have created what are often called "problem solving" courts, in which judges are authorized by court rules to act in nontraditional ways. For example, judges presiding in drug courts and monitoring the progress of participants in those courts' programs may be authorized, and even encouraged, to communicate directly with social workers, probation officers, and others outside the context of their usual judicial role as independent decision makers on issues of fact and law. When local rules specifically authorize conduct not otherwise permitted under these Rules, they take precedence over the provisions set forth in the Code. Nevertheless, judges serving on "problem solving" courts shall comply with this Code except to the extent local rules provide and permit otherwise.

II.   Retired Judge Subject to Recall

A retired judge subject to recall for service, who by law is not permitted to practice law, is not required to comply:

---

1. Each jurisdiction should consider the characteristics of particular positions within the administrative law judiciary in adopting, adapting, applying, and enforcing the Code for the administrative law judiciary. *See, e.g.,* Model Code of Judicial Conduct for Federal Administrative Law Judges (1989) and Model Code of Judicial Conduct for State Administrative Law Judges (1995). Both Model Codes are endorsed by the ABA National Conference of Administrative Law Judiciary.

(A) with Rule 3.9 (Service as Arbitrator or Mediator), except while serving as a judge; or

(B) at any time with Rule 3.8 (Appointments to Fiduciary Positions).

COMMENT

[1] For the purposes of this section, as long as a retired judge is subject to being recalled for service, the judge is considered to "perform judicial functions."

III.   Continuing Part-Time Judge

A judge who serves repeatedly on a part-time basis by election or under a continuing appointment, including a retired judge subject to recall who is permitted to practice law ("continuing part-time judge"),

(A) is not required to comply:

(1) with Rules 2.10(A), and 2.10(B) (Judicial Statements on Pending and Impending Cases), and 4.1 (Political and Campaign Activities of Judges and Judicial Candidates in General) (A)(1) through (7), except while serving as a judge; or

(2) at any time with Rules 3.4 (Appointments to Governmental Positions), 3.8 (A) (Appointments to Fiduciary Positions), 3.9 (Service as Arbitrator or Mediator), 3.10 (Practice of Law), and 3.11(B) (Financial, Business, or Remunerative Activities) 3.14 (Reimbursement of Expenses and Waivers of Fees or Charges), 3.15 (Reporting Requirements), 4.1 (Political and Campaign Activities of Judges and Judicial Candidates in General), 4.2 (Political and Campaign Activities of Judicial Candidates in Public Elections), 4.3 (Activities of Candidates for Appointive Judicial Office), 4.4 (Campaign Committees), and 4.5 (Activities of Judges Who Become Candidates for Nonjudicial Office); and

(B) shall not practice law in the court on which the judge serves, or in any court subject to the appellate jurisdiction of the court on which the judge serves, and shall not act as a lawyer in a proceeding in which the judge has served as a judge or in any other proceeding related thereto.

COMMENT

[1] When a person who has been a continuing part-time judge is no longer a continuing part-time judge, including a retired judge no longer subject to recall, that person may act as a lawyer in a proceeding in which he or she has served as a judge, or in any other proceeding related thereto only with the informed consent of all parties, and pursuant to any applicable Model Rules of Professional Conduct. An adopting jurisdiction should substitute a reference to its applicable rule.

IV.   Periodic Part-Time Judge

A periodic part-time judge who serves or expects to serve repeatedly on a part-time basis, but under a separate appointment for each limited period of service or for each matter,

    (A) is not required to comply:

        (1) with Rule 4.1 (Political and Campaign Activities of Judges and Judicial Candidates in General) (A)(1) through (7), except while serving as a judge; or

        (2) at any time with Rules 3.4 (Appointments to Governmental Positions), 3.8(A) (Appointments to Fiduciary Positions), 3.9 (Service as Arbitrator or Mediator), 3.10 (Practice of Law), and 3.11(B) (Financial, Business, or Remunerative Activities);

    (B) shall not practice law in the court on which the judge serves, or in any court subject to the appellate jurisdiction of the court on which the judge serves, and shall not act as a lawyer in a proceeding in which the judge has served as a judge or in any other proceeding related thereto.

V.   Pro Tempore Part-Time Judge

A pro tempore part-time judge who serves or expects to serve once or only sporadically on a part-time basis under a separate appointment for each period of service or for each case heard is not required to comply:

    (A) except while serving as a judge, with Rules 2.4 (External Influences on Judicial Conduct), 3.2 (Appearances before Governmental Bodies and Consultation with Government Officials), and 4.1 (Political and Campaign Activities of Judges and Judicial Candidates in General) (A)(1) through (7); or

    (B) at any time with Rules 3.4 (Appointments to Governmental Positions), 3.8(A) (Appointments to Fiduciary Positions), 3.9 (Service as Arbitrator or Mediator), 3.10 (Practice of Law), and 3.11(B) (Financial, Business, or Remunerative Activities).

VI.   Time for Compliance

A person to whom this Code becomes applicable shall comply immediately with its provisions, except that those judges to whom Rules 3.8 (Appointments to Fiduciary Positions) and 3.11 (Financial, Business, or Remunerative Activities) apply shall comply with those Rules as soon as reasonably possible, but in no event later than one year after the Code becomes applicable to the judge.

COMMENT

[1] If serving as a fiduciary when selected as judge, a new judge may, notwithstanding the prohibitions in Rule 3.8, continue to serve as fiduciary, but only for that period of time necessary to avoid serious adverse consequences to the beneficiaries of the fiduciary relationship and in no event longer than one year. Similarly, if engaged at the time of judicial selection in a business activity, a new judge may, notwithstanding the prohibitions in Rule 3.11, continue in that activity for a reasonable period but in no event longer than one year.

CANON 1. A JUDGE SHALL UPHOLD AND PROMOTE THE INDEPENDENCE, INTEGRITY, AND IMPARTIALITY OF THE JUDICIARY, AND SHALL AVOID IMPROPRIETY AND THE APPEARANCE OF IMPROPRIETY.

RULE 1.1   *Compliance with the Law*

A judge shall comply with the law,* including the Code of Judicial Conduct.

RULE 1.2   *Promoting Confidence in the Judiciary*

A judge shall act at all times in a manner that promotes public confidence in the independence,* integrity,* and impartiality* of the judiciary, and shall avoid impropriety and the appearance of impropriety.

COMMENT

[1] Public confidence in the judiciary is eroded by improper conduct and conduct that creates the appearance of impropriety. This principle applies to both the professional and personal conduct of a judge.

[2] A judge should expect to be the subject of public scrutiny that might be viewed as burdensome if applied to other citizens, and must accept the restrictions imposed by the Code.

[3] Conduct that compromises or appears to compromise the independence, integrity, and impartiality of a judge undermines public confidence in the judiciary. Because it is not practicable to list all such conduct, the Rule is necessarily cast in general terms.

[4] Judges should participate in activities that promote ethical conduct among judges and lawyers, support professionalism within the judiciary and the legal profession, and promote access to justice for all.

[5] Actual improprieties include violations of law, court rules or provisions of this Code. The test for appearance of impropriety is whether the conduct would

create in reasonable minds a perception that the judge violated this Code or engaged in other conduct that reflects adversely on the judge's honesty, impartiality, temperament, or fitness to serve as a judge.

[6] A judge should initiate and participate in community outreach activities for the purpose of promoting public understanding of and confidence in the administration of justice. In conducting such activities, the judge must act in a manner consistent with this Code.

RULE 1.3   *Avoiding Abuse of the Prestige of Judicial Office*

A judge shall not abuse the prestige of judicial office to advance the personal or economic interests* of the judge or others, or allow others to do so.

COMMENT

[1] It is improper for a judge to use or attempt to use his or her position to gain personal advantage or deferential treatment of any kind. For example, it would be improper for a judge to allude to his or her judicial status to gain favorable treatment in encounters with traffic officials. Similarly, a judge must not use judicial letterhead to gain an advantage in conducting his or her personal business.

[2] A judge may provide a reference or recommendation for an individual based upon the judge's personal knowledge. The judge may use official letterhead if the judge indicates that the reference is personal and if there is no likelihood that the use of the letterhead would reasonably be perceived as an attempt to exert pressure by reason of the judicial office.

[3] Judges may participate in the process of judicial selection by cooperating with appointing authorities and screening committees, and by responding to inquiries from such entities concerning the professional qualifications of a person being considered for judicial office.

[4] Special considerations arise when judges write or contribute to publications of for-profit entities, whether related or unrelated to the law. A judge should not permit anyone associated with the publication of such materials to exploit the judge's office in a manner that violates this Rule or other applicable law. In contracts for publication of a judge's writing, the judge should retain sufficient control over the advertising to avoid such exploitation.

CANON 2.   A JUDGE SHALL PERFORM THE DUTIES OF JUDICIAL OFFICE IMPARTIALLY, COMPETENTLY, AND DILIGENTLY.

RULE 2.1   *Giving Precedence to the Duties of Judicial Office*

The duties of judicial office, as prescribed by law,* shall take precedence over all of a judge's personal and extrajudicial activities.

COMMENT

[1] To ensure that judges are available to fulfill their judicial duties, judges must conduct their personal and extrajudicial activities to minimize the risk of conflicts that would result in frequent disqualification. See Canon 3.

[2] Although it is not a duty of judicial office unless prescribed by law, judges are encouraged to participate in activities that promote public understanding of and confidence in the justice system.

RULE 2.2   *Impartiality and Fairness*

A judge shall uphold and apply the law,* and shall perform all duties of judicial office fairly and impartially.*

COMMENT

[1] To ensure impartiality and fairness to all parties, a judge must be objective and open-minded.

[2] Although each judge comes to the bench with a unique background and personal philosophy, a judge must interpret and apply the law without regard to whether the judge approves or disapproves of the law in question.

[3] When applying and interpreting the law, a judge sometimes may make good-faith errors of fact or law. Errors of this kind do not violate this Rule.

[4] It is not a violation of this Rule for a judge to make reasonable accommodations to ensure pro se litigants the opportunity to have their matters fairly heard.

RULE 2.3   *Bias, Prejudice, and Harassment*

(A) A judge shall perform the duties of judicial office, including administrative duties, without bias or prejudice.

(B) A judge shall not, in the performance of judicial duties, by words or conduct manifest bias or prejudice, or engage in harassment, including but not limited to bias, prejudice, or harassment based upon race, sex, gender, religion, national origin, ethnicity, disability, age, sexual orientation, marital status, socioeconomic status, or political affiliation, and shall not permit court staff, court officials, or others subject to the judge's direction and control to do so.

(C) A judge shall require lawyers in proceedings before the court to refrain from manifesting bias or prejudice, or engaging in harassment, based upon attributes including but not limited to race, sex, gender, religion, national origin, ethnicity, disability, age, sexual orientation, marital status, socioeconomic status, or political affiliation, against parties, witnesses, lawyers, or others.

(D) The restrictions of paragraphs (B) and (C) do not preclude judges or lawyers from making legitimate reference to the listed factors, or similar factors, when they are relevant to an issue in a proceeding.

COMMENT

[1] A judge who manifests bias or prejudice in a proceeding impairs the fairness of the proceeding and brings the judiciary into disrepute.

[2] Examples of manifestations of bias or prejudice include but are not limited to epithets; slurs; demeaning nicknames; negative stereotyping; attempted humor based upon stereotypes; threatening, intimidating, or hostile acts; suggestions of connections between race, ethnicity, or nationality and crime; and irrelevant references to personal characteristics. Even facial expressions and body language can convey to parties and lawyers in the proceeding, jurors, the media, and others an appearance of bias or prejudice. A judge must avoid conduct that may reasonably be perceived as prejudiced or biased.

[3] Harassment, as referred to in paragraphs (B) and (C), is verbal or physical conduct that denigrates or shows hostility or aversion toward a person on bases such as race, sex, gender, religion, national origin, ethnicity, disability, age, sexual orientation, marital status, socioeconomic status, or political affiliation.

[4] Sexual harassment includes but is not limited to sexual advances, requests for sexual favors, and other verbal or physical conduct of a sexual nature that is unwelcome.

RULE 2.4   *External Influences on Judicial Conduct*

(A) A judge shall not be swayed by public clamor or fear of criticism.

(B) A judge shall not permit family, social, political, financial, or other interests or relationships to influence the judge's judicial conduct or judgment.

(C) A judge shall not convey or permit others to convey the impression that any person or organization is in a position to influence the judge.

COMMENT

[1] An independent judiciary requires that judges decide cases according to the law and facts, without regard to whether particular laws or litigants are popular or unpopular with the public, the media, government officials, or the judge's friends or family. Confidence in the judiciary is eroded if judicial decision making is perceived to be subject to inappropriate outside influences.

RULE 2.5   *Competence, Diligence, and Cooperation*

(A) A judge shall perform judicial and administrative duties, competently and diligently.

(B) A judge shall cooperate with other judges and court officials in the administration of court business.

COMMENT

[1] Competence in the performance of judicial duties requires the legal knowledge, skill, thoroughness, and preparation reasonably necessary to perform a judge's responsibilities of judicial office.

[2] A judge should seek the necessary docket time, court staff, expertise, and resources to discharge all adjudicative and administrative responsibilities.

[3] Prompt disposition of the court's business requires a judge to devote adequate time to judicial duties, to be punctual in attending court and expeditious in determining matters under submission, and to take reasonable measures to ensure that court officials, litigants, and their lawyers cooperate with the judge to that end.

[4] In disposing of matters promptly and efficiently, a judge must demonstrate due regard for the rights of parties to be heard and to have issues resolved without unnecessary cost or delay. A judge should monitor and supervise cases in ways that reduce or eliminate dilatory practices, avoidable delays, and unnecessary costs.

RULE 2.6   *Ensuring the Right to Be Heard*

(A) A judge shall accord to every person who has a legal interest in a proceeding, or that person's lawyer, the right to be heard according to law.*

(B) A judge may encourage parties to a proceeding and their lawyers to settle matters in dispute but shall not act in a manner that coerces any party into settlement.

COMMENT

[1] The right to be heard is an essential component of a fair and impartial system of justice. Substantive rights of litigants can be protected only if procedures protecting the right to be heard are observed.

[2] The judge plays an important role in overseeing the settlement of disputes, but should be careful that efforts to further settlement do not undermine any party's right to be heard according to law. The judge should keep in mind the effect that the judge's participation in settlement discussions may have, not only on the judge's own views of the case, but also on the perceptions of the lawyers and the parties if the case remains with the judge after settlement efforts are unsuccessful. Among the factors that a judge should consider when deciding upon an appropriate settlement practice for a case are (1) whether the parties have requested or voluntarily consented to a certain level of participation by the judge in settlement discussions, (2) whether the parties and their counsel are relatively sophisticated in legal matters,

(3) whether the case will be tried by the judge or a jury, (4) whether the parties participate with their counsel in settlement discussions, (5) whether any parties are unrepresented by counsel, and (6) whether the matter is civil or criminal.

[3] Judges must be mindful of the effect settlement discussions can have, not only on their objectivity and impartiality, but also on the appearance of their objectivity and impartiality. Despite a judge's best efforts, there may be instances when information obtained during settlement discussions could influence a judge's decision making during trial, and, in such instances, the judge should consider whether disqualification may be appropriate. See Rule 2.11(A)(1).

RULE 2.7 *Responsibility to Decide*

A judge shall hear and decide matters assigned to the judge, except when disqualification is required by Rule 2.11 or other law.*

COMMENT

[1] Judges must be available to decide the matters that come before the court. Although there are times when disqualification is necessary to protect the rights of litigants and preserve public confidence in the independence, integrity, and impartiality of the judiciary, judges must be available to decide matters that come before the courts. Unwarranted disqualification may bring public disfavor to the court and to the judge personally. The dignity of the court, the judge's respect for fulfillment of judicial duties, and a proper concern for the burdens that may be imposed upon the judge's colleagues require that a judge not use disqualification to avoid cases that present difficult, controversial, or unpopular issues.

RULE 2.8 *Decorum, Demeanor, and Communication with Jurors*

(A) A judge shall require order and decorum in proceedings before the court.

(B) A judge shall be patient, dignified, and courteous to litigants, jurors, witnesses, lawyers, court staff, court officials, and others with whom the judge deals in an official capacity, and shall require similar conduct of lawyers, court staff, court officials, and others subject to the judge's direction and control.

(C) A judge shall not commend or criticize jurors for their verdict other than in a court order or opinion in a proceeding.

COMMENT

[1] The duty to hear all proceedings with patience and courtesy is not inconsistent with the duty imposed in Rule 2.5 to dispose promptly of the business of the court. Judges can be efficient and businesslike while being patient and deliberate.

[2] Commending or criticizing jurors for their verdict may imply a judicial expectation in future cases and may impair a juror's ability to be fair and impartial in a subsequent case.

[3] A judge who is not otherwise prohibited by law from doing so may meet with jurors who choose to remain after trial but should be careful not to discuss the merits of the case.

RULE 2.9   *Ex Parte Communications*

(A) A judge shall not initiate, permit, or consider ex parte communications, or consider other communications made to the judge outside the presence of the parties or their lawyers, concerning a pending* or impending matter,* except as follows:

(1) When circumstances require it, ex parte communication for scheduling, administrative, or emergency purposes, which does not address substantive matters, is permitted, provided:

(a) the judge reasonably believes that no party will gain a procedural, substantive, or tactical advantage as a result of the ex parte communication; and

(b) the judge makes provision promptly to notify all other parties of the substance of the ex parte communication, and gives the parties an opportunity to respond.

(2) A judge may obtain the written advice of a disinterested expert on the law applicable to a proceeding before the judge, if the judge gives advance notice to the parties of the person to be consulted and the subject matter of the advice to be solicited, and affords the parties a reasonable opportunity to object and respond to the notice and to the advice received.

(3) A judge may consult with court staff and court officials whose functions are to aid the judge in carrying out the judge's adjudicative responsibilities, or with other judges, provided the judge makes reasonable efforts to avoid receiving factual information that is not part of the record, and does not abrogate the responsibility personally to decide the matter.

(4) A judge may, with the consent of the parties, confer separately with the parties and their lawyers in an effort to settle matters pending before the judge.

(5) A judge may initiate, permit, or consider any ex parte communication when expressly authorized by law* to do so.

(B) If a judge inadvertently receives an unauthorized ex parte communication bearing upon the substance of a matter, the judge shall make provision promptly to notify the parties of the substance of the communication and provide the parties with an opportunity to respond.

(C) A judge shall not investigate facts in a matter independently, and shall consider only the evidence presented and any facts that may properly be judicially noticed.

(D) A judge shall make reasonable efforts, including providing appropriate supervision, to ensure that this Rule is not violated by court staff, court officials, and others subject to the judge's direction and control.

COMMENT

[1] To the extent reasonably possible, all parties or their lawyers shall be included in communications with a judge.

[2] Whenever the presence of a party or notice to a party is required by this Rule, it is the party's lawyer, or if the party is unrepresented, the party, who is to be present or to whom notice is to be given.

[3] The proscription against communications concerning a proceeding includes communications with lawyers, law teachers, and other persons who are not participants in the proceeding, except to the limited extent permitted by this Rule.

[4] A judge may initiate, permit, or consider ex parte communications expressly authorized by law, such as when serving on therapeutic or problem-solving courts, mental health courts, or drug courts. In this capacity, judges may assume a more interactive role with parties, treatment providers, probation officers, social workers, and others.

[5] A judge may consult with other judges on pending matters, but must avoid ex parte discussions of a case with judges who have previously been disqualified from hearing the matter, and with judges who have appellate jurisdiction over the matter.

[6] The prohibition against a judge investigating the facts in a matter extends to information available in all mediums, including electronic.

[7] A judge may consult ethics advisory committees, outside counsel, or legal experts concerning the judge's compliance with this Code. Such consultations are not subject to the restrictions of paragraph (A)(2).

RULE 2.10 *Judicial Statements on Pending and Impending Cases*

(A) A judge shall not make any public statement that might reasonably be expected to affect the outcome or impair the fairness of a matter pending* or impending* in any court, or make any nonpublic statement that might substantially interfere with a fair trial or hearing.

(B) A judge shall not, in connection with cases, controversies, or issues that are likely to come before the court, make pledges, promises, or commitments that are inconsistent with the impartial* performance of the adjudicative duties of judicial office.

(C) A judge shall require court staff, court officials, and others subject to the judge's direction and control to refrain from making statements that the judge would be prohibited from making by paragraphs (A) and (B).

(D) Notwithstanding the restrictions in paragraph (A), a judge may make public statements in the course of official duties, may explain court procedures, and may comment on any proceeding in which the judge is a litigant in a personal capacity.

(E) Subject to the requirements of paragraph (A), a judge may respond directly or through a third party to allegations in the media or elsewhere concerning the judge's conduct in a matter.

COMMENT

[1] This Rule's restrictions on judicial speech are essential to the maintenance of the independence, integrity, and impartiality of the judiciary.

[2] This Rule does not prohibit a judge from commenting on proceedings in which the judge is a litigant in a personal capacity, **or represents a client as permitted by these Rules**. In cases in which the judge is a litigant in an official capacity, such as a writ of mandamus, the judge must not comment publicly.

[3] Depending upon the circumstances, the judge should consider whether it may be preferable for a third party, rather than the judge, to respond or issue statements in connection with allegations concerning the judge's conduct in a matter.

RULE 2.11   *Disqualification*

(A) A judge shall disqualify himself or herself in any proceeding in which the judge's impartiality* might reasonably be questioned, including but not limited to the following circumstances:

(1) The judge has a personal bias or prejudice concerning a party or a party's lawyer, or personal knowledge* of facts that are in dispute in the proceeding.

(2) The judge knows* that the judge, the judge's spouse or domestic partner,* or a person within the third degree of relationship* to either of them, or the spouse or domestic partner of such a person is:

(a) a party to the proceeding, or an officer, director, general partner, managing member, or trustee of a party;

(b) acting as a lawyer in the proceeding;

(c) a person who has more than a de minimis* interest that could be substantially affected by the proceeding; or

(d) likely to be a material witness in the proceeding.

(3) The judge knows that he or she, individually or as a fiduciary,* or the judge's spouse, domestic partner, parent, or child, or any other member of the judge's family residing in the judge's household,* has an economic interest* in the subject matter in controversy or in a party to the proceeding.

(4) The judge knows or learns by means of a timely motion that a party, a party's lawyer, or the law firm of a party's lawyer has within the previous [insert number] year[s] made aggregate* contributions* to the judge's campaign in an amount that [is greater than $[insert amount] for an individual or $[insert amount] for an entity] [is reasonable and appropriate for an individual or an entity].

(5) The judge, while a judge or a judicial candidate,* has made a public statement, other than in a court proceeding, judicial decision, or opinion, that commits or appears to commit the judge to reach a particular result or rule in a particular way in the proceeding or controversy.

(6) The judge:

(a) served as a lawyer in the matter in controversy, or was associated with a lawyer who participated substantially as a lawyer in the matter during such association;

(b) served in governmental employment, and in such capacity participated personally and substantially as a lawyer or public official concerning the proceeding, or has publicly expressed in such capacity an opinion concerning the merits of the particular matter in controversy;

(c) was a material witness concerning the matter; or

(d) previously presided as a judge over the matter in another court.

(B) A judge shall keep informed about the judge's personal and fiduciary economic interests, and make a reasonable effort to keep informed about the personal economic interests of the judge's spouse or domestic partner and minor children residing in the judge's household.

(C) A judge subject to disqualification under this Rule, other than for bias or prejudice under paragraph (A)(1), may disclose on the record the basis of the judge's disqualification and may ask the parties and their lawyers to consider, outside the presence of the judge and court personnel, whether to waive disqualification. If, following the disclosure, the parties and lawyers agree, without participation by the judge or court personnel, that the judge should not be disqualified, the judge may participate in the proceeding. The agreement shall be incorporated into the record of the proceeding.

COMMENT

[1] Under this Rule, a judge is disqualified whenever the judge's impartiality might reasonably be questioned, regardless of whether any of the specific provisions of paragraphs (A)(1) through (6) apply. In many jurisdictions, the term "recusal" is used interchangeably with the term "disqualification."

[2] A judge's obligation not to hear or decide matters in which disqualification is required applies regardless of whether a motion to disqualify is filed.

[3] The rule of necessity may override the rule of disqualification. For example, a judge might be required to participate in judicial review of a judicial salary statute, or might be the only judge available in a matter requiring immediate judicial action, such as a hearing on probable cause or a temporary restraining order. In matters that require immediate action, the judge must disclose on the record the basis for possible disqualification and make reasonable efforts to transfer the matter to another judge as soon as practicable.

[4] The fact that a lawyer in a proceeding is affiliated with a law firm with which a relative of the judge is affiliated does not itself disqualify the judge. If, however, the judge's impartiality might reasonably be questioned under paragraph (A), or the relative is known by the judge to have an interest in the law firm that could be substantially affected by the proceeding under paragraph (A)(2)(c), the judge's disqualification is required.

[5] A judge should disclose on the record information that the judge believes the parties or their lawyers might reasonably consider relevant to a possible motion for disqualification, even if the judge believes there is no basis for disqualification.

[6] "Economic interest," as set forth in the Terminology section, means ownership of more than a de minimis legal or equitable interest. Except for situations in which a judge participates in the management of such a legal or equitable interest, or the interest could be substantially affected by the outcome of a proceeding before a judge, it does not include:

> (1) an interest in the individual holdings within a mutual or common investment fund;

> (2) an interest in securities held by an educational, religious, charitable, fraternal, or civic organization in which the judge or the judge's spouse, domestic partner, parent, or child serves as a director, officer, advisor, or other participant;

> (3) a deposit in a financial institution or deposits or proprietary interests the judge may maintain as a member of a mutual savings association or credit union, or similar proprietary interests; or

> (4) an interest in the issuer of government securities held by the judge.

RULE 2.12 *Supervisory Duties*

(A) A judge shall require court staff, court officials, and others subject to the judge's direction and control to act in a manner consistent with the judge's obligations under this Code.

(B) A judge with supervisory authority for the performance of other judges shall take reasonable measures to ensure that those judges properly discharge their judicial responsibilities, including the prompt disposition of matters before them.

COMMENT

[1] A judge is responsible for his or her own conduct and for the conduct of others, such as staff, when those persons are acting at the judge's direction or

control. A judge may not direct court personnel to engage in conduct on the judge's behalf or as the judge's representative when such conduct would violate the Code if undertaken by the judge.

[2] Public confidence in the judicial system depends upon timely justice. To promote the efficient administration of justice, a judge with supervisory authority must take the steps needed to ensure that judges under his or her supervision administer their workloads promptly.

RULE 2.13   *Administrative Appointments*

(A) In making administrative appointments, a judge:

(1) shall exercise the power of appointment impartially* and on the basis of merit; and

(2) shall avoid nepotism, favoritism, and unnecessary appointments.

(B) A judge shall not appoint a lawyer to a position if the judge either knows* that the lawyer, or the lawyer's spouse or domestic partner,* has contributed more than $[insert amount] within the prior [insert number] year[s] to the judge's election campaign, or learns of such a contribution* by means of a timely motion by a party or other person properly interested in the matter, unless:

(1) the position is substantially uncompensated;

(2) the lawyer has been selected in rotation from a list of qualified and available lawyers compiled without regard to their having made political contributions; or

(3) the judge or another presiding or administrative judge affirmatively finds that no other lawyer is willing, competent, and able to accept the position.

(C) A judge shall not approve compensation of appointees beyond the fair value of services rendered.

COMMENT

[1] Appointees of a judge include assigned counsel, officials such as referees, commissioners, special masters, receivers, and guardians, and personnel such as clerks, secretaries, and bailiffs. Consent by the parties to an appointment or an award of compensation does not relieve the judge of the obligation prescribed by paragraph (A).

[2] Unless otherwise defined by law, nepotism is the appointment or hiring of any relative within the third degree of relationship of either the judge or the judge's spouse or domestic partner, or the spouse or domestic partner of such relative.

[3] The rule against making administrative appointments of lawyers who have contributed in excess of a specified dollar amount to a judge's election campaign includes an exception for positions that are substantially uncompensated, such as those for which the lawyer's compensation is limited to reimbursement for out-of-pocket expenses.

RULE 2.14   *Disability and Impairment*

A judge having a reasonable belief that the performance of a lawyer or another judge is impaired by drugs or alcohol, or by a mental, emotional, or physical condition, shall take appropriate action, which may include a confidential referral to a lawyer or judicial assistance program.

COMMENT

[1] "Appropriate action" means action intended and reasonably likely to help the judge or lawyer in question address the problem and prevent harm to the justice system. Depending upon the circumstances, appropriate action may include but is not limited to speaking directly to the impaired person, notifying an individual with supervisory responsibility over the impaired person, or making a referral to an assistance program.

[2] Taking or initiating corrective action by way of referral to an assistance program may satisfy a judge's responsibility under this Rule. Assistance programs have many approaches for offering help to impaired judges and lawyers, such as intervention, counseling, or referral to appropriate health care professionals. Depending upon the gravity of the conduct that has come to the judge's attention, however, the judge may be required to take other action, such as reporting the impaired judge or lawyer to the appropriate authority, agency, or body. See Rule 2.15.

RULE 2.15   *Responding to Judicial and Lawyer Misconduct*

(A) A judge having knowledge* that another judge has committed a violation of this Code that raises a substantial question regarding the judge's honesty, trustworthiness, or fitness as a judge in other respects shall inform the appropriate authority.*

(B) A judge having knowledge that a lawyer has committed a violation of the Rules of Professional Conduct that raises a substantial question regarding the lawyer's honesty, trustworthiness, or fitness as a lawyer in other respects shall inform the appropriate authority.

(C) A judge who receives information indicating a substantial likelihood that another judge has committed a violation of this Code shall take appropriate action.

(D) A judge who receives information indicating a substantial likelihood that a lawyer has committed a violation of the Rules of Professional Conduct shall take appropriate action.

COMMENT

[1] Taking action to address known misconduct is a judge's obligation. Paragraphs (A) and (B) impose an obligation on the judge to report to the

appropriate disciplinary authority the known misconduct of another judge or a lawyer that raises a substantial question regarding the honesty, trustworthiness, or fitness of that judge or lawyer. Ignoring or denying known misconduct among one's judicial colleagues or members of the legal profession undermines a judge's responsibility to participate in efforts to ensure public respect for the justice system. This Rule limits the reporting obligation to those offenses that an independent judiciary must vigorously endeavor to prevent.

[2] A judge who does not have actual knowledge that another judge or a lawyer may have committed misconduct, but receives information indicating a substantial likelihood of such misconduct, is required to take appropriate action under paragraphs (C) and (D). Appropriate action may include, but is not limited to, communicating directly with the judge who may have violated this Code, communicating with a supervising judge, or reporting the suspected violation to the appropriate authority or other agency or body. Similarly, actions to be taken in response to information indicating that a lawyer has committed a violation of the Rules of Professional Conduct may include but are not limited to communicating directly with the lawyer who may have committed the violation, or reporting the suspected violation to the appropriate authority or other agency or body.

RULE 2.16   *Cooperation with Disciplinary Authorities*

(A) A judge shall cooperate and be candid and honest with judicial and lawyer disciplinary agencies.

(B) A judge shall not retaliate, directly or indirectly, against a person known* or suspected to have assisted or cooperated with an investigation of a judge or a lawyer.

COMMENT

[1] Cooperation with investigations and proceedings of judicial and lawyer discipline agencies, as required in paragraph (A), instills confidence in judges' commitment to the integrity of the judicial system and the protection of the public.

CANON 3.   A JUDGE SHALL CONDUCT THE JUDGE'S PERSONAL AND EXTRAJUDICIAL ACTIVITIES TO MINIMIZE THE RISK OF CONFLICT WITH THE OBLIGATIONS OF JUDICIAL OFFICE.

RULE 3.1   *Extrajudicial Activities in General*

A judge may engage in extrajudicial activities, except as prohibited by law* or this Code. However, when engaging in extrajudicial activities, a judge shall not:

(A) participate in activities that will interfere with the proper performance of the judge's judicial duties;

(B) participate in activities that will lead to frequent disqualification of the judge;

(C) participate in activities that would appear to a reasonable person to undermine the judge's independence,* integrity,* or impartiality;*

(D) engage in conduct that would appear to a reasonable person to be coercive; or

(E) make use of court premises, staff, stationery, equipment, or other resources, except for incidental use for activities that concern the law, the legal system, or the administration of justice, or unless such additional use is permitted by law.

COMMENT

[1] To the extent that time permits, and judicial independence and impartiality are not compromised, judges are encouraged to engage in appropriate extrajudicial activities. Judges are uniquely qualified to engage in extrajudicial activities that concern the law, the legal system, and the administration of justice, such as by speaking, writing, teaching, or participating in scholarly research projects. In addition, judges are permitted and encouraged to engage in educational, religious, charitable, fraternal or civic extrajudicial activities not conducted for profit, even when the activities do not involve the law. See Rule 3.7.

[2] Participation in both law-related and other extrajudicial activities helps integrate judges into their communities, and furthers public understanding of and respect for courts and the judicial system.

[3] Discriminatory actions and expressions of bias or prejudice by a judge, even outside the judge's official or judicial actions, are likely to appear to a reasonable person to call into question the judge's integrity and impartiality. Examples include jokes or other remarks that demean individuals based upon their race, sex, gender, religion, national origin, ethnicity, disability, age, sexual orientation, or socioeconomic status. For the same reason, a judge's extrajudicial activities must not be conducted in connection or affiliation with an organization that practices invidious discrimination. See Rule 3.6.

[4] While engaged in permitted extrajudicial activities, judges must not coerce others or take action that would reasonably be perceived as coercive. For example, depending upon the circumstances, a judge's solicitation of contributions or memberships for an organization, even as permitted by Rule 3.7(A), might create the risk that the person solicited would feel obligated to respond favorably, or would do so to curry favor with the judge.

RULE 3.2   *Appearances Before Governmental Bodies and Consultation with Government Officials*

A judge shall not appear voluntarily at a public hearing before, or otherwise consult with, an executive or a legislative body or official, except:

(A) in connection with matters concerning the law, the legal system, or the administration of justice;

(B) in connection with matters about which the judge acquired knowledge or expertise in the course of the judge's judicial duties; or

(C) when the judge is acting pro se in a matter involving the judge's legal or economic interests, or when the judge is acting in a fiduciary* capacity.

COMMENT

[1] Judges possess special expertise in matters of law, the legal system, and the administration of justice, and may properly share that expertise with governmental bodies and executive or legislative branch officials.

[2] In appearing before governmental bodies or consulting with government officials, judges must be mindful that they remain subject to other provisions of this Code, such as Rule 1.3, prohibiting judges from using the prestige of office to advance their own or others' interests, Rule 2.10, governing public comment on pending and impending matters, and Rule 3.1(C), prohibiting judges from engaging in extrajudicial activities that would appear to a reasonable person to undermine the judge's independence, integrity, or impartiality.

[3] In general, it would be an unnecessary and unfair burden to prohibit judges from appearing before governmental bodies or consulting with government officials on matters that are likely to affect them as private citizens, such as zoning proposals affecting their real property. In engaging in such activities, however, judges must not refer to their judicial positions, and must otherwise exercise caution to avoid using the prestige of judicial office.

RULE 3.3   *Testifying as a Character Witness*

A judge shall not testify as a character witness in a judicial, administrative, or other adjudicatory proceeding or otherwise vouch for the character of a person in a legal proceeding, except when duly summoned.

COMMENT

[1] A judge who, without being subpoenaed, testifies as a character witness abuses the prestige of judicial office to advance the interests of another. See Rule 1.3. Except in unusual circumstances where the demands of justice require, a judge should discourage a party from requiring the judge to testify as a character witness.

RULE 3.4   *Appointments to Governmental Positions*

A judge shall not accept appointment to a governmental committee, board, commission, or other governmental position, unless it is one that concerns the law, the legal system, or the administration of justice.

COMMENT

[1] Rule 3.4 implicitly acknowledges the value of judges accepting appointments to entities that concern the law, the legal system, or the administration of justice. Even in such instances, however, a judge should assess the appropriateness of accepting an appointment, paying particular attention to the subject matter of the appointment and the availability and allocation of judicial resources, including the judge's time commitments, and giving due regard to the requirements of the independence and impartiality of the judiciary.

[2] A judge may represent his or her country, state, or locality on ceremonial occasions or in connection with historical, educational, or cultural activities. Such representation does not constitute acceptance of a government position.

RULE 3.5 *Use of Nonpublic Information*

A judge shall not intentionally disclose or use nonpublic information* acquired in a judicial capacity for any purpose unrelated to the judge's judicial duties.

COMMENT

[1] In the course of performing judicial duties, a judge may acquire information of commercial or other value that is unavailable to the public. The judge must not reveal or use such information for personal gain or for any purpose unrelated to his or her judicial duties.

[2] This rule is not intended, however, to affect a judge's ability to act on information as necessary to protect the health or safety of the judge or a member of a judge's family, court personnel, or other judicial officers if consistent with other provisions of this Code.

RULE 3.6 *Affiliation with Discriminatory Organizations*

(A) A judge shall not hold membership in any organization that practices invidious discrimination on the basis of race, sex, gender, religion, national origin, ethnicity, or sexual orientation.

(B) A judge shall not use the benefits or facilities of an organization if the judge knows* or should know that the organization practices invidious discrimination on one or more of the bases identified in paragraph (A). A judge's attendance at an event in a facility of an organization that the judge is not permitted to join is not a violation of this Rule when the judge's attendance is an isolated event that could not reasonably be perceived as an endorsement of the organization's practices.

COMMENT

[1] A judge's public manifestation of approval of invidious discrimination on any basis gives rise to the appearance of impropriety and diminishes public confidence in the integrity and impartiality of the judiciary. A judge's membership in an organization that practices invidious discrimination creates the perception that the judge's impartiality is impaired.

[2] An organization is generally said to discriminate invidiously if it arbitrarily excludes from membership on the basis of race, sex, gender, religion, national origin, ethnicity, or sexual orientation persons who would otherwise be eligible for admission. Whether an organization practices invidious discrimination is a complex question to which judges should be attentive. The answer cannot be determined from a mere examination of an organization's current membership rolls, but rather, depends upon how the organization selects members, as well as other relevant factors, such as whether the organization is dedicated to the preservation of religious, ethnic, or cultural values of legitimate common interest to its members, or whether it is an intimate, purely private organization whose membership limitations could not constitutionally be prohibited.

[3] When a judge learns that an organization to which the judge belongs engages in invidious discrimination, the judge must resign immediately from the organization.

[4] A judge's membership in a religious organization as a lawful exercise of the freedom of religion is not a violation of this Rule.

[5] This Rule does not apply to national or state military service.

RULE 3.7 *Participation in Educational, Religious, Charitable, Fraternal, or Civic Organizations and Activities*

(A) Subject to the requirements of Rule 3.1, a judge may participate in activities sponsored by organizations or governmental entities concerned with the law, the legal system, or the administration of justice, and those sponsored by or on behalf of educational, religious, charitable, fraternal, or civic organizations not conducted for profit, including but not limited to the following activities:

(1) assisting such an organization or entity in planning related to fund-raising, and participating in the management and investment of the organization's or entity's funds;

(2) soliciting* contributions* for such an organization or entity, but only from members of the judge's family,* or from judges over whom the judge does not exercise supervisory or appellate authority;

(3) soliciting membership for such an organization or entity, even though the membership dues or fees generated may be used to support the objectives of the organization or entity, but only if the organization or entity is concerned with the law, the legal system, or the administration of justice;

(4) appearing or speaking at, receiving an award or other recognition at, being featured on the program of, and permitting his or her title to be used in connection with an event of such an organization or entity, but if the event serves a fund-raising purpose, the judge may participate only if the event concerns the law, the legal system, or the administration of justice;

(5) making recommendations to such a public or private fund-granting organization or entity in connection with its programs and activities, but only if the organization or entity is concerned with the law, the legal system, or the administration of justice; and

(6) serving as an officer, director, trustee, or nonlegal advisor of such an organization or entity, unless it is likely that the organization or entity:

(a) will be engaged in proceedings that would ordinarily come before the judge; or

(b) will frequently be engaged in adversary proceedings in the court of which the judge is a member, or in any court subject to the appellate jurisdiction of the court of which the judge is a member.

(B) A judge may encourage lawyers to provide pro bono publico legal services.

COMMENT

[1] The activities permitted by paragraph (A) generally include those sponsored by or undertaken on behalf of public or private not-for-profit educational institutions, and other not-for-profit organizations, including law-related, charitable, and other organizations.

[2] Even for law-related organizations, a judge should consider whether the membership and purposes of the organization, or the nature of the judge's participation in or association with the organization, would conflict with the judge's obligation to refrain from activities that reflect adversely upon a judge's independence, integrity, and impartiality.

[3] Mere attendance at an event, whether or not the event serves a fund-raising purpose, does not constitute a violation of paragraph 4(A). It is also generally permissible for a judge to serve as an usher or a food server or preparer, or to perform similar functions, at fund-raising events sponsored by educational, religious, charitable, fraternal, or civic organizations. Such activities are not solicitation and do not present an element of coercion or abuse the prestige of judicial office.

[4] Identification of a judge's position in educational, religious, charitable, fraternal, or civic organizations on letterhead used for fund-raising or membership solicitation does not violate this Rule. The letterhead may list the judge's title or judicial office if comparable designations are used for other persons.

[5] In addition to appointing lawyers to serve as counsel for indigent parties in individual cases, a judge may promote broader access to justice by encouraging lawyers to participate in pro bono publico legal services, if in doing so the judge does not employ coercion, or abuse the prestige of judicial office. Such encouragement

may take many forms, including providing lists of available programs, training lawyers to do pro bono publico legal work, and participating in events recognizing lawyers who have done pro bono publico work.

RULE 3.8   *Appointments to Fiduciary Positions*

(A) A judge shall not accept appointment to serve in a fiduciary* position, such as executor, administrator, trustee, guardian, attorney in fact, or other personal representative, except for the estate, trust, or person of a member of the judge's family,* and then only if such service will not interfere with the proper performance of judicial duties.

(B) A judge shall not serve in a fiduciary position if the judge as fiduciary will likely be engaged in proceedings that would ordinarily come before the judge, or if the estate, trust, or ward becomes involved in adversary proceedings in the court on which the judge serves, or one under its appellate jurisdiction.

(C) A judge acting in a fiduciary capacity shall be subject to the same restrictions on engaging in financial activities that apply to a judge personally.

(D) If a person who is serving in a fiduciary position becomes a judge, he or she must comply with this Rule as soon as reasonably practicable, but in no event later than [one year] after becoming a judge.

COMMENT

[1] A judge should recognize that other restrictions imposed by this Code may conflict with a judge's obligations as a fiduciary; in such circumstances, a judge should resign as fiduciary. For example, serving as a fiduciary might require frequent disqualification of a judge under Rule 2.11 because a judge is deemed to have an economic interest in shares of stock held by a trust if the amount of stock held is more than de minimis.

RULE 3.9   *Service as Arbitrator or Mediator*

A judge shall not act as an arbitrator or a mediator or perform other judicial functions apart from the judge's official duties unless expressly authorized by law.*

COMMENT

[1] This Rule does not prohibit a judge from participating in arbitration, mediation, or settlement conferences performed as part of assigned judicial duties.

Rendering dispute resolution services apart from those duties, whether or not for economic gain, is prohibited unless it is expressly authorized by law.

RULE 3.10   *Practice of Law*

A judge shall not practice law. A judge may act pro se and may, without compensation, give legal advice to and draft or review documents for a member of the judge's family,* but is prohibited from serving as the family member's lawyer in any forum.

COMMENT

[1] A judge may act pro se in all legal matters, including matters involving litigation and matters involving appearances before or other dealings with governmental bodies. A judge must not use the prestige of office to advance the judge's personal or family interests. See Rule 1.3.

RULE 3.11   *Financial, Business, or Remunerative Activities*

(A) A judge may hold and manage investments of the judge and members of the judge's family.*

(B) A judge shall not serve as an officer, director, manager, general partner, advisor, or employee of any business entity except that a judge may manage or participate in:

(1) a business closely held by the judge or members of the judge's family; or

(2) a business entity primarily engaged in investment of the financial resources of the judge or members of the judge's family.

(C) A judge shall not engage in financial activities permitted under paragraphs (A) and (B) if they will:

(1) interfere with the proper performance of judicial duties;

(2) lead to frequent disqualification of the judge;

(3) involve the judge in frequent transactions or continuing business relationships with lawyers or other persons likely to come before the court on which the judge serves; or

(4) result in violation of other provisions of this Code.

COMMENT

[1] Judges are generally permitted to engage in financial activities, including managing real estate and other investments for themselves or for members of their families. Participation in these activities, like participation in other extrajudicial

activities, is subject to the requirements of this Code. For example, it would be improper for a judge to spend so much time on business activities that it interferes with the performance of judicial duties. See Rule 2.1. Similarly, it would be improper for a judge to use his or her official title or appear in judicial robes in business advertising, or to conduct his or her business or financial affairs in such a way that disqualification is frequently required. See Rules 1.3 and 2.11.

[2] As soon as practicable without serious financial detriment, the judge must divest himself or herself of investments and other financial interests that might require frequent disqualification or otherwise violate this Rule.

RULE 3.12   *Compensation for Extrajudicial Activities*

A judge may accept reasonable compensation for extrajudicial activities permitted by this Code or other law* unless such acceptance would appear to a reasonable person to undermine the judge's independence,* integrity,* or impartiality.*

COMMENT

[1] A judge is permitted to accept honoraria, stipends, fees, wages, salaries, royalties, or other compensation for speaking, teaching, writing, and other extrajudicial activities, provided the compensation is reasonable and commensurate with the task performed. The judge should be mindful, however, that judicial duties must take precedence over other activities. See Rule 2.1.

[2] Compensation derived from extrajudicial activities may be subject to public reporting. See Rule 3.15.

RULE 3.13   *Acceptance and Reporting of Gifts, Loans, Bequests, Benefits, or Other Things of Value*

(A) A judge shall not accept any gifts, loans, bequests, benefits, or other things of value, if acceptance is prohibited by law* or would appear to a reasonable person to undermine the judge's independence,* integrity,* or impartiality.*

(B) Unless otherwise prohibited by law, or by paragraph (A), a judge may accept the following without publicly reporting such acceptance:

    (1) items with little intrinsic value, such as plaques, certificates, trophies, and greeting cards;

    (2) gifts, loans, bequests, benefits, or other things of value from friends, relatives, or other persons, including lawyers, whose appearance or interest in a proceeding pending* or impending* before the judge would in any event require disqualification of the judge under Rule 2.11;

(3) ordinary social hospitality;

(4) commercial or financial opportunities and benefits, including special pricing and discounts, and loans from lending institutions in their regular course of business, if the same opportunities and benefits or loans are made available on the same terms to similarly situated persons who are not judges;

(5) rewards and prizes given to competitors or participants in random drawings, contests, or other events that are open to persons who are not judges;

(6) scholarships, fellowships, and similar benefits or awards, if they are available to similarly situated persons who are not judges, based upon the same terms and criteria;

(7) books, magazines, journals, audiovisual materials, and other resource materials supplied by publishers on a complimentary basis for official use; or

(8) gifts, awards, or benefits associated with the business, profession, or other separate activity of a spouse, a domestic partner,* or other family member of a judge residing in the judge's household,* but that incidentally benefit the judge.

(C) Unless otherwise prohibited by law or by paragraph (A), a judge may accept the following items, and must report such acceptance to the extent required by Rule 3.15:

(1) gifts incident to a public testimonial;

(2) invitations to the judge and the judge's spouse, domestic partner, or guest to attend without charge:

(a) an event associated with a bar-related function or other activity relating to the law, the legal system, or the administration of justice; or

(b) an event associated with any of the judge's educational, religious, charitable, fraternal or civic activities permitted by this Code, if the same invitation is offered to nonjudges who are engaged in similar ways in the activity as is the judge; and

(3) gifts, loans, bequests, benefits, or other things of value, if the source is a party or other person, including a lawyer, who has come or is likely to come before the judge, or whose interests have come or are likely to come before the judge.

COMMENT

[1] Whenever a judge accepts a gift or other thing of value without paying fair market value, there is a risk that the benefit might be viewed as intended to influence the judge's decision in a case. Rule 3.13 imposes restrictions upon the acceptance of such benefits, according to the magnitude of the risk. Paragraph (B) identifies circumstances in which the risk that the acceptance would appear to undermine the

judge's independence, integrity, or impartiality is low, and explicitly provides that such items need not be publicly reported. As the value of the benefit or the likelihood that the source of the benefit will appear before the judge increases, the judge is either prohibited under paragraph (A) from accepting the gift, or required under paragraph (C) to publicly report it.

[2] Gift-giving between friends and relatives is a common occurrence, and ordinarily does not create an appearance of impropriety or cause reasonable persons to believe that the judge's independence, integrity, or impartiality has been compromised. In addition, when the appearance of friends or relatives in a case would require the judge's disqualification under Rule 2.11, there would be no opportunity for a gift to influence the judge's decision making. Paragraph (B)(2) places no restrictions upon the ability of a judge to accept gifts or other things of value from friends or relatives under these circumstances, and does not require public reporting.

[3] Businesses and financial institutions frequently make available special pricing, discounts, and other benefits, either in connection with a temporary promotion or for preferred customers, based upon longevity of the relationship, volume of business transacted, and other factors. A judge may freely accept such benefits if they are available to the general public, or if the judge qualifies for the special price or discount according to the same criteria as are applied to persons who are not judges. As an example, loans provided at generally prevailing interest rates are not gifts, but a judge could not accept a loan from a financial institution at below-market interest rates unless the same rate was being made available to the general public for a certain period of time or only to borrowers with specified qualifications that the judge also possesses.

[4] Rule 3.13 applies only to acceptance of gifts or other things of value by a judge. Nonetheless, if a gift or other benefit is given to the judge's spouse, domestic partner, or member of the judge's family residing in the judge's household, it may be viewed as an attempt to evade Rule 3.13 and influence the judge indirectly. Where the gift or benefit is being made primarily to such other persons, and the judge is merely an incidental beneficiary, this concern is reduced. A judge should, however, remind family and household members of the restrictions imposed upon judges, and urge them to take these restrictions into account when making decisions about accepting such gifts or benefits.

[5] Rule 3.13 does not apply to contributions to a judge's campaign for judicial office. Such contributions are governed by other Rules of this Code, including Rules 4.3 and 4.4.

RULE 3.14   *Reimbursement of Expenses and Waivers of Fees or Charges*

(A) Unless otherwise prohibited by Rules 3.1 and 3.13(A) or other law,* a judge may accept reimbursement of necessary and reasonable expenses for travel, food, lodging, or other incidental expenses, or a waiver or partial waiver of fees or charges for registration, tuition, and similar items, from sources other than the judge's employing entity, if the expenses or charges are associated with the judge's participation in extrajudicial activities permitted by this Code.

(B) Reimbursement of expenses for necessary travel, food, lodging, or other incidental expenses shall be limited to the actual costs reasonably incurred by the judge and, when appropriate to the occasion, by the judge's spouse, domestic partner,* or guest.

(C) A judge who accepts reimbursement of expenses or waivers or partial waivers of fees or charges on behalf of the judge or the judge's spouse, domestic partner, or guest shall publicly report such acceptance as required by Rule 3.15.

COMMENT

[1] Educational, civic, religious, fraternal, and charitable organizations often sponsor meetings, seminars, symposia, dinners, awards ceremonies, and similar events. Judges are encouraged to attend educational programs, as both teachers and participants, in law-related and academic disciplines, in furtherance of their duty to remain competent in the law. Participation in a variety of other extrajudicial activity is also permitted and encouraged by this Code.

[2] Not infrequently, sponsoring organizations invite certain judges to attend seminars or other events on a fee-waived or partial-fee-waived basis, and sometimes include reimbursement for necessary travel, food, lodging, or other incidental expenses. A judge's decision whether to accept reimbursement of expenses or a waiver or partial waiver of fees or charges in connection with these or other extrajudicial activities must be based upon an assessment of all the circumstances. The judge must undertake a reasonable inquiry to obtain the information necessary to make an informed judgment about whether acceptance would be consistent with the requirements of this Code.

[3] A judge must assure himself or herself that acceptance of reimbursement or fee waivers would not appear to a reasonable person to undermine the judge's independence, integrity, or impartiality. The factors that a judge should consider when deciding whether to accept reimbursement or a fee waiver for attendance at a particular activity include:

(a) whether the sponsor is an accredited educational institution or bar association rather than a trade association or a for-profit entity;

(b) whether the funding comes largely from numerous contributors rather than from a single entity and is earmarked for programs with specific content;

(c) whether the content is related or unrelated to the subject matter of litigation pending or impending before the judge, or to matters that are likely to come before the judge;

(d) whether the activity is primarily educational rather than recreational, and whether the costs of the event are reasonable and comparable to those associated with similar events sponsored by the judiciary, bar associations, or similar groups;

(e) whether information concerning the activity and its funding sources is available upon inquiry;

(f) whether the sponsor or source of funding is generally associated with particular parties or interests currently appearing or likely to appear in the judge's court, thus possibly requiring disqualification of the judge under Rule 2.11;

(g) whether differing viewpoints are presented; and

(h) whether a broad range of judicial and nonjudicial participants are invited, whether a large number of participants are invited, and whether the program is designed specifically for judges.

RULE 3.15 *Reporting Requirements*

(A) A judge shall publicly report the amount or value of:

(1) compensation received for extrajudicial activities as permitted by Rule 3.12;

(2) gifts and other things of value as permitted by Rule 3.13(C), unless the value of such items, alone or in the aggregate with other items received from the same source in the same calendar year, does not exceed $[insert amount]; and

(3) reimbursement of expenses and waiver of fees or charges permitted by Rule 3.14(A), unless the amount of reimbursement or waiver, alone or in the aggregate with other reimbursements or waivers received from the same source in the same calendar year, does not exceed $[insert amount].

(B) When public reporting is required by paragraph (A), a judge shall report the date, place, and nature of the activity for which the judge received any compensation; the description of any gift, loan, bequest, benefit, or other thing of value accepted; and the source of reimbursement of expenses or waiver or partial waiver of fees or charges.

(C) The public report required by paragraph (A) shall be made at least annually, except that for reimbursement of expenses and waiver or partial waiver of fees or charges, the report shall be made within thirty days following the conclusion of the event or program.

(D) Reports made in compliance with this Rule shall be filed as public documents in the office of the clerk of the court on which the judge serves or other office designated by law,* and, when technically feasible, posted by the court or office personnel on the court's website.

CANON 4. A JUDGE OR CANDIDATE FOR JUDICIAL OFFICE SHALL NOT ENGAGE IN POLITICAL OR CAMPAIGN ACTIVITY THAT IS INCONSISTENT WITH THE INDEPENDENCE, INTEGRITY, OR IMPARTIALITY OF THE JUDICIARY.

RULE 4.1 *Political and Campaign Activities of Judges and Judicial Candidates in General*

(A) Except as permitted by law,* or by Rules 4.2, 4.3, and 4.4, a judge or a judicial candidate* shall not:

(1) act as a leader in, or hold an office in, a political organization;*

(2) make speeches on behalf of a political organization;

(3) publicly endorse or oppose a candidate for any public office;

(4) solicit funds for, pay an assessment to, or make a contribution* to a political organization or a candidate for public office;

(5) attend or purchase tickets for dinners or other events sponsored by a political organization or a candidate for public office;

(6) publicly identify himself or herself as a candidate of a political organization;

(7) seek, accept, or use endorsements from a political organization;

(8) personally solicit* or accept campaign contributions other than through a campaign committee authorized by Rule 4.4;

(9) use or permit the use of campaign contributions for the private benefit of the judge, the candidate, or others;

(10) use court staff, facilities, or other court resources in a campaign for judicial office;

(11) knowingly,* or with reckless disregard for the truth, make any false or misleading statement;

(12) make any statement that would reasonably be expected to affect the outcome or impair the fairness of a matter pending* or impending* in any court; or

(13) in connection with cases, controversies, or issues that are likely to come before the court, make pledges, promises, or commitments that are inconsistent with the impartial* performance of the adjudicative duties of judicial office.

(B) A judge or judicial candidate shall take reasonable measures to ensure that other persons do not undertake, on behalf of the judge or judicial candidate, any activities prohibited under paragraph (A).

COMMENT

General Considerations

[1] Even when subject to public election, a judge plays a role different from that of a legislator or executive branch official. Rather than making decisions based upon the expressed views or preferences of the electorate, a judge makes decisions based upon the law and the facts of every case. Therefore, in furtherance of this interest, judges and judicial candidates must, to the greatest extent possible, be free and appear to be free from political influence and political pressure. This Canon imposes narrowly tailored restrictions upon the political and campaign activities of all judges and judicial candidates, taking into account the various methods of selecting judges.

[2] When a person becomes a judicial candidate, this Canon becomes applicable to his or her conduct.

Participation in Political Activities

[3] Public confidence in the independence and impartiality of the judiciary is eroded if judges or judicial candidates are perceived to be subject to political influence. Although judges and judicial candidates may register to vote as members of a political party, they are prohibited by paragraph (A)(1) from assuming leadership roles in political organizations.

[4] Paragraphs (A)(2) and (A)(3) prohibit judges and judicial candidates from making speeches on behalf of political organizations or publicly endorsing or opposing candidates for public office, respectively, to prevent them from abusing the prestige of judicial office to advance the interests of others. See Rule 1.3. These Rules do not prohibit candidates from campaigning on their own behalf, or from endorsing or opposing candidates for the same judicial office for which they are running. See Rules 4.2(B)(2) and 4.2(B)(3).

[5] Although members of the families of judges and judicial candidates are free to engage in their own political activity, including running for public office, there is no "family exception" to the prohibition in paragraph (A)(3) against a judge or candidate publicly endorsing candidates for public office. A judge or judicial candidate must not become involved in, or publicly associated with, a family member's political activity or campaign for public office. To avoid public misunderstanding, judges and judicial candidates should take, and should urge members of their families to take, reasonable steps to avoid any implication that they endorse any family member's candidacy or other political activity.

[6] Judges and judicial candidates retain the right to participate in the political process as voters in both primary and general elections. For purposes of this Canon, participation in a caucus-type election procedure does not constitute public support for or endorsement of a political organization or candidate, and is not prohibited by paragraphs (A)(2) or (A)(3).

Statements and Comments Made during a Campaign for Judicial Office

[7] Judicial candidates must be scrupulously fair and accurate in all statements made by them and by their campaign committees. Paragraph (A)(11) obligates candidates and their committees to refrain from making statements that are false or misleading, or that omit facts necessary to make the communication considered as a whole not materially misleading.

[8] Judicial candidates are sometimes the subject of false, misleading, or unfair allegations made by opposing candidates, third parties, or the media. For example, false or misleading statements might be made regarding the identity, present position, experience, qualifications, or judicial rulings of a candidate. In other situations, false or misleading allegations may be made that bear upon a candidate's integrity or fitness for judicial office. As long as the candidate does not

violate paragraphs (A)(11), (A)(12), or (A)(13), the candidate may make a factually accurate public response. In addition, when an independent third party has
made unwarranted attacks on a candidate's opponent, the candidate may disavow
the attacks, and request the third party to cease and desist.

[9] Subject to paragraph (A)(12), a judicial candidate is permitted to respond
directly to false, misleading, or unfair allegations made against him or her during a
campaign, although it is preferable for someone else to respond if the allegations
relate to a pending case.

[10] Paragraph (A)(12) prohibits judicial candidates from making comments
that might impair the fairness of pending or impending judicial proceedings. This
provision does not restrict arguments or statements to the court or jury by a lawyer
who is a judicial candidate, or rulings, statements, or instructions by a judge that
may appropriately affect the outcome of a matter.

Pledges, Promises, or Commitments Inconsistent With Impartial Performance of the Adjudicative Duties of Judicial Office

[11] The role of a judge is different from that of a legislator or executive
branch official, even when the judge is subject to public election. Campaigns for
judicial office must be conducted differently from campaigns for other offices. The
narrowly drafted restrictions upon political and campaign activities of judicial candidates provided in Canon 4 allow candidates to conduct campaigns that provide
voters with sufficient information to permit them to distinguish between candidates
and make informed electoral choices.

[12] Paragraph (A)(13) makes applicable to both judges and judicial candidates the prohibition that applies to judges in Rule 2.10(B), relating to pledges,
promises, or commitments that are inconsistent with the impartial performance of
the adjudicative duties of judicial office.

[13] The making of a pledge, promise, or commitment is not dependent
upon, or limited to, the use of any specific words or phrases; instead, the totality of
the statement must be examined to determine if a reasonable person would believe
that the candidate for judicial office has specifically undertaken to reach a particular result. Pledges, promises, or commitments must be contrasted with statements
or announcements of personal views on legal, political, or other issues, which are
not prohibited. When making such statements, a judge should acknowledge the
overarching judicial obligation to apply and uphold the law, without regard to his
or her personal views.

[14] A judicial candidate may make campaign promises related to judicial
organization, administration, and court management, such as a promise to dispose
of a backlog of cases, start court sessions on time, or avoid favoritism in appointments and hiring. A candidate may also pledge to take action outside the courtroom, such as working toward an improved jury selection system, or advocating for
more funds to improve the physical plant and amenities of the courthouse.

[15] Judicial candidates may receive questionnaires or requests for interviews from the media and from issue advocacy or other community organizations
that seek to learn their views on disputed or controversial legal or political issues.

Paragraph (A)(13) does not specifically address judicial responses to such inquiries. Depending upon the wording and format of such questionnaires, candidates' responses might be viewed as pledges, promises, or commitments to perform the adjudicative duties of office other than in an impartial way. To avoid violating paragraph (A)(13), therefore, candidates who respond to media and other inquiries should also give assurances that they will keep an open mind and will carry out their adjudicative duties faithfully and impartially if elected. Candidates who do not respond may state their reasons for not responding, such as the danger that answering might be perceived by a reasonable person as undermining a successful candidate's independence or impartiality, or that it might lead to frequent disqualification. See Rule 2.11.

RULE 4.2   *Political and Campaign Activities of Judicial Candidates in Public Elections*

(A) A judicial candidate* in a partisan, nonpartisan, or retention public election* shall:

(1) act at all times in a manner consistent with the independence,* integrity,* and impartiality* of the judiciary;

(2) comply with all applicable election, election campaign, and election campaign fund-raising laws and regulations of this jurisdiction;

(3) review and approve the content of all campaign statements and materials produced by the candidate or his or her campaign committee, as authorized by Rule 4.4, before their dissemination; and

(4) take reasonable measures to ensure that other persons do not undertake on behalf of the candidate activities, other than those described in Rule 4.4, that the candidate is prohibited from doing by Rule 4.1.

(B) A candidate for elective judicial office may, unless prohibited by law,* and not earlier than [insert amount of time] before the first applicable primary election, caucus, or general or retention election:

(1) establish a campaign committee pursuant to the provisions of Rule 4.4;

(2) speak on behalf of his or her candidacy through any medium, including but not limited to advertisements, websites, or other campaign literature;

(3) publicly endorse or oppose candidates for the same judicial office for which he or she is running;

(4) attend or purchase tickets for dinners or other events sponsored by a political organization* or a candidate for public office;

(5) seek, accept, or use endorsements from any person or organization other than a partisan political organization; and

(6) contribute to a political organization or candidate for public office, but not more than $[insert amount] to any one organization or candidate.

(C) A judicial candidate in a partisan public election may, unless prohibited by law, and not earlier than [insert amount of time] before the first applicable primary election, caucus, or general election:

(1) identify himself or herself as a candidate of a political organization; and

(2) seek, accept, and use endorsements of a political organization.

COMMENT

[1] Paragraphs (B) and (C) permit judicial candidates in public elections to engage in some political and campaign activities otherwise prohibited by Rule 4.1. Candidates may not engage in these activities earlier than [insert amount of time] before the first applicable electoral event, such as a caucus or a primary election.

[2] Despite paragraphs (B) and (C), judicial candidates for public election remain subject to many of the provisions of Rule 4.1. For example, a candidate continues to be prohibited from soliciting funds for a political organization, knowingly making false or misleading statements during a campaign, or making certain promises, pledges, or commitments related to future adjudicative duties. See Rule 4.1(A), paragraphs (4), (11), and (13).

[3] In partisan public elections for judicial office, a candidate may be nominated by, affiliated with, or otherwise publicly identified or associated with a political organization, including a political party. This relationship may be maintained throughout the period of the public campaign, and may include use of political party or similar designations on campaign literature and on the ballot.

[4] In nonpartisan public elections or retention elections, paragraph (B)(5) prohibits a candidate from seeking, accepting, or using nominations or endorsements from a partisan political organization.

[5] Judicial candidates are permitted to attend or purchase tickets for dinners and other events sponsored by political organizations.

[6] For purposes of paragraph (B)(3), candidates are considered to be running for the same judicial office if they are competing for a single judgeship or if several judgeships on the same court are to be filled as a result of the election. In endorsing or opposing another candidate for a position on the same court, a judicial candidate must abide by the same rules governing campaign conduct and speech as apply to the candidate's own campaign.

[7] Although judicial candidates in nonpartisan public elections are prohibited from running on a ticket or slate associated with a political organization, they may group themselves into slates or other alliances to conduct their campaigns more effectively. Candidates who have grouped themselves together are considered to be running for the same judicial office if they satisfy the conditions described in Comment [6].

RULE 4.3   *Activities of Candidates for Appointive Judicial Office*

A candidate for appointment to judicial office may:

(A) communicate with the appointing or confirming authority, including any selection, screening, or nominating commission or similar agency; and

(B) seek endorsements for the appointment from any person or organization other than a partisan political organization.

COMMENT

[1] When seeking support or endorsement, or when communicating directly with an appointing or confirming authority, a candidate for appointive judicial office must not make any pledges, promises, or commitments that are inconsistent with the impartial performance of the adjudicative duties of the office. See Rule 4.1(A)(13).

RULE 4.4   *Campaign Committees*

(A) A judicial candidate* subject to public election* may establish a campaign committee to manage and conduct a campaign for the candidate, subject to the provisions of this Code. The candidate is responsible for ensuring that his or her campaign committee complies with applicable provisions of this Code and other applicable law.*

(B) A judicial candidate subject to public election shall direct his or her campaign committee:

(1) to solicit and accept only such campaign contributions* as are reasonable, in any event not to exceed, in the aggregate,* $[insert amount] from any individual or $[insert amount] from any entity or organization;

(2) not to solicit or accept contributions for a candidate's current campaign more than [insert amount of time] before the applicable primary election, caucus, or general or retention election, nor more than [insert number] days after the last election in which the candidate participated; and

(3) to comply with all applicable statutory requirements for disclosure and divestiture of campaign contributions, and to file with [name of appropriate regulatory authority] a report stating the name, address, occupation, and employer of each person who has made campaign contributions to the committee in an aggregate value exceeding $[insert amount]. The report must be filed within [insert number] days following an election, or within such other period as is provided by law.

COMMENT

[1] Judicial candidates are prohibited from personally soliciting campaign contributions or personally accepting campaign contributions. See Rule 4.1(A)(8). This Rule recognizes that in many jurisdictions, judicial candidates must raise

campaign funds to support their candidacies, and permits candidates, other than candidates for appointive judicial office, to establish campaign committees to solicit and accept reasonable financial contributions or in-kind contributions.

[2] Campaign committees may solicit and accept campaign contributions, manage the expenditure of campaign funds, and generally conduct campaigns. Candidates are responsible for compliance with the requirements of election law and other applicable law, and for the activities of their campaign committees.

[3] At the start of a campaign, the candidate must instruct the campaign committee to solicit or accept only such contributions as are reasonable in amount, appropriate under the circumstances, and in conformity with applicable law. Although lawyers and others who might appear before a successful candidate for judicial office are permitted to make campaign contributions, the candidate should instruct his or her campaign committee to be especially cautious in connection with such contributions, so they do not create grounds for disqualification if the candidate is elected to judicial office. See Rule 2.11.

RULE 4.5   *Activities of Judges Who Become Candidates for Nonjudicial Office*

(A) Upon becoming a candidate for a nonjudicial elective office, a judge shall resign from judicial office, unless permitted by law* to continue to hold judicial office.

(B) Upon becoming a candidate for a nonjudicial appointive office, a judge is not required to resign from judicial office, provided that the judge complies with the other provisions of this Code.

COMMENT

[1] In campaigns for nonjudicial elective public office, candidates may make pledges, promises, or commitments related to positions they would take and ways they would act if elected to office. Although appropriate in nonjudicial campaigns, this manner of campaigning is inconsistent with the role of a judge, who must remain fair and impartial to all who come before him or her. The potential for misuse of the judicial office, and the political promises that the judge would be compelled to make in the course of campaigning for nonjudicial elective office, together dictate that a judge who wishes to run for such an office must resign upon becoming a candidate.

[2] The "resign to run" rule set forth in paragraph (A) ensures that a judge cannot use the judicial office to promote his or her candidacy, and prevents post-campaign retaliation from the judge in the event the judge is defeated in the election. When a judge is seeking appointive nonjudicial office, however, the dangers are not sufficient to warrant imposing the "resign to run" rule.

Statutes on Disqualification and Discipline of Federal Judges

Editors' Introduction. This chapter reprints statutes governing the disqualification of federal judges for bias or prejudice or other reasons, and summarizes statutes governing discipline of federal judges who engage in improper conduct.

Regarding disqualification, the grounds on which federal judges may be disqualified are set forth in two federal statutes, 28 U.S.C. §§144 and 455, which we reprint below. (Section 144 is rarely the basis for a decision in view of the greater detail and modern language in §455, which is based on provisions in the 1990 ABA Model Code of Judicial Conduct.) Immediately following §455, we reprint an unusual press release entitled "Statement of Recusal Policy" in which seven Justices of the United States Supreme Court explained how they intend to interpret and apply §455 in certain situations. For a fascinating study of the application of §455 to Justices of the United States Supreme Court, see the Special Section at the end of the 2005 edition of this book, entitled "Should Justice Scalia Have Recused Himself in Vice President Cheney's Appeal to the Supreme Court?"

Regarding discipline, federal judges appointed under Article III of the Constitution enjoy life tenure and can be removed from office only through impeachment proceedings in Congress. This principle is established by Article III, §1 of the United States Constitution, which provides as follows:

> The judicial Power of the United States, shall be vested in one supreme Court, and in such inferior Courts as the Congress may from time to time ordain and establish. The Judges, both of the supreme and inferior Courts, shall hold their Offices during good Behaviour, and shall, at stated Times, receive for their Services, a Compensation, which shall not be diminished during their Continuance in Office.

However, federal judges who engage in conduct "prejudicial to the effective and expeditious administration of the business of the courts" (*see* 28 U.S.C. §351) may be disciplined by sanctions short of removal from office, such as public or private censure or an order that no new cases be assigned to a judge for a limited time. Provisions for discipline short of removal were formerly contained in 28 U.S.C. §372(c), but in 2002 Congress moved the substance of

§372(c), with minor amendments, to a series of sections designated 28 U.S.C. §§351 through 364. These statutes, which we do not reprint, permit anyone to file a complaint against a federal judge (but not a Justice of the Supreme Court) and also permit the chief judge of the circuit to invoke the discipline procedures without need for a complaint. There are provisions for investigation by a special committee and, where warranted, a due process hearing to determine if the alleged conduct merits discipline. Hearings are conducted before circuit and district judges in the circuit (called the Judicial Council). Review by the Judicial Conference of the United States in Washington (also composed of federal judges) is contemplated. Where the underlying conduct warrants impeachment, the Judicial Conference is instructed to inform Congress.

Resignation and retirement of judges is governed by 28 U.S.C. §§371 through 377, which we also do not reprint. Nor do we reprint the Code of Conduct for United States Judges, which is generally based on the 2007 ABA Model Code of Judicial Conduct, set out elsewhere in this volume, but differs from it in some significant ways.,

In September 2006, a committee appointed by former Chief Justice Rehnquist and chaired by Justice Breyer issued a lengthy report on the disciplinary system for federal judges and recommended changes to improve its accuracy and fairness. The report is at *www.fjc.gov/public/pdf.nsf/lookup/breyer06.pdf/$file/breyer06.pdf*. Since the last edition of this book went to press in October 2011, Congress has not amended any of the statutes reprinted below. (Indeed, §144 has not been amended since 1949, and §455 has not been amended since 1990.)

On March 11, 2008, the Judicial Conference of the United States approved a binding, nationwide set of rules for handling conduct and disability complaints against federal judges. The new rules, which took effect on April 10, 2008, respond to the recommendations of the Breyer committee. The rules cover such topics as complaint initiation and review, venue, confidentiality and publication, remedies, the conduct of investigations, and the rights and roles of participants in the process. Judicial councils in each circuit retain the power to adopt local rules regarding procedural details of the complaint-handling process, provided that those rules do not contradict the new uniform rules. The new rules are available online at *www.uscourts.gov/uscourts/News/2008/docs/jud_conduct_and_disability_308_app_B_rev.pdf*.

Contents

SELECTED STATUTES ON JUDICIAL DISQUALIFICATION

SELECTED STATUTES ON JUDICIAL DISQUALIFICATION

§144.   Bias or Prejudice of Judges

Whenever a party to any proceeding in a district court makes and files a timely and sufficient affidavit that the judge before whom the matter is pending has a personal bias or prejudice either against him or in favor of any adverse party, such judge shall proceed no further therein, but another judge shall be assigned to hear such proceeding.

The affidavit shall state the facts and the reasons for the belief that bias or prejudice exists, and shall be filed not less than ten days before the beginning of the term at which the proceeding is to be heard, or good cause shall be shown for failure to file it within such time. A party may file only one such affidavit in any case. It shall be accompanied by a certificate of counsel of record stating that it is made in good faith.

§455.   Disqualification of Justice, Judge, or Magistrate

(a) Any justice, judge, or magistrate of the United States shall disqualify himself in any proceeding in which his impartiality might reasonably be questioned.

(b) He shall also disqualify himself in the following circumstances:

(1) Where he has a personal bias or prejudice concerning a party, or personal knowledge of disputed evidentiary facts concerning the proceeding;

(2) Where in private practice he served as lawyer in the matter in controversy, or a lawyer with whom he previously practiced law served during such association as a lawyer concerning the matter, or the judge or such lawyer has been a material witness concerning it;

(3) Where he has served in governmental employment and in such capacity participated as counsel, adviser or material witness concerning the proceeding or expressed an opinion concerning the merits of the particular case in controversy;

(4) He knows that he, individually or as a fiduciary, or his spouse or minor child residing in his household, has a financial interest in the subject matter in controversy or in a party to the proceeding, or any other interest that could be substantially affected by the outcome of the proceeding;

(5) He or his spouse, or a person within the third degree of relationship to either of them, or the spouse of such a person:

(i) Is a party to the proceeding, or an officer, director, or trustee of a party;

(ii) Is acting as a lawyer in the proceeding;

(iii) Is known by the judge to have an interest that could be substantially affected by the outcome of the proceeding;

(iv) Is to the judge's knowledge likely to be a material witness in the proceeding.

(c) A judge should inform himself about his personal and fiduciary financial interests, and make a reasonable effort to inform himself about the personal financial interests of his spouse and minor children residing in his household.

(d) For the purposes of this section the following words or phrases shall have the meaning indicated:

(1) "Proceeding" includes pretrial, trial, appellate review, or other stages of litigation;

(2) the degree of relationship is calculated according to the civil law system;

(3) "fiduciary" includes such relationships as executor, administrator, trustee, and guardian;

(4) "financial interest" means ownership of a legal or equitable interest, however small, or a relationship as director, adviser, or other active participant in the affairs of a party, except that:

(i) Ownership in a mutual or common investment fund that holds securities is not a "financial interest" in such securities unless the judge participates in the management of the fund;

(ii) An office in an educational, religious, charitable, fraternal, or civic organization is not a "financial interest" in securities held by the organization;

(iii) The proprietary interest of a policyholder in a mutual insurance company, of a depositor in a mutual savings association, or a similar proprietary interest, is a "financial interest" in the organization only if the outcome of the proceeding could substantially affect the value of the interest;

(iv) Ownership of governmental securities is a "financial interest" in the issuer only if the outcome of the proceeding could substantially affect the value of the securities.

(e) No justice, judge, or magistrate shall accept from the parties to the proceeding a waiver of any ground for disqualification enumerated in subsection (b). Where the ground for disqualification arises only under subsection (a), waiver may be accepted provided it is preceded by a full disclosure on the record of the basis for disqualification.

(f) Notwithstanding the preceding provisions of this section, if any justice, judge, magistrate, or bankruptcy judge to whom a matter has been assigned would be disqualified, after substantial judicial time has been devoted to the matter, because of the appearance or discovery, after the matter was assigned to him or her, that he or she individually or as a fiduciary, or his or her spouse or minor child residing in his or her household, has a financial interest in a party (other than an interest that could be substantially affected by the outcome), disqualification is not required if the justice, judge, magistrate, bankruptcy judge, spouse or minor child, as the case may be, divests himself or herself of the interest that provides the grounds for the disqualification.

> **Editors' Note.** The Department of Justice has adopted the following regulation in 28 C.F.R. for procedures to follow before a Department lawyer seeks recusal of a federal judge.

§50.19. Procedures to Be Followed by Government Attorneys Prior to Filing Recusal or Disqualification Motions

The determination to seek for any reason the disqualification or recusal of a justice, judge, or magistrate is a most significant and sensitive decision. This is particularly true for government attorneys, who should be guided by uniform procedures in obtaining the requisite authorization for such a motion. This statement is designed to establish a uniform procedure.

(a) No motion to recuse or disqualify a justice, judge, or magistrate (see, e.g., 28 U.S.C. 144, 455) shall be made or supported by any Department of Justice attorney, U.S. Attorney (including Assistant U.S. Attorneys) or agency counsel conducting litigation pursuant to agreement with or authority delegated by the Attorney General, without the prior written approval of the Assistant Attorney General having ultimate supervisory power over the action in which recusal or disqualification is being considered.

(b) Prior to seeking such approval, Justice Department lawyer(s) handling the litigation shall timely seek the recommendations of the U.S. Attorney for the district in which the matter is pending, and the views of the client agencies, if any. Similarly, if agency attorneys are primarily handling any such suit, they shall seek the recommendations of the U.S. Attorney and provide them to the Department of Justice with the request for approval. In actions where the United States Attorneys are primarily handling the litigation in question, they shall seek the recommendation of the client agencies, if any, for submission to the Assistant Attorney General.

(c) In the event that the conduct and pace of the litigation does not allow sufficient time to seek the prior written approval by the Assistant Attorney General, prior oral authorization shall be sought and a written record fully reflecting that authorization shall be subsequently prepared and submitted to the Assistant Attorney General.

(d) Assistant Attorneys General may delegate the authority to approve or deny requests made pursuant to this section, but only to Deputy Assistant Attorneys General or an equivalent position.

(e) **This policy statement does not create or enlarge any legal obligations upon the Department of Justice in civil or criminal litigation, and it is not intended to create any private rights enforceable by private parties in litigation with the United States.**

> **Editors' Note.** On November 1, 1993, in an unusual press release, seven Justices of the Supreme Court issued the following announcement, entitled "Statement of Recusal Policy." The Statement was signed by Chief Justice Rehnquist and Justices Stevens, Scalia, Thomas, O'Connor, Kennedy, and Ginsburg. However, Justices Blackmun and Souter did not sign.

STATEMENT OF RECUSAL POLICY

We have spouses, children or other relatives within the degree of relationship covered by 28 U.S.C. §455 who are or may become practicing attorneys. In connection with a case four Terms ago, the Chief Justice announced his policy (with which we are all in accord) regarding recusal when a covered relative is "an associate in the law firm representing one of the parties before this Court" but has "not participated in the case before the Court or at previous stages of the litigation." [The letter concluded that recusal was not required.] We think it desirable to set forth what our recusal policy will be in additional situations—specifically, when the covered lawyer has participated in the case at an earlier stage of the litigation, or when the covered lawyer is a *partner* in a firm appearing before us. Determining and announcing our policy in advance will make it evident that future decisions to recuse or not to recuse are unaffected by irrelevant circumstances of the particular case, and will provide needed guidance to our relatives and the firms to which they belong.

The provision of the recusal statute that deals specifically with a relative's involvement as a lawyer in the case requires recusal only when the covered relative "[i]s acting as a lawyer in the proceeding." §455(b)(5)(ii). It is well established that this provision requires personal participation in the representation, and not just membership in the representing firm, see, e.g., Potashnick v. Port City Constr. Co., 609 F.2d 1101, 1113 (CA5), cert. denied, 449 U.S. 820 (1980). It is also apparent, from use of the present tense, that current participation as a lawyer, and not merely past involvement in earlier stages of the litigation, is required.

A relative's partnership status, or participation in earlier stages of the litigation, is relevant, therefore, only under one of two less specific provisions of §455, which require recusal when the judge knows that the relative has "an interest that could be substantially affected by the outcome of the proceeding," §455(b)(5)(iii), or when for any reason the judge's "impartiality might reasonably be questioned," §455(a). We think that a relative's partnership in the firm appearing before us, or his or her previous work as a lawyer on a case that later comes before us, does not *automatically* trigger these provisions. If that were the intent of the law, the per se "lawyer-related recusal" requirement of §455(b)(5)(ii) would have expressed it. Per se recusal for a relative's membership in the partnership appearing here, or for a relative's work on the case below, would render the limitation of §455(b)(5)(ii) to *personal* work, and to *present* representation, meaningless.

We do not think it would serve the public interest to go beyond the requirements of the statute, and to recuse ourselves, out of an excess of caution, whenever a relative is a partner in the firm before us or acted as a lawyer at an earlier stage. Even one unnecessary recusal impairs the functioning of the Court. Given the size and number of today's national law firms, and the frequent appearance before us of many of them in a single case, recusal might become a common occurrence, and opportunities would be multiplied for "strategizing" recusals, that is, selecting law firms with an eye to producing the recusal of particular Justices. In this Court, where the absence of one Justice cannot be made up by another, needless recusal deprives litigants of the nine Justices to which they are entitled, produces the possibility of an even division on the merits of the case, and has a distorting effect upon the certiorari process, requiring the petitioner to obtain (under our current practice) four votes out of eight instead of four out of nine.

Absent some special factor, therefore, we will not recuse ourselves by reason of a relative's participation as a lawyer in earlier stages of the case. One such special factor, perhaps the most common, would be the relative's functioning as lead counsel below, so that the litigation is in effect "his" or "her" case and its outcome even at a later stage might reasonably be thought capable of substantially enhancing or damaging his or her professional reputation. We shall recuse ourselves whenever, to our knowledge, a relative has been lead counsel below.

Another special factor, of course, would be the fact that the amount of the relative's compensation could be substantially affected by the outcome here. That would require our recusal even if the relative had not worked on the case, but was merely a partner in the firm that shared the profits. It seems to us that in virtually every case before us with retained counsel there exists a genuine possibility that success or failure will affect the amount of the fee, and hence a genuine possibility that the outcome will have a substantial effect upon each partner's compensation. Since it is impractical to assure ourselves of the absence of such consequences in each individual case, we shall recuse ourselves from all cases in which appearances on behalf of parties are made by firms in which our relatives are partners, unless we have received from the firm written assurance that income from Supreme Court litigation is, on a permanent basis, excluded from our relatives' partnership shares.

California Materials

California Rules of Professional Conduct

Editors' Introduction. California is the only state that has not adopted the framework of the ABA's Model Rules of Professional Conduct. California uses its own unique numbering system, and most California rules are followed by official "Discussion" paragraphs that serve roughly the same purpose as the Comments to the ABA Model Rules. In California Rule 1-100, the purpose of the Discussion paragraphs is described as follows:

> Because it is a practical impossibility to convey in black letter form all of the nuances of these disciplinary rules, the comments contained in the Discussions of the rules, while they do not add independent basis for imposing discipline, are intended to provide guidance for interpreting the rules and practicing in compliance with them.

California also regulates lawyers heavily by statute—see our chapter entitled Selected California Statutes. For an even broader compilation of various authorities that govern California attorneys, see California State Bar Publication 250, which can be found online at *http://ethics.calbar.ca.gov/Publications/Pub250.aspx.*

Ongoing comprehensive review of the Rules of Professional Conduct. California's unique status may not last much longer. The California State Bar's Special Commission for the Revision of the Rules of Professional Conduct has proposed comprehensive changes to the California Rules of Professional Conduct, including a move to the Model Rules framework. The Commission is an old committee that was reactivated in 2001 with the following charge:

> The Commission is to evaluate the existing California Rules of Professional Conduct in their entirety considering developments in the attorney professional responsibility field since the last comprehensive revision of the rules occurred in 1989 and 1992. In this regard, the Commission is to consider, along with judicial and statutory developments, the Final Report and Recommendations of the ABA Ethics 2000 Commission, the American Law Institute's Restatement of the Law Third, the Law Governing Lawyers, as well as other authorities relevant to the

development of professional responsibility standards. The Commission is specifically charged to also consider the work that has occurred at the local, state and national level with respect to multi-disciplinary practice, multi-jurisdictional practice, court facilitated *in propria persona* assistance, discrete task representation and other subjects that have a substantial impact upon the development of professional responsibility standards.

The Commission is to develop proposed amendments to the California Rules that . . . [e]liminate and avoid unnecessary differences between California and other states, fostering the evolution of a national standard with respect to professional responsibility issues.

After a nearly nine-year process, the Commission recently completed its work. The Commission developed rules that use the numbering, the format, and much of the language of the ABA Model Rules of Professional Conduct, but with numerous significant variations. During meetings in July and September 2010, the California Bar's Board of Governors adopted 67 of the Commission's proposed rules. At the time this book went to press in September 2012, the State Bar was preparing a petition for the California Supreme Court's consideration. For more information on developments relating to the California Rules of Professional Conduct, including a draft of the proposed rules, visit *http://ethics.calbar.ca.gov/Committees/RulesCommission.aspx.*

Changes to the California Rules of Professional Conduct since our last edition. Since our last edition went to press, there have been no significant changes to the California Rules of Professional Conduct. As explained above, however, the California Supreme Court may soon be considering substantial changes to the Rules.

Contents

CHAPTER 1.   PROFESSIONAL INTEGRITY IN GENERAL

Rule 1-100.   Rules of Professional Conduct, in General

(A) *Purpose and Function.*

The following rules are intended to regulate professional conduct of members of the State Bar through discipline. They have been adopted by the Board of Governors of the State Bar of California and approved by the Supreme Court of California pursuant to Business and Professions Code sections 6076 and 6077 to protect the public and to promote respect and confidence in the legal profession. These rules together with any standards adopted by the Board of Governors pursuant to these rules shall be binding upon all members of the State Bar.

For a willful breach of any of these rules, the Board of Governors has the power to discipline members as provided by law.

The prohibition of certain conduct in these rules is not exclusive. Members are also bound by applicable law including the State Bar Act (Bus. & Prof. Code, §6000 et seq.) and opinions of California courts. Although not binding, opinions of ethics committees in California should be consulted by members for guidance on proper professional conduct. Ethics opinions and rules and standards promulgated by other jurisdictions and bar associations may also be considered.

These rules are not intended to create new civil causes of action. Nothing in these rules shall be deemed to create, augment, diminish, or eliminate any substantive legal duty of lawyers or the non-disciplinary consequences of violating such a duty.

(B) *Definitions.*

(1) "Law Firm" means:

(a) two or more lawyers whose activities constitute the practice of law, and who share its profits, expenses, and liabilities; or

(b) a law corporation which employs more than one lawyer; or

(c) a division, department, office, or group within a business entity, which includes more than one lawyer who performs legal services for the business entity; or

(d) a publicly funded entity which employs more than one lawyer to perform legal services.

(2) "Member" means a member of the State Bar of California.

(3) "Lawyer" means a member of the State Bar of California or a person who is admitted in good standing of and eligible to practice before the bar of any United States court or the highest court of the District of Columbia or any state, territory, or insular possession of the United States, or is licensed to practice law in, or is admitted in good standing and eligible to practice before the bar of the highest court of, a foreign country or any political subdivision thereof.

(4) "Associate" means an employee or fellow employee who is employed as a lawyer.

(5) "Shareholder" means a shareholder in a professional corporation pursuant to Business and Professions Code section 6160 et seq.

(C) *Purpose of Discussions.*

Because it is a practical impossibility to convey in black letter form all of the nuances of these disciplinary rules, the comments contained in the Discussions of the rules, while they do not add independent basis for imposing discipline, are intended to provide guidance for interpreting the rules and practicing in compliance with them.

(D) *Geographic Scope of Rules.*

(1) As to members: These rules shall govern the activities of members in and outside this state, except as members lawfully practicing outside this state may be specifically required by a jurisdiction in which they are practicing to follow rules of professional conduct different from these rules.

(2) As to lawyers from other jurisdictions who are not members: These rules shall also govern the activities of lawyers while engaged in the performance of lawyer functions in this state; but nothing contained in these rules shall be deemed to authorize the performance of such functions by such persons in this state except as otherwise permitted by law.

(E) These rules may be cited and referred to as "Rules of Professional Conduct of the State Bar of California."

DISCUSSION

The Rules of Professional Conduct are intended to establish the standards for members for purposes of discipline. (See *Ames v. State Bar* (1973) 8 Cal. 3d 910 [106 Cal. Rptr. 489].) The fact that a member has engaged in conduct that may be contrary to these rules does not automatically give rise to a civil cause of action. (See *Noble v. Sears, Roebuck & Co.* (1973) 33 Cal. App. 3d 654 [109 Cal. Rptr. 269]; *Wilhelm v. Pray, Price, Williams & Russell* (1986) 186 Cal. App. 3d 1324 [231 Cal. Rptr. 355].) These rules are not intended to supersede existing law relating to members in non-disciplinary contexts. (See, e.g., *Klemm v. Superior Court* (1977) 75 Cal. App. 3d 893 [142 Cal. Rptr. 509] (motion for disqualification of counsel due to a conflict of interest); *Academy of California Optometrists, Inc. v. Superior Court* (1975) 51 Cal. App. 3d 999 [124 Cal. Rptr. 668] (duty to return client files); *Chronometrics, Inc. v. Sysgen, Inc.* (1980) 110 Cal. App. 3d 597 [168 Cal. Rptr. 196] (disqualification of member appropriate remedy for improper communication with adverse party).)

Law firm, as defined by subparagraph (B)(1), is not intended to include an association of lawyers who do not share profits, expenses, and liabilities. The subparagraph is not intended to imply that a law firm may include a person who is not a member in violation of the law governing the unauthorized practice of law.

Rule 1-110. Disciplinary Authority of the State Bar

A member shall comply with conditions attached to public or private reprovals or other discipline administered by the State Bar pursuant to Business and Professions Code sections 6077 and 6078 and rule 9.19, California Rules of Court.

Rule 1-120. Assisting, Soliciting, or Inducing Violations

A member shall not knowingly assist in, solicit, or induce any violation of these rules or the State Bar Act.

Rule 1-200. False Statement Regarding Admission to the State Bar

(A) A member shall not knowingly make a false statement regarding a material fact or knowingly fail to disclose a material fact in connection with an application for admission to the State Bar.

(B) A member shall not further an application for admission to the State Bar of a person whom the member knows to be unqualified in respect to character, education, or other relevant attributes.

(C) This rule shall not prevent a member from serving as counsel of record for an applicant for admission to practice in proceedings related to such admission.

DISCUSSION

For purposes of rule 1-200 "admission" includes readmission.

Rule 1-300. Unauthorized Practice of Law

(A) A member shall not aid any person or entity in the unauthorized practice of law.

(B) A member shall not practice law in a jurisdiction where to do so would be in violation of regulations of the profession in that jurisdiction.

> **Editors' Note.** The California Supreme Court has adopted four court rules to govern multijurisdictional practice (commonly called "MJP") by lawyers not admitted to practice in California. Most states are addressing MJP in their rules of professional conduct, but California has instead chosen to govern out-of-state lawyers through court rules. The rules were drafted by a Multijurisdictional Practice Implementation Committee appointed by the California Supreme Court. They grant limited privileges to practice law to four categories of lawyers who are not admitted in California: (1) public interest lawyers; (2) in-house lawyers; (3) litigators temporarily in California; and (4) non-litigators temporarily in California.

The rules were spurred by the California Supreme Court's decision in *Birbrower, Montalbano, Condon & Frank v. Superior Court,* 17 Cal. 4th 543a (1998), which held that a New York law firm violated California Business and Professions Code §6125 (Necessity of Active Membership in State Bar) — and therefore was not entitled to legal fees — for legal services performed in California for a California-based client in a matter governed by California law. The *Birbrower* decision also spurred the ABA to appoint its own Commission on Multijurisdictional Practice, which recommended the amendments to ABA Model Rules 5.5 and 8.5 that the ABA adopted in 2002. However, California's rules differ significantly from the ABA rules.

The MJP rules are too lengthy to reprint in full, but we reprint substantial excerpts of the rules here:

Rule 9.43.   Out-of-State Attorney Arbitration Counsel

(a) Definition

An "out-of-state attorney arbitration counsel" is an attorney who is:

(1) Not a member of the State Bar of California but who is a member in good standing of and eligible to practice before the bar of any United States court or the highest court in any state, territory, or insular possession of the United States, and who has been retained to appear in the course of, or in connection with, an arbitration proceeding in this state;

(2) Has served a certificate in accordance with the requirements of Code of Civil Procedure section 1282.4 on the arbitrator, the arbitrators, or the arbitral forum, the State Bar of California, and all other parties and counsel in the arbitration whose addresses are known to the attorney; and

(3) Whose appearance has been approved by the arbitrator, the arbitrators, or the arbitral forum.

(b) State Bar Out-of-State Attorney Arbitration Counsel Program

The State Bar of California must establish and administer a program to implement the State Bar of California's responsibilities under Code of Civil Procedure section 1282.4. The State Bar of California's program may be operative only as long as the applicable provisions of Code of Civil Procedure section 1282.4 remain in effect.

(c) Eligibility to appear as an out-of-state attorney arbitration counsel

To be eligible to appear as an out-of-state attorney arbitration counsel, an attorney must comply with all of the applicable provisions of Code of Civil Procedure section 1282.4 and the requirements of this rule and the related rules and regulations adopted by the State Bar of California.

(d) Discipline

An out-of-state attorney arbitration counsel who files a certificate containing false information or who otherwise fails to comply with the standards of professional conduct required of members of the State Bar of California is subject to the disciplinary jurisdiction of the State Bar with respect to any of his or her acts occurring in the course of the arbitration.

(e) Disqualification

Failure to timely file and serve a certificate or, absent special circumstances, appearances in multiple separate arbitration matters are grounds for disqualification from serving in the arbitration in which the certificate was filed.

(f) Fee

Out-of-state attorney arbitration counsel must pay a reasonable fee not exceeding $50 to the State Bar of California with the copy of the certificate that is served on the State Bar.

(g) Inherent power of Supreme Court

Nothing in these rules may be construed as affecting the power of the Supreme Court to exercise its inherent jurisdiction over the practice of law in California.

Rule 9.45. *Registered Legal Services Attorneys*

(a) Definitions

. . .

    (2) "Active member in good standing of the bar of a United States state, jurisdiction, possession, territory, or dependency" means an attorney who:

        (A) Is a member in good standing of the entity governing the practice of law in each jurisdiction in which the member is licensed to practice law;

        (B) Remains an active member in good standing of the entity governing the practice of law in at least one United States state, jurisdiction, possession, territory, or dependency other than California while practicing law as a registered legal services attorney in California; and

        (C) Has not been disbarred, has not resigned with charges pending, or is not suspended from practicing law in any other jurisdiction.

(b) Scope of practice

Subject to all applicable rules, regulations, and statutes, an attorney practicing law under this rule may practice law in California only while working, with or without pay, at a qualifying legal services provider, as defined in this rule, and, at that institution and only on behalf of its clients, may engage, under supervision, in all forms of legal practice that are permissible for a member of the State Bar of California.

(c) Requirements

For an attorney to practice law under this rule, the attorney must:

    (1) Be an active member in good standing of the bar of a United States state, jurisdiction, possession, territory, or dependency;

    (2) Register with the State Bar of California and file an Application for Determination of Moral Character;

    (3) Meet all of the requirements for admission to the State Bar of California, except that the attorney:

        (A) Need not take the California bar examination or the Multistate Professional Responsibility Examination; and

        (B) May practice law while awaiting the result of his or her Application for Determination of Moral Character;

    (4) Comply with the rules adopted by the Board of Governors relating to the State Bar Registered Legal Services Attorney Program;

    (5) Practice law exclusively for a single qualifying legal services provider, except that, if so qualified, an attorney may, while practicing under this rule, simultaneously practice law as registered in-house counsel;

    (6) Practice law under the supervision of an attorney who is employed by the qualifying legal services provider and who is a member in good standing of the State Bar of California;

    (7) Abide by all of the laws and rules that govern members of the State Bar of California, including the Minimum Continuing Legal Education (MCLE) requirements;

(8) Satisfy in his or her first year of practice under this rule all of the MCLE requirements, including ethics education, that members of the State Bar of California must complete every three years; and

(9) Not have taken and failed the California bar examination within five years immediately preceding application to register under this rule.

(d) Application

To qualify to practice law as a registered legal services attorney, the attorney must:

(1) Register as an attorney applicant and file an Application for Determination of Moral Character with the Committee of Bar Examiners;

(2) Submit to the State Bar of California a declaration signed by the attorney agreeing that he or she will be subject to the disciplinary authority of the Supreme Court of California and the State Bar of California and attesting that he or she will not practice law in California other than under supervision at a qualifying legal services provider during the time he or she practices law as a registered legal services attorney in California, except that, if so qualified, the attorney may, while practicing under this rule, simultaneously practice law as registered in-house counsel; and

(3) Submit to the State Bar of California a declaration signed by a qualifying supervisor on behalf of the qualifying legal services provider in California attesting that the applicant will work, with or without pay, as an attorney for the organization; that the applicant will be supervised as specified in this rule; and that the qualifying legal services provider and the supervising attorney assume professional responsibility for any work performed by the applicant under this rule.

(e) Duration of practice

An attorney may practice for no more than a total of three years under this rule.

(f) Application and registration fees

The State Bar of California may set appropriate application fees and initial and annual registration fees to be paid by registered legal services attorneys.

(g) State Bar Registered Legal Services Attorney Program

The State Bar may establish and administer a program for registering California legal services attorneys under rules adopted by the Board of Governors of the State Bar.

(h) Supervision

To meet the requirements of this rule, an attorney supervising a registered legal services attorney:

(1) Must be an active member in good standing of the State Bar of California;

(2) Must have actively practiced law in California and been a member in good standing of the State Bar of California for at least the two years immediately preceding the time of supervision;

(3) Must have practiced law as a full-time occupation for at least four years;

(4) Must not supervise more than two registered legal services attorneys concurrently;

(5) Must assume professional responsibility for any work that the registered legal services attorney performs under the supervising attorney's supervision;

(6) Must assist, counsel, and provide direct supervision of the registered legal services attorney in the activities authorized by this rule and review such activities with the supervised attorney, to the extent required for the protection of the client;

(7) Must read, approve, and personally sign any pleadings, briefs, or other similar documents prepared by the registered legal services attorney before their filing, and must read and approve any documents prepared by the registered legal services attorney for execution by any person who is not a member of the State Bar of California before their submission for execution; and

(8) May, in his or her absence, designate another attorney meeting the requirements of (1) through (7) to provide the supervision required under this rule.

(i) Inherent power of Supreme Court

Nothing in this rule may be construed as affecting the power of the Supreme Court of California to exercise its inherent jurisdiction over the practice of law in California.

(j) Effect of rule on multijurisdictional practice

Nothing in this rule limits the scope of activities permissible under existing law by attorneys who are not members of the State Bar of California.

Rule 9.46. Registered In-House Counsel

(a) Definitions

. . .

(1) "Qualifying institution" means a corporation, a partnership, an association, or other legal entity, including its subsidiaries and organizational affiliates. Neither a governmental entity nor an entity that provides legal services to others can be a qualifying institution for purposes of this rule. A qualifying institution must:

(A) Employ at least 10 employees full time in California; or

(B) Employ in California an attorney who is an active member in good standing of the State Bar of California.

(2) [Essentially the same as in Rule 9.45(a)(2)].

(b) Scope of practice

Subject to all applicable rules, regulations, and statutes, an attorney practicing law under this rule is:

(1) Permitted to provide legal services in California only to the qualifying institution that employs him or her;

(2) Not permitted to make court appearances in California state courts or to engage in any other activities for which *pro hac vice* admission is required if they are performed in California by an attorney who is not a member of the State Bar of California; and

(3) Not permitted to provide personal or individual representation to any customers, shareholders, owners, partners, officers, employees, servants, or agents of the qualifying institution.

(c) Requirements

For an attorney to practice law under this rule, the attorney must:

(1)-(3) [Identical to Rule 9.45(c)(1)-(3)].

(4) Comply with the rules adopted by the Board of Governors relating to the State Bar Registered In-House Counsel Program;

(5) Practice law exclusively for a single qualifying institution, except that, while practicing under this rule, the attorney may, if so qualified, simultaneously practice law as a registered legal services attorney;

(6) [Identical to Rule 9.45(c)(7)];

(7) Satisfy in his or her first year of practice under this rule all of the MCLE requirements, including ethics education, that members of the State Bar of California must complete every three years and, thereafter, satisfy the MCLE requirements applicable to all members of the State Bar; and

(8) Reside in California.

(d) Application

To qualify to practice law as registered in-house counsel, an attorney must:

(1) [Identical to Rule 9.45(d)(1)];

(2) [Essentially the same as in Rule 9.45(d)(2)]; and

(3) Submit to the State Bar of California a declaration signed by an officer, a director, or a general counsel of the applicant's employer, on behalf of the applicant's employer, attesting that the applicant is employed as an attorney for the employer, that the nature of the employment conforms to the requirements of this rule, that the employer will notify the State Bar of California within 30 days of the cessation of the applicant's employment in California, and that the person signing the declaration believes, to the best of his or her knowledge after reasonable inquiry, that the applicant qualifies for registration under this rule and is an individual of good moral character.

(e) Duration of practice

A registered in-house counsel must renew his or her registration annually. There is no limitation on the number of years in-house counsel may register under this rule. Registered in-house counsel may practice law under this rule only for as long as he or she remains employed by the same qualifying institution that provided the declaration in support of his or her application. If an attorney practicing law as registered in-house counsel leaves the employment of his or her employer or changes employers, he or she must notify the State Bar of California within 30 days. If an attorney wishes to practice law under this rule for a new employer, he or she must first register as in-house counsel for that employer.

(f) Eligibility

An application to register under this rule may not be denied because:

(1) The attorney applicant has practiced law in California as in-house counsel before the effective date of this rule.

(2) The attorney applicant is practicing law as in-house counsel at or after the effective date of this rule, provided that the attorney applies under this rule within six months of its effective date.

(g) Application and registration fees

The State Bar of California may set appropriate application fees and initial and annual registration fees to be paid by registered in-house counsel.

(h) State Bar Registered In-House Counsel Program

The State Bar must establish and administer a program for registering California in-house counsel under rules adopted by the Board of Governors.

(i)-(j) [Identical to Rule 9.45(i)-(j).]

Rule 9.47. Attorneys Practicing Law Temporarily in California as Part of Litigation

(a) Definitions

. . .

(1) "A formal legal proceeding" means litigation, arbitration, mediation, or a legal action before an administrative decision-maker.

(2) "Authorized to appear" means the attorney is permitted to appear in the proceeding by the rules of the jurisdiction in which the formal legal proceeding is taking place or will be taking place.

(3) [Essentially the same as Rule 9.45(a)(2)].

(b) Requirements

For an attorney to practice law under this rule, the attorney must:

(1) Maintain an office in a United States jurisdiction other than California and in which the attorney is licensed to practice law;

(2) Already be retained by a client in the matter for which the attorney is providing legal services in California, except that the attorney may provide legal advice to a potential client, at the potential client's request, to assist the client in deciding whether to retain the attorney;

(3) Indicate on any Web site or other advertisement that is accessible in California either that the attorney is not a member of the State Bar of California or that the attorney is admitted to practice law only in the states listed; and

(4) Be an active member in good standing of the bar of a United States state, jurisdiction, possession, territory, or dependency.

(c) Permissible activities

An attorney meeting the requirements of this rule, who complies with all applicable rules, regulations, and statutes, is not engaging in the unauthorized practice of law in California if the attorney's services are part of:

(1) A formal legal proceeding that is pending in another jurisdiction and in which the attorney is authorized to appear;

(2) A formal legal proceeding that is anticipated but is not yet pending in California and in which the attorney reasonably expects to be authorized to appear;

(3) A formal legal proceeding that is anticipated but is not yet pending in another jurisdiction and in which the attorney reasonably expects to be authorized to appear; or

(4) A formal legal proceeding that is anticipated or pending and in which the attorney's supervisor is authorized to appear or reasonably expects to be authorized to appear.

The attorney whose anticipated authorization to appear in a formal legal proceeding serves as the basis for practice under this rule must seek that authorization promptly after it becomes possible to do so. Failure to seek that authorization promptly, or denial of that authorization, ends eligibility to practice under this rule.

(d) Restrictions

To qualify to practice law in California under this rule, an attorney must not:

(1) Hold out to the public or otherwise represent that he or she is admitted to practice law in California;

(2) Establish or maintain a resident office or other systematic or continuous presence in California for the practice of law;

(3) Be a resident of California;

(4) Be regularly employed in California;

(5) Regularly engage in substantial business or professional activities in California; or

(6) Have been disbarred, have resigned with charges pending, or be suspended from practicing law in any other jurisdiction.

(e) Conditions

By practicing law in California under this rule, an attorney agrees that he or she is providing legal services in California subject to:

(1) The jurisdiction of the State Bar of California;

(2) The jurisdiction of the courts of this state to the same extent as is a member of the State Bar of California; and

(3) The laws of the State of California relating to the practice of law, the State Bar Rules of Professional Conduct, the rules and regulations of the State Bar of California, and these rules.

(f)-(g) [Identical to Rule 9.45(i)-(j).]

Rule 9.48.   Nonlitigating Attorneys Temporarily in
California to Provide Legal Services

(a) Definitions
The following definitions apply to terms used in this rule:
(1) "A transaction or other nonlitigation matter" includes any legal matter other than litigation, arbitration, mediation, or a legal action before an administrative decision-maker.
(2) [Essentially the same as Rule 9.45(a)(2)].
(b) [Identical to Rule 9.47(b).]
(c) [Permissible activities]
An attorney who meets the requirements of this rule and who complies with all applicable rules, regulations, and statutes is not engaging in the unauthorized practice of law in California if the attorney:
(1) Provides legal assistance or legal advice in California to a client concerning a transaction or other nonlitigation matter, a material aspect of which is taking place in a jurisdiction other than California and in which the attorney is licensed to provide legal services;
(2) Provides legal assistance or legal advice in California on an issue of federal law or of the law of a jurisdiction other than California to attorneys licensed to practice law in California; or
(3) Is an employee of a client and provides legal assistance or legal advice in California to the client or to the client's subsidiaries or organizational affiliates.
(d)-(e) [Identical to Rule 9.47(d)-(e).]
(f) Scope of practice
An attorney is permitted by this rule to provide legal assistance or legal services concerning only a transaction or other nonlitigation matter.
(g)-(h) [Identical to Rule 9.45(i)-(j).]

Rule 1-310.   Forming a Partnership with a Non-Lawyer

A member shall not form a partnership with a person who is not a lawyer if any of the activities of that partnership consist of the practice of law.

DISCUSSION

Rule 1-310 is not intended to govern members' activities which cannot be considered to constitute the practice of law. It is intended solely to preclude a member from being involved in the practice of law with a person who is not a lawyer.

Rule 1-311.   Employment of Disbarred, Suspended, Resigned, or Involuntarily Inactive Member

(A) For purposes of this rule:
(1) "Employ" means to engage the services of another, including employees, agents, independent contractors and consultants, regardless of whether any compensation is paid;

(2) "Involuntarily inactive member" means a member who is ineligible to practice law as a result of action taken pursuant to Business and Professions Code sections 6007, 6203(c), or California Rule of Court 9.31(d); and

(3) "Resigned member" means a member who has resigned from the State Bar while disciplinary charges are pending.

(B) A member shall not employ, associate professionally with, or aid a person the member knows or reasonably should know is a disbarred, suspended, resigned, or involuntarily inactive member to perform the following on behalf of the member's client:

(1) Render legal consultation or advice to the client;

(2) Appear on behalf of a client in any hearing or proceeding or before any judicial officer, arbitrator, mediator, court, public agency, referee, magistrate, commissioner, or hearing officer;

(3) Appear as a representative of the client at a deposition or other discovery matter;

(4) Negotiate or transact any matter for or on behalf of the client with third parties;

(5) Receive, disburse or otherwise handle the client's funds; or

(6) Engage in activities which constitute the practice of law.

(C) A member may employ, associate professionally with, or aid a disbarred, suspended, resigned, or involuntarily inactive member to perform research, drafting or clerical activities, including but not limited to:

(1) Legal work of a preparatory nature, such as legal research, the assemblage of data and other necessary information, drafting of pleadings, briefs, and other similar documents;

(2) Direct communication with the client or third parties regarding matters such as scheduling, billing, updates, confirmation of receipt or sending of correspondence and messages; or

(3) Accompanying an active member in attending a deposition or other discovery matter for the limited purpose of providing clerical assistance to the active member who will appear as the representative of the client.

(D) Prior to or at the time of employing a person the member knows or reasonably should know is a disbarred, suspended, resigned, or involuntarily inactive member, the member shall serve upon the State Bar written notice of the employment, including a full description of such person's current bar status. The written notice shall also list the activities prohibited in paragraph (B) and state that the disbarred, suspended, resigned, or involuntarily inactive member will not perform such activities. The member shall serve similar written notice upon each client on whose specific matter such person will work, prior to or at the time of employing such person to work on the client's specific matter. The member shall obtain proof of service of the client's written notice and shall retain such proof and a true and correct copy of the client's written notice for two years following termination of the member's employment with the client.

(E) A member may, without client or State Bar notification, employ a disbarred, suspended, resigned, or involuntarily inactive member whose sole function is to perform office physical plant or equipment maintenance, courier or delivery services, catering, reception, typing or transcription, or other similar support activities.

(F) Upon termination of the disbarred, suspended, resigned, or involuntarily inactive member, the member shall promptly serve upon the State Bar written notice of the termination.

DISCUSSION

For discussion of the activities that constitute the practice of law, see *Farnham v. State Bar* (1976) 17 Cal. 3d 605 [131 Cal. Rptr. 611]; *Bluestein v. State Bar* (1974) 13 Cal. 3d 162 [118 Cal. Rptr. 175]; *Baron v. City of Los Angeles* (1970) 2 Cal. 3d 535 [86 Cal. Rptr. 673]; *Crawford v. State Bar* (1960) 54 Cal. 2d 659 [7 Cal. Rptr. 746]; *People v. Merchants Protective Corporation* (1922) 189 Cal. 531, 535 [209 P. 363]; *People v. Landlords Professional Services* (1989) 215 Cal. App. 3d 1599 [264 Cal. Rptr. 548]; and *People v. Sipper* (1943) 61 Cal. App. 2d Supp. 844 [142 P. 2d 960].

Paragraph (D) is not intended to prevent or discourage a member from fully discussing with the client the activities that will be performed by the disbarred, suspended, resigned, or involuntarily inactive member on the client's matter. If a member's client is an organization, then the written notice required by paragraph (D) shall be served upon the highest authorized officer, employee, or constituent overseeing the particular engagement. (See rule 3-600.)

Nothing in rule 1-311 shall be deemed to limit or preclude any activity engaged in pursuant to rules 983, 983.1, 983.2, and 988 of the of the California Rules of Court, or any local rule of a federal district court concerning admission pro hac vice.

Rule 1-320.   Financial Arrangements with Non-Lawyers

(A) Neither a member nor a law firm shall directly or indirectly share legal fees with a person who is not a lawyer, except that:

(1) An agreement between a member and a law firm, partner, or associate may provide for the payment of money after the member's death to the member's estate or to one or more specified persons over a reasonable period of time; or

(2) A member or law firm undertaking to complete unfinished legal business of a deceased member may pay to the estate of the deceased member or other person legally entitled thereto that proportion of the total compensation which fairly represents the services rendered by the deceased member;

(3) A member or law firm may include non-member employees in a compensation, profit-sharing, or retirement plan even though the plan is based in whole or in part on a profit-sharing arrangement, if such plan does not circumvent these rules or Business and Professions Code section 6000 et seq.; or

(4) A member may pay a prescribed registration, referral, or participation fee to a lawyer referral service established, sponsored, and operated in accordance with the State Bar of California's Minimum Standards for a Lawyer Referral Service in California.

(B) A member shall not compensate, give, or promise anything of value to any person or entity for the purpose of recommending or securing employment of the member or the member's law firm by a client, or as a reward for having made a recommendation resulting in employment of the member or the member's law firm by a client. A member's offering of or giving a gift or gratuity to any person or entity having made a recommendation resulting in the employment of the member or the member's law firm shall not of itself violate this rule, provided that the gift or gratuity was not offered or given in consideration of any promise, agreement, or understanding that such a gift or gratuity would be forthcoming or that referrals would be made or encouraged in the future.

(C) A member shall not compensate, give, or promise anything of value to any representative of the press, radio, television, or other communication medium in anticipation of or in return for publicity of the member, the law firm, or any other member as such in a news item, but the incidental provision of food or beverage shall not of itself violate this rule.

DISCUSSION

Rule 1-320(C) is not intended to preclude compensation to the communications media in exchange for advertising the member's or law firm's availability for professional employment.

Rule 1-400.   Advertising and Solicitation

(A) For purposes of this rule, "communication" means any message or offer made by or on behalf of a member concerning the availability for professional employment of a member or a law firm directed to any former, present, or prospective client, including but not limited to the following:

(1) Any use of firm name, trade name, fictitious name, or other professional designation of such member or law firm; or

(2) Any stationery, letterhead, business card, sign, brochure, or other comparable written material describing such member, law firm, or lawyers; or

(3) Any advertisement (regardless of medium) of such member or law firm directed to the general public or any substantial portion thereof; or

(4) Any unsolicited correspondence from a member or law firm directed to any person or entity.

(B) For purposes of this rule, a "solicitation" means any communication:

(1) Concerning the availability for professional employment of a member or a law firm in which a significant motive is pecuniary gain; and

(2) Which is:

(a) delivered in person or by telephone, or

(b) directed by any means to a person known to the sender to be represented by counsel in a matter which is a subject of the communication.

(C) A solicitation shall not be made by or on behalf of a member or law firm to a prospective client with whom the member or law firm has no family or prior professional relationship, unless the solicitation is protected from abridgment by the Constitution of the United States or by the Constitution of the State of California. A solicitation to a former or present client in the discharge of a member's or law firm's professional duties is not prohibited.

(D) A communication or a solicitation (as defined herein) shall not:

(1) Contain any untrue statement; or

(2) Contain any matter, or present or arrange any matter in a manner or format which is false, deceptive, or which tends to confuse, deceive, or mislead the public; or

(3) Omit to state any fact necessary to make the statements made, in the light of circumstances under which they are made, not misleading to the public; or

(4) Fail to indicate clearly, expressly, or by context, that it is a communication or solicitation, as the case may be; or

(5) Be transmitted in any manner which involves intrusion, coercion, duress, compulsion, intimidation, threats, or vexatious or harassing conduct.

(6) State that a member is a "certified specialist" unless the member holds a current certificate as a specialist issued by the Board of Legal Specialization, or any other entity accredited by the State Bar to designate specialists pursuant to standards adopted by the Board of Governors, and states the complete name of the entity which granted certification.

Editors' Note. With respect to Rule 1-400(D)(6), the California State Bar Board of Governors has adopted Rules Governing the State Bar of California Program for Certifying Legal Specialists. These rules are too lengthy to reprint here. For more information about specialty certification in California, visit *www.CaliforniaSpecialist.org.*

(E) The Board of Governors of the State Bar shall formulate and adopt standards as to communications which will be presumed to violate this rule 1-400. The standards shall only be used as presumptions affecting the burden of proof in disciplinary proceedings involving alleged violations of these rules. "Presumption affecting the burden of proof" means that presumption defined in Evidence Code sections 605 and 606. Such standards formulated and adopted by the Board, as from time to time amended, shall be effective and binding on all members.

(F) A member shall retain for two years a true and correct copy or recording of any communication made by written or electronic media. Upon written request, the member shall make any such copy or recording available to the State Bar, and, if requested, shall provide to the State Bar evidence to support any factual or objective claim contained in the communication.

STANDARDS

Pursuant to rule 1-400(E) the Board of Governors of the State Bar has adopted the following standards, effective May 27, 1989, unless noted otherwise, as forms of "communication" defined in rule 1-400(A) which are presumed to be in violation of rule 1-400:

(1) A "communication" which contains guarantees, warranties, or predictions regarding the result of the representation.

(2) A "communication" which contains testimonials about or endorsements of a member unless such communication also contains an express disclaimer such as "this testimonial or endorsement does not constitute a guarantee, warranty, or prediction regarding the outcome of your legal matter."

(3) A "communication" which is delivered to a potential client whom the member knows or should reasonably know is in such a physical, emotional, or mental state that he or she would not be expected to exercise reasonable judgment as to the retention of counsel.

(4) A "communication" which is transmitted at the scene of an accident or at or en route to a hospital, emergency care center, or other health care facility.

(5) "communication," except professional announcements, seeking professional employment for pecuniary gain, which is transmitted by

mail or equivalent means which does not bear the words "Advertisement," "Newsletter" or words of similar import in 12 point print on the first page. If such communication, including firm brochures, newsletters, recent legal developments advisories, and similar materials, is transmitted in an envelope, the envelope shall bear the word "Advertisement," "Newsletter" or words of similar import on the outside thereof.

(6) A "communication" in the form of a firm name, trade name, fictitious name, or other professional designation which states or implies a relationship between any member in private practice and a government agency or instrumentality or a public or non-profit legal services organization.

(7) A "communication" in the form of a firm name, trade name, fictitious name, or other professional designation which states or implies that a member has a relationship to any other lawyer or a law firm as a partner or associate, or officer or shareholder pursuant to Business and Professions Code sections 6160-6172 unless such relationship in fact exists.

(8) A "communication" which states or implies that a member or law firm is "of counsel" to another lawyer or a law firm unless the former has a relationship with the latter (other than as a partner or associate, or officer or shareholder pursuant to Business and Professions Code sections 6160-6172) which is close, personal, continuous, and regular.

(9) A "communication" in the form of a firm name, trade name, fictitious name, or other professional designation used by a member or law firm in private practice which differs materially from any other such designation used by such member or law firm at the same time in the same community.

(10) A "communication" which implies that the member or law firm is participating in a lawyer referral service which has been certified by the State Bar of California or as having satisfied the Minimum Standards for Lawyer Referral Services in California, when that is not the case.

(11) [Repealed in 1997.]

(12) A "communication," except professional announcements, in the form of an advertisement primarily directed to seeking professional employment primarily for pecuniary gain transmitted to the general public or any substantial portion thereof by mail or equivalent means or by means of television, radio, newspaper, magazine or other form of commercial mass media which does not state the name of the member responsible for the communication. When the communication is made on behalf of a law firm, the communication shall state the name of at least one member responsible for it.

(13) A "communication" which contains a dramatization unless such communication contains a disclaimer which states "this is a dramatization" or words of similar import.

(14) A "communication" which states or implies "no fee without recovery" unless such communication also expressly discloses whether or not the client will be liable for costs.

(15) A "communication" which states or implies that a member is able to provide legal services in a language other than English unless the member can actually provide legal services in such language or the communication also states in the language of the communication (a) the employment title of the person who speaks such language and (b) that the person is not a member of the State Bar of California, if that is the case.

(16) An unsolicited "communication" transmitted to the general public or any substantial portion thereof primarily directed to seeking professional employment primarily for pecuniary gain which sets forth a specific fee or range of fees for a particular service where, in fact, the member charges a greater fee than advertised in such communication within a period of 90 days following dissemination of such communication, unless such communication expressly specifies a shorter period of time regarding the advertised fee. Where the communication is published in the classified or "yellow pages" section of telephone, business or legal directories or in other media not published more frequently than once a year, the member shall conform to the advertised fee for a period of one year from initial publication, unless such communication expressly specifies a shorter period of time regarding the advertised fee.

Rule 1-500. Agreements Restricting a Member's Practice

(A) A member shall not be a party to or participate in offering or making an agreement, whether in connection with the settlement of a lawsuit or otherwise, if the agreement restricts the right of a member to practice law, except that this rule shall not prohibit such an agreement which:

(1) Is a part of an employment, shareholders', or partnership agreement among members provided the restrictive agreement does not survive the termination of the employment, shareholder, or partnership relationship; or

(2) Requires payments to a member upon the member's retirement from the practice of law; or

(3) Is authorized by Business and Professions Code sections 6092.5 subdivision (i) or 6093.

(B) A member shall not be a party to or participate in offering or making an agreement which precludes the reporting of a violation of these rules.

DISCUSSION

Paragraph (A) makes it clear that the practice, in connection with settlement agreements, of proposing that a member refrain from representing other clients in similar litigation, is prohibited. Neither counsel may demand or suggest such provisions nor may opposing counsel accede or agree to such provisions.

Paragraph (A) permits a restrictive covenant in a law corporation, partnership, or employment agreement. The law corporation shareholder, partner, or associate may agree not to have a separate practice during the existence of the relationship; however, upon termination of the relationship (whether voluntary or involuntary), the member is free to practice law without any contractual restriction except in the case of retirement from the active practice of law.

Rule 1-600.   Legal Service Programs

(A) A member shall not participate in a nongovernmental program, activity, or organization furnishing, recommending, or paying for legal services, which allows any third person or organization to interfere with the member's independence of professional judgment, or with the client-lawyer relationship, or allows unlicensed persons to practice law, or allows any third person or organization to receive directly or indirectly any part of the consideration paid to the member except as permitted by these rules, or otherwise violates the State Bar Act or these rules.

(B) The Board of Governors of the State Bar shall formulate and adopt Minimum Standards for Lawyer Referral Services, which, as from time to time amended, shall be binding on members.

DISCUSSION

The participation of a member in a lawyer referral service established, sponsored, supervised, and operated in conformity with the Minimum Standards for a Lawyer Referral Service in California is encouraged and is not, of itself, a violation of these rules.

Rule 1-600 is not intended to override any contractual agreement or relationship between insurers and insureds regarding the provision of legal services.

Rule 1-600 is not intended to apply to the activities of a public agency responsible for providing legal services to a government or to the public.

For purposes of paragraph (A), "a nongovernmental program, activity, or organization" includes, but is not limited to group, prepaid, and voluntary legal service programs, activities, or organizations.

Editors' Note. Rule 1-600(B) refers to "Minimum Standards for Lawyer Referral Services." These Minimum Standards were originally adopted by the California Supreme Court in 1989 and were amended most recently in 1997, when they were clarified and renamed "Rules and Regulations of the State Bar of California Pertaining to Lawyer Referral Services." They are too lengthy to reprint here, but can be found in California statute books following §6155 of the Business and Professions Code.

Rule 1-650.   Limited Legal Services Programs

(A) A member who, under the auspices of a program sponsored by a court, government agency, bar association, law school, or nonprofit organization, provides short-term limited legal services to a client without expectation by either the member or the client that the member will provide continuing representation in the matter:

(1) is subject to rule 3-310 only if the member knows that the representation of the client involves a conflict of interest; and

(2) has an imputed conflict of interest only if the member knows that another lawyer associated with the member in a law firm would have a conflict of interest under rule 3-310 with respect to the matter.

(B) Except as provided in paragraph (A)(2), a conflict of interest that arises from a member's participation in a program under paragraph (A) will not be imputed to the member's law firm.

(C) The personal disqualification of a lawyer participating in the program will not be imputed to other lawyers participating in the program.

DISCUSSION

[1] Courts, government agencies, bar associations, law schools and various nonprofit organizations have established programs through which lawyers provide short-term limited legal services - such as advice or the completion of legal forms that will assist persons in addressing their legal problems without further representation by a lawyer. In these programs, such as legal-advice hotlines, advice-only clinics or pro se counseling programs, whenever a lawyer-client relationship is established, there is no expectation that the lawyer's representation of the client will continue beyond that limited consultation. Such programs are normally operated under circumstances in which it is not feasible for a lawyer to systematically screen for conflicts of interest as is generally required before undertaking a representation.

[2] A member who provides short-term limited legal services pursuant to rule 1-650 must secure the client's informed consent to the limited scope of the representation. If a short-term limited representation would not be reasonable under the circumstances, the member may offer advice to the client but must also advise the client of the need for further assistance of counsel. See rule 3-110. Except as provided in this rule 1-650, the Rules of Professional Conduct and the State Bar Act, including the member's duty of confidentiality under Business and Professions Code §6068(e)(1), are applicable to the limited representation. (Added by order of the Supreme Court, operative August 28, 2009.)

[3] A member who is representing a client in the circumstances addressed by rule 1-650 ordinarily is not able to check systematically for conflicts of interest.

Therefore, paragraph (A)(1) requires compliance with rule 3-310 only if the member knows that the representation presents a conflict of interest for the member. In addition, paragraph (A)(2) imputes conflicts of interest to the member only if the member knows that another lawyer in the member's law firm would be disqualified under rule 3-310.

[4] Because the limited nature of the services significantly reduces the risk of conflicts of interest with other matters being handled by the member's law firm, paragraph (B) provides that imputed conflicts of interest are inapplicable to a representation governed by this rule except as provided by paragraph (A)(2). Paragraph (A)(2) imputes conflicts of interest to the participating member when the member knows that any lawyer in the member's firm would be disqualified under rule 3-310. By virtue of paragraph (B), moreover, a member's participation in a short-term limited legal services program will not be imputed to the member's law firm or preclude the member's law firm from undertaking or continuing the representation of a client with interests adverse to a client being represented under the program's auspices. Nor will the personal disqualification of a lawyer participating in the program be imputed to other lawyers participating in the program.

[5] If, after commencing a short-term limited representation in accordance with rule 1-650, a member undertakes to represent the client in the matter on an ongoing basis, rule 3-310 and all other rules become applicable.

Rule 1-700.   Member as Candidate for Judicial Office

(A) A member who is a candidate for judicial office in California shall comply with Canon 5 of the Code of Judicial Ethics.

(B) For purposes of this rule, "candidate for judicial office" means a member seeking judicial office by election. The determination of when a member is a candidate for judicial office is defined in the terminology section of the California Code of Judicial Ethics. A member's duty to comply with paragraph (A) shall end when the member announces withdrawal of the member's candidacy or when the results of the election are final, whichever occurs first.

DISCUSSION

Nothing in rule 1-700 shall be deemed to limit the applicability of any other rule or law.

Rule 1-710.   Member as Temporary Judge, Referee,
or Court Appointed Arbitrator

A member who is serving as a temporary judge, referee, or court-appointed arbitrator, and is subject under the Code of Judicial Ethics to Canon 6D, shall comply with the terms of that canon.

DISCUSSION

This rule is intended to permit the State Bar to discipline members who violate applicable portions of the Code of Judicial Ethics while acting in a judicial capacity pursuant to an order or appointment by a court.

Nothing in rule 1-710 shall be deemed to limit the applicability of any other rule or law.

CHAPTER 2.   RELATIONSHIP AMONG MEMBERS

Rule 2-100.   Communication with a Represented Party

(A) While representing a client, a member shall not communicate directly or indirectly about the subject of the representation with a party the member knows to be represented by another lawyer in the matter, unless the member has the consent of the other lawyer.

(B) For purposes of this rule, a "party" includes:

(1) An officer, director, or managing agent of a corporation or association, and a partner or managing agent of a partnership; or

(2) An association member or an employee of an association, corporation, or partnership, if the subject of the communication is any act or omission of such person in connection with the matter which may be binding upon or imputed to the organization for purposes of civil or criminal liability or whose statement may constitute an admission on the part of the organization.

(C) This rule shall not prohibit:

(1) Communications with a public officer, board, committee, or body; or

(2) Communications initiated by a party seeking advice or representation from an independent lawyer of the party's choice; or

(3) Communications otherwise authorized by law.

DISCUSSION

Rule 2-100 is intended to control communications between a member and persons the member knows to be represented by counsel unless a statutory scheme or case law will override the rule. There are a number of express statutory schemes which authorize communications between a member and person who would otherwise be subject to this rule. These statutes protect a variety of other rights such as the right of employees to organize and to engage in collective bargaining, employee health and safety, or equal employment opportunity. Other applicable law also includes the authority of government prosecutors and investigators to conduct criminal investigations, as limited by the relevant decisional law.

Rule 2-100 is not intended to prevent the parties themselves from communicating with respect to the subject matter of the representation, and nothing in the rule prevents a member from advising the client that such communication can be made. Moreover, the rule does not prohibit a member who is also a party to a legal matter from directly or indirectly communicating on his or her own behalf with a represented party. Such a member has independent rights as a party which should not be abrogated because of his or her professional status. To prevent any possible abuse in such situations, the counsel for the opposing party may advise that party (1) about the risks and benefits of communications with a lawyer-party, and (2) not to accept or engage in communications with the lawyer-party.

Rule 2-100 also addresses the situation in which member A is contacted by an opposing party who is represented and, because of dissatisfaction with that party's counsel, seeks A's independent advice. Since A is employed by the opposition, the member cannot give independent advice.

As used in paragraph (A), "the subject of the representation," "matter," and "party" are not limited to a litigation context.

Paragraph (B) is intended to apply only to persons employed at the time of the communication.

Subparagraph (C)(2) is intended to permit a member to communicate with a party seeking to hire new counsel or to obtain a second opinion. A member contacted by such a party continues to be bound by other Rules of Professional Conduct. (See, e.g., rules 1-400 and 3-310.)

Rule 2-200. Financial Arrangements Among Lawyers

(A) A member shall not divide a fee for legal services with a lawyer who is not a partner of, associate of, or shareholder with the member unless:

(1) The client has consented in writing thereto after a full disclosure has been made in writing that a division of fees will be made and the terms of such division; and

(2) The total fee charged by all lawyers is not increased solely by reason of the provision for division of fees and is not unconscionable as that term is defined in rule 4-200.

(B) Except as permitted in paragraph (A) of this rule or rule 2-300, a member shall not compensate, give, or promise anything of value to any lawyer for the purpose of recommending or securing employment of the member or the member's law firm by a client, or as a reward for having made a recommendation resulting in employment of the member or the member's law firm by a client. A member's offering of or giving a gift or gratuity to any lawyer who has made a recommendation resulting in the employment of the member or the member's law firm shall not of itself violate this rule, provided that the gift or gratuity was not offered in consideration of any promise, agreement, or understanding that such a gift or gratuity would be forthcoming or that referrals would be made or encouraged in the future.

Rule 2-300.   Sale or Purchase of a Law Practice of a Member,
Living or Deceased

All or substantially all of the law practice of a member, living or
deceased, including goodwill, may be sold to another member or law
firm subject to all the following conditions:

(A) Fees charged to clients shall not be increased solely by reason
of such sale.

(B) If the sale contemplates the transfer of responsibility for work
not yet completed or responsibility for client files or information protected by Business and Professions Code section 6068, subdivision (e),
then:

(1) if the seller is deceased, or has a conservator or other person
acting in a representative capacity, and no member has been appointed
to act for the seller pursuant to Business and Professions Code section
6180.5, then prior to the transfer:

(a) the purchaser shall cause a written notice to be given to
the client stating that the interest in the law practice is being transferred to the purchaser; that the client has the right to retain other
counsel; that the client may take possession of any client papers
and property, as required by rule 3-700(D); and that if no response
is received to the notification within 90 days of the sending of such
notice, or in the event the client's rights would be prejudiced by a
failure to act during that time, the purchaser may act on behalf of
the client until otherwise notified by the client. Such notice shall
comply with the requirements as set forth in rule 1-400(D) and any
provisions relating to attorney-client fee arrangements, and

(b) the purchaser shall obtain the written consent of the client
provided that such consent shall be presumed until otherwise notified by the client if no response is received to the notification specified in subparagraph (a) within 90 days of the date of the sending of
such notification to the client's last address as shown on the records
of the seller, or the client's rights would be prejudiced by a failure
to act during such 90-day period.

(2) in all other circumstances, not less than 90 days prior to the
transfer;

(a) the seller, or the member appointed to act for the seller pursuant to Business and Professions Code section 6180.5, shall cause
a written notice to be given to the client stating that the interest in
the law practice is being transferred to the purchaser; that the client
has the right to retain other counsel; that the client may take possession of any client papers and property, as required by rule 3-700(D);
and that if no response is received to the notification within 90 days
of the sending of such notice, the purchaser may act on behalf of

the client until otherwise notified by the client. Such notice shall comply with the requirements as set forth in rule 1-400(D) and any provisions relating to attorney-client fee arrangements, and

(b) the seller, or the member appointed to act for the seller pursuant to Business and Professions Code section 6180.5, shall obtain the written consent of the client prior to the transfer provided that such consent shall be presumed until otherwise notified by the client if no response is received to the notification specified in subparagraph (a) within 90 days of the date of the sending of such notification to the client's last address as shown on the records of the seller.

(C) If substitution is required by the rules of a tribunal in which a matter is pending, all steps necessary to substitute a member shall be taken.

(D) All activity of a purchaser or potential purchaser under this rule shall be subject to compliance with rules 3-300 and 3-310 where applicable.

(E) Confidential information shall not be disclosed to a non-member in connection with a sale under this rule.

(F) Admission to or retirement from a law partnership or law corporation, retirement plans and similar arrangements, or sale of tangible assets of a law practice shall not be deemed a sale or purchase under this rule.

DISCUSSION

Paragraph (A) is intended to prohibit the purchaser from charging the former clients of the seller a higher fee than the purchaser is charging his or her existing clients.

"All or substantially all of the law practice of a member" means, for purposes of rule 2-300, that, for example, a member may retain one or two clients who have such a longstanding personal and professional relationship with the member that transfer of those clients' files is not feasible. Conversely, rule 2-300 is not intended to authorize the sale of a law practice in a piecemeal fashion except as may be required by subparagraph (B)(1)(a) or paragraph (D).

Transfer of individual client matters, where permitted, is governed by rule 2-200. Payment of a fee to a non-lawyer broker for arranging the sale or purchase of a law practice is governed by rule 1-320.

Rule 2-400.   Prohibited Discriminatory Conduct in a Law Practice

(A) For purposes of this rule:

(1) "law practice" includes sole practices, law partnerships, law corporations, corporate and governmental legal departments, and other entities which employ members to practice law;

(2) "knowingly permit" means a failure to advocate corrective action where the member knows of a discriminatory policy or practice which results in the unlawful discrimination prohibited in paragraph (B); and

(3) "unlawfully" and "unlawful" shall be determined by reference to applicable state or federal statutes or decisions making unlawful discrimination in employment and in offering goods and services to the public.

(B) In the management or operation of a law practice, a member shall not unlawfully discriminate or knowingly permit unlawful discrimination on the basis of race, national origin, sex, sexual orientation, religion, age or disability in:

(1) hiring, promoting, discharging or otherwise determining the conditions of employment of any person; or

(2) accepting or terminating representation of any client.

(C) No disciplinary investigation or proceeding may be initiated by the State Bar against a member under this rule unless and until a tribunal of competent jurisdiction, other than a disciplinary tribunal, shall have first adjudicated a complaint of alleged discrimination and found that unlawful conduct occurred. Upon such adjudication, the tribunal finding or verdict shall then be admissible evidence of the occurrence or non-occurrence of the alleged discrimination in any disciplinary proceeding initiated under this rule. In order for discipline to be imposed under this rule, however, the finding of unlawfulness must be upheld and final after appeal, the time for filing an appeal must have expired, or the appeal must have been dismissed.

DISCUSSION

In order for discriminatory conduct to be actionable under this rule, it must first be found to be unlawful by an appropriate civil administrative or judicial tribunal under applicable state or federal law. Until there is a finding of civil unlawfulness, there is no basis for disciplinary action under this rule.

A complaint of misconduct based on this rule may be filed with the State Bar following a finding of unlawfulness in the first instance even though that finding is thereafter appealed.

A disciplinary investigation or proceeding for conduct coming within this rule may be initiated and maintained, however, if such conduct warrants discipline under California Business and Professions Code sections 6106 and 6068, the California Supreme Court's inherent authority to impose discipline, or other disciplinary standard.

CHAPTER 3.   PROFESSIONAL RELATIONSHIP WITH CLIENTS

Rule 3-100.   Confidential Information of a Client

Editors' Note. The first rule in Chapter 3, Rule 3-100, governs confidentiality and its exceptions. Rule 3-100 took effect on July 1, 2004. Until that date, California was the only American jurisdiction whose Rules of Professional Conduct did not contain a rule setting forth an attorney's ethical duty of confidentiality. Before July 1, 2004, a California lawyer's duty of confidentiality was expressed solely in §6068(e) of the California Business and Professions Code (reprinted in the next chapter), which provided for more than a century that an attorney had a duty, without any exceptions, "[t]o maintain inviolate the confidence, and at every peril to himself or herself to preserve the secrets, of his or her client." (The gender neutral "his or her" language was added during the 1990s, but the essence of the statute traces back to 1872.)

The addition of Rule 3-100 in 2004 was the culmination of the California State Bar's repeated efforts, spanning more than 17 years, to gain the California Supreme Court's approval of a rule that would govern confidentiality. Those efforts are recounted in an Editors' Note to Rule 3-100 in our 2004, 2005, and 2006 editions.

In 2003, the California Legislature passed a bill adding a new §6068(e)(2) to the Business and Professions Code, which permits an attorney to reveal confidential information to the extent that the attorney reasonably believes necessary to prevent a criminal act likely to result in death or substantial bodily harm to an individual. The same bill invited the State Bar, in consultation with the California Supreme Court, to "appoint an advisory task force to study and make recommendations for a rule of professional conduct regarding professional responsibility issues related to the implementation" of the new "death or substantial bodily harm" exception in §6068(e)(2). The Legislature specified that the task force should consider the following issues:

(1) Whether an attorney must inform a client or a prospective client about the attorney's discretion to reveal the client's or prospective client's confidential information to the extent that the attorney reasonably believes that the disclosure is necessary to prevent a criminal act that the attorney reasonably believes is likely to result in the death of, or substantial bodily harm to, an individual.

(2) Whether an attorney must attempt to dissuade the client from committing the perceived criminal conduct prior to revealing the client's confidential information, and how those conflicts might be avoided or minimized.

(3) Whether conflict-of-interest issues between the attorney and client arise once the attorney elects to disclose the client's confidential information, and how those conflicts might be avoided or minimized.

(4) Other similar issues that are directly related to the disclosure of confidential information permitted by this act.

The California Supreme Court then appointed a 21-member task force, chaired by Professor Kevin Mohr of Western State University College of Law, which developed Rule 3-100. The State Bar circulated the proposed rule for public comment, made minor changes to the Discussion, and recommended the proposed rule to the California Supreme Court, which approved the rule.

(A) A member shall not reveal information protected from disclosure by Business and Professions Code section 6068, subdivision (e)(1) without the informed consent of the client, or as provided in paragraph (B) of this rule.

(B) A member may, but is not required to, reveal confidential information relating to the representation of a client to the extent that the member reasonably believes the disclosure is necessary to prevent a criminal act that the member reasonably believes is likely to result in death of, or substantial bodily harm to, an individual.

(C) Before revealing confidential information to prevent a criminal act as provided in paragraph (B), a member shall, if reasonable under the circumstances:

(1) make a good faith effort to persuade the client: (i) not to commit or to continue the criminal act or (ii) to pursue a course of conduct that will prevent the threatened death or substantial bodily harm; or do both (i) and (ii); and

(2) inform the client, at an appropriate time, of the member's ability or decision to reveal information as provided in paragraph (B).

(D) In revealing confidential information as provided in paragraph (B), the member's disclosure must be no more than is necessary to prevent the criminal act, given the information known to the member at the time of the disclosure.

(E) A member who does not reveal information permitted by paragraph (B) does not violate this rule.

DISCUSSION

[1] *Duty of confidentiality.* Paragraph (A) relates to a member's obligations under Business and Professions Code section 6068, subdivision (e)(1), which provides it is a duty of a member: "To maintain inviolate the confidence, and at every peril to himself or herself to preserve the secrets, of his or her client." A member's duty to preserve the confidentiality of client information involves public policies of paramount importance. (*In Re Jordan* (1974) 12 Cal. 3d 575, 580 [116 Cal. Rptr. 371].) Preserving the confidentiality of client information contributes to the trust that is the hallmark of the client-lawyer relationship. The client is thereby encouraged to seek legal assistance and to communicate fully and frankly with the lawyer even as to embarrassing or legally damaging subject matter. The lawyer needs this information to represent the client effectively and, if necessary, to advise the client to refrain from wrongful conduct. Almost without exception, clients come to lawyers in order to determine their rights and what is, in the complex of laws and

regulations, deemed to be legal and correct. Based upon experience, lawyers know that almost all clients follow the advice given, and the law is upheld. Paragraph (A) thus recognizes a fundamental principle in the client-lawyer relationship, that, in the absence of the client's informed consent, a member must not reveal information relating to the representation. (See, e.g., *Commercial Standard Title Co. v. Superior Court* (1979) 92 Cal. App. 3d 934, 945 [155 Cal. Rptr. 393].)

[2] *Client-lawyer confidentiality encompasses the attorney-client privilege, the work product doctrine and ethical standards of confidentiality.* The principle of client-lawyer confidentiality applies to information relating to the representation, whatever its source, and encompasses matters communicated in confidence by the client, and therefore protected by the attorney-client privilege, matters protected by the work product doctrine, and matters protected under ethical standards of confidentiality, all as established in law, rule and policy. (See *In the Matter of Johnson* (Rev. Dept. 2000) 4 Cal. State Bar Ct. Rptr. 179; *Goldstein v. Lees* (1975) 46 Cal. 3d 614, 621 [120 Cal. Rptr. 253].) The attorney-client privilege and work product doctrine apply in judicial and other proceedings in which a member may be called as a witness or be otherwise compelled to produce evidence concerning a client. A member's ethical duty of confidentiality is not so limited in its scope of protection for the client-lawyer relationship of trust and prevents a member from revealing the client's confidential information even when not confronted with such compulsion. Thus, a member may not reveal such information except with the consent of the client or as authorized or required by the State Bar Act, these rules, or other law.

[3] *Narrow exception to duty of confidentiality under this Rule.* Notwithstanding the important public policies promoted by lawyers adhering to the core duty of confidentiality, the overriding value of life permits disclosures otherwise prohibited under Business & Professions Code section 6068(e), subdivision (1). Paragraph (B), which restates Business and Professions Code section 6068, subdivision (e)(2), identifies a narrow confidentiality exception, absent the client's informed consent, when a member reasonably believes that disclosure is necessary to prevent a criminal act that the member reasonably believes is likely to result in the death of, or substantial bodily harm to, an individual. Evidence Code section 956.5, which relates to the evidentiary attorney-client privilege, sets forth a similar express exception. Although a member is not permitted to reveal confidential information concerning a client's past, completed criminal acts, the policy favoring the preservation of human life that underlies this exception to the duty of confidentiality and the evidentiary privilege permits disclosure to prevent a future or ongoing criminal act.

[4] *Member not subject to discipline for revealing confidential information as permitted under this Rule.* Rule 3-100, which restates Business and Professions Code section 6068, subdivision (e)(2), reflects a balancing between the interests of preserving client confidentiality and of preventing a criminal act that a member reasonably believes is likely to result in death or substantial bodily harm to an individual. A member who reveals information as permitted under this rule is not subject to discipline.

[5] *No duty to reveal confidential information.* Neither Business and Professions Code section 6068, subdivision (e)(2) nor this rule imposes an affirmative obligation on a member to reveal information in order to prevent harm. (See rule 1-100(A).) A member may decide not to reveal confidential information. Whether a member chooses to reveal confidential information as permitted under this rule is a matter

for the individual member to decide, based on all the facts and circumstances, such as those discussed in paragraph [6] of this discussion.

[6] *Deciding to reveal confidential information as permitted under paragraph (B).* Disclosure permitted under paragraph (B) is ordinarily a last resort, when no other available action is reasonably likely to prevent the criminal act. Prior to revealing information as permitted under paragraph (B), the member must, if reasonable under the circumstances, make a good faith effort to persuade the client to take steps to avoid the criminal act or threatened harm. Among the factors to be considered in determining whether to disclose confidential information are the following:

(1) the amount of time that the member has to make a decision about disclosure;

(2) whether the client or a third party has made similar threats before and whether they have ever acted or attempted to act upon them;

(3) whether the member believes the member's efforts to persuade the client or a third person not to engage in the criminal conduct have or have not been successful;

(4) the extent of adverse effect to the client's rights under the Fifth, Sixth and Fourteenth Amendments of the United States Constitution and analogous rights and privacy rights under Article 1 of the Constitution of the State of California that may result from disclosure contemplated by the member;

(5) the extent of other adverse effects to the client that may result from disclosure contemplated by the member; and

(6) the nature and extent of information that must be disclosed to prevent the criminal act or threatened harm.

A member may also consider whether the prospective harm to the victim or victims is imminent in deciding whether to disclose the confidential information. However, the imminence of the harm is not a prerequisite to disclosure and a member may disclose the information without waiting until immediately before the harm is likely to occur.

[7] *Counseling client or third person not to commit a criminal act reasonably likely to result in death or substantial bodily harm.* Subparagraph (C)(1) provides that before a member may reveal confidential information, the member must, if reasonable under the circumstances, make a good faith effort to persuade the client not to commit or to continue the criminal act, or to persuade the client to otherwise pursue a course of conduct that will prevent the threatened death or substantial bodily harm, or if necessary, do both. The interest protected by such counseling is the client's interest in limiting disclosure of confidential information and in taking responsible action to deal with situations attributable to the client. If a client, whether in response to the member's counseling or otherwise, takes corrective action — such as by ceasing the criminal act before harm is caused — the option for permissive disclosure by the member would cease as the threat posed by the criminal act would no longer be present. When the actor is a nonclient or when the act is deliberate or malicious, the member who contemplates making adverse disclosure of confidential information may reasonably conclude that the compelling interests of the member or others in their own personal safety preclude personal contact with the actor. Before counseling an actor who is a nonclient, the member should, if reasonable under the circumstances, first advise the client of the member's intended course of action. If a client or another person has already acted but the intended harm has not yet occurred, the member should consider, if reasonable under the circumstances,

efforts to persuade the client or third person to warn the victim or consider other appropriate action to prevent the harm. Even when the member has concluded that paragraph (B) does not permit the member to reveal confidential information, the member nevertheless is permitted to counsel the client as to why it may be in the client's best interest to consent to the attorney's disclosure of that information.

[8] *Disclosure of confidential information must be no more than is reasonably necessary to prevent the criminal act.* Under paragraph (D), disclosure of confidential information, when made, must be no more extensive than the member reasonably believes necessary to prevent the criminal act. Disclosure should allow access to the confidential information to only those persons who the member reasonably believes can act to prevent the harm. Under some circumstances, a member may determine that the best course to pursue is to make an anonymous disclosure to the potential victim or relevant law-enforcement authorities. What particular measures are reasonable depends on the circumstances known to the member. Relevant circumstances include the time available, whether the victim might be unaware of the threat, the member's prior course of dealings with the client, and the extent of the adverse effect on the client that may result from the disclosure contemplated by the member.

[9] *Informing client of member's ability or decision to reveal confidential information under subparagraph (C)(2).* A member is required to keep a client reasonably informed about significant developments regarding the employment or representation. Rule 3-500; Business and Professions Code, section 6068, subdivision (m). Paragraph (C)(2), however, recognizes that under certain circumstances, informing a client of the member's ability or decision to reveal confidential information under paragraph (B) would likely increase the risk of death or substantial bodily harm, not only to the originally-intended victims of the criminal act, but also to the client or members of the client's family, or to the member or the member's family or associates. Therefore, paragraph (C)(2) requires a member to inform the client of the member's ability or decision to reveal confidential information as provided in paragraph (B) only if it is reasonable to do so under the circumstances. Paragraph (C)(2) further recognizes that the appropriate time for the member to inform the client may vary depending upon the circumstances. (See paragraph [10] of this discussion.) Among the factors to be considered in determining an appropriate time, if any, to inform a client are:

(1) whether the client is an experienced user of legal services;

(2) the frequency of the member's contact with the client;

(3) the nature and length of the professional relationship with the client;

(4) whether the member and client have discussed the member's duty of confidentiality or any exceptions to that duty;

(5) the likelihood that the client's matter will involve information within paragraph (B);

(6) the member's belief, if applicable, that so informing the client is likely to increase the likelihood that a criminal act likely to result in the death of, or substantial bodily harm to, an individual; and

(7) the member's belief, if applicable, that good faith efforts to persuade a client not to act on a threat have failed.

[10] *Avoiding a chilling effect on the lawyer-client relationship.* The foregoing flexible approach to the member's informing a client of his or her ability or

decision to reveal confidential information recognizes the concern that informing a client about limits on confidentiality may have a chilling effect on client communication. (See Discussion paragraph [1].) To avoid that chilling effect, one member may choose to inform the client of the member's ability to reveal information as early as the outset of the representation, while another member may choose to inform a client only at a point when that client has imparted information that may fall under paragraph (B), or even choose not to inform a client until such time as the member attempts to counsel the client as contemplated in Discussion paragraph [7]. In each situation, the member will have discharged properly the requirement under subparagraph (C)(2), and will not be subject to discipline.

[11] *Informing client that disclosure has been made; termination of the lawyer-client relationship.* When a member has revealed confidential information under paragraph (B), in all but extraordinary cases the relationship between member and client will have deteriorated so as to make the member's representation of the client impossible. Therefore, the member is required to seek to withdraw from the representation (see rule 3-700(B)), unless the member is able to obtain the client's informed consent to the member's continued representation. The member must inform the client of the fact of the member's disclosure unless the member has a compelling interest in not informing the client, such as to protect the member, the member's family or a third person from the risk of death or substantial bodily harm.

[12] *Other consequences of the member's disclosure.* Depending upon the circumstances of a member's disclosure of confidential information, there may be other important issues that a member must address. For example, if a member will be called as a witness in the client's matter, then rule 5-210 should be considered. Similarly, the member should consider his or her duties of loyalty and competency (rule 3-110).

[13] *Other exceptions to confidentiality under California law.* Rule 3-100 is not intended to augment, diminish, or preclude reliance upon, any other exceptions to the duty to preserve the confidentiality of client information recognized under California law.

Rule 3-110. Failing to Act Competently

(A) A member shall not intentionally, recklessly, or repeatedly fail to perform legal services with competence.

(B) For purposes of this rule, "competence" in any legal service shall mean to apply the 1) diligence, 2) learning and skill, and 3) mental, emotional, and physical ability reasonably necessary for the performance of such service.

(C) If a member does not have sufficient learning and skill when the legal service is undertaken, the member may nonetheless perform such services competently by 1) associating with or, where appropriate, professionally consulting another lawyer reasonably believed to be competent, or 2) by acquiring sufficient learning and skill before performance is required.

DISCUSSION

The duties set forth in rule 3-110 include the duty to supervise the work of subordinate attorney and non-attorney employees or agents. (See, e.g., *Waysman v. State Bar* (1986) 41 Cal. 3d 452; *Trousil v. State Bar* (1985) 38 Cal. 3d 337, 342 [211 Cal. Rptr. 525]; *Palomo v. State Bar* (1984) 36 Cal. 3d 785 [205 Cal. Rptr. 834]; *Crane v. State Bar* (1981) 30 Cal. 3d 117, 122; *Black v. State Bar* (1972) 7 Cal. 3d 676, 692 [103 Cal. Rptr. 288; 499 P.2d 968]; *Vaughn v. State Bar* (1972) 6 Cal. 3d 847, 857-858 [100 Cal. Rptr. 713; 494 P.2d 1257]; *Moore v. State Bar* (1964) 62 Cal. 2d 74, 81 [41 Cal. Rptr. 161; 396 P.2d 577].)

In an emergency a lawyer may give advice or assistance in a matter in which the lawyer does not have the skill ordinarily required where referral to or consultation with another lawyer would be impractical. Even in an emergency, however, assistance should be limited to that reasonably necessary in the circumstances.

Rule 3-120.   Sexual Relations with Client

Editors' Note. California was the first state to adopt a rule of legal ethics expressly addressing sexual relationships with clients. The rule was a direct outgrowth of California Business and Professions Code §6106.8, which was enacted by the California Legislature in 1989. That statute, entitled "Sexual Involvement Between Lawyers and Clients; Rule of Professional Conduct," provided, in part, as follows:

(a) The Legislature hereby finds and declares that there is no rule that governs propriety of sexual relationships between lawyers and clients. The Legislature further finds and declares that it is difficult to separate sound judgment from emotion or bias which may result from sexual involvement between a lawyer and his or her client during the period that an attorney-client relationship exists, and that emotional detachment is essential to the lawyer's ability to render competent legal services. Therefore, in order to ensure that a lawyer acts in the best interest of his or her client, a rule of professional conduct governing sexual relations between attorneys and their clients shall be adopted.

Section 6106.8 also provided that, with the approval of the Supreme Court, the State Bar "shall adopt a rule of professional conduct governing sexual relations between attorneys and their clients in cases involving, but not limited to, probate matters and domestic relations, including dissolution proceedings, child custody cases, and settlement proceedings." The statute added that "[i]ntentional violation of this rule shall constitute a cause for suspension or disbarment."

The State Bar developed a proposed rule, and in August of 1992 the California Supreme Court adopted the rule almost as proposed. However, the Supreme Court deleted a proposed paragraph (E), which provided, in part, as follows:

(E) A member who engages in sexual relations with his or her client will be presumed to violate rule 3-120, paragraph (B)(3). This presumption shall only be used as a presumption affecting the burden of proof in disciplinary proceedings involving alleged violations of these rules. . . .

The Legislature was apparently not fully satisfied with Rule 3-120. Within weeks after Rule 3-120 took effect, the Legislature enacted another statute to govern the same subject. The new statute, §6106.9, entitled "Sexual Relations Between Attorney and Client; Cause for Discipline; Complaints to State Bar," provides, in pertinent part, as follows:

(a) It shall constitute cause for the imposition of discipline of an attorney within the meaning of this chapter for an attorney to do any of the following:

(1) Expressly or impliedly condition the performance of legal services for a current or prospective client upon the client's willingness to engage in sexual relations with the attorney.

(2) Employ coercion, intimidation, or undue influence in entering into sexual relations with a client.

(3) Continue representation of a client with whom the attorney has sexual relations if the sexual relations cause the attorney to perform legal services incompetently in violation of Rule 3-110 of the Rules of Professional Conduct of the State Bar of California, or if the sexual relations would, or would be likely to, damage or prejudice the client's case.

(b) Subdivision (a) shall not apply to sexual relations between attorneys and their spouses or persons in an equivalent domestic relationship or to ongoing consensual sexual relationships that predate the initiation of the attorney-client relationship.

To prevent groundless complaints against lawyers under the new law, §6106.9(e) also provides that any complaint made to the State Bar alleging a violation of subdivision (a) "shall be verified under oath by the person making the complaint." In addition, the statute requires the State Bar to "maintain statistical data regarding the number of complaints presented and the disposition or discipline imposed" pursuant to §6106.9, and required the State Bar to submit a statistical compilation of those data to the Legislature by January 1, 1996. Finally, §6106.9 required the State Bar to "develop and implement uniform standards" for implementing §6106.9, to develop "policies and procedures to ensure that complaints will be handled in a responsive and sensitive manner," and to "provide appropriate training to staff on the standards, policies, and practices." Section 6106.9 remains in effect today.

(A) For purposes of this rule, "sexual relations" means sexual intercourse or the touching of an intimate part of another person for the purpose of sexual arousal, gratification, or abuse.

(B) A member shall not:

(1) Require or demand sexual relations with a client incident to or as a condition of any professional representation; or

(2) Employ coercion, intimidation, or undue influence in entering into sexual relations with a client; or

(3) Continue representation of a client with whom the member has sexual relations if such sexual relations cause the member to perform legal services incompetently in violation of rule 3-110.

(C) Paragraph (B) shall not apply to sexual relations between members and their spouses or to ongoing consensual sexual relations which predate the initiation of the lawyer-client relationship.

(D) Where a lawyer in a firm has sexual relations with a client but does not participate in the representation of that client, the lawyers in the firm shall not be subject to discipline under this rule solely because of the occurrence of such sexual relations.

DISCUSSION

Rule 3-120 is intended to prohibit sexual exploitation by a lawyer in the course of a professional representation. Often, based upon the nature of the underlying representation, a client exhibits great emotional vulnerability and dependence upon the advice and guidance of counsel. Attorneys owe the utmost duty of good faith and fidelity to clients. (See, e.g., *Greenbaum v. State Bar* (1976) 15 Cal. 3d 893, 903 [126 Cal. Rptr. 785]; *Alkow v. State Bar* (1971) 3 Cal. 3d 924, 935 [92 Cal. Rptr. 278]; *Cutler v. State Bar* (1969) 71 Cal. 2d 241, 251 [78 Cal. Rptr. 172]; *Clancy v. State Bar* (1969) 71 Cal. 2d 140, 146 [77 Cal. Rptr. 657].) The relationship between an attorney and client is a fiduciary relationship of the very highest character and all dealings between an attorney and client that are beneficial to the attorney will be closely scrutinized with the utmost strictness for unfairness. (See, e.g., *Giovanazzi v. State Bar* (1980) 28 Cal. 3d 465, 472 [169 Cal. Rptr. 581]; *Benson v. State Bar* (1975) 13 Cal. 3d 581, 586 [119 Cal. Rptr. 297]; *Lee v. State Bar* (1970) 2 Cal. 3d 927, 939 [88 Cal. Rptr. 361]; *Clancy v. State Bar* (1969) 71 Cal. 2d 140, 146 [77 Cal. Rptr. 657].) Where attorneys exercise undue influence over clients or take unfair advantage of clients, discipline is appropriate. (See, e.g., *Magee v. State Bar* (1962) 58 Cal. 2d 423 [24 Cal. Rptr. 839]; *Lantz v. State Bar* (1931) 212 Cal. 213 [298 P. 497].) In all client matters, a member is advised to keep clients' interests paramount in the course of the member's representation.

For purposes of this rule, if the client is an organization, any individual overseeing the representation shall be deemed to be the client. (See rule 3-600.)

Although paragraph (C) excludes representation of certain clients from the scope of rule 3-120, such exclusion is not intended to preclude the applicability of other Rules of Professional Conduct, including rule 3-110.

Rule 3-200.   Prohibited Objectives of Employment

A member shall not seek, accept, or continue employment if the member knows or should know that the objective of such employment is:

(A) To bring an action, conduct a defense, assert a position in litigation, or take an appeal, without probable cause and for the purpose of harassing or maliciously injuring any person; or

(B) To present a claim or defense in litigation that is not warranted under existing law, unless it can be supported by a good faith argument for an extension, modification, or reversal of such existing law.

Rule 3-210.   Advising the Violation of Law

A member shall not advise the violation of any law, rule, or ruling of a tribunal unless the member believes in good faith that such law, rule, or ruling is invalid. A member may take appropriate steps in good faith to test the validity of any law, rule, or ruling of a tribunal.

DISCUSSION

Rule 3-210 is intended to apply not only to the prospective conduct of a client but also to the interaction between the member and client and to the specific legal service sought by the client from the member. An example of the former is the handling of physical evidence of a crime in the possession of the client and offered to the member. (See *People v. Meredith* (1981) 29 Cal. 3d 682 [175 Cal. Rptr. 612].) An example of the latter is a request that the member negotiate the return of stolen property in exchange for the owner's agreement not to report the theft to the police or prosecutorial authorities. (See *People v. Pic'l* (1982) 31 Cal. 3d 731 [183 Cal. Rptr. 685].)

Rule 3-300.   Avoiding Interests Adverse to a Client

A member shall not enter into a business transaction with a client; or knowingly acquire an ownership, possessory, security, or other pecuniary interest adverse to a client, unless each of the following requirements has been satisfied:

(A) The transaction or acquisition and its terms are fair and reasonable to the client and are fully disclosed and transmitted in writing to the client in a manner which should reasonably have been understood by the client; and

(B) The client is advised in writing that the client may seek the advice of an independent lawyer of the client's choice and is given a reasonable opportunity to seek that advice; and

(C) The client thereafter consents in writing to the terms of the transaction or the terms of the acquisition.

DISCUSSION

Rule 3-300 is not intended to apply to the agreement by which the member is retained by the client, unless the agreement confers on the member an ownership, possessory, security, or other pecuniary interest adverse to the client. Such an agreement is governed, in part, by rule 4-200.

Rule 3-300 is not intended to apply where the member and client each make an investment on terms offered to the general public or a significant portion thereof.

For example, rule 3-300 is not intended to apply where A, a member, invests in a limited partnership syndicated by a third party. B, A's client, makes the same investment. Although A and B are each investing in the same business, A did not enter into the transaction "with" B for the purposes of the rule.

Rule 3-300 is intended to apply where the member wishes to obtain an interest in client's property in order to secure the amount of the member's past due or future fees.

Rule 3-310. Avoiding the Representation of Adverse Interests

(A) For purposes of this rule:

(1) "Disclosure" means informing the client or former client of the relevant circumstances and of the actual and reasonably foreseeable adverse consequences to the client or former client;

(2) "Informed written consent" means the client's or former client's written agreement to the representation following written disclosure;

(3) "Written" means any writing as defined in Evidence Code section 250.

(B) A member shall not accept or continue representation of a client without providing written disclosure to the client where:

(1) The member has a legal, business, financial, professional, or personal relationship with a party or witness in the same matter; or

(2) The member knows or reasonably should know that:

(a) the member previously had a legal, business, financial, professional, or personal relationship with a party or witness in the same matter; and

(b) the previous relationship would substantially affect the member's representation; or

(3) The member has or had a legal, business, financial, professional, or personal relationship with another person or entity the member knows or reasonably should know would be affected substantially by resolution of the matter; or

(4) The member has or had a legal, business, financial, or professional interest in the subject matter of the representation.

(C) A member shall not, without the informed written consent of each client:

(1) Accept representation of more than one client in a matter in which the interests of the clients potentially conflict; or

(2) Accept or continue representation of more than one client in a matter in which the interests of the clients actually conflict; or

(3) Represent a client in a matter and at the same time in a separate matter accept as a client a person or entity whose interest in the first matter is adverse to the client in the first matter.

(D) A member who represents two or more clients shall not enter into an aggregate settlement of the claims of or against the clients, without the informed written consent of each client.

(E) A member shall not, without the informed written consent of the client or former client, accept employment adverse to the client or former client where, by reason of the representation of the client or former client, the member has obtained confidential information material to the employment.

(F) A member shall not accept compensation for representing a client from one other than the client unless:

(1) There is no interference with the member's independence of professional judgment or with the client-lawyer relationship; and

(2) Information relating to representation of the client is protected as required by Business and Professions Code section 6068, subdivision (e); and

(3) The member obtains the client's informed written consent, provided that no disclosure or consent is required if:

(a) such nondisclosure is otherwise authorized by law; or

(b) the member is rendering legal services on behalf of any public agency which provides legal services to other public agencies or the public.

DISCUSSION

Rule 3-310 is not intended to prohibit a member from representing parties having antagonistic positions on the same legal question that has arisen in different cases, unless representation of either client would be adversely affected.

Other rules and laws may preclude making adequate disclosure under this rule. If such disclosure is precluded, informed written consent is likewise precluded. (See, e.g., Business and Professions Code section 6068, subsection (e).)

Paragraph (B) is not intended to apply to the relationship of a member to another party's lawyer. Such relationships are governed by rule 3-320.

Paragraph (B) is not intended to require either the disclosure of the new engagement to a former client or the consent of the former client to the new engagement. However, both disclosure and consent are required if paragraph (E) applies.

While paragraph (B) deals with the issues of adequate disclosure to the present client or clients of the member's present or past relationships to other parties or witnesses or present interest in the subject matter of the representation, paragraph (E) is intended to protect the confidences of another present or former client. These two paragraphs are to apply as complementary provisions.

Paragraph (B) is intended to apply only to a member's own relationships or interests, unless the member knows that a partner or associate in the same firm as the member has or had a relationship with another party or witness or has or had an interest in the subject matter of the representation.

Subparagraphs (C)(1) and (C)(2) are intended to apply to all types of legal employment, including the concurrent representation of multiple parties in litigation or in a single transaction or in some other common enterprise or legal relationship. Examples of the latter include the formation of a partnership for several partners or a corporation for several shareholders, the preparation of an ante-nuptial agreement, or joint or reciprocal wills for a husband and wife, or the resolution of an "uncontested" marital dissolution. In such situations, for the sake of convenience or economy, the parties may well prefer to employ a single counsel, but a member must disclose the potential adverse aspects of such multiple representation (e.g., Evid. Code, §962) and must obtain the informed written consent of the clients thereto pursuant to subparagraph (C)(1). Moreover, if the potential adversity should become actual, the member must obtain the further informed written consent of the clients pursuant to subparagraph (C)(2).

Subparagraph (C)(3) is intended to apply to representations of clients in both litigation and transactional matters.

In *State Farm Mutual Automobile Ins. Co. v. Federal Ins. Co.* (1999), 72 Cal. App. 4th 1422, [86 Cal. Rptr. 2d 20], the court held that subparagraph (C)(3) was violated when a member, retained by an insurer to defend one suit, and while that suit was still pending, filed a direct action against the same insurer in an unrelated action without securing the insurer's consent. Notwithstanding *State Farm*, subparagraph (C)(3) is not intended to apply with respect to the relationship between an insurer and a member when in each matter the insurer's interest is only as an indemnity provider and not as a direct party to the action.

There are some matters in which the conflicts are such that written consent may not suffice for non-disciplinary purposes. (See *Woods v. Superior Court* (1983) 149 Cal. App. 3d 931 [197 Cal. Rptr. 185]; *Klemm v. Superior Court* (1977) 75 Cal. App. 3d 893 [142 Cal. Rptr. 509]; *Ishmael v. Millington* (1966) 241 Cal. App. 2d 520 [50 Cal. Rptr. 592].)

Paragraph (D) is not intended to apply to class action settlements subject to court approval.

Paragraph (F) is not intended to abrogate existing relationships between insurers and insureds whereby the insurer has the contractual right to unilaterally select counsel for the insured, where there is no conflict of interest. (See San Diego Navy Federal Credit Union v. Cumis Insurance Society (1984) 162 Cal. App. 3d 358 [208 Cal. Rptr. 494].)

> **Editors' Note.** In 2003, the California Supreme Court added a new paragraph to the Discussion following Rule 3-310, which is California's main provision governing conflicts of interest among multiple clients. (The court did not amend the text of Rule 3-310.) The amendment responds to *State Farm Mutual Insurance Co. v. Federal Insurance Co.*, 72 Cal. App. 4th 1422 (5th Dist. 1999). In *State Farm*, a law firm simultaneously (a) represented State Farm in a coverage action filed directly *against* Federal Insurance, and (b) represented a driver *insured by* Federal Insurance in an unrelated case. Federal Insurance moved to disqualify the law firm from opposing Federal Insurance in the *State Farm* case, arguing that the law firm had an attorney-client relationship with Federal Insurance by virtue of representing its insured in the unrelated case. The trial court denied the motion, but the intermediate appellate court reversed,

holding that "for purposes of disqualification, the attorney representing an insured is also representing the insurance company."

In 2001, the California Legislature enacted Business and Professions Code §6068.11, which ordered the California State Bar to study the professional responsibility issues posed by *State Farm*. The State Bar identified the "key issue" as whether *State Farm* could be expanded to disqualify an attorney from opposing a particular insurance company's insured in one case while representing a different insured of the same insurance company in a separate, unrelated matter. To discourage this expansion, the Bar proposed adding to the Discussion the new paragraph beginning, "In *State Farm Mutual Automobile Ins. Co. . . .*" The California Supreme Court approved the new paragraph, and it took effect on March 2, 2003.

Rule 3-320.   Relationship with Other Party's Lawyer

A member shall not represent a client in a matter in which another party's lawyer is a spouse, parent, child, or sibling of the member, lives with the member, is a client of the member, or has an intimate personal relationship with the member, unless the member informs the client in writing of the relationship.

DISCUSSION

Rule 3-320 is not intended to apply to circumstances in which a member fails to advise the client of a relationship with another lawyer who is merely a partner or associate in the same law firm as the adverse party's counsel, and who has no direct involvement in the matter.

Rule 3-400.   Limiting Liability to Client

A member shall not:

(A) Contract with a client prospectively limiting the member's liability to the client for the member's professional malpractice; or

(B) Settle a claim or potential claim for the member's liability to the client for the member's professional malpractice, unless the client is informed in writing that the client may seek the advice of an independent lawyer of the client's choice regarding the settlement and is given a reasonable opportunity to seek that advice.

DISCUSSION

Rule 3-400 is not intended to apply to customary qualifications and limitations in legal opinions and memoranda, nor is it intended to prevent a member from reasonably limiting the scope of the member's employment or representation.

Rule 3-410. Disclosure of Professional Liability Insurance

Editors' Note. Rule 3-410 became effective on January 1, 2010. It was a highly controversial rule that divided the profession. The California State Bar circulated proposed drafts of the rule for public comment three separate times before the State Bar's Board of Governors finally voted to forward a proposal to the California Supreme Court. Opponents of the rule argued that requiring public disclosure would stigmatize uninsured lawyers and force them to buy expensive malpractice coverage, which would drive up legal fees and price low-income clients out of the market. Proponents pointed to the lack of empirical evidence from other states to justify those fears, and argued that lack of insurance coverage was a material fact that prospective clients were entitled to know. The proposals were drafted by the State Bar's Insurance Disclosure Task Force, whose Chair is former State Bar President Jim Towery of San Jose.

(A) A member who knows or should know that he or she does not have professional liability insurance shall inform a client in writing, at the time of the client's engagement of the member, that the member does not have professional liability insurance whenever it is reasonably foreseeable that the total amount of the member's legal representation of the client in the matter will exceed four hours.

(B) If a member does not provide the notice required under paragraph (A) at the time of a client's engagement of the member, and the member subsequently knows or should know that he or she no longer has professional liability insurance during the representation of the client, the member shall inform the client in writing within thirty days of the date that the member knows or should know that he or she no longer has professional liability insurance.

(C) This rule does not apply to a member who is employed as a government lawyer or in-house counsel when that member is representing or providing legal advice to a client in that capacity.

(D) This rule does not apply to legal services rendered in an emergency to avoid foreseeable prejudice to the rights or interests of the client.

(E) This rule does not apply where the member has previously advised the client under Paragraph (A) or (B) that the member does not have professional liability insurance.

DISCUSSION

[1] The disclosure obligation imposed by Paragraph (A) of this rule applies with respect to new clients and new engagements with returning clients.

[2] A member may use the following language in making the disclosure required by Rule 3-410(A), and may include that language in a written fee agreement

with the client or in a separate writing: "Pursuant to California Rule of Professional Conduct 3-410, I am informing you in writing that I do not have professional liability insurance."

[3] A member may use the following language in making the disclosure required by Rule 3-410(B): "Pursuant to California Rule of Professional Conduct 3-410, I am informing you in writing that I no longer have professional liability insurance."

[4] Rule 3-410(C) provides an exemption for a "government lawyer or in-house counsel when that member is representing or providing legal advice to a client in that capacity." The basis of both exemptions is essentially the same. The purpose of this rule is to provide information directly to a client if a member is not covered by professional liability insurance. If a member is employed directly by and provides legal services directly for a private entity or a federal, state or local governmental entity, that entity presumably knows whether the member is or is not covered by professional liability insurance. The exemptions under this rule are limited to situations involving direct employment and representation, and do not, for example, apply to outside counsel for a private or governmental entity, or to counsel retained by an insurer to represent an insured.

Rule 3-500. Communication

A member shall keep a client reasonably informed about significant developments relating to the employment or representation, including promptly complying with reasonable requests for information and copies of significant documents when necessary to keep the client so informed.

DISCUSSION

Rule 3-500 is not intended to change a member's duties to his or her clients. It is intended to make clear that, while a client must be informed of significant developments in the matter, a member will not be disciplined for failing to communicate insignificant or irrelevant information. (See Bus. & Prof. Code, §6068, subd. (m).)

A member may contract with the client in their employment agreement that the client assumes responsibility for the cost of copying significant documents. This rule is not intended to prohibit a claim for the recovery of the member's expense in any subsequent legal proceeding.

Rule 3-500 is not intended to create, augment, diminish, or eliminate any application of the work product rule. The obligation of the member to provide work product to the client shall be governed by relevant statutory and decisional law. Additionally, this rule is not intended to apply to any document or correspondence that is subject to a protective order or non-disclosure agreement, or to override applicable statutory or decisional law requiring that certain information not be provided to criminal defendants who are clients of the member.

Rule 3-510.   Communication of Settlement Offer

(A) A member shall promptly communicate to the member's client:

(1) All terms and conditions of any offer made to the client in a criminal matter; and

(2) All amounts, terms, and conditions of any written offer of settlement made to the client in all other matters.

(B) As used in this rule, "client" includes a person who possesses the authority to accept an offer of settlement or plea, or, in a class action, all the named representatives of the class.

DISCUSSION

Rule 3-510 is intended to require that counsel in a criminal matter convey all offers, whether written or oral, to the client, as give and take negotiations are less common in criminal matters, and, even were they to occur, such negotiations should require the participation of the accused.

Any oral offers of settlement made to the client in a civil matter should also be communicated if they are "significant" for the purposes of rule 3-500.

Rule 3-600.   Organization as Client

(A) In representing an organization, a member shall conform his or her representation to the concept that the client is the organization itself, acting through its highest authorized officer, employee, body, or constituent overseeing the particular engagement.

(B) If a member acting on behalf of an organization knows that an actual or apparent agent of the organization acts or intends or refuses to act in a manner that is or may be a violation of law reasonably imputable to the organization, or in a manner which is likely to result in substantial injury to the organization, the member shall not violate his or her duty of protecting all confidential information as provided in Business and Professions Code section 6068, subdivision (e). Subject to Business and Professions Code section 6068, subdivision (e), the member may take such actions as appear to the member to be in the best lawful interest of the organization. Such actions may include among others:

(1) Urging reconsideration of the matter while explaining its likely consequences to the organization; or

(2) Referring the matter to the next higher authority in the organization, including, if warranted by the seriousness of the matter, referral to the highest internal authority that can act on behalf of the organization.

(C) If, despite the member's actions in accordance with paragraph (B), the highest authority that can act on behalf of the organization insists upon action or a refusal to act that is a violation of law and is likely to result in substantial injury to the organization, the member's response is limited to the member's right, and, where appropriate, duty to resign in accordance with rule 3-700.

(D) In dealing with an organization's directors, officers, employees, members, shareholders, or other constituents, a member shall explain the identity of the client for whom the member acts, whenever it is or becomes apparent that the organization's interests are or may become adverse to those of the constituent(s) with whom the member is dealing. The member shall not mislead such a constituent into believing that the constituent may communicate confidential information to the member in a way that will not be used in the organization's interest if that is or becomes adverse to the constituent.

(E) A member representing an organization may also represent any of its directors, officers, employees, members, shareholders, or other constituents, subject to the provisions of rule 3-310. If the organization's consent to the dual representation is required by rule 3-310, the consent shall be given by an appropriate constituent of the organization other than the individual or constituent who is to be represented, or by the shareholder(s) or organization members.

DISCUSSION

Rule 3-600 is not intended to enmesh members in the intricacies of the entity and aggregate theories of partnership.

Rule 3-600 is not intended to prohibit members from representing both an organization and other parties connected with it, as for instance (as simply one example) in establishing employee benefit packages for closely held corporations or professional partnerships.

Rule 3-600 is not intended to create or to validate artificial distinctions between entities and their officers, employees, or members, nor is it the purpose of the rule to deny the existence or importance of such formal distinctions. In dealing with a close corporation or small association, members commonly perform professional engagements for both the organization and its major constituents. When a change in control occurs or is threatened, members are faced with complex decisions involving personal and institutional relationships and loyalties and have frequently had difficulty in perceiving their correct duty. (See *People ex rel. Deukmejian v. Brown* (1981) 29 Cal. 3d 150 [172 Cal. Rptr. 478]; *Goldstein v. Lees* (1975) 46 Cal. App. 3d 614 [120 Cal. Rptr. 253]; *Woods v. Superior Court* (1983) 149 Cal. App. 3d 931 [197 Cal. Rptr. 185]; *In re Banks* (1978) 283 Ore. 459 [584 P.2d 284]; 1 A.L.R.4th 1105.) In resolving such multiple relationships, members must rely on case law.

Rule 3-700. Termination of Employment

(A) *In General.*

(1) If permission for termination of employment is required by the rules of a tribunal, a member shall not withdraw from employment in a proceeding before that tribunal without its permission.

(2) A member shall not withdraw from employment until the member has taken reasonable steps to avoid reasonably foreseeable prejudice to the rights of the client, including giving due notice to the client, allowing time for employment of other counsel, complying with rule 3-700(D), and complying with applicable laws and rules.

(B) *Mandatory Withdrawal.*

A member representing a client before a tribunal shall withdraw from employment with the permission of the tribunal, if required by its rules, and a member representing a client in other matters shall withdraw from employment, if:

(1) The member knows or should know that the client is bringing an action, conducting a defense, asserting a position in litigation, or taking an appeal, without probable cause and for the purpose of harassing or maliciously injuring any person; or

(2) The member knows or should know that continued employment will result in violation of these rules or of the State Bar Act; or

(3) The member's mental or physical condition renders it unreasonably difficult to carry out the employment effectively.

(C) *Permissive Withdrawal.*

If rule 3-700(B) is not applicable, a member may not request permission to withdraw in matters pending before a tribunal, and may not withdraw in other matters, unless such request or such withdrawal is because:

(1) The client

(a) insists upon presenting a claim or defense that is not warranted under existing law and cannot be supported by good faith argument for an extension, modification, or reversal of existing law, or

(b) seeks to pursue an illegal course of conduct, or

(c) insists that the member pursue a course of conduct that is illegal or that is prohibited under these rules or the State Bar Act, or

(d) by other conduct renders it unreasonably difficult for the member to carry out the employment effectively, or

(e) insists, in a matter not pending before a tribunal, that the member engage in conduct that is contrary to the judgment and advice of the member but not prohibited under these rules or the State Bar Act, or

(f) breaches an agreement or obligation to the member as to expenses or fees.

(2) The continued employment is likely to result in a violation of these rules or of the State Bar Act; or

(3) The inability to work with co-counsel indicates that the best interests of the client likely will be served by withdrawal; or

(4) The member's mental or physical condition renders it difficult for the member to carry out the employment effectively; or

(5) The client knowingly and freely assents to termination of the employment; or

(6) The member believes in good faith, in a proceeding pending before a tribunal, that the tribunal will find the existence of other good cause for withdrawal.

(D) *Papers, Property, and Fees.*

A member whose employment has terminated shall:

(1) Subject to any protective order or non-disclosure agreement, promptly release to the client, at the request of the client, all the client papers and property. "Client papers and property" includes correspondence, pleadings, deposition transcripts, exhibits, physical evidence, expert's reports, and other items reasonably necessary to the client's representation, whether the client has paid for them or not; and

(2) Promptly refund any part of a fee paid in advance that has not been earned. This provision is not applicable to a true retainer fee which is paid solely for the purpose of ensuring the availability of the member for the matter.

DISCUSSION

Subparagraph (A)(2) provides that "a member shall not withdraw from employment until the member has taken reasonable steps to avoid reasonably foreseeable prejudice to the rights of the clients." What such steps would include, of course, will vary according to the circumstances. Absent special circumstances, "reasonable steps" do not include providing additional services to the client once the successor counsel has been employed and rule 3-700(D) has been satisfied.

Paragraph (D) makes clear the member's duties in the recurring situation in which new counsel seeks to obtain client files from a member discharged by the client. It codifies existing case law. (See *Academy of California Optometrists v. Superior Court* (1975) 51 Cal. App. 3d 999 [124 Cal. Rptr. 668]; *Weiss v. Marcus* (1975) 51 Cal. App. 3d 590 [124 Cal. Rptr. 297].) Paragraph (D) also requires that the member "promptly" return unearned fees paid in advance. If a client disputes the amount to be returned, the member shall comply with rule 4-100(A)(2).

Paragraph (D) is not intended to prohibit a member from making, at the member's own expense, and retaining copies of papers released to the client, nor to prohibit a claim for the recovery of the member's expense in any subsequent legal proceeding.

CHAPTER 4.   FINANCIAL RELATIONSHIP WITH CLIENTS

Rule 4-100.   Preserving Identity of Funds and Property of a Client

(A) All funds received or held for the benefit of clients by a member or law firm, including advances for costs and expenses, shall be deposited in one or more identifiable bank accounts labeled "Trust Account," "Client's Funds Account" or words of similar import, maintained in the State of California, or, with written consent of the client, in any other jurisdiction where there is a substantial relationship between the client or the client's business and the other jurisdiction. No funds belonging to the member or the law firm shall be deposited therein or otherwise commingled therewith except as follows:

(1) Funds reasonably sufficient to pay bank charges.

(2) In the case of funds belonging in part to a client and in part presently or potentially to the member or the law firm, the portion belonging to the member or law firm must be withdrawn at the earliest reasonable time after the member's interest in that portion becomes fixed. However, when the right of the member or law firm to receive a portion of trust funds is disputed by the client, the disputed portion shall not be withdrawn until the dispute is finally resolved.

(B) A member shall:

(1) Promptly notify a client of the receipt of the client's funds, securities, or other properties.

(2) Identify and label securities and properties of a client promptly upon receipt and place them in a safe deposit box or other place of safekeeping as soon as practicable.

(3) Maintain complete records of all funds, securities, and other properties of a client coming into the possession of the member or law firm and render appropriate accounts to the client regarding them; preserve such records for a period of no less than five years after final appropriate distribution of such funds or properties; and comply with any order for an audit of such records issued pursuant to the Rules of Procedure of the State Bar.

(4) Promptly pay or deliver, as requested by the client, any funds, securities, or other properties in the possession of the member which the client is entitled to receive.

(C) The Board of Governors of the State Bar shall have the authority to formulate and adopt standards as to what "records" shall be maintained by members and law firms in accordance with subparagraph (B)(3). The standards formulated and adopted by the Board, as from time to time amended, shall be effective and binding on all members.

STANDARDS

Pursuant to rule 4-100(C) the Board of Governors of the State Bar adopted the following standards, effective January 1, 1993, as to what "records" shall be maintained by members and law firms in accordance with subparagraph (B)(3).

(1) A member shall, from the date of receipt of client funds through the period ending five years from the date of appropriate disbursement of such funds, maintain:

(a) written ledger for each client on whose behalf funds are held that sets forth:

(i) the name of such client,

(ii) the date, amount and source of all funds received on behalf of such client,

(iii) the date, amount, payee and purpose of each disbursement made on behalf of such client, and

(iv) the current balance for such client;

(b) a written journal for each bank account that sets forth

(i) the name of such account,

(ii) the date, amount and client affected by each debit and credit, and

(iii) the current balance in such account;

(c) all bank statements and cancelled checks for each bank account; and

(d) each monthly reconciliation (balancing) of (a), (b), and (c).

(2) A member shall, from the date of receipt of all securities and other properties held for the benefit of client through the period ending five years from the date of appropriate disbursement of such securities and other properties, maintain a written journal that specifies:

(a) each item of security and property held;

(b) the person on whose behalf the security or property is held;

(c) the date of receipt of the security or property;

(d) the date of distribution of the security or property; and

(e) person to whom the security or property was distributed.

Rule 4-200.   Fees for Legal Services

(A) A member shall not enter into an agreement for, charge, or collect an illegal or unconscionable fee.

(B) Unconscionability of a fee shall be determined on the basis of all the facts and circumstances existing at the time the agreement is entered into except where the parties contemplate that the fee will be affected by later events. Among the factors to be considered, where appropriate, in determining the conscionability of a fee are the following:

(1) The amount of the fee in proportion to the value of the services performed.

(2) The relative sophistication of the member and the client.

(3) The novelty and difficulty of the questions involved and the skill requisite to perform the legal service properly.

(4) The likelihood, if apparent to the client, that the acceptance of the particular employment will preclude other employment by the member.

(5) The amount involved and the results obtained.

(6) The time limitations imposed by the client or by the circumstances.

(7) The nature and length of the professional relationship with the client.

(8) The experience, reputation, and ability of the member or members performing the services.

(9) Whether the fee is fixed or contingent.

(10) The time and labor required.

(11) The informed consent of the client to the fee.

Editors' Note. Fees for legal services in California are also governed by various statutes. See California Business and Professions Code Article 8.5 (Fee Agreements), especially §§6146 through 6149 (reprinted below in our Selected California Statutes).

Rule 4-210. Payment of Personal or Business Expenses Incurred by or for a Client

(A) A member shall not directly or indirectly pay or agree to pay, guarantee, represent, or sanction a representation that the member or member's law firm will pay the personal or business expenses of a prospective or existing client, except that this rule shall not prohibit a member:

(1) With the consent of the client, from paying or agreeing to pay such expenses to third persons from funds collected or to be collected for the client as a result of the representation; or

(2) After employment, from lending money to the client upon the client's promise in writing to repay such loan; or

(3) From advancing the costs of prosecuting or defending a claim or action or otherwise protecting or promoting the client's interests, the repayment of which may be contingent on the outcome of the matter. Such costs within the meaning of this subparagraph (3) shall be limited to all reasonable expenses of litigation or reasonable expenses in preparation for litigation or in providing any legal services to the client.

(B) Nothing in rule 4-210 shall be deemed to limit rules 3-300, 3-310, and 4-300.

Rule 4-300. Purchasing Property at a Foreclosure or a Sale Subject to Judicial Review

(A) A member shall not directly or indirectly purchase property at a probate, foreclosure, receiver's, trustee's, or judicial sale in an action or proceeding in which such member or any lawyer affiliated by reason of personal, business, or professional relationship with that member or with that member's law firm is acting as a lawyer for a party or as executor, receiver, trustee, administrator, guardian, or conservator.

(B) A member shall not represent the seller at a probate, foreclosure, receiver, trustee, or judicial sale in an action or proceeding in which the purchaser is a spouse or relative of the member or of another lawyer in the member's law firm or is an employee of the member or the member's law firm.

Rule 4-400. Gifts from Client

A member shall not induce a client to make a substantial gift, including a testamentary gift, to the member or to the member's parent, child, sibling, or spouse, except where the client is related to the member.

DISCUSSION

A member may accept a gift from a member's client, subject to general standards of fairness and absence of undue influence. The member who participates in the preparation of an instrument memorializing a gift which is otherwise permissible ought not to be subject to professional discipline. On the other hand, where impermissible influence occurred, discipline is appropriate. (See *Magee v. State Bar* (1962) 58 Cal. 2d 423 [24 Cal. Rptr. 839].)

CHAPTER 5.   ADVOCACY AND REPRESENTATION

Rule 5-100. Threatening Criminal, Administrative, or Disciplinary Charges

(A) A member shall not threaten to present criminal, administrative, or disciplinary charges to obtain an advantage in a civil dispute.

(B) As used in paragraph (A) of this rule, the term "administrative charges" means the filing or lodging of a complaint with a federal, state, or local governmental entity which may order or recommend the loss or suspension of a license, or may impose or recommend the imposition of a fine, pecuniary sanction, or other sanction of a quasi-criminal nature but does not include filing charges with an administrative entity required by law as a condition precedent to maintaining a civil action.

(C) As used in paragraph (A) of this rule, the term "civil dispute" means a controversy or potential controversy over the rights and duties of two or more parties under civil law, whether or not an action has been commenced, and includes an administrative proceeding of a quasi-civil nature pending before a federal, state, or local governmental entity.

DISCUSSION

Rule 5-100 is not intended to apply to a member's threatening to initiate contempt proceedings against a party for a failure to comply with a court order.

Paragraph (B) is intended to exempt the threat of filing an administrative charge which is a prerequisite to filing a civil complaint on the same transaction or occurrence.

For purposes of paragraph (C), the definition of "civil dispute" makes clear that the rule is applicable prior to the formal filing of a civil action.

Rule 5-110.   Performing the Duty of Member in Government Service

A member in government service shall not institute or cause to be instituted criminal charges when the member knows or should know that the charges are not supported by probable cause. If, after the institution of criminal charges, the member in government service having responsibility for prosecuting the charges becomes aware that those charges are not supported by probable cause, the member shall promptly so advise the court in which the criminal matter is pending.

Rule 5-120.   Trial Publicity

Editors' Note. Rule 5-120 has a unique history. When O.J. Simpson was charged with murder in June 1994, California was the only state in the country without a rule restricting extrajudicial statements by lawyers, and public statements by lawyers involved in the case alarmed the California Legislature. The first bill developed by the Legislature to remedy the problem would have codified a version of ABA Model Rule 3.6 (as it then existed) as a California statute. Ultimately, however, the Legislature decided instead to let the State Bar draft its own rule, subject to approval by the California Supreme Court.

In June 1994, therefore, the California Legislature passed a statute commanding the State Bar to submit to the Supreme Court "a rule of professional conduct governing trial publicity and extrajudicial statements made by attorneys concerning adjudicative proceedings." Governor Pete Wilson signed the legislation into law on September 26, 1994, the first day of jury selection in the O.J. Simpson murder trial. (The statute is found at §6103.7 of the California Business and Professions Code.)

Obeying the statute, the State Bar submitted a proposal to the California Supreme Court in February 1995 but did so "without recommendation." The proposal would have applied only to jury trials and only to extrajudicial statements that posed a "clear and present danger" to trial proceedings. In March 1995, the Supreme Court wrote to the State Bar suggesting that the Bar either propose a trial publicity rule that it recommended "or particularly explain the reasons why it does not recommend approval of the rule already submitted."

In September 1995, after the Bar had explained its reasons for submitting a proposed rule without recommendation, the Supreme Court adopted a trial publicity rule that tracked ABA Model Rule 3.6 (which the ABA has since amended slightly) rather than the State Bar proposal. But California omitted Rule 3.6(d), which provides that "[n]o lawyer associated in a firm or government agency with a lawyer subject to paragraph (a) shall make a statement prohibited by paragraph (a)."

(A) A member who is participating or has participated in the investigation or litigation of a matter shall not make an extrajudicial statement that a reasonable person would expect to be disseminated by means of public communication if the member knows or reasonably should know that it will have a substantial likelihood of materially prejudicing an adjudicative proceeding in the matter.

(B) Notwithstanding paragraph (A), a member may state:

(1) the claim, offense or defense involved and, except when prohibited by law, the identity of the persons involved;

(2) the information contained in a public record;

(3) that an investigation of the matter is in progress;

(4) the scheduling or result of any step in litigation;

(5) a request for assistance in obtaining evidence and information necessary thereto;

(6) a warning of danger concerning the behavior of a person involved, when there is reason to believe that there exists the likelihood of substantial harm to an individual or to the public interest; and

(7) in a criminal case, in addition to subparagraphs (1) through (6):

(a) the identity, residence, occupation, and family status of the accused;

(b) if the accused has not been apprehended, information necessary to aid in apprehension of that person;

(c) the fact, time, and place of arrest; and

    (d) the identity of investigating and arresting officers or agencies and the length of the investigation.

    (C) Notwithstanding paragraph (A), a member may make a statement that a reasonable member would believe is required to protect a client from the substantial undue prejudicial effect of recent publicity not initiated by the member or the member's client. A statement made pursuant to this paragraph shall be limited to such information as is necessary to mitigate the recent adverse publicity.

DISCUSSION

    Rule 5-120 is intended to apply equally to prosecutors and criminal defense counsel.

    Whether an extrajudicial statement violates rule 5-120 depends on many factors, including:

    (1) whether the extrajudicial statement presents information clearly inadmissible as evidence in the matter for the purpose of proving or disproving a material fact in issue;

    (2) whether the extrajudicial statement presents information the member knows is false, deceptive, or the use of which would violate Business and Professions Code section 6068(d);

    (3) whether the extrajudicial statement violates a lawful "gag" order, or protective order, statute, rule of court, or special rule of confidentiality (for example, in juvenile, domestic, mental disability, and certain criminal proceedings); and

    (4) the timing of the statement.

    Paragraph (A) is intended to apply to statements made by or on behalf of the member.

    Subparagraph (B)(6) is not intended to create, augment, diminish, or eliminate any application of the lawyer-client privilege or of Business and Professions Code section 6068(e) regarding the member's duty to maintain client confidence and secrets.

Rule 5-200.   Trial Conduct

    In presenting a matter to a tribunal, a member:

    (A) Shall employ, for the purpose of maintaining the causes confided to the member such means only as are consistent with truth;

    (B) Shall not seek to mislead the judge, judicial officer, or jury by an artifice or false statement of fact or law;

    (C) Shall not intentionally misquote to a tribunal the language of a book, statute, or decision;

    (D) Shall not, knowing its invalidity, cite as authority a decision that has been overruled or a statute that has been repealed or declared unconstitutional; and

(E) Shall not assert personal knowledge of the facts at issue, except when testifying as a witness.

Rule 5-210.   Member as Witness

A member shall not act as an advocate before a jury which will hear testimony from the member unless:

(A) The testimony relates to an uncontested matter; or

(B) The testimony relates to the nature and value of legal services rendered in the case; or

(C) The member has the informed written consent of the client. If the member represents the People or a governmental entity, the consent shall be obtained from the head of the office or a designee of the head of the office by which the member is employed and shall be consistent with principles of recusal.

DISCUSSION

Rule 5-210 is intended to apply to situations in which the member knows or should know that he or she ought to be called as a witness in litigation in which there is a jury. This rule is not intended to encompass situations in which the member is representing the client in an adversarial proceeding and is testifying before a judge. In non-adversarial proceedings, as where the member testifies on behalf of the client in a hearing before a legislative body, rule 5-210 is not applicable.

Rule 5-210 is not intended to apply to circumstances in which a lawyer in an advocate's firm will be a witness.

Rule 5-220.   Suppression of Evidence

A member shall not suppress any evidence that the member or the member's client has a legal obligation to reveal or to produce.

Rule 5-300.   Contact with Officials

(A) A member shall not directly or indirectly give or lend anything of value to a judge, official, or employee of a tribunal unless the personal or family relationship between the member and the judge, official, or employee is such that gifts are customarily given and exchanged. Nothing contained in this rule shall prohibit a member from contributing to the campaign fund of a judge running for election or confirmation pursuant to applicable law pertaining to such contributions.

(B) A member shall not directly or indirectly communicate with or argue to a judge or judicial officer upon the merits of a contested matter pending before such judge or judicial officer, except:

(1) In open court; or

(2) With the consent of all other counsel in such matter; or

(3) In the presence of all other counsel in such matter; or

(4) In writing with a copy thereof furnished to such other counsel; or

(5) In ex parte matters.

(C) As used in this rule, "judge" and "judicial officer" shall include law clerks, research attorneys, or other court personnel who participate in the decision-making process.

Rule 5-310.   Prohibited Contact with Witnesses

A member shall not:

(A) Advise or directly or indirectly cause a person to secrete himself or herself or to leave the jurisdiction of a tribunal for the purpose of making that person unavailable as a witness therein.

(B) Directly or indirectly pay, offer to pay, or acquiesce in the payment of compensation to a witness contingent upon the content of the witness's testimony or the outcome of the case. Except where prohibited by law, a member may advance, guarantee, or acquiesce in the payment of:

(1) Expenses reasonably incurred by a witness in attending or testifying.

(2) Reasonable compensation to a witness for loss of time in attending or testifying.

(3) A reasonable fee for the professional services of an expert witness.

Rule 5-320.   Contact with Jurors

(A) A member connected with a case shall not communicate directly or indirectly with anyone the member knows to be a member of the venire from which the jury will be selected for trial of that case.

(B) During trial a member connected with the case shall not communicate directly or indirectly with any juror.

(C) During trial a member who is not connected with the case shall not communicate directly or indirectly concerning the case with anyone the member knows is a juror in the case.

(D) After discharge of the jury from further consideration of a case a member shall not ask questions of or make comments to a member of that jury that are intended to harass or embarrass the juror or to influence the juror's actions in future jury service.

(E) A member shall not directly or indirectly conduct an out of court investigation of a person who is either a member or the venire or a juror in a manner likely to influence the state of mind of such person in connection with present or future jury service.

(F) All restrictions imposed by this rule also apply to communications with, or investigations of, members of the family of a person who is either a member of the venire or a juror.

(G) A member shall reveal promptly to the court improper conduct by a person who is either a member of a venire or a juror, or by another toward a person who is either a member of a venire or a juror or a member of his or her family, of which the member has knowledge.

(H) This rule does not prohibit a member from communicating with persons who are members of a venire or jurors as a part of the official proceedings.

(I) For purposes of this rule, "juror" means any empaneled, discharged, or excused juror.

Selected California Statutes

Editors' Introduction. Perhaps more than any other state, California governs the conduct of lawyers by statute. Until 2004, for example, California's provision on confidentiality was not found in California's Rules of Professional Conduct, but in section 6068(e) of California's Business and Professions Code. The Business and Professions Code also contains provisions governing fee agreements, IOLTA accounts, paralegals, lawyer advertising, settlement offers, and many other matters that other states typically address in their Rules of Professional Conduct or via common law. In addition, California addresses by statute (in California Civil Code section 2860) the conflict of interest that arises when an insurance company provides a lawyer for the defense of an insured. California also governs the attorney-client privilege and work product protection through statutory provisions.

We include here the statutory materials that are most likely to be covered in a law school course on the law governing California attorneys. Most of these provisions come from Chapter 4 of California's Business and Professions Code, a chapter commonly known as the "State Bar Act."

Developments since our last edition. Since the last edition of this book went to press in September 2011, there have been relatively few changes to the statutes referenced below. One interesting development is the passage of section 6001.1, which describes the State Bar's "highest priority" as the "protection of the public." To this end, newly adopted section 6001.2 directs the State Bar to create a Public Interest Task Force. This Task Force, which is supposed to be created by February 1, 2013, will develop recommendations for "enhancing the protection of the public and ensuring that protection of the public is the highest priority in the licensing, regulation, and discipline of attorneys. . . ."

For updated information and for additional legislative history regarding California statutes and pending bills, visit the official website for California legislative information at *www.leginfo.ca.gov.* For bills related to attorneys, look in the index under the heading "attorneys" at the following website: *www. leginfo.ca.gov/legindexhtml/legindexALEAD.html.*

Contents

CALIFORNIA BUSINESS AND PROFESSIONS CODE: DIVISION 3 (PROFESSIONS AND VOCATIONS GENERALLY)

CHAPTER 4. ATTORNEYS

CALIFORNIA CIVIL CODE

CALIFORNIA CODE OF CIVIL PROCEDURE

CALIFORNIA EVIDENCE CODE

CALIFORNIA BUSINESS AND PROFESSIONS CODE

CHAPTER 4. ATTORNEYS

ARTICLE 4.   ADMISSION TO THE STATE BAR

§6001.1   State Bar — Protection of the Public as the Highest Priority

(a) Protection of the public shall be the highest priority for the State Bar of California and the board of trustees in exercising their licensing, regulatory, and disciplinary functions. Whenever the protection of the public is inconsistent with other interests sought to be promoted, the protection of the public shall be paramount.

§6001.2   State Bar Governance in the Public Interest Task Force

(a) On or before February 1, 2013, there shall be created within the State Bar a Governance in the Public Interest Task Force. . . .

(b) On or before May 15, 2014, and every three years thereafter, the task force shall prepare and submit a report to the Supreme Court, the Governor, and the Assembly and Senate Committees on Judiciary that includes its recommendations for enhancing the protection of the public and ensuring that protection of the public is the highest priority in the licensing, regulation, and discipline of attorneys, to be reviewed by the Assembly and Senate Committees on Judiciary in their regular consideration of the annual State Bar dues measure. . . .

§6060.   Qualifications; Examination and Fee

To be certified to the Supreme Court for admission and a license to practice law, a person who has not been admitted to practice law in a sister state, United States jurisdiction, possession, territory, or dependency or in a foreign country shall:

(a) Be of the age of at least 18 years.

(b) Be of good moral character.

(c) Before beginning the study of law, have done either of the following:

(1) Completed at least two years of college work, which college work shall be not less than one-half of the collegiate work acceptable for a bachelor's degree granted upon the basis of a four-year period of study by a college or university approved by the examining committee.

(2) Have attained in apparent intellectual ability the equivalent of at least two years of college work by taking any examinations in such subject matters and achieving the scores thereon as are prescribed by the examining committee.

(d) Have registered with the examining committee as a law student within 90 days after beginning the study of law. The examining committee, upon good cause being shown, may permit a later registration.

(e) Have done any of the following:

(1) Had conferred upon him or her a juris doctor (J.D.) degree or a bachelor of laws (LL.B.) degree by a law school accredited by the examining committee or approved by the American Bar Association.

(2) Studied law diligently and in good faith for at least four years in any of the following manners:

(A) In a law school that is authorized or approved to confer professional degrees and requires classroom attendance of its students for a minimum of 270 hours a year. A person who has received his or her legal education in a foreign state or country wherein the common law of England does not constitute the basis of jurisprudence shall demonstrate to the satisfaction of the examining committee that his or her education, experience, and qualifications qualify him or her to take the examination.

(B) In a law office in this state and under the personal supervision of a member of the State Bar of California who is, and for at least the last five years continuously has been, engaged in the active practice of law. It is the duty of the supervising attorney to render any periodic reports to the examining committee as the committee may require.

(C) In the chambers and under the personal supervision of a judge of a court of record of this state. It is the duty of the supervising judge to render any periodic reports to the examining committee as the committee may require.

(D) By instruction in law from a correspondence law school authorized or approved to confer professional degrees by this state, which requires 864 hours of preparation and study per year for four years.

(E) By any combination of the methods referred to in this paragraph (2) of this subdivision.

(f) Have passed any examination in professional responsibility or legal ethics as the examining committee may prescribe.

(g) Have passed the general bar examination given by the examining committee.

(h)(1) Have passed a law students' examination administered by the examining committee after completion of his or her first year of law study. Those who pass the examination within its first three administrations upon becoming eligible to take the examination shall receive credit for all law studies completed to the time the examination is passed. Those who do not pass the examination within its first three administrations upon becoming eligible to take the examination, but who subsequently pass the examination, shall receive credit for one year of legal study only.

(2) This requirement does not apply to a student who has satisfactorily completed his or her first year of law study at a law school accredited by the examining committee and who has completed at least two years of college work prior to matriculating in the accredited law school, nor shall this requirement apply to an applicant who has passed the bar examination of a sister state or of a country in which the common law of England constitutes the basis of jurisprudence.

The law students' examination shall be administered twice a year at reasonable intervals.

§6060.1 Violation of University or Law School Rules

(a) Any disciplinary action taken against an individual at a university or an accredited law school for violation of university or law school rules of conduct shall not be used as the sole basis for denying the individual admission to practice law in the State of California.

(b) This section shall not apply to university or law school violations which involve moral turpitude or that result in criminal prosecution under the laws of the State of California or any other state.

§6060.2 Confidentiality of Proceedings re Moral Character

All investigations or proceedings conducted by the State Bar concerning the moral character of an applicant shall be confidential unless the applicant, in writing, waives the confidentiality. However, the records of the proceeding may be subject to lawfully issued subpoenas.

§6061. Disclosure Statements — Unaccredited Law Schools

Any law school that is not accredited by the examining committee of the State Bar shall provide every student with a disclosure statement, subsequent to the payment of any application fee but prior to the payment of any registration fee, containing all of the following information:

(a) The school is not accredited. However, in addition, if the school has been approved by other agencies, that fact may be so stated.

(b) Where the school has not been in operation for 10 years, the assets and liabilities of the school. However, if the school has had prior affiliation with another school that has been in operation more than 10 years, has been under the control of another school that has been in operation more than 10 years, or has been a successor to a school in operation more than 10 years, this subdivision is not applicable.

(c) The number and percentage of students who have taken and who have passed the first year law student's examination and the final bar examination in the previous five years, or since the establishment of the school, whichever time is less, which shall include only those students who have been certified by the school to take the examinations.

(d) The number of legal volumes in the library. This subdivision does not apply to correspondence schools.

(e) The educational background, qualifications, and experience of the faculty, and whether or not the faculty members and administrators (e.g., the dean) are members of the California State Bar.

(f) The ratio of faculty to students for the previous five years or since the establishment of the school, whichever time is less.

(g) Whether or not the school has applied for accreditation, and, if so, the date of application and whether or not that application has been withdrawn, is currently pending, or has been finally denied. The school need only disclose information relating to applications made in the previous five years.

(h) That the education provided by the school may not satisfy the requirements of other states for the practice of law. Applicants should inquire regarding those requirements, if any, to the state in which they may wish to practice.

The disclosure statement required by this section shall be signed by each student, who shall receive as a receipt a copy of his or her signed disclosure statement. If any school does not comply with these requirements, it shall make a full refund of all fees paid by students.

Subject to approval by the board, the examining committee may adopt reasonable rules and regulations as are necessary for the purpose of ensuring compliance with this section.

§6062.   Out-of-State Attorneys

(a) To be certified to the Supreme Court for admission, and a license to practice law, a person who has been admitted to practice law in a sister state, United States jurisdiction, possession, territory, or dependency the United States may hereafter acquire shall:

(1) Be of the age of at least 18 years.

(2) Be of good moral character.

(3) Have passed the general bar examination given by the examining committee. However, if that person has been an active member in good standing of the bar of the admitting sister state or United States jurisdiction, possession, or territory for at least four years immediately preceding the first day of the examination applied for, he or she may elect to take the Attorneys' Examination rather than the general bar examination. Attorneys admitted less than four years and attorneys admitted four years or more in another jurisdiction but who have not been active members in good standing of their admitting jurisdiction for at least four years immediately proceeding the first day of the examination applied for must take the general bar examination administered to general applicants not admitted as attorneys in other jurisdictions.

(4) Have passed an examination in professional responsibility or legal ethics as the examining committee may prescribe.

(b) To be certified to the Supreme Court for admission, and a license to practice law, a person who has been admitted to practice law in a jurisdiction other than in a sister state, United States jurisdiction, possession, or territory shall:

(1) Be of the age of at least 18 years.

(2) Be of good moral character.

(3) Have passed the general bar examination given by the examining committee.

(4) Have passed an examination in professional responsibility or legal ethics as the examining committee may prescribe.

(c) The amendments to this section made at the 1997-98 Regular Session of the Legislature shall be applicable on and after January 1, 1997, and do not constitute a change in, but are declaratory of, existing law.

§6064.1 Advocacy of Overthrow of Government

No person who advocates the overthrow of the Government of the United States or of this State by force, violence, or other unconstitutional means, shall be certified to the Supreme Court for admission and a license to practice law.

§6065. Inspection of Papers and Grading

(a)(1) Any unsuccessful applicant for admission to practice, after he or she has taken any examination and within four months after the results thereof have been declared, has the right to inspect his or her examination papers at the office of the examining committee located nearest to the place at which the applicant took the examination.

(2) The applicant also has the right to inspect the grading of the papers whether the record thereof is marked upon the examination or otherwise.

(b) This section shall become operative on January 1, 2009.

§6068. Duties of Attorney

Editors' Note. For more than a century, §6068(e) provided, in substance: "It is the duty of an attorney to . . . maintain inviolate the confidence, and at every peril to himself or herself to preserve the secrets, of his or her client." (The gender-neutral "his or her" language took effect in the 1990s.) Thus, unlike every other jurisdiction in the United States, California had no exceptions to its duty of confidentiality.

Effective July 1, 2004, the California Legislature added §6068(e)(2), creating the first statutory exception to the duty of confidentiality. The amendment authorizes an attorney to reveal confidential information to the extent that the attorney reasonably believes disclosure is necessary to prevent a criminal act likely to result in death or substantial bodily harm to an individual. The amendment thus resembles the pre-2002 version of Rule 1.6(b)(1) of the ABA Model Rules of Professional Conduct.

It is the duty of an attorney to do all of the following:

(a) To support the Constitution and laws of the United States and of this state.

(b) To maintain the respect due to the courts of justice and judicial officers.

(c) To counsel or maintain those actions, proceedings, or defenses only as appear to him or her legal or just, except the defense of a person charged with a public offense.

(d) To employ, for the purpose of maintaining the causes confided to him or her those means only as are consistent with truth, and never to seek to mislead the judge or any judicial officer by an artifice or false statement of fact or law.

(e)(1) To maintain inviolate the confidence, and at every peril to himself or herself to preserve the secrets, of his or her client.

(2) Notwithstanding paragraph (1), an attorney may, but is not required to, reveal confidential information relating to the representation of a client to the extent that the attorney reasonably believes the disclosure is necessary to prevent a criminal act that the attorney reasonably believes is likely to result in death of, or substantial bodily harm to, an individual.

(f) To advance no fact prejudicial to the honor or reputation of a party or witness, unless required by the justice of the cause with which he or she is charged.

(g) Not to encourage either the commencement or the continuance of an action or proceeding from any corrupt motive of passion or interest.

(h) Never to reject, for any consideration personal to himself or herself, the cause of the defenseless or the oppressed.

(i) To cooperate and participate in any disciplinary investigation or other regulatory or disciplinary proceeding pending against himself or herself. However, this subdivision shall not be construed to deprive an attorney of any privilege guaranteed by the Fifth Amendment to the Constitution of the United States, or any other constitutional or statutory privileges. This subdivision shall not be construed to require an attorney to cooperate with a request that requires him or her to waive any constitutional or statutory privilege or to comply with a request for information or other matters within an unreasonable period of time in light of the time constraints of the attorney's practice. Any exercise by an attorney of any constitutional or statutory privilege shall not be used against the attorney in a regulatory or disciplinary proceeding against him or her.

(j) To comply with the requirements of Section 6002.1.

(k) To comply with all conditions attached to any disciplinary probation, including a probation imposed with the concurrence of the attorney.

(l) To keep all agreements made in lieu of disciplinary prosecution with the agency charged with attorney discipline.

(m) To respond promptly to reasonable status inquiries of clients and to keep clients reasonably informed of significant developments in matters with regard to which the attorney has agreed to provide legal services.

(n) To provide copies to the client of certain documents under time limits and as prescribed in a rule of professional conduct which the board shall adopt.

(o) To report to the agency charged with attorney discipline, in writing, within 30 days of the time the attorney has knowledge of any of the following:

(1) The filing of three or more lawsuits in a 12-month period against the attorney for malpractice or other wrongful conduct committed in a professional capacity.

(2) The entry of judgment against the attorney in any civil action for fraud, misrepresentation, breach of fiduciary duty, or gross negligence committed in a professional capacity.

(3) The imposition of any judicial sanctions against the attorney, except for sanctions for failure to make discovery or monetary sanctions of less than one thousand dollars ($1,000).

(4) The bringing of an indictment or information charging a felony against the attorney.

(5) The conviction of the attorney, including any verdict of guilty, or plea of guilty or no contest, of any felony, or any misdemeanor committed in the course of the practice of law, or in any manner in which a client of the attorney was the victim, or a necessary element of which, as determined by the statutory or common law definition of the misdemeanor, involves improper conduct of an attorney, including dishonesty or other moral turpitude, or an attempt or a conspiracy or solicitation of another to commit a felony or any misdemeanor of that type.

(6) The imposition of discipline against the attorney by any professional or occupational disciplinary agency or licensing board, whether in California or elsewhere.

(7) Reversal of judgment in a proceeding based in whole or in part upon misconduct, grossly incompetent representation, or willful misrepresentation by an attorney.

(8) As used in this subdivision, "against the attorney" includes claims and proceedings against any firm of attorneys for the practice of law in which the attorney was a partner at the time of the conduct complained of and any law corporation in which the attorney was a shareholder at the time of the conduct complained of unless the matter has to the attorney's knowledge already been reported by the law firm or corporation.

(9) The State Bar may develop a prescribed form for the making of reports required by this section, usage of which it may require by rule or regulation.

(10) This subdivision is only intended to provide that the failure to report as required herein may serve as a basis of discipline.

ARTICLE 5.   DISCIPLINARY AUTHORITY OF THE BOARD OF GOVERNORS

§6079.4.   Privilege; Exercise of Not Deemed Failure to Cooperate

The exercise by an attorney of his or her privilege under the Fifth Amendment to the Constitution of the United States, or of any other constitutional or statutory privileges shall not be deemed a failure to cooperate within the meaning of subdivision (i) of Section 6068.

§6086.1.   Disciplinary Proceeding Hearings and Records Shall Be Public

(a)(1) Subject to subdivision (b), and except as otherwise provided by law, hearings and records of original disciplinary proceedings in the State Bar Court shall be public, following a notice to show cause....

(b) All disciplinary investigations are confidential until the time that formal charges are filed. . . . This confidentiality requirement may be waived under [specified] exceptions....

§6086.7.   Court Notification to State Bar for Misconduct, Misrepresentation, Incompetent Representation and Imposition of Sanctions

(a) A court shall notify the State Bar of any of the following:

(1) A final order of contempt imposed against an attorney that may involve grounds warranting discipline under this chapter. The court entering the final order shall transmit to the State Bar a copy of the relevant minutes, final order, and transcript, if one exists.

(2) Whenever a modification or reversal of a judgment in a judicial proceeding is based in whole or in part on the misconduct, incompetent representation, or willful misrepresentation of an attorney.

(3) The imposition of any judicial sanctions against an attorney, except sanctions for failure to make discovery or monetary sanctions of less than one thousand dollars ($1,000).

(4) The imposition of any civil penalty upon an attorney pursuant to Section 8620 of the Family Code.

(b) In the event of a notification made under subdivision (a), (b), or (c), the court shall also notify the attorney involved that the matter has been referred to the State Bar.

(c) The State Bar shall investigate any matter reported under this section as to the appropriateness of initiating disciplinary action against the attorney.

§6086.8.   Reporting Requirements — Court, Insurers and
Attorneys

(a) Within 20 days after a judgment by a court of this state that a member of the State Bar of California is liable for any damages resulting in a judgment against the attorney in any civil action for fraud, misrepresentation, breach of fiduciary duty, or gross negligence committed in a professional capacity, the court which rendered the judgment shall report that fact in writing to the State Bar of California.

(b) Every claim or action for damages against a member of the State Bar of California for fraud, misrepresentation, breach of fiduciary duty, or negligence committed in a professional capacity shall be reported to the State Bar of California within 30 days of receipt by the admitted insurer or licensed surplus brokers providing professional liability insurance to that member of the State Bar.

(c) An attorney who does not possess professional liability insurance shall send a complete written report to the State Bar as to any settlement, judgment, or arbitration award described in subdivision (b), in the manner specified in that subdivision.

ARTICLE 5.5.   MISCELLANEOUS DISCIPLINARY
PROVISIONS

§6090.5.   Attorney/Client Agreement Not to File Complaint —
Cause for Discipline

(a) It is cause for suspension, disbarment, or other discipline for any member whether as a party or as an attorney for a party, to agree or seek agreement, that:

(1) The professional misconduct or the terms of a settlement of a claim for professional misconduct shall not be reported to the disciplinary agency.

(2) The plaintiff shall withdraw a disciplinary complaint or shall not cooperate with the investigation or prosecution conducted by the disciplinary agency.

(3) The record of any civil action for professional misconduct shall be sealed from review by the disciplinary agency.

(b) This section applies to all settlements, whether made before or after the commencement of a civil action.

ARTICLE 6.   DISCIPLINARY AUTHORITY OF THE COURTS

§6103.5.   Communicate Written Offer of Settlement to Client

(a) A member of the State Bar shall promptly communicate to the member's client all amounts, terms, and conditions of any written offer of settlement made by or on behalf of an opposing party. As used in this section, "client" includes any person employing the member of the State Bar who possesses the authority to accept an offer of settlement, or in a class action, who is a representative of the class.

(b) Any written offer of settlement or any required communication of a settlement offer, as described in subdivision (a), shall be discoverable by either party in any action in which the existence or communication of the offer of settlement is an issue before the trier of fact.

§6106.   Moral Turpitude, Dishonesty or Corruption Irrespective of Criminal Conviction

The commission of any act involving moral turpitude, dishonesty or corruption, whether the act is committed in the course of his relations as an attorney or otherwise, and whether the act is a felony or misdemeanor or not, constitutes a cause of disbarment or suspension.

If the act constitutes a felony or misdemeanor, conviction thereof in a criminal proceeding is not a condition precedent to disbarment or suspension from practice therefor.

§6106.1.   Advocacy of Overthrow of Government

Advocating the overthrow of the Government of the United States or of this State by force, violence, or other unconstitutional means, constitutes a cause for disbarment or suspension.

§6106.9.   Sexual Relations Between Attorney and Client; Cause for Discipline; Complaints to State Bar

(a) It shall constitute cause for the imposition of discipline of an attorney within the meaning of this chapter for an attorney to do any of the following:

(1) Expressly or impliedly condition the performance of legal services for a current or prospective client upon the client's willingness to engage in sexual relations with the attorney.

(2) Employ coercion, intimidation, or undue influence in entering into sexual relations with a client.

(3) Continue representation of a client with whom the attorney has sexual relations if the sexual relations cause the attorney to perform legal services incompetently in violation of Rule 3-110 of the Rules of Professional Conduct of the State Bar of California, or if the sexual relations would, or would be likely to, damage or prejudice the client's case.

(b) Subdivision (a) shall not apply to sexual relations between attorneys and their spouses or persons in an equivalent domestic relationship or to ongoing consensual sexual relationships that predate the initiation of the attorney-client relationship.

(c) Where an attorney in a firm has sexual relations with a client but does not participate in the representation of that client, the attorneys in the firm shall not be subject to discipline under this section solely because of the occurrence of those sexual relations.

(d) For the purposes of this section, "sexual relations" means sexual intercourse or the touching of an intimate part of another person for the purpose of sexual arousal, gratification, or abuse.

(e) Any complaint made to the State Bar alleging a violation of subdivision (a) shall be verified under oath by the person making the complaint.

ARTICLE 7. UNLAWFUL PRACTICE OF LAW

§6125. Necessity of Active Membership in State Bar

No person shall practice law in California unless the person is an active member of the State Bar.

> **Editors' Note.** Most states address multijurisdictional practice in their rules of professional conduct, but California governs out-of-state lawyers through court rules. For extensive excerpts from those rules, see the Editors' Note following Rule 1-300 of the California Rules of Professional Conduct. See also §1282.4 of the California Code of Civil Procedure, reprinted below, which permits attorneys not admitted in California to represent parties in California arbitration proceedings under certain circumstances.

§6126. Unauthorized Practice or Advertising as a Misdemeanor

(a) Any person advertising or holding himself or herself out as practicing or entitled to practice law or otherwise practicing law who is not an active member of the State Bar, or otherwise authorized pursuant to statute or court rule to practice law in this state at the time of doing so, is guilty of a misdemeanor punishable by up to one year in a county jail or by a fine of up to one thousand dollars ($1,000), or by both that fine and imprisonment. Upon a second or subsequent conviction, the person shall be confined in a county jail for not less than 90 days, except in an unusual case where the interests of justice would be served by imposition of a lesser sentence or a fine. If the court imposes only a fine or a sentence of less than 90 days for a second or subsequent conviction under this subdivision, the court shall state the reasons for its sentencing choice on the record.

(b) Any person who has been involuntarily enrolled as an inactive member of the State Bar, or has been suspended from membership from the State Bar, or has been disbarred, or has resigned from the State Bar with charges pending, and thereafter practices or attempts to practice law, advertises or holds himself or herself out as practicing or otherwise entitled to practice law, is guilty of a crime punishable by imprisonment . . . in the state prison or a county jail. . . .

(c) The willful failure of a member of the State Bar, or one who has resigned or been disbarred, to comply with an order of the Supreme Court to comply with Rule 9.20 of the California Rules of Court, constitutes a crime punishable by imprisonment in the state prison or a county jail.

(d) The penalties provided in this section are cumulative to each other and to any other remedies or penalties provided by law.

§6126.5.   Relief

(a) In addition to any remedies and penalties available in any enforcement action brought in the name of the people of the State of California by the Attorney General, a district attorney, or a city attorney, acting as a public prosecutor, the court shall award relief in the enforcement action for any person who obtained services offered or provided in violation of Section 6125 or 6126 or who purchased any goods, services, or real or personal property in connection with services offered or provided in violation of Section 6125 or 6126 against the person who violated Section 6125 or 6126, or who sold goods, services, or property in connection with that violation. The court shall consider the following relief:

(1) Actual damages.

(2) Restitution of all amounts paid.

(3) The amount of penalties and tax liabilities incurred in connection with the sale or transfer of assets to pay for any goods, services, or property.

(4) Reasonable attorney's fees and costs expended to rectify errors made in the unlawful practice of law.

(5) Prejudgment interest at the legal rate from the date of loss to the date of judgment.

(6) Appropriate equitable relief, including the rescission of sales made in connection with a violation of law.

(b) The relief awarded under paragraphs (1) to (6), inclusive, of subdivision (a) shall be distributed to, or on behalf of, the person for whom it was awarded or, if it is impracticable to do so, shall be distributed as may be directed by the court pursuant to its equitable powers.

(c) The court shall also award the Attorney General, district attorney, or city attorney reasonable attorney's fees and costs and, in the court's discretion, exemplary damages as provided in Section 3294 of the Civil Code.

(d) This section shall not be construed to create, abrogate, or otherwise affect claims, rights, or remedies, if any, that may be held by a person or entity other than those law enforcement agencies described in subdivision (a). The remedies provided in this section are cumulative to each other and to the remedies and penalties provided under other laws.

§6128.   Deceit, Collusion, Delay of Suit and Improper Receipt of Money as Misdemeanor

Every attorney is guilty of a misdemeanor who either:

(a) Is guilty of any deceit or collusion, or consents to any deceit or collusion, with intent to deceive the court or any party.

(b) Willfully delays his client's suit with a view to his own gain.

(c) Willfully receives any money or allowance for or on account of any money which he has not laid out or become answerable for.

Any violation of the provisions of this section is punishable by imprisonment in the county jail not exceeding six months, or by a fine not exceeding two thousand five hundred dollars ($2,500), or by both.

§6132.   Law Firm Name — Removal of Name of Disciplined Attorney

Any law firm, partnership, corporation, or association which contains the name of an attorney who is disbarred, or who resigned with charges pending, in its business name shall remove the name of that attorney from its business name, and from all signs, advertisements, letterhead, and other materials containing that name, within 60 days of the disbarment or resignation.

ARTICLE 8.5.   FEE AGREEMENTS

§6146.   Limitations; Periodic Payments; Definitions

(a) An attorney shall not contract for or collect a contingency fee for representing any person seeking damages in connection with an action for injury or damage against a health care provider based upon such person's alleged professional negligence in excess of the following limits:

(1) Forty percent of the first fifty thousand dollars ($50,000) recovered.

(2) Thirty-three and one-third percent of the next fifty thousand dollars ($50,000) recovered.

(3) Twenty-five percent of the next five hundred thousand dollars ($500,000) recovered.

(4) Fifteen percent of any amount on which the recovery exceeds six hundred thousand dollars ($600,000).

The limitations shall apply regardless of whether the recovery is by settlement, arbitration, or judgment, or whether the person for whom the recovery is made is a responsible adult, an infant, or a person of unsound mind. . . .

§6147.   Contingency Fee Contract: Contents; Effect of
          Noncompliance; Application to Contracts for
          Recovery of Workers' Compensation Benefits

(a) An attorney who contracts to represent a client on a contingency fee basis shall, at the time the contract is entered into, provide a duplicate copy of the contract, signed by both the attorney and the client, or the client's guardian or representative, to the plaintiff, or to the client's guardian or representative. The contract shall be in writing and shall include, but is not limited to, all of the following:

(1) A statement of the contingency fee rate that the client and attorney have agreed upon.

(2) A statement as to how disbursements and costs incurred in connection with the prosecution or settlement of the claim will affect the contingency fee and the client's recovery.

(3) A statement as to what extent, if any, the client could be required to pay any compensation to the attorney for related matters that arise out of their relationship not covered by their contingency fee contract. This may include any amounts collected for the plaintiff by the attorney.

(4) Unless the claim is subject to the provisions of Section 6146, a statement that the fee is not set by law but is negotiable between attorney and client.

(5) If the claim is subject to the provisions of Section 6146, a statement that the rates set forth in that section are the maximum limits for the contingency fee agreement, and that the attorney and client may negotiate a lower rate.

(b) Failure to comply with any provision of this section renders the agreement voidable at the option of the plaintiff, and the attorney shall thereupon be entitled to collect a reasonable fee.

(c) This section shall not apply to contingency fee contracts for the recovery of workers' compensation benefits.

(d) This section shall become operative on January 1, 2000.

§6147.5. Contingency Fee Contracts; Recovery of Claims Between Merchants

(a) Sections 6147 and 6148 shall not apply to contingency fee contracts for the recovery of claims between merchants . . . arising from the sale or lease of goods or services rendered, or money loaned for use, in the conduct of a business or profession if the merchant contracting for legal services employs 10 or more individuals.

(b)(1) In the instances in which no written contract for legal services exists as permitted by subdivision (a), an attorney shall not contract for or collect a contingency fee in excess of the following limits:

(A) Twenty percent of the first three hundred dollars ($300) collected.

(B) Eighteen percent of the next one thousand seven hundred dollars ($1,700) collected.

(C) Thirteen percent of sums collected in excess of two thousand dollars ($2,000).

(2) However, the following minimum charges may be charged and collected:

(A) Twenty-five dollars ($25) in collections of seventy-five dollars ($75) to one hundred twenty-five dollars ($125).

(B) Thirty-three and one-third percent of collections less than seventy-five dollars ($75).

§6148. Written Fee Contract: Contents; Effect of Noncompliance

(a) In any case not coming within Section 6147 in which it is reasonably foreseeable that total expense to a client, including attorney fees, will exceed one thousand dollars ($1,000), the contract for services in the case shall be in writing. At the time the contract is entered into, the attorney shall provide a duplicate copy of the contract signed by both the attorney and the client, or the client's guardian or representative, to the client or to the client's guardian or representative. The written contract shall contain all of the following:

(1) Any basis of compensation including, but not limited to, hourly rates, statutory fees or flat fees, and other standard rates, fees, and charges applicable to the case.

(2) The general nature of the legal services to be provided to the client.

(3) The respective responsibilities of the attorney and the client as to the performance of the contract.

(b) All bills rendered by an attorney to a client shall clearly state the basis thereof. Bills for the fee portion of the bill shall include the amount, rate, basis for calculation, or other method of determination of the attorney's fees and costs. Bills for the cost and expense portion of the bill shall clearly identify the costs and expenses incurred and the amount of the costs and expenses. Upon request by the client, the attorney shall provide a bill to the client no later than 10 days following the request. . . .

(c) Failure to comply with any provision of this section renders the agreement voidable at the option of the client, and the attorney shall, upon the agreement being voided, be entitled to collect a reasonable fee.

(d) This section shall not apply to any of the following:

(1) Services rendered in an emergency to avoid foreseeable prejudice to the rights or interests of the client or where a writing is otherwise impractical.

(2) An arrangement as to the fee implied by the fact that the attorney's services are of the same general kind as previously rendered to and paid for by the client.

(3) If the client knowingly states in writing, after full disclosure of this section, that a writing concerning fees is not required.

(4) If the client is a corporation.

(e) This section applies prospectively only to fee agreements following its operative date.

(f) This section shall become operative on January 1, 2000.

§6149.   Written Fee Contract Confidential Communication

A written fee contract shall be deemed to be a confidential communication within the meaning of subdivision (e) of Section 6068 and of Section 952 of the Evidence Code.

Editors' Note. Section 6068(e) of the Business and Professions Code is reprinted above in this chapter. Section 952 of the Evidence Code is reprinted below in this chapter.

ARTICLE 9.   UNLAWFUL SOLICITATION

§6151.   Runners and Cappers — Definitions

As used in this article:

(a) A runner or capper is any person, firm, association or corporation acting for consideration in any manner or in any capacity as an agent for an attorney at law or law firm, whether the attorney or any member of the law firm is admitted in California or any other jurisdiction, in the solicitation or procurement of business for the attorney at law or law firm as provided in this article.

(b) An agent is one who represents another in dealings with one or more third persons.

§6152. Prohibition of Solicitation

(a) It is unlawful for:

(1) Any person . . . to act as a runner or capper for any attorneys or to solicit any business for any attorneys in and about the state prisons, county jails, city jails, city prisons, or other places of detention of persons, city receiving hospitals, city and county receiving hospitals, county hospitals, superior courts, or in any public institution or in any public place or upon any public street or highway or in and about private hospitals, sanitariums or in and about any private institution or upon private property of any character whatsoever. . . .

(b) A general release from a liability claim obtained from any person during the period of the first physical confinement, whether as an inpatient or outpatient, in a clinic or health facility . . . as a result of the injury alleged to have given rise to the claim and primarily for treatment of the injury, is presumed fraudulent if the release is executed within 15 days after the commencement of confinement or prior to release from confinement, whichever occurs first. . . .

(d) Nothing in this section shall be construed to mean that a public defender or assigned counsel may not make known his or her services as a criminal defense attorney to persons unable to afford legal counsel whether such persons are in custody or otherwise.

§6153. Violation as Misdemeanor; Forfeiture of Public Office or Employment

Any person, firm, partnership, association, or corporation violating subdivision (a) of Section 6152 is punishable, upon a first conviction, by imprisonment in a county jail for not more than one year or by a fine not exceeding fifteen thousand dollars ($15,000), or by both that imprisonment and fine. Upon a second or subsequent conviction, a person, firm, partnership, association, or corporation is punishable by imprisonment pursuant to subdivision (h) of Section 1170 of the Penal Code for two, three, or four years, or by a fine not exceeding fifteen thousand dollars ($15,000), or by both that imprisonment and fine.

Any person employed either as an officer, director, trustee, clerk, servant or agent of this state or of any county or other municipal corporation or subdivision thereof, who is found guilty of violating any of the provisions of this article, shall forfeit the right to his office and employment in addition to any other penalty provided in this article.

§6154.   Invalidity of Contract for Services

(a) Any contract for professional services secured by any attorney at law or law firm in this state through the services of a runner or capper is void. . . .

ARTICLE 9.5.   LEGAL ADVERTISING

§6157.   Definitions

As used in this article, the following definitions apply: . . .

(c) "Advertise" or "advertisement" means any communication, disseminated by television or radio, by any print medium, including, but not limited to, newspapers and billboards, or by means of a mailing directed generally to members of the public and not to a specific person, that solicits employment of legal services provided by a member, and is directed to the general public and is paid for by, or on the behalf of, an attorney.

(d) "Electronic medium" means television, radio, or computer networks.

§6157.1.   Advertisements—False, Misleading or Deceptive

No advertisement shall contain any false, misleading, or deceptive statement or omit to state any fact necessary to make the statements made, in light of circumstances under which they are made, not false, misleading, or deceptive.

§6157.2.   Advertisements—Guarantees, Settlements, Impersonations, Dramatizations and Contingent Fee Basis

No advertisement shall contain or refer to any of the following:

(a) Any guarantee or warranty regarding the outcome of a legal matter as a result of representation by the member.

(b) Statements or symbols stating that the member featured in the advertisement can generally obtain immediate cash or quick settlements.

(c)(1) An impersonation of the name, voice, photograph, or electronic image of any person other than the lawyer, directly or implicitly purporting to be that of a lawyer.

(2) An impersonation of the name, voice, photograph, or electronic image of any person, directly or implicitly purporting to be a client of the member featured in the advertisement, or a dramatization of events, unless disclosure of the impersonation or dramatization is made in the advertisement.

(3) A spokesperson, including a celebrity spokesperson, unless there is disclosure of the spokesperson's title.

(d) A statement that a member offers representation on a contingent basis unless the statement also advises whether a client will be held responsible for any costs advanced by the member when no recovery is obtained on behalf of the client. If the client will not be held responsible for costs, no disclosure is required.

§6157.3. Advertisements—Disclosure of Payor Other Than Member

Any advertisement made on behalf of a member, which is not paid for by the member, shall disclose any business relationship, past or present, between the member and the person paying for the advertisement.

§6158. Electronic Media Advertisements; Compliance with Sections 6157.1 and 6157.2; Message May Not Be False, Misleading or Deceptive; Message Must Be Factually Substantiated

In advertising by electronic media, to comply with Sections 61571.1 and 6157.2, the message as a whole may not be false, misleading, or deceptive, and the message as a whole must be factually substantiated. The message means the effect in combination of the spoken word, sound, background, action, symbols, visual image, or any other technique employed to create the message. Factually substantiated means capable of verification by a credible source.

§6158.1. Rebuttable Presumptions; False, Misleading or Deceptive Message

There shall be a rebuttable presumption affecting the burden of producing evidence that the following messages are false, misleading, or deceptive within the meaning of Section 6158:

(a) A message as to the ultimate result of a specific case or cases presented out of context without adequately providing information as to the facts or law giving rise to the result.

(b) The depiction of an event through methods such as the use of displays of injuries, accident scenes, or portrayals of other injurious events which may or may not be accompanied by sound effects and which may give rise to a claim for compensation.

(c) A message referring to or implying money received by or for a client in a particular case or cases, or to potential monetary recovery for a prospective client. A reference to money or monetary recovery includes, but is not limited to, a specific dollar amount, characterization of a sum of money, monetary symbols, or the implication of wealth.

§6158.3.   Disclosures

. . . If an advertisement in the electronic media conveys a message portraying a result in a particular case or cases, the advertisement must state, in either an oral or printed communication, either of the following disclosures: The advertisement must adequately disclose the factual and legal circumstances that justify the result portrayed in the message, including the basis for liability and the nature of injury or damage sustained, or the advertisement must state that the result portrayed in the advertisement was dependent on the facts of that case, and that the results will differ if based on different facts.

§6450.   Paralegal Defined; Prohibited Activities; Qualifications; Continuing Legal Education

(a) "Paralegal" means a person who holds himself or herself out to be a paralegal, who is qualified by education, training, or work experience, and who either contracts with or is employed by an attorney, law firm, corporation, governmental agency, or other entity, and who performs substantial legal work under the direction and supervision of an active member of the State Bar of California, as defined in Section 6060, or an attorney practicing law in the federal courts of this state, that has been specifically delegated by the attorney to him or her. Tasks performed by a paralegal may include, but are not limited to, case planning, development, and management; legal research; interviewing clients; fact gathering and retrieving information; drafting and analyzing legal documents; collecting, compiling, and utilizing technical information to make an independent decision and recommendation to the supervising attorney; and representing clients before a state or federal administrative agency if that representation is permitted by statute, court rule, or administrative rule or regulation.

(b) Notwithstanding subdivision (a), a paralegal shall not do any of the following:

(1) Provide legal advice.

(2) Represent a client in court.

(3) Select, explain, draft, or recommend the use of any legal document to or for any person other than the attorney who directs and supervises the paralegal.

(4) Act as a runner or capper, as defined in Sections 6151 and 6152.

(5) Engage in conduct that constitutes the unlawful practice of law.

(6) Contract with, or be employed by, a natural person other than an attorney to perform paralegal services.

(7) In connection with providing paralegal services, induce a person to make an investment, purchase a financial product or service, or enter a transaction from which income or profit, or both, purportedly may be derived.

(8) Establish the fees to charge a client for the services the paralegal performs, which shall be established by the attorney who supervises the paralegal's work. This paragraph does not apply to fees charged by a paralegal in a contract to provide paralegal services to an attorney, law firm, corporation, governmental agency, or other entity as provided in subdivision (a).

(c) A paralegal shall possess at least one of the following:

(1) A certificate of completion of a paralegal program approved by the American Bar Association.

(2) A certificate of completion of a paralegal program at, or a degree from, a postsecondary institution that requires the successful completion of a minimum of 24 semester, or equivalent, units in law-related courses and that has been accredited by a national or regional accrediting organization or approved by the Bureau for Private Postsecondary and Vocational Education.

(3) A baccalaureate degree or an advanced degree in any subject, a minimum of one year of law-related experience under the supervision of an attorney who has been an active member of the State Bar of California for at least the preceding three years or who has practiced in the federal courts of this state for at least the preceding three years, and a written declaration from this attorney stating that the person is qualified to perform paralegal tasks.

(4) A high school diploma or general equivalency diploma, a minimum of three years of law-related experience under the supervision of an attorney who has been an active member of the State Bar of California for at least the preceding three years or who has practiced in the federal courts of this state for at least the preceding three years, and a written declaration from this attorney stating that the person

is qualified to perform paralegal tasks. This experience and training shall be completed no later than December 31, 2003.

(d) Every two years, commencing January 1, 2007, any person that is working as a paralegal shall be required to certify completion of four hours of mandatory continuing legal education in legal ethics and four hours of mandatory continuing legal education in either general law or in an area of specialized law. . . .

§6451. Paralegal; Unlawful Practices; Services for Consumers

It is unlawful for a paralegal to perform any services for a consumer except as performed under the direction and supervision of the attorney, law firm, corporation, government agency, or other entity that employs or contracts with the paralegal. Nothing in this chapter shall prohibit a paralegal who is employed by an attorney, law firm, governmental agency, or other entity from providing services to a consumer served by one of these entities if those services are specifically allowed by statute, case law, court rule, or federal or state administrative rule or regulation. "Consumer" means a natural person, firm, association, organization, partnership, business trust, corporation, or public entity.

§6452. Paralegal; Unlawful Practices; Persons Identifying
Themselves as Paralegals

(a) It is unlawful for a person to identify himself or herself as a paralegal on any advertisement, letterhead, business card or sign, or elsewhere unless he or she has met the qualifications of subdivision (c) of Section 6450 and performs all services under the direction and supervision of an attorney who is an active member of the State Bar of California or an attorney practicing law in the federal courts of this state who is responsible for all of the services performed by the paralegal. The business card of a paralegal shall include the name of the law firm where he or she is employed or a statement that he or she is employed by or contracting with a licensed attorney.

(b) An attorney who uses the services of a paralegal is liable for any harm caused as the result of the paralegal's negligence, misconduct, or violation of this chapter.

§6453. Duty of Paralegal; Confidentiality

A paralegal is subject to the same duty as an attorney specified in subdivision (e) of Section 6068 to maintain inviolate the confidentiality, and at every peril to himself or herself to preserve the attorney-client privilege, of a consumer for whom the paralegal has provided any of the services described in subdivision (a) of Section 6450.

CALIFORNIA CIVIL CODE

§2860.   Conflict of Interest; Duty to Provide Independent
          Counsel; Waiver; Qualifications of Independent Counsel;
          Fees; Disclosure of Information

(a) If the provisions of a policy of insurance impose a duty to defend upon an insurer and a conflict of interest arises which creates a duty on the part of the insurer to provide independent counsel to the insured, the insurer shall provide independent counsel to represent the insured unless, at the time the insured is informed that a possible conflict may arise or does exist, the insured expressly waives, in writing, the right to independent counsel. An insurance contract may contain a provision which sets forth the method of selecting that counsel consistent with this section.

(b) For purposes of this section, a conflict of interest does not exist as to allegations or facts in the litigation for which the insurer denies coverage; however, when an insurer reserves its rights on a given issue and the outcome of that coverage issue can be controlled by counsel first retained by the insurer for the defense of the claim, a conflict of interest may exist. No conflict of interest shall be deemed to exist as to allegations of punitive damages or be deemed to exist solely because an insured is sued for an amount in excess of the insurance policy limits.

(c) When the insured has selected independent counsel to represent him or her, the insurer may exercise its right to require that the counsel selected by the insured possess certain minimum qualifications which may include that the selected counsel have (1) at least five years of civil litigation practice which includes substantial defense experience in the subject at issue in the litigation, and (2) errors and omissions coverage. The insurer's obligation to pay fees to the independent counsel selected by the insured is limited to the rates which are actually paid by the insurer to attorneys retained by it in the ordinary course of business in the defense of similar actions in the community where the claim arose or is being defended. This subdivision does not invalidate other different or additional policy provisions pertaining to attorney's fees or providing for methods of settlement of disputes concerning those fees. Any dispute concerning attorney's fees not resolved by these methods shall be resolved by final and binding arbitration by a single neutral arbitrator selected by the parties to the dispute.

(d) When independent counsel has been selected by the insured, it shall be the duty of that counsel and the insured to disclose to the insurer all information concerning the action except privileged materials relevant to coverage disputes, and timely to inform and consult with the insurer on all matters relating to the action. Any claim of privilege asserted is subject to in camera review in the appropriate law and motion department of the superior court. Any information disclosed by the insured or by independent counsel is not a waiver of the privilege as to any other party.

(e) The insured may waive its right to select independent counsel by signing the following statement: "I have been advised and informed of my right to select independent counsel to represent me in this lawsuit. I have considered this matter fully and freely waive my right to select independent counsel at this time. I authorize my insurer to select a defense attorney to represent me in this lawsuit."

(f) Where the insured selects independent counsel pursuant to the provisions of this section, both the counsel provided by the insurer and independent counsel selected by the insured shall be allowed to participate in all aspects of the litigation. Counsel shall cooperate fully in the exchange of information that is consistent with each counsel's ethical and legal obligation to the insured. Nothing in this section shall relieve the insured of his or her duty to cooperate with the insurer under the terms of the insurance contract.

CALIFORNIA CODE OF CIVIL PROCEDURE

§206.   Criminal Actions; Discussion of Deliberation or Verdict After Discharge of Jury; Informing Jury; Violations

(a) Prior to discharging the jury from the case, the judge in a criminal action shall inform the jurors that they have an absolute right to discuss or not to discuss the deliberation or verdict with anyone. The judge shall also inform the jurors of the provisions set forth in subdivisions (b), (d), and (e).

(b) Following the discharge of the jury in a criminal case, the defendant, or his or her attorney or representative, or the prosecutor, or his or her representative, may discuss the jury deliberation or verdict with a member of the jury, provided that the juror consents to the discussion and that the discussion takes place at a reasonable time and place.

(c) If a discussion of the jury deliberation or verdict with a member of the jury pursuant to subdivision (b) occurs at any time more than 24 hours after the verdict, prior to discussing the jury deliberation or verdict with a member of a jury pursuant to subdivision (b), the defendant or his or her attorney or representative, or the prosecutor or his or her representative, shall inform the juror of the identity of the case, the party in that case which the person represents, the subject of the interview, the absolute right of the juror to discuss or not discuss the deliberations or verdict in the case with the person, and the juror's right to review and have a copy of any declaration filed with the court.

(d) Any unreasonable contact with a juror by the defendant, or his or her attorney or representative, or by the prosecutor, or his or her representative, without the juror's consent shall be immediately reported to the trial judge.

(e) Any violation of this section shall be considered a violation of a lawful court order and shall be subject to reasonable monetary sanctions. . . .

§284. Change or Substitution; Consent; Order of Court

The attorney in an action or special proceeding may be changed at any time before or after judgment or final determination, as follows:

(1) Upon the consent of both client and attorney, filed with the clerk, or entered upon the minutes.

(2) Upon the order of the court, upon the application of either client or attorney, after notice from one to the other.

§1282.4. Representation by Counsel

Editors' Note. In *Birbrower, Montalbano, Condon & Frank v. Superior Court*, 17 Cal. 4th 119 (1998), the California Supreme Court partially affirmed summary judgment denying legal fees to a New York law firm that had performed legal services in California for a California client in preparation for a California arbitration proceeding based on California law. The basis for denying fees was that the New York lawyers were not licensed to practice law in California as required by §6125 of the California Business and Professions Code. In response to *Birbrower*, the California Legislature soon amended §1282.4 of the California Code of Civil Procedure, which effectively overruled *Birbrower* and permitted out-of-state attorneys who meet certain conditions to appear in arbitration proceedings conducted in California — essentially a *pro hac vice* rule for arbitration proceedings.

Reflecting the controversial nature of the issue, §1282.4 has been scheduled to expire several times. Its expiration date was most recently extended in 2010, and it is now scheduled to expire on January 1, 2013. For this reason, §1282.4 contains two separate "sections," both of which are reprinted below: (1) the lengthy version of §1282.4 that will be in effect until January 1, 2013; and (2) the two-paragraph version of §1282.4 that will automatically take effect on January 1, 2013, unless the Legislature amends or extends the current version of §1282.4 before that date. (For more information about the enforcement concerns associated with this provision, see the Editors' Note on p. 768 of the 2006 edition of this book.)

In a related development, in 1999, the California Supreme Court adopted Rule 983.4 of the California Rules of Court to reinforce and amplify §1282.4. Effective January 1, 2007, the courts amended the rule and renumbered it as Rule 9.43. We reprint the amended rule in an Editors' Note immediately after §1282.4.

In another related development, the California Supreme Court adopted a series of new court rules in 2004 that govern temporary practice in California by four specific categories of out-of-state lawyers. These rules include Rule

9.47 (originally Rule 966), entitled "Attorneys Practicing Law Temporarily in California as Part of Litigation," which defines "litigation" to include "arbitration." Rule 9.47 is reprinted following Rule 1-300 (Unauthorized Practice of Law) in the California Rules of Professional Conduct portion of this book.

SEC. 1. (a) A party to the arbitration has the right to be represented by an attorney at any proceeding or hearing in arbitration under this title. A waiver of this right may be revoked; but if a party revokes such waiver, the other party is entitled to a reasonable continuance for the purpose of procuring an attorney.

(b) Notwithstanding any other provision of law, including Section 6125 of the Business and Professions Code, an attorney admitted to the bar of any other state may represent the parties in the course of, or in connection with, an arbitration proceeding in this state, provided that the attorney, if not admitted to the State Bar of California, satisfies all of the following:

(1) He or she timely serves the certificate described in subdivision (c).

(2) The attorney's appearance is approved in writing on that certificate by the arbitrator, the arbitrators, or the arbitral forum.

(3) The certificate bearing approval of the attorney's appearance is filed with the State Bar of California and served on the parties as described in this section.

(c) Within a reasonable period of time after the attorney described in subdivision (b) indicates an intention to appear in the arbitration, the attorney shall serve a certificate in a form prescribed by the State Bar of California on the arbitrator, arbitrators, or arbitral forum, the State Bar of California, and all other parties and counsel in the arbitration whose addresses are known to the attorney. The certificate shall state all of the following:

(1) The case name and number, and the name of the arbitrator, arbitrators, or arbitral forum assigned to the proceeding in which the attorney seeks to appear.

(2) The attorney's residence and office address.

(3) The courts before which the attorney has been admitted to practice and the dates of admission.

(4) That the attorney is currently a member in good standing of, and eligible to practice law before, the bar of those courts.

(5) That the attorney is not currently on suspension or disbarred from the practice of law before the bar of any court.

(6) That the attorney is not a resident of the State of California.

(7) That the attorney is not regularly employed in the State of California.

(8) That the attorney is not regularly engaged in substantial business, professional, or other activities in the State of California.

(9) That the attorney agrees to be subject to the jurisdiction of the courts of this state with respect to the law of this state governing the conduct of attorneys to the same extent as a member of the State Bar of California.

(10) The title of the court and the cause in which the attorney has filed an application to appear as counsel pro hac vice in this state or filed a certificate pursuant to this section in the preceding two years, the date of each application or certificate, and whether or not it was granted. If the attorney has made repeated appearances, the certificate shall reflect the special circumstances that warrant the approval of the attorney's appearance in the arbitration.

(11) The name, address, and telephone number of the active member of the State Bar of California who is the attorney of record.

(d) The arbitrator, arbitrators, or arbitral forum may approve the attorney's appearance if the attorney has complied with subdivision (c). Failure to timely file and serve the certificate described in subdivision (c) shall be grounds for disapproval of the appearance and disqualification from serving as an attorney in the arbitration in which the certificate was filed. In the absence of special circumstances, repeated appearances shall be grounds for disapproval of the appearance and disqualification from serving as an attorney in the arbitration in which the certificate was filed.

(e) Within a reasonable period of time after the arbitrator, arbitrators, or arbitral forum approves the certificate, the attorney shall file the certificate with the State Bar of California and serve the certificate as described in Section 1013a on all parties and counsel in the arbitration whose address is known to the attorney.

(f) An attorney who fails to file or serve the certificate required by this section or files or serves a certificate containing false information or who otherwise fails to comply with the standards of professional conduct required of members of the State Bar of California shall be subject to the disciplinary jurisdiction of the State Bar with respect to that certificate or any of his or her acts occurring in the course of the arbitration.

(g) Notwithstanding any other provision of law, including Section 6125 of the Business and Professions Code, an attorney who is a member in good standing of the bar of any state may represent the parties in connection with rendering legal services in this state in the course of and in connection with an arbitration pending in another state.

(h) Notwithstanding any other provision of law, including Section 6125 of the Business and Professions Code, any party to an arbitration arising under collective bargaining agreements in industries and provisions subject to either state or federal law may be represented in the course of, and in connection with, those proceedings by any person, regardless of whether that person is licensed to practice law in this state.

(i) Nothing in this section shall apply to Division 4 (commencing with Section 3201) of the Labor Code.

(j)(1) In enacting the amendments to this section made by Assembly Bill 2086 of the 1997-98 Regular Session, it is the intent of the Legislature to respond to the holding in Birbrower v. Superior Court (1998) 17 Cal. 4th 117, *as modified at* 17 Cal. 4th 643a (hereafter *Birbrower*), to provide a procedure for nonresident attorneys who are not licensed in this state to appear in California arbitration proceedings.

(2) In enacting subdivision (h), it is the intent of the Legislature to make clear that any party to an arbitration arising under a collective bargaining agreement governed by the laws of this state may be represented in the course of and in connection with those proceedings by any person regardless of whether that person is licensed to practice law in this state.

(3) Except as otherwise specifically provided in this section, in enacting the amendments to this section made by Assembly Bill 2086 of the 1997-98 Regular Session, it is the Legislature's intent that nothing in this section is intended to expand or restrict the ability of a party prior to the decision in *Birbrower* to elect to be represented by any person in a nonjudicial arbitration proceeding, to the extent those rights or abilities existed prior to that decision. To the extent that *Birbrower* is interpreted to expand or restrict that right or ability pursuant to the laws of this state, it is hereby abrogated except as specifically provided in this section.

(4) In enacting subdivision (i), it is the intent of the Legislature to make clear that nothing in this section shall affect those provisions of law governing the right of injured workers to elect to be represented by any person, regardless of whether that person is licensed to practice law in this state, as set forth in Division 4 (commencing with Section 3200) of the Labor Code.

(k) This section shall be operative until January 1, 2013, and on that date shall be repealed.

Editors' Note. The following version of §1282.4 will take effect on January 1, 2013, unless the California Legislature amends or extends the expiration date of the version that appears above.

SEC. 2. (a) A party to the arbitration has the right to be represented by an attorney at any proceeding or hearing in arbitration under this title. A waiver of this right may be revoked; but if a party revokes the waiver, the other party is entitled to a reasonable continuance for the purpose of procuring an attorney.

(b) This section shall become operative on January 1, 2013.

Editors' Note. In 1999, to reinforce and clarify §1282.4, the California Supreme Court promulgated Rule 983.4 of the California Rules of Court. Effective January 1, 2007, the courts renumbered the rule as Rule 9.43 and amended the rule to provide as follows:

Rule 9.43. Out-of-State Attorney Arbitration Counsel

(a) *Definition.* An "out-of-state attorney arbitration counsel" is an attorney who is:

(1) Not a member of the State Bar of California but who is a member in good standing of and eligible to practice before the bar of any United States court or the highest court in any state, territory, or insular possession of the United States, and who has been retained to appear in the course of, or in connection with, an arbitration proceeding in this state;

(2) Has served a certificate in accordance with the requirements of Code of Civil Procedure section 1282.4 on the arbitrator, the arbitrators, or the arbitral forum, the State Bar of California, and all other parties and counsel in the arbitration whose addresses are known to the attorney; and

(3) Whose appearance has been approved by the arbitrator, the arbitrators, or the arbitral forum.

(b) *State Bar Out-of-State Attorney Arbitration Counsel Program.* The State Bar of California must establish and administer a program to implement the State Bar of California's responsibilities under Code of Civil Procedure section 1282.4. The State Bar of California's program may be operative only as long as the applicable provisions of Code of Civil Procedure section 1282.4 remain in effect.

(c) *Eligibility to appear as an out-of-state attorney arbitration counsel.* To be eligible to appear as an out-of-state attorney arbitration counsel, an attorney must comply with all of the applicable provisions of Code of Civil Procedure section 1282.4 and the requirements of this rule and the related rules and regulations adopted by the State Bar of California.

(d) *Discipline.* An out-of-state attorney arbitration counsel who files a certificate containing false information or who otherwise fails to comply with the standards of professional conduct required of members of the State Bar of California is subject to the disciplinary jurisdiction of the State Bar with respect to any of his or her acts occurring in the course of the arbitration.

(e) *Disqualification.* Failure to timely file and serve a certificate or, absent special circumstances, appearances in multiple separate arbitration matters are grounds for disqualification from serving in the arbitration in which the certificate was filed.

(f) *Fee.* Out-of-state attorney arbitration counsel must pay a reasonable fee not exceeding $50 to the State Bar of California with the copy of the certificate that is served on the State Bar.

(g) *Inherent power of Supreme Court.* Nothing in these rules may be construed as affecting the power of the Supreme Court to exercise its inherent jurisdiction over the practice of law in California.

§2018.010.   "Client" Defined

For purposes of this chapter, "client" means a "client" as defined in Section 951 of the Evidence Code.

§2018.020.   Policy of the State

It is the policy of the state to do both of the following:

(a) Preserve the rights of attorneys to prepare cases for trial with that degree of privacy necessary to encourage them to prepare their cases thoroughly and to investigate not only the favorable but the unfavorable aspects of those cases.

(b) Prevent attorneys from taking undue advantage of their adversary's industry and efforts.

§2018.030. Writings and Written Documentation

(a) A writing that reflects an attorney's impressions, conclusions, opinions, or legal research or theories is not discoverable under any circumstances.

(b) The work product of an attorney, other than a writing described in subdivision (a), is not discoverable unless the court determines that denial of discovery will unfairly prejudice the party seeking discovery in preparing that party's claim or defense or will result in an injustice.

§2018.040. Restatement of Existing Law

This chapter is intended to be a restatement of existing law relating to protection of work product. It is not intended to expand or reduce the extent to which work product is discoverable under existing law in any action.

§2018.050. Participation in Crime or Fraud

Notwithstanding Section 2018.040, when a lawyer is suspected of knowingly participating in a crime or fraud, there is no protection of work product under this chapter in any official investigation by a law enforcement agency or proceeding or action brought by a public prosecutor in the name of the people of the State of California if the services of the lawyer were sought or obtained to enable or aid anyone to commit or plan to commit a crime or fraud.

§2018.060. In Camera Hearings

Nothing in this chapter is intended to limit an attorney's ability to request an in camera hearing as provided for in People v. Superior Court (Laff) (2001) 25 Cal. 4th 703.

§2018.070. Disciplinary Proceedings

(a) The State Bar may discover the work product of an attorney against whom disciplinary charges are pending when it is relevant to issues of breach of duty by the lawyer and requisite client approval has been granted.

(b) Where requested and for good cause, discovery under this section shall be subject to a protective order to ensure the confidentiality of the work product except for its use by the State Bar in disciplinary investigations and its consideration under seal in State Bar Court proceedings.

(c) For purposes of this chapter, whenever a client has initiated a complaint against an attorney, the requisite client approval shall be deemed to have been granted.

§2018.080   Breach of Duty; Actions Against Attorney by Client or Former Client

In an action between an attorney and a client or a former client of the attorney, no work product privilege under this chapter exists if the work product is relevant to an issue of breach by the attorney of a duty to the client arising out of the attorney-client relationship.

CALIFORNIA EVIDENCE CODE

§911.   General Rule as to Privileges

Except as otherwise provided by statute:
(a) No person has a privilege to refuse to be a witness.
(b) No person has a privilege to refuse to disclose any matter or to refuse to produce any writing, object, or other thing.
(c) No person has a privilege that another shall not be a witness or shall not disclose any matter or shall not produce any writing, object, or other thing.

§912.   Waiver of Privilege

(a) Except as otherwise provided in this section, the right of any person to claim a privilege provided by Section 954 (lawyer-client privilege), 980 (privilege for confidential marital communications), 994 (physician-patient privilege), 1014 (psychotherapist-patient privilege), 1033 (privilege of penitent), 1034 (privilege of clergyman), or 1035.8 (sexual assault counselor-victim privilege), or 1037.5 (domestic violence victim-counselor privilege), is waived with respect to a communication protected by the privilege if any holder of the privilege, without coercion, has disclosed a significant part of the communication or has consented to disclosure made by anyone. Consent to disclosure is manifested by any statement or other conduct of the holder of the privilege indicating consent to the disclosure, including failure to claim the privilege in any proceeding in which the holder has the legal standing and opportunity to claim the privilege.

(b) Where two or more persons are joint holders of a privilege provided by Section 954 (lawyer-client privilege), 994 (physician-patient privilege), 1014 (psychotherapist-patient privilege), 1035.8 (sexual assault counselor-victim privilege), or 1037.5 (domestic violence counselor-victim privilege), a waiver of the right of a particular joint holder of the privilege to claim the privilege does not affect the right of another joint holder to claim the privilege. In the case of the privilege provided by Section 980 (privilege for confidential marital communications), a waiver of the right of one spouse to claim the privilege does not affect the right of the other spouse to claim the privilege.

(c) A disclosure that is itself privileged is not a waiver of any privilege.

(d) A disclosure in confidence of a communication that is protected by a privilege provided by Section 954 (lawyer-client privilege), 994 (physician-patient privilege), 1014 (psychotherapist-patient privilege), 1035.8 (sexual assault counselor-victim privilege), or 1037.5 (domestic violence counselor-victim privilege) when disclosure is reasonably necessary for the accomplishment of the purpose for which the lawyer, physician, psychotherapist, sexual assault counselor, or domestic violence counselor was consulted, is not a waiver of the privilege.

§915. Disclosure of Privileged Information or Attorney Work Product in Ruling on Claim of Privilege

(a) Subject to subdivision (b), the presiding officer may not require disclosure of information claimed to be privileged under this division or attorney work product under subdivision (a) of Section 2018.030 of the Code of Civil Procedure in order to rule on the claim of privilege; provided, however, that in any hearing conducted pursuant to subdivision (c) of Section 1524 of the Penal Code in which a claim of privilege is made and the court determines that there is no other feasible means to rule on the validity of the claim other than to require disclosure, the court shall proceed in accordance with subdivision (b).

(b) When a court is ruling on a claim of privilege . . . under subdivision (b) of Section 2018.030 of the Code of Civil Procedure (attorney work product) and is unable to do so without requiring disclosure of the information claimed to be privileged, the court may require the person from whom disclosure is sought or the person authorized to claim the privilege, or both, to disclose the information in chambers out of the presence and hearing of all persons except the person authorized to claim the privilege and any other persons as the person authorized to claim the privilege is willing to have present. If the judge determines that the information is privileged, neither the judge nor any other person may ever disclose, without the consent of a person authorized to permit disclosure, what was disclosed in the course of the proceedings in chambers.

§917. Presumption That Certain Communications Are Confidential; Privileged Character of Electronic Communications

(a) If a privilege is claimed on the ground that the matter sought to be disclosed is a communication made in confidence in the course of the lawyer-client, physician-patient, psychotherapist-patient, clergy-penitent, husband-wife, sexual assault counselor-victim, or domestic violence counselor-victim relationship, the communication is presumed to have been made in confidence and the opponent of the claim of privilege has the burden of proof to establish that the communication was not confidential.

(b) A communication between persons in a relationship listed in subdivision (a) does not lose its privileged character for the sole reason that it is communicated by electronic means or because persons involved in the delivery, facilitation, or storage of electronic communication may have access to the content of the communication.

(c) For purposes of this section, "electronic" has the same meaning provided in Section 1633.2 of the Civil Code.

§950. "Lawyer"

As used in this article, "lawyer" means a person authorized, or reasonably believed by the client to be authorized, to practice law in any state or nation.

§951. "Client"

As used in this article, "client" means a person who, directly or through an authorized representative, consults a lawyer for the purpose of retaining the lawyer or securing legal service or advice from him in his professional capacity, and includes an incompetent (a) who himself so consults the lawyer or (b) whose guardian or conservator so consults the lawyer in behalf of the incompetent.

§952. "Confidential Communication Between Client and Lawyer"

As used in this article, "confidential communication between client and lawyer" means information transmitted between a client and his or her lawyer in the course of that relationship and in confidence by a means which, so far as the client is aware, discloses the information to no third persons other than those who are present to further the interest of the client in the consultation or those to whom disclosure is reasonably necessary for the transmission of the information or the accomplishment of the purpose for which the lawyer is consulted, and includes a legal opinion formed and the advice given by the lawyer in the course of that relationship.

§953. "Holder of the Privilege"

As used in this article, "holder of the privilege" means:

(a) The client, if the client has no guardian or conservator.

(b) A guardian or conservator of the client, if the client has a guardian or conservator.

(c) The personal representative of the client if the client is dead, including a personal representative appointed pursuant to Section 12252 of the Probate Code.

(d) A successor, assign, trustee in dissolution, or any similar representative of a firm, association, organization, partnership, business trust, corporation, or public entity that is no longer in existence.

§954. Lawyer-Client Privilege

Subject to Section 912 and except as otherwise provided in this article, the client, whether or not a party, has a privilege to refuse to disclose, and to prevent another from disclosing, a confidential communication between client and lawyer if the privilege is claimed by:

(a) The holder of the privilege;

(b) A person who is authorized to claim the privilege by the holder of the privilege; or

(c) The person who was the lawyer at the time of the confidential communication, but such person may not claim the privilege if there is no holder of the privilege in existence or if he is otherwise instructed by a person authorized to permit disclosure.

The relationship of attorney and client shall exist between a law corporation as defined in Article 10 (commencing with Section 6160) of Chapter 4 of Division 3 of the Business and Professions Code and the persons to whom it renders professional services, as well as between such persons and members of the State Bar employed by such corporation to render services to such persons. The word "persons" as used in this subdivision includes partnerships, corporations, limited liability companies, associations and other groups and entities.

§955. When Lawyer Required to Claim Privilege

The lawyer who received or made a communication subject to the privilege under this article shall claim the privilege whenever he is present when the communication is sought to be disclosed and is authorized to claim the privilege under subdivision (c) of Section 954.

§956. Exception: Crime or Fraud

There is no privilege under this article if the services of the lawyer were sought or obtained to enable or aid anyone to commit or plan to commit a crime or a fraud.

§956.5. Reasonable Belief That Disclosure of Confidential Communication Is Necessary to Prevent Criminal Act Resulting in Death or Bodily Harm; Exception to Privilege

There is no privilege under this article if the lawyer reasonably believes that disclosure of any confidential communication relating to representation of a client is necessary to prevent a criminal act that the lawyer reasonably believes is likely to result in death of, or substantial bodily harm to, an individual.

§957. Exception: Parties Claiming Through Deceased Client

There is no privilege under this article as to a communication relevant to an issue between parties all of whom claim through a deceased client, regardless of whether the claims are by testate or intestate succession, nonprobate transfer, or inter vivos transaction.

§958. Exception: Breach of Duty Arising out of Lawyer-Client Relationship

There is no privilege under this article as to a communication relevant to an issue of breach, by the lawyer or by the client, of a duty arising out of the lawyer-client relationship.

§959.   Exception: Lawyer as Attesting Witness

There is no privilege under this article as to a communication relevant to an issue concerning the intention or competence of a client executing an attested document of which the lawyer is an attesting witness, or concerning the execution or attestation of such a document.

§960.   Exception: Intention of Deceased Client Concerning Writing Affecting Property Interest

There is no privilege under this article as to a communication relevant to an issue concerning the intention of a client, now deceased, with respect to a deed of conveyance, will, or other writing, executed by the client, purporting to affect an interest in property.

§961.   Exception: Validity of Writing Affecting Property Interest

There is no privilege under this article as to a communication relevant to an issue concerning the validity of a deed of conveyance, will, or other writing, executed by a client, now deceased, purporting to affect an interest in property.

§962.   Exception: Joint Clients

Where two or more clients have retained or consulted a lawyer upon a matter of common interest, none of them, nor the successor in interest of any of them, may claim a privilege under this article as to a communication made in the course of that relationship when such communication is offered in a civil proceeding between one of such clients (or his successor in interest) and another of such clients (or his successor in interest).

District of Columbia Materials

District of Columbia Rules of Professional Conduct

Editors' Introduction. The District of Columbia Rules of Professional Conduct were first adopted by the D.C. Court of Appeals in 1990 and have been amended several times since then. Except for minor amendments to Rules 1.15 and 6.1 in 2011, the most recent amendments, which comprehensively revised the rules, took effect on August 1, 2010, and February 1, 2007. In adopting the 2007 amendments, the D.C. Court of Appeals accepted nearly all of the recommendations of a Rules of Professional Conduct Review Committee chaired by Professor Leah Wortham of Catholic University's Columbus School of Law. These rules have not been amended since our last edition went to press in October 2011. (We reprint the D.C. Rules without its table of contents because it is almost identical to the table of contents of the ABA Model Rules of Professional Conduct.) The 2010 amendment made changes to Rule 1.15.

The District of Columbia's rules, both before and after the 2007 amendments, track the ABA Model Rules in many places, but they also differ from them in significant ways. For example, both the text and comments of D.C.'s provisions governing core issues such as confidentiality, conflicts of interest, and candor to the court are lengthier and more detailed than their counterparts in the ABA Model Rules. At the same time, D.C.'s provisions governing advertising are far less detailed than their ABA counterparts—for example, D.C. has no equivalent to ABA Model Rules 7.2, 7.3, or 7.4. (In our Selected State Variations following the ABA Model Rules of Professional Conduct, we identify each D.C. rule that differs significantly from the corresponding ABA Model Rule.)

In a development closely related to the Rules of Professional Conduct, the D.C. Bar's Special Committee on Multijurisdictional Practice (the "MJP Committee") issued a report in Fall 2004 recommending that the D.C. Court of Appeals significantly amend the court's Rule 49, which governs the unauthorized practice of law. The amendments would bring Rule 49 more closely into line with ABA Model Rule 5.5 (Unauthorized Practice of Law;

Multijurisdictional Practice of Law) and ABA Model Rule 8.5 (Disciplinary Authority; Choice of Law). The MJP Committee was chaired by attorney James J. Sandman of Arnold & Porter. (We reprint substantial excerpts from the current version of Rule 49 after D.C. Rule 5.5 below.) The report is available online at *www.dcbar.org/inside_the_bar/structure/reports* (look for the heading "Special Committee on Multijurisdictional Practice"). In June 2007, the Board of Governors of the D.C. Bar submitted its own report on multijurisdictional practice to the D.C. Court of Appeals.

In March 2008, the court amended Rule 49 in response to the recommendation. See *www.dcappeals.gov/dccourts/docs/orders/M-231-07-DCAppR49 CompareVersion.pdf* and *www.dcappeals.gov/dccourts/docs/orders/M-231-07_2008-03-20.pdf.*

In another development, in 2003 the D.C. Court of Appeals established a special Disciplinary System Study Committee (the "DSS Committee"). The DSS Committee issued a report in February 2006 recommending major changes to D.C.'s lawyer disciplinary system. The report recommends nine separate changes that go far beyond concerns about expanding the disciplinary system to deal with lawyers who engage in multijurisdictional practice. The DSS Committee was chaired by former D.C. Bar President John Payton of WilmerHale. The DSS Committee's full 166-page report is available online at *www.dcbar.org/inside_the_bar/structure/reports* (look for the heading "Disciplinary System Study Committee").

In April 2008, the D.C. Court of Appeals responded to the Committee's recommendations. See *http://www.dcbar.org/inside_the_bar/structure/bar_rules/rule11.cfm.*

In 2010, the D.C. Bar was weighing a proposal to amend D.C. Rule 1.10 to allow screening of lateral lawyers who move between private practice settings. Comments on the proposed changes were received through August 2010. Progress on this proposal since then, if any, can be found by visiting the D.C. Bar website, *www.dcbar.org*, and following the links to legal ethics.

Updates on the District of Columbia Rules of Professional Conduct and full copies of the reports of the Rules of Professional Conduct Review Committee, the Special Committee on Multijurisdictional Practice, and the Disciplinary System Study Committee can also be found by visiting the District's website at *www.dcbar.org.*

SCOPE

[1] The Rules of Professional Conduct (Rules) are rules of reason. They should be interpreted with reference to the purposes of legal representation and of the law itself. Some of the Rules are imperatives, cast in the terms "shall" or "shall not." These define proper conduct for purposes of professional discipline. Others, generally cast in the term "may," are permissive and define areas under the Rules in which the lawyer has professional discretion. No disciplinary action should be taken when the lawyer chooses not to act or acts within the bounds of such discretion. Other Rules define the nature of relationships between the lawyer and others. The Rules are thus partly obligatory and disciplinary and partly constitutive and descriptive in

that they define a lawyer's professional role. Many of the Comments use the term "should." Comments do not add obligations to the Rules but provide guidance for interpreting the Rules and practicing in compliance with them.

[2] The Rules presuppose a larger legal context shaping the lawyer's role. That context includes court rules and statutes relating to matters of licensure, laws defining specific obligations of lawyers, and substantive and procedural law in general. Compliance with the Rules, as with all law in an open society, depends primarily upon understanding and voluntary compliance, secondarily upon reinforcement by peer and public opinion, and finally, when necessary, upon enforcement through disciplinary proceedings. The Rules do not, however, exhaust the moral and ethical considerations that should inform a lawyer, for no worthwhile human activity can be completely defined by legal rules. The Rules simply provide a framework for the ethical practice of law.

[3] Failure to comply with an obligation or prohibition imposed by a rule is a basis for invoking the disciplinary process. The Rules presuppose that disciplinary assessment of a lawyer's conduct will be made on the basis of the facts and circumstances as they existed at the time of the conduct in question and in recognition of the fact that a lawyer often has to act upon uncertain or incomplete evidence of the situation. Moreover, the Rules presuppose that whether or not discipline should be imposed for a violation, and the severity of a sanction, depend on all the circumstances, such as the willfulness and seriousness of the violation, extenuating factors and whether there have been previous violations.

[4] Nothing in these Rules, the Comments associated with them, or this Scope section is intended to enlarge or restrict existing law regarding the liability of lawyers to others or the requirements that the testimony of expert witnesses or other modes of proof must be employed in determining the scope of a lawyer's duty to others. Moreover, nothing in the Rules or associated Comments or this Scope section is intended to confer rights on an adversary of a lawyer to enforce the Rules in a proceeding other than a disciplinary proceeding. Some judicial decisions have considered the standard of conduct established in these Rules in determining the standard of care applicable in a proceeding other than a disciplinary proceeding. A tribunal presented with claims that the conduct of a lawyer appearing before that tribunal requires, for example, disqualification of the lawyer and/or the lawyer's firm may take such action as seems appropriate in the circumstances, which may or may not involve disqualification.

[5] In interpreting these Rules, the specific shall control the general in the sense that any rule that specifically addresses conduct shall control the disposition of matters and the outcome of such matters shall not turn upon the application of a more general rule that arguably also applies to the conduct in question. In a number of instances, there are specific rules that address specific types of conduct. The rule of interpretation expressed here is meant to make it clear that the general rule does not supplant, amend, enlarge, or extend the specific rule. So, for instance, the general terms of Rule 1.3 are not intended to govern conflicts of interest, which are particularly discussed in Rules 1.7, 1.8, and 1.9. Thus, conduct that is proper under the specific conflicts rules is not improper under the more general rule of Rule 1.3. Except where the principle of priority stated here is applicable, however, compliance with one rule does not generally excuse compliance with other rules. Accordingly, once a lawyer has analyzed the ethical considerations under a given

rule, the lawyer must generally extend the analysis to ensure compliance with all other applicable rules.

[6] The Comment accompanying each Rule explains and illustrates the meaning and purpose of the Rule. This note on Scope provides general orientation and general rules of interpretation. The Comments are intended as guides to interpretation, but the text of each Rule is controlling.

TERMINOLOGY

(a) "Belief" or "believes" denotes that the person involved actually supposed the fact in question to be true. A person's belief may be inferred from circumstances.

(b) "Consult" or "consultation" denotes communication of information reasonably sufficient to permit the client to appreciate the significance of the matter in question.

(c) "Firm" or "law firm" denotes a lawyer or lawyers in a law partnership, professional corporation, sole proprietorship or other association authorized to practice law; or lawyers employed in a legal services organization or the legal department of a corporation or other organization, but does not include a government agency or other government entity. *See* Comment, Rule 1.10.

(d) "Fraud" or "fraudulent" denotes conduct that is fraudulent under the substantive or procedural law of the applicable jurisdiction and has a purpose to deceive.

(e) "Informed consent" denotes the agreement by a person to a proposed course of conduct after the lawyer has communicated adequate information and explanation about the material risks of and reasonably available alternatives to the proposed course of conduct.

(f) "Knowingly," "known," or "knows" denotes actual knowledge of the fact in question. A person's knowledge may be inferred from circumstances.

(g) "Law clerk" denotes a person, typically a recent law school graduate, who acts, typically for a limited period, as confidential assistant to a judge or judges of a court; to an administrative law judge or a similar administrative hearing officer; or to the head of a governmental agency or to a member of a governmental commission, either of which has authority to adjudicate or to promulgate rules or regulations of general application.

(h) "Matter" means any litigation, administrative proceeding, lobbying activity, application, claim, investigation, arrest, charge or accusation, the drafting of a contract, a negotiation, estate or family relations practice issue, or any other representation, except as expressly limited in a particular rule.

(i) "Partner" denotes a member of a partnership, a shareholder in a law firm organized as a professional corporation or professional limited liability company, or a member of an association authorized to practice law.

(j) "Reasonable" or "reasonably" when used in relation to conduct by a lawyer denotes the conduct of a reasonably prudent and competent lawyer.

(k) "Reasonably should know" when used in reference to a lawyer denotes that a lawyer of reasonable prudence and competence would ascertain the matter in question.

(l) "Screened" denotes the isolation of a lawyer from any participation in a matter through the timely imposition of procedures within a firm that are reasonably adequate under the circumstances to protect information that the isolated lawyer is obligated to protect under these Rules or other law.

(m) "Substantial" when used in reference to degree or extent denotes a material matter of clear and weighty importance.

(n) "Tribunal" denotes a court, an arbitrator in a binding arbitration proceeding, or a legislative body, administrative agency, or other body acting in an adjudicative capacity. A legislative body, administrative agency or other body acts in an adjudicative capacity when a neutral official, after the presentation of evidence or legal argument by a party or parties, will render a binding legal judgment directly affecting a party's interests in a particular matter.

(o) "Writing" or "written" denotes a tangible or electronic record of a communication or representation, including handwriting, typewriting, printing, photo stating, photography, audio or video recording, and e-mail. A "signed" writing includes an electronic sound, symbol or process attached to or logically associated with a writing and executed or adopted by a person with the intent to sign the writing.

COMMENT

"Fraud" or "fraudulent"

[1] When used in these Rules, the terms "fraud" or "fraudulent" refer to conduct that is characterized as such under the substantive or procedural law of the applicable jurisdiction and has a purpose to deceive. This does not include merely negligent misrepresentation or negligent failure to apprise another of relevant information. For purposes of these Rules, it is not necessary that anyone has suffered damages or relied on the misrepresentation or failure to inform.

"Informed consent"

[2] Many of the Rules of Professional Conduct require the lawyer to obtain the informed consent of a client or other person (e.g., a former client or, under certain circumstances, a prospective client) before accepting or continuing representation or pursuing a course of conduct. *See, e.g.,* Rules 1.2(c), 1.6(e) and 1.7(c)(1). The communication necessary to obtain such consent will vary according to the Rule involved and the circumstances giving rise to the need to obtain informed consent. The lawyer must make reasonable efforts to ensure that the client or other person possesses information reasonably adequate to make an informed decision. Ordinarily, this will require communication that includes a disclosure of the facts and circumstances giving rise to the situation, any explanation reasonably necessary to inform the client or other person of the material advantages and disadvantages of the proposed course of conduct and a discussion of the client's or other person's options and alternatives. In some circumstances it may be appropriate for a lawyer to advise a client or other person to seek the advice of other counsel. A lawyer need

not inform a client or other person of facts or implications already known to the client or other person; nevertheless, a lawyer who does not personally inform the client or other person assumes the risk that the client or other person is inadequately informed and the consent is invalid. In determining whether the information and explanation provided are reasonably adequate, relevant factors include whether the client or other person is experienced in legal matters generally and in making decisions of the type involved, and whether the client or other person is independently represented by other counsel in giving the consent. Normally, such persons need less information and explanation than others, and generally a client or other person who is independently represented by other counsel in giving the consent should be assumed to have given informed consent. In all circumstances, the client's consent must be not only informed but also uncoerced by the lawyer or by any other person acting on the lawyer's behalf.

[3] Obtaining informed consent will usually require an affirmative response by the client or other person. In general, a lawyer may not assume consent from a client's or other person's silence. Consent may be inferred, however, from the conduct of a client or other person who has reasonably adequate information about the matter. A number of Rules require that a person's consent be in writing. *See* Rules 1.8(a)(3) and 1.8(g). For a definition of "writing," *see* Rule 1.0(o).

"Screened"

[4] This definition applies to situations where screening of a personally disqualified lawyer is permitted to remove imputation of a conflict of interest under Rules 1.11, 1.12 or 1.18.

[5] The purpose of screening is to assure the affected parties that confidential information known by the personally disqualified lawyer remains protected. The personally disqualified lawyer should acknowledge the obligation not to communicate with any of the other lawyers in the firm with respect to the matter. Similarly, other lawyers in the firm who are working on the matter should be informed that the screening is in place and that they may not communicate with the personally disqualified lawyer with respect to the matter. Additional screening measures that are appropriate for the particular matter will depend upon the circumstances. To implement, reinforce and remind all affected lawyers of the presence of the screening, it may be appropriate for the firm to undertake such procedures as a written undertaking by the screened lawyer to avoid any communication with other firm personnel and any contact with any firm files or other materials relating to the matter, written notice and instructions to all other firm personnel forbidding any communication with the screened lawyer relating to the matter, denial of access by the screened lawyer to firm files or other materials relating to the matter and periodic reminders of the screen to the screened lawyer and all other firm personnel. For a further explanation of screening, *see* D.C. Bar Legal Ethics Committee Opinion 279.

[6] In order to be effective, screening measures must be implemented as soon as practical after a lawyer or law firm knows or reasonably should know that there is a need for screening.

CLIENT-LAWYER RELATIONSHIP

Rule 1.1. Competence

(a) A lawyer shall provide competent representation to a client. Competent representation requires the legal knowledge, skill, thoroughness, and preparation reasonably necessary for the representation.

(b) A lawyer shall serve a client with skill and care commensurate with that generally afforded to clients by other lawyers in similar matters.

COMMENT

Legal Knowledge and Skill

[1] In determining whether a lawyer employs the requisite knowledge and skill in a particular matter, relevant factors include the relative complexity and specialized nature of the matter, the lawyer's general experience, the lawyer's training and experience in the field in question, the preparation and study the lawyer is able to give the matter, and whether it is feasible to refer the matter to, or associate or consult with, a lawyer of established competence in the field in question. In many instances, the required proficiency is that of a general practitioner. Expertise in a particular field of law may be required in some circumstances. One such circumstance would be where the lawyer, by representations made to the client, has led the client reasonably to expect a special level of expertise in the matter undertaken by the lawyer.

[2] A lawyer need not necessarily have special training or prior experience to handle legal problems of a type with which the lawyer is unfamiliar. A newly admitted lawyer can be as competent as a practitioner with long experience. Some important legal skills, such as the analysis of precedent, the evaluation of evidence, and legal drafting, are required in all legal problems. Perhaps the most fundamental legal skill consists of determining what kind of legal problems a situation may involve, a skill that necessarily transcends any particular specialized knowledge. A lawyer can provide adequate representation in a wholly novel field through necessary study. Competent representation can also be provided through the association of a lawyer of established competence in the field in question.

[3] In an emergency a lawyer may give advice or assistance in a matter in which the lawyer does not have the skill ordinarily required where referral to or consultation or association with another lawyer would be impractical. Even in an emergency, however, assistance should be limited to that reasonably necessary in the circumstances, for ill-considered action under emergency conditions can jeopardize the client's interest.

[4] A lawyer may accept representation where the requisite level of competence can be achieved by reasonable preparation. This applies as well to a lawyer who is appointed as counsel for an unrepresented person. *See also* Rule 6.2.

Thoroughness and Preparation

[5] Competent handling of a particular matter includes inquiry into and analysis of the factual and legal elements of the problem, and use of methods and procedures meeting the standards of competent practitioners. It also includes adequate preparation and continuing attention to the needs of the representation to assure that there is no neglect of such needs. The required attention and preparation are determined in part by what is at stake; major litigation and complex transactions ordinarily require more elaborate treatment than matters of lesser consequence.

Maintaining Competence

[6] To maintain the requisite knowledge and skill, a lawyer should keep abreast of changes in the law and its practice, and engage in such continuing study and education as may be necessary to maintain competence.

Rule 1.2.   Scope of Representation

(a) A lawyer shall abide by a client's decisions concerning the objectives of representation, subject to paragraphs (c), (d), and (e), and shall consult with the client as to the means by which they are to be pursued. A lawyer may take such action on behalf of the client as is impliedly authorized to carry out the representation. A lawyer shall abide by a client's decision whether to accept an offer of settlement of a matter. In a criminal case, the lawyer shall abide by the client's decision, after consultation with the lawyer, as to a plea to be entered, whether to waive jury trial, and whether the client will testify.

(b) A lawyer's representation of a client, including representation by appointment, does not constitute an endorsement of the client's political, economic, social, or moral views or activities.

(c) A lawyer may limit the objective of the representation if the client gives informed consent.

(d) A government lawyer's authority and control over decisions concerning the representation may, by statute or regulation, be expanded beyond the limits imposed by paragraphs (a) and (c).

(e) A lawyer shall not counsel a client to engage, or assist a client, in conduct that the lawyer knows is criminal or fraudulent, but a lawyer may discuss the legal consequences of any proposed course of conduct with a client and may counsel or assist a client to make a good-faith effort to determine the validity, scope, meaning, or application of the law.

(f) When a lawyer knows that a client expects assistance not permitted by the Rules of Professional Conduct or other law, the lawyer shall consult with the client regarding the relevant limitations on the lawyer's conduct.

COMMENT

Scope of Representation

[1] Both lawyer and client have authority and responsibility in the objectives and means of representation. The client has ultimate authority to determine the purposes to be served by legal representation, within the limits imposed by law and the lawyer's professional obligations. Within these limits, a client also has a right to consult with the lawyer about the means to be used in pursuing those objectives. At the same time, a lawyer is not required to pursue objectives or employ means simply because a client may wish that the lawyer do so. A clear distinction between objectives and means sometimes cannot be drawn, and in many cases the client-lawyer relationship partakes of a joint undertaking. In questions of means, the lawyer should assume responsibility for technical and legal tactical issues, but should defer to the client regarding such questions as the expense to be incurred and concern for third persons who might be adversely affected. Law defining the lawyer's scope of authority in litigation varies among jurisdictions.

[2] In a case in which the client appears to be suffering mental disability, the lawyer's duty to abide by the client's decisions is to be guided by reference to Rule 1.14.

Independence from Client's Views or Activities

[3] Legal representation should not be denied to people who are unable to afford legal services, or whose cause is controversial or the subject of popular disapproval. By the same token, representing a client does not constitute approval of the client's views or activities.

Services Limited in Objectives or Means

[4] The objectives or scope of services provided by the lawyer may be limited by agreement with the client or by terms under which the lawyer's services are made available to the client. For example, a retainer may be for a specifically defined purpose. Representation provided through a legal aid agency may be subject to limitations on the types of cases the agency handles. When a lawyer has been retained by an insurer to represent an insured, the representation may be limited to matters related to the insurance coverage. The terms upon which representation is undertaken may exclude specific objectives or means. Such limitations may exclude objectives or means that the lawyer regards as repugnant or imprudent. Rule 1.5(b) requires a lawyer to communicate the scope of the lawyer's representation when the lawyer establishes a new lawyer-client relationship, and it is generally prudent for the lawyer to explain in writing any limits on the objectives or scope of the lawyer's services.

[5] An agreement concerning the scope of representation must accord with the Rules of Professional Conduct and other law. Thus, the client may not be asked to agree to representation so limited in scope as to violate Rule 1.1, or to surrender

849

the right to terminate the lawyer's services or the right to settle litigation that the lawyer might wish to continue.

Criminal, Fraudulent, and Prohibited Transactions

[6] A lawyer is required to give an honest opinion about the actual consequences that appear likely to result from a client's conduct. The fact that a client uses advice in a course of action that is criminal or fraudulent does not, of itself, make a lawyer a party to the course of action. However, a lawyer may not knowingly assist a client in criminal or fraudulent conduct. There is a critical distinction between presenting an analysis of legal aspects of questionable conduct and recommending the means by which a crime or fraud might be committed with impunity.

[7] When the client's course of action has already begun and is continuing, the lawyer's responsibility is especially delicate. The lawyer is required to avoid assisting the client, for example, by drafting or delivering documents that the lawyer knows are fraudulent or by suggesting how the wrongdoing might be concealed. A lawyer may not continue assisting a client in conduct that the lawyer originally supposed was legally proper but then discovers is criminal or fraudulent. The lawyer must, therefore, withdraw from the representation of the client in the matter. *See* Rule 1.16(a). In some cases, withdrawal alone might be insufficient. It may be necessary for the lawyer to give notice of the fact of withdrawal and to disaffirm any opinion, document, affirmation or the like. *See* Rule 4.1.

[8] Where the client is a fiduciary, the lawyer may be charged with special obligations in dealings with a beneficiary.

[9] Paragraph (e) applies whether or not the defrauded party is a party to the transaction. Hence, a lawyer should not participate in a sham transaction, for example, a transaction to effectuate criminal or fraudulent escape of tax liability. Paragraph (e) does not preclude undertaking a criminal defense incident to a general retainer for legal services to a lawful enterprise. The last clause of paragraph (e) recognizes that determining the validity or interpretation of a statute or regulation may require a course of action involving disobedience of the statute or regulation or of the interpretation placed upon it by governmental authorities.

Rule 1.3.   Diligence and Zeal

(a) **A lawyer shall represent a client zealously and diligently within the bounds of the law.**

(b) **A lawyer shall not intentionally:**

(1) **Fail to seek the lawful objectives of a client through reasonably available means permitted by law and the disciplinary rules; or**

(2) **Prejudice or damage a client during the course of the professional relationship.**

(c) **A lawyer shall act with reasonable promptness in representing a client.**

COMMENT

[1] The duty of a lawyer, both to the client and to the legal system, is to represent the client zealously within the bounds of the law, including the Rules of Professional Conduct and other enforceable professional regulations, such as agency regulations applicable to lawyers practicing before the agency. This duty requires the lawyer to pursue a matter on behalf of a client despite opposition, obstruction, or personal inconvenience to the lawyer, and to take whatever lawful and ethical measures are required to vindicate a client's cause or endeavor. A lawyer should act with commitment and dedication to the interests of the client. However, a lawyer is not bound to press for every advantage that might be realized for a client. A lawyer has professional discretion in determining the means by which a matter should be pursued. *See* Rule 1.2. A lawyer's workload should be controlled so that each matter can be handled adequately.

[2] This duty derives from the lawyer's membership in a profession that has the duty of assisting members of the public to secure and protect available legal rights and benefits. In our government of laws and not of individuals, each member of our society is entitled to have such member's conduct judged and regulated in accordance with the law; to seek any lawful objective through legally permissible means; and to present for adjudication any lawful claim, issue, or defense.

[3] The bounds of the law in a given case are often difficult to ascertain. The language of legislative enactments and judicial opinions may be uncertain as applied to varying factual situations. The limits and specific meaning of apparently relevant law may be made doubtful by changing or developing constitutional interpretations, ambiguous statutes, or judicial opinions, and changing public and judicial attitudes.

[4] Where the bounds of law are uncertain, the action of a lawyer may depend on whether the lawyer is serving as advocate or adviser. A lawyer may serve simultaneously as both advocate and adviser, but the two roles are essentially different. In asserting a position on behalf of a client, an advocate for the most part deals with past conduct and must take the facts as the advocate finds them. By contrast, a lawyer serving as adviser primarily assists the client in determining the course of future conduct and relationships. While serving as advocate, a lawyer should resolve in favor of the client doubts as to the bounds of the law, but even when acting as an advocate, a lawyer may not institute or defend a proceeding unless the positions taken are not frivolous. *See* Rule 3.1. In serving a client as adviser, a lawyer, in appropriate circumstances, should give a lawyer's professional opinion as to what the ultimate decision of the courts would likely be as to the applicable law.

[5] To prevent neglect of client matters in the event that a sole practitioner ceases to practice law, each sole practitioner should prepare a plan, in conformity with applicable rules, that designates another competent lawyer to review client files, notify each client that the lawyer is no longer engaged in the practice of law, and determine whether there is a need for immediate protective action. *See* D.C. App. R. XI, §15(a) (appointment of counsel by District of Columbia Court of Appeals, on motion of Board on Professional Responsibility, where an attorney dies, disappears, or is suspended for incapacity or disability and no partner, associate or other responsible attorney is capable of conducting the attorney's affairs).

[6] In the exercise of professional judgment, a lawyer should always act in a manner consistent with the best interests of the client. However, when an action in the best interests of the client seems to be unjust, a lawyer may ask the client for permission to forgo such action. If the lawyer knows that the client expects assistance that is not in accord with the Rules of Professional Conduct or other law, the lawyer must inform the client of the pertinent limitations on the lawyer's conduct. *See* Rule 1.2(e) and (f). Similarly, the lawyer's obligation not to prejudice the interests of the client is subject to the duty of candor toward the tribunal under Rule 3.3 and the duty to expedite litigation under Rule 3.2.

[7] The duty of a lawyer to represent the client with zeal does not militate against the concurrent obligation to treat with consideration all persons involved in the legal process and to avoid the infliction of needless harm. Thus, the lawyer's duty to pursue a client's lawful objectives zealously does not prevent the lawyer from acceding to reasonable requests of opposing counsel that do not prejudice the client's rights, being punctual in fulfilling all professional commitments, avoiding offensive tactics, or treating all persons involved in the legal process with courtesy and consideration.

[8] Perhaps no professional shortcoming is more widely resented by clients than procrastination. A client's interests often can be adversely affected by the passage of time or the change of conditions; in extreme instances, as when a lawyer overlooks a statute of limitations, the client's legal position may be destroyed. Even when the client's interests are not affected in substance, however, unreasonable delay can cause a client needless anxiety and undermine confidence in the lawyer's trustworthiness. Neglect of client matters is a serious violation of the obligation of diligence.

[9] Unless the relationship is terminated as provided in Rule 1.16, a lawyer should carry through to conclusion all matters undertaken for a client. If a lawyer's employment is limited to a specific matter, the relationship terminates when the matter has been resolved. If a lawyer has served a client over a substantial period in a variety of matters, the client sometimes may assume that the lawyer will continue to serve on a continuing basis unless the lawyer gives notice of withdrawal. Doubt about whether a client-lawyer relationship still exists should be eliminated by the lawyer, preferably in writing, so that the client will not mistakenly suppose the lawyer is looking after the client's affairs when the lawyer has ceased to do so. For example, if a lawyer has handled a judicial or administrative proceeding that produced a result adverse to the client but has not been specifically instructed concerning pursuit of an appeal, the lawyer should advise the client of the possibility of appeal before relinquishing responsibility for the matter.

[10] Rule 1.3 is a rule of general applicability, and it is not meant to enlarge or restrict any specific rule. In particular, Rule 1.3 is not meant to govern conflicts of interest, which are addressed by Rules 1.7, 1.8, and 1.9.

Rule 1.4. Communication

(a) **A lawyer shall keep a client reasonably informed about the status of a matter and promptly comply with reasonable requests for information.**

(b) A lawyer shall explain a matter to the extent reasonably necessary to permit the client to make informed decisions regarding the representation.

(c) A lawyer who receives an offer of settlement in a civil case or proffered plea bargain in a criminal case shall inform the client promptly of the substance of the communication.

COMMENT

[1] The client should have sufficient information to participate intelligently in decisions concerning the objectives of the representation and the means by which they are to be pursued, to the extent the client is willing and able to do so. For example, a lawyer negotiating on behalf of a client should provide the client with facts relevant to the matter, inform the client of communications from another party, and take other reasonable steps that permit the client to make a decision regarding a serious offer from another party. A lawyer who receives from opposing counsel an offer of settlement in a civil controversy or a proffered plea bargain in a criminal case is required to inform the client promptly of its substance. *See* Rule 1.2(a). Even when a client delegates authority to the lawyer, the client should be kept advised of the status of the matter.

[2] A client is entitled to whatever information the client wishes about all aspects of the subject matter of the representation unless the client expressly consents not to have certain information passed on. The lawyer must be particularly careful to ensure that decisions of the client are made only after the client has been informed of all relevant considerations. The lawyer must initiate and maintain the consultative and decision-making process if the client does not do so and must ensure that the ongoing process is thorough and complete.

[3] Adequacy of communication depends in part on the kind of advice or assistance involved. The guiding principle is that the lawyer should fulfill reasonable client expectations for information consistent with (1) the duty to act in the client's best interests, and (2) the client's overall requirements and objectives as to the character of representation.

[4] Ordinarily, the information to be provided is that appropriate for a client who is a comprehending and responsible adult. However, fully informing the client according to this standard may be impracticable, for example, where the client is a child or suffers from mental disability. *See* Rule 1.14. When the client is an organization or group, it is often impossible or inappropriate to inform every one of its members about its legal affairs; ordinarily, the lawyer should address communications to the appropriate officials of the organization. *See* Rule 1.13. Where many routine matters are involved, a system of limited or occasional reporting may be arranged with the client. Practical exigency may also require a lawyer to act for a client without prior consultation. When the lawyer is conducting a trial, it is often not possible for the lawyer to consult with the client and obtain the client's acquiescence in tactical matters arising during the course of trial. It is sufficient if the lawyer consults with the client in advance of trial on significant issues that can be anticipated as arising during the course of the trial, and consults during trial to the extent practical, given the nature of the trial process.

Withholding Information

[5] In rare circumstances, a lawyer may be justified in delaying transmission of information when the client would be likely to react imprudently to an immediate communication. Thus, a lawyer might withhold a psychiatric diagnosis of a client when the examining psychiatrist indicates that disclosure would harm the client. Similarly, a lawyer may be justified, for humanitarian reasons, in not conveying certain information, for example, where the information would merely be upsetting to a terminally ill client. A lawyer may not withhold information to serve the lawyer's own interest or convenience. Rules or court orders governing litigation (such as a protective order limiting access to certain types of discovery material to counsel only) may provide that information supplied to a lawyer may not be disclosed to the client. Rule 3.4(c) directs compliance with such rules or orders.

Rule 1.5. Fees

(a) A lawyer's fee shall be reasonable. The factors to be considered in determining the reasonableness of a fee include the following:

(1) The time and labor required, the novelty and difficulty of the questions involved, and the skill requisite to perform the legal service properly;

(2) The likelihood, if apparent to the client, that the acceptance of the particular employment will preclude other employment by the lawyer;

(3) The fee customarily charged in the locality for similar legal services;

(4) The amount involved and the results obtained;

(5) The limitations imposed by the client or by the circumstances;

(6) The nature and length of the professional relationship with the client;

(7) The experience, reputation, and ability of the lawyer or lawyers performing the services; and

(8) Whether the fee is fixed or contingent.

(b) When the lawyer has not regularly represented the client, the basis or rate of the fee, the scope of the lawyer's representation, and the expenses for which the client will be responsible shall be communicated to the client, in writing, before or within a reasonable time after commencing the representation.

(c) A fee may be contingent on the outcome of the matter for which the service is rendered, except in a matter in which a contingent fee is prohibited by paragraph (d) or other law. A contingent fee agreement shall be in writing and shall state the method by which the fee is to be determined, including the percentage or percentages that shall accrue to the lawyer in the event of settlement, trial, or appeal, litigation, other expenses to be deducted from the recovery, whether such expenses are to be deducted before or after the contingent fee is calculated, and whether the client will be liable for expenses regardless of the outcome of the matter. Upon conclusion of a contingent fee matter, the lawyer shall provide the client with a written statement stating the outcome of the matter, and if there is a recovery, showing the remittance to the client and the method of its determination.

(d) A lawyer shall not enter into an arrangement for, charge, or collect a contingent fee for representing a defendant in a criminal case.

(e) A division of a fee between lawyers who are not in the same firm may be made only if:

(1) The division is in proportion to the services performed by each lawyer or each lawyer assumes joint responsibility for the representation.

(2) The client is advised, in writing, of the identity of the lawyers who will participate in the representation, of the contemplated division of responsibility, and of the effect of the association of lawyers outside the firm on the fee to be charged;

(3) The client gives informed consent to the arrangement; and

(4) The total fee is reasonable.

(f) Any fee that is prohibited by paragraph (d) above or by law is *per se* unreasonable.

COMMENT

Basis or Rate of Fee

[1] When the lawyer has regularly represented a client, they ordinarily will have evolved an understanding concerning the basis or rate of the fee. In a new client-lawyer relationship, however, an understanding as to the fee should be promptly established, together with the scope of the lawyer's representation and the expenses for which the client will be responsible. It is not necessary to recite all the factors that underlie the basis of the fee, but only those that are directly involved in its computation. It is sufficient, for example, to state that the basic rate is an hourly charge or a fixed amount or an estimated amount, or to identify the factors that may be taken into account in finally fixing the fee. When developments occur during the representation that render an earlier estimate substantially inaccurate, a revised estimate should be provided to the client.

[2] A written statement concerning the fee, required to be furnished in advance in most cases by paragraph (b), reduces the possibility of misunderstanding. In circumstances in which paragraph (b) requires that the basis for the lawyer's fee be in writing, an individualized writing specific to the particular client and representation is generally not required. Unless there are unique aspects of the fee arrangement, the lawyer may utilize a standardized letter, memorandum, or pamphlet explaining the lawyer's fee practices, and indicating those practices applicable to the specific representation. Such publications would, for example, explain applicable hourly billing rates, if billing on an hourly rate basis is contemplated, and indicate what charges (such as filing fees, transcript costs, duplicating costs, long-distance telephone charges) are imposed in addition to hourly rate charges.

[3] Where the services to be rendered are covered by a fixed fee schedule that adequately informs the client of the charges to be imposed, a copy of such schedule may be utilized to satisfy the requirement for a writing. Such services as routine real estate transactions, uncontested divorces, or preparation of simple wills, for example, may be suitable for description in such a fixed-fee schedule.

Terms of Payment

[4] A lawyer may require advance payment of a fee, but is obliged to return any unearned portion. *See* Rule 1.16(d). A lawyer may accept property in payment for services, such as an ownership interest in an enterprise. However, a fee paid in property instead of money may be subject to special scrutiny because it involves questions concerning both the value of the services and the lawyer's special knowledge of the value of the property.

[5] An agreement may not be made whose terms might induce the lawyer improperly to curtail services for the client or perform them in a way contrary to the client's interest. For example, a lawyer should not enter into an agreement whereby services are to be provided only up to a stated amount when it is foreseeable that more extensive services probably will be required, unless the situation is adequately explained to the client. Otherwise, the client might have to bargain for further assistance in the midst of a proceeding or transaction. However, it is proper to define the extent of services in the light of the client's ability to pay. A lawyer should not exploit a fee arrangement based primarily on hourly charges by using wasteful procedures.

Contingent Fees

[6] Generally, contingent fees are permissible in all civil cases. However, paragraph (d) continues the prohibition, imposed under the previous Code of Professional Responsibility, against the use of a contingent fee arrangement by a lawyer representing a defendant in a criminal case. Applicable law may impose other limitations on contingent fees, such as a ceiling on the percentage. And in any case, if there is doubt whether a contingent fee is consistent with the client's best interests, the lawyer should explain any existing payment alternatives and their implications.

[7] Contingent fees in domestic relations cases, while rarely justified, are not prohibited by Rule 1.5. Contingent fees in such cases are permitted in order that lawyers may provide representation to clients who might not otherwise be able to afford to contract for the payment of fees on a noncontingent basis.

[8] Paragraph (c) requires that the contingent fee arrangement be in writing. This writing must explain the method by which the fee is to be computed, as well as the client's responsibility for expenses. The lawyer must also provide the client with a written statement at the conclusion of a contingent fee matter, stating the outcome of the matter and explaining the computation of any remittance made to the client.

Division of Fee

[9] A division of fee is a single billing to a client covering the fee of two or more lawyers who are not in the same firm. A division of fee facilitates association

of more than one lawyer in a matter in which neither alone could serve the client as well, and most often is used when the fee is contingent and the division is between a referring lawyer and a trial specialist.

[10] Paragraph (e) permits the lawyers to divide a fee either on the basis of the proportion of services they render or by agreement between the participating lawyers if all assume responsibility for the representation as a whole. Joint responsibility for the representation entails the obligations stated in Rule 5.1 for purposes of the matter involved. Permitting a division on the basis of joint responsibility, rather than on the basis of services performed, represents a change from the basis for fee divisions allowed under the prior Code of Professional Responsibility. The change is intended to encourage lawyers to affiliate other counsel, who are better equipped by reason of experience or specialized background to serve the client's needs, rather than to retain sole responsibility for the representation in order to avoid losing the right to a fee.

[11] The concept of joint responsibility is not, however, merely a technicality or incantation. The lawyer who refers the client to another lawyer, or affiliates another lawyer in the representation, remains fully responsible to the client, and is accountable to the client for deficiencies in the discharge of the representation by the lawyer who has been brought into the representation. If a lawyer wishes to avoid such responsibility for the potential deficiencies of another lawyer, the matter must be referred to the other lawyer without retaining a right to participate in fees beyond those fees justified by services actually rendered.

[12] The concept of joint responsibility does not require the referring lawyer to perform any minimum portion of the total legal services rendered. The referring lawyer may agree that the lawyer to whom the referral is made will perform substantially all of the services to be rendered in connection with the representation, without review by the referring lawyer. Thus, the referring lawyer is not required to review pleadings or other documents, attend hearings or depositions, or otherwise participate in a significant and continuing manner. The referring lawyer does not, however, escape the implications of joint responsibility, *see* Comment [11], by avoiding direct participation.

[13] When fee divisions are based on assumed joint responsibility, the requirement of paragraph (a) that the fee be reasonable applies to the total fee charged for the representation by all participating lawyers.

[14] Paragraph (e) requires that the client be advised, in writing, of the fee division and states that the client must affirmatively give informed consent to the proposed fee arrangement. For the definition of "informed consent," *see* Rule 1.0(e). The Rule does not require disclosure to the client of the share that each lawyer is to receive but does require that the client be informed of the identity of the lawyers sharing the fee, their respective responsibilities in the representation, and the effect of the association of lawyers outside the firm on the fee charged.

Disputes over Fees

[15] If a procedure has been established for resolution of fee disputes, such as an arbitration or mediation procedure established by the Bar, the lawyer should conscientiously consider submitting to it. Law may prescribe a procedure for determining a lawyer's fee, for example, in representation of an executor or administrator,

a class, or a person entitled to a reasonable fee as part of the measure of damages. The lawyer entitled to such a fee and a lawyer representing another party concerned with the fee should comply with the prescribed procedure.

Rule 1.6. Confidentiality of Information

(a) Except when permitted under paragraph (c), (d), or (e), a lawyer shall not knowingly:

(1) reveal a confidence or secret of the lawyer's client;

(2) use a confidence or secret of the lawyer's client to the disadvantage of the client;

(3) use a confidence or secret of the lawyer's client for the advantage of the lawyer or of a third person.

(b) "Confidence" refers to information protected by the attorney-client privilege under applicable law, and "secret" refers to other information gained in the professional relationship that the client has requested be held inviolate, or the disclosure of which would be embarrassing, or would be likely to be detrimental, to the client.

(c) A lawyer may reveal client confidences and secrets, to the extent reasonably necessary:

(1) to prevent a criminal act that the lawyer reasonably believes is likely to result in death or substantial bodily harm absent disclosure of the client's secrets or confidences by the lawyer; or

(2) to prevent the bribery or intimidation of witnesses, jurors, court officials, or other persons who are involved in proceedings before a tribunal if the lawyer reasonably believes that such acts are likely to result absent disclosure of the client's confidences or secrets by the lawyer.

(d) When a client has used or is using a lawyer's services to further a crime or fraud, the lawyer may reveal client confidences and secrets, to the extent reasonably necessary:

(1) to prevent the client from committing the crime or fraud if it is reasonably certain to result in substantial injury to the financial interests or property of another; or

(2) to prevent, mitigate or rectify substantial injury to the financial interests or property of another that is reasonably certain to result or has resulted from the client's commission of the crime or fraud.

(e) A lawyer may use or reveal client confidences or secrets:

(1) with the informed consent of the client;

(2)(A) when permitted by these Rules or required by law or court order; and

(B) if a government lawyer, when permitted or authorized by law;

(3) to the extent reasonably necessary to establish a defense to a criminal charge, disciplinary charge, or civil claim, formally instituted against the lawyer, based upon conduct in which the client was involved,

or to the extent reasonably necessary to respond to specific allegations by the client concerning the lawyer's representation of the client;

(4) when the lawyer has reasonable grounds for believing that a client has impliedly authorized disclosure of a confidence or secret in order to carry out the representation;

(5) to the minimum extent necessary in an action instituted by the lawyer to establish or collect the lawyer's fee; or

(6) to the extent reasonably necessary to secure legal advice about the lawyer's compliance with law, including these Rules.

(f) A lawyer shall exercise reasonable care to prevent the lawyer's employees, associates, and others whose services are utilized by the lawyer from disclosing or using confidences or secrets of a client, except that such persons may reveal information permitted to be disclosed by paragraphs (c), (d), or (e).

(g) The lawyer's obligation to preserve the client's confidences and secrets continues after termination of the lawyer's employment.

(h) The obligation of a lawyer under paragraph (a) also applies to confidences and secrets learned prior to becoming a lawyer in the course of providing assistance to another lawyer.

(i) For purposes of this rule, a lawyer who serves as a member of the D.C. Bar Lawyer Counseling Committee, or as a trained intervenor for that committee, shall be deemed to have a lawyer-client relationship with respect to any lawyer-counselee being counseled under programs conducted by or on behalf of the committee. Information obtained from another lawyer being counseled under the auspices of the committee, or in the course of and associated with such counseling, shall be treated as a confidence or secret within the terms of paragraph (b). Such information may be disclosed only to the extent permitted by this rule.

(j) For purposes of this rule, a lawyer who serves as a member of the D.C. Bar Practice Management Service Committee, formerly known as the Lawyer Practice Assistance Committee,[1] or a staff assistant, mentor, monitor or other consultant for that committee, shall be deemed to have a lawyer-client relationship with respect to any lawyer-counselee being counseled under programs conducted by or on behalf of the committee. Communications between the counselor and the lawyer being counseled under the auspices of the committee, or made in the course of and associated with such counseling, shall be treated as a confidence or secret within the terms of paragraph (b). Such information may be disclosed only to the extent permitted by this rule. However, during the period in which the lawyer-counselee is subject to a probationary or monitoring order of the Court of Appeals or the Board on Professional Responsibility in a disciplinary

---

1. On May 10, 2005, the D.C. Bar Board of Governors approved a name change for the Lawyer Practice Assistance Committee. Effective July 1, 2005, the Committee will be known as the Practice Management Service Committee.

case instituted pursuant to Rule XI of the Rules of the Court of Appeals Governing the Bar, such information shall be subject to disclosure in accordance with the order.

(k) The client of the government lawyer is the agency that employs the lawyer unless expressly provided to the contrary by appropriate law, regulation, or order.

COMMENT

[1] The lawyer is part of a judicial system charged with upholding the law. One of the lawyer's functions is to advise clients so that they avoid any violation of the law in the proper exercise of their rights.

[2] The observance of the ethical obligation of a lawyer to hold inviolate confidential information of the client not only facilitates the full development of facts essential to proper representation of the client but also encourages people to seek early legal assistance.

[3] Almost without exception, clients come to lawyers in order to determine what their rights are and what is, in the maze of laws and regulations, deemed to be legal and correct. The common law recognizes that the client's confidences must be protected from disclosure. Based upon experience, lawyers know that almost all clients follow the advice given, and the law is upheld.

[4] A fundamental principle in the client-lawyer relationship is that the lawyer holds inviolate the client's secrets and confidences. The client is thereby encouraged to communicate fully and frankly with the lawyer even as to embarrassing or legally damaging subject matter.

[5] This rule prohibits a lawyer from revealing the confidences and secrets of a client except as provided in this rule or elsewhere in the Rules. Proper concern for professional duty should cause a lawyer to shun indiscreet conversations concerning clients. A lawyer's use of a hypothetical to discuss issues relating to the representation is permissible so long as there is no reasonable likelihood that the listener will be able to ascertain the identity of the client or the situation involved.

Relationship Between Rule 1.6 and
Attorney-Client Evidentiary Privilege and
Work Product Doctrine

[6] The principle of confidentiality is given effect in two related bodies of law: the attorney-client privilege and the work product doctrine in the law of evidence and the rule of confidentiality established in professional ethics. The attorney-client privilege and the work product doctrine apply in judicial and other proceedings in which a lawyer may be called as a witness or otherwise required to produce evidence concerning a client. This rule is not intended to govern or affect judicial application of the attorney-client privilege or work product doctrine. The privilege and doctrine were developed to promote compliance with law and fairness in litigation.

In reliance on the attorney-client privilege, clients are entitled to expect that communications within the scope of the privilege will be protected against compelled disclosure.

[7] The attorney-client privilege is that of the client and not of the lawyer. As a general matter, the client has a reasonable expectation that information relating to the client will not be voluntarily disclosed and that disclosure of such information may be judicially compelled only in accordance with recognized exceptions to the attorney-client privilege and work product doctrine.

[8] The rule of client-lawyer confidentiality applies in situations other than those where evidence is sought from the lawyer through compulsion of law; furthermore, it applies not merely to matters communicated in confidence by the client (i.e., confidences) but also to all information gained in the course of the professional relationship that the client has requested be held inviolate, or the disclosure of which would be embarrassing or would be likely to be detrimental to the client (i.e., secrets). This ethical precept, unlike the evidentiary privilege, exists without regard to the nature or source of the information or the fact that others share the knowledge. It reflects not only the principles underlying the attorney-client privilege, but the lawyer's duty of loyalty to the client.

The Commencement of the Client-Lawyer Relationship

[9] Principles of substantive law external to these Rules determine whether a client-lawyer relationship exists. Although most of the duties flowing from the client-lawyer relationship attach only after the client has requested the lawyer to render legal services and the lawyer has agreed to do so, the duty of confidentiality imposed by this rule attaches when the lawyer agrees to consider whether a client-lawyer relationship shall be established. Other duties of a lawyer to a prospective client are set forth in Rule 1.18.

Exploitation of Confidences and Secrets

[10] In addition to prohibiting the disclosure of a client's confidences and secrets, subparagraph (a)(2) provides that a lawyer may not use the client's confidences and secrets to the disadvantage of the client. For example, a lawyer who has learned that the client is investing in specific real estate may not seek to acquire nearby property where doing so would adversely affect the client's plan for investment. Similarly, information acquired by the lawyer in the course of representing a client may not be used to the disadvantage of that client even after the termination of the lawyer's representation of the client. However, the fact that a lawyer has once served a client does not preclude the lawyer from using generally known information about the former client when later representing another client. Under subparagraphs (a)(3) and (e)(1), a lawyer may use a client's confidences and secrets for the lawyer's own benefit or that of a third party only after the lawyer has obtained the client's informed consent to the use in question.

Authorized Disclosure

[11] A lawyer is impliedly authorized to make disclosures about a client when appropriate in carrying out the representation, except to the extent that the client's instructions or special circumstances limit that authority. In litigation, for example, a lawyer may disclose information by admitting a fact that cannot properly be disputed, or in negotiation by making a disclosure that facilitates a satisfactory conclusion.

[12] The obligation to protect confidences and secrets obviously does not preclude a lawyer from revealing information when the client gives informed consent, when necessary to perform the professional employment, when permitted by these Rules, or when required by law. For the definition of "informed consent," *see* Rule 1.0(e). Unless the client otherwise directs, a lawyer may disclose the affairs of the client to partners or associates of the lawyer's firm. It is a matter of common knowledge that the normal operation of a law office exposes confidential professional information to nonlawyer employees of the office, particularly secretaries and those having access to the files; and this obligates a lawyer to exercise care in selecting and training employees so that the sanctity of all confidences and secrets of clients may be preserved. If the obligation extends to two or more clients as to the same information, a lawyer should obtain the permission of all before revealing the information. A lawyer must always be sensitive to the rights and wishes of the client and act scrupulously in the making of decisions that may involve the disclosure of information obtained in the course of the professional relationship.

[13] A lawyer's confidentiality obligations do not preclude a lawyer from securing confidential legal advice about the lawyer's personal responsibilities to comply with these Rules. In most situations disclosing information to secure such advice will be impliedly authorized for the lawyer to carry out the representation. Even when disclosure is not impliedly authorized, paragraph (e)(6) permits such disclosure because of the importance of a lawyer's compliance with the Rules of Professional Conduct and other law.

[14] Unless the client otherwise directs, it is not improper for a lawyer to give limited information from client files to an outside agency necessary for statistical, bookkeeping, accounting, data processing, banking, printing, or other legitimate purposes, provided the lawyer exercises due care in the selection of the agency and warns the agency that the information must be kept confidential.

[15] Although the public interest is usually best served by a strict rule requiring lawyers to preserve the confidentiality of information relating to the representation of their clients, the confidentiality rule is subject to limited exceptions.

[16] Rule 1.6(c) describes situations presenting a sufficiently serious threat such that a client's confidences and secrets may be revealed to the extent reasonably necessary to prevent the harm described. Thus, a lawyer may reveal confidences and secrets to the extent necessary to prevent a criminal act that the lawyer reasonably believes is likely to result in death or substantial bodily harm absent disclosure and to prevent bribery or intimidation of witnesses, jurors, court officials, or other persons involved in proceedings before a tribunal.

[17] Rule 1.6(d) describes situations in which the client's usual expectation of confidentiality is not warranted because the client has abused the lawyer-client relationship by using the lawyer's services to further a crime or fraud. In these circumstances, Rule 1.6(d)(1) provides a limited exception to the rule of confidentiality,

which permits the lawyer to reveal information to the extent reasonably necessary to enable affected persons or appropriate authorities to prevent the client from committing a crime or fraud, as defined in Rule 1.0(d), if such crime or fraud is reasonably certain to result in substantial injury to the financial or property interests of another. The D.C. Court of Appeals has held that the crime-fraud exception to the attorney-client privilege requires that a lawyer's services were actually used to further a crime or fraud that occurred, not merely that the client sought to do so. *See In re Public Defender Service*, 831 A.2d 890 (D.C. 2003). The Rule 1.6(d) exception to the ethical duty of confidentiality also requires that the lawyer's services actually were used to further a crime or fraud. A client can prevent disclosure by refraining from the wrongful conduct or by not using the lawyer's services to further a crime or fraud. Although Rule 1.6(d)(1) does not require the lawyer to reveal the client's misconduct, the lawyer may not counsel or assist the client in conduct the lawyer knows is criminal or fraudulent. *See* Rule 1.2(e). Rule 1.16 addresses the lawyer's obligation or right to withdraw from the representation of the client in such circumstances if withdrawal is necessary to prevent the client from misusing the lawyer's services or if withdrawal would otherwise prevent, mitigate, or rectify substantial injury caused by the client who misused the lawyer's services. Rules 3.3(a)(1), 3.3(d) and 4.1(b) address circumstances in which disclosure may be mandatory. Rules 3.4(a), 8.1, and 8.3 do not require disclosure of information otherwise protected by Rule 1.6; disclosure that is permissive in the limited situations specified in Rule 1.6 is not mandatory under Rules 3.4(a), 8.1 or 8.3. Rule 1.6(d) applies to organizations as well as to individuals.

[18] Paragraph (d)(2) refers to situations in which the crime or fraud has already commenced and is on-going or completed such that complete prevention is not an option. Thus, the client no longer has the option of preventing disclosure by refraining from the wrongful conduct. In these circumstances, there may be situations in which the loss suffered by an affected person can be prevented, rectified, or mitigated. In such situations, the lawyer may disclose information relating to the representation to the extent necessary to enable the affected persons to prevent or mitigate reasonably certain losses or to attempt to recoup their losses. Paragraph (d)(2) does not apply to disclosure with regard to a crime or fraud committed prior to retaining the lawyer for representation concerning that offense.

[19] Rule 1.2, Comment [7] and Rule 4.1, Comment [3] acknowledge that, to avoid assisting in a client crime or fraud, a lawyer in some instances may be required to withdraw from representation, give notice of the fact of withdrawal, or disaffirm an opinion, document, affirmation or the like. In some instances when a lawyer's services have been or are being used to further a client's crime or fraud, a lawyer may conclude that more than withdrawal and disaffirmance is required to avoid assisting in the client's crime or fraud and that disclosure of client information protected by this rule is warranted. If the lawyer has such a reasonable belief, the lawyer may make such disclosures to the extent reasonably necessary to permit corrective action, for example, prompt initiation of proceedings in order to seize or recover assets fraudulently obtained by the client. Once the lawyer has disclosed information reasonably necessary to prevent, rectify, or mitigate loss, the lawyer may not take additional actions that would harm the client. Thus, a lawyer is not warranted under Rule 1.6(d) in providing legal advice or assistance to a victim as the victim's lawyer or voluntarily serving as a witness or otherwise cooperating in a proceeding brought by the victim or anyone else seeking compensation for the victim.

The lawyer also may not use or disclose information for the purpose of voluntarily assisting a law-enforcement agency to apprehend and prosecute the client, unless the lawyer reasonably believes that such disclosure would be reasonably necessary to prevent, rectify, or mitigate the victim's loss.

[20] This rule permits but does not require the disclosure of information relating to a client's representation to accomplish the purposes specified. In exercising the discretion conferred by this rule by paragraphs (c) and (d), the lawyer may consider such factors as the nature of the lawyer's relationship with the client and with those who might be injured by the client, the lawyer's own involvement in the transaction, and factors that may extenuate the conduct in question. The lawyer's exercise of discretion in determining whether to make disclosures that are reasonably likely to prevent the death or substantial bodily injury of another requires consideration of such factors as the client's tendency to commit violent acts or, conversely, to make idle threats. When a lawyer is given discretion to disclose under this rule, the lawyer's decision not to disclose as permitted by the Rule does not violate Rule 1.6. Other Rules may impose disclosure obligations. *See* Rules 1.2(e), 2.3, 3.3, 3.4(a), 4.1(b), 8.1, and 8.3 regarding the reconciliation of the confidentiality protections of this rule with disclosure provisions of those Rules.

[21] Paragraphs (c) and (d) permit disclosure only to the extent the lawyer reasonably believes the disclosure is necessary to accomplish one of the purposes specified. The "reasonably believes" standard is applied because it is difficult for a lawyer to "know" when acts with such potentially serious consequences will actually be carried out, for the client may have a change of mind. Where practicable, the lawyer should first seek to persuade the client to take suitable action to obviate the need for disclosure. In any case, a disclosure adverse to the client's interest should be no greater than the lawyer reasonably believes necessary to accomplish the purpose. If the disclosure will be made in connection with a judicial proceeding, the disclosure should be made in a manner that limits access to the information to the tribunal or other persons having a need to know it, and appropriate protective orders or other arrangements should be sought by the lawyer to the fullest extent practicable.

[22] Other law may require that a lawyer disclose information otherwise protected by Rule 1.6. Whether a law requires such disclosure is a question of law beyond the scope of these Rules. When such disclosure appears to be required by other law, the lawyer must discuss the matter with the client to the extent required by Rule 1.4. If, however, the other law requires disclosure, paragraph (e)(2)(A) permits the lawyer to make such disclosure as is necessary to comply with the law.

Dispute Concerning Lawyer's Conduct

[23] Where a legal claim or disciplinary charge alleges complicity of the lawyer in a client's conduct or other misconduct of the lawyer involving representation of the client, the lawyer may respond to the extent the lawyer reasonably believes necessary to establish a defense. The same is true with respect to a claim involving the conduct or representation of a former client. Charges, in defense of which a lawyer may disclose client confidences and secrets, can arise in a civil, criminal, or

professional disciplinary proceeding, and can be based on a wrong allegedly committed by the lawyer against the client, or on a wrong alleged by a third person; for example, a person claiming to have been defrauded by the lawyer and client acting together.

[24] The lawyer may not disclose a client's confidences or secrets to defend against informal allegations made by third parties; the Rule allows disclosure only if a third party has formally instituted a civil, criminal, or disciplinary action against the lawyer. Even if the third party has formally instituted such a proceeding, the lawyer should advise the client of the third party's action and request that the client respond appropriately, if this is practicable and would not be prejudicial to the lawyer's ability to establish a defense.

[25] If a lawyer's client, or former client, has made specific allegations against the lawyer, the lawyer may disclose that client's confidences and secrets in establishing a defense, without waiting for formal proceedings to be commenced. The requirement of subparagraph (e)(3) that there be "specific" charges of misconduct by the client precludes the lawyer from disclosing confidences or secrets in response to general criticism by a client; an example of such a general criticism would be an assertion by the client that the lawyer "did a poor job" of representing the client. But in this situation, as well as in the defense of formally instituted third-party proceedings, disclosure should be no greater than the lawyer reasonably believes is necessary to vindicate innocence, the disclosure should be made in a manner that limits access to the information to the tribunal or other persons having a need to know it, and appropriate protective orders or other arrangements should be sought by the lawyer to the fullest extent practicable.

Fee Collection Actions

[26] Subparagraph (e)(5) permits a lawyer to reveal a client's confidences or secrets if this is necessary in an action to collect fees from the client. This aspect of the rule expresses the principle that the beneficiary of a fiduciary relationship may not exploit it to the detriment of the fiduciary. Subparagraph (e)(5) should be construed narrowly; it does not authorize broad, indiscriminate disclosure of secrets or confidences. The lawyer should evaluate the necessity for disclosure of information at each stage of the action. For example, in drafting the complaint in a fee collection suit, it would be necessary to reveal the "secrets" that the lawyer was retained by the client, that fees are due, and that the client has failed to pay those fees. Further disclosure of the client's secrets and confidences would be impermissible at the complaint stage. If possible, the lawyer should prevent even the disclosure of the client's identity through the use of John Doe pleadings.

[27] If the client's response to the lawyer's complaint raised issues implicating confidences or secrets, the lawyer would be permitted to disclose confidential or secret information pertinent to the client's claims or defenses. Even then, the rule would require that the lawyer's response be narrowly tailored to meet the client's specific allegations, with the minimum degree of disclosure sufficient to respond effectively. In addition, the lawyer should continue, throughout the action, to make every effort to avoid unnecessary disclosure of the client's confidences and secrets and to limit the disclosure to those having the need to know it. To this end the

lawyer should seek appropriate protective orders and make any other arrangements that would minimize the risk of disclosure of the confidential information in question, including the utilization of *in camera* proceedings.

Disclosures Otherwise Required or Authorized

[28] The attorney-client privilege is differently defined in various jurisdictions. If a lawyer is called as a witness to give testimony concerning a client, absent waiver by the client, subparagraph (e)(2) requires the lawyer to invoke the privilege when it is applicable. The lawyer may comply with the final orders of a court or other tribunal of competent jurisdiction requiring the lawyer to give information about the client. But a lawyer ordered by a court to disclose client confidences or secrets should not comply with the order until the lawyer has personally made every reasonable effort to appeal the order or has notified the client of the order and given the client the opportunity to challenge it.

Former Client

[29] The duty of confidentiality continues after the client-lawyer relationship has terminated.

Services Rendered in Assisting Another Lawyer Before Becoming a Member of the Bar

[30] There are circumstances in which a person who ultimately becomes a lawyer provides assistance to a lawyer while serving in a nonlawyer capacity. The typical situation is that of the law clerk or summer associate in a law firm or government agency. Paragraph (h) addresses the confidentiality obligations of such a person after becoming a member of the Bar; the same confidentiality obligations are imposed as would apply if the person had been a member of the Bar at the time confidences or secrets were received. This resolution of the confidentiality obligation is consistent with the reasoning employed in D.C. Bar Legal Ethics Committee Opinion 84. For a related provision dealing with the imputation of disqualifications arising from prior participation as a summer associate or in a similar position, *see* Rule 1.10(b). For a provision addressing the imputation of disqualifications arising from prior participation as a law clerk, *see* Rule 1.12.

Bar Sponsored Counseling Programs

[31] Paragraph (i) adds a provision dealing specifically with the disclosure obligations of lawyers who are assisting in the counseling programs of the D.C. Bar's Lawyer Counseling Committee. Members of that committee, and lawyer-intervenors who assist the committee in counseling, may obtain information from lawyer-counselees who have sought assistance from the counseling programs offered

by the committee. It is in the interest of the public to encourage lawyers who have alcohol or other substance abuse problems to seek counseling as a first step toward rehabilitation. Some lawyers who seek such assistance may have violated provisions of the Rules of Professional Conduct, or other provisions of law, including criminal statutes such as those dealing with embezzlement. In order for those who are providing counseling services to evaluate properly the lawyer-counselee's problems and enhance the prospects for rehabilitation, it is necessary for the counselors to receive completely candid information from the lawyer-counselee. Such candor is not likely if the counselor, for example, would be compelled by Rule 8.3 to report the lawyer-counselee's conduct to Bar Counsel, or if the lawyer-counselee feared that the counselor could be compelled by prosecutors or others to disclose information.

[32] It is similarly in the interest of the public to encourage lawyers to seek the assistance of the D.C. Bar's Practice Management Service Committee to address management problems in their practices. In order for those who are providing counseling services through the Practice Management Service Committee to evaluate properly the lawyer-counselee's problems and enhance the prospects for self-improvement by the counselee, paragraph (j) adds a provision addressing the confidentiality obligations of lawyers who are assisting in the counseling programs of the Practice Management Service Committee.

[33] These considerations make it appropriate to treat the lawyer-counselee relationship as a lawyer-client relationship, and to create an additional limited class of information treated as secrets or confidences subject to the protection of Rule 1.6. The scope of that information is set forth in paragraph (i) and (j). The lawyer-client relationship is deemed to exist only with respect to the obligation of confidentiality created under Rule 1.6, and not to obligations created elsewhere in these Rules, including the obligation of zealous representation under Rule 1.3 and the obligation to avoid conflicts of interest set forth in Rules 1.7 and 1.9. The obligation of confidentiality extends to non-lawyer assistants of lawyers serving the committee. *See* Rule 5.1.

[34] Notwithstanding the obligation of confidentiality under paragraph (j), during the period in which a lawyer-counselee is subject to a probationary or monitoring order of the Court of Appeals or the Board on Professional Responsibility in a disciplinary case instituted pursuant to Rule XI of the Rules of the Court of Appeals Governing the Bar, communications between the counselor and the lawyer being counseled under the auspices of the Practice Management Service Committee shall be subject to disclosure in accordance with an Order of the Court or the Board, since the participation of the lawyer-counselee in the programs of the committee in such circumstances is not voluntary.

[35] Ethical rules established by the District of Columbia Court of Appeals with respect to the kinds of information protected from compelled disclosure may not be accepted by other forums or jurisdictions. Therefore, the protections afforded to lawyer-counselees by paragraphs (i) and (j) may not be available to preclude disclosure in all circumstances. Furthermore, lawyers who are members of the bar of other jurisdictions may not be entitled, under the ethics rules applicable to members of the bar in such other jurisdictions, to forgo reporting violations to disciplinary authorities pursuant to the other jurisdictions' counterparts to Rule 8.3.

Government Lawyers

[36] Subparagraph (e)(2) was revised, and paragraph (k) was added, to address the unique circumstances raised by attorney-client relationships within the government.

[37] Subparagraph (e)(2)(A) applies to both private and government attorney-client relationships. Subparagraph (e)(2)(B) applies to government lawyers only. It is designed to permit disclosures that are not required by law or court order under Rule 1.6(e)(2)(A), but which the government authorizes its attorneys to make in connection with their professional services to the government. Such disclosures may be authorized or required by statute, executive order, or regulation, depending on the constitutional or statutory powers of the authorizing entity. If so authorized or required, subparagraph (e)(2)(B) governs.

[38] The term "agency" in paragraph (j) includes, *inter alia,* executive and independent departments and agencies, special commissions, committees of the legislature, agencies of the legislative branch such as the Government Accountability Office, and the courts to the extent that they employ lawyers (e.g., staff counsel) to counsel them. The employing agency has been designated the client under this rule to provide a commonly understood and easily determinable point for identifying the government client.

[39] Government lawyers may also be assigned to provide an individual with counsel or representation in circumstances that make clear that an obligation of confidentiality runs directly to that individual and that subparagraph (e)(2)(A), not (e)(2)(B), applies. It is, of course, acceptable in this circumstance for a government lawyer to make disclosures about the individual representation to supervisors or others within the employing governmental agency so long as such disclosures are made in the context of, and consistent with, the agency's representation program. *See, e.g.,* 28 C.F.R. §§50.15 and 50.16. The relevant circumstances, including the agreement to represent the individual, may also indicate whether the individual client to whom the government lawyer is assigned will be deemed to have granted or denied informed consent to disclosures to the lawyer's employing agency. Examples of such representation include representation by a public defender, a government lawyer representing a defendant sued for damages arising out of the performance of the defendant's government employment, and a military lawyer representing a court-martial defendant.

Acting Competently to Preserve Confidences

[40] When transmitting a communication that includes information relating to the representation of a client, the lawyer must take reasonable precautions to prevent the information from coming into the hands of unintended recipients. This duty does not require that the lawyer use special security measures if the method of communication affords a reasonable expectation of privacy. Special circumstances, however, may warrant special precautions. Factors to be considered in determining the reasonableness of the lawyer's expectation of confidentiality include the sensitivity of the information and the extent to which the privacy of the communication is protected by law or by a confidentiality agreement. A client may require the

lawyer to implement special security measures not required by this rule or may give informed consent to the use of a means of communication that would otherwise be prohibited by this rule.

Rule 1.7.   Conflict of Interest: General

(a) A lawyer shall not advance two or more adverse positions in the same matter.

(b) Except as permitted by paragraph (c) below, a lawyer shall not represent a client with respect to a matter if:

(1) That matter involves a specific party or parties and a position to be taken by that client in that matter is adverse to a position taken or to be taken by another client in the same matter even though that client is unrepresented or represented by a different lawyer;

(2) Such representation will be or is likely to be adversely affected by representation of another client;

(3) Representation of another client will be or is likely to be adversely affected by such representation;

(4) The lawyer's professional judgment on behalf of the client will be or reasonably may be adversely affected by the lawyer's responsibilities to or interests in a third party or the lawyer's own financial, business, property, or personal interests.

(c) A lawyer may represent a client with respect to a matter in the circumstances described in paragraph (b) above if

(1) Each potentially affected client provides informed consent to such representation after full disclosure of the existence and nature of the possible conflict and the possible adverse consequences of such representation; and

(2) The lawyer reasonably believes that the lawyer will be able to provide competent and diligent representation to each affected client.

(d) If a conflict not reasonably foreseeable at the outset of representation arises under paragraph (b)(1) after the representation commences, and is not waived under paragraph (c), a lawyer need not withdraw from any representation unless the conflict also arises under paragraphs (b)(2), (b)(3), or (b)(4).

COMMENT

[1] Rule 1.7 is intended to provide clear notice of circumstances that may constitute a conflict of interest. Rule 1.7(a) sets out the limited circumstances in which representation of conflicting interests is absolutely prohibited even with the informed consent of all involved clients. Rule 1.7(b) sets out those circumstances in which representation is barred in the absence of informed client consent. For the definition of "informed consent," *see* Rule 1.0(e). The difference between Rule 1.7(a) and Rule 1.7(b) is that in the former, the lawyer is representing multiple interests in the same matter, while in the latter, the lawyer is representing a single

interest, but a client of the lawyer who is represented by different counsel has an interest adverse to that advanced by the lawyer. The application of Rules 1.7(a) and 1.7(b) to specific facts must also take into consideration the principles of imputed disqualification described in Rule 1.10. Rule 1.7(c) states the procedure that must be used to obtain the client's informed consent if representation is to commence or continue in the circumstances described in Rule 1.7(b). Rule 1.7(d) governs withdrawal in cases arising under Rule 1.7(b)(1).

Representation Absolutely Prohibited—Rule 1.7(a)

[2] Institutional interests in preserving confidence in the adversary process and in the administration of justice preclude permitting a lawyer to represent adverse positions in the same matter. For that reason, paragraph (a) prohibits such conflicting representations, with or without client consent.

[3] The same lawyer (or law firm, *see* Rule 1.10) should not espouse adverse positions in the same matter during the course of any type of representation, whether such adverse positions are taken on behalf of clients or on behalf of the lawyer or an association of which the lawyer is a member. On the other hand, for purposes of Rule 1.7(a), an "adverse" position does not include inconsistent or alternative positions advanced by counsel on behalf of a single client. Rule 1.7(a) is intended to codify the result reached in D.C. Bar Legal Ethics Committee Opinion 204, including the conclusion that a rulemaking whose result will be applied retroactively in pending adjudications is the same matter as the adjudications, even though treated as separate proceedings by an agency. However, if the adverse positions to be taken relate to different matters, the absolute prohibition of paragraph (a) is inapplicable, even though paragraphs (b) and (c) may apply.

[4] The absolute prohibition of paragraph (a) applies only to situations in which a lawyer would be called upon to espouse adverse positions for different clients in the same matter. It is for this reason that paragraph (a) refers to adversity with respect to a "position taken or to be taken" in a matter rather than adversity with respect to the matter or the entire representation. This approach is intended to reduce the costs of litigation in other representations where parties have common, non-adverse interests on certain issues, but have adverse (or contingently or possibly adverse) positions with respect to other issues. If, for example, a lawyer would not be required to take adverse positions in providing joint representation of two clients in the liability phase of a case, it would be permissible to undertake such a limited representation. Then, after completion of the liability phase, and upon satisfying the requirements of paragraph (c) of this rule, and of any other applicable Rules, the lawyer could represent either one of those parties as to the damages phase of the case, even though the other, represented by separate counsel as to damages, might have an adverse position as to that phase of the case. Insofar as the absolute prohibition of paragraph (a) is concerned, a lawyer may represent two parties that may be adverse to each other as to some aspects of the case so long as the same lawyer does not represent both parties with respect to those positions. Such a representation comes within paragraph (b), rather than paragraph (a), and is therefore subject to the consent provisions of paragraph (c).

[5] The ability to represent two parties who have adverse interests as to portions of a case may be limited because the lawyer obtains confidences or secrets

relating to a party while jointly representing both parties in one phase of the case. In some circumstances, such confidences or secrets might be useful, against the interests of the party to whom they relate, in a subsequent part of the case. Absent the informed consent of the party whose confidences or secrets are implicated, the subsequent adverse representation is governed by the "substantial relationship" test, which is set forth in Rule 1.9.

[6] The prohibition of paragraph (a) relates only to actual conflicts of positions, not to mere formalities. For example, a lawyer is not absolutely forbidden to provide joint or simultaneous representation if the clients' positions are only nominally but not actually adverse. Joint representation is commonly provided to incorporators of a business, to parties to a contract, in formulating estate plans for family members, and in other circumstances where the clients might be nominally adverse in some respect but have retained a lawyer to accomplish a common purpose. If no actual conflict of positions exists with respect to a matter, the absolute prohibition of paragraph (a) does not come into play. Thus, in the limited circumstances set forth in Opinion 143 of the D.C. Bar Legal Ethics Committee, this prohibition would not preclude the representation of both parties in an uncontested divorce proceeding, there being no actual conflict of positions based on the facts presented in Opinion 143. For further discussion of common representation issues, including intermediation, *see* Comments [14]-[18].

Representation Conditionally Prohibited—Rule 1.7(b)

[7] Paragraphs (b) and (c) are based upon two principles: (1) that a client is entitled to wholehearted and zealous representation of its interests, and (2) that the client as well as the lawyer must have the opportunity to judge and be satisfied that such representation can be provided. Consistent with these principles, paragraph (b) provides a general description of the types of circumstances in which representation is improper in the absence of informed consent. The underlying premise is that disclosure and informed consent are required before assuming a representation if there is any reason to doubt the lawyer's ability to provide wholehearted and zealous representation of a client or if a client might reasonably consider the representation of its interests to be adversely affected by the lawyer's assumption of the other representation in question. Although the lawyer must be satisfied that the representation can be wholeheartedly and zealously undertaken, if an objective observer would have any reasonable doubt on that issue, the client has a right to disclosure of all relevant considerations and the opportunity to be the judge of its own interests.

[8] A client may, on occasion, adopt unreasonable positions with respect to having the lawyer who is representing that client also represent other parties. Such an unreasonable position may be based on an aversion to the other parties being represented by a lawyer, or on some philosophical or ideological ground having no foundation in the Rules regarding representation of conflicting interests. Whatever difficulties may be presented for the lawyer in such circumstances as a matter of client relations, the unreasonable positions taken by a client do not fall within the circumstances requiring notification and informed consent. Clients have broad discretion to terminate their representation by a lawyer and that discretion may generally be exercised on unreasonable as well as reasonable grounds.

[9] If the lawyer determines or can foresee that an issue with respect to the application of paragraph (b) exists, the only prudent course is for the lawyer to make disclosure, pursuant to paragraph (c), to each affected client and enable each to determine whether in its judgment the representation at issue is likely to affect its interests adversely.

[10] Paragraph (b) does not purport to state a uniform rule applicable to cases in which two clients may be adverse to each other in a matter in which neither is represented by the lawyer or in a situation in which two or more clients may be direct business competitors. The matter in which two clients are adverse may be so unrelated or insignificant as to have no possible effect upon a lawyer's ability to represent both in other matters. The fact that two clients are business competitors, standing alone, is usually not a bar to simultaneous representation. Thus, in a matter involving a specific party or parties, paragraphs (b)(1) and (c) require notice and informed consent if the lawyer will take a position on behalf of one client adverse to another client even though the lawyer represents the latter client only on an unrelated position or in an unrelated matter. Paragraphs (b)(2), (3), (4) and (c) require disclosure and informed consent in any situation in which the lawyer's representation of a client may be adversely affected by representation of another client or by any of the factors specified in paragraph (b)(4).

Individual Interest Conflicts

[11] The lawyer's own interests should not be permitted to have an adverse effect on representation of a client. For example, if the probity of a lawyer's own conduct in a transaction is in serious question, it may be difficult or impossible for the lawyer to give a client detached advice. Similarly, when a lawyer has discussions concerning possible employment with an opponent of the lawyer's client, or with a law firm representing the opponent, such discussions could adversely affect the lawyer's representation of the client. *See* D.C. Bar Legal Ethics Committee Opinion No. 210 (defense attorney negotiating position with United States Attorney's Office). In addition, a lawyer may not allow related business interests to affect representation, for example, by referring clients to an enterprise in which the lawyer has an undisclosed financial interest. *See* Comment [34] for specific commentary concerning affiliated business interests; Rule 1.8 for specific Rules pertaining to a number of individual attorney's interest conflicts, including business transactions with clients; Rule 1.8(j) for the effect of firm-wide imputation upon individual attorney interests.

[12] For the effect of a blood or marital relationship between lawyers representing different clients, *see* Rule 1.8(h). Disqualification arising from a close family relationship is not imputed. *See* Rule 1.8(j).

Positional Conflicts

[13] Ordinarily a lawyer may take inconsistent legal positions in different forums at different times on behalf of different clients. The mere fact that advocating a legal position on behalf of one client might create precedent adverse to

the interests of a client represented by the lawyer in an unrelated matter does not, without more, create a conflict of interest. A conflict of interest exists, however, if there is a significant risk that a lawyer's action on behalf of one client in a given matter, as referred to in Rule 1.7(b), will adversely affect the lawyer's effectiveness in representing another client in the same or different matter; for example, when a decision favoring one client will create a precedent likely to seriously weaken the position being taken on behalf of the other client. Factors relevant in determining whether the clients need to be advised of the risk include: where the matters are pending, the temporal relationship between the matters, the significance of the issue to the immediate and long-term interests of the clients involved, and the clients' reasonable expectations in retaining the lawyer. If there is significant risk of material limitation, then, absent informed consent of the affected clients, the lawyer must refuse one of the representations or withdraw from one or both matters, subject to the exception provided in Rule 1.7(d). *See* D.C. Legal Ethics Committee Opinion No. 265.

Special Considerations in Common Representation

[14] In considering whether to represent multiple clients in the same matter, a lawyer should be mindful that if the common representation fails because the potentially adverse interests cannot be reconciled, the result can be additional cost, embarrassment and recrimination. In some situations, the risk of failure is so great that multiple representation is plainly impossible. For example, a lawyer cannot undertake common representation of clients where contentious litigation or negotiations between them are imminent or contemplated. Moreover, because the lawyer is required to be impartial between commonly represented clients, representation of multiple clients is improper when it is unlikely that impartiality can be maintained. Generally, if the relationship between the parties has already assumed antagonism, the possibility that the clients' interests can be adequately served by common representation is not very good. Other relevant factors are whether the lawyer subsequently will represent both parties on a continuing basis and whether the situation involves creating or terminating a relationship between the parties.

[15] A particularly important factor in determining the appropriateness of common representation is the effect on client-lawyer confidentiality and the attorney-client privilege. With regard to the attorney-client privilege, the prevailing rule is that, as between commonly represented clients, the privilege does not attach. Hence, it must be assumed that if litigation eventuates between the clients, the privilege will not protect any such communications, and the clients should be so advised.

[16] As to the duty of confidentiality, continued common representation will almost certainly be inadequate if one client asks the lawyer not to disclose to the other client information relevant to the common representation. This is so because the lawyer has an equal duty of loyalty to each client, and each client has the right to be informed of anything bearing on the representation that might affect that client's interests and the right to expect that the lawyer will use that information to that client's benefit. *See* Rule 1.4. The lawyer should, at the outset of the common representation and as part of the process of obtaining each client's informed consent, advise each client that information relevant to the common representation will

be shared, and explain the circumstances in which the lawyer may have to withdraw from any or all representations if one client later objects to continued common representation or sharing of such information. In limited circumstances, it may be appropriate for the lawyer to proceed with the representation when the clients have agreed, after being properly informed, that the lawyer will keep certain information confidential. For example, the lawyer may reasonably conclude that failure to disclose one client's trade secrets to another client will not adversely affect representation involving a joint venture between the clients and agree to keep that information confidential with the informed consent of both clients.

[17] When seeking to establish or adjust a relationship between clients, the lawyer should make clear that the lawyer's role is not that of partisanship normally expected in other circumstances and, thus, that the clients may be required to assume greater responsibility for decisions than when each client is separately represented. Any limitations on the scope of the representation made necessary as a result of the common representation should be fully explained to the clients at the outset of the representation. *See* Rule 1.2(c).

[18] Subject to the above limitations, each client in the common representation has the right to loyal and diligent representation and the protection of Rule 1.9 concerning the obligations to a former client. The client also has the right to discharge the lawyer as stated in Rule 1.16.

Lawyer's Duty to Make Inquiries to Determine Potential Conflicts

[19] The scope of and parties to a "matter" are typically apparent in on-the-record adversary proceedings or other proceedings in which a written record of the identity and the position of the parties exists. In Rule 1.7(b)(1), the phrase "matter involving a specific party or parties" refers to such situations. In other situations, however, it may not be clear to a lawyer whether the representation of one client is adverse to the interests of another client. For example, a lawyer may represent a client only with respect to one or a few of the client's areas of interest. Other lawyers, or non-lawyers (such as lobbyists), or employees of the client (such as government relations personnel) may be representing that client on many issues whose scope and content are unknown to the lawyer. Clients often have many representatives acting for them, including multiple law firms, nonlawyer lobbyists, and client employees. A lawyer retained for a limited purpose may not be aware of the full range of a client's other interests or positions on issues. Except in matters involving a specific party or parties, a lawyer is not required to inquire of a client concerning the full range of that client's interests in issues, unless it is clear to the lawyer that there is a potential for adversity between the interests of clients of the lawyer. Where lawyers are associated in a firm within the meaning of Rule 1.10(a), the rule stated in the preceding sentence must be applied to all lawyers and all clients in the firm. Unless a lawyer is aware that representing one client involves seeking a result to which another client is opposed, Rule 1.7 is not violated by a representation that eventuates in the lawyer's unwittingly taking a position for one client adverse to the interests of another client. The test to be applied here is one of reasonableness and may turn on whether the lawyer has an effective conflict checking system in place.

Situations That Frequently Arise

[20] A number of types of situations frequently arise in which disclosure and informed consent are usually required. These include joint representation of parties to criminal and civil litigation, joint representation of incorporators of a business, joint representation of a business or government agency and its employees, representation of family members seeking estate planning or the drafting of wills, joint representation of an insurer and an insured, representation in circumstances in which the personal or financial interests of the lawyer, or the lawyer's family, might be affected by the representation, and other similar situations in which experience indicates that conflicts are likely to exist or arise. For example, a lawyer might not be able to represent a client vigorously if the client's adversary is a person with whom the lawyer has longstanding personal or social ties. The client is entitled to be informed of such circumstances so that an informed decision can be made concerning the advisability of retaining the lawyer who has such ties to the adversary. The principles of disclosure and informed consent are equally applicable to all such circumstances, except that if the positions to be taken by two clients in a matter as to which the lawyer represents both are actually adverse, then, as provided in paragraph (a), the lawyer may not undertake or continue the representation with respect to those issues even if disclosure has been made and informed consent obtained.

Organization Clients

[21] As is provided in Rule 1.13, the lawyer who represents a corporation, partnership, trade association or other organization-type client is deemed to represent that specific entity, and not its shareholders, owners, partners, members or "other constituents." Thus, for purposes of interpreting this rule, the specific entity represented by the lawyer is the "client." Ordinarily that client's affiliates (parents and subsidiaries), other stockholders and owners, partners, members, etc., are not considered to be clients of the lawyer. Generally, the lawyer for a corporation is not prohibited by legal ethics principles from representing the corporation in a matter in which the corporation's stockholders or other constituents are adverse to the corporation. *See* D.C. Bar Legal Ethics Committee Opinion No. 216. A fortiori, and consistent with the principle reflected in Rule 1.13, the lawyer for an organization normally should not be precluded from representing an unrelated client whose interests are adverse to the interests of an affiliate (e.g., parent or subsidiary), stockholders and owners, partners, members, etc., of that organization in a matter that is separate from and not substantially related to the matter on which the lawyer represents the organization.

[22] However, there may be cases in which a lawyer is deemed to represent a constituent of an organization client. Such de facto representation has been found where a lawyer has received confidences from a constituent during the course of representing an organization client in circumstances in which the constituent reasonably believed that the lawyer was acting as the constituent's lawyer as well as the lawyer for the organization client. *See generally* ABA Formal Opinion 92-365. In general, representation may be implied where on the facts there is a reasonable belief by the constituent that there is individual as well as collective representation. *Id.* The

propriety of representation adverse to an affiliate or constituent of the organization client, therefore, must first be tested by determining whether a constituent is in fact a client of the lawyer. If it is, representation adverse to the constituent requires compliance with Rule 1.7. *See* ABA Opinion 92-365. The propriety of representation must also be tested by reference to the lawyer's obligation under Rule 1.6 to preserve confidences and secrets and to the obligations imposed by paragraphs (b)(2) through (b)(4) of this rule. Thus, absent informed consent under Rule 1.7(c), such adverse representation ordinarily would be improper if

(a) the adverse matter is the same as, or substantially related to, the matter on which the lawyer represents the organization client,

(b) during the course of representation of the organization client the lawyer has in fact acquired confidences or secrets (as defined in Rule 1.6(b)) of the organization client or an affiliate or constituent that could be used to the disadvantage of any of the organization client or its affiliate or constituents, or

(c) such representation seeks a result that is likely to have a material adverse effect on the financial condition of the organization client.

[23] In addition, the propriety of representation adverse to an affiliate or constituent of the organization client must be tested by attempting to determine whether the adverse party is in substance the "alter ego" of the organization client. The alter ego case is one in which there is likely to be a reasonable expectation by the constituents or affiliates of an organization that each has an individual as well as a collective client-lawyer relationship with the lawyer, a likelihood that a result adverse to the constituent would also be adverse to the existing organization client, and a risk that both the new and the old representation would be so adversely affected that the conflict would not be "consentable." Although the alter ego criterion necessarily involves some imprecision, it may be usefully applied in a parent-subsidiary context, for example, by analyzing the following relevant factors: whether (i) the parent directly or indirectly owns all or substantially all of the voting stock of the subsidiary, (ii) the two companies have common directors, officers, office premises, or business activities, or (iii) a single legal department retains, supervises and pays outside lawyers for both the parent and the subsidiary. If all or most of those factors are present, for conflict of interest purposes those two entities normally would be considered alter egos of one another and the lawyer for one of them should refrain from engaging in representation adverse to the other, even on a matter where clauses (a), (b) and (c) of the preceding paragraph [21] are not applicable. Similarly, if the organization client is a corporation that is wholly owned by a single individual, in most cases for purposes of applying this rule, that client should be deemed to be the alter ego of its sole stockholder. Therefore, the corporation's lawyer should refrain from engaging in representation adverse to the sole stockholder, even on a matter where clauses (a), (b) and (c) of the preceding paragraph [21] are not applicable.

[24] If representation otherwise appropriate under the preceding paragraphs seeks a result that is likely ultimately to have a material adverse effect on the financial condition of the organization client, such representation is prohibited by Rule 1.7(b)(3). If the likely adverse effect on the financial condition of the organization client is not material, such representation is not prohibited by Rule 1.7(b)(3). Obviously, however, a lawyer should exercise restraint and sensitivity in determining whether to undertake such representation in a case of that type, particularly if the organization client does not realistically have the option to discharge the lawyer as counsel to the organization client.

[25] The provisions of paragraphs [20] through [23] are subject to any contrary agreement or other understanding between the client and the lawyer. In particular, the client has the right by means of the original engagement letter or otherwise to restrict the lawyer from engaging in representations otherwise permissible under the foregoing guidelines. If the lawyer agrees to such restrictions in order to obtain or keep the client's business, any such agreement between client and lawyer will take precedence over these guidelines. Conversely, an organization client, in order to obtain the lawyer's services, may in the original engagement letter or otherwise give informed consent to the lawyer in advance to engage in representations adverse to an affiliate, owner or other constituent of the client not otherwise permissible under the foregoing guidelines so long as the requirements of Rule 1.7(c) can be met.

[26] In any event, in all cases referred to above, the lawyer must carefully consider whether Rule 1.7(b)(2) or Rule 1.7(b)(4) requires informed consent from the second client whom the lawyer proposes to represent adverse to an affiliate, owner or other constituent of the first client.

Disclosure and Consent

[27] Disclosure and informed consent are not mere formalities. Adequate disclosure requires such disclosure of the parties and their interests and positions as to enable each potential client to make a fully informed decision as to whether to proceed with the contemplated representation. If a lawyer's obligation to one or another client or to others or some other consideration precludes making such full disclosure to all affected parties, that fact alone precludes undertaking the representation at issue. Full disclosure also requires that clients be made aware of the possible extra expense, inconvenience, and other disadvantages that may arise if an actual conflict of position should later arise and the lawyer be required to terminate the representation.

[28] It is ordinarily prudent for the lawyer to provide at least a written summary of the considerations disclosed and to request and receive a written informed consent, although the rule does not require that disclosure be in writing or in any other particular form in all cases. Lawyers should also recognize that the form of disclosure sufficient for more sophisticated business clients may not be sufficient to permit less sophisticated clients to provide informed consent. Moreover, under the District of Columbia substantive law, the lawyer bears the burden of proof that informed consent was secured.

[29] The term "informed consent" is defined in Rule 1.0(e). As indicated in Comment [2] to that rule, a client's consent must not be coerced either by the lawyer or by any other person. In particular, the lawyer should not use the client's investment in previous representation by the lawyer as leverage to obtain or maintain representation that may be contrary to the client's best interests. If a lawyer has reason to believe that undue influence has been used by anyone to obtain agreement to the representation, the lawyer should not undertake the representation.

[30] The lawyer's authority to solicit and to act upon the client's consent to a conflict is limited further by the requirement that the lawyer reasonably believe that he or she will be able to provide competent and diligent representation to each affected client. Generally, it is doubtful that a lawyer could hold such a belief where the representation of one client is likely to have a substantial and material adverse effect upon the interests of another client, or where the lawyer's individual interests

make it likely that the lawyer will be adversely situated to the client with respect to the subject matter of the legal representation.

[31] Rule 1.7 permits advance waivers within certain limits and subject to certain client protections. Such waivers are permissible only if the prerequisites of the rule—namely "full disclosure of the existence and nature of the possible conflict and the possible adverse consequences of such representation"—are satisfied. Under the Rules' definition of "informed consent," the client must have "adequate information and explanation about the material risks of and reasonably available alternatives to the proposed course of action." *See* Rule 1.0(e). Ordinarily this will require that either (1) the consent is specific as to types of potentially adverse representations and types of adverse clients (e.g., a bank client for whom the lawyer performs corporate work waives the lawyer's representation of borrowers in mortgage loan transactions with that bank) or (2) the waiving client has available in-house or other current counsel independent of the lawyer soliciting the waiver.

[32] Rule 1.7(a) provides that a conflict arising from the lawyer's advancing adverse positions in the same matter cannot be waived in advance or otherwise. Although an advance waiver may permit the lawyer to act adversely to the waiving client in matters that are substantially related to the matter in which the lawyer represents that client, lawyers should take particular care in obtaining and acting pursuant to advance waivers where such a matter is involved.

Withdrawal

[33] It is much to be preferred that a representation that is likely to lead to a conflict be avoided before the representation begins, and a lawyer should bear this fact in mind in considering whether disclosure should be made and informed consent obtained at the outset. If, however, a conflict arises after a representation has been undertaken, and the conflict falls within paragraph (a), or if a conflict arises under paragraph (b) and informed and uncoerced consent is not or cannot be obtained pursuant to paragraph (c), then the lawyer should withdraw from the representation, complying with Rule 1.16. Where a conflict is not foreseeable at the outset of representation and arises only under Rule 1.7(b)(1), a lawyer should seek informed consent to the conflict at the time that the conflict becomes evident, but if such consent is not given by the opposing party in the matter, the lawyer need not withdraw. In determining whether conflict is reasonably foreseeable, the test is an objective one. In determining the reasonableness of a lawyer's conduct, such factors as whether the lawyer (or lawyer's firm) has an adequate conflict-checking system in place, must be considered. Where more than one client is involved and the lawyer must withdraw because a conflict arises after representation has been undertaken, the question of whether the lawyer may continue to represent any of the clients is determined by Rule 1.9.

Imputed Disqualification

[34] All of the references in Rule 1.7 and its accompanying Comment to the limitation upon a "lawyer" must be read in light of the imputed disqualification provisions of Rule 1.10, which affect lawyers practicing in a firm.

[35] In the government lawyer context, Rule 1.7(b) is not intended to apply to conflicts between agencies or components of government (federal, state, or local) where the resolution of such conflicts has been entrusted by law, order, or regulation to a specific individual or entity.

Businesses Affiliated with a Lawyer or Firm

[36] Lawyers, either alone or through firms, may have interests in enterprises that do not practice law but that, in some or all of their work, become involved with lawyers or their clients either by assisting the lawyer in providing legal services or by providing related services to the client. Examples of such enterprises are accounting firms, consultants, real estate brokerages, and the like. The existence of such interests raises several questions under this rule. First, a lawyer's recommendation, as part of legal advice, that the client obtain the services of an enterprise in which the lawyer has an interest implicates paragraph 1.7(b)(4). The lawyer should not make such a recommendation unless able to conclude that the lawyer's professional judgment on behalf of the client will not be adversely affected. Even then, the lawyer should not make such a recommendation without full disclosure to the client so that the client can make a fully informed choice. Such disclosure should include the nature and substance of the lawyer's or the firm's interest in the related enterprise, alternative sources for the non-legal services in question, and sufficient information so that the client understands that the related enterprise's services are not legal services and that the client's relationship to the related enterprise will not be that of a client to attorney. Second, such a related enterprise may refer a potential client to the lawyer; the lawyer should take steps to assure that the related enterprise will inform the lawyer of all such referrals. The lawyer should not accept such a referral without full disclosure of the nature and substance of the lawyer's interest in the related enterprise. *See also* Rule 7.1(b). Third, the lawyer should be aware that the relationship of a related enterprise to its own customer may create a significant interest in the lawyer in the continuation of that relationship. The substantiality of such an interest may be enough to require the lawyer to decline a proffered client representation that would conflict with that interest; at least Rule1.7(b)(4) and (c) may require the prospective client to be informed and to give informed consent before the representation could be undertaken. Fourth, a lawyer's interest in a related enterprise that may also serve the lawyer's clients creates a situation in which the lawyer must take unusual care to fashion the relationship among lawyer, client, and related enterprise to assure that the confidences and secrets are properly preserved pursuant to Rule 1.6 to the maximum extent possible. *See* Rule 5.3.

Sexual Relations Between Lawyer and Client

[37] The relationship between lawyer and client is a fiduciary one in which the lawyer occupies the highest position of trust and confidence. Because of this fiduciary duty to clients, combining a professional relationship with any intimate personal relationship may raise concerns about conflict of interest, impairment of the judgment of both lawyer and client, and preservation of attorney-client privilege.

These concerns may be particularly acute when a lawyer has a sexual relationship with a client. Such a relationship may create a conflict of interest under Rule 1.7(b)(4) or violate other disciplinary rules, and it generally is imprudent even in the absence of an actual violation of these Rules.

[38] Especially when the client is an individual, the client's dependence on the lawyer's knowledge of the law is likely to make the relationship between lawyer and client unequal. A sexual relationship between lawyer and client can involve unfair exploitation of the lawyer's fiduciary role and thereby violate the lawyer's basic obligation not to use the trust of the client to the client's disadvantage. In addition, such a relationship presents a significant risk that the lawyer's emotional involvement will impair the lawyer's independent professional judgment. Moreover, a blurred line between the professional and personal relationships may make it difficult to predict the extent to which client confidences will be protected by the attorney-client privilege, because client confidences are protected by privilege only when they are imparted in the context of the client-lawyer relationship. The client's own emotional involvement may make it impossible for the client to give informed consent to these risks.

[39] Sexual relationships with the representative of an organization client may not present the same questions of inherent inequality as the relationship with an individual client. Nonetheless, impairment of the lawyer's independent professional judgment and protection of the attorney-client privilege are still of concern, particularly if outside counsel has a sexual relationship with a representative of the organization who supervises, directs, or regularly consults with an outside lawyer concerning the organization's legal matters. An in-house employee in an intimate personal relationship with outside counsel may not be able to assess and waive any conflict of interest for the organization because of the employee's personal involvement, and another representative of the organization may be required to determine whether to give informed consent to a waiver. The lawyer should consider not only the disciplinary rules but also the organization's personnel policies regarding sexual relationships (for example, prohibiting such relationships between supervisors and subordinates).

Short-Term Limited Legal Services

[40] For the application of this rule and Rules 1.9 and 1.10 when the lawyer undertakes to provide short-term limited legal services to a client under the auspices of a program sponsored by a nonprofit organization or court, *see* Rule 6.5(a).

Rule 1.8.   Conflict of Interest: Specific Rules

(a) A lawyer shall not enter into a business transaction with a client or knowingly acquire an ownership, possessory, security, or other pecuniary interest adverse to a client unless:

(1) The transaction and terms on which the lawyer acquires the interest are fair and reasonable to the client and are fully disclosed and transmitted in writing to the client in a manner which can be reasonably understood by the client;

(2) The client is given a reasonable opportunity to seek the advice of independent counsel in the transaction; and

(3) The client gives informed consent in writing thereto.

(b) A lawyer shall not prepare an instrument giving the lawyer or a person related to the lawyer any substantial gift from a client, including a testamentary gift, except where the client is related to the donee. For purposes of this paragraph, related persons include a spouse, child, grandchild, parent, grandparent or other relative or individual with whom the lawyer or the client maintains a close familial relationship.

(c) Prior to the conclusion of representation of a client, a lawyer shall not make or negotiate an agreement giving the lawyer literary or media rights to a portrayal or account based in substantial part on information relating to the representation.

(d) While representing a client in connection with contemplated or pending litigation or administrative proceedings, a lawyer shall not advance or guarantee financial assistance to the client, except that a lawyer may pay or otherwise provide:

(1) The expenses of litigation or administrative proceedings, including court costs, expenses of investigation, expenses or medical examination, costs of obtaining and presenting evidence; and

(2) Other financial assistance which is reasonably necessary to permit the client to institute or maintain the litigation or administrative proceedings.

(e) A lawyer shall not accept compensation for representing a client from one other than the client unless:

(1) The client gives informed consent after consultation;

(2) There is no interference with the lawyer's independence of professional judgment or with the client-lawyer relationship; and

(3) Information relating to representation of a client is protected as required by Rule 1.6

(f) A lawyer who represents two or more clients shall not participate in making an aggregate settlement of the claims for or against the clients, or in a criminal case an aggregated agreement as to guilty or *nolo contendere* pleas, unless each client gives informed consent in a writing signed by the client after consultation, including disclosure of the existence and nature of all the claims or pleas involved and of the participation of each person in the settlement.

(g) A lawyer shall not:

(1) Make an agreement prospectively limiting the lawyer's liability to a client for malpractice; or

(2) Settle a claim or potential claim for malpractice arising out of the lawyer's past conduct with unrepresented client or former client unless that person is advised in writing of the desirability of seeking the advice of independent legal counsel and is given a reasonable opportunity to do so in connection therewith.

(h) A lawyer related to another lawyer as parent, child, sibling, or spouse shall not represent a client in a representation directly adverse to a person who the lawyer knows is represented by the other lawyer except upon informed consent by the client after consultation regarding the relationship.

(i) A lawyer may acquire and enforce a lien granted by law to secure the lawyer's fees or expenses, but a lawyer shall not impose a lien upon any part of a client's files, except upon the lawyer's own work product, and then only to the extent that the work product has not been paid for. This work product exception shall not apply when the client has become unable to pay, or when withholding the lawyer's work product would present a significant risk to the client of irreparable harm.

(j) While lawyers are associated in a firm, a prohibition in the foregoing paragraphs (a) through (g) and (i) that applies to any one of them shall apply to all of them.

COMMENT

Transactions Between Client and Lawyer

[1] A lawyer's legal skill and training, together with the relationship of trust and confidence between lawyer and client, create the possibility of overreaching when the lawyer participates in a business, property or financial transaction with a client, for example, a loan or sales transaction or a lawyer investment on behalf of a client. The requirements of paragraph (a) must be met even when the transaction is not closely related to the subject matter of the representation, as when a lawyer drafting a will for a client learns that the client needs money for unrelated expenses and offers to make a loan to the client. The rule applies to lawyers engaged in the sale of goods or services related to the practice of law, for example, the sale of title insurance or investment services to the existing clients of the lawyer's legal practice. *See* Rule 5.7. It also applies to lawyers purchasing property from estates they represent. It does not apply to ordinary fee arrangements between client and lawyer, which are governed by Rule 1.5, although the requirements of this rule must be met when the lawyer accepts an interest in the client's business or other non-monetary property as payment of all or part of a fee. In addition, the rule does not apply to standard commercial transactions between the lawyer and the client for products and services that the client generally markets to others; for example, banking or brokerage services, medical services, products manufactured or distributed by the client, and utility services. In such transactions, the lawyer has no advantage in dealing with the client, and the restrictions in paragraph (a) are unnecessary and impracticable.

[2] The client's consent need not be an actual or electronic signature but must be in written or electronic form and show the client's assent to the terms communicated by the lawyer, e.g., a return electronic mail. When necessary, the lawyer should discuss both the material risks of the proposed transaction, including any risk presented by the lawyer's involvement, and the existence of reasonably available

alternatives and, where appropriate, should explain that the client may wish to seek the advice of independent counsel.

[3] The risk to a client is greatest when the client expects the lawyer to represent the client in the transaction itself or when the lawyer's financial interest otherwise poses a significant risk that the lawyer's representation of the client will be adversely affected by the lawyer's financial interest in the transaction. Here the lawyer's role requires that the lawyer must comply not only with the requirements of paragraph (a), but also with the requirements of Rule 1.7. Under that rule, the lawyer must disclose the risks associated with the lawyer's dual role as both legal adviser and participant in the transaction, such as the risk that the lawyer will structure the transaction or give legal advice in a way that favors the lawyer's interests at the expense of the client. Moreover, the lawyer must obtain the client's informed consent. For the definition of "informed consent," *see* Rule 1.0(e). In some cases, the lawyer's interest may be such that Rule 1.7 will preclude the lawyer from seeking the client's consent to the transaction.

[4] The fact that the client was independently represented in the transaction is relevant in determining whether the agreement was fair and reasonable to the client, as paragraph (a)(1) requires.

[5] A lawyer may accept a gift from a client, if the transaction meets general standards of fairness. For example, a simple gift such as a present given at a holiday or as a token of appreciation is permitted. If effectuation of a substantial gift requires preparing a legal instrument such as a will or conveyance, however, the client should be advised by the lawyer to obtain the detached advice that another lawyer can provide. Paragraph (b) recognizes an exception where the client is a relative of the donee or the gift is not substantial.

[6] This rule does not prohibit a lawyer from seeking to have the lawyer or a partner or associate of the lawyer named as executor of the client's estate or to another potentially lucrative fiduciary position. Nevertheless, such appointments will be subject to the general conflict of interest provision in Rule 1.7 when there is a significant risk that the lawyer's interest in obtaining the appointment will adversely affect the lawyer's independent professional judgment in advising the client concerning the choice of an executor or other fiduciary. In obtaining the client's informed consent to the conflict, the lawyer should advise the client concerning the nature and extent of the lawyer's financial interest in the appointment, as well as the availability of alternative candidates for the position.

[7] This rule does not prevent a lawyer from entering into a contingent fee arrangement with a client in a civil case, if the arrangement satisfies all the requirements of Rule 1.5(c).

Literary Rights

[8] An agreement by which a lawyer acquires literary or media rights concerning the conduct of the representation creates a conflict between the interests of the client and the personal interests of the lawyer. Measures that might otherwise be taken in the representation of the client may detract from the publication value of an account of the representation. Paragraph (c) does not prohibit a lawyer representing a client in a transaction concerning literary property from agreeing that the lawyer's fee shall consist of a share in ownership in the property, if the arrangement conforms to Rule 1.5.

Paying Certain Litigation Costs and Client Expenses

[9] Historically, under the Code of Professional Responsibility, lawyers could only advance the costs of litigation. The client remained ultimately responsible, and was required to pay such costs even if the client lost the case. That rule was modified by this court in 1980 in an amendment to DR 5-103(B) that eliminated the requirement that the client remain ultimately liable for costs of litigation, even if the litigation was unsuccessful. The provisions of Rule 1.8(d) embrace the result of the 1980 modification, but go further by providing that a lawyer may also pay certain expenses of a client that are not litigation expenses. Thus, under Rule 1.8(d), a lawyer may pay medical or living expenses of a client to the extent necessary to permit the client to continue the litigation. The payment of these additional expenses is limited to those strictly necessary to sustain the client during the litigation, such as medical expenses and minimum living expenses. The purpose of permitting such payments is to avoid situations in which a client is compelled by exigent financial circumstances to settle a claim on unfavorable terms in order to receive the immediate proceeds of settlement. This provision does not permit lawyers to "bid" for clients by offering financial payments beyond those minimum payments necessary to sustain the client until the litigation is completed. Regardless of the types of payments involved, assuming such payments are proper under Rule 1.8(d), client reimbursement of the lawyer is not required. However, no lawyer is required to pay litigation or other costs to a client. The rule merely permits such payments to be made without requiring reimbursement by the client.

Person Paying for Lawyer's Services

[10] Lawyers are frequently asked to represent a client under circumstances in which a third person will compensate the lawyer, in whole or in part. The third person might be a relative or friend, an indemnitor (such as a liability insurance company) or a co-client (such as a corporation sued along with one or more of its employees). Because third-party payers frequently have interests that differ from those of the client, including interests in minimizing the amount spent on the representation and in learning how the representation is progressing, lawyers are prohibited from accepting or continuing such representations unless the lawyer determines that there will be no interference with the lawyer's independent professional judgment and there is informed consent from the client. In some circumstances, such as the relationship among insured, insurer, and defense counsel, substantive law regarding the role of the third-party payer may affect the applicability of this rule. Paragraph (e) requires disclosure of the fact that the lawyer's services are being paid for by a third party. Such an arrangement must also conform to the requirements of Rule 1.6 concerning confidentiality and Rule 1.7 concerning conflict of interest. Where the client is a class, consent may be obtained on behalf of the class by court-supervised procedure. *See also* Rule 5.4(c) (prohibiting interference with a lawyer's professional judgment by one who recommends, employs or pays the lawyer to render legal services for another). The requirements of Rule 1.8(e)(1) do not apply to lawyers appointed to represent indigent criminal defendants whose fees are paid under the Criminal Justice Act or any similar statute or rule.

[11] Sometimes, it will be sufficient for the lawyer to obtain the client's informed consent regarding the fact of the payment and the identity of the third-party payer. If, however, the fee arrangement creates a conflict of interest for the lawyer, then the lawyer must comply with Rule 1.7. The lawyer must also conform to the requirements of Rule 1.6 concerning confidentiality. Under Rule 1.7(b)(4), a conflict of interest exists if there is a significant risk that the lawyer's representation will be adversely affected by the lawyer's own interest in the fee arrangement or by the lawyer's responsibilities to the third-party payer (for example, when the third-party payer is a co-client). Under Rule 1.7, the lawyer may accept or continue the representation with the informed consent of each affected client, unless the conflict is nonconsentable under Rule 1.7(a).

Aggregate Settlements

[12] Differences in willingness to make or accept an offer of settlement are among the risks of common representation of multiple clients by a single lawyer. Under Rule 1.7, this is one of the risks that should be discussed before undertaking the representation, as part of the process of obtaining the clients' informed consent. In addition, Rule 1.2(a) protects each client's right to have the final say in deciding whether to accept or reject an offer of settlement and in deciding whether to enter a guilty or *nolo contendere* plea in a criminal case. The rule stated in paragraph (f) of this rule is a corollary of both Rules 1.7 and 1.2(a), and provides that, before any settlement offer or plea bargain is made or accepted on behalf of multiple clients, the lawyer must inform each of them about all the material terms of the settlement, including what the other clients will receive or pay if the settlement or plea offer is accepted. Lawyers representing a class of plaintiffs or defendants, or those proceeding derivatively, must comply with applicable rules regulating notification of class members, compensation of class counsel, and other procedural requirements designed to ensure adequate protection of the entire class.

Limiting Liability and Settling Malpractice Claims

[13] Agreements prospectively limiting a lawyer's liability for malpractice are prohibited because they are likely to undermine competent and diligent representation. Also, many clients are unable to evaluate the desirability of making such an agreement before a dispute has arisen. Rule 1.8(g) does not, however, prohibit a lawyer from entering into an agreement with the client to arbitrate legal malpractice claims, to the extent that such an agreement is valid and enforceable and the client is fully informed of the scope and effect of the agreement. Nor does the rule prohibit an agreement in accordance with Rule 1.2 that defines the scope of the representation, although a definition of scope that makes the obligations of representation illusory will amount to an attempt to limit liability.

[14] Agreements settling a claim or potential claim for malpractice arising out of the lawyer's past conduct are not prohibited by Rule 1.8(g). Nevertheless, in view of the danger that the lawyer will take unfair advantage of an unrepresented client or a former client, the lawyer must first advise such a person in writing of the

appropriateness of independent representation in connection with such a settlement. In addition, the lawyer must give the client or former client a reasonable opportunity to find and consult independent counsel. Settlement of a potential claim most often will occur in the context of the resolution of an actual dispute between the attorney and the client, whether concerning the claim itself or a dispute concerning fees. The rule does not authorize the lawyer to solicit a blanket release from the client as a routine incident of the conclusion of the legal representation.

[15] Paragraph (h) applies to related lawyers who are in different firms. Related lawyers in the same firm are governed by Rules 1.7, 1.9, and 1.10. Pursuant to the provisions of Rule 1.8(j), the disqualification stated in paragraph (h) is personal and is not imputed to members of firms with whom the lawyers are associated. Since each of the related lawyers is subject to paragraph (h), the effect is to require the informed consent of all materially affected clients. Romantic relationships between lawyers may create conflicts of interest under Rule 1.7(b)(4), likewise requiring informed consent of all materially affected clients.

[16] The substantive law of the District of Columbia has long permitted lawyers to assert and enforce liens against the property of clients. *See, e.g., Redevelopment Land Agency v. Dowdey,* 618 A.2d 153, 159-60 (D.C. 1992), and cases cited therein. Whether a lawyer has a lien on money or property belonging to a client is generally a matter of substantive law as to which the ethics rules take no position. Exceptions to what the common law might otherwise permit are made with respect to contingent fees and retaining liens. *See,* respectively, Rule 1.5(c) and Rule 1.8(i).

[17] Rule 1.16(d) requires a lawyer to surrender papers and property to which the client is entitled when representation of the client terminates. Paragraph (i) of this rule states a narrow exception to 1.16(d): a lawyer may retain anything the law permits — including property except for files. As to files, a lawyer may retain only the lawyer's own work product, and then only if the client has not paid for the work. However, if the client has paid for the work product, the client is entitled to receive it, even if the client has not previously seen or received a copy of the work product. Furthermore, the lawyer may not retain the work product for which the client has not paid, if the client has become unable to pay or if withholding the work product might irreparably harm the client's interest.

[18] Under Rule 1.16(d), for example, a lawyer would be required to return all papers received from a client, such as birth certificates, wills, tax returns, or "green cards." Rule 1.8(i) does not permit retention of such papers to secure payment of any fee due. Only the lawyer's own work product — results of factual investigations, legal research and analysis, and similar materials generated by the lawyer's own effort — could be retained. (The term "work product" as used in paragraph (i) is limited to materials falling within the "work product doctrine," but includes any material generated by the lawyer that would be protected under that doctrine whether or not created in connection with pending or anticipated litigation.) And a lawyer could not withhold all the work product merely because a portion of the lawyer's fees had not been paid.

[19] There are situations in which withholding the work product would not be permissible because of irreparable harm to the client. The possibility of involuntary incarceration or criminal conviction constitutes one category of irreparable harm. The realistic possibility that a client might irretrievably lose a significant right or become subject to a significant liability because of the withholding of the work

product constitutes another category of irreparable harm. On the other hand, the mere fact that the client might have to pay another lawyer to replicate the work product does not, standing alone, constitute irreparable harm. These examples are merely indicative of the meaning of the term "irreparable harm," and are not exhaustive.

Attribution of Prohibitions

[20] Under paragraph (j), a prohibition of conduct by an individual lawyer in paragraphs (a) through (g) and (i) applies also to all lawyers associated in a firm with the personally prohibited lawyer. For example, one lawyer in a firm may not enter into a business transaction with a client of another member of the firm without complying with paragraph (a), even if the first lawyer is not personally involved in the representation of the client. The prohibition set forth in paragraph (h) is personal and is not applied to associated lawyers.

Sexual Relationships with Clients

[21] Concerns about personal relationships, including sexual relationships, between lawyers and clients are addressed in Comments [37]-[39] to Rule 1.7.

Rule 1.9.   Conflict of Interest: Former Client

A lawyer who has formerly represented a client in a matter shall not thereafter represent another person in the same or a substantially related matter in which that person's interests are materially adverse to the interests of the former client unless the former client gives informed consent.

COMMENT

[1] After termination of client-lawyer relationship, a lawyer may not represent another client except in conformity with the Rule. The principles in Rule 1.7 determine whether the interests of the present and former client are adverse. Thus, a lawyer could not properly seek to rescind on behalf of a new client a contract drafted on behalf of the former client. Similarly, a lawyer who has defended a client against charges brought by a regulatory agency concerning a transaction may not later represent another client in a private lawsuit against the client involving the same transaction, absent the first client's informed consent. For the definition of "informed consent," *see* Rule 1.0(e).

[2] The scope of a "matter" for purposes of this rule may depend on the facts of a particular situation or transaction. The lawyer's involvement in a matter can also be a question of degree. When a lawyer has been directly involved in a specific transaction, subsequent representation of other clients with materially adverse

interests clearly is prohibited. On the other hand, a lawyer who recurrently handled a type of problem for a former client is not precluded from later representing another client in a wholly distinct problem of that type even though the subsequent representation involves a position adverse to the prior client. Similar considerations can apply to the reassignment of military lawyers between defense and prosecution functions within the same military jurisdiction. The underlying question is whether the lawyer was so involved in the matter that the subsequent representation can be justly regarded as a changing of sides in the matter in question. Rule 1.9 is intended to incorporate District of Columbia and federal case law defining the "substantial relationship" test. *See, e.g., Brown v. District of Columbia Board of Zoning Adjustment,* 486 A.2d 37 (D.C. 1984) (en banc); *T.C. Theatre Corp. v. Warner Brothers Pictures,* 113 F. Supp. 265 (S.D.N.Y. 1953), and its progeny.

[3] Matters are "substantially related" for purposes of this rule if they involve the same transaction or legal dispute or if there otherwise is a substantial risk that confidential factual information as would normally have been obtained in the prior representation would materially advance the client's position in the subsequent matter. For example, a lawyer who has represented a businessperson and learned extensive private financial information about that person may not then represent that person's spouse in seeking a divorce. Similarly, a lawyer who has previously represented a client in securing environmental permits to build a shopping center would be precluded from representing neighbors seeking to oppose rezoning of the property on the basis of environmental considerations; however, the lawyer would not be precluded, on the grounds of substantial relationship, from defending a tenant of the completed shopping center in resisting eviction for nonpayment of rent. Information that has been disclosed to the public or to other parties adverse to the former client ordinarily will not be disqualifying. Information acquired in a prior representation may have been rendered obsolete by the passage of time, a circumstance that may be relevant in determining whether two representations are substantially related. In the case of an organizational client, general knowledge of the client's policies and practices ordinarily will not preclude a subsequent representation; on the other hand, knowledge of specific facts gained in a prior representation that are relevant to the matter in question ordinarily will preclude such a representation. A former client is not required to reveal the confidential information learned by the lawyer in order to establish a substantial risk that the lawyer has confidential information to use in the subsequent matter. A conclusion about the possession of such information may be based on the nature of the services the lawyer provided the former client and information that would in ordinary practice be learned by a lawyer providing such services.

[4] Disqualification from subsequent representation is for the protection of clients and can be waived by them. A waiver is effective only if there is disclosure of the circumstances, including the lawyer's intended role in behalf of the new client. The question of whether a lawyer is personally disqualified from representation in any matter on account of successive government and private employment is governed by Rule 1.11 rather than by Rule 1.9.

[5] With regard to disqualification of a firm with which a lawyer is associated, *see* Rules 1.10; for former government lawyers, *see* Rule 1.11; for former judges and law clerks, *see* Rule 1.12.

Rule 1.10. Imputed Disqualification: General Rule

(a) While lawyers are associated in a firm, none of them shall knowingly represent a client when any one of them practicing alone would be prohibited from doing so by Rules 1.7 or 1.9, unless:

    (1) the prohibition of the individual lawyer's representation is based on an interest of the lawyer described in Rule 1.7(b)(4) and that interest does not present a significant risk of adversely affecting the representation of the client by the remaining lawyers in the firm; or

    (2) the representation is permitted by Rules 1.11, 1.12, or 1.18.

(b) When a lawyer becomes associated with a firm, the firm may not knowingly represent a person in a matter which is the same as, or substantially related to, a matter with respect to which the lawyer had previously represented a client whose interests are materially adverse to that person and about whom the lawyer has in fact acquired information protected by Rule 1.6 that is material to the matter. The firm is not disqualified if the lawyer participated in a previous representation or acquired information under the circumstances covered by Rule 1.6(h) or Rule 1.18.

(c) When a lawyer has terminated an association with a firm, the firm is not prohibited from thereafter representing a person with interests materially adverse to those of a client who was represented by the formerly associated lawyer during the association and is not currently represented by the firm, unless:

    (1) the matter is the same or substantially related to that in which the formerly associated lawyer represented the client; and

    (2) any lawyer remaining in the firm has information protected by Rule 1.6 that is material to the matter.

(d) A disqualification prescribed by this rule may be waived by the affected client under the conditions stated in Rule 1.7.

(e) A lawyer who, while affiliated with a firm, is made available to assist the Office of the Attorney General of the District of Columbia in providing legal services to that agency is not considered to be associated in a firm for purposes of paragraph (a), provided, however, that no such lawyer shall represent the Office of the Attorney General with respect to a matter in which the lawyer's firm appears on behalf of an adversary.

COMMENT

Definition of "Firm"

[1] Whether two or more lawyers constitute a firm within this definition can depend on the specific facts. *See* Rule 1.0(c). For purposes of this rule, the term "firm" includes lawyers in a private firm and lawyers employed in the legal department of a

corporation, legal services organization, or other organization, but does not include a government agency or other government entity. For example, two practitioners who share office space and occasionally consult or assist each other ordinarily would not be regarded as constituting a firm. However, if they present themselves to the public in a way suggesting that they are a firm or conduct themselves as a firm, they should be regarded as a firm for purposes of the Rules. The terms of any formal agreement between associated lawyers are relevant in determining whether they are a firm, as is the fact that they have mutual access to confidential information concerning the clients they serve. Furthermore, it is relevant in doubtful cases to consider the underlying purpose of the Rule that is involved. A group of lawyers could be regarded as a firm for purposes of the Rule that the same lawyer should not represent opposing parties in litigation, while it might not be so regarded for purposes of the Rule that information acquired by one lawyer is attributed to another.

[2] There is ordinarily no question that the members of the law department of an organization constitute a firm within the meaning of the Rules of Professional Conduct, but there can be uncertainty as to the identity of the client. For example, it may not be clear whether the law department of a corporation represents a subsidiary or an affiliated corporation, as well as the corporation by which the members of the department are directly employed. A similar question can arise concerning an unincorporated association and its local affiliates.

[3] Similar questions can also arise with respect to lawyers in legal aid organizations. Lawyers employed in the same unit of a legal service organization constitute a firm, but not necessarily those employed in separate units. As in the case of independent practitioners, whether the lawyers should be treated as associated with each other can depend on the particular Rule that is involved, and on the specific facts of the situation.

Principles of Imputed Disqualification

[4] The rule of imputed disqualification stated in paragraph (a) gives effect to the principle of loyalty to the client as it applies to lawyers who practice in a law firm. Such situations can be considered from the premise that a firm of lawyers is essentially one lawyer for purposes of the Rules governing loyalty to the client, or from the premise that each lawyer is vicariously bound by the obligation of loyalty owed by each lawyer with whom the lawyer is associated. Paragraph (a) operates only among the lawyers currently associated in a firm. When a lawyer moves from one firm to another, the situation is governed by paragraph (b) or (c).

[5] Where an individual lawyer is prohibited from engaging in certain transactions under Rule 1.8, paragraph (j) of that Rule, and not this Rule, governs whether that prohibition applies also to other lawyers in a firm with which that lawyer is associated. For issues involving prospective clients, see Rule 1.18.

[6] Where a lawyer has joined a private firm after having represented the government, the situation is governed by Rule 1.11.

[7] Different provisions are thus made for movement of a lawyer from one private firm to another and for movement of a lawyer from the government to a private firm. The government is entitled to protection of its client confidences, and therefore to the protections provided in Rules 1.6 and 1.11. Nevertheless, if the

more extensive disqualification in Rule 1.10 were applied to former government lawyers, the potential effect on the government would be unduly burdensome. The government deals with all private citizens and organizations, and thus has a much wider circle of adverse legal interests than does any private law firm. In these circumstances, the government's recruitment of lawyers would be seriously impaired if Rule 1.10 were applied to the government. On balance, therefore, the government is better served in the long run by the protections stated in Rule 1.11.

Exception for Personal Interest of the Disqualified Lawyer

[8] The rule in paragraph (a) does not prohibit representation by the firm where neither questions of client loyalty nor protection of confidential information are presented. Where an individual lawyer could not effectively represent a given client because of an interest described in Rule 1.7(b)(4), but that lawyer will do no work on the matter and the disqualifying interest of the lawyer will not adversely affect the representation by others in the firm, the firm should not be disqualified. For example, a lawyer's strong political beliefs may disqualify the lawyer from representing a client, but the firm should not be disqualified if the lawyer's beliefs will not adversely affect the representation by others in the firm. Similarly, representation of a client by the firm would not be precluded merely because the client's adversary is a person with whom one of the firm's lawyers has longstanding personal or social ties or is represented by a lawyer in another firm who is closely related to one of the firm's lawyers. See Rule 1.7, Comment [12] and Rule 1.8(h), Comment [7], respectively. Nor would representation by the firm be precluded merely because one of its lawyers is seeking possible employment with an opponent (e.g., U.S. Attorney's Office) or with a law firm representing the opponent of a firm client.

Lawyers Moving Between Firms

[9] When lawyers move between firms or when lawyers have been associated in a firm but then end their association, the fiction that the law firm is the same as a single lawyer is no longer wholly realistic. There are several competing considerations. First, the client previously represented must be reasonably assured that the principle of loyalty to the client is not compromised. Second, the rule of disqualification should not be so broadly cast as to preclude other persons from having reasonable choice of legal counsel. Third, the rule of disqualification should not unreasonably hamper lawyers from forming new associations and taking on new clients after having left a previous association, or unreasonably hamper the former firm from representing a client with interests adverse to those of a former client who was represented by a lawyer who has terminated an association with the firm. In this connection, it should be recognized that today many lawyers practice in firms, that many to some degree limit their practice to one field or another, and that many move from one association to another several times in their careers. If the concept of imputed disqualification were defined with unqualified rigor, the result would be radical curtailment of the opportunity of lawyers to move from one practice setting to another and of the opportunity of clients to change counsel.

[10] Reconciliation of these competing principles in the past has been attempted under two rubrics. One approach has been to seek *per se* rules of disqualification. For example, it has been held that a partner in a law firm is conclusively presumed to have access to all confidences concerning all clients of the firm. Under this analysis, if a lawyer has been a partner in one law firm and then becomes a partner in another law firm, there is a presumption that all confidences known by a partner in the first firm are known to all partners in the second firm. This presumption might properly be applied in some circumstances, especially where the client has been extensively represented, but may be unrealistic where the client was represented only for limited purposes. Furthermore, such a rigid rule exaggerates the difference between a partner and an associate in modern law firms.

[11] The other rubric formerly used for dealing with vicarious disqualification is the appearance of impropriety proscribed in Canon 9 of the Code of Professional Responsibility. Applying this rubric presents two problems. First, the appearance of impropriety can be taken to include any new client-lawyer relationship that might make a former client feel anxious. If that meaning were adopted, disqualification would become little more than a question of subjective judgment by the former client. Second, since "impropriety" is undefined, the term "appearance of impropriety" is question-begging. It therefore has to be recognized that the problem of imputed disqualification cannot be properly resolved either by simple analogy to a lawyer practicing alone or by the very general concept of appearance of impropriety.

[12] A rule based on a functional analysis is more appropriate for determining the question of vicarious disqualification. Two functions are involved: preserving confidentiality and avoiding positions adverse to a client.

Confidentiality

[13] Preserving confidentiality is a question of access to information. Access to information, in turn, is essentially a question of fact in particular circumstances, aided by inferences, deductions, or working presumptions that reasonably may be made about the way in which lawyers work together. A lawyer may have general access to files of all clients of a law firm and may regularly participate in discussions of their affairs; it should be inferred that such a lawyer in fact is privy to all information about all the firm's clients. In contrast, another lawyer may have access to the files of only a limited number of clients and participate in discussion of the affairs of no other clients; in the absence of information to the contrary, it should be inferred that such a lawyer in fact is privy to information about the clients actually served but not those of other clients.

[14] Application of paragraphs (b) and (c) depends on a situation's particular facts. In any such inquiry, the burden of proof should rest upon the firm whose disqualification is sought.

[15] The provisions of paragraphs (b) and (c) which refer to possession of protected information operate to disqualify the firm only when the lawyer involved has actual knowledge of information protected by Rule 1.6. Thus, if a lawyer while with one firm acquired no knowledge of information relating to a particular client of the firm, and that lawyer later joined another firm, neither the lawyer individually

nor the second firm is disqualified from representing another client in the same or a substantially related matter even though the interests of the two clients conflict.

[16] Independent of the question of disqualification of a firm, a lawyer changing professional association has a continuing duty to preserve confidentiality of information about a client formerly represented. *See* Rule 1.6.

Adverse Positions

[17] The second aspect of loyalty to a client is the lawyer's obligation to decline subsequent representations involving positions adverse to a former client arising in the same or substantially related matters. This obligation requires abstention from adverse representations by the individual lawyer involved, and may also entail abstention of other lawyers through imputed disqualification. Hence, this aspect of the problem is governed by the principles of Rule 1.9. Thus, under paragraph (b), if a lawyer left one firm for another, the new affiliation would preclude the lawyer's new firm from continuing to represent clients with interests materially adverse to those of the lawyer's former clients in the same or substantially related matters. In this respect paragraph (b) is at odds with—and thus must be understood to reject—the dicta expressed in the "second" hypothetical in the second paragraph of footnote 5 of *Brown v. District of Columbia Board of Zoning Adjustment*, 486 A.2d 37, 42 n.5 (D.C. 1984) (en banc), premised on *LaSalle National Bank v. County of Lake*, 703 F.2d 252, 257-59 (7th Cir. 1983).

[18] The concept of "former client" as used in paragraph (b) extends only to actual representation of the client by the newly affiliated lawyer while that lawyer was employed by the former firm. Thus, not all of the clients of the former firm during the newly affiliated lawyer's practice there are necessarily deemed former clients of the newly affiliated lawyer. Only those clients with whom the newly affiliated lawyer in fact personally had a lawyer-client relationship are former clients within the terms of paragraph (b).

[19] The last sentence of paragraph (b) limits the imputation rule in certain limited circumstances. Those circumstances involve situations in which any secrets or confidences obtained were received before the lawyer had become a member of the Bar, but during a time when such person was providing assistance to another lawyer. The typical situation is that of the part-time or summer law clerk, or so-called summer associate. Other types of assistance to a lawyer, such as working as a paralegal or legal assistant, could also fall within the scope of this sentence. The limitation on the imputation rule is similar to the provision dealing with judicial law clerks under Rule 1.12. Not applying the imputation rule reflects a policy choice that imputation in such circumstances could unduly impair the mobility of persons employed in such nonlawyer positions once they become members of the Bar. The personal disqualification of the former nonlawyer is not affected, and the lawyer who previously held the non-legal job may not be involved in any representation with respect to which the firm would have been disqualified but for the last sentence of paragraph (b). Rule 1.6(h) provides that the former nonlawyer is subject to the requirements of Rule 1.6 (regarding protection of client confidences and secrets) just as if the person had been a member of the Bar when employed in the prior position.

[20] Under certain circumstances, paragraph (c) permits a law firm to represent a person with interests directly adverse to those of a client represented by a lawyer who formerly was associated with the firm. The Rule applies regardless of when the formerly associated lawyer represented the client. The firm, however, may not represent a person in a matter adverse to a current client of the firm, which would violate Rule 1.7. Moreover, the firm may not represent the person where the matter is the same as, or substantially related to, that in which the formerly associated lawyer represented the client and any other lawyer currently in the firm has material information protected by Rule 1.6.

Lawyers Assisting the Office of the Attorney General of the District of Columbia

[21] The Office of the Attorney General of the District of Columbia may experience periods of peak need for legal services which cannot be met by normal hiring programs, or may experience problems in dealing with a large backlog of matters requiring legal services. In such circumstances, the public interest is served by permitting private firms to provide the services of lawyers affiliated with such private firms on a temporary basis to assist the Office of the Attorney General. Such arrangements do not fit within the classical pattern of situations involving the general imputation rule of paragraph (a). Provided that safeguards are in place which preclude the improper disclosure of client confidences or secrets, and the improper use of one client's confidences or secrets on behalf of another client, the public interest benefits of such arrangements justify an exception to the general imputation rule, just as Comment [1] excludes from the definition of "firm" lawyers employed by a government agency or other government entity. Lawyers assigned to assist the Office of the Attorney General pursuant to such temporary programs are, by virtue of paragraph (e), treated as if they were employed as government employees and as if their affiliation with the private firm did not exist during the period of temporary service with the Office of the Attorney General. *See* Rule 1.11(h) with respect to the procedures to be followed by lawyers participating in such temporary programs and by the firms with which such lawyers are affiliated after the participating lawyers have ended their participation in such temporary programs.

[22] The term "made available to assist the Office of the Attorney General in providing legal services" in paragraph (e) contemplates the temporary cessation of practice with the firm during the period legal services are being made available to the Office of the Attorney General, so that during that period the lawyer's activities which involve the practice of law are devoted fully to assisting the Office of the Attorney General.

[23] Rule 1.10(e) prohibits a lawyer who is assisting the Office of the Attorney General from representing that office in any matter in which the lawyer's firm represents an adversary. Rule 1.10(e) does not, however, by its terms, prohibit lawyers assisting the Office of the Attorney General from participating in every matter in which the Attorney General is taking a position adverse to that of a current client of the firm with which the participating lawyer was affiliated prior to joining the program of assistance to the Office of the Attorney General. Such an unequivocal

prohibition would be overly broad, difficult to administer in practice, and inconsistent with the purposes of Rule 1.10(e).

[24] The absence of such *a per se* prohibition in Rule 1.10(e) does not diminish the importance of a thoughtful and restrained approach to defining those matters in which it is appropriate for a participating lawyer to be involved. An appearance of impropriety in programs of this kind can undermine the public's acceptance of the program and embarrass the Office of the Attorney General, the participating lawyer, that lawyer's law firm and clients of that firm. For example, it would not be appropriate for a participant lawyer to engage in a representation adverse to a party who is known to be a major client of the participating lawyer's firm, even though the subject matter of the representation of the Office of the Attorney General bears no substantial relationship to any representation of that party by the participating lawyer's firm. Similarly, it would be inappropriate for a participating lawyer to be involved in a representation adverse to a party that the participating lawyer has been personally involved in representing while at the firm, even if the client is not a major client of the firm. The appropriate test is that of conservative good judgment; if any reasonable doubts concerning the unrestrained vigor of the participating lawyer's representation on behalf of the Office of the Attorney General might be created, the lawyer should advise the appropriate officials of the Office of the Attorney General and decline to participate. Similarly, if participation on behalf of the Office of the Attorney General might reasonably give rise to a concern on the part of a participating lawyer's firm or a client of the firm that its secrets or confidences (as defined by Rule 1.6) might be compromised, participation should be declined. It is not anticipated that situations suggesting the appropriateness of a refusal to participate will occur so frequently as to significantly impair the usefulness of the program of participation by lawyers from private firms.

[25] The primary responsibility for identifying situations in which representation by the participating lawyer might raise reasonable doubts as to the lawyer's zealous representation on behalf of the Office of the Attorney General must rest on the participating lawyer, who will generally be privy to nonpublic information bearing on the appropriateness of the lawyer's participation in a matter on behalf of the Office of the Attorney General. Recognizing that many representations by law firms are nonpublic matters, the existence and nature of which may not be disclosed consistent with Rule 1.6, it is not anticipated that law firms from which participating lawyers have been drawn would be asked to perform formal "conflicts checks" with respect to matters in which participating lawyers may be involved. However, consultations between participating lawyers and their law firms to identify potential areas of concern, provided that such consultations honor the requirements of Rule 1.6, are appropriate to protect the interests of all involved — the Office of the Attorney General, the participating lawyer, that lawyer's law firm, and any clients whose interests are potentially implicated.

Rule 1.11.   Successive Government and Private or Other Employment

(a) A lawyer shall not accept other employment in connection with a matter which is the same as, or substantially related to, a matter in which the lawyer participated personally and substantially as a public officer or employee. Such participation includes acting on the merits of a matter in a judicial or other adjudicative capacity.

(b) If a lawyer is required to decline or to withdraw from employment under paragraph (a) on account of a personal and substantial participation in a matter, no partner or associate of that lawyer, or lawyer with an of counsel relationship to that lawyer, may knowingly accept or continue such employment except as provided in paragraphs (c) and (d) below. The disqualification of such other lawyers does not apply if the sole form of participation was as a judicial law clerk.

(c) The prohibition stated in paragraph (b) shall not apply if the personally disqualified lawyer is timely screened from any form of participation in the matter or representation as the case may be, and from sharing in any fees resulting therefrom, and if the requirements of paragraphs (d) and (e) are satisfied.

(d) Except as provided in paragraph (e), when any of counsel, lawyer, partner, or associate of a lawyer personally disqualified under paragraph (a) accepts employment in connection with a matter giving rise to the personal disqualification, the following notifications shall be required:

(1) The personally disqualified lawyer shall submit to the public department or agency by which the lawyer was formerly employed and serve on each other party to any pertinent proceeding a signed document attesting that during the period of disqualification the personally disqualified lawyer will not participate in any manner in the matter or the representation, will not discuss the matter or the representation with any partner, associate, or of counsel lawyer, and will not share in any fees for the matter or the representation.

(2) At least one affiliated lawyer shall submit to the same department or agency and serve on the same parties a signed document attesting that all affiliated lawyers are aware of the requirement that the personally disqualified lawyer be screened from participating in or discussing the matter or the representation and describing the procedures being taken to screen the personally disqualified lawyer.

(e) If a client requests in writing that the fact and subject matter of a representation subject to paragraph (d) not be disclosed by submitting the signed statements referred to in paragraph (d), such statements shall be prepared concurrently with undertaking the representation and filed with Bar Counsel under seal. If at any time thereafter the fact and subject matter of the representation are disclosed to the public or become a part of the public record, the signed statements previously prepared shall be promptly submitted as required by paragraph (d).

(f) Signed documents filed pursuant to paragraph (d) shall be available to the public, except to the extent that a lawyer submitting a signed document demonstrates to the satisfaction of the public department or agency upon which such documents are served that public disclosure is inconsistent with Rule 1.6 or other applicable law.

(g) This rule applies to any matter involving a specific party or parties.

(h) A lawyer who participates in a program of temporary service to the Office of the District of Columbia Attorney General of the kind described in Rule 1.10(e) shall be treated as having served as a public officer or employee for purposes of paragraph (a), and the provisions of paragraphs (b)-(e) shall apply to the lawyer and to lawyers affiliated with the lawyer.

COMMENT

[1] This rule deals with lawyers who leave public office and enter other employment. It applies to judges and their law clerks as well as to lawyers who act in other capacities. It is a counterpart of Rule 1.9, as applied to an individual former government lawyer, and of Rule 1.10, as applied to a law firm.

[2] A lawyer representing a government agency, whether employed or specially retained by the government, is subject to the Rules of Professional Conduct, including the prohibition against representing adverse interests stated in Rule 1.7 and the protections afforded former clients in Rule 1.9. In addition, such a lawyer is subject to this Rule 1.11 and to statutes and government regulations concerning conflict of interest. In the District of Columbia, where there are many lawyers for the federal and D.C. governments and their agencies, a number of whom are constantly leaving government and accepting other employment, particular heed must be paid to the federal conflict-of-interest statutes. *See, e.g.,* 18 U.S.C. Chapter 11 and regulations and opinions thereunder.

[3] Rule 1.11, in paragraph (a), flatly forbids a lawyer to accept other employment in a matter in which the lawyer participated personally and substantially as a public officer or employee; participation specifically includes acting on a matter in a judicial capacity. Other than as noted in Comment [10] to this rule, there is no provision for waiver of the individual lawyer's disqualification. "Matter" is defined in paragraph (g) so as to encompass only matters that are particular to a specific party or parties. The making of rules of general applicability and the establishment of general policy will ordinarily not be a "matter" within the meaning of Rule 1.11. When a lawyer is forbidden by paragraph (a) to accept private employment in a matter, the partners and associates of that lawyer are likewise forbidden, by paragraph (b), to accept the employment unless the screening and disclosure procedures described in paragraphs (c) through (f) are followed.

[4] The rule forbids lawyers to accept other employment in connection with matters that are the same as or "substantially related" to matters in which they participated personally and substantially while serving as public officers or employees. The leading case defining "substantially related" matters in the context of former government employment is *Brown v. District of Columbia Board of Zoning Adjustment,* 486 A.2d 37 (D.C. 1984) (en banc). There the D.C. Court of Appeals, *en banc,* held that in the "revolving door" context, a showing that a reasonable person could infer that, through participation in one matter as a public officer or employee, the former government lawyer "may have had access to information legally relevant to, or

otherwise useful in" a subsequent representation, is *prima facie* evidence that the two matters are substantially related. If this *prima facie* showing is made, the former government lawyer must disprove any ethical impropriety by showing that the lawyer "could not have gained access to information during the first representation that might be useful in the later representation." *Id.* at 49-50. In *Brown,* the Court of Appeals announced the "substantially related" test after concluding that, under former DR 9-101(B), *see* "Revolving Door," 445 A.2d 615 (D.C. 1982) (en banc) (per curiam), the term "matter" was intended to embrace all matters "substantially related" to one another—a test that originated in "side-switching" litigation between private parties. *See* Rule 1.9, Comments [2] and [3]; *Brown,* 486 A.2d at 39-40 n.1, 41-42 & n.4. Accordingly, the words "or substantially related to" in paragraph (a) are an express statement of the judicial gloss in *Brown* interpreting "matter."

[5] Paragraph (a)'s absolute disqualification of a lawyer from matters in which the lawyer participated personally and substantially carries forward a policy of avoiding both actual impropriety and the appearance of impropriety that is expressed in the federal conflict-of-interest statutes and was expressed in the former Code of Professional Responsibility. Paragraph (c) requires the screening of a disqualified lawyer from such a matter as a condition to allowing any lawyers in the disqualified lawyer's firm to participate in it. This procedure is permitted in order to avoid imposing a serious deterrent to lawyers' entering public service. Governments have found that they benefit from having in their service both younger and more experienced lawyers who do not intend to devote their entire careers to public service. Some lawyers might not enter into short-term public service if they thought that, as a result of their active governmental practice, a firm would hesitate to hire them because of a concern that the entire firm would be disqualified from matters as a result.

[6] There is no imputed disqualification and consequently no screening requirement in the case of a judicial law clerk. But such clerks are subject to a personal obligation not to participate in matters falling within paragraph (a), since participation by a law clerk is within the term "judicial or other adjudicative capacity."

[7] Paragraph (d) imposes a further requirement that must be met before lawyers affiliated with a disqualified lawyer may participate in the representation. Except to the extent that the exception in paragraph (e) is satisfied, both the personally disqualified lawyer and at least one affiliated lawyer must submit to the agency signed documents basically stating that the personally disqualified lawyer will be screened from participation in the matter. The personally disqualified lawyer must also state that the lawyer will not share in any fees paid for the representation in question. And the affiliated lawyer must describe the procedures to be followed to ensure that the personally disqualified lawyer is effectively screened.

[8] Paragraph (e) makes it clear that the lawyer's duty, under Rule 1.6, to maintain client confidences and secrets may preclude the submission of any notice required by paragraph (d). If the client requests in writing that the fact and subject matter of the representation not be disclosed, the lawyer must comply with that request. If the client makes such a request, the lawyer must abide by the client's wishes until such time as the fact and subject matter of the representation become public through some other means, such as a public filing. Filing a pleading or making an appearance in a proceeding before a tribunal constitutes a public filing. Once information concerning the representation is public, the notifications called

for must be made promptly, and the lawyers involved may not honor a client request not to make the notifications. If a government agency has adopted rules governing practice before the agency by former government employees, members of the District of Columbia Bar are not exempted by Rule 1.11(e) from any additional or more restrictive notice requirements that the agency may impose. Thus the agency may require filing of notifications whether or not a client consents. While the lawyer cannot file a notification that the client has directed the lawyer not to file, the failure to file in accordance with agency rules may preclude the lawyer's representation of the client before the agency. Such issues are governed by the agency's rules, and Rule 1.11(e) is not intended to displace such agency requirements.

[9] Although paragraph (e) prohibits the lawyer from disclosing the fact and subject matter of the representation when the client has requested in writing that the information be kept confidential, the paragraph requires the lawyer to prepare the documents described in paragraph (d) as soon as the representation commences and to preserve the documents for possible submission to the agency and parties to any pertinent proceeding if and when the client does consent to their submission or the information becomes public.

[10] "Other employment," as used in paragraph (a) of this rule, includes the representation of a governmental body other than an agency of the government by which the lawyer was employed as a public officer or employee, but in the case of a move from one government agency to another the prohibition provided in paragraph (a) may be waived by the government agency with which the lawyer was previously employed. As used in paragraph (a), it would not be other employment for a lawyer who has left the employment of a particular government agency and taken employment with another government agency (e.g., the Department of Justice) or with a private law firm to continue or accept representation of the same government agency with which the lawyer was previously employed.

[11] Paragraph (c) does not prohibit a lawyer from receiving a salary or partnership share established by prior independent agreement. It prohibits directly relating the attorney's compensation in any way to the fee in the matter in which the lawyer is disqualified. *See* D.C. Bar Legal Ethics Committee Opinion 279.

[12] Rule 1.10(e) provides an exception to the general imputation imposed by Rule 1.10(a) for lawyers assisting the Office of the District of Columbia Attorney General on a temporary basis. Rule 1.10(e) provides that lawyers providing such temporary assistance are not considered to be affiliated with their law firm during such periods of temporary assistance. However, lawyers participating in such temporary assistance programs have a potential for conflicts of interest or the abuse of information obtained while participating in such programs. It is appropriate to subject lawyers participating in temporary assistance programs to the same rules which paragraphs (a)-(g) impose on former government employees. Paragraph (h) effects this result.

[13] In addition to ethical concerns, provisions of conflict of interest statutes or regulations may impose limitations on the conduct of lawyers while they are providing assistance to the Office of the District of Columbia Attorney or after they return from such assignments. *See, e.g.,* 18 U.S.C. §§207, 208. Compliance with the Rules of Professional Conduct does not necessarily constitute compliance with all of the obligations imposed by conflict of interest statutes or regulations.

Rule 1.12. Third-Party Neutrals

(a) Except as stated in paragraph (e), a lawyer shall not represent anyone in connection with a matter in which the lawyer participated personally and substantially as an arbitrator, mediator or other third-party neutral, unless all parties to the proceedings give their informed consent after disclosure.

(b) A lawyer shall not negotiate for employment with any person who is involved as a party or as a lawyer for a party in a matter in which the lawyer is participating personally and substantially as an arbitrator, mediator or other third-party neutral.

(c) If a lawyer is disqualified by paragraph (a), no lawyer in a firm with which that lawyer is associated may knowingly undertake or continue representation in the matter unless:

(1) The disqualified lawyer is timely screened from any participation in the matter and is apportioned no part of the fee therefrom; and

(2) Written notice is promptly given to the parties and any appropriate tribunal to enable them to ascertain compliance with the provisions of this rule.

(d) If a client requests in writing that the fact and subject matter of a representation subject to paragraph (a) not be disclosed by submitting the signed statements referred to in paragraph (c), such statements shall be prepared concurrently with undertaking the representation and filed with Bar Counsel under seal. If at any time thereafter the fact and subject matter of the representation are disclosed to the public or become a part of the public record, the signed statements previously prepared shall be promptly submitted as required by paragraph (c).

(e) An arbitrator selected as a partisan of a party in a multimember arbitration panel is not prohibited from subsequently representing that party.

COMMENT

[1] Lawyers who have served as arbitrators, mediators or other third-party neutrals may be asked to represent a client in a matter in which the lawyer participated personally and substantially. This rule forbids such representation unless all of the parties to the proceedings give their informed consent. For the definition of "informed consent," *see* Rule 1.0(e). Other law or codes of ethics governing third-party neutrals may impose more stringent standards of personal or imputed disqualification. *See* Rule 2.4.

[2] Although lawyers who serve as third-party neutrals do not have information concerning the parties that is protected under Rule 1.6, they typically owe the parties an obligation of confidentiality under law or codes of ethics governing third-party neutrals. Thus, paragraph (c) provides that conflicts of the personally disqualified lawyer will be imputed to other lawyers in a law firm unless the conditions of this paragraph are met.

[3] Requirements for screening procedures are stated in Rule 1.0(l). Paragraph (c)(1) does not prohibit the screened lawyer from receiving a salary or partnership share established by prior independent agreement, but that lawyer may not receive compensation directly related to the matter in which the lawyer is disqualified. *See* D.C. Bar Legal Ethics Committee Opinion 279.

[4] Notice, including a description of the screened lawyer's prior representation and of the screening procedures employed, generally should be given as soon as practicable after the need for screening becomes apparent.

[5] With respect to statements filed with Bar Counsel pursuant to paragraph (d), *see* Comments [8] and [9] to Rule 1.11.

Rule 1.13.   Organization as Client

(a) A lawyer employed or retained by an organization represents the organization acting through its duly authorized constituents.

(b) If a lawyer for an organization knows that an officer, employee, or other person associated with the organization is engaged in action, intends to act or refuses to act in a matter related to the representation that is a violation of a legal obligation, or a violation of law which reasonably might be imputed to the organization, and is likely to result in substantial injury to the organization, the lawyer shall proceed as is reasonably necessary in the best interest of the organization. Unless the lawyer reasonably believes that it is not necessary in the best interest of the organization to do so, the lawyer shall refer the matter to higher authority in the organization, including, if warranted by the circumstances, to the highest authority that can act on behalf of the organization as determined by applicable law.

(c) In dealing with an organization's directors, officers, employees, members, shareholders, or other constituents, a lawyer shall explain the identity of the client when it is apparent that the organization's interests may be adverse to those of the constituents with whom the lawyer is dealing.

(d) A lawyer representing an organization may also represent any of its directors, officers, employees, members, shareholders, or other constituents, subject to the provisions of Rule 1.7. If the organization's consent to the dual representation is required by Rule 1.7, the consent shall be given by an appropriate official of the organization other than the individual who is to be represented, or by the shareholders.

COMMENT

The Entity as the Client

[1] An organizational client is a legal entity, but it cannot act except through its officers, directors, employees, shareholders, and other constituents. Officers, directors, employees, and shareholders are the constituents of the corporate

organizational client. The duties defined in this Comment apply equally to unincorporated associations. "Other constituents" as used in this Comment means the positions equivalent to officers, directors, employees, and shareholders held by persons acting for organizational clients that are not corporations.

[2] When one of the constituents of an organizational client communicates with the organization's lawyer in that person's organizational capacity, the communication is protected by Rule 1.6. Thus, by way of example, if an organizational client requests its lawyer to investigate allegations of wrongdoing, interviews made in the course of that investigation between the lawyer and the client's employees or other constituents are covered by Rule 1.6. This does not mean, however, that constituents of an organizational client are the clients of the lawyer. The lawyer may not disclose to such constituents information relating to the representation except for disclosures explicitly or impliedly authorized by the organizational client in order to carry out the representation or as otherwise permitted by Rule 1.6.

[3] When constituents of the organization make decisions for it, the decisions ordinarily must be accepted by the lawyer even if their utility or prudence is doubtful. Decisions concerning policy and operations, including ones entailing serious risk, are not as such in the lawyer's province. Paragraph (b) makes clear, however, that when the lawyer knows that the organization is likely to be substantially injured by action of an officer or other constituent that violates a legal obligation to the organization or is in violation of law that might be imputed to the organization, the lawyer must proceed as reasonably necessary in the best interest of the organization. As defined in Rule 1.0(f), knowledge can be inferred from circumstances, and a lawyer cannot ignore the obvious.

[4] In determining how to proceed under paragraph (b), the lawyer should give due consideration to the seriousness of the violation and its consequences, the responsibility in the organization and the apparent motivation of the person involved, the policies of the organization concerning such matters, and any other relevant considerations. Ordinarily, referral to a higher authority would be necessary. In some circumstances, however, it may be appropriate for the lawyer to ask the constituent to reconsider the matter; for example, if the circumstances involve a constituent's innocent misunderstanding of law and subsequent acceptance of the lawyer's advice, the lawyer may reasonably conclude that the best interest of the organization does not require that the matter be referred to higher authority. If a constituent persists in conduct contrary to the lawyer's advice, it will be necessary for the lawyer to take steps to have the matter reviewed by a higher authority in the organization. If the matter is of sufficient seriousness and importance or urgency to the organization, referral to higher authority in the organization may be necessary even if the lawyer has not communicated with the constituent. Any measures taken should, to the extent practicable, minimize the risk of revealing information relating to the representation to persons outside the organization. Even in circumstances where a lawyer is not obligated by Rule 1.13 to proceed, a lawyer may bring to the attention of an organizational client, including its highest authority, matters that the lawyer reasonably believes to be of sufficient importance to warrant doing so in the best interest of the organization.

[5] When it is reasonably necessary to enable the organization to address the matter in a timely and appropriate manner, paragraph (b) requires the lawyer to refer the matter to higher authority, including, if warranted by the circumstances,

the highest authority that can act on behalf of the organization under applicable law. The organization's highest authority to whom a matter may be referred ordinarily will be the board of directors or similar governing body. However, applicable law may prescribe that under certain conditions the highest authority reposes elsewhere, for example, in the independent directors of a corporation.

[6] Although Model Rule 1.13 contains a "reporting out" requirement that authorizes disclosure of confidential client information concerning an organizational client that would be prohibited with respect to other types of clients, D.C. Rule 1.13 does not expand the kinds of disclosures that are permitted for organizational clients. Under the D.C. Rules, client confidences are protected to the same degree whether the client is an organization or an individual. If a lawyer has reported a matter to the highest appropriate authority in the organization, and that authority has determined not to take any action recommended by the lawyer, the lawyer should accept that authority's decision, just as the lawyer is required to abide by the decision of an individual client to maintain confidences and secrets — unless disclosure is authorized under Rule 1.6. If a binding judicial determination is made that the disclosure limitations under D.C. Rule 1.13 are pre empted by federal law conferring broader authority to disclose client confidences or secrets of certain types of organizational clients, a lawyer may exercise the broader authority granted by federal law. The strictures of the D.C. Rules, however, would continue to apply to protection of confidences and secrets of other types of organizational clients.

Relation to Other Rules

[7] This rule does not limit or expand the lawyer's responsibility under Rules 1.6, 1.8, 1.16, 3.3, and 4.1. If the lawyer's services are being used by an organization to further a crime or fraud by the organization, Rules 1.2(e) and 1.6(d) can be applicable.

Government Agency

[8] The duty defined in this rule encompasses the representation of governmental organizations. *See* Rule 1.6 comments [37] through [40].

Clarifying the Lawyer's Role

[9] There are times when the organization's interest may be or become adverse to those of one or more of its constituents. In such circumstances the lawyer should advise any constituent, whose interest the lawyer finds adverse to that of the organization, of the conflict or potential conflict of interest, that the lawyer cannot represent such constituent, and that such person may wish to obtain independent representation. Care must be taken to assure that the individual understands that, when there is such adversity of interest, the lawyer for the organization cannot provide legal representation for that constituent individual, and that discussions between the lawyer for the organization and the individual may not be privileged.

[10] Whether such a warning should be given by the lawyer for the organization to any constituent individual may turn on the facts of each case.

Dual Representation

[11] Paragraph (c) recognizes that a lawyer for an organization may also represent a principal officer or major shareholder.

Derivative Actions

[12] Under generally prevailing law, the shareholders or members of a corporation may bring suit to compel the directors to perform their legal obligations in the supervision of the organization. Members of unincorporated associations have essentially the same right. Such an action may be brought nominally by the organization, but usually is, in fact, a legal controversy over management of the organization.

[13] The question can arise whether counsel for the organization may defend such an action. The proposition that the organization is the lawyer's client does not alone resolve the issue. Most derivative actions are a normal incident of an organization's affairs, to be defended by the organization's lawyer like any other suit. However, if the claim involves serious charges of wrongdoing by those in control of the organization, a conflict may arise between the lawyer's duty to the organization and the lawyer's relationship with the board. In those circumstances, Rule 1.7 governs whether lawyers who normally serve as counsel to the corporation can properly represent both the directors and the organization.

Rule 1.14.   Client Under a Disability

(a) When a client's capacity to make adequately considered decisions in connection with a representation is diminished, whether because of minority, mental impairment or for some other reason, the lawyer shall, as far as reasonably possible, maintain a typical client-lawyer relationship with the client.

(b) When the lawyer reasonably believes that the client has diminished capacity, is at risk of substantial physical, financial or other harm unless action is taken and cannot adequately act in the client's own interest, the lawyer may take reasonably necessary protective action, including consulting with individuals or entities that have the ability to take action to protect the client and, in appropriate cases, seeking the appointment of a surrogate decision-maker.

(c) Information relating to the representation of a client with diminished capacity is protected by Rule 1.6. When taking protective action pursuant to paragraph (b), the lawyer is impliedly authorized under Rule 1.6(a) to reveal information about the client, but only to the extent reasonably necessary to protect the client's interests.

COMMENT

[1] The typical client-lawyer relationship is based on the assumption that the client, when properly advised and assisted, is capable of making decisions about important matters. When the client is a minor or suffers from a diminished mental capacity, however, maintaining the ordinary client-lawyer relationship may not be possible in all respects. In particular, a severely incapacitated person may have no power to make legally binding decisions. Nevertheless, a client with diminished capacity often has the ability to understand, deliberate upon, and reach conclusions about matters affecting the client's own well-being. For example, children as young as five or six years of age, and certainly those of ten or twelve, are regarded as having opinions that are entitled to weight in legal proceedings concerning their custody. So also, it is recognized that some persons of advanced age can be quite capable of handling routine financial matters while needing special legal protection concerning major transactions. Many people with intellectual disabilities, while lacking sufficient capacity to make binding decisions, have, and are capable of expressing, opinions about a wide range of matters that affect their lives.

[2] The fact that a client suffers a disability does not diminish the lawyer's obligation to treat the client with attention and respect. Even if the person has a surrogate decision-maker, the lawyer should as far as possible accord the represented person the status of client, particularly in maintaining communication. "Surrogate decision-maker" denotes an individual or entity appointed by a court or otherwise authorized by law to make important decisions on behalf of an individual who lacks capacity to make decisions in one or more significant areas of his or her life. The term "surrogate decision-maker" includes, but is not limited to, guardian ad litem, plenary or limited guardian or conservator, proxy decision-maker, or other legal representative.

[3] The client may wish to have family members, lay advocates, or other persons participate in discussions with the lawyer. When necessary to assist in the representation, the presence of such persons generally does not affect the applicability of the attorney-client evidentiary privilege. Nevertheless, the lawyer must keep the client's interests foremost and, except for protective action authorized under paragraph (b), must look to the client, and not family members or others, to make decisions on the client's behalf.

[4] If a surrogate decision-maker has already been appointed for the client, the lawyer should ordinarily look to that person for decisions on behalf of the client. In matters involving a minor, whether the lawyer should look to the parents as natural guardians may depend on the type of proceeding or matter in which the lawyer is representing the minor. In either case, the lawyer should consult with the represented person to the maximum extent possible, as indicated in comment [2] above.

Taking Protective Action

[5] If a lawyer reasonably believes that a client is at risk of substantial physical, financial or other harm unless action is taken, and that a typical client-lawyer relationship cannot be maintained as provided in paragraph (a) because the client lacks sufficient capacity to communicate or to make adequately considered

decisions in connection with the representation, then paragraph (b) permits the lawyer to take protective measures deemed necessary. Such measures could include: consulting with family members, using a reconsideration period to permit clarification or improvement of circumstances, using voluntary surrogate decision-making tools such as durable powers of attorney, or consulting with support groups, professional services, adult-protective agencies or other individuals or entities that have the ability to protect the client. In taking any protective action, the lawyer should be guided by such factors as the wishes and values of the client to the extent known, the client's best interests, the goals of intruding into the client's decision-making autonomy to the least extent feasible, maximizing client capacities and respecting the client's family and social connections.

[6] In determining the extent of the client's diminished capacity, the lawyer should consider and balance such factors as: the client's ability to articulate reasoning leading to a decision, variability of state of mind, ability to appreciate the consequences of a decision, the substantive fairness of a decision, the consistency of a decision with the known long-term commitments and values of the client. In appropriate circumstances, the lawyer may seek guidance from an appropriate diagnostician.

[7] If the client does not have a surrogate decision-maker, the lawyer should consider whether the appointment of a surrogate decision-maker is necessary to protect the client's interests. Thus, if a client with diminished capacity has substantial property that should be sold for the client's benefit, effective completion of the transaction may require appointment of a surrogate decision-maker. In addition, rules of procedure in litigation sometimes provide that minors or persons with diminished capacity must be represented by a guardian or next friend if they do not have a general guardian. In many circumstances, however, the appointment of at least some types of surrogate decision-makers may be more expensive, intrusive, or traumatic for the client than circumstances in fact require. Evaluation of such circumstances is a matter entrusted to the professional judgment of the lawyer. In considering alternatives, however, the lawyer should advocate on behalf of the client the least restrictive form of intervention in the client's decision-making.

Disclosure of the Client's Condition

[8] Disclosure of the client's diminished capacity could adversely affect the client's interests. For example, raising the question of diminished capacity could, in some circumstances, lead to proceedings for involuntary commitment. Information relating to the representation is protected by Rule 1.6. Therefore, unless authorized to do so, the lawyer may not disclose such information. When taking protective action pursuant to paragraph (b), the lawyer is impliedly authorized to make the necessary disclosures, even when the client directs the lawyer to the contrary. Nevertheless, given the risks of disclosure, paragraph (c) limits what the lawyer may disclose in consulting with other individuals or entities or seeking the appointment of a surrogate decision-maker. At the very least, the lawyer should determine whether it is likely that the person or entity consulted with will act adversely to the client's interests before discussing matters related to the client. The lawyer's position in such cases is an unavoidably difficult one.

Emergency Legal Assistance

[9] In an emergency where the health, safety or a financial interest of a person with seriously diminished capacity is threatened with imminent and irreparable harm, a lawyer may take legal action on behalf of such a person even though the person is unable to establish a client-lawyer relationship or to make or express considered judgments about the matter, when the person or another acting in good faith on that person's behalf has consulted with the lawyer. Even in such an emergency, however, the lawyer should not act unless the lawyer reasonably believes that the person has no other lawyer, agent or other representative available. The lawyer should take legal action on behalf of the person only to the extent reasonably necessary to maintain the status quo or otherwise avoid imminent and irreparable harm. A lawyer who undertakes to represent a person in such an exigent situation has the same duties under these Rules as the lawyer would with respect to a client.

[10] A lawyer who acts on behalf of a person with seriously diminished capacity in an emergency should keep the confidences of the person as if dealing with a client, disclosing them only to the extent necessary to accomplish the intended protective action. The lawyer should disclose to any tribunal involved and to any other counsel involved the nature of his or her relationship with the person. The lawyer should take steps to regularize the relationship or implement other protective solutions as soon as possible. Normally, a lawyer would not seek compensation for such emergency actions taken.

Rule 1.15. Safekeeping Property

(a) A lawyer shall hold property of clients or third persons that is in the lawyer's possession in connection with a representation separate from the lawyer's own property. Funds of clients or third persons that are in the lawyer's possession (trust funds) shall be kept in one or more trust accounts maintained in accordance with paragraph (b). Other property shall be identified as such and appropriately safeguarded. Complete records of such account funds and other property shall be kept by the lawyer and shall be preserved for a period of five years after termination of the representation.

(b) All trust funds shall be deposited with an "approved depository" as that term is defined in Rule XI of the Rules Governing the District of Columbia Bar. Trust funds that are nominal in amount or expected to be held for a short period of time, and as such would not be expected to earn income for a client or third-party in excess of the costs incurred to secure such income, shall be held at an approved depository and in compliance with the District of Columbia's Interest on Lawyers Trust Account (DC IOLTA) program. The title on each DC IOLTA account shall include the name of the lawyer or law firm that controls the account, as well as "DC IOLTA Account" or "IOLTA Account." The title on all other trust accounts shall include the name of the lawyer or law firm that

controls the account, as well as "Trust Account" or "Escrow Account." The requirements of this paragraph (b) shall not apply when a lawyer is otherwise compliant with the contrary mandates of a tribunal; or when the lawyer is participating in, and compliant with, the trust accounting rules and the IOLTA program of the jurisdiction in which the lawyer is licensed and principally practices.

(c) Upon receiving funds or other property in which a client or third person has an interest, a lawyer shall promptly notify the client or third person. Except as stated in this rule or otherwise permitted by law or by agreement with the client, a lawyer shall promptly deliver to the client or third person any funds or other property that the client or third person is entitled to receive and, upon request by the client or third person, shall promptly render a full accounting regarding such property, subject to Rule 1.6.

(d) When in the course of representation a lawyer is in possession of property in which interests are claimed by the lawyer and another person, or by two or more persons to each of whom the lawyer may have an obligation, the property shall be kept separate by the lawyer until there is an accounting and severance of interests in the property. If a dispute arises concerning the respective interests among persons claiming an interest in such property, the undisputed portion shall be distributed and the portion in dispute shall be kept separate by the lawyer until the dispute is resolved. Any funds in dispute shall be deposited in a separate account meeting the requirements of paragraphs (a) and (b).

(e) Advances of unearned fees and unincurred costs shall be treated as property of the client pursuant to paragraph (a) until earned or incurred unless the client gives informed consent to a different arrangement. Regardless of whether such consent is provided, Rule 1.16(d) applies to require the return to the client of any unearned portion of advanced legal fees and unincurred costs at the termination of the lawyer's services in accordance with Rule 1.16(d).

(f) Nothing in this rule shall prohibit a lawyer from placing a small amount of the lawyer's funds into a trust account for the sole purpose of defraying bank charges that may be made against that account.

COMMENT

[1] A lawyer should hold property of others with the care required of a professional fiduciary. Securities should be kept in a safe deposit box, except when some other form of safekeeping is warranted by special circumstances. All property that is the property of clients or third persons should be kept separate from the lawyer's business and personal property and, if monies, in one or more trust accounts maintained with financial institutions meeting the requirements of this rule. This rule, among other things, sets forth the longstanding prohibitions of the misappropriation of entrusted funds and the commingling of entrusted funds with the lawyer's property. This rule also requires that a lawyer safeguard "other property" of clients,

which may include client files. For guidance concerning the disposition of closed client files, *see* D.C. Bar Legal Ethics Committee Opinion No. 283.

[2] Paragraph (a) concerns trust funds arising from "a representation." The obligations of a lawyer under this rule are independent of those arising from activity other than rendering legal services. For example, a lawyer who serves as an escrow agent is governed by the applicable law relating to fiduciaries even though the lawyer does not render legal services in the transaction. Separate trust accounts may be warranted when administering estate monies or acting in similar fiduciary capacities.

[3] Paragraph (b) mandates where trust deposits shall be held and further mandates participation in the District of Columbia's IOLTA program. This paragraph is intended to reach every lawyer who is admitted in this jurisdiction regardless of where the lawyer practices, unless a stated exception applies. Thus, a lawyer should follow the contrary mandates of a tribunal regarding deposits that are subject to that tribunal's oversight. Similarly, if the lawyer principally practices in a foreign jurisdiction in which the lawyer is also licensed, and the lawyer maintains trust accounts compliant with that foreign jurisdiction's trust accounting rules, the lawyer may deposit trust funds to an approved depository or to a banking institution acceptable to that foreign jurisdiction. Finally, a lawyer is not obligated to participate in the District of Columbia IOLTA program if the lawyer is participating in, and compliant with, the IOLTA program in the jurisdiction in which the lawyer is licensed and principally practices. IOLTA programs are known by different names or acronyms in some jurisdictions; this rule and its exceptions apply to all such programs, however named. This rule anticipates that a law firm with lawyers admitted to practice in the District of Columbia may be obligated to maintain accounts compliant with the IOLTA rules of other jurisdictions where firm lawyers principally practice. A lawyer who is not participating in the IOLTA program of the jurisdiction in which the lawyer principally practices because the lawyer has exercised a right to opt out of, or not to opt into, the jurisdiction's IOLTA program, or because the jurisdiction does not have an IOLTA program, shall not thereby be excused from participating in the District of Columbia's IOLTA program. To the extent paragraph (b) does not resolve a multijurisdictional conflict, see Rule 8.5. Nothing in this rule is intended to limit the power of any tribunal to direct a lawyer in connection with a pending matter, including a lawyer who is admitted *pro hac vice*, to hold trust funds as may be directed by that tribunal. For a list of approved depositories and additional information regarding DC IOLTA program compliance, see Rule XI, Section 20, of the Rules Governing the District of Columbia Bar, and the D.C. Bar Foundation's website, *www.dcbarfoundation.org.*

[4] The exception to Rule 1.15(b) requires a lawyer to make a good faith determination of the jurisdiction in which the lawyer principally practices. The phrase "principally practices" refers to the conduct of an individual lawyer, not to the principal place of practice of his or her law firm (which might yield a different result for a lawyer with partners). For purposes of this rule, an individual lawyer principally practices in the jurisdiction where the lawyer is licensed and generates the clear majority of his or her income. If there is no such jurisdiction, then a lawyer should identify the physical location of the office where the lawyer devotes the largest portion of his or her time. In any event, the initial good faith determination of where the lawyer principally practices should be changed only if the lawyer's circumstances change significantly and the change is expected to continue indefinitely.

[5] The determination, under paragraph (b), whether trust funds are not expected to earn income in excess of costs, rests in the sound judgment of the lawyer. The lawyer should review trust practices at reasonable intervals to determine whether circumstances require further action with respect to the funds of any client or third party. Because paragraph (b) is a lawyer-specific obligation, this rule anticipates that a law firm may be obligated to maintain accounts compliant with the IOLTA rules of other jurisdictions, to the extent the lawyers in that firm do not all principally practice in the District of Columbia.

[6] Paragraphs (c) and (d) recognize that lawyers often receive funds from third parties from which the lawyer's fee will be paid. The lawyer is not required to remit to the client funds that the lawyer reasonably believes represent fees owed. However, a lawyer may not hold funds to coerce a client into accepting the lawyer's contention. The disputed portion of the funds should be kept in trust and the lawyer should suggest means for prompt resolution of the dispute, such as arbitration. The undisputed portion of the funds should be promptly distributed.

[7] Third parties, such as a client's creditors, may have just claims against funds or other property in a lawyer's custody. A lawyer may have a duty under applicable law to protect such third-party claims against wrongful interference by the client, and accordingly may refuse to surrender the property to the client. However, a lawyer should not unilaterally assume to arbitrate a dispute between the client and the third party. *See* D.C. Bar Legal Ethics Committee Opinion 293.

[8] Paragraph (e) permits advances against unearned fees and unincurred costs to be treated as either the property of the client or the property of the lawyer, but absent informed consent by the client to a different arrangement, the rule's default position is that such advances be treated as the property of the client, subject to the restrictions provided in paragraph (a). In any case, at the termination of an engagement, advances against fees that have not been incurred must be returned to the client as provided in Rule 1.16(d). For the definition of "informed consent," see Rule 1.0(e).

[9] With respect to property that constitutes evidence, such as the instruments or proceeds of crime, *see* Rule 3.4(a).

Rule 1.16.   Declining or Terminating Representation

(a) Except as stated in paragraph (c), a lawyer shall not represent a client or, where representation has commenced, shall withdraw from the representation of a client if

(1) The representation will result in violation of the Rules of Professional Conduct or other law;

(2) The lawyer's physical or mental condition materially impairs the lawyer's ability to represent the client; or

(3) The lawyer is discharged.

(b) Except as stated in paragraph (c), a lawyer may withdraw from representing a client if withdrawal can be accomplished without material adverse effect on the interests of the client, or if:

(1) The client persists in a course of action involving the lawyer's services that the lawyer reasonably believes is criminal or fraudulent;

(2) The client has used the lawyer's services to perpetrate a crime or fraud;

(3) The client fails substantially to fulfill an obligation to the lawyer regarding the lawyer's services and has been given reasonable warning that the lawyer will withdraw unless the obligation is fulfilled;

(4) The representation will result in an unreasonable financial burden on the lawyer or obdurate or vexatious conduct on the part of the client has rendered the representation unreasonably difficult;

(5) The lawyer believes in good faith, in a proceeding before a tribunal, that the tribunal will find the existence of other good cause for withdrawal.

(c) A lawyer must comply with applicable law requiring notice to or permission of a tribunal when terminating a representation. When ordered to do so by a tribunal, a lawyer shall continue representation notwithstanding good cause for terminating the representation.

(d) In connection with any termination of representation, a lawyer shall take timely steps to the extent reasonably practicable to protect a client's interests, such as giving reasonable notice to the client, allowing time for employment of other counsel, surrendering papers and property to which the client is entitled, and refunding any advance payment of fee or expense that has not been earned or incurred. The lawyer may retain papers relating to the client to the extent permitted by Rule 1.8(i).

COMMENT

[1] A lawyer should not accept representation in a matter unless it can be performed competently, promptly, without improper conflict of interest, and to completion.

Mandatory Withdrawal

[2] A lawyer ordinarily must decline or withdraw from representation if the client demands that the lawyer engage in conduct that is illegal or violates the Rules of Professional Conduct or other law. The lawyer is not obliged to decline or withdraw simply because the client suggests such a course of conduct; a client may make such a suggestion in the hope that a lawyer will not be constrained by a professional obligation.

[3] When a lawyer has been appointed to represent a client, withdrawal ordinarily requires approval of the appointing authority. *See also* Rule 6.2. Difficulty may be encountered if withdrawal is based on the client's demand that the lawyer engage in unprofessional conduct. The court may wish an explanation for the withdrawal, while the lawyer may be bound to keep confidential the facts that would constitute such an explanation. The lawyer's statement that irreconcilable differences between

the lawyer and client require termination of the representation ordinarily should be accepted as sufficient.

Discharge

[4] A client has a right to discharge a lawyer at any time, with or without cause, subject to liability for payment for the lawyer's services. Where future dispute about the withdrawal may be anticipated, it may be advisable to prepare a written statement reciting the circumstances.

[5] Whether a client can discharge appointed counsel may depend on applicable law. A client seeking to do so should be given a full explanation of the consequences. These consequences may include a decision by the appointing authority that appointment of successor counsel is unjustified, thus requiring the client to proceed *pro se*.

[6] If the client has diminished capacity, the client may lack the legal capacity to discharge the lawyer, and in any event the discharge may be seriously adverse to the client's interests. The lawyer should make a special effort to help the client consider the consequences and, in an extreme case, may initiate proceedings for the appointment of a surrogate decision maker or similar protection of the client. *See* Rule 1.14.

Optional Withdrawal

[7] A lawyer may withdraw from representation in some circumstances. The lawyer has the option to withdraw if the withdrawal can be accomplished without material adverse effect on the client's interests. Withdrawal is also justified if the client persists in a course of action that the lawyer reasonably believes is criminal or fraudulent, for a lawyer is not required to be associated with such conduct even if the lawyer does not further it. Withdrawal is also permitted if the lawyer's services were misused in the past even if that would materially prejudice the client.

[8] A lawyer may withdraw if the client refuses to abide by the terms of an agreement relating to the representation, such as an agreement concerning the timely payment of the lawyer's fees, court costs or other out-of-pocket expenses of the representation, or an agreement limiting the objectives of the representation.

Assisting the Client upon Withdrawal

[9] Even if the lawyer has been unfairly discharged by the client, a lawyer must take all reasonable steps to mitigate the consequences to the client. The lawyer may retain papers as security for a fee only to the extent permitted by Rule 1.8(i).

Compliance with Requirements of a Tribunal

[10] Paragraph (c) reflects the possibility that a lawyer may, by appearing before a tribunal, become subject to the tribunal's power in some circumstances

to prevent a withdrawal that would otherwise be proper. Paragraph (c) requires the lawyer who is ordered to continue a representation before a tribunal to do so. However, paragraph (c) is not intended to prevent the lawyer from challenging the tribunal's order as beyond its jurisdiction, arbitrary, or otherwise improper while, in the interim, continuing the representation.

Return of Client's Property or Money

[11] Paragraph (d) requires a lawyer to make timely return to the client of any property or money "to which the client is entitled." Where a lawyer holds property or money of a client at the termination of a representation and there is a dispute concerning the distribution of such property or money—whether such dispute is between the lawyer and a client, the lawyer and another lawyer who is owed a fee in the matter, or between either the lawyer or the client and a third party—the lawyer must segregate the disputed portion of such property or money, hold that property or money in trust as required by Rule 1.15, and promptly distribute any undisputed amounts. *See* Rule 1.15 and Comments [4] and [5] thereto; *see In re Haar,* 667 A.2d 1350 (D.C. 1995), 698 A.2d 412 (D.C. 1997). Notwithstanding the foregoing, where a lawyer has a valid lien covering undisputed amounts of property or money, the lawyer may continue to hold such property or money to the extent permitted by the substantive law governing the lien asserted. *See generally* Rules 1.8, 1.15(b).

Rule 1.17.　Sale of Law Practice

A lawyer or a law firm may sell or purchase a law practice, or an area of law practice, including good will, if the following conditions are satisfied:

(a) The seller ceases to engage in the private practice of law, or in the area of practice that has been sold, in the jurisdiction in which the practice has been conducted;

(b) The entire practice is sold to one or more lawyers or law firms or an entire area of practice is sold to one purchaser (either a solo practitioner or a single law firm);

(c) The seller gives a written notice to each of the seller's clients regarding:

(1) the proposed sale;

(2) the client's right to retain other counsel, to take possession of the file or of any funds or property to which the client is entitled; and

(3) the fact that the client's consent to the transfer to the purchasing lawyer or law firm of the client's files, of the representation and of any client funds held by the selling lawyer or law firm will be presumed if the client does not take any action or does not otherwise object within ninety (90) days of receipt of the notice.

If a client cannot be given notice, the representation of that client may be transferred to the purchaser only upon entry of an order so authorizing by a court having jurisdiction. The seller may disclose to the court *in camera* information relating to the representation only to the extent necessary to obtain an order authorizing the transfer of a file.

Once a client has consented to the transfer to the purchasing lawyer or law firm of the client's files, funds and representation or the client fails to take action or otherwise object within ninety (90) days of the notice, then the purchasing lawyer is responsible for the client's matter(s).

(d) The fees charged clients shall not be increased by reason of the sale.

COMMENT

[1] The practice of law is a profession, not merely a business. Clients are not commodities that can be purchased and sold at will. Pursuant to this rule, when a lawyer or an entire firm ceases to practice, or ceases to practice in an area of law, and other lawyers or firms take over the representation, the selling lawyer or firm may obtain compensation for the reasonable value of the practice as may withdrawing partners of law firms. *See* Rules 5.4 and 5.6.

Termination of Practice by the Seller

[2] The requirement that all of the private practice, or all of an area of practice, be sold is satisfied if the seller in good faith makes the entire practice, or the area of practice, available for sale to the purchasers. The fact that a number of the seller's clients decide not to be represented by the purchasers but take their matters elsewhere, therefore, does not result in a violation. Return to private practice as a result of an unanticipated change in circumstances does not necessarily result in a violation. For example, a lawyer who has sold the practice to accept an appointment to judicial office does not violate the requirement that the sale be attendant to cessation of practice if the lawyer later resumes private practice upon being defeated in a contested or a retention election for the office or resigns from a judiciary position.

[3] The requirement that the seller cease to engage in the private practice of law does not prohibit employment as a lawyer on the staff of a public agency or a legal services entity that provides legal services to the poor, or as in-house counsel to a business.

[4] The rule permits a sale of an entire practice attendant upon retirement from the private practice of law within the jurisdiction. Its provisions, therefore, accommodate the lawyer who sells the practice on the occasion of moving to another state.

[5] This rule also permits a lawyer or law firm to sell an area of practice, although, in contrast to the ABA Model Rule and to the provisions of this rule with respect to the sale of an entire practice, a sale of an area of practice can only be made to a single purchaser. If an area of practice is sold and the lawyer remains in the active practice of law, the lawyer must cease accepting any matters in the area of practice that has been sold, either as counsel or co-counsel or by assuming joint responsibility for a matter in connection with the division of a fee with another

lawyer as would otherwise be permitted by Rule 1.5(e). For example, a lawyer with a substantial number of estate planning matters and a substantial number of probate administration cases may sell the estate planning portion of the practice but remain in the practice of law by concentrating on probate administration; however, that practitioner may not thereafter accept any estate planning matters. Although a lawyer who leaves the jurisdiction typically would sell the entire practice, this rule permits the lawyer to limit the sale to one or more areas of the practice, thereby preserving the lawyer's right to continue practice in the areas of the practice that were not sold.

Sale of Entire Practice or Entire Area of Practice

[6] The rule requires that the seller's entire practice, or an entire area of practice, be sold. The prohibition against sale of less than an entire practice area protects those clients whose matters are less lucrative and who might find it difficult to secure other counsel if a sale could be limited to substantial fee-generating matters. The purchasers are required to undertake all client matters in the practice or practice area, subject to client consent. This requirement is satisfied, however, even if a purchaser is unable to undertake a particular client matter because of a conflict of interest.

Client Confidences, Consent and Notice

[7] Negotiations between seller and prospective purchaser prior to disclosure of information relating to a specific representation of an identifiable client no more violate the confidentiality provisions of Rule 1.6 than do preliminary discussions concerning the possible association of another lawyer or merger between firms, with respect to which client consent is not required. Providing the purchaser access to client-specific information relating to the representation and to the file, however, requires client consent. The rule provides that before such information may be disclosed by the seller to the purchaser, the client must be given actual written notice of the contemplated sale, including the identity of the purchaser, and must be told that the decision to consent or make other arrangements must be made within 90 days. If nothing is heard from the client within that time, consent to the sale is presumed, and the purchasing attorney is thereafter responsible for all aspects of the client representation for which the selling lawyer or law firm previously had responsibility. So long as the client does not object or instruct otherwise, the transfer of the representation includes the transfer of client funds or property held by the selling lawyer or law firm directly to the purchasing lawyer or law firm; the contrary guidance contained on the issue of client funds or property in D.C. Legal Ethics Committee Opinion 294 is not adopted. The provision concerning transfer of the representation is added to the ABA Model Rule to ensure that clients are fully aware and fully protected when a lawyer or law firm sells a law practice.

[8] A lawyer or law firm ceasing to practice cannot be required to remain in practice because some clients cannot be given actual notice of the proposed purchase. Since these clients cannot themselves consent to the purchase or direct any

other disposition of their files and of the representation generally, the rule requires an order from a court having jurisdiction authorizing their transfer or other disposition. The court can be expected to determine whether reasonable efforts to locate the client have been exhausted, and whether the absent client's legitimate interests will be served by authorizing the transfer of the file and representation so that the purchaser may continue the representation. Preservation of client confidences requires that the petition for a court order be considered *in camera*.

[9] All elements of client autonomy, including the client's absolute right to discharge a lawyer and transfer the representation to another, survive the sale of the practice or area of practice.

Fee Arrangements Between Client and Purchaser

[10] The sale may not be financed by increases in fees charged the clients of the practice. Existing arrangements between the seller and the client as to fees and the scope of the work must be honored by the purchaser. The purchasing lawyer must comply with all existing rules concerning fee arrangements, such as Rule 1.5.

Other Applicable Ethical Standards

[11] Lawyers participating in the sale of a law practice or a practice area are subject to the ethical standards applicable to involving another lawyer in the representation of a client. These include, for example, the seller's obligation to exercise competence in identifying a purchaser qualified to assume the practice and the purchaser's obligation to undertake the representation competently (*see* Rule 1.1); the obligation to avoid disqualifying conflicts, and to secure the client's informed consent for those conflicts that can be agreed to (*see* Rule 1.7 regarding conflicts and Rule 1.0(e) for the definition of informed consent); and the obligation to protect information relating to the representation (*see* Rules 1.6 and 1.9).

[12] If approval of the substitution of the purchasing lawyer for the selling lawyer is required by the rules of any tribunal in which a matter is pending, such approval must be obtained before the matter may be included in the sale (*see* Rule 1.16).

Applicability of the Rule

[13] This rule applies to the sale of a law practice of a deceased, disabled or disappeared lawyer. Thus, the seller may be represented by a non-lawyer representative not subject to these Rules. Since, however, no lawyer may participate in a sale of a law practice which does not conform to the requirements of this rule, the representatives of the seller as well as the purchasing lawyer may be expected to see to it that they are met.

[14] Admission to or retirement from a law partnership or professional association, retirement, plans and similar arrangements, and a sale of tangible assets of a law practice, do not constitute a sale or purchase governed by this rule.

[15] This rule does not apply to the transfers of legal representation between lawyers when such transfers are unrelated to the sale of a practice or an area of practice.

Other

[16] This rule generally follows the discussion and views concerning the sale of a law practice expressed in D.C. Bar Legal Ethics Committee Opinion 294. The provisions of that Opinion not inconsistent with this rule and Comments remain as appropriate guidance.

Rule 1.18. Duties to Prospective Client

(a) A person who discusses with a lawyer the possibility of forming a client-lawyer relationship with respect to a matter is a prospective client.

(b) Even when no client-lawyer relationship ensues, a lawyer who has had discussions with a prospective client shall not use or reveal information learned in the consultation, except as permitted by Rule 1.6.

(c) A lawyer subject to paragraph (b) shall not represent a client with interests materially adverse to those of a prospective client in the same or a substantially related matter if the lawyer received a confidence or secret from the prospective client, except as provided in paragraph (d). If a lawyer is disqualified from representation under this paragraph, no lawyer in a firm with which that lawyer is associated may knowingly undertake or continue representation in such a matter, except as provided in paragraph (d).

(d) When the lawyer has received a confidence or secret from the prospective client, representation is permissible if:

(1) both the affected client and the prospective client have given informed consent, or

(2) the disqualified lawyer is timely screened from any participation in the matter.

COMMENT

[1] Prospective clients, like clients, may disclose information to a lawyer, place documents or other property in the lawyer's custody, or rely on the lawyer's advice. A lawyer's discussions with a prospective client usually are limited in time and depth and leave both the prospective client and the lawyer free (and sometimes required) to proceed no further. The principle of loyalty diminishes in importance if the sole reason for an individual lawyer's disqualification is the lawyer's initial consultation with a prospective new client with whom no client-lawyer relationship was ever formed, either because the lawyer detected a conflict of interest as a result of an initial consultation, or for some other reason (e.g., the prospective client decided not to retain the firm). Hence, prospective clients should receive some but not all of the protection afforded clients.

[2] Not all persons who communicate information to a lawyer are entitled to protection under this rule. A person who communicates information unilaterally to a lawyer, without any reasonable expectation that the lawyer is willing to discuss the possibility of forming a client-lawyer relationship, is not a "prospective client" within the meaning of paragraph (a).

[3] It is often necessary for a prospective client to reveal information to the lawyer during an initial consultation prior to the decision about formation of a client-lawyer relationship. The client may disclose such information as part of the process of determining whether the client wishes to form a client-lawyer relationship. The lawyer often must learn such information to determine whether there is a conflict of interest with an existing client and whether the matter is one that the lawyer is willing to undertake. Such information is generally protected by Rule 1.6, even if the client or lawyer decides not to proceed with the representation. *See* Rule 1.6, Comment [9]. Paragraph (b) of Rule 1.18 prohibits the lawyer from using or revealing that information, except as permitted by Rule 1.6. The duty to protect confidences and secrets exists regardless of how brief the initial conference may be. The prohibition against use or disclosure of information received from the prospective client may in turn cause the individual lawyer to be disqualified pursuant to Rule 1.7(b)(4) from representing a current or future client of the firm adverse to the prospective client because that lawyer's inability to use or disclose information from the prospective client may adversely affect that lawyer's professional judgment on behalf of the current or future client of the firm whose interests are adverse to the interests of the prospective client.

[4] In order to avoid acquiring confidences and secrets from a prospective client, a lawyer considering whether or not to undertake a new matter may limit the initial interview only to information that does not constitute a confidence or secret, if the lawyer can do so and still determine whether a conflict of interest or other reason for non-representation exists. An individual lawyer of the firm who obtains information from a prospective client is permitted by Rule 1.6(a) to disclose that information to other persons in the lawyer's firm, but any such dissemination may cause additional individual lawyers of the firm to be personally disqualified. If a firm wishes to keep open the screening option under paragraph (d)(2) which permits lawyers who are not personally disqualified to represent clients in the same or substantially related matters, the firm must limit and control dissemination of information obtained from the prospective client. Where the information from the prospective client indicates that any reason for non-representation exists, the lawyer should so inform the prospective client or decline the representation. If the prospective client wishes to retain the lawyer, and if consent is possible under Rule 1.7, then informed consent from all affected present or former clients must be obtained before accepting the representation.

[5] A lawyer may condition conversations with a prospective client on the person's informed consent that no information disclosed during the consultation will prohibit the lawyer from representing a different client in the matter. For the definition of "informed consent," *see* Rule 1.0(e). If the agreement expressly so provides, the prospective client may also consent to the lawyer's subsequent use of information received from the prospective client.

[6] Even in the absence of an agreement, under paragraph (c), the lawyer is not prohibited from representing a client with interests adverse to those of the prospective client in the same or a substantially related matter unless the lawyer has

received confidences and secrets from the prospective client. ABA Model Rule 1.18 provides for personal disqualification only if the information received by the lawyer could be significantly harmful if used in the matter, but the trigger in D.C. Rule 1.18 is receipt of any confidence or secret because of the interest in more broadly protecting the prospective client and the difficulty of determining whether use of the information would be significantly harmful to the prospective client.

[7] Under paragraph (c), the prohibition in this rule is imputed to other lawyers as provided in Rule 1.10, but, under paragraph (d)(1), imputation may be avoided if the lawyer obtains the informed consent of both the prospective and affected clients. In the alternative, imputation may be avoided under paragraph (d)(2) if all disqualified lawyers are timely screened. *See* Rule 1.0(l) (requirements for screening procedures). When a firm may wish to rely on paragraph (d)(2) to avoid imputed disqualification of the firm as a whole, it should take affirmative steps—as soon as an actual or potential conflict is suspected—to prevent a personally disqualified lawyer from disseminating any information about the potential client that is protected by Rule 1.6, except as necessary to investigate potential conflicts of interest, to any other person in the firm, including non-lawyer staff. Any lawyer in the firm who actually receives, directly or indirectly, protected information provided by a prospective client is disqualified. Unlike ABA Model Rule 1.18, this rule does not condition use of screening on the taking of reasonable measures by the personally disqualified lawyer to avoid exposure to more disqualifying information than was reasonably necessary to determine whether to represent the prospective client; that is because the screen protects the prospective client regardless of the amount of information received by the personally disqualified lawyer, and this standard may be difficult to apply in practice. This rule does not prohibit the screened lawyer from receiving any part of the fee, in contrast to ABA Model Rule 1.18, because the substantial administrative burden of complying with such a prohibition exceeds any marginal benefit.

[8] This rule, unlike ABA Model Rule 1.18, does not require notice to the prospective client that lawyers in the firm who are not personally disqualified are representing a client adverse to the prospective client in the same or substantially related matters subject to the screening requirement, because the lack of such a notice requirement under the prior D.C. Rule concerning prospective clients (Rule 1.10(a)) did not prove problematic and it is not clear that the notice requirement materially advances any significant interest of the prospective client.

[9] For the duty of competence of a lawyer who gives assistance on the merits of a matter to a prospective client, *see* Rule 1.1. For a lawyer's duties when a prospective client entrusts valuables or papers to the lawyer's care, *see* Rule 1.15.

COUNSELOR

Rule 2.1. Advisor

In representing a client, a lawyer shall exercise independent professional judgment and render candid advice. In rendering advice, a lawyer may refer not only to law but to other considerations such as moral, economic, social, and political factors that may be relevant to the client's situation.

COMMENT

Scope of Advice

[1] A client is entitled to straightforward advice expressing the lawyer's honest assessment. Legal advice often involves unpleasant facts and alternatives that a client may be disinclined to confront. In presenting advice, a lawyer endeavors to sustain the client's morale and may put advice in as acceptable a form as honesty permits. However, a lawyer should not be deterred from giving candid advice by the prospect that the advice will be unpalatable to the client.

[2] Advice couched in narrowly legal terms may be of little value to a client, especially where practical considerations, such as cost or effects on other people, are predominant. Purely technical legal advice, therefore, can sometimes be inadequate. It is proper for a lawyer to refer to relevant moral and ethical considerations in giving advice. Although a lawyer is not a moral advisor as such, moral and ethical considerations impinge upon most legal questions and may decisively influence how the law will be applied.

[3] A client may expressly or impliedly ask the lawyer for purely technical advice. When such a request is made by a client experienced in legal matters, the lawyer may accept it at face value. When such a request is made by a client inexperienced in legal matters, however, the lawyer's responsibility as advisor may include indicating that more may be involved than strictly legal considerations.

[4] Matters that go beyond strictly legal questions may also be in the domain of another profession. Family matters can involve problems within the professional competence of psychiatry, clinical psychology, or social work; business matters can involve problems within the competence of the accounting profession or of financial specialists. Where consultation with a professional in another field is itself something a competent lawyer would recommend, the lawyer should make such a recommendation. At the same time, a lawyer's advice at its best often consists of recommending a course of action in the face of conflicting recommendations of experts.

Offering Advice

[5] In general, a lawyer is not expected to give advice until asked by the client. However, when a lawyer knows that a client proposes a course of action that is likely to result in substantial adverse legal consequences to the client, duty to the client under Rule 1.4 may require that the lawyer act if the client's course of action is related to the representation. Similarly, when a matter is likely to involve litigation, it may be necessary under Rule 1.4 to inform the client of forms of dispute resolution that might constitute reasonable alternatives to litigation. A lawyer ordinarily has no duty to initiate investigation of a client's affairs or to give advice that the client has indicated is unwanted, but a lawyer may initiate advice to a client when doing so appears to be in the client's interest.

Rule 2.3. Evaluation for Use by Third Persons

(a) A lawyer may provide an evaluation of a matter affecting a client for the use of someone other than the client if the lawyer reasonably believes

that making the evaluation is compatible with other aspects of the lawyer's relationship with the client.

(b) When the lawyer knows or reasonably should know that the evaluation is likely to affect the client's interests materially and adversely, the lawyer shall not provide the evaluation unless the client gives informed consent.

(c) Except as disclosure is authorized in connection with a report of an evaluation, information relating to the evaluation is otherwise protected by Rule 1.6.

COMMENT

Definition

[1] An evaluation may be performed at the client's direction or when impliedly authorized in order to carry out the representation. *See* Rule 1.2. Such an evaluation may be for the primary purpose of establishing information for the benefit of third parties; for example, an opinion concerning the title of property rendered at the behest of a vendor for the information of a prospective purchaser, or at the behest of a borrower for the information of a prospective lender. In some situations, the evaluation may be required by a government agency; for example, an opinion concerning the legality of the securities registered for sale under the securities laws. In other instances, the evaluation may be required by a third person, such as a purchaser of a business.

[2] A legal evaluation should be distinguished from an investigation of a person with whom the lawyer does not have a client-lawyer relationship. For example, a lawyer retained by a purchaser to analyze a vendor's title to property does not have a client-lawyer relationship with the vendor. So also, an investigation into a person's affairs by a government lawyer, or by special counsel employed by the government, is not an evaluation as that term is used in this rule. The question is whether the lawyer is retained by the person whose affairs are being examined. When the lawyer is retained by that person, the general rules concerning loyalty to client and preservation of confidences apply, which is not the case if the lawyer is retained by someone else. For this reason, it is essential to identify the person by whom the lawyer is retained. This should be made clear not only to the person under examination, but also to others to whom the results are to be made available.

Duties Owed to Third Person and Client

[3] When the evaluation is intended for the information or use of a third person, a legal duty to that person may or may not arise. That legal question is beyond the scope of this rule. However, since such an evaluation involves a departure from the normal client-lawyer relationship, careful analysis of the situation is required. The lawyer must be satisfied as a matter of professional judgment that making the evaluation is compatible with other functions undertaken on behalf of the client. For example, if the lawyer is acting as advocate in defending the client against charges of fraud, it would normally be incompatible with that responsibility for the lawyer to perform an evaluation for others concerning the same or a related transaction.

Assuming no such impediment is apparent, however, the lawyer should advise the client of the implications of the evaluation, particularly the lawyer's responsibilities to third persons and the duty to disseminate the findings.

Access to and Disclosure of Information

[4] The quality of an evaluation depends on the freedom and extent of the investigation upon which it is based. Ordinarily a lawyer should have whatever latitude of investigation seems necessary as a matter of professional judgment. Under some circumstances, however, the terms of the evaluation may be limited. For example, certain issues or sources may be categorically excluded, or the scope of search may be limited by time constraints or the noncooperation of persons having relevant information. Any such limitations that are material to the evaluation should be described in the report. If after a lawyer has commenced an evaluation, the client refuses to comply with the terms upon which it was understood the evaluation was to have been made, the lawyer's obligations are determined by law, having reference to the terms of the client's agreement and the surrounding circumstances. In no circumstances is the lawyer permitted to knowingly make a false statement of material fact or law in providing an evaluation under this rule. *See* Rule 4.1. If a lawyer learns that the client has used or will use an evaluation in a crime or fraud, the lawyer may have a duty under Rule 4.1(b) to take action to avoid assisting in the crime or fraud.

Obtaining Client's Informed Consent

[5] Information relating to an evaluation is protected by Rule 1.6. In many situations, providing an evaluation to a third party poses no significant risk to the client; thus, the lawyer may be impliedly authorized to disclose information to carry out the representation. *See* Rule 1.6(a). Where, however, it is reasonably likely that providing the evaluation will affect the client's interests materially and adversely, the lawyer must first obtain the client's consent after the client has been adequately informed concerning the important possible effects on the client's interests. *See* Rules 1.6(a) and 1.0(e).

Financial Auditors' Requests for Information

[6] When a question concerning the legal situation of a client arises at the instance of the client's financial auditor and the question is referred to the lawyer, the lawyer's response may be made in accordance with procedures recognized in the legal profession. Such a procedure is set forth in the American Bar Association Statement of Policy Regarding Lawyers' Responses to Auditors' Requests for Information, adopted in 1975.

Rule 2.4.   Lawyer Serving as Third-Party Neutral

(a) A lawyer serves as a third-party neutral when the lawyer assists two or more persons who are not clients of the lawyer to reach a resolution of

a dispute or other matter that has arisen between them. Service as a third-party neutral may include service as an arbitrator, a mediator or in such other capacity as will enable the lawyer to assist the parties to resolve the matter.

(b) A lawyer serving as a third-party neutral shall inform unrepresented parties that the lawyer is not representing them. When the lawyer knows or reasonably should know that a party does not understand the lawyer's role in the matter, the lawyer shall explain the difference between the lawyer's role as a third-party neutral and a lawyer's role as one who represents a client.

COMMENT

[1] Alternative dispute resolution has become a substantial part of the civil justice system. Aside from representing clients in dispute-resolution processes, lawyers often serve as third-party neutrals. A third-party neutral is a person, such as a mediator, arbitrator, conciliator or evaluator, who assists the parties, represented or unrepresented, in the resolution of a dispute or in the arrangement of a transaction. Whether a third-party neutral serves primarily as a facilitator, evaluator or decision-maker depends on the particular process that is either selected by the parties or mandated by a court.

[2] The role of a third-party neutral is not unique to lawyers, although, in some court-connected contexts, only lawyers are allowed to serve in this role or to handle certain types of cases. In performing this role, the lawyer may be subject to court rules or other law that applies either to third-party neutrals generally or to lawyers serving as third-party neutrals. Lawyer-neutrals may also be subject to various codes of ethics, such as the Code of Ethics for Arbitration in Commercial Disputes prepared by a joint committee of the American Bar Association and the American Arbitration Association or the Model Standards of Conduct for Mediators jointly prepared by the American Bar Association, the American Arbitration Association and the Society of Professionals in Dispute Resolution.

[3] Unlike non-lawyers who serve as third-party neutrals, lawyers serving in this role may experience unique problems as a result of differences between the role of a third-party neutral and a lawyer's service as a client representative. The potential for confusion is significant when the parties are unrepresented in the process. Thus, paragraph (b) requires a lawyer-neutral to inform unrepresented parties that the lawyer is not representing them. For some parties, particularly parties who frequently use dispute-resolution processes, this information will be sufficient. For others, particularly those who are using the process for the first time, more information will be required. Where appropriate, the lawyer should inform unrepresented parties of the important differences between the lawyer's role as third-party neutral and a lawyer's role as a client representative, including the inapplicability of the attorney-client evidentiary privilege. The extent of disclosure required under this paragraph will depend on the particular parties involved and the subject matter of the proceedings, as well as the particular features of the dispute-resolution process selected.

[4] A lawyer who serves as a third-party neutral subsequently may be asked to serve as a lawyer representing a client in the same matter. The conflicts of interest that arise for both the individual lawyer and the lawyer's law firm are addressed in Rule 1.12.

[5] Lawyers who represent clients in alternative dispute-resolution processes are governed by the Rules of Professional Conduct. When the dispute-resolution process takes place before a tribunal, as in binding arbitration (*see* Rule 1.0(n)), the lawyer's duty of candor is governed by Rule 3.3. Otherwise, the lawyer's duty of candor toward both the third-party neutral and other parties is governed by Rule 4.1.

ADVOCATE

Rule 3.1. Meritorious Claims and Contentions

A lawyer shall not bring or defend a proceeding, or assert or controvert an issue therein, unless there is a basis in law and fact for doing so that is not frivolous, which includes a good-faith argument for an extension, modification, or reversal of existing law. A lawyer for the defendant in a criminal proceeding, or for the respondent in a proceeding that could result in involuntary institutionalization, shall, if the client elects to go to trial or to a contested fact-finding hearing, nevertheless so defend the proceeding as to require that the government carry its burden of proof.

COMMENT

[1] The advocate has a duty to use legal procedure for the fullest benefit of the client's cause, but also a duty not to abuse legal procedure. The law, both procedural and substantive, establishes the limits within which an advocate may proceed. However, the law is not always clear and never is static. Accordingly, in determining the proper scope of advocacy, account must be taken of the law's ambiguities and potential for change.

[2] The filing of an action or defense or similar action taken for a client is not frivolous merely because the facts have not first been fully substantiated or because the lawyer expects to develop vital evidence only by discovery. Lawyers, however, are required to inform themselves about the facts of their clients' cases and the applicable law and determine that they can make good faith arguments in support of their clients' positions. Such action is not frivolous even though the lawyer believes that the client's position ultimately will not prevail. The action is frivolous if the lawyer is unable either to make a good-faith argument on the merits of the action taken or to support the action taken by a good-faith argument for an extension, modification, or reversal of existing law.

[3] In criminal cases or proceedings in which the respondent can be involuntarily institutionalized, such as juvenile delinquency and civil commitment cases, the lawyer is not only permitted, but is indeed required, to put the government to its proof whenever the client elects to contest adjudication. The lawyer's obligations under this rule are subordinate to federal or state law that entitles a defendant in a criminal matter to the assistance of counsel in presenting a claim or contention that otherwise would be prohibited by this rule.

Rule 3.2.   Expediting Litigation

(a) In representing a client, a lawyer shall not delay a proceeding when the lawyer knows or when it is obvious that such action would serve solely to harass or maliciously injure another.

(b) A lawyer shall make reasonable efforts to expedite litigation consistent with the interests of the client.

COMMENT

[1] Dilatory practices bring the administration of justice into disrepute. Delay should not be indulged merely for the convenience of the advocates, or for the purpose of frustrating an opposing party's attempt to obtain rightful redress or repose. It is not a justification that similar conduct is often tolerated by the bench and bar. The question is whether a competent lawyer acting in good faith would regard the course of action as having some substantial purpose other than delay. Realizing financial or other benefit from otherwise improper delay in litigation is not a legitimate interest of the client.

Rule 3.3.   Candor to Tribunal

(a) A lawyer shall not knowingly:

(1) Make a false statement of fact or law to a tribunal or fail to correct a false statement of material fact or law previously made to the tribunal by the lawyer, unless correction would require disclosure of information that is prohibited by Rule 1.6;

(2) Counsel or assist a client to engage in conduct that the lawyer knows is criminal or fraudulent, but a lawyer may discuss the legal consequences of any proposed course of conduct with a client and may counsel or assist a client to make a good-faith effort to determine the validity, scope, meaning, or application of the law;

(3) Fail to disclose to the tribunal legal authority in the controlling jurisdiction not disclosed by opposing counsel and known to the lawyer to be dispositive of a question at issue and directly adverse to the position of the client; or

(4) Offer evidence that the lawyer knows to be false, except as provided in paragraph (b). A lawyer may refuse to offer evidence, other than the testimony of a defendant in a criminal matter, that the lawyer reasonably believes is false.

(b) When the witness who intends to give evidence that the lawyer knows to be false is the lawyer's client and is the accused in a criminal case, the lawyer shall first make a good-faith effort to dissuade the client from presenting the false evidence; if the lawyer is unable to dissuade the client, the lawyer shall seek leave of the tribunal to withdraw. If the lawyer is unable to dissuade the client or to withdraw without seriously harming the client, the lawyer may put the client on the stand to testify in a narrative fashion, but the lawyer shall not examine the client in such manner as to elicit testimony which the lawyer knows to be false, and shall not argue the probative value of the client's testimony in closing argument.

(c) The duties stated in paragraph (a) continue to the conclusion of the proceeding.

(d) A lawyer who receives information clearly establishing that a fraud has been perpetrated upon the tribunal shall promptly take reasonable remedial measures, including disclosure to the tribunal to the extent disclosure is permitted by Rule 1.6(d).

COMMENT

[1] This rule defines the duty of candor to the tribunal. *See* Rule 1.0(l) for the definition of "tribunal." The rule also applies when the lawyer is representing a client in an ancillary proceeding conducted pursuant to the tribunal's adjudicative authority, such as a deposition. In dealing with a tribunal the lawyer is also required to comply with the general requirements of Rule 1.2(e) and (f). However, an advocate does not vouch for the evidence submitted in a cause; the tribunal is responsible for assessing its probative value.

Representations by a Lawyer

[2] An assertion purported to be made by the lawyer, as in an affidavit by the lawyer or in a statement in open court, may properly be made only when the lawyer knows the assertion is true or believes it to be true on the basis of a reasonably diligent inquiry. There may be circumstances where failure to make a disclosure is the equivalent of an affirmative misrepresentation. If the lawyer comes to know that a statement of material fact or law that the lawyer previously made to the tribunal is false, the lawyer has a duty to correct the statement, unless correction would require a disclosure of information that is prohibited by Rule 1.6. This provision in paragraph (a)(1) differs from ABA Model Rule 3.3(a)(1), which requires a lawyer to disclose information otherwise protected by Rule 1.6 if necessary to correct the lawyer's false statement. If Rule 1.6 permits a lawyer to disclose a client confidence or secret, D.C. Rule 3.3(a)(1) requires the lawyer to disclose that information to the extent reasonably necessary to correct a false statement of material fact or law. Nothing in D.C. Rule 3.3(a)(1) limits any disclosure duty under Rule 4.1(b) when substantive law requires a lawyer to disclose client information to avoid being deemed to have assisted the client's crime or fraud. The obligation prescribed in Rule 1.2(e) not to counsel a client to commit or assist the client in committing a fraud applies in litigation but is subject to Rule 3.3(b) and (d). Regarding compliance with Rule 1.2(e), see the Comment to that Rule. *See also* Rule 8.4.

Misleading Legal Argument

[3] Legal argument based on a knowingly false representation of law constitutes dishonesty toward the tribunal. A lawyer is not required to make a disinterested

exposition of the law, but must recognize the existence of pertinent legal authorities. Furthermore, as stated in subparagraph (a)(3), an advocate has a duty to disclose directly adverse authority in the controlling jurisdiction that has not been disclosed by the opposing party and that is dispositive of a question at issue. The underlying concept is that legal argument is a discussion seeking to determine the legal premises properly applicable to the case.

Offering Evidence

[4] When evidence that a lawyer knows to be false is provided by a person who is not the client, the lawyer must refuse to offer it regardless of the client's wishes. This duty is premised on the lawyer's obligation as an officer of the court to prevent the trier of fact from being misled by false evidence. A lawyer does not violate this rule if the lawyer offers the evidence for the purpose of establishing its falsity.

[5] When false evidence is offered by the client, however, a conflict may arise between the lawyer's duty to keep the client's revelations confidential and the duty of candor to the court. Upon ascertaining that material evidence is false, the lawyer should seek to persuade the client that the evidence should not be offered or, if it has been offered, that its false character should immediately be disclosed. Regardless of the client's wishes, however, a lawyer may not offer evidence of a client if the evidence is known by the lawyer to be false, except to the extent permitted by paragraph (b) where the client is a defendant in a criminal case. The lawyer is obligated not only to refuse to offer false evidence under subparagraph (a)(4) but also to take reasonable remedial measures under paragraph (d) if the false evidence has been offered.

[6] The prohibition against offering false evidence applies only if the lawyer knows that the evidence is false. A lawyer's knowledge that evidence is false can be inferred from the circumstances. *See* Rule 1.0(f). Thus, although a lawyer should resolve doubts about the veracity of testimony or other evidence in favor of the client, the lawyer cannot ignore an obvious falsehood.

[7] Although paragraph (a)(4) prohibits a lawyer from offering evidence only if the lawyer knows it to be false, it also permits the lawyer to refuse to offer testimony or other proof that the lawyer reasonably believes is false. Offering such proof may reflect adversely on the lawyer's ability to discriminate in the quality of evidence and thus impair the lawyer's effectiveness as an advocate. Because of the special protections historically provided criminal defendants, however, this rule does not permit a lawyer to refuse to offer the testimony of such a client where the lawyer reasonably believes but does not know that the testimony will be false. Unless the lawyer knows the testimony will be false, the lawyer must honor the client's decision to testify.

Remedial Measures

[8] Paragraph (d) provides that if a lawyer learns that a fraud has been perpetrated on the tribunal, the lawyer must take reasonable remedial measures. If the

lawyer's client is implicated in the fraud, the lawyer should ordinarily first call upon the client to rectify the fraud. If the client is unwilling to do so, the lawyer should consider other remedial measures. The lawyer may not, however, disclose information otherwise protected by Rule 1.6, unless the client has used the lawyer's services to further a crime or fraud and disclosure is permitted by Rule 1.6(d). In other cases, the lawyer may learn of the client's intention to present false evidence before the client has had a chance to do so. In this situation, paragraphs (a)(4) and (b) forbid the lawyer to present the false evidence, except in rare instances where the witness is the accused in a criminal case, the lawyer is unsuccessful in dissuading the client from going forward, and the lawyer is unable to withdraw without causing serious harm to the client. In addition, Rule 1.6(c) may permit disclosure of client confidences and secrets when the lawyer learns of a prospective fraud on the tribunal involving, for example, bribery or intimidation of witnesses. The terms "criminal case" and "criminal defendant" as used in Rule 3.3 and its Comment include juvenile delinquency proceedings and the person who is the subject of such proceedings.

Perjury by a Criminal Defendant

[9] Paragraph (b) allows the lawyer to permit a client who is the accused in a criminal case to present false testimony in very narrowly circumscribed circumstances and in a very limited manner. Even in a criminal case the lawyer must seek to persuade the defendant-client to refrain from perjurious testimony. There has been dispute concerning the lawyer's duty when that persuasion fails. Paragraph (b) requires the lawyer to withdraw rather than offer the client's false testimony, if this can be done without seriously harming the client.

[10] Serious harm to the client sufficient to prevent the lawyer's withdrawal entails more than the usual inconveniences that necessarily result from withdrawal, such as delay in concluding the client's case or an increase in the costs of concluding the case. The term should be construed narrowly to preclude withdrawal only where the special circumstances of the case are such that the client would be significantly prejudiced, such as by express or implied divulgence of information otherwise protected by Rule 1.6. If the confrontation with the client occurs before trial, the lawyer ordinarily can withdraw. Withdrawal before trial may not be possible, however, either because trial is imminent, or because the confrontation with the client does not take place until the trial itself, or because no other counsel is available. In those rare circumstances in which withdrawal without such serious harm to the client is impossible, the lawyer may go forward with examination of the client and closing argument subject to the limitations of paragraph (b).

Refusing to Offer Proof of a Non-client Known to Be False

[11] Generally speaking, a lawyer may not offer testimony or other proof, through a nonclient, that the lawyer knows to be false. Furthermore, a lawyer may not offer evidence of a client if the evidence is known by the lawyer to be false, except to the extent permitted by paragraph (b) where the client is a defendant in a criminal case.

Duration of Obligation

[12] A practical time limit on the obligation to take reasonable remedial measures concerning criminal and fraudulent conducted related to the proceeding is needed. The conclusion of the proceeding is an appropriate and reasonably definite point for the termination of the obligation. A proceeding has concluded within the meaning of this rule when a final judgment in the proceeding has been affirmed on appeal or the time for review has passed. If the lawyer withdraws before the conclusion of the proceeding, the lawyer's obligation ends at the time of withdrawal.

Withdrawal

[13] A lawyer's compliance with the duty of candor imposed by this rule might require that the lawyer withdraw from the representation of a client. The lawyer may, however, be required by Rule 1.16(a) to seek permission of the tribunal to withdraw if the lawyer's compliance with this rule's duty of candor, or with the requirements of Rule 1.6(c), results in the lawyer's inability to represent the client in accordance with these Rules. *See also* Rule 1.16(b) for the circumstances in which a lawyer will be permitted to seek a tribunal's permission to withdraw. In connection with a request for permission to withdraw that is premised on a client's misconduct, a lawyer may reveal information relating to the representation only to the extent permitted by Rule 1.6.

Rule 3.4.   Fairness to Opposing Party and Counsel

A lawyer shall not:

(a) Obstruct another party's access to evidence or alter, destroy, or conceal evidence, or counsel or assist another person to do so, if the lawyer reasonably should know that the evidence is or may be the subject of discovery or subpoena in any pending or imminent proceeding. Unless prohibited by law, a lawyer may receive physical evidence of any kind from the client or from another person. If the evidence received by the lawyer belongs to anyone other than the client, the lawyer shall make a good-faith effort to preserve it and to return it to the owner, subject to Rule 1.6;

(b) Falsify evidence, counsel or assist a witness to testify falsely, or offer an inducement to a witness that is prohibited by law;

(c) Knowingly disobey an obligation under the rules of a tribunal except for an open refusal based on an assertion that no valid obligation exists;

(d) In pretrial procedure, make a frivolous discovery request or fail to make reasonably diligent efforts to comply with a legally proper discovery request by an opposing party;

(e) In trial, allude to any matter that the lawyer does not reasonably believe is relevant or that will not be supported by admissible evidence, assert personal knowledge of facts in issue except when testifying as a witness, or state a personal opinion as to the justness of a cause, the credibility of a witness, the culpability of a civil litigant, or the guilt or innocence of an accused;

(f) Request a person other than a client to refrain from voluntarily giving relevant information to another party unless:

(1) The person is a relative or an employee or other agent of a client; and

(2) The lawyer reasonably believes that the person's interests will not be adversely affected by refraining from giving such information; or

(g) Peremptorily strike jurors for any reason prohibited by law.

COMMENT

[1] The procedure of the adversary system contemplates that the evidence in a case is to be marshaled competitively by the contending parties. Fair competition in the adversary system is secured by prohibitions against destruction or concealment of evidence, improperly influencing witnesses, obstructive tactics in discovery procedure, and the like.

[2] Documents and other items of evidence are often essential to establish a claim or defense. Subject to evidentiary privileges, the right of an opposing party, including the government, to obtain evidence through discovery or subpoena is an important procedural right. The exercise of that right can be frustrated if relevant material is altered, concealed, or destroyed. To the extent clients are involved in the effort to comply with discovery requests, the lawyer's obligations are to pursue reasonable efforts to assure that documents and other information subject to proper discovery requests are produced. Applicable law in many jurisdictions makes it an offense to destroy material for [the] purpose of impairing its availability in a pending proceeding or a proceeding whose commencement can be foreseen. Falsifying evidence is also generally a criminal offense. Paragraph (a) applies to evidentiary material generally, including computerized information.

[3] Paragraph (a) permits, but does not require, the lawyer to accept physical evidence (including the instruments or proceeds of crime) from the client or any other person. Such receipt is, as stated in paragraph (a), subject to other provisions of law and the limitations imposed by paragraph (a) with respect to obstruction of access, alteration, destruction, or concealment, and subject also to the requirements of paragraph (a) with respect to return of property to its rightful owner, and to the obligation to comply with subpoenas and discovery requests. The term "evidence" includes any document or physical object that the lawyer reasonably should know may be the subject of discovery or subpoena in any pending or imminent litigation. *See* D.C. Bar Legal Ethics Committee Opinion No. 119 (test is whether destruction of document is directed at concrete litigation that is either pending or almost certain to be filed).

[4] A lawyer should ascertain that the lawyer's handling of documents or other physical objects does not violate any other law. Federal criminal law may forbid the destruction of documents or other physical objects in circumstances not covered by the ethical rule set forth in paragraph (a). *See, e.g.,* 18 U.S.C. §1503 (obstruction of

justice); 18 U.S.C. §1505 (obstruction of proceedings before departments, agencies, and committees); 18 U.S.C. §1510 (obstruction of criminal investigations). And it is a crime in the District of Columbia for one who knows or has reason to know that an official proceeding has begun or is likely to be instituted to alter, destroy, or conceal a document with intent to impair its integrity or availability for use in the proceeding. D.C. Code §22-723 (2001). Finally, some discovery rules having the force of law may prohibit the destruction of documents and other material even if litigation is not pending or imminent. This rule does not set forth the scope of a lawyer's responsibilities under all applicable laws. It merely imposes on the lawyer an ethical duty to make reasonable efforts to comply fully with those laws. The provisions of paragraph (a) prohibit a lawyer from obstructing another party's access to evidence, and from altering, destroying, or concealing evidence. These prohibitions may overlap with criminal obstruction provisions and civil discovery rules, but they apply whether or not the prohibited conduct violates criminal provisions or court rules. Thus, the alteration of evidence by a lawyer, whether or not such conduct violates criminal law or court rules, constitutes a violation of paragraph (a).

[5] Because of the duty of confidentiality under Rule 1.6, the lawyer is generally forbidden to volunteer information about physical evidence received from a client without the client's informed consent. In some cases, the Office of Bar Counsel will accept physical evidence from a lawyer and then turn it over to the appropriate persons; in those cases this procedure is usually the best means of delivering evidence to the proper authorities without disclosing the client's confidences. However, Bar Counsel may refuse to accept evidence; thus lawyers should keep the following in mind before accepting evidence from a client, and should discuss with Bar Counsel's office the procedures that may be employed in particular circumstances.

[6] First, if the evidence received from the client is subpoenaed or otherwise requested through the discovery process while held by the lawyer, the lawyer will be obligated to deliver the evidence directly to the appropriate persons, unless there is a basis for objecting to the discovery request or moving to quash the subpoena. A lawyer should therefore advise the client of the risk that evidence may be subject to subpoena or discovery, and of the lawyer's duty to turn the evidence over in that event, before accepting it from the client.

[7] Second, if the lawyer has received physical evidence belonging to the client, for purposes of examination or testing, the lawyer may later return the property to the client pursuant to Rule 1.15, provided that the evidence has not been subpoenaed. The lawyer may not be justified in returning to a client physical evidence the possession of which by the client would be *per se* illegal, such as certain drugs and weapons. And if it is reasonably apparent that the evidence is not the client's property, the lawyer may not retain the evidence or return it to the client. Instead, the lawyer must, under paragraph (a), make a good-faith effort to return the evidence to its owner. Rule 3.4(a) makes this duty subject to Rule 1.6. Rules 1.6(c), (d) and (e) describe circumstances in which a lawyer may reveal information otherwise protected by Rule 1.6. If such circumstances exist, the lawyer may, but is not required to, reveal information otherwise protected by Rule 1.6 as part of a good-faith effort to preserve the evidence and return it to the owner pursuant to Rule 3.4(a).

[8] With regard to paragraph (b), it is not improper to pay a witness's expenses or to compensate a witness for loss of time in preparing to testify, in attending, or in testifying. A fee for the services of a witness who will be proffered as an expert may

be made contingent on the outcome of the litigation, provided, however, that the fee, while conditioned on recovery, shall not be a percentage of the recovery.

[9] Paragraph (f) permits a lawyer to advise employees of a client to refrain from giving information to another party, for the employees may identify their interests with those of the client. *See also* Rule 4.2.

[10] Paragraph (g) prohibits any lawyer from exercising peremptory challenges to prospective jurors on any impermissible ground. Impermissible grounds include race, sex, and other factors that have been determined in binding judicial decisions to be discriminatory in jury selection.

Rule 3.5.   Impartiality and Decorum of the Tribunal

A lawyer shall not:

(a) Seek to influence a judge, juror, prospective juror, or other official by means prohibited by law;

(b) Communicate ex parte with such a person during the proceeding unless authorized to do so by law or court order;

(c) Communicate, either ex parte or with opposing counsel, with a juror or prospective juror after discharge of the jury if:

(1) The communication is prohibited by law or court order;

(2) The juror or prospective juror has made known to the lawyer a desire not to communicate; or

(3) The communication involves misrepresentation, coercion, duress, or harassment; or

(d) Engage in conduct intended to disrupt any proceeding of a tribunal, including a deposition.

COMMENT

[1] Many forms of improper influence upon a tribunal are proscribed by criminal law. Others are specified in the Code of Judicial Conduct, with which an advocate should be familiar. A lawyer is required to avoid contributing to a violation of such provisions.

[2] During a proceeding a lawyer may not communicate ex parte with persons serving in an official capacity in the proceeding, such as judges, masters or jurors, unless authorized to do so by law or court order.

[3] A lawyer may on occasion want to communicate with a juror or prospective juror after the jury has been discharged, even though the proceeding has not ended. The lawyer may do so, either ex parte or with opposing counsel, unless the communication is prohibited by law or a court order. The lawyer, however, must respect the desire of the juror or prospective juror not to talk with the lawyer. The lawyer may not engage in improper conduct during the communication.

[4] The advocate's function is to present evidence and argument so that the cause may be decided according to law. Refraining from abusive or obstreperous conduct is a corollary of the advocate's right to speak on behalf of litigants. A lawyer

may stand firm against abuse by a judge but should avoid reciprocation; the judge's default is no justification for similar dereliction by an advocate. An advocate can present the cause, protect the record for subsequent review, and preserve professional integrity by patient firmness no less effectively than by belligerence or theatrics.

Rule 3.6.   Trial Publicity

A lawyer engaged in a case being tried to a judge or jury shall not make an extrajudicial statement that the lawyer knows or reasonably should know will be disseminated by means of mass public communication and will create a serious and imminent threat of material prejudice to the proceeding.

COMMENT

[1] It is difficult to strike a proper balance between protecting the right to a fair trial and safeguarding the right of free expression, which are both guaranteed by the Constitution. On one hand, publicity should not be allowed to influence the fair administration of justice. On the other hand, litigants have a right to present their side of a dispute to the public, and the public has an interest in receiving information about matters that are in litigation. Often a lawyer involved in the litigation is in the best position to assist in furthering these legitimate objectives. No body of rules can simultaneously satisfy all interests of fair trial and all those of free expression.

[2] The special obligations of prosecutors to limit comment on criminal matters involve considerations in addition to those implicated in this rule, and are dealt with in Rule 3.8(f). Furthermore, this rule is not intended to abrogate special court rules of confidentiality in juvenile or other cases. Lawyers are bound by Rule 3.4(c) to adhere to any such rules that have not been found invalid.

[3] Because administrative agencies should have the prerogative to determine the ethical rules for prehearing publicity, this rule does not purport to apply to matters before administrative agencies.

Rule 3.7.   Lawyer as Witness

(a) A lawyer shall not act as advocate at a trial in which the lawyer is likely to be a necessary witness except where:

(1) The testimony relates to an uncontested issue;

(2) The testimony relates to the nature and value of legal services rendered in the case; or

(3) Disqualification of the lawyer would work substantial hardship on the client.

(b) A lawyer may not act as advocate in a trial in which another lawyer in the lawyer's firm is likely to be called as a witness if the other lawyer would be precluded from acting as advocate in the trial by Rule

1.7 or Rule 1.9. The provisions of this paragraph (b) do not apply if the lawyer who is appearing as an advocate is employed by, and appears on behalf of, a government agency.

COMMENT

[1] Combining the roles of advocate and witness can prejudice the opposing party and can involve a conflict of interest between the lawyer and client.

[2] The opposing party has proper objection where the combination of roles may prejudice that party's rights in the litigation. A witness is required to testify on the basis of personal knowledge, while an advocate is expected to explain and comment on evidence given by others. It may not be clear whether a statement by an advocate-witness should be taken as proof or as an analysis of the proof.

[3] Subparagraph (a)(1) recognizes that if the testimony will be uncontested, the ambiguities in the dual role are purely theoretical. Subparagraph (a)(2) recognizes that where the testimony concerns the extent and value of legal services rendered in the action in which the testimony is offered, permitting the lawyers to testify avoids the need for a second trial with new counsel to resolve that issue. Moreover, in such a situation the judge has firsthand knowledge of the matter in issue; hence, there is less dependence on the adversary process to test the credibility of the testimony.

[4] Apart from these two exceptions, subparagraph (a)(3) recognizes that a balancing is required between the interests of the client and those of the opposing party. Whether the opposing party is likely to suffer prejudice depends on the nature of the case, the importance and probable tenor of the lawyer's testimony, and the probability that the lawyer's testimony will conflict with that of other witnesses. Even if there is risk of such prejudice, in determining whether the lawyer should be disqualified, due regard must be given to the effect of disqualification on the lawyer's client. It is relevant that one or both parties could reasonably foresee that the lawyer would probably be a witness.

[5] If the only reason for not permitting a lawyer to combine the roles of advocate and witness is possible prejudice to the opposing party, there is no reason to disqualify other lawyers in the testifying lawyer's firm from acting as advocates in that trial. In short, there is no general rule of imputed disqualification applicable to Rule 3.7. However, the combination of roles of advocate and witness may involve an improper conflict of interest between the lawyer and the client in addition to or apart from possible prejudice to the opposing party. Whether there is such a client conflict is determined by Rule 1.7 or 1.9. For example, if there is likely to be a significant conflict between the testimony of the client and that of the lawyer, the representation is improper by the standard of Rule 1.7(b) without regard to Rule 3.7(a). The problem can arise whether the lawyer is called as a witness on behalf of the client or is called by the opposing party. Determining whether such a conflict exists is, in the first instance, the responsibility of the lawyer involved. *See* Comment to Rule 1.7. Rule 3.7(b) states that other lawyers in the testifying lawyer's firm are disqualified only when there is such a client conflict and the testifying lawyer therefore could not represent the client under Rule 1.7 or 1.9. The principles of client consent, embodied in Rules 1.7 and 1.9, also apply to paragraph (b). Thus, the reference to Rules 1.7 and 1.9 incorporates the client consent aspects of those Rules.

Paragraph (b) is designed to provide protection for the client, not rights of disqualification to the adversary. Subject to the disclosure and consultation requirements of Rules 1.7 and 1.9, the client may consent to the firm's continuing representation, despite the potential problems created by the nature of the testimony to be provided by a lawyer in the firm.

[6] Even though a lawyer's testimony does not involve a conflict with the client's interests under Rule 1.7 or 1.9 and would not be precluded under Rule 3.7, the client's interests might nevertheless be harmed by the appearance as a witness of a lawyer in the firm that represents the client. For example, the lawyer's testimony would be vulnerable to impeachment on the grounds that the lawyer-witness is testifying to support the position of the lawyer's own firm. Similarly, a lawyer whose firm colleague is testifying in the case should recognize the possibility that the lawyer might not scrutinize the testimony of the colleague carefully enough and that this could prejudice the client's interests, whether the colleague is testifying for or against the client. In such instances, the lawyer should inform the client of any possible adverse effects on the client's interests that might result from the lawyer's relationship with the colleague-witness, so that the client may make a meaningful choice whether to retain the lawyer for the representation in question.

Rule 3.8.   Special Responsibilities of a Prosecutor

The prosecutor in a criminal case shall not:

(a) In exercising discretion to investigate or to prosecute, improperly favor or invidiously discriminate against any person;

(b) File in court or maintain a charge that the prosecutor knows is not supported by probable cause;

(c) Prosecute to trial a charge that the prosecutor knows is not supported by evidence sufficient to establish *a prima facie* showing of guilt;

(d) Intentionally avoid pursuit of evidence or information because it may damage the prosecution's case or aid the defense;

(e) Intentionally fail to disclose to the defense, upon request and at a time when use by the defense is reasonably feasible, any evidence or information that the prosecutor knows or reasonably should know tends to negate the guilt of the accused or to mitigate the offense, or in connection with sentencing, intentionally fail to disclose to the defense upon request any unprivileged mitigating information known to the prosecutor and not reasonably available to the defense, except when the prosecutor is relieved of this responsibility by a protective order of the tribunal;

(f) Except for statements which are necessary to inform the public of the nature and extent of the prosecutor's action and which serve a legitimate law enforcement purpose, make extrajudicial comments which serve to heighten condemnation of the accused; or

(g) In presenting a case to a grand jury, intentionally interfere with the independence of the grand jury, preempt a function of the grand jury, abuse the processes of the grand jury, or fail to bring to the attention of the grand jury material facts tending substantially to negate the existence of probable cause.

COMMENT

[1] A prosecutor has the responsibility of a minister of justice and not simply that of an advocate. This responsibility carries with it specific obligations to see that the defendant is accorded procedural justice and that guilt is decided upon the basis of sufficient evidence. Precisely how far the prosecutor is required to go in this direction is a matter of debate and varies in different jurisdictions. Many jurisdictions have adopted the ABA Standards of Criminal Justice Relating to Prosecution Function, which in turn are the product of prolonged and careful deliberation by lawyers experienced in both criminal prosecution and defense. This rule is intended to be a distillation of some, but not all, of the professional obligations imposed on prosecutors by applicable law. The rule, however, is not intended either to restrict or to expand the obligations of prosecutors derived from the United States Constitution, federal or District of Columbia statutes, and court rules of procedure.

[2] Apart from the special responsibilities of a prosecutor under this rule, prosecutors are subject to the same obligations imposed upon all lawyers by these Rules of Professional Conduct, including Rule 3.4 prohibiting the discriminatory use of peremptory strikes, and Rule 5.3, relating to responsibilities regarding nonlawyers who work for or in association with the lawyer's office. Indeed, because of the power and visibility of a prosecutor, the prosecutor's compliance with these Rules, and recognition of the need to refrain even from some actions technically allowed to other lawyers under the Rules, may, in certain instances, be of special importance. For example, Rule 3.6 prohibits extrajudicial statements that will have a substantial likelihood of destroying the impartiality of the judge or jury. In the context of a criminal prosecution, pretrial publicity can present the further problem of giving the public the incorrect impression that the accused is guilty before having been proven guilty through the due processes of the law. It is unavoidable, of course, that the publication of an indictment may itself have severe consequences for an accused. What is avoidable, however, is extrajudicial comment by a prosecutor that serves unnecessarily to heighten public condemnation of the accused without a legitimate law enforcement purpose before the criminal process has taken its course. When that occurs, even if the ultimate trial is not prejudiced, the accused may be subjected to unfair and unnecessary condemnation before the trial takes place. Accordingly, a prosecutor should use special care to avoid publicity, such as through televised press conferences, which would unnecessarily heighten condemnation of the accused.

[3] Nothing in this Comment, however, is intended to suggest that a prosecutor may not inform the public of such matters as whether an official investigation has ended or is continuing, or who participated in it, and the prosecutor may respond to press inquiries to clarify such things as technicalities of the indictment, the status of the matter, or the legal procedures that will follow. Also, a prosecutor should be free to respond, insofar as necessary, to any extrajudicial allegations by the defense of unprofessional or unlawful conduct on the part of the prosecutor's office.

Rule 3.9.   Advocate in Nonadjudicative Proceedings

A lawyer representing a client before a legislative or administrative body in a nonadjudicative proceeding shall disclose that the appearance is in a representative capacity and shall conform to the provisions of Rules 3.3, 3.4(a) through (c), and 3.5.

COMMENT

[1] In representation before bodies such as legislatures, municipal councils, and executive and administrative agencies acting in a rule-making or policy-making capacity, lawyers present facts, formulate issues, and advance argument in the matters under consideration. The decision-making body, like a court, should be able to rely on the integrity of the submissions made to it. A lawyer appearing before such a body should deal with it honestly and in conformity with applicable rules of procedure.

[2] Lawyers have no exclusive right to appear before nonadjudicative bodies, as they do before a court. The requirements of this rule therefore may subject lawyers to regulations inapplicable to advocates, such as nonlawyer lobbyists, who are not lawyers. However, legislatures and administrative agencies have a right to expect lawyers to deal with them as they deal with courts.

[3] This rule does not apply to representation of a client in a negotiation or other bilateral transaction with a government agency; representation in such a transaction is governed by Rules 4.1 through 4.4.

[4] This rule is closely related to Rules 3.3 through 3.5, which deal with conduct regarding tribunals. The term "tribunal," as defined Rule 1.0(n), refers to adjudicative or quasi-adjudicative bodies.

TRANSACTIONS WITH PERSONS OTHER THAN CLIENTS

Rule 4.1.   Truthfulness in Statements to Others

In the course of representing a client, a lawyer shall not knowingly:

(a) Make a false statement of material fact or law to a third person; or

(b) Fail to disclose a material fact to a third person when disclosure is necessary to avoid assisting a criminal or fraudulent act by a client, unless disclosure is prohibited by Rule 1.6.

COMMENT

Misrepresentation

[1] A lawyer is required to be truthful when dealing with others on a client's behalf, but generally has no affirmative duty to inform an opposing party of relevant

facts. A misrepresentation can occur if the lawyer incorporates or affirms a statement of another person that the lawyer knows is false. Misrepresentations can also occur by partially true but misleading statements or omissions that are the equivalent of affirmative false statements. For dishonest conduct that does not amount to a false statement or for misrepresentations by a lawyer other than in the course of representing a client, *see* Rule 8.4. The term "third person" as used in paragraphs (a) and (b) refers to any person or entity other than the lawyer's client.

Statements of Fact

[2] This rule refers to material statements of fact. Whether a particular statement should be regarded as material, and as one of fact, can depend on the circumstances. Under generally accepted conventions in negotiation, certain types of statements ordinarily are not taken as statements of material fact. Estimates of price or value placed on the subject of a transaction and a party's intentions as to an acceptable settlement of a claim are ordinarily in this category, and so is the existence of an undisclosed principal except where nondisclosure of the principal would constitute fraud. Lawyers should be mindful of their obligations under applicable law to avoid criminal and tortious misrepresentation. There may be other analogous situations.

Fraud by Client

[3] Under Rule 1.2(e), a lawyer is prohibited from counseling or assisting a client in conduct that the lawyer knows is criminal or fraudulent. Paragraph (b) states a specific application of the principle set forth in Rule 1.2(e) and addresses the situation where a client's crime or fraud takes the form of a lie or misrepresentation. Ordinarily, a lawyer can avoid assisting a client's crime or fraud by withdrawing from the representation. Sometimes it may be necessary for the lawyer to give notice of the fact of withdrawal and to disaffirm an opinion, document, affirmation or the like. In extreme cases, substantive law may require a lawyer to disclose client information to avoid being deemed to have assisted the client's crime or fraud. If the lawyer can avoid assisting a client's crime or fraud only by disclosing such client information, then under paragraph (b) the lawyer is required to do so, unless the disclosure is prohibited by Rule 1.6. If, in the particular circumstances in which the lawyer finds himself or herself, the lawyer has discretion to disclose a client confidence or secret under Rule 1.6(c), (d), or (e), disclosure is not prohibited by Rule 1.6, and the lawyer must disclose the information if otherwise required by this rule.

Rule 4.2.   Communication Between Lawyer and Person Represented by Counsel

(a) **During the course of representing a client, a lawyer shall not communicate or cause another to communicate about the subject of the** representation with a person known to be represented by another lawyer in the matter, unless the lawyer has the prior consent of the lawyer representing such other person or is authorized by law or a court order to do so.

(b) During the course of representing a client, a lawyer may communicate about the subject of the representation with a nonparty employee of an organization without obtaining the consent of that organization's lawyer. If the organization is an adverse party, however, prior to communicating with any such nonparty employee, a lawyer must disclose to such employee both the lawyer's identity and the fact that the lawyer represents a party that is adverse to the employee's employer.

(c) For purposes of this rule, the term "party" or "person" includes any person or organization, including an employee of an organization, who has the authority to bind an organization as to the representation to which the communication relates.

(d) This rule does not prohibit communication by a lawyer with government officials who have the authority to redress the grievances of the lawyer's client, whether or not those grievances or the lawyer's communications relate to matters that are the subject of the representation, provided that in the event of such communications the disclosures specified in (b) are made to the government official to whom the communication is made.

COMMENT

[1] This rule covers any person, whether or not a party to a formal proceeding, who is represented by counsel concerning the matter in question.

[2] This rule does not prohibit communication with a person or party, or an employee or agent of an organization, concerning matters outside the representation. For example, the existence of a controversy between two organizations does not prohibit a lawyer for either from communicating with representatives of the other regarding a separate matter. Also, parties to a matter may communicate directly with each other and a lawyer having independent justification for communicating with the other party is permitted to do so. In addition, a lawyer is not prohibited from advising a client concerning a communication that the client is legally entitled to make, provided that the client communication is not solely for the purpose of evading restrictions imposed on the lawyer by this rule.

[3] In the case of an organization, and other than as noted in Comment [5], this rule prohibits communication by a lawyer for one party concerning the matter in representation with persons having the power to bind the organization as to the particular representation to which the communication relates. If an agent or employee of the organization with authority to make binding decisions regarding the representation is represented in the matter by separate counsel, the consent by that agent's or employee's counsel to a communication will be sufficient for purposes of this rule.

[4] The rule does not prohibit a lawyer from communicating with employees of an organization who have the authority to bind the organization with respect

to the matters underlying the representation if they do not also have authority to make binding decisions regarding the representation itself. A lawyer may therefore communicate with such persons without first notifying the organization's lawyer. *See* D.C. Bar Legal Ethics Committee Opinion No. 129. But before communicating with such a "nonparty employee," the lawyer must disclose to the employee the lawyer's identity and the fact that the lawyer represents a party with a claim against the employer. It is preferable that this disclosure be made in writing. The notification requirements of Rule 4.2(b) apply to contacts with government employees who do not have the authority to make binding decisions regarding the representation.

[5]Because this rule is primarily focused on protecting represented persons unschooled in the law from direct communications from counsel for an adverse person, consent of the organization's lawyer is not required where a lawyer seeks to communicate with in-house counsel of an organization. If individual in-house counsel is represented separately from the organization, however, consent of that individual's personal counsel is required before communicating with that individual in-house counsel.

[6] Consent of the organization's lawyer is not required where a lawyer seeks to communicate with a former constituent of an organization. In making such contact, however, the lawyer may not seek to obtain information that is otherwise protected.

[7] This rule also does not preclude communication with a represented person who is seeking advice from a lawyer who is not otherwise representing a client in the matter.

[8] This rule applies even though the represented person initiates or consents to the communication. A lawyer must immediately terminate communication with a person if, after commencing communication, the lawyer learns that the person is one with whom communication is not permitted by this rule.

[9] This rule does not apply to the situation in which a lawyer contacts employees of an organization for the purpose of obtaining information generally available to the public, or obtainable under the Freedom of Information Act, even if the information in question is related to the representation. For example, a lawyer for a plaintiff who has filed suit against an organization represented by a lawyer may telephone the organization to request a copy of a press release regarding the representation, without disclosing the lawyer's identity, obtaining the consent of the organization's lawyer, or otherwise acting as paragraphs (a) and (b) of this rule require.

[10] Paragraph (d) recognizes that special considerations come into play when a lawyer is seeking to redress grievances involving the government. It permits communications with those in government having the authority to redress such grievances (but not with any other government personnel) without the prior consent of the lawyer representing the government in such cases. However, a lawyer making such a communication without the prior consent of the lawyer representing the government must make the kinds of disclosures that are required by paragraph (b) in the case of communications with nonparty employees.

[11] Paragraph (d) does not permit a lawyer to bypass counsel representing the government on every issue that may arise in the course of disputes with the government. It is intended to provide lawyers access to decision makers in government with respect to genuine grievances, such as to present the view that the government's

basic policy position with respect to a dispute is faulty, or that government personnel are conducting themselves improperly with respect to aspects of the dispute. It is not intended to provide direct access on routine disputes such as ordinary discovery disputes, extensions of time or other scheduling matters, or similar routine aspects of the resolution of disputes.

[12] This rule is not intended to enlarge or restrict the law enforcement activities of the United States or the District of Columbia which are authorized and permissible under the Constitution and law of the United States or the District of Columbia. The "authorized by law" proviso to Rule 4.2(a) is intended to permit government conduct that is valid under this law. The proviso is not intended to freeze any particular substantive law, but is meant to accommodate substantive law as it may develop over time.

Rule 4.3. Dealings with Unrepresented Parties

(a) In dealing on behalf of a client with a person who is not represented by counsel, a lawyer shall not:

(1) Give advice to the unrepresented person other than the advice to secure counsel, if the interests of such person are or have a reasonable possibility of being in conflict with the interests of the lawyer's client; or

(2) State or imply to unrepresented persons whose interests are not in conflict with the interests of the lawyer's client that the lawyer is disinterested.

(b) When the lawyer knows or reasonably should know that the unrepresented person misunderstands the lawyer's role in the matter, the lawyer shall make reasonable efforts to correct the misunderstanding.

COMMENT

[1] An unrepresented person, particularly one not experienced in dealing with legal matters, might assume that a lawyer will provide disinterested advice concerning the law even when the lawyer represents a client. In dealing personally with any unrepresented third party on behalf of the lawyer's client, a lawyer must take great care not to exploit these assumptions. *See* D.C. Bar Legal Ethics Committee Opinion 321.

[2] The rule distinguishes between situations involving unrepresented third parties whose interests may be adverse to those of the lawyer's client and those in which the third party's interests are not in conflict with the client's. In the former situation, the possibility of the lawyer's compromising the unrepresented person's interests is so great that the rule prohibits the giving of any advice, apart from the advice that the unrepresented person obtain counsel. A lawyer is free to give advice to unrepresented persons whose interests are not in conflict with those of the lawyer's client, but only if it is made clear that the lawyer is acting in the interests of the client. Thus the lawyer should not represent to such persons, either expressly or implicitly, that the lawyer is disinterested. Furthermore, if it becomes apparent that the unrepresented person misunderstands the lawyer's role in the matter, the

lawyer must take whatever reasonable, affirmative steps are necessary to correct the misunderstanding.

[3] This rule does not prohibit a lawyer from negotiating the terms of a transaction or settling a dispute with an unrepresented person. So long as the lawyer has explained that the lawyer represents an adverse party and is not representing the person, the lawyer may inform the person of the terms on which the lawyer's client will enter into an agreement or settle a matter, prepare documents that require the person's signature and explain the lawyer's own view of the meaning of the document or the lawyer's view of the underlying legal obligations.

[4] This rule is not intended to restrict in any way law enforcement efforts by government lawyers that are consistent with constitutional requirements and applicable federal law.

Rule 4.4.   Respect for Rights of Third Persons

(a) In representing a client, a lawyer shall not use means that have no substantial purpose other than to embarrass, delay, or burden a third person, or knowingly use methods of obtaining evidence that violate the legal rights of such a person.

(b) A lawyer who receives a writing relating to the representation of a client and knows, before examining the writing, that it has been inadvertently sent, shall not examine the writing, but shall notify the sending party and abide by the instructions of the sending party regarding the return or destruction of the writing.

COMMENT

[1] Responsibility to a client requires a lawyer to subordinate the interests of others to those of the client, but that responsibility does not imply that a lawyer may disregard the rights of third persons. It is impractical to catalogue all such rights, but they include legal restrictions on methods of obtaining evidence from third persons and unwarranted intrusions into privileged relationships, such as the client-lawyer relationship.

[2] Paragraph (b) addresses the obligations of a lawyer who receives writings containing client secrets or confidences in material delivered by an adversary lawyer and who knows that the sending lawyer inadvertently included these writings. As the D.C. Legal Ethics Committee noted in Opinion 256, this problem is "an unfortunate (but not uncommon) consequence of an increasingly electronic world, as when a facsimile or electronic mail transmission is mistakenly made to an unintended recipient." Consistent with Opinion 256, paragraph (b) requires the receiving lawyer to comply with the sending party's instruction about disposition of the writing in this circumstance, and also prohibits the receiving lawyer from reading or using the material. *See also* ABA Formal Opinion 92-368, which found that the receiving lawyer should not examine the materials once the inadvertence is discovered, should notify the sending lawyer of their receipt, and should abide by the

sending lawyer's instructions as to their disposition. ABA Model Rule 4.4 requires the receiving lawyer only to notify the sender in order to permit the sender to take protective measures, but Paragraph (b) of the D.C. Rule 4.4 requires the receiving lawyer to do more.

[3] On the other hand, where writings containing client secrets or confidences are inadvertently delivered to an adversary lawyer, and the receiving lawyer in good faith reviews the materials before the lawyer knows that they were inadvertently sent, the receiving lawyer commits no ethical violation by retaining and using those materials. *See* D.C. Legal Ethics Committee Opinion 256. Whether the privileged status of a writing has been waived is a matter of law beyond the scope of these Rules. Similarly, this rule does not address the legal duties of a lawyer who receives a writing that the lawyer knows or reasonably should know may have been wrongfully obtained by the sending person. *See* D.C. Bar Legal Ethics Committee Opinion 318.

LAW FIRMS AND ASSOCIATIONS

Rule 5.1.   Responsibilities of a Partner or Supervisory Lawyer

(a) A partner in a law firm, and a lawyer who individually or together with other lawyers possesses comparable managerial authority in a law firm or government agency, shall make reasonable efforts to ensure that the firm has in effect measures giving reasonable assurance that all lawyers in the firm or agency conform to the Rules of Professional Conduct.

(b) A lawyer having direct supervisory authority over another lawyer shall make reasonable efforts to ensure that the other lawyer conforms to the Rules of Professional Conduct.

(c) A lawyer shall be responsible for another lawyer's violation of the Rules of Professional Conduct if:

(1) The lawyer orders or, with knowledge of the specific conduct, ratifies the conduct involved; or

(2) The lawyer has direct supervisory authority over the other lawyer or is a partner or has comparable managerial authority in the law firm or government agency in which the other lawyer practices, and knows or reasonably should know of the conduct at a time when its consequences can be avoided or mitigated but fails to take reasonable remedial action.

COMMENT

[1] Paragraph (a) applies to lawyers who have managerial authority over the professional work of a firm or government agency. This includes members of a partnership, the shareholders in a law firm organized as a professional corporation and members of other associations authorized to practice law; lawyers having comparable managerial authority in a legal services organization or the law department of an enterprise or government agency; and lawyers who have intermediate

managerial responsibilities in a firm. For the broad definition of "firm," *see* Rule 1.0(c). Paragraph (b) applies to lawyers who have supervisory authority over the work of other lawyers.

[2] Paragraph (a) requires lawyers with managerial authority within a firm to make reasonable efforts to establish internal policies and procedures designed to provide reasonable assurance that all lawyers in the firm will conform to the Rules of Professional Conduct. Such policies and procedures include those designed to detect and resolve conflicts of interest, identify dates by which actions must be taken in pending matters, account for client funds and property and ensure that inexperienced lawyers are properly supervised.

[3] Other measures that may be required to fulfill the responsibility prescribed in paragraph (a), and measures that may be required to fulfill the responsibility prescribed in paragraph (b), can depend on the firm's structure and the nature of its practice. In a small firm, informal supervision and occasional admonition ordinarily might be sufficient. In a large firm, or in practice situations in which intensely difficult ethical problems frequently arise, more elaborate procedures may be necessary. Some firms, for example, have a procedure whereby junior lawyers can make confidential referral of ethical problems directly to a designated senior partner or special committee. *See* Rule 5.2. Firms, whether large or small, may also rely on continuing legal education in professional ethics. In any event, the ethical atmosphere of a firm can influence the conduct of all its members and a lawyer having authority over the work of another may not assume that the subordinate lawyer will inevitably conform to the Rules.

[4] Paragraph (c) sets forth general principles of imputed responsibility for the misconduct of others. Subparagraph (c)(1) makes any lawyer who orders or, with knowledge, ratifies misconduct responsible for that misconduct. *See also* Rule 8.4(a). Subparagraph (c)(2) extends that responsibility to any lawyer who is a partner or person in comparable managerial authority in the firm in which the misconduct takes place, or who has direct supervisory authority over the lawyer who engages in misconduct, when the lawyer knows or should reasonably know of the conduct and could intervene to ameliorate its consequences. Whether a lawyer has such supervisory authority in particular circumstances is a question of fact. A lawyer with direct supervisory authority is a lawyer who has an actual supervisory role with respect to directing the conduct of other lawyers in a particular representation. A lawyer who is technically a "supervisor" in organizational terms, but is not involved in directing the effort of other lawyers in a particular representation, is not a supervising lawyer with respect to that representation.

[5] The existence of actual knowledge is also a question of fact; whether a lawyer should reasonably have known of misconduct by another lawyer in the same firm is an objective standard based on evaluation of all the facts, including the size and organizational structure of the firm, the lawyer's position and responsibilities within the firm, the type and frequency of contacts between the various lawyers involved, the nature of the misconduct at issue, and the nature of the supervision or other direct responsibility (if any) actually exercised. The mere fact of partnership or a position as a principal in a firm is not sufficient, without more, to satisfy this standard. Similarly, the fact that a lawyer holds a position on the management committee of a firm, or heads a department of the firm, or has comparable management authority in some other form of organization or a government agency is not sufficient, standing alone, to satisfy this standard.

[6] Appropriate remedial action would depend on the immediacy of the involvement and the seriousness of the misconduct. The supervisor is required to intervene to prevent avoidable consequences of misconduct if the supervisor knows that the misconduct occurred. Thus, if a supervising lawyer knows that a subordinate misrepresented a matter to an opposing party in a negotiation, the supervisor as well as the subordinate has a duty to correct the resulting misapprehension.

[7] Professional misconduct by a lawyer under supervision could reveal a violation of paragraph (b) on the part of the supervisory lawyer even though it does not entail a violation of paragraph (c) because there was no direction, ratification, or knowledge of the violation.

[8] Apart from this rule and Rule 8.4(a), a lawyer does not have disciplinary liability for the conduct of a partner, associate, or subordinate. Whether a lawyer may be liable civilly or criminally for another lawyer's conduct is a question of law beyond the scope of these Rules.

[9] The duties imposed by this rule on managing and supervisory lawyers do not alter the personal duty of each lawyer in a firm to abide by the Rules of Professional Conduct. *See* Rule 5.2(a).

Rule 5.2.   Subordinate Lawyers

(a) A lawyer is bound by the Rules of Professional Conduct notwithstanding that the lawyer acted at the direction of another person.

(b) A subordinate lawyer does not violate the Rules of Professional Conduct if that lawyer acts in accordance with a supervisory lawyer's reasonable resolution of an arguable question of professional duty.

COMMENT

[1] Although a lawyer is not relieved of responsibility for a violation by the fact that the lawyer acted at the direction of a supervisor, that fact may be relevant in determining whether a lawyer had the knowledge required to render conduct a violation of the Rules. For example, if a subordinate filed a frivolous pleading at the direction of a supervisor, the subordinate would not be guilty of a professional violation unless the subordinate knew of the document's frivolous character.

[2] When lawyers in a supervisor-subordinate relationship encounter a matter involving professional judgment as to ethical duty, the supervisor may assume responsibility for making the judgment. Otherwise a consistent course of action or position could not be taken. If the question can reasonably be answered only one way, the duty of both lawyers is clear and they are equally responsible for fulfilling it. However, if the question is reasonably arguable, someone has to decide upon the course of action. That authority ordinarily reposes in the supervisor, and a subordinate may be guided accordingly. For example, if a question arises whether the interests of two clients conflict under Rule 1.7, the supervisor's reasonable resolution of the question should protect the subordinate professionally if the resolution is subsequently challenged.

Rule 5.3.   Responsibilities Regarding Nonlawyer Assistants

With respect to a nonlawyer employed or retained by or associated with a lawyer:

(a) A partner or a lawyer who individually or together with other lawyers possesses comparable managerial authority in a law firm or government agency shall make reasonable efforts to ensure that the firm or agency has in effect measures giving reasonable assurance that the person's conduct is compatible with the professional obligations of the lawyer;

(b) A lawyer having direct supervisory authority over the nonlawyer shall make reasonable efforts to ensure that the person's conduct is compatible with the professional obligations of the lawyer; and

(c) A lawyer shall be responsible for conduct of such a person that would be a violation of the Rules of Professional Conduct if engaged in by a lawyer if:

(1) The lawyer requests or, with knowledge of the specific conduct, ratifies the conduct involved; or

(2) The lawyer has direct supervisory authority over the person, or is a partner or a lawyer who individually or together with other lawyers possess comparable managerial authority in the law firm or government agency in which the person is employed, and knows of the conduct at a time when its consequences can be avoided or mitigated but fails to take reasonable remedial action.

COMMENT

[1] Lawyers generally employ assistants in their practice, including secretaries, investigators, law student interns, and paraprofessionals. Such assistants, whether employees or independent contractors, act for the lawyer in rendition of the lawyer's professional services. A lawyer should give such assistants appropriate instruction and supervision concerning the ethical aspects of their employment, particularly regarding the obligation not to disclose information relating to representation of the client, and should be responsible for their work product. The measures employed in supervising should take account of the fact that they do not have legal training and are not subject to professional discipline.

[2] Just as lawyers in private practice may direct the conduct of investigators who may be independent contractors, prosecutors and other government lawyers may effectively direct the conduct of police or other governmental investigative personnel, even though they may not have, strictly speaking, formal authority to order actions by such personnel, who report to the chief of police or the head of another enforcement agency. Such prosecutors or other government lawyers have a responsibility with respect to police or investigative personnel, whose conduct they effectively direct, equivalent to that of private lawyers with respect to investigators whom they retain. *See also* Comments [4], [5], and [6] to Rule 5.1, in particular, the concept of what constitutes direct supervisory authority, and the significance of

holding certain positions in a firm. Comments [4], [5], and [6] of Rule 5.1 apply as well to Rule 5.3.

Rule 5.4. Professional Independence of a Lawyer

(a) A lawyer or law firm shall not share legal fees with a nonlawyer, except that:

(1) An agreement by a lawyer with the lawyer's firm, partner, or associate may provide for the payment of money, over a reasonable period of time after the lawyer's death, to the lawyer's estate or to one or more specified persons;

(2) A lawyer who undertakes to complete unfinished legal business of a deceased lawyer may pay to the estate of the deceased lawyer that proportion of the total compensation which fairly represents the services rendered by the deceased lawyer. A lawyer who purchases the practice of a deceased, disabled, or disappeared lawyer may, pursuant to the provisions of Rule 1.17, pay to the estate or other representative of that lawyer the agreed-upon purchase price.

(3) A lawyer or law firm may include nonlawyer employees in a compensation or retirement plan, even though the plan is based in whole or in part on a profit-sharing arrangement;

(4) Sharing of fees is permitted in a partnership or other form of organization which meets the requirements of paragraph (b); and

(5) A lawyer may share legal fees, whether awarded by a tribunal or received in settlement of a matter, with a nonprofit organization that employed, retained, or recommended employment of the lawyer in the matter and that qualifies under Section 501(c)(3) of the Internal Revenue Code.

(b) A lawyer may practice law in a partnership or other form of organization in which a financial interest is held or managerial authority is exercised by an individual nonlawyer who performs professional services which assist the organization in providing legal services to clients, but only if:

(1) The partnership or organization has as its sole purpose providing legal services to clients;

(2) All persons having such managerial authority or holding a financial interest undertake to abide by these Rules of Professional Conduct;

(3) The lawyers who have a financial interest or managerial authority in the partnership or organization undertake to be responsible for the nonlawyer participants to the same extent as if nonlawyer participants were lawyers under Rule 5.1;

(4) The foregoing conditions are set forth in writing.

(c) A lawyer shall not permit a person who recommends, employs, or pays the lawyer to render legal services for another to direct or regulate the lawyer's professional judgment in rendering such legal services.

COMMENT

[1] The provisions of this rule express traditional limitations on sharing fees with nonlawyers. (On sharing fees among lawyers not in the same firm, *see* Rule 1.5(e).) These limitations are to protect the lawyer's professional independence of judgment. Where someone other than the client pays the lawyer's fee or salary, or recommends employment of the lawyer, that arrangement does not modify the lawyer's obligation to the client. As stated in paragraph (c), such arrangements should not interfere with the lawyer's professional judgment.

[2] Traditionally, the canons of legal ethics and disciplinary rules prohibited lawyers from practicing law in a partnership that includes nonlawyers or in any other organization where a nonlawyer is a shareholder, director, or officer. Notwithstanding these strictures, the profession implicitly recognized exceptions for lawyers who work for corporate law departments, insurance companies, and legal service organizations.

[3] As the demand increased for a broad range of professional services from a single source, lawyers employed professionals from other disciplines to work for them. So long as the nonlawyers remained employees of the lawyers, these relationships did not violate the disciplinary rules. However, when lawyers and nonlawyers considered forming partnerships and professional corporations to provide a combination of legal and other services to the public, they faced serious obstacles under the former rules.

[4] This rule rejects an absolute prohibition against lawyers and nonlawyers joining together to provide collaborative services, but continues to impose traditional ethical requirements with respect to the organization thus created. Thus, a lawyer may practice law in an organization where nonlawyers hold a financial interest or exercise managerial authority, but only if the conditions set forth in subparagraphs (b)(1), (b)(2), and (b)(3) are satisfied, and pursuant to subparagraph (b)(4), satisfaction of these conditions is set forth in a written instrument. The requirement of a writing helps ensure that these important conditions are not overlooked in establishing the organizational structure of entities in which nonlawyers enjoy an ownership or managerial role equivalent to that of a partner in a traditional law firm.

[5] Nonlawyer participants under Rule 5.4 ought not be confused with nonlawyer assistants under Rule 5.3. Nonlawyer participants are persons having managerial authority or financial interests in organizations that provide legal services. Within such organizations, lawyers with financial interests or managerial authority are held responsible for ethical misconduct by nonlawyer participants about which the lawyers know or reasonably should know. This is the same standard of liability contemplated by Rule 5.1, regarding the responsibilities of lawyers with direct supervisory authority over other lawyers.

[6] Nonlawyer assistants under Rule 5.3 do not have managerial authority or financial interests in the organization. Lawyers having direct supervisory authority over nonlawyer assistants are held responsible only for ethical misconduct by assistants about which the lawyers actually know.

[7] As the introductory portion of paragraph (b) makes clear, the purpose of liberalizing the Rules regarding the possession of a financial interest or the exercise of management authority by a nonlawyer is to permit nonlawyer professionals to work with lawyers in the delivery of legal services without being relegated to the role of an employee. For example, the rule permits economists to work in a firm with antitrust or public utility practitioners, psychologists or psychiatric social workers to

work with family law practitioners to assist in counseling clients, nonlawyer lobbyists to work with lawyers who perform legislative services, certified public accountants to work in conjunction with tax lawyers or others who use accountants' services in performing legal services, and professional managers to serve as office managers, executive directors, or in similar positions. In all of these situations, the professionals may be given financial interests or managerial responsibility, so long as all of the requirements of paragraph (c) are met.

[8] Paragraph (b) does not permit an individual or entity to acquire all or any part of the ownership of a law partnership or other form of law practice organization for investment or other purposes. It thus does not permit a corporation, an investment banking firm, an investor, or any other person or entity to entitle itself to all or any portion of the income or profits of a law firm or other similar organization. Since such an investor would not be an individual performing professional services within the law firm or other organization, the requirements of paragraph (b) would not be met.

[9] The term "individual" in subparagraph (b) is not intended to preclude the participation in a law firm or other organization by an individual professional corporation in the same manner as lawyers who have incorporated as a professional corporation currently participate in partnerships that include professional corporations.

[10] Some sharing of fees is likely to occur in the kinds of organizations permitted by paragraph (b). Subparagraph (a)(4) makes it clear that such fee sharing is not prohibited.

[11] Subparagraph (a)(5) permits a lawyer to share legal fees with a nonprofit organization that employed, retained, or recommended employment of the lawyer in the matter. A lawyer may decide to contribute all or part of legal fees recovered from the opposing party to a nonprofit organization. Such a contribution may or may not involve fee-splitting, but when it does, the prospect that the organization will obtain all or part of the lawyer's fees does not inherently compromise the lawyer's professional independence, whether the lawyer is employed by the organization or was only retained or recommended by it. A lawyer who has agreed to share legal fees with such an organization remains obligated to exercise professional judgment solely in the client's best interests. Moreover, fee-splitting in these circumstances may promote the financial viability of such nonprofit organizations and facilitate their public interest mission. Unlike the corresponding provision of Model Rule 5.4(a)(5), this provision is not limited to sharing of fees awarded by a court because that restriction would significantly interfere with settlement of cases, without significantly advancing the purpose of the exception. To prevent abuse of this broader exception, it applies only if the nonprofit organization qualifies under Section 501(c)(3) of the Internal Revenue Code.

Rule 5.5.   Unauthorized Practice

A lawyer shall not:
(a) Practice law in a jurisdiction where doing so violates the regulation of the legal profession in that jurisdiction; or
(b) Assist a person who is not a member of the bar in the performance of activity that constitutes the unauthorized practice of law.

COMMENT

[1] This rule concerns the unauthorized practice of law by District of Columbia Bar members in other jurisdictions and assistance by District of Columbia Bar members in the unauthorized practice of law by lawyers not admitted in this jurisdiction or by nonlawyers. The provisions concerning the unauthorized practice of law in the District of Columbia, including those activities in which a lawyer not admitted in the District of Columbia may and may not engage, are set forth in Rule 49 of the Rules of the District of Columbia Court of Appeals.

[2] The definition of the practice of law is established by law and varies from one jurisdiction to another. Whatever the definition, limiting the practice of law to members of the bar protects the public against rendition of legal services by unqualified persons. Paragraph (b) does not prohibit a lawyer from employing the services of paraprofessionals and delegating functions to them, so long as the lawyer supervises the delegated work and retains responsibility for their work. *See* Rule 5.3. Likewise, it does not prohibit lawyers from providing professional advice and instruction to nonlawyers whose employment requires knowledge of law; for example, claims adjusters, employees of financial or commercial institutions, social workers, accountants and persons employed in government agencies. In addition, a lawyer may counsel nonlawyers who wish to proceed *pro se.*

Editors' Note. Effective January 2, 2004, the D.C. Court of Appeals amended the court's Rule 49, which defines and governs the unauthorized practice of law in the District of Columbia. Rule 49 thus determines the scope of Rule 5.5(b), which prohibits a lawyer from assisting a person who is not a member of the D.C. Bar "in the performance of activity that constitutes the unauthorized practice of law." For a detailed commentary on Rule 49 written by the D.C. Bar's Examination of Rule 49 Committee, visit the D.C. Bar's website at *www.dcbar.org* (click on "For Lawyers," then on "Courts," then on "Rules of the D.C. Court of Appeals").

In September 2004, the D.C. Bar's Special Committee on Multijurisdictional Practice issued a report recommending significant amendments to Rule 49. The amendments were intended to bring Rule 49 more closely into line with ABA Model Rule 5.5 (Unauthorized Practice of Law; Multijurisdictional Practice of Law) and ABA Model Rule 8.5 (Disciplinary Authority; Choice of Law). The Committee was chaired by attorney James J. Sandman of Arnold & Porter. In June 2007, the Board of Governors of the D.C. Bar submitted its own report on multijurisdictional practice to the D.C. Court of Appeals. In March 2008, the court adopted amendments to Rule 49 to respond to the recommendations. D.C. Court of Appeals Rule 49 now provides in part:

The following activity in the District of Columbia is excepted from the prohibitions of section (a) of this Rule [prohibiting unauthorized practice], provided the person is not otherwise engaged in the practice of law or holding out as authorized or competent to practice law in the District of Columbia:

(6) Internal Counsel: Providing legal advice only to one's regular employer, where the employer does not reasonably expect that it is receiving advice from a person authorized to practice law in the District of Columbia. . . .

(13) Incidental and Temporary Practice: Providing legal services in the District of Columbia on an incidental and temporary basis, provided that the person is authorized to practice law by the highest court of a state or territory or by a foreign country, and is not disbarred or suspended for disciplinary reasons and has not resigned with charges pending in any jurisdiction or court.

See the full text of Rule 49 for, inter alia, exceptions for ADR, pro hac vice in court, and government lawyers.

Rule 5.6. Restrictions on Right to Practice

A lawyer shall not participate in offering or making:

(a) A partnership, shareholders, operating, employment, or other similar type of agreement that restricts the rights of a lawyer to practice after termination of the relationship, except an agreement concerning benefits upon retirement; or

(b) An agreement in which a restriction on the lawyer's right to practice is part of the settlement of a controversy between parties.

COMMENT

[1] An agreement restricting the right of partners or associates to practice after leaving a firm not only limits their professional autonomy but also limits the freedom of clients to choose a lawyer. Paragraph (a) prohibits such agreements except for restrictions incident to provisions concerning retirement benefits for service with the firm. Whether provisions limiting benefits are retirement provisions, excepted by this rule, will depend on a number of factors. *See Neuman v. Akman,* 715 A.2d 127 (D.C. 1998).

[2] Restrictions, other than those concerning retirement benefits, that impose a substantial financial penalty on a lawyer who competes after leaving the firm may violate paragraph (a).

[3] Paragraph (b) prohibits a lawyer from agreeing not to represent other persons in connection with settling a claim on behalf of a client.

[4] This rule does not prohibit restrictions that may be included in the terms of the sale of a law practice pursuant to Rule 1.17.

Rule 5.7. Responsibilities Regarding Law-Related Services

(a) A lawyer shall be subject to the Rules of Professional Conduct with respect to the provision of law-related services, as defined in paragraph (b), if the law-related services are provided:

(1) by the lawyer in circumstances that are not distinct from the lawyer's provision of legal services to clients; or

(2) in other circumstances by an entity controlled by the lawyer individually or with others if the lawyer fails to take reasonable measures to

assure that a person obtaining the law-related services knows that the services are not legal services and that the protections of the client-lawyer relationship do not exist.

(b) The term law-related services denotes services that might reasonably be performed in conjunction with and in substance are related to the provision of legal services, and that are not prohibited as unauthorized practice of law when provided by a nonlawyer.

COMMENT

[1] When a lawyer performs law-related services or controls an organization that does so, there exists the potential for ethical problems. Principal among these is the possibility that the person for whom the law-related services are performed fails to understand that the services may not carry with them the protections normally afforded as part of the client-lawyer relationship. The recipient of the law-related services may expect, for example, that the protection of client confidences, prohibitions against representation of persons with conflicting interests, and obligations of a lawyer to maintain professional independence apply to the provision of law-related services when that may not be the case.

[2] Rule 5.7 applies to the provision of law-related services by a lawyer even when the lawyer does not provide any legal services to the person for whom the law-related services are performed and whether the law-related services are performed through a law firm or a separate entity. The rule identifies the circumstances in which all the Rules of Professional Conduct apply to the provision of law-related services. Even when those circumstances do not exist, however, the conduct of a lawyer involved in the provision of law-related services is subject to those Rules that apply generally to lawyer conduct, regardless of whether the conduct involves the provision of legal services. *See, e.g.,* Rule 8.4.

[3] When law-related services are provided by a lawyer under circumstances that are not distinct from the lawyer's provision of legal services to clients, the lawyer in providing the law-related services must adhere to the requirements of the Rules of Professional Conduct as provided in paragraph (a)(1). Even when the law-related and legal services are provided in circumstances that are distinct from each other, for example through separate entities or different support staff within the law firm, the Rules of Professional Conduct apply to the lawyer as provided in paragraph (a)(2) unless the lawyer takes reasonable measures to assure that the recipient of the law-related services knows that the services are not legal services and that the protections of the client-lawyer relationship do not apply.

[4] Law-related services also may be provided through an entity that is distinct from that through which the lawyer provides legal services. If the lawyer individually or with others has control of such an entity's operations, the rule requires the lawyer to take reasonable measures to assure that each person using the services of the entity knows that the services provided by the entity are not legal services and that the Rules of Professional Conduct that relate to the client-lawyer relationship do not apply. A lawyer's control of an entity extends to the ability to direct its operation. Whether a lawyer has such control will depend upon the circumstances of the particular case.

[5] When a client-lawyer relationship exists with a person who is referred by a lawyer to a separate law-related service entity controlled by the lawyer, individually or with others, the lawyer must comply with Rule 1.8(a).

[6] In taking the reasonable measures referred to in paragraph (a)(2) to assure that a person using law-related services understands the practical effect or significance of the inapplicability of the Rules of Professional Conduct, the lawyer should communicate to the person receiving the law-related services, in a manner sufficient to assure that the person understands the significance of the fact, that the relationship of the person to the business entity will not be a client-lawyer relationship. The communication should be made before entering into an agreement for provision of or providing law-related services, and preferably should be in writing.

[7] The burden is upon the lawyer to show that the lawyer has taken reasonable measures under the circumstances to communicate the desired understanding. For instance, a sophisticated user of law-related services, such as a publicly held corporation, may require a lesser explanation than someone unaccustomed to making distinctions between legal services and law-related services, such as an individual seeking tax advice from a lawyer-accountant or investigative services in connection with a lawsuit.

[8] Regardless of the sophistication of potential recipients of law-related services, a lawyer should take special care to keep separate the provision of law-related and legal services in order to minimize the risk that the recipient will assume that the law-related services are legal services. The risk of such confusion is especially acute when the lawyer renders both types of services with respect to the same matter. Under some circumstances the legal and law-related services may be so closely entwined that they cannot be distinguished from each other, and the requirement of disclosure and consultation imposed by paragraph (a)(2) of the rule cannot be met. In such a case a lawyer will be responsible for assuring that both the lawyer's conduct and, to the extent required by Rule 5.3, that of nonlawyer employees in the distinct entity that the lawyer controls complies in all respects with the Rules of Professional Conduct.

[9] A broad range of economic and other interests of clients may be served by lawyers engaging in the delivery of law-related services. Examples of law-related services include providing title insurance, financial planning, accounting, trust services, real estate counseling, legislative lobbying, economic analysis, social work, psychological counseling, tax preparation, and patent, medical or environmental consulting.

[10] When a lawyer is obliged to accord the recipients of such services the protections of those Rules that apply to the client-lawyer relationship, the lawyer must take special care to heed the proscriptions of the Rules addressing conflict of interest (Rules 1.7 through 1.11, especially Rules 1.7(b)(2)-(4) and 1.8(a) and (e)), and to scrupulously adhere to the requirements of Rule 1.6 relating to disclosure and use of confidential information. *See also* Comment [26] to Rule 1.7. The promotion of the law-related services must also in all respects comply with Rule 7.1, dealing with advertising and solicitation. In that regard, lawyers should take special care to identify the obligations that may be imposed as a result of a jurisdiction decisional law. Rule 1.8 addresses a lawyer's provision of non law-related services to a client.

[11] When the full protections of all the Rules of Professional Conduct do not apply to the provision of law-related services, principles of law external to the Rules, for example, the law of principal and agent, govern the legal duties owed to

those receiving the services. Those other legal principles may establish a different degree of protection for the recipient with respect to confidentiality of information, conflicts of interest and permissible business relationships with clients. Rule 5.7 does not limit the protection provided by any other Rule, including but not limited to Rule 8.4, which prohibits, among other things, conduct involving dishonesty or fraud whether or not the lawyer engages in such conduct in connection with the rendering of law-related services.

PUBLIC SERVICE

Rule 6.1.   Pro Bono Publico Service

A lawyer should participate in serving those persons, or groups of persons, who are unable to pay all or a portion of reasonable attorney's fees or who are otherwise unable to obtain counsel. A lawyer may discharge this responsibility by providing professional services at no fee, or at a substantially reduced fee, to persons and groups who are unable to afford or obtain counsel, or by active participation in the work of organizations that provide legal services to them. When personal representation is not feasible, a lawyer may discharge this responsibility by providing financial support for organizations that provide legal representation to those unable to obtain counsel.

COMMENT

[1] This rule reflects the long-standing ethical principle underlying Canon 2 of the previous Code of Professional Responsibility that "A lawyer should assist the legal profession in fulfilling its duty to make legal counsel available." The rule incorporates the legal profession's historical commitment to the principle that all persons in our society should be able to obtain necessary legal services. The rule also recognizes that the rights and responsibilities of individuals and groups in the United States are increasingly defined in legal terms and that, as a consequence, legal assistance in coping with the web of statutes, rules, and regulations is imperative for persons of modest and limited means, as well as for the relatively well-to-do. The rule also recognizes that a lawyer's pro bono services are sometimes needed to assert or defend public rights belonging to the public generally where no individual or group can afford to pay for the services.

[2] This rule carries forward the ethical precepts set forth in the Code. Specifically, the rule recognizes that the basic responsibility for providing legal services for those unable to pay ultimately rests upon the individual lawyer, and that every lawyer, regardless of professional prominence or professional work load, should find time to participate in or otherwise support the provision of legal services to the disadvantaged.

[3] The rule also acknowledges that while the provision of free legal services to those unable to pay reasonable fees continues to be an obligation of each lawyer

as well as the profession generally, the efforts of individual lawyers are often not enough to meet the need. Thus, it has been necessary for the profession and government to institute additional programs to provide legal services. Accordingly, legal aid offices, lawyer referral services, and other related programs have been developed, and others will be developed by the profession and government. Every lawyer should support all proper efforts to meet this need for legal services. A lawyer also should not refuse a request from a court or bar association to undertake representation of a person unable to obtain counsel except for compelling reasons such as those listed in Rule 6.2.

[4] This rule expresses the profession's traditional commitment to make legal counsel available, but it is not intended that the rule be enforced through disciplinary process. Neither is it intended to place any obligation on a government lawyer that is inconsistent with laws such as 18 U.S.C. §§203 and 205 limiting the scope of permissible employment or representational activities.

[5] In determining their responsibilities under this rule, lawyers admitted to practice in the District of Columbia should be guided by the Resolutions on Pro Bono Services passed by the Judicial Conferences of the District of Columbia and the D.C. Circuit as amended from time to time. Those resolutions as adopted in 2009 and 2010, respectively, call on members of the D.C. Bar, at a minimum, each year to (1) accept one court appointment, (2) provide 50 hours of pro bono legal service, or (3) when personal representation is not feasible, contribute the lesser of $750 or 1 percent of earned income to a legal assistance organization that services the community's economically disadvantaged, including pro bono referral and appointment offices sponsored by the Bar and the courts.

[6] Law firms and other organizations employing lawyers should act reasonably to enable and encourage all lawyers in the organization to provide the pro bono legal services called for by this rule.

Rule 6.2.   Accepting Appointments

A lawyer shall not seek to avoid appointment by a tribunal to represent a person except for good cause, such as:

(a) Representing the client is likely to result in violation of the Rules of Professional Conduct or other law;

(b) Representing the client is likely to result in a substantial and unreasonable burden on the lawyer; or

(c) The client or the cause is so repugnant to the lawyer as to be likely to impair the client-lawyer relationship or the lawyer's ability to represent the client.

COMMENT

[1] A lawyer ordinarily is not obliged to accept a client whose character or cause the lawyer regards as repugnant. The lawyer's freedom to select clients is, however, qualified. All lawyers have a responsibility to assist in providing pro bono

public service. *See* Rule 6.1. An individual lawyer fulfills this responsibility by accepting a fair share of unpopular matters or indigent or unpopular clients. A lawyer may also be subject to appointment by a court to serve unpopular clients or persons unable to afford legal services.

Appointed Counsel

[2] For good cause a lawyer may seek to decline an appointment to represent a person who cannot afford to retain counsel or whose cause is unpopular. Good cause exists if the lawyer could not handle the matter competently, *see* Rule 1.1, or if undertaking the representation would result in an improper conflict of interest; for example, when the client or the cause is so repugnant to the lawyer as to be likely to impair the client-lawyer relationship or the lawyer's ability to represent the client. A lawyer may also seek to decline an appointment if acceptance would be substantially and unreasonably burdensome, such as when it would impose a financial sacrifice so great as to be unjust.

[3] An appointed lawyer has the same obligations to the client as retained counsel, including the obligations of loyalty and confidentiality, and is subject to the same limitations on the client-lawyer relationship, such as the obligation to refrain from assisting the client in violation of the Rules.

Rule 6.3.   Membership in Legal Services Organization

A lawyer may serve as a director, officer, or member of a legal services organization, apart from the law firm in which the lawyer practices, notwithstanding that the organization serves persons having interests adverse to a client of the lawyer. The lawyer shall not knowingly participate in a decision or action of the organization:

(a) If participating in the decision would be incompatible with the lawyer's obligations to a client under Rule 1.7; or

(b) Where the decision could have a material adverse effect on the representation of a client of the organization whose interests are adverse to a client of the lawyer.

COMMENT

[1] Lawyers should be encouraged to support and participate in legal service organizations. A lawyer who is an officer or a member of such an organization does not thereby have a client-lawyer relationship with persons served by the organization. However, there is potential conflict between the interests of such persons and the interests of the lawyer's clients. If the possibility of such conflict disqualified a lawyer from serving on the board of a legal services organization, the profession's involvement in such organizations would be severely curtailed.

[2] It may be necessary in appropriate cases to reassure a client of the organization that the representation will not be affected by conflicting loyalties of a member of the board. Established, written policies in this respect can enhance the credibility of such assurances.

Rule 6.4.   Law Reform Activities Affecting Client Interests

(a) A lawyer should assist in improving the administration of justice. A lawyer may discharge this requirement by rendering services in activities for improving the law, the legal system, or the legal profession.

(b) A lawyer may serve as a director, officer, or member of an organization involved in reform of the law or its administration notwithstanding that the reform may affect the interests of a client of the lawyer. When the lawyer knows that the interests of a client may be materially benefited by a decision in which the lawyer participates, the lawyer shall disclose that fact but need not identify the client.

COMMENT

[1] Changes in human affairs and imperfections in human institutions make necessary constant efforts to maintain and improve our legal system. This system should function in a manner that commands public respect and fosters the use of legal remedies to achieve redress of grievances. By reason of education and experience, lawyers are especially qualified to recognize deficiencies in the legal system and to initiate corrective measures therein. Thus, they should participate in proposing and supporting legislation and programs to improve the system, without regard to the general interests or desires of clients or former clients. Rules of law are deficient if they are not just, understandable, and responsive to the needs of society. If a lawyer believes that the existence or absence of a rule of law, substantive or procedural, causes or contributes to an unjust result, the lawyer should endeavor by lawful means to obtain appropriate changes in the law. This rule expresses the policy underlying Canon 8 of the previous Code of Professional Responsibility that "A lawyer should assist in improving the legal system," but it is not intended that it be enforced through disciplinary process.

[2] Lawyers involved in organizations seeking law reform generally do not have a client-lawyer relationship with the organization. Otherwise, it might follow that a lawyer could not be involved in a bar association law reform program that might indirectly affect a client. *See also* Rule 1.2(b). For example, a lawyer specializing in antitrust litigation might be regarded as disqualified from participating in drafting revisions of rules governing that subject. In determining the nature and scope of participation in such activities, a lawyer should be mindful of obligations to clients under other Rules, particularly Rule 1.7. A lawyer is professionally obligated to protect the integrity of the program by making an appropriate disclosure within the organization when the lawyer knows a private client might be materially benefited.

Rule 6.5.   Nonprofit and Court-Annexed Limited Legal Services Programs

(a) A lawyer who, under the auspices of a program sponsored by a nonprofit organization or court, provides short-term limited legal services to a client without expectation by either the lawyer or the client that the lawyer will provide continuing representation in the matter:

(1) is subject to Rules 1.7 and 1.9 only if the lawyer knows that the representation of the client involves a conflict of interest; and

(2) is subject to Rule 1.10 only if the lawyer knows that another lawyer associated with the lawyer in a law firm is disqualified by Rule 1.7 or 1.9 with respect to the matter.

(b) Except as provided in paragraph (a)(2), Rule 1.10 is inapplicable to a representation governed by this rule.

COMMENT

[1] Legal services organizations, courts, and various nonprofit organizations have established programs through which lawyers provide short-term limited legal services, such as advice or the completion of legal forms, that will assist persons to address their legal problems without further representation by a lawyer. In these programs, such as legal-advice hotlines, advice-only clinics or pro se counseling programs, a client-lawyer relationship is established, but there is no expectation that the lawyer's representation of the client will continue beyond the limited consultation. Such programs are normally operated under circumstances in which it is not feasible for a lawyer to systematically screen for conflicts of interest as is generally required before undertaking a representation. *See, e.g.,* Rules 1.7, 1.9 and 1.10. For the purposes of this rule, short-term limited legal services normally do not include appearing before a tribunal on behalf of a client.

[2] A lawyer who provides short-term limited legal services pursuant to this rule must secure the client's informed consent to the limited scope of the representation. *See* Rule 1.2(c). If a short-term limited representation would not be reasonable under the circumstances, the lawyer may offer advice to the client but must also advise the client of the need for further assistance of counsel. Except as provided in this rule, the Rules of Professional Conduct, including Rule 1.6, are applicable to the limited representation.

[3] Because a lawyer who is representing a client in the circumstances addressed by this rule ordinarily is not able to check systematically for conflicts of interest, paragraph (a) requires compliance with Rules 1.7 or 1.9 only if the lawyer knows that the representation presents a conflict of interest for the lawyer, and with Rule 1.10 only if the lawyer knows that another lawyer in the lawyer's firm is disqualified by Rules 1.7 or 1.9 in the matter.

[4] Because the limited nature of the services significantly reduces the risk of conflicts of interest with other matters being handled by the lawyer's firm, paragraph (b) provides that Rule 1.10 is inapplicable to a representation governed by this rule except as provided by paragraph (a)(2). Paragraph (a)(2) requires the participating

lawyer to comply with Rule 1.10 when the lawyer knows that the lawyer's firm is disqualified by Rules 1.7 or 1.9. By virtue of paragraph (b), however, a lawyer's participation in a short-term limited legal services program will not preclude the lawyer's firm from undertaking or continuing the representation of a client with interests adverse to a client being represented under the program's auspices. Nor will the personal disqualification of a lawyer participating in the program be imputed to other lawyers participating in the program.

[5] If, after commencing a short-term limited representation in accordance with this rule, a lawyer undertakes to represent the client in the matter on an ongoing basis, Rules 1.7, 1.9 and 1.10 become applicable.

[6] This rule serves the public interest by making it easier for lawyers affiliated with firms to provide pro bono legal services. Rule 1.10(e) contains a similarly motivated exception from imputation for attorneys who, while affiliated with a firm, assist the District of Columbia Attorney General with certain matters.

INFORMATION ABOUT LEGAL SERVICES

Rule 7.1. Communications Concerning a Lawyer's Services

(a) A lawyer shall not make a false or misleading communication about the lawyer or the lawyer's services. A communication is false or misleading if it:

(1) Contains a material misrepresentation of fact or law, or omits a fact necessary to make the statement considered as a whole not materially misleading; or

(2) Contains an assertion about the lawyer or the lawyer's services that cannot be substantiated.

(b)(1) A lawyer shall not seek by in-person contact, employment (or employment of a partner or associate) by a nonlawyer who has not sought the lawyer's advice regarding employment of a lawyer, if:

(A) The solicitation involves use of a statement or claim that is false or misleading, within the meaning of paragraph (a);

(B) The solicitation involves the use of coercion, duress or harassment; or

(C) The potential client is apparently in a physical or mental condition which would make it unlikely that the potential client could exercise reasonable, considered judgment as to the selection of a lawyer.

(2) A lawyer shall not give anything of value to a person (other than the lawyer's partner or employee) for recommending the lawyer's services through in-person contact.

(c) A lawyer shall not knowingly assist an organization that furnishes or pays for legal services to others to promote the use of the lawyer's services or those of the lawyer's partner or associate, or any other lawyer affiliated with the lawyer or the lawyer's firm, as a private practitioner, if the promotional activity involves the use of coercion, duress, compulsion, intimidation, threats, or vexatious or harassing conduct.

(d) No lawyer or any person acting on behalf of a lawyer shall solicit or invite or seek to solicit any person for purposes of representing that person for a fee paid by or on behalf of a client or under the Criminal Justice Act, D.C. Code Ann. §11-2601 (2001) et seq., in any present or future case in the District of Columbia Courthouse, on the sidewalks on the north, south, and west sides of the courthouse, or within 50 feet of the building on the east side.

(e) Any lawyer or person acting on behalf of a lawyer who solicits or invites or seeks to solicit any person incarcerated at the District of Columbia Jail, the Correctional Treatment Facility or any District of Columbia juvenile detention facility for the purpose of representing that person for a fee paid by or on behalf of that person or under the Criminal Justice Act, D.C. Code Ann. §11-2601 (2001) et seq., in any then-pending criminal case in which that person is represented, must provide timely and adequate notice to the person's then-current lawyer prior to accepting any fee from or on behalf of the incarcerated person.

COMMENT

[1] This rule governs all communications about a lawyer's services, including advertising. It is especially important that statements about a lawyer or the lawyer's services be accurate, since many members of the public lack detailed knowledge of legal matters. Certain advertisements such as those that describe the amount of a damage award, the lawyer's record in obtaining favorable verdicts, or those containing client endorsements, unless suitably qualified, have a capacity to mislead by creating an unjustified expectation that similar results can be obtained for others. Advertisements comparing the lawyer's services with those of other lawyers are false or misleading if the claims made cannot be substantiated.

Advertising

[2] To assist the public in obtaining legal services, lawyers should be allowed to make known their services not only through reputation but also through organized information campaigns in the form of advertising. Advertising involves an active quest for clients, contrary to the tradition that a lawyer should not seek clientele. However, the public's need to know about legal services can be fulfilled in part through advertising. This need is particularly acute in the case of persons of limited means who have not made extensive use of legal services. The interest in expanding public information about legal services ought to prevail over considerations of tradition.

[3] This rule permits public dissemination of information concerning a lawyer's name or firm name, address, and telephone number; the kinds of services the

lawyer will undertake; the basis on which the lawyer's fees are determined, including prices for specific services and payment and credit arrangements; a lawyer's foreign language ability; names of references and, with their consent, names of clients regularly represented; and other information that might invite the attention of those seeking legal assistance.

[4] Questions of effectiveness and taste in advertising are matters of speculation and subjective judgment. Some jurisdictions have rules regulating the type and content of advertising by lawyers that go beyond prohibitions against false or misleading statements. Such regulations create unneeded barriers to the flow of information about lawyers' services to persons needing such services, and so this rule subjects advertising by lawyers only to the requirement that it not be false or misleading.

[5] There is no significant distinction between disseminating information and soliciting clients through mass media or through individual personal contact. In-person solicitation (which would include telephone contact but not electronic mail) can, however, create problems because of the particular circumstances in which the solicitation takes place. This rule prohibits in-person solicitation in circumstances or through means that are not conducive to intelligent, rational decisions. Such circumstances and means could be the harassment of early morning or late night telephone calls to a prospective client to solicit legal work, or repeated calls at any time of day, and solicitation of an accident victim or the victim's family shortly after the accident or while the victim is still in medical distress. A lawyer is no longer permitted to conduct in-person solicitation through the use of a paid intermediary, i.e., a person who is neither the lawyer's partner (as defined in Rule 1.0(i)) nor employee (*see* Rule 5.3) and who is compensated for such services. This prohibition represents a change in Rule 7.1(b), which had previously authorized payments to intermediaries for recommending a lawyer. Experience under the former provision showed it to be unnecessary and subject to abuse. *See* Rules 5.3, 8.4(a), and 8.4(c) regarding a lawyer's responsibility for abusive or deceptive solicitation of a client by the lawyer's employee.

Payments for Advertising

[6] A lawyer is allowed to pay for advertising or marketing permitted by this rule. Likewise, a lawyer may participate in lawyer referral programs and pay the usual fees charged by such programs.

Solicitations in the Vicinity of the District of Columbia Courthouse

[7] Paragraph (d) is designed to prohibit unseemly solicitations of prospective clients in and around the District of Columbia Courthouse. The words "for a fee paid by or on behalf of a client or under the Criminal Justice Act" have been added to paragraph (d) as it was originally promulgated by the District of Columbia Court of Appeals in 1982. The purpose of the addition is to permit solicitation in the District of Columbia Courthouse for the purposes of pro bono representation. For the purposes of this rule, pro bono representation, whether by individual lawyers or

nonprofit organizations, is representation undertaken primarily for purposes other than a fee. That representation includes providing services free of charge for individuals who may be in need of legal assistance and may lack the financial means and sophistication necessary to have alternative sources of aid. Cases where fees are awarded under the Criminal Justice Act do not constitute pro bono representation for the purposes of this rule. However, the possibility that fees may be awarded under the Equal Access to Justice Act and Civil Rights Attorneys' Fees Awards Act of 1976, as amended, or other statutory attorney fee statutes, does not prevent representation from constituting pro bono representation.

Solicitations of Inmates

[8] Paragraph (e) is designed to address the vulnerability of incarcerated persons to lawyers seeking fee-paying representations. It applies only to situations where the incarcerated person has not initiated contact with the lawyer. In such situations, the lawyer may have contact with the individual but may not accept a fee unless and until timely notice is provided to current counsel for such incarcerated person.

Rule 7.5.   Firm Names and Letterheads

(a) A lawyer shall not use a firm name, letterhead, or other professional designation that violates Rule 7.1. A trade name may be used by a lawyer in private practice if it does not imply a connection with a government agency or with a public or charitable legal services organization and is not otherwise in violation of Rule 7.1.

(b) A law firm with offices in more than one jurisdiction may use the same name or other professional designation in each jurisdiction, but identification of the lawyers in an office of the firm shall indicate the jurisdictional limitations on those not licensed to practice in the jurisdiction where the office is located.

(c) The name of a lawyer holding a public office shall not be used in the name of a law firm, or in communications on its behalf, during any substantial period in which the lawyer is not actively and regularly practicing with the firm.

(d) Lawyers may state or imply that they practice in a partnership or other organization only when that is the fact.

COMMENT

[1] A firm may be designated by the names of all or some of its members, by the names of deceased members where there has been a continuing succession in the firm's identity, or by a trade name such as the "ABC Legal Clinic." A lawyer or law firm may also be designated by a distinctive website address or comparable professional designation. Although the United States Supreme Court has held that

legislation may prohibit the use of trade names in professional practice, use of such names in law practice is acceptable so long as it is not misleading. If a private firm uses a trade name that includes a geographical name such as "Springfield Legal Clinic," an express disclaimer that it is a public legal aid agency may be required to avoid a misleading implication. It may be observed that any firm name including the name of a deceased partner is, strictly speaking, a trade name. The use of such names to designate law firms has proven a useful means of identification. However, it is misleading to use the name of a lawyer not associated with the firm or a predecessor of the firm. It is also misleading to continue to use the name of a lawyer formerly associated with the firm who currently is practicing elsewhere. *See* D.C. Bar Legal Ethics Committee Opinion 277.

[2] With regard to paragraph (d), lawyers sharing office facilities, but who are not in fact associated with each other in a law firm, may not denominate themselves as, for example, "Smith and Jones," for that title suggests that they are practicing law together in a firm.

MAINTAINING THE INTEGRITY OF THE PROFESSION

Rule 8.1. Bar Admission and Disciplinary Matters

An applicant for admission to the Bar, or a lawyer in connection with a Bar admission application or in connection with a disciplinary matter, shall not:

(a) Knowingly make a false statement of fact; or

(b) Fail to disclose a fact necessary to correct a misapprehension known by the lawyer or applicant to have arisen in the matter, or knowingly fail to respond reasonably to a lawful demand for information from an admissions or disciplinary authority, except that this rule does not require disclosure of information otherwise protected by Rule 1.6.

COMMENT

[1] The duty imposed by this rule extends to persons seeking admission to the Bar as well as to lawyers. Hence, if a person knowingly makes a false statement of fact in connection with an application for admission, it may be the basis for subsequent disciplinary action if the person is admitted, and in any event may be relevant in a subsequent admission application. Lack of materiality does not excuse a knowingly false statement of fact. The duty imposed by this rule applies to a lawyer's own admission or discipline as well as that of others. Thus, it is a separate professional offense for a lawyer knowingly to make a misrepresentation or omission in connection with a disciplinary investigation of the lawyer's own conduct. Paragraph (b) of this rule also requires correction of any prior factual misstatement in the matter that the lawyer or applicant may have made, including affirmative clarification of any factual misunderstanding on the part of the admissions or disciplinary authority of which the person involved becomes aware.

[2] This rule is subject to the provisions of the Fifth Amendment of the United States Constitution and corresponding provisions of state constitutions. A person relying on such a provision in response to a question, however, should do so openly and not use the right of nondisclosure as a justification for failure to comply with this rule.

[3] A lawyer representing an applicant for admission to the Bar, or representing a lawyer who is the subject of a disciplinary inquiry or proceeding, is governed by the Rules applicable to the client-lawyer relationship. For example, Rule 1.6 may prohibit disclosures, which would otherwise be required, by a lawyer serving in such representative capacity. Information that is a client confidence or secret under Rule 1.6 is "protected by Rule 1.6" within the meaning of Rule 8.1(b), even if a permissive disclosure option applies. Rule 1.6(c), (d), and (e) describe circumstances in which a lawyer may reveal information otherwise protected by 1.6. In such circumstances, a lawyer acting in a representative capacity may, but is not required to, make disclosures otherwise required by this rule. This rule refers to demands for information from an admissions or disciplinary authority. If a lawyer appears in an adjudicative proceeding regarding admission or bar discipline as a witness or client representative, the lawyer's conduct is governed by Rule 3.3.

Rule 8.3. Reporting Professional Misconduct

(a) A lawyer who knows that another lawyer has committed a violation of the Rules of Professional Conduct that raises a substantial question as to that lawyer's honesty, trustworthiness, or fitness as a lawyer in other respects, shall inform the appropriate professional authority.

(b) A lawyer who knows that a judge has committed a violation of applicable rules of judicial conduct that raises a substantial question as to the judge's fitness for office shall inform the appropriate authority.

(c) This rule does not require disclosure of information otherwise protected by Rule 1.6 or other law.

COMMENT

[1] Self-regulation of the legal profession requires that members of the profession initiate disciplinary investigation when they know of a violation of the Rules of Professional Conduct. Lawyers have a similar obligation with respect to judicial misconduct. An apparently isolated violation may indicate a pattern of misconduct that only a disciplinary investigation can uncover. Reporting a violation is especially important where the victim is unlikely to discover the offense.

[2] A report about misconduct is not required where it would involve violation of Rule 1.6. However, a lawyer should encourage a client to consent to disclosure where prosecution would not substantially prejudice the client's interests. Information that is a client confidence or secret under Rule 1.6 is "otherwise protected by Rule 1.6" within the meaning of Rule 8.3(c). Rule 1.6(c), (d), and (e) describe circumstances in which a lawyer may reveal information otherwise

protected by Rule 1.6. In such circumstances, a lawyer may, but is not required to, make disclosures otherwise required by this rule.

[3] If a lawyer were obliged to report every violation of the Rules, the failure to report any violation would itself be a professional offense. Such a requirement existed in many jurisdictions but proved to be unenforceable. This rule limits the reporting obligation to those offenses that a self-regulating profession must vigorously endeavor to prevent. A measure of judgment is, therefore, required in complying with the provisions of this rule. The term "substantial" refers to the seriousness of the possible offense and not the quantum of evidence of which the lawyer is aware. A report should be made to the Office of Bar Counsel. A lawyer who believes that another lawyer has a significant problem of alcohol or other substance abuse which does not require reporting to Bar Counsel under this rule, may nonetheless wish to report the perceived situation to the Lawyer Counseling Committee, operated by the D.C. Bar, which assists lawyers having such problems.

[4] The duty to report professional misconduct does not apply to a lawyer retained to represent a lawyer whose professional conduct is in question. Such a situation is governed by the Rules applicable to the client-lawyer relationship. Rule 1.6(c), (d), and (e) give a lawyer discretion to reveal information otherwise protected by Rule 1.6 in some circumstances, despite a client-lawyer relationship. If such circumstances exist, the lawyer may, but is not required, to reveal the information as part of a report of misconduct under this rule. The duty to report may also be limited by other law, including court rules or orders, protective orders, and laws restricting disclosure of grand jury or tax information.

[5] Rule 1.6(h) brings within the protections of Rule 1.6 certain types of information gained by lawyers participating in lawyer counseling programs of the D.C. Bar Lawyer Counseling Committee. To the extent information concerning violations of the Rules of Professional Conduct falls within the scope of Rule 1.6(h), a lawyer-counselor would not be required or permitted to inform the "appropriate professional authority" referred to in Rule 8.3. Where disclosure is permissive under Rule 1.6 (*see* paragraph 1.6(c), (d), and (e) for cases of permitted disclosures), discretion to disclose to the "appropriate professional authority" would also exist pursuant to paragraph 8.3(c). *See also* Comment to Rule 1.6, paragraphs [29], [30], and [31].

Rule 8.4. Misconduct

It is professional misconduct for a lawyer to:

(a) Violate or attempt to violate the Rules of Professional Conduct, knowingly assist or induce another to do so, or do so through the acts of another;

(b) Commit a criminal act that reflects adversely on the lawyer's honesty, trustworthiness, or fitness as a lawyer in other respects;

(c) Engage in conduct involving dishonesty, fraud, deceit, or misrepresentation;

(d) Engage in conduct that seriously interferes with the administration of justice;

(e) State or imply an ability to influence improperly a government agency or official;

(f) Knowingly assist a judge or judicial officer in conduct that is a violation of applicable rules of judicial conduct or other law; or

(g) Seek or threaten to seek criminal charges or disciplinary charges solely to obtain an advantage in a civil matter.

COMMENT

[1] Many kinds of illegal conduct reflect adversely on fitness to practice law, such as offenses involving fraud and the offense of willful failure to file an income tax return. However, some kinds of offenses carry no such implication. Traditionally, the distinction was drawn in terms of offenses involving "moral turpitude." That concept can be construed to include offenses concerning some matters of personal morality, such as adultery and comparable offenses, that have no specific connection to fitness for the practice of law. Although a lawyer is personally answerable to the entire criminal law, a lawyer should be professionally answerable only for offenses that indicate lack of those characteristics relevant to law practice. Offenses involving violence, dishonesty, breach of trust, or serious interference with the administration of justice are in that category. A pattern of repeated offenses, even ones of minor significance when considered separately, can indicate indifference to legal obligation.

[2] Paragraph (d)'s prohibition of conduct that "seriously interferes with the administration of justice" includes conduct proscribed by the previous Code of Professional Responsibility under DR 1-102(A)(5) as "prejudicial to the administration of justice." The cases under paragraph (d) include acts by a lawyer such as: failure to cooperate with Bar Counsel; failure to respond to Bar Counsel's inquiries or subpoenas; failure to abide by agreements made with Bar Counsel; failure to appear in court for a scheduled hearing; failure to turn over the assets of a conservatorship to the court or to the successor conservator; failure to keep the Bar advised of respondent's changes of address, after being warned to do so; and tendering a check known to be worthless in settlement of a claim against the lawyer or against the lawyer's client. Paragraph (d) is to be interpreted flexibly and includes any improper behavior of an analogous nature to these examples.

[3] A lawyer violates paragraph (d) by offensive, abusive, or harassing conduct that seriously interferes with the administration of justice. Such conduct may include words or actions that manifest bias or prejudice based upon race, sex, religion, national origin, disability, age, sexual orientation, or socioeconomic status.

Rule 8.5.   Disciplinary Authority; Choice of Law

(a) Disciplinary Authority. A lawyer admitted to practice in this jurisdiction is subject to the disciplinary authority of this jurisdiction, regardless of where the lawyer's conduct occurs. A lawyer may be subject to the disciplinary authority of both this jurisdiction and another jurisdiction where the lawyer is admitted for the same conduct.

(b) **Choice of Law.** In any exercise of the disciplinary authority of this jurisdiction, the Rules of Professional Conduct to be applied shall be as follows:

(1) For conduct in connection with a matter pending before a tribunal, the rules to be applied shall be the rules of the jurisdiction in which the tribunal sits, unless the rules of the tribunal provide otherwise, and

(2) For any other conduct,

(i) If the lawyer is licensed to practice only in this jurisdiction, the rules to be applied shall be the rules of this jurisdiction, and

(ii) If the lawyer is licensed to practice in this and another jurisdiction, the rules to be applied shall be the rules of the admitting jurisdiction in which the lawyer principally practices; provided, however, that if particular conduct clearly has its predominant effect in another jurisdiction in which the lawyer is licensed to practice, the rules of that jurisdiction shall be applied to that conduct.

COMMENT

Disciplinary Authority

[1] Paragraph (a) restates long-standing law.

Choice of Law

[2] A lawyer may be potentially subject to more than one set of rules of professional conduct which impose different obligations. The lawyer may be licensed to practice in more than one jurisdiction with differing rules, or may be admitted to practice before a particular court with rules that differ from those of the jurisdiction or jurisdictions in which the lawyer is licensed to practice. In the past, decisions have not developed clear or consistent guidance as to which rules apply in such circumstances.

[3] Paragraph (b) seeks to resolve such potential conflicts. Its premise is that minimizing conflicts between rules, as well as uncertainty about which rules are applicable, is in the best interest of both clients and the profession (as well as the bodies having authority to regulate the profession). Accordingly, it takes the approach of (i) providing that any particular conduct of an attorney shall be subject to only one set of rules of professional conduct, and (ii) making the determination of which set of rules applies to particular conduct as straightforward as possible, consistent with recognition of appropriate regulatory interests of relevant jurisdictions.

[4] Paragraph (b) provides that as to a lawyer's conduct relating to a matter pending before a tribunal the lawyer shall be subject only to the rules of professional conduct of that tribunal. As to all other conduct, paragraph (b) provides that

a lawyer licensed to practice only in this jurisdiction shall be subject to the rules of professional conduct of this jurisdiction, and that a lawyer licensed in multiple jurisdictions shall be subject only to the rules of the jurisdiction where he or she (as an individual, not his or her firm) principally practices, but with one exception: if particular conduct clearly has its predominant effect in another admitting jurisdiction, then only the rules of that jurisdiction shall apply. The intention is for the latter exception to be a narrow one. It would be appropriately applied, for example, to a situation in which a lawyer admitted in, and principally practicing in, State A, but also admitted in State B, handled an acquisition by a company whose headquarters and operations were in State B of another similar such company. The exception would not appropriately be applied, on the other hand, if the lawyer handled an acquisition by a company whose headquarters and operations were in State A of a company whose headquarters and main operations were in State A, but which also had some operations in State B.

[5] If two admitting jurisdictions were to proceed against a lawyer for the same conduct, they should, applying this rule, identify the same governing ethics rules. They should take all appropriate steps to see that they do apply the same rule to the same conduct, and in all events should avoid proceeding against a lawyer on the basis of two inconsistent rules.

[6] The choice of law provision applies to lawyers engaged in transnational practice, unless international law, treaties or other agreements between competent regulatory authorities in the affected jurisdictions provide otherwise.

NONDISCRIMINATION BY MEMBERS OF THE BAR

Rule 9.1.   Nondiscrimination

A lawyer shall not discriminate against any individual in conditions of employment because of the individual's race, color, religion, national origin, sex, age, marital status, sexual orientation, family responsibility, or physical handicap.

COMMENT

[1] This provision is modeled after the D.C. Human Rights Act, D.C. Code §2-1402.11 (2001), though in some respects is more limited in scope. There are also provisions of federal law that contain certain prohibitions on discrimination in employment. The Rule is not intended to create ethical obligations that exceed those imposed on a lawyer by applicable law.

[2] The investigation and adjudication of discrimination claims may involve particular expertise of the kind found within the D.C. Office of Human Rights and the federal Equal Employment Opportunity Commission. Such experience may involve, among other things, methods of analysis of statistical data regarding discrimination claims. These agencies also have, in appropriate circumstances, the

power to award remedies to the victims of discrimination, such as reinstatement or back pay, which extend beyond the remedies that are available through the disciplinary process. Remedies available through the disciplinary process include such sanctions as disbarment, suspension, censure, and admonition, but do not extend to monetary awards or other remedies that could alter the employment status to take into account the impact of prior acts of discrimination.

[3] If proceedings are pending before other organizations, such as the D.C. Office of Human Rights or the Equal Employment Opportunity Commission, the processing of complaints by Bar Counsel may be deferred or abated where there is substantial similarity between the complaint filed with Bar Counsel and material allegations involved in such other proceedings. *See* §19(d) of Rule XI of the Rules Governing the District of Columbia Bar.

New York Materials

New York Rules of
Professional Conduct
As amended through August 2012

Editors' Introduction. Effective April 1, 2009, New York adopted the New York Rules of Professional Conduct, using the numbering system and much of the language of the ABA Model Rules of Professional Conduct. New York thus became the last jurisdiction in the United States to abandon the format and numbering system of the old ABA Model Code of Professional Responsibility. However, the New York Rules retain the language of almost every Disciplinary Rule of the old New York Code of Professional Responsibility, most of which was based (with periodic updates) on the ABA Model Code of Professional Responsibility. The New York Rules of Professional Conduct also borrow extensively from the ABA Model Rules (though often with significant modifications), but the New York Rules augment the ABA Model Rules with many provisions unique to New York.

The Comments to New York's Rules also have many unique features. They often track the Comments to the ABA Model Rules, but the New York State Bar Association has modified or omitted many of the Comments and has written several dozen new Comments as well. (New Comments unique to New York are generally designated with a capital letter after the number — *e.g.,* Comment [5A] or Comment [9B]. Comments that New York has omitted are marked "[Reserved.]"). The New York Rules of Professional Conduct are thus a *sui generis* amalgam of the ABA Model Rules, the old ABA Model Code, and original language found only in New York.

The new Rules and Comments are the product of many years of work. For details of the six-year-long process of drafting by the State Bar and adoption by the Courts, see the Editors' Introduction to the New York Rules of Professional Conduct in our 2010 edition. Roy Simon (a co-author of this book) served as Chief Reporter and Vice-Chair of the New York State Bar Association Committee on Standards of Attorney Conduct (COSAC), which drafted the rules that the State Bar recommended to the Courts in 2008.

Developments since our previous edition. Since our previous edition went to press in September 2011, the New York Courts have approved minor amendments to Rule 1.2 (Scope of Representation and Allocation of Authority Between Attorney and Client), and have approved major amendments to Rule 3.8 (Special Responsibilities of Prosecutors and Other Government Lawyers). In addition, the Second Circuit has struck down a sentence in Rule 7.4 (Identification of Practice and Specialty) on First Amendment grounds. To be more specific:

Regarding Rule 1.2, effective July 1, 2012, the Courts replaced the phrase "A lawyer does not violate *this Rule* by being punctual" (etc.) in Rule 1.2(g) with the phrase "A lawyer does not violate *these Rules* by being punctual. . . ." This tiny change makes clear that being punctual (etc.) does not violate *any* provision in the Rules of Professional Conduct.

Regarding Rule 3.8, effective July 1, 2012, the Courts added three new paragraphs to articulate a prosecutor's duties upon receiving evidence that a person has been wrongfully convicted. The amendments generally bring New York into line with ABA Model Rule 3.8(g) and (h). This is fitting because the proposals to add post-conviction responsibilities to ABA Model Rule 3.8 in 2008 originated with the New York City Bar Association, and Professors Bruce Green of Fordham and Ellen Yaroshefsky of Cardozo played key roles in persuading the ABA to add post-conviction responsibilities to Rule 3.8.

Regarding Rule 7.4, in *Hayes v. New York Attorney Grievance Committee of the Eighth Judicial District,* 672 F.3d 158 (2d Cir. 2012), the court held that a required disclaimer, "Certification is not a requirement for the practice of law in the State of New York and does not necessarily indicate greater competence than other attorneys experienced in this field of law," was unconstitutional under the First Amendment. The New York Attorney General did not petition for certiorari in the Supreme Court, so the Second Circuit's decision is final. By the time we went to press, the New York Courts had approved an amendment to Rule 7.4 deleting the unconstitutional disclaimer, but the Courts had not yet published their Order, which was expected in November 2012. (The *Hayes* decision also held the requirement that a different disclaimer be "prominently made" was unconstitutional as applied. The Courts are studying the implications of that ruling but are not expected to amend the language of Rule 7.4.)

Another important development in New York's regulation of lawyers occurred outside the Rules of Professional Conduct. On May 1, 2012 (Law Day), Chief Judge Jonathan Lippman announced that, starting on January 1, 2015, all applicants for admission to the New York Bar will be required to show that they have performed at least 50 hours of law-related pro bono service prior to admission. A few weeks later, Chief Judge Lippman created an advisory committee charged with recommending how to implement the pro bono service requirement. In September 2012, based on the advisory committee's recommendations, the Court of Appeals approved new rules to govern the pro bono requirement. New York's pro bono requirement is expected to have nationwide impact because it applies to all applicants to the New York Bar, whether they attended law school in New York or elsewhere. The pro bono requirement should have a long-term impact on the goal expressed in Rule 6.1 (Voluntary Pro Bono Service) that every lawyer should aspire to "provide at least 20 hours of pro bono legal services each year to poor persons."

Looking ahead, when we went to press the Courts were on the verge of adopting a proposed amendment to Rule 4.2 that was approved by the New York State Bar Association House of Delegates in January 2012 and forwarded to the Courts for their consideration in February 2012. The proposed amendment would add the following new paragraph (c) to Rule 4.2 to govern lawyers who are parties to a matter:

> (c) A lawyer who is acting *pro se* or is represented by counsel in a matter is subject to paragraph (a), but may communicate with a represented person, unless otherwise prohibited by law and unless the represented person is not legally competent, provided the lawyer or the lawyer's counsel gives reasonable advance notice to the represented person's counsel that such communications will be taking place.

The new provision, which would be unique to New York, would be accompanied by the following new Comment to Rule 4.2, which the State Bar approved contingent on the Courts' adoption of proposed Rule 4.2(c):

> [12A] When a lawyer is proceeding *pro se* in a matter, or is being represented by his or own counsel with respect to a matter, the lawyer's direct communications with a counterparty are subject to the no-contact rule, Rule 4.2. Unless authorized by law, the lawyer must not engage in direct communications with a party the lawyer knows to be represented by counsel without either (i) securing the prior consent of the represented party's counsel under Rule 4.2(a), or (ii) providing opposing counsel with reasonable advance notice that such communications will be taking place.

The Courts circulated proposed Rule 4.2(c) for public comment on April 19, 2012. Shortly before we went to press, the Courts approved the proposed new paragraph (c), and they were expected to publish an Order amending the black letter text of Rule 4.2 accordingly in November 2012. The proposal, together with the report submitted by State Bar President Vincent E. Doyle, III, is available online on the website of New York's Unified Court System at *http://www.nycourts.gov/rules/comments/Rule%204.2%20PC%20packet.pdf.*

Also pending when we went to press were proposals jointly developed and proposed by the New York State Bar Association, the New York City Bar Association, and the New York County Lawyers' Association asking the New York Court of Appeals to promulgate new rules of court patterned on ABA Model Rule 5.5. The new rules would permit lawyers admitted and in good standing in another United States jurisdiction — as well as foreign legal consultants authorized to practice foreign law in another U.S. jurisdiction — to provide temporary legal services in New York in limited circumstances. The proposed rules would also give New York disciplinary jurisdiction over these out-of-state and foreign lawyers. In most jurisdictions, temporary practice rules of this type are found in Rule 5.5 of the Rules of Professional Conduct, but New York's Appellate Divisions (which control the Rules of Professional Conduct) rejected versions of Rule 5.5 in 2003 and 2008, so the sponsoring bar associations are taking a different approach, recommending that these rules be codified as a new Part 523 of the Rules of the Court of Appeals. The proposed rules were approved by the New York State Bar Association House of Delegates at its June 2012 quarterly meeting and were forwarded to the Courts shortly afterwards. At our press time the Courts had not yet circulated the proposed rules for public comment, and it was not known if they would do so.

General information about the New York Rules. New York's black letter Rules of Professional Conduct are codified as court rules at 22 N.Y.C.R.R. Part 1200. Both the original Rules as promulgated by the Courts and the Rules with Comments as promulgated by the State Bar are available on the website of the New York State Bar Association at *www.nysba.org* (click on "For Attorneys," then scroll down and click on "Professional Standards for Attorneys"). We reprint below the version of the Rules published by the New York State Bar Association on its website, which includes not only the black letter Rules adopted by the Courts but also the influential Preamble, Scope, and Comments adopted only by the State Bar. Language that has been amended since our last edition is reprinted in legislative style, underscoring additions and striking through deletions. (Readers who want to know about earlier amendments should consult our 2011 and 2012 editions, which reprinted the numerous 2010 and 2011 amendments to the Rules and Comments in legislative style.)

The State Bar's website includes the following helpful guidance at the beginning of its online version of the Rules of Professional Conduct:

> The New York Rules of Professional Conduct have been adopted by the Appellate Divisions of the New York State Supreme Court and are published as Part 1200 of the Joint Rules of the Appellate Divisions (22 N.Y.C.R.R. Part 1200). The Appellate Divisions have not enacted the Preamble, Scope and Comments, which are published solely by the New York State Bar Association to provide guidance for attorneys in complying with the Rules. Where a conflict exists between a Rule and the Preamble, Scope or a Comment, the Rule controls.

New York also heavily regulates lawyers by statute. Accordingly, the next chapter of this book (Selected New York Statutes) reprints some important provisions from New York's extensive body of legislation governing lawyers and the legal profession. For additional developments in New York relating to the regulation of lawyers, see the New York entry in the section entitled "What's New Since Our Last Edition" in our introduction to this book.

Contents

PREAMBLE: A LAWYER'S RESPONSIBILITIES

[1] A lawyer, as a member of the legal profession, is a representative of clients and an officer of the legal system with special responsibility for the quality of justice. As a representative of clients, a lawyer assumes many roles, including advisor, advocate, negotiator, and evaluator. As an officer of the legal system, each lawyer has a duty to uphold the legal process; to demonstrate respect for the legal system; to seek improvement of the law; and to promote access to the legal system and the administration of justice. In addition, a lawyer should further the public's understanding of and confidence in the rule of law and the justice system because, in a constitutional democracy, legal institutions depend on popular participation and support to maintain their authority.

[2] The touchstone of the client-lawyer relationship is the lawyer's obligation to assert the client's position under the rules of the adversary system, to maintain the client's confidential information except in limited circumstances, and to act with loyalty during the period of the representation.

[3] A lawyer's responsibilities in fulfilling these many roles and obligations are usually harmonious. In the course of law practice, however, conflicts may arise among the lawyer's responsibilities to clients, to the legal system and to the lawyer's own interests. The Rules of Professional Conduct often prescribe terms for resolving such conflicts. Nevertheless, within the framework of the Rules, many difficult issues of professional discretion can arise. The lawyer must resolve such issues through the exercise of sensitive professional and moral judgment, guided by the basic principles underlying the Rules.

[4] The legal profession is largely self-governing. An independent legal profession is an important force in preserving government under law, because abuse of legal authority is more readily challenged by a profession whose members are not dependent on government for the right to practice law. To the extent that lawyers meet these professional obligations, the occasion for government regulation is obviated.

[5] The relative autonomy of the legal profession carries with it special responsibilities of self-governance. Every lawyer is responsible for observance of the Rules of Professional Conduct and also should aid in securing their observance by other lawyers. Neglect of these responsibilities compromises the independence of the profession and the public interest that it serves. Compliance with the Rules depends primarily upon the lawyer's understanding of the Rules and desire to comply with the professional norms they embody for the benefit of clients and the legal system, and, secondarily, upon reinforcement by peer and public opinion. So long as its practitioners are guided by these principles, the law will continue to be a noble profession.

SCOPE

[6] The Rules of Professional Conduct are rules of reason. They should be interpreted with reference to the purposes of legal representation and of the law itself. Some of the Rules are imperatives, cast in the terms "shall" or "shall not." These Rules define proper conduct for purposes of professional discipline. Others, generally cast in the term "may," are permissive and define areas under the Rules in which the lawyer has discretion to exercise professional judgment. No disciplinary action should be taken when the lawyer chooses not to act or acts within the

bounds of such discretion. Other Rules define the nature of relationships between the lawyer and others. The Rules are thus partly obligatory and disciplinary and partly constitutive and descriptive in that they define a lawyer's professional role. Many of the Comments use the term "should." Comments do not add obligations to the Rules but provide guidance for practicing in compliance with the Rules. The Rules state the minimum level of conduct below which no lawyer can fall without being subject to disciplinary action.

[7] The Rules presuppose a larger legal context shaping the lawyer's role. That context includes court rules and statutes relating to matters of licensure, laws defining specific obligations of lawyers, and substantive and procedural law in general. The Comments are sometimes used to alert lawyers to their responsibilities under such other law.

[8] The Rules provide a framework for the ethical practice of law. Compliance with the Rules, as with all law in an open society, depends primarily upon understanding and voluntary compliance, secondarily upon reinforcement by peer and public opinion and finally, when necessary, upon enforcement through disciplinary proceedings. The Rules do not, however, exhaust the moral and ethical considerations that should inform a lawyer, for no worthwhile human activity can be completely defined by legal rules.

[9] Furthermore, for purposes of determining the lawyer's authority and responsibility, principles of substantive law external to these Rules determine whether a client-lawyer relationship exists. Most of the duties flowing from the client-lawyer relationship attach only after the client has requested the lawyer to render legal services and the lawyer has agreed to do so. But there are some duties, such as that of confidentiality under Rule 1.6, that attach when the lawyer agrees to consider whether a client-lawyer relationship shall be established. *See* Rule 1.18. Whether a client-lawyer relationship exists for any specific purpose can depend on the circumstances and may be a question of fact.

[10] Under various legal provisions, including constitutional, statutory and common law, the responsibilities of government lawyers may include authority concerning legal matters that ordinarily reposes in the client in private client-lawyer relationships. For example, a lawyer for a government agency may have authority on behalf of the government to decide whether to agree to a settlement or to appeal from an adverse judgment. Such authority in various respects is generally vested in the attorney general and the state's attorney in state government, and in their federal counterparts, and the same may be true of other government law officers. Also, lawyers under the supervision of these officers may be authorized to represent several government agencies in intragovernmental legal controversies in circumstances where a private lawyer could not represent multiple private clients. These Rules do not abrogate any such authority.

[11] Failure to comply with an obligation or prohibition imposed by a Rule is a basis for invoking the disciplinary process. The Rules presuppose that disciplinary assessment of a lawyer's conduct will be made on the basis of the facts and circumstances as they existed at the time of the conduct in question and in recognition of the fact that a lawyer often has to act upon uncertain or incomplete evidence of the situation. Moreover, the Rules presuppose that whether discipline should be imposed for a violation, and the severity of a sanction, depend on all the circumstances, such as the willfulness and seriousness of the violation, extenuating factors and whether there have been previous violations.

[12] Violation of a Rule should not itself give rise to a cause of action against a lawyer nor should it create any presumption in such a case that a legal duty has been breached. In addition, violation of a Rule does not necessarily warrant any other nondisciplinary remedy, such as disqualification of a lawyer in pending litigation. The Rules are designed to provide guidance to lawyers and to provide a structure for regulating conduct through disciplinary agencies. They are not designed to be a basis for civil liability. Furthermore, the purpose of the Rules can be subverted when they are invoked by opposing parties as procedural weapons. The fact that a Rule is a just basis for a lawyer's self-assessment, or for sanctioning a lawyer under the administration of a disciplinary authority, does not imply that an antagonist in a collateral proceeding or transaction has standing to seek enforcement of the Rule. Nevertheless, because the Rules do establish standards of conduct by lawyers, a lawyer's violation of a Rule may be evidence of breach of the applicable standard of conduct.

[13] The Comment accompanying each Rule explains and illustrates the meaning and purpose of the Rule. The Preamble and this note on Scope provide general orientation. The Comments are intended as guides to interpretation, but the text of each Rule is authoritative.

Rule 1.0   Terminology

(a) "Advertisement" means any public or private communication made by or on behalf of a lawyer or law firm about that lawyer or law firm's services, the primary purpose of which is for the retention of the lawyer or law firm. It does not include communications to existing clients or other lawyers.

(b) "Belief" or "believes" denotes that the person involved actually believes the fact in question to be true. A person's belief may be inferred from circumstances.

(c) "Computer-accessed communication" means any communication made by or on behalf of a lawyer or law firm that is disseminated through the use of a computer or related electronic device, including, but not limited to, web sites, weblogs, search engines, electronic mail, banner advertisements, pop-up and pop-under advertisements, chat rooms, list servers, instant messaging, or other internet presences, and any attachments or links related thereto.

(d) "Confidential information" is defined in Rule 1.6.

(e) "Confirmed in writing" denotes (i) a writing from the person to the lawyer confirming that the person has given consent, (ii) a writing that the lawyer promptly transmits to the person confirming the person's oral consent, or (iii) a statement by the person made on the record of any proceeding before a tribunal. If it is not feasible to obtain or transmit the writing at the time the person gives oral consent, then the lawyer must obtain or transmit it within a reasonable time thereafter.

(f) "Differing interests" include every interest that will adversely affect either the judgment or the loyalty of a lawyer to a client, whether it be a conflicting, inconsistent, diverse, or other interest.

(g) "Domestic relations matter" denotes representation of a client in a claim, action or proceeding, or preliminary to the filing of a claim, action or proceeding, in either Supreme Court or Family Court, or in any court of appellate jurisdiction, for divorce, separation, annulment, custody, visitation, maintenance, child support or alimony, or to enforce or modify a judgment or order in connection with any such claim, action or proceeding.

(h) "Firm" or "law firm" includes, but is not limited to, a lawyer or lawyers in a law partnership, professional corporation, sole proprietorship or other association authorized to practice law; or lawyers employed in a qualified legal assistance organization, a government law office, or the legal department of a corporation or other organization.

(i) "Fraud" or "fraudulent" denotes conduct that is fraudulent under the substantive or procedural law of the applicable jurisdiction or has a purpose to deceive, provided that it does not include conduct that, although characterized as fraudulent by statute or administrative rule, lacks an element of scienter, deceit, intent to mislead, or knowing failure to correct misrepresentations that can be reasonably expected to induce detrimental reliance by another.

(j) "Informed consent" denotes the agreement by a person to a proposed course of conduct after the lawyer has communicated information adequate for the person to make an informed decision, and after the lawyer has adequately explained to the person the material risks of the proposed course of conduct and reasonably available alternatives.

(k) "Knowingly," "known," "know," or "knows" denotes actual knowledge of the fact in question. A person's knowledge may be inferred from circumstances.

(l) "Matter" includes any litigation, judicial or administrative proceeding, case, claim, application, request for a ruling or other determination, contract, controversy, investigation, charge, accusation, arrest, negotiation, arbitration, mediation or any other representation involving a specific party or parties.

(m) "Partner" denotes a member of a partnership, a shareholder in a law firm organized as a professional legal corporation or a member of an association authorized to practice law.

(n) "Person" includes an individual, a corporation, an association, a trust, a partnership, and any other organization or entity.

(o) "Professional legal corporation" means a corporation, or an association treated as a corporation, authorized by law to practice law for profit.

(p) "Qualified legal assistance organization" means an office or organization of one of the four types listed in Rule 7.2(b)(1)-(4) that meets all of the requirements thereof.

(q) "Reasonable" or "reasonably," when used in relation to conduct by a lawyer, denotes the conduct of a reasonably prudent and competent lawyer. When used in the context of conflict of interest determinations, "reasonable lawyer" denotes a lawyer acting from the perspective of a reasonably prudent and competent lawyer who is personally disinterested in commencing or continuing the representation.

(r) "Reasonable belief" or "reasonably believes," when used in reference to a lawyer, denotes that the lawyer believes the matter in question and that the circumstances are such that the belief is reasonable.

(s) "Reasonably should know," when used in reference to a lawyer, denotes that a lawyer of reasonable prudence and competence would ascertain the matter in question.

(t) "Screened" or "screening" denotes the isolation of a lawyer from any participation in a matter through the timely imposition of procedures within a firm that are reasonably adequate under the circumstances to protect information that the isolated lawyer or the firm is obligated to protect under these Rules or other law.

(u) "Sexual relations" denotes sexual intercourse or the touching of an intimate part of the lawyer or another person for the purpose of sexual arousal, sexual gratification or sexual abuse.

(v) "State" includes the District of Columbia, Puerto Rico, and other federal territories and possessions.

(w) "Tribunal" denotes a court, an arbitrator in an arbitration proceeding or a legislative body, administrative agency or other body acting in an adjudicative capacity. A legislative body, administrative agency or other body acts in an adjudicative capacity when a neutral official, after the presentation of evidence or legal argument by a party or parties, will render a legal judgment directly affecting a party's interests in a particular matter.

(x) "Writing" or "written" denotes a tangible or electronic record of a communication or representation, including handwriting, typewriting, printing, photocopying, photography, audio or video recording and email. A "signed" writing includes an electronic sound, symbol or process attached to or logically associated with a writing and executed or adopted by a person with the intent to sign the writing.

COMMENT

Confirmed in Writing

[1] Some Rules require that a person's oral consent be "confirmed in writing." *E.g.*, Rules 1.5(g)(2) (client's consent to division of fees with lawyer in another firm must be confirmed in writing), 1.7(b)(4) (client's informed consent to conflict of interest must be confirmed in writing) and 1.9(a) (former client's informed consent to conflict of interest must be confirmed in writing). The definition of "confirmed in writing" provides three distinct methods of confirming a person's consent: (i) a writing from the person to the lawyer, (ii) a writing from the lawyer to the person, or (iii) consent by the person on the record in any proceeding before a tribunal. The confirming writing need not recite the information that the lawyer communicated to the person in order to obtain the person's consent. For the

definition of "informed consent" *see* Rule 1.0(j). If it is not feasible for the lawyer to obtain or transmit a written confirmation at the time the client gives oral consent, then the lawyer must obtain or transmit the confirming writing within a reasonable time thereafter. If a lawyer has obtained a client's informed oral consent, the lawyer may act in reliance on that consent so long as it is confirmed in writing within a reasonable time thereafter.

Firm

[2] Whether two or more lawyers constitute a firm within paragraph (h) will depend on the specific facts. For example, two practitioners who share office space and occasionally consult or assist each other ordinarily would not be regarded as constituting a firm. However, if they present themselves to the public in a way that suggests that they are a firm or conduct themselves as a firm, they should be regarded as a firm for purposes of the Rules. The terms of any formal agreement between associated lawyers are relevant in determining whether they are a firm, as is the fact that they have mutual access to information concerning the clients they serve. Furthermore, it is relevant in doubtful cases to consider the underlying purpose of the Rule that is involved. For example, a group of lawyers could be regarded as a firm for purposes of determining whether a conflict of interest exists but not for application of the advertising rules.

[3] With respect to the law department of an organization, there is ordinarily no question that the members of the department constitute a firm within the meaning of the Rules of Professional Conduct. There can be uncertainty, however, as to the identity of the client. For example, it may not be clear whether the law department of a corporation represents a subsidiary or an affiliated corporation, as well as the corporation by which the members of the department are directly employed. A similar question can arise concerning an unincorporated association and its local affiliates. Whether lawyers in a government agency or department constitute a firm may depend upon the issue involved or be governed by other law.

[4] Similar questions can also arise with respect to lawyers in legal aid and legal services organizations. Depending upon the structure of the organization, the entire organization or components of it may constitute a firm or firms for purposes of these Rules.

Fraud

[5] When used in these Rules, the terms "fraud" and "fraudulent" refer to conduct that is characterized as such under the substantive or procedural law of the applicable jurisdiction or has a purpose to deceive. This does not include merely negligent misrepresentation or negligent failure to apprise another of relevant information. For purposes of these Rules, it is not necessary that anyone has suffered damages or relied on the misrepresentation or failure to inform, so long as the necessary scienter is present and the conduct in question could be reasonably expected to induce detrimental reliance.

Informed Consent

[6] Many of the Rules of Professional Conduct require the lawyer to obtain the informed consent of a client or other person (*e.g.*, a former client or, under certain circumstances, a prospective client) before accepting or continuing representation or pursuing a course of conduct. *E.g.*, Rules 1.2(c), 1.6(a) and 1.7(b). The communication necessary to obtain such consent will vary according to the Rule involved and the circumstances giving rise to the need to obtain informed consent. The lawyer must make reasonable efforts to ensure that the client or other person possesses information reasonably adequate to make an informed decision. Ordinarily, this will require communication that includes a disclosure of the facts and circumstances giving rise to the situation, any explanation reasonably necessary to inform the client or other person of the material advantages and disadvantages of the proposed course of conduct, and a discussion of the client's or other person's options and alternatives. In some circumstances it may be appropriate for a lawyer to advise a client or other person to seek the advice of other counsel. A lawyer need not inform a client or other person of facts or implications already known to the client or other person; nevertheless, a lawyer who does not personally inform the client or other person assumes the risk that the client or other person is inadequately informed and the consent is invalid. In determining whether the information and explanation provided are reasonably adequate, relevant factors include whether the client or other person is experienced in legal matters generally and in making decisions of the type involved, and whether the client or other person is independently represented by other counsel in giving the consent. Normally, such persons need less information and explanation than others, and generally a client or other person who is independently represented by other counsel in giving the consent should be assumed to have given informed consent. Other considerations may apply in representing impaired clients. *See* Rule 1.14.

[7] Obtaining informed consent will usually require an affirmative response by the client or other person. In general, a lawyer may not assume consent from a client's or other person's silence. Consent may be inferred, however, from the conduct of a client or other person who has reasonably adequate information about the matter. A number of Rules require that a person's consent be confirmed in writing. *E.g.*, Rules 1.7(b) and 1.9(a). For definitions of "writing" and "confirmed in writing" see paragraphs (x) and (e), respectively. Other Rules require that a client's consent be obtained in a writing signed by the client. *E.g.*, Rules 1.8(a) and (g). For the meaning of "signed," see paragraph (x).

Screened or Screening

[8] The definition of "screened" or "screening" applies to situations where screening of a personally disqualified lawyer is permitted to remove imputation of a conflict of interest under Rule 1.11, 1.12 or 1.18. See those Rules for the particular requirements of establishing effective screening.

[9] The purpose of screening is to ensure that confidential information known by the personally disqualified lawyer remains protected. The personally disqualified lawyer should acknowledge the obligation not to communicate with any of the other

lawyers in the firm with respect to the matter. Similarly, other lawyers in the firm who are working on the matter should promptly be informed that the screening is in place and that they may not communicate with the personally disqualified lawyer with respect to the matter. Additional screening measures that are appropriate for the particular matter will depend on the circumstances. In any event, procedures should be adequate to protect confidential information.

[10] In order to be effective, screening measures must be implemented as soon as practicable after a lawyer or law firm knows or reasonably should know that there is a need for screening.

Rule 1.1 Competence

(a) A lawyer should provide competent representation to a client. Competent representation requires the legal knowledge, skill, thoroughness and preparation reasonably necessary for the representation.

(b) A lawyer shall not handle a legal matter that the lawyer knows or should know that the lawyer is not competent to handle, without associating with a lawyer who is competent to handle it.

(c) A lawyer shall not intentionally:

(1) fail to seek the objectives of the client through reasonably available means permitted by law and these Rules; or

(2) prejudice or damage the client during the course of the representation except as permitted or required by these Rules.

COMMENT

Legal Knowledge and Skill

[1] In determining whether a lawyer employs the requisite knowledge and skill in a particular matter, relevant factors include the relative complexity and specialized nature of the matter, the lawyer's general experience, the lawyer's training and experience in the field in question, the preparation and study the lawyer is able to give the matter, and whether it is feasible to associate with a lawyer of established competence in the field in question. In many instances, the required proficiency is that of a general practitioner. Expertise in a particular field of law may be required in some circumstances. One such circumstance would be where the lawyer, by representations made to the client, has led the client reasonably to expect a special level of expertise in the matter undertaken by the lawyer.

[2] A lawyer need not necessarily have special training or prior experience to handle legal problems of a type with which the lawyer is unfamiliar. A newly admitted lawyer can be as competent as a practitioner with long experience. Some important legal skills, such as the analysis of precedent, the evaluation of evidence and legal drafting, are required in all legal problems. Perhaps the most fundamental legal skill consists of determining what kinds of legal problems a situation may involve, a skill that necessarily transcends any particular specialized knowledge. A

lawyer can provide adequate representation in a wholly novel field through necessary study. Competent representation can also be provided through the association of a lawyer of established competence in the field in question.

[3] [Reserved.]

[4] A lawyer may accept representation where the requisite level of competence can be achieved by adequate preparation before handling the legal matter. This applies as well to a lawyer who is appointed as counsel for an unrepresented person.

Thoroughness and Preparation

[5] Competent handling of a particular matter includes inquiry into and analysis of the factual and legal elements of the problem, and use of methods and procedures meeting the standards of competent practitioners. It also includes adequate preparation. The required attention and preparation are determined in part by what is at stake; major litigation and complex transactions ordinarily require more extensive treatment than matters of lesser complexity and consequence. An agreement between the lawyer and the client may limit the scope of the representation if the agreement complies with Rule 1.2(c).

Maintaining Competence

[6] To maintain the requisite knowledge and skill, a lawyer should keep abreast of changes in the law and its practice, engage in continuing study and education, and comply with all continuing legal education requirements to which the lawyer is subject. *See* 22 N.Y.C.R.R. Part 1500.

Rule 1.2   Scope of Representation and Allocation of Authority Between Client and Lawyer

Editors' Note. Effective July 1, 2012, on the recommendation of the New York State Bar Association's Committee on Standards of Attorney Conduct (COSAC), the Courts amended Rule 1.2(g). Specifically, the Courts changed the phrase "A lawyer does not violate *this Rule* by being punctual" (etc.) into the phrase "A lawyer does not violate *these Rules* by being punctual. . . ." The change makes clear that being punctual (etc.) does not violate any provision in the Rules of Professional Conduct. We reprint amended Rule 1.2(g) in legislative style.

(a) Subject to the provisions herein, a lawyer shall abide by a client's decisions concerning the objectives of representation and, as required by Rule 1.4, shall consult with the client as to the means by which they are to be pursued. A lawyer shall abide by a client's decision whether to settle a

matter. In a criminal case, the lawyer shall abide by the client's decision, after consultation with the lawyer, as to a plea to be entered, whether to waive jury trial and whether the client will testify.

(b) A lawyer's representation of a client, including representation by appointment, does not constitute an endorsement of the client's political, economic, social or moral views or activities.

(c) A lawyer may limit the scope of the representation if the limitation is reasonable under the circumstances, the client gives informed consent and where necessary notice is provided to the tribunal and/or opposing counsel.

(d) A lawyer shall not counsel a client to engage, or assist a client, in conduct that the lawyer knows is illegal or fraudulent, except that the lawyer may discuss the legal consequences of any proposed course of conduct with a client.

(e) A lawyer may exercise professional judgment to waive or fail to assert a right or position of the client, or accede to reasonable requests of opposing counsel, when doing so does not prejudice the rights of the client.

(f) A lawyer may refuse to aid or participate in conduct that the lawyer believes to be unlawful, even though there is some support for an argument that the conduct is legal.

(g) A lawyer does not violate ~~this Rule~~ these Rules by being punctual in fulfilling all professional commitments, by avoiding offensive tactics, and by treating with courtesy and consideration all persons involved in the legal process.

COMMENT

Allocation of Authority Between Client and Lawyer

[1] Paragraph (a) confers upon the client the ultimate authority to determine the purposes to be served by legal representation, within the limits imposed by law and the lawyer's professional obligations. The decisions specified in paragraph (a), such as whether to settle a civil matter, must also be made by the client. See Rule 1.4(a)(1) for the lawyer's duty to communicate with the client about such decisions. The lawyer shall consult with the client with respect to the means by which the client's objectives are to be pursued. *See* Rule 1.4(a)(2).

[2] Clients normally defer to the special knowledge and skill of their lawyer with respect to the means to be used to accomplish their objectives, particularly with respect to technical, legal and tactical matters. On the other hand, lawyers usually defer to their clients regarding such questions as the expense to be incurred and concern for third persons who might be adversely affected. On occasion, however, a lawyer and a client may disagree about the means to be used to accomplish the client's objectives. Because of the varied nature of the matters about which a lawyer and client might disagree, and because the actions in question may implicate the

interests of a tribunal or other persons, this Rule does not prescribe how such disagreements are to be resolved. Other law, however, may be applicable and should be consulted by the lawyer. The lawyer should also consult with the client and seek a mutually acceptable resolution of the disagreement. If such efforts are unavailing and the lawyer has a fundamental disagreement with the client, the lawyer may withdraw from the representation. *See* Rule 1.16(c)(4). Likewise, the client may resolve the disagreement by discharging the lawyer, in which case the lawyer must withdraw from the representation. *See* Rule 1.16(b)(3).

[3] At the outset of a representation, the client may authorize the lawyer to take specific action on the client's behalf without further consultation. Absent a material change in circumstances and subject to Rule 1.4, a lawyer may rely on such an advance authorization. The client, however, may revoke such authority at any time.

[4] In a case in which the client appears to be suffering diminished capacity, the lawyer's duty to abide by the client's decisions is to be guided by reference to Rule 1.14.

Independence from Client's Views or Activities

[5] Legal representation should not be denied to any person who is unable to afford legal services, or whose cause is controversial or the subject of popular disapproval. By the same token, representing a client does not constitute approval of the client's views or activities.

Agreements Limiting Scope of Representation

[6] The scope of services to be provided by a lawyer may be limited by agreement with the client or by the terms under which the lawyer's services are made available to the client. When a lawyer has been retained by an insurer to represent an insured, for example, the representation may be limited to issues related to the insurance coverage. A limited representation may be appropriate because the client has limited objectives for the representation. In addition, the terms upon which representation is undertaken may exclude specific means that might otherwise be used to accomplish the client's objectives. Such limitations may exclude actions that the client thinks are too costly or that the lawyer regards as repugnant or imprudent.

[6A] In obtaining consent from the client, the lawyer must adequately disclose the limitations on the scope of the engagement and the matters that will be excluded. In addition, the lawyer must disclose the reasonably foreseeable consequences of the limitation. In making such disclosure, the lawyer should explain that if the lawyer or the client determines during the representation that additional services outside the limited scope specified in the engagement are necessary or advisable to represent the client adequately, then the client may need to retain separate counsel, which could result in delay, additional expense, and complications.

[7] Although this Rule affords the lawyer and client substantial latitude to limit the representation, the limitation must be reasonable under the circumstances. If, for example, a client's objective is limited to securing general information about the

law the client needs in order to handle a common and typically uncomplicated legal problem, the lawyer and client may agree that the lawyer's services will be limited to a brief telephone consultation. Such a limitation, however, would not be reasonable if the time allotted were not sufficient to yield advice upon which the client could rely. Although an agreement for a limited representation does not exempt a lawyer from the duty to provide competent representation, the limitation is a factor to be considered when determining the legal knowledge, skill, thoroughness and preparation reasonably necessary for the representation. *See* Rule 1.1.

[8] All agreements concerning a lawyer's representation of a client must accord with the Rules of Professional Conduct and other law. *See* Rules 1.1, 1.8 and 5.6.

Illegal and Fraudulent Transactions

[9] Paragraph (d) prohibits a lawyer from counseling or assisting a client in conduct that the lawyer knows is illegal or fraudulent. This prohibition, however, does not preclude the lawyer from giving an honest opinion about the consequences that appear likely to result from a client's conduct. Nor does the fact that a client uses advice in a course of action that is illegal or fraudulent of itself make a lawyer a party to the course of action. There is a critical distinction between presenting an analysis of legal aspects of questionable conduct and recommending the means by which a crime or fraud might be committed with impunity.

[10] When the client's course of action has already begun and is continuing, the lawyer's responsibility is especially delicate. The lawyer is required to avoid assisting the client, for example, by drafting or delivering documents that the lawyer knows are fraudulent or by suggesting how the wrongdoing might be concealed. When the representation will result in violation of the Rules of Professional Conduct or other law, the lawyer must advise the client of any relevant limitation on the lawyer's conduct and remonstrate with the client. *See* Rules 1.4(a)(5) and 1.16(b)(1). Persuading a client to take necessary preventive or corrective action that will bring the client's conduct within the bounds of the law is a challenging but appropriate endeavor. If the client fails to take necessary corrective action and the lawyer's continued representation would assist client conduct that is illegal or fraudulent, the lawyer is required to withdraw. *See* Rule 1.16(b)(1). In some circumstances, withdrawal alone might be insufficient. In those cases the lawyer may be required to give notice of the fact of withdrawal and to disaffirm any opinion, document, affirmation or the like. *See* Rule 1.6(b)(3); Rule 4.1, Comment [3].

[11] Where the client is a fiduciary, the lawyer may be charged with special obligations in dealings with a beneficiary.

[12] Paragraph (d) prohibits a lawyer from assisting a client's illegal or fraudulent activity against a third person, whether or not the defrauded party is a party to the transaction. Paragraph (d) does not preclude undertaking a criminal defense incident to a general retainer for legal services to a lawful enterprise, but does preclude such a retainer for an enterprise known to be engaged in illegal or fraudulent activity.

[13] If a lawyer comes to know or reasonably should know that a client expects assistance not permitted by the Rules of Professional Conduct or other law, or if the lawyer intends to act contrary to the client's instructions, the lawyer must consult with the client regarding the limitations on the lawyer's conduct. *See* Rule 1.4(a)(5).

Exercise of Professional Judgment

[14] Paragraph (e) permits a lawyer to exercise professional judgment to waive or fail to assert a right of a client, or accede to reasonable requests of opposing counsel in such matters as court proceedings, settings, continuances, and waiver of procedural formalities, as long as doing so does not prejudice the rights of the client. Like paragraphs (f) and (g), paragraph (e) effectively creates a limited exception to the lawyer's obligations under Rule 1.1(c) (a lawyer shall not intentionally "fail to seek the objectives of the client through reasonably available means permitted by law and these Rules" or "prejudice or damage the client during the course of the representation except as permitted or required by these Rules"). If the lawyer is representing the client before a tribunal, the lawyer is required under Rule 3.3(f)(1) to comply with known local customs of courtesy or practice of the bar or a particular tribunal unless the lawyer gives opposing counsel timely notice of the intent not to comply.

Refusal to Participate in Conduct a Lawyer Believes to Be Unlawful

[15] In some situations such as those described in paragraph (d), a lawyer is prohibited from aiding or participating in a client's improper or potentially improper conduct; but in other situations, a lawyer has discretion. Paragraph (f) permits a lawyer to refuse to aid or participate in conduct the lawyer *believes* to be unlawful, even if the conduct is arguably legal. In addition, under Rule 1.16(c)(2), the lawyer *may* withdraw from representing a client when the client persists in a course of action involving the lawyer's services that the lawyer reasonably *believes* is criminal or fraudulent, even if the course of action is arguably legal. In contrast, when the lawyer *knows* (or reasonably should know) that the representation will result in a violation of law or the Rules of Professional Conduct, the lawyer *must* withdraw from the representation under Rule 1.16(b)(1). If the client "insists" that the lawyer pursue a course of conduct that is illegal or prohibited under the Rules, the lawyer must not carry out those instructions and, in addition, may withdraw from the representation under Rule 1.16(c)(13). If the lawyer is representing the client before a tribunal, additional rules come into play. For example, the lawyer may be required to obtain the tribunal's permission to withdraw under Rule 1.16(d), and the lawyer may be required to take reasonable remedial measures under Rule 3.3 with respect to false evidence or other criminal or fraudulent conduct relating to a proceeding.

Fulfilling Professional Commitments and Treating Others with Courtesy

[16] Both Rule 1.1(c)(1) and Rule 1.2(a) require generally that a lawyer seek the client's objectives and abide by the client's decisions concerning the objectives of the representation; but those rules do not require a lawyer to be offensive, discourteous, inconsiderate or dilatory. Paragraph (g) specifically affirms that a lawyer does not violate Rule 1.2 by being punctual in fulfilling professional commitments,

avoiding offensive tactics and treating with courtesy and consideration all persons involved in the legal process. Lawyers should be aware of the New York State
Standards of Civility adopted by the courts to guide the legal profession (22 NYCRR
Part 1200 Appendix A). Although the Standards of Civility are not intended to be
enforced by sanctions or disciplinary action, conduct before a tribunal that fails to
comply with known local customs of courtesy or practice, or that is undignified or
discourteous, may violate Rule 3.3(f). Conduct in a proceeding that serves merely
to harass or maliciously injure another would be frivolous in violation of Rule 3.1.
Dilatory conduct may violate Rule 1.3(a), which requires a lawyer to act with reasonable diligence and promptness in representing a client.

Rule 1.3   Diligence

**(a) A lawyer shall act with reasonable diligence and promptness in rep-
resenting a client.**

(b) A lawyer shall not neglect a legal matter entrusted to the lawyer.

**(c) A lawyer shall not intentionally fail to carry out a contract of employ-
ment entered into with a client for professional services, but the lawyer may
withdraw as permitted under these Rules.**

COMMENT

[1] A lawyer should pursue a matter on behalf of a client despite opposition,
obstruction or personal inconvenience to the lawyer, and take whatever lawful and
ethical measures are required to vindicate a client's cause or endeavor. A lawyer
must also act with commitment and dedication to the interests of the client and
in advocacy upon the client's behalf. A lawyer is not bound, however, to press for
every advantage that might be realized for a client. For example, a lawyer may have
authority to exercise professional discretion in determining the means by which a
matter should be pursued. *See* Rule 1.2. Notwithstanding the foregoing, the lawyer
should not use offensive tactics or fail to treat all persons involved in the legal process with courtesy and respect.

[2] A lawyer's work load must be controlled so that each matter can be handled diligently and promptly. Lawyers are encouraged to adopt and follow effective
office procedures and systems; neglect may occur when such arrangements are not
in place or are ineffective.

[3] Perhaps no professional shortcoming is more widely resented than procrastination. A client's interests often can be adversely affected by the passage of
time or the change of conditions; in extreme instances, as when a lawyer overlooks
a statute of limitations, the client's legal position may be destroyed. Even when the
client's interests are not affected in substance, unreasonable delay can cause a client
needless anxiety and undermine confidence in the lawyer's trustworthiness. A lawyer's duty to act with reasonable promptness, however, does not preclude the lawyer
from agreeing to a reasonable request for a postponement that will not prejudice
the lawyer's client.

[4] Unless the relationship is terminated, as provided in Rule 1.16, a lawyer should carry through to conclusion all matters undertaken for a client. If a lawyer's employment is limited to a specific matter, the relationship terminates when the matter has been resolved. If a lawyer has served a client over a substantial period in a variety of matters, the client sometimes may assume that the lawyer will continue to serve on a continuing basis unless the lawyer gives notice of withdrawal. Doubt about whether a client-lawyer relationship still exists should be clarified by the lawyer, preferably in writing, so that the client will not mistakenly suppose the lawyer is looking after the client's affairs when the lawyer has ceased to do so. If a lawyer has handled a judicial or administrative proceeding that produced a result adverse to the client and the lawyer and the client have not agreed that the lawyer will handle the matter on appeal, Rule 1.16(e) may require the lawyer to consult with the client about the possibility of appeal before relinquishing responsibility for the matter. Whether the lawyer is obligated to prosecute the appeal for the client depends on the scope of the representation the lawyer has agreed to provide to the client. *See* Rule 1.2.

[5] To avoid possible prejudice to client interests, a sole practitioner is well advised to prepare a plan that designates another competent lawyer to review client files, notify each client of the lawyer's death or disability, and determine whether there is a need for immediate protective action.

Rule 1.4   Communication

(a) **A lawyer shall:**

(1) **promptly inform the client of:**

(i) **any decision or circumstance with respect to which the client's informed consent, as defined in Rule 1.0(j), is required by these Rules;**

(ii) **any information required by court rule or other law to be communicated to a client; and**

(iii) **material developments in the matter including settlement or plea offers.**

(2) **reasonably consult with the client about the means by which the client's objectives are to be accomplished;**

(3) **keep the client reasonably informed about the status of the matter;**

(4) **promptly comply with a client's reasonable requests for information; and**

(5) **consult with the client about any relevant limitation on the lawyer's conduct when the lawyer knows that the client expects assistance not permitted by these Rules or other law.**

(b) **A lawyer shall explain a matter to the extent reasonably necessary to permit the client to make informed decisions regarding the representation.**

COMMENT

[1] Reasonable communication between the lawyer and the client is necessary for the client to participate effectively in the representation.

Communicating with Client

[2] In instances where these Rules require that a particular decision about the representation be made by the client, paragraph (a)(1) requires that the lawyer promptly consult with the client and secure the client's consent prior to taking action, unless prior discussions with the client have resolved what action the client wants the lawyer to take. For example, paragraph (a)(1)(iii) requires that a lawyer who receives from opposing counsel an offer of settlement in a civil controversy or a proffered plea bargain in a criminal case must promptly inform the client of its substance unless the client has previously made clear that the proposal will be acceptable or unacceptable or has authorized the lawyer to accept or to reject the offer. *See* Rule 1.2(a).

[3] Paragraph (a)(2) requires that the lawyer reasonably consult with the client about the means to be used to accomplish the client's objectives. In some situations — depending on both the importance of the action under consideration and the feasibility of consulting with the client — this duty will require consultation prior to taking action. In other circumstances, such as during a trial when an immediate decision must be made, the exigency of the situation may require the lawyer to act without prior consultation. In such cases, the lawyer must nonetheless act reasonably to inform the client of actions the lawyer has taken on the client's behalf. Likewise, for routine matters such as scheduling decisions not materially affecting the interests of the client, the lawyer need not consult in advance, but should keep the client reasonably informed thereafter. Additionally, paragraph (a)(3) requires that the lawyer keep the client reasonably informed about the status of the matter, such as significant developments affecting the timing or the substance of the representation.

[4] A lawyer's regular communication with clients will minimize the occasions on which a client will need to request information concerning the representation. When a client makes a reasonable request for information, however, paragraph (a)(4) requires prompt compliance with the request, or if a prompt response is not feasible, that the lawyer or a member of the lawyer's staff acknowledge receipt of the request and advise the client when a response may be expected. Client telephone calls should be promptly returned or acknowledged.

Explaining Matters

[5] The client should have sufficient information to participate intelligently in decisions concerning the objectives of the representation and the means by which they are to be pursued, to the extent the client is willing and able to do so. Adequacy of communication depends in part on the kind of advice or assistance that is involved. For example, when there is time to explain a proposal made in a negotiation, the lawyer should review all important provisions with the client before proceeding to an agreement. In litigation a lawyer should explain the general strategy and prospects of success and ordinarily should consult the client on tactics that are likely to result in significant expense or to injure or coerce others. On the other hand, a lawyer ordinarily will not be expected to describe trial or negotiation strategy in detail. The guiding principle is that the lawyer should fulfill reasonable client

expectations for information consistent with the duty to act in the client's best interest and the client's overall requirements as to the character of representation. In certain circumstances, such as when a lawyer asks a client to consent to a representation affected by a conflict of interest, the client must give informed consent, as defined in Rule 1.0(j).

[6] Ordinarily, the information to be provided is that appropriate for a client who is a comprehending and responsible adult. However, fully informing the client according to this standard may be impracticable, for example, where the client is a child or suffers from diminished capacity. *See* Rule 1.14. When the client is an organization or group, it is often impossible or inappropriate to inform every one of its members about its legal affairs; ordinarily, the lawyer should address communications to those who the lawyer reasonably believes to be appropriate persons within the organization. *See* Rule 1.13. Where many routine matters are involved, a system of limited or occasional reporting may be arranged with the client.

Withholding Information

[7] In some circumstances, a lawyer may be justified in delaying transmission of information when the client would be likely to react imprudently to an immediate communication. Thus, a lawyer might withhold a psychiatric diagnosis of a client when the examining psychiatrist indicates that disclosure would harm the client. A lawyer may not withhold information to serve the lawyer's own interest or convenience or the interests or convenience of another person. Rules or court orders governing litigation may provide that information supplied to a lawyer may not be disclosed to the client. Rule 3.4(c) directs compliance with such rules or orders.

Rule 1.5   Fees and Division of Fees

(a) A lawyer shall not make an agreement for, charge, or collect an excessive or illegal fee or expense. A fee is excessive when, after a review of the facts, a reasonable lawyer would be left with a definite and firm conviction that the fee is excessive. The factors to be considered in determining whether a fee is excessive may include the following:

(1) the time and labor required, the novelty and difficulty of the questions involved, and the skill requisite to perform the legal service properly;

(2) the likelihood, if apparent or made known to the client, that the acceptance of the particular employment will preclude other employment by the lawyer;

(3) the fee customarily charged in the locality for similar legal services;

(4) the amount involved and the results obtained;

(5) the time limitations imposed by the client or by circumstances;

(6) the nature and length of the professional relationship with the client;

(7) the experience, reputation and ability of the lawyer or lawyers performing the services; and

(8) whether the fee is fixed or contingent.

(b) A lawyer shall communicate to a client the scope of the representation and the basis or rate of the fee and expenses for which the client will be responsible. This information shall be communicated to the client before or within a reasonable time after commencement of the representation and shall be in writing where required by statute or court rule. This provision shall not apply when the lawyer will charge a regularly represented client on the same basis or rate and perform services that are of the same general kind as previously rendered to and paid for by the client. Any changes in the scope of the representation or the basis or rate of the fee or expenses shall also be communicated to the client.

(c) A fee may be contingent on the outcome of the matter for which the service is rendered, except in a matter in which a contingent fee is prohibited by paragraph (d) or other law. Promptly after a lawyer has been employed in a contingent fee matter, the lawyer shall provide the client with a writing stating the method by which the fee is to be determined, including the percentage or percentages that shall accrue to the lawyer in the event of settlement, trial or appeal; litigation and other expenses to be deducted from the recovery; and whether such expenses are to be deducted before or, if not prohibited by statute or court rule, after the contingent fee is calculated. The writing must clearly notify the client of any expenses for which the client will be liable regardless of whether the client is the prevailing party. Upon conclusion of a contingent fee matter, the lawyer shall provide the client with a writing stating the outcome of the matter and, if there is a recovery, showing the remittance to the client and the method of its determination.

(d) A lawyer shall not enter into an arrangement for, charge or collect:

(1) a contingent fee for representing a defendant in a criminal matter;

(2) a fee prohibited by law or rule of court;

(3) a fee based on fraudulent billing;

(4) a nonrefundable retainer fee; provided that a lawyer may enter into a retainer agreement with a client containing a reasonable minimum fee clause if it defines in plain language and sets forth the circumstances under which such fee may be incurred and how it will be calculated; or

(5) any fee in a domestic relations matter if:

(i) the payment or amount of the fee is contingent upon the securing of a divorce or of obtaining child custody or visitation or is in any way determined by reference to the amount of maintenance, support, equitable distribution, or property settlement;

(ii) a written retainer agreement has not been signed by the lawyer and client setting forth in plain language the nature of the relationship and the details of the fee arrangement; or

(iii) the written retainer agreement includes a security interest, confession of judgment or other lien without prior notice being provided to the client in a signed retainer agreement and approval from a tribunal after notice to the adversary. A lawyer shall not foreclose on a mortgage placed on the marital residence while the spouse who consents to the mortgage remains the titleholder and the residence remains the spouse's primary residence.

(e) In domestic relations matters, a lawyer shall provide a prospective client with a Statement of Client's Rights and Responsibilities at the initial conference and prior to the signing of a written retainer agreement.

(f) Where applicable, a lawyer shall resolve fee disputes by arbitration at the election of the client pursuant to a fee arbitration program established by the Chief Administrator of the Courts and approved by the Administrative Board of the Courts.

(g) A lawyer shall not divide a fee for legal services with another lawyer who is not associated in the same law firm unless:

(1) the division is in proportion to the services performed by each lawyer or, by a writing given to the client, each lawyer assumes joint responsibility for the representation;

(2) the client agrees to employment of the other lawyer after a full disclosure that a division of fees will be made, including the share each lawyer will receive, and the client's agreement is confirmed in writing; and

(3) the total fee is not excessive.

(h) Rule 1.5(g) does not prohibit payment to a lawyer formerly associated in a law firm pursuant to a separation or retirement agreement.

COMMENT

[1] Paragraph (a) requires that lawyers not charge fees that are excessive or illegal under the circumstances. The factors specified in paragraphs (a)(1) through (a)(8) are not exclusive, nor will each factor be relevant in each instance. The time and labor required for a matter may be affected by the actions of the lawyer's own client or by those of the opposing party and counsel. Paragraph (a) also requires that expenses for which the client will be charged must not be excessive or illegal. A lawyer may seek payment for services performed in-house, such as copying, or for other expenses incurred in-house, such as telephone charges, either by charging an amount to which the client has agreed in advance or by charging an amount that reflects the cost incurred by the lawyer, provided in either case that the amount charged is not excessive.

[1A] A billing is fraudulent if it is knowingly and intentionally based on false or inaccurate information. Thus, under an hourly billing arrangement, it would be fraudulent to knowingly and intentionally charge a client for more than the actual number of hours spent by the lawyer on the client's matter; similarly, where the client has agreed to pay the lawyer's cost of in-house services, such as for photocopying or telephone calls, it would be fraudulent knowingly and intentionally to charge a client more than the actual costs incurred. Fraudulent billing requires an element of scienter and does not include inaccurate billing due to an innocent mistake.

[1B] A supervising lawyer who submits a fraudulent bill for fees or expenses to a client based on submissions by a subordinate lawyer has not automatically violated this Rule. In this situation, whether the lawyer is responsible for a violation must be determined by reference to Rules 5.1, 5.2 and 5.3. As noted in Comment [8] to Rule 5.1, nothing in that Rule alters the personal duty of each lawyer in a firm to abide by these Rules and in some situations, other rules may impose upon a supervising lawyer a duty to ensure that the books and records of a firm are accurate. *See* Rule 1.15(j).

Basis or Rate of Fee

[2] When the lawyer has regularly represented a client, they ordinarily will have evolved an understanding concerning the basis or rate of the fee and the expenses for which the client will be responsible. In a new client-lawyer relationship, however, an understanding as to fees and expenses must be promptly established. Court rules regarding engagement letters require that such an understanding be memorialized in writing in certain cases. *See* 22 N.Y.C.R.R. Part 1215. Even where not required, it is desirable to furnish the client with at least a simple memorandum or copy of the lawyer's customary fee arrangements that states the general nature of the legal services to be provided, the basis, rate or total amount of the fee, and whether and to what extent the client will be responsible for any costs, expenses or disbursements in the course of the representation. A written statement concerning the terms of the engagement reduces the possibility of misunderstanding.

[3] Contingent fees, like any other fees, are subject to the excessiveness standard of paragraph (a). In determining whether a particular contingent fee is excessive, or whether it is excessive to charge any form of contingent fee, a lawyer must consider the factors that are relevant under the circumstances. Applicable law may impose limitations on contingent fees, such as a ceiling on the percentage allowable, or may regulate the type or amount of the fee that may be charged.

Terms of Payment

[4] A lawyer may require advance payment of a fee, but is obliged to return any unearned portion. *See* Rule 1.16(e). A lawyer may charge a minimum fee, if that fee is not excessive, and if the wording of the minimum fee clause of the retainer agreement meets the requirements of paragraph (d)(4). A lawyer may accept property in payment for services, such as an ownership interest in an enterprise, providing this does not involve acquisition of a proprietary interest in the cause of action or subject matter of the litigation contrary to Rule 1.8(i). A fee paid in property instead of money may, however, be subject to the requirements of Rule 1.8(a), because such fees often have the essential qualities of a business transaction with the client.

[5] An agreement may not be made if its terms might induce the lawyer improperly to curtail services for the client or perform them in a way contrary to the

client's interest. For example, a lawyer should not enter into an agreement whereby services are to be provided only up to a stated amount when it is foreseeable that more extensive services probably will be required, unless the situation is adequately explained to the client. Otherwise, the client might have to bargain for further assistance in the midst of a proceeding or transaction. In matters in litigation, the court's approval for the lawyer's withdrawal may be required. *See* Rule 1.16(d). It is proper, however, to define the extent of services in light of the client's ability to pay. A lawyer should not exploit a fee arrangement based primarily on hourly charges by using wasteful procedures.

[5A] The New York Court Rules require every lawyer with an office located in New York to post in that office, in a manner visible to clients of the lawyer, a "Statement of Client's Rights." *See* 22 N.Y.C.R.R. §1210.1. Paragraph (e) requires a lawyer in a domestic relations matter, as defined in Rule 1.0(g), to provide a prospective client with the "Statement of Client's Rights and Responsibilities," as further set forth in 22 N.Y.C.R.R. §1400.2, at the initial conference and, in any event, prior to the signing of a written retainer agreement.

Prohibited Contingent Fees

[6] Paragraph (d) prohibits a lawyer from charging a contingent fee in a domestic relations matter when payment is contingent upon the securing of a divorce or upon the amount of alimony or support or property settlement to be obtained or upon obtaining child custody or visitation. This provision does not preclude a contract for a contingent fee for legal representation in connection with the recovery of post-judgment balances due under support, alimony or other financial orders because such contracts do not implicate the same policy concerns. *See* Rule 1.0(g) (defining "domestic relations matter" to include an action to enforce such a judgment).

Division of Fee

[7] A division of fee is a single billing to a client covering the fee of two or more lawyers who are not affiliated in the same firm. A division of fee facilitates association of more than one lawyer in a matter in which neither alone could serve the client as well. Paragraph (g) permits the lawyers to divide a fee either on the basis of the proportion of services they render or if each lawyer assumes responsibility for the representation as a whole in a writing given to the client. In addition, the client must agree to the arrangement, including the share that each lawyer is to receive, and the client's agreement must be confirmed in writing. Contingent fee arrangements must comply with paragraph (c). Joint responsibility for the representation entails financial and ethical responsibility for the representation as if the lawyers were associated in a partnership. *See* Rule 5.1. A lawyer should refer a matter only to a lawyer who the referring lawyer reasonably believes is competent to handle the matter. *See* Rule 1.1.

[8] Paragraph (g) does not prohibit or regulate division of fees to be received in the future for work done when lawyers were previously associated in a law firm.

Paragraph (h) recognizes that this Rule does not prohibit payment to a previously associated lawyer pursuant to a separation or retirement agreement.

Disputes over Fees

[9] A lawyer should seek to avoid controversies over fees with clients and should attempt to resolve amicably any differences on the subject. The New York courts have established a procedure for resolution of fee disputes through arbitration and the lawyer must comply with the procedure when it is mandatory. Even when it is voluntary, the lawyer should conscientiously consider submitting to it.

Rule 1.6   Confidentiality of Information

(a) A lawyer shall not knowingly reveal confidential information, as defined in this Rule, or use such information to the disadvantage of a client or for the advantage of the lawyer or a third person, unless:

(1) the client gives informed consent, as defined in Rule 1.0(j);

(2) the disclosure is impliedly authorized to advance the best interests of the client and is either reasonable under the circumstances or customary in the professional community; or

(3) the disclosure is permitted by paragraph (b).

"Confidential information" consists of information gained during or relating to the representation of a client, whatever its source, that is (a) protected by the attorney-client privilege, (b) likely to be embarrassing or detrimental to the client if disclosed, or (c) information that the client has requested be kept confidential. "Confidential information" does not ordinarily include (i) a lawyer's legal knowledge or legal research or (ii) information that is generally known in the local community or in the trade, field or profession to which the information relates.

(b) A lawyer may reveal or use confidential information to the extent that the lawyer reasonably believes necessary:

(1) to prevent reasonably certain death or substantial bodily harm;

(2) to prevent the client from committing a crime;

(3) to withdraw a written or oral opinion or representation previously given by the lawyer and reasonably believed by the lawyer still to be relied upon by a third person, where the lawyer has discovered that the opinion or representation was based on materially inaccurate information or is being used to further a crime or fraud;

(4) to secure legal advice about compliance with these Rules or other law by the lawyer, another lawyer associated with the lawyer's firm or the law firm;

(5) (i) to defend the lawyer or the lawyer's employees and associates against an accusation of wrongful conduct; or

(ii) to establish or collect a fee; or

(6) when permitted or required under these Rules or to comply with other law or court order.

(c) A lawyer shall exercise reasonable care to prevent the lawyer's employees, associates, and others whose services are utilized by the lawyer from disclosing or using confidential information of a client, except that a lawyer may reveal the information permitted to be disclosed by paragraph (b) through an employee.

COMMENT

Scope of the Professional Duty of Confidentiality

[1] This Rule governs the disclosure of information protected by the professional duty of confidentiality. Such information is described in these Rules as "confidential information" as defined in this Rule. Other rules also deal with confidential information. See Rules 1.8(b) and 1.9(c)(1) for the lawyer's duties with respect to the use of such information to the disadvantage of clients and former clients; Rule 1.9(c)(2) for the lawyer's duty not to reveal information relating to the lawyer's prior representation of a former client; Rule 1.14(c) for information relating to representation of a client with diminished capacity; Rule 1.18(b) for the lawyer's duties with respect to information provided to the lawyer by a prospective client; Rule 3.3 for the lawyer's duty of candor to a tribunal; and Rule 8.3(c) for information gained by a lawyer or judge while participating in an approved lawyer assistance program.

[2] A fundamental principle in the client-lawyer relationship is that, in the absence of the client's informed consent, or except as permitted or required by these Rules, the lawyer must not knowingly reveal information gained during and related to the representation, whatever its source. See Rule 1.0(j) for the definition of informed consent. The lawyer's duty of confidentiality contributes to the trust that is the hallmark of the client-lawyer relationship. The client is thereby encouraged to seek legal assistance and to communicate fully and frankly with the lawyer, even as to embarrassing or legally damaging subject matter. The lawyer needs this information to represent the client effectively and, if necessary, to advise the client to refrain from wrongful conduct. Typically, clients come to lawyers to determine their rights and what is, in the complex of laws and regulations, deemed to be legal and correct. Based upon experience, lawyers know that almost all clients follow the advice given, and the law is thereby upheld.

[3] The principle of client-lawyer confidentiality is given effect in three related bodies of law: the attorney-client privilege of evidence law, the work-product doctrine of civil procedure and the professional duty of confidentiality established in legal ethics codes. The attorney-client privilege and the work-product doctrine apply when compulsory process by a judicial or other governmental body seeks to compel a lawyer to testify or produce information or evidence concerning a client. The professional duty of client-lawyer confidentiality, in contrast, applies to a lawyer in all settings and at all times, prohibiting the lawyer from disclosing confidential information unless permitted or required by these Rules or to comply with other

law or court order. The confidentiality duty applies not only to matters communicated in confidence by the client, which are protected by the attorney-client privilege, but also to all information gained during and relating to the representation, whatever its source. The confidentiality duty, for example, prohibits a lawyer from volunteering confidential information to a friend or to any other person except in compliance with the provisions of this Rule, including the Rule's reference to other law that may compel disclosure. *See* Comments [12]-[13]; *see also* Scope.

[4] Paragraph (a) prohibits a lawyer from knowingly revealing confidential information as defined by this Rule. This prohibition also applies to disclosures by a lawyer that do not in themselves reveal confidential information but could reasonably lead to the discovery of such information by a third person. A lawyer's use of a hypothetical to discuss issues relating to the representation with persons not connected to the representation is permissible so long as there is no reasonable likelihood that the listener will be able to ascertain the identity of the client.

[4A] Paragraph (a) protects all factual information "gained during or relating to the representation of a client." Information relates to the representation if it has any possible relevance to the representation or is received because of the representation. The accumulation of legal knowledge or legal research that a lawyer acquires through practice ordinarily is not client information protected by this Rule. However, in some circumstances, including where the client and the lawyer have so agreed, a client may have a proprietary interest in a particular product of the lawyer's research. Information is generally known in the local community or in the trade, field or profession to which the information relates is also not protected, unless the client and the lawyer have otherwise agreed. Information is not "generally known" simply because it is in the public domain or available in a public file.

Use of Information Related to Representation

[4B] The duty of confidentiality also prohibits a lawyer from using confidential information to the advantage of the lawyer or a third person or to the disadvantage of a client or former client unless the client or former client has given informed consent. See Rule 1.0(j) for the definition of "informed consent." This part of paragraph (a) applies when information is used to benefit either the lawyer or a third person, such as another client, a former client or a business associate of the lawyer. For example, if a lawyer learns that a client intends to purchase and develop several parcels of land, the lawyer may not (absent the client's informed consent) use that information to buy a nearby parcel that is expected to appreciate in value due to the client's purchase, or to recommend that another client buy the nearby land, even if the lawyer does not reveal any confidential information. The duty also prohibits disadvantageous use of confidential information unless the client gives informed consent, except as permitted or required by these Rules. For example, a lawyer assisting a client in purchasing a parcel of land may not make a competing bid on the same land. However, the fact that a lawyer has once served a client does not preclude the lawyer from using generally known information about that client, even to the disadvantage of the former client, after the client-lawyer relationship has terminated. *See* Rule 1.9(c)(1).

Authorized Disclosure

[5] Except to the extent that the client's instructions or special circumstances limit that authority, a lawyer may make disclosures of confidential information that are impliedly authorized by a client if the disclosures (i) advance the best interests of the client and (ii) are either reasonable under the circumstances or customary in the professional community. In some situations, for example, a lawyer may be impliedly authorized to admit a fact that cannot properly be disputed or to make a disclosure that facilitates a satisfactory conclusion to a matter. In addition, lawyers in a firm may, in the course of the firm's practice, disclose to each other information relating to a client of the firm, unless the client has instructed that particular information be confined to specified lawyers. Lawyers are also impliedly authorized to reveal information about a client with diminished capacity when necessary to take protective action to safeguard the client's interests. *See* Rules 1.14(b) and (c).

Disclosure Adverse to Client

[6] Although the public interest is usually best served by a strict rule requiring lawyers to preserve the confidentiality of information relating to the representation of their clients, the confidentiality rule is subject to limited exceptions that prevent substantial harm to important interests, deter wrongdoing by clients, prevent violations of the law, and maintain the impartiality and integrity of judicial proceedings. Paragraph (b) permits, but does not require, a lawyer to disclose information relating to the representation to accomplish these specified purposes.

[6A] The lawyer's exercise of discretion conferred by paragraphs (b)(1) through (b)(3) requires consideration of a wide range of factors and should therefore be given great weight. In exercising such discretion under these paragraphs, the lawyer should consider such factors as: (i) the seriousness of the potential injury to others if the prospective harm or crime occurs, (ii) the likelihood that it will occur and its imminence, (iii) the apparent absence of any other feasible way to prevent the potential injury, (iv) the extent to which the client may be using the lawyer's services in bringing about the harm or crime, (v) the circumstances under which the lawyer acquired the information of the client's intent or prospective course of action, and (vi) any other aggravating or extenuating circumstances. In any case, disclosure adverse to the client's interest should be no greater than the lawyer reasonably believes necessary to prevent the threatened harm or crime. When a lawyer learns that a client intends to pursue or is pursuing a course of conduct that would permit disclosure under paragraphs (b)(1), (b)(2) or (b)(3), the lawyer's initial duty, where practicable, is to remonstrate with the client. In the rare situation in which the client is reluctant to accept the lawyer's advice, the lawyer's threat of disclosure is a measure of last resort that may persuade the client. When the lawyer reasonably believes that the client will carry out the threatened harm or crime, the lawyer may disclose confidential information when permitted by paragraphs (b)(1), (b)(2) or (b)(3). A lawyer's permissible disclosure under paragraph (b) does not waive the client's attorney-client privilege; neither the lawyer nor the client may be forced to testify about communications protected by the privilege, unless a tribunal or body with authority to compel testimony makes a determination that the crime-fraud exception to the privilege, or some other exception, has been satisfied by a party to the proceeding. For a lawyer's duties when representing an organizational client engaged in wrongdoing, see Rule 1.13(b).

[6B] Paragraph (b)(1) recognizes the overriding value of life and physical integrity and permits disclosure reasonably necessary to prevent reasonably certain death or substantial bodily harm. Such harm is reasonably certain to occur if it will be suffered imminently or if there is a present and substantial risk that a person will suffer such harm at a later date if the lawyer fails to take action necessary to eliminate the threat. Thus, a lawyer who knows that a client has accidentally discharged toxic waste into a town's water supply may reveal this information to the authorities if there is a present and substantial risk that a person who drinks the water will contract a life-threatening or debilitating disease and the lawyer's disclosure is necessary to eliminate the threat or reduce the number of victims. Wrongful execution of a person is a life-threatening and imminent harm under paragraph (b)(1) once the person has been convicted and sentenced to death. On the other hand, an event that will cause property damage but is unlikely to cause substantial bodily harm is not a present and substantial risk under paragraph (b)(1); similarly, a remote possibility or small statistical likelihood that any particular unit of a mass-distributed product will cause death or substantial bodily harm to unspecified persons over a period of years does not satisfy the element of reasonably certain death or substantial bodily harm under the exception to the duty of confidentiality in paragraph (b)(1).

[6C] Paragraph (b)(2) recognizes that society has important interests in preventing a client's crime. Disclosure of the client's intention is permitted to the extent reasonably necessary to prevent the crime. In exercising discretion under this paragraph, the lawyer should consider such factors as those stated in Comment [6A].

[6D] Some crimes, such as criminal fraud, may be ongoing in the sense that the client's past material false representations are still deceiving new victims. The law treats such crimes as continuing crimes in which new violations are constantly occurring. The lawyer whose services were involved in the criminal acts that constitute a continuing crime may reveal the client's refusal to bring an end to a continuing crime, even though that disclosure may also reveal the client's past wrongful acts, because refusal to end a continuing crime is equivalent to an intention to commit a new crime. Disclosure is not permitted under paragraph (b)(2), however, when a person who may have committed a crime employs a new lawyer for investigation or defense. Such a lawyer does not have discretion under paragraph (b)(2) to use or disclose the client's past acts that may have continuing criminal consequences. Disclosure is permitted, however, if the client uses the new lawyer's services to commit a further crime, such as obstruction of justice or perjury.

[6E] Paragraph (b)(3) permits a lawyer to withdraw a legal opinion or to disaffirm a prior representation made to third parties when the lawyer reasonably believes that third persons are still relying on the lawyer's work and the work was based on "materially inaccurate information or is being used to further a crime or fraud." See Rule 1.16(b)(1), requiring the lawyer to withdraw when the lawyer knows or reasonably should know that the representation will result in a violation of law. Paragraph (b)(3) permits the lawyer to give only the limited notice that is implicit in withdrawing an opinion or representation, which may have the collateral effect of inferentially revealing confidential information. The lawyer's withdrawal of the tainted opinion or representation allows the lawyer to prevent further harm to third persons and to protect the lawyer's own interest when the client has abused the professional relationship, but paragraph (b)(3) does not permit explicit disclosure of the client's past acts unless such disclosure is permitted under paragraph (b)(2).

[7] [Reserved.]

[8] [Reserved.]

[9] A lawyer's confidentiality obligations do not preclude a lawyer from securing confidential legal advice about compliance with these Rules and other law by the lawyer, another lawyer in the lawyer's firm, or the law firm. In many situations, disclosing information to secure such advice will be impliedly authorized for the lawyer to carry out the representation. Even when the disclosure is not impliedly authorized, paragraph (b)(4) permits such disclosure because of the importance of a lawyer's compliance with these Rules, court orders and other law.

[10] Where a claim or charge alleges misconduct of the lawyer related to the representation of a current or former client, the lawyer may respond to the extent the lawyer reasonably believes necessary to establish a defense. Such a claim can arise in a civil, criminal, disciplinary or other proceeding and can be based on a wrong allegedly committed by the lawyer against the client or on a wrong alleged by a third person, such as a person claiming to have been defrauded by the lawyer and client acting together or by the lawyer acting alone. The lawyer may respond directly to the person who has made an accusation that permits disclosure, provided that the lawyer's response complies with Rule 4.2 and Rule 4.3, and other Rules or applicable law. A lawyer may make the disclosures authorized by paragraph (b)(5) through counsel. The right to respond also applies to accusations of wrongful conduct concerning the lawyer's law firm, employees or associates.

[11] A lawyer entitled to a fee is permitted by paragraph (b)(5) to prove the services rendered in an action to collect it. This aspect of the rule expresses the principle that the beneficiary of a fiduciary relationship may not exploit it to the detriment of the fiduciary.

[12] Paragraph (b) does not mandate any disclosures. However, other law may require that a lawyer disclose confidential information. Whether such a law supersedes Rule 1.6 is a question of law beyond the scope of these Rules. When disclosure of confidential information appears to be required by other law, the lawyer must consult with the client to the extent required by Rule 1.4 before making the disclosure, unless such consultation would be prohibited by other law. If the lawyer concludes that other law supersedes this Rule and requires disclosure, paragraph (b)(6) permits the lawyer to make such disclosures as are necessary to comply with the law.

[13] A tribunal or governmental entity claiming authority pursuant to other law to compel disclosure may order a lawyer to reveal confidential information. Absent informed consent of the client to comply with the order, the lawyer should assert on behalf of the client nonfrivolous arguments that the order is not authorized by law, the information sought is protected against disclosure by an applicable privilege or other law, or the order is invalid or defective for some other reason. In the event of an adverse ruling, the lawyer must consult with the client to the extent required by Rule 1.4 about the possibility of an appeal or further challenge, unless such consultation would be prohibited by other law. If such review is not sought or is unsuccessful, paragraph (b)(6) permits the lawyer to comply with the order.

specific Rules regarding certain concurrent conflicts of interest, see Rule 1.8. For former client conflicts of interest, see Rule 1.9. For conflicts of interest involving prospective clients, see Rule 1.18. For definitions of "differing interests," "informed consent" and "confirmed in writing," see Rules 1.0(f), (j) and (e), respectively.

[2] Resolution of a conflict of interest problem under this Rule requires the lawyer, acting reasonably, to: (i) identify clearly the client or clients, (ii) determine whether a conflict of interest exists, *i.e.*, whether the lawyer's judgment may be impaired or the lawyer's loyalty may be divided if the lawyer accepts or continues the representation, (iii) decide whether the representation may be undertaken despite the existence of a conflict, *i.e.*, whether the conflict is consentable under paragraph (b); and if so (iv) consult with the clients affected under paragraph (a) and obtain their informed consent, confirmed in writing. The clients affected under paragraph (a) include all of the clients who may have differing interests under paragraph (a)(1) and any clients whose representation might be adversely affected under paragraph (a)(2).

[3] A conflict of interest may exist before representation is undertaken, in which event the representation must be declined, unless the lawyer obtains the informed consent of each client under the conditions of paragraph (b). *See* Rule 1.10(e), which requires every law firm to create, implement and maintain a conflict-checking system.

[4] If a conflict arises after representation has been undertaken, the lawyer ordinarily must withdraw from the representation unless the lawyer has obtained the informed consent of the client under the conditions of paragraph (b). *See* Rule 1.16(b)(1). Where more than one client is involved, whether the lawyer may continue to represent any of the clients is determined both by the lawyer's ability to comply with duties owed to the former client and by the lawyer's ability to represent adequately the remaining client or clients, given the lawyer's duties to the former client. *See* Rule 1.9; *see also* Comments [5], [29A].

[5] Unforeseeable developments, such as changes in corporate and other organizational affiliations or the addition or realignment of parties in litigation, might create conflicts in the midst of a representation, as when a company sued by the lawyer on behalf of one client is acquired by another client represented by the lawyer in an unrelated matter. Depending on the circumstances, the lawyer may have the option to withdraw from one of the representations in order to avoid the conflict. The lawyer must seek court approval where necessary and take steps to minimize harm to the clients. *See* Rules 1.16(d) and (e). The lawyer must continue to protect the confidences of the client from whose representation the lawyer has withdrawn. *See* Rule 1.9(c).

Identifying Conflicts of Interest

[6] The duty to avoid the representation of differing interest prohibits, among other things, undertaking representation adverse to a current client without that client's informed consent. For example, absent consent, a lawyer may not advocate in one matter against another client that the lawyer represents in some other matter, even when the matters are wholly unrelated. The client as to whom the representation is adverse is likely to feel betrayed and the resulting damage to the client-lawyer

relationship is likely to impair the lawyer's ability to represent the client effectively. In addition, the client on whose behalf the adverse representation is undertaken may reasonably fear that the lawyer will pursue that client's case less effectively out of deference to the other client, that is, that the lawyer's exercise of professional judgment on behalf of that client will be adversely affected by the lawyer's interest in retaining the current client. Similarly, a conflict may arise when a lawyer is required to cross-examine a client appearing as a witness in a lawsuit involving another client, as when the testimony will be damaging to the client represented in the lawsuit. On the other hand, simultaneous representation in unrelated matters of clients whose interests are only economically adverse, such as representation of competing economic enterprises in unrelated litigation, does not ordinarily constitute a conflict of interest and thus may not require consent of the respective clients.

[7] Differing interests can also arise in transactional matters. For example, if a lawyer is asked to represent the seller of a business in negotiations with a buyer represented by the lawyer, not in the same transaction but in another, unrelated matter, the lawyer could not undertake the representation without the informed consent of each client.

[8] Differing interests exist if there is a significant risk that a lawyer's exercise of professional judgment in considering, recommending or carrying out an appropriate course of action for the client will be adversely affected or the representation would otherwise be materially limited by the lawyer's other responsibilities or interests. For example, the professional judgment of a lawyer asked to represent several individuals operating a joint venture is likely to be adversely affected to the extent that the lawyer is unable to recommend or advocate all possible positions that each client might take because of the lawyer's duty of loyalty to the others. The conflict in effect forecloses alternatives that would otherwise be available to the client. The mere possibility of subsequent harm does not itself require disclosure and consent. The critical questions are the likelihood that a difference in interests will eventuate and, if it does, whether it will adversely affect the lawyer's professional judgment in considering alternatives or foreclose courses of action that reasonably should be pursued on behalf of the client.

Lawyer's Responsibilities to Former Clients and Other Third Persons

[9] In addition to conflicts with other current clients, a lawyer's duties of loyalty and independence may be adversely affected by responsibilities to former clients under Rule 1.9, or by the lawyer's responsibilities to other persons, such as fiduciary duties arising from a lawyer's service as a trustee, executor or corporate director.

Personal-Interest Conflicts

[10] The lawyer's own financial, property, business or other personal interests should not be permitted to have an adverse effect on representation of a client. For example, if the probity of a lawyer's own conduct in a transaction is in serious question, it may be difficult or impossible for the lawyer to give a client detached advice.

Similarly, when a lawyer has discussions concerning possible employment with an opponent of the lawyer's client or with a law firm representing the opponent, such discussions could materially limit the lawyer's representation of the client. In addition, a lawyer may not allow related business interests to affect representation, for example, by referring clients to an enterprise in which the lawyer has an undisclosed financial interest. See Rule 5.7 on responsibilities regarding nonlegal services and Rule 1.8 pertaining to a number of personal-interest conflicts, including business transactions with clients.

[11] When lawyers representing different clients in the same matter or in substantially related matters are closely related, there may be a significant risk that client confidences will be revealed and that the lawyer's family relationship will interfere with both loyalty and professional judgment. As a result, each client is entitled to know of the existence and implications of the relationship between the lawyers, before the lawyer agrees to undertake the representation. Thus, a lawyer who has a significant intimate or close family relationship with another lawyer ordinarily may not represent a client in a matter where that other lawyer is representing another party, unless each client gives informed consent, as defined in Rule 1.0(j).

[12] A lawyer is prohibited from engaging in sexual relations with a client in domestic relations matters. In all other matters a lawyer's sexual relations with a client are circumscribed by the provisions of Rule 1.8(j).

Interest of Person Paying for Lawyer's Services

[13] A lawyer may be paid from a source other than the client, including a co-client, if the client is informed of that fact and consents and the arrangement does not compromise the lawyer's duty of loyalty or independent judgment to the client. *See* Rule 1.8(f). If acceptance of the payment from any other source presents a significant risk that the lawyer's exercise of professional judgment on behalf of a client will be adversely affected by the lawyer's own interest in accommodating the person paying the lawyer's fee or by the lawyer's responsibilities to a payer who is also a co-client, then the lawyer must comply with the requirements of paragraph (b) before accepting the representation, including determining whether the conflict is consentable and, if so, that the client has adequate information about the material risks of the representation.

Prohibited Representations

[14] Ordinarily, clients may consent to representation notwithstanding a conflict. As paragraph (b) indicates, however, some conflicts are nonconsentable. If a lawyer does not reasonably believe that the conditions set forth in paragraph (b) can be met, the lawyer should neither ask for the client's consent nor provide representation on the basis of the client's consent. A client's consent to a nonconsentable conflict is ineffective. When the lawyer is representing more than one client, the question of consentability must be resolved as to each client.

[15] Consentability is typically determined by considering whether the interests of the clients will be adequately protected if the clients consent to representation

burdened by a conflict of interest. Thus, under paragraph (b)(1), notwithstanding client consent, a representation is prohibited if, in the circumstances, the lawyer cannot reasonably conclude that the lawyer will be able to provide competent and diligent representation. See Rule 1.1 regarding competence and Rule 1.3 regarding diligence.

[16] Paragraph (b)(2) describes conflicts that are nonconsentable because the representation is prohibited by applicable law. For example, federal criminal statutes prohibit certain representations by a former government lawyer despite the informed consent of the former governmental client. In addition, there are some instances where conflicts are nonconsentable under decisional law.

[17] Paragraph (b)(3) describes conflicts that are nonconsentable because of the institutional interest in vigorous development of each client's position when the clients are aligned directly against each other in the same litigation or other proceeding before a tribunal. Whether clients are aligned directly against each other within the meaning of this paragraph requires examination of the context of the proceeding. Although this paragraph does not preclude a lawyer's multiple representation of adverse parties to mediation (because mediation is not a proceeding before a ''tribunal'' as defined in Rule 1.0(w)), such representation may be precluded by paragraph (b)(1).

Informed Consent

[18] Informed consent requires that each affected client be aware of the relevant circumstances, including the material and reasonably foreseeable ways that the conflict could adversely affect the interests of that client. Informed consent also requires that the client be given the opportunity to obtain other counsel if the client so desires. See Rule 1.0(j). The information that a lawyer is required to communicate to a client depends on the nature of the conflict and the nature of the risks involved, and a lawyer should take into account the sophistication of the client in explaining the potential adverse consequences of the conflict. There are circumstances in which it is appropriate for a lawyer to advise a client to seek the advice of a disinterested lawyer in reaching a decision as to whether to consent to the conflict. When representation of multiple clients in a single matter is undertaken, the information must include the implications of the common representation, including possible effects on loyalty, confidentiality and the attorney-client privilege, and the advantages and risks involved. See Comments [30] and [31] concerning the effect of common representation on confidentiality.

[19] Under some circumstances it may be impossible to make the disclosure necessary to obtain consent. For example, when the lawyer represents different clients in related matters and one client refuses to consent to the disclosure necessary to permit the other client to make an informed decision, the lawyer cannot properly ask the latter to consent. In some cases the alternative to common representation is that each party obtains separate representation with the possibility of incurring additional costs. These costs, along with the benefits of securing separate representation, are factors that may be considered by the affected client in determining whether common representation is in the client's interests. Where the fact, validity or propriety of client consent is called into question, the lawyer has the burden of establishing that the client's consent was properly obtained in accordance with the Rule.

Client Consent Confirmed in Writing

[20] Paragraph (b) requires the lawyer to obtain the informed consent of the client, confirmed in writing. Such a writing may consist of (i) a document from the client, (ii) a document that the lawyer promptly transmits to the client confirming an oral informed consent, or (iii) a statement by the client made on the record of any proceeding before a tribunal, whether before, during or after a trial or hearing. *See* Rule 1.0(e) for the definition of "confirmed in writing." *See also* Rule 1.0(x) ("writing" includes electronic transmission). If it is not feasible to obtain or transmit the writing at the time the client gives informed consent, then the lawyer must obtain or transmit it within a reasonable time thereafter. The Rule does not require that the information communicated to the client by the lawyer necessary to make the consent "informed" be in writing or in any particular form in all cases. *See* Rules 1.0(e) and (j). The requirement of a writing does not supplant the need in most cases for the lawyer to talk with the client to explain the risks and advantages, if any, of representation burdened with a conflict of interest, as well as reasonably available alternatives, and to afford the client a reasonable opportunity to consider the risks and alternatives and to raise questions and concerns. Rather, the writing is required in order to impress upon clients the seriousness of the decision the client is being asked to make and to avoid disputes or ambiguities that might later occur in the absence of a writing. *See* Comment [18].

Revoking Consent

[21] A client who has given consent to a conflict may revoke the consent and, like any other client, may terminate the lawyer's representation at any time. Whether revoking consent to the client's own representation precludes the lawyer from continuing to represent other clients depends on the circumstances, including the nature of the conflict, whether the client revoked consent because of a material change in circumstances, the reasonable expectations of the other clients, and whether material detriment to the other clients or the lawyer would result.

Consent to Future Conflict

[22] Whether a lawyer may properly request a client to waive conflicts that might arise in the future is subject to the conditions set forth in paragraph (b). The effectiveness of advance waivers is generally determined by the extent to which the client reasonably understands the material risks that the waiver entails. At a minimum, the client should be advised generally of the types of possible future adverse representations that the lawyer envisions, as well as the types of clients and matters that may present such conflicts. The more comprehensive the explanation and disclosure of the types of future representations that might arise and the actual and reasonably foreseeable adverse consequences of those representations, the greater the likelihood that the client will have the understanding necessary to make the consent "informed" and the waiver effective. *See* Rule 1.0(j). The lawyer should also disclose the measures that will be taken to protect the client should a conflict

arise, including procedures such as screening that would be put in place. See Rule 1.0(t) for the definition of "screening." The adequacy of the disclosure necessary to obtain valid advance consent to conflicts may also depend on the sophistication and experience of the client. For example, if the client is unsophisticated about legal matters generally or about the particular type of matter at hand, the lawyer should provide more detailed information about both the nature of the anticipated conflict and the adverse consequences to the client that may ensue should the potential conflict become an actual one. In other instances, such as where the client is a child or an incapacitated or impaired person, it may be impossible to inform the client sufficiently, and the lawyer should not seek an advance waiver. On the other hand, if the client is an experienced user of the legal services involved and is reasonably informed regarding the risk that a conflict may arise, an advance waiver is more likely to be effective, particularly if, for example, the client is independently represented or advised by in-house or other counsel in giving consent. Thus, in some circumstances, even general and open-ended waivers by experienced users of legal services may be effective.

[22A] Even if a client has validly consented to waive future conflicts, however, the lawyer must reassess the propriety of the adverse concurrent representation under paragraph (b) when an actual conflict arises. If the actual conflict is materially different from the conflict that has been waived, the lawyer may not rely on the advance consent previously obtained. Even if the actual conflict is not materially different from the conflict the client has previously waived, the client's advance consent cannot be effective if the particular circumstances that have created an actual conflict during the course of the representation would make the conflict nonconsentable under paragraph (b). *See* Comments [14]-[17] and [28] addressing nonconsentable conflicts.

Conflicts in Litigation

[23] Paragraph (b)(3) prohibits representation of opposing parties in the same litigation, regardless of the clients' consent. On the other hand, simultaneous representation of parties whose interests in litigation may conflict, such as co-plaintiffs or co-defendants, is governed by paragraph (a)(1). A conflict may exist by reason of substantial discrepancy in the parties' testimony, incompatibility in positions in relation to an opposing party or the fact that there are substantially different possibilities of settlement of the claims or liabilities in question. Such conflicts can arise in criminal as well as civil cases. Some examples are those in which a lawyer is asked to represent co-defendants in a criminal case, co-plaintiffs or co-defendants in a personal injury case, an insured and insurer, or beneficiaries of the estate of a decedent. In a criminal case, the potential for conflict of interest in representing multiple defendants is so grave that ordinarily a lawyer should decline to represent more than one co-defendant. On the other hand, multiple representation of persons having similar interests in civil litigation is proper if the requirements of paragraph (b) are met.

[24] Ordinarily a lawyer may take inconsistent legal positions in different tribunals at different times on behalf of different clients. The mere fact that advocating a legal position on behalf of one client might create precedent adverse to the interests of a client represented by the lawyer in an unrelated matter does not create

a conflict of interest. A conflict of interest exists, however, if there is a significant risk that a lawyer's action on behalf of one client will materially limit the lawyer's representation of another client in a different case; for example, when a decision favoring one client will create a precedent likely to weaken seriously the position taken on behalf of the other client. Factors relevant in determining whether the clients need to be advised of this risk include: (i) where the cases are pending, (ii) whether the issue is substantive or procedural, (iii) the temporal relationship between the matters, (iv) the significance of the issue to the immediate and long-term interests of the clients involved, and (v) the clients' reasonable expectations in retaining the lawyer. Similar concerns may be present when lawyers advocate on behalf of clients before other entities, such as regulatory authorities whose regulations or rulings may significantly implicate clients' interests. If there is significant risk of an adverse effect on the lawyer's professional judgment, then absent informed consent of the affected clients, the lawyer must decline the representation.

[25] When a lawyer represents or seeks to represent a class of plaintiffs or defendants in a class-action lawsuit, unnamed members of the class are ordinarily not considered to be clients of the lawyer for purposes of applying paragraph (a)(1). Thus, the lawyer does not typically need to get the consent of such a person before representing a client suing the person in an unrelated matter. Similarly, a lawyer seeking to represent an opponent in a class action does not typically need the consent of an unnamed member of the class whom the lawyer represents in an unrelated matter.

Nonlitigation Conflicts

[26] Conflicts of interest under paragraph (a)(1) arise in contexts other than litigation. For a discussion of such conflicts in transactional matters, see Comment [7]. Regarding paragraph (a)(2), relevant factors in determining whether there is a significant risk that the lawyer's professional judgment will be adversely affected include: (i) the importance of the matter to each client, (ii) the duration and intimacy of the lawyer's relationship with the client or clients involved, (iii) the functions being performed by the lawyer, (iv) the likelihood that significant disagreements will arise, (v) the likelihood that negotiations will be contentious, (vi) the likelihood that the matter will result in litigation, and (vii) the likelihood that the client will suffer prejudice from the conflict. The issue is often one of proximity (how close the situation is to open conflict) and degree (how serious the conflict will be if it does erupt). *See* Comments [8], [29] and [29A].

[27] For example, conflict questions may arise in estate planning and estate administration. A lawyer may be called upon to prepare wills for several family members, such as husband and wife, and, depending upon the circumstances, a conflict of interest may be present at the outset or may arise during the representation. In order to avoid the development of a disqualifying conflict, the lawyer should, at the outset of the common representation and as part of the process of obtaining each client's informed consent, advise each client that information will be shared (and regardless of whether it is shared, may not be privileged in a subsequent dispute between the parties) and that the lawyer will have to withdraw from one or both representations if one client decides that some matter material to the representation should be kept secret from the other. *See* Comment [31].

[28] Whether a conflict is consentable depends on the circumstances. For example, a lawyer may not represent multiple parties to a negotiation if their interests are fundamentally antagonistic to one another, but common representation is permissible where the clients are generally aligned in interest, even though there is some difference in interest among them. Thus, a lawyer may seek to establish or adjust a relationship between clients on an amicable and mutually advantageous basis. Examples include helping to organize a business in which two or more clients are entrepreneurs, working out the financial reorganization of an enterprise in which two or more clients have an interest, and arranging a property distribution in settlement of an estate. The lawyer seeks to resolve potentially adverse interests by developing the parties' mutual interests. Otherwise, each party might have to obtain separate representation, with the possibility of incurring additional cost, complication or even litigation. Given these and other relevant factors, the clients may prefer that the lawyer act for all of them.

Special Considerations in Common Representation

[29] In civil matters, two or more clients may wish to be represented by a single lawyer in seeking to establish or adjust a relationship between them on an amicable and mutually advantageous basis. For example, clients may wish to be represented by a single lawyer in helping to organize a business, working out a financial reorganization of an enterprise in which two or more clients have an interest, arranging a property distribution of an estate or resolving a dispute between clients. The alternative to common representation can be that each party may have to obtain separate representation, with the possibility of incurring additional cost, complication or even litigation that might otherwise be avoided, or that some parties will have no lawyer at all. Given these and other relevant factors, clients may prefer common representation to separate representation or no representation. A lawyer should consult with each client concerning the implications of the common representation, including the advantages and the risks involved, and the effect on the attorney-client privilege, and obtain each client's informed consent, confirmed in writing, to the common representation.

[29A] Factors may be present that militate against a common representation. In considering whether to represent multiple clients in the same matter, a lawyer should be mindful that if the common representation fails because the potentially adverse interests cannot be reconciled, the result can be additional cost, embarrassment and recrimination. Ordinarily, absent the informed consent of all clients, the lawyer will be forced to withdraw from representing all of the clients if the common representation fails. *See* Rule 1.9(a). In some situations, the risk of failure is so great that multiple representation is plainly impossible. For example, a lawyer cannot undertake common representation of clients where contentious litigation or negotiations between them are imminent or contemplated. Moreover, because the lawyer is required to be impartial between or among commonly represented clients, representation of multiple clients is improper when it is unlikely that impartiality can be maintained. Generally, if the relationship between the parties has already assumed antagonism, it is unlikely that the clients' interests can be adequately served by common representation. For example, a lawyer who has represented one of the clients for a long period or in multiple matters might have difficulty being impartial between that client and one to whom the lawyer has only recently been introduced.

[30] A particularly important factor in determining the appropriateness of common representation is the effect on client-lawyer confidentiality and the attorney-client privilege. With regard to the attorney-client privilege, the prevailing rule is that, as between commonly represented clients, the privilege does not attach. It must therefore be assumed that if litigation eventuates between the clients, the privilege will not protect any such communications, and the clients should be so advised.

[31] As to the duty of confidentiality, continued common representation will almost certainly be inadequate if one client asks the lawyer not to disclose to the other client information relevant to the common representation. This is so because the lawyer has an equal duty of loyalty to each client, and each client has the right to be informed of anything bearing on the representation that might affect that client's interests and the right to expect that the lawyer will use that information to that client's benefit. *See* Rule 1.4. At the outset of the common representation and as part of the process of obtaining each client's informed consent, the lawyer should advise each client that information will be shared and that the lawyer will have to withdraw if one client decides that some matter material to the representation should be kept from the other. In limited circumstances, it may be appropriate for the lawyer to proceed with the representation when the clients have agreed, after being properly informed, that the lawyer will keep certain information confidential even as among the commonly represented clients. For example, the lawyer may reasonably conclude that failure to disclose one client's trade secrets to another client will not adversely affect representation involving a joint venture between the two clients and agree to keep that information confidential with the informed consent of both clients.

[32] When seeking to establish or adjust a relationship between clients, the lawyer should make clear that the lawyer's role is not that of partisanship normally expected in other circumstances and, thus, that the clients may be required to assume greater responsibility for decisions than when each client is separately represented. Any limitation on the scope of the representation made necessary as a result of the common representation should be fully explained to the clients at the outset of the representation. *See* Rule 1.2(c).

[33] Subject to the above limitations, each client in the common representation has the right to loyal and diligent representation and the protection of Rule 1.9 concerning the obligations to a former client. The client also has the right to discharge the lawyer as stated in Rule 1.16.

Organizational Clients

[34] A lawyer who represents a corporation or other organization does not, simply by virtue of that representation, necessarily represent any constituent or affiliated organization, such as a parent or subsidiary. *See* Rule 1.13(a). Although a desire to preserve good relationships with clients may strongly suggest that the lawyer should always seek informed consent of the client organization before undertaking any representation that is adverse to its affiliates, Rule 1.7 does not require the lawyer to obtain such consent unless: (i) the lawyer has an understanding with the

organizational client that the lawyer will avoid representation adverse to the client's affiliates, (ii) the lawyer's obligations to either the organizational client or the new client are likely to adversely affect the lawyer's exercise of professional judgment on behalf of the other client, or (iii) the circumstances are such that the affiliate should also be considered a client of the lawyer. Whether the affiliate should be considered a client will depend on the nature of the lawyer's relationship with the affiliate or on the nature of the relationship between the client and its affiliate. For example, the lawyer's work for the client organization may be intended to benefit its affiliates. The overlap or identity of the officers and boards of directors, and the client's overall mode of doing business, may be so extensive that the entities would be viewed as "alter egos." Under such circumstances, the lawyer may conclude that the affiliate is the lawyer's client despite the lack of any formal agreement to represent the affiliate.

[34A] Whether the affiliate should be considered a client of the lawyer may also depend on: (i) whether the affiliate has imparted confidential information to the lawyer in furtherance of the representation, (ii) whether the affiliated entities share a legal department and general counsel, and (iii) other factors relating to the legitimate expectations of the client as to whether the lawyer also represents the affiliate. Where the entities are related only through stock ownership, the ownership is less than a controlling interest, and the lawyer has had no significant dealings with the affiliate or access to its confidences, the lawyer may reasonably conclude that the affiliate is not the lawyer's client.

[34B] Finally, before accepting a representation adverse to an affiliate of a corporate client, a lawyer should consider whether the extent of the possible adverse economic impact of the representation on the entire corporate family might be of such a magnitude that it would materially limit the lawyer's ability to represent the client opposing the affiliate. In those circumstances, Rule 1.7 will ordinarily require the lawyer to decline representation adverse to a member of the same corporate family, absent the informed consent of the client opposing the affiliate of the lawyer's corporate client.

Lawyer as Corporate Director

[35] A lawyer for a corporation or other organization who is also a member of its board of directors should determine whether the responsibilities of the two roles may conflict. The lawyer may be called on to advise the corporation in matters involving actions of the directors. Consideration should be given to the frequency with which such situations may arise, the potential intensity of the conflict, the effect of the lawyer's resignation from the board, and the possibility of the corporation's obtaining legal advice from another lawyer in such situations. If there is material risk that the dual role will compromise the lawyer's professional judgment, the lawyer should not serve as a director or should cease to act as the corporation's lawyer when conflicts of interest arise. The lawyer should advise the other members of the board that, in some circumstances, matters discussed at board meetings while the lawyer is present in the capacity of director might not be protected by the attorney-client privilege and that conflict of interest considerations might require the lawyer's recusal as a director or might require the lawyer and the lawyer's firm to decline representation of the corporation in a matter.

1016

Rule 1.8   Current Clients: Specific Conflict of Interest Rules

(a) A lawyer shall not enter into a business transaction with a client if they have differing interests therein and if the client expects the lawyer to exercise professional judgment therein for the protection of the client, unless:

(1) the transaction is fair and reasonable to the client and the terms of the transaction are fully disclosed and transmitted in writing in a manner that can be reasonably understood by the client;

(2) the client is advised in writing of the desirability of seeking, and is given a reasonable opportunity to seek, the advice of independent legal counsel on the transaction; and

(3) the client gives informed consent, in a writing signed by the client, to the essential terms of the transaction and the lawyer's role in the transaction, including whether the lawyer is representing the client in the transaction.

(b) A lawyer shall not use information relating to representation of a client to the disadvantage of the client unless the client gives informed consent, except as permitted or required by these Rules.

(c) A lawyer shall not:

(1) solicit any gift from a client, including a testamentary gift, for the benefit of the lawyer or a person related to the lawyer; or

(2) prepare on behalf of a client an instrument giving the lawyer or a person related to the lawyer any gift, unless the lawyer or other recipient of the gift is related to the client and a reasonable lawyer would conclude that the transaction is fair and reasonable.

For purposes of this paragraph, related persons include a spouse, child, grandchild, parent, grandparent or other relative, or individual with whom the lawyer or the client maintains a close, familial relationship.

(d) Prior to conclusion of all aspects of the matter giving rise to the representation or proposed representation of the client or prospective client, a lawyer shall not negotiate or enter into any arrangement or understanding with:

(1) a client or a prospective client by which the lawyer acquires an interest in literary or media rights with respect to the subject matter of the representation or proposed representation; or

(2) any person by which the lawyer transfers or assigns any interest in literary or media rights with respect to the subject matter of the representation of a client or prospective client.

(e) While representing a client in connection with contemplated or pending litigation, a lawyer shall not advance or guarantee financial assistance to the client, except that:

(1) a lawyer may advance court costs and expenses of litigation, the repayment of which may be contingent on the outcome of the matter;

(2) a lawyer representing an indigent or pro bono client may pay court costs and expenses of litigation on behalf of the client; and

(3) a lawyer, in an action in which an attorney's fee is payable in whole or in part as a percentage of the recovery in the action, may pay on the lawyer's own account court costs and expenses of litigation. In such case, the fee paid to the lawyer from the proceeds of the action may include an amount equal to such costs and expenses incurred.

(f) A lawyer shall not accept compensation for representing a client, or anything of value related to the lawyer's representation of the client, from one other than the client unless:

(1) the client gives informed consent;

(2) there is no interference with the lawyer's independent professional judgment or with the client-lawyer relationship; and

(3) the client's confidential information is protected as required by Rule 1.6.

(g) A lawyer who represents two or more clients shall not participate in making an aggregate settlement of the claims of or against the clients, absent court approval, unless each client gives informed consent in a writing signed by the client. The lawyer's disclosure shall include the existence and nature of all the claims involved and of the participation of each person in the settlement.

(h) A lawyer shall not:

(1) make an agreement prospectively limiting the lawyer's liability to a client for malpractice; or

(2) settle a claim or potential claim for such liability with an unrepresented client or former client unless that person is advised in writing of the desirability of seeking, and is given a reasonable opportunity to seek, the advice of independent legal counsel in connection therewith.

(i) A lawyer shall not acquire a proprietary interest in the cause of action or subject matter of litigation the lawyer is conducting for a client, except that the lawyer may:

(1) acquire a lien authorized by law to secure the lawyer's fee or expenses; and

(2) contract with a client for a reasonable contingent fee in a civil matter subject to Rule 1.5(d) or other law or court rule.

(j)(1) A lawyer shall not:

(i) as a condition of entering into or continuing any professional representation by the lawyer or the lawyer's firm, require or demand sexual relations with any person;

(ii) employ coercion, intimidation or undue influence in entering into sexual relations incident to any professional representation by the lawyer or the lawyer's firm; or

(iii) in domestic relations matters, enter into sexual relations with a client during the course of the lawyer's representation of the client.

(2) Rule 1.8(j)(1) shall not apply to sexual relations between lawyers and their spouses or to ongoing consensual sexual relationships that predate the initiation of the client-lawyer relationship.

(k) Where a lawyer in a firm has sexual relations with a client but does not participate in the representation of that client, the lawyers in the firm shall not be subject to discipline under this Rule solely because of the occurrence of such sexual relations.

COMMENT

Business Transactions Between Client and Lawyer

[1] A lawyer's legal skill and training, together with the relationship of trust and confidence between lawyer and client, create the possibility of overreaching when the lawyer participates in a business, property or financial transaction with a client, for example, a loan or sales transaction or a lawyer's investment on behalf of a client. For these reasons business transactions between a lawyer and client are not advisable. If a lawyer nevertheless elects to enter into a business transaction with a current client, the requirements of paragraph (a) must be met if the client and lawyer have differing interests in the transaction and the client expects the lawyer to exercise professional judgment therein for the benefit of the client. This will ordinarily be the case even when the transaction is not related to the subject matter of the representation, as when a lawyer drafting a will for a client learns that the client needs money for unrelated expenses and offers to make a loan to the client. The Rule applies to lawyers engaged in the sale of goods or services related to the practice of law, such as the sale of title insurance or investment services to existing clients of the lawyer's legal practice. *See* Rule 5.7. It also applies to lawyers purchasing property from estates they represent.

[2] Paragraphs (a)(1), (a)(2) and (a)(3) set out the conditions that a lawyer must satisfy under this Rule. Paragraph (a)(1) requires that the transaction itself be fair to the client and that its essential terms be communicated in writing to the client in a manner that can be reasonably understood. Paragraph (a)(2) requires that the client also be advised in writing of the desirability of seeking the advice of independent legal counsel. It also requires that the client be given a reasonable opportunity to obtain such advice. Paragraph (a)(3) requires that the lawyer obtain the client's informed consent, in a writing signed by the client, both to the essential terms of the transaction and to the lawyer's role. When necessary, the lawyer should discuss both the material risks of the proposed transaction, including any risk presented by the lawyer's involvement and the existence of reasonably available alternatives, and should explain why the advice of independent legal counsel is desirable. *See* Rule 1.0(j) for the definition of "informed consent."

[3] The risk to a client is greatest when the client expects the lawyer to represent the client in the transaction itself or when the lawyer's financial interest otherwise poses a significant risk that the lawyer's representation of the client will be materially adversely affected by the lawyer's financial interest in the transaction. Here the lawyer's role requires that the lawyer must comply, not only with the requirements of paragraph (a), but also with the requirements of Rule 1.7. Under that Rule, the lawyer must disclose the risks associated with the lawyer's dual role as both legal adviser and participant in the transaction, such as the risk that the lawyer will structure the transaction or give legal advice in a way that favors the

lawyer's interests at the client's expense. Moreover, the lawyer must obtain the client's informed consent. In some cases, the lawyer's interest may be such that Rule 1.7 will preclude the lawyer from seeking the client's consent to the transaction. A lawyer has a continuing duty to monitor the inherent conflicts of interest that arise out of the lawyer's business transaction with a client or because the lawyer has an ownership interest in property in which the client also has an interest. A lawyer is also required to make such additional disclosures to the client as are necessary to obtain the client's informed consent to the continuation of the representation.

[3A] The self-interest of a lawyer resulting from a business transaction with a client may interfere with the lawyer's exercise of independent judgment on behalf of the client. If such interference will occur should a lawyer agree to represent a prospective client, the lawyer should decline the proffered employment. After accepting employment, a lawyer should not acquire property rights that would adversely affect the lawyer's professional judgment in representing the client. Even if the property interests of a lawyer do not presently interfere with the exercise of independent judgment, but the likelihood of interference can be reasonably foreseen by the lawyer, the lawyer should explain the situation to the client and should decline employment or withdraw unless the client gives informed consent to the continued representation, confirmed in writing. A lawyer should not seek to persuade a client to permit the lawyer to invest in an undertaking of the client nor make improper use of a professional relationship to influence the client to invest in an enterprise in which the lawyer is interested.

[4] If the client is independently represented in the transaction, paragraph (a)(2) is inapplicable, and the requirement of full disclosure in paragraph (a)(1) is satisfied by a written disclosure by either the lawyer involved in the transaction or the client's independent counsel. The fact that the client was independently represented in the transaction is relevant in determining whether the agreement was fair and reasonable to the client, as paragraph (a)(1) further requires.

[4A] Rule 1.8(a) does not apply to business transactions with former clients, but the line between current and former clients is not always clear. A lawyer entering into a business transaction with a former client may not use information relating to the representation to the disadvantage of the former client unless the information has become generally known. *See* Rule 1.9(c).

[4B] The Rule does not apply to standard commercial transactions between the lawyer and the client for products or services that the client generally markets to others, for example, banking or brokerage services, medical services, products manufactured or distributed by the client, and utilities services. In such transactions, the lawyer has no advantage in dealing with the client, and the restrictions in paragraph (a) are unnecessary and impracticable.

[4C] This Rule also does not apply to ordinary fee arrangements between client and lawyer reached at the inception of the client-lawyer relationship, which are governed by Rule 1.5. The requirements of the Rule ordinarily must be met, however, when the lawyer accepts an interest in the client's business or other non-monetary property as payment of all or part of the lawyer's fee. For example, the requirements of paragraph (a) must ordinarily be met if a lawyer agrees to take stock (or stock options) in the client in lieu of cash fees. Such an exchange creates a risk that the lawyer's judgment will be skewed in favor of closing a transaction to such an extent that the lawyer may fail to exercise professional judgment as to whether it is in the client's best interest for the transaction to close. This may occur where the client expects the lawyer to provide professional advice in structuring a securities-for-services exchange. If the lawyer is expected to play any role in advising the client regarding the securities-for-services exchange, especially if the client lacks sophistication, the requirements of fairness, full disclosure and written consent set forth in paragraph (a) must be met. When a lawyer represents a client in a transaction concerning literary property, Rule 1.8(d) does not prohibit the lawyer from agreeing that the lawyer's fee shall consist of a share of the ownership of the literary property or a share of the royalties or license fees from the property, but the lawyer must ordinarily comply with Rule 1.8(a).

[4D] An exchange of securities for legal services will also trigger the requirements of Rule 1.7 if the lawyer's ownership interest in the client would, or reasonably may, affect the lawyer's exercise of professional judgment on behalf of the client. For example, where a lawyer has agreed to accept securities in a client corporation as a fee for negotiating and documenting an equity investment, or for representing a client in connection with an initial public offering, there is a risk that the lawyer's judgment will be skewed in favor of closing the transaction to such an extent that that the lawyer may fail to exercise professional judgment. (The lawyer's judgment may be skewed because unless the transaction closes, the securities will be worthless.) Unless a lawyer reasonably concludes that he or she will be able to provide competent, diligent and loyal representation to the client, the lawyer may not undertake or continue the representation, even with the client's consent. To determine whether a reasonable possibility of such an adverse effect on the representation exists, the lawyer should analyze the nature and relationship of the particular interest and the specific legal services to be rendered. Some salient factors may be (i) the size of the lawyer's investment in proportion to the holdings of other investors, (ii) the potential value of the investment in relation to the lawyer's or law firm's earnings or other assets, and (iii) whether the investment is active or passive.

[4E] If the lawyer reasonably concludes that the lawyer's representation of the client will not be adversely affected by the agreement to accept client securities as a legal fee, the Rules permit the representation, but only if full disclosure is made to the client and the client's informed consent is obtained and confirmed in writing. See Rules 1.0(e) (defining "confirmed in writing"), 1.0(j) (defining "informed consent"), and 1.7.

[4F] A lawyer must also consider whether accepting securities in a client as payment for legal services constitutes charging or collecting an unreasonable or excessive fee in violation of Rule 1.5. Determining whether a fee accepted in the form of securities is unreasonable or excessive requires a determination of the value of the securities at the time the agreement is reached and may require the lawyer to engage the services of an investment professional to appraise the value of the securities to be given. The lawyer and client can then make their own advised decisions as to whether the securities-for-fees exchange results in a reasonable fee.

[5] A lawyer's use of information relating to the representation to the disadvantage of the client violates the lawyer's duty of loyalty. Paragraph (b) applies when the information is used to benefit either the lawyer or a third person, such as another client or a business associate of the lawyer, at the expense of a client. For example, if a lawyer learns that a client intends to purchase and develop several parcels of land, the lawyer may not use that information to purchase one of the parcels in competition with the client or to recommend that another client make such a purchase. But

the rule does not prohibit uses that do not disadvantage the client. For example, a lawyer who learns a government agency's interpretation of trade legislation during the representation of one client may properly use that information to benefit other clients. Paragraph (b) prohibits use of client information to the disadvantage of the client unless the client gives informed consent, except as permitted or required by these Rules. Rules that permit or require use of client information to the disadvantage of the client include Rules 1.6, 1.9(c), and 3.3.

Gifts to Lawyers

[6] A lawyer may accept a gift from a client if the transaction meets general standards of fairness. If a client offers the lawyer a gift, paragraph (c) does not prohibit the lawyer from accepting it, although such a gift may be voidable by the client. Before accepting a gift offered by a client, a lawyer should urge the client to secure disinterested advice from an independent, competent person who is cognizant of all of the circumstances. In any event, due to concerns about overreaching and imposition on clients, a lawyer may not suggest that a gift be made to the lawyer or for the lawyer's benefit.

[6A] This Rule does not apply to success fees, bonuses and the like from clients for legal services. These are governed by Rule 1.5.

[7] If effectuation of a gift requires preparing a legal instrument such as a will or conveyance, the client should have the detached advice that another lawyer can provide. The sole exception to this Rule is where the client is related to the donee and a reasonable lawyer would conclude that the transaction is fair and reasonable, as set forth in paragraph (c).

[8] This Rule does not prohibit a lawyer or a partner or associate of the lawyer from being named as executor of the client's estate or named to another fiduciary position. Nevertheless, such appointments will be subject to the general conflict of interest provision in Rule 1.7 when there is a significant risk that the lawyer's interest in obtaining the appointment will adversely affect the lawyer's professional judgment in advising the client concerning the choice of an executor or other fiduciary. In obtaining the client's informed consent to the conflict, the lawyer should advise the client concerning the nature and extent of the lawyer's financial interest in the appointment, as well as the availability of alternative candidates for the position.

Literary or Media Rights

[9] An agreement by which a lawyer acquires literary or media rights concerning the subject matter of the representation creates a conflict between the interest of the client and the personal interests of the lawyer. The lawyer may be tempted to subordinate the interests of the client to the lawyer's own anticipated pecuniary gain. For example, a lawyer in a criminal case who obtains from the client television, radio, motion picture, newspaper, magazine, book, or other literary or media rights with respect to the case may be influenced, consciously or unconsciously, to a course of conduct that will enhance the value of the literary or media rights to the prejudice of the client. To prevent this adverse impact on the representation,

such arrangements should be scrupulously avoided prior to the termination of all aspects of the matter giving rise to the representation, even though the representation has previously ended. Likewise, arrangements with third parties, such as book, newspaper or magazine publishers or television, radio or motion picture producers, pursuant to which the lawyer conveys whatever literary or media rights the lawyer may have, should not be entered into prior to the conclusion of all aspects of the matter giving rise to the representation.

[9A] Rule 1.8(d) does not prohibit a lawyer representing a client in a transaction concerning intellectual property from agreeing that the lawyer's fee shall consist of an ownership share in the property, if the arrangement conforms to paragraph (a) and Rule 1.5.

Financial Assistance

[9B] Paragraph (e) eliminates the former requirement that the client remain "ultimately liable" to repay any costs and expenses of litigation that were advanced by the lawyer regardless of whether the client obtained a recovery. Accordingly, a lawyer may make repayment from the client contingent on the outcome of the litigation, and may forgo repayment if the client obtains no recovery or a recovery less than the amount of the advanced costs and expenses. A lawyer may also, in an action in which the lawyer's fee is payable in whole or in part as a percentage of the recovery, pay court costs and litigation expenses on the lawyer's own account. However, like the former New York rule, paragraph (e) limits permitted financial assistance to court costs directly related to litigation. Examples of permitted expenses include filing fees, expenses of investigation, medical diagnostic work connected with the matter under litigation and treatment necessary for the diagnosis, and the costs of obtaining and presenting evidence. Permitted expenses do not include living or medical expenses other than those listed above.

[10] Lawyers may not subsidize lawsuits or administrative proceedings brought on behalf of their clients, including making or guaranteeing loans to their clients for living expenses, because to do so would encourage clients to pursue lawsuits that might not otherwise be brought and because such assistance gives lawyers too great a financial stake in the litigation. These dangers do not warrant a prohibition against a lawyer lending a client money for court costs and litigation expenses, including the expenses of medical examination and testing and the costs of obtaining and presenting evidence, because these advances are virtually indistinguishable from contingent fee agreements and help ensure access to the courts. Similarly, an exception is warranted permitting lawyers representing indigent or pro bono clients to pay court costs and litigation expenses whether or not these funds will be repaid.

Person Paying for a Lawyer's Services

[11] Lawyers are frequently asked to represent clients under circumstances in which a third person will compensate them, in whole or in part. The third person might be a relative or friend, an indemnitor (such as a liability insurance company)

or a co-client (such as a corporation sued along with one or more of its employees). Third-party payers frequently have interests that may differ from those of the client. A lawyer is therefore prohibited from accepting or continuing such a representation unless the lawyer determines that there will be no interference with the lawyer's professional judgment and there is informed consent from the client. *See also* Rule 5.4(c), prohibiting interference with a lawyer's professional judgment by one who recommends, employs or pays the lawyer to render legal services for another.

[12] Sometimes it will be sufficient for the lawyer to obtain the client's informed consent regarding the fact of the payment and the identity of the third-party payer. If, however, the fee arrangement creates a conflict of interest for the lawyer, then the lawyer must comply with Rule 1.7. The lawyer must also conform to the requirements of Rule 1.6 concerning confidentiality. Under Rule 1.7(a), a conflict of interest may exist if the lawyer will be involved in representing differing interests or if there is a significant risk that the lawyer's professional judgment on behalf of the client will be adversely affected by the lawyer's own interest in the fee arrangement or by the lawyer's responsibilities to the third-party payer (for example, when the third-party payer is a co-client). Under Rule 1.7(b), the lawyer may accept or continue the representation with the informed consent of each affected client, unless the conflict is nonconsentable under that paragraph. Under Rule 1.7(b), the informed consent must be confirmed in writing. See Rules 1.0(e) (definition of "confirmed in writing"), 1.0(j) (definition of "informed consent"), and 1.0(x) (definition of "writing" or "written").

Aggregate Settlements

[13] Differences in willingness to make or accept an offer of settlement are among the risks of common representation of multiple clients by a single lawyer. Under Rule 1.7, this is one of the risks that should be discussed before undertaking the representation, as part of the process of obtaining the clients' informed consents. In addition, Rule 1.2(a) protects each client's right to have the final say in deciding whether to accept or reject an offer of settlement. Paragraph (g) is a corollary of both these Rules and provides that, before any settlement offer is made or accepted on behalf of multiple clients, the lawyer must inform each of them about all the material terms of the settlement, including what the other clients will receive or pay if the settlement is accepted. *See also* Rule 1.0(j) (definition of "informed consent"). Lawyers representing a class of plaintiffs or defendants, or those proceeding derivatively, may not have a full client-lawyer relationship with each member of the class; nevertheless, such lawyers must comply with applicable rules regulating notification of class members and other procedural requirements designed to ensure adequate protection of the entire class.

Limiting Liability and Settling Malpractice Claims

[14] Agreements prospectively limiting a lawyer's liability for malpractice are prohibited because they are likely to undermine competent and diligent representation. Also, many clients are unable to evaluate the desirability of making such an agreement before a dispute has arisen, particularly if they are currently represented

by the lawyer seeking the agreement. This paragraph does not, however, prohibit a lawyer from entering into an agreement with the client to arbitrate legal malpractice claims, provided such agreements are enforceable and the client is fully informed of the scope and effect of the agreement. Nor does this paragraph limit the ability of lawyers to practice in the form of a limited-liability entity, where permitted by law, provided that each lawyer remains personally liable to the client for the lawyer's own conduct and the firm complies with any conditions required by law, such as provisions requiring client notification or maintenance of adequate liability insurance. Nor does it prohibit an agreement in accordance with Rule 1.2 that defines the scope of the representation, although a definition of scope that makes the obligations of representation illusory will amount to an attempt to limit liability.

[15] Agreements settling a claim or a potential claim for malpractice are not prohibited by this Rule. Nevertheless, in view of the danger that a lawyer will take unfair advantage of an unrepresented client or former client, the lawyer must first advise such a person in writing of the appropriateness of independent representation in connection with such a settlement. In addition, the lawyer must give the client or former client a reasonable opportunity to find and consult independent counsel.

Acquiring Proprietary Interest in Litigation

[16] Paragraph (i) states the traditional general rule that lawyers are prohibited from acquiring a proprietary interest in litigation. Like paragraph (e), the general rule has its basis in common law champerty and maintenance and is designed to avoid giving the lawyer too great an interest in the representation. In addition, when the lawyer acquires an ownership interest in the subject of the representation, it will be more difficult for a client to discharge the lawyer if the client so desires. The rule is subject to specific exceptions developed in decisional law and continued in these Rules. The exception for certain advances of the costs of litigation is set forth in paragraph (e). In addition, paragraph (i) sets forth exceptions for liens authorized by law to secure the lawyer's fees or expenses and contracts for reasonable contingent fees. These may include liens granted by statute, liens originating in common law and liens acquired by contract with the client. When a lawyer acquires by contract a security interest in property other than that recovered through the lawyer's efforts in the litigation, such an acquisition is a business or financial transaction with a client and is governed by the requirements of paragraph (a). Contracts for contingent fees in civil matters are governed by Rule 1.5.

Client-Lawyer Sexual Relationships

[17] The relationship between lawyer and client is a fiduciary one in which the lawyer occupies the highest position of trust and confidence. The relationship is often unequal; thus, a sexual relationship between lawyer and client can involve unfair exploitation of the lawyer's fiduciary role, in violation of the lawyer's basic ethical obligation not to use the trust of the client to the client's disadvantage. In addition, such a relationship presents a significant danger that if the sexual relationship leads to the lawyer's emotional involvement, the lawyer will be unable to

represent the client without impairing the lawyer's exercise of professional judgment. Moreover, a blurred line between the professional and personal relationships may make it difficult to predict the extent to which client confidences will be protected by the attorney-client evidentiary privilege. A client's sexual involvement with the client's lawyer, especially if the sexual relations create emotional involvement, will often render it unlikely that the client could rationally determine whether to consent to the conflict created by the sexual relations. If a client were to consent to the conflict created by the sexual relations without fully appreciating the nature and implications of that conflict, there is a significant risk of harm to client interests. Therefore, sexual relations between lawyers and their clients are dangerous and inadvisable. Out of respect for the desires of consenting adults, however, paragraph (j) does not flatly prohibit client-lawyer sexual relations in matters other than domestic relations matters. Even when sexual relations between a lawyer and client are permitted under paragraph (j), however, they may lead to incompetent representation in violation of Rule 1.1. Because domestic relations clients are often emotionally vulnerable, domestic relations matters entail a heightened risk of exploitation of the client. Accordingly, lawyers are flatly prohibited from entering into sexual relations with domestic relations clients during the course of the representation even if the sexual relationship is consensual and even if prejudice to the client is not immediately apparent. For a definition of "sexual relations" for the purposes of this Rule, see Rule 1.0(u).

[17A] The prohibitions in paragraph (j)(1) apply to all lawyers in a firm who know of the representation, whether or not they are personally representing the client. The Rule prohibits any lawyer in the firm from exploiting the client-lawyer relationship by directly or indirectly requiring or demanding sexual relations as a condition of representation by the lawyer or the lawyer's firm. Paragraph (j)(1)(i) thus seeks to prevent a situation where a client may fear that a willingness or unwillingness to have sexual relations with a lawyer in the firm may have an impact on the representation, or even on the firm's willingness to represent or continue representing the client. The Rule also prohibits the use of coercion, undue influence or intimidation to obtain sexual relations with a person known to that lawyer to be a client or a prospective client of the firm. Paragraph (j)(1)(ii) thus seeks to prevent a lawyer from exploiting the professional relationship between the client and the lawyer's firm. Even if a lawyer does not know that the firm represents a person, the lawyer's use of coercion or intimidation to obtain sexual relations with that person might well violate other Rules or substantive law. Where the representation of the client involves a domestic relations matter, the restrictions stated in paragraphs (j)(1)(i) and (j)(1)(ii), and not the per se prohibition imposed by paragraph (j)(1)(iii), apply to lawyers in a firm who know of the representation but who are not personally representing the client. Nevertheless, because domestic relations matters may be volatile and may entail a heightened risk of exploitation of the client, the risk that a sexual relationship with a client of the firm may result in a violation of other Rules is likewise heightened, even if the sexual relations are not per se prohibited by paragraph (j).

[17B] A law firm's failure to educate lawyers about the restrictions on sexual relations—or a firm's failure to enforce those restrictions against lawyers who violate them—may constitute a violation of Rule 5.1, which obligates a law firm to make reasonable efforts to ensure that all lawyers in the firm conform to these Rules.

[18] Sexual relationships between spouses or those that predate the client-lawyer relationship are not prohibited. Issues relating to the exploitation of the fiduciary relationship and client dependency are diminished when the sexual relationship existed prior to the commencement of the client-lawyer relationship. However, before proceeding with the representation in these circumstances, the lawyer should consider whether the lawyer's ability to represent the client will be materially limited by the sexual relationship and therefore constitute an impermissible conflict of interest. *See* Rule 1.7(a)(2).

[19] When the client is an organization, paragraph (j) applies to sexual relations between a lawyer for the organization (whether inside counsel or outside counsel) and a constituent of the organization who supervises, directs or regularly consults with that lawyer or a lawyer in that lawyer's firm concerning the organization's legal matters.

Imputation of Prohibitions

[20] Where a lawyer who is not personally representing a client has sexual relations with a client of the firm in violation of paragraph (j), the other lawyers in the firm are not subject to discipline solely because those improper sexual relations occurred. There may be circumstances, however, where a violation of paragraph (j) by one lawyer in a firm gives rise to violations of other Rules by the other lawyers in the firm through imputation. For example, sexual relations between a lawyer and a client may give rise to a violation of Rule 1.7(a), and such a conflict under Rule 1.7 may be imputed to all other lawyers in the firm under Rule 1.10(a).

Rule 1.9   Duties to Former Clients

(a) A lawyer who has formerly represented a client in a matter shall not thereafter represent another person in the same or a substantially related matter in which that person's interests are materially adverse to the interests of the former client unless the former client gives informed consent, confirmed in writing.

(b) Unless the former client gives informed consent, confirmed in writing, a lawyer shall not knowingly represent a person in the same or a substantially related matter in which a firm with which the lawyer formerly was associated had previously represented a client:

(1) whose interests are materially adverse to that person; and

(2) about whom the lawyer had acquired information protected by Rules 1.6 or paragraph (c) of this Rule that is material to the matter.

(c) A lawyer who has formerly represented a client in a matter or whose present or former firm has formerly represented a client in a matter shall not thereafter:

(1) use confidential information of the former client protected by Rule 1.6 to the disadvantage of the former client, except as these Rules

would permit or require with respect to a current client or when the information has become generally known; or

(2) reveal confidential information of the former client protected by Rule 1.6 except as these Rules would permit or require with respect to a current client.

COMMENT

[1] After termination of a client-lawyer relationship, a lawyer has certain continuing duties with respect to confidentiality and conflicts of interest and thus may not represent another client except in conformity with these Rules. Under this Rule, for example, a lawyer could not properly seek to rescind on behalf of a new client a contract drafted on behalf of a former client. So also, a lawyer who has prosecuted an accused person could not properly represent that person in a subsequent civil action against the government concerning the same transaction. Nor could a lawyer who has represented multiple clients in a matter represent one of the clients against the others in the same or a substantially related matter after a dispute arose among the clients in that matter, unless all affected clients give informed consent. *See* Comment [9]. Current and former government lawyers must comply with this Rule to the extent required by Rule 1.11.

[2] The scope of a "matter" for purposes of this Rule depends on the facts of a particular situation or transaction. The lawyer's involvement in a matter can also be a question of degree. When a lawyer has been directly involved in a specific transaction, subsequent representation of other clients with materially adverse interests in that transaction clearly is prohibited. On the other hand, a lawyer who recurrently handled a type of problem for a former client is not precluded from later representing another client in a factually distinct problem of that type, even though the subsequent representation involves a position adverse to the prior client. Similar considerations can apply to the reassignment of military lawyers between defense and prosecution functions within the same military jurisdictions. The underlying question is whether the lawyer was so involved in the matter that the subsequent representation can be justly regarded as a changing of sides in the matter in question.

[3] Matters are "substantially related" for purposes of this Rule if they involve the same transaction or legal dispute or if, under the circumstances, a reasonable lawyer would conclude that there is otherwise a substantial risk that confidential factual information that would normally have been obtained in the prior representation would materially advance the client's position in the subsequent matter. For example, a lawyer who has represented a businessperson and learned extensive private financial information about that person may not then represent that person's spouse in seeking a divorce. Similarly, a lawyer who has previously represented a client in securing environmental permits to build a shopping center would be precluded from representing neighbors seeking to oppose rezoning of the property on the basis of environmental considerations; however, the lawyer would not be precluded, on the grounds of substantial relationship, from defending a tenant of the completed shopping center in resisting eviction for nonpayment of rent. Information that has been disclosed to the public or to other parties adverse to the former client ordinarily will not be disqualifying. Information acquired in a

prior representation may have been rendered obsolete by the passage of time, a circumstance that may be relevant in determining whether two representations are substantially related. In the case of an organizational client, general knowledge of the client's policies and practices ordinarily will not preclude a subsequent representation. On the other hand, knowledge of specific facts gained in a prior representation that are relevant to the matter in question ordinarily will preclude such a representation. A former client is not required to reveal the confidential information learned by the lawyer in order to establish a substantial risk that the lawyer has confidential information to use in the subsequent matter. A conclusion about the possession of such information may be based on the nature of the services the lawyer provided the former client and information that would in ordinary practice be learned by a lawyer providing such services.

[4] [Moved to Comment to Rule 1.10.]

[5] [Moved to Comment to Rule 1.10.]

[6] [Moved to Comment to Rule 1.10.]

[7] Independent of the prohibition against subsequent representation, a lawyer changing professional association has a continuing duty to preserve confidentiality of information about a client formerly represented. *See* Rules 1.6, 1.9(c).

[8] Paragraph (c) generally extends the confidentiality protections of Rule 1.6 to a lawyer's former clients. Paragraph (c)(1) provides that information acquired by the lawyer in the course of representing a client may not subsequently be used by the lawyer to the disadvantage of the client. However, the fact that a lawyer has once served a client does not preclude the lawyer from using generally known information about that client when later representing another client. Paragraph (c)(2) provides that a lawyer may not reveal information acquired in the course of representing a client except as these Rules would permit or require with respect to a current client. *See* Rules 1.6, 3.3.

[9] The provisions of this Rule are for the protection of former clients and can be waived if the client gives informed consent, which consent must be confirmed in writing under paragraph (a). *See also* Rule 1.0(j) for the definition of "informed consent." With regard to the effectiveness of an advance waiver, see Rule 1.7, Comments [22]-[22A]. With regard to disqualification of a firm with which a lawyer is or was formerly associated, see Rule 1.10.

Rule 1.10   Imputation of Conflicts of Interest

(a) While lawyers are associated in a firm, none of them shall knowingly represent a client when any one of them practicing alone would be prohibited from doing so by Rule 1.7, 1.8 or 1.9, except as otherwise provided therein.

(b) When a lawyer has terminated an association with a firm, the firm is prohibited from thereafter representing a person with interests that the firm knows or reasonably should know are materially adverse to those of a client represented by the formerly associated lawyer and not currently represented by the firm if the firm or any lawyer remaining in the firm has information protected by Rule 1.6 or Rule 1.9(c) that is material to the matter.

(c) When a lawyer becomes associated with a firm, the firm may not knowingly represent a client in a matter that is the same as or substantially

related to a matter in which the newly associated lawyer, or a firm with which that lawyer was associated, formerly represented a client whose interests are materially adverse to the prospective or current client unless the newly associated lawyer did not acquire any information protected by Rule 1.6 or Rule 1.9(c) that is material to the current matter.

(d) A disqualification prescribed by this Rule may be waived by the affected client or former client under the conditions stated in Rule 1.7.

(e) A law firm shall make a written record of its engagements, at or near the time of each new engagement, and shall implement and maintain a system by which proposed engagements are checked against current and previous engagements when:

(1) the firm agrees to represent a new client;

(2) the firm agrees to represent an existing client in a new matter;

(3) the firm hires or associates with another lawyer; or

(4) an additional party is named or appears in a pending matter.

(f) Substantial failure to keep records or to implement or maintain a conflict-checking system that complies with paragraph (e) shall be a violation thereof regardless of whether there is another violation of these Rules.

(g) Where a violation of paragraph (e) by a law firm is a substantial factor in causing a violation of paragraph (a) by a lawyer, the law firm, as well as the individual lawyer, shall be responsible for the violation of paragraph (a).

(h) A lawyer related to another lawyer as parent, child, sibling or spouse shall not represent in any matter a client whose interests differ from those of another party to the matter who the lawyer knows is represented by the other lawyer unless the client consents to the representation after full disclosure and the lawyer concludes that the lawyer can adequately represent the interests of the client.

COMMENT

Definition of "Firm"

[1] For purposes of these Rules, the term "firm" includes, but is not limited to, (i) a lawyer or lawyers in a law partnership, professional corporation, sole proprietorship or other association authorized to practice law, and (ii) lawyers employed in a legal services organization, a government law office or the legal department of a corporation or other organization. *See* Rule 1.0(h). Whether two or more lawyers constitute a "firm" within this definition will depend on the specific facts. *See* Rule 1.0, Comments [2]-[4].

Principles of Imputed Disqualification

[2] The rule of imputed disqualification stated in paragraph (a) gives effect to the principle of loyalty to the client as it applies to lawyers who practice in a law firm.

Such situations can be considered from the premise that a firm of lawyers is essentially one lawyer for purposes of the rules governing loyalty to the client, or from the premise that each lawyer is vicariously bound by the obligation of loyalty owed by each lawyer with whom the lawyer is associated. Paragraph (a) operates only among the lawyers currently associated in a firm. When a lawyer moves from one firm to another, the situation is governed by paragraphs (b) and (c).

[3] [Reserved]

[4] The rule in paragraph (a) also does not prohibit representation by others in the law firm where the person prohibited from involvement in a matter is a non-lawyer, such as a paralegal or legal secretary. Such persons, however, ordinarily must be screened from any personal participation in the matter to avoid communication to others in the firm of confidential information that both the nonlawyers and the firm have a legal duty to protect. *See* Rules 1.0(t), 5.3.

Lawyers Moving Between Firms

[4A] The principles of imputed disqualification are modified when lawyers have been associated in a firm and then end their association. The nature of contemporary law practice and the organization of law firms have made the fiction that the law firm is the same as a single lawyer unrealistic in certain situations. In crafting a rule to govern imputed conflicts, there are several competing considerations. First, the former client must be reasonably assured that the client's confidentiality interests are not compromised. Second, the principles of imputed disqualification should not be so broadly cast as to preclude others from having reasonable choice of counsel. Third, the principles of imputed disqualification should not unreasonably hamper lawyers from forming new associations and taking on new clients after leaving a firm. In this connection, it should be recognized that today most lawyers practice in firms, that many limit their practice to, or otherwise concentrate in, one area of law, and that many move from one association to another multiple times in their careers. If the principles of imputed disqualification were defined too strictly, the result would be undue curtailment of the opportunity of lawyers to move from one practice setting to another, of the opportunity of clients to choose counsel, and of the opportunity of firms to retain qualified lawyers. For these reasons, a functional analysis that focuses on preserving the former client's reasonable confidentiality interests is appropriate in balancing the competing interests.

[5] Paragraph (b) permits a law firm, under certain circumstances, to represent a client with interests adverse to those of a client represented by a lawyer who formerly was associated with the firm. The Rule applies regardless of when the formerly associated lawyer represented the client. However, under Rule 1.7 the law firm may not represent a client with interests adverse to those of a current client of the firm. Moreover, the firm may not represent the client where the matter is the same or substantially related to a matter in which (i) the formerly associated lawyer represented the client, and (ii) the firm or any lawyer currently in the firm has information protected by Rule 1.6 and Rule 1.9(c) that is material to the matter.

[5A] In addition to information that may be in the possession of one or more of the lawyers remaining in the firm, information in documents or files retained by the firm itself may preclude the firm from opposing the former client in the same or substantially related matter if the information is protected by Rule 1.6 and Rule 1.9(c) and is material to the current matter.

[5B] Rule 1.10(c) permits a law firm to represent a client in a matter that is the same as or substantially related to a matter in which the newly associated lawyer, or the firm with which the lawyer was previously associated, represented a client whose interests are materially adverse to that client, provided the newly associated lawyer did not acquire any confidential information of the previously represented client that is material to the current matter.

Client Consent

[6] Rule 1.10(d) removes imputation with the informed consent of the affected client or former client under the conditions stated in Rule 1.7. The conditions stated in Rule 1.7 require the lawyer to determine that the representation is not prohibited by Rule 1.7(b) and that each affected client or former client has given informed consent to the representation, confirmed in writing. In some cases, the risk may be so severe that the conflict cannot be cured by client consent. For a discussion of the effectiveness of client waivers of conflicts that might arise in the future, see Rule 1.7, Comments [22]-[22A]. For a definition of "informed consent," see Rule 1.0(j).

Former Government Lawyers

[7] Where a lawyer has joined a private firm after having represented the government, imputation is governed by Rule 1.11(b), not this Rule.

Relationship Between This Rule and Rule 1.8(k)

[8] Where a lawyer is prohibited from engaging in certain transactions under Rule 1.8(a) through (i), this Rule imputes that prohibition to other lawyers associated in a firm with the personally prohibited lawyer. Under Rule 1.8(k), however, where a lawyer in a firm has sexual relations with a client but does not participate in the representation of that client, the other lawyers in the firm are not subject to discipline under Rule 1.8 solely because such sexual relations occur.

Conflict-Checking Procedures

[9] Under paragraph (e), every law firm, no matter how large or small (including sole practitioners), is responsible for creating, implementing and maintaining a system to check proposed engagements against current and previous engagements and against new parties in pending matters. The system must be adequate to detect conflicts that will or reasonably may arise if: (i) the firm agrees to represent a new client, (ii) the firm agrees to represent an existing client in a new matter, (iii) the firm hires or associates with another lawyer, or (iv) an additional party is named or

appears in a pending matter. The system will thus render effective assistance to lawyers in the firm in avoiding conflicts of interest. *See also* Rule 5.1.

[9A] Failure to create, implement and maintain a conflict-checking system adequate for this purpose is a violation of this Rule by the firm. In cases in which a lawyer, despite reasonably diligent efforts to do so, could not acquire the information that would have revealed a conflict because of the firm's failure to maintain an adequate conflict-checking system, the firm shall be responsible for the violation. However, a lawyer who knows or should know of a conflict in a matter that the lawyer is handling remains individually responsible for the violation of these Rules, whether or not the firm's conflict-checking system has identified the conflict. In cases in which a violation of paragraph (e) by the firm is a substantial factor in causing a violation of these Rules by a lawyer, the firm, as well as the individual lawyer, is responsible for the violation. As to whether a client-lawyer relationship exists or is continuing, see Scope [9]-[10]; Rule 1.3, Comment [4].

[9B] The records required to be maintained under paragraph (e) must be in written form. *See* Rule 1.0(x) for the definition of "written," which includes tangible or electronic records. To be effective, a conflict-checking system may also need to supplement written information with recourse to the memory of the firm's lawyers through in-person, telephonic, or electronic communications. An effective conflict-checking system as required by this Rule may not, however, depend solely on recourse to lawyers' memories or other such informal sources of information.

[9C] The nature of the records needed to render effective assistance to lawyers will vary depending on the size, structure, history, and nature of the firm's practice. At a minimum, however, a firm must record information that will enable the firm to identify (i) each client that the firm represents, (ii) each party in a litigated, transactional or other matter whose interests are materially adverse to the firm's clients, and (iii) the general nature of each matter.

[9D] To the extent that the records made and maintained for the purpose of complying with this Rule contain confidential information, a firm must exercise reasonable care to protect the confidentiality of these records. *See* Rule 1.6(c).

[9E] The nature of a firm's conflict-checking system may vary depending on a number of factors, including the size and structure of the firm, the nature of the firm's practice, the number and location of the firm offices, and the relationship among the firm's separate offices. In all cases, however, an effective conflict-checking system should record and maintain information in a way that permits the information to be checked systematically and accurately when the firm is considering a proposed engagement. A small firm or a firm with a small number of engagements may be able to create and maintain an effective conflict-checking system through the use of hard-copy rather than electronic records. But larger firms, or firms with a large number of engagements, may need to create and maintain records in electronic form so that the information can be accessed quickly and efficiently.

Organizational Clients

[9F] Representation of corporate or other organizational clients makes it prudent for a firm to maintain additional information in its conflict-checking system. For example, absent an agreement with the client to the contrary, a conflict may arise when a firm desires to oppose an entity that is part of a current or former client's corporate family (*e.g.*, an affiliate, subsidiary, parent or sister organization). *See* Rule 1.7, Comments [34]-[34B]. Although a law firm is not required to maintain records showing every corporate affiliate of every corporate client, if a law firm frequently represents corporations that belong to large corporate families, the law firm should make reasonable efforts to institute and maintain a system for alerting the firm to potential conflicts with the members of the corporate client's family.

[9G] Under certain circumstances, a law firm may also need to include information about the constituents of a corporate client. Although Rule 1.13 provides that a firm is the lawyer for the entity and not for any of its constituents, confusion may arise when a law firm represents small or closely held corporations with few shareholders, or when a firm represents both the corporation and individual officers or employees but bills the corporate client for the legal services. In other situations, a client-lawyer relationship may develop unintentionally between the law firm and one or more individual constituents of the entity. Accordingly, a firm that represents corporate clients may need a system for determining whether or not the law firm has a client-lawyer relationship with individual constituents of an organizational client. If so, the law firm should add the names of those constituents to the database of its conflict-checking system.

Rule 1.11   Special Conflicts of Interest for Former and Current Government Officers and Employees

(a) Except as law may otherwise expressly provide, a lawyer who has formerly served as a public officer or employee of the government:

(1) shall comply with Rule 1.9(c); and

(2) shall not represent a client in connection with a matter in which the lawyer participated personally and substantially as a public officer or employee, unless the appropriate government agency gives its informed consent, confirmed in writing, to the representation. This provision shall not apply to matters governed by Rule 1.12(a).

(b) When a lawyer is disqualified from representation under paragraph (a), no lawyer in a firm with which that lawyer is associated may knowingly undertake or continue representation in such a matter unless:

(1) the firm acts promptly and reasonably to:

(i) notify, as appropriate, lawyers and nonlawyer personnel within the firm that the personally disqualified lawyer is prohibited from participating in the representation of the current client;

(ii) implement effective screening procedures to prevent the flow of information about the matter between the personally disqualified lawyer and the others in the firm;

(iii) ensure that the disqualified lawyer is apportioned no part of the fee therefrom; and

(iv) give written notice to the appropriate government agency to enable it to ascertain compliance with the provisions of this Rule; and

(2) there are no other circumstances in the particular representation that create an appearance of impropriety.

(c) Except as law may otherwise expressly provide, a lawyer having information that the lawyer knows is confidential government information about a person, acquired when the lawyer was a public officer or employee, may not represent a private client whose interests are adverse to that person in a matter in which the information could be used to the material disadvantage of that person. As used in this Rule, the term "confidential government information" means information that has been obtained under governmental authority and that, at the time this Rule is applied, the government is prohibited by law from disclosing to the public or has a legal privilege not to disclose, and that is not otherwise available to the public. A firm with which that lawyer is associated may undertake or continue representation in the matter only if the disqualified lawyer is timely and effectively screened from any participation in the matter in accordance with the provisions of paragraph (b).

(d) Except as law may otherwise expressly provide, a lawyer currently serving as a public officer or employee shall not:

(1) participate in a matter in which the lawyer participated personally and substantially while in private practice or nongovernmental employment, unless under applicable law no one is, or by lawful delegation may be, authorized to act in the lawyer's stead in the matter; or

(2) negotiate for private employment with any person who is involved as a party or as lawyer for a party in a matter in which the lawyer is participating personally and substantially.

(e) As used in this Rule, the term "matter" as defined in Rule 1.0(l) does not include or apply to agency rulemaking functions.

(f) A lawyer who holds public office shall not:

(1) use the public position to obtain, or attempt to obtain, a special advantage in legislative matters for the lawyer or for a client under circumstances where the lawyer knows or it is obvious that such action is not in the public interest;

(2) use the public position to influence, or attempt to influence, a tribunal to act in favor of the lawyer or of a client; or

(3) accept anything of value from any person when the lawyer knows or it is obvious that the offer is for the purpose of influencing the lawyer's action as a public official.

COMMENT

[1] A lawyer who has served or is currently serving as a public officer or employee is personally subject to the Rules of Professional Conduct, including the prohibition against concurrent conflicts of interest stated in Rule 1.7. In addition, such a lawyer may be subject to statutes and government regulations regarding conflicts of interest. Such statutes and regulations may circumscribe the extent to which the government agency may give consent under this Rule. See Rule 1.0(j) for the definition of "informed consent."

[2] Paragraphs (a), (d) and (f) restate the obligations of an individual lawyer who has served or is currently serving as an officer or employee of the government toward a former government or private client. Paragraph (b) sets forth special imputation rules for former government lawyers, with screening and notice provisions, and Rule 1.10 is not applicable to these conflicts. *See* Comments [6]-[7B] concerning imputation of the conflicts of former government lawyers.

[3] Paragraphs (a)(2), (d) and (f) apply regardless of whether a lawyer is adverse to a former client and are thus designed not only to protect the former client, but also to prevent a lawyer from exploiting public office for the advantage of another client. For example, a lawyer who has pursued a claim on behalf of the government may not pursue the same claim on behalf of a private client after the lawyer has left government service, except when authorized to do so by the government agency under paragraph (a). Similarly, a lawyer who has pursued a claim on behalf of a private client may not pursue the claim on behalf of the government, except when authorized to do so.

[4] This Rule represents a balancing of interests. On the one hand, where the successive clients are a government agency and another client, public or private, the risk exists that power or discretion vested in that agency might be used for the special benefit of the other client. A lawyer should not be in a position where benefit to the other client might affect performance of the lawyer's professional functions on behalf of the government. Also, unfair advantage could accrue to the other client by reason of access to confidential government information about the client's adversary obtainable only through the lawyer's government service. On the other hand, the rules governing lawyers presently or formerly employed by a government agency should not be so restrictive as to inhibit transfer of employment to and from the government. The government has a legitimate need to attract qualified lawyers as well as to maintain high ethical standards. A former government lawyer is therefore disqualified only from particular matters in which the lawyer participated personally and substantially. The provisions for screening and waiver in paragraph (b) are necessary to prevent the disqualification rule from imposing too severe a deterrent to entering public service. The limitation on disqualification in paragraphs (a)(2) and (d) to matters involving a specific party or specific parties, rather than extending disqualification to all substantive issues on which the lawyer worked, serves a similar function.

[4A] By requiring a former government lawyer to comply with Rule 1.9(c), Rule 1.11(a)(1) protects information obtained while working for the government to the same extent as information learned while representing a private client. Accordingly, unless the information acquired during government service is "generally known" or these Rules would otherwise permit or require its use or disclosure, the information may not be used or revealed to the government's disadvantage. This provision applies regardless of whether the lawyer was working in a "legal" capacity. Thus, information learned by the lawyer while in public service in an administrative, policy or advisory position also is covered by Rule 1.11(a)(1). Paragraph (c) of Rule 1.11 adds further protections against exploitation of confidential information. Paragraph (c) prohibits a lawyer who has information about a person acquired when the lawyer was a public officer or employee, that the lawyer knows is confidential government information, from representing a private client whose interests are adverse to that person in a matter in which the information could be used to that person's material disadvantage. A firm with which the lawyer is associated may undertake or continue representation in the matter only if the lawyer who possesses the confidential government information is timely and effectively screened. Because Rule 1.11 is not among the Rules enumerated in Rule 1.10, Rule 1.10 is not applicable to (and therefore does not impute) conflicts arising under Rule 1.11. Thus, the purpose and effect of the prohibitions contained in Rule 1.11(c) are to prevent the private client of a law firm with which the former public officer or official is associated from obtaining an unfair advantage by using the lawyer's confidential government information about the private client's adversary.

[5] When a lawyer has been employed by one government agency and then moves to a second government agency, it may be appropriate to treat that second agency as another client for purposes of this Rule, as when a lawyer is employed by a municipality and subsequently is employed by a federal agency. The question whether two government agencies should be regarded as the same or different clients for conflict of interest purposes is beyond the scope of these Rules. *See* Rule 1.13, Comment [9].

Former Government Lawyers: Using Screening to Avoid Imputed Disqualification

[6] Paragraphs (b) and (c) contemplate the use of screening procedures that permit the law firm of a personally disqualified former government lawyer to avoid imputed disqualification. Nevertheless, there may be circumstances where, despite screening, representation by the personally disqualified lawyer's firm could still undermine the public's confidence in the integrity of the legal system. Such a circumstance may arise, for example, where the personally disqualified lawyer occupied a highly visible government position prior to entering private practice, or where other facts and circumstances of the representation itself create an appearance of impropriety. Where the particular circumstances create an appearance of impropriety, a law firm must decline the representation. See Rule 1.0(t) for the definition of "screened" and "screening."

[7] A firm seeking to avoid disqualification under this Rule should also consider its ability to implement, maintain, and monitor the screening procedures permitted by paragraphs (b) and (c) before undertaking or continuing the representation. In deciding whether the screening procedures permitted by this Rule will be effective to avoid imputed disqualification, a firm should consider a number of factors, including how the size, practices and organization of the firm will affect the likelihood that any confidential information acquired about the matter by the personally disqualified lawyer can be protected. If the firm is large and is organized into separate departments, or maintains offices in multiple locations, or for any reason the structure of the firm facilitates preventing the sharing of information with lawyers not participating in the particular matter, it is more likely that the requirements of this Rule can be met and imputed disqualification avoided. Although a large firm will find it easier to maintain effective screening, lack of timeliness in instituting, or lack of vigilance in maintaining, the procedures required by this Rule may make those procedures ineffective in avoiding imputed disqualification. If a personally disqualified lawyer is working on other matters with lawyers who are participating in

a matter requiring screening, it may be impossible to maintain effective screening procedures. Although the size of the firm may be considered as one of the factors affecting the firm's ability to institute and maintain effective screening procedures, it is not a dispositive factor. A small firm may need to exercise special care and vigilance to maintain effective screening but, if appropriate precautions are taken, small firms can satisfy the requirements of paragraphs (b) and (c).

[7A] In order to prevent any lawyer in the firm from acquiring confidential information about the matter from the newly associated lawyer, it is essential that notification be given and screening procedures implemented promptly. If the matter requiring screening is already pending before the personally disqualified lawyer joins the firm, the procedures required by this Rule should be implemented before the lawyer joins the firm. If a newly associated lawyer joins a firm before a conflict requiring screening arises, the requirements of this Rule should be satisfied as soon as practicable after the conflict arises. If any lawyer in the firm acquires confidential information about the matter from the personally disqualified lawyer, the requirements of this Rule cannot be met, and any subsequent efforts to institute or maintain screening will not be effective in avoiding the firm's disqualification. Other factors may affect the likelihood that screening procedures will be effective in preventing the flow of confidential information between the personally disqualified lawyer and other lawyers in the firm in a given matter.

[7B] To enable the government agency to determine compliance with the Rule, notice to the appropriate government agency generally should be given as soon as practicable after the need for screening becomes apparent.

[8] Paragraph (c) operates only when the lawyer in question has actual knowledge of the information. It does not operate with respect to information that merely could be imputed to the lawyer.

[9] Paragraph (a) does not prohibit a lawyer from representing a private party and a government agency jointly when doing so is permitted by Rule 1.7 and is not otherwise prohibited by law.

[9A] Paragraph (d)(1) prohibits a lawyer currently serving as a government officer or employee from participating in a matter in which the lawyer participated personally and substantially while in private practice or other non-governmental employment, unless under applicable law no one else is, or by lawful designation could be, authorized to act in the lawyer's stead. Informed consent on the part of the government agency is not required where such necessity exists. Conversely, informed consent does not suffice to overcome the conflict in the absence of necessity.

[9B] Unlike paragraphs (a) and (c), paragraph (d)(1) contains no special rules providing for imputation of the conflict addressed in paragraph (d)(1) to other lawyers in the same agency. Moreover, Rule 1.10 by its terms does not apply to conflicts under paragraph (d)(1). Thus, even where paragraph (d)(1) bars one lawyer in a government law office from working on a matter, other lawyers in the office may ordinarily work on the matter unless prohibited by other law. Where a government law office's representation is materially adverse to a government lawyer's former private client, however, the representation would, absent informed consent of the former client, also be prohibited by Rule 1.9. Rule 1.10 remains applicable to that former client conflict so as to impute the conflict to all lawyers associated in the same government law office. In applying Rule 1.10 to such conflicts, see Rule1.0(h) (defining "firm" and "law firm").

[10] For purposes of paragraph (e), a "matter" may continue in another form. In determining whether two particular matters are the same, the lawyer should consider the extent to which (i) the matters involve the same basic facts, (ii) the matters involve the same or related parties, and (iii) time has elapsed between the matters.

Rule 1.12   Specific Conflicts of Interest for Former Judges, Arbitrators, Mediators or Other Third-Party Neutrals

(a) A lawyer shall not accept private employment in a matter upon the merits of which the lawyer has acted in a judicial capacity.

(b) Except as stated in paragraph (e), and unless all parties to the proceeding give informed consent, confirmed in writing, a lawyer shall not represent anyone in connection with a matter in which the lawyer participated personally and substantially as:

(1) an arbitrator, mediator or other third-party neutral; or

(2) a law clerk to a judge or other adjudicative officer or an arbitrator, mediator or other third-party neutral.

(c) A lawyer shall not negotiate for employment with any person who is involved as a party or as lawyer for a party in a matter in which the lawyer is participating personally and substantially as a judge or other adjudicative officer or as an arbitrator, mediator or other third-party neutral.

(d) When a lawyer is disqualified from representation under this Rule, no lawyer in a firm with which that lawyer is associated may knowingly undertake or continue representation in such a matter unless:

(1) the firm acts promptly and reasonably to:

(i) notify, as appropriate, lawyers and nonlawyer personnel within the firm that the personally disqualified lawyer is prohibited from participating in the representation of the current client;

(ii) implement effective screening procedures to prevent the flow of information about the matter between the personally disqualified lawyer and the others in the firm;

(iii) ensure that the disqualified lawyer is apportioned no part of the fee therefrom; and

(iv) give written notice to the parties and any appropriate tribunal to enable it to ascertain compliance with the provisions of this Rule; and

(2) there are no other circumstances in the particular representation that create an appearance of impropriety.

(e) An arbitrator selected as a partisan of a party in a multimember arbitration panel is not prohibited from subsequently representing that party.

COMMENT

[1] A lawyer acts in a "judicial capacity" within the meaning of paragraph (a) when the lawyer serves as a judge or other adjudicative officer. Where a judge or

other adjudicative officer in a multimember court leaves judicial office to practice law, the former judge or adjudicative officer is not prohibited from representing a client in a matter that was pending in the court if the former judge or adjudicative officer did not act upon the merits in that matter. So also, the fact that a former judge or adjudicative officer exercised administrative responsibility in a court does not prevent the former judge or adjudicative officer from acting as a lawyer in a matter where the judge or adjudicative officer had previously exercised remote or incidental administrative responsibility that did not affect the merits. *See* Rule 1.11, Comment [4] (a former government lawyer is disqualified "only from particular matters in which the lawyer participated personally and substantially"). A former judge or adjudicative officer may not, however, accept private employment in a matter upon the merits of which the judge or adjudicative officer has acted in a judicial capacity, and—unlike conflicts for lawyers who have acted in a capacity listed in Rule 1.12(b)—a conflict arising under paragraph (a) cannot be waived. The term "adjudicative officer" includes such officials as judges pro tempore, referees, special masters, hearing officers and other parajudicial officers.

[2] A lawyer who has served as an arbitrator, mediator or other third-party neutral may be asked to represent a client in a matter in which the lawyer participated personally and substantially. This Rule forbids such representation unless all of the parties to the proceedings give their informed consents, confirmed in writing. See Rules 1.0(j), (e). Other law or codes of ethics governing third-party neutrals may impose more stringent standards of personal or imputed disqualification. *See* Rule 2.4.

[3] Although lawyers who serve as third-party neutrals do not obtain information concerning the parties that is protected under Rule 1.6, they typically owe the parties an obligation of confidentiality under law or codes of ethics governing third-party neutrals. Paragraph (d) therefore provides that conflicts of the personally disqualified lawyer will be imputed to other lawyers in a law firm unless the conditions of this paragraph are met.

[4] Requirements for screening procedures are stated in paragraph (d). "Screened" and "screening" are defined in Rule 1.0(t).

[4A] A firm seeking to avoid imputed disqualification under this Rule must prohibit the personally disqualified lawyer from sharing in the fees in the matter.

[4B] A firm seeking to avoid disqualification under this Rule should also consider its ability to implement, maintain, and monitor the screening procedures permitted by paragraph (d) before undertaking or continuing the representation. In deciding whether the screening procedures permitted by this Rule will be effective to avoid imputed disqualification, a firm should consider a number of factors, including how the size, practices and organization of the firm will affect the likelihood that any confidential information acquired about the matter by the personally disqualified lawyer can be protected. If the firm is large and is organized into separate departments, or maintains offices in multiple locations, or for any reason the structure of the firm facilitates preventing the sharing of information with lawyers not participating in the particular matter, it is more likely that the requirements of this Rule can be met and imputed disqualification avoided. Although a large firm will find it easier to maintain effective screening, lack of timeliness in instituting, or lack of vigilance in maintaining, the procedures required by this Rule may make those procedures ineffective in avoiding imputed disqualification. If a personally disqualified lawyer is working on other matters with lawyers who are participating in a matter requiring screening, it may be impossible to maintain effective screening procedures. The size of the firm may be considered as one of the factors affecting the firm's ability to institute and maintain effective screening procedures, it is not a dispositive factor. A small firm may need to exercise special care and vigilance to maintain effective screening but, if appropriate precautions are taken, small firms can satisfy the requirements of paragraph (d).

[4C] In order to prevent any lawyer in the firm from acquiring confidential information about the matter from the newly associated lawyer, it is essential that notification be given and screening procedures implemented promptly. If the matter requiring screening is already pending before the personally disqualified lawyer joins the firm, the procedures required by this Rule should be implemented before the lawyer joins the firm. If a newly associated lawyer joins a firm before a conflict requiring screening arises, the requirements of this Rule should be satisfied as soon as practicable after the conflict arises. If any lawyer in the firm acquires confidential information about the matter from the personally disqualified lawyer, the requirements of this Rule cannot be met, and any subsequent efforts to institute or maintain screening will not be effective in avoiding the firm's disqualification. Other factors may affect the likelihood that screening procedures will be effective in preventing the flow of confidential information between the personally disqualified lawyer and others in the firm in a given matter.

[5] To enable the tribunal to determine compliance with the Rule, notice to the parties and any appropriate tribunal generally should be given as soon as practicable after the need for screening becomes apparent.

Rule 1.13   Organization as Client

(a) When a lawyer employed or retained by an organization is dealing with the organization's directors, officers, employees, members, shareholders or other constituents, and it appears that the organization's interests may differ from those of the constituents with whom the lawyer is dealing, the lawyer shall explain that the lawyer is the lawyer for the organization and not for any of the constituents.

(b) If a lawyer for an organization knows that an officer, employee or other person associated with the organization is engaged in action or intends to act or refuses to act in a matter related to the representation that (i) is a violation of a legal obligation to the organization or a violation of law that reasonably might be imputed to the organization, and (ii) is likely to result in substantial injury to the organization, then the lawyer shall proceed as is reasonably necessary in the best interest of the organization. In determining how to proceed, the lawyer shall give due consideration to the seriousness of the violation and its consequences, the scope and nature of the lawyer's representation, the responsibility in the organization and the apparent motivation of the person involved, the policies of the organization concerning such matters and any other relevant considerations. Any measures taken shall be designed to minimize disruption of the organization and the risk of revealing information relating to the representation to persons outside the organization. Such measures may include, among others:

(1) asking reconsideration of the matter;

(2) advising that a separate legal opinion on the matter be sought for presentation to an appropriate authority in the organization; and

(3) referring the matter to higher authority in the organization, including, if warranted by the seriousness of the matter, referral to the highest authority that can act in behalf of the organization as determined by applicable law.

(c) If, despite the lawyer's efforts in accordance with paragraph (b), the highest authority that can act on behalf of the organization insists upon action, or a refusal to act, that is clearly in violation of law and is likely to result in a substantial injury to the organization, the lawyer may reveal confidential information only if permitted by Rule 1.6, and may resign in accordance with Rule 1.16.

(d) A lawyer representing an organization may also represent any of its directors, officers, employees, members, shareholders or other constituents, subject to the provisions of Rule 1.7. If the organization's consent to the concurrent representation is required by Rule 1.7, the consent shall be given by an appropriate official of the organization other than the individual who is to be represented, or by the shareholders.

COMMENT

The Entity as the Client

[1] An organizational client is a legal entity, but it cannot act except through its officers, directors, employees, members, shareholders and other constituents. Officers, directors, employees and shareholders are the constituents of the corporate organizational client. The duties defined in this Rule apply equally to unincorporated associations. "Other constituents" as used in this Rule means the positions equivalent to officers, directors, employees, and shareholders held by persons acting for organizational clients that are not corporations.

[2] When one of the constituents of an organizational client communicates with the organization's lawyer in that person's organizational capacity, the communication is protected by Rule 1.6. Thus, for example, if an organizational client requests its lawyer to investigate allegations of wrongdoing, interviews between the lawyer and the client's employees or other constituents made in the course of that investigation are covered by Rule 1.6. This does not mean, however, that constituents of an organizational client are the clients of the lawyer. The lawyer may not disclose to such constituents information relating to the representation except for disclosures explicitly or impliedly authorized by the organizational client in order to carry out the representation or as otherwise permitted by Rule 1.6.

[2A] There are times when the organization's interests may differ from those of one or more of its constituents. In such circumstances, the lawyer should advise any constituent whose interest differs from that of the organization: (i) that a conflict or potential conflict of interest exists, (ii) that the lawyer does not represent the constituent in connection with the matter, unless the representation has been approved in accordance with Rule 1.13(d), (iii) that the constituent may wish to obtain independent representation, and (iv) that any attorney-client privilege that applies to discussions between the lawyer and the constituent belongs to the organization and may be waived by the organization. Care must be taken to ensure that the constituent understands that, when there is such adversity of interest, the lawyer for the organization cannot provide legal representation for that constituent, and that discussions between the lawyer for the organization and the constituent may not be privileged.

[2B] Whether such a warning should be given by the lawyer for the organization to any constituent may turn on the facts of each case.

Acting in the Best Interest of the Organization

[3] When constituents of the organization make decisions for it, the decisions ordinarily must be accepted by the lawyer, even if their utility or prudence is doubtful. Decisions concerning policy and operations, including ones entailing serious risk, are not as such in the lawyer's province. Paragraph (b) makes clear, however, that when the lawyer knows that the organization is likely to be substantially injured by action of an officer or other constituent that violates a legal obligation to the organization or is in violation of law that might be imputed to the organization, the lawyer must proceed as is reasonably necessary in the best interest of the organization. Under Rule 1.0(k), a lawyer's knowledge can be inferred from circumstances, and a lawyer cannot ignore the obvious. The terms "reasonable" and "reasonably" connote a range of conduct that will satisfy the requirements of Rule 1.13. In determining what is reasonable in the best interest of the organization, the circumstances at the time of determination are relevant. Such circumstances may include, among others, the lawyer's area of expertise, the time constraints under which the lawyer is acting, and the lawyer's previous experience and familiarity with the client.

[4] In determining how to proceed under paragraph (b), the lawyer should give due consideration to the seriousness of the violation and its consequences, the scope and nature of the lawyer's representation, the responsibility within the organization and the apparent motivation of the person involved, the policies of the organization concerning such matters, and any other relevant considerations. Measures to be taken may include, among others, asking the constituent to reconsider the matter. For example, if the circumstances involve a constituent's innocent misunderstanding of law and subsequent acceptance of the lawyer's advice, the lawyer may reasonably conclude that the best interest of the organization does not require that the matter be referred to higher authority. If a constituent persists in conduct contrary to the lawyer's advice, it may be necessary for the lawyer to take steps to have the matter reviewed by a higher authority in the organization. If the matter is of sufficient seriousness and importance or urgency to the organization, referral to higher authority in the organization may be necessary even if the lawyer has not communicated with the constituent. Any measures taken should, to the extent practicable, minimize the risk of revealing information relating to the

representation to persons outside the organization. Even in circumstances where a lawyer is not obligated by Rule 1.13 to proceed, a lawyer may bring to the attention of an organizational client, including its highest authority, matters that the lawyer reasonably believes to be of sufficient importance to warrant doing so in the best interest of the organization. *See* Rule 1.4.

[5] The organization's highest authority to which a matter may be referred ordinarily will be the board of directors or similar governing body. However, applicable law may prescribe that under certain conditions the highest authority reposes elsewhere, for example, in the independent directors of a corporation.

Relation to Other Rules

[6] The authority and responsibility provided in this Rule are concurrent with the authority and responsibility provided in other Rules. In particular, this Rule does not limit or expand the lawyer's responsibility under Rule 1.6, Rule 1.8, Rule 1.16, Rule 3.3 or Rule 4.1. Rules 1.6(b)(2) and (b)(3) may permit the lawyer in some circumstances to disclose confidential information. In such circumstances Rule 1.2(d) may also be applicable, in which event withdrawal from the representation under Rule 1.16(b)(1) may be required.

[7] The authority of a lawyer to disclose information relating to a representation under Rule 1.6 does not apply with respect to information relating to a lawyer's engagement by an organization to investigate an alleged violation of law or to defend the organization or an officer, employee or other person associated with the organization against a claim arising out of an alleged past violation of law. Having a lawyer who cannot disclose confidential information concerning past acts relevant to the representation for which the lawyer was retained enables an organizational client to enjoy the full benefits of legal counsel in conducting an investigation or defending against a claim.

[8] A lawyer for an organization who reasonably believes that the lawyer's discharge was because of actions taken pursuant to paragraph (b), or who withdraws in circumstances that require or permit the lawyer to take action under paragraph (b), must proceed as "reasonably necessary in the best interest of the organization." Under some circumstances, the duty of communication under Rule 1.4 and the duty under Rule 1.16(e) to protect a client's interest upon termination of the representation, in conjunction with this Rule, may require the lawyer to inform the organization's highest authority of the lawyer's discharge or withdrawal, and of what the lawyer reasonably believes to be the basis for the discharge or withdrawal.

Government Agency

[9] The duties defined in this Rule apply to governmental organizations. Defining precisely the identity of the client and prescribing the resulting obligations of such lawyers may be more difficult in the government context. Although in some circumstances the client may be a specific agency, it may also be a branch of government, such as the executive branch, or the government as a whole. For example, if the action or failure to act involves the head of a bureau, either the

department of which the bureau is a part or the relevant branch of government may be the client for purposes of this Rule. Defining or identifying the client of a lawyer representing a government entity depends on applicable federal, state and local law and is a matter beyond the scope of these Rules. *See* Scope [9]. Moreover, in a matter involving the conduct of government officials, a government lawyer may have greater authority under applicable law to question such conduct than would a lawyer for a private organization in similar circumstances. Thus, when the client is a governmental organization, a different balance may be appropriate between maintaining confidentiality and assuring that the wrongful act is prevented or rectified. In addition, duties of lawyers employed by the government or lawyers in military service may be defined by statutes and regulation. This Rule does not limit that authority. *See* Scope [10].

[10] See Comment [2A].

[11] See Comment [2B].

Concurrent Representation

[12] Paragraph (d) recognizes that a lawyer for an organization may also represent a principal officer or major shareholder, subject to the provisions of Rule 1.7. If the corporation's informed consent to such a concurrent representation is needed, the lawyer should advise the principal officer or major shareholder that any consent given on behalf of the corporation by the conflicted officer or shareholder may not be valid, and the lawyer should explain the potential consequences of an invalid consent.

Derivative Actions

[13] Under generally prevailing law, the shareholders or members of a corporation may bring suit to compel the directors to perform their legal obligations in the supervision of the organization. Members of unincorporated associations have essentially the same right. Such an action may be brought nominally by the organization, but usually is, in fact, a legal controversy over management of the organization.

[14] The question can arise whether counsel for the organization may defend such an action. The proposition that the organization is the lawyer's client does not alone resolve the issue. Most derivative actions are normal incidents of an organization's affairs, to be defended by the organization's lawyer like any other suits. However, if the claim involves serious charges of wrongdoing by those in control of the organization, a conflict may arise between the lawyer's duty to the organization and the lawyer's relationship with the board. In those circumstances, Rule 1.7 governs who should represent the directors and the organization.

Rule 1.14   Client with Diminished Capacity

(a) When a client's capacity to make adequately considered decisions in connection with a representation is diminished, whether because of minority,

mental impairment or for some other reason, the lawyer shall, as far as reasonably possible, maintain a conventional relationship with the client.

(b) When the lawyer reasonably believes that the client has diminished capacity, is at risk of substantial physical, financial or other harm unless action is taken and cannot adequately act in the client's own interest, the lawyer may take reasonably necessary protective action, including consulting with individuals or entities that have the ability to take action to protect the client and, in appropriate cases, seeking the appointment of a guardian ad litem, conservator or guardian.

(c) Information relating to the representation of a client with diminished capacity is protected by Rule 1.6. When taking protective action pursuant to paragraph (b), the lawyer is impliedly authorized under Rule 1.6(a) to reveal information about the client, but only to the extent reasonably necessary to protect the client's interests.

COMMENT

[1] The responsibilities of a lawyer may vary according to the intelligence, experience, mental condition or age of a client, the obligation of a public officer, or the nature of a particular proceeding. The conventional client-lawyer relationship is based on the assumption that the client, when properly advised and assisted, is capable of making decisions about important matters. Any condition that renders a client incapable of communicating or making a considered judgment on the client's own behalf casts additional responsibilities upon the lawyer. When the client is a minor or suffers from a diminished mental capacity, maintaining the conventional client-lawyer relationship may not be possible in all respects. In particular, a severely incapacitated person may have no power to make legally binding decisions. Nevertheless, a client with diminished capacity often has the ability to understand, deliberate upon and reach conclusions about matters affecting the client's own well-being.

[2] The fact that a client suffers a disability does not diminish the lawyer's obligation to treat the client attentively and with respect.

[3] The client may wish to have family members or other persons participate in discussions with the lawyer. The lawyer should consider whether the presence of such persons will affect the attorney-client privilege. Nevertheless, the lawyer must keep the client's interests foremost and, except for protective action authorized under paragraph (b), must look to the client, and not family members, to make decisions on the client's behalf.

[4] If a legal representative has already been appointed for the client, the lawyer should ordinarily look to the representative for decisions on behalf of the client. In matters involving a minor, with or without a disability, the question whether the lawyer should look to the parents as natural guardians may depend on the type of proceeding or matter in which the lawyer is representing the minor. If the lawyer represents the guardian as distinct from the ward, and reasonably believes that the guardian is acting adversely to the ward's interest, the lawyer may have an obligation to prevent or rectify the guardian's misconduct. *See* Rule 1.2(d).

Taking Protective Action

[5] If a lawyer reasonably believes that a client is at risk of substantial physical, financial or other harm unless action is taken, and that a conventional client-lawyer relationship cannot be maintained as provided in paragraph (a) because the client lacks sufficient capacity to communicate or to make adequately considered decisions in connection with the representation, then paragraph (b) permits the lawyer to take reasonably necessary protective measures. Such measures could include: consulting with family members, using a reconsideration period to permit clarification or improvement of circumstances, using voluntary surrogate decision-making tools such as durable powers of attorney, or consulting with support groups, professional services, adult-protective agencies or other individuals or entities that have the ability to protect the client. In taking any protective action, the lawyer should be guided by such factors as the wishes and values of the client to the extent known, the client's best interest, and the goals of minimizing intrusion into the client's decision-making autonomy and maximizing respect for the client's family and social connections.

[6] In determining the extent of the client's diminished capacity, the lawyer should consider and balance such factors as: (i) the client's ability to articulate reasoning leading to a decision, (ii) variability of state of mind and ability to appreciate consequences of a decision; the substantive fairness of a decision, and (iii) the consistency of a decision with the known long-term commitments and values of the client. In appropriate circumstances, the lawyer may seek guidance from an appropriate diagnostician.

[7] If a legal representative has not been appointed, the lawyer should consider whether appointment of a guardian ad litem, conservator or guardian is necessary to protect the client's interests. Thus, if a client with diminished capacity has substantial property that should be sold for the client's benefit, effective completion of the transaction may require appointment of a legal representative. In addition, rules of procedure in litigation sometimes provide that a minor or a person with diminished capacity must be represented by a guardian or next friend if they do not have a general guardian. In many circumstances, however, appointment of a legal representative may be unnecessarily expensive or traumatic for the client. Seeking a guardian or conservator without the client's consent (including doing so over the client's objection) is appropriate only in the limited circumstances where a client's diminished capacity is such that the lawyer reasonably believes that no other practical method of protecting the client's interests is readily available. The lawyer should always consider less restrictive protective actions before seeking the appointment of a guardian or conservator. The lawyer should act as petitioner in such a proceeding only when no other person is available to do so.

[7A] Prior to withdrawing from the representation of a client whose capacity is in question, the lawyer should consider taking reasonable protective action. *See* Rule 1.16(e).

Disclosure of the Client's Condition

[8] Disclosure of the client's diminished capacity could adversely affect the client's interests. For example, raising the question of diminished capacity could, in

some circumstances, lead to proceedings for involuntary commitment. Information relating to the representation is protected by Rule 1.6. Therefore, unless authorized to do so, the lawyer may not disclose such information. When taking protective action pursuant to paragraph (b), the lawyer is impliedly authorized to make the necessary disclosures, even when the client directs the lawyer to the contrary. Nevertheless, given the risks of disclosure, paragraph (c) limits what the lawyer may disclose in consulting with other individuals or entities or in seeking the appointment of a legal representative. At the very least, the lawyer should determine whether it is likely that the person or entity consulted will act adversely to the client's interests before discussing matters related to the client.

Rule 1.15 Preserving Identity of Funds and Property of Others; Fiduciary Responsibility; Commingling and Misappropriation of Client Funds or Property; Maintenance of Bank Accounts; Record Keeping; Examination of Records

(a) *Prohibition Against Commingling and Misappropriation of Client Funds or Property.*

A lawyer in possession of any funds or other property belonging to another person, where such possession is incident to his or her practice of law, is a fiduciary, and must not misappropriate such funds or property or commingle such funds or property with his or her own.

(b) *Separate Accounts.*

(1) A lawyer who is in possession of funds belonging to another person incident to the lawyer's practice of law shall maintain such funds in a banking institution within New York State that agrees to provide dishonored check reports in accordance with the provisions of 22 N.Y.C.R.R. Part 1300. "Banking institution" means a state or national bank, trust company, savings bank, savings and loan association or credit union. Such funds shall be maintained, in the lawyer's own name, or in the name of a firm of lawyers of which the lawyer is a member, or in the name of the lawyer or firm of lawyers by whom the lawyer is employed, in a special account or accounts, separate from any business or personal accounts of the lawyer or lawyer's firm, and separate from any accounts that the lawyer may maintain as executor, guardian, trustee or receiver, or in any other fiduciary capacity; into such special account or accounts all funds held in escrow or otherwise entrusted to the lawyer or firm shall be deposited; provided, however, that such funds may be maintained in a banking institution located outside New York State if such banking institution complies with 22 N.Y.C.R.R. Part 1300 and the lawyer has obtained the prior written approval of the person to whom such funds belong specifying the name and address of the office or branch of the banking institution where such funds are to be maintained.

(2) A lawyer or the lawyer's firm shall identify the special bank account or accounts required by Rule 1.15(b)(1) as an "Attorney Special Account," "Attorney Trust Account," or "Attorney Escrow Account," and shall obtain checks and deposit slips that bear such title. Such title may be accompanied by such other descriptive language as the lawyer may deem appropriate, provided that such additional language distinguishes such special account or accounts from other bank accounts that are maintained by the lawyer or the lawyer's firm.

(3) Funds reasonably sufficient to maintain the account or to pay account charges may be deposited therein.

(4) Funds belonging in part to a client or third person and in part currently or potentially to the lawyer or law firm shall be kept in such special account or accounts, but the portion belonging to the lawyer or law firm may be withdrawn when due unless the right of the lawyer or law firm to receive it is disputed by the client or third person, in which event the disputed portion shall not be withdrawn until the dispute is finally resolved.

(c) *Notification of Receipt of Property; Safekeeping; Rendering Accounts; Payment or Delivery of Property.*

A lawyer shall:

(1) promptly notify a client or third person of the receipt of funds, securities, or other properties in which the client or third person has an interest;

(2) identify and label securities and properties of a client or third person promptly upon receipt and place them in a safe deposit box or other place of safekeeping as soon as practicable;

(3) maintain complete records of all funds, securities, and other properties of a client or third person coming into the possession of the lawyer and render appropriate accounts to the client or third person regarding them; and

(4) promptly pay or deliver to the client or third person as requested by the client or third person the funds, securities, or other properties in the possession of the lawyer that the client or third person is entitled to receive.

(d) *Required Bookkeeping Records.*

(1) A lawyer shall maintain for seven years after the events that they record:

(i) the records of all deposits in and withdrawals from the accounts specified in Rule 1.15(b) and of any other bank account that concerns or affects the lawyer's practice of law; these records shall specifically identify the date, source and description of each item deposited, as well as the date, payee and purpose of each withdrawal or disbursement;

(ii) a record for special accounts, showing the source of all funds deposited in such accounts, the names of all persons for whom the funds are or were held, the amount of such funds, the description and amounts, and the names of all persons to whom such funds were disbursed;

(iii) copies of all retainer and compensation agreements with clients;

(iv) copies of all statements to clients or other persons showing the disbursement of funds to them or on their behalf;

(v) copies of all bills rendered to clients;

(vi) copies of all records showing payments to lawyers, investigators or other persons, not in the lawyer's regular employ, for services rendered or performed;

(vii) copies of all retainer and closing statements filed with the Office of Court Administration; and

(viii) all checkbooks and check stubs, bank statements, prenumbered canceled checks and duplicate deposit slips.

(2) Lawyers shall make accurate entries of all financial transactions in their records of receipts and disbursements, in their special accounts, in their ledger books or similar records, and in any other books of account kept by them in the regular course of their practice, which entries shall be made at or near the time of the act, condition or event recorded.

(3) For purposes of Rule 1.15(d), a lawyer may satisfy the requirements of maintaining "copies" by maintaining any of the following items: original records, photocopies, microfilm, optical imaging, and any other medium that preserves an image of the document that cannot be altered without detection.

(e) *Authorized Signatories.*

All special account withdrawals shall be made only to a named payee and not to cash. Such withdrawals shall be made by check or, with the prior written approval of the party entitled to the proceeds, by bank transfer. Only a lawyer admitted to practice law in New York State shall be an authorized signatory of a special account.

(f) *Missing Clients.*

Whenever any sum of money is payable to a client and the lawyer is unable to locate the client, the lawyer shall apply to the court in which the action was brought if in the unified court system, or, if no action was commenced in the unified court system, to the Supreme Court in the county in which the lawyer maintains an office for the practice of law, for an order directing payment to the lawyer of any fees and disbursements that are owed by the client and the balance, if any, to the Lawyers' Fund for Client Protection for safeguarding and disbursement to persons who are entitled thereto.

(g) *Designation of Successor Signatories.*

(1) Upon the death of a lawyer who was the sole signatory on an attorney trust, escrow or special account, an application may be made to the Supreme Court for an order designating a successor signatory for such trust, escrow or special account, who shall be a member of the bar in good standing and admitted to the practice of law in New York State.

(2) An application to designate a successor signatory shall be made to the Supreme Court in the judicial district in which the deceased lawyer maintained an office for the practice of law. The application may be made by the legal representative of the deceased lawyer's estate; a lawyer who was affiliated with the deceased lawyer in the practice of law; any person who has a beneficial interest in such trust, escrow or special account; an officer of a city or county bar association; or counsel for an attorney disciplinary committee. No lawyer may charge a legal fee for assisting with an application to designate a successor signatory pursuant to this Rule.

(3) The Supreme Court may designate a successor signatory and may direct the safeguarding of funds from such trust, escrow or special account, and the disbursement of such funds to persons who are entitled thereto, and may order that funds in such account be deposited with the Lawyers' Fund for Client Protection for safeguarding and disbursement to persons who are entitled thereto.

(h) *Dissolution of a Firm.*

Upon the dissolution of any firm of lawyers, the former partners or members shall make appropriate arrangements for the maintenance, by one of them or by a successor firm, of the records specified in Rule 1.15(d).

(i) *Availability of Bookkeeping Records: Records Subject to Production in Disciplinary Investigations and Proceedings.*

The financial records required by this Rule shall be located, or made available, at the principal New York State office of the lawyers subject hereto, and any such records shall be produced in response to a notice or subpoena duces tecum issued in connection with a complaint before or any investigation by the appropriate grievance or departmental disciplinary committee, or shall be produced at the direction of the appropriate Appellate Division before any person designated by it. All books and records produced pursuant to this Rule shall be kept confidential, except for the purpose of the particular proceeding, and their contents shall not be disclosed by anyone in violation of the attorney-client privilege.

(j) *Disciplinary Action.*

A lawyer who does not maintain and keep the accounts and records as specified and required by this Rule, or who does not produce any such records pursuant to this Rule, shall be deemed in violation of these Rules and shall be subject to disciplinary proceedings.

COMMENT

[1] A lawyer should hold the funds and property of others using the care required of a professional fiduciary. Securities and other property should be kept in a safe deposit box, except when some other form of safekeeping is warranted by special circumstances. All property that is the property of clients or third persons, including prospective clients, must be kept separate from the lawyer's business

and personal property and, if monies, in one or more trust accounts, including an account established pursuant to the "Interest on Lawyer Accounts" law where appropriate. *See* State Finance Law §97-v(4)(a); Judiciary Law §497(2); 21 N.Y.C.R.R. §7000.10. Separate trust accounts may be warranted or required when administering estate monies or acting in similar fiduciary capacities.

[2] While normally it is impermissible to commingle the lawyer's own funds with client funds, paragraph (b)(3) provides that it is permissible when necessary to pay bank service charges on that account. Accurate records must be kept regarding which portion of the funds belongs to the lawyer.

[3] Lawyers often receive funds from which the lawyer's fee will or may be paid. The lawyer is not required to remit to the client funds that the lawyer reasonably believes represent fees owed to the lawyer. However, a lawyer may not withhold the client's share of the funds to coerce the client into accepting the lawyer's claim for fees. While a lawyer may be entitled under applicable law to assert a retaining lien on funds in the lawyer's possession, a lawyer may not enforce such a lien by taking the lawyer's fee from funds that the lawyer holds in an attorney's trust account, escrow account or special account, except as may be provided in an applicable agreement or directed by court order. Furthermore, the disputed portion of the funds must be kept in or transferred into a trust account, and the lawyer should suggest means for prompt resolution of the dispute, such as arbitration. Notice to the client of the right to arbitrate fee disputes is required in some circumstances. The undisputed portion of the funds is to be distributed promptly.

[4] Paragraph (c)(4) also recognizes that third parties may have lawful claims against specific funds or other property in a lawyer's custody, such as a client's creditor who has a lien on funds recovered in a personal injury action. A lawyer may have a duty under applicable law to protect such third-party claims against wrongful interference by the client. In such cases, when the third-party claim is not frivolous under applicable law, the lawyer must refuse to surrender the property to the client until the claims are resolved. A lawyer should not unilaterally assume to arbitrate a dispute between the client and the third party, but, when there are substantial grounds for dispute as to the person entitled to the funds, the lawyer may file an action to have a court resolve the dispute.

[5] The obligations of a lawyer under this Rule are independent of those arising from activity other than rendering legal services. For example, a lawyer who serves only as an escrow agent is governed by the applicable law relating to fiduciaries even though the lawyer does not render legal services in the transaction and is not governed by this Rule.

Rule 1.16   Declining or Terminating Representation

(a) A lawyer shall not accept employment on behalf of a person if the lawyer knows or reasonably should know that such person wishes to:

(1) bring a legal action, conduct a defense, or assert a position in a matter, or otherwise have steps taken for such person, merely for the purpose of harassing or maliciously injuring any person; or

(2) present a claim or defense in a matter that is not warranted under existing law, unless it can be supported by a good faith argument for an extension, modification, or reversal of existing law.

(b) Except as stated in paragraph (d), a lawyer shall withdraw from the representation of a client when:

(1) the lawyer knows or reasonably should know that the representation will result in a violation of these Rules or of law;

(2) the lawyer's physical or mental condition materially impairs the lawyer's ability to represent the client;

(3) the lawyer is discharged; or

(4) the lawyer knows or reasonably should know that the client is bringing the legal action, conducting the defense, or asserting a position in the matter, or is otherwise having steps taken, merely for the purpose of harassing or maliciously injuring any person.

(c) Except as stated in paragraph (d), a lawyer may withdraw from representing a client when:

(1) withdrawal can be accomplished without material adverse effect on the interests of the client;

(2) the client persists in a course of action involving the lawyer's services that the lawyer reasonably believes is criminal or fraudulent;

(3) the client has used the lawyer's services to perpetrate a crime or fraud;

(4) the client insists upon taking action with which the lawyer has a fundamental disagreement;

(5) the client deliberately disregards an agreement or obligation to the lawyer as to expenses or fees;

(6) the client insists upon presenting a claim or defense that is not warranted under existing law and cannot be supported by good faith argument for an extension, modification, or reversal of existing law;

(7) the client fails to cooperate in the representation or otherwise renders the representation unreasonably difficult for the lawyer to carry out employment effectively;

(8) the lawyer's inability to work with co-counsel indicates that the best interest of the client likely will be served by withdrawal;

(9) the lawyer's mental or physical condition renders it difficult for the lawyer to carry out the representation effectively;

(10) the client knowingly and freely assents to termination of the employment;

(11) withdrawal is permitted under Rule 1.13(c) or other law;

(12) the lawyer believes in good faith, in a matter pending before a tribunal, that the tribunal will find the existence of other good cause for withdrawal; or

(13) the client insists that the lawyer pursue a course of conduct which is illegal or prohibited under these Rules.

(d) If permission for withdrawal from employment is required by the rules of a tribunal, a lawyer shall not withdraw from employment in a matter before that tribunal without its permission. When ordered to do so by a tribunal, a lawyer shall continue representation notwithstanding good cause for terminating the representation.

(e) Even when withdrawal is otherwise permitted or required, upon termination of representation, a lawyer shall take steps, to the extent reasonably practicable, to avoid foreseeable prejudice to the rights of the client, including giving reasonable notice to the client, allowing time for employment of other counsel, delivering to the client all papers and property to which the client is entitled, promptly refunding any part of a fee paid in advance that has not been earned and complying with applicable laws and rules.

COMMENT

[1] A lawyer should not accept representation in a matter unless it can be performed competently, promptly, without improper conflict of interest and to completion. Ordinarily, a representation in a matter is completed when the agreed-upon assistance has been concluded. *See* Rules 1.2(c), 6.5; *see also* Rule 1.3, Comment [4].

Mandatory Withdrawal

[2] A lawyer ordinarily must decline or withdraw from representation under paragraph (a), (b)(1) or (b)(4), as the case may be, if the client demands that the lawyer engage in conduct that is illegal or that violates these Rules or other law. The lawyer is not obliged to decline or withdraw simply because the client suggests such a course of conduct; a client may make such a suggestion in the hope that a lawyer will not be constrained by a professional obligation.

[3] Court approval or notice to the court is often required by applicable law, and when so required by applicable law is also required by paragraph (d), before a lawyer withdraws from pending litigation. Difficulty may be encountered if withdrawal is based on the client's demand that the lawyer engage in unprofessional conduct. The court may request an explanation for the withdrawal, while the lawyer may be bound to keep confidential the facts that would constitute such an explanation. The lawyer's statement that professional considerations require termination of the representation ordinarily should be accepted as sufficient. Lawyers should be mindful of their obligations to both clients and the court under Rule 1.6 and Rule 3.3.

Discharge

[4] As provided in paragraph (b)(3), a client has a right to discharge a lawyer at any time, with or without cause, subject to liability for payment for the lawyer's

services. Where future dispute about the withdrawal may be anticipated, it may be advisable to prepare a written statement reciting the circumstances.

[5] Whether a client can discharge appointed counsel may depend on applicable law. A client seeking to do so should be given a full explanation of the consequences. These consequences may include a decision by the appointing authority that appointment of successor counsel is unjustified, thus requiring self-representation by the client.

[6] If the client has severely diminished capacity, the client may lack the legal capacity to discharge the lawyer, and in any event the discharge may be seriously adverse to the client's interests. The lawyer should make special effort to help the client consider the consequences and may take reasonably necessary protective action as provided in Rule 1.14(b).

Optional Withdrawal

[7] Under paragraph (c), a lawyer may withdraw from representation in some circumstances. The lawyer has the option to withdraw if withdrawal can be accomplished without material adverse effect on the client's interests. Withdrawal is also justified if the client persists in a course of action that the lawyer reasonably believes is criminal or fraudulent, for a lawyer is not required to be associated with such conduct even if the lawyer does not further it. Withdrawal is also permitted if the lawyer's services were misused in the past, even if withdrawal would materially prejudice the client. The lawyer may also withdraw where the client insists on taking action with which the lawyer has a fundamental disagreement.

[7A] In accordance with paragraph (c)(4), a lawyer should use reasonable foresight in determining whether a proposed representation will involve client objectives or instructions with which the lawyer has a fundamental disagreement. A client's intended action does not create a fundamental disagreement simply because the lawyer disagrees with it. *See* Rule 1.2 regarding the allocation of responsibility between client and lawyer. The client has the right, for example, to accept or reject a settlement proposal; a client's decision on settlement involves a fundamental disagreement only when no reasonable person in the client's position, having regard for the hazards of litigation, would have declined the settlement. In addition, the client should be given notice of intent to withdraw and an opportunity to reconsider.

[8] Under paragraph (c)(5), a lawyer may withdraw if the client refuses to abide by the terms of an agreement concerning fees or court costs (or other expenses or disbursements).

[8A] Continuing to represent a client may impose an unreasonable burden unexpected by the client and lawyer at the outset of the representation. However, lawyers are ordinarily better suited than clients to foresee and provide for the burdens of representation. The burdens of uncertainty should therefore ordinarily fall on lawyers rather than clients unless they are attributable to client misconduct. That a representation will require more work or significantly larger advances of expenses than the lawyer contemplated when the fee was fixed is not grounds for withdrawal under paragraph (c)(5).

Assisting the Client upon Withdrawal

[9] Even if the lawyer has been unfairly discharged by the client, under paragraph ~~(e)~~ (e) a lawyer must take all reasonable steps to mitigate the consequences to the client. The lawyer may retain papers as security for a fee only to the extent permitted by law. *See* Rule 1.8(i)(1).

Rule 1.17   Sale of Law Practice

(a) A lawyer retiring from a private practice of law; a law firm, one or more members of which are retiring from the private practice of law with the firm; or the personal representative of a deceased, disabled or missing lawyer, may sell a law practice, including goodwill, to one or more lawyers or law firms, who may purchase the practice. The seller and the buyer may agree on reasonable restrictions on the seller's private practice of law, notwithstanding any other provision of these Rules. Retirement shall include the cessation of the private practice of law in the geographic area, that is, the county and city and any county or city contiguous thereto, in which the practice to be sold has been conducted.

(b) *Confidential information.*

(1) With respect to each matter subject to the contemplated sale, the seller may provide prospective buyers with any information not protected as confidential information under Rule 1.6.

(2) Notwithstanding Rule 1.6, the seller may provide the prospective buyer with information as to individual clients:

(i) concerning the identity of the client, except as provided in paragraph (b)(6);

(ii) concerning the status and general nature of the matter;

(iii) available in public court files; and

(iv) concerning the financial terms of the client-lawyer relationship and the payment status of the client's account.

(3) Prior to making any disclosure of confidential information that may be permitted under paragraph (b)(2), the seller shall provide the prospective buyer with information regarding the matters involved in the proposed sale sufficient to enable the prospective buyer to determine whether any conflicts of interest exist. Where sufficient information cannot be disclosed without revealing client confidential information, the seller may make the disclosures necessary for the prospective buyer to determine whether any conflict of interest exists, subject to paragraph (b)(6). If the prospective buyer determines that conflicts of interest exist prior to reviewing the information, or determines during the course of review that a conflict of interest exists, the prospective buyer shall not review or continue to review the information unless the seller shall have obtained the consent of the client in accordance with Rule 1.6(a)(1).

(4) Prospective buyers shall maintain the confidentiality of and shall not use any client information received in connection with the proposed sale in the same manner and to the same extent as if the prospective buyers represented the client.

(5) Absent the consent of the client after full disclosure, a seller shall not provide a prospective buyer with information if doing so would cause a violation of the attorney-client privilege.

(6) If the seller has reason to believe that the identity of the client or the fact of the representation itself constitutes confidential information in the circumstances, the seller may not provide such information to a prospective buyer without first advising the client of the identity of the prospective buyer and obtaining the client's consent to the proposed disclosure.

(c) Written notice of the sale shall be given jointly by the seller and the buyer to each of the seller's clients and shall include information regarding:

(1) the client's right to retain other counsel or to take possession of the file;

(2) the fact that the client's consent to the transfer of the client's file or matter to the buyer will be presumed if the client does not take any action or otherwise object within 90 days of the sending of the notice, subject to any court rule or statute requiring express approval by the client or a court;

(3) the fact that agreements between the seller and the seller's clients as to fees will be honored by the buyer;

(4) proposed fee increases, if any, permitted under paragraph (e); and

(5) the identity and background of the buyer or buyers, including principal office address, bar admissions, number of years in practice in New York State, whether the buyer has ever been disciplined for professional misconduct or convicted of a crime, and whether the buyer currently intends to resell the practice.

(d) When the buyer's representation of a client of the seller would give rise to a waivable conflict of interest, the buyer shall not undertake such representation unless the necessary waiver or waivers have been obtained in writing.

(e) The fee charged a client by the buyer shall not be increased by reason of the sale, unless permitted by a retainer agreement with the client or otherwise specifically agreed to by the client.

COMMENT

[1] The practice of law is a profession, not merely a business. Clients are not commodities that can be purchased and sold at will. Pursuant to this Rule, when a lawyer or an entire firm ceases to practice, and other lawyers or firms take over the

representation, the selling lawyer or firm may obtain compensation for the reasonable value of the practice, as may withdrawing partners of law firms.

Termination of Practice by Seller

[2] The requirement that all of the private practice be sold is satisfied if the seller in good faith makes the entire practice available for sale to the buyers. The fact that a number of the seller's clients decide not to be represented by the buyers but take their matters elsewhere, therefore, does not result in a violation. Return to private practice as a result of an unanticipated change in circumstances does not necessarily result in a violation. For example, a lawyer who has sold the practice to accept an appointment to judicial office does not violate the requirement that the sale be attendant to cessation of practice if the lawyer later resumes private practice upon being defeated in a contested or a retention election for the office or resigns from a judiciary position. Although the requirements of this Rule may not be violated in these situations, contractual provisions in the agreement governing the sale of the practice may contain reasonable restrictions on a lawyer's resuming private practice. *See* Rule 5.6, Comment [1], regarding restrictions on right to practice.

[3] The private practice of law refers to a private law firm or lawyer, not to a public agency, legal services entity, or in-house counsel to a business. The requirement that the seller cease to engage in the private practice of law therefore does not prohibit employment as a lawyer on the staff of a public agency or a legal services entity that provides legal services to the poor, or as in-house counsel to a business.

[4] The Rule permits a sale of an entire practice attendant upon retirement from the private practice of law within a geographic area, defined as the county and city and any county or city contiguous thereto, in which the practice to be sold has been conducted. Its provisions therefore accommodate the lawyer who sells the practice on the occasion of moving to another city and county that does not border on the city or county.

[5] [Reserved.]

Sale of Entire Practice

[6] The Rule requires that the seller's entire practice be sold. The prohibition against sale of less than an entire practice protects those clients whose matters are less lucrative and who might find it difficult to secure other counsel if a sale could be limited to substantial fee-generating matters. The buyers are required to undertake all client matters in the practice, subject to client consent. This requirement is not violated even if a buyer is unable to undertake a particular client matter because of a conflict of interest and the seller therefore remains as attorney of record for the matter in question.

Client Confidences, Consent and Notice

[7] Giving the buyer access to client-specific information relating to the representation and to the file requires client consent. Rule 1.17 provides that before

such information can be disclosed by the seller to the buyer, the client must be given actual written notice of the contemplated sale, including the identity of the buyer, and must be told that the decision to consent or make other arrangements must be made within 90 days. If nothing is heard from the client within that time, consent to the sale is presumed under paragraph (c)(2).

[8] A lawyer or law firm ceasing to practice cannot be required to remain in practice because some clients cannot be given actual notice of the proposed purchase. The selling lawyer must make a good-faith effort to notify all of the lawyer's current clients. Where clients cannot be given actual notice and therefore cannot themselves consent to the purchase or direct any other disposition of their files, they are nevertheless protected by the fact that the buyer has the duty to maintain their confidences under paragraph (b)(4).

[9] All elements of client autonomy, including the client's absolute right to discharge a lawyer and transfer the representation to another, survive the sale of the practice.

Fee Arrangements Between Client and Buyer

[10] The sale may not be financed by increases in fees charged to the clients of the purchased practice except to the extent permitted by subparagraph (e) of this Rule. Under subparagraph (e), the buyer must honor existing arrangements between the seller and the client as to fees unless the seller's retainer agreement with the client permits a fee increase or the buyer obtains a client's specific agreement to a fee increase in compliance with the strict standards of Rule 1.8(a) (governing business transactions between lawyers and clients).

Other Applicable Ethical Standards

[11] Lawyers participating in the sale or purchase of a law practice are subject to the ethical standards applicable to involving another lawyer in the representation of a client. Examples include (i) the seller's obligation to exercise competence in identifying a buyer qualified to assume the practice and the buyer's obligation to undertake the representation competently under Rule 1.1, (ii) the obligation of the seller and the buyer to avoid disqualifying conflicts, and to secure the client's informed consent for those conflicts that can be agreed to under Rule 1.7, and (iii) the obligation of the seller and the buyer to protect information relating to the representation under Rule 1.6 and Rule 1.9. *See also* Rule 1.0(j) for the definition of "informed consent."

[12] If approval of the substitution of the purchasing lawyer for the selling lawyer is required by the rules of any tribunal in which a matter is pending, such approval must be obtained before the matter can be included in the sale. *See* Rule 1.16. If a tribunal refuses to give its permission for the substitution and the seller therefore must continue in the matter, the seller does not thereby violate the portion of this Rule requiring the seller to cease practice in the described geographic area.

Applicability of the Rule

[13] [Reserved.]

[14] This Rule does not apply to: (i) admission to or retirement from a law partnership or professional association, (ii) retirement plans and similar arrangements, (iii) a sale of tangible assets of a law practice, or (iv) the transfers of legal representation between lawyers when such transfers are unrelated to the sale of a practice. This Rule governs the sale of an entire law practice upon retirement, which is defined in paragraph (a) as the cessation of the private practice of law in a given geographic area. Rule 5.4(a)(2) provides for the compensation of a lawyer who undertakes to complete one or more unfinished pieces of legal business of a deceased lawyer.

Rule 1.18 Duties to Prospective Clients

(a) A person who discusses with a lawyer the possibility of forming a client-lawyer relationship with respect to a matter is a "prospective client."

(b) Even when no client-lawyer relationship ensues, a lawyer who has had discussions with a prospective client shall not use or reveal information learned in the consultation, except as Rule 1.9 would permit with respect to information of a former client.

(c) A lawyer subject to paragraph (b) shall not represent a client with interests materially adverse to those of a prospective client in the same or a substantially related matter if the lawyer received information from the prospective client that could be significantly harmful to that person in the matter, except as provided in paragraph (d). If a lawyer is disqualified from representation under this paragraph, no lawyer in a firm with which that lawyer is associated may knowingly undertake or continue representation in such a matter, except as provided in paragraph (d).

(d) When the lawyer has received disqualifying information as defined in paragraph (c), representation is permissible if:

(1) both the affected client and the prospective client have given informed consent, confirmed in writing; or

(2) the lawyer who received the information took reasonable measures to avoid exposure to more disqualifying information than was reasonably necessary to determine whether to represent the prospective client; and

(i) the firm acts promptly and reasonably to notify, as appropriate, lawyers and nonlawyer personnel within the firm that the personally disqualified lawyer is prohibited from participating in the representation of the current client;

(ii) the firm implements effective screening procedures to prevent the flow of information about the matter between the disqualified lawyer and the others in the firm;

(iii) the disqualified lawyer is apportioned no part of the fee there-from; and

(iv) written notice is promptly given to the prospective client; and

(3) a reasonable lawyer would conclude that the law firm will be able to provide competent and diligent representation in the matter.

(e) A person who:

(1) communicates information unilaterally to a lawyer, without any reasonable expectation that the lawyer is willing to discuss the possibility of forming a client-lawyer relationship; or

(2) communicates with a lawyer for the purpose of disqualifying the lawyer from handling a materially adverse representation on the same or a substantially related matter, is not a prospective client within the meaning of paragraph (a).

COMMENT

[1] Prospective clients, like current clients, may disclose information to a lawyer, place documents or other property in the lawyer's custody, or rely on the lawyer's advice. A lawyer's discussions with a prospective client usually are limited in time and depth and leave both the prospective client and the lawyer free (and sometimes required) to proceed no further. Prospective clients should therefore receive some, but not all, of the protection afforded clients.

[2] Not all persons who communicate information to a lawyer are entitled to protection under this Rule. As provided in paragraph (e), a person who communicates information unilaterally to a lawyer, without any reasonable expectation that the lawyer is willing to discuss the possibility of forming a client-lawyer relationship, is not a "prospective client" within the meaning of paragraph (a). Similarly, a person who communicates with a lawyer for the purpose of disqualifying the lawyer from handling a materially adverse representation on the same or a substantially related matter is not entitled to the protection of this Rule. A lawyer may not encourage or induce a person to communicate with a lawyer or lawyers for that improper purpose. *See* Rules 3.1(b)(2), 4.4, 8.4(a).

[3] It is often necessary for a prospective client to reveal information to the lawyer during an initial consultation prior to the decision about formation of a client-lawyer relationship. The lawyer often must learn such information to determine whether there is a conflict of interest with an existing client and whether the matter is one that the lawyer is willing to undertake. Paragraph (b) prohibits the lawyer from using or revealing that information, except as permitted by Rule 1.9, even if the client or lawyer decides not to proceed with the representation. The duty exists regardless of how brief the initial conference may be.

[4] In order to avoid acquiring disqualifying information from a prospective client, a lawyer considering whether to undertake a new matter should limit the initial interview to only such information as reasonably appears necessary for that purpose. Where the information indicates that a conflict of interest or other reason for non-representation exists, the lawyer should so inform the prospective client or decline the representation. If the prospective client wishes to retain the lawyer, and

if consent is possible under Rule 1.7 or Rule 1.9, then consent from all affected current or former clients must be obtained before accepting the representation. The representation must be declined if the lawyer will be unable to provide competent, diligent and adequate representation to the affected current and former clients and the prospective client.

[5] A lawyer may condition conversations with a prospective client on the person's informed consent that no information disclosed during the consultation will prohibit the lawyer from representing a different client in the matter. See Rule 1.0(j) for the definition of "informed consent," and with regard to the effectiveness of an advance waiver see Rule 1.7, Comments [22]-[22A] and Rule 1.9, Comment [9]. If permitted by law and if the agreement expressly so provides, the prospective client may also consent to the lawyer's subsequent use of information received from the prospective client.

[6] Under paragraph (c), even in the absence of an agreement the lawyer is not prohibited from representing a client with interests adverse to those of the prospective client in the same or a substantially related matter unless the lawyer has received from the prospective client information that could be significantly harmful if used in that matter.

[7] Under paragraph (c), the prohibition in this Rule is imputed to other lawyers as provided in Rule 1.10, but, under paragraph (d)(1), imputation may be avoided if the lawyer obtains the informed consent, confirmed in writing, of both the prospective and affected clients. In the alternative, imputation may be avoided if the conditions of paragraph (d)(2) are met and all disqualified lawyers are timely screened, and written notice is promptly given to the prospective client. *See* Rule 1.10. Paragraph (d)(2)(i) does not prohibit the screened lawyer from receiving a salary or partnership share established by prior independent agreement, but that lawyer may not receive compensation directly related to the matter in which the lawyer is disqualified. Before proceeding under paragraph (d)(1) or paragraph (d)(2), however, a lawyer must be mindful of the requirement of paragraph (d)(3) that "a reasonable lawyer would conclude that the law firm will be able to provide competent and diligent representation in the matter."

[7A] Paragraph (d)(2) sets out the basic procedural requirements that a law firm must satisfy to ensure that a personally disqualified lawyer is effectively screened from participation in the matter. This Rule requires that the firm promptly: (i) notify, as appropriate, lawyers and relevant nonlawyer personnel within the firm that the personally disqualified lawyer is prohibited from participating in the representation of the current client, and (ii) implement effective screening procedures to prevent the flow of information about the matter between the personally disqualified lawyer and others in the firm.

[7B] A firm seeking to avoid disqualification under this Rule should also consider its ability to implement, maintain, and monitor the screening procedures permitted by paragraph (d)(2) before undertaking or continuing the representation. In deciding whether the screening procedures permitted by this Rule will be effective to avoid imputed disqualification, a firm should consider a number of factors, including how the size, practices and organization of the firm will affect the likelihood that any confidential information acquired about the matter by the personally disqualified lawyer can be protected. If the firm is large and is organized into separate departments, or maintains offices in multiple locations, or for any reason the structure of the firm facilitates preventing the sharing of information with lawyers not participating in the particular matter, it is more likely that the requirements of this Rule can be met and imputed disqualification avoided. Although a large firm will find it easier to maintain effective screening, lack of timeliness in instituting, or lack of vigilance in maintaining, the procedures required by this Rule may make those procedures ineffective in avoiding imputed disqualification. If a personally disqualified lawyer is working on other matters with lawyers who are participating in a matter requiring screening, it may be impossible to maintain effective screening procedures. The size of the firm may be considered as one of the factors affecting the firm's ability to institute and maintain effective screening procedures, but it is not a dispositive factor. A small firm may need to exercise special care and vigilance to maintain effective screening but, if appropriate precautions are taken, small firms can satisfy the requirements of paragraph (d)(2).

[7C] In order to prevent any other lawyer in the firm from acquiring confidential information about the matter from the disqualified lawyer, it is essential that notification be given and screening procedures implemented promptly. If any lawyer in the firm acquires confidential information about the matter from the disqualified lawyer, the requirements of this Rule cannot be met, and any subsequent efforts to institute or maintain screening will not be effective in avoiding the firm's disqualification. Other factors may affect the likelihood that screening procedures will be effective in preventing the flow of confidential information between the disqualified lawyer and other lawyers in the firm in a given matter.

[8] Notice under paragraph (d)(2), including a general description of the subject matter about which the lawyer was consulted and of the screening procedures employed, generally should be given as soon as practicable after the need for screening becomes apparent.

[9] For the duty of competence of a lawyer who gives assistance on the merits of a matter to a prospective client, see Rule 1.1. For a lawyer's duties when a prospective client entrusts valuables or papers to the lawyer's care, see Rule 1.15.

Rule 2.1   Advisor

In representing a client, a lawyer shall exercise independent professional judgment and render candid advice. In rendering advice, a lawyer may refer not only to law but to other considerations such as moral, economic, social, psychological, and political factors that may be relevant to the client's situation.

COMMENT

Scope of Advice

[1] A client is entitled to straightforward advice expressing the lawyer's honest assessment. Legal advice often involves unpleasant facts and alternatives that a client may be disinclined to confront. In presenting advice, a lawyer endeavors to

sustain the client's morale and may put advice in as acceptable a form as honesty permits. Nevertheless, a lawyer should not be deterred from giving candid advice by the prospect that the advice will be unpalatable to the client.

[2] Advice couched in narrow legal terms may be of little value to a client, especially where practical considerations, such as cost or effects on other people, are predominant. Purely technical legal advice, therefore, can sometimes be inadequate. It is proper for a lawyer to refer to relevant moral and ethical considerations in giving advice. Although a lawyer is not a moral advisor as such, moral and ethical considerations impinge upon most legal questions and may decisively influence how the law will be applied.

[3] A client may expressly or impliedly ask the lawyer for purely technical advice. When such a request is made by a client experienced in legal matters, the lawyer may accept it at face value. When such a request is made by a client inexperienced in legal matters, however, the lawyer's responsibilities as advisor may include the responsibility to indicate that more may be involved than strictly legal considerations. For the allocation of responsibility in decision making between lawyer and client, see Rule 1.2.

[4] Matters that go beyond strictly legal questions may also be in the domain of another profession. Family matters can involve problems within the professional competence of psychiatry, clinical psychology or social work; business matters can involve problems within the competence of the accounting profession or of financial or public relations specialists. Where consultation with a professional in another field is itself something a competent lawyer would recommend, the lawyer should make such a recommendation. At the same time, a lawyer's advice at its best often consists of recommending a course of action in the face of conflicting recommendations of experts.

Offering Advice

[5] In general, a lawyer is not expected to give advice until asked by the client. However, when a lawyer knows that a client proposes a course of action that is likely to result in substantial adverse legal consequences to the client, the lawyer's duty to the client under Rule 1.4 may require that the lawyer offer advice if the client's course of action is related to the representation. Similarly, when a matter is likely to involve litigation, it may be advisable under Rule 1.4 to inform the client of forms of dispute resolution that might constitute reasonable alternatives to litigation. A lawyer ordinarily has no duty to initiate investigation of a client's affairs or to give advice that the client has indicated is unwanted, but a lawyer may initiate advice to a client when doing so appears to be in the client's interest.

Rule 2.2   [Reserved]

Rule 2.3   Evaluation for Use by Third Persons

(a) A lawyer may provide an evaluation of a matter affecting a client for the use of someone other than the client if the lawyer reasonably believes

that making the evaluation is compatible with other aspects of the lawyer's relationship with the client.

(b) When the lawyer knows or reasonably should know that the evaluation is likely to affect the client's interests materially and adversely, the lawyer shall not provide the evaluation unless the client gives informed consent.

(c) Unless disclosure is authorized in connection with a report of an evaluation, information relating to the evaluation is protected by Rule 1.6.

COMMENT

Definition

[1] An evaluation may be performed at the client's direction or if the lawyer reasonably believes that making the evaluation is compatible with other aspects of the lawyer's relationship with the client. Such an evaluation may be for the primary purpose of establishing information for the benefit of third parties: for example, an opinion concerning the title of property rendered at the behest of a vendor for the information of a prospective purchaser, or at the behest of a borrower for the information of a prospective lender. In some situations, the evaluation may be required by a government agency: for example, an opinion concerning the legality of securities registered for sale under the securities laws. In other instances, the evaluation may be required by a third person, such as a purchaser of a business, or of intellectual property or a similar asset.

[2] A legal evaluation should be distinguished from an investigation of a person with whom the lawyer does not have a client-lawyer relationship. For example, a lawyer retained by a purchaser to analyze a vendor's title to property does not have a client-lawyer relationship with the vendor. So also, an investigation into a person's affairs by a government lawyer or by special counsel employed by the government is not an "evaluation" as that term is used in this Rule. The question is whether the lawyer is retained by the person whose affairs are being examined. When the lawyer is retained by that person, the general rules concerning loyalty to a client and preservation of confidences apply, which is not the case if the lawyer is retained by someone else. For this reason, it is essential to identify the person by whom the lawyer is retained. This should be made clear not only to the person under examination, but also to others to whom the results are to be made available.

Duties Owed to Third Person and Client

[3] When the evaluation is intended for the information or use of a third person, a legal duty to that person may or may not arise. That legal question is beyond the scope of this Rule. However, because such an evaluation involves a departure from the normal client-lawyer relationship, careful analysis of the situation is required. The lawyer must be satisfied as a matter of professional judgment that making the evaluation is compatible with other functions undertaken on behalf of the client. For example, if the lawyer is acting as advocate in defending

the client against charges of fraud, it would normally be incompatible with that responsibility for the lawyer to perform an evaluation for others concerning the same or a related transaction. Assuming no such impediment is apparent, however, the lawyer should advise the client of the implications of the evaluation, particularly the lawyer's responsibilities to third persons and the duty to disseminate the findings.

Access to and Disclosure of Information

[4] The quality of an evaluation depends on the freedom and extent of the investigation upon which it is based. Ordinarily a lawyer should have whatever latitude of investigation seems necessary as a matter of professional judgment. Under some circumstances, however, the terms of the evaluation may be limited. For example, certain issues or sources may be categorically excluded, or the scope of the search may be limited by time constraints or the non-cooperation of persons having relevant information. Any such limitations that are material to the evaluation should be described in the report. If, after a lawyer has commenced an evaluation, the client refuses to comply with the terms upon which it was understood the evaluation was to have been made, the lawyer's obligations are determined by law having reference to the terms of the client's agreement and the surrounding circumstances. In no circumstances is the lawyer permitted knowingly to make a false statement of fact or law in providing an evaluation under this Rule. *See* Rule 4.1. A knowing omission of information that must be disclosed to make statements in the evaluation not false or misleading may violate this Rule.

Obtaining Client's Informed Consent

[5] Information relating to an evaluation is protected by Rule 1.6. In many situations, providing an evaluation to a third party poses no significant risk to the client; thus, the lawyer may be impliedly authorized to disclose information to carry out the representation, if the disclosures (i) advance the best interests of the client and (ii) are either reasonable under the circumstances or customary in the professional community. *See* Rule 1.6(a)(2). Where, however, it is reasonably likely that providing the evaluation will affect the client's interests materially and adversely, the lawyer must first obtain the client's consent after the lawyer has consulted with the client and the client has been adequately informed concerning the conditions of the evaluation, the nature of the information to be disclosed and important possible effects on the client's interests. *See* Rules 1.0(j), 1.6(a).

Financial Auditors' Requests for Information

[6] When a question is raised by the client's financial auditor concerning the legal situation of a client, and the question is referred to the lawyer, the lawyer's response may be made in accordance with procedures recognized in the legal profession. Such a procedure is set forth in the American Bar Association Statement

of Policy Regarding Lawyers' Responses to Auditors' Requests for Information, adopted in 1975.

Rule 2.4 Lawyer Serving as Third-Party Neutral

(a) A lawyer serves as a "third-party neutral" when the lawyer assists two or more persons who are not clients of the lawyer to reach a resolution of a dispute or other matter that has arisen between them. Service as a third-party neutral may include service as an arbitrator, a mediator or in such other capacity as will enable the lawyer to assist the parties to resolve the matter.

(b) A lawyer serving as a third-party neutral shall inform unrepresented parties that the lawyer is not representing them. When the lawyer knows or reasonably should know that a party does not understand the lawyer's role in the matter, the lawyer shall explain the difference between the lawyer's role as a third-party neutral and a lawyer's role as one who represents a client.

COMMENT

[1] Alternative dispute resolution has become a substantial part of the civil justice system. In addition to representing clients in dispute-resolution processes, lawyers often serve as third-party neutrals. A "third-party neutral" is a person such as a mediator, arbitrator, conciliator or evaluator or a person serving in another capacity that assists the parties, represented or unrepresented, in the resolution of a dispute or in the arrangement of a transaction. Whether a third-party neutral serves primarily as a facilitator, evaluator or decision maker depends on the particular process that is either selected by the parties or mandated by a court.

[2] The role of a third-party neutral is not unique to lawyers although, in some court-connected contexts, only lawyers are permitted to serve in this role or to handle certain types of cases. In performing this role, the lawyer may be subject to court rules or other law that applies either to third-party neutrals generally or to lawyers serving as third-party neutrals. Lawyer-neutrals may also be subject to various codes of ethics, such as the Code of Ethics for Arbitration in Commercial Disputes prepared by a joint committee of the American Bar Association and the American Arbitration Association or the Model Standards of Conduct for Mediators jointly prepared by the American Bar Association, the American Arbitration Association and the Society of Professionals in Dispute Resolution.

[3] Unlike nonlawyers who serve as third-party neutrals, lawyers serving in this role may experience unique problems as a result of differences between the role of a third-party neutral and a lawyer's service as a client representative. The potential for confusion is significant when the parties are unrepresented in the process. Thus, paragraph (b) requires a lawyer-neutral to inform unrepresented parties that the lawyer is not representing them. For some parties, particularly parties who frequently use dispute-resolution processes, this information will be sufficient. For others, particularly those who are using the process for the first time, more information

will be required. Where appropriate, the lawyer should inform unrepresented parties of the important differences between the lawyer's role as a third-party neutral and as a client representative, including the inapplicability of the attorney-client evidentiary privilege. The extent of disclosure required under this paragraph will depend on the particular parties involved and the subject matter of the proceeding, as well as the particular features of the dispute-resolution process selected.

[4] A lawyer who serves as a third-party neutral may be asked subsequently to serve as a lawyer representing a client in the same matter. The conflicts of interest that arise for both the lawyer and the lawyer's law firm are addressed in Rule 1.12.

[5] Lawyers who represent clients in alternative dispute-resolution processes are governed by the Rules of Professional Conduct. When the dispute-resolution process takes place before a tribunal, as in binding arbitration (*see* Rule 1.0(w)), the lawyer's duty of candor is governed by Rule 3.3. Otherwise, the lawyer's duty of candor toward both the third-party neutral and other parties is governed by Rule 4.1.

Rule 3.1   Non-Meritorious Claims and Contentions

(a) A lawyer shall not bring or defend a proceeding, or assert or controvert an issue therein, unless there is a basis in law and fact for doing so that is not frivolous. A lawyer for the defendant in a criminal proceeding or for the respondent in a proceeding that could result in incarceration may nevertheless so defend the proceeding as to require that every element of the case be established.

(b) A lawyer's conduct is "frivolous" for purposes of this Rule if:

(1) the lawyer knowingly advances a claim or defense that is unwarranted under existing law, except that the lawyer may advance such claim or defense if it can be supported by good faith argument for an extension, modification, or reversal of existing law;

(2) the conduct has no reasonable purpose other than to delay or prolong the resolution of litigation, in violation of Rule 3.2, or serves merely to harass or maliciously injure another; or

(3) the lawyer knowingly asserts material factual statements that are false.

COMMENT

[1] The advocate has a duty to use legal procedure for the fullest benefit of the client's cause, but also a duty not to abuse legal procedure. The law, both procedural and substantive, establishes the limits within which an advocate may proceed. However, the law is not always clear and is never static. Accordingly, in determining the proper scope of advocacy, account must be taken of the law's ambiguities and potential for change.

[2] The filing of a claim or defense or similar action taken for a client is not frivolous merely because the facts have not first been fully substantiated or because the lawyer expects to develop vital evidence only by discovery. Lawyers are required,

however, to inform themselves about the facts of their clients' cases and the applicable law, and determine that they can make good-faith arguments in support of their clients' positions. Such action is not frivolous even though the lawyer believes that the client's position ultimately will not prevail. The action is frivolous, however, if the action has no reasonable purpose other than to harass or maliciously injure a person, or if the lawyer is unable either to make a good-faith argument on the merits of the action taken or to support the action taken by a good-faith argument for an extension, modification or reversal of existing law (which includes the establishment of new judge-made law). The term ''knowingly,'' which is used in Rule 3.1(b)(1) and (b)(3), is defined in Rule 1.0(k).

[3] The lawyer's obligations under this Rule are subordinate to federal or state constitutional law that entitles a defendant in a criminal matter to the assistance of counsel in presenting a claim or contention that otherwise would be prohibited by this Rule.

Rule 3.2   Delay of Litigation

In representing a client, a lawyer shall not use means that have no substantial purpose other than to delay or prolong the proceeding or to cause needless expense.

COMMENT

[1] Dilatory practices bring the administration of justice into disrepute. Such tactics are prohibited if their only substantial purpose is to frustrate an opposing party's attempt to obtain rightful redress or repose. It is not a justification that such tactics are often tolerated by the bench and bar. The question is whether a competent lawyer acting in good faith would regard the course of action as having some substantial purpose other than delay or needless expense. Seeking or realizing financial or other benefit from otherwise improper delay in litigation is not a legitimate interest of the client.

Rule 3.3   Conduct Before a Tribunal

(a) A lawyer shall not knowingly:

(1) make a false statement of fact or law to a tribunal or fail to correct a false statement of material fact or law previously made to the tribunal by the lawyer;

(2) fail to disclose to the tribunal controlling legal authority known to the lawyer to be directly adverse to the position of the client and not disclosed by opposing counsel; or

(3) offer or use evidence that the lawyer knows to be false. If a lawyer, the lawyer's client, or a witness called by the lawyer has offered material evidence and the lawyer comes to know of its falsity, the lawyer shall take reasonable remedial measures, including, if necessary, disclosure to the

tribunal. A lawyer may refuse to offer evidence, other than the testimony of a defendant in a criminal matter, that the lawyer reasonably believes is false.

(b) A lawyer who represents a client before a tribunal and who knows that a person intends to engage, is engaging or has engaged in criminal or fraudulent conduct related to the proceeding shall take reasonable remedial measures, including, if necessary, disclosure to the tribunal.

(c) The duties stated in paragraphs (a) and (b) apply even if compliance requires disclosure of information otherwise protected by Rule 1.6.

(d) In an ex parte proceeding, a lawyer shall inform the tribunal of all material facts known to the lawyer that will enable the tribunal to make an informed decision, whether or not the facts are adverse.

(e) In presenting a matter to a tribunal, a lawyer shall disclose, unless privileged or irrelevant, the identities of the clients the lawyer represents and of the persons who employed the lawyer.

(f) In appearing as a lawyer before a tribunal, a lawyer shall not:

(1) fail to comply with known local customs of courtesy or practice of the bar or a particular tribunal without giving to opposing counsel timely notice of the intent not to comply;

(2) engage in undignified or discourteous conduct;

(3) intentionally or habitually violate any established rule of procedure or of evidence; or

(4) engage in conduct intended to disrupt the tribunal.

COMMENT

[1] This Rule governs the conduct of a lawyer who is representing a client in the proceedings of a tribunal. See Rule 1.0(w) for the definition of "tribunal." It also applies when the lawyer is representing a client in an ancillary proceeding conducted pursuant to the tribunal's adjudicative authority, such as a deposition. Thus, for example, paragraph (a)(3) requires a lawyer to take reasonable remedial measures if the lawyer comes to know that a client has offered false evidence in a deposition.

[2] This Rule sets forth the special duties of lawyers as officers of the court to avoid conduct that undermines the integrity of the adjudicative process. A lawyer acting as an advocate in an adjudicative proceeding has an obligation to present the client's case with persuasive force. Performance of that duty while maintaining confidences of the client, however, is qualified by the advocate's duty of candor to the tribunal. Consequently, although a lawyer in an adversary proceeding is not required to present an impartial exposition of the law and may not vouch for the evidence submitted in a cause, the lawyer must not allow the tribunal to be misled by false statements of law or fact or by evidence that the lawyer knows to be false.

Representations by a Lawyer

[3] An advocate is responsible for pleadings and other documents prepared for litigation, but is usually not required to have personal knowledge of matters asserted

therein because litigation documents ordinarily present assertions by the client or by someone on the client's behalf and not assertions by the lawyer. Compare Rule 3.1. However, an assertion purporting to be based on the lawyer's own knowledge, as in an affidavit or declaration by the lawyer or in a statement in open court, may properly be made only when the lawyer knows the assertion is true or believes it to be true on the basis of a reasonably diligent inquiry. There are circumstances where failure to make a disclosure is the equivalent of an affirmative misrepresentation. The obligation prescribed in Rule 1.2(d) not to counsel a client to commit or assist the client in committing a fraud applies in litigation. *See also* Rule 8.4(b), Comments [2]-[3].

Legal Argument

[4] Although a lawyer is not required to make a disinterested exposition of the law, legal argument based on a knowingly false representation of law constitutes dishonesty toward the tribunal. Paragraph (a)(2) requires an advocate to disclose directly adverse and controlling legal authority that is known to the lawyer and that has not been disclosed by the opposing party. A tribunal that is fully informed on the applicable law is better able to make a fair and accurate determination of the matter before it.

Offering or Using False Evidence

[5] Paragraph (a)(3) requires that the lawyer refuse to offer or use evidence that the lawyer knows to be false, regardless of the client's wishes. This duty is premised on the lawyer's obligation as an officer of the court to prevent the trier of fact from being misled by false evidence. A lawyer does not violate this Rule if the lawyer offers the evidence for the purpose of establishing its falsity.

[6] If a lawyer knows that the client intends to testify falsely or wants the lawyer to introduce or use false evidence, the lawyer should seek to persuade the client that the evidence should not be offered. If the persuasion is ineffective and the lawyer continues to represent the client, the lawyer must refuse to offer the false evidence. If only a portion of a witness's testimony will be false, the lawyer may call the witness to testify but may not (i) elicit or otherwise permit the witness to present testimony that the lawyer knows is false or (ii) base arguments to the trier of fact on evidence known to be false.

[6A] The duties stated in paragraphs (a) and (b) — including the prohibitions against offering and using false evidence — apply to all lawyers, including lawyers for plaintiffs and defendants in civil matters, and to both prosecutors and defense counsel in criminal cases. In criminal matters, therefore, Rule 3.3(a)(3) requires a prosecutor to refrain from offering or using false evidence, and to take reasonable remedial measures to correct any false evidence that the government has already offered. For example, when a prosecutor comes to know that a prosecution witness has testified falsely, the prosecutor should either recall the witness to give truthful testimony or should inform the tribunal about the false evidence. At the sentencing stage, a prosecutor should correct any material errors in a presentence report. In addition, prosecutors are subject to special duties and prohibitions that are set out in Rule 3.8.

[7] If a criminal defendant insists on testifying and the lawyer knows that the testimony will be false, the lawyer may have the option of offering the testimony in a narrative form, though this option may require advance notice to the court or court approval. The lawyer's ethical duties under paragraphs (a) and (b) may be qualified by judicial decisions interpreting the constitutional rights to due process and to counsel in criminal cases. The obligation of the advocate under the Rules of Professional Conduct is subordinate to such requirements.

[8] The prohibition against offering or using false evidence applies only if the lawyer knows that the evidence is false. A lawyer's reasonable belief that evidence is false does not preclude its presentation to the trier of fact. A lawyer's knowledge that evidence is false, however, can be inferred from the circumstances. *See* Rule 1.0(k) for the definition of "knowledge." Thus, although a lawyer should resolve doubts about the veracity of testimony or other evidence in favor of the client, the lawyer cannot ignore an obvious falsehood.

[9] Although paragraph (a)(3) prohibits a lawyer from offering or using evidence the lawyer knows to be false, it permits the lawyer to refuse to offer testimony or other proof that the lawyer reasonably believes to be false. Offering such proof may impair the integrity of an adjudicatory proceeding. Because of the special protections historically provided criminal defendants, however, this Rule does not permit a lawyer to refuse to offer the testimony of a criminal defense client where the lawyer reasonably believes, but does not know, that the testimony will be false. Unless the lawyer knows the testimony will be false, the lawyer must honor the criminal defendant's decision to testify.

Remedial Measures

[10] A lawyer who has offered or used material evidence in the belief that it was true may subsequently come to know that the evidence is false. Or, a lawyer may be surprised when the lawyer's client or another witness called by the lawyer offers testimony the lawyer knows to be false, either during the lawyer's direct examination or in response to cross-examination by the opposing lawyer. In such situations, or if the lawyer knows of the falsity of testimony elicited from the client during a deposition, the lawyer must take reasonable remedial measures. The advocate's proper course is to remonstrate with the client confidentially, advise the client of the lawyer's duty of candor to the tribunal, and seek the client's cooperation with respect to the withdrawal or correction of the false statements or evidence. If that fails, the advocate must take further remedial action. If withdrawal from the representation is not permitted or will not undo the effect of the false evidence, the advocate must make such disclosure to the tribunal as is reasonably necessary to remedy the situation, even if doing so requires the lawyer to reveal confidential information that otherwise would be protected by Rule 1.6. It is for the tribunal then to determine what should be done, such as making a statement about the matter to the trier of fact, ordering a mistrial, taking other appropriate steps or doing nothing.

[11] The disclosure of a client's false testimony can result in grave consequences to the client, including not only a sense of betrayal but also loss of the case and perhaps a prosecution for perjury. But the alternative is for the lawyer to cooperate in deceiving the court, thereby subverting the truth-finding process, which the adversary system is designed to implement. *See* Rule 1.2(d). Furthermore, unless it

is clearly understood that the lawyer will act upon the duty to disclose the existence of false evidence, the client can simply reject the lawyer's advice to reveal the false evidence and insist that the lawyer keep silent. The client could therefore in effect coerce the lawyer into being a party to a fraud on the court.

Preserving Integrity of the Adjudicative Process

[12] Lawyers have a special obligation as officers of the court to protect a tribunal against criminal or fraudulent conduct that undermines the integrity of the adjudicative process. Accordingly, paragraph (b) requires a lawyer who represents a client in an adjudicative proceeding to take reasonable remedial measures, including disclosure if necessary, whenever the lawyer knows that a person, including the lawyer's client, intends to engage, is engaging or has engaged in criminal or fraudulent conduct related to the proceeding. Such conduct includes, among other things, bribing, intimidating or otherwise unlawfully communicating with a witness, juror, court official or other participant in the proceeding; unlawfully destroying or concealing documents or other evidence related to the proceeding; and failing to disclose information to the tribunal when required by law to do so. For example, under some circumstances a person's omission of a material fact may constitute a crime or fraud on the tribunal.

[12A] A lawyer's duty to take reasonable remedial measures under paragraph (b) does not apply to another lawyer who is retained to represent a person in an investigation or proceeding concerning that person's conduct in the prior proceeding.

[13] Judicial hearings ought to be conducted through dignified and orderly procedures designed to protect the rights of all parties. A lawyer should not engage in conduct that offends the dignity and decorum of proceedings or that is intended to disrupt the tribunal. While maintaining independence, a lawyer should be respectful and courteous in relations with a judge or hearing officer before whom the lawyer appears. In adversary proceedings, ill feeling may exist between clients, but such ill feeling should not influence a lawyer's conduct, attitude, and demeanor towards opposing lawyers. A lawyer should not make unfair or derogatory personal reference to opposing counsel. Haranguing and offensive tactics by lawyers interfere with the orderly administration of justice and have no proper place in our legal system.

Ex Parte Proceedings

[14] Ordinarily, an advocate has the limited responsibility of presenting one side of the matters that a tribunal should consider in reaching a decision; the opposing position is expected to be presented by the adverse party. However, in any ex parte proceeding, such as an application for a temporary restraining order, there may be no presentation by opposing advocates. The object of an ex parte proceeding is nevertheless to yield a substantially just result. The judge has an affirmative responsibility to accord the opposing party, if absent, just consideration. The lawyer for the represented party has the correlative duty to make disclosures of material facts known to the lawyer that the lawyer reasonably believes are necessary to an informed decision.

Withdrawal

[15] A lawyer's compliance with the duty of candor imposed by this Rule does not automatically require that the lawyer withdraw from the representation of a client whose interests will be or have been adversely affected by the lawyer's disclosure. The lawyer, however, may be required by Rule 1.16(d) to seek permission of the tribunal to withdraw if the lawyer's compliance with this Rule's duty of candor results in such an extreme deterioration of the client-lawyer relationship that the lawyer can no longer competently represent the client. *See also* Rule 1.16(c) for the circumstances in which a lawyer will be permitted to seek a tribunal's permission to withdraw. In connection with a request for permission to withdraw that is premised on a client's misconduct, a lawyer may reveal information relating to the representation only to the extent reasonably necessary to comply with this Rule or as otherwise permitted by Rule 1.6.

Rule 3.4 Fairness to Opposing Party and Counsel

A lawyer shall not:

(a)(1) suppress any evidence that the lawyer or the client has a legal obligation to reveal or produce;

(2) advise or cause a person to hide or leave the jurisdiction of a tribunal for the purpose of making the person unavailable as a witness therein;

(3) conceal or knowingly fail to disclose that which the lawyer is required by law to reveal;

(4) knowingly use perjured testimony or false evidence;

(5) participate in the creation or preservation of evidence when the lawyer knows or it is obvious that the evidence is false; or

(6) knowingly engage in other illegal conduct or conduct contrary to these Rules;

(b) offer an inducement to a witness that is prohibited by law or pay, offer to pay or acquiesce in the payment of compensation to a witness contingent upon the content of the witness's testimony or the outcome of the matter. A lawyer may advance, guarantee or acquiesce in the payment of:

(1) reasonable compensation to a witness for the loss of time in attending, testifying, preparing to testify or otherwise assisting counsel, and reasonable related expenses; or

(2) a reasonable fee for the professional services of an expert witness and reasonable related expenses;

(c) disregard or advise the client to disregard a standing rule of a tribunal or a ruling of a tribunal made in the course of a proceeding, but the lawyer may take appropriate steps in good faith to test the validity of such rule or ruling;

(d) in appearing before a tribunal on behalf of a client:

(1) state or allude to any matter that the lawyer does not reasonably believe is relevant or that will not be supported by admissible evidence;

(2) assert personal knowledge of facts in issue except when testifying as a witness;

(3) assert a personal opinion as to the justness of a cause, the credibility of a witness, the culpability of a civil litigant or the guilt or innocence of an accused but the lawyer may argue, upon analysis of the evidence, for any position or conclusion with respect to the matters stated herein; or

(4) ask any question that the lawyer has no reasonable basis to believe is relevant to the case and that is intended to degrade a witness or other person; or

(e) present, participate in presenting, or threaten to present criminal charges solely to obtain an advantage in a civil matter.

COMMENT

[1] The procedure of the adversary system contemplates that the evidence in a case is to be marshaled competitively by the contending parties. Fair competition in the adversary system is secured by prohibitions against destruction or concealment of evidence, improperly influencing witnesses, obstructionist tactics in discovery procedure, and the like. The Rule applies to any conduct that falls within its general terms (for example, "obstruct another party's access to evidence") that is a crime, an intentional tort or prohibited by rules or a ruling of a tribunal. An example is "advis[ing] or caus[ing] a person to hide or leave the jurisdiction of a tribunal for the purpose of making the person unavailable as a witness therein."

[2] Documents and other evidence are often essential to establish a claim or defense. Subject to evidentiary privileges, the right of an opposing party, including the government, to obtain evidence through discovery or subpoena is an important procedural right. The exercise of that right can be frustrated if relevant material is altered, concealed or destroyed. Paragraph (a) protects that right. Evidence that has been properly requested must be produced unless there is a good-faith basis for not doing so. Applicable state and federal law may make it an offense to destroy material for the purpose of impairing its availability in a pending or reasonably foreseeable proceeding, even though no specific request to reveal or produce evidence has been made. Paragraph (a) applies to evidentiary material generally, including computerized information.

[2A] Falsifying evidence, dealt with in paragraph (a), is also generally a criminal offense. Of additional relevance is Rule 3.3(a)(3), dealing with use of false evidence in a proceeding before a tribunal. Applicable law may permit a lawyer to take temporary possession of physical evidence of client crimes for the purpose of conducting a limited examination that will not alter or destroy material characteristics of the evidence. In such a case, applicable law may require the lawyer to turn the evidence over to the police or other prosecuting authority, depending on the circumstances.

[3] Paragraph (b) applies generally to any inducement to a witness that is prohibited by law. It is not improper to pay a witness's reasonable expenses or to

compensate an expert witness on terms permitted by law. However, any fee contingent upon the content of a witness' testimony or the outcome of the case is prohibited.

[3A] Paragraph (d) deals with improper statements relating to the merits of a case when representing a client before a tribunal: alluding to irrelevant matters, asserting personal knowledge of facts in issue, and asserting a personal opinion on issues to be decided by the trier of fact. *See also* Rule 4.4, prohibiting the use of any means that have no substantial purpose other than to embarrass or harm a third person. However, a lawyer may argue, upon analysis of the evidence, for any position or conclusion supported by the record. The term "admissible evidence" refers to evidence considered admissible in the particular context. For example, admission of evidence in an administrative adjudication or an arbitration proceeding may be governed by different standards than those applied in a jury trial.

[4] In general, a lawyer is prohibited from giving legal advice to an unrepresented person, other than the advice to secure counsel, when the interests of that person are or may have a reasonable possibility of being in conflict with the interests of the lawyer's client. *See* Rule 4.3.

[5] The use of threats in negotiation may constitute the crime of extortion. However, not all threats are improper. For example, if a lawyer represents a client who has been criminally harmed by a third person (for example, a theft of property), the lawyer's threat to report the crime does not constitute extortion when honestly claimed in an effort to obtain restitution or indemnification for the harm done. But extortion is committed if the threat involves conduct of the third person unrelated to the criminal harm (for example, a threat to report tax evasion by the third person that is unrelated to the civil dispute).

Rule 3.5   Maintaining and Preserving the Impartiality of Tribunals and Jurors

(a) A lawyer shall not:

(1) **seek to or cause another person to influence a judge, official or employee of a tribunal by means prohibited by law or give or lend anything of value to such judge, official, or employee of a tribunal when the recipient is prohibited from accepting the gift or loan but a lawyer may make a contribution to the campaign fund of a candidate for judicial office in conformity with Part 100 of the Rules of the Chief Administrator of the Courts;**

(2) **in an adversarial proceeding communicate or cause another person to do so on the lawyer's behalf, as to the merits of the matter with a judge or official of a tribunal or an employee thereof before whom the matter is pending, except:**

(i) **in the course of official proceedings in the matter;**

(ii) **in writing, if the lawyer promptly delivers a copy of the writing to counsel for other parties and to a party who is not represented by a lawyer;**

(iii) orally, upon adequate notice to counsel for the other parties and to any party who is not represented by a lawyer; or

(iv) as otherwise authorized by law, or by Part 100 of the Rules of the Chief Administrator of the Courts;

(3) seek to or cause another person to influence a juror or prospective juror by means prohibited by law;

(4) communicate or cause another to communicate with a member of the jury venire from which the jury will be selected for the trial of a case or, during the trial of a case, with any member of the jury unless authorized to do so by law or court order;

(5) communicate with a juror or prospective juror after discharge of the jury if:

(i) the communication is prohibited by law or court order;

(ii) the juror has made known to the lawyer a desire not to communicate;

(iii) the communication involves misrepresentation, coercion, duress or harassment; or

(iv) the communication is an attempt to influence the juror's actions in future jury service; or

(6) conduct a vexatious or harassing investigation of either a member of the venire or a juror or, by financial support or otherwise, cause another to do so.

(b) During the trial of a case a lawyer who is not connected therewith shall not communicate with or cause another to communicate with a juror concerning the case.

(c) All restrictions imposed by this Rule also apply to communications with or investigations of members of a family of a member of the venire or a juror.

(d) A lawyer shall reveal promptly to the court improper conduct by a member of the venire or a juror, or by another toward a member of the venire or a juror or a member of his or her family of which the lawyer has knowledge.

COMMENT

[1] Many forms of improper influence upon a tribunal are proscribed by criminal law. In addition, gifts and loans to judges and judicial employees, as well as contributions to candidates for judicial election, are regulated by the New York Code of Judicial Conduct, with which an advocate should be familiar. *See* New York Code of Judicial Conduct, Canon 4(D)(5), 22 N.Y.C.R.R. §100.4(D)(5) (prohibition of a judge's receipt of a gift, loan, etc., and exceptions) and Canon 5(A)(5), 22 N.Y.C.R.R. §100.5(A)(5) (concerning lawyer contributions to the campaign committee of a candidate for judicial office). A lawyer is prohibited from aiding a violation of such provisions. Limitations on contributions in the Election Law may also be relevant.

[2] Unless authorized to do so by law or court order, a lawyer is prohibited from communicating ex parte with persons serving in a judicial capacity in an adjudicative proceeding, such as judges, masters or jurors, or to employees who assist them, such as law clerks. *See* New York Code of Judicial Conduct, Canon 3(B)(6), 22 N.Y.C.R.R. §100.3(B)(6).

[3] A lawyer may on occasion want to communicate with a juror or prospective juror after the jury has been discharged. Paragraph (a)(5) permits a lawyer to do so unless the communication is prohibited by law or a court order, but the lawyer must respect the desire of a juror not to talk with the lawyer. The lawyer may not engage in improper conduct during the communication.

[4] The advocate's function is to present evidence and argument so that the cause may be decided according to law. Refraining from abusive or obstreperous conduct is a corollary of the advocate's right to speak on behalf of litigants. A lawyer may stand firm against abuse by a judge but should avoid reciprocation; the judge's misbehavior is no justification for similar dereliction by an advocate. An advocate can present the cause, protect the record for subsequent review and preserve professional integrity by patient firmness no less effectively than by belligerence or theatrics.

[4A] Paragraph (b) prohibits lawyers who are not connected with a case from communicating (or causing another to communicate) with jurors concerning the case.

[4B] Paragraph (c) extends the rules concerning communications with jurors and members of the venire to communications with family members of the jurors and venire members.

[4C] Paragraph (d) imposes a reporting obligation on lawyers who have knowledge of improper conduct by or toward jurors, members of the venire, or family members thereof.

Rule 3.6   Trial Publicity

(a) A lawyer who is participating in or has participated in a criminal or civil matter shall not make an extrajudicial statement that the lawyer knows or reasonably should know will be disseminated by means of public communication and will have a substantial likelihood of materially prejudicing an adjudicative proceeding in the matter.

(b) A statement ordinarily is likely to prejudice materially an adjudicative proceeding when it refers to a civil matter triable to a jury, a criminal matter or any other proceeding that could result in incarceration, and the statement relates to:

(1) the character, credibility, reputation or criminal record of a party, suspect in a criminal investigation or witness, or the identity of a witness or the expected testimony of a party or witness;

(2) in a criminal matter that could result in incarceration, the possibility of a plea of guilty to the offense or the existence or contents of any confession, admission or statement given by a defendant or suspect, or that person's refusal or failure to make a statement;

(3) the performance or results of any examination or test, or the refusal or failure of a person to submit to an examination or test, or the identity or nature of physical evidence expected to be presented;

(4) any opinion as to the guilt or innocence of a defendant or suspect in a criminal matter that could result in incarceration;

(5) information the lawyer knows or reasonably should know is likely to be inadmissible as evidence in a trial and would, if disclosed, create a substantial risk of prejudicing an impartial trial; or

(6) the fact that a defendant has been charged with a crime, unless there is included therein a statement explaining that the charge is merely an accusation and that the defendant is presumed innocent until and unless proven guilty.

(c) Provided that the statement complies with paragraph (a), a lawyer may state the following without elaboration:

(1) the claim, offense or defense and, except when prohibited by law, the identity of the persons involved;

(2) information contained in a public record;

(3) that an investigation of a matter is in progress;

(4) the scheduling or result of any step in litigation;

(5) a request for assistance in obtaining evidence and information necessary thereto;

(6) a warning of danger concerning the behavior of a person involved, when there is reason to believe that there exists the likelihood of substantial harm to an individual or to the public interest; and

(7) in a criminal matter:

(i) the identity, age, residence, occupation and family status of the accused;

(ii) if the accused has not been apprehended, information necessary to aid in apprehension of that person;

(iii) the identity of investigating and arresting officers or agencies and the length of the investigation; and

(iv) the fact, time and place of arrest, resistance, pursuit and use of weapons, and a description of physical evidence seized, other than as contained only in a confession, admission or statement.

(d) Notwithstanding paragraph (a), a lawyer may make a statement that a reasonable lawyer would believe is required to protect a client from the substantial prejudicial effect of recent publicity not initiated by the lawyer or the lawyer's client. A statement made pursuant to this paragraph shall be limited to such information as is necessary to mitigate the recent adverse publicity.

(e) No lawyer associated in a firm or government agency with a lawyer subject to paragraph (a) shall make a statement prohibited by paragraph (a).

COMMENT

[1] It is difficult to strike a balance between protecting the right to a fair trial and safeguarding the right of free expression. Preserving the right to a fair trial necessarily entails some curtailment of the information that may be disseminated about a party prior to trial, particularly where trial by jury is involved. If there were no such limits, the result would be the practical nullification of the protective effect of the rules of forensic decorum and the exclusionary rules of evidence. On the other hand, there are vital social interests served by the free dissemination of information about events having legal consequences and about legal proceedings themselves. The public has a right to know about threats to its safety and measures aimed at assuring its security. It also has a legitimate interest in the conduct of judicial proceedings, particularly in matters of general public concern. Furthermore, the subject matter of legal proceedings is often of direct significance in debate and deliberation over questions of public policy.

[2] Special rules of confidentiality may validly govern proceedings in juvenile, domestic relations and mental disability proceedings and perhaps other types of litigation. Rule 3.4(c) requires compliance with such rules.

[3] The Rule sets forth a basic general prohibition against a lawyer making statements that the lawyer knows or reasonably should know will have a substantial likelihood of materially prejudicing an adjudicative proceeding. It recognizes that the public value of informed commentary is great and that the likelihood of prejudice to a proceeding because of the commentary of a lawyer who is not involved in the proceeding is small. Thus, the Rule applies only to lawyers who are participating or have participated in the investigation or litigation of a matter and their associates.

[4] There are certain subjects that are more likely than not to have a material prejudicial effect on a proceeding, particularly when they refer to a civil matter triable to a jury, a criminal matter or any other proceeding that could result in incarceration. Paragraph (b) specifies certain statements that ordinarily will have prejudicial effect.

[5] Paragraph (c) identifies specific matters about which a lawyer's statements would not ordinarily be considered to present a substantial likelihood of material prejudice. Nevertheless, some statements in criminal cases are also required to meet the fundamental requirements of paragraph (a), for example, those identified in paragraph (c)(7)(iv). Paragraph (c) is not intended to be an exhaustive listing of the subjects upon which a lawyer may make a statement; statements on other matters may be permissible under paragraph (a).

[6] Another relevant factor in determining prejudice is the nature of the proceeding involved. Criminal jury trials will be most sensitive to extrajudicial speech. Civil trials may be less sensitive. Non-jury hearings and arbitration proceedings may be even less affected. The Rule will still place limitations on prejudicial comments in these cases, but the likelihood of prejudice may be different depending on the type of proceeding.

[7] Extrajudicial statements that might otherwise raise a question under this Rule may be permissible when they are made in response to statements made publicly by another party, another party's lawyer or third persons, where a reasonable lawyer would believe a public response is required in order to avoid prejudice to the lawyer's client. When prejudicial statements have been publicly made by others,

responsive statements may have the salutary effect of lessening any resulting adverse impact on the adjudicative proceeding. Paragraph (d) permits such responsive statements, provided they contain only such information as is necessary to mitigate undue prejudice created by the statements made by others.

[8] See Rule 3.8 Comment [5] for additional duties of prosecutors in connection with extrajudicial statements about criminal proceedings.

Rule 3.7   Lawyer as Witness

(a) A lawyer shall not act as advocate before a tribunal in a matter in which the lawyer is likely to be a witness on a significant issue of fact unless:

(1) the testimony relates solely to an uncontested issue;

(2) the testimony relates solely to the nature and value of legal services rendered in the matter;

(3) disqualification of the lawyer would work substantial hardship on the client;

(4) the testimony will relate solely to a matter of formality, and there is no reason to believe that substantial evidence will be offered in opposition to the testimony; or

(5) the testimony is authorized by the tribunal.

(b) A lawyer may not act as advocate before a tribunal in a matter if:

(1) another lawyer in the lawyer's firm is likely to be called as a witness on a significant issue other than on behalf of the client, and it is apparent that the testimony may be prejudicial to the client; or

(2) the lawyer is precluded from doing so by Rule 1.7 or Rule 1.9.

COMMENT

[1] Combining the roles of advocate and witness can prejudice the tribunal and the opposing party and also can create a conflict of interest between the lawyer and client.

Advocate-Witness Rule

[2] The tribunal may properly object when the trier of fact may be confused or misled by a lawyer's serving as both advocate and witness. The opposing party may properly object where the combination of roles may prejudice that party's rights in the litigation. A witness is required to testify on the basis of personal knowledge, while an advocate is expected to explain and comment on evidence given by others. It may not be clear whether a statement by an advocate-witness should be taken as proof or as an analysis of the proof. The requirement that the testimony of the advocate-witness be on a significant issue of fact provides a materiality limitation.

[3] To protect the tribunal, the Rule prohibits a lawyer from simultaneously serving as advocate and witness except in those circumstances specified in paragraph (a). Paragraph (a)(1) recognizes that if the testimony will be uncontested, the ambiguities in the dual role are purely theoretical. Testimony relating solely to a formality is uncontested when the lawyer reasonably believes that no substantial evidence will be offered in opposition to the testimony. Paragraph (a)(2) recognizes that where the testimony concerns the extent and value of legal services rendered in the action in which the testimony is offered, permitting the lawyer to testify avoids the need for a second trial with new counsel to resolve that issue. Moreover, in such a situation the judge has firsthand knowledge of the matter in issue; hence, there is less dependence on the adversary process to test the credibility of the testimony.

[4] Apart from these two exceptions, paragraph (a)(3) recognizes that a balancing is required among the interests of the client, of the tribunal, and of the opposing party. Whether the tribunal is likely to be misled or the opposing party is likely to suffer prejudice depends on the nature of the case, the importance and probable tenor of the lawyer's testimony and the probability that the lawyer's testimony will conflict with that of other witnesses. Even if there is risk of such prejudice, in determining whether the lawyer should be disqualified, due regard must be given to the effect of disqualification on the lawyer's client. It is relevant that one or both parties could reasonably foresee that the lawyer would probably be a witness. The conflict of interest principles stated in Rule 1.7, 1.9 and 1.10, which may separately require disqualification of the lawyer-advocate, have no application to the tribunal's determination of the balancing of judicial and party interests required by paragraph (a)(3).

[5] The tribunal is not likely to be misled when a lawyer acts as advocate before a tribunal in a matter in which another lawyer in the lawyer's firm testifies as a witness. Therefore, paragraph (b) permits the non-testifying lawyer to act as advocate before the tribunal except (1) when another lawyer in the lawyer's firm is likely to be called as a witness on a significant issue other than on behalf of the client, and it is apparent that the testimony may be prejudicial to the client, or (2) when either Rule 1.7 or Rule 1.9 would prohibit the non-testifying lawyer from acting as advocate before the tribunal. Moreover, unless Rules 1.7 or 1.9 preclude it, the non-testifying lawyer and the testifying lawyer may continue to represent the client outside of the tribunal, with the client's informed consent, in pretrial activities such as legal research, fact gathering, and preparation or argument of motions and briefs on issues of law, and may be consulted during the trial by the lawyer serving as advocate.

Conflict of Interest

[6] In determining whether it is permissible to act as advocate before a tribunal in which the lawyer will be a witness, the lawyer must also consider that the dual role may give rise to a conflict of interest that will require compliance with Rule 1.7 or Rule 1.9. For example, if there is likely to be substantial conflict between the testimony of the client and that of the lawyer, the representation involves a conflict of interest that requires compliance with Rule 1.7. This would be true even though the lawyer might not be prohibited by paragraph (a) from simultaneously serving as advocate and witness because the lawyer's disqualification would work a substantial

hardship on the client. Similarly, a lawyer who might be permitted to serve simultaneously as an advocate and a witness by paragraph (a)(3) might be precluded from doing so by Rule 1.9. The problem can arise whether the lawyer is called as a witness on behalf of the client or is called by the opposing party. Determining whether such a conflict exists is primarily the responsibility of the lawyer involved. If there is a conflict of interest, the lawyer must secure the client's informed consent, confirmed in writing. In some cases, the lawyer will be precluded from seeking the client's consent. *See* Rule 1.7. See Rule 1.0(e) for the definition of ''confirmed in writing'' and Rule 1.0(j) for the definition of ''informed consent.''

Rule 3.8   Special Responsibilities of Prosecutors and Other Government Lawyers

> **Editors' Note.**   Effective July 1, 2012, the Courts added paragraphs (c), (d), and (e) to Rule 3.8. The new paragraphs articulate a prosecutor's duties upon receiving evidence that a person has been wrongfully convicted. The amendments bring New York into line with ABA Model Rule 3.8(g) and (h), though with some differences in language. The changes were originally developed by the New York City Bar Association's Committee on Professional Responsibility in 2005, with the assistance of Professors Bruce Green of Fordham and Ellen Yaroshefsky of Cardozo, who then played key roles in persuading the ABA to add post-conviction responsibilities to ABA Model Rule 3.8.
>
> In 2008, the New York State Bar Association's Committee on Standards of Attorney Conduct (COSAC) recommended similar changes as part of the comprehensive package of proposed amendments to the former Code of Professional Responsibility, but the Courts rejected the proposal. The New York City Bar persisted in negotiating with federal and state prosecutors from around the state, however, and in July 2012 the New York Courts issued an order amending Rule 3.8. We reprint the changes below in legislative style, underscoring all of paragraphs (c), (d), and (e) to indicate that they are new. COSAC was also reviewing the Comment to Rule 3.8 to determine whether any changes were necessary or advisable to reflect the adoption of Rule 3.8(c)-(e).

(a) A prosecutor or other government lawyer shall not institute, cause to be instituted or maintain a criminal charge when the prosecutor or other government lawyer knows or it is obvious that the charge is not supported by probable cause.

(b) A prosecutor or other government lawyer in criminal litigation shall make timely disclosure to counsel for the defendant or to a defendant who has no counsel of the existence of evidence or information known to the prosecutor or other government lawyer that tends to negate the guilt of the accused, mitigate the degree of the offense, or reduce the sentence, except when relieved of this responsibility by a protective order of a tribunal.

(c) When a prosecutor knows of new, credible and material evidence creating a reasonable likelihood that a convicted defendant did not commit an offense of which the defendant was convicted, the prosecutor shall within a reasonable time:

    (1) disclose that evidence to an appropriate court or prosecutor's office; or

    (2) if the conviction was obtained by that prosecutor's office,

        (A) notify the appropriate court and the defendant that the prosecutor's office possesses such evidence unless a court authorizes delay for good cause shown;

        (B) disclose that evidence to the defendant unless the disclosure would interfere with an ongoing investigation or endanger the safety of a witness or other person, and a court authorizes delay for good cause shown; and

        (C) undertake or make reasonable efforts to cause to be undertaken such further inquiry or investigation as may be necessary to provide a reasonable belief that the conviction should or should not be set aside.

    (d) When a prosecutor knows of clear and convincing evidence establishing that a defendant was convicted, in a prosecution by the prosecutor's office, of an offense that the defendant did not commit, the prosecutor shall seek a remedy consistent with justice, applicable law, and the circumstances of the case.

    (e) A prosecutor's independent judgment, made in good faith, that the new evidence is not of such nature as to trigger the obligations of sections (c) and (d), though subsequently determined to have been erroneous, does not constitute a violation of this rule.

COMMENT

    [1] A prosecutor has the responsibility of a minister of justice and not simply that of an advocate. This responsibility carries with it specific obligations to see that the defendant is accorded procedural justice and that guilt is decided upon the basis of sufficient evidence. Applicable state or federal law may require other measures by the prosecutor, and knowing disregard of those obligations or a systematic abuse of prosecutorial discretion could constitute a violation of Rule 8.4. A government lawyer in a criminal case is considered a "prosecutor" for purposes of this Rule.

    [2] A defendant who has no counsel may waive a preliminary hearing or other important pretrial rights and thereby lose a valuable opportunity to challenge probable cause. Accordingly, prosecutors should not seek to obtain waivers of preliminary hearings or other important pretrial rights from unrepresented accused persons. This would not be applicable, however, to an accused appearing pro se with the approval of the tribunal, or to the lawful questioning of an uncharged suspect who has knowingly waived the rights to counsel and silence.

    [3] The exception in paragraph (b) recognizes that a prosecutor may seek an appropriate protective order from the tribunal if disclosure of information to the defense could result in substantial harm to an individual or to the public interest.

    [4] [Reserved.]

    [5] Rule 3.6 prohibits extrajudicial statements that have a substantial likelihood of prejudicing an adjudicatory proceeding. In the context of a criminal prosecution,

a prosecutor's extrajudicial statement can create the additional problem of increasing public condemnation of the accused. Although the announcement of an indictment, for example, will necessarily have severe consequences for the accused, a prosecutor can, and should, avoid comments that have no legitimate law enforcement purpose and have a substantial likelihood of increasing public opprobrium against the accused. A prosecutor in a criminal case should make reasonable efforts to prevent persons under the prosecutor's supervisory authority, which may include investigators, law enforcement personnel, employees and other persons assisting or associated with the prosecutor, from making extrajudicial statements that the prosecutor would be prohibited from making under Rule 3.6. *See* Rule 5.3. Nothing in this Comment is intended to restrict the statements that a prosecutor may make that comply with Rule 3.6(c) or Rule 3.6(d).

[6] Like other lawyers, prosecutors are subject to Rule 5.1 and Rule 5.3, which relate to responsibilities regarding lawyers and nonlawyers who work for or are associated with the lawyer's office. Prosecutors should bear in mind the importance of these obligations in connection with the unique dangers of improper extrajudicial statements in a criminal case, and should exercise reasonable care to prevent persons assisting or associated with the prosecutor from making improper extrajudicial statements. Ordinarily, the reasonable care standard will be satisfied if the prosecutor issues the appropriate cautions to law enforcement personnel and other relevant individuals.

[6A] Reference to a "prosecutor" in this Rule includes the office of the prosecutor and all lawyers affiliated with the prosecutor's office who are responsible for the prosecution function. Like other lawyers, prosecutors are subject to Rule 3.3, which requires a lawyer to take reasonable remedial measures to correct material evidence that the lawyer has offered when the lawyer comes to know of its falsity. *See* Rule 3.3, Comment [6A].

[6B] The prosecutor's duty to seek justice has traditionally been understood not only to require the prosecutor to take precautions to avoid convicting innocent individuals, but also to require the prosecutor to take reasonable remedial measures when it appears likely that an innocent person was wrongly convicted. Accordingly, though not required by these Rules, when a prosecutor comes to know of new and material evidence creating a reasonable likelihood that a person was wrongly convicted, the prosecutor should examine the evidence and undertake such further inquiry or investigation as may be necessary to determine whether the conviction was wrongful. The scope of the inquiry will depend on the circumstances. In some cases, the prosecutor may recognize the need to reinvestigate the underlying case; in others, it may be appropriate to await development of the record in collateral proceedings initiated by the defendant. The nature of the inquiry or investigation should be such as to provide a reasonable belief that the conviction should or should not be set aside.

[6C] Likewise, when a prosecutor comes to know of clear and convincing evidence establishing that a conviction was wrongful, the prosecutor should disclose the new evidence to the defendant so that defense counsel may conduct any necessary investigation and make any appropriate motions directed at setting aside the verdict, and should disclose the new evidence to the court or other appropriate authority so that the court can determine whether to initiate its own inquiry. The evidence should be disclosed in a timely manner, depending on the particular circumstances. For example, disclosure of the evidence might be deferred where it could prejudice the prosecutor's investigation into the matter. If the convicted defendant is unrepresented and cannot afford to retain counsel, the prosecutor should request that the court appoint counsel for purposes of these post-conviction proceedings. This Comment applies to new and material evidence of innocence, regardless of whether it could previously have been discovered by the defense.

[6D] If the prosecutor comes to know of clear and convincing evidence that the defendant was convicted of an offense that the defendant did not commit, the prosecutor should seek to remedy the injustice by taking appropriate steps to remedy the wrongful conviction. These steps may include, depending on the particular circumstances, disclosure of the evidence to the defendant, requesting that the court appoint counsel for an unrepresented indigent defendant and, where appropriate, notifying the court that the prosecutor believes that the defendant was wrongfully convicted.

[6E] Comments [6B], [6C] and [6D] apply whether the new evidence comes to the attention of the prosecutor who obtained the defendant's conviction or to a different prosecutor. If the evidence comes to the attention of a prosecutor in a different prosecutor's office, the prosecutor should notify the office of the prosecutor who obtained the conviction.

Rule 3.9 Advocate in Non-Adjudicative Matters

A lawyer communicating in a representative capacity with a legislative body or administrative agency in connection with a pending non-adjudicative matter or proceeding shall disclose that the appearance is in a representative capacity, except when the lawyer seeks information from an agency that is available to the public.

COMMENT

[1] In representation before bodies such as legislatures, municipal councils and executive and administrative agencies acting in a rule-making or policy-making capacity, lawyers present facts, formulate issues and advance arguments regarding the matters under consideration. The legislative body or administrative agency is entitled to know that the lawyer is appearing in a representative capacity. Ordinarily the client will consent to being identified, but if not, such as when the lawyer is appearing on behalf of an undisclosed principal, the governmental body at least knows that the lawyer is acting in a representative capacity as opposed to advancing the lawyer's personal opinion as a citizen. Representation in such matters is governed by Rules 4.1 through 4.4, and 8.4.

[1A] Rule 3.9 does not apply to adjudicative proceedings before a tribunal. Court rules and other law require a lawyer, in making an appearance before a tribunal in a representative capacity, to identify the client or clients and provide other information required for communication with the tribunal or other parties.

[2] [Reserved.]

[3] [Reserved.]

Rule 4.1 Truthfulness in Statements to Others

In the course of representing a client, a lawyer shall not knowingly make a false statement of fact or law to a third person.

COMMENT

Misrepresentation

[1] A lawyer is required to be truthful when dealing with others on a client's behalf, but generally has no affirmative duty to inform an opposing party of relevant facts. A misrepresentation can occur if the lawyer incorporates or affirms a statement of another person that the lawyer knows is false. Misrepresentations can also occur by partially true but misleading statements or omissions that are the equivalent of affirmative false statements. As to dishonest conduct that does not amount to a false statement or for misrepresentations by a lawyer other than in the course of representing a client, see Rule 8.4.

Statements of Fact

[2] This Rule refers to statements of fact. Whether a particular statement should be regarded as one of fact can depend on the circumstances. Under generally accepted conventions in negotiation, certain types of statements ordinarily are not taken as statements of fact. Estimates of price or value placed on the subject of a transaction and a party's intentions as to an acceptable settlement of a claim are ordinarily in this category; so is the existence of an undisclosed principal, except where nondisclosure of the principal would constitute fraud. Lawyers should be mindful of their obligations under applicable law to avoid criminal and tortious misrepresentation.

Illegal or Fraudulent Conduct by Client

[3] Under Rule 1.2(d), a lawyer is prohibited from counseling or assisting a client as to conduct that the lawyer knows is illegal or fraudulent. Ordinarily, a lawyer can avoid assisting a client's illegality or fraud by withdrawing from the representation. *See* Rule 1.16(c)(2). Sometimes it may be necessary for the lawyer to give notice of the fact of withdrawal and to disaffirm an opinion, document, affirmation or the like. *See* Rules 1.2(d), 1.6(b)(3).

Rule 4.2 Communication with Person Represented by Counsel

(a) In representing a client, a lawyer shall not communicate or cause another to communicate about the subject of the representation with a party

the lawyer knows to be represented by another lawyer in the matter, unless the lawyer has the prior consent of the other lawyer or is authorized to do so by law.

(b) Notwithstanding the prohibitions of paragraph (a), and unless otherwise prohibited by law, a lawyer may cause a client to communicate with a represented person unless the represented person is not legally competent, and may counsel the client with respect to those communications, provided the lawyer gives reasonable advance notice to the represented person's counsel that such communications will be taking place.

> **Editors' Note.** Shortly before we went to press, New York's Courts approved a new paragraph (c) to Rule 4.2 that would provide as follows:
>
> > (c) A lawyer who is acting *pro se* or is represented by counsel in a matter is subject to paragraph (a), but may communicate with a represented person, unless otherwise prohibited by law and unless the represented person is not legally competent, provided the lawyer or the lawyer's counsel gives reasonable advance notice to the represented person's counsel that such communications will be taking place.
>
> The Courts were expected to publish an Order adding the new paragraph in November 2012. For additional information, and for the text of a new Comment [12A] that the State Bar wrote to explain paragraph (c), see the Editors' Introduction at the beginning of the New York Rules of Professional Conduct.

COMMENT

[1] This Rule contributes to the proper functioning of the legal system by protecting a person who has chosen to be represented by a lawyer in a matter against possible overreaching by other lawyers who are participating in the matter, interference by those lawyers with the client-lawyer relationship, and un-counseled disclosure of information relating to the representation.

[2] Paragraph (a) applies to communications with any party who is represented by counsel concerning the matter to which the communication relates.

[3] Paragraph (a) applies even though the represented party initiates or consents to the communication. A lawyer must immediately terminate communication with a party if after commencing communication, the lawyer learns that the party is one with whom communication is not permitted by this Rule.

[4] This Rule does not prohibit communication with a represented party or person or an employee or agent of such a party or person concerning matters outside the representation. For example, the existence of a controversy between a government agency and a private party or person or between two organizations does not prohibit a lawyer for either from communicating with nonlawyer representatives of the other regarding a separate matter. Nor does this Rule preclude communication with a represented party or person who is seeking advice from a lawyer who is not otherwise representing a client in the matter. A lawyer having independent justification or legal authorization for communicating with a represented party or person is permitted to do so.

[5] Communications authorized by law may include communications by a lawyer on behalf of a client who is exercising a constitutional or other legal right to communicate with the government. Communications authorized by law may also include investigative activities of lawyers representing governmental entities, directly or through investigative agents, prior to the commencement (as defined by law) of criminal or civil enforcement proceedings. When communicating with the accused in a criminal matter, a government lawyer must comply with this Rule in addition to honoring the state or federal rights of the accused. The fact that a communication does not violate a state or federal right is insufficient to establish that the communication is permissible under this Rule. This Rule is not intended to effect any change in the scope of the anti-contact rule in criminal cases.

[6] [Reserved.]

[7] In the case of a represented organization, paragraph (a) ordinarily prohibits communications with a constituent of the organization who: (i) supervises, directs or regularly consults with the organization's lawyer concerning the matter, (ii) has authority to obligate the organization with respect to the matter, or (iii) whose act or omission in connection with the matter may be imputed to the organization for purposes of civil or criminal liability. Consent of the organization's lawyer is not required for communication with a former unrepresented constituent. If an individual constituent of the organization is represented in the matter by the person's own counsel, the consent by that counsel to a communication will be sufficient for purposes of this Rule. In communicating with a current or former constituent of an organization, a lawyer must not use methods of obtaining evidence that violate the legal rights of the organization. See Rules 1.13, 4.4.

[8] The prohibition on communications with a represented party applies only in circumstances where the lawyer knows that the party is in fact represented in the matter to be discussed. This means that the lawyer has actual knowledge of the fact of the representation; but such knowledge may be inferred from the circumstances. See Rule 1.0(k) for the definition of "knowledge." Thus, the lawyer cannot evade the requirement of obtaining the consent of counsel by ignoring the obvious.

[9] In the event the party with whom the lawyer communicates is not known to be represented by counsel in the matter, the lawyer's communications are subject to Rule 4.3.

[10] A lawyer may not make a communication prohibited by paragraph (a) through the acts of another. See Rule 8.4(a).

Client-to-Client Communications

[11] Persons represented in a matter may communicate directly with each other. A lawyer may properly advise a client to communicate directly with a represented person, and may counsel the client with respect to those communications, provided the lawyer complies with paragraph (b). Agents for lawyers, such as investigators, are not considered clients within the meaning of this Rule even where the represented entity is an agency, department or other organization of the government, and therefore a lawyer may not cause such an agent to communicate with a represented person, unless the lawyer would be authorized by law or a court order to do so. A lawyer

may also counsel a client with respect to communications with a represented person, including by drafting papers for the client to present to the represented person. In advising a client in connection with such communications, a lawyer may not advise the client to seek privileged information or other information that the represented person is not personally authorized to disclose or is prohibited from disclosing, such as a trade secret or other information protected by law, or to encourage or invite the represented person to take actions without the advice of counsel.

[12] A lawyer who advises a client with respect to communications with a represented person should be mindful of the obligation to avoid abusive, harassing, or unfair conduct with regard to the represented person. The lawyer should advise the client against such conduct. A lawyer shall not advise a client to communicate with a represented person if the lawyer knows that the represented person is legally incompetent. *See* Rule 4.4.

Rule 4.3   Communicating with Unrepresented Persons

In communicating on behalf of a client with a person who is not represented by counsel, a lawyer shall not state or imply that the lawyer is disinterested. When the lawyer knows or reasonably should know that the unrepresented person misunderstands the lawyer's role in the matter, the lawyer shall make reasonable efforts to correct the misunderstanding. The lawyer shall not give legal advice to an unrepresented person other than the advice to secure counsel if the lawyer knows or reasonably should know that the interests of such person are or have a reasonable possibility of being in conflict with the interests of the client.

COMMENT

[1] An unrepresented person, particularly one not experienced in dealing with legal matters, might assume that a lawyer is disinterested in loyalties or is a disinterested authority on the law even when the lawyer represents a client. In order to avoid a misunderstanding, a lawyer will typically need to identify the lawyer's client and, where necessary, explain that the client has interests opposed to those of the unrepresented person. As to misunderstandings that sometimes arise when a lawyer for an organization deals with an unrepresented constituent, see Rule 1.13(a), Comment [2A].

[2] The Rule distinguishes between situations involving unrepresented parties whose interests may be adverse to those of the lawyer's client and those in which the person's interests are not in conflict with the client's. In the former situation, the possibility that the lawyer will compromise the unrepresented person's interests is so great that the Rule prohibits the giving of any advice apart from the advice to obtain counsel. Whether a lawyer is giving impermissible advice may depend on the experience and sophistication of the unrepresented party, as well as the setting in which the behavior and comments occur. This Rule does not prohibit a lawyer from negotiating the terms of a transaction or settling a dispute with an unrepresented person. So long as the lawyer has explained that the lawyer represents an adverse

party and is not representing the person, the lawyer may inform the person of the terms on which the lawyer's client will enter into an agreement or settle a matter, prepare documents that require the person's signature, and explain the lawyer's own view of the meaning of the document or the lawyer's view of the underlying legal obligations.

Rule 4.4   Respect for Rights of Third Persons

(a) In representing a client, a lawyer shall not use means that have no substantial purpose other than to embarrass or harm a third person or use methods of obtaining evidence that violate the legal rights of such a person.

(b) A lawyer who receives a document relating to the representation of the lawyer's client and knows or reasonably should know that the document was inadvertently sent shall promptly notify the sender.

COMMENT

[1] Responsibility to a client requires a lawyer to subordinate the interests of others to those of the client, but that responsibility does not imply that a lawyer may disregard the rights of third persons. It is impractical to catalogue all such rights, but they include legal restrictions on methods of obtaining evidence from third persons and unwarranted intrusions into privileged relationships, such as the client-lawyer relationship.

[2] Paragraph (b) recognizes that lawyers sometimes receive documents that were mistakenly sent, produced, or otherwise inadvertently made available by opposing parties or their lawyers. One way to resolve this situation is for lawyers to enter into agreements containing explicit provisions as to how the parties will deal with inadvertently sent documents. In the absence of such an agreement, however, if a lawyer knows or reasonably should know that such a document was sent inadvertently, this Rule requires only that the lawyer promptly notify the sender in order to permit that person to take protective measures. Although this Rule does not require that the lawyer refrain from reading or continuing to read the document, a lawyer who reads or continues to read a document that contains privileged or confidential information may be subject to court-imposed sanctions, including disqualification and evidence-preclusion. Whether the lawyer is required to take additional steps, such as returning the original document, is a matter of law beyond the scope of these Rules, as is the question whether the privileged status of a document has been waived. Similarly, this Rule does not address the legal duties of a lawyer who receives a document that the lawyer knows or reasonably should know may have been wrongfully obtained by the sending person. For purposes of this Rule, "document" includes email and other electronically stored information subject to being read or put into readable form.

[3] Refraining from reading or continuing to read a document once a lawyer realizes that it was inadvertently sent to the wrong address and returning the document to the sender honors the policy of these Rules to protect the principles of

client confidentiality. Because there are circumstances where a lawyer's ethical obligations should not bar use of the information obtained from an inadvertently sent document, however, this Rule does not subject a lawyer to professional discipline for reading and using that information. Nevertheless, substantive law or procedural rules may require a lawyer to refrain from reading an inadvertently sent document, or to return the document to the sender, or both. Accordingly, in deciding whether to retain or use an inadvertently received document, some lawyers may take into account whether the attorney-client privilege would attach. But if applicable law or rules do not address the situation, decisions to refrain from reading such documents or to return them, or both, are matters of professional judgment reserved to the lawyer. *See* Rules 1.2, 1.4.

Rule 4.5 Communication After Incidents Involving Personal Injury or Wrongful Death

(a) In the event of a specific incident involving potential claims for personal injury or wrongful death, no unsolicited communication shall be made to an individual injured in the incident or to a family member or legal representative of such an individual, by a lawyer or law firm, or by any associate, agent, employee or other representative of a lawyer or law firm representing actual or potential defendants or entities that may defend and/or indemnify said defendants, before the 30th day after the date of the incident, unless a filing must be made within 30 days of the incident as a legal prerequisite to the particular claim, in which case no unsolicited communication shall be made before the 15th day after the date of the incident.

(b) An unsolicited communication by a lawyer or law firm, seeking to represent an injured individual or the legal representative thereof under the circumstance described in paragraph (a) shall comply with Rule 7.3(e).

COMMENT

[1] Paragraph (a) imposes a 30-day (or 15-day) restriction on unsolicited communications directed to potential claimants relating to a specific incident involving potential claims for personal injury or wrongful death, by lawyers or law firms who represent actual or potential defendants or entities that may defend or indemnify those defendants. However, if potential claimants are represented by counsel, it is proper for defense counsel to communicate with potential plaintiffs' counsel even during the 30-day (or 15-day) period. *See also* Rule 7.3(e).

Rule 5.1 Responsibilities of Law Firms, Partners, Managers and Supervisory Lawyers

(a) A law firm shall make reasonable efforts to ensure that all lawyers in the firm conform to these Rules.

(b)(1) A lawyer with management responsibility in a law firm shall make reasonable efforts to ensure that other lawyers in the law firm conform to these Rules.

(2) A lawyer with direct supervisory authority over another lawyer shall make reasonable efforts to ensure that the supervised lawyer conforms to these Rules.

(c) A law firm shall ensure that the work of partners and associates is adequately supervised, as appropriate. A lawyer with direct supervisory authority over another lawyer shall adequately supervise the work of the other lawyer, as appropriate. In either case, the degree of supervision required is that which is reasonable under the circumstances, taking into account factors such as the experience of the person whose work is being supervised, the amount of work involved in a particular matter, and the likelihood that ethical problems might arise in the course of working on the matter.

(d) A lawyer shall be responsible for a violation of these Rules by another lawyer if:

(1) the lawyer orders or directs the specific conduct or, with knowledge of the specific conduct, ratifies it; or

(2) the lawyer is a partner in a law firm or is a lawyer who individually or together with other lawyers possesses comparable managerial responsibility in a law firm in which the other lawyer practices or is a lawyer who has supervisory authority over the other lawyer; and

(i) knows of such conduct at a time when it could be prevented or its consequences avoided or mitigated but fails to take reasonable remedial action; or

(ii) in the exercise of reasonable management or supervisory authority should have known of the conduct so that reasonable remedial action could have been taken at a time when the consequences of the conduct could have been avoided or mitigated.

COMMENT

[1] Paragraph (a) applies to law firms; paragraph (b) applies to lawyers with management responsibility in a law firm or a lawyer with direct supervisory authority over another lawyer.

[2] Paragraph (b) requires lawyers with management authority within a firm or those having direct supervisory authority over other lawyers to make reasonable efforts to establish internal policies and procedures designed to provide reasonable assurance that all lawyers in the firm will conform to these Rules. Such policies and procedures include those designed (i) to detect and resolve conflicts of interest (*see* Rule 1.10(e)), (ii) to identify dates by which actions must be taken in pending matters, (iii) to account for client funds and property, and (iv) to ensure that inexperienced lawyers are appropriately supervised.

[3] Other measures that may be required to fulfill the responsibility prescribed in paragraph (b) can depend on the firm's structure and the nature of its practice.

In a small firm of experienced lawyers, informal supervision and periodic review of compliance with the required systems ordinarily will suffice. In a large firm, or in practice situations in which difficult ethical problems frequently arise, more elaborate measures may be necessary. Some firms, for example, have a procedure whereby junior lawyers can make confidential referral of ethical problems directly to a designated senior partner or special committee. *See* Rule 5.2. Firms, whether large or small, may also rely on continuing legal education in professional ethics. In any event, the ethical atmosphere of a firm can influence the conduct of all its members and lawyers with management authority may not assume that all lawyers associated with the firm will inevitably conform to the Rules.

[4] Paragraph (d) expresses a general principle of personal responsibility for acts of other lawyers in the law firm. *See also* Rule 8.4(a).

[5] Paragraph (d) imposes such responsibility on a lawyer who orders, directs or ratifies wrongful conduct and on lawyers who are partners or who have comparable managerial authority in a law firm who know or reasonably should know of the conduct. Whether a lawyer has supervisory authority in particular circumstances is a question of fact. Partners and lawyers with comparable authority have at least indirect responsibility for all work being done by the firm, while a partner or manager in charge of a particular matter ordinarily also has supervisory responsibility for the work of other firm lawyers engaged in the matter. Partners and lawyers with comparable authority, as well as those who supervise other lawyers, are indirectly responsible for improper conduct of which they know or should have known in the exercise of reasonable managerial or supervisory authority. Appropriate remedial action by a partner or managing lawyer would depend on the immediacy of that lawyer's involvement and the seriousness of the misconduct. A supervisor is required to intervene to prevent misconduct or to prevent or mitigate avoidable consequences of misconduct if the supervisor knows that the misconduct occurred.

[6] Professional misconduct by a lawyer under supervision could reveal a violation of paragraph (a), (b) or (c) on the part of a law firm, partner or supervisory lawyer even though it does not entail a violation of paragraph (d) because there was no direction, ratification or knowledge of the violation or no violation occurred.

[7] Apart from this Rule and Rule 8.4(a), a lawyer does not have disciplinary liability for the conduct of another lawyer. Whether a lawyer may be liable civilly or criminally for another lawyer's conduct is a question of law beyond the scope of these Rules.

[8] The duties imposed by this Rule on managing and supervising lawyers do not alter the personal duty of each lawyer in a firm to abide by these Rules. *See* Rule 5.2(a).

Rule 5.2   Responsibilities of a Subordinate Lawyer

(a) A lawyer is bound by these Rules notwithstanding that the lawyer acted at the direction of another person.

(b) A subordinate lawyer does not violate these Rules if that lawyer acts in accordance with a supervisory lawyer's reasonable resolution of an arguable question of professional duty.

COMMENT

[1] Although a lawyer is not relieved of responsibility for a violation by the fact that the lawyer acted at the direction of a supervisor, that fact may be relevant in determining whether a lawyer had the knowledge required to render conduct a violation of these Rules. For example, if a subordinate filed a frivolous pleading at the direction of a supervisor, the subordinate would not be guilty of a professional violation unless the subordinate knew of the document's frivolous character.

[2] When lawyers in a supervisor-subordinate relationship encounter a matter involving professional judgment as to ethical duty, the supervisor may assume responsibility for making the judgment. Otherwise, a consistent course of action or position could not be taken. If the question can reasonably be answered only one way, the duty of both lawyers is clear, and they are equally responsible for fulfilling it. However, if the question is reasonably arguable, someone has to decide upon the course of action. That authority ordinarily reposes in the supervisor, and a subordinate may be guided accordingly. To evaluate the supervisor's conclusion that the question is arguable and the supervisor's resolution of it is reasonable in light of applicable law, it is advisable that the subordinate lawyer undertake research, consult with a designated senior partner or special committee, if any (*see* Rule 5.1, Comment [3]), or use other appropriate means. For example, if a question arises whether the interests of two clients conflict under Rule 1.7, the supervisor's reasonable resolution of the question should protect the subordinate professionally if the resolution is subsequently challenged.

Rule 5.3   Lawyer's Responsibility for Conduct of Nonlawyers

(a) A law firm shall ensure that the work of nonlawyers who work for the firm is adequately supervised, as appropriate. A lawyer with direct supervisory authority over a nonlawyer shall adequately supervise the work of the nonlawyer, as appropriate. In either case, the degree of supervision required is that which is reasonable under the circumstances, taking into account factors such as the experience of the person whose work is being supervised, the amount of work involved in a particular matter and the likelihood that ethical problems might arise in the course of working on the matter.

(b) A lawyer shall be responsible for conduct of a nonlawyer employed or retained by or associated with the lawyer that would be a violation of these Rules if engaged in by a lawyer, if:

(1) the lawyer orders or directs the specific conduct or, with knowledge of the specific conduct, ratifies it; or

(2) the lawyer is a partner in a law firm or is a lawyer who individually or together with other lawyers possesses comparable managerial responsibility in a law firm in which the nonlawyer is employed or is a lawyer who has supervisory authority over the nonlawyer; and

(i) knows of such conduct at a time when it could be prevented or its consequences avoided or mitigated but fails to take reasonable remedial action; or

(ii) in the exercise of reasonable management or supervisory authority should have known of the conduct so that reasonable remedial action could have been taken at a time when the consequences of the conduct could have been avoided or mitigated.

COMMENT

[1] This Rule requires a law firm to ensure that work of nonlawyers is appropriately supervised. In addition, a lawyer with direct supervisory authority over the work of nonlawyers must adequately supervise those nonlawyers. Comments [2] and [3] to Rule 5.1, which concern supervision of lawyers, provide guidance by analogy for the methods and extent of supervising nonlawyers.

[2] With regard to nonlawyers, who are not themselves subject to these Rules, the purpose of the supervision is to give reasonable assurance that the conduct of all nonlawyers employed by or retained by or associated with the law firm is compatible with the professional obligations of the lawyers and firm. Lawyers generally employ assistants in their practice, including secretaries, investigators, law student interns and paraprofessionals. Such assistants, whether they are employees or independent contractors, act for the lawyer in rendition of the lawyer's professional services. A law firm must ensure that such assistants are given appropriate instruction and supervision concerning the ethical aspects of their employment, particularly regarding the obligation not to disclose information relating to representation of the client, and should be responsible for their work product. The measures employed in supervising nonlawyers should take account of the fact that they do not have legal training and are not subject to professional discipline. A law firm should make reasonable efforts to establish internal policies and procedures designed to provide reasonable assurance that nonlawyers in the firm will act in a way compatible with these Rules. A lawyer with direct supervisory authority over a nonlawyer has a parallel duty to provide appropriate supervision of the supervised nonlawyer.

[3] Paragraph (b) specifies the circumstances in which a lawyer is responsible for conduct of a nonlawyer that would be a violation of these Rules if engaged in by a lawyer. For guidance by analogy, see Rule 5.1, Comments [5]-[8].

Rule 5.4   Professional Independence of a Lawyer

(a) A lawyer or law firm shall not share legal fees with a nonlawyer, except that:

(1) an agreement by a lawyer with the lawyer's firm or another lawyer associated in the firm may provide for the payment of money, over a reasonable period of time after the lawyer's death, to the lawyer's estate or to one or more specified persons;

(2) a lawyer who undertakes to complete unfinished legal business of a deceased lawyer may pay to the estate of the deceased lawyer that

portion of the total compensation that fairly represents the services rendered by the deceased lawyer; and

(3) a lawyer or law firm may compensate a nonlawyer employee or include a nonlawyer employee in a retirement plan based in whole or in part on a profit-sharing arrangement.

(b) A lawyer shall not form a partnership with a nonlawyer if any of the activities of the partnership consist of the practice of law.

(c) Unless authorized by law, a lawyer shall not permit a person who recommends, employs or pays the lawyer to render legal service for another to direct or regulate the lawyer's professional judgment in rendering such legal services or to cause the lawyer to compromise the lawyer's duty to maintain the confidential information of the client under Rule 1.6.

(d) A lawyer shall not practice with or in the form of an entity authorized to practice law for profit, if:

(1) a nonlawyer owns any interest therein, except that a fiduciary representative of the estate of a lawyer may hold the stock or interest of the lawyer for a reasonable time during administration;

(2) a nonlawyer is a member, corporate director or officer thereof or occupies a position of similar responsibility in any form of association other than a corporation; or

(3) a nonlawyer has the right to direct or control the professional judgment of a lawyer.

COMMENT

[1] The provisions of this Rule express traditional limitations on sharing fees. These limitations are to protect the lawyer's professional independence of judgment. Where someone other than the client pays the lawyer's fee or salary, or recommends employment of the lawyer, that arrangement does not modify the lawyer's obligation to the client. As stated in paragraph (c), such arrangements should not interfere with the lawyer's professional judgment.

[1A] Paragraph (a)(2) governs the compensation of a lawyer who undertakes to complete one or more unfinished pieces of legal business of a deceased lawyer. Rule 1.17 governs the sale of an entire law practice upon retirement, which is defined as the cessation of the private practice of law in a given geographic area.

[1B] Paragraph (a)(3) permits limited fee sharing with a nonlawyer employee, where the employee's compensation or retirement plan is based in whole or in part on a profit-sharing arrangement. Such sharing of profits with a nonlawyer employee must be based on the total profitability of the law firm or a department within a law firm and may not be based on the fee resulting from a single case.

[2] This Rule also expresses traditional limitations on permitting a third party to direct or regulate the lawyer's professional judgment in rendering legal services to another. See also Rule 1.8(f), providing that a lawyer may accept compensation from a third party as long as there is no interference with the lawyer's professional judgment and the client gives informed consent.

Rule 5.5   Unauthorized Practice of Law

(a) A lawyer shall not practice law in a jurisdiction in violation of the regulation of the legal profession in that jurisdiction.

(b) A lawyer shall not aid a nonlawyer in the unauthorized practice of law.

COMMENT

[1] A lawyer may practice law only in a jurisdiction in which the lawyer is authorized to practice. A lawyer may be admitted to practice law in a jurisdiction on a regular basis or may be authorized by court rule or order or by law to practice for a limited purpose or on a restricted basis. Paragraph (a) applies to unauthorized practice of law in another jurisdiction by a lawyer through the lawyer's direct action, and paragraph (b) prohibits a lawyer from aiding a nonlawyer in the unauthorized practice of law.

[2] The definition of the "practice of law" is established by law and varies from one jurisdiction to another. Whatever the definition, limiting the practice of law to members of the bar protects the public against rendition of legal services by unqualified persons. This Rule does not prohibit a lawyer from employing the services of paraprofessionals and delegating functions to them, so long as the lawyer supervises the delegated work and retains responsibility for their work. *See* Rule 5.3.

Rule 5.6   Restrictions on Right to Practice

(a) A lawyer shall not participate in offering or making:

(1) a partnership, shareholder, operating, employment, or other similar type of agreement that restricts the right of a lawyer to practice after termination of the relationship, except an agreement concerning benefits upon retirement; or

(2) an agreement in which a restriction on a lawyer's right to practice is part of the settlement of a client controversy.

(b) This Rule does not prohibit restrictions that may be included in the terms of the sale of a law practice pursuant to Rule 1.17.

COMMENT

[1] An agreement restricting the right of lawyers to practice after leaving a firm not only limits their professional autonomy but also limits the freedom of clients to choose a lawyer. Paragraph (a) prohibits such agreements except for restrictions incident to provisions concerning retirement benefits for service with the firm.

[2] Paragraph (a)(2) prohibits a lawyer from agreeing not to represent other persons in connection with settling a claim on behalf of a client.

[3] This Rule does not apply to prohibit restrictions that may be included in the terms of the sale of a law practice pursuant to Rule 1.17.

Rule 5.7   Responsibilities Regarding Nonlegal Services

(a) With respect to lawyers or law firms providing nonlegal services to clients or other persons:

(1) A lawyer or law firm that provides nonlegal services to a person that are not distinct from legal services being provided to that person by the lawyer or law firm is subject to these Rules with respect to the provision of both legal and nonlegal services.

(2) A lawyer or law firm that provides nonlegal services to a person that are distinct from legal services being provided to that person by the lawyer or law firm is subject to these Rules with respect to the nonlegal services if the person receiving the services could reasonably believe that the nonlegal services are the subject of a client-lawyer relationship.

(3) A lawyer or law firm that is an owner, controlling party or agent of, or that is otherwise affiliated with, an entity that the lawyer or law firm knows to be providing nonlegal services to a person is subject to these Rules with respect to the nonlegal services if the person receiving the services could reasonably believe that the nonlegal services are the subject of a client-lawyer relationship.

(4) For purposes of paragraphs (a)(2) and (a)(3), it will be presumed that the person receiving nonlegal services believes the services to be the subject of a client-lawyer relationship unless the lawyer or law firm has advised the person receiving the services in writing that the services are not legal services and that the protection of a client-lawyer relationship does not exist with respect to the nonlegal services, or if the interest of the lawyer or law firm in the entity providing nonlegal services is *de minimis*.

(b) Notwithstanding the provisions of paragraph (a), a lawyer or law firm that is an owner, controlling party, agent, or is otherwise affiliated with an entity that the lawyer or law firm knows is providing nonlegal services to a person shall not permit any nonlawyer providing such services or affiliated with that entity to direct or regulate the professional judgment of the lawyer or law firm in rendering legal services to any person, or to cause the lawyer or law firm to compromise its duty under Rule 1.6(a) and Rule 1.6(c) with respect to the confidential information of a client receiving legal services.

(c) For purposes of this Rule, "nonlegal services" shall mean those services that lawyers may lawfully provide and that are not prohibited as an unauthorized practice of law when provided by a nonlawyer.

COMMENT

[1] For many years, lawyers have provided nonlegal services to their clients. By participating in the delivery of these services, lawyers can serve a broad range of economic and other interests of clients. Whenever a lawyer directly provides nonlegal services, the lawyer must avoid confusion on the part of the client as to the nature of the lawyer's role, so that the person for whom the nonlegal services are

performed understands that the services may not carry with them the legal and ethical protections that ordinarily accompany a client-lawyer relationship. The recipient of the nonlegal services may expect, for example, that the protection of client confidences and secrets, prohibitions against representation of persons with conflicting interests, and obligations of a lawyer to maintain professional independence apply to the provision of nonlegal services when that may not be the case. The risk of confusion is especially acute when the lawyer renders both legal and nonlegal services with respect to the same matter. Under some circumstances, the legal and nonlegal services may be so closely entwined that they cannot be distinguished from each other. In this situation, the recipient is likely to be confused as to whether and when the relationship is protected as a client-lawyer relationship. Therefore, where the legal and nonlegal services are not distinct, paragraph (a)(1) requires that the lawyer providing nonlegal services adhere to all of the requirements of these Rules with respect to the nonlegal services. Paragraph (a)(1) applies to the provision of nonlegal services by a law firm if the person for whom the nonlegal services are being performed is also receiving legal services from the firm that are not distinct from the nonlegal services.

[2] Even when the lawyer believes that the provision of nonlegal services is distinct from any legal services being provided, there is still a risk that the recipient of the nonlegal services might reasonably believe that the recipient is receiving the protection of a client-lawyer relationship. Therefore, paragraph (a)(2) requires that the lawyer providing the nonlegal services adhere to these Rules, unless the person understands that the nonlegal services are not the subject of a client-lawyer relationship. Nonlegal services also may be provided through an entity with which a lawyer is affiliated, for example, as owner, controlling party or agent. In this situation, there is still a risk that the recipient of the nonlegal services might reasonably believe that the recipient is receiving the protection of a client-lawyer relationship. Therefore, paragraph (a)(3) requires that the lawyer involved with the entity providing nonlegal services adhere to all of these Rules with respect to the nonlegal services, unless the person understands that the nonlegal services are not the subject of a client-lawyer relationship.

[3] These Rules will be presumed to apply to a lawyer who directly provides or is otherwise involved in the provision of nonlegal services unless the lawyer complies with paragraph (a)(4) by communicating in writing to the person receiving the nonlegal services that the services are not legal services and that the protection of a client-lawyer relationship does not exist with respect to the nonlegal services. Such a communication should be made before entering into an agreement for the provision of nonlegal services in a manner sufficient to ensure that the person understands the significance of the communication. In certain circumstances, however, additional steps may be required to ensure that the person understands the distinction. For example, while the written disclaimer set forth in paragraph (a)(4) will be adequate for a sophisticated user of legal and nonlegal services, a more detailed explanation may be required for someone unaccustomed to making distinctions between legal services and nonlegal services. Where appropriate and especially where legal services are provided in the same transaction as nonlegal services, the lawyer should counsel the client about the possible effect of the proposed provision of services on the availability of the attorney-client privilege. The lawyer or law firm will not be required to comply with these requirements if its interest in the entity providing the nonlegal services is so small as to be de minimis.

[4] Although a lawyer may be exempt from the application of these Rules with respect to nonlegal services on the face of paragraph (a), the scope of the exemption is not absolute. A lawyer who provides or who is involved in the provision of nonlegal services may be excused from compliance with only those Rules that are dependent upon the existence of a representation or client-lawyer relationship. Other Rules, such as those prohibiting lawyers from misusing the confidences or secrets of a former client (*see* Rule 1.9), requiring lawyers to report certain lawyer misconduct (*see* Rule 8.3), and prohibiting lawyers from engaging in illegal, dishonest, fraudulent or deceptive conduct (*see* Rule 8.4), apply to a lawyer irrespective of the existence of a representation, and thus govern a lawyer not covered by paragraph (a). A lawyer or law firm rendering legal services is always subject to these Rules.

Provision of Legal and Nonlegal Services in the Same Transaction

[5] In some situations it may be beneficial to a client to purchase both legal and nonlegal services from a lawyer, law firm or affiliated entity in the same matter or in two or more substantially related matters. Examples include: (i) a law firm that represents corporations and also provides public lobbying, public relations, investment banking and business relocation services, (ii) a law firm that represents clients in environmental matters and also provides engineering consulting services to those clients, and (iii) a law firm that represents clients in litigation and also provides consulting services relating to electronic document discovery. In these situations, the lawyer may have a financial interest in the nonlegal services that would constitute a conflict of interest under Rule 1.7(a)(2), which governs conflicts between a client and a lawyer's personal interests.

[5A] Under Rule 1.7(a)(2), a concurrent conflict of interest exists when a reasonable lawyer would conclude that there is a significant risk that the lawyer's professional judgment on behalf of a client will be adversely affected by the lawyer's own financial, business, property or personal interests. When a lawyer or law firm provides both legal and nonlegal services in the same matter (or in substantially related matters), a conflict with the lawyer's own interests will nearly always arise. For example, if the legal representation involves exercising judgment about whether to recommend nonlegal services and which provider to recommend, or if it involves overseeing the provision of the nonlegal services, then a conflict with the lawyer's own interests under Rule 1.7(a)(2) is likely to arise. However, when seeking the consent of a client to such a conflict, the lawyer should comply with both Rule 1.7(b) regarding the conflict affecting the legal representation of the client and Rule 1.8(a) regarding the business transaction with the client.

[5B] Thus, the client may consent if: (i) the lawyer complies with Rule 1.8(a) with respect to the transaction in which the lawyer agrees to provide the nonlegal services, including obtaining the client's informed consent in a writing signed by the client, (ii) the lawyer reasonably believes that the lawyer can provide competent and diligent legal representation despite the conflict within the meaning of Rule 1.7(b), and (iii) the client gives informed consent pursuant to Rule 1.7(b), confirmed in writing. In certain cases, it will not be possible to provide both legal and nonlegal services because the lawyer could not reasonably believe that he or she can represent the client competently and diligently while providing both legal and nonlegal services in the same or substantially related matters. Whether providing dual services gives rise to an impermissible conflict must be determined on a case-by-case basis, taking into account all of the facts and circumstances, including factors such as: (i) the experience and sophistication of the client in obtaining legal and nonlegal services of the kind being provided in the matter, (ii) the relative size of the anticipated fees for the legal and nonlegal services, (iii) the closeness of the relationship between the legal and nonlegal services, and (iv) the degree of discretion the lawyer has in providing the legal and nonlegal services.

[6] In the context of providing legal and nonlegal services in the same transaction, Rule 1.8(a) first requires that: (i) the nonlegal services be provided on terms that are fair and reasonable to the client, (ii) full disclosure of the terms on which the nonlegal services will be provided be made in writing to the client in a manner understandable by the client, (iii) the client is advised to seek the advice of independent counsel about the provision of the nonlegal services by the lawyer, and (iv) the client gives informed consent, as set forth in Rule 1.8(a)(3), in a writing signed by the client, to the terms of the transaction in which the nonlegal services are provided and to the lawyer's inherent conflict of interest.

[7] In addition, in the context of providing legal and nonlegal services in the same transaction, Rule 1.8(a) requires a full disclosure of the nature and extent of the lawyer's financial interest or stake in the provision of the nonlegal services. By its terms, Rule 1.8(a) requires that the nonlegal services be provided on terms that are fair and reasonable to the client. (Where the nonlegal services are provided on terms generally available to the public in the marketplace, that requirement is ordinarily met.) Consequently, as a further safeguard against conflicts that may arise when the same lawyer provides both legal and nonlegal services in the same or substantially related matters, a lawyer may do so only if the lawyer not only complies with Rule 1.8(a) with respect to the nonlegal services, but also obtains the client's informed consent, pursuant to Rule 1.7(b), confirmed in writing, after fully disclosing the advantages and risks of obtaining legal and nonlegal services from the same or affiliated providers in a single matter (or in substantially related matters), including the lawyer's conflict of interest arising from the lawyer's financial interest in the provision of the nonlegal services.

[8] [Reserved.]

[9] [Reserved.]

[10] [Reserved.]

[11] [Reserved.]

Rule 5.8   Contractual Relationships Between Lawyers and Nonlegal Professionals

(a) The practice of law has an essential tradition of complete independence and uncompromised loyalty to those it serves. Recognizing this tradition, clients of lawyers practicing in New York State are guaranteed "independent professional judgment and undivided loyalty uncompromised by conflicts of interest." Indeed, these guarantees represent the very foundation of the profession and allow and foster its continued role as a protector of the system of law. Therefore, a lawyer must remain completely

responsible for his or her own independent professional judgment, maintain the confidences and secrets of clients, preserve funds of clients and third parties in his or her control, and otherwise comply with the legal and ethical principles governing lawyers in New York State.

Multi-disciplinary practice between lawyers and nonlawyers is incompatible with the core values of the legal profession and therefore, a strict division between services provided by lawyers and those provided by nonlawyers is essential to protect those values. However, a lawyer or law firm may enter into and maintain a contractual relationship with a nonlegal professional or nonlegal professional service firm for the purpose of offering to the public, on a systematic and continuing basis, legal services performed by the lawyer or law firm as well as other nonlegal professional services, notwithstanding the provisions of Rule 1.7(a), provided that:

(1) the profession of the nonlegal professional or nonlegal professional service firm is included in a list jointly established and maintained by the Appellate Divisions pursuant to Section 1205.3 of the Joint Appellate Division Rules;

(2) the lawyer or law firm neither grants to the nonlegal professional or nonlegal professional service firm, nor permits such person or firm to obtain, hold or exercise, directly or indirectly, any ownership or investment interest in, or managerial or supervisory right, power or position in connection with the practice of law by the lawyer or law firm, nor, as provided in Rule 7.2(a)(1), shares legal fees with a nonlawyer or receives or gives any monetary or other tangible benefit for giving or receiving a referral; and

(3) the fact that the contractual relationship exists is disclosed by the lawyer or law firm to any client of the lawyer or law firm before the client is referred to the nonlegal professional service firm, or to any client of the nonlegal professional service firm before that client receives legal services from the lawyer or law firm; and the client has given informed written consent and has been provided with a copy of the "Statement of Client's Rights In Cooperative Business Arrangements" pursuant to section 1205.4 of the Joint Appellate Divisions Rules.

(b) For purposes of paragraph (a):

(1) each profession on the list maintained pursuant to a Joint Rule of the Appellate Divisions shall have been designated sua sponte, or approved by the Appellate Divisions upon application of a member of a nonlegal profession or nonlegal professional service firm, upon a determination that the profession is composed of individuals who, with respect to their profession:

(i) have been awarded a bachelor's degree or its equivalent from an accredited college or university, or have attained an equivalent combination of educational credit from such a college or university and work experience;

(ii) are licensed to practice the profession by an agency of the State of New York or the United States Government; and

(iii) are required under penalty of suspension or revocation of license to adhere to a code of ethical conduct that is reasonably comparable to that of the legal profession;

(2) the term "ownership or investment interest" shall mean any such interest in any form of debt or equity, and shall include any interest commonly considered to be an interest accruing to or enjoyed by an owner or investor.

(c) This Rule shall not apply to relationships consisting solely of non-exclusive reciprocal referral agreements or understandings between a lawyer or law firm and a nonlegal professional or nonlegal professional service firm.

COMMENT

Contractual Relationships Between Lawyers and Nonlegal Professionals

[1] Lawyers may enter into interprofessional contractual relationships for the systematic and continuing provision of legal and nonlegal professional services, provided the nonlegal professional or nonlegal professional service firm with which the lawyer or law firm is affiliated does not own, control, supervise or manage, directly or indirectly, in whole or in part, the lawyer's or law firm's practice of law. The nonlegal professional or nonlegal professional service firm may not play a role in, for example, (i) deciding whether to accept or terminate an engagement to provide legal services in a particular matter or to a particular client, (ii) determining the manner in which lawyers are hired or trained, (iii) assigning lawyers to handle particular matters or to provide legal services to particular clients, (iv) deciding whether to undertake pro bono and other public-interest legal work, (v) making financial and budgetary decisions relating to the legal practice, and (vi) determining the compensation and advancement of lawyers and of persons assisting lawyers on legal matters.

[2] The contractual relationship permitted by this Rule may include the sharing of premises, general overhead or administrative costs and services on an arm's length basis. Such financial arrangements, in the context of an agreement between lawyers and other professionals to provide legal and other professional services on a systematic and continuing basis, are permitted subject to the requirements of paragraph (a) and Rule 7.2(a). Similarly, lawyers participating in such arrangements remain subject to general ethical principles in addition to those set forth in this Rule including, at a minimum, Rule 1.7, Rule 1.8(f), Rule 1.9, Rule 5.7(b) and Rule 7.5(a). Thus, the lawyer or law firm may not, for example, include in its firm name the name of the nonlegal professional service firm or any individual nonlegal professional, enter into formal partnerships with nonlawyers, or practice in an organization authorized to practice law for a profit in which nonlawyers own any interest. Moreover, a lawyer or law firm may not enter into an agreement or arrangement for

the use of a name in respect of which a nonlegal professional or nonlegal professional service firm has or exercises a proprietary interest if, under or pursuant to the agreement or arrangement, that nonlegal professional or firm acts or is entitled to act in a manner inconsistent with paragraph (a)(2) or Comment [1]. More generally, the existence of a contractual relationship permitted by this Rule does not by itself create a conflict of interest in violation of Rule 1.8(a). Whenever a law firm represents a client in a matter in which the nonlegal professional service firm's client is also involved, the law firm's interest in maintaining an advantageous relationship with a nonlegal professional service firm might, in certain circumstances, adversely affect the professional judgment of the law firm.

[3] Each lawyer and law firm having a contractual relationship under paragraph (a) has an ethical duty to observe these Rules with respect to the lawyer's or law firm's own conduct in the context of that relationship. For example, the lawyer or law firm cannot permit the obligation to maintain client confidences, as required by Rule 1.6, to be compromised by the contractual relationship or by its implementation by or on behalf of nonlawyers involved in the relationship. In addition, the prohibition in Rule 8.4(a) against circumventing a Rule through actions of another applies generally to the lawyer or law firm in the contractual relationship.

[4] The contractual relationship permitted by paragraph (a) may provide for the reciprocal referral of clients by and between the lawyer or law firm and the nonlegal professional or nonlegal professional service firm. When in the context of such a contractual relationship a lawyer or law firm refers a client to the nonlegal professional or nonlegal professional service firm, the lawyer or law firm shall observe the ethical standards of the legal profession in verifying the competence of the nonlegal professional or nonlegal professional services firm to handle the relevant affairs and interests of the client. Referrals should be made only when requested by the client or deemed to be reasonably necessary to serve the client. Thus, even if otherwise permitted by paragraph (a), a contractual relationship may not require referrals on an exclusive basis. *See* Rule 7.2(a).

[5] To ensure that only appropriate professional services are involved, a contractual relationship for the provision of services is permitted under paragraph (a) only if the nonlegal party thereto is a professional or professional service firm meeting appropriate standards regarding ethics, education, training and licensing. The Appellate Divisions maintain a public list of eligible professions at 22 N.Y.C.R.R. §1205.5. A member of the nonlegal profession or a professional service firm may apply for the inclusion of particular professions on the list or professions may be added to the list by the Appellate Divisions sua sponte. A lawyer or law firm not wishing to affiliate with a nonlawyer on a systematic and continuing basis, but only to engage a nonlawyer on an ad hoc basis to assist in a specific matter, is not governed by this Rule when so dealing with the nonlawyer. Thus, a lawyer advising a client in connection with a discharge of chemical wastes may engage the services of and consult with an environmental engineer on that matter without the need to comply with this Rule. Likewise, the requirements of this Rule need not be met when a lawyer retains an expert witness in a particular litigation.

[6] Depending upon the extent and nature of the relationship between the lawyer or law firm, on the one hand, and the nonlegal professional or nonlegal professional service firm, on the other hand, it may be appropriate to treat the parties to a contractual relationship permitted by paragraph (a) as a single law firm for purposes of these Rules, as would be the case if the nonlegal professional or

nonlegal professional service firm were in an "of counsel" relationship with the lawyer or law firm. If the parties to the relationship are treated as a single law firm, the principal effects would be that conflicts of interest are imputed as between them pursuant to Rule 1.10(a) and that the law firm would be required to maintain systems for determining whether such conflicts exist pursuant to Rule 1.10(f). To the extent that the rules of ethics of the nonlegal profession conflict with these Rules, the rules of the legal profession will still govern the conduct of the lawyers and the law firm participants in the relationship. A lawyer or law firm may also be subject to legal obligations arising from a relationship with nonlawyer professionals, who are themselves subject to regulation.

Rule 6.1   Voluntary Pro Bono Service

Lawyers are strongly encouraged to provide pro bono legal services to benefit poor persons.

(a) Every lawyer should aspire to:

(1) provide at least 20 hours of pro bono legal services each year to poor persons; and

(2) contribute financially to organizations that provide legal services to poor persons.

(b) Pro bono legal services that meet this goal are:

(1) professional services rendered in civil matters, and in those criminal matters for which the government is not obliged to provide funds for legal representation, to persons who are financially unable to compensate counsel;

(2) activities related to improving the administration of justice by simplifying the legal process for, or increasing the availability and quality of legal services to, poor persons; and

(3) professional services to charitable, religious, civic and educational organizations in matters designed predominantly to address the needs of poor persons.

(c) Appropriate organizations for financial contributions are:

(1) organizations primarily engaged in the provision of legal services to the poor; and

(2) organizations substantially engaged in the provision of legal services to the poor, provided that the donated funds are to be used for the provision of such legal services.

(d) This Rule is not intended to be enforced through the disciplinary process, and the failure to fulfill the aspirational goals contained herein should be without legal consequence.

COMMENT

[1] As our society has become one in which rights and responsibilities are increasingly defined in legal terms, access to legal services has become of critical

importance. This is true for all people, rich, poor or of moderate means. However, because the legal problems of the poor often involve areas of basic need, their inability to obtain legal services can have dire consequences. The vast unmet legal needs of the poor in New York have been recognized in several studies undertaken over the past two decades. Each lawyer—including members of the judiciary and government lawyers, and regardless of professional prominence or professional work load—is strongly encouraged to provide or to assist in providing pro bono legal services to the poor.

[2] Paragraph (a) urges all lawyers to provide a minimum of 20 hours of pro bono legal service annually without fee or expectation of fee, either directly to poor persons or to organizations that serve the legal or other basic needs of persons of limited financial means. It is recognized that in some years a lawyer may render greater or fewer hours than the annual standard specified, but during the course of the lawyer's career, the lawyer should render on average per year, the number of hours set forth in this Rule. Services can be performed in civil matters or in criminal or quasi-criminal matters for which there is no government obligation to provide funds for legal representation, such as post-conviction death penalty appeal cases.

[2A] Paragraph (a)(2) provides that, in addition to providing the services described in paragraph (a), lawyers should provide financial support to organizations that provide legal services to the poor. This goal is separate from and not a substitute for the provision of legal services described in paragraph (a). To assist the funding of civil legal services for low income people, when selecting a bank for deposit of funds into an ''IOLA'' account pursuant to Judiciary Law §497, a lawyer should take into consideration the interest rate offered by the bank on such funds.

[2B] Paragraphs (a)(1) and (a)(2) recognize the critical need for legal services that exists among poor persons. Legal services under these paragraphs consist of a full range of activities, including individual and class representation, the provision of legal advice, legislative lobbying, administrative rulemaking and the provision of free training or mentoring to those who represent poor persons.

[3] ''Poor persons'' under paragraphs (a)(1) and (a)(2) include both (i) individuals who qualify for participation in programs funded by the Legal Services Corporation and (ii) individuals whose incomes and financial resources are slightly above the guidelines utilized by Legal Services Corporation programs but nevertheless cannot afford counsel. To satisfy the goal of paragraph (a)(1), lawyers may provide legal services to individuals in either of those categories, or, pursuant to paragraph (b)(3), may provide legal services to organizations such as homeless shelters, battered women's centers, and food pantries that serve persons in either of those categories.

[4] To qualify as pro bono service within the meaning of paragraph (a)(1) the service must be provided without fee or expectation of fee, so the intent of the lawyer to render free legal services is essential. Accordingly, services rendered cannot be considered pro bono if an anticipated fee is uncollected, but the award of statutory attorneys' fees in a case originally accepted as pro bono would not disqualify such services from inclusion under this Rule. Lawyers who do receive fees in such cases are encouraged to contribute an appropriate portion of such fees to organizations or projects that benefit persons of limited means.

[5] Constitutional, statutory or regulatory restrictions may prohibit or impede government and public sector lawyers and judges from performing the pro bono service outlined in paragraph (b)(1). Accordingly, where those restrictions apply, government and public sector lawyers and judges may fulfill their pro bono responsibility by making financial contributions to organizations that help meet the legal and other basic needs of the poor, as described in paragraphs (a)(2), (c)(1) and (c)(2) or by performing some of the services outlined in paragraph (b)(2) or (b)(3).

[6] [Reserved.]

[7] In addition to rendering pro bono services directly to the poor and making financial contributions, lawyers may fulfill the goal of rendering pro bono services by serving on the boards or giving legal advice to organizations whose mission is helping poor persons. While a lawyer may fulfill the annual goal to perform pro bono service exclusively through activities described in paragraphs (a)(1) and (a)(2), all lawyers are urged to render public-interest and pro bono service in addition to assisting the poor.

[8] Paragraphs (c)(1) and (c)(2) essentially reiterate the goal as set forth in (a)(2) with the further provision that the lawyer should seek to ensure that the donated money be directed to providing legal assistance to the poor rather than the general charitable objectives of such organizations.

[9] Law firms should act reasonably to enable and encourage all lawyers in the firm to provide the pro bono legal service called for by this Rule.

Rule 6.2   [Reserved]

Editors' Note. New York has not adopted any version of ABA Model Rule 6.2. To preserve uniformity with the numbering system of the ABA Model Rules of Professional Conduct, the rule is marked "Reserved."

Rule 6.3   Membership in a Legal Services Organization

A lawyer may serve as a director, officer or member of a not-for-profit legal services organization, apart from the law firm in which the lawyer practices, notwithstanding that the organization serves persons having interests that differ from those of a client of the lawyer or the lawyer's firm. The lawyer shall not knowingly participate in a decision or action of the organization:

(a) if participating in the decision or action would be incompatible with the lawyer's obligations to a client under Rules 1.7 through 1.13; or

(b) where the decision or action could have a material adverse effect on the representation of a client of the organization whose interests differ from those of a client of the lawyer or the lawyer's firm.

COMMENT

[1] Lawyers should be encouraged to support and participate in legal services organizations. A lawyer who is an officer or a member of such an organization does

not thereby have a client-lawyer relationship with persons served by the organization. However, there is potential conflict between the interests of such persons and the interests of the lawyer's clients. If the possibility of such conflict disqualified a lawyer from serving on the board of a legal services organization, the profession's involvement in such organizations would be severely curtailed.

[1A] This Rule applies to legal services organizations organized and operating on a not-for-profit basis.

[2] It may be necessary in appropriate cases to reassure a client of the organization that the representation will not be affected by conflicting loyalties of a member of the board. Established, written policies in this respect can enhance the credibility of such assurances.

Rule 6.4   Law Reform Activities Affecting Client Interests

> **Editors' Note.** Rule 6.4 was amended by the Courts in 2010. The amendment deleted the original last sentence of the rule and replaced it with the current last sentence. (The original last sentence of Rule 6.4 said: "When the lawyer knows that the interests of a client may be adversely affected by a decision in which the lawyer actively participates, the lawyer shall disclose that fact to the client.")

A lawyer may serve as a director, officer or member of an organization involved in reform of the law or its administration, notwithstanding that the reform may affect the interests of a client of the lawyer. When the lawyer knows that the interests of a client may be materially benefitted by a decision in which the lawyer actively participates, the lawyer shall disclose that fact to the organization, but need not identify the client. In determining the nature and scope of participation in such activities, a lawyer should be mindful of obligations to clients under other Rules, particularly Rule 1.7.

COMMENT

[1] Lawyers involved in organizations seeking law reform generally do not have a client-lawyer relationship with the organization. Otherwise, it might follow that a lawyer could not be involved in a bar association law reform program that might indirectly affect a client. For example, a lawyer concentrating in antitrust litigation might be regarded as disqualified from participating in drafting revisions of rules governing that subject. In determining the nature and scope of participation in such activities, a lawyer should be mindful of obligations to clients. A lawyer's identification with the organization's aims and purposes, under some circumstances, may give rise to a personal-interest conflict with client interests implicating the lawyer's obligations under other Rules, particularly Rule 1.7. A lawyer is also professionally obligated to protect the integrity of the law reform program by making an appropriate disclosure within the organization when the lawyer knows a private client might be materially affected.

Rule 6.5   Participation in Limited Pro Bono Legal Services Programs

(a) A lawyer who, under the auspices of a program sponsored by a court, government agency, bar association or not-for-profit legal services organization, provides short-term limited legal services to a client without expectation by either the lawyer or the client that the lawyer will provide continuing representation in the matter:

(1) shall comply with Rules 1.7, 1.8 and 1.9, concerning restrictions on representations where there are or may be conflicts of interest as that term is defined in these Rules, only if the lawyer has actual knowledge at the time of commencement of representation that the representation of the client involves a conflict of interest; and

(2) shall comply with Rule 1.10 only if the lawyer has actual knowledge at the time of commencement of representation that another lawyer associated with the lawyer in a law firm is affected by Rules 1.7, 1.8 and 1.9.

(b) Except as provided in paragraph (a)(2), Rule 1.7 and Rule 1.9 are inapplicable to a representation governed by this Rule.

(c) Short-term limited legal services are services providing legal advice or representation free of charge as part of a program described in paragraph (a) with no expectation that the assistance will continue beyond what is necessary to complete an initial consultation, representation or court appearance.

(d) The lawyer providing short-term limited legal services must secure the client's informed consent to the limited scope of the representation, and such representation shall be subject to the provisions of Rule 1.6.

(e) This Rule shall not apply where the court before which the matter is pending determines that a conflict of interest exists or, if during the course of the representation, the lawyer providing the services becomes aware of the existence of a conflict of interest precluding continued representation.

COMMENT

[1] Legal services organizations, courts, government agencies, bar associations and various non-profit organizations have established programs through which lawyers provide free short-term limited legal services, such as advice or the completion of legal forms, to assist persons to address their legal problems without further representation by a lawyer. In these programs, such as legal-advice hotlines, advice-only clinics or pro se counseling programs, a client-lawyer relationship is established, but there is no expectation that the lawyer's representation of the client will continue beyond the limited consultation. Such programs are normally operated under circumstances in which it is not feasible for a lawyer to utilize the conflict-checking system required by Rule 1.10(e) before providing the short-term limited legal services contemplated by this Rule. *See also* Rules 1.7, 1.8, 1.9, 1.10.

[2] A lawyer who provides short-term limited legal services pursuant to this Rule must secure the client's informed consent to the limited scope of the

representation. *See* Rule 1.2(c). If a short-term limited representation would not be reasonable under the circumstances, the lawyer may offer advice to the client, but must also advise the client of the need for further assistance of counsel. Except as provided in this Rule, these Rules, including Rules 1.6 and Rule 1.9(c), are applicable to the limited representation.

[3] Because a lawyer who is representing a client in the circumstances addressed by this Rule ordinarily is not able to check systematically for conflicts of interest, paragraph (a) requires compliance with Rules 1.7, 1.8 and 1.9 only if the lawyer knows that the representation presents a conflict of interest for the lawyer, and with Rule 1.10 only if the lawyer knows that another lawyer in the lawyer's firm is affected by these Rules.

[4] Because the limited nature of the services significantly reduces the risk of conflicts of interest with other matters being handled by the lawyer's firm, paragraph (b) provides that Rules 1.7 and 1.9 are inapplicable to a representation governed by this Rule, except as provided by paragraph (a)(2). Paragraph (a)(2) requires the participating lawyer to comply with Rule 1.10 only when the lawyer knows that the lawyer's firm is affected by Rules 1.7, 1.8 or 1.9.

[5] If, after commencing a short-term limited representation in accordance with this Rule, a lawyer undertakes to represent the client in the matter on an ongoing basis, Rules 1.7, 1.9(a) and 1.10 become applicable.

Rule 7.1   Advertising

Editors' Note. In *Alexander v. Cahill*, 634 F. Supp. 2d 239 (N.D.N.Y. 2007), *aff'd in part and rev'd in part*, 598 F.3d 79 (2d Cir.), *cert. denied*, 131 U.S. 820 (2010), the courts declared that provisions formerly found at Rule 7.1(c)(1), (c)(3), (c)(5), (c)(7), and (g)(1) violated the First Amendment to the United States Constitution. On April 15, 2011, effective immediately, the New York Appellate Divisions amended or deleted the unconstitutional provisions, renumbered the remaining provisions, and amended related provisions in Rule 7.1(d) and (e). For details, see our Editors' Notes immediately before Rule 7.1(c) and (g).

(a) A lawyer or law firm shall not use or disseminate or participate in the use or dissemination of any advertisement that:

(1) contains statements or claims that are false, deceptive or misleading; or

(2) violates a Rule.

(b) Subject to the provisions of paragraph (a), an advertisement may include information as to:

(1) legal and nonlegal education, degrees and other scholastic distinctions; dates of admission to any bar; areas of the law in which the lawyer or law firm practices, as authorized by these Rules; public offices and teaching positions held; publications of law-related matters authored by the lawyer; memberships in bar associations or other professional societies or organizations, including offices and committee assignments therein; foreign language fluency; and bona fide professional ratings;

(2) names of clients regularly represented, provided that the client has given prior written consent;

(3) bank references; credit arrangements accepted; prepaid or group legal services programs in which the lawyer or law firm participates; non-legal services provided by the lawyer or law firm or by an entity owned and controlled by the lawyer or law firm; the existence of contractual relationships between the lawyer or law firm and a nonlegal professional or nonlegal professional service firm, to the extent permitted by Rule 5.8, and the nature and extent of services available through those contractual relationships; and

(4) legal fees for initial consultation; contingent fee rates in civil matters, when accompanied by a statement disclosing the information required by paragraph (p); range of fees for legal and nonlegal services, provided that there be available to the public free of charge a written statement clearly describing the scope of each advertised service, hourly rates, and fixed fees for specified legal and nonlegal services.

> **Editors' Note.** On February 1, 2007, the New York Appellate Divisions radically amended New York's rules governing lawyer advertising and solicitation. On the same day, a plaintiffs' personal injury firm (Alexander & Catalano), its lead partner (James Alexander), and a public interest group (Public Citizen, Inc.) filed a lawsuit in the United States District Court for the Northern District of New York challenging numerous provisions on First Amendment grounds.
>
> In July 2007, the district court held that the provisions formerly found at Rule 7.1(c)(1), (c)(3), (c)(5), (c)(7) and (g)(1) violated the First Amendment. The Second Circuit affirmed the district court's decision except as to language in Rule 7.1(c)(3) providing that an advertisement shall not include "the portrayal of a fictitious law firm, the use of a fictitious name to refer to lawyers not associated together in a law firm, or otherwise imply that lawyers are associated in a law firm if that is not the case." (The Second Circuit agreed with the district court, however, that the clause in subparagraph (c)(3) banning "the portrayal of a judge" was unconstitutional.) *See Alexander v. Cahill*, 634 F. Supp. 2d 239 (N.D.N.Y. 2007), *aff'd in part and rev'd in part*, 598 F.3d 79 (2d Cir.), *cert. denied*, 131 U.S. 820 (2010) On April 15, 2011, effective immediately, the New York Appellate Divisions amended or deleted the unconstitutional provisions, renumbered the remaining provisions in Rule 7.1(c), amended a related provision in Rule 7.1(d), and added a new Rule 7.1(e)(4). (If readers want to see the precise changes, our 2012 edition reprinted the amended provisions in legislative style.)

(c) An advertisement shall not:

(1) include a paid endorsement of, or testimonial about, a lawyer or law firm without disclosing that the person is being compensated therefor;

(2) include the portrayal of a fictitious law firm, the use of a fictitious name to refer to lawyers not associated together in a law firm, or

otherwise imply that lawyers are associated in a law firm if that is not the case;

(3) use actors to portray a judge, the lawyer, members of the law firm, or clients, or utilize depictions of fictionalized events or scenes, without disclosure of same; or

(4) be made to resemble legal documents.

(d) An advertisement that complies with paragraph (e) may contain the following:

(1) statements that are reasonably likely to create an expectation about results the lawyer can achieve;

(2) statements that compare the lawyer's services with the services of other lawyers;

(3) testimonials or endorsements of clients, and of former clients; or

(4) statements describing or characterizing the quality of the lawyer or law firm's services.

(e) It is permissible to provide the information set forth in paragraph (d) provided:

(1) its dissemination does not violate paragraph (a);

(2) it can be factually supported by the lawyer or law firm as of the date on which the advertisement is published or disseminated; and

(3) it is accompanied by the following disclaimer: "Prior results do not guarantee a similar outcome."; and

(4) in the case of a testimonial or endorsement from a client with respect to a matter still pending, the client gives informed consent confirmed in writing.

(f) Every advertisement other than those appearing in a radio, television or billboard advertisement, in a directory, newspaper, magazine or other periodical (and any web sites related thereto), or made in person pursuant to Rule 7.3(a)(1), shall be labeled "Attorney Advertising" on the first page, or on the home page in the case of a web site. If the communication is in the form of a self-mailing brochure or postcard, the words "Attorney Advertising" shall appear therein. In the case of electronic mail, the subject line shall contain the notation "ATTORNEY ADVERTISING."

> **Editors' Note.** In *Alexander v. Cahill*, 634 F. Supp. 2d 239 (N.D.N.Y. 2007), *aff'd in part and rev'd in part*, 598 F.3d 79 (2d Cir.), *cert. denied*, 131 U.S. 820 (2010), the courts held that Rule 7.1(g)(1) violated the First Amendment to the United States Constitution. On April 15, 2011, effective immediately, the New York Appellate Divisions deleted former subparagraph (g)(1) and merged subparagraph (g)(2) with the introductory language, making Rule 7.1(g) a single paragraph. (If readers want to study the precise changes, our 2012 edition reprinted the amended rule in legislative style.)

(g) A lawyer or law firm shall not utilize meta-tags or other hidden computer codes that, if displayed, would violate these Rules.

(h) All advertisements shall include the name, principal law office address and telephone number of the lawyer or law firm whose services are being offered.

(i) Any words or statements required by this Rule to appear in an advertisement must be clearly legible and capable of being read by the average person, if written, and intelligible if spoken aloud. In the case of a web site, the required words or statements shall appear on the home page.

(j) A lawyer or law firm advertising any fixed fee for specified legal services shall, at the time of fee publication, have available to the public a written statement clearly describing the scope of each advertised service, which statement shall be available to the client at the time of retainer for any such service. Such legal services shall include all those services that are recognized as reasonable and necessary under local custom in the area of practice in the community where the services are performed.

(k) All advertisements shall be pre-approved by the lawyer or law firm, and a copy shall be retained for a period of not less than three years following its initial dissemination. Any advertisement contained in a computer-accessed communication shall be retained for a period of not less than one year. A copy of the contents of any web site covered by this Rule shall be preserved upon the initial publication of the web site, any major web site redesign, or a meaningful and extensive content change, but in no event less frequently than once every 90 days.

(l) If a lawyer or law firm advertises a range of fees or an hourly rate for services, the lawyer or law firm shall not charge more than the fee advertised for such services. If a lawyer or law firm advertises a fixed fee for specified legal services, or performs services described in a fee schedule, the lawyer or law firm shall not charge more than the fixed fee for such stated legal service as set forth in the advertisement or fee schedule, unless the client agrees in writing that the services performed or to be performed were not legal services referred to or implied in the advertisement or in the fee schedule and, further, that a different fee arrangement shall apply to the transaction.

(m) Unless otherwise specified in the advertisement, if a lawyer publishes any fee information authorized under this Rule in a publication that is published more frequently than once per month, the lawyer shall be bound by any representation made therein for a period of not less than 30 days after such publication. If a lawyer publishes any fee information authorized under this Rule in a publication that is published once per month or less frequently, the lawyer shall be bound by any representation made therein until the publication of the succeeding issue. If a lawyer publishes any fee information authorized under this Rule in a publication that has no fixed date for publication of a succeeding issue, the lawyer shall be bound by any representation made therein for a reasonable period of time after publication, but in no event less than 90 days.

(n) Unless otherwise specified, if a lawyer broadcasts any fee information authorized under this Rule, the lawyer shall be bound by any representation made therein for a period of not less than 30 days after such broadcast.

(o) A lawyer shall not compensate or give anything of value to representatives of the press, radio, television or other communication medium in anticipation of or in return for professional publicity in a news item.

(p) All advertisements that contain information about the fees charged by the lawyer or law firm, including those indicating that in the absence of a recovery no fee will be charged, shall comply with the provisions of Judiciary Law §488(3).

(q) A lawyer may accept employment that results from participation in activities designed to educate the public to recognize legal problems, to make intelligent selection of counsel or to utilize available legal services.

(r) Without affecting the right to accept employment, a lawyer may speak publicly or write for publication on legal topics so long as the lawyer does not undertake to give individual advice.

COMMENT

Advertising

[1] The need of members of the public for legal services is met only if they recognize their legal problems, appreciate the importance of seeking assistance, and are able to obtain the services of competent legal counsel. Hence, important functions of the legal profession are to educate people to recognize their problems, to facilitate the process of intelligent selection of lawyers, and to assist in making legal services fully available.

[2] The public's need to know about legal services can be fulfilled in part through advertising. People of limited means who have not made extensive use of legal services in many instances rely on advertising to find appropriate counsel. While a lawyer's reputation may attract some clients, lawyers may also make the public aware of their services by advertising to obtain work.

[3] Advertising by lawyers serves two principal purposes. First, it educates potential clients regarding their need for legal advice and assists them in obtaining a lawyer appropriate for those needs. Second, it enables lawyers to attract clients. To carry out these two purposes and because of the critical importance of legal services, it is of the utmost importance that lawyer advertising not be false, deceptive or misleading. Truthful statements that are misleading are prohibited by this Rule. A truthful statement is misleading if it omits a fact necessary to make the lawyer's communication, considered as a whole, not materially misleading. A truthful statement is also misleading if there is a substantial likelihood that it will lead a reasonable person to formulate a specific conclusion about the lawyer or the lawyer's services, or about the results a lawyer can achieve, for which there is no reasonable factual foundation. For example, a lawyer might truthfully state, "I have never lost a

case," but that statement would be misleading if the lawyer settled virtually all cases that the lawyer handled. A communication to anyone that states or implies that the lawyer has the ability to influence improperly a court, court officer, governmental agency or government official is improper under Rule 8.4(e).

[4] To be effective, advertising must attract the attention of viewers, readers or recipients and convey its content in ways that will be understandable and helpful to them. Lawyers may therefore use advertising techniques intended to attract attention, such as music, sound effects, graphics and the like, so long as those techniques do not render the advertisement false, deceptive or misleading. Lawyer advertising may use actors or fictionalized events or scenes for this purpose, provided appropriate disclosure of their use is made. Some images or techniques, however, are highly likely to be misleading. So, for instance, legal advertising should not be made to resemble legal documents.

[5] The "Attorney Advertising" label serves to dispel any confusion or concern that might be created when nonlawyers receive letters or emails from lawyers. The label is not necessary for advertising in newspapers or on television, or similar communications that are self-evidently advertisements, such as billboards or press releases transmitted to news outlets, and as to which there is no risk of such confusion or concern. The ultimate purpose of the label is to inform readers where they might otherwise be confused.

[6] Not all communications made by lawyers about the lawyer or the law firm's services are advertising. Advertising by lawyers consists of communications made in any form about the lawyer or the law firm's services, the primary purpose of which is retention of the lawyer or law firm for pecuniary gain as a result of the communication. However, non-commercial communications motivated by a not-for-profit organization's interest in political expression and association are generally not considered advertising. Of course, all communications by lawyers, whether subject to the special rules governing lawyer advertising or not, are governed by the general rule that lawyers may not engage in conduct involving dishonesty, fraud, deceit or misrepresentation, or knowingly make a material false statement of fact or law. By definition, communications to existing clients are excluded from the Rules governing advertising. A client who is a current client in any matter is an existing client for all purposes of these Rules. (Whether a client is a current client for purposes of conflicts of interest and other issues may depend on other considerations. Generally, the term "current client" for purposes of the advertising exemption should be interpreted more broadly than it is for determining whether a client is a "current client" for purposes of a conflict of interest analysis.)

[7] Communications to former clients that are germane to the earlier representation are not considered to be advertising. Likewise, communications to other lawyers, including those made in bar association publications and other publications targeted primarily at lawyers, are excluded from the special rules governing lawyer advertising even if their purpose is the retention of the lawyer or law firm. Topical newsletters, client alerts, or blogs intended to educate recipients about new developments in the law are generally not considered advertising. However, a newsletter, client alert, or blog that provides information or news primarily about the lawyer or law firm (for example, the lawyer or law firm's cases, personnel, clients or achievements) generally would be considered advertising. Communications, such as proposed retainer agreements or ordinary correspondence with a prospective client

who has expressed interest in, and requested information about, a lawyer's services, are not advertising. Accordingly, the special restrictions on advertising and solicitation would not apply to a lawyer's response to a prospective client who has asked the lawyer to outline the lawyer's qualifications to undertake a proposed retention or the terms of a potential retention.

[8] The circulation or distribution to prospective clients by a lawyer of an article or report published about the lawyer by a third party is advertising if the lawyer's primary purpose is to obtain retentions. In circulating or distributing such materials the lawyer should include information or disclaimers as necessary to dispel any misconceptions to which the article may give rise. For example, if a lawyer circulates an article discussing the lawyer's successes that is reasonably likely to create an expectation about the results the lawyer will achieve in future cases, a disclaimer is required by paragraph (e)(3). If the article contains misinformation about the lawyer's qualifications, any circulation of the article by the lawyer should make any necessary corrections or qualifications. This may be necessary even when the article included misinformation through no fault of the lawyer or because the article is out of date, so that material information that was true at the time is no longer true. Some communications by a law firm that may constitute marketing or branding are not necessarily advertisements. For example, pencils, legal pads, greeting cards, coffee mugs, T-shirts or the like with the law firm name, logo, and contact information printed on them do not constitute "advertisements" within the definition of this Rule if their primary purpose is general awareness and branding, rather than the retention of the law firm for a particular matter.

Recognition of Legal Problems

[9] The legal professional should help the public to recognize legal problems because such problems may not be self-revealing and might not be timely noticed. Therefore, lawyers should encourage and participate in educational and public-relations programs concerning the legal system, with particular reference to legal problems that frequently arise. A lawyer's participation in an educational program is ordinarily not considered to be advertising because its primary purpose is to educate and inform rather than to attract clients. Such a program might be considered to be advertising if, in addition to its educational component, participants or recipients are expressly encouraged to hire the lawyer or law firm. A lawyer who writes or speaks for the purpose of educating members of the public to recognize their legal problems should carefully refrain from giving or appearing to give a general solution applicable to all apparently similar individual problems, because slight changes in fact situations may require a material variance in the applicable advice; otherwise, the public may be misled and misadvised. Talks and writings by lawyers for nonlawyers should caution them not to attempt to solve individual problems on the basis of the information contained therein.

[10] As members of their communities, lawyers may choose to sponsor or contribute to cultural, sporting, charitable or other events organized by not-for-profit organizations. If information about the lawyer or law firm disseminated in connection with such an event is limited to the identification of the lawyer or law firm, the lawyer's or law firm's contact information, a brief description of areas of practice,

and the fact of sponsorship or contribution, the communication is not considered advertising.

Statements Creating Expectations, Characterizations of Quality, and Comparisons

[11] Lawyer advertising may include statements that are reasonably likely to create an expectation about results the lawyer can achieve, statements that compare the lawyer's services with the services of other lawyers, or statements describing or characterizing the quality of the lawyer's or law firm's services, only if they can be factually supported by the lawyer or law firm as of the date on which the advertisement is published or disseminated and are accompanied by the following disclaimer: "Prior results do not guarantee a similar outcome." Accordingly, if true and accompanied by the disclaimer, a lawyer or law firm could advertise "Our firm won 10 jury verdicts over $1,000,000 in the last five years," "We have more Patent Lawyers than any other firm in X County," or "I have been practicing in the area of divorce law for more than 10 years." Even true factual statements may be misleading if presented out of the context of additional information needed to properly understand and evaluate the statements. For example, a truthful statement by a lawyer that the lawyer's average jury verdict for a given year was $100,000 may be misleading if that average was based on a large number of very small verdicts and one $10,000,000 verdict. Likewise, advertising that truthfully recites judgment amounts would be misleading if the lawyer failed to disclose that the judgments described were overturned on appeal or were obtained by default.

[12] Descriptions of characteristics of the lawyer or law firm that are not comparative and do not involve results obtained are permissible even though they cannot be factually supported. Such statements are understood to be general descriptions and not claims about quality, and would not be likely to mislead potential clients. Accordingly, a law firm could advertise that it is "Hard-Working," "Dedicated," or "Compassionate" without the necessity to provide factual support for such subjective claims. On the other hand, descriptions of characteristics of the law firm that compare its services with those of other law firms and that are not susceptible of being factually supported could be misleading to potential clients. Accordingly, a lawyer may not advertise that the lawyer is the "Best," "Most Experienced," or "Hardest Working." Similarly, some claims that involve results obtained are not susceptible of being factually supported and could be misleading to potential clients. Accordingly, a law firm may not advertise that it will obtain "Big $$$," "Most Money," or "We Win Big."

Bona Fide Professional Ratings

[13] An advertisement may include information regarding bona fide professional ratings by referring to the rating service and how it has rated the lawyer, provided that the advertisement contains the "past results" disclaimer as required under paragraphs (d) and (e). However, a rating is not "bona fide" unless it is unbiased and nondiscriminatory. Thus, it must evaluate lawyers based on objective

criteria or legitimate peer review in a manner unbiased by the rating service's economic interests (such as payment to the rating service by the rated lawyer) and not subject to improper influence by lawyers who are being evaluated. Further, the rating service must fairly consider all lawyers within the pool of those who are purported to be covered. For example, a rating service that purports to evaluate all lawyers practicing in a particular geographic area or in a particular area of practice or of a particular age must apply its criteria to all lawyers within that geographic area, practice area, or age group.

Meta-Tags

[14] Meta-tags are hidden computer software codes that direct certain Internet search engines to the web site of a lawyer or law firm. For example, if a lawyer places the meta-tag "NY personal injury specialist" on the lawyer's web site, then a person who enters the search term "personal injury specialist" into a search engine will be directed to that lawyer's web page. That particular meta-tag is prohibited because Rule 7.4(a) generally prohibits the use of the word "specialist." However, a lawyer may use an advertisement employing meta-tags or other hidden computer codes that, if displayed, would not violate a Rule.

Advertisements Referring to Fees and Advances

[15] All advertisements that contain information about the fees or expenses charged by the lawyer or law firm, including advertisements indicating that in the absence of a recovery no fee will be charged, must comply with the provisions of section 488(3) of the Judiciary Law. However, a lawyer or law firm that offers any of the fee and expense arrangements permitted by section 488(3) must not, either directly or in any advertisement, state or imply that the lawyer's or law firm's ability to advance or pay costs and expenses of litigation is unique or extraordinary when that is not the case. For example, if an advertisement promises that the lawyer or law firm will advance the costs and expenses of litigation contingent on the outcome of the matter, or promises that the lawyer or law firm will pay the costs and expenses of litigation for indigent clients, then the advertisement must not say that such arrangements are "unique in the area," "unlike other firms," available "only at our firm," "extraordinary," or words to that effect, unless that is actually the case. However, if the lawyer or law firm can objectively demonstrate that this arrangement is unique or extraordinary, then the lawyer or law firm may make such a claim in the advertisement.

Retention of Copies; Filing of Copies; Designation of Principal Office

[16] Where these Rules require that a lawyer retain a copy of an advertisement or file a copy of a solicitation or other information, that obligation may be satisfied by any of the following: original records, photocopies, microfilm, optical imaging,

and any other medium that preserves an image of the document that cannot be altered without detection.

[17] A law firm that has no office it considers its principal office may comply with paragraph (h) by listing one or more offices where a substantial amount of the law firm's work is performed.

Rule 7.2   Payment for Referrals

(a) A lawyer shall not compensate or give anything of value to a person or organization to recommend or obtain employment by a client, or as a reward for having made a recommendation resulting in employment by a client, except that:

(1) a lawyer or law firm may refer clients to a nonlegal professional or nonlegal professional service firm pursuant to a contractual relationship with such nonlegal professional or nonlegal professional service firm to provide legal and other professional services on a systematic and continuing basis as permitted by Rule 5.8, provided however that such referral shall not otherwise include any monetary or other tangible consideration or reward for such, or the sharing of legal fees; and

(2) a lawyer may pay the usual and reasonable fees or dues charged by a qualified legal assistance organization or referral fees to another lawyer as permitted by Rule 1.5(g).

(b) A lawyer or the lawyer's partner or associate or any other affiliated lawyer may be recommended, employed or paid by, or may cooperate with one of the following offices or organizations that promote the use of the lawyer's services or those of a partner or associate or any other affiliated lawyer, or request one of the following offices or organizations to recommend or promote the use of the lawyer's services or those of the lawyer's partner or associate, or any other affiliated lawyer as a private practitioner, if there is no interference with the exercise of independent professional judgment on behalf of the client:

(1) a legal aid office or public defender office:

(i) operated or sponsored by a duly accredited law school;

(ii) operated or sponsored by a bona fide, non-profit community organization;

(iii) operated or sponsored by a governmental agency; or

(iv) operated, sponsored, or approved by a bar association;

(2) a military legal assistance office;

(3) a lawyer referral service operated, sponsored or approved by a bar association or authorized by law or court rule; or

(4) any bona fide organization that recommends, furnishes or pays for legal services to its members or beneficiaries provided the following conditions are satisfied:

(i) Neither the lawyer, nor the lawyer's partner, nor associate, nor any other affiliated lawyer nor any nonlawyer, shall have initiated or promoted such organization for the primary purpose of providing financial or other benefit to such lawyer, partner, associate or affiliated lawyer;

(ii) Such organization is not operated for the purpose of procuring legal work or financial benefit for any lawyer as a private practitioner outside of the legal services program of the organization;

(iii) The member or beneficiary to whom the legal services are furnished, and not such organization, is recognized as the client of the lawyer in the matter;

(iv) The legal service plan of such organization provides appropriate relief for any member or beneficiary who asserts a claim that representation by counsel furnished, selected or approved by the organization for the particular matter involved would be unethical, improper or inadequate under the circumstances of the matter involved; and the plan provides an appropriate procedure for seeking such relief;

(v) The lawyer does not know or have cause to know that such organization is in violation of applicable laws, rules of court or other legal requirements that govern its legal service operations; and

(vi) Such organization has filed with the appropriate disciplinary authority, to the extent required by such authority, at least annually a report with respect to its legal service plan, if any, showing its terms, its schedule of benefits, its subscription charges, agreements with counsel and financial results of its legal service activities or, if it has failed to do so, the lawyer does not know or have cause to know of such failure.

COMMENT

Paying Others to Recommend a Lawyer

[1] Lawyers are not permitted to pay others for channeling professional work. Paragraph (a)(3), however, allows a lawyer to pay for advertising and communications permitted by these Rules, including the costs of print directory listings, online directory listings, newspaper ads, television and radio airtime, domain name registrations, sponsorship fees, banner ads and group advertising. A lawyer may compensate employees, agents and vendors who are engaged to provide marketing or client development services, such as publicists, public-relations personnel, marketing personnel and web site designers. See Rule 5.3 for the duties of lawyers and law firms with respect to the conduct of nonlawyers who prepare marketing materials for them.

[2] A lawyer may pay the usual charges of a qualified legal assistance organization. A lawyer so participating should make certain that the relationship with a qualified legal assistance organization in no way interferes with independent professional representation of the interests of the individual client. A lawyer should avoid situations in which officials of the organization who are not lawyers attempt to direct lawyers concerning the manner in which legal services are performed for individual

members and should also avoid situations in which considerations of economy are given undue weight in determining the lawyers employed by an organization or the legal services to be performed for the member or beneficiary, rather than competence and quality of service.

[3] A lawyer who accepts assignments or referrals from a qualified legal assistance organization must act reasonably to ensure that the activities of the plan or service are compatible with the lawyer's professional obligations. *See* Rule 5.3. The lawyer must ensure that the organization's communications with prospective clients are in conformity with these Rules. Thus, advertising must not be false or misleading, as would be the case if the communications of a qualified legal assistance organization would mislead prospective clients to think that it was a lawyer referral service sponsored by a state agency or bar association. Nor could the lawyer allow in-person, telephonic or real-time interactive electronic contacts that would violate Rule 7.3.

[4] A lawyer also may agree to refer clients to another lawyer or a nonlawyer in return for the undertaking of that person to refer clients or customers to the lawyer. Such reciprocal referral arrangements must not interfere with the lawyer's professional judgment as to making referrals or as to providing substantive legal services. *See* Rules 2.1, 5.4(c). Except as provided in Rule 1.5(e), a lawyer who receives referrals from a lawyer or nonlawyer must not pay anything solely for the referral, but the lawyer does not violate paragraph (a) by agreeing to refer clients to the other lawyer or nonlawyer so long as the reciprocal referral agreement is not exclusive and the client is informed of the referral agreement. A lawyer may enter into such an arrangement only if it is nonexclusive on both sides, so that both the lawyer and the nonlawyer are free to refer clients to others if that is in the best interest of those clients. Conflicts of interest created by such arrangements are governed by Rule 1.7. A lawyer's interest in receiving a steady stream of referrals from a particular source must not undermine the lawyer's professional judgment on behalf of clients. Reciprocal referral agreements should not be of indefinite duration and should be reviewed periodically to determine whether they comply with these Rules. This Rule does not restrict referrals or divisions of revenues or net income among lawyers within firms comprising multiple entities.

[5] Campaign contributions by lawyers to government officials or candidates for public office who are, or may be, in a position to influence the award of a legal engagement may threaten governmental integrity by subjecting the recipient to a conflict of interest. Correspondingly, when a lawyer makes a significant contribution to a public official or an election campaign for a candidate for public office and is later engaged by the official to perform legal services for the official's agency, it may appear that the official has been improperly influenced in selecting the lawyer, whether or not this is so. This appearance of influence reflects poorly on the integrity of the legal profession and government as a whole. For these reasons, just as the Code prohibits a lawyer from compensating or giving anything of value to a person or organization to recommend or obtain employment by a client, the Code prohibits a lawyer from making or soliciting a political contribution to any candidate for government office, government official, political campaign committee or political party, if a disinterested person would conclude that the contribution is being made or solicited for the purpose of obtaining or being considered eligible to obtain a government legal engagement. This would be true even in the absence

of an understanding between the lawyer and any government official or candidate that special consideration will be given in return for the political contribution or solicitation.

[6] In determining whether a disinterested person would conclude that a contribution to a candidate for government office, government official, political campaign committee or political party is or has been made for the purpose of obtaining or being considered eligible to obtain a government legal engagement, the factors to be considered include (a) whether legal work awarded to the contributor or solicitor, if any, was awarded pursuant to a process that was insulated from political influence, such as a "Request for Proposal" process, (b) the amount of the contribution or the contributions resulting from a solicitation, (c) whether the contributor or any law firm with which the lawyer is associated has sought or plans to seek government legal work from the official or candidate, (d) whether the contribution or solicitation was made because of an existing personal, family or non-client professional relationship with the government official or candidate, (e) whether prior to the contribution or solicitation in question, the contributor or solicitor had made comparable contributions or had engaged in comparable solicitations on behalf of governmental officials or candidates for public office for which the lawyer or any law firm with which the lawyer is associated did not perform or seek to perform legal work, (f) whether the contributor has made a contribution to the government official's or candidate's opponent(s) during the same campaign period and, if so, the amounts thereof, and (g) whether the contributor is eligible to vote in the jurisdiction of the governmental official or candidate, and if not, whether other factors indicate that the contribution or solicitation was nonetheless made to further a genuinely held political, social or economic belief or interest rather than to obtain a legal engagement.

Rule 7.3   Solicitation and Recommendation of Professional Employment

(a) A lawyer shall not engage in solicitation:

(1) by in-person or telephone contact, or by real-time or interactive computer-accessed communication unless the recipient is a close friend, relative, former client or existing client; or

(2) by any form of communication if:

(i) the communication or contact violates Rule 4.5, Rule 7.1(a), or paragraph (e) of this Rule;

(ii) the recipient has made known to the lawyer a desire not to be solicited by the lawyer;

(iii) the solicitation involves coercion, duress or harassment;

(iv) the lawyer knows or reasonably should know that the age or the physical, emotional or mental state of the recipient makes it unlikely that the recipient will be able to exercise reasonable judgment in retaining a lawyer; or

(v) the lawyer intends or expects, but does not disclose, that the legal services necessary to handle the matter competently will be performed primarily by another lawyer who is not affiliated with the soliciting lawyer as a partner, associate or of counsel.

(b) For purposes of this Rule, "solicitation" means any advertisement initiated by or on behalf of a lawyer or law firm that is directed to, or targeted at, a specific recipient or group of recipients, or their family members or legal representatives, the primary purpose of which is the retention of the lawyer or law firm, and a significant motive for which is pecuniary gain. It does not include a proposal or other writing prepared and delivered in response to a specific request of a prospective client.

(c) A solicitation directed to a recipient in this State shall be subject to the following provisions:

(1) A copy of the solicitation shall at the time of its dissemination be filed with the attorney disciplinary committee of the judicial district or judicial department wherein the lawyer or law firm maintains its principal office. Where no such office is maintained, the filing shall be made in the judicial department where the solicitation is targeted. A filing shall consist of:

(i) a copy of the solicitation;

(ii) a transcript of the audio portion of any radio or television solicitation; and

(iii) if the solicitation is in a language other than English, an accurate English-language translation.

(2) Such solicitation shall contain no reference to the fact of filing.

(3) If a solicitation is directed to a predetermined recipient, a list containing the names and addresses of all recipients shall be retained by the lawyer or law firm for a period of not less than three years following the last date of its dissemination.

(4) Solicitations filed pursuant to this subdivision shall be open to public inspection.

(5) The provisions of this paragraph shall not apply to:

(i) a solicitation directed or disseminated to a close friend, relative, or former or existing client;

(ii) a web site maintained by the lawyer or law firm, unless the web site is designed for and directed to or targeted at a prospective client affected by an identifiable actual event or occurrence or by an identifiable prospective defendant; or

(iii) professional cards or other announcements the distribution of which is authorized by Rule 7.5(a).

(d) A written solicitation shall not be sent by a method that requires the recipient to travel to a location other than that at which the recipient ordinarily receives business or personal mail or that requires a signature on the part of the recipient.

(e) No solicitation relating to a specific incident involving potential claims for personal injury or wrongful death shall be disseminated before the 30th day after the date of the incident, unless a filing must be made within 30 days of the incident as a legal prerequisite to the particular claim, in which case no unsolicited communication shall be made before the 15th day after the date of the incident.

(f) Any solicitation made in writing or by computer-accessed communication and directed to a pre-determined recipient, if prompted by a specific occurrence involving or affecting a recipient, shall disclose how the lawyer obtained the identity of the recipient and learned of the recipient's potential legal need.

(g) If a retainer agreement is provided with any solicitation, the top of each page shall be marked "SAMPLE" in red ink in a type size equal to the largest type size used in the agreement and the words "DO NOT SIGN" shall appear on the client signature line.

(h) Any solicitation covered by this section shall include the name, principal law office address and telephone number of the lawyer or law firm whose services are being offered.

(i) The provisions of this Rule shall apply to a lawyer or members of a law firm not admitted to practice in this State who shall solicit retention by residents of this State.

COMMENT

Solicitation

[1] In addition to seeking clients through general advertising (either by public communications in the media or by private communications to potential clients who are neither current clients nor other lawyers), many lawyers attempt to attract clients through a specialized category of advertising called "solicitation." Not all advertisements are solicitations within the meaning of this Rule. All solicitations, however, are advertisements with certain additional characteristics. By definition, a communication that is not an advertisement is not a solicitation. Solicitations are subject to all of the Rules governing advertising and are also subject to additional Rules, including filing a copy of the solicitation with the appropriate attorney disciplinary authority (including a transcript of the audio portion of any radio or television solicitation and, if the solicitation is in a language other than English, an accurate English language translation). These and other additional requirements will facilitate oversight by disciplinary authorities.

[2] A "solicitation" means any advertisement: (i) that is initiated by a lawyer or law firm (as opposed to a communication made in response to an inquiry initiated by a potential client), (ii) with a primary purpose of persuading recipients to retain the lawyer or law firm (as opposed to providing educational information about the law, *see* Rule 7.1, Comment [7]), (iii) that has as a significant motive for the lawyer to make money (as opposed to a public-interest lawyer offering pro bono services), and (iv) that is directed to or targeted at a specific recipient or group of recipients, or their family members or legal representatives. Any advertisement that meets all four of these criteria is a solicitation, and is governed not only by the Rules that govern all advertisements but also by special Rules governing solicitation.

Directed or Targeted

[3] An advertisement may be considered to be directed to or targeted at a specific recipient or recipients in two different ways. First, an advertisement is considered "directed to or targeted at" a specific recipient or recipients if it is made by in-person or telephone contact or by real-time or interactive computer-accessed communication or if it is addressed so that it will be delivered to the specific recipient or recipients or their families or agents (as with letters, emails, express packages). Advertisements made by in-person or telephone contact or by real-time or interactive computer-accessed communication are prohibited unless the recipient is a close friend, relative, former client or current client. Advertisements addressed so that they will be delivered to the specific recipient or recipients or their families or agents (as with letters, emails, express packages) are subject to various additional rules governing solicitation (including filing and public inspection) because otherwise they would not be readily subject to disciplinary oversight and review. Second, an advertisement in public media such as newspapers, television, billboards, web sites or the like is a solicitation if it makes reference to a specific person or group of people whose legal needs arise out of a specific incident to which the advertisement explicitly refers. The term "specific incident" is explained in Comment [5].

[4] Unless it falls within Comment [3], an advertisement in public media such as newspapers, television, billboards, web sites or the like is presumed not to be directed to or targeted at a specific recipient or recipients. For example, an advertisement in a public medium is not directed to or targeted at "a specific recipient or group of recipients" simply because it is intended to attract potential clients with needs in a specified area of law. Thus, a lawyer could advertise in the local newspaper that the lawyer is available to assist homeowners in reducing property tax assessments. Likewise, an advertisement by a patent lawyer is not directed or targeted within the meaning of the definition solely because the magazine is geared toward inventors. Similarly, a lawyer could advertise on television or in a newspaper or web site to the general public that the lawyer practices in the area of personal injury or Workers' Compensation law. The fact that some recipients of such advertisements might actually be in need of specific legal services at the time of the communication does not transform such advertisements into solicitations.

Solicitations Relating to a Specific Incident Involving Potential Claims for Personal Injury or Wrongful Death

[5] Solicitations relating to a specific incident involving potential claims for personal injury or wrongful death are subject to a further restriction, in that they may not be disseminated until 30 days (or in some cases 15 days) after the date of the incident. This restriction applies even where the recipient is a close friend, relative, or former client, but not where the recipient is a current client. A "specific incident" is a particular identifiable event (or a sequence of related events occurring at approximately the same time and place) that causes harm to one or more people. Specific incidents include such events as traffic accidents, plane or train crashes, explosions, building collapses, and the like.

[6] A solicitation that is intended to attract potential claims for personal injury or wrongful death arising from a common cause but at disparate times and places, does not relate to a specific incident and is not subject to the special 30-day (or 15-day) rule, even though it is addressed so that it will be delivered to specific recipients or their families or agents (as with letters, emails, express packages), or is made in a public medium such as newspapers, television, billboards, web sites or the like and makes reference to a specific person or group of people, *see* Comments [3]-[4]. For example, solicitations intended to be of interest only to potential claimants injured over a period of years by a defective medical device or medication do not relate to a specific incident and are not subject to the special 30-day (or 15-day) rule.

[7] An advertisement in the public media that makes no express reference to a specific incident does not become a solicitation subject to the 30-day (or 15-day) rule solely because a specific incident has occurred within the last 30 (or 15) days. Thus, a law firm that advertises on television or in newspapers that it can "help injured people explore their legal rights" is not violating the 30-day (or 15-day) rule by running or continuing to run its advertisements even though a mass disaster injured many people within hours or days before the advertisement appeared. Unless an advertisement in the public media explicitly refers to a specific incident, it is not a solicitation subject to the 30-day (or 15-day) blackout period. However, if a lawyer causes an advertisement to be delivered (whether by mail, email, express service, courier, or any other form of direct delivery) to a specific recipient (i) with knowledge that the addressee is either a person killed or injured in a specific incident or that person's family member or agent, and (ii) with the intent to communicate with that person because of that knowledge, then the advertisement is a solicitation subject to the 30-day (or 15-day) rule even if it makes no reference to a specific incident and even if it is part of a mass mailing.

Extraterritorial Application of Solicitation Rules

[8] All of the special solicitation rules, including the special 30-day (or 15-day) rule, apply to solicitations directed to recipients in New York State, whether made by a lawyer admitted in New York State or a lawyer admitted in any another jurisdiction. Solicitations by a lawyer admitted in New York State directed to or targeted at a recipient or recipients outside of New York State are not subject to the filing and related requirements set out in Rule 7.3(c). Whether such solicitations are subject to the special 30-day (or 15-day) rule depends on the application of Rule 8.5.

In-Person, Telephone and Real-Time or Interactive Computer-Accessed Communication

[9] Paragraph (a) generally prohibits in-person solicitation, which has historically been disfavored by the bar because it poses serious dangers to potential clients. For example, in-person solicitation poses the risk that a lawyer, who is trained in the arts of advocacy and persuasion, may pressure a potential client to hire the lawyer without adequate consideration. These same risks are present in

telephone contact or by real-time or interactive computer-accessed communication and are regulated in the same manner. The prohibitions on in-person or telephone contact and by real-time or interactive computer-accessed communication do not apply if the recipient is a close friend, relative, former or current client. Communications with these individuals do not pose the same dangers as solicitations to others. However, when the special 30-day (or 15-day) rule applies, it does so even where the recipient is a close friend, relative, or former client. Ordinary email and web sites are not considered to be real-time or interactive communication. Similarly, automated pop-up advertisements on a web site that are not a live response are not considered to be real-time or interactive communication. Instant messaging, chat rooms, and other similar types of conversational computer-accessed communication are considered to be real-time or interactive communication.

Rule 7.4   Identification of Practice and Specialty

> **Editors' Note.** in *Hayes v. New York Attorney Grievance Committee of the Eighth Judicial District*, 672 F.3d 158 (2d Cir. 2012), the Second Circuit struck down on First Amendment grounds the last sentence of the disclaimer required by Rule 7.4(c)(1) ("Certification is not a requirement for the practice of law in the State of New York and does not necessarily indicate greater competence than other attorneys experienced in this field of law."). The identical language appears in Rule 7.4(c)(2) as well. The defendant did not seek review in the United States Supreme Court, and shortly before our press deadline the New York Courts approved an amendment to Rule 7.4(c) deleting the unconstitutional language from subparagraphs (c)(1) and (c)(2). The Courts were expected to issue an Order formalizing that amendment n November 2012, but they had not yet done so when we went to press, so we have left the unconstitutional language in the rule.

(a) A lawyer or law firm may publicly identify one or more areas of law in which the lawyer or the law firm practices, or may state that the practice of the lawyer or law firm is limited to one or more areas of law, provided that the lawyer or law firm shall not state that the lawyer or law firm is a specialist or specializes in a particular field of law, except as provided in Rule 7.4(c).

(b) A lawyer admitted to engage in patent practice before the United States Patent and Trademark Office may use the designation "Patent Attorney" or a substantially similar designation.

(c) A lawyer may state that the lawyer has been recognized or certified as a specialist only as follows:

(1) A lawyer who is certified as a specialist in a particular area of law or law practice by a private organization approved for that purpose by the American Bar Association may state the fact of certification if, in conjunction therewith, the certifying organization is identified and the following statement is prominently made: "The [name of the private certifying organization] is not affiliated with any governmental authority. Certification is not a requirement for the practice of law in the State of New York and

does not necessarily indicate greater competence than other attorneys experienced in this field of law;"

(2) A lawyer who is certified as a specialist in a particular area of law or law practice by the authority having jurisdiction over specialization under the laws of another state or territory may state the fact of certification if, in conjunction therewith, the certifying state or territory is identified and the following statement is prominently made: "Certification granted by the [identify state or territory] is not recognized by any governmental authority within the State of New York. Certification is not a requirement for the practice of law in the State of New York and does not necessarily indicate greater competence than other attorneys experienced in this field of law."

COMMENT

[1] Paragraph (a) permits a lawyer to indicate areas of practice in which the lawyer practices, or that his or her practice is limited to those areas.

[2] Paragraph (b) recognizes the long-established policy of the Patent and Trademark Office for the designation of lawyers practicing before the Office.

[3] Paragraph (c) permits a lawyer to state that the lawyer specializes or is certified as a specialist in a field of law if such certification is granted by an organization approved or accredited by the American Bar Association or by the authority having jurisdiction over specialization under the laws of another jurisdiction provided that the name of the certifying organization or authority must be included in any communication regarding the certification together with the disclaimer required by paragraph (c).

Rule 7.5 Professional Notices, Letterheads and Signs

(a) A lawyer or law firm may use internet web sites, professional cards, professional announcement cards, office signs, letterheads or similar professional notices or devices, provided the same do not violate any statute or court rule and are in accordance with Rule 7.1, including the following:

(1) a professional card of a lawyer identifying the lawyer by name and as a lawyer, and giving addresses, telephone numbers, the name of the law firm, and any information permitted under Rule 7.1(b) or Rule 7.4. A professional card of a law firm may also give the names of members and associates;

(2) a professional announcement card stating new or changed associations or addresses, change of firm name, or similar matters pertaining to the professional offices of a lawyer or law firm or any nonlegal business conducted by the lawyer or law firm pursuant to Rule 5.7. It may state biographical data, the names of members of the firm and associates, and the names and dates of predecessor firms in a continuing line of succession. It may state the nature of the legal practice if permitted under Rule 7.4;

(3) a sign in or near the office and in the building directory identifying the law office and any nonlegal business conducted by the lawyer or law firm pursuant to Rule 5.7. The sign may state the nature of the legal practice if permitted under Rule 7.4; or

(4) a letterhead identifying the lawyer by name and as a lawyer, and giving addresses, telephone numbers, the name of the law firm, associates and any information permitted under Rule 7.1(b) or Rule 7.4. A letterhead of a law firm may also give the names of members and associates, and names and dates relating to deceased and retired members. A lawyer or law firm may be designated "Of Counsel" on a letterhead if there is a continuing relationship with a lawyer or law firm, other than as a partner or associate. A lawyer or law firm may be designated as "General Counsel" or by similar professional reference on stationery of a client if the lawyer or the firm devotes a substantial amount of professional time in the representation of that client. The letterhead of a law firm may give the names and dates of predecessor firms in a continuing line of succession.

(b) A lawyer in private practice shall not practice under a trade name, a name that is misleading as to the identity of the lawyer or lawyers practicing under such name, or a firm name containing names other than those of one or more of the lawyers in the firm, except that the name of a professional corporation shall contain "PC" or such symbols permitted by law, the name of a limited liability company or partnership shall contain "LLC," "LLP" or such symbols permitted by law and, if otherwise lawful, a firm may use as, or continue to include in its name the name or names of one or more deceased or retired members of the firm or of a predecessor firm in a continuing line of succession. Such terms as "legal clinic," "legal aid," "legal service office," "legal assistance office," "defender office" and the like may be used only by qualified legal assistance organizations, except that the term "legal clinic" may be used by any lawyer or law firm provided the name of a participating lawyer or firm is incorporated therein. A lawyer or law firm may not include the name of a nonlawyer in its firm name, nor may a lawyer or law firm that has a contractual relationship with a nonlegal professional or nonlegal professional service firm pursuant to Rule 5.8 to provide legal and other professional services on a systematic and continuing basis include in its firm name the name of the nonlegal professional service firm or any individual nonlegal professional affiliated therewith. A lawyer who assumes a judicial, legislative or public executive or administrative post or office shall not permit the lawyer's name to remain in the name of a law firm or to be used in professional notices of the firm during any significant period in which the lawyer is not actively and regularly practicing law as a member of the firm and, during such period, other members of the firm shall not use the lawyer's name in the firm name or in professional notices of the firm.

(c) Lawyers shall not hold themselves out as having a partnership with one or more other lawyers unless they are in fact partners.

(d) A partnership shall not be formed or continued between or among lawyers licensed in different jurisdictions unless all enumerations of the members and associates of the firm on its letterhead and in other permissible listings make clear the jurisdictional limitations on those members and associates of the firm not licensed to practice in all listed jurisdictions; however, the same firm name may be used in each jurisdiction.

(e) A lawyer or law firm may utilize a domain name for an internet web site that does not include the name of the lawyer or law firm provided:

(1) all pages of the web site clearly and conspicuously include the actual name of the lawyer or law firm;

(2) the lawyer or law firm in no way attempts to engage in the practice of law using the domain name;

(3) the domain name does not imply an ability to obtain results in a matter; and

(4) the domain name does not otherwise violate these Rules.

(f) A lawyer or law firm may utilize a telephone number which contains a domain name, nickname, moniker or motto that does not otherwise violate these Rules.

COMMENT

Professional Status

[1] In order to avoid the possibility of misleading persons with whom a lawyer deals, a lawyer should be scrupulous in the representation of professional status. Lawyers should not hold themselves out as being partners or associates of a law firm if that is not the fact, and thus lawyers should not hold themselves out as being a partners or associates if they only share offices.

Trade Names and Domain Names

[2] A lawyer may not practice under a trade name. Many law firms have created Internet web sites to provide information about their firms. A web site is reached through an Internet address, commonly called a "domain name." As long as a law firm's name complies with other Rules, it is always proper for a law firm to use its own name or its initials or some abbreviation or variation of its own name as its domain name. For example, the law firm of Able and Baker may use the domain name www.ableandbaker.com, or www.ab.com, or www.able.com, or www.ablelaw.com. However, to make domain names easier for clients and potential clients to remember and to locate, some law firms may prefer to use terms other than the law firm's name. If Able and Baker practices real estate law, for instance, it may prefer a descriptive domain name such as www.realestatelaw.com or www.ablerealestatelaw.com or a colloquial domain name such as www.dirtlawyers.com. Accordingly, a law firm may utilize a domain name for an Internet web site that does not include the name of the law firm, provided the domain name meets four conditions: First, all pages of the web site created by the law firm must clearly and conspicuously include the actual name of the law firm. Second, the law firm must in no way attempt to engage in the practice of law using the domain name. This restriction is parallel to the general

prohibition against the use of trade names. For example, if Able and Baker uses the domain name www.realestatelaw.com, the firm may not advertise that people buying or selling homes should "contact www.realestatelaw.com" unless the firm also clearly and conspicuously includes the name of the law firm in the advertisement. Third, the domain name must not imply an ability to obtain results in a matter. For example, a personal injury firm could not use the domain name www.win-your-case. com or www.settle-for-more.com because such names imply that the law firm can obtain favorable results in every matter regardless of the particular facts and circumstances. Fourth, the domain name must not otherwise violate a Rule. If a domain name meets the three criteria listed here but violates another Rule, then the domain name is improper under this Rule as well. For example, if Able and Baker are each solo practitioners who are not partners, they may not jointly establish a web site with the domain name www.ableandbaker.com because the lawyers would be holding themselves out as having a partnership when they are in fact not partners.

Telephone Numbers

[3] Many lawyers and law firms use telephone numbers that spell words, because such telephone numbers are generally easier to remember than strings of numbers. As with domain names, lawyers and law firms may always properly use their own names, initials, or combinations of names, initials, numbers, and legal words as telephone numbers. For example, the law firm of Red & Blue may properly use phone numbers such as RED-BLUE, 4-RED-LAW, or RB-LEGAL.

[4] Some lawyers and firms may instead (or in addition) wish to use telephone numbers that contain a domain name, nickname, moniker, or motto. A lawyer or law firm may use such telephone numbers as long as they do not violate any Rules, including those governing domain names. For example, a personal injury law firm may use the numbers 1-800-ACCIDENT, 1-800-HURT-BAD, or 1-800-INJURY-LAW, but may not use the numbers 1-800-WINNERS, 1-800-2WIN-BIG, or 1-800-GET-CASH. (Phone numbers with more letters than the number of digits in a phone number are acceptable as long as the words do not violate a Rule.) *See* Rule 7.1, Comment [12].

Rule 8.1   Candor in the Bar Admission Process

(a) A lawyer shall be subject to discipline if, in connection with the lawyer's own application for admission to the bar previously filed in this state or in any other jurisdiction, or in connection with the application of another person for admission to the bar, the lawyer knowingly:

(1) has made or failed to correct a false statement of material fact; or

(2) has failed to disclose a material fact requested in connection with a lawful demand for information from an admissions authority.

COMMENT

[1] If a person makes a material false statement in connection with an application for admission, it may be the basis for subsequent disciplinary action if the person is admitted and in any event may be relevant in a subsequent admission

application. The duty imposed by this Rule applies to a lawyer's own admission as well as that of another.

[2] This Rule is subject to the provisions of the Fifth Amendment to the United States Constitution and corresponding provisions of state constitutions. A person relying on such a provision in response to a question, however, should do so openly and not use the right of nondisclosure as a justification for failure to comply with this Rule.

Rule 8.2   Judicial Officers and Candidates

(a) A lawyer shall not knowingly make a false statement of fact concerning the qualifications, conduct or integrity of a judge or other adjudicatory officer or of a candidate for election or appointment to judicial office.

(b) A lawyer who is a candidate for judicial office shall comply with the applicable provisions of Part 100 of the Rules of the Chief Administrator of the Courts.

COMMENT

[1] Assessments by lawyers are relied on in evaluating the professional or personal fitness of persons being considered for election or appointment to judicial office. Expressing honest and candid opinions on such matters contributes to improving the administration of justice. False statements of fact by a lawyer can unfairly undermine public confidence in the administration of justice.

[2] When a lawyer seeks judicial office, the lawyer may engage in constitutionally protected speech, but is bound by valid limitations on speech and political activity.

[3] To maintain the fair and independent administration of justice, lawyers are encouraged to continue traditional efforts to defend judges and courts unjustly criticized.

Rule 8.3   Reporting Professional Misconduct

(a) A lawyer who knows that another lawyer has committed a violation of the Rules of Professional Conduct that raises a substantial question as to that lawyer's honesty, trustworthiness or fitness as a lawyer shall report such knowledge to a tribunal or other authority empowered to investigate or act upon such violation.

(b) A lawyer who possesses knowledge or evidence concerning another lawyer or a judge shall not fail to respond to a lawful demand for information from a tribunal or other authority empowered to investigate or act upon such conduct.

(c) This Rule does not require disclosure of:

(1) information otherwise protected by Rule 1.6; or

(2) information gained by a lawyer or judge while participating in a bona fide lawyer assistance program.

COMMENT

[1] Self-regulation of the legal profession requires that members of the profession initiate disciplinary investigation when they know of a violation of the Rules of Professional Conduct. Lawyers have a similar obligation to cooperate with authorities empowered to investigate judicial misconduct. An apparently isolated violation may indicate a pattern of misconduct that only a disciplinary investigation can uncover. Reporting a violation is especially important where the victim is unlikely to discover the offense.

[2] A report about misconduct is not required where it would result in violation of Rule 1.6. However, a lawyer should encourage a client to consent to disclosure where prosecution would not substantially prejudice the client's interests.

[3] If a lawyer were obliged to report every violation of the Rules, the failure to report any violation would itself be a professional offense. Such a requirement existed in many jurisdictions, but proved to be unenforceable. This Rule limits the reporting obligation to those offenses that a self-regulating profession must vigorously endeavor to prevent. A measure of judgment is therefore required in complying with the provisions of this Rule. The term "substantial" refers to the seriousness of the possible offense and not the quantum of evidence of which the lawyer is aware. A report should be made to a tribunal or other authority empowered to investigate or act upon the violation.

[3A] Paragraph (b) requires a lawyer in certain situations to respond to a lawful demand for information concerning another lawyer or a judge. This Rule is subject to the provisions of the Fifth Amendment to the United States Constitution and corresponding provisions of state law. A person relying on such a provision in response to a question, however, should do so openly and not use the right of nondisclosure as a justification for failure to comply with this Rule.

[4] The duty to report professional misconduct does not apply to a lawyer retained to represent a lawyer whose professional conduct is in question. Such a situation is governed by the Rules applicable to the client-lawyer relationship.

[5] Information about a lawyer's or judge's misconduct or fitness may be received by a lawyer in the course of that lawyer's participation in a bona fide assistance program for lawyers or judges. In that circumstance, providing for an exception to the reporting requirements of paragraphs (a) and (b) encourages lawyers and judges to seek assistance and treatment through such a program. Without such an exception, lawyers and judges may hesitate to seek assistance and treatment from these programs, and this may result in additional harm to their professional careers and additional injury to the welfare of clients and the public.

Rule 8.4 Misconduct

A lawyer or law firm shall not:

(a) violate or attempt to violate the Rules of Professional Conduct, knowingly assist or induce another to do so, or do so through the acts of another;

(b) engage in illegal conduct that adversely reflects on the lawyer's honesty, trustworthiness or fitness as a lawyer;

(c) engage in conduct involving dishonesty, fraud, deceit or misrepresentation;

(d) engage in conduct that is prejudicial to the administration of justice;

(e) state or imply an ability:

(1) to influence improperly or upon irrelevant grounds any tribunal, legislative body or public official; or

(2) to achieve results using means that violate these Rules or other law;

(f) knowingly assist a judge or judicial officer in conduct that is a violation of applicable rules of judicial conduct or other law;

(g) unlawfully discriminate in the practice of law, including in hiring, promoting or otherwise determining conditions of employment on the basis of age, race, creed, color, national origin, sex, disability, marital status or sexual orientation. Where there is a tribunal with jurisdiction to hear a complaint, if timely brought, other than a Departmental Disciplinary Committee, a complaint based on unlawful discrimination shall be brought before such tribunal in the first instance. A certified copy of a determination by such a tribunal, which has become final and enforceable and as to which the right to judicial or appellate review has been exhausted, finding that the lawyer has engaged in an unlawful discriminatory practice shall constitute prima facie evidence of professional misconduct in a disciplinary proceeding; or

(h) engage in any other conduct that adversely reflects on the lawyer's fitness as a lawyer.

COMMENT

[1] Lawyers are subject to discipline when they violate or attempt to violate the Rules of Professional Conduct, knowingly assist or induce another to do so, or do so through the acts of another, as when they request or instruct an agent to do so on their behalf. Paragraph (a), however, does not prohibit a lawyer from advising a client concerning action the client is legally entitled to take.

[2] Many kinds of illegal conduct reflect adversely on fitness to practice law. Illegal conduct involving violence, dishonesty, fraud, breach of trust, or serious interference with the administration of justice is illustrative of illegal conduct that reflects adversely on fitness to practice law. A pattern of repeated offenses, even ones of minor significance when considered separately, can indicate indifference to legal obligation.

[3] The prohibition on conduct prejudicial to the administration of justice is generally invoked to punish conduct, whether or not it violates another ethics rule, that results in substantial harm to the justice system comparable to those caused by obstruction of justice, such as advising a client to testify falsely, paying a witness to be unavailable, altering documents, repeatedly disrupting a proceeding, or failing to cooperate in an attorney disciplinary investigation or proceeding. The assertion of the lawyer's constitutional rights consistent with Rule 8.1, Comment [2] does not constitute failure to cooperate. The conduct must be seriously inconsistent with a lawyer's responsibility as an officer of the court.

[4] A lawyer may refuse to comply with an obligation imposed by law if such refusal is based upon a reasonable good-faith belief that no valid obligation exists

because, for example, the law is unconstitutional, conflicts with other legal or professional obligations, or is otherwise invalid. As set forth in Rule 3.4(c), a lawyer may not disregard a specific ruling or standing rule of a tribunal, but can take appropriate steps to test the validity of such a rule or ruling.

[4A] A lawyer harms the integrity of the law and the legal profession when the lawyer states or implies an ability to influence improperly any officer or agency of the executive, legislative or judicial branches of government.

[5] Lawyers holding public office assume legal responsibilities going beyond those of other citizens. A lawyer's abuse of public office can suggest an inability to fulfill the professional role of lawyers. The same is true of abuse of positions of private trust such as trustee, executor, administrator, guardian, agent and officer, director or manager of a corporation or other organization.

[5A] Unlawful discrimination in the practice of law on the basis of age, race, creed, color, national origin, sex, disability, marital status, or sexual orientation is governed by paragraph (g).

Rule 8.5   Disciplinary Authority and Choice of Law

(a) A lawyer admitted to practice in this state is subject to the disciplinary authority of this state, regardless of where the lawyer's conduct occurs. A lawyer may be subject to the disciplinary authority of both this state and another jurisdiction where the lawyer is admitted for the same conduct.

(b) In any exercise of the disciplinary authority of this state, the rules of professional conduct to be applied shall be as follows:

(1) For conduct in connection with a proceeding in a court before which a lawyer has been admitted to practice (either generally or for purposes of that proceeding), the rules to be applied shall be the rules of the jurisdiction in which the court sits, unless the rules of the court provide otherwise; and

(2) For any other conduct:

(i) If the lawyer is licensed to practice only in this state, the rules to be applied shall be the rules of this state, and

(ii) If the lawyer is licensed to practice in this state and another jurisdiction, the rules to be applied shall be the rules of the admitting jurisdiction in which the lawyer principally practices; provided, however, that if particular conduct clearly has its predominant effect in another jurisdiction in which the lawyer is licensed to practice, the rules of that jurisdiction shall be applied to that conduct.

COMMENT

Disciplinary Authority

[1] It is longstanding law that the conduct of a lawyer admitted to practice in this state is subject to the disciplinary authority of this state, regardless of where the conduct occurs.

Choice of Law

[2] A lawyer may be potentially subject to more than one set of rules of professional conduct, imposing different obligations. The lawyer may be licensed to practice in more than one jurisdiction with differing rules, or may be admitted to practice before a particular court with rules that differ from those of the jurisdiction or jurisdictions in which the lawyer is licensed to practice. Additionally, the lawyer's conduct may involve significant contacts with more than one jurisdiction.

[3] Paragraph (b) seeks to resolve such potential conflicts. Its premise is that minimizing conflicts between rules, as well as uncertainty about which rules are applicable, is in the best interest of clients and the profession (as well as the bodies having authority to regulate the profession). Accordingly, it takes the approach of (i) providing that any particular conduct of a lawyer shall be subject to only one set of rules of professional conduct, and (ii) making the determination of which set of rules applies to particular conduct as straightforward as possible, consistent with recognition of appropriate regulatory interests of relevant jurisdictions.

[4] Paragraph (b)(1) provides that as to a lawyer's conduct relating to a proceeding pending before a court before which the attorney is admitted to practice either generally or for purposes of that proceeding, the lawyer shall be subject only to the rules of the jurisdiction in which the court sits unless the rules of the court, including its choice-of-law rules, provide otherwise. As to all other conduct, paragraph (b)(2) provides that a lawyer shall be subject to the rules of the admitting jurisdiction in which the lawyer-principally practices or, if the predominant effect of the conduct is clearly in another jurisdiction in which the lawyer is licensed to practice, the rules of that jurisdiction shall be applied to the conduct. In the case of conduct in anticipation of a proceeding that is likely to be before a court, the predominant effect of such conduct could be where the lawyer principally practices, where the conduct occurred, where the court in which the proceeding is ultimately brought sits, or in another jurisdiction.

[5] When a lawyer is licensed to practice in New York and another jurisdiction and the lawyer's conduct involves significant contacts with more than one jurisdiction, it may not be clear whether the predominant effect of the lawyer's conduct will occur in an admitting jurisdiction other than the one in which the lawyer principally practices. For conduct governed by paragraph (b)(2), as long as the lawyer's conduct conforms to the rules of the jurisdiction in which the lawyer principally practices, the lawyer should not be subject to discipline unless the predominant effect of the lawyer's conduct will clearly occur in another admitting jurisdiction.

[6] If two admitting jurisdictions were to proceed against a lawyer for the same conduct, they should, applying this Rule, identify the same governing ethics rules. They should take all appropriate steps to see that they do apply the same rule to the same conduct, and in all events should avoid proceeding against a lawyer on the basis of two inconsistent rules.

[7] The choice-of-law provision applies to lawyers engaged in transnational practice, unless international law, treaties or other agreements between or among competent regulatory authorities in the affected jurisdictions provide otherwise.

Selected New York Statutes

Editors' Introduction. In New York State, topics such as admission to the bar, the attorney-client privilege, work product protection, professional discipline, solicitation of new clients, and the unauthorized practice of law are heavily governed by statute, especially by the New York Judiciary Law and by the Civil Practice Law and Rules (the "CPLR"). We reprint many sections of the Judiciary Law and a few sections of the CPLR that we consider most relevant to law students who are studying professional responsibility.

Since the previous edition of this book went to press in September 2011, two of the statutes reprinted below — §§475 and 475-a — were amended. The amendments took effect on January 1, 2013. They provide that "charging liens," which protect attorney fees, attach to the proceeds of out-of-court settlements and to awards obtained by arbitration or other means of alternative dispute resolution. We reprint the amended statutes below in legislative style.

Other statutes are also likely to be amended in the foreseeable future. In 2012, both the Assembly and the Senate passed legislation (A. 5700 and S. 1998-A) that would have amended Judiciary Law §§478, 485, 486, and 495, and would have added a new §485-a. Specifically, the bills would have amended §478 (Practicing or Appearing as Attorney-at-Law Without Being Admitted and Registered) by making it gender neutral and by acknowledging that out-of-state lawyers who are admitted pro hac vice by a New York court are not engaged in the unauthorized practice of law. In addition, the bills would have enacted a new §485-a (Violation of Certain Sections a Class E Felony), which would have provided that a violation of specified unauthorized practice of law statutes constitutes a Class E felony (rather than a misdemeanor as the same violation is under §485) if the person committing the violation "(1) either impersonates an attorney or offers legal services to the public under a title other than attorney; and (2) causes another person to suffer monetary loss or damages exceeding one thousand dollars or other material damage resulting from impairment of a legal right to which he or she is entitled according to law." Senator Charles Fuschillo, the sponsor of the Senate bill (S. 1998-A), provided the following justification for the proposed amendments:

> Currently, those persons who hold themselves out as an attorney-at-law or counselor-at-law without being admitted and registered are guilty of a misdemeanor.

1139

The purpose of this legislation is to provide consistency within the law regarding the unauthorized practice of a profession. Under section 6512 of the Education Law, anyone not authorized to practice . . . who practices or holds himself (or herself) out as being able to practice in any profession for which a license is required commits a class E felony. Examples of those professionals licensed under Title VIII of the Education Law include physicians, chiropractors, dentists, veterinarians, physical therapists, pharmacists, registered professional nurses, licensed practical nurses, licensed master social workers, certified public accountants, landscape architects, certified shorthand reporters, etc.

Licenses and registration ensure the public that a certain level of competency has been achieved to practice within a profession. Certainly, the unlawful practice of law should constitute a crime equivalent to the unauthorized practice of other professions.

However, Governor Cuomo had not signed the bill into law by the time we went to press, and the lengthy delay suggested that he might not do so. Readers should stay alert for further developments regarding §§478, 485, 485-a, 486, and 495.

Also affecting the New York statutes reprinted below is the decision in *Schoenefeld v. New York*, 2011 WL 3957282 (N.D.N.Y. 2011), a suit brought by a lawyer who lives in New Jersey. In *Schoenefeld*, the court struck down §470 of the New York Judiciary Law, which has been interpreted to require New York lawyers who reside in other states to maintain a law office in New York. The court held that the statute "infringes on nonresident attorneys' right to practice law in violation of the Privileges and Immunities Clause." On October 5, 2011, however, the New York Attorney General filed a Notice of Appeal to the Second Circuit. When we went to press with this edition in September 2012, the appeal was still pending and the Legislature had not repealed §470, so for now, §470 remains on the books.

For updates on New York legislation, visit the New York State Bar Association's website at *www.nysba.org* (click on "For Attorneys," then scroll down to "Legislation") — or visit *http://public.leginfo.state.ny.us/menuf.cgi*, which permits searches of Assembly and Senate bills either by keyword or by bill number.

Contents

NEW YORK JUDICIARY LAW

NEW YORK CIVIL PRACTICE LAW AND RULES

NEW YORK JUDICIARY LAW

§90. Admission to and Removal from Practice by Appellate Division; Character Committees

(1)(a) Upon the state board of law examiners certifying that a person has passed the required examination, or that the examination has been dispensed with, the appellate division of the supreme court in the department to which such person shall have been certified by the state board of law examiners, if it shall be satisfied that such person possesses the character and general fitness requisite for an attorney and counsellor-at-law, and has satisfied the requirements of section 3-503 of the general obligations law, shall admit him to practice as such attorney and counsellor-at-law in all the courts of this state, provided that he has in all respects complied with the rules of the court of appeals and the rules of the appellate divisions relating to the admission of attorneys.

(b) Upon the application, pursuant to the rules of the court of appeals, of any person who has been admitted to practice law in another state or territory or the District of Columbia of the United States or in a foreign country, to be admitted to practice as an attorney and counsellor-at-law in the courts of this state without taking the regular bar examination, the appellate division of the supreme court, if it shall be satisfied that such person is currently admitted to the bar in such other jurisdiction or jurisdictions, that at least one such jurisdiction in which he is so admitted would similarly admit an attorney or counsellor-at-law admitted to practice in New York state to its bar without examination and that such person possesses the character and general fitness requisite for an attorney and counsellor-at-law, and has satisfied the requirements of section 3-503 of the general obligations law, shall admit him to practice as such attorney and counsellor-at-law in all the courts of this state, provided, that he has in all respects complied with the rules of the court of appeals and the rules of the appellate divisions relating to the admission of attorneys. Such application, which shall conform to the requirements of section 3-503 of the general obligations law, shall be submitted to the appellate division of the supreme court in the department specified in the rules of the court of appeals.

> **Editors' Note.** Section 3-503 of New York General Obligations Law, which is referred to in §90(1)(a) and (b), requires every applicant for a license or the renewal of a license — including a law license — to certify under oath that "he or she is (or is not) under an obligation to pay child support," and to reveal whether he or she is four months or more in arrears in paying child support. If the applicant is more than four months in arrears and does not fall within one of the narrow exceptions to §3-503, then a license may be issued or renewed but it must expire within six months unless the applicant certifies under oath within that time either that the violation has been corrected or that he or she qualifies for an exception. Thereafter, any licensees who are "four months or more in arrears in child support may be subject to suspension of their business, professional and/or driver's license." "License" is defined in §3-503 to include "any . . . profession."

(c) . . .

(2) The supreme court shall have power and control over attorneys and counsellors-at-law and all persons practicing or assuming to practice law, and the appellate division of the supreme court in each department is authorized to censure, suspend from practice or remove from office any attorney and counsellor-at-law admitted to practice who is guilty of professional misconduct, malpractice, fraud, deceit, crime or misdemeanor, or any conduct prejudicial to the administration of justice; and the appellate division of the supreme court is hereby authorized to revoke such admission for any misrepresentation or suppression of any information in connection with the application for admission to practice.

It shall be the duty of the appellate division to insert in each order of suspension or removal hereafter rendered a provision which shall command the attorney and counsellor-at-law thereafter to desist and refrain from the practice of law in any form, either as principal or as agent, clerk or employee of another. In addition it shall forbid the performance of any of the following acts, to wit:

(a) The appearance as an attorney or counsellor-at-law before any court, judge, justice, board, commission or other public authority.

(b) The giving to another of an opinion as to the law or its application, or of any advice in relation thereto.

In case of suspension only, the order may limit the command to the period of time within which such suspension shall continue, and if justice so requires may further limit the scope thereof.

If an attorney and counsellor-at-law has been heretofore removed from office, the appellate division shall upon application of any attorney and counsellor-at-law, or of any incorporated bar association, and upon such notice to the respondent as may be required, amend the order of removal by adding thereto as a part thereof, provisions similar to those required to be inserted in orders hereafter made.

If a certified copy of such order or of such amended order, be served upon the attorney and counsellor-at-law suspended or removed from office, a violation thereof may be punished as a contempt of court.

(2-a)(a) The provisions of this subdivision shall apply in all cases of an attorney licensed, registered or admitted to practice in this state who has failed after receiving appropriate notice, to comply with a summons, subpoena or warrant relating to a paternity or child support proceeding involving him or her personally, or who is in arrears in payment of child support or combined child and spousal support which matter shall be referred to the appropriate appellate division by a court pursuant to the requirements of section two hundred forty-four-c of the domestic relations law or pursuant to section four hundred fifty-eight-b or five hundred forty-eight-b of the family court act.

(b) Upon receipt of an order from the court based on arrears in payment of child support or combined child and spousal support pursuant to one of the foregoing provisions of law, the appropriate appellate division within thirty days of receipt of such order, if it finds such person to be so licensed, registered or admitted, shall provide notice to such attorney of, and initiate, a hearing which shall be held by it at least twenty days and no more than thirty days after the sending of such notice to the attorney. The hearing shall be held solely for the purpose of determining whether there exists as of the date of the hearing proof that full payment of all arrears of support established by the order of the court to be due from the licensed, registered or admitted attorney have been paid. Proof of such payment shall be a certified check showing full payment of established arrears or a notice issued by the court or the support collection unit, where the order is payable to the support collection unit designated by the appropriate social services district. Such notice shall state that full payment of all arrears of support established by the order of the court to be due have been paid. The licensed attorney shall be given full opportunity to present such proof of payment at the hearing in person or by counsel. The only issue to be determined as a result of the hearing is whether the arrears have been paid. No evidence with respect to the appropriateness of the court order or ability of the respondent party in arrears to comply with such order shall be received or considered by the disciplinary committee.

(c) Upon receipt of an order from the court based on failure to comply with a summons, subpoena, or warrant relating to a paternity or child support proceeding, the appropriate appellate division within thirty days of receipt of such order, if it finds such person to be so licensed, registered or admitted, shall provide notice to such attorney that his or her license shall be suspended within sixty days of such notice to the attorney unless the conditions in paragraph e of this section are met.

(d) Notwithstanding any inconsistent provision of this section or of any other provision of law to the contrary, the license to practice law in this state of an attorney admitted to practice shall be suspended by the appellate division if, at the hearing provided for by paragraph b of this subdivision, the licensed attorney fails to present proof of payments as required by such subdivision. Such suspension shall not be lifted unless the original court or the support collection unit, where the court order is payable to the support collection unit designated by the appropriate social services district, issues notice to the appellate division that full payment of all arrears of support established by the order of the original court to be due have been paid.

(e) Notwithstanding any inconsistent provision of this section or of any other provision of law to the contrary, the license of an attorney admitted to practice law in this state shall be suspended by the appellate division, in accordance with paragraph c of this subdivision unless the court terminates its order to commence suspension proceedings. Such suspension shall not be lifted unless the court issues an order to the appellate division terminating its order to commence suspension proceedings.

(f) The appellate division shall inform the original court of all actions taken hereunder.

(g) This subdivision two-a applies to paternity and child support proceedings commenced under, and support obligations paid pursuant to any order of child support or child and spousal support issued under provisions of section two hundred thirty-six or two hundred forty of the domestic relations law, or article four, five, five-A or five-B of the family court act.

(h) Notwithstanding any inconsistent provision of this section or of any other provision of law to the contrary, the provisions of this subdivision two-a shall apply to the exclusion of any other requirements of this section and to the exclusion of any other requirement of law to the contrary.

(3) The suspension or removal of an attorney or counsellor-at-law, by the appellate division of the supreme court, operates as a suspension or removal in every court of the state.

(4)(a) Any person being an attorney and counsellor-at-law who shall be convicted of a felony as defined in paragraph e of this subdivision shall upon such conviction, cease to be an attorney and counsellor-at-law, or to be competent to practice law as such.

(b) Whenever any attorney and counsellor-at-law shall be convicted of a felony as defined in paragraph e of this subdivision, there may be presented to the appellate division of the supreme court certified or exemplified copy of the judgment of such conviction, and thereupon the name of the person so convicted shall, by order of the court, be struck from the roll of attorneys.

(c) Whenever an attorney shall be convicted of a crime in a court of record of the United States or of any state, territory or district, including this state, whether by a plea of guilty or nolo contendere or from a verdict after trial or otherwise, the attorney shall file, within thirty days thereafter, with the appellate division of the supreme court, the record of such conviction.

The failure of the attorney to so file shall be deemed professional misconduct provided, however, that the appellate division may upon application of the attorney, grant an extension upon good cause shown.

(d) For purposes of this subdivision, the term serious crime shall mean any criminal offense denominated a felony under the laws of any state, district or territory or of the United States which does not constitute a felony under the laws of this state, and any other crime a necessary element of which, as determined by statutory or common law definition of such crime, includes interference with the administration of justice, false swearing, misrepresentation, fraud, willful failure to file income tax returns, deceit, bribery, extortion, misappropriation, theft, or an attempt or conspiracy or solicitation of another to commit a serious crime.

(e) For purposes of this subdivision, the term felony shall mean any criminal offense classified as a felony under the laws of this state or any criminal offense committed in any other state, district, or territory of the United States and classified as a felony therein which if committed within this state, would constitute a felony in this state.

(f) Any attorney and counsellor-at-law convicted of a serious crime, as defined in paragraph d of this subdivision, whether by plea of guilty or nolo contendere or from a verdict after trial or otherwise, shall be suspended upon the receipt by the appellate division of the supreme court of the record of such conviction until a final order is made pursuant to paragraph g of this subdivision.

Upon good cause shown the appellate division of the supreme court may, upon application of the attorney or on its own motion, set aside such suspension when it appears consistent with the maintenance of the integrity and honor of the profession, the protection of the public and the interest of justice.

(g) Upon a judgment of conviction against an attorney becoming final the appellate division of the supreme court shall order the attorney to show cause why a final order of suspension, censure or removal from office should not be made.

(h) If the attorney requests a hearing, the appellate division of the supreme court shall refer the proceeding to a referee, justice or judge appointed by the appellate division for hearing, report and recommendation.

After said hearing, the appellate division may impose such discipline as it deems proper under the facts and circumstances.

(5)(a) If such removal or debarment was based upon conviction for a serious crime or upon a felony conviction as defined in subdivision four of this section, and such felony conviction was subsequently reversed or pardoned by the president of the United States, or governor of this or another state of the United States, the appellate division shall have power to vacate or modify such order or debarment, provided, however, that if such attorney or counsellor-at-law has been removed from practice in another jurisdiction, a pardon in said jurisdiction shall not be a basis for application for re-admission in this jurisdiction unless he shall have been readmitted in the jurisdiction where pardoned.

(b) If such removal or debarment was based upon conviction for a felony as defined in subdivision four of this section, the appellate division shall have power to vacate or modify such order or debarment after a period of seven years provided that such person has not been convicted of a crime during such seven-year period.

(c) An attorney and counsellor-at-law who has been convicted of a felony without the state and whose name has been struck from the roll of attorneys prior to July thirteenth, nineteen hundred seventy-nine by virtue of the provisions of subdivision four of this section may, if he alleges that such felony committed without the state would not constitute a felony if committed within the state, petition the appellate division to vacate or modify such debarment. If the appellate division finds that the felony of which the attorney and counsellor-at-law has been convicted without the state would not constitute a felony if committed within the state, it shall grant a hearing and may retroactively vacate or modify such debarment and impose such discipline as it deems just and proper under the facts and circumstances.

The attorney and counsellor-at-law shall petition for reinstatement by filing in the appellate division a copy of the order of removal together with a request for a hearing pursuant to the provisions of this paragraph.

Upon such application, the order of removal shall be deemed an order of suspension for the purposes of a proceeding pursuant to this paragraph.

(6) Before an attorney or counsellor-at-law is suspended or removed as prescribed in this section, a copy of the charges against him must be delivered to him personally within or without the state or, in case it is established to the satisfaction of the presiding justice of the appellate division of the supreme court to which the charges have been presented, that he cannot with due diligence be served personally, the same may be served upon him by mail, publication or otherwise as the said presiding justice may direct, and he must be allowed an opportunity of being heard in his defense. In all cases where the charges are served in any manner other than personally, and the attorney and counsellor-at-law so served does not appear, an application may be made by such attorney or in his behalf to the presiding justice of the appellate division of the supreme court to whom the charges were presented at any time within one year after the rendition of the judgment, or final order of suspension or removal, and upon good cause shown and upon such terms as may be deemed just by such presiding justice, such attorney and counsellor- at-law must be allowed to defend himself against such charges.

The justices of the appellate division in any judicial department, or a majority of them, may make an order directing the expenses of any disciplinary proceedings, and the necessary costs and disbursements of the petitioner in prosecuting such charges, including the expense of any preliminary investigation in relation to professional conduct of an attorney and counsellor-at-law, to be paid out of funds appropriated to the office of court administration for that purpose.

(a) Where the appellate division of [the] supreme court orders the censure, suspension from practice or removal from office of an attorney or counsellor-at-law following disciplinary proceedings at which it found, based upon a preponderance of the legally admissible evidence, that such attorney or counsellor-at-law wilfully misappropriated or misapplied money or property in the practice of law, its order may require him or her to make monetary restitution in accordance with this subdivision. Its order also may require that he or she reimburse the lawyers' fund for client protection of the state of New York for awards made to the person whose money or property was wilfully misappropriated or misapplied.

(b) Monetary restitution, as authorized hereunder, shall be made to the person whose money or property was wilfully misappropriated or misapplied and shall be for the amount or value of such money or property, as found in the disciplinary proceedings. In the event that such person dies prior to completion of such restitution, any amount remaining to be paid shall be paid to the estate of the deceased.

(c) Any payment made as restitution pursuant to this subdivision shall not limit, preclude or impair any liability for damages in any civil action or proceeding for an amount in excess of such payment; nor shall any order of the appellate division made hereunder deprive a criminal court of any authority pursuant to article sixty of the penal law.

(d) An order issued pursuant to this subdivision may be entered as a civil judgment. Such judgment shall be enforceable as a money judgment in any court of competent jurisdiction by any person to whom payments are due thereunder, or by the lawyers' fund for client protection where it has been subrogated to the rights of such person.

(e) Where an attorney or counsellor-at-law is permitted to resign from office, the appellate division may, if appropriate, issue an order as provided herein requiring him or her to make payments specified by this subdivision.

(f) Notwithstanding any other provision of this subdivision, no order may be issued hereunder unless the person required to make payments under such order first is given an opportunity to be heard in opposition thereto.

(7) In addition to the duties prescribed by section seven hundred of the county law, it shall be the duty of any district attorney within a department, when so designated by the justices of the appellate division of the supreme court in such department, or a majority of them, to prosecute all proceedings for the removal or suspension of attorneys and counsellors-at-law or the said justices, or a majority of them, may appoint any attorney and counsellor-at-law to conduct a preliminary investigation and to prosecute any disciplinary proceedings and, during or upon the termination of the investigation or proceedings, may fix the compensation to be paid to such attorney and counsellor-at-law for the services rendered, which compensation shall be a charge against the county specified in his certificate and shall be paid thereon.

(8) Any petitioner or respondent in a disciplinary proceeding against an attorney or counsellor-at-law under this section, including a bar association or any other corporation or association, shall have the right to appeal to the court of appeals from a final order of any appellate division in such proceeding upon questions of law involved therein, subject to the limitations prescribed by section three of article six of the constitution of this state.

(9) No objection shall be taken to the appointment of any member of the bar to act as referee or judge in a disciplinary proceeding under this section on the ground that he is a member of a bar association or other corporation or association which is the petitioner therein.

(10) Any statute or rule to the contrary notwithstanding, all papers, records and documents upon the application or examination of any person for admission as an attorney and counsellor-at-law and upon any complaint, inquiry, investigation or proceeding relating to the conduct or discipline of an attorney or attorneys, shall be sealed and be deemed private and confidential. However, upon good cause being shown, the justices of the appellate division having jurisdiction are empowered, in their discretion, by written order, to permit to be divulged all or any part of such papers, records and

documents. In the discretion of the presiding or acting presiding justice of said appellate division, such order may be made either without notice to the persons or attorneys to be affected thereby or upon such notice to them as he may direct. In furtherance of the purpose of this subdivision, said justices are also empowered, in their discretion, from time to time to make such rules as they may deem necessary. Without regard to the foregoing, in the event that charges are sustained by the justices of the appellate division having jurisdiction in any complaint, investigation or proceeding relating to the conduct or discipline of any attorney, the records and documents in relation thereto shall be deemed public records.

§460. Examination and Admission of Attorneys

An applicant for admission to practice as an attorney or counsellor in this state, must be examined and licensed to practice as prescribed in this chapter and in the rules of the court of appeals. Race, creed, color, national origin, alienage or sex shall constitute no cause for refusing any person examination or admission to practice.

§460-a. Disclosure with Respect to Loans Made or Guaranteed by the New York State Higher Education Services Corporation

Every application for admission to practice as an attorney or counsellor in the courts in this state issued pursuant to the provisions of this chapter shall contain a question inquiring whether the applicant has any loans made or guaranteed by the New York state higher education services corporation currently outstanding, and if so, whether such applicant is presently in default on any such loan. The name and address of any applicant who answers either or both of such questions in the affirmative shall be transmitted to such corporation by the appellate division prior to the date on which such license is issued.

§466. Attorney's Oath of Office

Each person, admitted as prescribed in this chapter must, upon his admission, take the constitutional oath of office in open court, and subscribe the same in a roll or book, to be kept in the office of the clerk of the appellate division of the supreme court for that purpose. . . .

Editors' Note. The "constitutional oath of office" referred to in §466 is found in the New York State Constitution at Article 13, §1, which provides, in relevant part, as follows:

Members of the legislature, and all officers, executive and judicial, except such inferior officers as shall be by law exempted, shall, before they enter on the duties of their respective offices, take and subscribe the following oath or affirmation: "I do solemnly swear (or affirm) that I will support the constitution of the United States, and the constitution of the State of New York, and that I will faithfully discharge the duties of the office of . . . . , according to the best of my ability"; and no other oath, declaration or test shall be required as a qualification for any office of public trust. . . .

§470. Attorneys Having Offices in This State May Reside in Adjoining State

Editors' Note. In *Schoenefeld v. New York*, 2011 WL 3957282 (N.D.N.Y. 2011), the district court struck down §470 on grounds that the statute "infringes on nonresident attorneys' right to practice law in violation of the Privileges and Immunities Clause." However, the New York Attorney General filed a Notice of Appeal on October 5, 2011, and the Legislature has not repealed §470, so the law remains on the books.

A person, regularly admitted to practice as an attorney and counsellor, in the courts of record of this state, whose office for the transaction of law business is within the state, may practice as such attorney or counsellor, although he resides in an adjoining state.

§474. Compensation of Attorney or Counsellor

The compensation of an attorney or counsellor for his services is governed by agreement, express or implied, which is not restrained by law, except that no agreement made hereafter between an attorney and a guardian of an infant for the compensation of such attorney, dependent upon the success of the prosecution by said attorney of a claim belonging to said infant, or by which such attorney is to receive a percentage of any recovery or award in behalf of such infant or a sum equal to a percentage of any such recovery or award, shall be valid or enforceable unless made as hereinafter provided. . . .

§474-a. Contingent Fees for Attorneys in Claims or Actions for Medical, Dental or Podiatric Malpractice

1. For the purpose of this section, the term "contingent fee" shall mean any attorney's fee in any claim or action for medical, dental or podiatric malpractice, whether determined by judgment or settlement, which is dependent in whole or in part upon the success of the prosecution by the attorney of such claim or action, or which is to consist of a percentage of any recovery, or a sum equal to a percentage of any recovery, in such claim or action.

2. Notwithstanding any inconsistent judicial rule, a contingent fee in a medical, dental or podiatric malpractice action shall not exceed the amount of compensation provided for in the following schedule:

30 percent of the first $250,000 of the sum recovered;

25 percent of the next $250,000 of the sum recovered;

20 percent of the next $500,000 of the sum recovered;

15 percent of the next $250,000 of the sum recovered;

10 percent of any amount over $1,250,000 of the sum recovered.

3. Such percentages shall be computed on the net sum recovered after deducting from the amount recovered expenses and disbursements for expert testimony and investigative or other services properly chargeable to the enforcement of the claim or prosecution of the action. In computing the fee, the costs as taxed, including interest upon a judgment, shall be deemed part of the amount recovered. For the following or similar items there shall be no deduction in computing such percentages: liens, assignments or claims in favor of hospitals, for medical care, dental care, podiatric care and treatment by doctors and nurses, or of self-insurers or insurance carriers.

4. In the event that claimant's or plaintiff's attorney believes in good faith that the fee schedule set forth in subdivision two of this section, because of extraordinary circumstances, will not give him adequate compensation, application for greater compensation may be made upon affidavit with written notice and an opportunity to be heard to the claimant or plaintiff and other persons holding liens or assignments on the recovery. . . .

5. Any contingent fee in a claim or action for medical, dental or podiatric malpractice brought on behalf of an infant shall continue to be subject to the provisions of section four hundred seventy-four of this chapter.

§475. Attorney's Lien in Action, Special or Other Proceeding.

Editors' Note. On October 3, 2012, Governor Andrew Cuomo signed into law a bill (A. 5275, S. 1546) amending §§475 and 475-a of the New York Judiciary Law. Those two statutes create so-called "charging liens" that protect an attorney's fees by attaching to the proceeds of any "action, special or other proceeding" in a court or government department. However, courts consistently held that the two statutes in their pre-amendment form did not create liens on settlements or awards obtained through arbitration or other forms of alternative dispute resolution. The amendments fill this gap by giving attorneys the same protection for their fees *even if* a dispute is resolved using any form of alternative dispute resolution or is settled via negotiations before any suit is filed. The amendments took effect on January 1, 2013. We reprint §§475 and 475-a in legislative style, underscoring new language and striking through deleted language.

From the commencement of an action, special or other proceeding in any court or before any state, municipal or federal department, except a department of labor, or the service of an answer containing a counterclaim, or the initiation of any means of alternative dispute resolution including, but not limited to, mediation or arbitration, or the provision of services in a settlement negotiation at any stage of the dispute, the attorney who appears for a party has a lien upon his or her client's cause of action, claim or counterclaim, which attaches to a verdict, report, determination, decision, award, settlement, judgment or final order in his or her client's favor, and the proceeds thereof in whatever hands they may come; and the lien cannot be affected by any settlement between the parties before or after judgment, final order or determination. The court upon the petition of the client or attorney may determine and enforce the lien.

§475-a. Notice of Lien.

If prior to the commencement of an action, arbitration, mediation or a form of alternative dispute resolution, or a special or other proceeding, an attorney serves a notice of lien upon the person or persons against whom his or her client has or may have a claim or cause of action, the attorney has a lien upon the claim or cause of action from the time such notice is given, which attaches to a verdict, report, determination, decision, award, settlement or final order in his or her client's favor of any court, arbitral tribunal or of any state, municipal or federal department, except a department of labor, and to any money or property which may be recovered on account of such claim or cause of action in whatever hands they may come; and the lien cannot be affected by any settlement between the parties after such notice of lien is given. . . . A lien obtained under this section shall otherwise have the same effect and be enforced in the same manner as a lien obtained under section four hundred seventy-five of this ~~chapter~~ article.

§476-a. Action for Unlawful Practice of the Law

1. The attorney-general may maintain an action upon his or her own information or upon the complaint of a private person or of a bar association organized and existing under the laws of this state against any person, partnership, corporation, or association, and any employee, agent, director, or officer thereof who commits any act or engages in any conduct prohibited by law as constituting the unlawful practice of the law. The term "action" as used in this subdivision shall be construed to include both civil actions and criminal actions.

The term "unlawful practice of the law" as used in this article shall include, but is not limited to,

(a) any act prohibited by penal law sections two hundred seventy, two hundred seventy-a, two hundred seventy-e, two hundred seventy-one, two hundred seventy-five, two hundred seventy-five-a, two hundred seventy-six, two hundred eighty or fourteen hundred fifty-two, or

(b) any other act forbidden by law to be done by any person not regularly licensed and admitted to practice law in this state, or

(c) any act punishable by the supreme court as a criminal contempt of court under section seven hundred fifty-B of this chapter.

2. Such a civil action may also be maintained by a bar association organized and existing under the laws of the state of New York, upon an application to the supreme court of the state of New York, or a justice thereof, for leave to bring the same by such bar association on good cause shown therefor and proof that a written request was made upon the attorney-general to bring such an action and that more than twenty days have elapsed since the making of such request and he or she has failed or refused to bring such an action.

§477. Settlement of Actions for Personal Injury

If, in an action commenced to recover damages for a personal injury or for death as the result of a personal injury, an attorney having or claiming to have a lien for services performed or to be performed who shall have appeared for the person or persons having or claiming to have a right of action for such injury or death, no settlement or adjustment of such action shall be valid, unless consented to in writing by such attorney and by the person or persons for whom he shall have appeared, or approved by an order of the court in which such action is brought.

§478. Practicing or Appearing as Attorney-at-Law Without Being Admitted and Registered

Editors' Note. In 2012, the New York State Senate and Assembly passed bills (A. 5700 and S. 1998-A) that would have amended §478 to make make clear that lawyers from other U.S. jurisdictions or from foreign countries who are admitted pro hac vice in New York courts are not engaged in the unlawful practice of law. However, Governor Cuomo had not signed the bill into law by the time we went to press, and the lengthy delay suggested that he might not do so. Readers should stay alert for further developments regarding §478.

It shall be unlawful for any natural person to practice or appear as an attorney-at-law or as an attorney and counselor-at-law for a person other than himself in a court of record in this state, or to furnish attorneys or counsel or an attorney and counsel to render legal services, or to hold himself out to the public as being entitled to practice law as aforesaid, or in any other manner, or to assume to be an attorney or counselor-at-law, or to assume, use, or advertise the title of lawyer, or attorney and counselor-at-law, or attorney-at-law or counselor-at-law, or attorney, or counselor, or attorney and counselor, or equivalent terms in any language, in such manner as to convey the impression that he is a legal practitioner of law or in any manner to advertise that he either alone or together with any other persons or person has, owns, conducts or maintains a law office or law and collection office, or office of any kind for the practice of law, without having first been duly and regularly licensed and admitted to practice law in the courts of record of this state, and without having taken the constitutional oath. Provided, however, that nothing in this section shall be held to apply . . . (2) to law students who have completed at least two semesters of law school or persons who have graduated from a law school, who have taken the examination for admittance to practice law in the courts of record in the state immediately available after graduation from law school, or the examination immediately available after being notified by the board of law examiners that they failed to pass said exam, and who have not been notified by the board of law examiners that they have failed to pass two such examinations, acting under the supervision of a legal aid organization when such students and persons are acting under a program approved by the appellate division . . . ; or (3) to law students who have completed at least two semesters of law school, or to persons who have graduated from a law school . . . and who have taken the examination for admission to practice as an attorney and counselor-at-law immediately available after graduation from law school or the examination immediately available after being notified by the board of law examiners that they failed to pass said exam, and who have not been notified by the board of law examiners that they have failed to pass two such examinations, when such students or persons are acting under the supervision of the state or a subdivision thereof . . . pursuant to a program approved by the appellate division of the supreme court of the department within which such activities are taking place and specifying the extent to which they may engage in activities otherwise prohibited by this statute. . . .

§479. Soliciting Business on Behalf of an Attorney

It shall be unlawful for any person or his agent, employee or any person acting on his behalf, to solicit or procure through solicitation either directly or indirectly legal business, or to solicit or procure through solicitation a retainer, written or oral, or any agreement authorizing an attorney to perform or render legal services, or to make it a business so to solicit or procure such business, retainers or agreements.

§480. Entering Hospital to Negotiate Settlement or Obtain Release or Statement

It shall be unlawful for any person to enter a hospital for the purpose of negotiating a settlement or obtaining a general release or statement, written or oral, from any person confined in said hospital or sanitarium as a patient, with reference to any personal injuries for which said person is confined in said hospital or sanitarium within fifteen days after the injuries were sustained, unless at least five days prior to the obtaining or procuring of such general release or statement such injured party has signified in writing his willingness that such general release or statement be given. This section shall not apply to a person entering a hospital for the purpose of visiting a person therein confined, as his attorney or on behalf of his attorney.

§481. Aiding, Assisting or Abetting the Solicitation of Persons or the Procurement of a Retainer for or on Behalf of an Attorney

It shall be unlawful for any person in the employ of or in any capacity attached to any hospital, sanitarium, police department, prison or court, or for a person authorized to furnish bail bonds, to communicate directly or indirectly with any attorney or person acting on his behalf for the purpose of aiding, assisting or abetting such attorney in the solicitation of legal business or the procurement through solicitation of a retainer, written or oral, or any agreement authorizing the attorney to perform or render legal services.

§482. Employment by Attorney of Person to Aid, Assist or Abet in the Solicitation of Business or the Procurement Through Solicitation of a Retainer to Perform Legal Services

It shall be unlawful for an attorney to employ any person for the purpose of soliciting or aiding, assisting or abetting in the solicitation of legal business or the procurement through solicitation either directly or indirectly of a retainer, written or oral, or of any agreement authorizing the attorney to perform or render legal services.

§483. Signs Advertising Services as Attorney at Law

It shall be unlawful for any person to maintain on real property or to permit or allow any other person to maintain, on such property a sign, in any language, to the effect that an attorney-at-law or legal services are available therein unless the full name of the attorney-at-law or the firm rendering such services is set forth thereon. In any prosecution for violation of the provisions of this section the existence of such a sign on real property shall be presumptive evidence that it was placed or permitted to exist thereon with the knowledge and consent of the person or persons in possession of said premises.

§484. None but Attorneys to Practice in the State

No natural person shall ask or receive, directly or indirectly, compensation for appearing for a person other than himself as attorney in any court or before any magistrate, or for preparing deeds, mortgages, assignments, discharges, leases or any other instruments affecting real estate, wills, codicils, or any other instrument affecting the disposition of property after death, or decedents' estates, or pleadings of any kind in any action brought before any court of record in this state, or make it a business to practice for another as an attorney in any court or before any magistrate unless he has been regularly admitted to practice, as an attorney or counselor, in the courts of record in the state; but nothing in this section shall apply (1) to officers of societies for the prevention of cruelty to animals, duly appointed, when exercising the special powers conferred upon such corporations under section fourteen hundred three of the not-for-profit corporation law; or (2) to law students who have completed at least two semesters of law school or persons who have graduated from a law school, who have taken the examination for admittance to practice law in the courts of record in the state immediately available after graduation from law school, or the examination immediately available after being notified by the board of law examiners that they failed to pass said exam, and who have not been notified by the board of law examiners that they have failed to pass two such examinations, acting under the supervision of a legal aid organization, when such students and persons are acting under a program approved by the appellate division of the supreme court of the department in which the principal office of such organization is located and specifying the extent to which such students and persons may engage in activities prohibited by this statute; or (3) to persons who have graduated from a law school approved pursuant to the rules of the court of appeals for the admission of attorneys and counsellors-at-law and who have taken the examination for admission to practice as an attorney and counsellor-at-law immediately available after graduation from law school or the examination immediately available after being notified by the board of law examiners that they failed to pass said exam, and who have not been notified by the board of law examiners that they have failed to pass two such examinations, when such persons are acting under the supervision of the state or a subdivision thereof or of any officer or agency of the state or a subdivision thereof, pursuant to a program approved by the appellate division of the supreme court of the department within which such activities are taking place and specifying the extent to which they may engage in activities otherwise prohibited by this statute and those powers of the supervising governmental entity or officer in connection with which they may engage in such activities.

§485. Violation of Certain Preceding Sections a Misdemeanor

Editors' Note. Under Judiciary Law §485, a violation of New York's various statutes governing the unauthorized practice of law is currently a misdemeanor. In 2012, however, the New York State Senate and Assembly passed bills (A. 5700 and S. 1998-A) that would have amended §485 to make a violation of §485-a Class E felony in specified circumstances. However, Governor Cuomo had not signed the bill into law by the time we went to press, and the lengthy delay suggested that he might not do so. Readers should check online sources for further developments regarding §485 and related statutes.

Any person violating the provisions of sections four hundred seventy-eight, four hundred seventy-nine, four hundred eighty, four hundred eighty-one, four hundred eighty-two, four hundred eighty-three or four hundred eighty-four, shall be guilty of a misdemeanor.

§486. Practice of Law by Attorney Who Has Been Disbarred, Suspended, or Convicted of a Felony

Editors' Note. In 2012, the New York State Senate and Assembly passed bills (A. 5700 and S. 1998-A) that would have amended §486 to make a violation a Class E felony in specified circumstances. However, Governor Cuomo had not signed the bill into law by the time we went to press, and the lengthy delay suggested that he might not do so. Readers should check online sources for further developments regarding §486.

Any person whose admission to practice as an attorney and counselor-at-law has been revoked or who has been removed from office as attorney and counselor-at-law or, being an attorney and counselor-at-law, has been convicted of a felony or has been suspended from practice and has not been duly and regularly reinstated, who does any act forbidden by the provisions of this article to be done by any person not regularly admitted to practice law in the courts of record of this state, unless the judgment, decree or order suspending him shall permit such act, shall be guilty of a misdemeanor.

§487. Misconduct by Attorneys

An attorney or counsellor who:

(1) Is guilty of any deceit or collusion, or consents to any deceit or collusion, with intent to deceive the court or any party; or,

(2) Wilfully delays his client's suit with a view to his own gain; or, wilfully receives any money or allowance for or on account of any money which he has not laid out, or becomes answerable for,

Is guilty of a misdemeanor, and in addition to the punishment prescribed therefor by the penal law, he forfeits to the party injured treble damages, to be recovered in a civil action.

§488. Buying Demands on Which to Bring Action

An attorney or counselor shall not:

(1) Directly or indirectly, buy, take an assignment of or be in any manner interested in buying or taking an assignment of a bond, promissory note, bill of exchange, book debt, or other thing in action, with the intent and for the purpose of bringing an action thereon.

(2) By himself or herself, or by or in the name of another person, either before or after action brought, promise or give, or procure to be

promised or given, a valuable consideration to any person, as an inducement to placing, or in consideration of having placed, in his or her hands, or in the hands of another person, a demand of any kind, for the purpose of bringing an action thereon, or of representing the claimant in the pursuit of any civil remedy for the recovery thereof. But this subdivision does not apply to:

(a) an agreement between attorneys and counselors, or either, to divide between themselves the compensation to be received;

(b) a lawyer representing an indigent or pro bono client paying court costs and expenses of litigation on behalf of the client;

(c) a lawyer advancing court costs and expenses of litigation, the repayment of which may be contingent on the outcome of the matter; or

(d) a lawyer, in an action in which an attorney's fee is payable in whole or in part as a percentage of the recovery in the action, paying on the lawyer's own account court costs and expenses of litigation. In such case, the fee paid to the attorney from the proceeds of the action may include an amount equal to such costs and expenses incurred.

(3) A lawyer that offers services as described in paragraphs b, c and d of subdivision two of this section shall not, either directly or through any media used to advertise or otherwise publicize the lawyer's services, promise or advertise his or her ability to advance or pay costs and expenses of litigation in such manner as to state or imply that such ability is unique or extraordinary when such is not the case.

(4) An attorney or counselor who violates the provisions of this section is guilty of a misdemeanor.

§491. Sharing of Compensation by Attorneys Prohibited

(1) It shall be unlawful for any person, partnership, corporation, or association to divide with or receive from, or to agree to divide with or receive from, any attorney-at-law or group of attorneys-at-law, whether practicing in this state or elsewhere, either before or after action brought, any portion of any fee or compensation, charged or received by such attorney-at-law or any valuable consideration or reward, as an inducement for placing, or in consideration of having placed, in the hands of such attorney-at-law, or in the hands of another person, a claim or demand of any kind for the purpose of collecting such claim, or bringing an action thereon, or of representing claimant in the pursuit of any civil remedy for the recovery thereof. But this section does not apply to an agreement between attorneys and counsellors-at-law to divide between themselves the compensation to be received.

(2) Any person violating any of the provisions of this section is guilty of a misdemeanor.

§493. Attorneys Forbidden to Defend Criminal Prosecutions Carried on by Their Partners, or Formerly by Themselves

An attorney, who directly or indirectly advises in relation to, or aids or promotes the defense of any action or proceeding in any court, the prosecution of which is carried on, aided or promoted by a person as district attorney or other public prosecutor, with whom such attorney is directly or indirectly connected as a partner; or who, having himself prosecuted or in any manner aided or promoted any action or proceeding in any court, as district attorney or other public prosecutor, afterwards directly or indirectly advises in relation to, or takes any part in, the defense thereof, as attorney or otherwise; or who takes or receives any valuable consideration from or on behalf of any defendant in any such action, upon any understanding or agreement whatever, express or implied, having relation to the defense thereof, is guilty of a misdemeanor.

§494. Attorneys May Defend Themselves

The last section does not prohibit an attorney from defending himself in person, as attorney or as counsel, when prosecuted either civilly or criminally.

§495. Corporations and Voluntary Associations Not to Practice Law

Editors' Note. In 2012, the New York State Senate and Assembly passed bills (A. 5700 and S. 1998-A) that would have amended §495(3) to make a violation a Class E felony in specified circumstances. However, Governor Cuomo had not signed the bill into law by the time we went to press, and the lengthy delay suggested that he might not do so. Readers should check online sources for further developments regarding §495(3).

(1) No corporation or voluntary association shall

(a) practice or appear as an attorney-at-law for any person in any court in this state or before any judicial body, nor

(b) make it a business to practice as an attorney-at-law, for any person, in any of said courts, nor

(c) hold itself out to the public as being entitled to practice law, or to render legal services or advice, nor

(d) furnish attorneys or counsel, nor

(e) render legal services of any kind in actions or proceedings of any nature or any other way or manner, nor

(f) assume in any other manner to be entitled to practice law, nor

(g) assume, use or advertise the title of lawyer or attorney, attorney-at-law, or equivalent terms in any language in such manner as to convey the impression that it is entitled to practice law or to furnish legal advice, services or counsel, nor

(h) advertise that either alone or together with or by or through any person whether or not a duly and regularly admitted attorney-at-law, it has, owns, conducts or maintains a law office or an office for the practice of law, or for furnishing legal advice, services or counsel. . . .

(3) No voluntary association or corporation shall ask or receive directly or indirectly, compensation for preparing deeds, mortgages, assignments, discharges, leases, or any other instruments affecting real estate, wills, codicils, or any other instruments affecting disposition of property after death or decedents' estates, or pleadings of any kind in actions or proceedings of any nature. Any association or corporation violating the provisions of this subdivision is guilty of a misdemeanor. . . .

(7) This section does not apply to organizations which offer prepaid legal services; to non-profit organizations whether incorporated or unincorporated, organized and operating primarily for a purpose other than the provision of legal services and which furnish legal services as an incidental activity in furtherance of their primary purpose; or to organizations which have as their primary purpose the furnishing of legal services to indigent persons.

§496.   [Prepaid Legal Services Plans; Registration Statement]

An organization described in subdivision seven of section four hundred ninety-five of this article shall file with the appellate division department in which its principal office is located a statement describing the nature and purposes of the organization, the composition of its governing body, the type of legal services being made available, and the names and addresses of any attorneys and counselors-at-law employed by the organization or with whom commitments have been made. An updating of this information shall be furnished to the appropriate appellate division on or before July first of each year and the names and addresses of attorneys and counsellors-at-law who rendered legal services during that year shall be included.

§498.   Professional Referrals

(1) There shall be no cause of action for damages arising against any association or society of attorneys and counsellors at law authorized to practice in the state of New York for referring any person or persons to a member of the profession for the purpose of obtaining legal services, provided that such referral was made without charge and as a public service by said association or society, and without malice, and in the reasonable belief that such referral was warranted, based upon the facts disclosed.

(2) For the purposes of this section, "association or society of attorneys or counsellors at law" shall mean any such organization, whether incorporated or unincorporated, which offers professional referrals as an incidental service in the normal course of business, but which business does not include the providing of legal services.

§499. Lawyer Assistance Committees

(1) *Confidential information privileged.* The confidential relations and communications between a member or authorized agent of a lawyer assistance committee sponsored by a state or local bar association and any person, firm or corporation communicating with such committee, its members or authorized agents shall be deemed to be privileged on the same basis as those provided by law between attorney and client. Such privilege may be waived only by the person, firm or corporation which has furnished information to the committee.

(2) *Immunity from liability.* Any person, firm or corporation in good faith providing information to, or in any other way participating in the affairs of, any of the committees referred to in subdivision one of this section shall be immune from civil liability that might otherwise result by reason of such conduct. For the purpose of any proceeding, the good faith of any such person, firm or corporation shall be presumed.

NEW YORK CIVIL PRACTICE LAW AND RULES

§3101. Scope of Disclosure

(a) *Generally.* There shall be full disclosure of all matter material and necessary in the prosecution or defense of an action, regardless of the burden of proof. . . .

(b) *Privileged matter.* Upon objection by a person entitled to assert the privilege, privileged matter shall not be obtainable.

(c) *Attorney's work product.* The work product of an attorney shall not be obtainable.

(d) *Trial preparation.*

1. *Experts.*

(i) Upon request, each party shall identify each person whom the party expects to call as an expert witness at trial and shall disclose in reasonable detail the subject matter on which each expert is expected to testify, the substance of the facts and opinions on which each expert is expected to testify, the qualifications of each expert witness and a summary of the grounds for each expert's opinion. However, where a party for good cause shown retains an expert an insufficient period of time before the commencement of trial to give appropriate notice thereof, the party shall not thereupon be precluded from introducing the expert's testimony at the trial solely on grounds of noncompliance with this paragraph. In that instance, upon motion of any party, made before or at trial, or on its own initiative, the court may make whatever order may be just. . . .

(iii) Further disclosure concerning the expected testimony of any expert may be obtained only by court order upon a showing of special circumstances and subject to restrictions as to scope and provisions concerning fees and expenses as the court may deem appropriate. . . .

2. *Materials.* Subject to the provisions of paragraph one of this subdivision, materials otherwise discoverable under subdivision (a) of this section and prepared in anticipation of litigation or for trial by or for another party, or by or for that other party's representative (including an attorney, consultant, surety, indemnitor, insurer or agent), may be obtained only upon a showing that the party seeking discovery has substantial need of the materials in the preparation of the case and is unable without undue hardship to obtain the substantial equivalent of the materials by other means. In ordering discovery of the materials when the required showing has been made, the court shall protect against disclosure of the mental impressions, conclusions, opinions or legal theories of an attorney or other representative of a party concerning the litigation.

(e) *Party's statement.* A party may obtain a copy of his own statement. . . .

§4503. Attorney

(a)(1) *Confidential communication privileged.* Unless the client waives the privilege, an attorney or his or her employee, or any person who obtains without the knowledge of the client evidence of a confidential communication made between the attorney or his or her employee and the client in the course of professional employment, shall not disclose, or be allowed to disclose such communication, nor shall the client be compelled to disclose such communication, in any action, disciplinary trial or hearing, or administrative action, proceeding or hearing conducted by or on behalf of any state, municipal or local governmental agency or by the legislature or any committee or body thereof. Evidence of any such communication obtained by any such person, and evidence resulting therefrom, shall not be disclosed by any state, municipal or local governmental agency or by the legislature or any committee or body thereof. The relationship of an attorney and client shall exist between a professional service corporation organized under article fifteen of the business corporation law to practice as an attorney and counselor- at-law and the clients to whom it renders legal services.